Following the casing of the brigade, battalion and division colors, Soldiers assigned to the 1st Cavalry Division Horse Detachment perform a cavalry charge accompanied by a helicopter flyover performed by the 1st Cavalry Division Air Cavalry Brigade at Fort Hood, Texas, Dec. 12, 2008. U.S. Army photo by Pfc. Phillip Turner.

Reapers Unit, B/227th. Courtesy of Carl Fox.

1st Cavalry Division

1921-2017

Acclaim Press
MORLEY, MISSOURI

1st Cav (Airmobile) insertion, Vietnam. Courtesy of Walter C. Smith.

Acclaim Press
— Your Next Great Book —

P.O. Box 238
Morley, MO 63767
(573) 472-9800
www.acclaimpress.com

1st Cavalry Division Association Liaison: 1SG (Ret) Dara Wydler
Publishing Consultant: Duane A. Sikes
Editor: Randy Baumgardner
Book Design: Ron Eifert
Cover Design: M. Frene Melton

ISBN: 978-1-942613-80-0 | 1-942613-80-6
Library of Congress Control Number: 2017913878

First Printing: 2017
Printed in the United States of America
10 9 8 7 6 5 4 3 2 1

Contents

This history book is dedicated to the 10,921 men and women of the 1st Cavalry Division who unselfishly gave their lives in the name of freedom and to the Families and Friends who keep their memories alive.

Letter from the Association President

1st Cavalry Division Association

As we publish this History of the 1st Cavalry Division and its Veterans containing the names, stories, and photos of our members, we have several teams involved in this undertaking. This is your history and much to be proud of is contained in these pages.

First, I want to congratulate our publisher, Acclaim Press, for preserving our history and bringing it to print. When they brought this proposal to the Association and our Board of Governors, Duane Sikes of Acclaim Press answered the many questions about why we would want to do this project. Their insight and support for this undertaking was evident throughout this work. Additionally, our submissions were hand written and most of our handwriting defies imagination and requires an interpreter. Acclaim Press labored to transform our writing and properly relate our words to the presentation. We salute your team and say, "Thank You, Acclaim Press!" We also recognize Duane and Zelma Sikes of Acclaim Press, who spent so much time with us gathering our stories and convincing us that they were important to this venture. They visited our 2017 Reunion in Texas and were always available to speak with the members, encouraging everyone to submit their information because it was important. We enjoyed our time with both of them, especially watching them with our Veterans as they listened to their stories and convinced them to elaborate on some items for their submissions. The success of this book is a credit to their outgoing personalities in bringing these personal life travels to print.

I would be remiss not to thank our Veterans for this publication. This history would not be what it is without you and your memories. You made the First Team what it has become today with your willingness to bring these stories to life, detailing each of your experiences, and allowing others to see what we saw firsthand. I thank you for searching the very essence of your being in relating the excitement, and the sorrow, you keep in special places. Thank you for opening your hearts and sharing our history together.

Lastly, I want to thank our 1st Cavalry Division Association staff. They have been responsible for handling the many questions you have had in both "When will the book be available?" and "Why is it taking so long?" In addition to conducting their daily duties, they were essential in securing the Division's history and getting our stories presented to the publisher. The final publishing of this history is a testament to their devotion to the Veterans of the Association in all aspects of their performance. We all can be proud of this work.

Sincerely,
Allen O. Norris
President, 1st Cavalry Division Association

1ST CAVALRY DIVISION INSIGNIA

1st Cavalry Division Shoulder Sleeve Insignia

Description — On a yellow triangular Norman shield with rounded corners 5 1/4 inches (13.34 cm) in height overall, a black diagonal stripe extending over the shield from upper left to lower right and in the upper right a black horse's head cut off diagonally at the neck all within a 1/8 inch (.32 cm) green border.

Symbolism — The color yellow, the traditional Cavalry color, and the horse's head refer to the Division's original Cavalry structure. Black, symbolic of iron, alludes to the transition to tanks and armor. The black diagonal stripe represents a sword baldric and is a mark of military honor; it also implies movement "up the field" and thus symbolizes aggressive élan and attack. The one diagonal bend, as well as the one horse's head, also alludes to the Division's numerical designation.

Background — The shoulder sleeve insignia was originally approved for the 1st Cavalry Division on 3 January 1921, with several variations in colors of the bend and horse's head to reflect the subordinate elements of the division. The current design was authorized for wear by all subordinate elements of the Division on 11 December 1934, and previous authorization for the variations was cancelled. The insignia was redesignated for the 1st Air Cavalry Division on 5 August 1968. It was redesignated for 1st Cavalry Division (Airmobile) on 10 September 1968. The insignia was redesignated for the 1st Cavalry Division on 24 May 1971.

1st Cavalry Division Combat Service Identification Badge

Description — A gold color metal and enamel device 2 inches (5.08 cm) in height consisting of a design similar to the shoulder sleeve insignia.

Distinctive Unit Insignia

Description — A metal and enameled device 1 inch (2.54 cm) in height overall consisting of a gold colored Norman shield with a black horse's head couped in sinister chief, and a black bend charged with two five-pointed stars.

Symbolism — The device is a miniature reproduction of the 1st Cavalry Division's shoulder sleeve insignia with the addition of two five-pointed stars. The Division Commander and the Division Staff wore the distinctive insignia design from 1922 to 1934 as a shoulder sleeve insignia.

Background — The distinctive unit insignia was originally approved for the 1st Cavalry Division on 25 August 1965. It was redesignated for the 1st Air Cavalry Division on 5 August 1968. It was redesignated for the 1st Cavalry Division (Airmobile) on 10 September 1968. The insignia was redesignated for the 1st Cavalry Division on 24 May 1971.

"The big yellow patch does something to an individual that makes him a better Soldier, a better team member, and a better American than he otherwise would have been."
—General Creighton Abrams, while commander of all U.S. Forces in Southeast Asia

"Wearing the largest patch in the Army inventory also brings with it a responsibility to be the best."
—General Peter Chiarelli at his change of command.

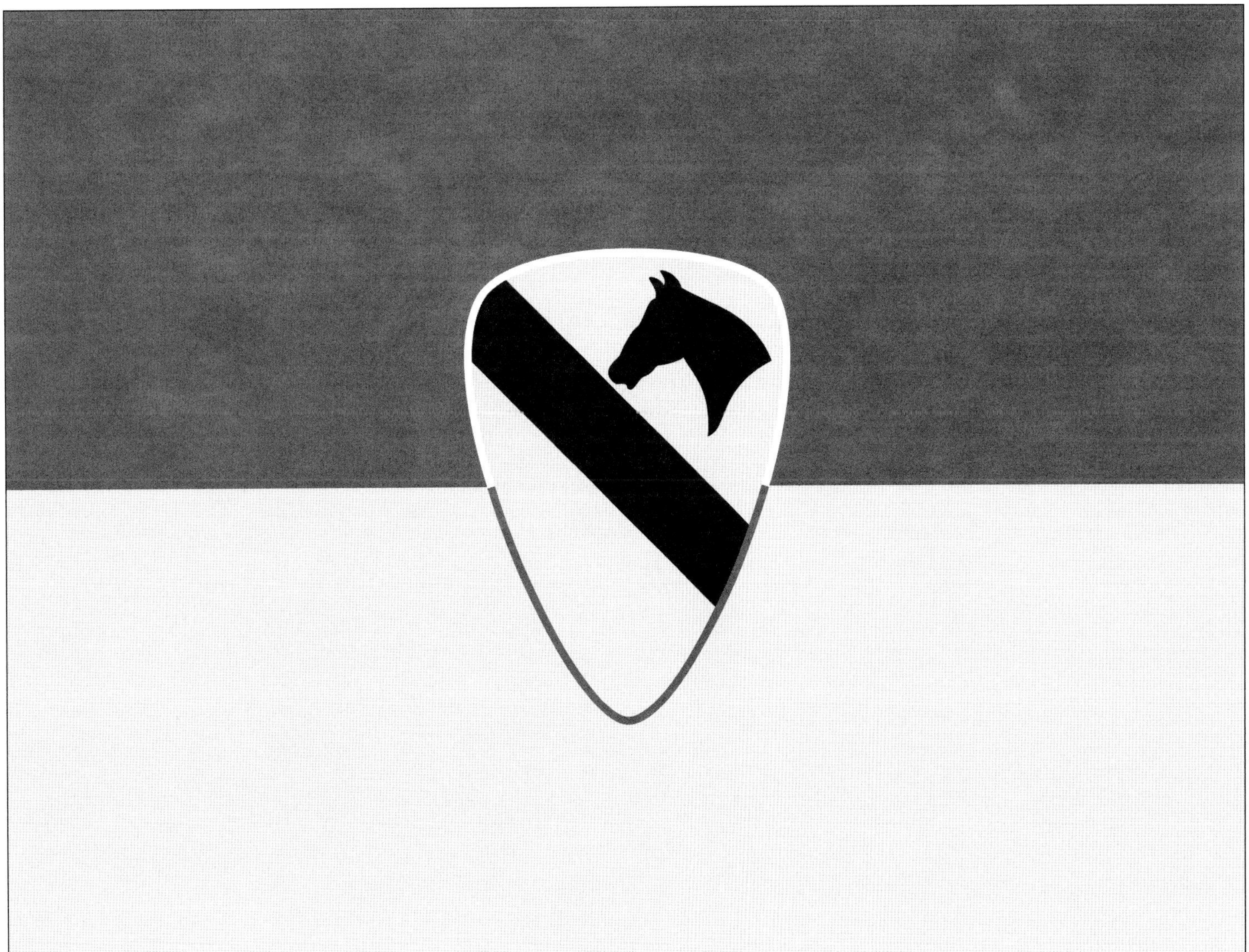

LINEAGE AND HONORS OF THE 1ST CAVALRY DIVISION AS OF 25 MAY 2011

HEADQUARTERS AND HEADQUARTERS BATTALION, 1ST CAVALRY DIVISION (THE FIRST TEAM)

LINEAGE

Constituted 20 August 1921 in the Regular Army as Headquarters, 1st Cavalry Division.

Activated 13 September 1921 at Fort Bliss, Texas

Reorganized and redesignated 4 December 1943 as Headquarters, 1st Cavalry Division, Special

Reorganized and redesignated 25 March 1949 as Headquarters, 1st Cavalry Division (Infantry)

Reorganized and redesignated 1 July 1960 as Headquarters and Headquarters Company, 1st Cavalry Division

Reorganized and redesignated 16 October 2005 as Headquarters and Tactical Command Posts, 1st Cavalry Division

Reorganized and redesignated 16 April 2010 as Headquarters and Headquarters Battalion, 1st Cavalry Division

CAMPAIGN PARTICIPATION CREDIT

World War II
New Guinea
Bismarck Archipelago
Leyte (with arrowhead)
Luzon

Korean War
UN Defensive
UN Offensive
CCF Intervention
First UN Counteroffensive
CCF Spring Offensive
UN Summer-Fall Offensive
Second Korean Winter

Vietnam War
Defense
Counteroffensive
Counteroffensive, Phase II
Counteroffensive, Phase III
Tet Counteroffensive
Counteroffensive, Phase IV
Counteroffensive, Phase V
Counteroffensive, Phase VI
Tet 69/Counteroffensive
Summer-Fall 1969
Winter-Spring 1970
Sanctuary Counteroffensive
Counteroffensive, Phase VII

Southwest Asia
Defense of Saudi Arabia
Liberation and Defense of Kuwait

War on Terrorism
Iraq
Transition of Iraq
Iraqi Governance
Afghanistan

DECORATIONS

- Presidential Unit Citation (Army), Streamer embroidered PLEIKU PROVINCE
- Valorous Unit Award, Streamer embroidered FISH HOOK
- Meritorious Unit Commendation (Army), Streamer embroidered SOUTHWEST ASIA 1990-1991
- Meritorious Unit Commendation (Army), Streamer embroidered IRAQ 2009-2010
- Philippine Presidential Unit Citation, Streamer embroidered 17 OCTOBER 1944 TO 4 JULY 1945
- Republic of Korea Presidential Unit Citation, Streamer embroidered WAEGWAN-TEAGU
- Chryssoun Aristion Andrias (Bravery Gold Medal of Greece), Streamer embroidered KOREA
- Republic of Vietnam Cross of Gallantry with Palm, Streamer embroidered VIETNAM 1965-1969
- Republic of Vietnam Cross of Gallantry with Palm, Streamer embroidered VIETNAM 1969-1970
- Republic of Vietnam Cross of Gallantry with Palm, Streamer embroidered VIETNAM 1970-1971
- Republic of Vietnam Civil Action Honor Medal, First Class, Streamer embroidered VIETNAM 1969-1970

HAT & SPURS

The same MOI that covers the "Cav Hat" covers the qualifications required for the present troopers of the First Team to "earn their spurs" and also describes the spurs authorized for wear and how to wear them. Many veterans of the First Team will have no remembrance of earning their spurs since most of the unit spur programs came into being after the Division arrived at Fort Hood. Those troopers that rode horses in West Texas with the Division and rode horses earned their spurs learning to be a horse cavalry trooper. Those troopers that have been fortunate enough to serve in the Horse Cavalry Detachment have been earning the right to wear spurs for many years.

The Division's MOI states, "The 'Order of the Spur' will not be awarded to any Trooper based on arbitrary or meritless criteria such as rank, time in service, branch, and ability to endure hazing or other degrading behavior. Rather, Troopers must be in good standing within their formation (i.e. have no incidents of misconduct, record of adverse actions, or failures in obtaining basic Army standards) and then 'earn' the right to wear Cavalry Spurs through their demonstrated proficiency at both technical and tactical skills expected of Troopers assigned to the Division." Troopers may lose their right to wear spurs if they "fail to remain in good standing such as demonstrating an act of indiscipline." The Troopers are awarded a certificate and are able to wear 'Silver Spurs' once they have completed the Spur Ride (test) and been approved.

Those who have earned their spurs may also be awarded "Combat Spurs" if they conduct at least two combat patrols or missions outside of the Forward Operating Base, Combat Outpost, or camp. Being flown from one secure location to another does not constitute a patrol, but does apply to pilots or air crewman with the primary duty of flying combat missions. Combat Spurs are "Gold Spurs," while those earned in peacetime are "Silver Spurs." Neither the Silver nor the Gold Spur is more prestigious than the other. The wearer may wear either color, but the spurs being worn must match.

When are the Spurs Appropriate for Wear?

The answer to that question is whenever you are wearing a "Cav Hat" or riding a horse — unless you are presently an active duty Trooper. Active duty Troopers are bound by uniform policies, and wearing of the Spurs is covered in the Memorandum of Instruction. All former Cav Troopers may wear their Spurs at their own pleasure, but are encouraged to wear them to all gatherings of Cavalry veterans and unit reunions. The "Cav Hat" is always appropriate at patriotic observances like Veterans Day, Independence Day and Memorial Day. As with the "Cav Hat," never wear your Spurs in circumstances that would bring discredit to the Cavalry or your unit.

When is a "Cav Hat" Appropriate for Wear?

The answer to that question is always — unless you are presently an active duty Trooper. Active duty Troopers are bound by uniform policies and wear of the "Cav Hat" is covered in the MOI. All former Cav Troopers may wear their "Cav Hat" at their own pleasure, but are encouraged to wear them to all gatherings of Cavalry veterans and unit reunions. The "Cav Hat" is always appropriate at patriotic observances like Veterans Day, Independence Day, and Memorial Day. Of course, never wear your "Cav Hat" in circumstances that would bring discredit to the Cavalry or your unit.

Cavalry Traditions

The tradition of the "Cav Hat" began in the early days before the Vietnam War. The 11th Air Assault Division cavalry scout pilots were looking to distinguish themselves from other troops when they adopted the Model 1876 campaign hat for wear. They felt a need to return to the traditions of the Cavalry so long forgotten. LTC John B. Stockton, commander of the 3rd Battalion, 17th Cavalry Regiment, is given credit for establishing the tradition of wearing the Cavalry Stetson, much to the chagrin of the Division

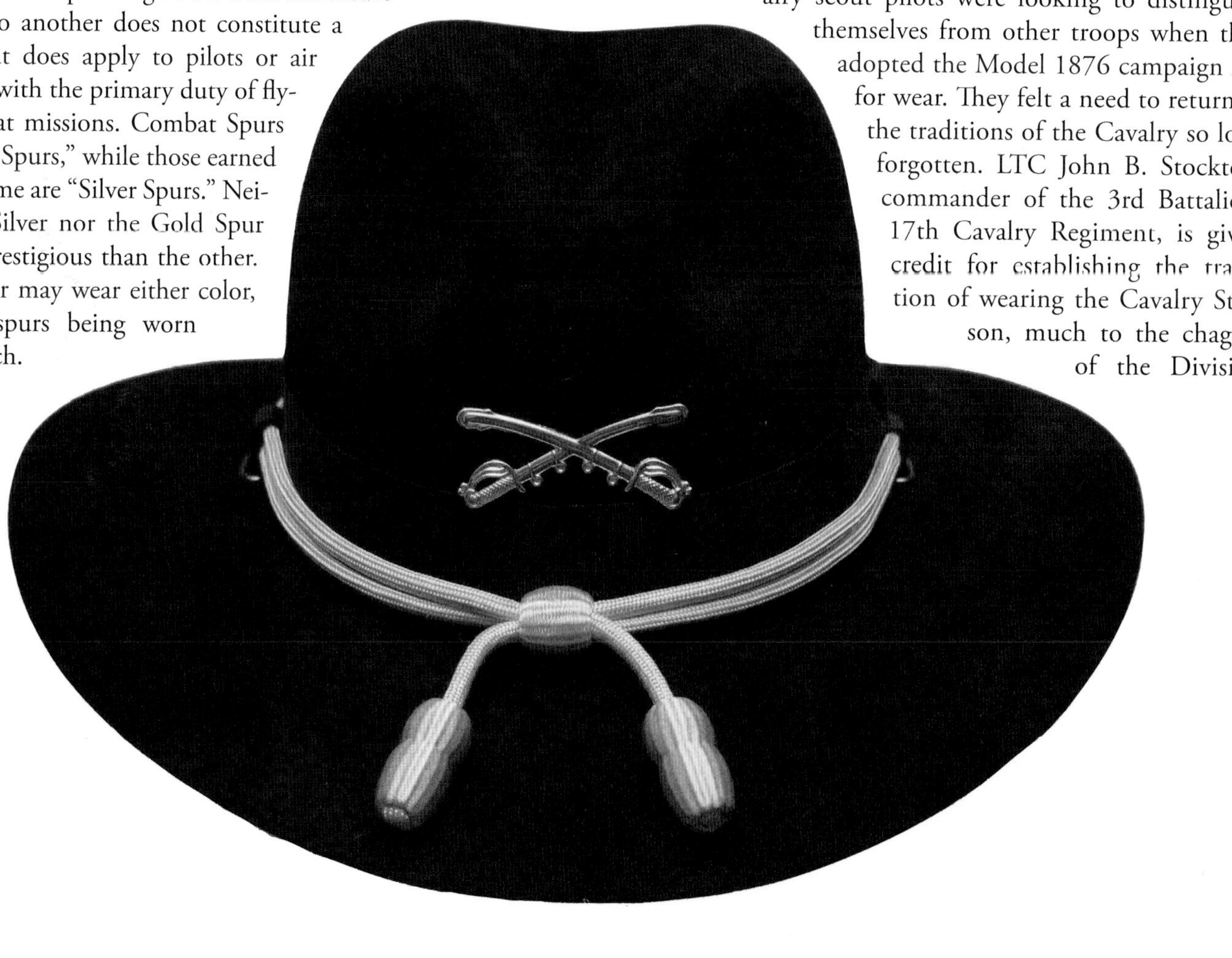

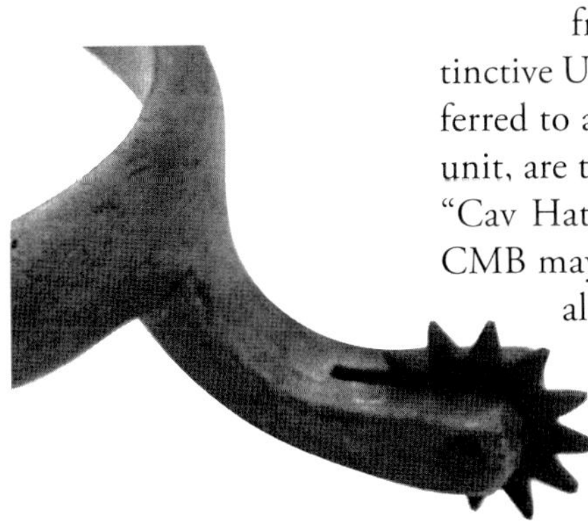

command group. By the time the 11th Air Assault Division was redesignated as the 1st Cavalry Division (Airmobile), the members of his unit, the 1st Squadron of the 9th Cavalry Regiment, were wearing the hat. LTC Stockton transferred the "Cav Hat" tradition to the 1st Cavalry Division in Vietnam. By the end of the Vietnam War, many air and ground units were wearing the hat. The tradition was continued after Vietnam and has become the standard for all cavalry units in the Army.

The "Cav Hat" is not an issued item and it is not covered in any of the uniform regulations. However, the Troopers of the 1st Cavalry Division, and many other cavalry units, wear it for ceremonies and special cavalry events. The type and number of items worn on the "Cav Hat" vary greatly and demonstrate the individuality and style of the wearer. The 1st Cavalry Division has published a Memorandum of Instruction (MOI) that covers the wearing of the "Cav Hat" and spurs for those currently serving with the First Team, but for veterans the MOI is only a guideline of what right looks like. A link to the MOI is provided on the 1st Cavalry Division Association web page.

The "Cav Hat" is a standard black Cavalry hat, Stetson, or other appropriate brand, with a 3-inch brim and a black leather chinstrap. The chinstrap is fastened to the hat cord and goes through the brim. The chinstrap is worn behind the wearer's head unless mounted. When mounted the chinstrap may be worn under the chin to maintain the hat's position on your head and keep it from falling off. If your "Cav Hat" does not have a chinstrap, it is just a black hat commonly referred to as a "cowboy hat."

Hat cords are worn and represent the rank of the wearer. General officers wear solid gold cords, field and company grade officers wear black and gold hat cords, warrant officers wear black and silver hat cords, and enlisted troopers wear Cavalry yellow hat cords. The hat cords should be adjusted so that the acorn on the ends of the cord comes to the edge of the brim. Cords may be knotted if the wearer wishes. While many refer to the knots in the cords as "combat knots," there is no documentation available to support this idea. The Division MOI prohibits any other type of hat cords for those troopers currently on active duty with the 1st Cavalry Division.

Normally, the branch insignia of the Cavalry, crossed sabers, are worn on the front along with the rank of the wearer. The rank is worn above the branch insignia evenly spaced. Both are centered on the front of the hat. Regular sized Distinctive Unit Insignias (DUI), commonly referred to as unit crests or miniatures of your unit, are traditionally put on the back of the "Cav Hat." Additional items like a CIB or CMB may also be placed on the "Cav Hat," along with reunion pins or other items, if you are a veteran. Some of the "Cav Hats" worn by our veterans are festooned with numerous pins, miniature medals, and other items. Active Duty Troopers assigned to the First Team must follow the guidelines of the MOI.

While Cavalry is not the oldest branch in the Army, it is a branch steeped in history, tradition, and colorful tales of daring. The flash of a saber in the sunlight, the bugler sounding the charge, a red and white guidon flapping in the breeze, and the thunder of horses hooves pounding the ground come to mind when one thinks of Cavalry. The tales of Cavalry troopers told in books and movies and the brisk tune of "Garryowen" remind us of the dust covered troopers on horseback and the dashing officers with bold ideas and tactics that turned the tide of battle. In all of these things, the Cav trooper, with his Cavalry Hat (Stetson) and Spurs, stands out as the epitome of excellence. A heroic figure with ties to the history of our nation and a focus on the future greatness yet to come.

What follows is a history of the "Cav Hat" and the Spurs that each Cavalry Trooper of today strives to attain. Not only because they look good, but also they strive for the recognition of excellence that marks those that wear the Cavalry Hat and wear Spurs earned by test and in battle.

> "The tradition of awarding spurs has its roots in knighthood, where the awarding of spurs symbolized entry into the ranks - and fraternity - of mounted warriors. Usually the squire aspiring to knighthood had to perform some task or deed on the battlefield or tournament field (tournaments were considered like our training maneuvers) to "win their spurs." The spurs themselves where buckled on during the investiture to knighthood, usually during a Mass or some other religious ceremony (Knighthood itself was considered sacramental, if not a sacrament itself). Thereafter, it was the spurs that symbolized that a man was a knight - not his sword, horse, or armor. No matter how financially destitute, a poor knight would

part with everything else before his spurs. The primary act of degradation (removing someone from the knightly class) was to have another knight cut off the offending knight's spurs. So much for the mists of time.... It is not known when the ceremony for awarding spurs for outstanding performance started in the U.S. Cavalry. Today, the Order of the Spur recognizes individual qualifications for those in a Cavalry unit. The privilege of being awarded spurs in any Cavalry unit comes with hard work and challenges. For an individual to qualify and compete for the Order of the Spur within the unit, the Cavalry Soldier must first meet or exceed established standards of performance. Once documented as having achieved the performance objectives, the candidate is designated to participate in the Spur Ride exercise. This exercise requires completion of numerous additional tasks. Upon successful accomplishment of the requirements, the senior officer awards the spurs to be proudly worn throughout the trooper's Cavalry career."

—*Source: The cover liner of the book,* 1st Cavalry Division - A Spur Ride Through the 20th Century, "From Horses to the Digital Battlefield".

Division MOI 29 Feb 2016

Troopers may purchase Spurs anywhere that sells them, but we strongly recommend that you purchase your Spurs from the Crossed Sabers Souvenir Shop, located in the 1st Cavalry Division Museum at Fort Hood, Texas. For those of you that live elsewhere, the Souvenir Shop has an online catalog (http://www.crossedsabers-chapter-giftshop.com/) and you can order your Spurs from them and have them shipped to your home. The Crossed Sabers Souvenir Shop sells the Prince of Wales Spur in both silver and gold color. Spurs come with black straps. Tan straps may be ordered separately.

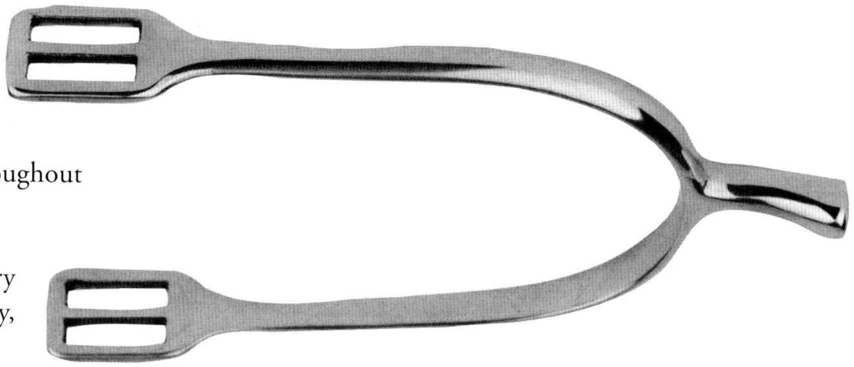

Another proud day at Fort Hood as these Troopers get their spurs!

COMMANDING GENERALS OF THE 1ST CAVALRY DIVISION

The 1st Cavalry Division was formed at Fort Bliss, Texas on 13 September 1921 and is normally commanded by a Major General (MG). The listing below includes those officers, which served in an interim position and normally only for a very short period

MG Robert L. Howze 1921-1925
BG Joseph C. Castner 1925-1926
MG Edwin B. Winans 1926-1927
BG Samuel D. Rockenback 1927
MG G. Van Horn Moseley 1927-1929
BG Charles J. Symmonds 1929-1930
BG George C. Barnhardt 1930
MG Ewing E. Booth 1930-1932
BG Walter C. Short 1932-1933
MG Frank R. McCoy 1933
BG Walter C. Short 1933-1934
BG Hamilton S. Hawkins 1934-1936
BG George Vidmer 1936
BG Francis LeJ. Parker 1936
MG Ben Lear 1936-1938
MG Kenyon A. Joyce 1938-1940
MG Robert C. Richardson, Jr. 1940-1941
MG Innis Palmer Swift 1941-1944
MG Verne D. Mudge 1944-1945
BG Hugh F. T. Hoffman 1945
MG William C. Chase 1945-1949
BG William B. Bradford 1949
MG John M. Devine 1949
BG Henry I. Hodes 1949
MG Hobart R. Gay 1949-1951
MG Charles D. Palmer 1951
MG Thomas L. Harrold 1951-1952
MG Arthur G. Trudeau 1952-1953
BG William J. Bradley 1953
MG Joseph P. Cleland 1953
MG Armistead D. Mead 1953-1954
BG Orlando C. Troxel, Jr. 1954-1955
MG Edward J. McGaw 1955-1956
MG Edwin H. J. Carns 1956-1957
MG Ralph W. Zwicker 1957-1958
MG George E. Bush 1958-1959
MG Charles E. Beauchamp 1959-1960
MG Charles G. Dodge 1960
MG Frank H. Britton 1960-1961
MG James K. Woolnough 1961-1962
BG D. C. Clayman 1962
MG Clifton F. von Kann 1962-1963
BG Charles P. Brown 1963
MG Charles F. Leonard, Jr. 1963-1964
MG Hugh Exton 1964-1965
MG Harry W. O. Kinnard 1965-1966
MG John Norton 1966-1967
MG John J. Tolson 1967-1968
BG Richard L. Irby 1968

MG George I. Forsythe 1968-1969
MG Elvy B. Roberts 1969-1970
MG George W. Casey 1970
MG George W. Putnam 1970-1971
MG James C. Smith 1971-1973
MG Robert M. Shoemaker 1973-1975
MG Julius W. Becton, Jr. 1975-1976
MG W. Russell Todd 1976-1978
MG Paul S. Williams, Jr. 1978-1980
MG Richard D. Lawrence 1980-1982
MG Andrew P. Chambers 1982-1984
MG Michael J. Conrad 1984-1986
MG John J. Yeosock 1986-1988
MG William F. Streeter 1988-1990
MG John H. Tilelli, Jr. 1990-1992
MG Wesley K. Clark 1992-1994
MG Eric K. Shinseki 1994-1995
MG Leon J. LaPorte 1995-1997
MG Kevin P. Byrnes 1997-1999
MG David D. McKiernan 1999-2001
MG Joseph F. H. Peterson 2001-2003
MG Peter W. Chiarelli 2003-2005
MG Joseph F. Fil, Jr. 2005-2008
BG Vincent K. Brooks 2008
MG Daniel P. Bolger 2008-2010
MG Daniel B. Allyn 2010-2012
MG Anthony R. Ierardi 2012-2014
MG Michael A. Bills 2014-2016
MG John C. Thomson, III 2016-2017

Major General Robert L. Howze

Major General John C. Thomson III

COMMAND SERGEANT MAJORS OF THE 1ST CAVALRY DIVISION

The position of Command Sergeant Major was not established until July 1967. Prior to that time the senior enlisted rank was Sergeant Major. While units were assigned a Sergeant Major, records often do not indicate the name of the Sergeant Major. The list attempts to identify the names of the senior enlisted Soldier of the 1st Cavalry Division. Dates from many of the sergeants major listed may be inaccurate and anyone that has documentation that can provide more accurate data should contact the 1st Cavalry Division Association.

CSM Chester R. Westervelt	July 1965 - June 1966
CSM Kenneth W. Cooper	June 1966 - July 1967
CSM William O. Marshall	July 1967 - May 1968
CSM Jack B. Moore	May 1968 - October 1968
CSM Vern O. Peters	October 1968 - April 1969
CSM Lawrence Kennedy	April 1969 - April 1970
CSM Kenneth W. Cooper	April 1970 - July 1970
Unknown (1st Brigade CSM) *	July 1970 - May 1971 (in Vietnam)
CSM Arnold E. Orr	May 1971 - January 1972 (Fort Hood)
CSM William Corn	January 1972 - July 1973
CSM Homer R. Moss	July 1973 - January 1975
CSM Walter W. Krueger	February 1975 - November 1977
CSM Douglas B. Hayes	November 1977 - February 1983
CSM Kenneth E. Parsons	February 1983 - July 1983
CSM Delbert O. Jennings	July 1983 - February 1985
CSM A. C. Cotton	February 1985 - November 1988
CSM Robert E. Wilson	November 1988 - February 1991
CSM Gilbert Paez	February 1991 - July 1992
CSM Charles M. Gee	July 1992 - November 1994
CSM Johnny D. Duncan	November 1994 - December 1995
CSM Dennis E. Webster	January 1996 - August 1998
CSM Paul M. Inman	August 1998 - April 2001
CSM John D. Sparks	June 2001 - February 2003
CSM Richard Hernandez	February 2003 - June 2004
CSM Gerald R. Schindler**	June 2004 - August 2004
CSM Neil L. Ciotola	August 2004 - October 2005
CSM Donald R. Sanders**	October 2005 - March 2006
CSM Philip F. Johndrow	March 2006 - April 2008
CSM Donald Felt**	April 2008 - June 2008
CSM Rory L. Malloy	June 2008 - April 2011
CSM Isaia T. Vimoto	April 2011 - July 2012
CSM James P. Norman, III	August 2012 - September 2013
CSM Andrew L. Barteky	November 2013 - November 2015
CSM Maurice Jackson	November 2015 - October 2017

*The death of CSM Cooper along with the death of MG Casey resulted in the appointment of the 1st Brigade CSM to fill the position until a replacement could be identified and assigned. This sergeant major's name is unknown.

**Interim – Served in position pending the selection and assignment of a new Division Sergeant Major, received an evaluation report for time in position.

History of the 1st Cavalry Division Band

The Early Years, 1855 – 1921

On 3 March 1855, one of the oldest units in the 1st Cavalry Division, the 1st Cavalry Band was constituted in the Second Regiment of Cavalry. Later in the year, in December, the unit was organized at Camp Verde, Texas. The band, assigned to the 2nd Cavalry Regiment, spent several years in Texas. With the Civil War on the horizon, on 29 March 1861, the Band along with the 2nd Cavalry Regiment left their last post in Texas, Fort Mason, which was turned over to the Texas Confederate Authorities.

Arriving at their destination of Carlisle Barracks, Pennsylvania, the 2nd Cavalry Regiment was reorganized with new officers and recruits and was assigned to the Union "Army of the Potomac" that was organized under General George McClellen. The band members, as infantrymen, fought its first battle of the Civil War and its last designated as the 2nd Cavalry Regiment, at the first Battle of Bull Run (1st Manassas) on 21 July 1861. By an act of congress, dated 3 August 1861, and a general order, dated 10 August 1861, the 2nd US Cavalry Regiment was reorganized and, along with the Band, was redesignated as the 5th U.S. Cavalry Regiment.

Reorganized as the 5th Cavalry Regiment Band, it supported the regiment throughout the war. In December 1866, following the end of the Civil War, the Band was disbanded at Camp Sedgwick, Washington, DC. Three years later, in 1869, the band was reconstituted, reorganized, and remained assigned to the 5th Cavalry Regiment. It again participated in the Indian Wars (1869-77) against the Sioux, Cheyenne, Utes, and Apache. In 1916, the band participated in General Pershing's Mexican Expeditionary Force.

Following the organization of the 1st Cavalry Division in 1921, the Band would not become a member until 18 December 1922, when the 5th Cavalry Regiment (and its Band) was assigned to the Division, relieving the 10th Cavalry Regiment.

World War II, 1941 – 1945

The band remained with the 5th Cavalry Regiment until 3 June 1945, when it was reorganized into its modern form, using the battle-scarred remains of three regimental bands: the 5th Cavalry Regimental Band, the 7th Cavalry Regimental Band, and the 1st Cavalry Division Artillery Band. It remained assigned to the 1st Cavalry Division and the primary station of the band was Camp Drake, outside Tokyo, Japan. In keeping with a long tradition of wartime service, the new 1st Cavalry Division Band served at several different posts. While enhancing morale, the band promoted American popular music to both US Troops and the Japanese during the post-war occupational period.

Korean War, 1950 – 1952

It happened before dawn on 25 June 1950. Less than 5 years after the terrible devastations of World War II, a new war broke out from a distant land whose name means "Morning Calm". On 18 July, the 1st Cavalry Division was ordered to Korea. The band followed the 1st Cavalry Division to Korea, setting aside their musical instruments to fight as infantrymen as they had done in previous wars. By December 1951, the Division, after 549 days of continuous fighting, began planning for rotation back to Hokkaido, Japan.

Return to Japan, 1952 – 1957

The band, along with the First Team returned to the northern island of Japan, Hokkaido, and was stationed outside Sapporo, the capital city of the island, at Camp Crawford with its steam heated, red brick barracks. Camp Crawford had been constructed in 1946 on the location of the Makomanai National Dairy, which was the largest dairy farm in Japan operated by the Japanese Agricultural Ministry. A highlight of the band was its presentation of "Jazz on Parade," which was given on tours to military bases in Hokkaido. On two occasions, the band combined forces with a local Japanese band to give a large concert for the local townsfolk. In October 1953, the band Table of Organization was downsized from the authorized 96 to 48 troopers. The surplus band members were transferred to the 5th, 7th, and 8th Regiments and were allowed to form a Drum and Bugle Corps, which represented the Regiments at various functions. In July 1954, the Band, in line with their alternate security mission of the Division, was assigned a secondary mission as a Smoke Generator Unit.

In 1954, the Japanese assumed responsibility for defending Hokkaido and on 13 September, the 1st Cavalry Division, with the band, returned to the main Island of Honshu, Japan. Its new duty station was Camp Schimmelpfennig, Sandai, Japan. In February 1956, the band was relieved of its smoke generation duties. On 14 March 1956, the 1st Cavalry Band moved to its new duty station at Camp Drake, outside of Tokyo, Japan. Soon afterwards, on 4 May 1956, the band absorbed the members of the deactivated 293rd Army Band. In addition to its primary duty, the band was assigned the mission of Defense Platoon of Headquarters, 1st Cavalry Division, which it held until May 1957.

On 26 June 1956, a Provisional Unit of 12 band members was constituted to supply music for Armed Service personnel arriving and departing at the Port of Yokohama. In April 1957, this contingent returned to the main unit at Camp Drake. Throughout its duty in Japan, the 1st Cavalry Band performed many concerts and parades dedicated to strengthening relations between the occupying Americans and the Japanese. On 20 August 1957, the Band, along with the 1st Cavalry Division transferred to Korea. In the subsequent reorganization, the 1st Cavalry Division Band was assigned under the command of the "Trains," a unified concept of divisional support.

Demilitarized Zone, 1957 – 1965

When reorganizing the Regular Army Infantry and Armored Divisions in 1957, under the changing world conditions, several changes were necessary in the force levels to accommodate a reduction of 100,000 Soldiers. In the Far East, the United States agreed to withdraw all ground troops from Japan.

Specifically, as these changes were applied on 15 October in ceremonies held in Tonggu, Korea, the colors of the 24th Infantry Division were retired and the colors of the 1st Cavalry Division were passed to the Commanding General of the former 24th Infantry Division, Major General Ralph W. Zwicker. "The First Team" had returned, standing ready to defend Korea against Communist aggression.

On 1 September 1963, the Division Band was consolidated with the 1st Cavalry Division Trains and the Trains were redesignated as Headquarters, Headquarters Company and Band, 1st Cavalry Division Support Command. In June 1965, the Division Support Command and its subordinate units began rotation back to the United States along with other units of the 1st Cavalry Division.

Vietnam War, 1965 – 1972

The 1st Cavalry Division went home, but only long enough to be reorganized and be prepared for a new mission. On 3 July 1965, in Doughboy Stadium at Fort Benning, Georgia, the colors of the 11th Air Assault Division (Test) were cased and retired. As the band played the rousing strains of Garryowen, the colors of the 1st Cavalry Division were moved onto the field. As part of the reorganization, the Headquarters and Headquarters Company and Band, 11th Air Assault Division Support Command was redesignated as Headquarters, Headquarters Company and Band, 1st Cavalry Division, Support Command.

In 1965, the Support Command accompanied the 1st Cavalry Division when it was deployed to Vietnam, arriving on 12 September. The band continued in its multitask of being musicians and infantryman as in previous wars. In November 1969, the band was giving one of its firebase concerts, which were designed to give variety and entertainment to the otherwise repetitive days of jungle outposts. Upon being fired on, from the

nearby jungle, the band had to drop their instruments and take up their M-16s. Following the firefight, they returned to continue their concert.

26 March 1971 officially marked the end of duties in Vietnam for the majority of the 1st Cavalry Division. On 29 April, the Band along with the Division Support Command departed Vietnam for Fort Hood, Texas.

TriCap to Armor, 1971 – 1990

In the fall of 1983, the 1st Cavalry Division deployed to Europe for the annual Return of Forces to Germany (REFORGER) exercises. The band accompanied the division to Germany for REFORGER '83 and REFORGER '87. During these two large-scale exercises, the band served the division by promoting Esprit de Corps throughout Germany and the Netherlands.

Persian Gulf War, 1990 – 1991

In August 1990, the 1st Cavalry Division was alerted for deployment to Southwest Asia as part of the joint forces participating in Operation Desert Shield. The focus at that time was the defense of Saudi Arabia against potential Iraqi attack. In Octo-

ber 1990, the Band accompanied the Division when it deployed in support of Desert Shield.

Upon the return of the 1st Cavalry Division to the United States, the band joined in leading the whirlwind celebrations by parading down a dozen avenues of Atlanta, Houston, Dallas, Washington, D.C., and New York. The visit to New York City was a tremendous welcome from the public, press, and police.

At Battery Park, the parade formation turned into Broadway, a wide red carpet. There on Broadway, under a sunlit snowstorm of paper, the 1st Cavalry Division Band, lead by Bandmaster SFC Gary Flake, took the Big Apple by storm when they played the swaggering melody of the division song, "Garryowen".

Bosnia Peacekeepers, 1998 – 1999

In November 1989, a detachment of the Cavalry Division Band from Fort Hood, Texas, deployed to Bosnia to provide musical entertainment for the troopers of the division and the citizens at the Bosnian Cultural Center in Tuzla. The three-month tour of the band in Bosnia included a series of concerts for SFOR Soldiers and citizens. The 39-member band delighted their audiences with a musical sampling of rock-n-roll, Dixieland, country western, and classical music. In addition, the holiday concerts included combined performances with the Turkish and Russian military bands.

At Christmas, the brass players performed tree lighting ceremony at the 1st Cavalry Division Headquarters, complete with Santa Claus in a Hummer and a bag full of gifts. After the ceremony, the band, trading their battle dress uniforms for "dress blues", held a concert for MG Byrnes and the staff. Throughout the tour and at all the concerts, the band served the division well by promoting Esprit de Corps throughout Bosnia.

Iraqi Freedom and Operation Enduring Freedom, 2003 – 2012

Since the War on Terror began, the 1st Cavalry Division Band has deployed to Iraq three times as part of Operation Iraqi Freedom (OIF), and to Afghanistan once, as part of Operation Enduring Freedom (OEF). The band deployed with the 1st Cavalry Division during OIF II, where they performed over 550 missions. The band again deployed with the Division to Iraq in support of OIF 06-08 where they surpassed the number of missions from the previous deployment. The Cavalry Band deployed again to Iraq for OIF 09-10 and deployed to Afghanistan in 2011 in support of OEF, returning to Fort Hood in 2012.

Today's First Team Band

Stationed at Fort Hood, Texas, the 1st Cavalry Division Band is comprised of 61 Soldier-musicians who perform regularly in concert and ceremonial bands on Fort Hood, throughout Central Texas, and in nationally televised events.

The First Team Band is a modern professional organization equipped to perform a variety of music, including marches, pop tunes, top 40, big band jazz, and concert band literature. Within the organization there are several small ensembles, such as the jazz combo brass quintet and woodwind quintet, each increasing the variety of music that is performed by the band. The mission of the band is threefold: 1.) To promote morale and Esprit de Corps throughout the division and Fort Hood by providing traditional music for military ceremonies and special events; 2.) To enhance community relations through participation in the local community events throughout the Central Texas area; and 3.) To enhance recruiting efforts of the U.S. Army.

The 1st Cavalry Division Band, over its history, has distinguished itself in combat and in the performance of its mission in garrison. Its success is due to the hard charging spirit of the men and women who serve in it. The First Team Band continues to promote the traditions and Spirit of the Cavalry wherever it performs.

Information compiled and composed by William H. Boudreau. Edited to update changes in the Band's history by the Association staff.

Garryowen

"Garryowen" is an old Irish quick-step that can be traced back to the early 1860s. The Regimental Song "Garryowen" came informally into the Army between 1861 and 1866 as a quickstep, but its use was first documented in 1867 when "Garryowen" was adopted by the 7th US Cavalry Regiment as the official Air (tune) of the Regiment, and the historical nickname given to the 7th Cavalry Regiment and troopers. As it is generally portrayed, George Armstrong Custer did not, himself, bring the song to the regiment, but Brevet Lieutenant Colonel (Captain) Myles W. Keogh and several other officers with ties to the Fifth Royal Irish Lancers and the Papal Guard, two Irish regiments in the British Army, were believed to be instrumental in bringing the air to the regiment.

The geographical area that provided the inspiration and the name of one of the most popular, rollicking folk songs of Ireland is situated on the upward slope of a hill in Limerick County, near the City of Limerick. Local traditions and folklore have preserved the historical significance of the area and the origin of its name "Garryowen", a compounded word composed of two Irish words, which means "Garden of Owen".

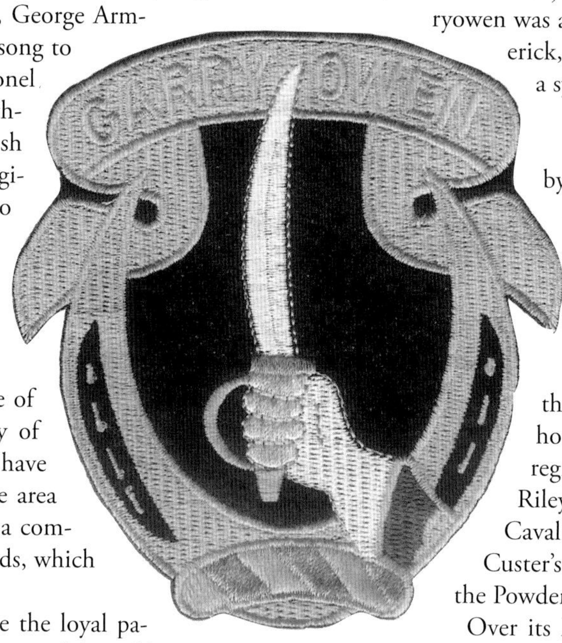

The terrain features of Garryowen gave the loyal patrons of the garden a broad, commanding view of the richly cultivated surrounding countryside, the old town of Limerick and the valley of the Shannon River which gently washes the battered, fortified towers of King John's castle which was constructed in the late 1180's to control traffic along the river. The cottage of Owen and surrounding plot of ground soon became a favorite holiday resort with the near-by citizens of Limerick because the atmosphere and accommodations were somewhat similar to those offered to the London mechanic by the Battersea tea gardens.

A review of Irish literature reveals that:

> "Owen's garden was a general rendezvous for those who sought simple pleasure and amusement. The elderly drank together under the shade of trees and the young played at ball, goal, or other athletic activities on the green; while a few lingered in the near-by hedge-rows with their fair acquaintances. Owen's garden soon became as famous for scenes of strife as it was for mirth and humor; and broken arms, legs and heads became a staple article of manufacture in the neighborhood.
>
> "These new diversions were encouraged by a number of young people having a greater supply of animal spirits than wisdom to control themselves. The young gentlemen being fond of wit, amused themselves by having parties at night to wring the heads off all the geese, and tearing knockers off the doors in the neighborhood. They sometimes suffered their genius to soar as high as the breaking of a street lamp, and even resorting to the physical violence of a watchman. But, this type of joking was found a little too serious to be repeated very frequently, for few achievements of so daring a violence were documented in the records. They were obliged to content themselves with less ambitious distinction of destroying the door knockers and storelocks, annoying the peace of the neighborhood, with long continued assaults on the front doors, terrifying the quiet onlookers with every species of insult and provocation, and indulging their fratricidal propensities against all the geese in Garryowen.
>
> "The fame of the 'Garryowen Boys' soon spread far and wide. Their deeds were celebrated by some inglorious minstrel of the day in that melody which has, since, resounded over the world; and even symbolically competed for national popularity with 'St. Patrick's Day'. A string of verses were appended to the tune, which soon enjoyed equal notoriety. The name of Garryowen was as well known as that of the city of Limerick, itself, and Owen's garden became almost a synonym for Ireland."

"Garryowen" is known to have been used by Irish regiments as a drinking song. As the story goes, one of the Irish "melting pot" troopers of the 7th Cavalry, under the influence of "spirits", was singing the song. By chance Custer heard the melody, liked the cadence, and soon began to hum the tune himself. The tune has a lively beat, that accentuates the cadence of marching horses, and for that reason was adopted as the regimental song soon after Custer arrived at Ft. Riley, Kansas to take over command of the 7th Cavalry Regiment. It was the last song played for Custer's men as they left General Terry's column at the Powder River and rode into history.

Over its history, continuing the Regimental legacy, the 7th Cavalry Regiment has formed 3 Garryowen Bagpipe and drum bands.

1954 — The 7th Cavalry Regiment Bagpipe & Drum Band organized by SSG Robert J. Scroggie at Camp Haugen, Japan. The Tartan had 7 colors: Dark Blue and Yellow of the US Cavalry; Light Blue to signify the present day infantry role in the cavalry; Red for action; and White for honor along with Green and Lavender.

1959 — The 2nd Reconnaissance Squadron, 7th Cavalry formed a BagPipe and Drum Band, under the guidance of LTC Roger Rawley and CPT John L. Lindgren. The original members were sent to a British regiment, the 1st Battalion Royal Inniskilling Fusiliers at Wuppertal, where they were given preliminary training by Irish pipers and drummers.

1963 — The 3rd Reconnaissance Squadron, 7th Cavalry at Ledward Barracks, Schweinfurt West Germany.

Today units of the 7th Cavalry still use Bagpipers. As they march and play, we think of all of those glorious memories of the past.

"Garryowen" has become undoubtedly the most famous of all the regimental marches in the Army. It became the Official Song of the 1st Cavalry Division in 1981. During "First Team" ceremonies, at Cooper Field, Fort Hood the song is not sung; however, it is customary for the song to be played at the conclusion of the ceremonial activities and the guests stand and clap.

In closing out of the Gulf War and returning home to the United States, in 1991, the 1st Cavalry Division the band joined in leading the whirlwind celebrations by parading down a dozen avenues of Atlanta, Houston, Dallas, Washington, DC and New York.

The visit to New York City was a tremendous welcome from the public, press and police. At Battery Park, the parade formation turned into Broadway, which became a wide "red" carpet for the Band to perform. There on Broadway, under a sunlit snowstorm of paper, the 1st Cavalry Division Band, lead by Bandmaster SFC Gary Flake, took the Big Apple by storm when they played the swaggering melody of the Division song, "Garryowen".

Information compiled and composed by William H. Boudreau.

LYRICS TO *GARRYOWEN*

[Verse 1]
Let Bacchus's sons be not dismayed,
but join with me each jovial blade,
come booze and sing and lend your aid,
to help me with the chorus:

[Chorus[
Instead of spa we'll drink down ale
and pay the reckoning on the nail,
for debt no man shall go to jail
from Garry Owen in glory.

[Verse 2]
We are the boys who take delight
in smashing Limerick lamps at night,
and through the street like sportsters fight,
tearing all before us. (Chorus)

[Verse 3]
We'll break windows, we'll break doors,
the watch knock down by threes and fours,
then let the doctors work their cures,
and tinker up our bruises, (Chorus)

[Verse 4]
We'll beat the bailiffs out of fun,
we'll make the mayor and sheriffs run,
we are the boys no man dare dun,
if he regards a whole skin. (Chorus)

[Verse 5]
Our hearts so stout have got us fame,
for soon 'tis known from whence we came,
where're we go they dread the name,
of Garry Owen in glory. (Chorus)

There was a special set of lyrics written for the 7th Cavalry Regiment in 1905. For those special troopers of the 7th:

[Verse 1]
We are the pride of the Army
and a regiment of great renown,
Our name's on the pages of history.
From sixty-six on down.
If you think we stop or falter
While into the fray we're going
Just watch the steps with our heads erect,
While our band plays Garryowen. (Chorus)

[Chorus]
In the Fighting Seventh's the place for me,
It's the cream of all the Cavalry;
No other regiment ever can claim
Its pride, honor, glory and undying fame.

[Verse 2]
We know fear when stern duty
Calls us far away from home,
Our country's flag shall safely o'er us wave,
No matter where we roam.
"Tis the gallant 7th Cavalry
It matters not where we are going"
Such you'll surely say as we march away;
And our band plays Garryowen. (Chorus)

[Verse 3]
Then hurrah for our brave commanders!
Who led us into the fight.
We'll do or die in our country's cause,
And battle for the right.
And when the war is o'er,
And to our home we're goin
Just watch your step, with our heads erect,
When our band plays Garryowen. (Chorus)

Reference: "From Custer to MacArthur, the 7th US Cavalry"

HISTORY OF THE 1ST CAVALRY DIVISION

Troop lift over the Bong Son Plain, Viet Nam, 1967.

HISTORY OF THE 1ST CAVALRY DIVISION

"THE FIRST TEAM"

The history of the 1st Cavalry Division is a colorful tale of Troopers on horseback in the desert areas around Fort Bliss, Texas; fighting in World War II; occupation duty in Japan; combat in the Korean War; service in Hokkaido; patrols along the Korean DMZ; Airmobile warfare in Vietnam; the Cold War with service at Fort Hood; desert fighting in the Gulf War; peacekeeping in Bosnia; and fighting the War on Terror in Iraq and Afghanistan. The following pages provide a brief history of the First Team from its inception in 1921 through 2017.

Troopers develop their skills at the 1st Cavalry Operations Training Center, 1938.

Division review at Ft. Bliss, TX

Officers of the 82nd Field Artillery BN, Ft. Bliss, TX, March 1932.

82nd Field Artillery camp at Toyahvale, TX, during 1st Cav maneuvers, 1938.

Formation

The 1st Cavalry Division was formally activated on 13 September 1921 at Fort Bliss, Texas. Its early duties in West Texas included rough-riding and patrolling the Mexican border. Technological progress of the 1940s diminished the usefulness of horse-mounted Soldiers, and the division turned in its horses and prepared to serve as dismounted cavalry in World War II's Pacific Theater.

Division review, 1923

1921

The 1st Cavalry Division is formally activated at Fort Bliss, Texas, on Sept. 13.

Horse artillery on parade at Ft. Bliss, 1938.

Firing cannons in the field.

1930s

The division provides training for the Civilian Conservation Corps, which constructed barracks for 20,000 anti-aircraft troops at Fort Bliss.

Prior to World War II, the 1st Cav communicated with troops in the field via horse pack radio system.

1st Cavalry Division Wagon Train in Toyahvale, TX.

Troopers on maneuvers in the Texas desert make room for a lone automobile.

1940-41
The 1st Cavalry Division participates in the 3rd Army Louisiana Maneuvers from April-October, designed to evaluate U.S. training, logistics, doctrine and overall effectiveness. Horses are used in the exercises in addition to tanks and vehicles, but would later be phased out due to advancing technology. Japan attacks Pearl Harbor on December 7, and U.S. Congress declares war on Japan on December 8.

7/20 Cav Motor Pool in the Philippines, with plenty of mud for everyone.

Elements of the 5th Cavalry and the 8th Engineers load a landing craft at Cape Sudest, New Guinea, bound for the Admiralty Islands, March 13, 1944.

Troopers having a laugh while stationed in Tokyo, ca. 1945

1942
The 1st Cavalry Division participates in the VIII Corps Louisiana Maneuvers near Mansfield, Louisiana during the months of August and September.

Famous photo of General Douglas MacArthur landing at Leyte, Philippines.

A Trooper moving under fire on Admiralty Island.

1st Signal Company running wire on Luzon.

World War II

In February 1943, the 1st Cavalry Division was alerted for overseas assignment and closed at Strathpine in Queensland, Australia on 26 July to train for jungle and amphibious operations. On 29 February 1944, the 1st Cavalry Division had its first combat as the Troopers stormed the beaches of Los Negros Island, fighting a fierce campaign that took some 7,000 Japanese casualties. The division's next action was a few months later on the Philippine Island of Leyte. When the last Japanese stronghold was eliminated, the division moved to Luzon.

The 1st Cavalry Division was first into Manila in February 1945 following one of the most important actions of the war, which is known as the "Flying Column." The Division's Troopers entered Manila and freed the internees at Santo Tomas University. Two Troopers of the 1st Cavalry Division were awarded the Medal of Honor posthumously during World War II. Major General William C. Chase officially took command months later, and his nickname for the division, "First Team," was well-received and remains today.

1943

The 1st Cavalry Division is officially dismounted and prepares for deployment to the South Pacific as foot cavalry. Echelons of the Division depart for the Pacific Theater in July.

Gen. Douglas MacArthur signs the formal surrender from Japan to end World War II.

7th CAV Guardhouse and NCO.

Sgt. Otis Higgins, 8th Engineering Battalion, 1944.

1944

On February 29, the division sails to the Admiralty Islands for its first combat engagement of World War II. After fighting in Operation King II on the island of Leyte, the Division moves onto the main island of the Philippines, Luzon, where the division's accomplishments lead Gen. Douglas MacArthur to nickname it the "First Team."

8th Engineers field inspection, 1943.

View from a landing craft during D-Day in Europe.

Under fire in Manila China Town.

The 8th Engineering Battalion rafting on Manus Island.

In September 1945, the "First Team" led occupational forces into Japan's capital city, earning the distinction of "First in Tokyo." The 1st Cavalry Division spent the next five years in Japan on Occupation Duty. First quartered on the Yoyogi Parade Grounds, the Division moved to the outskirts of the city and occupied Camp Drake in September 1945.

The Division's first mission in Tokyo was to assume control of the central portion of the city. Daily patrols began the long task of locating, investigating, and reporting all Japanese installations that had contributed to the nation's war effort. All arsenals, factories, barracks, and storage grounds had to be examined and reports made of their contents. In addition, the Division was concerned with the status of demobilization of the Japanese armed forces. The 1st Cavalry Division's occupation jurisdiction extended over 5,000 square miles.

Troopers following the capture of the Admiralty Islands. Photo courtesy of Robert Garretson.

Robert Garretson in a pup tent

1945

On Feb. 11, two squadrons of the 1st Cavalry Brigade form a "flying column" to cut a 100-mile path through Japanese-held territory, breaking through the gates of the Santo Tomas internment camp to free its prisoners. The division is the "First in Manila." When the war suddenly comes to an end after the atomic bombing of Hiroshima and Nagasaki, the "First Team" leads the Allied Occupation Army into Tokyo in September.

First in Tokyo – Major General William C. Chase and PFC Paul Davis, D 12C.

The First Cavalry Band marches in a parade through the streets of Tokyo.

G 8C Robert Garretson with friends riding in a Jeep.

The years 1946 to 1950 saw further easing of tensions between Japanese and Americans. Whenever floods or earthquakes hit the Japanese mainland, the Cavalrymen joined the rescue efforts. Once every few weeks, the Division staged colorful parades in the Imperial Plaza in the heart of Tokyo. Division Troopers contributed time, money and their talents to a number of Japanese orphanages and other social relief agencies. In June 1950, North Korea invaded South Korea and despite woeful manning and equipment shortages, the First Team prepared for their next combat.

Locals of Samar welcome American troopers.

1950
The 1st Cavalry Division leaves Japan, and, on July 18, carries out the first amphibious landing of the Korean War along the shores of Pohang Dong, South Korea. There, they help stop the North Korean army at the Pusan Perimeter.

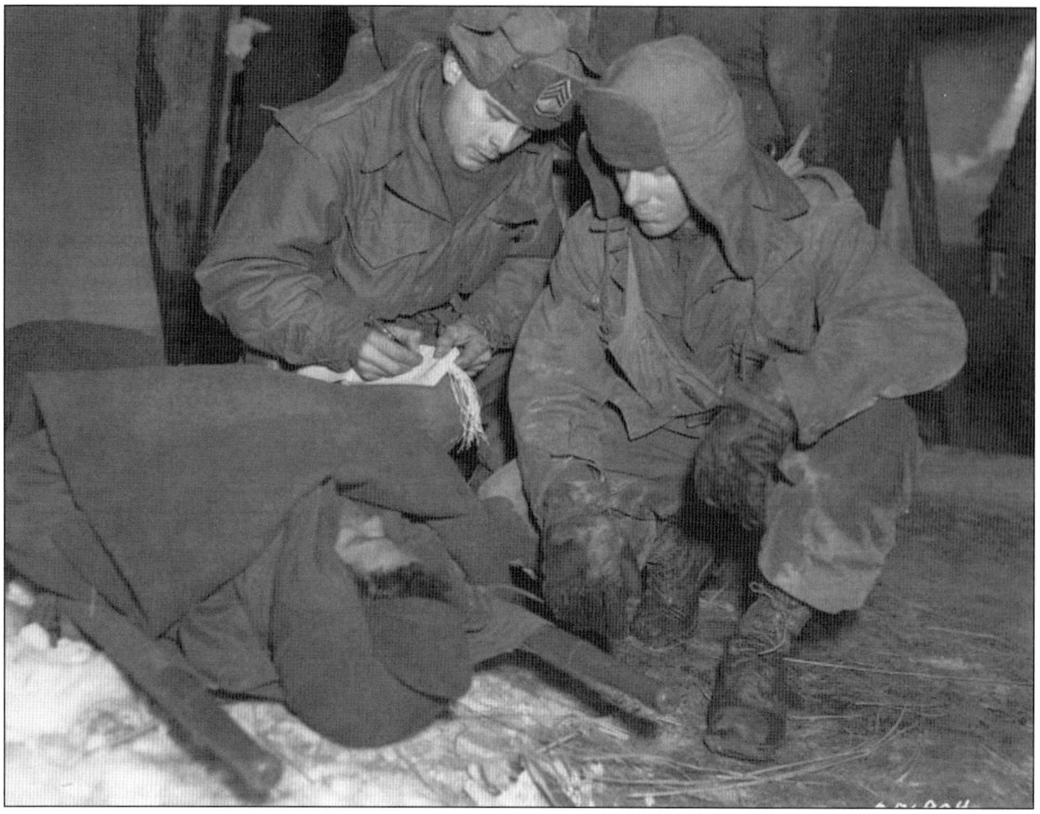
KOR Medical Company 8C preparing to evac a patient.

1951
Allied forces withdraw south of Seoul. In a spring offensive, the division moves north and engages enemy forces throughout the mountains of central Korea.

545MP streets of Chunchon.

LTJG James Brewer Crane Couch, a U.S. Navy surgeon with the 99th FA, killed in action in Korea, April 5, 1951.

Cavalry Troopers on the road to Pyongyang.

Korea, 8C Kapaun — Captain Jerome Dolan assists the wounded, 1950.

Korea

The 1st Cavalry Division stormed ashore at Pohang Dong, South Korea, in the Korean War's first amphibious landing. By July 1950, the division began offensive operations to the north and crossed the 38th parallel on October 9th. Closing on North Korea's capital ten days later, the "First Team" was "First in Pyongyang." With the war almost won and U.S. forces just south of the Chinese border, the Chinese Communist Forces entered the war and the onslaught of numerically superior forces overran and encircled the 8th Cavalry Regiment at Unsan. United Nation's forces began a withdrawal and were pushed past the 38th Parallel and below Seoul. The UN forces counterattacked and the 1st Cavalry Division again crossed the 38th parallel as fighting settled along that area. After 549 days of continuous combat, the division began planning to return to Japan. The division established a defensive military presence in the northern island of Hokkaido. Several units of the division returned to serve in Korea. During the Korean War, eleven Troopers of the First Team were awarded the Medal of Honor for their actions.

5C CPT J W Finley (F Co) suffered a neck wound in combat, 22 February 1951.

Major General Hobart R. Gay awards the Silver Star to 2LT Raymond Whelan, 25 August 1950.

1952
After 18 months of combat, the 1st Cavalry Division returns to Hokkaido, Japan, where troopers replace equipment and retrain.

KOR DMZ 9C B Troop, September 1962.

The 1st Cavalry pursues North Korean troops north of Kaesong, 13 October 1950.

1953
Korean Armistice signed on July 27.

1957
The division deploys again to Korea to patrol the Demilitarized Zone.

5C trooper PFC William Stinnett at his post.

5C PFC Dwight Exe, 15 November 1951.

At the end of the Korean War, the division remained on duty in Japan until its move back to the Korean Peninsula and duty along the Demilitarized Zone in 1957. The division spent the majority of its time in the field operations patrolling the southern border of the DMZ and adjacent areas in observation and listening posts that were manned 24 hours a day until departing for Fort Benning, Georgia in July 1965.

7C 50CAL covers Greek troops north of Uijongbu 9 May 1951.

13 Sig mail call, 25 July 1950 in Korea.

1965

Troopers leave Korea for the division's new home at Fort Benning, Ga., where they become the Army's first airmobile division. After a few months of preparation for the Pleiku Campaign, the division engages enemy forces in South Vietnam. On October 29, troopers destroy two of three regiments of a North Vietnamese division, earning the division the only Presidential Unit Citation given to a division in Vietnam.

7th Cav Vietnam B-W-1.

Left: VN B 2-12 Cavalry, 1970.

A 2-8 waiting for lift into a mountainous area for snatch ops, October 1968.

Bob Hope makes an appearance, 1966.

Vietnam

Reorganized and equipped as an airmobile division the "First Team" was quickly shipped to Vietnam becoming the first fully committed division in country. The division became the first division to earn the Presidential Unit Citation during the thirty-five day Pleiku Campaign. Airmobile tactics permitted fast movement on the battlefield as the "Sky Troopers" of the 1st Cavalry Division rode their helicopters into numerous battles. The enemy launched the famous Tet Offensive in late January 1968. Already on the move, the "First Team" rushed north, liberating cities and boldly repelling the enemy offensive. The division's "Sky Troopers" flew in to relieve the besieged Marine base at Khe Sahn and the division was first into Cambodia in May 1970.

Left: SP4 Martin Rodgers A 2-7, February 1969. Below: VN 2-5C III Corps area.

1970

In May, the 1st Cavalry Division is the first into Cambodia.

1971

The division returns home to its new headquarters at Fort Hood, Texas, on May 5. There it is reorganized into the Triple Capability (TRI-CAP) Division.

The 191st MI Lietenant Little and a pilot of LOH prepare hand held photo reconnaissance, 1968.

CWO A C Joe Freeman 2-20 ARA, 1965.

Below: The USS Boxer *leaves for Vietnam.*

B 2-8C VUC award MG John J. Tolson.

The first full division into Vietnam was the last full division to leave Vietnam. Thirty Troopers of the 1st Cavalry Division were awarded the Medal of Honor for their valor during the Vietnam War. Redeployment to Fort Hood, Texas began in 1971, where the "First Team" reorganized into a "Triple Capability" or "Tricap" Division, incorporating an armor brigade, an air mobility brigade, and an air cavalry brigade. While the Division colors left Vietnam in 1971, the 3rd Brigade, 1st Cavalry Division (Separate) remained in Vietnam until June 1972.

9 Cav assault outside Tay Ninh by Bob Griffin, 1970.

1-FA 30 Firing FSB Noble, 1971.

1975
In January, the division is reorganized once again into the Army's newest armored division.

1980
The 1st Cavalry Division is the first to field the M1 Abrams tank.

Operation Granadero, 1984.

Operation Granadero, 1984.

1982
The division opens the National Training Center at Fort Irwin, Calif., and begins rotations of realistic desert battle training.

1983
The "First Team" becomes the first U.S. force to deploy to Holland and northern Germany since World War II. Approximately 9,000 Troopers conduct exercises as part of Return of Forces to Germany.

DMZ 1-9C, post-war Korea.

Above: The 9 Cav lines up to move out in the DMZ. Below: 8C Ship returning from Japan, 1957.

Cold War

In the following years the First Team fought the "Cold War" as they trained and readied for combat in any area of the world. Training at Fort Hood, deploying to Germany as part of Return of Forces to Germany (REFORGER), and fighting the Opposing Force at the National Training Center at Fort Irwin, California became the routine of America's only Cavalry Division.

1990-91

In August, the 1st Cavalry Division prepares to deploy to the Middle East as part of Operation Desert Shield.

Entertainer Dolly Parton visits the First Team.

Command and staff during the Desert Shield/Desert Storm campaign.

Laundry time while deployed for Desert Shield/Desert Storm.

Operation Desert Shield

In August 1990, the 1st Cavalry Division was alerted for deployment to Southwest Asia as part of the joint forces participating in Operation Desert Shield. The focus at that time was the defense of Saudi Arabia against a potential Iraqi attack.

In January 1991, the division was attached to VII (US) Corps and the focus of the First Team clearly began to shift toward offensive action. The division moved nearly 500 kilometers to another assembly area near King Khalid Military city (KKMC) in northern Saudi Arabia. This put the division in a key strategic location covering the historic Wadi al Batin approach into Saudi Arabia. The stay near KKMC was short and the division jumped north toward the juncture of the Saudi, Iraq, and Kuwait borders beginning a calculated war of deception along the Saudi border.

Above: The 5 Cav holds a Chapel service in the desert. Left: M-109A2, 1-82 FA.

1991-92

The division returns to the United States and, with the reactivation of the 3rd "Greywolf" Battle Team on May 21, 1991, becomes the largest division in the Army.

1CD 82 FA Desert Storm

Artillery on the march during the Gulf War.

A 1-5C.

The deception caused Iraq to focus their forces along the Wadi and on 20 February, prior to the main attack by coalition forces the First Team's 2nd Brigade mounted the first major mounted ground attack 10 miles into Iraq ensuring that the Iraqi Army thought the main attack was to be through the Wadi al Batin.

On February 26, the commander of the Allied forces, General Norman Schwartzkopf directed, "send in the First Team. Destroy the Republican Guard. Let's go home." The entire division, minus the 2nd Armored Division's "Tiger" Brigade who was with the Marines moving into Kuwait, pausing only to refuel before passing through the breeches continued north, then east, moving in a vast armada of armor and went 300 kilometers in 24 hours, slicing deep into the enemy's rear.

Fire trench remnants

PFC David Webster and actress Brooke Shields meet during R&R, December 1990.

BG Robles and staff

1998
The 1st Cavalry Division conducts peace support operations in Bosnia and Herzegovina as part of Task Force Eagle. In October, the Division takes over the Multinational Division North area of operations.

MND N Chng of Cmd Shinseki, Brynes Larry Ellis 1AD.

1-5C truck coming in.

C 1-8 Bosnia Patrol.

Bosnia-Herzegovina

In 1998, the 1st Cavalry Division assumed the mission of Task Force Eagle, conducting peace support operations in Bosnia-Herzegovina. Following four months of highly successful and intensive planning, training, and maintaining, America's "First Team" assumed the mission of ensuring peace and stability throughout Bosnia-Herzegovina for over a year, transferring authority to the 10th Mountain Division in August 1999.

Above: First Cavalry meets a Russian soldier. Below: Eagle Base Nines. Photo courtesy of Juan Gaitan.

2001

After the September 11 attacks, elements of the 1st Cavalry Division join the joint task force charged with protecting key national assets in Washington, D.C., as part of Operation Clear Skies. On December 15, the Division's 545th Military Police Company deploys to Bagram, Afghanistan, where they interrogate and process approximately 2,500 detainees as part of Operation Enduring Freedom.

C 4-9 Haifa St, 13 February 2007.

D Trp 1-82FA going to a meeting in Assiriyah, Iraq, December 2007.

D 1-5C Michael Howard, 11 December 2007.

Reacting to a sniper attack.

Awarding Spurs

Operation Iraqi Freedom

In early 2003, select divisional units were designated to deploy in support of Operation Iraqi Freedom through the initial phase of combat culminating in the liberation of the Iraqi people from the tyrannical rule of Saddam Hussein. In the fall of 2003, the division as a whole was ordered to prepare for deployment in Operation Iraqi Freedom II. Assuming control of Task Force Baghdad in April 2004, the division engaged the enemy across multiple lines of operation, helping the Iraqi people forge a new, democratic government — the first in the nation's history. Two major events occurred during the division's year in the Iraqi capital: first, the coalition returned sovereignty to the people of Iraq in June 2004; and second, the national elections of January 2005 demonstrated the resolve of the Iraqi people to gain control of their country. The division transferred authority to the 3rd Infantry Division in February 2005 and completed their return to Fort Hood on April 2, 2005.

After returning from Iraq in 2005, the Division underwent a transformation to the Army's new modular design becoming a combined arms division. Many of our units were inactivated or redesignated, as the Division reorganized into a more deployable and lethal configuration. Adding a fourth maneuver brigade that was temporarily located at Fort Bliss, Texas, the Division began a training program to prepare for a return to Iraq in 2006.

1-227 AVN Apaches land after mission over Baghdad

2003

At the beginning of the year, select units deploy in support of Operation Iraqi Freedom. In the fall, the entire division prepares for deployment.

2-162 INF Dismounted on patrol.

20ENG Christmas Tree in MP, 2004.

SGM Della St.Louis Avn Bdes

2004

In April, the division assumes command of Task Force Baghdad.

2005

The division transfers authority to the 3rd Infantry Division and returns to the United States. In July, the division moves to its current brigade combat team format.

2-7 Fallujah

On 15 November, 2006 the 1st Cavalry Division assumed control of Baghdad for the second time and leadership of Multi-National Division Baghdad. Two of our brigades, the 3rd and 4th Brigade Combat Teams, were attached to the 25th Infantry Division working in a different area of Iraq while the ranks of the First Team were expanded by the attachment of brigades from divisions across the Army. The surge in Iraq brought the assigned and attached strength of the First Team and MND-Baghdad to over 100,000 Soldiers.

Returning to Fort Hood in late 2007, the division relocated the 4th Brigade Combat Team from Fort Bliss to Fort Hood and saw the departure of the 15th Sustainment Brigade from division control in 2008. The 4th BCT again deployed to Iraq, leaving the rest of the division to train and prepare for a third deployment in 2009.

3-8C Medics treat a wounded Iraqi, December 2004.

1st BCT UAV returning from a mission, June 2009.

2006-07
The 1st Cavalry Division deploys to Iraq a second time.

D 2-12C setting up checkpoint

1-12C raid on sports complex OPN Soprano Sunset eastern Baghdad, 6 December 2004.

115 BSB carry water pipe to repair water access point 2 in Mushada, 28 December 2006.

2008
The United States and Iraq sign a security agreement to withdraw U.S. forces and organize U.S. troops' activities during their temporary stay in the country. The 1st Cavalry Division is the first to take command of Multinational Division Baghdad.

Sgt. Mike Gmitter conducts a cordon and search with Shadow, 21 April 2007.

In late 2008, the 3rd Brigade Combat Team deployed to Iraq followed by the 2nd BCT, 1st BCT and the Division Headquarters in early 2009. The First Team once again accepted the control on MND-Baghdad from the 4th Infantry Division on 10 February, 2009. Only the 1st BCT remained assigned to the Division, with the other three Heavy Brigade Combat Teams being attached to other divisions in Iraq. The 1st Air Cavalry Brigade deployed to Iraq in the spring of 2009 for a one-year deployment and was the last 1st Cavalry Division unit to participate in Operation Iraqi Freedom.

The 4th BCT was one of the first units to deploy for Operation New Dawn with the mission to train and assist Iraqi Security Forces in September, 2010. The other three brigades followed on to Iraq for Operation New Dawn and the movement out of Iraq and into Kuwait. On the morning of 18 December 2011, after almost nine years, the 3rd Special Troops Battalion of the 3rd Brigade Combat Team (Grey Wolf) was the last unit to leave Iraq. The units of the First Team had completed a flawless movement involving multiple passages of lines conducted without incident. After leaving Iraq, the 1st Brigade Combat Team remained in Kuwait for several months as a contingency force for the CENTCOM area.

PFC Glenn Linder D 2-8 Cavalry.

4BCT Casing

2011

The Division begins deployment from Fort Hood to Afghanistan in support of Operation Enduring Freedom and, on May 19, assumes command of Regional Command-East.

2012

The division turns command over to the 1st Infantry Division in April and begins its return to the United States. The 1st Air Cavalry Brigade returns in June, completing the division's split deployment.

D 1-12 foot patrol Khalis, 23 February 2007.

3-82 FA Colors Uncasing, 4 August 2013.

Bon Apetit BSTB, March/April 2013.

2-82 FA Paladin firing, January 2005.

15 BSB cases colors for redeployment back to Ft Hood, 14 January 2014.

Afghanistan

On 19 May 2011, in continuing to expand its role in the mid-eastern theater of operations, the 1st Cavalry Division unfurled the unit's new colors in a transfer of authority ceremony with the 101st Airborne Division (Air Assault) on Bagram Airfield, Afghanistan.

During a pivotal time in the war on terror and in Afghanistan's history, the command authority of the Regional Command – East (RC-E) shifted from Combined Joint Task Force-101 to CJTF-1. In this new mission, the 1st Cavalry Division took control of over 35,000 Soldiers from eight US, French and Polish task forces and 14 provinces that, combined, provide safety and security in an area populated by approximately 7.5 million Afghans. The Area of Command consists of 43,000 square miles and shares 450 miles of border with Pakistan. The Division's Air Cavalry Brigade also deployed to Afghanistan and conducted operations in almost all areas of Afghanistan for a full year.

1-8 CAV Troopers inspect suicide bombing site outside base, January 2014.

2013

The 2nd Armored Brigade Combat Team (The Black Jack Brigade) and its subordinate units deploy as part of a force rotation in Afghanistan. The units assist with base closures and the withdrawal of forces and equipment.

Returning 2nd BCT Family, 2014

3-82 FA fires in Afghanistan, August 2013.

Deric M. Rasmussen, CW2, died of non-battle related causes, May 2014.

15 BSB work on turret of M-ATV at Bagram, November 2013.

In 2014, a portion of the Division Headquarters headed to Afghanistan where it took over the training of Afghan units as the Headquarters for Train, Advise, Assist Command – South. They conducted train, advise, and assist missions so that the Afghan National Security Forces would be sustainable and capable of protecting their population and government into the future. The final Troopers from this deployment returned to Fort Hood in June 2015.

LTC Phil Brooks 3-82 FA, 2013

4-9 CAV near FOB Fenty presence patrol, PFC Nicholas Peterson in foreground, 22 August 2013.

C 1-8 CAV Cobras in Uruzgan, January 2014.

Soldiers from B 2-8C receive instruction about the 120mm used in the M-1A1 Abrams

7-17 CAV activated 22 Oct 16 LTC Scott Myers CSM Maurice Thibodeaux.

6-9CAV A Troop firing, Sharm of Sheikh Egypt.

1SG Moss, SGT Core HCD in creek.

1-12 Cav Air Assault training at Ft Hood, October 2013.

The Division began aligning its brigades in different areas and sending, first 2-12 Cavalry and then 3-8 Cavalry to Korea, which led to the 2nd BCT, 1st Cavalry Division (Black Jack) deployment to Korea in 2015 to replace a brigade of the 2nd Infantry Division, which was inactivated. When the 2nd BCT's nine month deployment ended in 2016 they were replaced by the 1st BCT, 1st Cavalry Division (Iron Horse) which ended in October 2016. The 1st BCT had sent units to Europe, similar to the old REFORGER exercises after Russian Troops invaded Ukraine in 2014. 1st Cavalry units trained with old Cold War foes and demonstrated the ability to deploy heavy forces quickly. In the fall of 2015, the 3rd Battalion, 227th Aviation deployed to support operations in Europe.

Reorganization in the Division continued with the return of the Division Artillery (Red Team) and the activation and assignment of the 1st Sustainment Brigade (Wagon Masters), which carries the lineage and history of the Division Support Command. Both DIVARTY and DISCOM had been inactivated in 2005.

The 1st Cavalry Division, along with the 1st Cavalry Division Sustainment Brigade, cased their colors on 25 August 2016 in preparation for their deployment to Afghanistan in support of Operation Freedom's Sentinel, marking the Division Headquarters return to Afghanistan for the third time. The 1st Cavalry Division uncased their colors in Bagram on 13 September 2016, 95 years after the Division was formed at Fort Bliss, Texas in 1921.

With the Army's finest Soldiers and best equipment, the hard-riding spirit of the United States Cavalry is alive and well in the 1st Cavalry Division. Our more than 24,000 Soldiers combine the spirit of the Cav's heritage with challenges facing an alert, combat-ready division. The "First Team" remains ready to fight anywhere, anytime, and win.

"Live the Legend"

Taji R&S, May 30, 2004. Courtesy of Carl Fox.

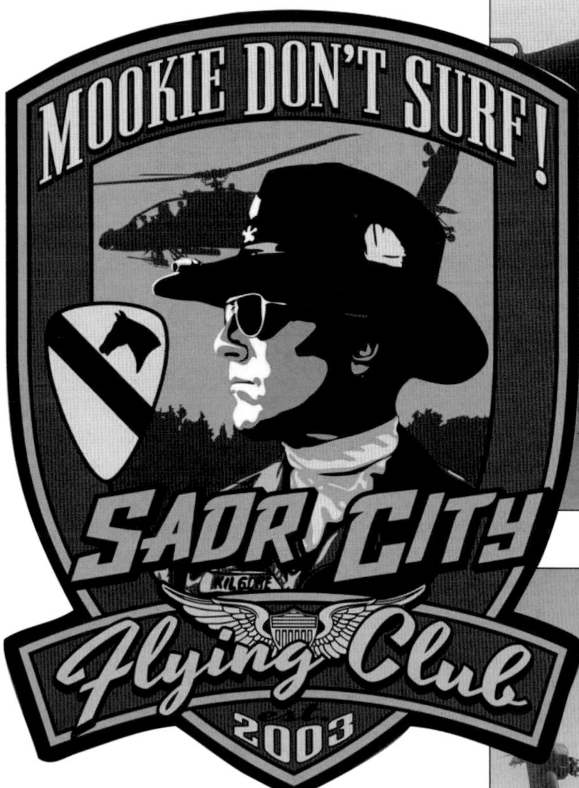

Patch honoring 1st Cav pilots at Sadr City, Iraq, 2003. Courtesy of Carl Fox.

Reapers assigned to I MEF at FOB Duke, An Najaf, August 15, 2004. Courtesy of Carl Fox.

CW4 Carl Fox at Camp Udairi, March 2004.

Right: AH-64D landing beneath crossed sabers – Baghdad, 2004.

Pyle and Potochick. Courtesy of Mike Cahalan.

Unknown, Ron Righton, Unknown, Casmier, Ronald Cheek, Unknown. Courtesy of Mike Cahalan.

Terry Morgan, Vignoli, Mike Cahalan, Wilbert Kell. Courtesy of Mike Cahalan.

Rex Johnston. Courtesy of Mike Cahalan.

Ray Martinez and Ricardo Rosonet. Courtesy of Reynaldo Martinez and Mike Cahalan.

HHC at An Khe Golf Course. Courtesy of Mike Cahalan.

Wade Clark. Courtesy of Mike Cahalan.

Right: An Khe Pass. Courtesy of Mike Cahalan.

Sunrise at An Khe Pass. Courtesy of Mike Cahalan.

Father Phil Lucide, Chaplin, An Khe, 1966. Courtesy of Mike Cahalan.

Joe Barlak, William Prater, and Frisbee. Courtesy of Mike Cahalan.

Leaving for An Khe, Camp Radcliff from Qui Nhon by trucks and Chinook helicopters. Photo by Joseph Barlak, Gorden Caughiull, and Flip Heilig courtesy of Mike Cahalan.

Left: Courtesy of Mike Cahalan.

Photos from Qui Nhon Harbor, South China Sea, Vietnam. Photo by Joseph Barlak, Gorden Caughiull, and Flip Heilig courtesy of Mike Cahalan.

Waiting to convoy out. Courtesy of Mike Cahalan.

Above: Entertainer Sammy Davis Jr. checks out a Cobra gunship during a USO stop with the 1st Cav. Courtesy of Bill Corsair.

Left: Bill Ellis in Vietnam.

Below: Bill Ellis performs for members of the First Team.

"The Rose" - Panama Canal, on the way to Viet Nam, 1965. Courtesy of Donald R. Davis.

Joe E. Gray ready for action, ca. 1960s.

SP4 Edward Belec, of the 1st Cav's 1st Battalion, 5th Cavalry, is helped out of a 20-foot concealed well after falling in while on patrol. Photo by Robert Sharp courtesy of Bill Corsair.

Harding at LZ English. Courtesy of Mike Cahalan.

Plei Me, 1966. Courtesy of Thomas Gorman.

Bon Song, 1967. Courtesy of Thomas W. Gorman.

Kontum Province, 1966. Courtesy of Thomas W. Gorman.

Courtesy of Terry Morgan and Mike Cahalan.

Ia Drang Valley, 1966-67. Courtesy of Thomas Gorman.

Over the berm, and onto the firebase (quickly)! Courtesy of Richard Cameron.

Courtesy of Mike Cahalan.

Coming into a fire support base — the only way in was by helicopter. Courtesy of Richard Cameron.

Left: Chaplain Acker administers the oath for reenlistment to his NCO at 1st Cav, 2d Bgd Chapel, Ft Hood, 1978. Courtesy of Raymond Acker.

Children of the wire — they exemplify the large numbers of Vietnamese who were forced by the fighting to flee from contested areas, living a hand-to-mouth existence. Courtesy of Richard Cameron.

Headquarters and Headquarters Company and Air Evac area of the 15th Medical Battalion, 1st Cavalry Division at Phuoc Vinh. Courtesy of Richard Cameron.

This mileage marker reflects a strong sense of dislocation that affects Troopers fighting a war halfway around the world, far from home and the familiar. Courtesy of Richard Cameron.

Maj. Richard Cameron on a MEDCAP Mission (Medical Civilian Action Program) designed to "win the hearts and minds, and loyalty of villagers."

Medical staff transport a wounded Trooper in for evaluation. Note: he was previously treated in a forward battalion or by medics on the air ambulance. Courtesy of Richard Cameron.

John Albert Quay, US Army Air Corps ca. 1916, was the father of 1st Cav member Matthew Quay. Both joined the service before turning 16! Courtesy of Matthew Quay.

Don Greer and Parunak.

Back to the Horse Cavalry, Korea, 1950. Courtesy of Matthew Quay

Matthew Quay is pictured on the far left.

CW3 Trenholm & LT Smith Touring the Ruins of Babylon. Courtesy of Carl Fox.

CW4 Carl Fox is inducted into the American Combat Airman Hall of Fame.

SP4 Duane D. Grenz brushes the giant teeth of a Cobra gunship, Troop C, 1/9th Cav. Photo by Terry Moon courtesy of Bill Corsair.

Donald Swan with some heavy firepower.

Rosonet. Courtesy of Flip Heilig and Mike Cahalan.

Getting the Jeep washed in the Song Ba River. Courtesy of Flip Heilig and Mike Cahalan.

Terry Morgan, Bong Son, 1966. Courtesy of Mike Cahalan.

Tim Carey, Jackson Gibson, Jose A. Ramos, Charles Emmons, Mike Cahalan, and Tim Taylor. Courtesy of Mike Cahalan.

Qui Nhon Harbor, South China Sea, Vietnam. Photo by Joseph Barlak, Gorden Caughiull, and Flip Heilig courtesy of Mike Cahalan.

Qui Nhon Harbor, South China Sea, Vietnam. Photo by Joseph Barlak, Gorden Caughiull, and Flip Heilig courtesy of Mike Cahalan.

Calvin Strong. Courtesy of Flip Heilig and Mike Cahalan.

Flip Heilig and an ROK. Courtesy of Flip Heilig and Mike Cahalan.

Lt. Bohonakat Duc Co. SF Camp. Courtesy of Flip Heilig and Mike Cahalan.

Capt. Carl Groth – Postn Bird. Courtesy of Mike Cahalan.

Operation "All The Way". Courtesy of Mike Cahalan.

Sgt. Stanfield (Stanfill). Courtesy of Flip Heilig and Mike Cahalan.

CURRENT UNITS OF THE 1ST CAVALRY DIVISION

Headquarters & Headquarters Battalion (Maverick)
Headquarters Service Company
Operations Company
Intelligence & Sustainment Company
Signal Company
1st Cavalry Division Band
Horse Cavalry Detachment

2nd Brigade Combat Team (Black Jack)
HHC, 2nd BCT
4th Squadron, 9th Cavalry "Darkhorse"
1st Battalion, 5th Cavalry "Black Knights"
1st Battalion, 8th Cavalry "Mustangs"
1st Battalion, 9th Cavalry "Head Hunters"
8th Brigade Engineer Battalion "Trojan Horse"
3rd Battalion, 16th Field Artillery "Rolling Thunder"
15th Brigade Support Battalion "Gambler"

1st Brigade Combat Team (Iron Horse)
HHC, 1st BCT
1st Squadron, 7th Cavalry "Garryowen"
2nd Battalion, 5th Cavalry "Lancers"
2nd Battalion, 8th Cavalry "Stallions"
2nd Battalion, 12th Cavalry "Thunder Horse"
91st Brigade Engineer Battalion "Sabers"
1st Battalion, 82nd Field Artillery "Dragons"
115th Brigade Support Battalion "Muleskinners"

3rd Brigade Combat Team (Grey Wolf)
HHC, 2nd BCT
6th Squadron, 9th Cavalry "Saber"
2nd Battalion, 7th Cavalry "Ghost"
3rd Battalion, 8th Cavalry "Warhorse"
1st Battalion, 12th Cavalry "Chargers"
3rd Brigade Engineer Battalion "Beavers"
2nd Battalion, 82nd Field Artillery "Steel Dragons"
215th Brigade Support Battalion "Blacksmiths"

1st Air Cavalry Brigade
(Warrior)
HHC, 1st ACB
1st Battalion, 227th Aviation "First Attack"
2nd Battalion, 227th Aviation "Lobos"
3rd Battalion, 227th Aviation "Spearhead"
7th Squadron, 17th Cavalry "Palehorse"
615th Brigade Support Battalion "Cold Steel"

1st Cavalry Division Artillery
(Red Team)
HHB, DIVARTY

1st Cavalry Division Sustainment Brigade
(Wagon Master)
1st Special Troops Battalion, 1CDSB "Wranglers"
553rd Combat Sustainment Support Battalion "Gunslingers"
124th Transportation Company (OKARNG)
249th Transportation Company (TXARNG)

3d Cavalry Regiment (Attached) (Brave Rifles)
RHHT, 3d Cavalry "Remington"
1st Squadron, 3d Cavalry "Tiger"
2nd Squadron 3d Cavalry "Sabre"
3rd Squadron, 3d Cavalry "Thunder"
4th Squadron, 3d Cavalry "Longknife"
Engineer Squadron, 3d Cavalry "Pioneer"
Fires Squadron, 3d Cavalry "Steel"
Support Squadron, 3d Cavalry "Muleskinner"

9th Air Support Operations Squadron (USAF)

1st Cavalry Division Book of Honor "Our Honored Dead"

"The nation that forgets its defenders, will itself be forgotten."
—President Calvin Coolidge

We call to mind with deepest gratitude and highest praise those gallant Troopers who gave their lives on the field of battle. The roll is long, for the battles are many and the fighting hard.

The number of Troopers from the 1st Cavalry Division—our honored dead—are listed below in conflict order. We will never forget these valiant Troopers and their sacrifice.

World War II
1,152

Korea
3,812

Vietnam
5,621

Operation Desert Storm & Operation Desert Shield
12

Operation Inherent Resolve
1

Operation New Dawn
16

Operation Iraqi Freedom
715

Afghanistan
107

Total 1st Cavalry Troopers Lost
11,436

Field ceremony for CW4 Keith Yoakum and CW2 Jason DeFrenn, ca. 5 February 2007, Camp Taji, Iraq. Yoakum was awarded the Distinguished Service Cross (posthumously) and DeFrenn the Distinguished Flying Cross (posthumously). Courtesy of Brian Carbone.

Troopers pay their final respects for Gen. Robert M. Shoemaker.

1st Cavalry Division Medal of Honor Recipients

Forty-three Troopers of the 1st Cavalry Division have been awarded the Medal of Honor for gallantry in three different wars. Twenty-nine of the medals were awarded posthumously. Eight of the 1st Cavalry Division's recipients of the Medal of Honor are still living.

The Medal of Honor is the highest medal awarded by the United States. The following excerpt from Army Regulation 600-8-22 (Military Awards) describes the eligibility criteria for the award of the Medal of Honor.

"The Medal of Honor [Army], section 3741 title 10, United States Code (10 USC 3741), was established by Joint Resolution of Congress, 12 July 1862 (amended by acts 9 July 1918 and 25 July 1963).

"The Medal of Honor is awarded by the President, in the name of Congress, to a person who, while a member of the Army, distinguishes himself or herself conspicuously by gallantry and intrepidity at the risk of his or her life above and beyond the call of duty while engaged in action against an enemy of the United States; while engaged in military operations involving conflict with an opposing foreign force; or while serving with friendly foreign forces engaged in an armed conflict against an opposing armed force in which the United States is not a belligerent party. The deed performed must have been one of personal bravery or self-sacrifice so conspicuous as to clearly distinguish the individual above his or her comrades and must have involved risk of life. Incontestable proof of the performance of the service will be exacted and each recommendation for the award of this decoration will be considered on the standard of extraordinary merit. "

A gold five-pointed star, each point tipped with trefoils, 1½ inches wide, surrounded by a green laurel wreath and suspended from a gold bar inscribed "VALOR", surmounted by an eagle. In the center of the star, Minerva's head surrounded by the words "UNITED STATES OF AMERICA." On each ray of the star is a green oak leaf. On the reverse is a bar engraved "THE CONGRESS TO" with a space for engraving the name of the recipient.

Medal of Honor Recipients by War and Date Earned

World War II

SGT Troy A. McGill, G Troop, 5th Cavalry Regiment. Awarded posthumously for actions on Los Negros Island, Admiralty Group on 4 March 1944.

PFC William J. Grabiarz, E Troop, 5th Cavalry Regiment. Awarded posthumously for actions in Manila, Philippine Islands on 23 February 1945.

Korean War

SGT Eduardo C. Gomez, L Company, 8th Cavalry Regiment. Awarded posthumously for actions in Tabu-dong, Korea on 3 September 1950.

PFC Melvin L. Brown, D Company, 8th Engineer Battalion. Awarded posthumously for actions near Kasan, Korea on 4 September 1950.

MSG Mike C. Pena, F Company, 5th Cavalry Regiment. Awarded posthumously for actions near Waegwan, Korea on 4 September 1950.

CPL Gordon M. Craig, 16th Reconnaissance Company. Awarded posthumously for actions near Kasan, Korea on 10 September 1950.

PFC Robert H. Young, E Company, 8th Cavalry Regiment. Awarded posthumously for actions North of Kaesong, Korea on 9 October 1950.

1LT Samuel S. Coursen, C Company, 5th Cavalry Regiment. Awarded posthumously for actions near Kaesong, Korea on 12 October 1950.

Chaplain (CPT) Emil J. Kapaun, HQ, 8th Cavalry Regiment. Awarded posthumously for actions near Unsan, Korea on 1 and 2 November 1950.

1LT Robert M. McGovern, A Company, 5th Cavalry Regiment. Awarded posthumously for actions near Kamyangian-ni, Korea on 30 January, 1951.

1LT Lloyd L. Burke, G Company, 5th Cavalry Regiment. Awarded for actions near Chong-dong, Korea on 28 October 1951.

1LT James L. Stone, F Company, 8th Cavalry Regiment. Awarded for actions near Sokkogae, Korea on 21 and 22 November 1951.

CPL Tibor Rubin, I Company, 8th Cavalry Regiment. Awarded for actions in Korea and as a Prisoner of War between 23 July 1950 and 20 April 1953.

Vietnam War

MAJ Bruce P. Crandall, A Company, 229th Assault Helicopter Battalion. Awarded for actions in the Ia Drang Valley, Vietnam on 14 November 1965.

CPT Ed W. Freeman, A Company, 229th Assault Helicopter Battalion. Awarded for actions in the Ia Drang Valley, Vietnam on 14 November 1965.

1LT Walter Joseph Marm, A Company, 1-7th Cavalry. Awarded for actions in the Ia Drang Valley, Vietnam on 14 November 1965.

SSG Jimmy G. Stewart, B Company, 2-12th Cavalry. Awarded posthumously for actions in the Vinh Thanh Valley, Vietnam on 18 May 1966.

SP4 David C. Dolby, B Company, 1-8th Cavalry (Airborne). Awarded for actions in the vicinity of the Vinh Thanh Valley, Vietnam on 21 May 1966.

PFC Billy L. Lauffer, C Company, 2-5th Cavalry. Awarded posthumously for actions near Bon Son, Vietnam on 21 September 1966.

PFC Lewis Albanese, B Company, 5-7th Cavalry. Awarded posthumously for actions near Phu Huu 2, Vietnam on 1 December 1966.

SSG Delbert O. Jennings, C Company, 1-12th Cavalry (Airborne). Awarded for actions in the Kim Song Valley, Vietnam on 27 December 1966.

PFC James H. Monroe, HHC, 1-8th Cavalry. Awarded posthumously for actions near Bong Son, Vietnam on 16 February 1967.

SP4 Charles C. Hagemeister, HHC, 1-5th Cavalry. Awarded for actions in Binh Dinh Province, Vietnam on 20 March 1967.

SP4 George A. Ingalls, A Company, 2-5th Cavalry. Awarded posthumously for actions near Duc Pho, Vietnam on 16 April 1967.

SP4 Carmel B. Harvey, Jr., B Company, 1-5th Cavalry. Awarded posthumously for actions in Binh Dinh Province, Vietnam on 21 June 1967.

SP5 Edgar L. McWethy, B Company, 1-5th Cavalry. Awarded posthumously for actions in Binh Dinh Province, Vietnam on 21 June 1967.

SGT Allen J. Lynch, D Company, 1-12th Cavalry. Awarded for actions near My An, Vietnam on 15 December 1967.

SGT William D. Port, C Company, 5-7th Cavalry. Awarded posthumously for actions in the Que Son Valley, Vietnam on 12 January 1968.

CWO Fredrick E. Ferguson, C Company, 227th Aviation Battalion. Awarded for actions near Hue, Vietnam on 31 January 1968.

CPT James M. Sprayberry, D Company, 5-7th Cavalry. Awarded for actions in the A Shau Valley, Vietnam on 25 April 1968.

1LT Douglas B. Fournet, B Company, 1-7th Cavalry. Awarded posthumously for actions in the A Shau Valley, Vietnam on 4 May 1968.

SP4 Hector Santiago-Colon, B Company, 5-7th Cavalry. Awarded posthumously for actions in the Quang Tri Province, Vietnam on 28 June 1968.

SGT John N. Holcomb, D Company, 2-7th Cavalry. Awarded posthumously for actions near Quan Loi, Vietnam on 3 December 1968.

SP4 Donald R. Johnston, D Company, 1-8th Cavalry. Awarded posthumously for actions in Tay Ninh Province, Vietnam on 21 March 1969.

SP4 Jesus S. Duran, E Company, 2-5th Cavalry. Awarded posthumously for actions in the Republic of Vietnam on 10 April 1969.

1LT Robert L. Poxon, B Troop, 1-9th Cavalry. Awarded posthumously for actions in Tay Ninh Province, Vietnam on 2 June 1969.

SGT Rodney J. Evans, D Company, 1-12th Cavalry. Awarded posthumously for actions in Tay Ninh Province, Vietnam on 18 July 1969.

SP4 Leonard L. Alvarado, D Company, 2-12th Cavalry. Awarded posthumously for actions in Phouc Long Province, Vietnam on 12 August 1969.

SGT Donald S. Skidgel, D Troop, 1-9th Cavalry. Awarded posthumously for actions near Bong Son, Vietnam on 14 September 1969.

2LT Robert R. Leisy, B Company, 1-8th Cavalry. Awarded posthumously for actions in Phuoc Long Province, Vietnam on 2 December 1969.

SP4 John P. Baca, D Company, 1-12th Cavalry. Awarded for actions in Phouc Long Province, Vietnam on 10 February 1970.

SGT Peter C. Lemon, E Company, 2-8th Cavalry. Awarded for actions in Tay Ninh Province, Vietnam on 1 April 1970.

CPT Jon E. Swanson, B Troop, 1-9th Cavalry. Awarded posthumously for actions in the Kingdom of Cambodia on 26 February 1971.

1st Cavalry Division Distinguished Service Cross

The Distinguished Service Cross (DSC) is the second highest military decoration that can be awarded to a member of the United States Army (and previously, the United States Army Air Forces). It is awarded for extraordinary heroism:

While engaged in action against an enemy of the United States; While engaged in military operations involving conflict with an opposing foreign force; or While serving with friendly foreign forces engaged in an armed conflict against an opposing armed force in which the United States is not a belligerent party.

Actions that merit the Distinguished Service Cross must be of such a high degree that they are above those required for all other U.S. combat decorations but do not merit award of the Medal of Honor. The Distinguished Service Cross is equivalent to the Navy Cross (Navy and Marine Corps, and Coast Guard when operating under the authority of the Department of the Navy) and the Air Force Cross (Air Force).

Troopers of the 1st Cavalry Division have been awarded 261 Distinguished Service Crosses in four wars, with 113 of them being awarded posthumously. There were no Distinguished Service Crosses awarded to First Team Troopers during the Gulf War or from service in Afghanistan.

All Troopers are listed by rank, name, unit and date of action. An asterisk denotes that the Distinguished Service Cross was awarded posthumously.

We honor these brave Troopers.

World War II

CPL Peter J. Armstrong, A Troop 1-8th Cavalry, March 19, 1944
BG William G. Chase, HQ 1st Cavalry Brigade, February 2-3, 1945
LTC Haskett L. Conner, HQ 2-8th Cavalry, February 3, 1945
1LT Shirley Davidson, 1st Cavalry Division, February 12-24, 1945
T-SGT Harold W. Deitrick, 1st Cavalry Division, February 25, 1945
*SGT Harold L. Finney, Weapons Troop 5th Cavalry, November 22, 1944
T-SGT John J. Gallagher, G Troop 2-8th Cavalry, February 3, 1945
MAJ James C. Gerhart, HQ 2-8th Cavalry, February 3, 1945
*2LT Marvin J. Henshaw, G Troop 2-5th Cavalry, February 29, 1944
CPL Grover S. Jordan, C Troop 1-12th Cavalry, March 20, 1944
*PFC Calvin T. Lewis, B Troop 1-7th Cavalry, March 9, 1945
LTC William E. Lobit, HQ 2-5th Cavalry, March 4, 1944
PFC Margarito G. Lopez, E Troop 2-7th Cavalry, December 20, 1944
*PFC Malcolm E. Lott, F Troop 2-5th Cavalry, October 20, 1944
*SGT Randolph F. Mattison, Anti-Tank Platoon 2-8th Cavalry, February 3, 1945
SSG Winfred E. McAdoo, A Troop 1-12th Cavalry, December 10, 1944
1LT John L. Nichols, B Troop 1-12th Cavalry, February 19-20, 1945
*PVT Nelson D. Palmer, G Troop 2-8th Cavalry, April 3, 1945
PFC Louis Testa, D Troop 1-7th Cavalry, March 29, 1945
CPT Joseph Q. Tuck, HQ 1st Cavalry Brigade, March 1, 1944
CPL Manuel Urenda, D Troop 1-7th Cavalry, March 29, 1945
CPL Armando V. Valencia, A Troop 1-8th Cavalry, March 19, 1944
SGT Louis Zalusky, G Troop 2-12th Cavalry, March 12, 1945

Korean War

Eighty Troopers of the 1st Cavalry Division were awarded the Distinguished Service Cross for their actions during the Korean War, with 41 of them being awarded posthumously. One Trooper received the award twice. The recipients of the DSC are listed below in alphabetical order. Citations may be viewed on the DSC Korean War Citations page.

CPT Clarence L. Anderson, 3-8th Cavalry, November 1-2, 1950
*SGT Alton M. Ashworth, I Company 3-8th Cavalry, December 2, 1950
*2LT Virgil M. Atwood, K Company 3-5th Cavalry, June 3, 1951
*SFC Earl R. Baxter, L Company 3-8th Cavalry, September 15, 1950
*PVT Lloyd E. Beltz, K Company 3-7th Cavalry, October 5, 1951
*1LT Marinus Bruinooge, G Company 2-7th Cavalry, February 14, 1951
2LT Lloyd L. Burke, F Company 2-5th Cavalry, November 26, 1950
*1LT James L. Caldwell, L Company 3-7th Cavalry, October 5, 1951
1LT Howard W. Cardoza, HQ & SVC Co. 70th Tank Battalion, August 16, 1950
*PVT Donald L. Chaney, B Company 1-7th Cavalry, August 9, 1950
*CPL Willard L. Clinch, C Company 1-8th Cavalry, February 12, 1951
*SGT Stephen A. Condon, F Company 2-5th Cavalry, October 19, 1950
MSG Aron E. Cook, K Company 3-7th Cavalry, February 14, 1951
CPL Lee E. Copeland, 1-8th Cavalry, July 22, 1950
COL Marcel G. Crombez, HQ 5th Cavalry Regiment, February 15-16, 1951
*2LT Courtenay C. Davis, Jr., B Company 1-5th Cavalry, September 12, 1950
*CPL Marvin L. Davis, H Company 2-7th Cavalry, September 3, 1950
*CPT Fred P. DePalma, G Company 2-7th Cavalry, September 19, 1950
*1LT Stephen Dubinsky, A Company 1-8th Cavalry, July 24, 1950
*1LT Richard O. Eiler, D Company 8th Engineer Battalion, September 5, 1950
SGT Hubert P. Flerchinger, B Company 1-7th Cavalry, September 10-11, 1950
MG Hobart R. Gay, HQ 1st Cavalry Division, July 18 to October 1. 1950
*CPL Frank D. Hagan, K Company 3-7th Cavalry, September 28, 1951
LTC William A. Harris, HQ 7th Cavalry Regiment - September 26-27, 1950
*PVT Paulino E. Hernaez, A Company 1-5th Cavalry, May 30, 1951
MAJ John G. Hill, Jr., HQ 7th Cavalry Regiment, September 26-27, 1950
*MAJ Omar T. Hitchner, HQ 2-7th Cavalry, September 6, 1950
*SFC Willard H. Hopkins, HQ 3-7th Cavalry, September 26-27, 1950
LTC Gilmon A. Huff, HQ 2-7th Cavalry, October 10, 1950
1LT David R. Hughes, K Company 3-7th Cavalry, October 7, 1951
*CPL Coleman C. Hundley, F Company 2-7th Cavalry, August 6, 1950
*PVT David A. Hurr, E Company 2-5th Cavalry, August 1-2, 1950
1LT Charles V. Ickes, Heavy Mortar Co. 5th Cavalry Regiment, August 15, 1950
2LT Tylee N. James, A Company 1-8th Cavalry, January 26, 1951
CPL James B. Jenkins, I Company 3-5th Cavalry, September 14, 1950
1LT Raymond A. Jensen, K Company 3-8th Cavalry, October 10, 1951
LTC Harold K. Johnson, HQ 3-8th Cavalry, September 4, 1950
*1LT James B. Johnson, L Company 3-5th Cavalry, September 6, 1951
1LT Wayne D. Jones, L Company 3 8th Cavalry, October 11, 1951
PFC Duane E. Litzinger, K Company 3-8th Cavalry, October 11-12, 1951
PFC Francis Loviska, B Battery 99th Field Artillery, July 24, 1950
LTC James H. Lynch, HQ 3-7th Cavalry, September 21-22, 1950
LTC James H. Lynch, HQ 3-7th Cavalry, September 27, 1950
*1LT Elmy L. Matta, F Company 2-8th Cavalry, August 3, 1950
*2LT Green B. Mayo, B Company 1-5th Cavalry, January 29, 1951
1LT John S. McKim, K Company 3-8th Cavalry, February 14, 1951
*PFC Robert B. McKim, B Company 1-7th Cavalry, August 9, 1950
*PFC Paul J. McLaughlin, L Company 3-5th Cavalry, February 15, 1951
*SGT Johnny J. Miller, H Company 2-7th Cavalry, September 3, 1950
SGT Edward W. Minnick, G Company 2-5th Cavalry, September 10 and 12, 1950
*MSG John H. Mitchell, I Company 3-7th Cavalry, September 12, 1950
CPT Howard M. Moore, C Battery 61st Field Artillery, November 5, 1950
*CPL Charles E. Nichols, F Company 2-7th Cavalry, September 18, 1950
MSG Edward P. Nonnweiler, D Company 1-7th Cavalry, August 13, 1950
PFC Roberto Pacheco, Jr., B Company 1-7th Cavalry, August 9, 1950
(Roberto Siqueiros-Gamez, Jr.)
*SFC Clarence E. Postlethwait, C Company 8th Engineer Battalion, November 2, 1950
PFC Michael Radice, E Company 2-7th Cavalry, May 10, 1951

CPL Edward G. Rector, Heavy Mortar Co. 5th Cavalry Regiment, August 2, 1950
*CPL Billy F. Reddick, 8th Cavalry Regiment, October 10, 1951
CPL Robert D. Roberts, G Company 2-7th Cavalry, June 8, 1951
*1LT Robert S. Roberts, K Company 3-7th Cavalry, September 5, 1950
SFC Leroy Robinson, G Company 2-8th Cavalry, September 11, 1950
*PFC Donald E. Rodstrom, Med Company 7th Cavalry Regiment, September 12, 1950
CPL Homer E. Sanderford, C Company 1-5th Cavalry, September 21, 1950
*SFC Theodore A. Schierman, G Company 2-7th Cavalry, August 10, 1950
PFC Buster Shell, L Company 3-7th Cavalry, October 18, 1950
*PFC Reginald D. Smith, K Company 3-8th Cavalry, October 8, 1951
PFC Willard V. Swing, Jr., D Company 1-7th Cavalry, August 13, 1950
*PFC Clarice C. Swinney, H Company 2-7th Cavalry, September 3, 1950
*SFC Burton A. Wagner, A Company 8th Engineer Battalion, December 2, 1950
*CPT Robert B. Walker, L Company 3-7th Cavalry, September 12 & 24, 1950
CPT James B. Webel, HQ 7th Cavalry Regiment, September 26-27, 1950
*SFC Dave W. Wentzel, F Company 2-8th Cavalry, November 21, 1951
CPT Herman L. West, HQ 2-7th Cavalry, September 7, 1950
*1LT Edward A. White, F Company 2-5th Cavalry, August 2, 1950
*2LT William H. Wilbur, I Company 3-8th Cavalry, August 28 to Sept 4, 1950
PFC Norman E. Wilson, M Company 3-5th Cavalry, September 6, 1951
SGT Royal A. Wisemore, I Company 3-5th Cavalry, November 28, 1950
*2LT Theodore R. Woo, E Company 2-5th Cavalry, October 3, 1951
1LT William W. Woodside, L Company 3-7th Cavalry, September 26-27, 1950
SFC Howard C. Wurst, A Company 1-8th Cavalry, July 14, 1951

Vietnam War

The names of the 145 Troopers of the 1st Cavalry Division who were awarded the Distinguished Service Cross for actions during the Vietnam War are listed below. The 66 that were awarded posthumously are marked with an asterisk. To view the citations visit the Vietnam War DSC Citations page.

*SP4 Walther T. Bahl, D Company 2-7th Cavalry, December 3, 1968
MAJ Leon D. Bieri, HHC 1-12th Cavalry, December 17, 1966
PFC Thomas D. Bouchard, HHC 1-8th Cavalry, December 7, 1967
SP4 Steven R. Branham, C Company 1-5th Cavalry, November 29, 1969
*PFC Kenneth J. Brenner, A Company 2-5th Cavalry, March 29, 1969
*SGT Darrell E. Burns, B Company 5-7th Cavalry, June 22, 1970
MAJ George D. Burrow, B Troop 1-9th Cavalry, December 9, 1967
*SFC Guy A. Byrd, C Company 2-7th Cavalry, April 5, 1967
SP4 Darrell W. Campbell, A Company 1-5th Cavalry, February 13, 1968
*SSG Martin J. Canavan, Jr., A Company 2-5th Cavalry, March 29, 1969
SP4 Patrick S. Carmichael, B Company 227th Aviation, March 11, 1969
*CPT Robert H. Carroll, B Company 2-5th Cavalry, May 12, 1968
*SGT Eddie E. Chervony, A Battery 1-77th Field Artillery, May 5, 1968
PFC Jerry D. Clayton, D Company 2-7th Cavalry, March 23, 1968
MSG William A. Clemmons, D Company 2-5th Cavalry, June 14, 1971
*SFC Hubbard D. Cobb, A Company 2-5th Cavalry, January 14, 1968
*PFC Noah C. Collier, A Company 1-8th Cavalry, October 26, 1966
SP4 Billy R. Comer, D Company 2-5th Cavalry, June 22, 1970
SFC Carroll V. Crain, A Battery 2-19th Field Artillery, December 27, 1966
PFC Gary E. Crews, C Company 2-12th Cavalry, July 29, 1968
SSG John E. Darnell, Jr., C Company 2-12th Cavalry, January 2, 1968
PFC Mitchell Davis, HHC 2-8th Cavalry, March 6, 1970
*PFC Stephen W. Day, B Company 5-7th Cavalry, December 1, 1966
SP4 Joseph D. Deleo, C Company 5-7th Cavalry, July 21, 1968
SP4 David D. Dentinger, A Company 2-12th Cavalry, February 21, 1968
*2LT Thomas E. Dobrinska, B Company 2-12th Cavalry, February 9, 1968
*SP4 Clark R. Douglas, C Company 1-5th Cavalry, November 11, 1969
*PFC Leo P. Dunsmore, A Company 5-7th Cavalry, February 12, 1968
*PFC John W. Eutsler, B Company 1-8th Cavalry, January 31, 1969
*PFC Donald P. Evans, D Company 5-7th Cavalry, November 20, 1968
*SP4 Jerry D. Evans, A Company 5-7th Cavalry, February 23, 1968
*PVT Jerry L. Ewing, E Company 1-8th Cavalry, February 23, 1969
*SP4 Michael A. Fontaine, C Company 2-7th Cavalry, January 10, 1969
SGT Sherman G. Fuller, A Company 1-12th Cavalry, December 17, 1966
SP4 Gordon W. Gaskin, HHC 2-12th Cavalry, January 3, 1968

*PFC Allen B. Glines, A Company 5-7th Cavalry, January 3, 1968
SP4 Larry E. Godlewski, D Company 2-7th Cavalry, November 6, 1968
*SGT Gary B. Gorton, B Company 2-5th Cavalry, February 17, 1966
SP4 Stanley E. Greene, C Troop 1-9th Cavalry, October 12, 1967
*LTC Bob L. Gregory, HHC 2-12th Cavalry, January 2-3. 1969
*CPT Patrick L. Haley, A Troop 1-9th Cavalry, October 2, 1966
SGT Sequoyah Hall, B Company 2-12th Cavalry, April 21, 1970
PFC George E. Hamilton, A Company 1-7th Cavalry, August 8, 1966
1LT Martin J. Hammer, A Company 2-7th Cavalry, May 6, 1966
*SFC Roy G. Harris, Jr., A Company 2-7th Cavalry, September 19, 1967
*SP4 Paul J. Harrison, C Company 1-12th Cavalry, May 21, 1966
MAJ Thomas H. Harvey, B Troop 1-9th Cavalry, April 16, 1967
PFC Roger K. Hattersley, D Company 1-12th Cavalry, December 17, 1966
SP4 Harris R. Haynie, B Troop 1-9th Cavalry, May 27, 1967
CPT Robert L. Helvey, A Company 2-12th Cavalry, January 7, 1968
*1LT Daniel A. Hennessy, B Company 1-8th Cavalry, December 28, 1966
1LT Ferdinand Hepp, C Company 1-5th Cavalry, October 21, 1966
CPT Thomas K. Hightower, A Company 2-12th Cavalry, February 14, 1967
*SSG Richard G. Hill, E Company 1-7th Cavalry, December 9, 1969
CPT John L. Hitti, B Company 5-7th Cavalry, November 1, 1966
1LT George W Hughes, D Company 1-7th Cavalry, May 5, 1966
SP4 Tom C. Hunt, HHC 1-8th Cavalry, July 12, 1970
CW2 Warren G. Jackson, Med Company 215th Support Battalion, June 28, 1971
LTC Wilbur G. Jenkins, Jr., HHC 1-8th Cavalry, September 24, 1967
*SSG Edward N. Kaneshiro, C Troop 1-9th Cavalry, December 1, 1966
*1LT John K. Kauhaihao, B Company 2-8th Cavalry, September 5, 1969
*PFC Alton R. Kennedy, HHC 1-12th Cavalry, December 17, 1966
WO1 Raymond A. Kerns, A Troop 1-9th Cavalry, September 19, 1967
*SSG Dennis D. Kiger, B Company 8th Enginners, May 7, 1970
*1LT Raymond J. Krupinski, B Company 1-12th Cavalry, April 30, 1969
SP4 Bobby W. Kyles, A Company 2-7th Cavalry, February 27, 1967
*CPT Luther M. Lasater, III, F Troop 9th Cavalry, February 13, 1972
1LT John J. Lewis, B Company 2-12th Cavalry, February 3-4, 1968
*SP4 Larry J. Loncon, HHC 1-8th Cavalry, April 27, 1970
SP5 Charles R. Lose, B Company 1-7th Cavalry, November 14-15, 1965
1LT Thomas E. Lutchendorf, D Company 2-7th Cavalry, December 9, 1967
CPT James E. Mace, A Company 2-5th Cavalry, December 2-4, 1968
SSG Martin A. Manglona, A Company 1-12th Cavalry, February 23, 1969
CPT Roy D. Martin, B Company 1-8th Cavalry, May 21, 1966
*PFC Thomas H. Maynard, C Company 2-8th Cavalry, November 6, 1965
CPT Barry R. McCaffrey, B Company 2-7th Cavalry, March 9, 1969
*1LT Douglas M. McCrary, C Company 5-7th Cavalry, February 16, 1967
SFC Hugh J. McQuiston. Jr., A Company 1-8th Cavalry, July 2, 1967
*CPT William D. Meara, B Company 2-7th Cavalry, November 2, 1968
*PFC Charles T. Moore, D Company 2-5th Cavalry, January 5, 1970
LTC Harold G. Moore, HHC 1-7th Cavalry, November 14-16, 1965
1LT Norman A. Mordue, C Company 1-12th Cavalry - May 31, 1967
*PFC Dan L. Neely, B Company 2-7th Cavalry, March 1, 1968
SFC Charles E. Nelson, A Company 1-5th Cavalry, January 10, 1969
*SP4 William D. Nelson, D Company 2-7th Cavalry, November 6, 1968
CPT Oscar L. O'Connor, D Company 2-7th Cavalry, November 4, 1967
*2LT Henry J. O'Kusky, Jr., D Company 2-7th Cavalry, July 1, 1968
*SP4 Fruto J. Oquendo, C Company 2-8th Cavalry, May 6, 1969
CPT Donald A. Orsini, D Company 1-12th Cavalry, December 15, 1967
SP4 Raymond Ortiz, A Company 1-8th Cavalry, November 3-5, 1965
*SFC Wilfredo Pagan-Lozada, D Company 2-5th Cavalry, February 9, 1967
*1LT Robert C. Peda, A Troop 1-9th Cavalry, April 7, 1968
SP4 William Phifer, A Company 5-7th Cavalry, February 23, 1968
*PFC Alfred Pickard, B Company 1-8th Cavalry, December 2, 1969
1LT John D. Piper, A Battery 2-19th Field Artillery, December 27, 1966
*SP5 James F. Polusney, HHC 2-7th Cavalry, November 17, 1969
*PFC Thomas D. Poole, A Company 5-7th Cavalry, February 12, 1968
PFC Jean D. Poutrain, HHC 2-5th Cavalry, February 9, 1967
*SP4 Richard F. Quinn, HHC 1-8th Cavalry, July 12, 1970

*PFC Lorenzo Ramirez, Jr., D Company 1-5th Cavalry, June 28, 1968
*SSG Thomas G. Reyes, A Company 1-7th Cavalry, November 9, 1967
MAJ Archie A. Rider, A Troop 1-9th Cavalry, December 3, 1967
1LT Ronald J. Riley, D Company 1-5th Cavalry, February 16-17, 1967
2LT George M. Ring, C Company 2-12th Cavalry, June 7, 1968
SP4 Paul J. Rock, B Company 1-12th Cavalry, October 26, 1967
*SP4 Onsby R. Rose, D Company 1-5th Cavalry, May 18, 1966
SFC Edgar A. Ross, D Company 1-8th Cavalry, March 30, 1969
2LT John R. Rowland, D Company 2-5th Cavalry, June 22, 1970
SGT Clyde E. Savage, B Company 1-7th Cavalry, November 14, 1965
1LT James Schlottman, A Troop 1-9th Cavalry, October 2, 1966
SGM James A. Scott, HHC 2-7th Cavalry, November 17, 1965
*SFC Otto W. See, A Troop 1-9th Cavalry, March 11, 1968
WO1 Richard D. Sellers, E Troop 1-9th Cavalry, January 5, 1971
*1SG Earl T. Shaffer, A Company 5-7th Cavalry, December 9, 1968
*CPT Marvin I Siders, D Company 2-7th Cavalry, November 6, 1968
1LT James P. Simons, A Troop 1-9th Cavalry, December 17, 1966
SGT Harold M. Snoddy, D Company 2-12th Cavalry, May 12, 1969
*1LT Richard M. Speer, D Company 2-12th Cavalry, April 22, 1970
SP4 Noble L. Steeley, A Troop 1-9th Cavalry, August 20, 1968
1LT Rufus Stephens, B Company 2-5th Cavalry, February 17, 1966
LTC Robert D. Stevenson, HHC 2-5th Cavalry, March 11, 1967
*PFC Michael H. Stoflet, A Company 5-7th Cavalry, November 1, 1966
*1LT James M. Stone, C Company 2-12th Cavalry, January 7, 1968
*SP4 Brent A. Street, E Company 2-8th Cavalry, April 1, 1970
*SP4 Johnnie D. Swann, B Company 2-8th Cavalry, September 5, 1969
LTC Richard S. Sweet, HHC 2-12th Cavalry, February 3-5, 1968
LTC Thomas H. Tackaberry, HHC 2-8th Cavalry, September 19, 1966
1LT Ronald S. Taylor, C Company 2-12th Cavalry, January 7, 1968
*CPT William E. Taylor, B Company 2-5th Cavalry, August 14-15, 1966
*SP4 Brian E. Tierney, D Company 1-12th Cavalry, May 21, 1968
*SP4 Robert A. Tillquist, B Company 2-12th Cavalry, November 4, 1965
MG John J. Tolson, HHC 1st Cavalry Division, February 14-27 March, 1968
SP4 Robert L. Towles, D Company 2-7th Cavalry, November 17, 1965
CW2 Ronald L. Tusi, F Battery 79th Artillery (AFA), April 15, 1972
*SP4 Michael G. Vinassa, C Company 1-8th Cavalry, May 21, 1966
SGT Raymond F. Waite, D Company 229th Aviation, April 8, 1972
*SP4 Casey O. Waller, E Company 2-8th Cavalry, April 1, 1970
SFC Albert R. Watts, D Company 2-12th Cavalry, September 23, 1966
*SP4 Richard L. Waycaster, A Company 2-8th Cavalry, February 19, 1969
SP5 Thomas E. West, 1st Cavalry Division, May 2, 1970
CPT John B. Whitehead, D Company 229th Aviation, April 8, 1972
*SSG Elvin J. Wideman, A Company 5-7th Cavalry, November 19, 1966
SP5 Larry D. Wright, A Troop 1-9th Cavalry, October 2, 1966
CPT Merrill F. Wymer, Jr., HHC 2-12th Cavalry, April 21, 1967
*SP4 Kent M. Zerr, B Troop 1-9th Cavalry, March 6, 1970

Operation Iraqi Freedom
The President of the United States
Takes Pride in Presenting
The Distinguished Service Cross
(Posthumously) To
Keith Yoakum
Chief Warrant Officer Four, U.S. Army

Citation:

For extraordinary heroism in action while serving with Company A, 1st Battalion, 227th Aviation Regiment, 1st Air Cavalry Brigade, Multi-National Corps-Iraq. Chief Warrant Officer Four Yoakum distinguished himself as a Pilot of an AH-64D Longbow Apache Helicopter on 2 February 2007 while engaged in aerial operations in Baghdad, Iraq, during Operation IRAQI FREEDOM. During a reconnaissance mission, Chief Warrant Officer Four Yaokum's aircraft was seriously damaged by heavy enemy machine gun fire, which required him to land immediately. Without regard for his own safety and to protect his comrades, Chief Warrant Officer Four Yoakum chose to remain with his wingman to destroy the enemy. With his main gun inoperable, his only option was to climb in altitude and then dive while firing his Apache's rockets. Ultimately the aircraft succumbed to its battle damage and crashed. Chief Warrant Officer Four Yoakum's distinctive accomplishments and dedication to service to his country are in keeping with the finest traditions of the military service, reflecting great credit upon himself, the 1st Cavalry Division, the Multi-National Corps-Iraq, and the United States Army.

Col. Hal Moore being presented the Distinguished Service Cross by Gen. Westmoreland. Photo courtesy of Donald R. Davis.

HISTORY OF THE 1ST CAVALRY DIVISION ASSOCIATION

On 17 July 1944, a group of First Team Soldiers in the Admiralty Islands agreed to form an Association of 1st Cavalry Division Soldiers and Veterans to preserve old friendships and conduct periodic reunions. The first reunion of the 1st Cavalry Division Association was held in 1948 at El Paso, Texas where the 1st Cavalry Division was organized in 1921 at Fort Bliss. Today the 1st Cavalry Division Association is a non-political, non-sectarian, non-profit, Soldiers and Veterans fraternal organization that has over 28,600 active members. Our membership consists of Troopers who rode horses in the 1940's through Troopers who ride Abrams tanks and Apache helicopters today. Our equipment, tactics and the locations where we served may be different, but we all share a commonality of serving in the best Division in the United States Army – the 1st Cavalry Division.

The Association unanimously adopted a Constitution in November 1948 during its first reunion and was incorporated in Washington, D.C. on 1 September 1949. The Constitution begins by listing the aims and objectives of the Association. It states, "The 1st Cavalry Division Association was organized in the Admiralty Islands with the common aims: to perpetuate the fine traditions and the gallant accomplishments of the Division; to provide a suitable memorial dedicated to the memory of our fallen comrades; to establish an endowment program to continue as a lasting reminder in their memory; to preserve and strengthen the fine friendships that found root during war service in the 1st Cavalry Division; and to be mutually helpful to one another in the years which lie ahead."

Perpetuation of the fine traditions and the gallant accomplishments of the Division remain one of the objectives of the Association. The 1st Cavalry Division Band, Honor Guard, and Horse Cavalry Detachment maintain that tradition as the Battle Streamers on the unit Colors flutter in the breeze on Cooper Field during ceremonies at Fort Hood. The Association has a close tie to the Horse Cavalry Detachment since it provided funds to assist the Division Commander, MG Jim Smith, in equipping the Horse Platoon in 1971. Since that time, the Association has remained in close contact with the unit that has ridden in Rose Bowl Parades and Presidential Inaugurations. Association members maintain contact with their old units and often conduct briefings or leader development classes for them during the reunions conducted at Fort Hood. This helps to bring the Division's history to life for the present day Troopers. The Association Historian and other members of the Association undertook the task of updating and recording the history of the Division. The resulting book, 1st Cavalry Division, A Spur Ride Through the 20th Century, is another way the Association ensures that the accomplishments of the Division are remembered.

The Association formed the 1st Cavalry Division Association Museum Foundation in 2004 to provide support to the 1st Cavalry Division Museum. The Museum Foundation helps the Museum preserve, maintain, and present the history of the First Team for generations of Troopers yet to come. The Museum Foundation currently is trying to fund a new museum building to house the historical artifacts and exhibits that detail the Division's glorious history. Contributions to the 1st Cavalry Division Association Museum Foundation are tax deductible.

The names of our honored dead from previous wars are set in long bronze tablets that surround those who enter the 1st Cavalry Division Memorial Chapel on Fort Hood. The tablets affixed to the inner walls of the Chapel are a fulfillment of the pledge to dedicate a fitting memorial to the 10,383 Troopers assigned to units of the 1st Cavalry Division who gave their lives during World War II, the Korean War, the Vietnam War, and Desert Storm. The dedication plaque near the entrance of the Chapel states, "This Memorial is dedicated by the Troopers past and present of the 1st Cavalry Division to those of our ranks who have fallen in battle. We record their names here as a perpetual roll call in honor of their selfless sacrifice. We, your comrades in arms, salute you and rededicate ourselves to the principles of duty, honor, and country for which you gave the last full measure of devotion." The memorial was dedicated during the 1995 reunion and continues to be a focus of our Memorial Service during reunions held in Killeen. Names of the war in Iraq will be added at a later date. Additionally, the Museum Foundation organized an effort to build a Division Memorial to honor the Troopers of the Division that were killed during the Division's first deployment to Iraq. This Memorial stands on Cooper Field adjacent to the Division Headquarters to honor those who died. The names of the honored dead from the Division's subsequent deployments to Iraq and Afghanistan have been added to the Memorial.

In 1967, the Sergeants Major of the Division asked the 1st Cavalry Division Association to provide support for the children of Troopers who had been killed in action in Vietnam in the form of scholarships. In August of 1968 a trust agreement was signed that established the Foundation of the 1st Cavalry Division Association. Since that time, the Foundation has provided in excess of $1,000,000 in scholarship grants to over 768 eligible applicants. Scholarships are awarded to children of Soldiers of the 1st Cavalry Division who died or were totally and permanently disabled as a result of wounds received or diseases contracted while serving with the 1st Cavalry Division in any armed conflict. The children of Association members who die while serving with the 1st Cavalry Division during peacetime and active duty Soldiers, currently serving in the Division, who are members of the Association and their Family members are also eligible. Since the Foundation started providing scholarships no student has been turned away due to lack of funds. Donations by individual Association members, fund drives within the Division and an investment portfolio managed by the Foundation Trustees provide the corpus that supports the program. Contributions to the Foundation of the 1st Cavalry Division Association are tax deductible.

Presidents of the 1st Cavalry Division Association 1944-2017

Innis Palmer Swift 1944
William C. Chase 1945
Verne D. Mudge 1948
William J. Bradley 1949
Charles C. Young 1950
Hobart R. Gay 1951
Rex E. Chandler 1952
Rodger D. Schoch 1953
Carl Milchen 1954
Alfred E. Stevens 1955
Charles A. Sheldon 1956
Rowland O. Huddleston 1957
Chester H. Chambers 1958
James B. Corbett 1959
Charles E. Brady 1960
Eugene J. Field 1961
William H. Nealing 1962
John J. Naughton 1963
John J. O'Connell 1964
Hughes Seewald 1965
Mitchell Piperski 1966
Ignacio Passos 1967
Sherman P. Haight 1968
Donald H. Walton 1970
William A. Becker 1972
Horace G. Goodrich 1974
Harry W.O. Kinnard 1976
Robert P. Cooper 1978
John R. Hall, Jr. 1980
James C. Smith 1982
Robert M. Shoemaker 1984
Hugh L.C. Millar, Jr. 1986
Thomas E. Hartin 1988
Norman R. Osterby 1990
Peter Tattersall 1992
William K. Kreischer 1994
Ernest P. Terrell, Jr. 1995
William A. Richardson 1996
Roy C. Blumenauer 1998
John T. Hodes 2000
Peter Tattersall 2002
Robert D. Johnson 2004
William J. Richardson, Jr. 2006
James W. Booth 2008
Lyman C. Duryea 2010
Jerry F. Eller 2012
James R. Stokely 2014
Scott B. Smith 2016
Allan O. Norris 2017

Annual Reunion Sites

1948 – El Paso, Texas
1949 – Louisville, Kentucky
1950 – New York, New York
1951 – San Antonio, Texas
1952 – Cleveland, Ohio
1953 – El Paso, Texas
1954 – Washington, DC
1955 – Detroit, Michigan
1956 – Denver, Colorado
1957 – Chicago, Illinois
1958 – El Paso, Texas
1959 – San Francisco, Calif.
1960 – Washington, DC
1961 – San Antonio, Texas
1962 – Louisville, Kentucky
1963 – El Paso, Texas
1964 – New York, New York
1965 – Kansas City, Kansas
1966 – Miami, Florida
1967 – Los Angeles, California
1968 – El Paso, Texas
1969 – Fort Benning, Georgia
1970 – Boston, Massachusetts
1971 – San Antonio, Texas
1972 – Fort Hood, Texas
1973 – El Paso, Texas
1974 – Fort Benning, Georgia
1975 – Norfolk, Virginia
1976 – Fort Hood, Texas
1977 – Los Angeles, California
1978 – Fort Hood, Texas
1979 – El Paso, Texas
1980 – Fort Hood, Texas
1981 – Colorado Springs, Colorado
1982 – Washington, DC
1983 – Fort Hood, Texas
1984 – El Paso, Texas
1985 – Fort Hood, Texas
1986 – Las Vegas, Nevada
1987 – Fort Hood, Texas
1988 – Orlando, Florida
1989 – Fort Hood, Texas
1990 – Fort Benning, Georgia
1991 – Fort Hood, Texas
1992 – Billings, Montana
1993 – Fort Hood, Texas
1994 – Orlando, Florida
1995 – Fort Hood, Texas
1996 – Milwaukee, Wisconsin
1997 – Fort Hood, Texas
1998 – Buffalo, New York
1999 – Fort Hood, Texas
2000 – Fayetteville, North Carolina
2001 – Fort Hood, Texas
2002 – Colorado Springs, Colorado
2003 – Fort Hood, Texas
2004 – Milwaukee, Wisconsin
2005 – Fort Hood, Texas
2006 – Louisville, Kentucky
2007 – Riverside, California
2008 – Jacksonville, Florida
2009 – Fort Hood, Texas
2010 – Bloomington, Minn.
2011 – Fort Hood, Texas
2012 – Portland, Oregon
2013 – Fort Hood, Texas
2014 – Oak Brook, Illinois (DuPage County)
2015 – Fort Hood, Texas
2016 – Las Vegas, Nevada
2017 – Fort Hood, Texas
2018 – Charleston, West Virginia (20-24 June)
2019 – Fort Hood, Texas (12-16 June)
2020 – Louisville, Kentucky (30 June - 5 July)
2021 – Fort Hood, Texas (TBD)

1C-5C

Stories, Reflections, and Photos

5th Cavalry Troopers take a break — Korea, 1950.

Stories of the 1st Cavalry Division

My Most Memorable Experience

By Terry Wilson

My most memorable experience was at Camp Evans May 19, 1968. It was about 6:00 P.M., when an enemy rocket attack began. One rocket hit our ammo dump. It started off slow, sounding like small arms fire. We initially thought we were under a ground assault. But then, larger explosions began. C-4 (Plastic explosives) began to detonate, hurling pallets of artillery canisters at least 400 to 500 feet into the air causing airbursts of hot shrapnel to rain down on us. As I lay in an open trench, I could not help but think how much it looked like a 4th of July fireworks display. Hot shrapnel landed on huge fuel bladders that, when ignited, sent a destructive wave of concussion blasts filled with dirt and rocks across the entire encampment. In general, there were minimal casualties, which I considered a major miracle. Almost nothing was left standing by morning. It took weeks to haul out all the damaged helicopters and vehicles.

My most vivid memory though, was what I observed the next morning. The explosions during the night set off large tear gas supplies so massive that clouds of tear gas settled over the entire camp like early morning fog; not bad enough to merit wearing a gas mask, but enough to burn your eyes and irritate your throat.

At day break, I crawled out of the trench and made my way down to the communications bunker about 300 yards from my position. I was needed there to fix damaged equipment and help re-establish Division communications. On my way, I had to walk by what remained of the Senior Officers' Mess tent. There, standing at a wooden table, was a cook wearing a gas mask and tossing a salad for the officers. A photo of that would have been priceless. None of us, including the officers, had seen or eaten fresh food for months, and here was the Senior Officers' cook mixing tear gas residue into their fresh salad.

Bon Appetite Sir! Waste not, want not.

A Triumphant Election Day

By Frank Caponio

Two days before the first national election since the fall of Saddam, I pleaded with the Division Chief of Staff to let me go out with the 1st Brigade commander, who had offered me the opportunity to spend election day with him traveling around his area of operations: Sadr City and other areas on the east side of the Tigress River. January 30th proved to be the most memorable and significant day of my tour. Throughout that day, I rode and walked the streets of many neighborhoods in Baghdad with the 1st BCT Commander and several of his battalion commanders.

On Election Day, Iraqi National Guard Soldiers, with help from the police, were providing security at the polling sites. U.S. forces were providing an outer ring of security and responding to attacks as they occurred. The bravery and courage of the Iraqi citizens, demonstrated by their refusal to stay away from the polls despite the threat of death, particularly the women, was incredible. On one occasion, I witnessed a long line of people, mostly females, continuing to wait in line until the bodies of a suicide bomber and the policeman he had killed could be cleaned up and the polling station reopened. These Iraqis were risking their lives to cast a vote and move their country forward. The feeling was infectious and our Soldiers all felt it.

Not only had American Soldiers reduced the threat of an Iraq armed with weapons of mass destruction and eliminated a tyrannical government, they were also agents of change, providing the people of Iraq the chance for a more democratic government. They were the ones paying the tremendous cost in blood and personal sacrifice, and many of them felt that, just as in previous wars, American society was supporting them after summoning them to answer in the aftermath of 9/11. They had rid the world of a horrible tyrant. And if they stayed with it, would be able to foster democracy in this corner of the world that was in desperate need of an end to the bloodshed and injustice that had plagued it for so many decades. They knew what they were fighting and sacrificing for, and it seemed to be worth it.

As we walked the streets of a certain section of Sadr City, the exact block where we had seen the first significant losses of the deployment, I couldn't help but notice the expression on the battalion commander's face. During one evening in April, he had lost five men with 50 more wounded on this very street. Now, children were surrounding him and chanting his name with joy and excitement. There was music and dancing and an absence of the menacing scowls that typified the faces of the poor residents of the slum. This time, the battalion commander's eyes reflected his undeniable pride in the accomplishments and progress of his Soldiers. As we returned to the rallying point at sunset, we were anxious to find out how the rest of the city and country had voted, but at least in this part of Baghdad, Election Day had been a great success.

The Voice of G.I. Joe

By Bill Corsair (McGroarty)

For the most part, you were older, by a few years, than the rest of the passengers on Flight 703. At 28, you were one of the Old Timers. On landing, you follow the long green line of anxious faces out into the blinding, yellow-tinted sunlight of Bien Hoa and feel the 120° heat push heavy on your lungs. Then it climbs aboard your already damp shoulders for a yearlong ride. A ride that will be, for the most part, aboard the choppers and fixed wing aircraft of the "Sky Troopers" of the fabled 1st Cavalry Division, Airmobile. You'll travel across three of the four tactical areas of Vietnam and elsewhere, when necessary, as part of the division's assignment to interdict the build-up and execution of the second Tet Offensive, by the NVA, and what was left of the VC.

Less than a year before, I recorded the voice of Hasbro's "Talking G.I. Joe." The company had decided to add a voice to the soon to be iconic figures. Pull the dog tags and "G.I. Joe, U.S. Army, reporting for duty", "Enemy planes, hit the dirt," and so on, would be the response. It was sometime in 1967, and I was a rock & roll deejay at a RI radio station. Hasbro is Rhode Island based, so when their Sam Speers asked everyone on the air staff to audition for "something new we're going to try", I cut a tape and got the job. I recorded, edited and voiced all branches of the services. Handing the tape to Sam, he gave me the princely sum of $100.

Not long after that, on 13 May 1968, the five Officers and one hundred twenty-one enlisted men of my company, the 115th Military Police, RING were mobilized for active duty and stationed at the United States Military Academy, West Point, NY. We were to act as a personnel pool, under the Levy System, to fill slots in the major combat divisions in Vietnam. Special training included night infiltration, reconnaissance and field maneuvers against the 82nd Airborne.

I was assigned to the FWD Headquarters of the 1st Cav, one of three from the 115th (with Sergeant Piatek and Specialist Nicholson) to serve with the "Sky Troopers". I was based at Phouc Vinh, close to the Cambodian border.

I wrote to Hasbro for some of the "Talking G.I. Joe's" to pass out to the kids in the nearby village. They had nothing and were great little heroes in their own right.

Seemed like a natural to me, but the response from the PR guy in R.I. was "sorry Bill, but Hasbro is trying to distance itself from their war toys." Well it was 1969, but I was still disappointed with the response. The kids in the Village had to make do with playing with, what some considered the real "G.I. Joe," whenever I could grab a few minutes in between rockets, mortars and angry men in black pajamas. That was pretty much the last I ever heard from anybody at Hasbro.

Late in my tour I was sent TDY to AFVN-TV/Radio Network in Saigon, to write, produce and give voice to the combat footage shot with my team (Specialists Hufford & Newsome), in the field. I was to tell the story of "The 1st Team" in combat in Vietnam via the AFVN TV/Radio Network newscasts and features. Completing that assignment, I left Country and rejoined the 115th MPC at the USMA and ended my service in RI, after the Company was returned to state control, in December 1969.

So, now you know. "G.I. Joe" was a Staff Sergeant with the 1st Cavalry Division in Vietnam....or at least his voice was. Who better than a Sky Trooper?

The Medic, the MOH, and Me

By Donald Swan

I boarded a red-eye out of Oakland, crossed the International Date Line and was still in the air when I spotted a fighter jet, port side, flying close enough that I recognized it as a USAF F-4 Phantom II. The pilot saluted smartly, split left, went wet with after burners, belched two trails of JP-4 and disappeared. An escort? All right.

Half an hour later, I stepped from the cool comfort of a USAF C-141 Starlifter, thinking I'd walked into a sauna with bad breath, body odor and maybe someone breaking wind. Unless severely wounded or killed, Vietnam was my home for the next 365 days or 364 and wake-up from 7 January 1967.

The USAF C-130 Hercules landed hard on the PSP, of the too short runway, in An Khe. Before me was a sight to behold, headquarters for the elite 1st Cavalry Division (Airmobile) with sixteen thousand men and more than four hundred helicopters. I was temporally assigned to the Cav's forward operating post, a short C7-A hop northeast to Bong Son.

On 20 March 1967, our small PIO Detachment there heard about an ambushed Cav company in jeopardy of losing contact with its battalion in the Northern Dinh Binh Providence.

My OIC gave me tacit approval, thinking I couldn't get a lift, to go to the scene. Within the hour late that afternoon, I was ass-deep in elephant grass after leaping from a hovering D model Huey with a squad of six pissed-off 11Bs laden with M-60s, M-79s, M-16s, a crap load of ammo and a bunch of other stuff. Less than two hours ago one of these GIs had to fold a good poker hand, another was daydreaming about a can of lukewarm Falstaff, still others were just sleeping when they got word they were going north to supplement a replacement platoon for the beleaguered unit. But now these 18-20 year-olds were gung-ho and I was going in with them.

After a few hundred meters of tactical movement toward the objective, we heard sporadic gunfire in the distance, around Tan An or Don Song village, and rushed toward it low-crawling the last few yards. Amongst a line of palms and graveyard mounds is where we saw it; a sandy field littered with our own dead and wounded. The smoke. The smell. The scent I won't forget, the smell of battle.*

Of all the emotions that could arise from this devastating scene; the men preparing for another attack, during a brief respite, were all talking about just one thing: the heroics one SP4 medic.

Evidently just one Soldier saw enough to realize what was coming, and a split-second after yelling "Ambush!" was dead. Blazing from three positions a company of dug-in NVA was overwhelming the 27 men of 1st Platoon; bullets flying twice the speed of sound—laying waste to soft skin—pulverizing bones—dropping men screaming-scattering the platoon. The SP4 medic reacted instantly by grabbing an M-16 from a seriously wounded comrade, took out an enemy sniper, machine gun position, and three or four more NVA. To aid his wounded Soldiers, he ran and crawled across the ambush zone again and again totally exposed, refusing cover through the withering enemy fire as bullets ripped through his poncho and struck all around him. His Platoon leader was dead from a shot to the head, one of his two machine gunners was killed and several other Soldiers badly wounded. He pulled the M-60 from his dead gunner and gave it to a rifleman for more firepower, ran for help and brought men from other platoons. Finding his RTO, wounded, he finally reached his Company Commander who told him they were in the shit too and had no one to send.

The sun had set and darkness was near, yet there were hours to go before relief. The Soldier, still too young to vote, had saved at least a dozen of his fellow Sky Troopers by killing the enemy, encouraging and directing his men, treating the wounded and supervising the evacuation. For six hours the 20 year-old SP4 from Lincoln, Nebraska held together what was left of his 1st Platoon.

News of the heroics travelled fast and it caught the attention of one MG John Norton, Commander of 1st Cav, who arrived the next morning by chopper. The two star General pinned the Silver Star on SP4 Charles C. Hagemeister's tattered uniform, for his heroics the previous day while serving as a medic with A Company, 1st Battalion of the 5th Cavalry Regiment (Black Knights). As he shook his hand, Gen. Norton said to Hagemeister, "I'm about to rotate back to the states and I'm gonna' put you in for the Medal of Honor, boy."

I was excited, I had the story and what a story it became. (Think: May '68) After that, I continued going where the troops were for their stories and escorting U.S. news media to show the Cav in action. I was also a DJ and newscaster on AFVN An Khe.

I hadn't thought much about Gen Norton's declaration until I was safely back in the States in May 1968 and saw, on TV, President Johnson at the White House placing the Medal of Honor around Hagemeister's neck! (His MOH citation is on Wikipedia.)

A few months later I received word that my replacement at PIO-VN was KIA. Now I count my blessings every night lying in a comfortable bed—not worried about Incoming. And every now and then I think about Hagemeister and other brave men of the 1st Cav who got no medal at all, the wounded and

Black Knights of A Company's 1st Platoon, 1st of 5th Cav, on the offensive (right) after taking cover behind grave mounds. A company-sized force of NVA ambushed the 27-man platoon, 20 March 1967, near Don Song/Tan An village. Medic Charles C. Hagemeister earned the Medal of Honor for his heroics that day (1st Cav. PIO).

those who gave it all. As we enter our twilight years and begin to reflect, let's take a breath and raise our chests once more and remember; however the Vietnam outcome, we served with honor. Indeed, we served on The First Team.

*Note: my depiction of these events is based solely on my recollections from 49 years. Any misrepresentations or mistakes are mine and unintentional.

Hanoi Hannah Gave Unbelievable News

By Ted Cogut

November 1965, somewhere east of An Khe in South Vietnam's Central Highlands....daylight had completely faded. It was not a place or a date that would otherwise be remembered—just a hill with no name on a day like many others and yet not like them. At the start of full-scale warfare, our First Cavalry Division was battling two enemies—the invading North Vietnamese Army (NVA) and their highly organized puppet guerillas, the Viet Cong (VC). We looked for the moon. If it were full, we could face a little less exciting night. It was believed the VC would stand down in full moon; though the NVA would indeed be there. But a thick cloud deck blocked all skylight. We could not see the moon. While tuning the ANGRC-19, the AM radio, out of the dark a female voice broke in. Sounding almost American, she said New York City lost all electrical power. Could it be true? Electrical power in America was as reliable as a rising moon. Then, talking directly to us, she said the First Cavalry Division was losing its current battle and was headed for complete defeat. Someone said: "Where was that coming from? Who was it?" A Soldier guessing: "Hanoi." A chuckle, followed by: "Hanoi Hannah."

Typical of Soldiers in all wars, we were in the dark with respect to the overall battle, but we were fortified in belief of our capabilities and confident she didn't know American Soldiers and their "First Cav." Of course, we believed her report was mere propaganda. Still, even if only for a fleeting instant, one had to wonder—was anything happening on the battlefield that we should know? In a week or two, letters and newspapers from home confirmed a power failure in New York, on November 9-10. Widespread, it also affected nearby states and Canada.

I don't know if that was the first time she was called "Hanoi Hannah." In any case, in my two tours in South Vietnam the only time I heard her was on that night with no visible moon—in the Central Highlands, on a hill with no name. She had been right about the power failure and quite wrong about First Cav. First, Cav took the war directly to the invading NVA; inevitably and sadly, First Cav would suffer casualties, though far less than the enemy, as it decisively defeated and repulsed the invader in all those battles.

Notes: Adapted from Ted Cogut's book, Forecaster! Battling the Weather Odds in Peace and War.

1st Cavalry Division LRRP/Rangers

by Ronald Lee Christopher

In late October 1966 with approval from the Department of the Army, the 1st Cavalry Division was authorized to form an experimental Long Range Reconnaissance Patrol (LRRP). On October 31, 1966, I was called to the Division rear (An Khe) by the G2 to be interviewed as the team leader of that experimental team. So, on November 1st, I stood before the Division G2 listening to a proposal that the G2 wanted. I accepted the mission and from that time until January 1, 1967, I built the Division LRRP camp with mostly scrounged material because we were not TO&E. However, the LRRP unit was attached to the 191st Military Intelligence for logistical purposes, so the 191st got me the military supplies I needed. Another part of my mission was to test new equipment for the Division per the desires of the Division G3. What is interesting is that the G2 and G3 both knew me, as I had worked for the G3 for a few weeks. So when the G2 was searching for someone to train and lead the experimental team, the G3 recommended me. A phone call was made by the G2 to my troop commander, Lt. Col George (Blake) McIlwain. Col McIlwain ended that phone call in this manner. "If you want the job done, then Staff Sergeant Christopher is the Trooper to do the job."

On January 1, 1967, four Troopers showed up at the LRRP camp to be the rest of my experimental LRRP team. From that date until January 6th, I trained those four Troopers as to what I felt they needed to know to accomplish the mission and of course, stay alive. On January 7, 1967, me and my team, Sergeant John Simones, assistant team leader; SP4 Douglas Fletcher, senior scout; SP4 Geoffrey Koper, medic and SP4 Arthur Guerrero, rear scout, were inserted at night into the An Lao Valley. The only words from Captain Jim James, the CO of our unit, were these: "Chris, you have to stay the full seven days or there will be no LRRPs. If you get into trouble, you are on your own. There is no support."

Our mission was to find the enemy and report back, but more important, we were to stay in the An Lao Valley for seven days and eight nights, living off what we carried on our backs. And of course, we were not to be seen by the enemy because we had no backup support whatsoever. An interesting side note is when Lieutenant Ronald Hall, the XO, did not unpack his bags because he said, "nobody has stayed in the An Loa Valley." It is worth noting that the pilot who flew us into the An Lao Valley for insertion was Warrant Officer Jim Bracewell, and he did that with no other helicopter support.

I had come from the reconnaissance platoon of A Troop, 9th Cavalry at LZ Hammond, where I was a squad leader and the assistant platoon sergeant, and on a few occasions I was the platoon sergeant. Being a Ranger school graduate, I knew the importance of how to run reconnaissance missions. I had one standing order, which I informed my new members on the day they arrived at the LRRP camp. That order was, "Do exactly as I tell you to do. If you cannot do that then you are free to leave with no hard feelings." They all stayed. I felt such an order was necessary, because none of those four Troopers had reconnaissance experience.

After conducting a successful seven-day mission for the Cavalry Division, Captain James began recruiting additional volunteers to expand the unit. After completing three, seven-day, eight-night missions in January, my team and I were again inserted into the An Lao Valley on February 2, 1967 to conduct the first official mission of the Cavalry Division's LRRP unit, another seven-day, eight-night mission. We were official and TO&E to the Division. My team and I went on to run seven-day, eight-night missions with only one day off between missions. I left the LRRPs in the middle of April, satisfied that I had completed what the G2 wanted done.

On December 20, 1967 our LRRP unit was redesignated Company E, 52nd Infantry. On February 1, 1969, Company E was redesignated Company H (Ranger), 75th Infantry (Airborne). The 1st Cavalry Division LRRP/Ranger unit was the longest serving LRRP/Ranger unit of the Vietnam War. Today's 2nd Battalion 75th Rangers is carrying our colors.

At the undertaking of the first experimental LRRP mission I was a Staff Sergeant, Ranger School graduate, 29 years of age, with 10 years of Army service (and I might mention, I had a broken back). After my tour in Vietnam, I became a US Army Counterintelligence Agent. I retired with over 20 years' service as a Sergeant First Class.

Over the course of years, since 1987, I have had eight books published. The first two are about me and my Troopers in Vietnam. Its title: *A Troop, 9th Cavalry, (The boldest cavalrymen the world has ever known)*. My second book is about the beginning of the 1st Cavalry Division's LRRPs, the building of the camp, the training of my team and the missions we conducted. The other book of interest, concerning the 1st Cavalry Division is: *LURPS AT WAR VIETNAM*. It is the history of the 1st Cavalry Division LRRPs from beginning to end.

Some Experiences

By J.M. Hilts

Beyond the Wire

Crouching in my black pit, I intently studied the concertina wire some 60 yards away, straining to pick-up the slightest motion of the enemy. That wire became a towering brick wall in my mind, keeping me safe, allowing my thoughts to drift off to life beyond it. Yet, it was never far from my thoughts, that during a dark monsoon downpour an enemy could slither through and take away the life that I sought beyond the wire.

Oh, my life beyond the wire would be so full. I would marry her. I would return to school and become someone great. We would have children and a very good life.

My buddy nudged me, pointing to a perceived motion, bringing me back to within the wire. Time passed and nothing happened, thank God! He said he needed to get some sleep. Okay, I said. He quietly sank into the hole. I wondered how far beyond the wire his thoughts were. Time passed, nothing happened. Dawn started to break and the wire slowly became transparent; once more showing that no one was there.

Jumping the Gun

Guarding the perimeter of Camp Evans, I was on top of a bunker with a cook extremely anxious to fire his M79 grenade launcher. He kept seeing movement along the perimeter. I finally requested a flare and cautioned the cook to be sure of his target before firing. The flare went up, so did the cook and let loose a grenade which hit a dead tree only 75 feet in front of us. We both hit the deck, luckily without shrapnel wounds. A second later the officer of the guard called yelling, "What the hell is going on?" I replied, "Nothing sir," but the cook smiled.

A Lot of Beer

My company had come in for an extended rest at Camp Evans. It was monsoon season and very few supply choppers were making it in through the bad weather. The PX was out of beer and we were a mighty thirst crew. So the guys in my platoon decided to take things into our own hands. We pooled our money and talked a Sikorsky flying crane pilot into going to Da Nang to buy a full skid load of beer and deliver it to us. I don't quite remember how many cases of beer that was, but it stood four or five feet high. It was a lot of beer. My platoon decided to have a party. We traded some beer for some Air Force steaks since they always had good chow. We had the beer hidden under a tarp, but it was still pretty conspicuous in the company area that is shown in Figure 5. It wasn't long before someone spilled the beans. The company commander came over and asked me what was under the tarp. Well, it's very difficult to lie to your commander when he's leaning against the tarp. "Uh, we bought some beer sir." "Oh, I see, and what were you going to do with it?" "Well, we were going to have a party, sir." "And who were you inviting to the party?" "Well, sir, just the guys in the platoon." "Looks like you have enough for the whole company." "Uh, yes sir, but the guys all chipped in the money for it." "Well, that's very generous of them but here is what we are going to do. You either invite the entire company to your party, or I confiscate the whole skid and give it back to you one can a day." It was a great party while it lasted!

Sweet Coolness

Having just come out of the bush for a rest at Camp Evans, my platoon was suddenly sent out on a mission to provide security for a small unit coming to a hill about five klicks away. We were not happy campers. Air assaulting to the hill, we formed a defensive perimeter and waited. Finally, on the third day a Sikorsky flying crane with a large building-sized box slung below it landed: It was an ice cream factory! Of course, needing some confirmation of the product's quality, we spent the rest of the day devouring five gallon containers, which made up for the shortness of our camp stay.

Hot Time on the Old LZ

A couple of us radio men were sent to a temporary fire base on LZ MIGUEL, to establish a relay station over the mountains for an upcoming operation. Since we were going to be there for a week or so, I decided to build a little hooch to protect myself from the weather and have some privacy. I found a good spot between two big boulders. I scrounged some ammo boxes, sand bags and a few tarps and built a cozy hooch. At the end of this first day, I was pretty wiped out so I decided to get some sleep. Even though I was exhausted, I couldn't close my eyes because big rats were crawling in and out of my hooch. I felt like taking my 45 and shooting them, but it would just be my luck that the round would ricochet off of a boulder and kill me. Finally, I fell asleep. I woke with a start to the sound of a tremendous battle going on. I grabbed my rifle and ran to the perimeter, thinking we were being overrun. Everybody and their brother were blasting away at the wire, but there was no incoming fire. I asked someone what was going on, and he said they were having a "mad minute" expending old ammunition. Nobody had bothered to tell me, but I joined in on the fun.

The Night of the Rocket

I had just come off duty at the battalion TOC radio room and was bone tired. I lay on my cot in the tent where the radio guys slept and was soon fast asleep. The tent was located about 50 feet behind and to the side of the radio room end of the TOC. There was a small ventilation window in the radio room sand bag wall. I hadn't been asleep for more than an hour, when a 122 mm rocket slammed right into that small ventilation window of the TOC. My cot was at the end of the tent furthest from the TOC. The blast blew me about 15-20 feet out of the tent. I picked myself up and realizing I wasn't hit, ran down into the TOC, which was filled with smoke and dust. Most of the shrapnel had gone through the window and out the door of the radio room and pinned the duty officer against the sand bag wall. He was bleeding from what looked like every part of his body. I helped carry him outside to be flown to an off-shore hospital ship. I don't know if he survived or not. The two men in the radio room were seriously wounded but survived. Two men in the tent with me were seriously wounded, but also survived. After the excitement calmed down, I went back to sleep. I woke up with a start and realized I was having problems breathing. I got the attention of the guy next to me. They put me in a jeep and drove me to the small field hospital at Camp Evans. The doctors immediately knew that I had gone into shock from what had happened the previous night. My heart was threatening to stop, so the doctor gave me a shot of adrenalin to boost my heart rate. Later, he told me that it may have actually stopped beating for a few seconds. That was the closest I ever came to being killed in Viet Nam.

A Lucky Shot

While working out of the battalion TOC (tactical operations center); I would make trips out to our companies on a "mule", when they were within a klick or two outside of Camp Evans to check on radios, bring out new batteries and distribute the latest code sheets. However, between guys being killed, wounded or rotating back home we were critically short of company radio men or RTO's (radio telephone operators). Since I had been promoted to buck sergeant and was familiar with all our companies, I was immediately transferred to C Company; thus, starting my career as a true grunt. "Charley" Company was bivouacked on some low lying hills outside Camp Evans. The VC would harass the camp by randomly firing 122 mm rockets at it, then taking off before we could get to the launch sites. As C Company was preparing to start a new mission, an NVA gunner got lucky. We heard the rocket go over our heads and land right on top of our main ammo dump. The whole dump went up like a fourth of July finale. Since there was nothing we could do, we just sat back and enjoyed the show. It was at least three days until the dump was safe enough to start cleaning up.

The Long and the Short of It

I was walking along a path through a Michelin rubber plantation. The trees were extremely tall with high grass all around. I was really hungry and headed for some chow. I saw this log up ahead, just about the same diameter as the trees and wondered why it had been cut down. I then became cautious. Drawing closer, I realized that the "log" was moving. I stood there for what seemed an eternity watching the log slither across the path. I took a wide detour in the opposite direction while keeping my rifle at the ready and hoping the snake had already had his lunch.

Night Ambush

My platoon was patrolling along the Bong Son River and had been ordered to stop at a backwater, which extended maybe a football field length into the jungle. The previous spring another American patrol had lost some equipment trying to cross the backwater when the river was high and turbulent. Since it was late in the day, the bulk of the platoon bivouacked at the head of the backwater. My platoon leader prudently set up a three-man ambush at the mouth of the backwater, to catch any night traffic on the river. My lieutenant and I called in preplanned fire zones for the night. These were coordinates that a nearby firebase would use to place artillery fire on in case we were attacked.

About 3:00 AM all hell broke loose. I awoke to machine gun tracers flying over my head. I immediately grabbed the radio, identified myself and within 15 seconds artillery shells started coming in like freight trains. Although they were landing hundreds of feet from our position, we could hear the shrapnel shrieking through the air. Then our ambush started lobbing grenades at the enemy and as suddenly as it began, it was all over. We nervously waited for the dawn. We found a little blood and footprints. We figured a small NVA or VC patrol had heard us and started shooting toward the noise. We searched the backwater to try to locate the lost equipment but to no avail. That afternoon we moved out on our patrol again.

A Scary Night

My platoon was once again patrolling along a river, hoping to set up night ambushes to catch VC infiltrating on boats or rafts. The mountains came right down to the river along this stretch. There was no real good spot to establish an ambush, so we set up a night perimeter a couple of hundred feet up the mountainside. The hillside was so steep we sat or slept against the trunks of the trees to keep from rolling or sliding down hill. I dug out a shallow foxhole the best that I could and crouched down for the night. Soon after, I started my watch an eerie cry started. It was as if an animal was in deep pain; I was hoping it was not a human. The terrible crying and moaning continued for hours. My buddy said it was probably an animal wounded by artillery fire. Even after my watch finished I could not sleep, the ghostly moans seemed to penetrate my very soul. I was so glad when morning came and we left that place.

Jungle Rot and Other Inconveniences

One of the routine tasks we had to perform when on patrol was to check for bloodsuckers. Those little buggers could get anywhere and you had to be careful in taking them off. If you just ripped them off, they could leave their heads in you, which could lead to infections. What you wanted was to have them cleanly let go of you. The best ways were to touch them with a hot cigarette or squirt them with mosquito repellent. In either case they would just shrivel up and drop off. But they were nowhere near as bad as jungle rot. I woke up one morning with pain in my left foot and a severe itch in my crotch area and thighs. I could hardly walk. I had a pretty good case of jungle rot. My left middle toe had turned black and my crotch and thighs were enflamed and very sensitive to the touch.

I was flown out on a chopper and taken to a field hospital. The doctor said he would have to lance my toe and squeeze the puss out. The lancing wasn't bad, but the squeezing of the puss was excruciating. They had to hold me down on the table. I was given a shot of penicillin, some pills and an antiseptic paint that I had to apply each day for two weeks and it burned like hell. Finally, I was back to normal, but my toe remained discolored for many years.

The Friends of Jiminy C.

By Joe Cox

My story begins on a Huey helicopter flying at over 2,000 feet, as I am being airlifted to my infantry unit in Vietnam. I am a new replacement, better known by grunts as an FNG (F'n New Guy) and I am being airlifted to my unit's forward firebase, Dragonhead. I am not alone on this aerial sojourn. There are three other FNGs making the trip with me. The Huey is used by my unit, the 1st Cavalry AirMobile Division, as the primary method of transporting troops and supplies. When transporting troops (grunts, as we are called), the protocol is to sit on the floor of the chopper facing outward, legs dangling over the skids of the bird. When airborne, this positioning produces a feeling of exhilaration such as one might experience on a thrilling amusement park ride. However, on my first such ride I was somewhat alarmed since my front was completely exposed to the outside, thousands of feet in the air. The thought of falling out of the bird does cross my mind, and that thought was especially true for me on my first "Huey Ride."

As the bird lifts off, the main rooter blade, which is above the chopper, pulls the craft along as though it is trying to outrace the front of the chopper. The effect is that the nose of the chopper is straining to become perpendicular to the ground. Eventually, sooner rather than later, equilibrium is established between whatever competing forces of physics are in play, and the bird levels off and begins its smooth climb. As the bird climbs, a rush of cooler air hits me and the ever present oppressive heat is whisked away. I am suddenly aware that I'm thousands of feet above the tree line, as the ground rushes by! Below are the verdant vistas of Vietnam's lush foliage, as far as the eye can see! I wonder about my destination and how I will fit in with my unit. As I look down, I see this little brown patch of cleared space. It looks no bigger than a postage stamp. I sigh and say to myself, "I'm sure glad that I am not going to that little god forsaken place", when all of a sudden the Huey banks hard to the left! At that instant, two competing thoughts race to gain primacy in my brain. "Oh my god, that's my destination!" Followed by, "F---, I am going to fall out of this f'n bird!! I can feel myself slipping through the open door. As I frantically try to lean back, I realize that I have only marginally gained on whatever force it is that is trying to expel me from the bird. I cannot use my hands since they are in front of me, clasped tightly around my M16 rifle. I have visions of my untimely demise and how my death will be received back home. I am experiencing sheer terror, when suddenly the pilot stops the bird's steep banking and slowly sets the chopper on a more gradual decent to the safety of the ground. To this day, I am not sure whether the pilot purposely exaggerated that banking maneuver aware, as he must have been, of our FNG status, or that he simply had to pilot the Huey in that manner in order to make his approach to the firebase. My lingering suspicion however, is that he was trying to scare the shit out of us, and he almost succeeded with me!!

Did I say safety of the ground? Dragonhead was hardly bigger than its aerial appearance indicated. It was less than the length of a football field and not much wider! My unit, Charlie Co. 1st of the 8thReg., was out on a mission and would not be back for a day or two. My foreboding about this place was intensified as I looked around and saw less than a company of men on the base. How the hell this was place secure enough to withstand a ground assault with so few in number, I thought?

As the bird drops us off, it settles down on its skids. The pilot and crewmembers take on some outgoing mail bags and were soon airborne again. As the chopper takes off, it whips up a miniature dust storm. We are far enough from the LZ (landing zone) to avoid the dust storm that follows. Unfortunately, some of the base personnel are showering under unenclosed showers; as a result, they are unceremoniously covered with a fine red dust. Their animated and creative cussing can be heard above the whirring of the Huey's turbine and across the firebase. The sudden change of events for those naked washed/now unwashed poor suckers, produces chortle of laughter from the knowing occupants of the base.

We are met by the base sergeant who is in charge of incoming personnel. He takes us to an area that will serve as our temporary sleeping quarters until our unit finishes its mission in the field and returns to Dragonhead. The sleeping area is close to one side of the berm, which forms the perimeter of the base. The berm consisted of a mound of dirt, no more than three feet high, which encloses the base. Our sleeping area consisted of a group of steel culverts about four feet high covered by sandbags. Inside the culvert is a floor made from scavenged wooded pallets. We have been given air mattresses, which will serve as our bed. On the other side of the firebase, directly across from our sleeping area is the mess tent, where we will go to eat.

After settling in but before our evening meal, the sergeant who had assigned us our sleeping area returns to give us specific times we will pull guard duty that evening. I am assigned guard duty from 12 mid. until 2 A.M. (graveyard shift). The sergeant tells me that he will come around and wake me up when it's my turn for guard duty. At that time he says he will go over the protocol for pulling guard.

The rest of what was left of the afternoon is spent walking around the firebase, familiarizing myself with what limited amenities the base possesses (location of the open air showers) and getting acquainted with the other three FNG's. Soon it is time to eat dinner and then catch some sleep before guard duty. In Nam, when night descends it is pitch black and it is impossible to penetrate the sheer blackness of that experience.

As I settled into my culvert, I began to drift into a type of exhausted half sleep. I can feel the effects of my drifting off with the weird sense of my surroundings. It is while I am in this semi-dream like state that I begin to feel that I am not alone in my culvert. Something runs over me, then again, only this time it's over my face. What was it, I wonder in my dull druglike state? And then suddenly, I realize that I am being visited by rats. I am so tired, knowing that soon I will face my first challenge of being on guard duty, that I make no attempt to protect myself against these unwanted intruders or get out of my sleeping area. In fact, I think that if I am bitten by one of these rats it might result in an early exit from this nightmare experience and that fleeting thought produces some solace. With that comforting thought, I soon fall into a deep sleep until I am awakened by the base sergeant for my turn on guard.

Alright, he says, it's time for you to pull guard duty. Get your 16 (M-16) and follow me. He has a flashlight with him, so I am able to follow in his footsteps as he leads me to the guard position on the perimeter. He explains to me that the guard position is very low on flares; only two were there, so that I am not to fire any. I asked him nervously how I am going to know if I have enemy movement to my front, if I cannot shoot off a flare. His answer is not very reassuring. He says that I am to use the radio, which is at the guard position, to call him. In addition, he says he will be circling inside the perimeter on a vehicle he calls a mule. It is a little motorized vehicle that is used to carry supplies and other items from place to place on the firebase. This proves to be a little more comforting, since he adds that the mule he will be riding is equipped with a mini-gun, capable of firing over 3,000 rounds a minute. With that explanation, he is off and I am completely and utterly alone in the dark. As I parse over his words, it strikes me that having a radio did not fundamentally alter the fact that I have no reasonable way of knowing if the enemy is indeed sneaking up on me and would get to me before I could get to my radio!

Since I cannot see anything in the blackness that enveloped me, I begin to use my ears. How will I be able to discern which sounds in the darkness are threatening ones and which are part of the nightly cacophony? As I strain to hear every sound, one in particular has a familiar ring to it. It is the sound of crickets. And then it hits me! I remembered as kids the difficulty we had in trying to catch these little noisemakers. They would stop their chirping as we would approach them. NOW I HAD IT! I HAD MY EARLY WARNING SYSTEM—CRICKETS!!! I selected crickets at various distances, based on the strength of their chirping, and did so while placing them on a mentally constructed semicircle grid. Then I tested my early warning system. When a cricket in my constructed grid stopped chirping, I listened for any additional sounds that might signal a hostile approach. If the cricket began to chirp again than I assured myself that indeed nothing of hostile intent was approaching. My improvised early cricket warning system went on like that all throughout my guard duty. At 2 A.M. I was relieved of my guard and headed back to my sleeping area. As I did so, ironically, from across the base near the mess tent a flare is sent skyward and as that flare ascends I stop and I am transfixed by the visual in front of me. There about 30 meters before me is the mess tent, and on the ground around the mess tent is the surreal sight of hundreds if not thousands of rats scurrying around under the glare of that flare. It's as though I had been placed by central casting in some weird movie in which I had to improvise my own script, develop my character and the role he was going to play in this movie that was to last for the next year!

But at least I had cast my part cleverly that evening, or so I thought. Based on my experience that evening, one aspect of my character's persona that I was completely committed to was the lifelong debt I owed to my crickets. Right then and there I made a pact with those little guys. And the pact was simple: in recognition of their invaluable service to me on that evening of my first guard duty, I would from that day/night forward protect and save any cricket that was in danger or in distress. It is a promise that I have kept, even to this day! As for the rats, screw 'em!

Scary Times During the Rainy Season

By Harley Hawkins

It was the rainy season and we stopped working out of our APC and were running missions using choppers and walking. We were working just north and west of Uplift. We started in the brush country, with tall elephant grass and brush, and worked our way up into the jungle.

It was very humid and hot, and a few days walking in there I got rid of my socks as there wasn't any water to wash them in, and I also got rid of my undershorts.

The medic gave me some foot powder. We were cutting and clawing our way through the jungle, and it was slow going at best. We made so much noise we could not sneak up on anyone, as we sounded like a herd of elephants walking in the jungle, and it was hard work and slow going. I didn't see it; if the NVA were up here, let's leave them alone. They stay up here. We stay down there and we will shoot them if they come down. Oh well, it gave you something to think about while you chopped your way through the jungle.

Our backpacks were very heavy. It seemed we had everything with us. My straps on my pack had rubbed on the chain of my dog tags and had dug into my shoulder. I went to Randy Smith, the medic, and he patched me up. I would say our packs weighted about 70-80 lbs. We had our tent, 400 rounds of M16 (some only 200), I carried a claymore mine, two sticks of C4, C rations, four trip flares, two concussion grenades, four hand grenades, wire, mosquito juice (great for removing leaches – not much for mosquitos), water, mosquito net, and rope. We took turns packing the M70 grenade launcher, and everyone packed a few shells for it.

After a few days of chopping around the jungle and not finding much, we set up in an area that kind of opened up from the jungle we had been in. There were still trees and not grass, but trees not as close and no vines (damn, I hated those vines).

Sgt. Ward came over and told me I had LP tonight with John Hoya. LP is a listening point where you set up about 150-200 yards out in front of the platoon night perimeter. You checked in every hour by keying the mike on the radio, so those on guard at the perimeter will know everything is okay. If you see something, you key the mike twice, meaning you are coming in and they won't shoot you and can disarm their trip flares; they click twice to let you know they received your click.

John and I moved out just before dark, and it was raining hard. We didn't talk, just walked. After we had walked a while, John stopped and said this looked like a good place. I said, "Suits me. I'm tired."

The area of trees had opened up kind of in a circle, where we could see in all directions, but the undergrowth was not so heavy, so as to allow us a good field of fire, which I really hoped we wouldn't need.

Christmas '68

By Terry A. Moon

In 1968, I arrived at the 1st Air Cavalry (1st Cav) base camp at Phuoc Vinh (PV), 50 kilometers (km) north of Saigon. After a sweat-soaked week of endlessly filling sandbags and repairing greenline (base perimeter defensive zone) bunkers, I worked for three weeks at the 1st Cav photo lab at Bien Hoa, and then returned to PV ready for my inevitable assignment as a photographer with a combat brigade. Four of our photographers had gone home while I was away on my "vacation" with the Rear Echelon Mother F-ers (REMFs).

In the early afternoon, 1st Cav information officer Major Fox McCarthy called me into his office and introduced me to Lieutenant (Lt.) Tim Millar, Officer In Charge of our 3rd Brigade information office. I immediately jumped to the conclusion that I was being sent to 3rd Brigade with the 7th Cavalry grunts, Custer's famous unit.

The major was a small man with a large forehead. He paused to look at some papers, then looked straight at me and said, "You will accompany Lt. Millar to Quan Loi now. Early tomorrow you will fly to a Song Be area fire support base for a special job, but I can't tell you what it is. You will be briefed by the battalion commander when you arrive at the LZ (landing zone)."

"Thank you, sir," I replied, surprised. What! This must be an important job. Why me? I'm the FNG (F'n New Guy). There are several other photographers. Excited, I ran to get all of my camera gear.

Lt. Millar and I bumped along in a jeep to the 15th Med area at PV to catch a Huey flight to Quan Loi. Soon a light observation helicopter (LOH; see preceding photograph) landed nearby. Lt. Millar knew the pilot and after a short, laugh-filled conversation, the pilot flew us to Quan Loi, 35 km to the north. This was my first flight in the smallest of the military helicopters. We zoomed around, just above the treetops, turning abruptly like an aerial sports car. The pilot showed off. I sat in the back, with one leg dangling out into space. This is fun. What seat belt? After an exhilarating flight, we descended onto the Snoopy pad at Quan Loi, so named because the famous beagle flying his doghouse was painted on the perforated steel surface of the pad.

Up early on Christmas Eve day for my exciting mystery job, I caught a Huey at 6:30 a.m. to LZ Buttons, a Song Be area fire support base 40 km east of Quan Loi. I joined two dog teams in the Huey. One of the huge German shepherds liked me, licking my face like a giant puppy.

As we landed outside the perimeter wire, I thought to myself, this place looks menacing. I could see all the deadly Claymores and the two tangled layers of nasty concertina wire in front of the defensive bunkers. A four-foot-high berm encircled the entire LZ, with the bunkers a part of it. I walked through the narrow gate into the LZ. Guards escorted me to the command bunker.

Lieutenant Colonel John B. Blount, battalion commander of 2/12, briefed me quickly as we stepped outside the bunker, "You will be photographing the Christmas Eve good will tour of South Vietnamese president Nguyen Van Thieu," he said calmly.

My heart rate jumped. What! I can't believe this.

"He will arrive in an hour or so and quickly tour the LZ. Take as many pictures as you can of him with my Sky Troopers," he said.

"Yes sir, that's my job," I replied.

He smiled. "You can have the run of the place. Go to the mess tent and get something to eat. How long have you been over here?"

"Five weeks, sir," I said.

"I thought so. Good luck son," he said, smiling again as he returned to the bunker.

FNG must be painted on my back.

I stopped at the mess tent for toast and a welcome cup of coffee. It was a tiny area, only about a half-mile around the greenline. I quickly walked around the entire base. A very tight defensive perimeter surrounded us; the bunkers were close together. I could feel an intensity here that was new to me.

Shortly, the sky was filled with the thunder of Hueys and Cobras descending. The VIP entourage had arrived. The tour moved along quickly, 1st Cav Commanding General George Forsythe escorting the VIP. I had to run to stay in good position for photographing the diminutive President Thieu, casual in his white shirt and baseball cap. He talked to several different Sky Troopers, having animated exchanges with each one. I hustled to obtain all the grunts' names; these photos would be great hometown news releases for them. He also spoke with LTC Blount about PSYOPS operations. I didn't see any CBS or NBC news reporters. This tour was a well-kept secret. I had learned quickly that you couldn't trust the media here. Suddenly, it was over and the swarm of helicopters departed.

Returning to PV was my responsibility. I convinced a pilot that I was important enough to overload his LOH for the flight to Quan Loi. He flew so high, I froze up there, and was relieved to reach Quan Loi. The helpful controller at the "terminal" there found a flight to PV for me as the lone passenger on a Huey.

President Thieu toured only four places that day. Fred, our photo coordinator, covered him at PV. I covered him at LZ Buttons (Song Be). He also visited two other LZs. I was pleased that Major McCarthy gave me a shot at this important job.

Late in the evening, I walked in the light rain to take photos of Christmas dinner preparations at the nearby 15th Admin Company mess hall. Upon entering, I sensed the holiday spirit; everyone was smiling. Frivolity reigned as I took the pictures; plenty of goodies covered one of the tables. Soon, I stashed my camera and helped them make the rolls; the aroma was heavenly. We had a blast. An instant camaraderie blossomed there.

inside of card

A few hours later I left, the fatigue from my long day finally grabbing hold of me. It was raining hard; I should have brought my poncho. I slogged out into the torrent. A no-win situation: if you walked, you were soaked; if you ran, you slipped in the mud. I also had to learn quickly how to better protect my cameras in the heavy rain.

In the red glow of the dawn on Christmas morning, I headed to greenline guard at tower eight. The tower stood forty feet high and had an unencumbered view of the southern greenline. It stood by the rubber trees about 200 yards from our office. Later, I saw movement far down the line, but couldn't tell what it was; nothing was supposed to be there. I grabbed the big binoculars. No problem; the cows looked friendly. They told me nothing ever happened on day guard. Another guy, fresh from his Christmas feast, struggled up the many steps and relieved me shortly after noon. As he reached the top, he gasped, "You won't believe all the food."

I jogged to the mess hall for the much-anticipated Christmas dinner. The menu looked like one from a fancy restaurant. Our cooks did a great job, almost like home. I ate so much that I had to take a siesta; I understood now why my replacement on the tower today had struggled to reach the top. Work details were split up so everyone had at least a half-day off to enjoy the festivities. Smiles appeared everywhere. I could sense the camaraderie here among all the guys, no matter what their job was. We had been strangers, but after our Christmas dinner we were like old friends. From the commanding general to the logistics people to the mess hall cooks, they all did a fine job to make holidays here seem like real holidays.

To top off the day, a big goodie package arrived in the mail from my girlfriend, Sally. Perfect timing; inside were several wrapped gifts. I carefully opened them under our gleaming seven-foot Christmas tree, lovingly made out of beer cans.

For a Public Information Office assignment, I took pictures of APO (post office) clerks sorting huge piles of holiday packages. Three of the photographs appeared in the Christmas edition of our Cavalair newspaper.

My pleasant holiday came to a soggy ending late in the evening, after I returned to the grubby tent where the FNGs slept. I had just settled in, when my corner of the tent collapsed. What a mess; of course it was raining. I got soaked as I pulled it back up and quickly pounded a couple of pegs in with a shovel.

As I dried off and reclined on my cot ready to sleep, with my mostly dry poncho liner, partially inflated air mattress and two precious dry towels, I thought about the instant camaraderie between the guys here. What a great Christmas it turned out to be for an FNG in a war zone, more than eight thousand miles from home.

Merry Christmas to all, and to all a good night.

Classified Memories

By Ora Arlan Smith

Due to the classified nature of my work, most of my memorable experiences can't be discussed, but, some things really stand out, such as working in the NSA HQ Building, working in the CIA HQ Building, the Khe Sanh intelligence report, the night Captain John Casey was killed, expanding the Utah National Guard 142 MI Co to a Battalion, then to a Brigade, submitting the paperwork to add Fort Douglas, Utah to the National Register of Historic Places, getting calls from the Whitehouse Communications Office to provide interpreters (almost all of the 142 MI Soldiers were fluent in a foreign language as a result of their Mormon missionary training and assignments, and some of them were fluent in languages not taught at the Defense Language Institute) for President Reagan when visited by Middle Eastern heads of state.

Also, during my assignment at HQ INSCOM, I had the unusual privilege of writing an Army Regulation — AR 350-3 REDTRAIN (Tactical Intelligence Readiness Training) — and an extensive update/rewrite of AR 380-5 Department of the Army Information Security Program.

I also got to travel quite a lot, to provide training to USAR Intel units, (the deputy undersecretary of the interior was a lieutenant in one of my USAR Intel Units) and the Utah National Guard 142nd MI (the Utah NG 142nd MI was the only NG Intelligence unit, and was initially formed only with special approval of the Army Chief of Staff as existing regulations prohibited intelligence units in the National Guard to prevent them being activated and employed by state governors).

The Khe Sanh Intelligence Report: On the first day of the Cav's Operation Pegasus, the 371 RRC had a three man team equipped with a radio-teletype machine (think they were called Martin 95's) accompanying the Div Hq element so we could transmit classified intelligence information to the CG. However, we were unable to establish communications with them. Then, in the very early evening hours, I came into possession of classified intelligence about how, when, and where the enemy units planned to ambush CAV units the next day when the second day of Operation Pegasus began. A last ditch emergency effort to establish the teletype link (they were out of range of our voice radios) with our team failed. WHAT TO DO! I knew something had to be done, but what. Then the idea came. I sat down and punched the intelligence data that I wanted to send to the CG onto a seven level paper tape.

I then walked down the road inside the Camp Evans base camp to the 15th Signal Battalion. I made my way into their operations center and found only one signal operator (I believe he was a sergeant). I asked if he had communications with the forward command post. He pointed to a single radio-teletype machine obviously receiving messages and punching them onto paper tape, and said that was the only link to the forward command center.

Although I was only an acting sergeant (3 striper), I held out my paper tape and asked him to transmit it to the CG. He informed me that the messages coming in were from the CG, requesting B-52 support for the next day. I told him that my tape was more important and that he should break the incoming messages and send my tape.

Needless to say, he was quite amused at first, but with the help of my M-16 rifle, I soon convinced him to do as I asked. When the tape had been transmitted, I took my tape, thanked him, and left, wondering all the while if the MP's were going to arrest me before I made it back to the 371 RRC ops center.

Strangely enough, I never heard anything about the incident until a few weeks later when the Div G2 approached me while I was delivering classified intelligence reports to DIV HQ. He thanked me, and told me that the CG USASA Pacific (ASA Pacific HQ in Hawaii) had started to initiate disciplinary proceedings against me for transmitting classified data over a non-secure communications circuit, but that General Tolson had intervened and told him "Look, you only got one star on your collar and I got two. Don't you dare touch a hair on that boy's head." I never tried to confirm this, but needless to say, it made me feel like the risks that I had taken, had been worthwhile, and 45 years later, the memory still holds a special place in my heart.

The night Captain Casey was killed. Upon my arrival at Camp Evans just after TET 68, I was introduced to the 371 RRC Company Commander. There was something about his name that was a bit familiar, and he had a Southern Accent very similar to mine. Being a very curious type, I got up the courage (I was only an SP5) to ask where he was from. He told me he was from Cookeville, TN. Then it hit met. He had been a high school basketball star, and his team played against two of our six Warren County high schools. Each time, he was written up as a star player in our local newspaper. I had read about him several times. Over the next few weeks, I discovered that he was also a good company commander.

The 371 RRC compound at Camp Evans was very small, and when I arrived, all the sandbagged tents were full. However, at a right angle adjacent to the officers tent was a supply tent that was only a little over half full, but did not have any sandbags around it. (The officers tent was also without sandbags, but had a sandbag bunker at the rear.) We found a medical stretcher and set it on top of wooden pallets in the supply tent. This was my home for several weeks.

When I went to bed at night, I laid my M-16 on the ground beside the pallet. One night, I was almost asleep when I heard a mortar round explode several yards away. I immediately rolled off my stretcher and hugged the ground beside my M-16. Over the next few minutes, three or four more went off inside the 371 RRC compound.

Then there was an extremely loud explosion very close by. A few more minutes went by and somehow everyone knew it was over and got up and started assessing the damage. That is when we discovered that Captain Casey had not survived. When the first round hit, instead of running for the bunker, he had grabbed his boots and was sitting on his cot putting them on. The mortar round had hit one of the 2 x 4 frame boards supporting the tent and had exploded just a few feet above his head, and about 18-20 feet from me.

The next day, I discovered some small shrapnel holes in the supply tent, and that the handguard on my M-16 which had been near my cheek as I lay on the ground, was cracked and a small chip missing. Although there is no way to prove it, I will always believe that a piece of shrapnel from the round that exploded over Captain Casey's head cracked that handguard lying beside my cheek. The only way I can explain it is that GOD was right there beside me on that ground.

When I returned home a few months later, my mom surprised be by telling me that his mother (Cookeville is over 50 miles from where we lived, and to this day I still do not understand how my mom ever had any contact with his mom) had been real upset when his body was brought home in a closed casket, and the army would not let her open it. I told my mom what had happened and that was the reason his casket could not be opened. She said that wasn't the problem, that John's mom believed that the casket was empty and he might still be alive.

I assured her that the casket had not been empty, and told her to tell his mom that I had been only a few feet away when he was killed, and that I knew for sure that it had happened, and that the reason the army would not let her open it was to protect her from a sight that no mother should ever have to see.

Christmas (1983) at Diogenes Station, Sinop, Turkey is also a very special memory. The base was built on top of an ancient Volcano mountain in the Dead Sea, and connected to the mainland by a two lane land bridge just a few feet above the water. On the top edge facing the mainland, near the NCO club was the remains of what appeared to be an ancient Roman Fort. On Christmas eve night, I remember setting on one of the ramparts under a clear starry sky, and looking at the stars over the mainland, and wondering if Roman Soldiers had been on those same ramparts 2,000 years ago, and if they could have seen the Star of Bethlehem moving across the sky and then stopping over the stable as it announced the birth of Jesus. What must have they thought if they saw such a heavenly phenomenon, and having no idea what or why it was happening.

Another special memory from Sinop occurred on October 23, 1983. I was on duty as Officer of the Day, and was called to the communications center to receive the critical incident notification of the bombing of the Marine barracks in Lebanon. Although I knew the message was for real, it was just so unbelievable that such a tragedy could happen.

Although most of my memories are rather pleasantly satisfying, there are some, usually as a result of my own stupidity that I am not very proud of, but they are still part of me. One of these is about the time I did something really stupid during my time in Vietnam. It was after the CAV had moved to Phouc Vinh. We each had ration cards that permitted us to buy a limited number of bottles of hard liquor at the PX each month. However the PX at Phuoc Vinh did not carry liquor. We had to drive to Bien Hoa to use our ration cards.

One day one of my comrades and I collected several friend's ration cards and got in a 3/4 truck to make a "booze run" to Bien Hoa. The drive took a little over two hours each way along a road that was considered a "safe" road so we did not take our rifles. The only thing we had weapon wise was my nine-inch Bowie Knife.

We were close to halfway back to Phuoc Vinh, and very near a small Vietnamese village with our cargo of 23 bottles of whiskey when our truck quit running and would not re-start. It was between 3-4 p.m. There was very little traffic, however after several minutes another 3/4 with several Soldiers and equipment came by and stopped. They tried to help us start our jeep, but to no avail. They only had room for one of us, so I stayed with our truck and 23 bottles of whiskey, and my buddy went with them. They promised to send someone back from Phuoc Vinh to get me as soon as they got there.

No other vehicles passed that afternoon, and soon it was getting dark. I was sitting in the 3/4 drifting off to sleep when I heard a noise. I turned and looked out the driver window and went into immediate shock. In the early moonlight, I could see two people a few feet from my door. They were dressed in baggy clothes and wearing the coolie hats typically associated with the Viet Cong, and my heart fluttered as I tried not to scream.

They began trying to communicate. Between my very limited Vietnamese words and their very limited English, after a few minutes, they understood my truck would not start, and began to push it. Fortunately there was a very, very slight downhill grade, and after a few feet, I popped the clutch and the truck started. I floored it and never looked back.

I had to swerve around a couple of barbed wire barricades as I went through the little village, but made it to the gate at Phuoc Vinh in probably about half an hour without getting shot. Looking back, I sincerely believe I had another weapon that night in addition to my nine inch Bowie knife. His name is GOD!

A Day in the Life of a Combat Photographer

By Frank Smart

The grunts did the dirty, dangerous work of ferreting out the enemy and killing them.

The helicopter pilots and door gunners did their part, often displaying uncommon valor.

The medics risked their lives to save others.

Someone had to tell their stories so the people back home would know.

In Vietnam, as in other wars, that job fell to the Combat Reporter/Photographer. That was my Army job in Vietnam.

To get these stories we had to hump the boonies with the grunts, suffer the agonizing cries of pain alongside the medics, and we rode with the chopper pilots and door gunners to bring those stories to life.

This then, is the story of a day in the life of Army men who performed these duties with the First Cavalry Division (Airmobile) in the Republic of South Vietnam. I served from April 1968 to April 1969, as a staff reporter/photographer for the Cavalair newspaper, the official organ for my unit.

And while the day I describe is not necessarily a typical day, it is nevertheless a close approximation of those days we spent plying our military trade during the Vietnam War.

Military journalists did not have the freedom of our civilian counterparts. Regardless of what went down in the field during any given day, we still had the military to contend with and all that entails.

We could not, for instance, return to Saigon each day, file our stories and head to the Caravel Hotel rooftop bar for cocktails and dinner as they did.

The best we could hope for, if we were in the field, was warmed-up C-Rations, a quick smoke before dark on some small Night Defensive Position (NDP) on a hilltop and a couple of hours fitful sleep before being roused for our stint on radio watch or foxhole guard duty.

If we were back at our main base camp we would probably get a hot meal, a shower, maybe a couple of cold sodas or a beer, after we filed our stories.

And then, of course, the Army extracted its pound of flesh with KP, guard duty, Charge-of-Quarters and the soulful, character-building duty of shit-burning detail. Vietnam had no sewer system outside of the major cities, so all feces was burned using kerosene. This was a day-long duty in which the Soldier pulled a can from under the latrine, poured kerosene on, lit it and stood there and stirred it until all the feces was turned to ashes. Then on to the next can.

Working out of a Brigade Public Information Office, of which I was NCOIC of the 2nd Brigade PIO, required spending time in the field with the infantry companies to get our stories and photographs.

Normally we would team up with an Army photographer who was assigned to my office and we would spend three to five days in the field with the grunts.

When enough cameras and film were available we did our own photography, as we were cross-trained.

Each Army Brigade consisted of three battalions of five companies each, plus support units.

Our Brigade office attempted to cover as many of these units as possible with the three or four reporters and one or two photographers available to us.

Our articles and photographs were primarily written for the Division newspaper, "The Cavalier", but were also made available to the mainstream media in the US and to other military publications such as "The Stars and Stripes".

One factor we had to contend with was trying to be self-sustaining while in the field with the infantry.

Logistic support for the troops in the field was always a problem and each additional mouth to feed and water was just another burden on that system.

The key was the proper loading of the field pack and that became an art, to keep it light as possible and yet contain the minimum necessitates of life. The rule of thumb was to take enough food for three days and enough water for two days.

Of course you wanted to keep your pack light since you had to hump it all day through often times severe terrain in tropical heat.

To accomplish this you stripped the C-Rations down to one can of Fruit Cocktail and coffee for breakfast, a main meal for lunch and supper, a few heat tabs to warm things up, plenty of Tabasco sauce to liven up the meal, matches, toilet paper and you were basically set. Another necessity from home was Kool-Aid. You were required to put purification tablets in your canteen and that produced a terrible taste. Kool-Aid solved that problem.

In addition you carried an Army .45 sidearm, your M-16 rifle, a bandoleer of ammo, (200 rounds) a bayonet, an entrenching tool, several fragmentation and smoke grenades, a couple of pen flares, a medical field kit, a poncho and liner, smokes, a bar of soap, toothbrush, toothpaste, your steel pot, writing material, and one, two and sometimes, three cameras, both personal and military.

And depending on the company you were traveling with, how the company commander felt and the situation, perhaps a Gas Mask and a Flak Jacket.

At best your pack would weigh about 50 pounds and at the worst about 70 pounds.

There were other goodies you could bring along, like a pair of clean socks (we didn't wear underwear) mosquito repellant and some candy.

Checking with the Brigade Tactical Operations Center (BTOC) to see where the various units were and what they were doing was next and then a trip to that company's area to arrange a ride on the next outbound chopper to their location and your mission was on.

Normally we took more than the required 200 rounds of M-16 ammo and plenty of hand grenades and anything else we could get our hands on to give to the grunts in the field. They never turned down ammo, clothing, food, writing materials, candy, smokes, and they always seemed grateful.

Arriving in the field the Reporter/Photographer introduced himself to the Company Commander or the Platoon Leader and explained what he was doing there and how long he expected to stay.

Sometimes we were welcomed, especially if we were well-known to the company as honest and fair journalists and had proven that we were not a liability in the field. We had to carry out own weight and not burden the operation in any way. We were often viewed as another gun in the foxhole.

When the unit moved out on that day's mission, we took our assigned position (with a particular squad or platoon) and moved out with them.

What ever the unit was assigned to do, search and cordon, patrolling, ambushes, etc., we tried to assist them in any way. More than a liability, we tried to provide that extra gun on the line or in the foxhole.

All of us had undergone basic training, plus our specialty training and we knew the fundamentals of fire and maneuver and enough field craft to take care of our selves in the field. In my case, I had originally been trained as a Combat Engineer. That's basically just an Infantryman who blows things up and builds portable, temporary bridges.

In a nutshell, whatever befell the unit we were with, befell us, for better or worse.

If they were on a stand-down (a 3 to 5 day break from the field) at a Fire Support Base, or at a Main Base Camp, then so were we. That break from the field generally gave us a chance to get caught up on those interminable Hometown News Releases the Army required us to produce. You've seen them in your local newspaper: PFC Joe Smokes, son of John and Susie Smokes, is currently serving with the First Cavalry Division in South Vietnam. Smokes a 1967 graduate of......"

The more adventurous of our kind went out on night ambushes and night combat assaults. I went out on several, but that's another story for another time.

Some of our fellows followed Special Forces and SEAL units on combat missions and a number of them were wounded and some were killed-in-action and still other received medals for valorous actions while doing their jobs.

I was one of the lucky ones who made it through the longest year of my life, unscathed, physically and mentally.

Returning from the field we wrote our stories and turned them in to our main office at Camp Evans or Ben Hoa, sent out film to the photo lab for processing and started thinking about our next trip to the field.

All in all the Combat Reporter/Photographers plied their trade pretty much the way everyone did in Vietnam. They did their best under trying, uncomfortable and dangerous conditions.

In no way is this story intended to portray our jobs as being as dangerous as those who actually did the fighting, although we also fought when necessary.

But, our jobs were important, and it was dangerous and dirty at times.

It required great stamina, fortitude and a nose for news.

We were not heroes.

But, we were there in the foxholes, on the jungle trails and in the villes with the real heroes, taking their pictures and getting their stories for the world to know.

And those stories will live for time immemorial, in print and film.

An Abbreviated History of the 27th Maintenance Battalion in Vietnam

By Ed Jones

The 27th Maintenance Battalion deployed with the 1st Cavalry Division arriving at An Khe on September 17, 1965. The mission of the 27th was to repair and provide repair parts for all ground equipment of the 1st Cavalry Division. This included rifles, machine guns, artillery, forklifts, vehicles, communications equipment, night vision equipment, and generators. The Battalion was organized into a Headquarters and Main Support Company, three Forward Support Detachments, and was authorized 334 personnel.

Although hampered by heavy rains, the Battalion was able to set up its repair shops and by the end of December, 1965 had completed over 3600 repair jobs and had ordered over 42,000 repair parts. In 1966, the Forward Support Detachments were constantly on the move as the combat Brigades moved to engage the enemy in the II Corps operational area.

Although the 27th Maintenance Battalion was able to do its mission to keep the CAV moving, shooting, and communicating, the repair parts situation continued to be perilous. In spite of repair parts shortages, the 27th in 1966 completed some 22,000 jobs including 6200 armament items, 4000 vehicles items, and some 2500 engineer items ¬– mostly generators.

In 1967, the 27th received the new automated NCR 500, an early large computer using punch cards, to keep track of repair parts. The NCR 500 was located in a semi-trailer. As the CAV moved more units to the Coastal area of the II Corps operational area, the 27th Forward Support Detachments were deployed to LZ English, LZ Two Bits, LZ Hammond, and LZ Uplift. By October, elements of Hq and Main Support Company were also located at LZ English. A major problem had occurred with the M-16 Rifle and the 27th worked with all the units of the Division to install new buffers and to replace all older M16's with the new chrome chambered rifles. Also during this period, all older M102 Howitzers had to be retubed, and 30 new M102 howitzers were issued to the Division through the 27th. In addition, the 27th was engaged in a priority training program to assist units in better taking care of their equipment. These training programs included over 550 weapons clinics and 190 commo clinic, as well as generator clinics.

1968 was a year of movement. In January the CAV started moving North to the I Corps operational area. Moving by sea and air, the 27th found its way to Quang Tri, Camp Evans, and LZ Jane. Tet 68 was in full swing and the CAV and the 27th were involved immediately. Maintenance and supply operations in I Corps were difficult as this had been a US Marine Corps area of operation. US Army supply and maintenance support were lacking. The 27th supported operations to relieve the Marines at Khe Sanh, and had troops assisting in the operations in the A Shau Valley. Helicopters, Caribou's, and trucks were used to move personnel and repair parts to the various units within the 27th, spread out throughout northern I Corps. September was a particularly difficult month as the unit was hit by an unannounced typhoon on September 4/5, 1968 and then the crash of a CH 47 helicopter on September 17, that took out part of the Tech Supply area. Then on October 26, the Battalion was alerted that the entire Division was being moved South to the III Corps operational area. By mid-November, the entire 27th Maintenance Battalion was in place in III Corps, having moved by sea and air. The Battalion Headquarters and part of Hq and Main Support Company ended up in Bien Hoa, B Detachment and the other part of Hq and Main Support Company at Phuoc Vinh, A Detachment at Tay Ninh, and C Detachment at Quan Loi. The supply situation in the new area was a vast improvement over that previously encountered in II Corps and I Corps. The Battalion was near the logistics center of Long Bien and the repair parts situation began to improve.

If 1968 was the year of moving, 1969 was the year of stability. The Battalion instituted the concept of "area support" which allowed the detachments to stay in place and support whichever CAV units were in that area at the time. Problem areas were primarily generators, 105 Howitzers, commo equipment, and the AN/PPS 5 ground radar. Part of the solution to these problem areas was better education of the user on how to perform preventive maintenance. In addition to 27th personnel visiting units and conducting training, the 27th obtained a full time Tech Rep from Army Material Command to inspect and conduct training on generators. With this assistance and training, and the hard work put in by all 27th Maintenance Battalion Personnel, the Division achieved a readiness rate of over 98% on equipment serviced by the 27th.

1970 saw support of the Cambodian operation. Although the Forward Support Detachment located at Tay Ninh provided the bulk of the support it was supplemented by personnel from Hq and Main Support Company, as well as contact teams from the other Forward Support Detachments. During 1970, a reorganization of the MTOE was finally approved recognizing the need for Hq and Main Support Company to be split into two organizations. They in fact had been operating this way since early 1968. Hq and Main Support Company remained but was reduced in strength to formally organize the Main Support Detachment.

Following the incursion into Cambodia, efforts started to have ARVN units take on more operations. The Division and the 27th Maintenance Battalion began to consolidate in and around Bien Hoa, with the exception of C Detachment being at Song Be to support the 2nd Brigade. Maintenance problems remained for generators, commo equipment, forklifts, and vehicles, all of which were showing their age and the effects of the climate and rough handling.

1971 saw the end of the of the 27th Maintenance Battalion's time in Vietnam. The Division, minus the 3rd Brigade, was moving back to Ft. Hood. The official date of departure for the 27th Maintenance Battalion was April 8, 1971. During its over 5 years in Vietnam, the 27th Maintenance Battalion distinguished itself by providing outstanding maintenance and supply support to all elements of the 1st Cavalry Division, under the most severe conditions. The 27th participated in ten campaigns in Vietnam and was awarded the Presidential Unit Citation, the Valorous Unit Award, three Meritorious Unit Commendations, three awards of the Republic of Vietnam Cross of Gallantry with Palm, and one award of the Republic of Vietnam Civil Action Medal, First Class. In addition, C Detachment was awarded a separate Valorous Unit Award.

All members of the 27th Maintenance Battalion should be extremely proud of their service during the Vietnam War and know they were a part of a valiant history.

Defending FB David

By Joel Chase

In early May 1970, the U.S. launched an "incursion" into Cambodia to disrupt the flow of materials being brought south to wage the prolonged war against the south. The mission was to capture, destroy and dismantle the NVA's supplies in Cambodia in preparation to the U.S. withdrawal of troops from the region.

The 1st Cav was the primary force to enter Cambodia, and it established a number of Fire Support Bases in the area as operations centers to support one another. One of those FSB's was originally named Terri Lynn but later changed to North One and then David. For whatever illogical reason, David was located beyond supporting fire from friendly fire so it was alone and dependent on organic mortar and 105 howitzer defense. Perhaps the strategy was that air support would take the place of fan artillery from other bases, but that proved to be a command miscalculation. We built secondary fighting positions in the berm between the main bunkers and installed 50 trip flares in front of each bunker. The claymores were brought in from the wire and dug onto the berm. Fields of fire were assigned each man on the perimeter, and extra ammo was provided everyone and fighting position. We were as ready as we could be for an assault. My instructions were to avoid the bunkers unless you wanted to die because they were magnets for B40 rockets.

At about 0300 hours on June 14th, a trip in from of a bunker went off and the guard fired on round at a shape he thought had moved. Nothing else happened, and when I arrived I decided something was up so called my CO and advised him to go 100% perimeter alert, which we did. We attempted to scan the area visually but the fog allowed only about 50 feet visibility. After about 30 minutes of searching with no enemy sighted, most of our guys wanted to pack it in, but I was still suspicious. One of my guys standing next to me behind the berm said he thought he saw something and pointed to a spot about 30 to our front. I still saw nothing, but then he yelled "it's a gook he's gonna shoot." The NVA did in fact shoot but rather than give me a new belly button he hit the berm and the rounds grazed my head. Then all hell broke loose on both sides of the berm.

I wasn't badly hurt but bleeding pretty good. I gave a sit-rep to my CO and had the mortars crank up their preplanned fires. Then a grenade rolled up along beside me and blew up. That was the end of my fight, but not that of the other Troopers defending David. The NVA had sent an estimated 300 of their best fighters to take David and kill the approximate 250 defendants of the base. The enemy had underestimated the resolve and determination of the Cav.

When the sun rose that morning the enemy retreated dragging their dead and wounded comrades away to be buried or treated leaving 28 of their best behind. The U.S. lost ZERO killed during that three-hour battle for David and there were no lack of heroics in the process. A total of nine Silver Star medals were awarded as a result of gallantry by the defenders of David. The organic mortars had shot over 1,600 rounds of HE and 1,200 rounds of illumination during the night. They had a handful of each at first light. No air support was possible during the fight due to the dense fog.

I am honored to have been associated with the brave personnel of the 1/5 Cav that saved a firebase from disaster on that fateful night.

Last Stand at the Bien Hoa Officer's Club 1972

By Charles Lee

The Bien Hoa Officer's Club was one of the permanent facilities built in South Vietnam in the 1960s. At that time the chiefs in Washington felt the successful completion of the "police action" in Southeast Asia was a sure thing. Consequently, well thought out structures received the very best engineering and materials. In retrospect, we now know the US politicians in charge of the war underestimated the Vietnamese resistance, mistakenly determined we were winning and would be there for a long time resulting in immeasurable waste of effort, money, and lives. Certain facilities, headquarters, hospitals, BXs and Officer's Clubs, received more attention in construction than other buildings such as, transient quarters and enlisted barracks. Many of the favored structures were set on solid concrete foundations, surrounded by blast protection walls and built with permanent framing complete with heat and air-conditioning.

Charles R. Lee, USAF, on the revetment across from the Cavalry mess hall.

Only an hour cyclo ride north of Saigon, the officer's club at Bien Hoa Air Base was a fine example of the well constructed buildings, examples of the best Army engineering. Austere in outward appearance for security reasons, inside the building embodied all the amenities of the best stateside military club. Members and guests entered through large double doors into a cool air conditioned facility. Comfortable tables and chairs for dining or relaxing were spread out in a large room with high ceilings. Other doors in the main area gave access to restrooms and the kitchen area. Across one wall a bar extended to accommodate a crowd of rowdy drinkers. Safety, in case of incoming, dictated the absence of windows, but state-of-the-art lighting made the dining/bar area a comfortable place for war weary Soldiers to relax, have a beverage, or enjoy a nice meal. I remember the strip steaks were excellent, a result of the months spent aging on the boat traveling across the Pacific on their way to the club kitchen.

By contrast, on the north side of Bien Hoa was one of the many provisional containment locations where remnants of the 1st Calvary, 3rd Brigade bivouacked to conduct their last operations before shipping out for home. This was the time when the Army, along with other forces, preparing to leave Southeast Asia in an orderly fashion, consolidated troops on or close to well defended bases. The facilities and conditions here were markedly different from those on the main base just a few miles away. Positioned on the extreme base perimeter in an area lined with dirt streets (mud when it rained) most of the Troopers lived in wooden temporary hooches. Still flying helicopter combat missions, despite the plans to leave the country in a few days or weeks, Cavalry crews and support teams continued to bivouac in rough conditions on that far edge of Bien Hoa Air Base.

I arrived in Bien Hoa in early 1972 after five years of flying missions in support of the war effort, and was assigned to a ground job. Moreover, unbeknownst to me, the decision had been made to pull out. America, growing weary of the protracted war, decided not to continue the effort, thus everything invested was soon to be abandoned. Unaware of political decision making back home, I started working twelve hour shifts at an Air Force radar site on the north edge of the base adjacent to where the Cavalry was camped. My little radar facility tasked to direct air strikes was just a speck compared to the large encampment located just across a dirt roadway. Nice thing was, when my shift was over, I returned back to the luxury facilities on the main base for a hot shower and a cold beverage at the club.

It was one afternoon in the Officer's Club after my work shift that I had the opportunity to encounter several Army officers that may have been members of the 3rd Brigade, fondly referred to as: The Cav.

Only ten degrees north of the equator, Bien Hoa was extremely hot outside as I wandered into the pleasant air-conditioned O club bar around 1800 hours. It was a day when little drips of sweat would trickle down your back, helping the green baggy fatigues stick to your skin, so I was happy to get inside. There, surprisingly, no one, I mean, no one else was there, it was empty, except for several bartenders very busy arranging for what looked like might be a party. I eased up to the bar to order a drink. In a few moments as my waiter served up a Jack Daniels and water he said, "It would be good if you'd drink up and leave now." I was a little curious, but more interested in a cool drink, so his suggestion went by without a response from me. A few moments later when another bar tender moved in behind the bar, he, too, suggested I leave; now curious, I sat my glass down and asked why?

The first waiter's eyebrows went up, looked at me like I was some kind of dummy, and replied, "It's Cav Night!" When I said I was ignorant of what "Cav Night" was, he went on to educate me about how, because of their previous unruly conduct, Cav officers—Troopers as they were known—were only allowed in the club once a month, and this evening was their night. If I didn't want trouble, I'd best leave, pronto!

Still sublimely unconcerned, I took another sip of Jack and was about to continue the discussion when the double doors burst open on the other side of the room. Outside, the low setting sun sent rays of blinding light across the dark room, backlighting a silhouette of a huge gentleman decked out in a black flight suit, topped off with a black western hat trimmed with yellow braid. I can't recall for sure, but I believe he wore western boots? There was a brief moment of silence as he puffed up like a toad about to croak and then bellowed out:

If you ain't Cav,
You ain't shit,
If you ain't Cav,
You better git!

Stunned by the blast of sunlight in my face, along with the brash commandment issued by the cowboy, I wasn't exactly sure what was happening. But after a moment's consideration, I

Bien Hoa, Vietnam, after the 1st Cav pulled out. Courtesy of Charles Lee.

thought it best to sacrifice the rest of my drink and turned back to the counter to toss a buck onto the bar for the keeper before I would leave. But before I could even step away from the bar, a host of Troopers rumbled into the room immediately pressing in to order drinks. I was flanked shoulder to shoulder on each side by a couple of similarly uniformed Troopers, sunburned dark brown, except around their eyes scrupulously protected by GI issue sunglasses, each man sporting handlebar mustaches of various designs. Strangely, quietly, beers were flying onto the bar, but not much noise other than the sounds of mugs banging down and men guzzling. No one was talking. The bartender eyed me with an, "I told you so," look. The big guy on my right raised his mug, took a gulp, sat the mug down and then quietly stared into the bar top. On my left a shorter, thickset man took a drink turned his head toward me to give me a menacing look with his bloodshot eye capped by bushy eyebrow.

Now this was when I really began to experience what psychologists describe as "the fight or flight response" — your body's primitive, automatic, inborn response that prepares the body to "fight" or "flee" from perceived attack, harm or threat to your survival."

I was contemplating my escape, checking to see if my hand shook as I pretended to confidently lift my glass to take a sip then make my exit, when the Vietnamese band made an entrance through a back door with their instruments and a couple of cute go-go girls in skimpy outfits. Usually chattering in an unintelligible foreign language they were strangely silent; they must have been bewildered by the silence in the typically boisterous bar on any night.

It was about that moment aTrooper three down on my left shifted his stance to lift his leg to unlace a well worn boot, remove it and thump it down on the bar. The impact of his foot gear caused some of the finest Vietnamese compost caked in the waffle patterned sole to become dislodged and mix with spilled beer. He ceremoniously lifted his beer mug, tilted it, half filling the rice paddy wader with the frothy beverage. Uh oh, now I was curious, what kind of custom is this? Right then the crowd grew silent. The bartenders stood mute, watching as the Trooper hoisted boot to lips with laces over his nose and the toe pointed to the ceiling, he chugged a few hearty Adams Apple bobbing swallows. The bar remained ominously quiet, and without comment he slammed the boot down and slid it smartly to his right in front of the Trooper standing there, who reverently repeated the previous man's ritual, dumped his beer in and took several big slurps. Next it was the fellow on my immediate left. I think it was about this time that I got the idea of what was about to be expected of me. The Trooper on my left with no hesitation lifted his beer, took a big gulp that left a coating of froth in his mustache, looked at me and moved the boot directly in front of me. As I looked down at the wader, I could feel his huge eye glaring at me; if that wasn't bad enough, I had a feeling the entire room was anxiously watching, waiting for my next move.

I must have known that a delay would be disaster, without hesitation and with as much aplomb as I could muster I dumped my Jack and water in the leather and canvas vessel, lifted it smartly (suspecting if I didn't pull this off there might be bruises), and took a big swig. Then sent boot down the bar to the big guy on my right.

With that I never heard such uproar. I must have passed some sacred ritual, because the house came down with cheers, claps on the back, more beers all round, and the band cranked up. The rest of the night was complete with more booze, go-go girls, several rounds of, "We Gotta Get Outta This Place," and a lot of broken-up club furniture. I was able to sneak out a side door before the fights began.

A few weeks later, in June 1972, the last of the 3rd Brigade left Vietnam, taking with them a record of sacrifice, courage, and dedication that stands in history as one of the finest. The Cav had been the first of the Army to enter Vietnam and the last to leave.

Back then I escaped my encounter with the "The Cav," but now, more than four decades later, I wonder: who is it that really ever wins a war? I see the Sioux, Cheyenne and Arapaho nations each have rewarding casinos, and for lunch I'm opening a can of Vietnamese sardines.

A Hot LZ

By Henry Kowalski

On July 12, 1969, we picked up A Company, 2/12 Cav at LZ Barbara to be inserted in a tight, one ship LZ. We were three lift ships, with Cobra and Loach cover. Multiple insertions were needed. Only one ship could land at a time. My ship was UH-1D #910.

About the second or third time into the LZ, while in hover, we were ambushed point blank just as the last grunt jumped

Henry Kowalski with UH-1D #910 back at Phuoc Vinh after it was hoisted out by a CH-47. Note the bullet holes to the front right winshield, which were just above the head of Zastrow.

Henry Kowalski's flight helmet shows where a round hit his head; the bullet didn't penetrate!

off. The A/C (Grundy) pulled us out, while we continued to exchange fire with the NVA. We flew about a mile, when I noticed smoke (which turned out to be fuel vapor) pouring out of the back. We made it to a small clearing where the gunship covered us until we got extracted.

Our crew included Grundy – A/C, Zastrow – Pilot, Bill Dillon – Crew Chief, and Henry Kowalski – Door Gunner.

The photographs show the damage from that day. Later, there were 45 bullet holes counted in the cockpit, plus a shot to the push-pull tubes that control the pitch of the rotor blades. C-Troop maintenance said this bird should not have flown out of there…we were very lucky that day!

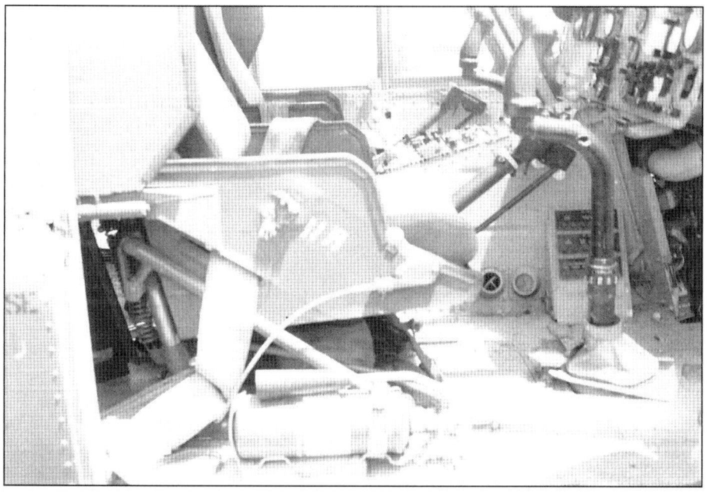

(Above three photos) Bullet damage to the cockpit. Note where the bullets hit the armored seat and the perfect hole through the cyclic, which wounded Zastrow.

The Experience of a Cav Forward Observer in RVN 1967

By Walter C. Smith

In February 1967, I joined the 1/21st FA in An Khe as a newly promoted field artillery 1LT, having been in the US Army an entire year and having completed Jungle Warfare School at the School of the Americas in Panama. Somehow the powers to be felt this qualified (sic) me for a tour in Vietnam, but, I wasn't so sure about that! Regardless, I was at Camp Radcliff, Home of the 1st Cavalry Division (Airmobile).

Walter C. Smith, RVN 1967

I was assigned to Bravo Battery (M102s), which was task organized in DS of the 2/7th CAV and had attached FO teams for fire support to their infantry companies. The battery was in Bong Son, wherever that was, but the 2/7th was in Phan Thiet on the South China Sea, where it was conducting operations with the 101st Abn as part of a Task Force in Operation Thayer and that was where I was headed as a forward observer. I was ushered to a C130, flying out of the 'golf course', and flown to join my comrades.

Now, all of the FO parties with the 2/7th were from B Btry, but A battery was supporting the battalion in Phan Thiet. This battery was split between LZ Betty (base camp) on the coast, which had an uphill or down hill, determined whether you were landing or departing, functional airstrip, and LZ Virginia, 10 clicks north in nowhere. Three guns in each location provided mutual support and extended the fire coverage for operations.

Stepping off the C130 with my newly issued M16, I was met by CPT Haines, the Arty LNO who introduced me to the A Btry BC, CPT Foley, who attached me to Delta Company. This company was not a traditional weapons company with their 106-gun jeep platoon, 4 deuce mortar platoon and my FO jeep, but a reconstituted infantry company with CPT Adams as CO. He was also an Army aviator, who proved this when he replaced

Henry Kowalski and Beverly, the rat chasing mascot of Lift Platoon.

a wounded OH13 pilot who had made an "emergency" landing on top of the company and preceded to lead us from the air against the guys who had caused the pilot to land, but that is another historic event. Lt Westphalen (1st Plt), Lt Spenser (2d Plt) and Lt Blanchard (3d Plt) made up the officer cadre; the weapons platoon leader was a very good 60mm mortar Sergeant, who humped a recaptured US knee mortar. These were the gentlemen I would meet shortly out in the field.

Artillery Lieutenants were scarce on the hill and not too numerous elsewhere…I often wondered why…I was soon to find out! But at this time, I was replacing LT Dan Staber who was sunbathing with the company on the side of a mountain, 50 clicks to the north on an LZ called Pall Mall, securing a couple of howitzers. As I arrived on the resupply bird, I met CPL Hope, the Recon Sergeant, (pic 1) and SP4 Pillot (his real name is twelve letters and I could not pronounce it, so we settled on Pillot), my RTO (pic 2) and Dan, who subsequently got on the aircraft as I got off. So much for the transition! He was headed back to A Btry as the XO/FDO. Seems that you have to spend time 'on the hill' before being eligible for Battery leisure life and one did not waste time delaying that security. I learned that of the 2/7th's four FO teams only one other officer, LT Jerry Johnson was 'on the hill' and he left shortly thereafter causing CPL, soon to be SGT, Hope to be his replacement. Consequently, all other parties were headed by Recon Sergeants, all 'volunteers' from the firing battery.

Over the next six months, we conducted continuous operations either in the flat plains to the northwest of Phan Thiet, donning a helmet, or in the mountains north of the area, wearing a striker hat, where the French had established their unsupportable forts. But you could see the South China Sea, so I guess that gave them some relief, because they were not going to survive the journey down those mountain roads once they got up there. I became very appreciative of our air mobile concept. We also secured the artillery fire support LZ's while other companies did the sweeps. We normally did not operate outside the support ring of A/1/21st even though we had gun ships, ARA and, occasionally, fast movers. I do not believe that I ever knew where we were in relationship to the country's worldly features; only the gun target line from the FS base. Our 1:50,000 scale maps were all green with blue streams/rivers and very close together brown contour lines and superimposed grid lines; checking your location was by high streamer smoke and sound. Our trusty LNO would deliver new maps into the LZ's when we were alerted for a new combat assault somewhere, God knows where. I think we were playing chess with the VC and NVA who were recently in the neighborhood.

Regardless A/1/21st was always within range whether they were positioned with two guns or three guns. Mutual support was mandatory.

Death Valley Resupply. Photo courtesy of Walter C. Smith

Essentially LZ Virginia was our home base. SP4 Pillot and I made like infantrymen and accompanied the security patrols, slept or coordinated from our FO post. (Pic 3). A few of our leisure strolls enabled Lt Spenser and I (pic 4) to chat before an ant hill which was ideal hiding places for weapons and snipers. We can also attest that Agent Orange was effective in defoliation. Then there was the wet feet approach to finding the bad guys. That's me (pic 5) and next is Pillot (pic 6) with the rest of 1st Plt. SP4 Pillot was issued one of those AR15 with the short barrel and he was determined to show the infantry how to engage the enemy. Unfortunately, he had the PRC25 on his back

LZ Baldy, B1 of the 21st, 1967. Photo courtesy of Walter C. Smith.

and was constantly out of my reach, so I taught him how to call for fire. Normally, the Recon Sgt walked with the point platoon HQ and we with the Company CO, but Recon Sgt were hard to keep, so most of the time we walk with the point; but it really didn't matter because the whole company wasn't more than a reinforced platoon (about 80 guys) and in that terrain, we were nothing more then a column of grunts. So, we were all in this together, rallying on the guy with the most firepower at his finger tips or who had the PRC. Those few seconds of indirect firepower determined your survival.

We were privileged to have a 175 battery move into the area to support an interdiction effort along the trails in the mountains. Their range was approximately 32 km, which meant we were way out there. Boy, watch the PE range on that gun, as bad as naval gunfire close support employed while operating in the Le Hong Phong forest, which buttressed the coast. We ran into a SEAL team in that forest, a very dense scrub area around 40x40 km northeast of Phan Thiet River. I think they were looking for Uncle Ho. Someone told me Ho Chi Minh had guerrilla'd out of it against the French in 1953. Evidently, they never got him and I can understand why. With all that activity, the TF staff had the brainy idea to send a SP 40mm platoon from LZ Betty to help the infantryman clean out the area. This developed into a recovery effort to protect and extract the vehicles while keeping snipers at bay. Ever see what a 40-mike-mike does to a guy hiding behind a tree? Battery A also conducted 2 gun raids into the forest unsupported, fire and scat. But again, another story. Many, many events between February and July 1967 in Phan Thiet, but must move on and not bore the Troopers.

Next time, it's back to B Battery in August 1967 and many LZ's; terminating at a place called LZ Leslie up north when we were OPCON to the Americal Division west of Tam Ky and I was the XO with CPT Conroy as BC. The battery was awarded a Presidential valorous unit award for action on LZ Leslie in January 1968 at the beginning of TET68.

The Talk We Never Had

By Bill Corsair (McGroarty)

My brother Patrick was in his early teens when, in 1969, I went to serve, as a SSG, with the 1st Cavalry Division, Airmobile, at the Forward Headquarters, Phuoc Vinh, RVN. Within a year, of my return, my wife and I were off on a seven state odyssey, pursuing our career paths and he made a name for himself in theater stage management in Florida.

We never had that "what did you do in the war, Brother" talk. When he moved to Manhattan, a few years ago, where my wife Janis and I had lived and worked for over three decades, we became very close, but even then, that talk never happened. So when, on Memorial Day 2016, I received this email from Patrick , I was moved by the understanding he had, of words never spoken, an experience never related and the pride of service deep and everlasting but never flaunted. How loud and clear the silence between brothers can be.

My Dear Brother,

I was reminded today that there were previous generations of men who were called to duty to serve our country. Most didn't have a choice with the "draft" in those years. Many of us were either not born or old enough to be effected by the draft - and so we just went on with our lives, never really knowing or experiencing the sacrifice that those people from those generations had to make, what they had to remember and live with in the years following. We couldn't know the strength and the fatigue, the weaknesses, the sicknesses, the fears, or the hellish environment they had to survive in - or not survive.

My brother is a member of the radio, television, film, and theatrical communities. Fortunate enough to be a long standing part of a profession he chose, he has been recognized, written about, awarded, and tributed. Yet, I know that the proudest accomplishment he has above all, is that he is a Veteran who served our country.

My brother is a Veteran, which makes my brother an actual hero. So today, and always, on behalf of the rest of us who may take our freedom for granted at times, and who will never know what it takes to be a Soldier:

Thank you to Bill Corsair McGroarty for your service.

Thank you for your heroism.

Bill Corsair (left) and his brother, Patrick McGroarty

Dear Patrick,

I want to let you know how much I appreciate what you wrote.

I remember standing with my Mother the day I left for Vietnam. She cried and said: "No one in the Family has ever been through anything like this." I hugged her and said: "Don't worry, I'll be alright and when I come home we'll all have something to be proud of." That wasn't the homecoming any of us got, but my wife, Mom, my Daughter and now you make my prediction a fact. A small group of Family, admittedly, but I've always felt quality was more important than quantity. You've always been quality.

I don't talk about my time in country. First, because nobody wanted to hear about it and, second, on the rare occasions when it did come up, it usually led to negative conversations or, more accurately, confrontation. That's why most of us keep it inside and the other, perhaps more significant reason, for me is, I was privileged to serve with giants, whose courage was inspiring, even as I fought beside them. How do you tell your story when it pales compared to so many of theirs?

The sad part of the Vietnam War is that the victory we won on the ground was given away in the halls of Washington. I have no hope that history will redeem us because the accepted analysis of the war, almost without exception, is written by those who stayed home. Their investment in a story of failure is a search for vindication of their own actions. It's a longer story but those are the basics. When the last of us are gone, sadly their story will stand unchallenged.

All wars are hard but what was unique about what we "had to remember and live with in the years following" was, and is, the homecoming. The first inkling of what was awaiting us, came when in our instructions about returning home they included the warning: "It's not a good idea to wear your uniform when you return stateside, there have been a lot of problems. Some attacks, and that sort of thing by groups of civilians on Soldiers." Amazing what courage a coward can find when with an overpowering group.

All of this is why most Vietnam Veterans when meeting say: "Welcome Home." For some it's the first time they've heard those words. I'm sure all this is TMI but I thought I'd share a little. It doesn't keep me awake at night, it just brings me sadness when remembering all those who answered the call when others walked away and, of course, the bewilderment our Southeast Asian allies must have felt when, "Stateside heroes" insisted on abandoning them.

I'm fine but I wonder how those who sit in wheelchairs and those whose Family heroes never made it home, handle some of what I mentioned. God bless them all.

In short, it was the bravest, most unselfish and patriotic thing I've ever done. I could never top it. I can't imagine my life if I hadn't gone.

And your tribute, my brother, fulfills my prediction: "...we'll all have something to be proud of." As good as any medal I received.

See you soon,
Brother Bill

Air Evac unit mascot, wounded the night before in a mortar attack. Much to the delight of the unit, he made a full recovery. Courtesy of Richard Cameron.

Doctors of A Company, 15th Medical Company, LZ Evans, 1968. Pictured from left are Bill Couser, O.B. Johnson, Don Barton (C.O.), and Paul Sizemore. Courtesy of Don Barton.

Flip Heilig and Alejandro Villarreal. Courtesy of Flip Heilig and Mike Cahalan.

Lt. Charles Campanella (left) and Sgt. James Abram meet for the first time in over 40 years at a 1st Cavalry Reunion at Fort Hood. Campanella had saved Abram's life at LZ Bird on Dec. 26, 1966. Courtesy of James Abram.

Emperor Hirotito steps out of his Mercedes. The photographer, James K. Mellow, was the only American present, 1947.

Living conditions on Firebase "Hotel Hilton" — high heat, confined living quarters, limited amenities, and persistent threat of enemy attack — took a special breed of strong "1st Team" Troopers. Courtesy of Richard Cameron.

Members of the 70th Tank BN,Sherman M4A3E8 Tank #31 "Mary Jane", Gerald Wood - Tank Commander, Korean War. Courtesy of Jason Wood.

CW4 Carl Fox launching on a mission over Baghdad, October 2006.

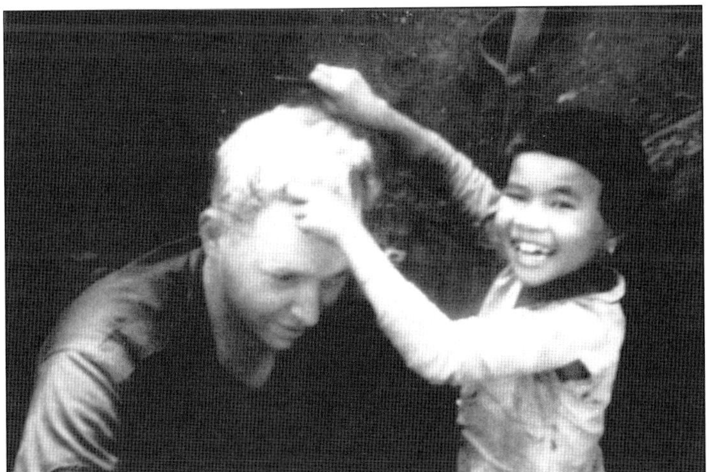

Thomas Gorman and friend, Kontum Province, 1966. Photo courtesy of Thomas W. Gorman.

Biographies

Spec 4 Larry Guenther, Major Don Munson, and PFC Richard Chamberlain comprise the S-3, Operations Forward element during Operation Pegasus, the relief of the Khe Sahn combat base, Republic of South Vietnam, 7 April 1968. Courtesy of Don Munson.

JOE ABODEELY was born and raised in Tucson, Arizona, graduated as a Distinguished Military Graduate and commissioned as a 2nd Lieutenant, Infantry, from the University of Arizona in 1965. He remained in college until called to active duty in 1967, went to Fort Benning's Combat Platoon Leaders' Course, and later trained infantry troops at Fort Polk, Louisiana. In January 1968, he served as a platoon leader in the 1st Air Cavalry Division--an entire airmobile division with infantry, support units, and aviation units assigned as part of the division.

Abodeely wrote a book about his experience in Vietnam—*Dear Mom and Dad, Love from Vietnam,* which won three Global E-book awards.

The *Los Angeles Herald Examiner* on April 8 reported:

"A two-mile victorious march by the Army 1st Air Cavalry Division formally ended the 78-day Communist siege of the fort Hanoi vowed it would take and American generals pledged would never be lost. The siege was over but the battle for control of South Vietnam's Communist-infested northern frontier roared on…

"At Khe Sanh, where around the clock Communist artillery fire had driven 6000 Marine defenders underground, the Leathernecks Sunday whooped it up as Army 1st Lt. Joe Abodeely's unit walked the last two miles into the camp. Abodeely, 24 of Tucson, Ariz. and his platoon formed the 1st Air Cavalry spearhead of the 20,000-man Operation Pegasus drive that broke the Communist grip around Khe Sanh in a week-long drive that covered 12 miles of jungle, hills and minefields…"

Joe (kneeling left front) and his platoon RVN 1968

Abodeely returned from Vietnam in January 1969, finished law school, and became a JAG officer serving in the National Guard and the Army Reserve while practicing law, first as a county prosecutor for 15 years, and then as a criminal defense attorney in city, state, federal, and military courts. Abodeely's last Army Reserve assignment was Chief, Law Branch, Military Police Operations Agency. He retired as O-6, Colonel. His decorations include Combat Infantryman's Badge, Bronze Star, Air Medal, Vietnam Service Medal, Vietnam Campaign Medal with Silver Star device, Vietnamese Cross of Gallantry with Palm, and others.

As labors of love, he operates the Arizona Military Museum (since 1980) and presents dinners/events each year honoring Vietnam Veterans as part of the Commemoration of the Vietnam War. He hosts Buddhist youth for their annual gathering in October and an annual event for Vietnam Veterans called Base Camp on his acreage each April. He serves as a gubernatorial appointee on the Board of Directors of the Arizona Historical Society. Colonel Joe Abodeely designed and encouraged the Arizona legislature to install a Vietnam memorial at the state capitol which honors and respects all those who honorably served in the Vietnam War.

Colonel Joe (as his friends call him) married Donna in 1974, and they live on 20 acres in the desert about 40 miles south of Phoenix, Arizona with three dogs and eight cats.

JAMES EDWARD "POINT MAN" ABRAM was born July 27, 1945 in Marion, SC, and graduated from Johnakin High School in June 1964. He was drafted on Feb. 2, 1966 and attended boot camp at Fort Dix, NJ, with special training as an Ammunition Storage Specialist. Abram was stationed at Redstone Arsenal in Huntsville, AL prior to assignment to Vietnam, where he served in the Central Highlands, the Battle of Hoa Hoi, Operation Irving, and LZ Bird.

He received two Presidential Unit Citations (Operation Irving and LZ Bird), the Valorous Unit Award, National Defense Service Medal, Vietnam Service Medal, and Vietnam Campaign Medal w/ 60 device.

Abram was discharged on Feb. 3, 1968 with the rank of Sgt. E-5. He is a member of Teamsters Local 115, retiring on April 25, 2002. He formed a Veterans group called Pointman Soldiers Heart Ministry to help Veterans form a right relationship with the Lord Jesus Christ, to help them overcome addictions through counseling and caring, and to receive earned benefits for serving their country to support themselves and their families.

He has been married to Claudette for over 51 years. They have three children, Michael Anthony Abram (deceased), Yolanda Stevens, and Myeashia Abram, three grandchildren, Tayhan Abram, Ayana Stevens, and Amira Stevens, and three great-grandchildren, Tayhan Abram Jr., Gemair James Abram, and Nalia (Queen) Walker.

RAYMOND A. ACKER was born January 4, 1932 in Hartford, CT, and graduated from Bulkeley High School in 1950. He also received a bachelor's degree from Philadelphia College of Bible in 1959; a master's of divinity from Reformed Episcopal Seminary in 1962; THM from Dallas Theological Seminary in 1964; and a master's degree from Long Island University in 1973.

He enlisted in March 1953 in Montgomery, AL, with boot camp at Fort Jackson, SC, then to Fort Gordon, GA, Southeastern Signal School, Intermediate Radio Operator, June 1953. Separated from service in February 1955, Camp Kilmer, NJ, with the rank of PFC (E-3), and discharged in March 1961. He later received his commission in July 1963 in Dallas, TX, with reserve training from 1963-65, US Army Chaplain School, Fort Hamilton, NY; Officer Career Course, Fort Hamilton, 1972-73; Hospital Ministry Course, Walter Reed Medical Center, 1978; Army Management Course (3 weeks), Fort Lee, VA, 1980; and Plans, Program & Budget Course, Ft. Benjamin, Harrison, IN, 1981; active duty 1965-83.

He served as a radio operator while stationed in Greenland for an anti-aircraft artillery battalion. As a chaplain, he served in the Pacific and in Vietnam during three major battle periods with a boat battalion whose mission was to man and maintain the harbors and conduct supply missions in the Delta.

Acker was awarded the Bronze Star, Meritorious Service Medal, Army Commendation Medal w/three OLC, Good Conduct Medal, National Defense Service Medal with one OLC, Vietnam Service Medal with three battle stars, Vietnam Gallantry Medal with Palm, Armed Forces Service Medal, Overseas Service Medal with three stars; Army Reserve Medal with 20 year devise; Meritorious Unit Citation with OLC; Vietnamese Award for work with an orphanage, and numerous letters of commendation and appreciation.

He retired from service in May 1983 at Fort Meade, MD, with the rank of LTC (O-5). He was the Alumni Director for the Philadelphia College of Bible, Langhorne, PA, 1983-84; Assistant to the General Director, Biblical Ministries Worldwide, Langhorne, 1984-89; Director, Worldwide Bible Institutes, Grace & Truth Evangelistic Assoc., South Gibson, PA, 1990-95.

Acker married Jean R. Acker in 1960. They have two children, Thomas and Douglas, six grandchildren, Felicia, Douglas Jr., Robbin, Nolita, Bethanie, and Briley, and eight great-grandchildren.

KENNETH ALLEN was born August 16, 1942 in Peoria, IL, and attended boot camp at Fort Leonard Wood, MO. He also trained at Aberdeen Proving Grounds as a Ca. Narcotics Officer and Background Investigator.

Allen was assigned to Vietnam in 1965-66 with the Military Police Platoon, then to Fort Leonard Wood as a Drill Sergeant (1967), Traffic Safety Investigator in West Germany (1977), and Traffic Safety Administration, Test and Licensing Agent (1978).

He received the following awards: Air Medal, Army Commendation Medal, Good Conduct Medal, National Defense Service Medal, Vietnam Service Medal, NCO Professional Development Ribbon, Army Service Ribbon, Republic of Vietnam Campaign Medal, Vietnam Cross of Gallantry with Palm, and Combat Infantry Badge.

He was discharged on Feb. 29, 1984 at Oakland Army Base, with the rank of SFC (E7). He then worked for the Santa Clara County Sheriff's Dept., retiring in 1998. He is a member of the Lion's Club of W.S.J., Veterans of Foreign Wars, Moose Lodge, Masonic Lodge, and the Auto Association.

He is married to Luzvismin P. Allen with one child, Tracie W.G. Allen, and grandchildren Samuel, Jacob, Elijah, and Daniel.

FRANK L. ALVERSON JR. was commissioned in July 1963. After boot camp at Fort Benning (college junior), additional training was at Jump School, Flight School, Commands Gen Staff and Air Defense Career Course. He was stationed at Fort Bliss, TX; Fort Benning, GA; Fort Wolters, TX; Fort Rucker, AL; Nellis AFB, NV; West Germany and Vietnam. He served in the Cuban Missile Crisis (1964) and Vietnam (1965 and 1968).

Alverson received the Distinguished Flying Cross, Bronze Star Medal, Purple Heart, Defense Meritorious Service Medal, Vietnam Service Medal w/one Silver Star and two Bronze Stars, Air Medal w/V Device (Numeral 24), National Defense Service Medal, Republic of Vietnam Campaign Medal, Vietnamese Cross of Gallantry w/ Palm, Army Service Ribbon, Meritorious Unit Commendation, Combat Infantry Badge, Master Army Aviator Badge, Parachutist Badge, Presidential Unit Citation (Army), Overseas Service Ribbon and Armed Forces Reserve Medal.

Memorable experiences were serving two tours in Vietnam and fighting for his country.

LTC Alverson was discharged in July 1985 at Fort Rucker, AL.

Civilian jobs were with Allied Signal and Comarco before he retired in 1988.

Activities in retirement include a bowling coach; Palm Bay, FL City Council; DAV Commander, Palm Bay; Brevard Veterans Council; Vietnam Vets of Brevard, Brevard Community College Bowling Teacher.

Frank and Mary have two children, Frank III (Tre) and Robin and three grandchildren: Carson, Kayla and Megan.

SABAS AMAYA JR., born in October 1941 in Bishop, TX, was drafted in November 1963 and inducted into the Army in December. He took his basic training in Fort Leonard Wood, MO. Amaya was then sent to Fort Benning, GA for his A.I.T. His unit was then designated 11th Air Assault Division, and was the first to train with the Helicopters. They then became the 1st Cavalry Division Air Mobile Unit. They trained until June 1965 and then the entire Division shipped to Viet Nam, 30 days at sea.

Based at An Khe, his company, 1st of the 5th Cavalry, spent all of our time in the Central Highlands; Amaya's rank, E-4 Specialist Machine Gunner.

On November 16, they marched to LZ X-Ray in the Ia Drang Valley to reinforce the 1st of the 7th. They suffered heavy casualties, defended the night and then ordered to LZ Columbus, but redirected to LZ Albany where they were ambushed. The conflict was the largest battle of Viet Nam.

Amaya received the Purple Heart, Presidential Unit Citation among other Viet Nam Medals. He came home wounded, unable to walk, recovered, married and had two daughters. He worked for a Ford dealership, then the United States Postal Service.

Amaya retired in 2007; he joined the Military Order of the Purple Heart, serving as an Officer and is now an Officer in Vets Helping Vets Inc, a 501c3 organization who assists Veterans in obtaining their VA Benefits.

JOHN K. ANDERSON, COL. (RETIRED), was born Dec 8, 1947 to Karl and Ardythe (Holcomb) Anderson. He graduated as the Salutatorian in the first graduating class of Pine River Area High School in 1966. He attended NW Michigan College for one year before entering the United States Military Academy at West Point, NY.

Colonel (Retired) Anderson was commissioned a Second Lieutenant in Field Artillery upon graduating from the U.S. Military Academy in 1971. During his initial years on active duty, he served as a Forward Observer, a Fire Direction Officer, and as an Executive Officer in Battery A, lst Battalion, 83d Field Artillery. He subsequently served as an Assistant Division Artillery S1, Baumholder, Federal Republic of Germany (FRG), and as a Task Force Fire Support Officer in the 2d Armored Division Artillery, Fort Hood, Texas.

In December 1976, he took command of Battery C, 1st Battalion, 14th Field Artillery. While in command, his battery deployed to Grafenwoeher, FRG, for six months, and later redeployed back to Fort Hood. In July 1978, he took command of the Milwaukee Area, Milwaukee District Recruiting Command, U.S. Army Recruiting Command, relinquishing command in March 1980. From March 1980 to July 1981, he served as Operations Officer for Milwaukee District Recruiting Command.

From July 1981 to July 1984, he was assigned to the 194th Separate Armored Brigade, Fort Knox, Kentucky, as Brigade Fire Support Officer, Brigade Assistant S3, and S3 for 3d Battalion, 3d Field Artillery. From July 1985 to June 1988, he was assigned as Operations Officer for Technical Inspections Division, USAREUR Inspector General, Heidelberg, FRG.

From June 1988 to March 1989, he served as the 1st Cavalry Division Artillery S3. In March 1989, Colonel (Retired) Anderson assumed command of 1st Battalion, 82d Field Artillery, 1st Cavalry Division, Fort Hood, Texas. While in command, he deployed his battalion to Southwest Asia in support of Operation Desert Shield and Desert Storm. He relinquished command in June 1991. In July 1992, he became the Senior Fire Support Trainer at the National Training Center (NTC), Fort Irwin, California. From June 1994 to July 1996, he served as Deputy Commander, Operations Group, at NTC. In July 1996 Colonel (Retired) Anderson was assigned to Fort Sill, Oklahoma, to serve as Director, Gunnery Department, U.S. Army Field Artillery School. In October 1998 he moved to the Test and Experimentation Command (redesignated U.S. Army Operational Test Command) Fire Support Test Directorate where he served as Director/Commander until his retirement in June 2000. After retiring from the Army he served as the Director of Doctrine and Training for Tec-Masters, Inc. in Lawton, Oklahoma.

His overseas tours include Germany and Southwest Asia. His decorations include the Legion of Merit, Bronze Star Medal, Meritorious Service Medal with three OLCs, Army Commendation Medal, National Defense Service Medal with Service Star, and Southwest Asia Service Medal with two Service Stars.

Colonel (Retired) Anderson is a graduate of the Field Artillery Officer Basic Course, Field Artillery Officer Advanced Course, Command and General Staff College, and the National War College. He is married to the former Julie Meyers, also a graduate of the class of 1966 at Pine River Area High School.

LUIS M. ARAGON enlisted in the Army on August 4, 1964 entering service at Fort Ord, California. Following basic training, he was selected to attend medical corpsman training at Fort Sam Houston, Texas. After graduating, he was assigned to the 14th Field Hospital, Bad Kreuznach, Germany as a hospital corpsman. While assigned to the 14th, Aragon learned of the Vietnam conflict and volunteered for service. After leave, Aragon reported to Oakland Army Terminal and was advised that he could not deploy because he was not a US citizen. Aragon was then assigned to the 5th Medical Battalion at Fort Carson, Colorado. While providing down range medical support, Aragon learned of the 5th Battalion, 7th Cavalry, 1st Cavalry Division and their upcoming deployment to Vietnam. Aragon again volunteered and was successful in deploying to Vietnam for the first of three tours. Aragon's first tour was as a platoon medic, 2d platoon, Company B, 5/7th. His second tour was as a Med-E-Vac medic with the 15th Medical Battalion, Division Support Command, 1st Cavalry Division (Airmobile). Aragon deployed for a third tour serving as Noncommissioned Officer in Charge, Clearing Platoon, Company A, 15th Medical Battalion, DISCOM, 1st Cavalry Division.

During Aragon's 20 years of service, his most cherished assignments were as Senior Instructor, Tactics Committee, 5th Army NCO Academy, Fort Riley, Kansas; First Sergeant, 43rd Mobile Army Surgical Hospital (MASH), Camp Humphreys, Korea; Full Time Active Duty Advisor, 804th Medical Center, Hanscom Air Force Base, New Bedford, Massachusetts; Station Commander, USA Recruiting Command, Madera, California; and Administrative Assistant to Commander, 7th Special Forces Group and Security Assistance Force for Latin America (SAFLA), Fort Gulick, Canal Zone (Panama), Platform Instructor, Nursing Department, Medical Training Center (MTC), Fort Sam Houston, Texas. Among Aragon's many awards are the Combat Medical Badge, Aircraft Crewmans Badge, Recruiting Command Badge with Gold Stars, four Bronze Stars (two for Valor in combat operations); three Army Commendation Medals (one for Valor in air combat operations) and the Air Medal 5th Award. Aragon retired from active duty with the grade of First Sergeant, on 1 September 1984.

In 1967, Aragon married his high school sweetheart, Julie and they have two children, Luis and Sergi along with nine grandchildren, Luis, Janie, Renee, Christopher, Toni, Gabriel, Jacob, Nevaeh, Isabella, and three great-grandchildren, Gavin, Irvin, and Zaylen.

BRIAN HERBERT ARCHIE enlisted March 3, 1984 at Fort Jackson, SC. Additional training was: Infantryman 11B, Bradley Fighting Vehicle Transition Training Course, Primary Leadership Development Course, Basic non-Commissioned Officer Course for Combat Arms, Military Operations on Urban Terrain, Bradley Infantry Fighting Vehicle Master Gunner Course, Instructor Operator Course-UCOFT, Instructor Training Course, Combat Lifesaver Course, Tactical Certification Course and Bradley Master Gunner Instructor.

He was stationed at Schweinfurt, FRG, Ledward Barracks, C 1/30th INF, 2BDE, 3rd INF DIV; Fort Hood, TX, A co. 1/5 CAV and HHC 1/5 CAV, 2BDE, 1st CAV DIV; Erlangen, FRG, Ferris Barracks, C Co. 1/30th INF, 2BDE, 3rd INF DIV; Fort Hood, TX, A Co. 2/5CAV, 1BDE, 1st CAV DIV, Fort Benning, GA, BIC 1/29INF, 11 REGT, CATD, Bradley Instructional Company, HHC 1/11th INF, 11th REGT.

Desert Shield/Desert Storm, Knight Strike 1, Reconnaissance in Force, Deception of Wadi al Batin were battles he was engaged in.

Archie received the Meritorious Service Medal, Army Commendation medal with Combat Distinguishing Device "V", Army Commendation Medal (5th Award), Army Achievement Medal (8th Award), Joint Meritorious Unit Award, Army Good Conduct Medal (6th Award), Army Lapel Button, Valorous Unit Award, Southwest Asia Service Medal (2nd Award), Noncommissioned Officers Professional Development Ribbon with Numeral (two), Overseas Service Ribbon (2nd Award), Combat Infantryman Badge, Expert Infantryman Badge, Driver and Mechanic Badge with driver-T Bar.

Memorable experiences were the loss of a fallen comrade, SGT Randy Randazzo during Knight Strike 1. SGT Randazzo received a Red Cross message about his father the evening prior, to operation Knight Strike 1. He chose to go to battle with the Black Knights. During Desert Shield, he was tasked as part of the Master Gunner Team, to build a multi-purpose range, in the Desert. The range was named Pegasus Range. This allowed Tanks, Bradleys and other combat units to live-fire their weapon systems prior to Desert Storm.

SSG Archie was discharged on Oct. 31, 2003 at Fort Benning, GA. He worked private security at Fort Jackson, SC and retired from Vance Federal Security in 2007.

In retirement he enjoys fishing, traveling and spending time with Family.

He and Deborah have four children: Shalaine, Desmond, Pam and James, and two grandchildren, Brionna and Keyshaun.

RAYMOND B. ARMER II enlisted for Basic Training in June 1959 at Fort Leonard Wood, MO. He trained as a Combat Engineer. In 1961 he was chosen as a candidate for NCO Academy and graduated the same year in Munich, Germany.

During his time in the Army, he was stationed in Vicenza, Italy in 1960; Olathe N.A.S. Kansas in 1963; Fort Leonard Wood in 1967; Korea in 1967; Fort Benning, GA 1967 to attend OCS and again in 1973 and Fort Polk, LA in 1970.

He received his commission in February 1968 as a 2nd Lieutenant in the Infantry at Ft. Benning, GA. He was an instructor at the Infantry School and volunteered for early assignment to Vietnam.

He arrived in Vietnam November 1968 and served 18 months. During his time in Vietnam, he was promoted to Captain and assumed command of Co A 2/8 in January 1970.

Armer received the Combat Infantry Badge; four Bronze Stars, two with "V" Device; Purple Heart with two OLC; Air Metal with two OLC; Vietnam Service Metal with one Silver Star and 1 Bronze Star; Presidential Unit Citation; Army Valorous Unit Citation; RVN Gallantry Cross with Palm; RVN Civic Action Honor Metal Unit Citation as well as other service metals. Armer and his unit are portrayed in three books written about Vietnam: *The Anonymous Battle*, *Black Horse Rider* and *Fire Base Illingworth*. He is also featured along with several other Veterans in the documentary film Against All Odds, Cavalry to the Rescue at the Dog's Head.

After release from active duty, Armer continued to serve in the Army Reserve until he retired as a Major. He graduated from the University of South Carolina. After leaving the corporate sector, he and his wife owned and operated a restaurant, catering service and bed and breakfast in Georgia.

He is married to Donna Keel Armer. They live and enjoy retirement in Beaufort, SC.

ROBERT M. ATKINS JR. was born on Oct. 4, 1946 in Miami, FL and graduated from Grandy High School in Norfolk, VA, in 1964. He later received a BA from Chaminade University in 1972 and an MA from the University of Illinois Springfield in 1980.

Atkins enlisted into the service at Richmond, VA in March 1965, with basic training at Fort Gordon, GA. He was stationed at Phan Thiet, Pleiku, Ia Drang, Khe Sanh, A Shau, and Quan Tri, and also spent time in Germany, Alaska and various other posts in the U.S.

He received the Combat Infantryman Badge, Vietnam Service Medal, Vietnam Campaign Medal, Purple Heart, Bronze Star, Good Conduct, and other awards. He left the service on June 1, 1990 with the rank of Major, and then became a Drug and Alcohol Counselor and Probation and Parole Officer for the State of Florida, retiring in 2006.

He married Linda S. Atkins on May 22, 1971, and they have three children, Sean Atkins, Chris Atkins, and Maj. Ryan Atkins (U.S. Army), and five grandchildren, Tyler, Katey, Jake, Mickey, and Zoey.

ROBERT "BOB" D. BABCOCK graduated from high school in 1952 and from college in 1982. He enlisted at Lansing, MI and took Boot Camp at Fort Knox, KY. Additional training was in Airborne and Ranger. He says he was stationed all over the world.

Babcock was engaged in battles in Korea and Viet Nam.

He received a Purple Heart, Wings, Ranger Tab, Combat Infantry Badge and Bronze Star.

Memorable experiences were as a Scout for the 10th Recon, 7th Cav in 1952.

CSM Babcock was discharged in 1978 at Fort Hood, TX.

After retiring in 2010, he has enjoyed hunting and fishing.

Bob and Thach have three children and seven grandchildren: Cooper, Same, Owen, Braxton, Collin and Audery.

LYLE J. BACKEN was inducted into the Army, September 1950. His Basic Training was at Camp Atterbury, IN. Following training, he left for Japan. Then he went from Japan to Pusan, Korea, March 1951 and was assigned to I Company, 5th Cavalry Regiment, 4th Platoon, 1st Cavalry Division.

Backen was in the 57 mm Recoilless Rifle Squad, as ammo bearer and later as assistant gunner. Later he was assigned as I Company Mail Clerk.

In December he left Korea for Camp Chitosse, Japan. He returned to the US in February 1952, and was assigned to Camp McCoy, WI until June 1952, when he was put on inactive service. He received his honorable discharge in December 1956.

Medals Backen received were: Good Conduct Medal, National Defense Medal, United Nation's Service Medal, Combat Infantry Badge, Army of Occupational Medal, Republic of Korea Presidential Medal and Korean Service Medal.

When he returned home, he returned to farming until August 1966, when he began working at Fisher Controls in Marshalltown, IA, until his retirement in 1986.

Backen married Mildred Hess in 1952 and has four children: Duane, Donna, John and Judith, along with eight grandchildren: Darren, Karen, Chad, Nathan, Derrick, Julia, Christopher and Curtis. Backen passed away November 2001.

CSM DAVID O. BAILLIE was born in November 1934 in New York City, the son of a World War I and World War II Veteran, plus other Family Veterans including five uncles and two aunts and several cousins (only two uncles and one aunt came back from World War II) and about four cousins.

He joined under age in 1949 at 15 years old in New York City and spent his first night on Governor's Island (just outside New York City) and then went to Fort Dix, NJ for medical inspection (shots) and some very basic military training; manual of arms and close order drill (marching) (1st Army provisional), then to Fort Benning GA, (3rd Army) for basic and advanced training. 3rd Inf. Division, 30th Inf. Regt. 3rd Platoon, (provisional). He was in the top 1% of his class and qualified as Expert with the M-l rifle and was one of the top three in the battalion. He then went to advanced training and was taught how to lay mines, hand to hand combat and fired Expert with the 45 cal pistol and 32 cal M-l and M-2 carbine and Expert with Bayonet training, and Bazooka and Hand grenades. Was again in the top 1% of his class, (third). This group was then picked for special training with the 3rd Tank Ban, where they learned all the positions within the tank. He also qualified for all tank weapons as Expert: .30 cal machine gun, .50 cal machine gun, .45 cal grease gun and the tank .37 mm, .75 mm and .90 mm gun. He again was one of the outstanding students and was picked and transferred to ISD/ Inf. School Detachment, Infantry School as an Ass't. Instructor. His duties were to instruct officers from the USA and friendly countries in armor infantry tactics BOTC/ Basic Officer Training Course. The team also helped write the army manuals on Tank specifications for the M-26, M-46 and M-48 tanks/ their capability etc. The team would present 'problems' to BOTC learners over a 72-hour period and report on their findings. Here he also qualified in driving a staff car ('49 Chevy), jeep, 3/4 ton truck, duce and half, 5 ton wheeled wrecker, and half track and many tanks, from the M-4, M-4al, M-37, M-41, M-26, M-46, M-48 and others.

He volunteered for overseas service and was sent to Japan and then in early spring of 1950 to Korea with the 34th Inf. Regt/24th Inf. Division. It was the first full regiment to land on Korean soil and enter the Korean War. He was assigned to the 34th Tank Company/24th Inf. Div. near the town of Poedigree, South Korea. (Just northeast of Seoul) He was an E-4 (Cpl.) and upon arrival became acting section Sgt. in the 3rd platoon (the heavy section of the platoon/two tanks for a total of 5). He saw action with this unit until it was reduced in strength to a paper unit. The 34th Inf. Regt. landed with 1,900+ men in June and but August there were only 183 that were still standing (all others were KIA, WIA, POWs, MIA.) CSM Baillie, now S/Sgt and acting platoon Sgt. after the Pusan perimeter, was transferred to the 1st Cav. Div., recon Sqdn. Troop B. It did recon work over and above the 38th Parallel for some months. In all CSM Baillie was in seven out of the 10 campaigns in Korea. After the war in Korea he went state side to go to NCO school (Sgt. Maj. academy) and on leave for 30 days. He reenlisted and went to Fort Hood, TX, where he rejoined the 1st Cav. Div. again and was sent to Vietnam as a recon member and did several special ops assignments in the northern part of Vietnam (attached to 23rd Div.) and then back to Fort Hood, TX where he was called in by his battalion commander and promoted to E-8 (M/S) and asked to take the role of 1st Sgt with a new unit, it was headed for Nam (this would be his 4th tour). He took it; CSM was promoted to Sgt. Maj. during this tour and then after a few years was raised to CSM, then came state side again, this time he went into the Army Reserve and National Guard for 10 years. After active duty he entered college and attained degrees in Phcy. Soc., Education, and became an educator for about 20 years.

His thesis was on the 'un-met needs of the Non-traditional Student 'and later started a Counseling agency on UMass campus to help these students (many returning Veterans). He retired from that and is now an author and poet (published) in 1999, *Dry Tears* and *Line Kansas*, he was awarded the Studs Truckle award from the state of Illinois and named poet laureate of the town of Elburn, IL. The Mayor of Elburn presented him with the Key to the City in 2001. He has been active with both the American Legion and the VFW for over 30 years. He has also been active with The Boy Scout of America for over 60 years; four of his sons are Eagle Scouts, as is he.

His military awards and decorations include; Silver Star (two) Bronze Star (three) with 'V' and Legion of Merit (three) and Army Commendation Medal (four) with 'V', Purple Heart (two) Army Achievement Medal (four), Army Soldiers Medal, Meritorious Service Medal (three) Joint Service Command Medal with 'V', Army Occupation Medal with' Japan' bar, Outstanding Volunteer Service Medal (two), National Defense Medal with one star, Korean service medal with one silver star and four bronze stars, UN Korean Service Medal, ROK Korean War Service Medal, Army Expeditionary Force Medal with two stars, Vietnam service Medal with three stars, Good conduct medal with silver bar and three knots, Expert in tank weapon's medal, Combat Infantry Badge with star (two), Expert Infantry Bar, Tanker of the year three times, NCO of the month and Tank crew proficiency award for (42nd Inf. Div.), State of New York Cross for Combat Veterans, and several Unit awards. He was also awarded the 'Ambassador for Peace Medal' from the South Korean government and a plaque from the Korean Association of Asheville NC. "Thank you for your Service" and a letter of appreciation from the President of South Korea for his service in the defense of South Korea. The Korean USA Association also awarded him a 'special plaque' for his service to South Korea during the Korean War.

RAYMOND D. "RAY" BANNING enlisted in the Army on July 1, 1960. After Basic and AIT training in the 2nd Armored Division at Fort Hood, TX, he reported to Fort Benning, GA for Infantry OCS.

Pictured l-r: Bde Commander Col. "Sly" Meyer, Bn Commander Lt. Col. Hal Iverson, Div. Commander Maj. E. Roberts, and Bn. XO Major Ray Banning.

Ray was commissioned as a second lieutenant in June 1961. His first assignment was with the 24th Infantry Division in Germany, where between 1961 and 1964 he served as a platoon leader, an .81mm mortar platoon leader, a Fire Direction Officer in a 4.2-inch mortar platoon and as a Brigade Communications Officer. Returning to Fort Hood in 1964 for an assignment with the 1st Armored Division, he served as a Company Executive Officer and a Company Commander.

In June 1966 he reported to MACV for a year as an adviser to the South Vietnamese Army, at II Corps Headquarters as an Operations Officer and as an adviser with an ARVN Regiment. Ray next completed the Infantry Officer's Advanced Course at Fort Benning before returning to Vietnam in January 1969 to serve with the 1st Cavalry Division, first on the 1st Brigade staff then as the Executive Officer of the 2/12 Cavalry. Ray then returned to Germany for an assignment with the 1st Armored Division where he was the Executive Officer of a Mech. Infantry Battalion, a Brigade Staff Officer and the Division G-5. Returning to Fort Benning in 1974, he served as the Infantry Center Protocol Officer for two years. Next he reported to Fort Leavenworth, KS to attend the Army Command and General Staff College. He served with the Army Training and Doctrine command at Fort Leavenworth until retiring as a lieutenant colonel in July 1980.

He received the National Defense Service Medal; Vietnam Service Medal with 1 Silver Service Star; Republic of Vietnam Campaign Medal; Combat Infantryman Badge; Purple Heart; Army Commendation Medal; four Overseas Bars; Republic of Vietnam Armed Forces Honor Medal, First Class; Meritorious Service Medal (2nd Oak Leaf Cluster); Bronze Star Medal (4th Oak Leaf Cluster) with V Device; Air Medal (Num 3); Republic of Vietnam Gallantry Cross with Palm.

Ray's civilian career was in the Aerospace Business, first in a marketing position with the Lockheed Georgia Company in Marietta, GA from July 1980 to January 1989. While with Lockheed, Ray worked on identifying what the replacement for the C-130 should be, answer more C-130s. In 1989 Ray moved to Wichita to work for Boeing. While with Boeing, Ray worked in Wichita, Seattle and Philadelphia. He was a Regional Marketing Manager selling CH-47 helicopters.

Ray retired in 2000 and moved to Springfield, MO where he lives on a small farm with Shari, his wife of 56 years. They have two children, Tina and Scott and five grandchildren: Kaci, Logan, Tory, Faith and Gabe and two great-grandchildren, Evie and Thea.

ALEJANDRO M. BARRAZA was born in 1939 in Empalme, Sonora, Mexico. He enlisted on Jan. 26, 1962 and took Boot Camp at Fort Ord, CA. He also trained at Guerrilla Warfare School and Jump School.

In addition to Fort Ord, Barraza was stationed at Camp Casey, Korea; Fort Hood, TX; Fort Benning, GA, Vietnam and again at Fort Benning, GA. He received a Bronze Star with V, Combat Infantry Badge, Airborne.

After military service, he worked as a mechanic.

Alejandro and Esperanza have four children: Alejandro, David, Ada and Rocio. Their grandchildren are Alejandro, Marcos, Carlos, David, Carolina, Sofia, Mia, Maxim, Milano and Dolce.

DONALD C. BARTON, M.D. was born March 23, 1935 in Salem, KY and graduated from Williamsburg (Ky) High School in 1952. He then attended the University of Louisville for eight years, earning a Bachelor of Arts degree and later, his M.D.

Don entered military service in June 1956 and received basic training at Fort Sam Houston. He was assigned to the 1st Air Cavalry and became the company commander for A Co., Medical Battalion. In 1966 he was assigned to Fort Campbell, KY before transferring to Vietnam in 1967.

He participated in numerous engagements including: An Khe, LZ Baldy, LZ Evans, LZ Stud to support the liberation of Khe Sanh, Au Shau Valley, and LZ Sharon at Quang Tri. He received the Air Medal, Bronze Star (1968), Comm. Service Award (1995). He served on the KMDAC Board from 1998-2000.

Don was discharged in Seattle, Washington in June 1968 with the rank of Captain.

In civilian life, he was a family practice physician, retiring in June 2000. He was named to the GOP Hall of Fame in 1997, was President of the Kentucky Medical Association from 1987-98, was a delegate to the American Medical Association for ten years, and was named Doctor of the Year in 1991. In retirement he enjoys golf, hunting, and travel.

He is married to Joan and they have four children — Donna, Becky, Toni, and David — and nine grandchildren — Amber, Kari, Heather, Tanner, John David, Kelly, Tia, Donnie, and Nikki.

CLAUD A. BASKIN was born in 1934 in Lebanon, TN, graduated from Lebanon Senior High in 1953 and enlisted in January 1957 at Lebanon, TN. He attended Boot Camp at Fort Carson, CO. Additional training was Methods of Instruction, Radar Operators Course, NCO Academy, Demotions and Mine Warfare.

Baskin was stationed at Camp Hanford, WI; Fort Huachuca, AZ; Fort Knox, KY; Fort Mead, MD; Fort Hood, TX; Fort Rucker, AL; Fort Leonard Wood, MO; Germany and Korea.

He served in Vietnam with Bravo Troop, 1st Squadron 9th Cavalry.

Memorable experiences included serving with the elite 1st of the 9th Cavalry, First Cavalry Division in 1967, Vietnam.

Baskin was discharged Jan. 1, 1979 as SFC E7.

Awards received were Combat Infantry Badge, Air Assault Badge, Silver Star, a Bronze Star, two Purple Hearts and Air Medal.

He and Jimmie Sue have four children: Mark, Rory, LaQuita and Regina. Grandchildren are Crystan, Dewayne, Mellisa and Heather.

RICHARD "RICK" BASSUK was born in 1949 in Chicago and graduated from Niles North High School in 1967. He entered the Army on March 23, 1971 and took Boot Camp at Fort Lewis, WA.

He graduated first in class "Trainee of the Cycle." Bassuk took training at Fort Sill, OK, Field Radio Mechanic 31B20.

Bassuk entered Vietnam on August 23, 1971. He was stationed out of Bien Hoa but spent the entire time at Fire Support Bases Andrews, Makowski and Melanie. He was RTO for Base Commander. Rick was awarded a Bronze Star.

He received an honorable discharge on April 15, 1972 as E4 Specialist 4th Class.

Bassuk attained a B.S. in Industrial Marketing in 1973 from Southern Illinois University. He spent 40 years as an outdoor salesman selling electrical products, and retired in 2013. He and Peggy have two children, Cynthia and Phillip.

Bassuk loves playing golf. He is a Lifetime Member of 1st Cavalry Division and Vietnam Veterans of America and belongs to Sheridan's Cavalry Chapter – Greater Chicago.

CLINTON D. BATCHELLER enlisted April 3, 1964 from Denver, CO. Basic Training at Fort Polk, AIT at Fort Knox. Assigned to Company C 1st. Bn. 70th Armor at Gablingen, Germany. Volunteered for assignment to Vietnam 1965. December 1965 assigned to D Co. 2nd Bn. 12th Cavalry l Cavalry Division as a crewman on 106 recoilless rifle, later to gunner on M2 .50 machine gun. Transferred to B Co. 2/12 Infantry Platoon. Wounded May 17, 1966 on operation Crazy Horse, evacuated to 7th Field Hospital, Japan. January 1967 assigned to Fort Carson A Co. 1/77 Armor. Volunteered for duty with 1st Cavalry June 1968, assigned to A Trp. 1/9 Cavalry as a scout on OH 13 and OH6a. Assigned to Fort Knox, served as DI training Armor Crewmen. Other assignments were Fort Wolters, Fort Meade, Fort Dix, Fort Knox, Baumholder, Germany, Ansbach, Germany. He retired MSG E-8 from active duty in 1984.

Batcheller went to Boyce College at The Southern Baptist Seminary and studied for Pastoral Ministry. In 1987 he pastored the Olive Branch Baptist Church in Martinsville, IL. In 1998 he pastored the First Baptist Church in Robinson, IL and pastored the Heartland Baptist in Hutsonville, IL. He is presently retired at Robinson, IL.

His military awards are BZ, two PH, 31 Air Medals, two Army Commendations, six Good Conduct, National Defense, American Campaign, RVCM, Vietnamese Cross of Gallantry, three Service Ribbons, Drill Sergeant 10 Badge, CIB, Aircraft Crewman Badge.

He married Effie "Micky" Bennett from Benton, IL, June 1969; they have three children: Shawn, Angela and Hannah; and five grandchildren: Callie, Ashtyn, Emma, Eli and Ethan.

FRANKLIN L. BAYER was born June 30, 1950 in Portland, OR, and graduated from Central High School in 1968. He entered the army on Sept. 26, 1969 and then did basic training and AIT at Ft. Lewis, WA and was given an MOS of 11Bravo. Arriving in Vietnam on March 4, 1970 he was assigned to A2/5 second platoon. Their company was along the Cambodian border west of Saigon. He also took part in the invasion of Cambodia in May and June 1970.

Most of his time was spent with the gun team, where he carried the M-60 for many months.

Bayer says he should have been killed or wounded several times, but he survived unhurt. And for a while he wondered why he made it and others did not. Looking back, he says he has no human explanation except for God's grace, and he want to thank his precious Lord and Savior, Jesus Christ, for bringing him back to know Him and enjoy life. Franklin has a wonderful wife, grandchildren, and great-grandchildren.

He spent the last six months of his time at Fort Hood, TX. Bayer left the army on Sept. 24, 1971 and returned to his hometown of Portland, OR, where he lives today.

MARGARITO R. "BJ" BEJARANO was born Feb. 23, 1946 in Virden, NM, and graduated from Duncan High School in 1966. He enlisted on Feb. 8, 1966 in Duncan and attended basic training at Fort Ord, CA, later transitioning to Fort Polk, LA, and then Vietnam as part of Headquarters & Headquarters Co., 1st Brigade (Abn), 1st Cavalry Division (Airmobile).

Bajarano received the CBI, National Defense Medal, Professional Infantry Corps, Sharpshooter, Vietnam Air Service, Vietnam Campaign, Vietnam Service Medal, Air Medal, Vietnam Civil Action, Vietnam Cross of Gallantry (Individual) and Vietnam Cross of Gallantry (Unit).

He was discharged on Feb. 7, 1969 at Fort Polk, LA, with the rank of sergeant (E5). He worked for Phelps Dodge for 11 years, BHP for 13 years, and Asarco for 10 years, and served with the National Guard for 22 years, 12 days. He officially retired in 2011, and enjoys deer hunting and visiting casinos.

He is married to Guadalupe, with three children – Margarito Jr., Judy, and Beverley – and eight grandchildren – Angle, Frankie, Bedelia, Renae, Kayla, Rhianna, Oceanana, and Illy.

JOSEPH H. BELSHA III was selected for the Warrant Officer Flight Training program at the age of 17, and enlisted at Fort Knox, KY in June 2003. Following Basic Training, he completed flight training at Fort Rucker, AL as an Apache attack helicopter pilot. Belsha served two combat tours to Iraq with the 1st Battalion, 227th Aviation Regiment, including the Troop Surge of OIF 06-

08, and OIF 09-10. Following his second deployment, Belsha served as a Platoon Leader for the Apache Aircraft Qualification Course (FSXXI) at Fort Rucker, AL, and later as a Standardization Instructor Pilot/Instrument Examiner/Master Gunner for 2nd Battalion, 10th Aviation, 10th Mountain Division in Afghanistan.

Belsha's awards include the Combat Action Badge, Senior Aviator Badge, Parachutist Badge, Air Medal (3rd Award), Army Commendation Medal (3rd Award), Iraq Campaign Medal (3 Combat Stars), and the Afghanistan Campaign Medal (1 Combat Star).

Belsha's transition from the Army to civilian Helicopter Air Ambulance in 2014, and has held the positions of Site Safety and Lead Pilot/Base Manager. He is currently a Pilot and Program Safety Chairman for a multi-aircraft Air Ambulance operation, and resides in Texas with his high school sweetheart wife and their two sons.

BRUCE BERGSTROM enlisted in February 1979 and attended Basic and AIT at Fort Jackson, SC. After training as a Unit Supply Clerk, he was assigned to HQ Company, Fort Wainwright, AK. In January 1981 he transferred to Fort Huachuca, serving at the S4 of the Intelligence School. In September 1986 he was reclassified as a Patient Administration Specialist and trained at Fort Sam Houston, TX. In December 1986 he transferred to Martin Army Hospital at Fort Benning, GA. In September 1991 he transferred to 130th Station Hospital, Heidelberg, Germany. In July 1994 he transferred to Evans Army Hospital at Fort Carson, CO.

In August 1997 he attended Army Recruiting School and assigned to Minot, ND. In June 1998 he transferred to the Medical Operations Center of the 1st Cavalry Division at Fort Hood, TX, serving as a manager of immunization and panorex records. In August 2000 he transferred to the Medical Information Systems Agency at Fort Sam Houston, TX. In December 2003 he transferred to Bassett Army Hospital, Fort Wainwright, AK. In May 2004 he was sent as an augmentee to the 31st Combat Support Hospital in Balad, Iraq and later moved to Mosul, Iraq. He retired in 2007.

Since the 1st Cavalry Division was in the Iraq theater at the time, many of the medical evacuation patients that we coordinated came from the 1st Cavalry. In Balad, the hospital actually had a full time representative from the 1st Cavalry sitting in the Patient Administration tent. They were mainly there to maintain accountability of patients, personal effects and weapons of 1st Cavalry personnel.

ALBERT "BEEZEL" BIERLY JR. was born in 1945 at Durham, NC and graduated from John Marshall High School in 1963.

He enlisted on March 27, 1964 at Rochester, MN and attended Boot Camp at Fort Leonard Wood. He attended Nuclear Weapon Assembly/Artillery Liaison School in Korea, Artillery School at Fort Sill, OK and Map Reading in Korea. He was stationed at Fort Leonard Wood, MO; Fort Sill and Fort Benning, GA.

Bierly served in Korea in 1964 and in Vietnam from 1965-1966. He was discharged as CPL. E4 on June 9, 1966 at Oakland, CA.

He was awarded the Air Assault Badge, Combat Artillery Badge and Vietnam Service Medal/OSBAR.

After military service "Beezel" was a truck driver and business owner, union drywall finisher and belonged to Painters & Allied Trades Union, retiring in 2007. He is affiliated with the National Federation Independent Business.

He now does volunteer work, attends church, travels, enjoys hunting and fishing. He has two children, Todd and Troy; two grandchildren, Robert and Danielle; and great-grandson Rylan.

RONALD M. BLACK went through basic training at Fort Polk, Louisiana, then to flight school at Fort Wolters and Fort Rucker, flight class 69-21.

In Vietnam, he was assigned to Alpha Troop, 1st Squadron, 9th Cavalry, 1st Cavalry Division, based at Tay Ninh, flying as a scout pilot in OH-6A from August 1969 through March 1970 and as a lift pilot in UH-1H from March 1970 through August 1970. He participated in Operation Shoemaker in the Cambodian incursion in May 1970.

His awards include the Distinguished Flying Cross with one oak leaf cluster; 47 Air Medals, one with "V" device; Army Commendation Medal with "V" device; Purple Heart; Bronze Star. After returning stateside, he taught Instrument Methods of Instruction at Fort Rucker until my discharge from the Army on April 1, 1971.

As a civilian, he continued to fly helicopters, working in Indonesia, Egypt, and the western U.S., transitioning into management in the 1980s. He's been fortunate to have great flying experiences fighting wildfires, flying high altitude operations over mountainous jungle terrain on New Guinea, and participating in vertical replenishment with the Navy's Military Sealift Command.

He currently is an aviation management consultant, living in Oregon, where he and his wife will eventually live in retirement.

PHILLIP L. BLAKE graduated from the US Military Academy in 1960 and was commissioned an Infantry officer. He took parachute and Ranger training and was then assigned as a platoon leader in the 101st Airborne Division, Fort Campbell. He subsequently commanded a company until reassigned in 1963 to the 173rd Airborne Brigade on Okinawa. After duty as platoon leader, staff officer and company commander, he deployed with the brigade to Vietnam in early 1965.

Blake returned to Vietnam in 1966 and was assigned to the 1st Battalion (Airborne), 12th Cavalry as the adjutant. After four months, he assumed command of Company A.

Upon return to CONUS in 1967, he attended graduate school and served a tour on the faculty at West Point. In 1972 he began his last tour in Vietnam as advisor to a Vietnamese airborne battalion. Later assigned as aide to COMUSMACV, he departed on March 29, 1973, the last day of US military involvement.

Among his later assignments, Blake served as a battalion XO in the 101st, a battalion CO in the 24th Infantry Division and on the DA Staff. He retired as a colonel in 1988.

Blake's decorations include the Soldiers Medal, the Purple Heart, two awards of the Bronze Star (Valor) and the Legion of Merit. He is a master parachutist and a pathfinder.

Blake married Red Wallace in 1962. They have two children and five grandchildren.

PAUL N. "NORM" BLANKENBECKLER (BB) was married to his lovely wife, Donna; graduated from the University of Tennessee-Knoxville (BS Education); was commissioned an Infantry Lieutenant and arrived at Ft. Benning, all in December 1972. Assigned to the 1st CAVALRY DIVISION (TRICAP) in mid-1973, he became a platoon leader in CSC/2-7 CAV (AMBL) (INF) then later Assistant S2, 3rd BDE and transferred to the Military Intelligence Corps. He returned to 2-7 CAV (MECH) (INF) as the S2. In Europe, he was S2, 10th EGR BN then S2, 3rd DIV ARTY in 3rd ID. Stateside he became the Senior Intelligence Instructor then SSO at the Infantry School. Upon reassignment he became the DSE Chief/G2 Plans, then the S2, 1st BDE, 24th ID. Returning to Europe, he became S1, 207th MI BDE, then served two years as S3, 307th MI BN in VII CORPS watching the Iron Curtain crumble.

In July 1990, he returned stateside assigned as S3, 525th MI BDE (CEWI) (ABN), XVIII AIRBORNE CORPS, directing deployment and operations in support of DESERT SHIELD and executing standard and non-standard intelligence operations during DESERT STORM. After redeployment and recovery, Norm became the 525 MI Deputy Commanding Officer. Selected ACofS G2 in the summer of 1992, he returned to the 1st CAVALRY DIVISION, preparing and training for contingency operations, testing/fielding the All Source Analysis System, and integrating unmanned aerial vehicles. Retiring as G2 in the fall of 1993, Norm's decorations include the Bronze Star, MSM (four OLC), ARCOM (two OLC), AAM (one OLC) and Parachutist Badge.

From 1993 till 1998 he was the Customer Service Manager, Wells Fargo Alarm Services, in Memphis, TN. Since August 1998, Norm served Northrop Grumman as a Training and Behavioral Research Manager in Columbus, GA. His efforts support the US Army Research Institute for the Behavioral and Social Sciences. Norm has authored or coauthored over 30 published studies informing Army leaders and decision makers on issues related to training, leadership, technology integration, situational awareness, and decision-making. Norm and Donna have two children and three wonderful grandchildren. Living in Midland, they are active in Cavalry Baptist Church. Norm remains active in the Masonic Fraternity and has been honored with membership in the Red Cross of Constantine and coroneted a 33° Inspector General (Honorary) in the Scottish Rite.

CW4 GEOFFREY M. BOEHM (RET.) enlisted in the Delayed Entry Program for Warrant Officer

Candidate and Flight School program in Hempstead, NY in May 1968. In July 1968, he received Basic Training at Fort Polk, LA. In September 1968, he attended WOC and Primary Helicopter School, Fort Wolters, TX. Attended Advanced Helicopter School Hunter AAF/Fort Stewart, GA in November 1968. In July 1969 he graduated from Flight School (Rotary Wing) and was promoted to Warrant Officer 1. From August 1969 to August 1970, he was in Republic of Vietnam assigned to Company C, 227th Assault Helicopter Battalion, 1st Cavalry Division, Phouc Vinh, RVN with call sign "Ghostrider 28."

Born June 15, 1948 in New York, graduated from Paul D. Schreiber High School, Port Washington, NY in 1966. He attended Nassau Community College, Hempstead, NY; Bunker Hill Community College AAS, Boston, MA and University of Massachusetts attaining a BS Business Administration.

Boehm was Executive Director City of Boston Air Pollution Control Commission; Staff Assistant for Veterans and Military Personnel US Senator John F. Kerry; currently property manager for a 324-unit condominium complex for The Dartmouth Group.

He is married to Sharon Burke and has two sons from a previous marriage, Ryan F. Boehm and Eric M. Boehm, both living and working in Massachusetts.

RICHARD E. BOND was born in 1938 in Akron, IA. He graduated from Denver South High School and in 1961 attained a BS BA at Denver University.

Bond enlisted at Denver in 1956 and attended Boot Camp at Fort Leonard Wood, MO. Additional training was Radio Operator and FA Basic. He was stationed at Fort Sill and Fort Dix and served in Viet Nam. Bond was awarded a Bronze Star and Air Medal. His memorable experience was Khe Sahn Rehab.

Bond was discharged as a colonel at Denver, CO in 1976.

In civilian life he was a business owner and now enjoys hunting and fishing in his retirement.

He has one daughter, Sharla J., and two grandchildren, Amilia and Jonah.

STEPHEN F. "BOZ" BOSMA enlisted on Nov. 30, 1953 at Sioux Falls, SD and took Boot Camp at Fort Riley, KS. In January 1956 he enlisted in the South Dakota National Guard. In June 1959 he was discharged as Master Sergeant E-7 from enlisted service at Huron, SD. In November 1979 he was discharged as 0-5 LTC from commissioned service in San Jose, CA.

Additional Training was: Advanced Infantry Basic Training, Officer Candidate School, Ordnance Officers Orientation Course, Ordnance Career Course, Engineer Basic Officer Course, Engineer Career Officers Course, Command and General Staff College, Chemical, Biological, and Radiological Course, California Specialized Training Institute (Civil Disturbances), Engineer Equipment Officer Course.

Bosma was stationed at Fort Funston, Fort Riley, Fort Leavenworth in Kansas, Fort Lewis, WA; Camp Drake, Camp Drew, Camp Weir, Camp Whittington, all Honshu, Japan; Camp Chitose and Camp Crawford of Hokkaido, Japan. Fort Ord, Camp Hunter Leggett, Camp Roberts, Camp Irwin, Camp San Luis Obispo, Camp Parks, Camp Baker, and Sharp Army Depot in California; Aberdeen Proving Ground, MD; Fort Belvoir, VA; Camp J. Hugo, Aronson, MT; Camp McCoy, WI and Camp Rapid, SD. He was also stationed at armories in Huron, SD; Miles City, MT; San Lorenzo, Fort Funston, Mission Street in San Francisco and Santa Rosa and US Army Reserve Training Center in Sunnyvale, CA and University of Nevada, Reno.

He was engaged in: Pacific Theater of Operations (Korea), United Nations Peace Keeping Mission. As a California National Guard Officer served missions and/or provided support for all 1960s Civil Disturbances, including First Watts Riot, Berkeley Free Speech Movement, May Day Riot, Hunter's Point Riot, Angela Davis Shootout at Marin County Courthouse. Led National Guard Engineers with Metal Detector into San Quentin to search for weapons and ammunitions.

All medals were based on weapons qualifications, all as an enlisted man: Rifle, Pistol, B.A.R., Carbine, 60MM Mortar, WWII Occupation medal (Japan), Army Good Conduct, US National Service, Korean Service, UN Korean Service, Korean Presidential Unit Citation, US Presidential Unit Service, NG Achievement, Ambassador for Peace, State of California Active Duty medal.

Memorable experiences were: Battalion Soldier of the week and Colonel's Orderly on the same day, 8th Cav. Rgt., 1955. He set a record as Enlisted Man five times, selected opportunities as Colonel's Order in eight days, also 8th Cav Rgt, 1955. Was promoted to Master Sergeant E-7 as Engineer Platoon Sergeant within four years of total active duty and National Guard time served. Was Honor Graduate of International Engineer Equipment Officer Course at Fort Belvoir, VA, 1972. Was an O (outstanding) rated instructor for both Non Commissioned Officers and Officer Candidates at the California Military Academy, 1965-1975. In May, 1954 he was a Replacement Soldier on the ill-fated railroad *Toya Maru* ferry four months before it was sunk by a typhoon in one of the most destructive maritime disasters in recorded history. (September 1954) Over 1,000 persons were killed including 1st Cavalry Division Soldiers, their wives and children.

Bosma was a Public School Teacher and Counselor (1959-1992) in the Union School District. Steve was selected as Teacher of the Year (1972) in Union School District, San Jose, CA. He was selected as the Union Leader of the year in 1992 for Santa Clara County, CA

Steve is affiliated with California Teachers Association, National Education Association, American Legion, Veterans of Foreign Wars plus many more charities and Service entities.

Activities in retirement include family history, golf, duplicate bridge, homeowner's organization leadership and travel. Plus many military Veterans organizations including the founding of the Veterans Club in his retirement community, along with military reunions in various parts of the US and South Korea.

Steve and Gloria Jean Shea-Bosma have four children: Walter R., Wayde R., Wendee R. Brumwell and Wisti R. Quenneville. Grandchildren are Melanee Sanchez, Kelly Brumwell, Carly Quenneville and Joe Quenneville. Great-grandchildren are Trinity Pichardo, Harmonee Brumwell, Sienna Sanchez, Mariah Sanchez and Caitlyn Posey.

STANLEY BOTTS was born May 28, 1947 in Okeene, OK and graduated from Enid High School in 1965. He enlisted at Enid, OK Aug. 29, 1966 and attended Boot Camp at Fort Bliss, TX. He attended Officer Basic Course and FA Officer Candidate School. He was stationed at Fort Gordon, GA and served in Germany (4th Armored Division, 2/4th Cavalry) and Vietnam (3rd Bde. 1/12th Cavalry).

He was commissioned an Officer/Command and General Staff Officer Course, during Desert Shield.

He was awarded the Legion of Merit (1st Cav. Div.), Bronze Medal, Army Commendation Medal, Combat Medic Badge, Vietnam Service Medal, Vietnam Campaign Medal w/60 device, National Defense Service Medal and Army Valorous Unit Award.

After 20 years active military and nine years National Guard, Stan was discharged in February 1996 at Myer, VA as LTC. He was a system analyst for 20 years and teacher for seven years, retiring in 2016. Botts is a church pastor and Royal Rangers Coordinator in retirement.

Stan and Corinne were married in 1967 and have three children: Teresa, Stan Jr. and Tina. Grandchildren are Raymond, Julea, Zoe, Miguel, Kaimi and Brooklyn. Amelia is their great-grandchild.

HAROLD O. BOURNE left Yakima, WA to enlist in the Army in February 1951 at Portland, OR and was sent to Camp Rucker, AL for basic training with the 47th Infantry Division (MN/NO NG). Bourne graduated from Infantry OCS in October 1952. A year later he was selected for flight training, graduating in 1954. In 1957 Bourne was assigned to Korea with the 1st Cavalry Division, organized similar to a 1952 field test at Camp Hood, in which Bourne participated. Following other assignments, Bourne was assigned to the 11th Air Assault Division in 1964, which was designated the 1st Cavalry Division, Air Mobile in July 1965 and sent to Vietnam. He was part of a team of 28 that selected An Khe as the base camp, named Camp Radcliff in honor of the first in-country division casualty, who was one of the team. His second tour in Vietnam was in 1969-1970 with the 1st Aviation Brigade/USARV HQ.

Following assignments to the Pentagon, Germany, Fort Huachuca, AZ and New York Bourne retired to Milwaukee, WI in 1980 where he worked for Astronautics Corporation of America for 20 years, retired again, but continued working

as a news-helicopter and charter pilot for 10 years and finally retired in 2010.

Bourne and his wife, Anne (Roach), married for 65 years, live in Brown Deer, WI. They have five children, 10 grandchildren and 21 great-grandchildren. They spend their time traveling to visit family and with church projects when at home.

TERENCE "TERRY" M. BRAIN was drafted May 28, 1968 in Washington State. He did basic training/AIT at Fort Lewis. He made a game of it, did great at what they had us do.

Headed to Nam, got assigned to the 1/5th CAV/ACO Air Mobile at An Khe, late October of 1968 when Division moved south to Phuoc Vinh. He was in the 3rd Platoon, was squad leader and a 6'5" point man. During a mission with the 11th armored unit, while on the move, they got caught in an ambush. They were under heavy fire and a round his helmet and knocked him out. He doesn't remember being medevac'd out. Had a severe concussion and blackouts for 10 days or so. That was Jan. 13, 1969, his first Purple Heart.

Brain was raised outdoors, a lot of hunting, fishing and hiking. CPT Davidson paid attention to his awareness, like when he pointed out Elephant tracks and then tuffs of coarse hair eye level in trees. Got laughed at, but later one of the ambushes reported heavy movement near an inlet of water. About 30 minutes later they all heard several elephant trumpets. Come morning, he wore the big smile. They were assigned to these bases: Quan Loi, The Fishook, Tay Ninh, LZ Grant, several out of and on LZ Dolly, Michelin Rubber Plantation and a bit in Cambodia. On LZ Dolly, Brain became CPT Davidson's paceman and bodyguard. He was a good man. "We didn't salute officers in field operations, good rule." His unit dealt with a lot of trauma, but together they created a great bond and he still stays in contact with many of his fellow Soldiers.

He made it to Aug. 26, 1969. While performing base security for a new base under construction, they were hit hard with a heavy rocket attack and small arms that night. Terry was hit with shrapnel in his lower left back and lost his left kidney. He came to in a military hospital in Saigon, was later sent to Japan hospital where he turned 21 years old. Wow, what a party…yeah right. Final stop was Madigan Hospital, Fort Lewis.

Brain was stationed at Fort Presidio, San Francisco. Assigned to the Military Postal Unit for his last 10 months, where he received his second Purple Heart and Bronze Star at revelry. He was discharged on May 27, 1970.

Terry went to work at the Post Office as a Maintenance Tech. When he hit 55, his wife Ann, together now 36 years, said, "Hey retire." So he left with 35-1/2 years. He still goes to the mountains to hunt, but shoots more with his camera. They are proud of their son, Trevor, who is 26 years old. Terry has taken them to meet a very good friend of his since basic training and from the same 3rd platoon with 1/5th ACO. "I'm sure you all know of him, Bill Ellis. So glad he got pulled from the field to play his music. He had his guitar sent to him, so he could play and write when on base. Bill is still at it."

From a Former Hired Gun – Welcome Home All Vietnam Veterans.

TRUITT D. "BREEZE" BREAZEALE was born in 1940 in Philadelphia, MS. He graduated from Neshoba Central High School in 1959 and in 1979 attained his BS from Columbus College. He enlisted July 13, 1958 in Philadelphia and attended Boot Camp at Fort Benning, GA. He also took Airborne Training.

"Breeze" was stationed at Fort Benning, Fort Bragg, Fort Riley, Fort Greeley, Fort Jackson, in Korea and Germany. He served one tour with MACU and one tour with 1/8 Cavalry.

Breazeale received a Purple Heart, Combat Infantry Badge, BS/U, MSM, and Good Conduct Medal.

His memorable experiences included the travel, excitement and togetherness.

Breazeale was discharged on July 31, 1990 at Cpt. 03E. He taught JROTC for 22 years.

Truitt and Vonnell have three children: Dewayne, Gwendolyn and Jeffrey. Grandchildren are Brittany, Benjamin, Christene, Madison, Olivia and Juliana.

ALVIE "AL" L. BREWER was born June 25, 1926 in Ruston, LA and graduated from Ruston High School in 1943. He enlisted in 1944 at Shreveport, LA and attended Boot Camp at Joseph T. Robinson, AR. He took the Transportation Officers Course and Advanced Course and Highway Transportation Course.

"Al" was stationed at Fort Sill, OK; Fort Eustis, VA; Supreme Hqs. Allied Powers in Europe; Paris, France; Bad Kreuznach, Germany; Istanbul, Turkey and Fort Polk, LA.

He served in World War II, Korea and Vietnam. Brewer received a Battle Field Commission to second lieutenant in Korea, Feb. 14, 1951 and served as 1st Cavalry Division Transportation Officer from 1965-1966.

Brewer received a Bronze Star with Oak Leaf Cluster, Army Commendation Medal, Infantry Combat Badge, Philippine Liberation Medal, Korean Service Medal, Republic of Korea Presidential Unit Citation Badge, Vietnam Service Medal, Republic of Vietnam Campaign Ribbon, Republic of Vietnam Gallantry Cross w/Palm Unit Citation Badge, plus 11 additional medals and awards.

He was discharged with the rank of Major at Fort Polk, LA in 1969.

"Al" served as Director of Public Works, city of Ruston, LA, 1976 until retiring in 1997. He now serves as Church Finance Chairman and on Fort Polk Retiree Advisory Council. He is affiliated with 1st Cavalry Assn., Military Officers Association, VFW and American Legion.

"Al" and Billie were married in 1951 and have two children, Ginger and Douglas; grandchildren Brandon, Jeremy, Matthew and Michael and great-grandchild Austin.

JAMES BUFORD BRIGGS was commissioned a second lieutenant of Artillery from Texas A&M University, College Station, TX in 1964. Without attending the basic course, he was assigned directly to 4/3rd Arty, First Armored Division, Fort Hood, TX, which was located 27 miles from his hometown of Lampasas, TX. Briggs saw the 4/3rd go from a full TO&E Unit, ready to deploy for combat in two hours, to a third of its TO&E strength conducting BCT, AIT, riot control duty (Detroit, MI) and lastly as the Site Support unit at North Fort Hood for National Guard Summer Camp. During this time Briggs, married his sweetheart Dorothy Ann Reed, was a Communications Platoon Leader, HqHq&Svc Battery Commander with 66 additional duties which included acting S-l, S-2, S-3 and communications officer. Next he commanded B Battery 4/3rd and the final months he served as Battalion XO. First SG Herbert L. Baker and LTC Samuel Stapleton of the 4/3rd were major influences on Briggs making the army a career.

In 1968 Briggs deployed to Vietnam, serving in PCV /XXIV Corps Arty S-3 Section, then commanded B Btry 1-83FA. B Btry 1/83FA served in Quang Tri and Thua Thien-Hue provinces. The next assignment was FAOAC at Fort Sill, OK, followed by a year at Texas A&M University where he received his Masters Degree. The next three years he was Tactical Officer for Company A-1 at USMA, West Point, NY. This was followed with an assignment as S-3, 1/15FA, 2nd Infantry Division, Camp Stanley, Korea. He then returned to Ft Hood where he served as XO of 1/77F A, 1st Cav. and S-4 of the 1st Cavalry Division Artillery. The unit spent extensive time in the field (close to 300 days one year) while involved in the Division Restructure Test, TacFire implementation etc.

He then served as assistant professor of military science at Texas A&I University in Kingsville, TX; attended CGSC at Fort Leavenworth, KS where he was a section leader and an honor graduate. In Germany he served with the 8th Infantry Division as Divarty S-3 and then as Commander of 1-83rd FA Battalion. The Battalion Command was the most fun of a lot of really enjoyable assignments. Returning to Fort Hood, he served as XO of 1st Cavalry Division Artillery and then as III Corps G-3 - Chief of the Exercise Division and later as acting G-3 for PO&E.

In 1986 James retired as a LTC(P) with almost 22 years of service. After retirement he returned home to Lampasas, TX. James, a certified arborist, started his own business, Briggs Oak Wilt Service and travels all over central Texas treating oak trees for the Oak Wilt disease. He and Dorothy are avid volunteers in the community and were selected as the Grand Marshals of the 2013 Lampasas Spring Ho Festival.

James and Dorothy were blessed with one beautiful daughter, Marcia Ann.

LLOYD J. BROCKNEY enlisted October 1965, Basic Training Fort Dix, NJ and graduated Dec.

24, 1965. He was posted to Fort Sam Houston, Texas, in February 1966 for AIT medical corpsman training. He was then assigned April 1966 to 546th Medical Company (CLR), 7th Medical Brigade, 7th Army, Germany. Stationed in Heilbronn and Crailsheim. Returned to the States early 1968, stationed at Fort Benning, GA until orders for Vietnam.

He entered Vietnam Dec. 15, 1968 and received orders for Alpha Troop 1st Squadron, 9th Cavalry, 1st Cavalry Division (Airmobile). He processed to Alpha Troop Headhunters in Tay Ninh as Troop medic. Alpha Troop was involved in combat mission on Feb. 15, 1969 resulting in two lift ships shot down. Over 20 WIA's including himself and five of their Brothers KIA — Francis Kulbatski, James Fields, Dennis North, Franklin Gilbert and Harold Tyson. He was hospitalized and returned home in the spring of 1970.

He received a Bachelor of Science Degree from State University of New York and retired from Essex County, NY as Social Services Caseworker in 2006.

He received the Valorous Unit Award, Combat Medical Badge, Purple Heart, Good Conduct Medal, Vietnam Service Medal, National Defense Service Medal, South Vietnamese Armed Services Honor Medal 1st Class, Gallantry Cross with Palm, Vietnam Campaign Medal, New York State Meritorious Service Medal.

NEVER FORGET OUR FALLEN
ONCE CAV ALWAYS CAV

GENE E. BROWN was born September 3, 1930 in Burkburnett, TX, and graduated from Burkburnett High School in 1948. He enlisted in Texas in 1950 and attended Boot Camp at Camp Chaffe, AR. Additional training was with the 82nd Airborne (serving four years as a paratrooper), Special Forces, Aviation School, Command and General Staff College.

He was stationed at Fort Bragg; Fort Rucker; Schofield Barracks, HI; Taiwan; Hunter Army Airfield, Savannah, GA. From 1967-68 he served in Vietnam, commanding the 229th Assault Helicopter Battalion.

Brown received two Legion of Merit Awards, the Distinguished Flying Cross, Silver Star, Bronze Star with "V" device, Air Medal with 12 OLC and Vietnamese Cross of Gallantry.

While stationed in Hawaii in September 1957, he discovered the highest lake atop Mauna Kea.

He earned a bachelor of business administration degree from University of Southern Mississippi and completed graduate work at Georgia Southern University.

Brown was discharged on Dec. 31, 1970 at Hunter Army Airfield as a lieutenant colonel.

Brown was a custom home builder for 20 years following his military service retirement.

Gene and wife Regina have two children, Patrick and Michael and four grandchildren: Abby, Luke, Lydia and Phoebe.

JAMES "JIM" H. BROWN was born August 25, 1942 in Sunbury, PA and graduated from Bound Brook High School in June 1961. He enlisted on Oct. 14, 1961 at Newark, NJ and attended Boot Camp at Fort Dix, NJ. He took Photo Lithographer training at Fort Belvoir, VA.

He was stationed in Japan (1962-1964), Fort Bragg (1964-1966 and 1979-1981), Korea (1965-1967), Frankfurt, Germany (1967-1970), Fort Hood (1970-1976) and Heidelberg, (1976-1979).

Brown received six Good Conduct Medals, National Defense, Expedition Medal, Korea SM and Commendation Medal. Memorable experiences were serving overseas and basically seeing the world.

On Oct. 31, 1981 Brown was discharged as SSG.

In 2005 Jim retired after working for the State of New Jersey as UMDNJ printer.

He is a life member of VFW, American Legion, DAV, and VVA.

"Jim" and wife Taka, from Japan, were married Feb. 13, 1964. They have two children, Margaret "Peggy" and James E. and two grandchildren, Nicole and Michael.

MICHAEL "MIKE" BROWN was drafted Dec. 12, 1965 (Los Angeles). After basic training and AIT at Fort Hood, spent four months in an artillery battery. He got orders for Vietnam in October 1966. After a 30-day leave, flew to Vietnam, being assigned to HQ Battery of the 1/2 FA. After two months in AnKhe, then to LZ English on the Bong Son plain. Most of the next months were spent in the Central Highlands and one firebase at Kontum. Then they moved to an ex-marine base between Tam Ky and Chu Lai. While on radio watch one morning, they got a call for counter-mortar fire from Charley battery. The VC hit the BOQ, killing their liaison. Brown was awakened one morning by the Section Chief, who told him he was going out as an RTO with his grunts. The S-3 was mad because he left his M/6 by the chow tent. Brown humped the hills for three days, even making a combat assault, thankfully on a cold LZ. He left Vietnam on Dec. 5, 1967 and went to Fort Lewis, WA, where he was discharged.

"Mike" received the Air Medal, Army Commendation, Army Good Conduct, National Defense, Vietnam Service, Vietnam Campaign, Meritorious Unit Citation, RVN Gallantry Cross Unit Citation.

He was a group insurance underwriter for 25 years and an escrow officer with his own company for 10 years, retiring in 2010.

He is active in Rotary and his church, enjoying his children and granddaughters.

"Mike" and Carolyn have three children: David, Greg and Philip and grandchildren Penelope, Adelaide and a grandson due in January 2017.

CARL FREDRICK "BUGGER" BRUGMANN was born Jan. 16, 1918 in Lexington, KY, and graduated from Caterina (TX) High School in 1936. He enlisted in January 1936 at Fort Brown, TX, with the 12th Cavalry, and was discharged in January 1939 at Fort Brown, with the rank of PFC. He reenlisted in Feb. 1941 at Fort Sam Houston, TX, with the 12th Cavalry, station at Fort Bliss, TX.

Brugmann served in the South Pacific Theatre and Philippines, including New Guinea, Bismark Archipelago, and Luzon. He was awarded the Philippine Liberation Ribbon w/ 2 Bronze Stars, Asiatic Pacific Campaign Medal w/ 4 Bronze Stars, American Defense Service Medal, and Good Conduct Medal.

He service ended in September 1945 upon his discharge at Fort Sam Houston, with the rank of S/Sgt. Following the service, he was an equipment operator/mechanic/shop foreman at Victoria Machine Works in Victoria, TX, retiring in 1983. He was a life member of the US Horse Cavalry Association.

He married Bernice Garrett in June 1947, and they had one son, Lester, who was born in May 1950. Brugmann passed away in March 1997.

ALLAN "AL" A. BUCHOLZ enlisted at Fort Lewis, WA and attended Boot Camp at Fort Custer, MI. He was trained as a Rifleman – Basic Training – MP.

Al served in Bismarck – Archipelago, New Guinea, South Philippines and Luzon.

He received the Philippine Liberation Medal, two Bronze Service Stars, Victory Medal, Asiatic Pacific Service Medal.

Memorable experiences were entering Japan as occupation, carrying a BAR in Philippines and Luzon as point man.

Al was discharged as PFC at Fort Lewis in 1946.

He worked 20 years for Monites Cabinets and as an architect on contemporary homes. He retired and started building "Tide Runner Boats." In retirement he enjoys fishing and traveling.

Al has been married twice, first to Dorothy Kroll and second to Joanne Rice. He has two children, Susan Jensen and Jeffery Bucholz. Grandchildren are Gretchen, Adam, Erin, Lauren, P.J., and Sara.

CRYSTAL ELIZABETH BUMGARDNER enlisted in the Signal Corps in March 1979 and entered service at Fort Gordon, GA for basic training and AIT for O5C.

From 1979-1981, Co A, 9th Signal Battalion, Mannheim, Germany, as a RAT Rig Operator. From 1981-1983, 5th Signal BN, Fort Polk, LA as Motor Sergeant. Reenlisted for Executive secretary (71C). 1983-1984, HHC, 7th Infantry Division, Fort Ord, CA as a Secretary and Assistant Community Relations Specialist with the Public Affairs office. She earned a position with the *Army Soldiers Showcase* on Tour as a singer, touring various Army bases in the US. 1984-1986, Taegu, Korea, HHC, 19th SUPCOM, IG office. Toured with the

Journey show as a singer throughout Korea. 1986-1989, SHAPE HQ, Mons, Belgium, Community Affairs Office. 1989-1991, HHC, 1st Cavalry Division, Fort Hood, TX, as NCOIC, SGS and 1990-1991, proudly served her country during Desert Storm/Gulf War.

1997-1999, Command and General Staff College, US Army Student Division, Fort Leavenworth, KS. She retired as a SSG in 1999.

Awards include AFSM, BSM, DMSM, MSM, JSCM (third award), ARCOM, JSAM, AAM third award, JMUA, MUC, ACM 6th award, NDSM, SWA with 2, NCOPD with numeral 2, ASR, ALB, NATO Medal, OSR with fourth award. KLM (K), KLM (SA), and Expert Marksmanship with rifle bar.

She was a civilian government employee from 1999-2014 with the Command and General Staff School and International Military Student Division, CGSc.

Crystal married William Bumgardner Jr. in 1988. They have two children, Reneé and Ashley and one step-child, Bonnie and two grandchildren, Jaymes and Lauren.

DEAN LEWIS "BEANIE" BUNNELL was born April 17, 1951 in West Stewartstown, NH, and graduated from Canaan Memorial (VT) High School in 1969. He enlisted on March 16, 1970 and went through basic training at Ft. Dix, also receiving 11 Bravo, 17 kilo Redeye and Tow training. Bunnell spent time at Ft. Carson, Ft. Stewart, FSB Sauffy, FSB Betty, FSB Buttons, FB Sandra, FB Evelyn, and FB Otter.

He was assigned to the III Corps area, Post Cambodian Theatre during the Vietnam War, and received the Bronze Star, Republic of Vietnam Service Medal, Good Conduct Medal, Armed Forces Expeditionary Medal, Expert Infantryman Badge, two Overseas Service Bars, National Defense Medal, Republic of Vietnam Campaign Ribbon, and Aircraft Crewman Badge.

One memorable experience was flying on a Chinook to FB Snuffy, his first assignment in Vietnam. As they approached the base and descended to about 500 feet, small arms fire struck the rear of the copter so we quickly regained altitude. Upon landing, he quickly low crawled from the Chinook into the safety of the firebase. As he looked around, he noticed men outside the wire doing their duties, and there were many grins and murmurings including the phrase, "Another FNG!"

Bunnell was discharged from service on Dec. 12, 1977 with the rank of E-6. He went on to work for the United States Postal Service as a rural mail carrier, retiring in 2017. In retirement he enjoys bicycling, hiking, snowmobiling, camping, and working with his portable sawmill.

He is married to Janet, with four children — Deanna, Richard, Katie, and Jonathan — and three grandchildren — Josef, Sean, and Shael.

WYNDELL E. BURDEN quit college in his freshman year in 1960, to pursue his goal of becoming an aviator. Three years later he was on his way to flight school at Camp Wolters, TX. He graduated in February 1964 at Fort Rucker as a Warrant Officer.

He was assigned to the 611th Bn, 11th Air Assault Division at Fort Benning, GA. In a year and a half this division would become the 1st Air Cav Div and under President Johnson's orders would become the first division to enter the war in Vietnam. CW2 Burden was assigned to D Co, 15th TC Bn, but spent most of the tour shadowing the 1/9th Air Cav Sqdn, under LTC Stockton, commanding a detachment to pull on-site maintenance.

In July 1966, Wyndell was assigned to the 507th General Support Company, Fort Knox, KY. He received his direct appointment to 2LT TC and became the executive officer. In January 1968 he was assigned to B Co, 15th Bn with a Cobra transition en-route. Most of his duties were the same as his first tour but this time he got to see most all the country, from the DMZ to the Delta in Tay Ninh. (Participated in a total of eight major campaigns for both tours.)

In 1969, Cpt. Burden returned to the Aircraft Maintenance Brigade, Hunter Army Airfield. His time was spent as XO, CO and Bde Staff. In late 1973, he attended a course at Fort Lee and another at Fort Eustis. He was assigned to Fort Eustis to attend Transportation Officers Advanced Course (TOAC).

In February 1974, Wyndell was assigned as Chief, General Subjects Branch, Department of Academic Training (DOAT), Fort Rucker, AL. He was responsible for the training of all enlisted training and all the system courses for the officer's rotary and fixed wing aircraft transition.

In June 1977, Wyndell was promoted to Major. After taking another course at Fort Lee, he was on his way to South Korea as Plans and Operations Officer for the Assistant Chief of Staff (AC of S) J4, UN Command. In 1979, he returned to Fort Rucker where he retired in January 1980.

Wyndell spent the next 22 years as an Instrument Flight Instructor, where he taught US military and Allied Officers from a total of 10 countries.

RICHARD A. BURNSIDE was born August 16, 1939 in Ely, NY, and graduated from Mater Dei High School in 1957. He enlisted in 1958 at Los Angeles, CA and attended Boot Camp at Fort Ord, CA. He received additional training in RTO-MC, LRP, NCOA.

Richard was stationed in California, North Carolina, Maine, Korea, Texas, Germany, Alabama, Vietnam, Washington, and Germany. He was engaged in battles in Korea and Vietnam.

He received the Meritorious Service Medal, BSM, Army Commendation Medal, Good Conduct Medal, NDSM, AFEM – Korea, Vietnam Service Medal, VCM, VGC, and PUS. He was discharged in 1979 at Fort Ord, CA as PSG.

He worked at ROLM, SEIMEN and IBM, retiring in 1994.

Married to Tong and to Sharon, his children are Linda and Barbara. Grandchildren are Amanda, Christian, Kaitlyn and Chase. Great-grandchildren are Aizen and Locklyn.

COL. GEORGE DONELSON BURROW, RETIRED completed 39 years of military service. He entered the Texas National Guard in 1950 and subsequently enlisted in the Regular Army as an enlisted Soldier. He attended the Sixth army Leadership School in 1953. In 1955 he was named the 4th Infantry Division N.C.O. of the year. In 1957 he was the Honor Graduate of The Seventh Army N.C.O. Academy and recommended for attendance at Infantry Officer Candidate School (O.C.S.) by the Commanding General. He graduated from O.C.S. as a Distinguished Military Graduate in 1958 with a Regular Army commission. Following O.C.S., he became airborne and aviator qualified. Burrow served as Infantry Company Commander, Air Cavalry Troop Commander, Air Cavalry Squadron Commander-all in the 1st Cavalry Division in Korea, Vietnam, and the Continental US (CONUS).

Burrow has served in high level staff positions in the Anny, Joint Chief of Staff (JCS) and The European Command. These include Air Cavalry Brigade Executive Officer, War Plans Officer, J5, European Command, VII Corps Inspector General, Fifth Army Deputy Chief of Staff, Operations and President, Physical Evaluation Board (PEB). He served five tours overseas – Germany from 1953-1957, Korea from 1961-1962, Germany from 1965-1967, Vietnam from 1967-1968 and Germany from 1978-1981.

His military education as an officer includes Infantry O.C.S., Airborne School, Flight Aviation Staff Officer's Course, Command and General Staff College, Department of the Army Inspector General Course and National War College.

His awards include: Distinguished Service Cross, Silver Star, Distinguished Flying Cross x3, Legion of Merit, Bronze Star x2, Air Medal x34, Purple Heart x3, DOD Meritorious Service Medal x3, good Conduct Medal, National Defense Service Medal x2, army Occupation Medal, NCO Achievement Medal, Overseas Medal x5, Vietnam Service Medal, Vietnam Campaign Medal Vietnam Cross of Gallantry, Combat Infantry Badge, Expert Infantry Badge, Master Army Aviator Wings, Parachute Badge, and Joint Chief of Staff Badge. Burrow was inducted into the Infantry Officers Hall of Fame in 1979.

WILLIAM O. BURROW was born 1942 in Mobile, Alabama and graduated from Wakefield High

School in 1962, and later attended the University of Mississippi. He enlisted at Fort Gordon, GA, and following boot camp received additional training in as a radio operator at Fort Monmouth.

He was stationed in the Canal Zone Fort Clayton and DIA, Washington, DC. In 1969 and 1970 he was stationed at RVN with the 1st Signal Bn, 2/19th, 1st Cav.

Burrow was awarded Three Bronze Stars, Air Medal, Army Commendation, Joint Service Command, etc.

Memorable experiences include the E.O. Office for the Chairmen CJCS – Adm. Thomas Moorer. Burrow was discharged as LTC in 2002 at St. Louis, MO.

He served as Postmaster in Myrtle, MS, retiring in 2002 and enjoys working on family history.

William and Gloria Ann have one child, Olivia Louis and two grandchildren, Jake and John.

FRANK BUTORYAK was drafted on Dec. 28, 1942 and was shipped to a station in eastern Pennsylvania. After all the shots, then the uniform, I became a Soldier. After a few days, they put me on a train with a lot of other Soldiers and after many days we arrived at Camp Hale, CO.

We were ushered into a large arena. They started calling all the names and the outfit they were assigned to. After all the names were called off, they asked if there was anyone not called. I was the only one not called so they put me in the 99th Field Artillery, which was a mountain outfit. This outfit was made up of mules packing 75 MM artillery cannons. The colonel told me later that I was supposed to be at an advance Air Force Base in California. He said I would have to have Basic Training so I might as well do it there and after that see him and he would transfer me to the right base.

After Basic Training, I went to him for my transfer and he said, "I'm sorry but all transfers were stopped because the outfit was attached to the First Cavalry Division based in El Paso, TX." He told me to reapply when we got there but when we got to Texas and I reapplied for my transfer, I was again told that the First Cavalry was alerted for overseas duty and no transfers were to be given. I was put into the air section as their second mechanic. The aircrafts were Piper Cubs and Aeroncas. These were small single engine planes to be used as fire control (controlling cannon fire from the air).

After a short stay, we got on a train going to Pittsburg, PA, to California, then on a ship from San Francisco. After 21 days, we arrived in Brisbane, Australia. We stayed there for about two months getting re-outfitted from a mountain pack outfit to jungle equipment. What a change! Snow to heat! I had a nice time in Australia and met some very nice people. We shipped out to New Guinea and trained for jungle operations. During our stay there, I went to the Air Force field and talked to the general in charge and told him my story of why I was where I was and where I should have been. He wrote me a letter to give to my commanding officer explaining that he would like to have me with his group with a promotion to Second Lieutenant. I gave the request to my commanding officer and he said great and he would pass it on to the Division Commander named General Mudge. The request for transfer was rejected.

One day General Mudge was at our field walking down the landing strip, so I caught up to him and told him who I was and asked why he rejected my transfer. He told me being here was more important than a dozen bombers. I told the general if I was that important why was I only a Private when I could be an officer in the Air Force, but he kept saying how important my job was and walked to his jeep. While this was going on, the whole aircrew section was listening to the verbal argument I had with the general, and they told me that you don't argue with a general. They expected I would be taken off to the brig. So that was my last attempt for a transfer.

Later on, we left that base and made an invasion on the Admiralty Islands. We went on shore on the second landing, because they wanted the aircraft in the air as soon as possible to direct the battleship's shells ahead of our troops. After we got on shore and reassembled the planes, we dug our hole and stayed there because the front troops were only about 50 yards ahead of us fighting the Japs. During one of these battles, I went up with another flier, Masona, to drop blood plasma and ammunition to our troops on one of the islands and on our return back to the airfield, the aircraft went into a spin and the pilot was bent over forward. Not realizing that he may have been shot, I didn't take over the controls soon enough and crashed into the water, all I remember saying to myself was, "I have to get the hell out of here."

When we hit the water I hit the back of the forward seat, and the next thing I remember was the cabin was full of water. I opened the door and tried to get out but forgot to release my safety belt. I relaxed, unbuckled the belt and swam out from under the aircraft. I went back under the wings to the cabin twice to try and pull out the pilot, but was unable to reach him before the aircraft sank below the waves. I was about half a mile or so from shore, but I knew I had to try and swim to land. In front of me was one of the wheels with an attached strut, so I swam to it and removed my shoes and leggings for the long swim. I was bleeding from the mouth, but didn't know the cause. As I was about to remove my jump suit, I saw a large ship coming at me but then went right by. I thought it didn't see me. The next thing, there was a lifeboat beside me and two sailors grabbed me and pulled me into the boat. Later in the hospital, I was told that there were many sharks swimming around me and the captain of the Australian sub chaser went through the sharks and lowered the lifeboat as he got near me. Thank God for the smart thinking of that captain.

The crew of the lifeboat wrapped me in a long bamboo mat, got next to the ship and they pushed me up. The sailors on board the large ship tried to pull me up and almost dropped me back into the water. When on board, they took me to what I believe to be the bridge of the ship. At that time, when I was safe, my body relaxed and all the pain in my lips, back and legs came rushing in. The captain offered me rum, whiskey, gin and some other hard drink and I said, "No." He asked me what I wanted and I asked for cold water. The captain looked at me and said, "You're the first damn Yank I know that doesn't drink."

I don't remember anything after that (I must have passed out). I came to in the Evac hospital with a doctor looking at me and he said, "Hi, you're back with us." He had a needle in his hand and started to sew my upper lip back together. He told me that only the outer skin was holding my upper lip together. They took me to the X-ray tent and took pictures of my back. The next thing I know they put a body stocking on me and wrapped me up in wide strips of wet gauze. When they were through, I was wrapped from under my arms to my knees with my legs spread apart and my back arched. They told me I had fractured vertebrae. I looked like a mummy.

The Evac hospital sent me to Port Moresby, New Guinea (the largest city in Papaua New Guinea) where they took more X-rays and told me there was no fracture and put me on a Liberty ship (a cargo ship) back to my base. When I got back to my outfit, our doctor sent me back to the Evac hospital and I saw the doctor that treated me the first time. He asked me what was I doing back and that I should have been sent stateside. When I told him what happened at Port Moresby, he said they were wrong and took more X-rays and said this will show them the fracture and sent me back to Port Moresby. More X-rays were taken saying no fracture could be found and sent me back to my outfit on another Liberty ship. On the ship, I was on one of the cargo doors that they had a little shack tied to with a box of C rations. I had two bad trips going back and forth. When the doctor saw me again he wanted me to return again but I told him that no way was I going on another Liberty ship under those conditions and that I would stay with the outfit no matter how much my back hurt.

The following are some of my moments in the Admiralty Islands. We had a bunker built in a side of an aircraft repair area. It was well concealed, luckily, because one night the enemy infiltrated our area. As I watched them pass our bunker, they were throwing hand grenades. As they left, the artillery began shelling us. A Soldier with us began to cry out because he didn't have his helmet, so I put my hands around his head and my head on his head until it was over. Sometime later we were told to get everything together because we were to board the last landing craft. When we were on our way, they told us we were to make an invasion on the Philippine Island of Leyte. When we arrived at daybreak, the Navy was shelling the island. We made shore on the second landing. We pushed our aircraft off and started assembling them on the beach. The higher ups wanted the planes in the air as soon as possible. The aircraft took off from the beach and started to direct the Navy battleships, cruisers and destroyers. The positions were relayed to the ships so the shells fell ahead of the troops and on the enemy. The front troops secured the airport and we moved our operation from the beach to a safer place. Shortly after that, we were told to get all our personal items and armament and be ready to leave for the mountains because enemy ships may try a landing, but they canceled our move because our naval F ships destroyed theirs.

At one point in this engagement, one of our aircraft carriers was destroyed. That meant they had to land at our airport, which had many bombed holes. In a rush the holes were filled and then as many trucks as possible were lined up at the edge of the runway with their lights on to give the returning aircraft a look at the runway from beginning to end. When some aircraft hit a soft spot and turned over a truck hooked up a cable to it and dragged it off the runway so other aircraft were able to land. Every Soldier of our air section did all we could to help the Naval flight crews.

One of the torpedo bombers with a bell gunner came in with a shell lying across his hands with his fingers still gripped onto his gun. The unexploded shell was removed from the gunner's hands and they had to pry his fingers from his own gun, he was so frozen with fear.

After the inland, we got a well-deserved rest. Some place in the campaign I received the Bronze Star for service beyond normal battle. We were told again to get ready for another campaign and this one would be on the main island, which was Luzon (the largest island in the Philippines).

When we got on shore we made a mad dash to the capital city, which is Manila. As the front troops started moving, we the ground crew for the aircrafts, were right behind them and at dusk we had to find a level area for the planes to land and set up a perimeter for that night. We did this for the next two days and we were in enemy territory all the time. We set up on a good long paved road in a city called Grace Park.

We were getting prepared for the invasion of Japan when the enemy surrendered. We were on a landing craft in the harbor when the enemy signed the armistice. While in Japan, I met a Japanese Air Force officer and the only way we could talk to each other was by looking at a book with cross meanings for each word. But we both learned a little about each other. One day, word came down that some of us were going home. The very next morning I was on a ship going home and my first thoughts were that I would see Jean (my girlfriend) again. When I got home, we continued our relationship, married and had six children that I am proud of. One of my sons was in the Army and one of my grandsons made a career in the Air Force.

TEDDY L. "EL' HEFE" BUZBEE was born on Dec. 12, 1951 in Fort Worth, TX and graduated from Grace Davis High School in 1971 and St. Martins' University in 1994.

In 1971 he enlisted at Fort Lewis, WA. Memorable experiences included planning and executing the many successful missions of the 1st Cavalry Division. Buzbee was discharged in 1994 at Fort Lewis, WA with the rank of CW3.

He retired in 2013 after working as Washington State HCA. He is affiliated with Disabled American Veterans, VFW and American Legion.

In retirement Buzbee enjoys competitive senior softball and golf.

He and Linda have two children, Dawn and Hillary and two grandchildren, Jaden and Shaley.

RICHARD "DICK" D. CAMERON says:

July 1969 - Upon completion of my graduate medical education, I was ready at last for my first real job in the Army. I told the assignment folks I liked the outdoors and would be willing to go to Alaska! "You like the outdoors? Then you will love Vietnam."

July 1970 - Here I am, standing on a hot dusty road one afternoon in Phouc Vin, Republic of Vietnam. A proud member of the First Air Cavalry Division, quartered with the 15th Medical Battalion and Air Evac and I had no idea what was in store.

That muggy evening shortly after dark, all hell broke loose in our area. Suddenly we were under a well coordinated mortar barrage. Explosions marched up and down the revetments housing our air evac ships. Many were damaged or destroyed.

In the aftermath, our medical clearing station was a scene of organized chaos as we worked to stabilize Troopers with shrapnel wounds. IV's were started, wounds cleansed, dressings applied and chest tubes inserted. During the commotion, I felt a firm tug on my t-shirt from the chaplain: "Doc, get over here right away, you have to do something for this boy." I hurried to a cot where a young Trooper lay. I realized he was already triaged with a mortal wound. The back of his head was shattered, blood and brain matter were seeping onto the cot. At that moment a multitude of emotions flooded over me. Simultaneously I felt empathy, sorrow, anger and utter dismay as there was obviously nothing to be done. "Chaplain, there is nothing we can do here. Pray for the young Soldier and then comfort others." My eyes swept the room crowded with wounded Soldiers, feeling a sense of pride for them. At that moment I knew that my future efforts in the Army would be to promote and provide the finest medical care possible for our brave men and women in uniform.

Forty-six years later the actual chain of events are a little blurry, but the feelings and emotions I felt that night still well up and are crystal clear. So, I stuck around the Army for the next 26 years serving in a number of assignments (could not keep a job!). These assignments came with greater responsibility and, more importantly, greater influence to positively support Soldiers from a medical standpoint. To that end I was able to be a part of the largest reorganization in the history of the US Army Medical Department. To support field units, we fought for and obtained the Blackhawk Air Ambulance and upgraded radio capability to provide enhanced communication in the field. Newly designed field hospitals were procured to be deployed as needed. As the Middle East heated up, our medical units were better prepared and ready to support the Army in Iraq, Afghanistan and Africa.

Retirement caught up with me in 1995. Today I'm pushing the big 80. I'm still healthy and on the go chasing after six very active grandchildren. I also still ride real, long-ear mules with my shotgun rider of 56 years, "Miss Kay" in the beautiful mountains of Arkansas.

The First Team will always hold a special place in my heart for instilling the motivation and passion that sustained me in many uphill battles to obtain the best resources and care for the finest Soldiers in the world.

THOMAS JOSEPH MARTIN CAMPBELL, JR. was born on the first day of September in the year 1931, in Brooklyn, New York, to an Irish-German immigrant family. Raised in the turbulent environment of the Great Depression and World War II, Thomas was given over to the state at the age of 3, along with his two sisters, Katherine (the elder) and Dorothy (the younger), both of whom have pre-deceased him, and spent his youth in the Brooklyn Orphanage where he began his career as a crooner, rivaled only by Frank and Bing. A few years later he was sent to the Brookwood Hall Orphanage in Islip, Long Island. Here he honed his singing skills, learned to play stick ball, and kick-the-can (and broke his toe when someone played a trick on him by hiding a sizable rock inside the can!). Dad also learned the meaning of giving of oneself, and of having very little.

His real parents must have still yet loved each other, for they died within a month of one another. Marilyn only met them once or twice. His children never met them for they died when they (the two eldest) were still babies. A tragic loss to family connection. Ironic that Tom's own father (and his father's siblings), were to be raised in an orphanage as well when their parents (Tom's grandparents) died tragically and unexpectedly. And, not just his father, but also Tom's grandfather served in World War I.

Tom joined the Army (1st CAV) in 1947, at the age of 17 years. He told me that he came to a crossroad in his life and had to make a decision, which would affect his very survival. You see, sleeping in friends cars, running the streets with other boys, sometimes running for his life down the alleys between the tenements to the railroad tracks, and it was during one of these flights for the tracks that he found himself close to being at the losing end of a fist & knife fight with a rival gang.

By 1948 he was in Denver, CO (Fort Carson). By January 1949, Tom was in Okinawa, just north of Toguchi. Assigned to "A" Company 808th Engineers SCARWAF. He spoke of landing at Inchon, not fully remembering how he made it down the ropes from the transport into the small landing boats and then to the mainland. Remembering salt spray and waves and the mayhem of it all, but nothing else, or at least no memories would surface to share with his daughter. Three days of his life lost. And, they wouldn't be the last. So many details missing, so many suppressed memories. A body's way of protecting itself.

He spoke of spending time in Japan and reminisced of both funny stories and tragic tales. There was the flash flood when he lost his M1Grand and he and his boys had to spend the night on top of their transports; sure he got a new, lighter carbine, but it would never take the place of his M1, it might have been faster, and it may have been better at short distance, but it didn't come close to the M1's long range accuracy (he spoke fondly of his M1). And, in the heart of the bitter cold of the winter of 1951, being issued surplus WWII flight jackets. Then there was the haircut in Japan, when he said "scochi, scochi" to the old barber, and he soon lost his Elvis-style pompadour. There was the tagging, the body bags, and collecting personal effects. The chaplain who was his friend, who left the camp to head to another, and when the Jeep was out of sight and had gone around the bend in the road, Dad heard the explosion. And, somewhere in the middle of Korea, there was the water tower and rock cliff face painted with the 1st Cav insignia.

In the Army, he would see the world and experience the horrors of war, the tragedy of loss of life, loss of friends. It would haunt him for the rest of his life. He never ceased in his pride for his Troop, had many good and jolly stories to tell, yet bittersweet, still felt sorrow and pain for the loss of friends, and buried gruesome memories. He rarely spoke of the sorrows, and not until later years, when Honor Roll would be called, did he share his tears. He came home from Korea a changed man, who wouldn't have? Tom left the army a 1Sgt, due to wound injuries, which (at the time) prevented him from continuing in his duties, and so, re-enlisted into the Air Force, less than year later, but lost a stripe for waiting a few too many days.

He served in New Foundland, where he drank coffee with Elvis. Fort Dix / McGuire AFB in New Jersey. Anderson AFB on Guam (he was almost sent to Alaska-but swapped orders with a friend!). Yet, it was always the Cav that held sway on his heart. The mental and emotional ties so closely binding him to his Troop.

Retiring from the U.S. Air Force as a SSGT, he had made a career out of the military. It was the best thing he ever did. For himself. For his family. He relocated his family to Florida in 1970, and joined the U.S. Postal Service. He was a life member of the Florida Chapter 1st Cav Division, and served nearly 30 years as the Secretary and Treasurer. He was also a member of the Korean War Veterans Assoc., Veterans of Foreign Wars, American Legion, Air Force Sergeants Assoc., and SCARWAF.

He and his wife, Marilyn, have four children — Dr. Thomas B. Campbell, Kathleen M. Campbell-Connor, Douglas M. Campbell, and Patrick G. Campbell — seven grandchildren, and four great-grandchildren. Thomas died 24 January 2017 at the age of 85.

JAMES D. "DAVE" CANFIELD was born Jan. 19, 1937 in Keyser, WV. As soon as he was 17 he joined the Army "Airborne Unassigned" (parents' permission needed at that time) and after advanced Infantry training and a year of Infantry duty, and still with a Light Weapons Infantry MOS, he was selected for assignment to the Office of the Army Chief of Staff in the Pentagon. From there, as a 20-year-old sergeant he was sent to Infantry OCS at Fort Benning, GA. He followed OCS with a tour at Fort Knox, KY, first as an Infantry Platoon Leader then as Foreign Liaison Officer, G2.

Dave graduated from flight school in 1960 and after two aviation assignments and an infantry company command in Germany, he joined the 1st Air Cav. at Chu Pong in 1966, first flying "slicks" with Bravo Company, then gunships with Delta Company, 227th Aviation Battalion. Canfield ("Cobra 3") was shot down on his 30th birthday near Bong Son. He later returned in a second aircraft, neutralized several enemy targets and was again downed, but with only minor damage. He received the Distinguished Flying Cross for this eventful eight-hour day.

After a tour as a flight commander at Fort Wolters, TX, he returned to Vietnam as an intelligence officer, first in counterinsurgency operations, then as Commanding Officer, 144th Aviation Company (RR). Promoted to Colonel at 39, Canfield filled several key intelligence posts, including G2, 82n Airborne Division, Commanding officer, 1st Military Intelligence Battalion, and Group Commander before retiring from the Staff and Faculty of the Army War College in 1980. He holds a bachelors degree from The University of Nebraska and a masters from The University of Oklahoma.

In addition to the Distinguished Flying Cross for Heroism, he also received the Legion of Merit with 2 OLCs, Bronze Star with 2 OLCs, Air MedaV30 with "V" device, Army Commendation Medal, and the Vietnamese Cross of Gallantry with Palm.

After retirement, Canfield worked in the nuclear industry in the Three Mile Island area, then as Editorial Director of *Bowhunter* magazine. He retired as a publisher with *Cowles Magazines* in 1997. At the time of this printing, he and his wife, Ina, have five children, 11 grandchildren, 18 great-grandchildren, and one great-great grandson.

COL. FRANK CAPONIO, USA, Ret., enlisted in the Army Reserve in 1980 as an Intelligence Analyst and was subsequently commissioned as a second lieutenant in the USAR serving as the Assistant S-3, Air, with the 5th Psychological Operations Group, and later, Detainee, Evacuee and Refugee Officer with the 478th Civil Affairs Battalion.

He retired from the Pentagon in 2013, where he served as the Chief, Individual Readiness Division, Army G1. Previously, he served with NATO as the Director, Support of Staff after Commanding the HQ Support Group, Allied Joint Force Command–Brunssum, Netherlands. Other assignments include Deputy Commander-West, United States Army Recruiting Command, after two years in Command of the U.S. Army 5th Recruiting Brigade at Fort Sam Houston, Texas.

He served two years with the 1st Cavalry Division at Fort Hood, Texas. As the Division and Task Force Baghdad G1 during the deployment of the "First Team" in Iraq in 2004–05, he was responsible for all G1 functions supporting more than 30,000 U.S. and Iraqi Soldiers.

He commanded the 43rd Adjutant General Battalion at Fort Leonard Wood, Missouri, following time with the EPMD, Army's Human Resources Command, where he served as Chief, Army Restructuring Branch; Chief, Combat Arms Distribution, Career Management Field Branch; Chief, Command Strength Branch; and Chief, Adjutant General Branch. He also served on the Army Chief of Staff's Turbulence Task Force.

Overseas assignments include Executive Officer of the 38th Personnel Services Battalion in Gibelstadt, Germany; Deputy G1/AG, Personnel Operations, and Chief of Officer Management with the 3rd Infantry Division, in Wurzburg, Germany; and Chief, Personnel Plans and Exercises Division, Assistant Chief of Staff for Personnel for the 21st Theater Army Area Command in Kaiserslautern, Germany. Chief, Plans and Operations, Theater Personnel Operations Directorate in the Republic of Korea, following a tour as Commander, HHC, 8th PERSCOM.

His awards include the Defense Superior Service Medal, Legion of Merit (2nd Award), the Bronze Star Medal, Meritorious Service Medal (6th Award), the Joint Services Commendation Medal, Army Commendation Medal, Army Achievement Medal, Meritorious Unit Commendation, Army Superior Unit Award (2nd Award), Iraq Campaign Ribbon with Campaign Star), National Defense Service Medal (2nd Award), Global War on Terrorism Service Medal, the Korean Defense Service Medal, Armed Forces Reserve Medal, Overseas Service Ribbon (4th Award), the Combat Action Badge, and Army Staff Identification Badge.

Born in Washington, DC, his military education includes ICAF, CGSC, AGOAC, and OBC. His civilian education includes a BS from Shenandoah University, an MS from Florida International University, and an MS from National Defense University.

He is married to the former Ileana Loria of Costa Rica, with two sons: Joseph and Daniel.

BOB R. CARPENTER was born in 1944 in Mansfield, OH. He enlisted at Columbus, OH and attended boot camp at Fort Knox, KY. He received additional training in heavy weapons. He obtained a military GED.

Carpenter was stationed at Fort Ord, CA and also served in the South Korea DMZ.

He was discharged as SP-4 at Fort Lewis, WA.

Carpenter retired in 2002 after working with heavy equipment – long haul.

Bob and Madalene Elaine have two children, Diana and Wendy and two grandchildren, Danielle and Nicholas.

In retirement he says he does whatever he wants!

DAVID LEE "GOMER" CARPENTER was born Nov. 18, 1947 in Mattoon, IL, and graduated from Neago High School in 1965. He enlisted on Sept. 13, 1967 at St. Louis, MO. In addition to Boot Camp at Fort Leonard Wood, MO he had 12 weeks Infantry Training at Fort Polk, LA.

Biggest battles he was in were: May 10, 1968, four miles in Demilitarized Zone, 19 years old; Khe Sanh; June 27, 1968 – battle lasted 24 hours – over 400 Viet Cong killed, 45 prisoners; in Laos and Cambodia in 1968. He was in over 82 missions where he rode a helicopter.

He was awarded the Combat Infantry Badge; Air Medal, two Bronze Stars, one with V (for saving 1st Sergeant Ron Hayworth) and one without; Army Commendation, Army Good Conduct, National Defense, Vietnam Service, Vietnam Campaign and Sharpshooter Medal.

Carpenter was discharged as Sergeant E5 at Fort Lewis, WA on Sept. 12, 1969.

He worked at General Electric in Mattoon, IL from Oct. 20, 1969 to Nov. 30, 2011, as machine adjustor and packing operator.

KING W. CARTER enlisted in the United States Army at Fort Mead on Nov. 22, and served 22 years, six months, eight days.

King first served in Japan with the 11th Airborne. He later served in Germany as an Infantry Soldier. He made Master Sgt. at age 25. He served in Korea, E Company, 19th Infantry, and afterwards taught ROTC at the University of Alaska. In 1965, as Sgt. Major, King went to Bowdoin College in Maine to teach Army History with the ROTC Attachment there. He served two tours in Vietnam with the 1st Cavalry Division (1966-1967). His last assignment was at the Pentagon. He retired in 1968, returning to Maine.

One of his proudest moments was when he was one of 100 chosen to serve as Honor Guard at President Kennedy's inauguration.

King earned many medals while serving our country, including the Bronze Star for Bravery.

In 1976 he earned his Bachelor of Science degree in Criminal Justice at the University of Southern Maine. He then began a new career in security, loss prevention and investigations.

In retirement King enjoyed traveling, camping, fishing, gardening and spending time with his family.

ROSEMARY "ROSEY" CARTER was born in September 1963 in Queens, NY, and graduated from Paul M. Dorman High School in Spartanburg, SC, in 1981. She earned a BS in engineering from the University of South Carolina (1985), a Masters of Science in Information Systems from Hawaii Pacific University (1995), and a Master of Military Art and Science from US Army Command and General Staff College (1999).

Col. Rosey Carter commissioned into the Signal Corps in 1985 and served for over 29 years. Her assignments include six years at Fort Bragg, NC, where she earned the Master Parachutist Badge and deployed as Company Commander to Operation Desert Shield/Desert Storm. She also served as the 25th ID DIVARTY SIGO and O/C at JRTC prior to her Ft. Hood assignment. During her First Cav. Time from 1999-2002, she served as Assistant Division Signal Officer (ADSO), 13th Signal BN XO, Div. SGS, and Div G6. On her arrival in June 1999, then-MajorJ Carter joined the Division HQ at Eagle Base, Tuzla, Bosnia, completed the division's deployment as ADSO and flying out on the last C-130 with the Div Cdr and staff – Trigger was on an earlier plane.

After completing her tour with the Cav, Colonel Carter served as a battalion commander, FORSCOM staff officer, Deputy Chief of Plans for CSTC-A at Camp Eggers, in Kabul, Afghanistan, brigade commander, and HQDA staff officer. Her awards include two Bronze Stars and Cav Spurs.

Since retirement in 2014, Colonel (Ret.) Carter is working as a Management Consultant and operating a small cattle ranch in Central Texas. Her daughter, who attended Harker Heights Elementary School for four years, is now an archivist.

ROBERT C. CASPER began his military service in January 1968 at Fort Dix, NJ. AIT at Fort Lee, VA. May of 1968 assigned to the First Infantry Division at Lai Khe, Vietnam, refueling helicopters. When the 1st Division left Vietnam in early 1970, he was reassigned to the 227th Assault Helicopter Battalion of The First Cavalry Division at Lai Khe. With the 227th he refueled helicopters and was an occasional helicopter door gunner. He returned to the United States on Sept. 6, 1970 and was honorably discharged from military service.

Bob attained the rank of Sergeant and received the Bronze Star medal, Air Medal, Army Commendation Medal with three OLC, Good Conduct Medal, National Defense Service Medal, Vietnam Service Medal with four Bronze service stars, Vietnam Campaign Medal with 60 device, Meritorious unit emblem, Vietnam Gallantry Cross with palm unit citation, and Republic of Vietnam Civil Actions Honor Medal First Class.

After discharge Bob opened a retail coin and jewelry store that lasted 40 years until he retired. He married Denise Allard on the first of May 1971. They have two children, Tiffany and Matthew, along with three grandchildren: Crista, Mackenzie and Carson.

In 2006 Bob helped design and dedicate the black granite obelisk Vietnam Veterans Memorial for the town of Chelmsford, MA.

JIM M. CHAFFIN, a Distinguished Military Graduate at the Henderson State Teachers College ROTC program, began his 26-year military career on June 18, 1953. He retired with the rank of Colonel on July 31, 1979.

Chaffin served with the 1st Cavalry Division on three occasions. First, Korea (1961- 1962); second, Vietnam (1965-1966); third, Fort Hood, TX (1970 - 1971). He was proud to describe himself as a "muddy boots logistician who was richly blessed to have had the opportunity to volunteer and be detailed to serve as an Infantry Officer while serving in Vietnam."

Chaffin served with distinction as both a commander and staff officer. He commanded troops at the Battalion level.

Chaffin was the first certified professional logistician to serve as the Deputy Chief of Staff for Logistics at the Army Security Agency, a major US Army Command Headquarters. Serving as the ASA DCSLOG in the mid 1970s. He often said "Being engaged with the enemy 24/7 made this particular cold war intelligence assignment the most challenging and best five years of my entire career. We always operated with a war environment sense of urgency."

Chaffin received the Bronze Star Medal with one oak leaf cluster, the Legion of Merit with one OLC, the Air Medal with two OLC, the Meritorious Service Medal with two OLC, the Army Commendation Medal, the National Defense Service Medal, the European Army Occupation Medal, Vietnam Service Medal, Vietnam Cross of Gallantry with Palm, Vietnam Armed Forces Honor 1/C Medal, Vietnam Campaign Medal, Army Meritorious Unit Citation, Presidential Unit Citation, Combat Infantryman's Badge, Master Parachute Badge, Rigger Badge, The Department of Army Staff Badge, The Canadian Parachute Badge, Vietnam Parachute Badge and Jungle Expert Certification.

Chaffin's formal civilian education included the following: Henderson State Teachers College, Bachelor of Arts, 1953; Ohio State University, Master of Arts, 1961; Louisville Presbyterian Theological Seminary, Master of Divinity, 1982; McCormick Theological Seminary, Doctor of Ministry, 1997; San Francisco Theological Seminary, Diploma in the Art of Spiritual Direction, 2001.

Chaffin was inducted as a Hall of Fame Member of the US Army Quartermaster Corp Regiment on June 6, 2013.

After retiring from the Army, Chaffin served a 25-year career as a Presbyterian Church (USA) Minister and Pastor. On May 11, 2011 he was honored as a Henderson State University Distinguished Alumni.

Chaffin married Cynthia Caldwell in 1953 and they have two children, James and Cyndi, along with four grandchildren, Jade, Clay, K.C. and Kim.

GEORGE G. CHAPMAN was born Feb. 24, 1930 in Pontiac, Michigan. He enlisted on Oct. 6, 1947 at Detroit, MI. After basic training at Fort Knox, KY he received additional training as Inf. OCS, Armor Officer Basic, Armor Officer Advanced, Airborne, and Rangers. He was stationed at Command and General Staff College and fought in the Korean War.

Chapman retired in 1982 as a lieutenant colonel.

RONALD S. CHASTAIN was commissioned as an Infantry Officer at Arkansas Tech in 1972, receiving a B.S. in Biology. In 1974, he joined the Army National Guard and also began working for the U.S. Department of Agriculture's Farm Service Agency.

During DS/DS, LTC Chastain commanded the 25th rear area operations center under the XVIII Abn. Corps in Saudi Arabia and Iraq.

BG Chastain commanded the 39th BCT attached to 1CD during OIF-II. The 39th detached one light Infantry battalion (1-153 IN) to the 3rd BCT, 1CD, and then attached 2/7 Cav, in order to provide the 39th an armor capability. Headquartered in Taji, the 39th AO stretched from central Baghdad to Tarmiyah.

The 39th's 3-153 IN was in Baghdad's Adhamiyah district, while the 2-162 IN was in the Rusafa District.

After OIF-II, Chastain was promoted to major general and served as chief of staff (wartime), U.S. forces Korea. He then became the Adjutant General, Arkansas National Guard. Chastain's final assignment was as Deputy Commander (Reserve Component) U.S. Army Forces Command.

Chastain and his wife, Pam, live in Conway, Arkansas. They have two children, Lana and Lance (Stormey), and three grandsons, Jack, Sawyer, and Beau.

LYLE E. "CHAD" CHEADLE enlisted on August 25, 1956 at Billings, MT. Boot Camp was with 9th Division, Fort Carson. Additional training was as a Ranger, with Airborne and Special Forces.

Chad was stationed at Fort Carson, Fort Campbell, Fort Bragg, Fort Benning, in Korea, Vietnam (three tours), Taiwan and Germany. He was at Ia Drang, Bong Son, Happy Valley and Lam Son 719.

Cheadle was awarded SS, LOM, Bronze Star with V, Bronze Star Svc one OLC, AM 20 LC, PH 20 LC, MSM 3 OLS, ACM 3 OLC, EIB, Ranger and Master Parachutist.

A memorable experience for Cheadle was serving with the best Soldiers in the world.

He was discharged as CW3 on April 30, 1981 at Oakland, CA.

From 1981 to 1997 he was a GS 15 with Civil Service. Now he is a farmer/rancher.

He and Sukim have six children: Jacqueline, David, Larry, Robert, Janet and Laura. Grandchildren are John, Cristine, Kyle, Cody, and Josh.

ROBERT J. "BOB" CHILD graduated from Mapleton High School, Denver, CO, 1961 and from University of Denver, BSBA 1965.

He enlisted in the US Army October 1965, took Basic and AIT at Fort Gordon, GA; Artillery O.C.S. at Ft. Sill, OK and then 5/4 Artillery at Ft. Carson, CO.

Bob spent one year in Vietnam, 1967-1968, with 1st Air Cavalry Division, Forward Observer with B CO 5/7 Cavalry and then FDO with C Battery, 1/21 Artillery. He left as a 1LT.

Medals received for his service were Cross of Gallantry, Bronze Star, Air Medal, etc.

Major battles he was in were LZ Colt, Quang Tri, Battle of Hue, Tet Offensive, Khe Sahn and A Shau Valley.

Bob met his wife, Joan, a registered nurse, in Colorado Springs and got married in 1967, still married.

In civilian life he was a Purchasing Manager, Director and Vice President of Supply Chain Management in the Computer Storage Manufacturing Industry from 1973-2008. He earned Lifetime C.P.M. Certification with ISM and retired in 2008. He also worked as a Real Estate Investor (1968-2016) with Joan as the Property Manager.

They have two children, Julie and Brad and two grandchildren, McKenna and John.

They now spend their time managing property, traveling, volunteer work and Golf.

Child is currently Senior Vice President for Vets Helping Vets in Colorado, a non-profit, volunteer organization.

ANDREW PAUL CHURA enlisted on June 8, 1965 in Jamaica, NY and took Boot Camp at Fort Hood, TX. He received an honorable discharge at the end of his service.

He received the Vietnam Service Medal w/ two Bronze Service Stars, National Defense Service Medal, Republic of Vietnam Campaign Medal, Air Medal, Combat Infantryman Badge, Sharpshooter (Rifle) and Expert (81MM Mortar).

After discharge he worked for Department of Sanitation, New York City and at Nassau Coliseum.

Andrew and Mary Ann were married when he returned from Vietnam and had a wonderful life together. They were blessed with four beautiful healthy children: Robert, Bridget, Andrew and John. The grandchildren are Ashley, Bob, Connor, Caitlen, Shannon, Andy, Danny, Marisa, Daniella and John. Great-grandchildren are Hailey and Danny.

Andrew passed on August 13, 2008. When he was passing, his bed was put by the window so he could look out to the wooded area of their yard. He said he was going home to see his guys. *Submitted by Mary Ann E. Chura.*

DAVID A. CIOSEK belongs to Sheridan's Chapter of 1st Cavalry Association. He was born on Oct. 3, 1949 in Chicago IL and attended Proviso West, graduating in 1967. He enlisted at Chicago on July 31, 1967, with Basic and AIT at Ft. Leonard Wood, MO.

He went to Vietnam on Dec. 18, 1967 with the 87th Engineer Battalion stationed at Phan Rang Airbase, came home on Dec. 18, 1968 and went to Ft. Hood, TX. He was in the 1st of the 9th Armored Cavalry, 2nd Armored Division.

Ciosek went back to Vietnam in August 1969 with the 8th Engineer Battalion as an air mobile bulldozer operator building LZ's in Tay Ninh Province. He was also at LZ Buttons, LZ Ike, Jaimie Carolyn Grant, among others, plus Quan Loi, Phuoc Vinh and the first stages of the Cambodian invasion. He came back home on May 24, 1970.

He was awarded the National Defense, Vietnam Service, Vietnam Campaign, and Air Medals, Presidential Unit Citation, Meritorious Unit Citation, RVN Cross of Galantry w/Palm, and RVN Civil Action Honor Medal. Campaigns involved in were 1969 Tet Counter Offensive Summer and Fall, Sanctuary Counter Offensive, and Counter Offensive Phase VII.

He was discharged on May 24, 1970 at Ft. Ord, CA, as a Pfc, and worked on the railroad as a freight conductor for 37 years before retiring in 2009. A lifetime member of VFW and American Legion, his hobby is fishing.

Ciosek married Karen in 1971 and had three daughters, Tara, Nicole and Kimberly, and three grandchildren, Jason, Autumn and Jaxon.

NEIL L. CIOTOLA enlisted Aug. 3, 1976 at Newark, NJ and took Boot Camp at Fort Knox, KY.

Additional Training was Armor crewman (1976); Primary NCO Course (PNCOC); Basic NCO Course (BNCOC); Advanced NCO Course (ANCOC); Battalion Training Management Course; Leadership and Management Development Course; Nuclear, Biological and Chemical Defense Course; M60A3 Master Gunner Course; M1 and M1Al Master Gunner Course; Airborne School, Air Assault School, Operations and Intelligence Course; United States Army Sergeants Major Course; Command Sergeant Major designee course; Joint Forces Command Senior Enlisted Advisor Course (Keystone); and The Army Senior Leader Development Course Chapel Hill, North Carolina.

He was stationed at Fort Knox, KY; Sullivan Barracks, FRG; Fort Hood, TX; Coleman Barracks, FRG; Fort Stewart, GA; Coleman Kasserne, FRG; Fort Knox, KY; Fort MacPherson, GA; Fort Knox, KY; Fort Lewis, WA; The Pentagon and Fort Sam Houston, TX.

Ciotola received Distinguished Service Medal, Defense Superior Service Medal, Legion of Merit, Bronze Star Medal (2OLC), Meritorious Service Medal (60LC), Army Commendation Medal (40LC), Army Achievement Medal (20LC), Good Conduct Medal (12th Award), National Defense Service Medal (w/Bronze Star), Iraq Campaign Medal, Southwest Asia Service Medal (w/three Bronze Stars), Global War on Terrorism Service Medal, Military Outstanding Volunteer Service Medal, Noncommissioned Officer Professional Development Ribbon (w/numeral Four), Army Service Ribbon, Overseas Service Ribbon (w/numeral Three), Kuwait Liberation Medal (Saudi Arabia), Kuwait Liberation Medal (Kuwait), Parachutist Badge, Air Assault Badge, German Armed Forces Marksmanship Medal in Silver and Combat Action Badge.

Memorable experiences included Tank Commander (M60A1, M60A3, MHP, MIAl); Tank Commander, B Company, 1st Battalion, 8th Cavalry; Operations Sergeant/Master Gunner,

2nd Battalion 66th Armor Regiment, Operation Desert Shield/Desert Storm; Cavalry Troop First Sergeant; Command Sergeant Major of the 2nd Battalion, 46th Infantry (BCT); Command Sergeant Major of the 5th Squadron, 15th Cavalry Regiment (OSUT); Command Sergeant Major of the 1st Battalion, 33rd Armor; Command Sergeant Major of the 2nd Brigade Combat Team, First Cavalry Division; Command Sergeant Major of the First Cavalry Division (The First Team); Command Sergeant Major of Multi-National Division Baghdad; Command Sergeant Major of III Corps and Fort Hood; Command Sergeant Major of the Multi-National Corp in Iraq and Command Sergeant Major of Installation Management Command (IMCOM).

CSM Ciotola was discharged June 1, 2012 at Fort Sam Houston.

He and Beth have one child, Stanley.

EMMITT CLARK was born in 1948 in DeQuincy, LA. After graduating from DeQuincy High in 1966, he enlisted on Oct. 30, 1967 and attended Boot Camp at Fort Polk, LA. He also attended Fixed/Rotary Wing School.

He was stationed at Fort Polk, Fort Benning, Fort Rucker, Fort Eustus and Fort Sam Houston. He also serviced in Vietnam with Troop A-1-9.

During his service, Clark was awarded a Purple Heart, Bronze Star, Air Medal and DFC Award. He was discharged on Oct. 30, 1970 at Fort Polk, LA with the rank of E6.

After military service, Emmitt worked as a millwright. Emmitt and Janet have one son, Justin and two grandchildren.

JOHN WAYNE CLARKE enlisted in the US Army at Fort Jackson, SC in October 1965 to become a Helicopter pilot. However, he received orders to attend aircraft electronic school at Fort Eustice, VA. After graduation, waiting for orders to attend flight school, he received orders to report to Vietnam. Clarke was assigned to the 15th TC battalion of the 1st Cavalry Division and reported for duty in June 1966. During his tour he repaired helicopters, performed perimeter guard duty and participated in search and destroy missions.

A memorable moment occurred in the middle of the night at Camp Radcliff in An Khe when a gunship returned from a mission and during landing a misfired rocket was launched and exploded in their tent. They all thought it was just another mortar attack and did not find out what really happened until the next morning.

Clarke left Vietnam in June of 1967 and reported for duty at Fort Sill, OK. At Fort Sill his duties included Air Traffic Control, Finance and a stint as a Lifeguard. He joined the Red Leg flying club and flew to different states in the area. He requested an early out for college and was discharged in August 1968 to attend LaSalle University.

Back in Philadelphia he got a job as a flight instructor and applied to become an air traffic controller at the New York Center. He was accepted and started work in September 1970. At the same time Clarke finished his BS degree at Dowling College and received a MS at SUNY Stony Brook. He transferred to the Philadelphia TRACON in January 1976 to work in the Tower and Radar room. John continued his education and received a MA at West Chester University. He also applied and received a direct commission as a Warrant Officer on a special program to recruit pilots in the Pennsylvania National Guard.

Clarke returned to New York Center in August 1984 and was discharged from the Guard. He was promoted to Supervisor Air Traffic Controller and retired in April of 1998. John moved to Ventnor, NJ and was hired by a contractor as a Software Engineer in support of the program that supports the FAA Air Traffic Control system. Clarke retired from this position in February 2014.

He received an Aviators Badge, Sharpshooters Badge, National Defense Service Medal, Vietnam Campaign Medal, Vietnam Service Medal, Army Service Ribbon, Army Overseas Service Ribbon, Republic of Vietnam Gallantry Cross, and the Pennsylvania General Stewart Medal.

John married Eileen Beccaria in 1970 and they have three daughters: Jennifer, Susan and Colleen along with grandchildren Jessica, Jocelyn, Jackie, Ava, David and Jack and step-grandchildren Willow and Wyatt.

THEODORE L. "TED" COGUT, upon graduation from Detroit's John J. Pershing High School in 1944, was too young to enlist and was hired in a World War II War Production Plant to inspect B-29 parts. That was where he met beautiful Miss Marie Nordstrom, another teenage B-29 parts inspector. They would one day be married, a strong contract now in its 71st year.

Ted enlisted in the Army Air Corps/Air Force on 6 February 1946. A year later, the Air Force separated from the Army. In 1948, then probably the youngest USAF forecaster, he was awarded the skilled weather forecaster MOS and began briefing aircrews, including those flying the Berlin Airlift. Back when planes could not cope well with weather – weather radar, computers, satellites and good navigation aids were just dreams – he briefed thousands of aircrews at airfields in Massachusetts, Michigan, Saudi Arabia, Bermuda, and New Hampshire. Yet, even now, one may hear Marie say: "He never lost a plane due to weather."

When an enlistment ended in 1953, he joined the reserve and was recalled to active duty, in 1956. While at a Strategic Air Command base Ted voluntarily undertook a number of studies to find reliable answers to common queries, such as: "will the field be socked-in when we get back (after 12 to 14 hour missions)?" Transferred to the USAF Climatic Center in Washington DC, he produced answers to a vast number of other meteorology-related questions.

In February 1965, Ted, then a USAF master sergeant, was sent back to the Army, reporting as a warrant officer and serving as an instructor at Ft. Sill's Artillery and Missile School. In October 1965, in Vietnam, he was chief of the 13-man, 3/18 Battalion Artillery (heavy) Meteorology Section, providing artillery trajectory correction data for First Cavalry Division. He and his section were at the battle sites for operations Clean House, Black Horse, Masher/White Wing, Crazy Horse. Though the battles were critical, no medals were awarded. The war was too new and the battle sites too far from battalion's HQ bunker. Ted is most proud of that assignment.

In 1966, he was back at Ft. Sill writing instructional material, developing new courses, revising FM-615, the Manual for Artillery Meteorology; and then, in 1968, it was a return to Vietnam for operational control of six 13-man Army and one Marine Corps artillery meteorology sections. At the end of that tour, having 20 years on active duty, he took military retirement.

Among his second Vietnam-tour decorations are the Legion of Merit, Bronze Star Medal, Army Commendation Medal, and a unit award of the Vietnam Cross of Gallantry with Palm. He also holds, among other medals, the World War II Victory Medal with American Campaign Medal. After the military, Ted started up environmental controls at the Morenci, Arizona, mine, North America's largest copper producer. He holds a bachelor's degree from University of Maryland and a master's degree from Wayne State University. Ted has had articles published in national magazines, has had a book about his military experiences published and has coauthored three other published non-fiction books, these about the Southwest.

MERVIN "MERV" CORDER was born April 24, 1941 in Orofino, Idaho and graduated from Orofino High School in 1960. He enlisted in Jacksonville, FL and took Boot Camp at Fort Jackson, SC. He also trained as a Radio Repairman and Calibration Specialist.

He was stationed at Augsburg, Germany; Boblingen, Germany; Fort Gordon, GA; An Khe, RVN; Fort Benning, GA; Saigon, RVN; Aberdeen Proving Grounds, MD and Redstone Arsenal, AL x 2.

Merv received the National Defense Service Medal, Vietnam Service Medal, Republic of Vietnam Campaign Medal, Vietnam Cross of Gallantry w/Palm (Unit) and Good Conduct Medal (fifth award).

Memorable experiences were meeting many new people and traveling to many different countries.

SFC Corder (Ret.) was discharged on July 31, 1981.

He was a letter carrier for 20 years, and retired on Dec. 31, 2004. He is a member of American Legion, VFW and DAV.

Merv says he met his lovely wife, Dona, in 1963, married her in 1964 and she's still with me. They have two children, John and Sheila. Grandchildren are Brett, Chase, Alexis and Morgan. Ezekiel is their great-grandchild.

TERRY C. CORNEIL was commissioned a 2nd Lieutenant in the Infantry when he graduated from the University of Alabama in 1969. After Infantry Officer Basic Course and Airborne School at Fort Benning, GA, he was assigned to the 5th Mechanized Division at Fort Carson, CO where he was a Platoon Leader and S-3, Air. He graduated from Ranger School enroute to Viet Nam.

Corneil served with the 2nd Battalion (Airmobile), 5th Cav. Regiment, 1st Cavalry Division (Airmobile) as a Platoon Leader, Company XO, Battalion S-4 and Company Commander of Bravo Company. Operating primarily out of Firebase

Mace, his company conducted search-and-destroy missions against elements of the 33rd NVA Regiment.

After Viet Nam, he was assigned to the NATO/SHAPE Support Group in Belgium. Subsequent assignments included Defense Language Institute (DLI) (Russian), US Army Russian Institute, Foreign Language Training Advisor (Russian) at DLI and Combat Developments Officer at TRADOC. While at TRADOC, he also served on the personal staff of the CG, TRADOC and was the CG's Speechwriter. Corneil's last assignment was with the On-Site Inspection Agency where he served as an Inspection Team Chief inspecting Soviet nuclear weapons inside the former Soviet Union. LTC Corneil retired in June 1992.

Some of his awards include the Defense Superior Service Medal, four Bronze Stars (two with V devices), Defense Meritorious Service Medal, Meritorious Service Medal with Oak Leaf, Joint Service Commendation Medal, the CIB, Ranger Tab and Airborne Wings.

Corneil has a Bachelor of Science Degree from the University of Alabama and a Master's of Science (International Relations) from Boston University.

Corneil married Mary Neal Shope in 1968 and they have two daughters, Kimmon and Kasey and four grandchildren, Parker, Kailer, Harrison and Mason.

WILLIAM "BILL" CORSAIR (McGROARTY) joined the 115th MPC, RING in 1964, did basic at Ft. Jackson and AIT at Fort Dix.

In May 1968, the five officers and 121 enlisted men of the 115th Military Police Company, RING, were mobilized for active duty, stationed at the USMA, West Point, NY. The men were to act as a personnel pool, under the Levy System, to fill slots in major combat divisions in Vietnam. Special training included night infiltration and reconnaissance, with field maneuvers against the 82nd Airborne.

Bill was one of three (along with Sgt. Piatek and Specialist Nicholson) who served with the 1st Cav. Airmobile, RVN.

In January 1969, he was assigned to the FWD Headquarters of the 1st Cav, in Phuoc Vinh, where he served as NCOICCI until being sent TDY by then Commanding General EB Roberts, to AFVN-TV/Radio in Saigon to write, produce and give voice to the combat footage shot with his team (Specialists Hufford & Newsome), in the field. His mission was to tell the story of The 1st Team, in combat, in Vietnam via the AFVN TV/Radio Network newscasts and features. Mission accomplished, he returned to Phuoc Vinh to sign out and then processed at Ben Hoa, leaving Country in November 1969. He rejoined the 115th MPC at USMA, ending his service in Rhode Island in December 1969 when the Company returned to State control.

Bill was an on-air personality with a number of radio stations in numerous states before and after activation. A credit to be noted is he created, produced, engineered and gave voice to the original "Talking G.I. Joe" before beginning his active tour. So the original GI Joe, it could be said, was a SSG with the 1st team.

A pioneer of talk radio, with a show on WCAU-AM, in Philadelphia, which reached 38 states and Canada, he was in the Guinness Book of Records, for "Most Calls To A Show," for 20 years, from 1974-1994. He was declared "Humanitarian of the Year" by the city of Philadelphia during the Bicentennial Year.

Wife Janis, a former CBS producer, and Bill co-hosted a live audience, entertainment/information syndicated TV Show, "Corsair & Co." for Post-Newsweek before they segued into successful NYC-based film, TV and theater acting careers, including notable commercial and corporate credits. Bill is in "The Hall of Fame" of his high school, and is a member of The Rhode Island Radio Hall of Fame.

Bill was presented with a 2003 SAG Award for his "1920s Newsreel Announcer" in the Oscar winning film, "Chicago" and wife Janis, in 2014, received the same award for her performance in another Oscar winner, "Birdman." The couple, based in Manhattan for over three decades, continues frequent character work on "SNL" among other venues. Bill's "Depends Legends" parody is a heralded classic, available on youtube.com.

Bill's daughter, Robin, her daughters Lindsay and April, and their husbands, presented him with a total of three great-granddaughters and a great-grandson, rounding out a full family tree.

Robin's husband, Jim, an Army Veteran with service in Korea, and April's husband, Petty Officer 1st Class Ryan, on his second tour with the Navy, continue the family tradition of military service.

McGroarty's awards and decorations include the Bronze Star, with Oak Leaf Cluster, the Combat Air Medal, Vietnam Service and Vietnam Campaign Medal, along with the Vietnamese Cross of Gallantry with Palm, Army Valorous Unit Award and Presidential Unit Citation Division awards. Three Combat Stars for "Tet 69 Counteroffensive", "Vietnam Summer-Fall 1969" and "Vietnam Winter-Spring 1970."

LTC C.M. CRAWFORD was born and raised in Athens, TX. He graduated from Texas A&M College and received a Regular Army commission in 1956.

In 1963 he commanded A Troop, 1st Reconnaissance Squadron 9th Cavalry, along and within the Demilitarized Zone (DMZ) of Korea. Unit experienced two killed and one wounded on July 29, 1963. A DMZ OP was renamed OP Dessart in honor of Pfc Charles T. Dessart III.

In 1965 Crawford returned to Vietnam as an Armored Cavalry Troop Advisor (M-113), and in October 1970 he was en route to Vietnam for a second tour. Because of his prior experience, he was assigned as Armored Cavalry Brigade Senior Advisor and was awarded the Legion for Merit signed by General Crighton Abrams. From Vietnam to the Pentagon and Army General Staff (DCSOPS), he met General Abrams. Next, on to Fort Hood to command a converted airmobile unit to armor, First Battalion, Eighth Cavalry. Tank gunnery was a challenge, yet all 54 M60Al tank crews qualified. Better yet, in 1975 the "Mustangs" qualified all 54 crews with 37 attaining distinguished scores. The unit also attained an III Corps Superior Unit in 1975.

LTC Crawford was selected to attend the Army War College in 1976 but chose to retire to his Texas Historic Home built in 1868.

GEORGE S. CRAWFORD was born June 10, 1933 in Waukegan, IL, and graduated from Waukegan High School in 1951. He enlisted in 1952; basic training, 85th Infantry Regiment, 10th Infantry Division, Fort Riley, KS. Upon graduation, he was assigned to Company L, 167th Infantry Regiment, 31st Infantry Division, redesignated Company L, 28th Infantry Regiment, 8th Infantry Division.

Crawford was transferred to the Far East to the 9th Corps Mountain Warfare Training School, Japan. He was then assigned to K and E Companies, 8th Cavalry Regiment, 1st Cavalry Division, Japan.

Discharged in 1956 as a Regular Army Sergeant First Class, he attended and graduated from the University of Wisconsin in 1959 and was commissioned a Regular Army Second Lieutenant, Infantry.

Crawford attended the Infantry Officer Basic Course, then was assigned the 1st Battle Group, 11th Infantry; followed by attendance at Rotary Wing Flight School, Camp Wolters, TX and Fort Rucker, AL.

Upon graduation in December 1959, he was assigned to the 8th Aviation Company, 8th Infantry Division, Germany. He served three months in central Africa's Congo flying refugee rescue missions in 1960; his Sikorsky 19-D helicopter took 14 bullet holes in that period. Back in Germany, Crawford was an instructor pilot in the Sikorsky H-34 and UH1 Huey and also a helicopter instrument instructor pilot.

1963, he returned to USA and was assigned as Company Commander, B Company, 38th infantry, 2nd Infantry Division, and after a year, the battalion staff of 2nd Bn. 23 Infantry Battalion 11th Air Assault Division, and 1st Battalion 7th Cavalry, 1st Cavalry Division.

In 1966 Crawford was assigned to Republic of Vietnam, C Troop, 9th Cavalry, 1st Cavalry Division. The night of Dec. 17, 1966, he was WIA and was medically evacuated to the An Khe Mobile Army Surgical Hospital, the Evacuation Hospital at Qui Non, the 249th General Hospital, Japan and in March, 1967 to Martin Army Hospital, Fort Benning, GA.

In 1969, he was released from the hospital and was assigned for a year as Company Commander, 197th Aviation Company, Fort Benning, GA.

In 1970, his second tour in Vietnam, he was assigned as Company Commander of the 170th Aviation Company Assault Helicopter, Kontum, Vietnam, located on the tri-county border of Vietnam, Laos and Cambodia.

In April 1971, he returned to Fort Devens, MA, as the Infantry Instructor at the Army Security Agency School where he earned a Master's Degree in Education and attended Command and General Staff School, Fort Leavenworth, KS.

In 1974, Crawford was reassigned to the Lexington Blue Grass Depot, Lexington/Richmond, KY. He was Director of the Maintenance Directorate and then Commander of the Depot.

In 1978, he was assigned to Germany to the 3rd Armored Brigade, 3rd Armored Division and later to the division staff.

His final assignment was The United States Readiness Command, MacDill AFB, FL as the NATO Plans officer. Crawford retired from the US Army in January 1983.

He was awarded the Combat Infantry Badge, Master Army Aviator, the Purple Heart, and other valor and meritorious awards. He was also awarded three Presidential Unit Citations for service in combat.

WILLIAM SCOTT CRAWFORD enlisted at Thomasville, GA and took Boot Camp at Fort Benning, GA. He took Panama Jungle Training at Fort Polk, LA.

Crawford was based at HHC 15SS FSB Mace and engaged in battles in Vietnam.

He received the National Defense Service Medal one O/S Bar, Combat Infantry Badge, Republic of Vietnam NCM W/60 DEV, Vietnam Service Medal with two Bronze Stars, Republic of Vietnam Gallantry Cross with Palm Unit Citation, Sharpshooter Badge with Rifle Bar and Marksman Badge with Auto Rifle Bar with Machine Gun Bar.

PFC Crawford was discharged at Fort Benning, GA on March 1, 1972.

Since then he has worked as a correctional officer at Thomas County C.I., Colquitt County C.I., patrol officer for Ochlocknee Police Department and Pelham Police Department.

His wife is Donna and stepson is Micheal Owens. Grandchildren are Micayla Owens, John Micheal Owens and Harley Madison Owens.

His retirement activities are fishing and watching the grandchildren grow up.

THOMAS R. DANIELS enlisted in the Army on 4 August 1964 and completed basic training at Fort Polk, LA. Following basic training, he completed medical corpsman training (91A) at Fort Sam Houston, TX. Daniels served briefly at Fort Chaffee, AR and Fort Sill, OK before being stationed in Korea with 7th Infantry Division from 1965 to 1966. Returning from Korea, Tom was assigned to the hospital at Fort Polk. He requested EKG training and completed EKG technician training (91N) at Portsmouth Naval Hospital in Virginia. After returning to Fort Polk, Daniels received orders for Vietnam.

Daniels served in the Republic of Vietnam from July 1967 to July 1968 as a combat field medic. He was initial assigned to 11th ACR then transferred to 3rd Sq., 5th Cavalry, 9th Infantry Division. His unit helped the 5th Marines clear out Hue during the Tet Offensive before being attached to 1st Cavalry Division (Airmobile) for brief period. After Vietnam, he was assigned to William Beaumont General Hospital at Fort Bliss, TX where he finished his enlistment. After a 3 months break, Tom reenlisted for Europe and was stationed at 196th Station Hospital in SHAPE, Belgium as an EKG tech from 1969 to 1972.

Upon returning from Belgium, Daniels was assigned to the hospital at Fort Polk from 1972 to December 1974. Then he got orders for Letterman Army Medical Center at the Presidio of San Francisco, CA from January 1975 to September 1980 as an EKG tech. From 1980 to 1981, he would do his second tour of Korea with 2nd Medical Battalion of the 2nd Infantry Division. Daniels return orders would be that of Fort Hood, TX.

Tom reported to Fort Hood in September 1981 and was assigned as ambulance platoon sergeant of HHC, 1st Bn., 12th Cavalry, 1st Cavalry Division. After 2 years he was assigned to HHC, 2nd Bde, 1st Cav Div and which the brigade was the first to defeat the OPFOR at NTC. In 1985 Daniels became acting First Sergeant of Company Charlie, 1st Forward Support Battalion, 1st Cav Div. After that he was assigned to Med Ops, HHC, DISCOM, 1st Cav Div until November 1988. Daniels was involved with REFORGER 83 and 87 and an evaluator of the Expert Field Medical Badge tests within the 1st Cav. Half of his personal award ribbons were earned with the 1st Cavalry Division at Fort Hood. The last two years of service, Tom was assigned as a First Sergeant to a medical company of 1st Armored Division and then to HHC, DISCOM, USAREUR in Germany. Tom Daniels retired as First Sergeant to Fort Hood 1 September 1990.

Daniels' military awards include the Purple Heart, Meritorious Service Medal, Army Commendation Medal with two OLC, Army Achievement Medal with two OLC, Good Conduct Medal (8th Award), National Defense Service Medal, Vietnam Service Medal with four Bronze Service Stars, Army Services Medal, Overseas Service Ribbon Numeral 4, Republic Of Vietnam Campaign Medal, Combat Medical Badge, Valorous Unit Award, Republic Of Vietnam Gallantry Cross Unit Citation Badge with Palm (2nd Award), Expert Badge Rifle, and NCO Professional Ribbon.

Thomas married Ginger Schumann in 1969, and they have three children, Thomas (Teddy), Jennifer and Brittany. Tom has five grandchildren and one great-grandchild. He also has two "military adopted" children, Willie Arausa and Martha Wall. Thomas R. Daniels was born 2 August 1947 and passed away 14 January 2016 from complications of Agent Orange cancer.

DONALD RICHARD DAVIS was born to Mary Davis Snyder and Harman Cecil Davis in Cleveland, OH. He was known as "Davey" by some classmates, "Dad" by four children, variously "Pop-Pop" or "Pop-So" by seven grandchildren, and both "Don" and "friend" by those who knew him.

He graduated from Mentor High School in 1955 and, because of his demonstrated abilities, was recruited by Coach "Red" Blaik to play Army football. He joined the Class of '59 on a hot July on the Plain overlooking the majestic Hudson.

Don was a large man and was proud to have resided in the heaviest room in the Corps for three years. His unconquerable spirit, easygoing nature and unfailing sense of humor sustained him well and these traits characterized him throughout his life. His healthy skepticism about the cadet system significantly reduced the stresses of cadet life. As a result, he is remembered for his frequent successful bouts with the Academic Department and was never one to waste either a tenth or a minute out of the sack.

On Graduation Day, Don married his partner for life, Madeline Fowler, in the West Point Cadet Chapel and began a successful and fulfilling career in the Army Field Artillery.

His active duty service to his country included assignments in Germany, Thailand, Iran and two combat tours in Viet Nam. He served as an Artillery battery commander in combat, an instructor in the Department of Tactics at West Point, a student, and later the chief of plans and operations at CGSC and an advisor to the Imperial Iranian Army and to the Royal Thai Armed Forces, He wore his Ranger Tab and Airborne Wings with great pride and distinction. Along the way, Don earned a Master of Arts degree in personnel and supply management.

He was recognized for his military service by two awards of each of the following: the Bronze Star, the Meritorious Service Medal, the Joint Services Commendation Medal, the Army Commendation Medal and the Air Medal. He received one award of the Legion of Merit

Don was involved in the early formative years of the airmobile concept and was a charter member of 1st Cavalry Division (airmobile), deploying with it to Viet Nam in 1965. He was the battery commander of A Battery, 1-21 Artillery during the renowned Battle of the la Drang Valley, memorialized in *We Were Soldiers Once...and Young*, written by LTG Harold Moore, the battalion commander of the 1st Battalion, 7th Cavalry. Don's Artillery battery, located at LZ Falcon, provided direct support to two Infantry battalions, firing virtually nonstop during the four days of intense combat at LZ X-Ray and LZ Albany. Then-LTC Moore wrote a personal note about Don, stating that he was a superlative Artillery officer. "He helped keep us alive."

In Iran, Don had the interesting misfortune to have been held prisoner in the American embassy, along with many others – including two classmates – during a brief revolt on Valentine's Day 1979 by distraught Iranians who were not particularly impressed with Don's diplomatic status. Fortunately, there was a happy ending to that adventure.

In 1980 Don retired from the Army and moved to Lubbock, TX, where he worked for many years in the insurance industry and was responsible for ensuring the safety compliance of cotton gins and other insured properties across the South Plains. Later, he worked for the Texas Work Force Development Office, helping persons displaced by military base closures to find jobs in the civilian world,

Don's lifelong love was his family. He was a generous, loving yet stern father. He coached, cheered, or refereed each of his four children while they swam, and/or played softball or basketball. His love of sports also was experienced by his seven grandchildren, who fondly remember his yells of encouragement from the sidelines at football, hockey, basketball, volleyball and soccer games.

Don, a young man from Ohio, became a model Soldier and was clearly molded by West Point's creed of' "Duty, Honor, Country." Don died after a short battle with pancreatitis and diabetes, triggered in all likelihood by multiple exposures to Agent Orange in Viet Nam.

Any attempts to eulogize Don here will pale in comparison to the words delivered by his children at his memorial service at the Leavenworth National Cemetery, where he was interred with full military honors beside his daughter, Katherine, who preceded him in death. In poignant tribute, his children expressed their love, respect, admiration, and grief for their father in a thoughtful, loving, courageous and sometimes humorous way. No man could receive any greater tribute or leave any greater legacy.

KENNETH R. DEBES, born in 1946 at Great Bend, KS, graduated in 1964 from Odin High School. In 1974 he attended Kansas State University.

Debes enlisted at Great Bend, KS on Dec. 5, 1966 and attended Boot Camp at Fort Jackson, SC. He received additional training in Light Weapons Infantry and Drill Sgt. School. Debes was stationed in Germany, South Vietnam and Fort Ord, CA. He served with Company C and D, 2nd Battalion, 7th Cavalry in Khe Sanh, A Shau Valley and others from February 1968 through January 1969.

Debes was awarded the Bronze Star with V Device, Combat Infantry Badge and Purple Heart. He was discharged with the rank of E6 on Dec. 6, 1969 at Fort Ord, CA.

He retired in 2016. Kenneth and Deborah have three children: Anna, Stephen and Rachel. Charles is their grandchild.

NELSON RICHARD DeMILLE was born in New York City on Aug. 22, 1943 to Huron and Antonia (Panzera) DeMille, then moved with his parents to Long Island. He graduated from Elmont Memorial High School, where he played football and ran track.

DeMille spent three years at Hofstra University, then joined the Army where he attended Officer Candidate School and was commissioned a Lieutenant in the US Army (1966-69). He saw action in Vietnam as an infantry platoon leader with the First Cavalry Division and was decorated with the Air Medal, Bronze Star and the Vietnamese Cross of Gallantry.

After his discharge, DeMille returned to Hofstra University where he received his bachelor's degree in Political Science and History in 1970. He has three children: Lauren, Alexander and James, and he and his wife reside on Long Island.

DeMille's first major novel was *By the Rivers of Babylon,* published in 1978 and is still in print, as are all his succeeding novels. He is a member of American Mensa, The Authors Guild, and is past president of the Mystery Writers of America. He is also a member of International Thriller Writers and was chosen as ThrillerMaster of the Year 2015. He holds three honorary doctorates: Doctor of Humane Letters from Hofstra University, Doctor of Literature from Long Island University and Doctor of Humane Letters from Dowling College.

Nelson DeMille is the author of *By the Rivers of Babylon, Cathedral, The Talbot Odyssey, Word of Honor, The Charm School, The Gold Coast, The General's Daughter, Spencerville, Plum Island, The Lion's Game, Up Country, Night Fall, Wild Fire, The Gate House, The Lion, The Panther, The Quest* and *Radiant Angel. He* also co-authored *Mayday* with Thomas Block and has contributed short stories to anthologies and book reviews and articles to magazines and newspapers.

PASQUALE DI MATTIO was born on July 4, 1925 and drafted at the age of 18 in the Army in July 1943. He received basic training at Fort Riley, KS. His detachment, M Troop, was a Cavalry Troop and took basic training on horses.

In January 1944, he shipped out to Oro Bay, New Guinea. Private Di Mattio was a replacement waiting to be assigned to the 1st Cavalry Division prior to the invasion of the Philippines. While waiting to be assigned to a Regiment, Di Mattio saw MacArthur and the President of the Philippines land in Leyte. He was assigned to a machine gun squad in H Troop, 5th Cavalry Regiment during the invasion of the Philippines as an ammunition carrier for the water-cooled .30 caliber machine gun and saw action in the hills of the Philippines.

In February 1945 Di Mattio's troop was ordered by MacArthur to San Tomas University to protect 4,300 civilians rumored to be in danger of being slaughtered by the Japanese. After leaving San Tomas, Di Mattio's Troop helped US Soldiers in Manila City drive the Japanese out of Manila. Di Mattio once again saw MacArthur when he raised the flag after the Battle of Manilla.

After the surrender of the Japanese in the Philippines, Di Mattio trained for the invasion of Japan. He earned the rank of Corporal in Japan as his Captain's jeep driver.

Pat returned to the United States in January 1946 and was honorably discharged from the Army. While serving with the 1st Cavalry, Di Mattio received two Bronze Stars, the Combat Infantry Badge, the Expert Marksman Badge, the Philippine Liberation medal and other various medals.

Di Mattio met and married the love of his life, Frances Steen, in 1948. He has two beautiful daughters, four grandchildren, (one of which became an Army Ranger and also earned a Bronze Star) and five great-grandchildren.

SAMUEL C. DIXON was born on May 20, 1950 in Maryland, and graduated from Rising Sun High School in 1969. He enlisted in 1970 and received basic training at Fort Dix, NJ, with infantry training at Ft. Polk, LA, Special Jungle Training at Ft. Sherman, Panama.

Dixon did a tour in Vietnam, during which time he was awarded the Purple Heart, National Defense, Combat Infantry Badge, and Vietnam Service Medal. He received his discharge in Feb. 1972 at Fort Hood, with the rank of E-4.

From 1973-2007 he worked at Aberdeen Proving Grounds where he retired as Program Manager on June 29, 2007. He is a member of the 1st Cav. Div. Assn. and the NRA.

He is married to Cathy Ann Dixon.

MARK A. "DOC" DOCKTER was born May 11, 1953 in Jamestown, ND, and attended Streeter High School. He enlisted in the U.S. Army in May 1971 and attended boot camp at Ford Ord, CA, where he also received 2nd BDE AIT.

He was stationed at FB Bunker Hill (between Tay Ninh and An Loc near Sai Gon River) and the 3rd BDE rear at Bien Hoa, Republic of South Vietnam. He was "In Country" during the "NVA Easter Offensive" in 1972, assigned to A Co., 1st Battalion, 12th Cavalry, 3rd BDE "Separate", 1st Cavalry Division (Airmobile). He holds a roster for 21 air combat assaults with this company. In June 1972, 3rd BDE "Separate" stood down and became B Co., 1st Battalion, 7th Cavalry, Task Force "Garry Owen". He holds the roster (22 July 1972) for the last two combat assaults undertaken by the 1st Cavalry Division (Airmobile) in Vietnam. He left Vietnam in 05 September 1972.

Doc was awarded the Air Medal and Combat Infantry Badge. He was discharged in September 2007 at Fort Douglas, UT, with the rank of SFC/E8. He served three years in the Army and 18½ years in the Army Reserve.

In retirement, he is a rancher, enjoys his Harley Davidson, works with the American Legion, and is a rural firefighter. Doc is married to Kathy, with two children, Micah and Lucas, and one grandson, Madison.

DONALD O. DOLES was born January 26, 1947 in Vinton County, Ohio, and graduated from high school in 1965. He enlisted on May 28, 1965 and book Boot Camp at Fort Knox, KY. Additional training was Combat Medic and Jungle and Arctic Survival.

He was stationed in Germany, Honduras, Panama, Alaska and Vietnam. Donald was in Bong Son Plains RVN, TET-1968, RVN and Task Force 16 – Honduras.

He was awarded a Bronze Star – Valor, Purple Heart, AACM-OLD, CMB, EMB, Air Crew Wings, AAM, GDM – US – four stars.

Memorable experience was coming home from Vietnam. SP5 Doles was discharged on April 19, 1968.

He worked as a CSX-T railroad conductor for B&O and retired in 1996. In 1997, he retired from the Ohio National Guard as a SSgt.

In retirement he goes to Wyoming every chance he gets.

Doles' first wife was Judy Kaye; his second wife was Edith M. He has four children: Donald II, Lance (an Iraq Veteran), Travis and Scott. Grandchildren are Allison, Hanna, Josh, Andy, Taylor, Shylie and Gabe.

EUGENE DOLFI was born June 22, 1931 in Webster, PA and graduated from Rostraver High School in 1949. He enlisted for Infantry School in September 1952. During basic training at Camp Breckenridge, KY, he was selected as a candidate for Infantry School and was eventually commissioned as a second lieutenant and shipped to Korea. Prior to going to Korea he married his high school sweetheart, Shirley.

Gene served with the 27th Maintenance Battalion, 1st Cav Division as Executive Officer, during the years 1966-1967 in the Republic of Vietnam.

After returning to the States, he was assigned to various duty stations including Redstone Arsenal in Alabama, Fort Leavenworth, KS (Command and General Staff College) and second tour to Germany.

He received the Legion of Merit Medal, Bronze Star, RVN Commendation Medal, Vietnam Service Medal, Korean Service Medal, UN Service Medal and Air Medal (RVN).

After retirement from service in 1982, he worked as a civilian contractor doing tasks for the Marine Corps at Quantico, VA. The Dolfi family is enjoying the "retirement life" in Springfield, VA.

Eugene and Shirley have two children, Lori and Shari.

ARTHUR J. DORN was born Jan. 29, 1945 in Glen Cove, NY and graduated from Locust Valley High School in 1963. He enlisted Aug. 23, 1965 at Whitehall Street, NYC and took Boot Camp at Fort Dix, NJ. Additional training was 67A10, 67N20 Helicopter Single Engine Rotary Wing MOS Helicopter Technical Inspector 67W20

He was stationed at Fort Rucker, AL; Fort Eustis, VA; An Khe, Binh Dinh Province Vietnam; Chu Lai Quang Nam Province, Vietnam; 123rd Aviation Company, Fort Campbell, KY; Fort Benning, GA; Fort Stewart, GA; Hunter Army Airfield, GA; 609th Transportation company, Hanau, Germany; assigned JFK Kennedy CTR, Multan, Pakistan; Norfolk, VA and Jacksonville, FL.

He was assigned to H.H.C 3rd Bde as Helicopter Crew Chief for 1st of the 7th Cavalry Regiment, further assigned to Col. Daniels and Col. Johnathan Burton as Crew Chief on UH-1 Helicopter flew over and above men of the 1st Cavalry Division 1966 to 1967. Returned to Vietnam assigned to Americal Division 23rd Div A Company 123rd as Helicopter Technical Inspector. Provided 23rd Division UH-1H Helicopters to General Powell and many others from 1968 to 1969.

He was awarded the Senior Air Crew Man Badge, Bronze Star, Air Medals with V device, Army Commendation Medals (two) with V device, Vietnam Service, National Defense Service.

Dorn's memorable experience was spending over 20 years in US Army, by far the experience of being assigned to the First Cavalry Division in Combat in Republic of Vietnam with the best military personnel in the world. His opportunity to be assigned to a team of true American Hero's that fought and died for what they believed in to protect the country they loved. He has always reflected back on this experience as his best years of life. Officers, Enlisted – they all cared about each other and protected each other. He was discharged in February 1989 at Fort Eustis, VA.

He has been a Training Instructor GS 1712 Attack Helicopter Branch, Fort Eustis, VA both AH-1(M) and AH-64 Qualified Airframe and Armament Instructor. Transferred to US Navy NADEP Norfolk, VA Quality Assurance Specialist GS-1910 on A6E Intruder Program, EA-6B Prowler Program moving to FRCSE Jacksonville, FL as work moved to NAS Jacksonville continued on EA-6B Prowler; now Quality Assurance GS-1910 on T-44 Program since 2011 to date.

AJ and Ritia have two children, Michael and Denise, and two grandchildren, Serria and Gage.

TOMMY L. DORSEY enlisted August 7, 1964 at Los Angeles, CA with Boot Camp at Fort Ord, CA. Additional training was Technology Aircraft Maintenance – Inglewood, CA and Aircraft Maintenance, Fort Rucker, AL.

He was stationed with 17th Air Assault, and 1st Cav (Air Mobile) Fort Benning, GA. He was involved in battles in Vietnam, Battle LZ-X-Ray, Albany (3) Bon Song One – WIA LZ Byrd.

Dorsey was awarded Expert Rifle, Vietnam Service Medal, Purple Heat and Air Medal.

Dorsey was discharged on Nov. 18, 1968 as SP/5 at Valley Forge Hospital, Valley Forge, PA.

Tommy and Doris have two children, Scott and Sean and two grandchildren, Joshua and Jonathan.

MATTHEW "MATT" DRAGICEVIC was born in 1935 at Milwaukee, WI. After graduating from Pius XI High School, he enlisted on March 23, 1953 and attended Boot Camp at Camp Chaffee, AR. He also attended 1st Cavalry NCO School, Class #26 15 QM Company.

He was stationed at Camp Crawford, Hokkaido, Japan and Camp Schimmelpfennig, Sendai, Japan.

Matt was awarded the National Defense Medal. His memorable experience was at Projectionist School at Camp Schimmelpfennig, Sendai, Japan.

On March 12, 1956 he was discharged at Fort Sheridan, IL with the rank of Pvt. 2.

Matt retired in 2014 after working as industrial packaging distributor/owner. He and wife Mary have no children.

KENNETH E. DUNCAN was born Feb. 23, 1939 in Thomaston, GA and graduated from Robert E. Lee Institute, 1957; Gordon Military College, 1962; University of Georgia, 1964, Magna Cum Laude; Advanced ROTC University of Georgia. He was Second in Command his senior year.

He reported to Fort Benning, GA in June 1964 and took Infantry Officer Basic Course. Assigned to the 11th Air Assault Division, which later became First Cavalry Division. He left Fort Benning with an advanced party in August 1965 on *Lykes Liners* with equipment for Vietnam.

Standing l-r: Sgt. Maj. Basil Plumbley, Capt. Matt Dillon, Lt. Dick Merchant, Lt. Ken Duncan, Capt. John Herren. Kneeling: Lt. Col. Hal Moore, and an unknown Trooper.

Ken was in the Ia Drang battle, Bon Son I and II.

Duncan was awarded the Combat Infantry Badge, Bronze Star Medal with V Device and Bronze Star (First Oak Leaf Cluster), Vietnam Campaign Medal, Vietnam Gallantry Cross with Silver Star, one Overseas Bar, National Defense Service Medal and Vietnam Service Medal.

He was relieved of active duty on August 7, 1966 at Oakland, CA.

After service, he was manager of Industrial Division Sales at Thomaston Mills.

In retirement he enjoys golf and hunting.

Ken and Mimi (Minor) Duncan have two children, Kelly and John. Grandsons are Christopher Thomas and Chase Andrew.

GARRY DUNLOW was born on July 14, 1946 in Colerain, NC and graduated from Windsor High School. He enlisted at Ahoskie, NC and took Boot Camp at Fort Gordon, GA. AIT training was at Fort Benning, GA with 11th Air Assault.

He was stationed at An Khe, Vietnam; Fort Benning; Fort Jackson and was engaged in battle at Pleiku campaign and Ia Drang.

Medals Garry received are the National Defense Service, Vietnam Service, Combat Infantryman Badge, Republic of Vietnam Campaign Ribbon with Device, Expert Badge, Presidential Unit Citation.

Memorable experience was the Ia Drang Valley battle.

E-4 Dunlow was discharged at Oakland, CA. He works as Purchasing Manager for American Fire Technologies.

Garry is married to Beverly Dunlow.

HENRY L. DUNN was commissioned as a 2nd Lieutenant upon graduation from the University of Georgia in March, 1964. He spent nine weeks of Artillery training at Ft. Sill, OK, March – June 1964. He was assigned to A/2/42 Artillery, 11th Air Assault Division at Ft. Benning, GA, 6/64 – 6/65. He was then assigned to B/1/21 Artillery, 1st Cavalry Division and attached to A/2/7 Cav as a forward observer. Henry was shipped to Vietnam with the 1st Cav in August, 1965, and completed his service in March, 1966.

While in Vietnam, Henry was a part of the Ia Drang Valley Campaign during November, 1965. He flew into LZ X-Ray early on the morning of 11/15/65. His unit walked out of LZ X-Ray and into LZ Albany on 11/17/65. Henry was transferred back to the Artillery in January, 1966 and was the battalion air observer for Bong Son I.

Dunn received the Bronze Star Medal with V Device, 2 Air Medals, Vietnam Service Medal, and the Presidential Unit Citation.

Upon his return to Albany, GA, he married Sara Pattison. They have two children, Devin and Dena, and four grandchildren, Hank, Pace, Cannon and Coleman. Dunn retired in December

2005 from his professional career as a Certified Public Accountant.

MAX L. DUNN served with the 43rd Area Support Group, 68th Transportation Bn. 183rd Maintenance Company, Ft . Carson, CO, as a SGT. and was attached to the 1st Cavalry Division during Desert Storm. He served under Chief Warrant Officer 5 James Rathburn, and was apart of Task Force Coffer. First Team.

DENNIS ANTHONY DUNNE was born in Detroit, MI on July 24, 1946. He graduated from Benedictine High School, going on to college at Wayne State University.

He was drafted on July 31, 1968. He went to boot camp at Fort Knox, KY then on to Infantry School at Fort Polk, LA and NCO School at Fort Benning, GA.

He landed at Cam Ranh Bay and joined the 1st Cavalry Division, then on to Fire Base Grant where he joined Bravo Company 2/12th. During his tour the company moved to Tay Nihn, then further north, leaving country at Song Be. He walked point with Jim Jordan for over 90 days through the monsoons to the dry season.

Dunne was awarded a National Defense Service Medal, Vietnam Service Medal, Vietnam Campaign Medal, Bronze Star Medal, Air Medal and Combat Infantrymen Badge.

He returned to the US and earned a Bachelor of Arts degree. He utilized his degree throughout a career working in the film industry from New York City to Los Angeles. He divides his time between Fort Worth, FL and Grosse Point, MI in his retirement years.

PETER JOSEPH DURNO was born Oct. 7, 1940 in Boston, MA, and enlisted in South Naples, FL. He completed boot camp at Ft. Benning, GA, prior to assignment in Vietnam. He was a cook in the Army (also assigned to an Infantry company) from the time he went in until the time he got out, and he still cooks SOS to this day.

After returning home from Vietnam, he married Alice Avery Durno in January 1968. He worked in the Pepperell Mass Paper Mills until the company closed and forced his retirement. He and Alice moved to Colebrook, NH. They have one daughter, Lori, who lives in Pepperell and attends reunions with her father annually.

He has been a life member of Pepperell VFW for over 50 years, and is also a member of the American Legion in Canaan, VT. He enjoys fishing in retirement.

LYMAN C. DURYEA graduated from West Point and was commissioned on June 8, 1960. He completed the Infantry Officer Basic Course, Airborne School and Ranger School at Fort Benning and was stationed in Germany for three years. In Germany he served in a variety of positions at company, battalion and Division level, completing the following courses: CBR, Armored Reconnaissance Officer and Motor Officer.

From Germany it was back to Fort Benning and an assignment with the Infantry Board until he volunteered for Vietnam. In February 1966 he spent the first of two Vietnam tours in the 1st Cavalry Division, the majority of that tour as a Company Commander. This was his most rewarding and exciting year of service. From Vietnam it was back to Fort Benning for the Advanced Infantry Course. There followed another brief period with the Infantry Board and then Vietnamese Language training. His second Vietnam tour as an adviser in the Delta began in August 1968.

His next tour was for three years as the Plans and Programs Officer in the Military Assistance Group in the Congo following a brief refresher course in French and a course on Security Assistance. From the Congo he was assigned to the 1st Infantry Division at Fort Riley as the Operations Officer, 1st Battalion, 63rd Armor. His next tour was at Fort Leavenworth where he graduated from and completed a Master's Degree in Military Art and Science at the Command and General Staff College in 1974. From Fort Leavenworth to Paris for two years where he completed a Master's in Modern Languages from Middlebury College in 1976. Next up was three years on the faculty at West Point where he taught French. This was followed by a three-year tour at the School of the Americas at Fort Gulick, Panama, where he served as Instructor, Department Director and Director of Instruction. From Panama to Haiti as Defense and Army Attaché following completion of the Defense Attaché Course and a short course in Haitian Creole. During this assignment he completed the requirements for graduation from the Army War College. Next up was a two year assignment as Defense and Army Attaché in El Salvador where the country confronted a very violent insurgency and the music of gunfire livened the nights. From El Salvador followed his final assignment on the faculty of the Army War College from which he retired with the grade of Colonel on July 31, 1989.

Colonel Duryea received the following individual awards: Silver Star, Legion of Merit, Bronze Star with "V" device, Bronze Star with Oak Leaf Cluster for meritorious service, Defense Meritorious Service Medal, Meritorious Service Medal with Oak Leaf Cluster, Air Medal with "two" numeral, Army Commendation Medal with Oak Leaf Cluster, National Defense Service Medal, Armed Forces Expeditionary Medal, Vietnam Service Medal with stars for six campaigns, Army Service Ribbon, Overseas Service Ribbon with "six" numeral, Vietnamese Gallantry Cross with Silver Star, Vietnamese Honor Medal, First Class, Salvadoran Gold Medal for Distinguished Service, Republic of Vietnam Campaign Medal, and the Combat Infantry Badge (CIB). He received the following unit awards: the Presidential Unit Citation and the Vietnamese Gallantry Cross with Palm.

Upon retirement, he completed a PhD in Military History from Temple University in 1983, a program he had begun while on the War College faculty. He is on the Board of Governors of the 1st Cavalry Division Association and a former Association President. Among other activities he has been a translator, author and editor. His interests include classical and military history, both classical and modern languages, evolutionary theory and the theory of relativity. He is an active skier, SCUBA diver, backpacker and kayaker.

He was married to Gisela "Gigi" Duryea and they have three children: Robert Lyman Duryea, Gwynne Elizabeth Butcher and Dominique Erika Rattner. He has 12 grandchildren: Kay, Rachel, Rebekah, Robert, Mark, Joseph, John, Josh and Sylvia Duryea; Benjamin and Mathew Butcher; Emilie Rattner. One great grandson is expected as of this writing.

JEFF EARLEY was born June 18, 1954 in Cincinnati, OH and graduated from Valley Forge Military Academy in 1972. He also attended Monmouth College, IL (BA Business Admin), Webster University (MA Business Management) and US Army War College.

Earley enlisted June 5, 1976 and attended Boot Camp at Fort Riley, KS. He also received training with the Airborne, as Jumpmaster, Air Assault and Rigger.

Earley was stationed at Fort Knox, Fort Lee, Korea, Fort Bragg, MDW, Germany and Fort Campbell. He took part in Urgent Fury – Grenada and Desert Storm.

He was on the East German border in November 1989 when the wall came down. From 1993 to 1995 Earley commanded the 27th MSB.

He was awarded the DSSM, BSM, LOM, KSM w/4 OLC and ARCOM 3 OLC.

Colonel Earley was discharged on Jan. 1, 2002 at Fort Belvoir, VA.

He is a Board Member of Joseph House for Homeless Veterans and is affiliated with AVSA, MOAA and NDIA.

JOHN D. EDMUNDS (CW4, USA Ret) was born in 1951 in Alexandria, VA, the son of a career Army officer. Following high school graduation in 1969, he enlisted in the Army and completed basic training at Fort Polk, LA and Warrant Officer Flight Training at Fort Wolters, TX and Fort Rucker, AL. Completing OH-6A transition en route to Vietnam, WO1 Edmunds was initially assigned as a UH-1 pilot with C Company, 229th AHB, First Cavalry Division. In June 1971 he transferred to D Troop (Co) 229th AHB, 3rd BDE SEP, First Cavalry Division, where he served as a Scout Pilot and Instructor Pilot in the OH-6A until February 1972.

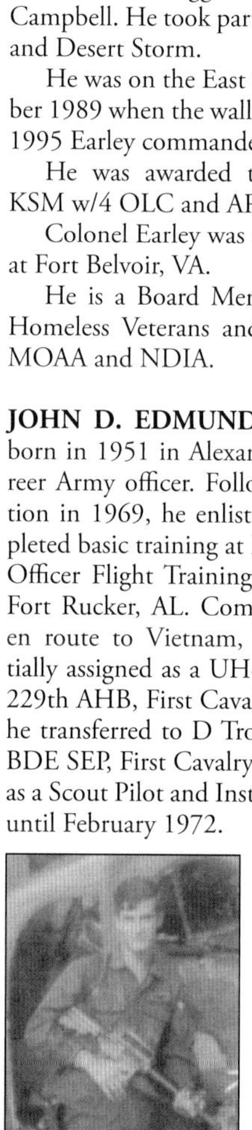

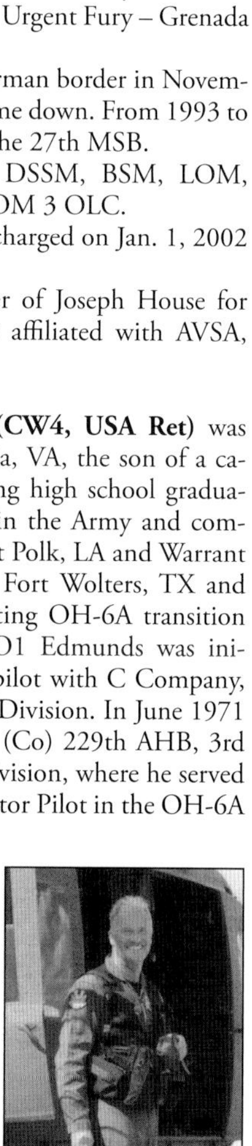

Released from active duty after returning from overseas, CW2 Edmunds served in the PA Army National Guard as a UH-1 Pilot and OH-6 Instructor while pursuing a Logistics degree at the Pennsylvania State University. After graduation in 1976, he was employed by Bell Helicopter Isfahan, Iran, as an Air Rescue Pilot, flying the Bell 214A/C, until the Islamic revolution in 1979. He has since been employed at Fort Rucker, AL as a Flight Instructor teaching the Rotary Wing Qualification Course and most recently as an Instructor Pilot for the USAF Specialized Undergraduate Pilot Training, Helicopter in the UH-1H/V and currently in the TH-1H (Huey II). CW4 Edmunds retired from the Army Reserves in 1996 after 27 years of active duty, National Guard and Reserve service, last serving as the 991st Medical Detachment, Helicopter Ambulance, Standardization Instructor Pilot, flying the UH-1V.

As of this writing (March 2017), Mr. Edmunds has been flying helicopters for 47 years accumulating just over 20,000 hours, approximately 16,000 as a flight instructor, and over 1,000 combat hours in the OH-6A, UH-1H, and AH-1G Cobra. Mr. Edmunds lives in Enterprise, AL and is married to the former Jenny Lynn Ingram of Enterprise. They have one married daughter, Jennifer (Mike) and two grandsons, Alden and Emmett.

ROBERT BROOKE ELDRIDGE was drafted, May 1966, into the United States Army and completed Basic and Advanced Individual Training at Fort Dix New Jersey! "Brooke" graduated, top of his class and was promoted to PFC, one month later, promoted to E4. He attended Armor Officer Training at Fort Knox Ky., and 360 days, after being inducted, he graduated as a Second Lieutenant, Armor Officer.

Joe Bowen, Brooke Eldridge, and ___ Iverson.

He obtained his BSC Degree from University of Louisville in 1976 and his Masters Degree from Central Michigan University in 1980, along with graduating the same year, from the Army, Command and General Staff College, Fort Leavenworth, KS.

Eldridge was selected for and went to Helicopter Flight Training at Enterprise Alabama and graduated as a helicopter pilot in May 1967. Graduating, in the top 5 percent of his class, he was selected for Cobra Training at Savannah Ga. Promoted to First Lieutenant in May 1968, he saw combat in Vietnam from March 1969 to March 1970. He has over 750 Vietnam, Combat Flight hours and accumulated approximately 1000 combat missions. A mission equates to, you used up all your fuel or all your ammunition, or both, so could be a 15-minute flight or up to one and one half hours, give or take! Shot down three times and took so many bullets that it is impossible to count them, "Needless to say, many!" Eldridge was assigned to Alpha Troop, 1/9, First Cavalry and Assigned as the Cobra Section Leader to start, promoted to Captain, May 1969 and later that year, assigned as Cobra Platoon Leader.

He was awarded the Bronze Star, Meritorious Service Medal, with two OLC, Air Medal, along with 14 Clusters for Combat Missions and an Additional award, of the Air Medal, for Valor, the Army Commendation Medal, National Defense Service Medal, Army Service Medal, Vietnam Service Medal, Over Seas Service Ribbon, Republic of Vietnam Campaign Medal, Republic of Vietnam Gallantry Cross, Unit Citation and Master Army Aviator, with Palm.

Captain Eldridge commanded a Cavalry Unit at Fort Knox, KY, and as a Major, commanded an aviation unit in Germany, with the 2nd Armored Cavalry Regiment and was also assigned as the 2nd ACR's Adjutant. His final assignment was Inspector General, for Fifth United States Army, Fort Sam Houston, San Antonio, TX, where he retired as a Lieutenant Colonel!

After Army retirement, he moved to San Diego, California and opened a Surf, Bike and Blade, Rental and Sales Company, Brooke "N" Bri's, Inc. It was located, oceanfront, on the Pacific Beach Boardwalk. Eldridge, ran Brooke "N" Bri's for 12 years and finally sold it in 2000. He did home remodeling sales for seven years and in early 2007, he opened a hauling, moving and demolition company, San Diego Hauling Hunks, which he still operates today (www.sandiegohaulinghunks.com).

Early in 2013, he got involved in the television reality industry and became the executive producer of a show called "The Romance" (www.theromance.tv). It is a reality TV show that followed 30 singles, dating each other, for over one year. "The Romance" went live in San Diego in January 2016 and will air, again in San Diego in November 2016, along with airing in Los Angeles in November 2016. It is pending viewing in several others major areas, such as Chicago and New York!

Additionally, he was producer of a short film, "Flowers of the Night," which aired in the Spring 2015 and won several awards for Best New Film, Best Martial Arts Film, etc. He is presently working on a full featured film, "Violet," concerning human sex trafficking. He has a well-known, martial arts, A-Listed, Hollywood actor, whose name he cannot reveal pending final contract agreement, but who you will immediately recognize, unfortunately, not in time, for this book's publication! The website for his movie is www.sunshineproductions.com.

BILL ELLIS grew up on the west coast and was performing in a Bay Area rock band on the verge of its first release when he received his draft notice in 1968. Following boot camp and advanced infantry training, Ellis was sent to Vietnam and assigned to Alpha Company 1/5 Air Cavalry as a grunt.

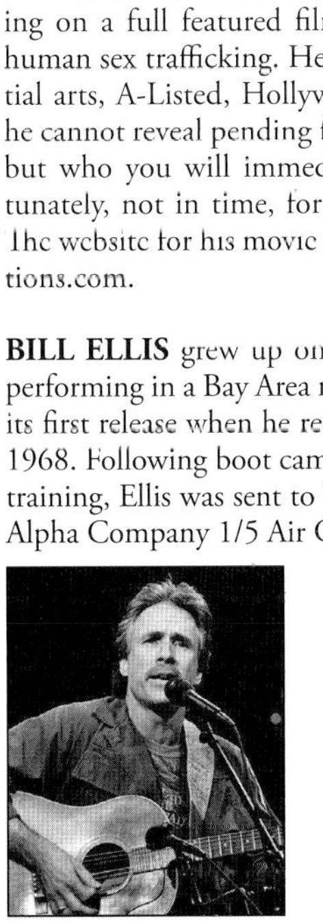

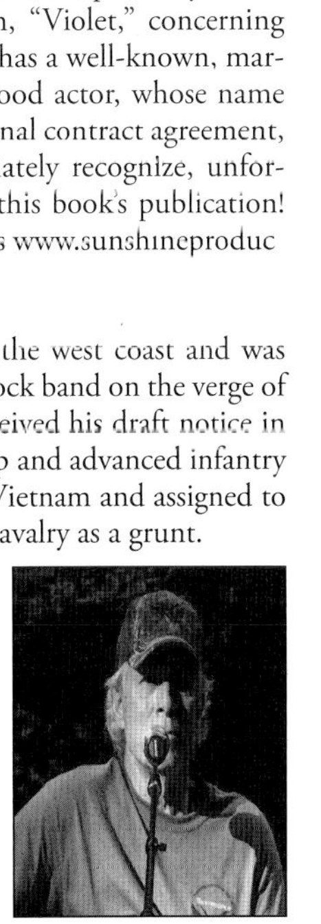

Four months into his tour in March 1969, it was discovered that he wrote and sang music, and he was assigned to travel to firebases and LZ's throughout Southeast Asia to play music for the troops. In 1969, four of his songs were recorded and an EP record was produced under the title "Impressions of a Skytrooper." A copy (30,000 produced) was given to each Trooper in the Cav when they left Vietnam to return home.

Upon returning home, Ellis made a career out of performing and writing music. In 1984 after attending a 1st Cav reunion, he began to develop a concept album and later rock musical titled "Beyond the Wall," which centers on the emotions and memories felt by all Vietnam Veterans.

He still travels and performs his latest show, Skytrooper.

JAMES F. ELLIS (JIM) volunteered for Warrant Officer Candidate Flight Program (Fall 1967) after 18 months at Texas A&M, graduating with class 68-21 January 1969. Jim attended Cobra transition in route to his assignment with Apache Troop 1st Sqdn 9th Cav 1st Cav Div in Tay Ninh, So Viet Nam March, 1969. Jim served as pilot/gunner/navigator, later as Apache 24 (Cobra Aircraft Commander), as Weapons Systems Maintenance Officer and Brigade Liaison Officer after a battlefield commission to second lieutenant.

Jim separated from active duty at Fort Hood, TX (Fall 1971) shortly after marrying Jean Hollerbach whom he met in 1969 when he shipped out overseas via Travis AFB, CA. Jim received a BS in Physics from Texas A&M and was elected to the Sigma Pi Sigma Honor Society. Jim worked for Sperry Flight Systems and Lockheed Martin while supporting The Army Digital Avionics System, MILSTAR I Satellite as CSE, IKONOS (CSE), SBIRS (Deputy CSE), and CSE on several classified programs for the CIA and NRO. From 1971-1987 Jim also held various National Guard/ Reserve assignments flying Hueys, CH-47s, and Satellite Operations Officer for the USAF at Onizuka AFS.

Jim and Jean have two sons, one daughter-in-law, and their first grandchild. They currently live in Camp Connell, California but are planning a move to Denver, CO to be closer to family and granddaughter!

JOSEPH L. "JERRY" ENGLISH enlisted in Los Angeles, CA on Aug. 5, 1965. In addition to Boot Camp at Fort Ord, he also trained in Radio Communications.

He was stationed at Fort Bragg and Germany and served in Vietnam. "Jerry" received the CIB, a Purple Heart, Good Conduct and VSM.

Memorable experiences were the world travel including Japan, Korea, Vietnam, Germany and Austria.

English was discharged as a first sergeant on April 11, 2008 at Priest River, ID.

"Jerry" was a Peace Officer in California, retiring in 1999. He remains active as a Reserve Sheriff Deputy and with Veterans groups.

English and Annie B. have two children, Karen and Annette, and two grandchildren.

DAVID ENYART was born and grew up in Whittier, California, and attended California High School and Mt. San Antonio Jr. College. He was drafted in 1964, but enlisted to attend The Army School of Aviation at Ft. Rucker, AL. He trained to be a crew chief on the UH-1 helicopter, and was sent to Ft. Bennings 11th Air Assault Div (Test) to train in helicopter warfare tactics. In 1965 they changed into the 1st Air Cav Div and were sent to Vietnam by ships. He sailed on the Simon B Buckner, then transferred over to the USS Boxer aircraft carrier where their helicopters departed to An Khe and built their new base camp.

His company was the D Co 227th AHB, 1st Cavalry Div., and he was with it the whole year in Vietnam. His company was a gunship company, and they were pretty much up and down the 11CTZ. After his year in Vietnam, he was sent to Ft.Carson's 5th Inf Div, Colorado Springs, Colorado, where he separated from the Army.

David stayed in Colorado Springs, where he met and married his wife, Judy, and they raised three children, Tasha, Adam and Paige.

MICHAEL "DIVISION POLACK" FALKOWSKI entered the ROTC in 1967 and attended Boot Camp at Fort Bliss, TX.

He attended University of Delaware (1967, BA) and Stetson College of Law (1973, JD). He also took ADA Basic – Military Intel at Fort Holabird, MD.

Falkowski was stationed at Mangil-san, Korea and Selfridge AFB, MI. He was involved at Phuc Vinh, Song Be, An Loc, and the Cho Hoi Program – Pacification Run.

He was awarded the Purple Heart, Merit Bronze Star with cluster and Air Medal.

Memorable experiences were serving his country and seeing Korea and Vietnam.

Falkowski was discharged with the rank of Captain at Fort Ord, CA.

He has served as an attorney since 1973, being affiliated with the American Bar Association, Florida Bar – Trial Lawyer.

Falkowski has three children: Rebecca, Jessica and Michael Jr. and one grandchild, Penelope.

WALTER A. "DUKE" FARRELL was born Feb. 9, 1947 in Philadelphia, PA, and attended South Philadelphia High School. He enlisted on Oct. 20, 1964 in Philadelphia, and was sent to Ft. Jackson for basic training and AIT, later attending Airborne School/Air Assault.

Farrell was stationed at Ft. Benning, GA with the 187th Inf., 11th AAD, then was transferred to the 1/12 Cavalry AirMobile for assignment to Vietnam from Sept. 21, 1965 to Sept. 20, 1966. Stations included Happy Valley, Shinny Bayonet, Pleiku, Ia Drang Valley, and LZ X-ray.

He was awarded the National Defense Service Medal, Combat Infantryman Badge, Purple Heart, Vietnam Service Medal, Vietnamese Campaign Medal with Device, and Presidential Citation. He was discharged on Oct. 20, 1967 at Ft. Campbell, KY with the rank of Sgt. E-5.

Farrell was the owner/operator of S&W Specialty Tooling, retiring in 2012. He is married to Marcella S. Farrell and has two children, Cynthia and Jeanette, and seven grandchildren, Crystal, Britnay, Kyle, Ashley, Angela, Austin, and Andrea.

GERALD E. FERGUSON JR., COLONEL (Ret.) was Commander, 1/12 Cavalry from June 1994 to June 1996; First Team G-3, June 1996 to August 1997; and First Team Chief of Staff, June 2001 to Sept. 2003. Awards include the Distinguished Service Medal and multiple awards of the Legion of Merit. Both of his grandfathers were members of the First Team during World War II and the Korean War.

WALLACE R. FISCHER enlisted in the Army on Feb. 11, 1948 at Watertown, WI. He was sent to Fort Sheridan, IL to be sworn in, then was sent to Fort Ord, CA for Basic Training – after a short delay en route, went on the *General Pope* with 4,500 other military and went to Japan, where he was assigned to the 5th Cavalry Regt. at Camp McGill, Takeyama, Japan. It had been a Japanese Sea Plane and Submarine base. They repaired the submarines in a military barracks. He was allowed to go in one before they bulldozed the entrance closed. The 1st Cavalry Division took its winter and summer training at the base of Mt. Fujiyama, Japan. Winters were like Minnesota and Wisconsin.

In July 1950, we loaded on LST's for Korea from Camp McGill. We landed at Jo-Hang Dong, Korea on July 18, 1950. Three days later we were on the front lines. In hot weather all you could smell was death.

The 5th Cavalry Regiment took a short halt south of "Pyongyang" – the capital of North Korea. A captain came to me and gave me some money. He said the Regiment Commander said there was a British Unit 3-4 miles south. He was to take a jeep, go to their unit and ask for some "refreshment for medicinal purposes" they may have. At their area, the sentry asked why he was at their camp. He told him to see Chuck Story, the postman. Fischer went to a tent near the top of the hill and talked to the postman. He said everything was OK. After about 15 minutes he said, "You will see a lorry go down on the road. When it stops, you go and then you will know 'the sale is on.'" The transfer then took place.

Also, around the first of July 1950 Fischer was told his enlistment would be close to being up and he received a one-year extension on his enlistment from President Harry S. Truman. With a short delay, he was one of the last to load on the LST. He was told to go in a compartment in the lower part of the LST. All compartments had already been taken. He then took his duffle bag and full field pack, put them in a 1-ton trailer on the main deck where he stayed during the trip from Japan to Korea. It was wonderful and/or spectacular to see all the Naval escort ships, minesweepers, etc. protecting them.

CHARLES M. "MIKE" FISHER graduated from Fork Union Military Academy in 1970 and Virginia Military Institute in 1974. Additional training was Armor Officer Basic.

Mike was stationed in Germany (12 years), Fort Knox, KY; Fort Benning, GA; and Fort Hood, TX. He was in Desert Storm. Mike was awarded the Bronze Star M&M (four). Memorable experiences were movement to Desert Storm with 1/8 Cav. OS XO

LTC Fisher was discharged at the Pentagon. After service he served as a State Magistrate. He is affiliated with the American Legion and spends retirement time farming.

Mike and Sarah have one daughter, Melissa and two grandchildren, Ava and Ospen.

BLAINE T. FLEMING graduated from Penn State University (BS degree), commissioned Regular Army 2nd Lieutenant as Distinguished Military Graduate (DMG) from ROTC and Private pilot fixed wing license June 6, 1959.

July 26 1959-Nov. 15, 1959 – USA Arty and MSL School, Fort Sill, OK and Fort Bliss, TX.

April 2, 1960-Dec. 5, 1960 – Primary USA Helicopter School, Camp Wolters, TX and Fort Rucker, AL.

Dec. 7, 1960-Oct. 16, 1961 – Arty Officer/Rotary Wing Aviator, Trp A, 1st Recon Sq (SKY CA V), 2nd USA Msl Cmd, Fort Carson, CO w/TDY

April 10, 1960-June 19, 1960 – spt OPERATION RED EYE (Hel armament and Survivability Expert) cdt by USACDEC, Camp Hunter Liggett, CA.

Oct. 17, 1961-Sept. 30, 1962 – Rotary Wing Aviator, 504th Avn Co., 4th Armored Div., Fuerth, Germany.

Oct. 1, 1962-Oct. 1, 1963 – 2nd How Bn., 14th Arty, 4th Armored Div. w/TDY

Nov. 27, 1962-Dec. 7, 1962 – attended 7th USA Combined Arms Sch., Btry XO/Cmdr, Btry C, 105 mm How Bn 14th Arty, 4th Arm Div.

Oct. 1, 1963-Sept. 27, 1964 – Rotary Wing Aviator, A Co, 504th Avn Bn., 4th Arm Div, Fuerth, Germany.

Oct. 15, 1964-June 10, 1965 – Arty Off Career Crs, Fort Sill, OK and USAMSL Sch, Fort Bliss, TX.

July 15, 1965 – RW Aviator, 1st Cav. Div. (AM), Fort Benning, GA.

July 23, 1965-May 1, 1966 – RW Aviator/Asst OPNS Off/Commo Off, Avn Co/, 7th Sp SF GP, 1st Cav. Div (AM) ch to Co A, 229th Aslt Hel Bn, 1st Cav. Div. (AM), participated in various combat assault campaigns under fire including "Happy Valley," Plei Me-IA Drang Valley, Bong Son and delivering supplies/extracting dead/wounded Soldiers to/from LZ X-Ray and LZ Albany, RVN.

May 2, 1966-August 13, 1966 – 13th Avn Bde, Co. A, 101st Avn Bn., RVN.

Sept. 30, 1966 – Resigned Regular Commission, commissioned Reserve Captain in USAR Control Gp.

July 1, 1966-June 5, 1989 – Active Reserve, 98th Div. (Tng) (AIT), Co OPns Off, Bn XO, Bn Cmdr, Bde S-I, Bde S-2/3, Opns/Tng Directorate, IG, Cmd/Gen Staff College, Advanced Engr Off Cr.

June 6, 1989 – Retired after 30 years, Col/AUS.

Fleming received the following awards: Air Medal (11th Oak leaf cluster), RVN Gallantry Cross with palm, Presidential Unit Citation, Army Commendation Medal, Vietnam Service Medal, Viet Nam Campaign Medal, National Defense Service Medal, Armed Forces Reserve Medal with 10-year device, Army Reserve Components Achievement Medal with two OLC, Army Service Ribbon, NY State Conspicuous Service Cross, Meritorious Unit Commendation with oak leaf cluster and NY State Conspicuous Service star.

Memorable experiences included participation in Armed Helicopter/Survivability Experiment, assault and extraction of troops from combat LZ's under fire, flood relief assistance from Hurricane Agnus in 1972 in Elmire/Corning, NY, loss of helicopter and crew for 43 years in RVN in 1965.

Dates/Places of discharge: 30 Sept 1966-Valley Forge, PA (Active duty)-Captain; June 6, 1989-Syracuse, NY (Reserve duty)-Colonel

Fleming held various management positions with Corning Glass, Westinghouse Electric, and Miller Brewing, retiring in December 1993.

CARL U. FOX III entered military service on 8 March 1993 at The Ohio State University, where he pursued a B.A. in Aviation Management. He completed basic training at Fort Jackson, SC and proceeded to Fort Rucker, AL to complete his flight training in the UH-1 and OH-58 aircraft. Fox graduated and received his coveted wings in June 1994. Subsequently, he was assigned to Fort Hood, TX to join the illustrious 1st Air Cavalry. He would spend 18 years in this storied unit as an AH-64 Apache pilot; deploying five times to engage in combat operations, while supporting the Global War on Terror.

Fox served in many assignments within the 1-227th Aviation Regiment over his distinguished career. However, the majority of his career, and all of his combat deployments were spent assigned to the "Reapers" of Bravo Company, 1-227th ARB. During his first combat tour, Fox was assigned as an AH-64D Standardization Instructor Pilot and Air Mission Commander. He was the flight lead for a team of four aircraft from the Regiment assigned to engage elements of the Medina Division of the Iraqi Republican Guard during the initial invasion of Iraq on the 23rd of March, 2003. During the Battle of Al Hillah, the Regiments aircraft were heavily damaged in a hornet's nest of anti-aircraft fire. One of his team's aircraft was shot down and the pilots captured by Iraqi forces. The other three were heavily damaged; two of which returned to base making emergency landings, while Fox's severely damaged aircraft remained on station attempting to engage targets amidst the intense fire.

Fox experienced intensified fighting across all regions of Iraq, during his second and third tours, as part of Task Force Attack during "The Insurgency" and the 1st Air Cavalry Brigade during "The Surge". Fox fought over Baghdad, Fallujah, An Najaf, Karbala, Ramadi, Al Kut and many other locations. During that time the 1st AIR CAV fortified its historical reputation as the force to call to honor and preserve the sacred bond of trust with the forces they support on the ground. His fourth tour to Iraq saw the comparatively peaceful transition to Iraqi governance and more of a security role emerging.

Fox completed his time in service at Fort Hood as the Command Chief Warrant Officer and Brigade Standardization Instructor Pilot for the 166th Aviation Brigade, Division West. His unit was responsible for the mobilization, training and deployment of National Guard and Reserve aviation forces to the theater. His deployment to Afghanistan in this role had him in numerous locations including Kabul, Kandahar, Jalalabad and Mazari Sharif.

Fox's complete operational history includes deployments supporting missions along the DMZ in South Korea; Operation Intrinsic Action; Operation Iraqi Freedom; OIF II; OIF 06-08; OIF 09-10; and Operation Enduring Freedom XI. His flight qualifications include the UH-1 Iroquois, OH-58A/CS Kiowa and AH-64A/D/E variants of the Longbow Apache. He is multi-engine turbine rated, Standardization Instructor Pilot, Instrument Flight Examiner and Forward Air Controller (Airborne) qualified. He has logged in excess of 5,000 flight hours with a large portion accumulated during combat operations.

CW4 Fox's awards and decorations include: The Bronze Star Medal, three awards of the Air Medal for "Valor", three additional awards of the Air Medal, two Meritorious Service Medals, the Army Commendation Medal for "Valor", five additional awards of the Army Commendation Medal, six awards of the Army Achievement Medal, two awards of the National Defense Service Medal, the Afghanistan Campaign Medal with Campaign Star, the Iraqi Campaign Medal with Six Campaign Stars, the Global War On Terrorism Expeditionary Medal, the Global War On Terrorism Service Medal, the Korean Defense Service Medal, the NATO ISAF Medal, the Joint Meritorious Unit Award, the Meritorious Unit Citation, and the Navy Unit Commendation. He earned the Combat Action Badge, the Master Army Aviator Wings and the Air Assault Badge. He has also been inducted into the American Combat Aviation Hall of Fame and awarded the Bronze Order of Saint Michael.

Fox retired in November 2013 after 21 years of service. He now trains pilots for the US Army and foreign countries who fly the AH-64E Apache helicopter. He married Amy Fox in 1997, and they have two children, Sydney and Carl.

DAVID H. FOX was born in 1949 at Monroe, MI. He graduated from Airport High School in 1967, enlisted at Fort Wayne, Detroit, MI and attended Boot Camp at Fort Knox, KY. He took Inf. Training at Fort Polk, LA. He was stationed with 793rd BN at Bamburg, Germany, and served with Infantry in Vietnam, 1st Cavalry plus spent six weeks in Cambodia.

Fox received the following medals: CIB, ARCOM "V," Air Medal and three BSM.

Memorable experience was finding a cache buried in Cambodia of fragmentation grenades and rifles.

Fox was discharged as Sgt. E-5 at Fort Dix, NJ

He worked as a machine repairman for Ford Motor Company until retiring in august 2007.

David and Robin Fox have two children, David D. Fox and Shawna L. Poore and granddaughter Olivia.

WILLIAM W. "BILL" FRANKLIN enlisted in the Regular Army on Jan. 5, 1959, out of Florida State University and reported to Fort Jackson, SC for Basic Training. He was born in Miami, FL on Oct. 7, 1939, graduated from Miami Senior High, attended FSU and later graduated from the University of Miami under the GI Bill.

In 1959 he met his future wife, Sara Walker, while attending Ordnance Guided Missile School at Redstone Arsenal, AL. They were married on June 11, 1960 in Guntersville, AL while he was assigned to White Sands Missile Range, NM. Their son, Mike, was born in El Paso, TX in 1961 and their daughter, Kim, in 1963 in Huntsville, AL.

He reached the rank of E-5, before being commissioned a 2nd Lt. Infantry through OCS in June 1964. In 1965 he was assigned to the 2nd Infantry Div. (11th Air Assault Test) at Fort Benning, GA. His unit was reflagged as the 1st Cavalry Division Airmobile in July 1965 and at that time he became the 3rd Platoon Leader, Company C, 1st Battalion, 7th Cavalry Regiment. He deployed to South Vietnam in August 1965 where he was severely wounded during the Battle of the la Drang Valley at Landing Zone Xray, Nov. 14-16, 1965. A book entitled *We Were Soldiers Once and Young* by LTG Harold Moore and civilian Joseph Galloway makes mention several places about Lt. Franklin. A Mel Gibson/Randy Wallace movie, "We Were Soldiers" told the story of the 1/7th at LZ Xray. Through the years Bill has spent many hours speaking to various groups about this story, especially to high school students and civic organizations.

Franklin holds a Combat Infantryman Badge, Bronze Star with V for Valor, Purple Heart, Army Commendation Medal, Vietnam Campaign Medal w/60 Device, National Defense Service Medal, Vietnam Cross of Gallantry with palm, Presidential Unit Citation, Good Conduct Medal, Aviator and Parachutist Badges, proudly has an early Green Beret made of wool in the USA, and in November 2015 was inducted into the Order of St. Maurice (Centurion) at Fort Benning, GA.

Franklin was a Private Pilot before he was both a Fixed Wing and a Rotor *Wing Pilot.* He was also a Sport Parachutist before he was a military parachutist. He left active duty Dec. 29, 1967 as a Captain to pursue a career in both business and aviation. He was an A Team Commander in the 20th Special Forces (Reserves), while continuing his college education. Later he became an Airline Transport Pilot and worked for both Pan American World Airways and Delta Airlines. Before, after and in between the airlines he flew as a corporate and a charter pilot. He has been a Flight Instructor for some 45 plus years and continued in the Army Reserves, retiring in December 1990 as a LTC/O-5. His last years in aviation were spent as an FAA Aviation Safety Inspector (Pilot) working out of the Miami, FL office. It seems that he went full circle as he was born and raised there and started his flying as a senior in high school. Now he and his wife of 56 years reside in Melbourne, FL and he continues to fly his Mooney, M20K airplane. In Orlando, he enjoys his grandchildren, Hannah and Sarah "Abby" and visits often Jennifer and Kristin, who reside in Huntsville, AL.

RALPH C. "COREY" FRATES JR. was born in San Francisco, CA and graduated form Fullerton Union High School in 1961. He later graduated from Stanford University (1965) and the Tulane University School of Medicine (1969).

Corey enlisted at Ft. Sam Houston, TX and attended AMEDD Officer Basic Training and Parachute Training. He was stationed at Ft. Bragg, NC, Phu Bai, RVN, and was in RVN during the Easter Offensive, 1972.

He received the Bronze Star, ARCOM with "V" device, Novice Parachute Badge, and Combat Medic Badge. He was discharged at Oakland Army Terminal in April 1972.

Corey is married to Sarah A. Burnett.

GORDON M. GARNER was born in a log house in Gordon County, GA, on 12 March 1941. In 1946, his family moved to a farm in Whitfield County, GA, where he, his brothers and sisters attended Valley Point School. On 3 Nov. 1959, he enlisted in the US Army and was sent to Ft. Jackson, SC for basic training, then to Ft. Benning, GA for advanced infantry training (AIT). After AIT, he was sent to Korea and served as a gunner on the 4.2 inch mortar and Forward Observer (FO) for the 81 mm. mortar in Mortar Battery and E Co., 2nd BG, 4th Cavalry, 1st Cavalry Division.

He went back to Ft. Benning to 1st Infantry Bde and served as gunner on 4.2 inch mortar and squad leader in combat support company. He served another tour in Korea with HHC 2nd BG 34th Infantry as Fire Direction Center (FDC) for 4.2 inch mortar. In September 1963, he returned to Ft. Benning to help form the 11th Air Assault Division (AAD) and served as squad leader and FDC for 4.2 inch mortar in D Co., 188th Infantry, 11th AAD.

In August 1965, Garner, along with the entire 1st Cavalry Division, went to Vietnam and set up base camp near An Khe in central highlands. He served with B Co., 2nd Battalion, 5th Cavalry, the first relief unit for the 1st Battalion, 7th Cavalry Regiment in the Battle of Ia Drang Valley at and near LZ X-ray in November. In Feb. 1966, his battalion was involved in Operation Tiger Paw near Bong Son, where many men were killed and wounded.

Garner received shrapnel wounds to both legs, arms, his face and chest, with such severe damage to his head and ears from the explosions that he was medically reclassified and served the next 18 years with the Army Corps of Engineers, where he served as instructor at the Army Engineer School at Ft. Belvoir, VA, from 1975-80, and finishing his career at Redstone Arsenal, AL, as technical advisor to the Alabama, Mississippi, and Tennessee Army Reserve and National Guard.

His awards and decorations include the VN Service Medal, CIB, Purple Heart, RVN Campaign Medal, RVN Cross of Gallantry with Palm, MSM, Good Conduct Medal 8th Award, Army Commendation Medal with 3 OLC, Expert Badge with Rifle, M1, M16, BAR, 81 mm, and 4.2 inch mortar.

Garner married Louise Manis on June 5, 1962. They have two grown children: Billy, who is a Veteran of Desert Storm with an artillery unit, and Janice.

He retired from the Army in November 1983 with the rank of Master Sergeant. After retirement, he worked for Carriage Carpets and spent several years working for Outboard Marine Corporation (OMC) in Calhoun, GA. After OMC closed, Garner enrolled in college and got a degree in Construction Management at Coosa Valley Technical College, where he graduated with highest honors with a GPA of 4.0.

He is a lifetime member of the American Legion, DAV, VFW, and Military Order of the Purple Heart, where he has served as Commander of Chapter 525 in Rome, GA, for the past four years. In his spare time he hunts, fishes, and volunteers with Habitat for Humanity, helping the organization plan and build safe, affordable houses for deserving families

ROBERT W. GAUTIER, SR. enlisted in 1941 and briefly served with the 117th Infantry, 30th Infantry Division. After attending OCS, he was then sent to the 346th Infantry, 87th Infantry Division in the Eastern Theater of Operations.

Robert W. Gautier, Sr., Robert W. Gautier, Jr., and Robert W. Gautier III.

He left active duty in October 1945. He was recalled in September 1950, assigned to the 61st Infantry, 8th Infantry Division. He served in Far East Command (FECOM), both in Japan and Korea, with the 7th Cavalry Regiment (Garry Owen), 1st Cavalry Division until May 1952. Later assignments were with the Mississippi Military District, ADSEC (Advanced Section/European Theater of Operations) in Verdun, France, and the 3241st USAR Logistical Command. He retired as a Lieutenant Colonel commanding the 486th Chemical Battalion. He received the Combat Infantryman's Badge (2nd award), Bronze Star Medal, Army Commendation Medal, ETO Campaign Medal, Korean Service Medal, United Nations Korea Service Medal, and numerous other awards. In civilian life, he worked for Hamilton Beach-Scoville and retired as a plant manager.

ROBERT W. GAUTIER, JR. enlisted in February 1966. After attending OCS, he went to Vietnam in December 1967, serving with the 34th General Support Group. He then extended my tour and was assigned to A Company, 159th Assault Support Helicopter Battalion, 101st Airborne Division. He extended again and was assigned to HHC, 3rd Brigade (Garry Owen), 1st Cavalry Division. He returned from Vietnam in February 1970 and left active duty in March 1972, returning to the active reserve in 1974.

After completion of the Special Forces Qualification Course, Gautier was assigned to C Co, 3rd Battalion, 11th Special Forces Group, in April 1975. Upon promotion to Major, he was assigned to the United States Army Institute for Military Assistance as an instructor at the Special Forces School. In December 1980, he vacated his commission and reverted back to my NCO grade, returning to C/3/11 SFGA, as a light weapons sergeant. In June 1981, he transferred to the 824th Quartermaster Company (AD) and became Rigger qualified, attending Pathfinder school in 1984.

He deployed to Desert Storm in December 1990, as a Platoon Sergeant with the 861st Quartermaster Company. During this deployment, he was assigned as the NCOIC of a small provisional Pathfinder detachment assigned to the US Embassy in Kuwait. Upon return from Desert Storm, he was promoted to Master Sergeant and assigned to the 360th Civil Affairs Brigade (Airborne) as the Senior Intelligence Sergeant. In May 1994, he returned to the 824th QM Co as the First Sergeant. In August 1997, he transferred to HHC, United States Army Civil Affairs Command (Airborne) as an Operations Sergeant.

Gautier retired in June 2000 as a Major. He received the Combat Infantry Badge, Air Crewmember Badge, Master Parachute Badge, Rigger Badge, Pathfinder Badge, Special Forces tab, Bronze Star (1 OLC), Air Medal (3), Army Commendation Medal (1 OLC), Army Achievement Medal (3 OLC), Viet Nam Service Medal, Viet Nam Campaign Medal with 60 device, Southwest Asia Service Medal, Kuwait Liberation Medal, Vietnam Cross of Gallantry with palm, and numerous other awards. He has also been awarded Navy/USMC, Spanish, Australian, Belgian, German, and Ecuadorian jump wings.

He graduated from North Carolina Wesleyan College, in 1980, with a BA in Business Administration and retired as a Production Manager from Abbott Laboratories. His son, Major Robert W. Gautier III, enlisted in the Army in June 1992 and served four years with the 82nd Abn. Division, later serving as a rigger with the 824th Quartermaster Co. (AD) while attending East Carolina University, before graduating from Naval OCS and serving in the submarine service with the US *Parche* (SSN683). In 2005, Gautier III returned to the Army as an Intelligence Officer, serving two tours in Iraq with the 1st Infantry Division and 502nd Military Intelligence Battalion. He retired as a Major in October 2015 and is pursuing a career as an Army JROTC instructor.

RONALD D. GAYLER enlisted in the Army in 1968 after graduating from Northwest Missouri State University. After basic and AIT training, he entered Infantry OCS at Fort Benning, GA receiving his commission as an infantry second lieutenant. He then entered Army Rotary Wing flight school at Fort Wolters, TX finishing at Fort Rucker, AL. After receiving his wings, Ron was sent to Vietnam where he spent a year flying for A/229th AHB, First Cavalry Division. After 30 days in country, he was made aircraft commander and spent the rest of his tour flying as A/229's flight leader (Yellow One).

Returning to the States, he spent a year at Fort Riley, KS where he received his discharge. After a short time crop dusting in Missouri, Ron joined PHI in Lafayette, LA and flew in support of the offshore oil industry. During his career, he flew in the Gulf of Mexico, Saudi Arabia, Egypt, Somalia, California and Ghana, Africa. Retiring from PHI he formed RG International and does consulting work for the offshore helicopter industry.

An avid golfer Ron and his wife, Barbara, live in south Louisiana ("Where I can play golf 12 months out of the year"). They have three grown children: Randy, Erin and Jessica plus two grandchildren.

JOHN G. "JOHNNY" GERGULIS was commissioned in the US Army INFANTRY upon graduation from The Citadel in 1959, entering active military service at Fort Jackson, SC upon completion of Basic INFANTRY Officer's Course and AIRBORNE Training, Fort Benning, GA. He had no intention at the time to remain in the Army!

As a young lieutenant, he COMMANDED several Training Companies, served as Training Battalion XO, Regimental S-3 and Headquarters Commandant. Requesting Viet Nam duty, he was instead sent to Korea. There he served as Battle Group S-2/Assistant S-3, Company COMMANDER and later, Battalion Headquarters Commandant. Returning to CONUS, was assigned to the 11th Air Assault Division (TEST), 1st Battalion (AIRBORNE), 18th Infantry ('Rakkasans'), Fort Benning, GA. After duty as Company XO, S-2/Assistant S-3, took COMMAND of 'Delta' Company, July 1964. Deferred from attending Advanced INFANTRY Course, he COMMANDED 'Delta' Company (Reorganized as 'D' Company, 1st Battalion (AIRBORNE-Air Assault), 12th Cavalry, 1st Cavalry Division (AIRMOBILE). 'D' Company deployed to RVN summer 1965, debarking USNS *Geiger*, being first unit to put AIRBORNE 'Boots on the beaches of Qui Nhon', en-route base camp Anke, central highlands, Hwy 19. Gergulis COMMANDED 'D' Company until 1966 when he was assigned as Battalion S-4. Medically evacuated to the States summer 1966, he completed deferred schooling at Fort Benning and was selected for Aide de Camp duties in Washington, DC. Requesting voluntary re-assignment to Viet Nam, 1968, he served as Senior Battalion Advisor, 21st ARVN Division, Soc Trang (Can Tho), Four Corps Tactical Zone. Medically evacuated to Saigon, he was re-assigned to COMUSMACV Command Center, as Three Corps 'Operations Officer.' Attended Command & General Staff College, Fort Leavenworth, KS, 1969.

He was assigned as US Army INFANTRY (AIRBORNE-Air Assault) Exchange Officer to British Army, served two years in office of Director, British Army Infantry, British Army Infantry School. Gergulis was reassigned to Washington, DC duty in office of Deputy CIS (Operations), Pentagon, summer 1972. Served as Chief, Capitol Rotunda Detail and Escort Officer, Joint Chiefs of Staff (JCS), State Funeral, President L.B. Johnson. Late 1974, selected for Battalion COMMAND, reported for duty with Berlin Brigade, assigned as COMMANDER, 2d Battalion (Reinforced-'C' Battery, 94th Artillery), 6th US INFANTRY (Mechanized). Selected to attend Army War College (AWC), Carlisle Barracks, Pennsylvania; reported for schooling summer 1976. While there, earned graduate degree (MS, Public Administration) from Shippensburg University. Reporting to Headquarters XVIII AIRBORNE Corps-Fort Bragg, NC, served as Corps Chief of Plans. Duty as Command Briefer, his 'Team' developed the Rapid Deployment Corps concept that led to the Rapid Deployment Joint Task Force (RDJTF) [Today, Central Command & Special Operations Command] development. Reassigned to MacDill, Air Force Base as 'Special Assistant', Commander, RDJTF, 1980, was selected to serve as EXECUTIVE OFFICER, office CINC US Readiness Command/Joint Deployment Agency (JDA)/RDJTF. Selected for BRIGADE Command, Gergulis COMMANDED the Armor Heavy 'Thundering Third Herd' (Mechanized), Mannheim, FRG 1981-1983. Reassigned again to Pentagon Army Staff duty, he requested early retirement, retiring from Dwight D. Eisenhower Medical Center, Fort Gordon, GA, 1985 as Colonel (0-6).

He was awarded COMBAT INFANTRY Badge, Expert INFANTRY Badge, MASTER Parachutist Badge, AIR ASSAULT Badge, Army STAFF Badge, British Paratrooper Badge, German Paratrooper Badge/Legion of Merit/Bronze Star Medal w/V and three Clusters/Air Medal w/V and two clusters, Army Commendation Medal w/four clusters, Army Meritorious Service Medal w/four Clusters, Viet Nam Gallantry Cross w/Palm, Viet Nam Gallantry Cross w/Gold Star, Defense Meritorious Service Medal, Joint Services Commendation Medal, Korean Defense Service Medal, Viet Nam Defense Service Medal, Presidential Unit Citation w/cluster, Army Meritorious Unit Citation, Korean Presidential Unit Citation, ARVN Gallantry Cross Unit Citation, National Defense Service Medal, World War II Occupation Medal, and numerous other Ribbons.

Post retirement, he taught at local public schools, at undergraduate and graduate college programs, served in operations-business management positions, Florida Department of Corrections, and finally 'retired-retired' from defense contracting management in 1992. Until his wife's death, together they operated three small businesses (book store, antiques-collectibles, ceramics) in the Tampa area.

Married to Helen English Gergulis in 1961, Manning, SC. Son, Kenneth, was born 1964. Mrs. Gergulis unexpectedly passed away in 1995. In 2005, Colonel John G. Gergulis married Babes Struhs. Their extended family includes son Kenneth, Tampa, FL; step-daughter Alisa K. S. McLean; step-son Craig H. Struhs, SC and numerous (too many to attempt to name here!!) nephews, nieces, grandchildren and great-grandchildren.

Colonel and Mrs. Gergulis reside in Columbia, SC, a short distance from Fort Jackson.

Both remain active in Military (Veteran) affairs, attending 1st Cavalry Division, 12th Cavalry Regiment and 'D' Company, 1st Battalion (AIRBORNE-Air Assault), 1st Cavalry Division (AIRMOBILE), annual 'REUNIONS' with Our Viet Nam 'Brothers'.

In their spare time (?), they enjoy travelling, boating-fishing, hunting, participating in Church activities and attending official functions at The Citadel in Charleston, SC.

ROY "CHIEF" GIBBENS enlisted Jan. 25, 1967 at Denver MEPS, Denver, CO. After Boot Camp at Fort Bliss, TX he took AIT Artillery Basic Training at Fort Sill, OK in 1967.

Other bases Gibbens assigned to: Fort Bliss, TX; Fort Sill, OK; Fort Carson, CO; 25th Infantry Division, Vietnam; Bamberg, Germany; 1st Cavalry Division, HHC 1st CAV, Division HQ, Vietnam and Fort Carson, CO.

He was in battles at Fire Base Dusty Danger, A Battery 1st BN 11th ARTY, 1969; Vietnam Counter Offensive Phase III, 1967-1968; two years Vietnam Service; TET Counter Offensive, 1968 and Unnamed Campaign. 1968.

Gibbens received Air Metal, Army Commendation, Army Achievement, Army Good Conduct, NDSM(2), Army Reserve Compo Ach. Medal with one oak leaf, Vietnam Service Medal with one silver star, Republic of Vietnam Campaign Medal, Army Service Medal, NCO Professional Development with three devices, Air Force Longevity with 3 oak leaves and Republic of Vietnam Gallantry Cross with PALM Unit Citation.

Gibbens was discharged in September 1997,153 CES, Cheyenne, WY with the rank of E-7 Master Sergent.

Others jobs included Larmier County Sheriff's Department, Fort Collins, CO; Conway County Sheriff's Department, Morrilton, AR; Hill Creek Fire Department, Plumerville, AR and Conway County Hospital Security, Conway, AR.

He is a Member of National Sheriffs Association, American Jailers Association, National Hospital Safety and Security and a Life member of VFW and DAV.

Having retired in 2012 he is active in Church, raising a granddaughter, HAM radio and travel.

Children of Roy and Linda are Roy Gene Gibbens, Mark Gibbens, Connie Gibbens, Leah Griffin and Ryan Griffin. Grandchildren are Anthony, Jadon, Tokah, Gabby, Rosemarie, Gianna, Anica, Annelisse, Penner, Charles, Michael and Hunter.

CHUCK GIETZ began his military career at Ft. Hamilton, NY, in 1966. WO Flight School was not available at this time so the enlisted Flight Operations Specialist was selected. During basic training at Ft. Jackson, SC, he qualified for Office Candidate School (OCS) and Rotary Wing Flight Training. Upon completion of Advanced Infantry Training and OCS Prep school at Ft. Ord, CA, Gietz was transferred to Ft. Sill, OK for Artillery and Missile OCS in November 1966.

After receiving his Commission as a 2nd Lieutenant in May 1967, Gietz spent six months serving in various position in the 2/36 FA Battalion before flight training began at Ft. Wolters, TX and Ft. Rucker, AL in November 1967. Gietz completed flight training and was designated an Army Aviator in July 1968. Gietz's Vietnam tour with the 1st Air Cavalry Division began in August 1968. Assignment with C/227 Avn Bn began at the Division HQ in An Khe in II Corp, continued at Camp Evans in I Corp and finished at Phouc Vinh, just north of Bien Hoa in III Corp. Counteroffensive, Phase IV, Phase V, Phase VI and Tet 69/ Counteroffensive were the four Campaigns Gietz supported as a mission pilot of a UH-1H (HUEY) helicopter. Both combat and combat support missions were a daily occurrence. Gietz flew missions as the Reaction Force Flight Leader (Yellow One) as well as logistical resupply, command and control and medical evacuation missions. He served as a Flight Section Leader, Platoon Leader and Flight Operations Officer before his tour was complete in August 1969.

Gietz was awarded the Bronze Star Medal and 33 Air Medals and the Valorous Unit Citation for his efforts in Vietnam. Gietz retired from the military in April 2000 after serving as an AGR Officer and Executive Officer in the Aviation Brigade, 42 Infantry Division of the New York Army National Guard.

He has two sons, Steven and Adam, four grandchildren and resides with his wife Linda in Florida.

RICHARD "DICK" H. GILL enlisted in May 1961 in Chicago, IL and took Boot Camp at Fort Leonard Wood, MO. He received his high school GED in 1962 at USAFI Japan, attended Rockford, IL College (1966), Bailey Technical School, St. Louis, MO (1967), Central Community College, Columbus, NE (1972) and Southeast Community College, Milford, NE (1985). He also took MOS 632.20 at Armor School, Fort Knox, KY.

He served with the 23rd Trans. Bn. in Korea and 3rd Prov Armored Maint in Germany.

Dick received the National Defense Medal and Marksman .30 CAL Carbine medal.

Memorable experiences included travel in the Far East and Europe while in the military on transport planes and troop transport ships.

PFC E-3 Gill was discharged in May 1964 at New York Port Authority.

He worked for 38 years as a drafting tech for Nebraska Public Power District, retiring in 2008. He is affiliated with Institute for Certification of Engineering Technicians.

He spends retirement time on woodcarving, yard work and his "to do list."

Dick and Patricia were married in 1969 and have five children: Kathleen, Richard, Sarah, Elisabeth and Heather. Grandchildren are Alex, Alana, Gabrielle, Emma, Madelyn and Harlen.

ALBERT "TONY" A. GILLETTE, born in 1949, graduated in 1967 from St. Mary's High School and obtained an Associate Degree from Oakland Community College in 1973.

On Sept. 10, 1969 Gillette enlisted at Royal Oak, MI. After Boot Camp at Fort Knox, KY he also attended Radio/Telephone School.

He was stationed at Fort Gordon, GA and was in battle Bearcat in Vietnam.

He was awarded the Army Commendation.

His memorable experience was flying in Chinooks.

On April 21, 1971 Gillette was discharged with the rank of E-4 at Oakland, CA.

Tony worked in Michigan and California and affiliated with American Trucking Association.

Retiring in 2003, he enjoys fishing, travel and model railroading.

He is married to Holly.

ARTHUR "ART" S. GINSBERG, born in 1949 in Bronx, NY, graduated from Columbus High School in 1967. He attended New York University, obtaining a BS in February 1976 and MA in June 1977.

Ginsberg was drafted in March 1969 in New York City. After AIT and Boot Camp at Fort Jackson, SC he took training at Fort Benning, GA in August 1969. In March 1970 he was at the Cambodian border – Viet Nam.

He was awarded a Purple Heart and Army Commendation with V device (March 15, 1970), CIB, Vietnam Campaign and Service Medal, Good Conduct and National Defense Service Medal.

Ginsberg was discharged August 21, 1970 as a corporal.

In retirement he enjoys traveling in the US and Canada and target shooting.

Art and Genevieve were married in 1973.

PAUL "TOP" GIRARD was born in 1939 in Providence, RI. He graduated from Mt. Pleasant in 1956.

After enlisting at Providence, RI and Boot Camp at Fort Dix, NJ, he had training in Advanced Infantry.

Girard was stationed at Fort Benning, GA, among others, and was engaged in battles in Pleiku, Vietnam.

He was awarded a Bronze Star, Good Conduct Medal, National Defense Medal, CIB and Jump Wings.

His memorable experience was being a dog handler with combat tracker, Scout.

Girard was discharged in 1986 at Fort Devens, MA as a first sergeant – E8.

BRUCE GLEASON enlisted in the Army band program in Fargo, North Dakota in September 1988 after serving for six years as a school band and choir director in Kennedy, Minnesota—and after completing a B.A. in music from Crown College and a B.S. and M.A. in music education from the University of Minnesota. Following basic training at Fort Dix, New Jersey, he completed the Army Basic Course at the Armed Forces School of Music at the Naval Amphibious Base in Norfolk, Virginia. From there he headed for Berlin, Germany in May 1989 where he played euphonium and trombone for military and civic ceremonies, parades and concerts with the 298th U.S. Army Band.

Memorable Army experiences include witnessing the opening of the Berlin Wall on the evening of 9 November 1989 with Tom Brokaw and the NBC cameras broadcasting to the world that history was in the making.

A year later during reunification week in October 1990, Gleason was part of a concert featuring the massed bands of the four Allied Powers comprised of the 298th U.S. Army Band, the British Light Infantry Corunna Band, the French La Musique du 46 éme Régiment d'infanterie and the U.S.S.R. Grand Ensemble of the West Forces. Performing for an audience of an estimated one million people, this band of two hundred musicians played a variety of music in the historic Lustgarten, across Unter den Linden from where Hitler had hosted book burnings at the Opernplatz, which in turn was next to the site of the Stadtschloss from where Frederick the Great and other Hohenzollerns had ruled.

Gleason received the Army Service Ribbon; National Defense Service Medal; Overseas Service Ribbon; Army of Occupation Medal (Army-Air Force); Sharpshooter Marksmanship Badge Rifle, M-16; Sharpshooter Marksmanship Badge Grenade; and the German Marksmanship Badge, Bronze.

Following his Army discharge, Gleason completed a Ph.D. in music education at the University of Iowa in 1995. Since 1999 he has lived in St. Paul, Minnesota where he is a professor of music education and music history at the University of St. Thomas.

For the past 30 years, Dr. Gleason has researched and written on the tradition of military music—resulting in over 25 publications, including the article, "Bands and Music" in the *Encyclopedia of Military Science* (Sage, 2013) and the book, *Sound the Trumpet, Beat the Drums: Horse-Mounted Bands of the U.S. Army, 1820 – 1940* (University of Oklahoma Press, 2016). He has been a member of the 1st Cavalry Division Association with the Walter H. Westman – Northland Chapter in Blaine, Minnesota for 15 years.

THOMAS N. GORMAN was born Oct. 14, 1944 in Brackton, MA and graduated from Albany Union High School in 1963. He enlisted at Albany, OR and took Boot Camp at Fort Ord, CA. Additional training was 13A10.

He was stationed with "1" Air Cav at An Khe and engaged in L.Q., Phu Cat and Kontum Prov., Pleiku Prov., Plei Me, and Bong Son.

He received the Army Commendation Medal for service.

Memorable experience was being a 1/77 FA, and Concret-19 out.

E-6 Gorman was discharged at Salem, OR.

He worked for Marion Auto Glass, retiring in 2004. His retirement activities include the Northwest Veterans Motorcycle Club. Thomas has two children, Cory and Cherae.

CHRISTOPHER JAMES "KIPPY" GRAY was born on Oct. 27, 1949 in Seattle WA. Kippy, as his family called him, was the fourth son of Wayne and Priscilla Gray. On August 6 1967, Kippy graduated from Queen Anne High School in Seattle, WA. The day after graduation Kippy went to a local Seattle recruiter and enlisted in the US Army.

Kippy's first set of orders were to report to Company A, 2nd Battalion, 2nd Brigade for eight weeks of basic at Fort Lewis, WA. After graduation from basic training, PVT Gray reported to transportation school for UH-IA helicopter repair at Fort Eustis, VA on Oct. 13, 1967. This school consisted of 11 weeks of single-rotor turbine utility helicopter repair, which Kippy completed on Feb. 5, 1968. His training continued at Hunter Army Airfield, Fort Stewart, GA on Feb. 12, 1968. Kippy was assigned to Co. "L" 4th Aircraft Maintenance Battalion. Following his training at Hunter Army Airfield, newly rank PFC3 Gray was given a leave to visit his family in Seattle. On Sept. 5, 1968, Kippy left McChord Air Force Base in Lakewood, WA and arrived in Cam Ranh Bay, Vietnam.

Soon after arriving PFC3 Gray received orders to report to the 1st Air Cav. Division, stationed at Quang Tri. We understand Kippy was originally with 1st of the 5th in weapons but later volunteered for Scouts with troop A, 1st of the 9th.

Kippy completed his first tour of duty in September 1969. He then requested an extension of his combat duty an additional six months. At the time Kippy stated, "To do more than the minimum effort," as his reasoning for the request.

Specialist 5, Chris Gray, was killed in action on Dec. 21, 1969 near Tay Ninh Province. Kippy was a door gunner of a scout helicopter when it was shot down. Those who died with Kippy were the pilot, Warrant Officer Thaddeus Yonika, and Specialist 4 Barry Kaletta, working as an observer. Kippy rests at Fort Lawton Military Cemetery in Seattle, WA. Fort Lawton Cemetery is just two miles from the home where Kippy was raised.

Kippy left behind a grieving but very proud Gold Star Family. His family includes his parents, Wayne and Priscilla, three brothers and two sisters, one of whom is his twin. Some of his family has attended reunions of the 1st Cav. at Ft. Hood, TX and for Troop A 1st of the 9th in Whitefish, MT. A constant theme of these reunions was the warm welcome of the Gray family with open arms by the Troopers. The family has always considered it a great honor and privilege to meet many of Kippy's fellow Troopers.

Staff Sergeant Chris Gray was awarded the following medals for his service: two Air Medals, Aircraft Crewman Badge, Distinguished Flying Cross 1st Oak leaf Cluster 32 to Follow, two Purple Hearts, Bronze Star and Military Merit Medal from the Republic of Vietnam.

COL. JOE E. GRAY was born Nov. 19, 1929, in Lawrenceville, IL. He received a Bachelor of Science degree from the Missouri School of Mines and Metallurgy He was a member of Sigma Nu fraternity and Theta Tau engineering fraternity.

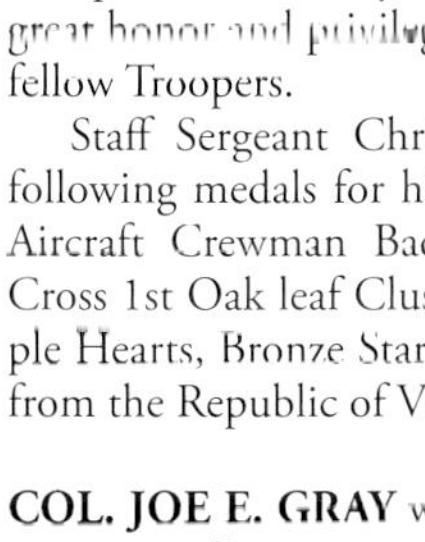

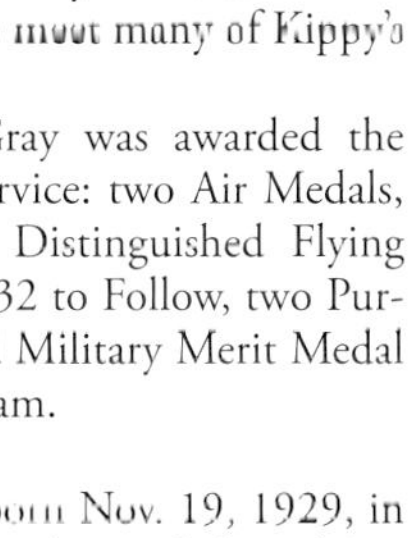

Colonel Gray, a Corps of Engineers officer, retired after an active and reserve duty career spanning 32 years. He served overseas tours in Germany, Libya, Iran, Central America and Vietnam as a member of the First Cavalry Division Col. Gray was awarded the Bronze Star with V device, Presidential Unit Citation, Vietnam Cross of Gallantry, Vietnam Campaign Medal, Air Medal with 18 OLC, Army Commendation Medal, Army of Occupation Medal, Meritorious Service Medal, US Army Reserve Achievement Medal, Armed Forces Reserve Medal, Government of Guatemala Honor al Merito Medal, and the 2012 Congressional Veteran Commendation.

Colonel Gray joined Bell Helicopter Textron in 1968 and held many marketing management positions during his 26 years working in Fort Worth, California and Singapore. He was instrumental in the introduction of the Bell models 212, 412, 222 and the 214ST. He retired in 1993.

Joe was a 2012 world record setter with the Masters of South Texas Relay Team in the 4-x-200 free relay.

Joe went to Heaven on Sept. 11, 2015. Survivors include his wife of 60 years, Edith Krisel Gray, two sons and a daughter, and four grandchildren.

CHARLES GREEN was one of twelve children, with two older brothers already in the military, who grew up on an Indiana farm. Since his father had passed away and his mother was trying to keep the rest of the family safe on the farm, it was decided that he should enlist in the army. He was later told that he was the second youngest master sergeant in the far eastern command, at age seventeen, which was a lot of responsibility for a young man.

While attending NCO Leadership School, he stood honor guard for General Douglas Macarthur and Sigmon Rea. In about the second wave to Korea, on an LST, he became chief of the 99th artillery firing battery, with over 1,000 men under his command.

His tour was extended by then president Truman, and many of his experiences were to painful to talk about — the friends and comrades that were lost, no food, no clothes for the freezing weather, and all the other trauma of war. His records were destroyed in a fire in St Louis.

Charles died on Oct. 19, 2015 and suffered from PTSD after 50 years. It has also been determined that he had a Silver Star and possibility a Purple Heart that were never been awarded. *Submitted by his wife.*

MELVIN L. GREGORY entered basic training Fort Leonard Wood, MO September 1963. AIT at Fort Polk, LA jump school and 11th Air Assault at Fort Benning, GA. Constant training at Fort Benning , GA, including: advanced communications, crypto/repair. MOS's: light weapons, heavy weapons and communications. Cadred: US Colt 45, mines and booby traps and communication.

He served with A CO 2/5th Cavalry at Fort Benning, GA and Vietnam, 1965-1966. Arrived Qui Nhon, Vietnam Sept. 18, 1965 aboard the troop ship, *USS Buckner*.

He was involved in creation of 1st Air Cavalry base camp, Camp Radclif, An Khe Vietnam. The 1st Air Cavalry went to war minus an entire BTN of the 3rd Brigade. Due to the missing 3rd Brigade BTN, the 2nd Cavalry 5th (Black Knights) did double duty. Serving the assignment to the 2nd Brigade while also tasked with the duties of the missing BTN 3rd Brigade.

He participated in major campaigns: Silver Bayonet, Pleiku, Ia Drang, the book *We Were Soldiers Once and Young, Masher/White Wing*, Bong Son campaign; Kontum province; Bin Din province.

After discharge, June 18, 1966, majored in electronic engineering; minored in automatic control engineering.

Worked 34 years for McDonnell-Douglas aerospace and Boeing aerospace, in various capacities, requiring high level DOD security clearances. The first 18 years were spent in R & D (Research and Development).

Worked as a system analyst robotics - computer systems. Worked in lower level management. Worked on numerous missile, rocket and stealth projects. Worked in check out of Gemini space capsules. Worked on the first Heads Up Display (HUD) still being utilized by DOD 45 years later. Involved in training of systems analysts and lower level managers.

Worked for eight months for Monsanto in the development and manufacture of ICS's (integrated circuit chips).

Worked six months as manager of CATV, a local cable TV company.

F. DONALD "DON" GRIFFITH enlisted on Oct. 7, 1943 at Fort Benjamin Harrison, IN and took Boot Camp at Fort Sill, OK. He was stationed at Fort Sill, OK; Fort Ord, CA and Camp Stoneman, CA. He served in Asia – Pacific Theater, Bismarck Archipelago, New Guinea, Admiralty Island – Norilo, Philippine Islands Leyte and Luzon.

He was awarded the Asiatic-Pacific Theater with four Bronze Stars, Philippine Islands Liberation with two Bronze Stars, Good Conduct, World War II Victory Medal.

Memorable experiences included combat on Leyte and Luzon, seeing the masses of dead Japanese. On Luzon, being the first US personnel into Manila. And being in Tokyo Bay on Sept. 2, 1945 for the Japanese surrender. The sky full of US fighters and bombers, the bay crowded with US Navy ships including battleship *Missouri* where the surrender was signed.

Griffith was discharged on Jan. 31, 1946 at Camp Atterbury, IN as Corporal.

After graduating from Indiana Technical College in 1950, he joined the Engineering Unit of the local International Harvester Truck Plant. He retired in 1981.

Donald and Kate have two children, Beth Anne Adams and Michael Griffith, and two grandchildren, Donny and Ted Adams.

WILLIAM GROGAN was born 12 March 1949 in Passaic, NJ, and graduated from Vianney High in Kirkwood, MO, later earning a degree in Civil Engineering from Southern Illinois University – Edwardsville.

He enlisted in St. Louis, MO, in June 1968, taking basic and AIT at Ft. Leonard Wood, MO. Infantry OCS was a Ft. Benning, GA, from Nov. 1968 – Feb. 1969, until forced to resign due to injury. He arrived at Ahn Kae, Vietnam, March 1969 assigned to 3rd Platoon Co C 8th Engineer Bn Ist Air Cav Div.

He was then sent to Quanloi, Vietnam to join his company, and spent rest of year with line company constructing firebases and supporting our infantry companies when needed. Promoted to Sgt E5 and assigned to a squad in the 2nd Platoon. After Jan. 1969, was assigned as Company Operations Sgt to assist in coordinating unit missions in the field. Extended tour twice during 1970 and finally went home early Jan 1971. He was there for Tet 1969 Counter Offensive, Vietnam Summer Fall 1969, Vietnam Winter Spring 1970, Cambodia May 1970.

Discharged at Ft Leonard Wood Jan. 1971. Reenlisted in MO National Guard late 1983 assigned to S3 1138 Engineer BNH (Combat). Accepted a full time active duty position as Operations Sgt/Training NCO for Co D, 1138th EN BN Stayed active for about five years then returned to reserve status. By this time he was promoted to Sgt First Class (E7) as platoon Sgt for a combat engineer platoon. They were deployed to Central America numerous times to construct roads to remote villages. Also was sent to Alaska for road construction. His last mission with the guard was being sent with his unit to the 2002 Olympics in Salt Lake to support law Enforcement as security. Stayed with Missouri Guard until March 2002, when he retired as an E7. His total years with the military is 26.

Grogan's military awards include Bronze Star, Purple Heart, Awarded Army Commendation medal 4 times one time with "H" device for Heroism, Air Medal, Army Achievement Medal 3 times

In his retired life, he enjoyed riding his bicycle all over the United States. As of this writing, he has only eight states to go to have ridden in all 50 states. His proudest achievement was riding up over the Rocky Mountains in Colorado. He likes to fly fish and kayak on rivers in Missouri and soon in other parts of the country, and enjoys spending as much time with his grandchildren as he can.

DICK DeWAYNE GRUBE was born Feb. 9, 1933 in Punxsutawney, PA (the home of the groundhog) of Everett Norman Grube and Margaret Florence Van Kuren Grube Smith.

After graduating from Punxsutawney High School in 1951 he went to work for J.C. Penney. In 1952 he was drafted into the Army. After boot camp at Fort Indiantown Gap he was chosen for officer's candidate school (Fort Campbell, KY) and afterwards completed engineering school (Fort Belvoir, VA) and flight school, fixed and rotor (Fort Sill, OK). As Dick liked to say, "J.C. Penney's loss was The Army's gain."

A constant throughout all of Dick's life was his love for antiques and history. In all of his assignments he volunteered to help with museum displays - this will become more important in Dick's life post-retirement.

Dick met his future bride, Deanna Almina Cook, while in Colombia, South America. They married in 1958 and returned to the States in 1960.

Upon his return he assumed command of Corps of Engineers Company B stationed in Fort Meade, MD, spent that cold winter clearing the grandstands of snow for JFK's inauguration before heading to Korea in 1963.

In 1965 he went to Viet Nam, serving in the 1/9 Air Cav as Adjutant Sl/S2 and more importantly personal handler for "Maggie the Mule," the controversial mascot and Col. John Stockton's pride and joy. Upon Maggie's untimely demise at the hands of the USN, he gathered what was left of her droppings, varnished them and saved them to present to exiting dignitaries. During this assignment he was exposed to Agent Orange, which would eventually rob him of his hobbies, passion and life.

In 1966 he was stationed at Fort Rucker, AL on Boot Strap, where he earned his bachelor's degree at Troy University. In 1968 he and the family moved to Fort Amador, Canal Zone, Panama where he established the Garrison Museum at the end of the causeway. Those artifacts were later transferred to the National Infantry Museum at Fort Benning.

His terminal station of duty was Fort Benning, GA, where he was in charge of the range and became involved with the National Infantry Museum, which was housed in a small old wooden structure with a leaky roof.

In 1973, after his retirement as Lieutenant Colonel, he became the curator of this museum. In 1975, he oversaw the relocation to the former Martin Army Hospital building. The museum was a showplace as Grube often said, built, "not to glorify war but to honor the Soldier and allow the public to understand the Soldier as a human being." During his time as Curator and later Director, he personally oversaw the accumulation of most of the artifacts added to the National Infantry Museum's historic collection.

One of his proudest accomplishments was saving the World War II era buildings where General George Patton's troops lived and trained. These barracks, mess hall, orderly room, supply room and chapel are the only fully preserved set of Series 700 buildings in existence. They are located at the World War II Company Street exhibit at the new National Infantry Museum and Soldier Center, Fort Benning, GA. The museum was recently voted the number 1 free museum in the nation.

Grube was a member of MOWW, MOM, Friday Friars, Executive Club, former Chair of the Historical Chattahoochee Commission. He served on the boards of Columbus Symphony, Columbus Arts Council, Port Columbus (Civil War Naval Museum), the Golden Boys Investment Club, the Chattahoochee River Club, Westville, Toastmaster's and was a 32nd degree Mason. He was named an honorary member of the Punxsutawney Groundhog Society for promotion of prognostication throughout the world celebrating Groundhog's day (Feb. 2) everywhere he lived including Colombia, Korea, Vietnam, Panama and Columbus, GA where he hosted an annual celebration at their home.

Medals he received were US Commendation Medal, multiple Bronze Stars, Air Medal, Legion of Merit, three overseas bars, National Defense Service Medal with OLC, Army Aviators Badge, Armed Forces Reserve Medal (second award), Good Conduct Medal, Sr. Army Aviator Badge, Army Commendation Medal with Oak Leaf Cluster, Master Army Aviator Badge, Presidential Unit Citation, Meritorious Service Medal and The Order of Saint Maurice, Primicerius — the highest level medal the National Infantry Association awards to Civilians.

He was married to Deanna Almina Cook Grube for 51 years. Children (spouses) are: Elizabeth Arthur Grube Cullinan (Steven Paul Sr.), Margaret Ann Grube Taylor (Michael Dowd) and Jennifer Deanna Grube Brown (Richard). Grandchildren are Kathryn Deanna Cullinan Moore (Christopher), Steven Paul Cullinan Jr. (Marissa), Kevin Patrick Cullinan, Meredith Welch Taylor, Elizabeth Abigail Brown and Andrew Pelham.

JON K. GUTIERREZ graduated from East Tennessee State University in 1996.

He served in Bosnia, Stabilization Force – 5, in 1999.

LTC HENRY "HANK" S. HALE JR. was born May 29, 1947 in St. Louis, MO, and graduated from Webster Groves High School in 1965. He enlisted in the Army Nov. 19, 1966 in St. Louis. MO. Having been selected for officer training during Basic, Hank took Advanced Individual Training in Artillery at Fort Sill, OK, followed by Artillery Officer Candidate School. Following assignments with the Army Artillery Aviation Battalion and 3rd Battalion, 32nd Artillery (Honest John), he was assigned to Viet Nam.

In Viet Nam, Hank was assigned to Bravo Battery, 1st Battalion/77th Artillery. He was attached to Bravo Company/1st Battalion/5th Cavalry as their Forward Observer and joined them in July 1969. From that time until January 1970 he supported Infantry operations in III Corps, participating in 35 Combat Assaults. He was promoted to Captain and served as B/1/77 Artillery S-1 and as Intelligence Officer with the 191st Military Intelligence Company before leaving Viet Nam. Hank's last active duty assignment was as Commanding Officer, Alpha Company/1st Battalion, 3rd Training Brigade at Fort Leonard Wood, MO.

After completing his Bachelors and Masters degrees, Hank joined the Active Reserve where he served in various capacities in various units until his retirement. His final Reserve assignment was as the Army Reserve Ground Liaison Officer to the 13lst Fighter Wing in St. Louis, MO.

Hank is married to Mary Ann Hale and has a son, Matthew, and two grandchildren, Matthew Jr. and Savannah.

TYRONE A. HAMBY was commissioned through the Army ROTC scholarship program as a DMG May 1972 at NDSU Fargo, ND. After Infantry Officer training at Fort Benning and Aerial Surveillance Officer training at Fort Huachuca - assigned to 1st MI Bn (ARS) Fort Bragg (1972-76) as an Air Recon Liaison Officer and later Chief, FORSCOM II Training Team. After completing the Intel Officer Advanced Course at Ft Huachuca (1977) his follow-on assignment was to the Sioux Falls AFEES (MEPS) as Processing Officer and Commander (1977-1980). Afterward he was assigned as a Warrant Officer Senior Course and Officer Advanced Course Instructor with the 5043rd USAR School (1980-83). In 1983 he is assigned to Ft Lewis with the 9th Infantry Division HQ Staff serving as the G2 Plans and G2 Operations Officer (1983-86). At Camp Red Cloud, South Korea (1986-87) he was Chief, Combined All-Source Intelligence Center. After returning stateside he is assigned to US Space Command on the J2 staff and was selected as an Intel Watch Crew Commander in Cheyenne Mountain AFS and later served as the J2 Plans and Exercise Officer at Peterson AFB (1987-1990). CGSC graduate 1988.

When Iraq invaded Kuwait in August 1990, Hamby is assigned to the 1st Cavalry Division at Ft Hood. He deployed with 1 CAV to Saudi Arabia in September 1990 with the Division HQ Staff as the Deputy G2 and served throughout DESERT SHIELD/STORM operations until re-deployment to Fort Hood in May 1991. Hamby received the honor of participating as the G2 representative with the 1 CAV contingent in the DS Victory Parades in Washington, DC and New York City - June 1991.

Final active duty assignment was to the National Security Agency at Fort Meade in August 1991 as the NSA Cryptologic Acquisition Oversight Officer for all Army Tactical Cryptologic Systems, retiring from active duty in October 1994.

Hamby received the Bronze Star Medal, Defense Meritorious Service Medal (20LC), Army Meritorious Service Medal, Joint Service Commendation Medal, Army Commendation Medal, Army Achievement Medal, Air Force Combat Readiness Medal, SWA Service Medal (3bs), Korea Service Medal, USAR Service Medal, National Defense Service Medal (lbs), Saudi Arabia Liberation of Kuwait Medal, Kuwait Liberation Medal, Army Aircrewmember Badge and the Air Force Senior Space Operations Badge.

In civilian life he became a high school educator in Beulah, ND teaching history and geography for nine years. In May 2005 Hamby was called upon to assist the anti-terrorism effort in Afghanistan. In June 2005 he was stationed at Camp Eggers as a member of the CJ2, CSTC-A staff and became a civilian advisor to the Afghan Ministry of Defense G2 Staff in Kabul continuously until July 2010 - receiving the NATO ISAF Medal.

Hamby is retired and together with his wife, Svitlana, divide their time between a home in Kiev, Ukraine and their ranch near Beulah, ND.

LESTER "RAY" HAMILTON was born Feb. 28, 1948 in Wake County, NC and graduated from Southern High School in Durham, NC. He enlisted Jan. 3, 1970, with Boot Camp at Fort Bragg, NC followed by Airborne School. He was stationed at Fort Bragg, NC; Fort McClellan, AL; Vietnam; Fort Rucker, AL and St. Louis, MO.

He served as a Ranger in Vietnam from June 1969 to June 1970. Ray received two Army Commendations, four Purple Hearts, two Bronze Stars and Air Medal.

Sgt E-5 Hamilton was discharged Dec. 18, 1970 at Fort Rucker, AL.

He spent 31 years as salesman, estimator and VP of Proctor Flooring and also as driver for Duke Med. Univ. He was affiliated with PCEA, a volunteer fireman and little league coach.

He and Marie C. were married in October 1970, four months after he returned from Vietnam. In November 1990 he started getting symptoms of Agent Orange. He was 100 percent service connected but not disabled until May 2009. He passed away in September 2013 at the age of 64.

His life was being with his son, David Ray, and grandsons Landen, Noah and Wesley.

He is a hero of his army service and a hero in the eyes of his family. *Submitted by Marie C. Hamilton*

DAVID L. HANCOCK was born in Bland, Virginia on 15 February 1942. He entered the U.S. Army in October 1961 and was assigned to Fort Chaffee, Arkansas where he completed Basic and Advanced Individual Training in March 1962. Hancock was assigned a Military Occupational Skill (MOS) of 112 indirect Fire Crewman (mortars, now MOS 11C).

In April 1962, Hancock received orders for Korea, where he was assigned to the 2nd Battle Group, 12th Cavalry, 15th Cavalry Division as an 81mm mortar crewman and in April 1963, was promoted to Sergeant E-5. Departing from Korea, in April 1963, his next assignment was to the 2nd Battalion, 2nd Infantry Division, Fort Benning, GA as a Squad Leader for a 4.2 inch mortar squad.

In November 1963, he transferred to the 15th Battalion, 2nd infantry Division, at which time the unit was being deployed to Germany to participate in Long Thrust number 9, which was later called reforger. In March 1964, the unit returned to Fort Benning and was redesignated as Headquarters Company, 2nd Bn, 9th Infantry, 2nd Inf Div. In November 1964, he reenlisted and was assigned to A Company, 2nd Battalion, 54th Infantry, Bamberg Germany as an 81mm mortar squad leader. During this assignment, his Company was selected to participate in Cold Weather Survival training under the 10th Special Forces Group, Bad, Toelz, Germany (six weeks ski training), and 17 days in Bardafuss, Norway.

In June 1966 he returned to the States, and was assigned to Fort Polk, LA. In December 1966, received orders for Viet Nam, and was assigned to the 81 mm Mortar Platoon, as Chief, Fire Direction Center, D Company, 2nd Battalion, 7th Cavalry, 13' Cavalry Division. In May, 1967 was promoted to Staff Sergeant and assumed duties as Platoon Sergeant/Platoon Leader for the 81mm mortar Platoon.

In December 1967, he was reassigned to Fort Leonard Wood, MO, where he attended/graduated from Drill Sergeant School and performed the duties of a Drill instructor. He was selected as Drill Sergeant of the Cycle in November 1969, and April 1970.

In February 1971, he reenlisted and was assigned to Headquarters Company, 2nd Battalion, 64th Armor, 3rd Infantry Division, Schweinfurt Germany as the 4.2 inch Mortar Platoon Sergeant. In 1971 and 1972, his Platoon achieved first in the Division Mortar Gunnery tests conducted by the 3rd Infantry Division.

In March 1974, he returned to the States and was assigned to Charlie Company, 3'" Battalion, 7th Infantry, Fort Benning, GA as the 81mm mortar Platoon Sergeant/First Sergeant of the Company.

In November 1974, he reenlisted and was transferred from FORSCOM Command to TRADOC Command for reassignment to Headquarters, 2nd Training Battalion, The School Brigade (TSB), and assigned to the Mortar Committee on 20 December 1974. After attending and receiving his Diploma from the Infantry Mortar Platoon Course in May 1975, through August 1978, Hancock was the Noncommissioned Officer in charge of the Fire Direction Center, Infantry Mortar Platoon Officer Course (IMPOC), now Infantry Mortar Leader Course IMLC).

In August 1978, received orders for Korea, and from August 1978 to July, 1979, was chief of Training/Operations Sergeant for the 8 Army Noncommissioned Officer Academy, Camp Jackson, Korea. He returned to back to the States in August 1979 and reassumed the duties of Noncommissioned Officer in charge of the infantry Mortar Platoon Officer Course until May 1980.

From May 1980 through April 1981, was reassigned as the Chief Instructor of the Anti-armor Missile Division, Weapons, Gunnery and Maintenance Department the School Brigade, Fort Benning, GA.

In April 1981, he was reassigned to the US Army Readiness And Mobilization, Region IV, Fort Gillem, GA. with duties at Readiness Group Patrick, Patrick Air Force Base, FL. He was the Senior Enlisted Advisor, Infantry Team, for the 53rd Infantry Brigade Separate, Tampa, FL.

In June 1983, Hancock was reassigned to the 2nd Training Battalion, The School Brigade, Fort Benning, GA, with duties as the Battalion Operations Sergeant, First Sergeant and Sergeant Major, respectively, for the Infantry Officers Basic Course (IOBC).

Hancock retired from the Army as a First Sergeant E-8, 30 September 1985. In October 1985, he began working in the Directorate of Training as a contractors representative writing Training Extension Course lessons for the M23 Mortar Ballistic Computer. In Dec 1986, he entered Civil Service as a GS-9 and worked in the Directorate of Evaluation and Standardization, Fort Benning, GA. In Jan 1987, was promoted to GS-11 and assigned to the Firepower Branch, Directorate of Combat Developments (DCD) as a Project Officer for the TOW weapon System. In August 1992, Hancock was assigned as the DCD Project Officer for all mortar system and was promoted to GS-12 in September 1993.

Hancock was later promoted to GS-13, and became the Deputy, Firepower Branch, Soldier Requirements Division, Capabilities, Development, & Integration Directorate, Fort Benning, GA. His Branch was responsible for the development of requirements for Mortars, Shoulder Launched Munitions, Close Combat Missiles, Soldier Munitions, and Tactical Non-Lethal Munitions. Hancock retired from Civil Service as a GS-13, 31 December 2011 after 25 years of sentence, with 49 years combined Military and Federal service.

Hancock's awards and decorations include the Bronze Star Medal with Oak Leaf Cluster (OLC), Meritorious Service Medal with 3 OLC, Army Commendation with 3 OLC, Air Medal, and Combat Infantryman's Badge (CIB).

Hancock's education includes a Bachelor of Science Degree, a minor in business management, and a minor in Military Science from Troy State University, the Drill Sergeant Academy, Infantry Mortar Platoon Officer Course and First Sergeant Course.

Hancock is married to Gertrud Hancock (10 September 1965). They have one son, Michael, and twin daughters, Pamela and Patricia. They have eight grandchildren and four great-grandchildren.

GUY L HANKINS began his army career as a 2d Lt Armor branch in 1963 upon graduating DMG from Lincoln University. Following training at Fort Knox, KY and Fort Benning, GA, Guy was assigned as a tank platoon leader in the 1st Armored Division, Fort Hood, TX.

Upon completing company level duties at Fort Hood and Fort Bliss, TX, Guy was assigned to MACV in 1966 as a district advisor in An Xuyen Province. Upon rotation from MACV in 1967, Guy reported to the Armor School is a student in the AGC Course, followed by aviation training at Fort Wolters, TX and Hunter AAF, GA. This was followed by assignment to the First Team in Viet Nam in 1969 during his First Team tour, Guy performed command and staff duties in the 227th AHB and the 11th CAG.

Upon completion of this second VN tour, Guy was posted to the staff and faculty of the Primary Helicopter School, Fort Wolters, serving until facility closure in 1973 and his selection to The Armed Forces Staff College Norfolk, VA. Upon graduation Guy was assigned to the 25th ID in Hawaii, where he performed command and staff duties in the 3/4 Cav and division headquarters.

Following the tour in paradise, Guy was assigned as PAG of TRADGC Combined Arms Test Activity, Fort Hood. Among duties performed at the test center, Guy participated in the evaluation of the 1st Cav Div during the Division Restructure Study of 1978-1979.

Major Guy Hankins ended military service in 1979 and began a civilian career in the hospitality industry, retiring in 2007.

JOHN CLIFFORD HANSEN JR. drafted out of school on Sept. 8, 1966 and entered Boot Camp on Nov. 22, 1966 at Fort Polk, LA. He took additional training at US Army Quartermaster Center.

He was stationed at Fort Lee, VA and served at AIT Fort Hood, TX, 501 AG Admin. 1st Armor Div. Supply Co.

Memorable experience was serving from September 1967 to September 1969 in the Republic of Vietnam.

Hansen was awarded the Army Commendation Medal, Vietnam Service Medal, Vietnam Campaign Medal, National Defense Medal, Army Valorous Unit Award and the Presidential Unit Citation.

He was discharged on Sept. 2, 1968 at Fort Lewis, WA as E-4 SP4.

Hanson retired in 2006 after working 40 years at Robbins Flooring Mill.

JAMES RANDY HARRIS was born July 30, 1949 in Rockwood, TN and graduated from Cumberland Co. High School. He enlisted Nov. 7, 1967 and entered military service at Fort Campbell, KY. Following basic training, he transferred to Fort Huachuca, AZ and advanced training at Fort Gordon, GA in communications field.

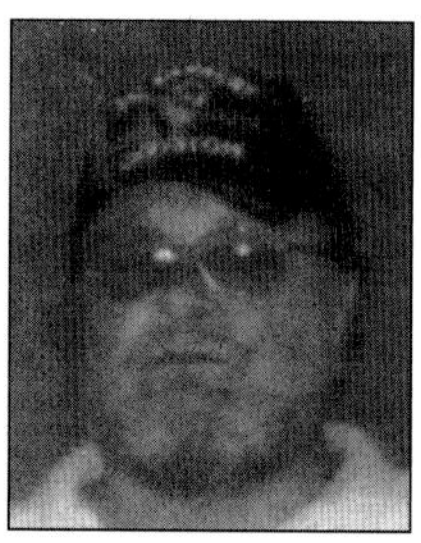

He arrived in Cam Rahn Bay, Vietnam, May 23, 1968. From there was assigned to 1st Cavalry Division and transferred to An Khe Province. Later arrived at Camp Evans in I Corp area with 13th Signal Corp. Volunteered for door gunner with 227th Aviation for two to four weeks and from there joined 1/12th Cav. Spent approximately four months in the field off and on. Awarded CIB and Bronze Star. Participated in Operation Liberty Canyon where 1st Cavalry entire division moved 571 miles by air and 627 miles by sea and air to Phoc Vinh as main base. Operated from Phoc Vinh to Serge's Jungle Highway, LZ Eleanor and LZ Carolyn. Departed Vietnam on May 23, 1969 via Bear Cat to Bien Hoa. Next assignment after 30 day leave back to good old Crossville, TN was Fort Lewis, WA where he served the last 17 months until was Honorably Discharged Nov. 7, 1970.

He says he would do it all over again "because we did not lose the war, our politicians did." "Garry Owen" coming and going. God bless the USA.

Married 33 years on Sept. 30, 2016 to Brenda, "the love of my life."

LEROY E. HARSHBERGER was born Jan. 23, 1947 in Goshen, IN, and graduated from Goshen High School in 1965. He was drafted on June 4, 1970 and, in addition to Boot Camp, took special training in AIT and AIT at Fort Polk, LA, and Track, APC and tank training at Fort Knox, KY.

He served in the III Corps area – Bien Hoa, Saigon, Long Binh areas. Even though he had track, APC and tank training, he was in the infantry because the mechanized units had gone home. He was assigned to Co. C 2d Btn. 5th Cav., 1st Cav. Div (Airmobile).

He was awarded Combat Infantry Badge, Purple Heart, National Defense Service Medal, Vietnam Service Medal; Vietnam Campaign Medal; Army Commendation Medal; Army Commendation Medal with "V" Device; Bronze Star; Bronze Star with Oak Leaf Cluster; Expert Marksman M-16, Pistol, Rifle; Air Medal and RVN Gall Cross.

Sgt. E5 Harshberger was discharged on Dec. 7, 19717 at Fort Dix, NJ.

Harshberger retired in 2000 after working as a Mason Contractor/Construction. In retirement he travels to reunions of Army Unit, fishing and attending Veterans Day dinners. He is a life member of DAV and VFW.

LeRoy and Nancy were married in 1973.

CLIFTON G. "CLIFF" HASKINS was born Sept. 28, 1940 in Kinston, NC, and graduated from Millbrook High School. He enlisted in December 1959 at Raleigh, NC, was a Distinguished Graduate at the Fifth United States Army and III Corps Noncommissioned Officer Academy, made the Commandan't List at the Infantry Armor Noncommissioned Officer Advanced Course – United States Infantry School at Fort Benning, GA, and was an Honor Graduate at Drill Sergeant School at Fort Polk, LA.

Bases and locations where he was stationed include 2nd Battle Group 21st Infantry 25th Infantry Division Schofield Barracks, Hawaii; 2nd Battalion 38th Infantry 2nd Infantry Division, Fort Benning, GA; 2nd Battalion 38th Infantry 11th Air Assault Division, Fort Benning, GA; 2nd Battalion 5th Cavalry 1st Cavalry Division, Fort Benning & Vietnam; 5th Battalion 12th Infantry 199th Light Infantry Brigade, Vietnam; 2nd Battalion 501st Infantry 101st Airborne Division, Vietnam; 2nd Battalion 41st Infantry 2nd Armored Division, Fort Hood, TX; 3rd Battalion 1st Infantry Training Brigade, Fort Polk, LA; III Corp NCO Academy Fort Hood, TX; 1st Battalion 13th Infantry 8th Infantry Division, Baumholder, Germany.

He fought at the Battle of Ia Drang, LZ XRay and LZ Columbus, Operation Silver Bayonet; the Cambodian Campaign, Battle at LZ Brown; and ground operations around Firebase Bastogne and Rifle in the I Corps area.

Awards include Bronze Star with two OLC, Meritorious Service Medal, Air Medal, Army Commendation Medal with one OLC, Good Conduct Medal 4th Award, National Defense Service Medal, Vietnam Service Medal, Republic of Vietnam Campaign Medal, Combat Infantryman Badge, Presidential Unit Citation, Air Assault Badge, and RVN Gallantry Cross Medal with Palm.

He retired from the service in January 1981 at Fort Bragg, NC, with the rank of SFC E-7, then worked for IBM Corp. at Research Triangle Park, NC, until retiring in 2006. He is a member of the 1st Cavalry Division Association, USO, VFW, and Association of the United States Army.

He has been married to Martha Haskins for over 45 years. Their daughter, Catherine, is married to husband Stacey Joyner.

HARLEY MICK HAWKINS was born Dec. 19, 1947 in South Gifford, MO, to Harley Jr. Hawkins and Theta Bell (McCollum) Hawkins. Mick graduated high school in 1965 at Browning Liberty High in Browning, MO.

Mick was drafted in September 1966 in Kansas City, MO, and shipped to Fort Leonard Wood, MO, to be inducted into the Army. From there he was transferred to Fort Hood, TX, for basic training and then AIT in infantry heavy weapons.

The 1st and 50th was shipped to Vietnam as an infantry unit in September 1967, and attached to the 1st Cavalry Division at An Khe, and their operating LZ was Uplift. Here they were engaged in many firefights and battles including the Battle of Tam Quan, Operation Pershing, and others.

Mick received the CIB, Purple Heart, Air Medal, Bronze Star with V device, Vietnam Campaign, Army Commendation, and various unit and other medals.

Mick was discharged in 1968 and married Carolyn Ervie of Marceline, MO. They have three children, Ronda, Jason and Josh, and eight grandchildren, Nick and Jacob Giger, Serena, Harley Brady, and Elaine Hawkins, and Gunnar, Hayden and Sophia Hawkins.

DOUGLAS B. HAYES began his military career in February 1953, receiving basic training at North Fort Hood, TX.

From 1953-54 he was Squad Leader with K Company, 7th Cavalry Regiment, Camp Haugen, Hokadiaho, Japan. 1956-57 was Squad Leader/Platoon Sergeant with 1st Squadron, 12th Cavalry, Armored Division, Fort Polk, LA. 1971, was the first Sergeant of a 200-man company with HQ & HQ Company, 7th Cavalry Regiment, Fort Hood, TX. 1971-73 G3 Operations Sergeant Major for the Division, then promoted to Sergeant Major and then Command Sergeant Major with HQ & HQ Company, 1st Cavalry Regiment, Fort Hood, TX. 1973-76, Command Sergeant Major with HQ & HQ Company, 1st Squadron, 9th Cavalry, 1st Cavalry Division. 1977-83 selected for Command Sergeant Major to serve with a two-star general officer to oversee leadership of 12,000 Soldiers, HQ & HQ Company, 1st Cavalry Division, Fort Hood, TX. Was Division Command Sergeant Major, serving with four two-star general officers for a period of almost six years – then retired in February 1983.

Ribbons and Awards he earned were Combat Infantry Badge, Legion of Merit, Bronze Star with three OLC, Army Commendation with three OLC, Meritorious Service Medal with OLC, Purple Heart, Good Conduct with four Silver Loops, Army Service Medal, Armed Forces Expeditionary, Army Overseas Service, National Defense, Air Medal, Vietnam Service Medal wirh one Silver and one Bronze Service Star, Vietnam Presidential Unit Citation, Valorous Unit Citation, Army Meritorious Unit Award, Army Gallantry Unit with Palm and Expert Rifle Badge.

WILBURN EUGENE "GENE" HENLEY was born August 24, 1932 in Covington County, AL and received his GED from LBW College in 1996. He enlisted Sept. 7, 1948 at Montgomery, AL and took Boot Camp at Fort Benning, GA. He was engaged in CE Infantry School Det TIS, and SFW Left Ankle, Sept. 11, 1950, Korea.

Henley received the Korean Service Medal, Bronze Service Stars, Service Medal, Combat Infantry Badge, PAR 21 So 200 Hq 7th Cavalry Regiment.

PFC Henley was discharged on Oct. 25, 1952 after serving three years, one month and 16 days.

Gene owned Henley's Heating AC until retiring in 1998. He passed on Nov. 19, 1998.

He was Mayor of Libertyville, AL; member of American Legion, DAV; a Mason, member of Scottish Rite and Shriners.

Gene and Elizabeth A. have children John, Gina and Judy. Grandchildren are Katharine, Riley, Brittany and Aaron. Two great-grandchildren are Princeton and Edyn.

FERNANDO HERNANDEZ was born in June 1948 in El Paso, TX and graduated from St. Joseph High School in 1967. He enlisted at Denver, CO and took Boot Camp at Fort Campbell, KY. He also took AIT, Fort Lee, VA - Supply and Armorer.

He was stationed with 1st Cav. in Vietnam and at Fort Sill, OK. His Vietnam service was from December 1967 to November 1968. Hernandez was awarded the NDSM, AM, AR Com., O/S Bars (2), RVN.

Memorable experience was with the men he served with.

SSG. Hernandez was discharged on July 2, 1970 at Fort Sill, OK.

He served as a State Patrol Trooper until retiring in 2000. Retirement activities include being a caregiver, traveling, reading and target shooting.

Fernando and Linda have two children, Nicholas and Rachel. Grandchildren are Ariel, Jonathan, Alexander, Elizabeth and Atticus. Thomas is their great-grandchild.

COLONEL ARVILLE L. "HICK" HICKERSON (RET.) resides in Belleair, FL, was born in Haverhill, MA on 31 December 1934, and grew up in Painesville, OH, graduating from Harvey High School in 1952.

A graduate of Dartmouth College/Thayer School, he was commissioned a 2LT RA, graduated from BIOC, Airborne and Ranger schools and was a 1970 USACGSC and 1977 NWC graduate.

He served in the 82nd Airborne Division as Company Commander, 6th Infantry, Berlin, Germany when the Berlin Wall was built on Aug. 13, 1961 and as a SF Team Commander. He served in RVN 27 consecutive months, eight campaigns and the TET Offensives of 1968 and 1969 - as Advisor in Phu Yen Province and Executive Officer and Commander of the 1st Battalion, 7th Cavalry, 1st Air Cavalry Division (Airmobile). He was awarded the Combat Infantryman Badge, six valor decorations and a Purple Heart. He was the 23rd Infantry Battalion Commander, 2nd Infantry Division in Korea during the 1973 world oil crisis, later serving on the Army Chief of Staff and Inspector General staffs. He was medically retired in 1983.

He received the LOM (two awards); BSM (four awards, one Valor), two MSM, five AM (one Valor), two ACM, the Master Parachutist Badge and Ranger Tab. RVN valor decorations include two CoG, one Palm and one Silver Star.

JOSE (JOE) A. HIDALGO JR. was commissioned a 2nd Lieutenant, Ordnance Corps with Combat Arms detail to the Infantry in May 1974. He reported to Fort Benning in June 1974 after graduation from the University of Houston. He attended the Infantry Officer Basic Course, graduating in August 1974, with subsequent assignment to the 1st Cavalry Division. On arrival to Fort Hood, Texas in September 1974, he was assigned as a Mechanized Infantry Platoon Leader with B Co, 1/12th Cav (Blue Lancers), 1st BDE. Hidalgo was then assigned to the 27th Maintenance Battalion in September 1975 after his year detail in the Infantry concluded and reported to the Missile Maintenance Unit – G Company. Hidalgo served in various unit positions ultimately commanding G Company from October 1977 to March 1979.

After PCS from Fort Hood, other world-wide assignments followed with highlights being: Commander, 4th Ordnance Company, 3rd Ordnance Battalion, 32nd Army Air Defense Command at Miesau Army Depot, Germany, January 1982 to April 1983; Chief, Contracting Office, Joint Task Force-Bravo at Palmerola AB, Honduras, June 1985 to December 1985; Commander, 41st Ordnance Company, 3rd Ordnance Battalion, 59th Ordnance Brigade at Rhine Ordnance Barracks,

Germany April 1986 to April 1988. An assignment at the US Army Missile Command (MICOM) at Redstone Arsenal, AL as a Contracting Officer was next from July 1990 to September 1992. Subsequent to the MICOM assignment, Hidalgo was sent on a tour of duty at the US Embassy-Cairo, Office of Military Cooperation. At the US Embassy, he was the Director of Defense Industrial Cooperation on all Defense Co-Production programs between the United States and Egypt, serving in country from October 1992 to March 1994.

Upon retirement from the US Army as a Lieutenant Colonel. Hidalgo joined the private sector and worked 18 years for different corporations in positions of increasing responsibility. On June 1, 2012, he founded FIRST TEAM Solutions, LLC — a consulting firm helping start-ups and small business navigate the Federal Government contracts process.

During his time in service, he earned the Legion of Merit Medal, Meritorious Service Medal (2D OLC), Joint Service Commendation Medal, Army Commendation Medal, Army Achievement Medal, National Defense Service Medal (2D AWD), Joint Meritorious Unit Award, Parachutist Badge and Expert Badge-Pistol.

Hidalgo married Frances Hammond in 1980 and they reside in Alabama with their five cats.

JAMES "JIM" M. HILTS entered the US Army in July 1967 at Buffalo, NY. He took his basic training at Fort Dix, NJ and then went on to radio school at Dix also. After radio school, he went to the South Eastern Signal School at Fort Gordon, GA where he learned about advanced communication techniques used at US embassies. He left Fort Gordon as a specialist 4 and was immediately sent to Viet Nam as a radio telephone operator (RTO), for the Army needed more RTO's than embassy communication experts.

Jim landed in Cam Ranh Bay, Vietnam on March 15, 1968 and was sent to the 1st BN of the 7th Cavalry of the 1st Air Cav Division at Camp Evans. His year in Viet Nam was spent either at the 1/7 BN HQ TOC, on patrol with Charley company or back at the 13th signal BN. As an RTO at the BN TOC, he monitored the BN and company nets and also performed courier duty flying in L4's. He would also establish relay stations over the mountains such as at LZ Miguel for upcoming operations. When a number of company RTO's were lost due to being killed, wounded or rotating back home he was assigned to Charlie Company of the 1/7. Finally, his last few months were spent with Alpha Company of the 13th Signal BN. Jim returned to the US in March of 1969 as a SGT and was discharged from service. Jim received the Bronze Star Medal, Vietnam Service Medal, Vietnam Campaign Medal w/60 Device and the Presidential Unit Citation.

After discharge, Jim returned to the SUNY at Buffalo and received a BS and MS in structural engineering. In 1996 Jim started a consulting company named Kingsway Engineering Services, selling it in 2014 and retiring. Jim also spent 14 years in the US Army Reserves finishing as a Major.

Jim married his high school sweetheart, Chris, in 1969 and lives with her in Coraopolis, PA. Jim and Chris have three children — Paul, David and Rebecca and five grandchildren — Matthew, Daniel, Andrew, Samuel and Rachel.

JESSE RUFFIN HINSON was born Nov. 23, 1939 in Wayne County, NC. Before entering the service, he worked for his father at Hinson's Grocery in Mt. Olive, NC. He joined the U.S. Army on March 6, 1951 in Fayetteville, NC and following basic was assigned to G Co., 5th Cav. Regt., 1st Cavalry Division.

Jesse fought in the Korean War and was involved in the battles of Hill 272 and 270 in October 1951, during which G Co. lost many of the 200+ men it started with, plus replacements. He received the Korean Service Medal with 2 Bronze Service Stars, United Nations Service Medal, Occupation Medal (Japan), and Combat Infantry Badge.

Jesse was discharged on Feb. 19, 1953 in Fort Jackson, SC, and worked for Dupont in Kinston, NC from April 3, 1953 until Jan. 31, 1986.

ODEAN E. HJELTER was born June 25, 1929 in Opheim, MT and graduated from Northfield High School in 1948. He enlisted at Great Fall, MT and took Boot Camp at Fort Ord, CA. On June 25, 1950 he was stationed at Camp McGill, Japan. The 1st Cavalry Division was ordered to Korea. The 5th Cavalry boarded LST on the shoreline of Camp McGill. They landed in Po Hang Dong, Korea three days later where they board rail cars and were moved to the center of Korea. After getting off the train, they walked half a day and dug in on a small mountain. Two days later F Company attacked a mountain. F Company was an over-strength company of 262 men. When the afternoon came, there were only 26 men still standing. The 2nd Battalion moved to the area near hill 303, F Company fought several in this area. The 2nd Battalion stayed in this area until the Inchon Landing. A few weeks later, the 2nd Battalion moved north into North Korea. The 2nd Battalion stopped in Pyongyang, the capital of North Korea. The 2nd stayed there for two weeks. The Bob Hope Company put on a show they attended. They stayed in an area near a brewery. Everyone drank their fill of beer. Then they moved farther north as the 8th Regt. of the 1st Cavalry was being surrounded. They were ordered to South Korea. The trucks they rode on after they reached there were on a single highway. They rode on the back of tanks. They spent January and February near the hill. In the spring they moved to Seoul where Hjelter was rotated.

TERRY A. HODOUS was born March 23, 1946 in Berwyn, IL and graduated from Brother Rice High School, and later St. Xavier College (1980). He enlisted in the U.S. Army in December 1965 at Chicago, IL, and went through boot camp at Fort Hood, TX. He also attended Radio Relay School at Fort Gordon, GA.

Terry was assigned to Fort Hood 2nd SG from June 1966 – Dec. 1967, then to Bong Son from Dec. 1966 – Dec. 1967, A Co. 13th SIG, 1st Cav Airmobile. He received the Army Commendation Medal and the Vietnam Campaign Medal. He was discharged from service at Fort Lewis, WA with the rank of Sgt. E-5.

Terry was the Director of Global Purchasing of Corn Products, retiring in 2000. He then became a tour greeter in Chicago. He is married to Dee and has one daughter, Carolyn, and two grandchildren, Stephanie and Vincent. He is a member of the Sheridan's Cavalry Chapter of the 1st Cavalry Division Association.

FRANCIS HOLLAND "BARRY" HOLLAND was commissioned an Infantry officer from Loyola College Baltimore in 1964.

His first assignment was with the 1/501st Parachute Infantry, 101st Airborne Division. The unit transferred to RVN and formed the 4thBattalion 503rd Infantry, 173rd Airborne Bde.

After his initial tour in RVN Holland returned to the 1st Cavalry Division in RVN, 1970-71, commanding in the 15th S & S Battalion. Holland completed CGSC in 1980 and was assigned to the 1st Corps Support Command commanding the 1st Material Management Center. His battalion commands spanned two battalions in Germany. The 64th Support Battalion, 4th Infantry Division and the 1st Forward Support Battalion in the 8th Infantry Division. After the Industrial College, Holland commanded the Central District of the Contract Management Command. During his five years in that position he settled the largest contract fraud case at over $200 million till that time. Holland is in the Quartermaster Hall of Fame.

During retirement he worked as an operations manager and international marketing manager for SAIC, retiring in 2013.

He resides with his wife Cindy in Williamsburg, VA. Cindy and Barry have four children (Col Joe Holland is the serving family member) and 13 grandchildren.

JOSEPH C. "JOE" HOLLAND was commissioned an Armor officer from Loyola University Chicago in May 1990.

He initially served in 2-68 Armor in Baumholder, Germany, then commanded Team C/3-66 Armor during the Army's Advanced Warfighting Experiment at Fort Hood, Texas. Following a tenure in a variety of positions at the Armor Center, Fort Knox, Kentucky, Colonel Holland served as an observer/controller at the National Training Center, and then again in 4th Infantry Division at Fort Hood, Texas and Iraq, as the Division Chief of Plans, and Executive Officer for 1-22 Infantry, and then 1st Brigade Combat Team. Colonel Holland commanded a combined arms battalion, 2-12 Cavalry in 1st Cavalry Division, at Fort Hood, Texas and in combat in Kirkuk, Iraq. Following battalion command, Colonel Holland served as the Future Operations Chief for III Corps at Fort Hood, and later as the Chief of Plans, US Army Europe in Wiesbaden, Germany. He currently commands

US Army Garrison Humphreys, in Pyeongtaek, Republic of Korea, where he leads the effort to provide services, facilities, and infrastructure at the future home of US Forces Korea, 8th US Army, and 2nd Infantry Division.

MERRILL M. "DUTCH" HOLLAND was born in Grand Meadow, MN, on June 21, 1926, and graduated from New Richmond High School in 1944. He enlisted on Dec. 23, 1944 and went through basic training at Camp Joseph T. Robinson. Following basic, he was assigned to Far East Command Intelligence School, then Camp Drake, Japan, HHB 271st FA BN, also spending time in Luzon and IPODAM.

Holland received the Combat Infantryman Badge and Asiatic Pacific Theater with Bronze Arrowhead. He was discharged on Oct. 16, 1946 at Fort Sheridan, IL, with the rank of Technical Sergeant.

He and his wife, Connie, have one child, Mark.

ROBERT "DUTCH" G. HOLLAND received his commission on June 14, 1954, 2nd Lt., Field Artillery, from Cornell University ROTC. He entered active duty Dec. 1, 1954 at Fort Sill, OK.

Holland received additional training in Primary Flight School, Aviation Tactical Course, Assoc. Field Artillery Basic Officer Course #4, Primary Helicopter Course #6, USA Instrument Flight Training Course #6 and Assoc. Field Artillery Officer Career Course #1.

He was assigned to 89th FA BN, 11th Abn Div., 24th Combat Avn Co, 24th Inf. Div., 2nd How Bn, 31st Arty, 55th Avn Co., 1st Rkt How Bn, 20th Arty, Btry E (Avn), 26th Arty, 11th AAD, Btry E (Avn), 82nd Arty, 1st Cay Div (AM), Btry D, 25th Arty, USAREUR, Hq VII Corps Arty, USAREUR, 199th Avn Co, USARPAC-RVN, 307th Cmbt Avn Bn, USARPAC, Casual Hold Det USAG, HHC 46th Gen Supt Group, Readiness Group, Fort Devens, MA

On Jan. 1, 1975, he retired at Fort Devens, MA as Major (04).

Memorable experience was flying the air observer of the 21st FA Bn, 1st Air Cav. Div during the Ia Drang Valley operation, November 1965.

He was awarded the Distinguished Flying Cross, Bronze Star with "V," Meritorious Service Medal, Air Medal, RVN Gallantry Cross with Silver Star and RVN Gallantry Cross with Bronze Star.

He held the position of Process Engineer with Lucent Technologies, Orlando, FL, retiring in December 1999. He moved back to home state of New York in February 2000.

Robert and Carole Bernier Holland had four children: Archie Anthony Holland (deceased) Melanie Catherine Holland (deceased) Robert John Holland and Stratton Daniel Holland (deceased).

MASON HOLMES, a college graduate draftee, was inducted from Buffalo NY in September 1969, completed basic training at Fort Dix in November 1969, then worked in the Post Finance Office through April 1970. On June 3rd, he shipped out to Vietnam from Fort Lewis, assigned to the 1st Cav's Public Information Office (PIO) in Phuoc Vinh. His duties were in Finance & Accounting (MOS 73D20) at the First Team Scholarship Gift Shop. They sold Cav logoed lighters, photo albums, pocket knives, etc. plus the *1965-1969 Cav History Book* to Troopers. With sale proceeds, we funded college scholarships for sons and daughters of fallen Troopers. Although a "REMF," I believe this helped boost the morale of infantry and other combat troops.

After discharge in April 1971, he had a career in government contractor financial management. Now semi-retired, he is active with Sheridan's Cavalry Chapter, as Chapter President, and organized the campaign to bring the Association's 67th Reunion to the Chicago area in 2014. Their members support Veterans' initiatives, including CARE packages to deployed Troopers. Also, they want to ensure that all military Veterans are welcomed home by their fellow citizens. They are now the 1 percent who protect the other 99 percent of our population.

WAYBURN DAWSON HOUCHIN was born on Feb. 12, 1930 in Hart County, KY, to Lester and Francis Houchin. It was a joyous day for the couple, who had previously only had a daughter, Pauline.

It was in 1948 that Wayburn decided to change his life to help his country for the better. He was stationed in Japan for approximately 18 months. When the Korean War commenced on June 25, 1950, the 1st Cavalry Division was alerted and on the 18th of July, they landed at Pohang-Dong, Korea.

They were constantly in combat, rarely ever seeing rest. They were pushed to the Naktong River, which they called the Naktong Perimeter. Wayburn was wounded in September of 1951, left Korea, and was discharged. He received a Purple Heart medal for his wounds in battle.

Shortly after he was discharged, Wayburn married the love of his life, Roma Graham on October 30, 1953. They had four children together: Patricia, Katherine, Daniel, and Leslie.

On October 25, 2002, Wayburn passed away peacefully, surrounded by the ones he loved. Everyone who had met him said he was a great man. When someone needed help, he was always there to help.

EDWARD LEE "HUCK" HUCKABEE was born June 30, 1947 in Delaplaine, AR, and graduated from Delaplaine High School in 1965. He enlisted on May 11, 1967 and took his basic training and AIT at Fort Polk, then on to Fort Benning for Neo School. In 1969 he was in Vietnam at LZ Grant.

Huckabee received the Vietnam Service Medal, National Defense, Air Medal, Vietnam Campaign, Bronze Star, and Army Commendation with V device. He was discharged on May 15, 1969 at Fort Ord, CA, with the rank of Sgt. E-5.

After the service, he worked in machine repair for GM for 34½ years, retiring in 1999. In retirement he has worked as a crewman on a NASCAR team.

He married Deborah A. Huckabee in 1969 and they have two children, Cathy and Micahel, and four grandchildren, Amber, Noah, Cooper, and Wyatt.

HADDON HUFFORD was born Nov. 29, 1949 in White Plains, NY and graduated from Irvington High School in 1967. He enlisted on Aug. 26, 1968 at White Hall St., NYC. After Boot Camp at Fort Gordon, GA he took AIT 84C20 – motion picture camera operator training at Fort Monmouth, NJ. He was based at 4th Army Photo Lab, Fort Sam Houston, TX and then traveled on assignment all over 1st Cav. A.O.

He filmed front seat of Cobra gunship – Blue Max; filmed for one week with Medevac out of Tay Ninh and many times in the boonies with grunts after combat assaults and the staging area for Cambodian invasion.

He was awarded the National Defense Service Medal, Bronze Star, Army Commendation Medal, Air Medal, Vietnam Campaign Medal and Vietnam Service Medal.

SP5 Hufford was discharged on June 4, 1971 at Fort Sam Houston, TX.

He spent 28 years in the film business – set builder, dolly and crane grip. He changed to silver smithing, spending 20 years in a studio.

He and wife Taylor Pape have been together 43 years. They lived in "Union Chapel," an 1875 chapel they renovated. They enjoy traveling worldwide and spending time with their four dogs — Wenlh, Knickerbocker, Slapstick and Inka.

DAVID L. HUGHART was drafted in September 1967. After boot camp and Advanced Infantry Training, he joined the 4th Platoon of B Company, 1/12, 1st Cavalry Division in Vietnam in February 1968. Hughart was promoted five times during his tour and finished as Platoon Sergeant (SSgt E6) of the 4th Platoon. He participated in combat operations in I Corp and III Corp including combat assaults in the Ashau Valley and Operation Pegasus for the relief of Khe Sanh.

Hughart completed his Vietnam tour in February 1969 and completed his military obligation as the Weapons Platoon Sergeant of A Company, 1/10, 5th Mechanized Division at Fort Carson. He was discharged in September of 1969.

Hughart received the Bronze Star with V device and 1st Oak Leaf Cluster, Vietnam Service Medal with Bronze Service Star, Vietnam Campaign Medal with "60" device, Air Medal, Combat Infantryman Badge, and the Good Conduct Medal.

After discharge, Hughart held numerous executive level positions in the telecommunications internet services industries. He has taught writing and literature as an Adjunct Professor at St. Edwards University for the last 10 years.

Hughart married Renate Stankiewicz in 1965. They live in Austin Texas, as does their daughter Elisabeth.

DAVID R. HUGHES served a year in Korean War Combat as a Rifle Platoon leader and Company Commander of Company K, 7th US Cavalry, immediately after graduating from West Point. That included the brutal winter retreat from the Yalu River in December 1950. Then in the 1951 offensives, he led his men as they pushed both the Chinese and North Korean Armies back over the 38th Parallel. He was awarded the Silver Star and two Purple Hearts during that spring push.

In the fall he then successfully defended Hill 339 from heavy Chinese attacks, being awarded his second Silver Star for one seven-day series of battles. After that he lost all six of his officers, and all but 15 Company K enlisted men, killed or wounded, before seizing assigned Hill 347 – Bloody Baldy – and capturing 192 Chinese Soldiers. He was awarded the Distinguished Service Cross for that action. That hill is now inside the Demilitarized Zone that divides the now free and prosperous South Korea from the dictatorship of the Communist North.

He served in different Army units until retiring in 1972 after 27 years in uniform as a Colonel, and attending Korean War 7th Cav vet reunions.

NORMAN F.S. HUGHES was born Dec. 7, 1934 in Orange, NJ, and graduated from Seton Hall Prep in 1953, earning his B.S. from Seton Hall University in 1958. He enlisted in February 1952 in the 199th F.A. BN, 50th Armored Div., East Orange, NJ, and in 1956 transferred to inactive Reserve. He was commissioned a 2nd Lieutenant at Seton Hall University ROTC.

He completed Officers Basic Course at Fort Bliss, TX, on 6 June 1958. Other training included: Advanced Course, Fort Sill, OK and Fort Bliss, TX; Vietnam Orientation Course, Fort Bragg, NC and Lang School, Monterey, CA; and ICM 1st Class, Oakland, CA and Club Management Course, Fort Lee, VA.

Stations included Fort Bliss, TX (June 1958); Bad Kissingen, Germany (Dec. 1960); Schweinfurt, Germany (1962); Fort Sill, OK and Fort Bliss, TX (1963); Fort Hood, TX (1964); MACV Tieu Can, Vietnam (Nov. 1965); ROTC at Fordham University, NYC (Dec. 1966); Phuoc Vinh, Vietnam, 1st Cav Arty (Nov. 1969); Fort Hood, TX (Nov. 1970); and Fort Polk, LA (1977). He was a MACV Subsector Advisor in Vietnam from November 1965 to November 1966.

Awards/Medals received: Bronze Star (2 OLC), Air Medal, Meritorious Service Medal, ARCOM (3 OLC), VC of G with Palm, VC of C with Palm (Unit), CIB, M-14 (SPS) Rifle, Pistol 45 (EXP), M-16 Rile (EXP), 30 Cal CBN (SPS).

He retired on 31 May 1979 at Fort Polk, LA, after 26 years of military duty, with the rank of Major. In civilian life, he was a MW WOOD Food Service Manager at Drew University, and an Installation Club Manager at Naval Weapons Station EARLE, retiring in 1998. He served on the Retiree Council at Fort Monmouth, NJ, for 16 years.

Norman has been married to Mary A. Hughes for over 58 years. They have four children – Patrick, Mary E., Brian, and Kathleen – and eight grandchildren – Dylan, Kyle, Jasmine, Connor, Zachary, Fiona, Sienna, and Shane.

BILL HUNT enlisted in the Army in September 1967, after graduating from New Bern High School (NC) and UNC at Chapel Hill with a degree in Business Administration.

He was assigned to Ft. Dix, N.J for Basic and AIT training. Upon completion, he was assigned to Infantry OCS at Ft. Benning, GA. He was commissioned on 28 Sep 68. Bill was then assigned to the Armor and Mine Subcommittee at Ft. Benning. He completed the Instructor Training course and taught mine warfare to OCS classes.

Hunt was next assigned to attend the Jungle Warfare School in Panama. After graduation in May, 1969, he was assigned to the First Air Cavalry Division in III Corps, South Vietnam. Hunt was further assigned to be a platoon leader in Delta Co, 1/8 Cav. He served in this capacity until October, 1969, when he was assigned to be the XO of B Co. 1/8 Cav. The primary area of operations was the jungle around Quan Loi and Song Be. Hunt was awarded the Combat Infantry Badge, 3 Bronze Stars, the Air Medal, Army Commendation Medal, Vietnam Campaign Ribbon, Vietnamese Cross of Gallantry and the Presidential Unit Citation among others. Bill voluntarily served in the Army Reserves for seven years, attaining the rank of captain.

Bill Hunt had civilian careers as a bank officer and Real Estate Broker in Atlanta and North Carolina. He retired in 2006 and now lives in North Carolina. Bill stays busy playing tennis, working out, reading, travel and going to numerous plays and UNC basketball games. He and his wife, Linda, love to spend time with their daughter, Jen, son-in-law Brandon and their two grandchildren, Miles and Scarlett.

JACK M. HUNTER II graduated from Colorado College (1967, BA) and University of South Dakota (MBA, 1981) and enlisted on May 30, 1967 as an ROTC graduate. He had additional training as a Ranger and C & GS. He was stationed at Fort Riley, Fort Carson and Fort Lewis and from October 1968 to October 1969 served in RVN.

Hunter was awarded the BS, RVN Cross of Gallantry, Air Medal and MSM.

Memorable experience was the Middle East and Africa projects office (Corps of Engineers), 1989-1992.

On August 1992 he was discharged as LTC.

Hunter retired in August 2014 after working in higher education at Missouri State University and South Dakota School of Mines.

Retirement activities include golf, fishing and volunteering.

He and Sheryl "Sheri" K have two children, Russell (deceased – US Army) and Craig. Grandchildren are Aviana and Alexander "Lex."

RAY D. IRBY, born Nov. 9, 1924 at Meridian, MS. He graduated from Meridian High School in July 1943, Meridian Jr. College and Mississippi State University, earning three years.

Irby enlisted in July 1943 at Camp Shelby, MS. He took basic training at Fort Riley, KS, then Fort Ord, CA. He served in the Asiatic-Pacific Theater, 1943 to September 1945 and at New Guinea, Oro Bay. He was at Admiralty Islands, D-Day Feb. 29, 1944; Leyte-Samar, A-Day, Oct. 20, 1944; Luzon-Manila, the 1st was First Landed; Lingayen Gulf, Jan. 27, 1945; first to enter Manila, Feb. 3, 1945; JAPAN-Tokyo Bay-Yokohama-Sept. 7, 1945-First Troops in Tokyo–Sept. 8, 1945. He returned to the United States in December 1945.

Irby served with the Army's 1st Cavalry Division from New Guinea to Tokyo, and then the Korean War as CO of Battery B 85 AAA Gun Bn., 1952-1953.

He has been employed with 3M, State Farm and then Sears for 28 years. He spent 17 years with SCORE, a nonprofit association of the Small Business Administration, where he served as a counselor advisor and mentor to aspiring entrepreneurs and potential business owners. Now a widower, Irby has three sons and seven grandchildren and traveling is his hobby.

ROBERT E. "JAKE" JACOBS was drafted on July 1, 1969. After basic training at Fort Dix, NJ he was sent to Fort Lewis, WA for Light Weapons Infantry (11B). Then he was sent to Vietnam and assigned to the 1st Cav.

While in-processing at Bien Hoa, he was put on hold to be retrained as a Personnel Specialist (71H) and then sent to Division HQ in Phuoc Vinh. Although originally to work in G-3, he was commandeered by the HQ Co 1SG to be a company clerk. After the head clerk rotated back to the states, he became the head clerk of Div HQ Company. In the spring of 1970, he was part of a small group who manned the operation for Taskforce Shoemaker, the Cambodian Incursion. They operated out of Quan Loi, their 3rd Bde HQ, which was near the Cambodian border. As the clerk for the operation, he was given the "honor" of typing the operation order that made Taskforce Shoemaker an official military operation. After R&R in Bangkok, he returned stateside and was assigned to Military Ocean Terminal Bayonne (MOTBY) and married his wife of now 45 years.

Prior to being drafted, he earned a BS in education from Temple University and in 1975 he earned an MS in education from Trenton State College.

After getting out of the Army in June 1971, he returned to the teaching job he held before being drafted. In the early 1980s, he enlisted in the NJ National Guard and later transferred to the USAR. He did a total of 22 years service as a clerk, supply sergeant and Lanes Trainer. His military medals include: Bronze Star, Air Medal, ARCOM, Army Achievement Medal, Good Conduct, National Defense, VN Campaign, VN Service and various Reserve component medals.

Including the two-year break for military service, he taught for 35 years and belonged to NJEA and NEA. He is active in Veterans groups and is a Past State Commander of the Jewish War Veterans of NJ. He is also a member of VVA, DAV and the 1st Cav. Association. He is married to Marcia for 45 years and they have a son, Matthew, along with one grandson, Jordan.

STEVEN R. JANSEN (DOC) was born 12 January 1951 in Appleton, WI, graduating from St. John High School in 1969. He enlisted in the US Army on 29 July 1969 in Appleton, and was sent to Fort Campbell, KY for boot camp and Combat Medic Training. Other stateside bases include Fort Sam Houston, TX, and Fort Leonard Wood, MO.

He went on to serve in the Republic of Vietnam during the Cambodia campaign with the 1st Cavalry Division. He received the Bronze Star with V device, CBM, Army Commendation Medal with V device and two OLC, Air Medal, Vietnam Service Medal, Vietnam Campaign with 60 device, National Defense, Air Medal, Expert Rifle badge, and Presidential Unit Citation. His most vivid memory is saving the life of George Avery.

Steven was discharged on 28 July 1969 at Fort Leonard Wood with the rank of SP/4. He worked for Appleton Papers as a bailer operator for 26 years, retiring on 30 January 2013. He is a member of Post 258 American Legion, the Legion Rid ers and Patriot Guard, and volunteers at High Cliff State Park cutting grass, and also for the American Red Cross and Senior Center.

In 2010, he and his wife along with her brother (who served with the 129th Assault Helicopter Co. in 1968-1969) and sister-in-law went back to Vietnam for a two-week tour. The first thing he and his brother-in-law noticed getting off the plane was that "it still smells the same." The people were very friendly and the country was beautiful. The bomb craters were still evident near Hue and the wall at the Citadel still had holes and damage from the intense fighting. They felt very safe and couldn't get over the new roads and highways, especially in Hanoi.

He is married to Diane M. Jansen, and they have two sons, Eric (deceased) and Brian, and two grandchildren, Gabrielle and Preston.

JERRY L. JENKINS enlisted on August 6, 1962 at Little Rock, AR. In Basic Training at Fort Polk, LA he broke the record for entire Army PT. Additional training was Scout Training, Fort Knox, KY; NCO Academy and 1st Sgt. Course, and was Featherweight on All Army Boxing Team (Champion in 1964).

He was stationed at Fort Stewart, GA; Augsburg, Germany, Vietnam C Troop 1/9 CAV, 1st Sgt, HQ – Company CO., HCR, Fulda, West Germany. He was an Air Scout in Vietnam (H-13), over 700 combat hours in a helicopter and WIA Jan. 2, 1968 on the coast of Bong Son, Vietnam.

Jenkins received DFC, Bronze Star, Air Medal/27 awards, one with "V" device, MSM, Purple Heart, Army Achievement Medals and 7 awards – Good Conduct Medal.

He was discharged on Dec. 1984 at Fort Campbell, KY as 1SG – E-8.

Jenkins retired in 2008 from Dickson Auto Parts. He spends time visiting nursing homes and speaking at schools for Veterans Day.

Jerry and Judy have one child, Lori and one grandchild, Ridley.

ALVIN B. "AL" JOHNSON was born June 14, 1938 in Galveston, TX, and graduated from Fortier High School in New Orleans, LA, and also attended Louisiana State University. He entered the Army through ROTC as a 2nd LT, and received special training with Special Forces/10th Special Forces Group, Airborne, Infantry Officer's Basic/Infantry Officer's Advanced Course.

He was stationed at Ft. Benning, Ft. Campbell, Ft. Hood, Ft. Monroe, Ft. McPherson, Ft. Lewis, Ft. Ord, Korea, Germany, and Vietnam. He did two tours in Vietnam (June 1967 – June 1968, and Dec. 1969 – Nov. 1970). June-Dec. 1967: Bin Dinh Province (D/1-5 Cav), Jan-June 1968: Quang Tri Province (HHC/2-8 Cav). Dec. 1969-Nov. 1970: Bin Dinh Province (SF Detachment).

Awards/Medals include: Legion of Merit, Vietnamese Honor Medal 1st Class, Vietnamese Gallantry Cross, Bronze Star, Bronze Star w/V, Distinguished Flying Cross, Air Medal (2), and Combat Infantry Badge.

He retired at Ft. Ord, CA, in June 1989 and was released from service in July 1989 at Ft. McPherson, GA, with the rank of Colonel. He spent 11 years with the GA Dept. of Veteran Services, and is the owner of Johnson Hall Fine Art in Roswell, Ga.

Al is married to Cheryle Hall Johnson; they have four children, Greg, Jeff, Heath, and Heather, and seven grandchildren, Lance, Merideth, Tori, Toni, Jessica, Nicholas, and Morgan.

JAMES P. JOHNSON graduated Jefferson High School in 1967 and then attended one year at Portland Community College. He married his wife, Charlene Kincaid Johnson, on March 15, 1969, and on June 11, 1969 he was inducted in the U.S. Army as a draftee in Portland, Oregon. At that time, Fort Lewis, WA was the base location he thought he would go to. Because Fort Lewis was having an outbreak of meningitis, their group was sent to Ft. Bliss, Texas. Basic Training at 125 degrees was common while doing maneuvers. They were up every morning at 4:30am to go running. It was a totally different climate, but he enjoyed it.

After Basic Training, he was sent to Ft. Huachuca AZ for AIT Training. He was trained as a Communication Tech, MOS 05B learning Morse Code and the use of all Army Radios.

After a short leave over Thanksgiving with his wife and family, he was sent to Vietnam for a one-year vacation in the sun. All accommodations were free. He arrived December 14th 1969 and was in a Holding area until February 1970. He was then sent to Tay Ninh where the 1st Air Cavalry 2nd Battalion 19th Artillery assigned him to HHB Communications section as an O5C for the colonel. He became responsible for all his reports.

In May, their communication center packed up and went into Cambodia for two weeks. When they returned, their HHB had moved to Ben Hoa/Long Binh.

The last six months he was in charge of radio call signs, and when compromised had to generate new ones and deliver to the field. He flew in Boeing CH-47 Chinooks, OH-6A "Cayuse" Scout Loaches and UH-1 Hueys to almost every Firebase and LZ, (Landing Zones with 3 105 howitzers or more); all in the 3 Corps area of South Vietnam during this time.

He received the National Defense Service Medal, Vietnam Service Medal, Vietnam Campaign Medal, Army Commendation Medal and the Air Medal.

He was discharged on December 19, 1970 in Oakland, CA as a SP4, and returned home to his wonderful wife. They have two children, Jason and Jamie, and three grandsons. He went to work for Pacific Northwest Bell and retired after 28 years. He worked another 10 years at Comcast, then retired again.

JOEL D. JONES was commissioned a Second Lieutenant upon graduation from the University of Iowa in 1960. After becoming Ranger and Airborne qualified, he served in Germany followed by two assignments with the Ranger Training Command at Eglin AFB, FL.

Jones was assigned to combat duty in 1966 as an advisor with the Military Assistance Command, Vietnam. During this assignment, Jones was awarded the Combat Infantry Badge, Bronze Star, Air Medal and the Vietnam Commendation Medal.

In 1969, he was assigned to the 2nd Brigade, First Cavalry Division. He served as Brigade XO and S-3 while at FSB Buttons, Song Ba. He later became Assistant to the Chief of Staff at Division HQ.

During his one year tour with the 1st Cavalry, he was awarded the Silver Star, Legion of Merit, Bronze Star with 2OLC, Air Medal with 9OLC, Vietnamese Cross of Gallantry with Silver Star, Presidential Unit Citation, and Valorous Unit Award.

Following Vietnam (1970-1978) Jones completed Command and General Staff College, served with DCSPER/Training and Doctrine Command and The Military Personnel Center.

From 1978-82, Jones served as Commander, 3 Bn, 36th Infantry, and G-1, 3rd AD in Germany. He was later assigned to DCSPER at US Army HQ, Washington, DC and to J-3 Central Command at Mc Dill AFB, Tampa, FL. He was promoted to Colonel in 1981. Colonel Jones retired in 1984, due to Service Connected Disabilities.

During retirement, he was founder and CEO of multiple non-profit organizations helping children in Central Florida. He retired from these positions in 2000.

Colonel Jones enjoyed 58 years of marriage to Gail Jones (deceased in 2016). He resides in Altamonte Springs, FL with four children, nine grandchildren and 11 great grandchildren.

WALKER A. JONES entered the Warrant Officer Rotary Winged Aviator Course in April, 1969 at Ft. Wolters, TX following Basic Training at Ft. Polk, LA. After graduating from advanced helicopter pilot training at Ft. Rucker, Jones served in Vietnam with C Troop, 1st Squadron, 9th Cavalry as both an OH-6A scout pilot and a Cobra gunship pilot in their Hunter-Killer Teams in support of the 1st Cav Division brigades. He was involved in both Cambodia Incursions.

Following early discharge upon returning from Vietnam in April 1971, Jones returned to college at the University of Mississippi. Afterward, he entered graduate school at Clemson University, obtaining M.S. and Ph.D. degrees in the biological sciences. Jones was recruited by the Agricultural Research Service of the U.S. Department of Agriculture and spent over 35 years conducting research at locations in Mississippi, Arizona, Texas and Europe. He has been Research Leader and Director of three research facilities. He married Linda Bell while living in Paris and has two children, Wendy Walker Jones and Jay Livingston Jones along with five grandchildren, Emma, Jay, Zoe, Penelope and Phoenix.

Beginning in the mid-1990s, Jones began tracking down former members of C-1/9th and organized their first large reunion in 1999. He is a life member in the Vietnam Helicopter Pilots Association, the Vietnam Helicopter Crewmembers Association as well the 1st Cavalry Division Association.

JAMES WOLF JORDAN was born Dec. 18, 1946 in Bedford, PA and graduated from Sarasota High School in 1966. He was drafted on April 21, 1968 reporting to Fort Jackson, SC for testing. Passing all with flying colors he went to Fort Gordon, GA for basic training. He followed with Advanced Infantry Training, Fort Dix, NY and shipped out to Vietnam in April 1969 having been assigned to the 1st Cavalry Division.

He started at Fire Base Grant as an Infantryman carrying the M-60, 7.62 MM ammunition. Next moved to Point Man for Bravo Company (Bad bet) 2nd of the 12th for over 100 days. All combat was with North Vietnam Army in full uniform. Next he became the company commanders Radio Telephone Operator, then promoted to the Battalion Radio Telephone Operator assigned to tactical operations center. He left Vietnam in April 1970 and was discharged.

Jim graduated in 1974 from the University of South Florida with a Bachelor of Arts in history. He was a Veterans Advisor there. After graduation he worked for the Sarasota Guidance Clinic. He moved to Albuquerque, NM and learned to fly hot air balloons. He worked for World Balloon Corporation, earning his Commercial Pilot Instructor license. He traveled across the US for Anheuser-Busch, Labatt's, Kraft and Sears flying their hot air balloons. After several years ballooning, Jim joined Public Service Company in customer service.

Jim joined the New Mexico National Guard Hawk Battalion and then transferred to the Army Reserves and became an instructor of BNOC, ANOC, Supplies and Instructor Training.

In 2013 he moved to Portland, OR and soon joined the 1st Cavalry Association, having found true friends and camaraderie with his fellow brothers.

HOWARD KALACHMAN was drafted May 1967 and served in Nam with the Cav 2/12 A & HHQ 11/67-12/68. He was awarded the Bronze Star, GCM, CIB, VSM, VCM, and NYS CSC, and is the author of *Hi Mom, I'm O.K and Other Lies From Vietnam*, dedicated to the sacrifices made by Vets and their loved ones.

After returning from Vietnam, he was briefly involved in politics and went on to earn B.A. in psychology, M.S., and Professional Diploma (P.D.). He spent 23 years in the business world as a manager in law, airfreight claims, collections, personnel, hypnotherapy, and counseling before finding his true calling in education. He retired from NYC Department of Education after 22 years of service as an assistant principal, computer, math, and classroom teacher.

Kalachman is a Life member of the DAV, VFW, & Legion; Past Commander, Victor Murtha Post 972; Treasurer & Past Commander of Joint Veterans Org of Long Beach; was Veteran consultant/liaison for the NYIT's & NYS, "Troop to Teachers" program; and volunteers at the V.A. hospital, Veteran Stand-downs and organizations serving Veterans.

A Big Brother since 2007, he is a Volunteer Veteran Mentor and public speaker at various volunteer events for Make-A-Wish & others, as well as City of Long Beach Veterans' events.

He was awarded the Legionnaire of the Year Award in 2014 for service to Veterans.

KERMIT D. KARR enlisted in February 1969 at London, KY. After Boot Camp at Fort Knox, KY he had AIT training at Fort Polk, LA. He was stationed in Vietnam, Cambodia and at Fort Carson, CO.

Karr was with III Corp. in Vietnam and in the invasion of Cambodia in May 1970.

Memorable experiences was an all night battle near LZ Cauldwell, Vietnam on August 12, 1969 and being wounded in action, August 24, 1969.

He was awarded the ARCOM with V device, Purple Heart, Bronze Star, Air Medal, Combat Inf. Badge, Vietnam Service Medal and Campaign Medal.

Karr was discharged at Fort Carson, CO on Feb. 12, 1971 as Sergeant E-5.

He retired in 2012 as an electrician after working in Kentucky, Florida, Pennsylvania and Louisiana.

Kermit and Kathy Heuser Karr have five children: Christopher, Phillip, Mary, Ada and Jacob. Grandchildren are Ashley, Katie, Trevor, Jason, Lucus, Trent, Aiden, Alex, Maddie and Jaxon.

JIM A. KEETON was born Nov. 19, 1946 in Colorado Springs, CO, and graduated from Fountain High School in 1964, later earning his BS (1968) and MS (1975) from Colorado State University. He enlisted for the Medical Corps in August 1969 and entered military service at Fort Campbell, KY on 3 September 1969. Following basic training, he was transferred to Fort Sam Houston Medical Center for Medical Corpsman training, where he graduated with honors. Keeton applied and was accepted into the Clinical Specialist Program (early PA school), and graduated from Clinical Specialist Program in 1971 at the top of the class.

Keeton served with the 101st Airborne Division 1/321 Artillery in charge of the Battalion Aide Station in Phu Bai, Vietnam, where conducted Civilian Med Cap operations on the Perfume River as well as medical operations on Fire Base Bastogne and others firebases in I corps.

As the 101st Airborne was leaving Vietnam, Keeton was transferred to the HHC 2ND BM 8 CAV 3 BDE (SEP) First Cavalry Division, where he was in charge of the Battalion Aide Station on Fire Base Melanie. Jim worked with Dr. William J. Osheroff (Battalion Surgeon), where Osheroff and Keeton maned the aide station on Fire Base Melanie 24/7 during operations of the 1st Cav Division, 2/8 th Cav. He returned to the US in late 1972 and was discharged from service in April 1973 with the rank of SP6/WO1.

Keeton received the Bronze Star Medal, Combat Medical Badge, Army Commendation Medal, Vietnam Service Medal, Vietnam Campaign Medal with 60 Device, National Defense Service Medal, Vietnam Cross of Gallantry with palm,

Army Valorous Unit Award and the Presidential Unit Citation.

After discharge, he returned to graduate school at Colorado State University in 1973 and started Keeton Industries, Inc. that same year; he serves as Chief Scientist and Aquaculture Engineer for the company. He served as president of the 101st Airborne Division Association.

Keeton married Linda Keeton in 1969, and they have two children, Luke and Jennifer, along with four grandchildren, Peyton, Braden, Stella and Grier.

BARBARA ELISE "BOBBIE" KEITH, an Army brat, was born in Winthrop, MA and grew up in five countries and seven states. Her dad, John D. Keith, was with the First Cav in North Korea; she wears his patch on her vest. Bobbie graduated from Narimasu High School at Grant Heights AFB and received an AA at Sophia University in Tokyo, Japan, before embarking on an assignment with the U.S. Agency for International Development (USAID) for a 3-year tour of duty in Viet Nam (1967-69).

During that time, Bobbie was asked to audition as a weather girl for the Armed Forces TV network, which started her volunteer career as "Bobbie the Weather Girl" (not paid but worth more than a million dollars because of the experiences of visiting the troops out in the boonies). The First CAV made her an honorary member of the First Team in 1968.

Upon her DEROS out of Viet Nam, she spent five years decompressing - leading a gypsy life - working and living in seven countries before returning to the United States. She had had a 30-year career in the Foreign Service of the Department of State and worked overseas in 14 embassies until retiring to Melbourne, FL. She has been a yellow hat volunteer for 16 years at the Viet Nam Veterans Memorial Wall.

JUAN KELLOGG graduated from Portsmouth Abbey in 1966 and was inducted on Sept. 22, 1969 at Fort Jackson, SC. He attained his AA in 1985 and AS in 1998 from Southwest Florida State.

Kellogg received the National Defense Medal, Vietnam Service, Air Medal, Army Commendation (two) and CIB.

He was discharged at Travis AFB, CA on April 29, 1971 as SP4.

Kellogg performed custodial work.

Juan and Joyce Kellogg have one daughter, Megan Ann.

GARRY O. KENDRICK enlisted in July 1971 for the Armor Corps and entered military service at Fort Lewis, WA on August 1, 1971. Following basic training, he was transferred to Fort Knox Armor Center for armor Crewman training. Later in his career, Garry attended every leadership course and served in every leadership position in the Armor Corps from Tank Commander to Command Sergeant Major.

During his service in the Army, Garry was assigned to the following units in Germany, the 1st Armored Division, the 1st and 3rd Infantry Divisions and the Combat Maneuver Training Center. In the US, he served at Fort Knox, KY and lastly at Fort Hood, TX with the 1st Cavalry Division.

In August 1995, Garry was assigned to the 2nd Battalion 12th Cavalry as the Command Sergeant Major. During his two years in the division, the unit was tasked twice to deploy over half of its Soldiers to Kuwait supporting other units. The Battalion conducted a National Training Center rotation and was commended for its performance during the live fire phase. The Battalion transferred their M1Al Abrams Tanks to the US Marine Corp. The Commanding General commended the unit for their hard work and untiring effort ensuring the Marine Corps received the best maintained equipment while ensuring repair costs were the lowest in the Division. Afterwards, Garry oversaw the execution of New Equipment Training and Tank Crew Qualification Course firing for the M1A2. This live fire exercise was the culminating/qualification event ensuring that the Soldiers were properly trained on their major weapon system, the Army's most modern Abram's Tanks.

In July 1997, Garry retired from the Army. He received the following awards during his service: Legion of Merit, Meritorious Service Medal w/OLC #2, Army Commendation Medal w/OLC #2, Army Achievement Medal, National Defense Service Medal 2nd award, Noncommissioned Officer Development Ribbon (4th Award), Army Service Ribbon and the Overseas Service Ribbon (4th Award).

While serving in the Army, Garry attended Central Texas College where he received an Associate Degree. After retiring from the Army, he attended Sullivan University, obtaining both a Bachelor and a Master of Science degrees.

In March 2015, Garry finally retired, having spent 43 years working of the Army as enlisted and in other civilian capacities; 26 years as a Soldier, six years as a support contractor and 11 years as a Department of the Army civilian. Today Garry enjoys working around his house and traveling.

Garry married Maria Paulus in 1974 and they have two children, Wolfgang and Jeffery.

STANLEY C. KENT was commissioned as a 2nd Lieutenant, Field Artillery, upon graduation from Indiana University in June 1967. He entered active duty at Fort Sill on June 19, 1967. After completion of the Officer Basic Course, Kent served with the 5th Infantry Division, Fort Carson and then attended Ranger School at Fort Benning, receiving the Ranger Tab in May 1968.

Kent served with 1st Cavalry Division in Vietnam from June 1968 to May 1969. He was assigned to B Battery, 1/30 Artillery as forward observer and executive officer and then HHB, 1/30 Artillery as S-l and air observer. Kent served on LZs Stella, Sharon, Anne, Rita, Ellen and Odessa and at Phouc Vinh.

After Vietnam, Kent was assigned to the Artillery School at Fort Sill. He was discharged from active duty at Fort Sill as a Captain on August 21, 1970.

Kent received the Bronze Star Medal, Army Accommodation Medal, Air Medal, Vietnam Service Medal, Vietnam Campaign Medal and National Defense Service Medal.

After discharge, Kent attended Indiana University School of Law, graduating in 1973. He has practiced law in Colorado Springs since 1974.

Kent is married to Peggy Richen Kent. They have two children, Alison Richen Kent and James Todd Kent.

TOMMY R. KETTERER was born Nov. 8, 1984 and graduated from Lyman High School in Longwood, FL, in 2003. He graduated from Jacksonville University in Florida in 2007, with a bachelor's degree in history and geography, and was also a Division 1AA college football player.

He enlisted on 30 January 2008 in Jacksonville, and was shipped to Fort Benning, GA, for boot camp. Enlisted Infantryman, OCS and Infantry Officer training was received at Fort Hood, TX. Ketterer served with B Co. 3-8 CAV, 3rd Brigade, 1ST Cavalry Division (MAY 2008- SEP 2010); HHC 1-7 CAV, 1ST Brigade, 1ST Cavalry Division (JUL 2011- DEC 2011); A CO. 2-8 CAV, 1ST Brigade, 1ST Cavalry Division (DEC 2011- NOV 2013); and HHC 2-8 CAV, 1ST Brigade, 1ST Cavalry Division (NOV 2013- SEP 2014).

During his service, Ketterer fought during Operation Iraqi Freedom (OIF), DEC 2008-DEC 2009, Mosul, Iraq; Operation New Dawn (OND), JULY 2011-DEC 2011, Balad, Iraq; and Operation Spartan Shield (OSS) DEC 2011-JUL 2012, Camp Buchring, Kuwait. He was awarded the Combat Infantryman Badge among others.

He was discharged at Fort Hood, TX, on 30 September 2014 with the rank of 1LT.

WILLIAM P. KIMREY was born Dec. 31, 1946 in High Point, NC and graduated from Ragsdale High School in 1965. He enlisted in July 1968.

After Boot Camp at Fort Bragg, additional training was TigerLand – NCOS – Fort Benning.

From May 1969 to November 1969, he served with B Company, 1/7. He was engaged in battles at Budop among others.

He was awarded the Combat Infantry Badge and Purple Heart.

SP4 Kimrey was discharged in April 1970 at Oakland, CA.

He worked in an automotive machine shop until retiring in 2010.

William and Jane have four children – Molly, Kate, Mary and Jonathon. Their grandchildren are Cameron, Hannah, Lillian, Payton, Adrienne, Addison, Mallory, William, Caroline and Parker.

MELBOURNE "MEL" E. KNOWLES was born Sept. 11, 1922 in Flint, MI and enlisted Sept. 10, 1942, took Boot Camp at Fort Bragg, NC and was also stationed at Fort Bliss, TX.

He was in New Guinea, Bismarck Archipelago, the Western Pacific and Southern Philippines, Luzon.

Knowles was awarded the Bronze Star.

His memorable experience was the push from Lingayen Gulf to Manila to free the POWs.

T-5 Knowles was discharged at Camp Grant, IL on Oct. 28, 1945.

He attended General Motor Institute and was a General Supervisor in Manufacturing for Buick Motor Div., GM, retiring August 1, 1980.

Retirement activities include bird watching, hunting and fishing the Great Lakes.

Mel and Joyce (deceased September 2014) have two children, Jack and Janet. Grandchildren are Jennifer, Gregory, Mark and Matthew.

ORVAL W. KOLDEN enlisted for the 1st Cav. Div. in early 1947. Basic training at Fort Knox, KY with Advanced Infantry Training at Fort Lewis, WA with 2d Inf. Div. Next, Army of Occupation in Tokyo with 7th Cav. Regt., later on detached service to HQ1CX in Camp Drake, north of Tokyo. Returned to CONUS December 1948 and spent the night of Dec. 23 at his buddy's outfit, Sugamo Prison, where the Class "A" war criminals were hanged that night.

In 1949 he re-upped for 1CX and assigned to G-2. His OIC was 1st Lt. Dale Buis, who in early 1960s, would become the first officer to be killed in Vietnam when he was an advisor there.

1CX was notified they would be making an amphibious behind-the-lines invasion on South Korea's east coast which they did July 18, 1950 – no shooting!! They made the drive north near Manchuria when the Chinese entered the war and US/UN armies pulled back down south. Kolden left 1st Cav. Div. in July 1951.

After some more interesting assignments he spent a tour in Vietnam as 1SGT and Operations Sgt. with military advisor team with the VN Army. He retired in 1974 with 27 years service.

Kolden was awarded Bronze Star Medal, Meritorious Svc. Medal, Joint Svcs. Commendation Medal, Good Conduct Medal with 9 knots, Army of Occupation Medal, Natl. Svc. Medal, Korean Service Medal with 5 stars, Vietnam Service Medal with 3 stars, US Pres. Meritorious Unit Citation, UN KSM, Korean Defense Medal (Korean Govt. Award). Korean Pres. Meritorious Unit Citation, Vietnam Pres. Meritorious Unit Citation and Vietnam Defense Medal.

CLINTON M. KOUNK enlisted in the U.S. Army in May 1964 and attended basic training at Fort Ord, CA. Following basic training, he attended training as a Helicopter Mechanic at Fort Eustis, VA. He was then transferred to Nuremburg, Germany where he was assigned to B Company, 126th Maintenance Battalion, 4th Armored Division. Kounk then received orders to attend the Warrant Officer Rotary Wing Aviator Course (66-11WFA) at Fort Wolters, TX and graduated as a WO1 in June 1966 at Fort Rucker, AL. From there he attended the Aircraft Maintenance Officer Course (AMOC) at Fort Eustis, VA. He then joined the 205th Assault Support Helicopter Company (Geronimo's) at Fort Sill, OK where he transitioned to the CH-47A and deployed with the aircraft on the MSTS Britton to Vũng Tàu, Vietnam arriving in May 1967.

Upon arrival in Vietnam, Kounk was transferred to the 180th Assault Support Helicopter Company (Big Windy) where he served as a Maintenance Officer in the 403rd Transportation Detachment in Phú Hiệp, Vietnam (just South of Tuy Hòa). Following his tour in 1967-68, he returned to Fort Eustis, VA and became an instructor in the CH-47 Maintenance Repair Course and also attended the CH-47 Test Pilot Course. Subsequently, he received a direct appointment to First Lieutenant Infantry.

Following attendance at the Infantry Officer's Basic Course, Fort Benning, GA and the U.S. Army Aircraft Accident Investigation Course, University of Southern California, Kounk returned to Vietnam in June 1970 and was assigned as the Battalion Aviation Safety Office for the 229th Assault Helicopter Battalion (Stacked Deck), 1st Cavalry Division at Bien Hoa Airbase, Vietnam. He returned to the U.S. in May 1971 and was assigned to the Flight Simulator Division, U.S. Army Aviation Center, Fort Rucker, AL. He received a Branch Transfer to the Transportation Corps and subsequently to the Aviation Branch. He attended the Transportation Officer's Advanced Course, Command and General Staff College; and was assigned as a National Guard Advisor to the Iowa National Guard in Davenport, Iowa.

Major Kounk was subsequently assigned to the U.S. Army Computer Science School at Fort Benjamin Harrison in Indianapolis, IN; and then to Headquarters, United States Army Europe, Heidelberg, Germany in August 1983 where he served as an Automation Systems Management Officer, Office of the Deputy Chief of Staff for Information Management. Kounk retired from the U.S. Army in March 1986 with 22 years of service. He continued to work for the U.S. Army in Germany as a Government Contractor returning to Colorado Springs, CO in August 1997 having served 14 years in Heidelberg, Germany.

Kounk received the Legion of Merit, several Bronze Stars, Air Medals, Army Commendation Medals, the Vietnam Service Medal, Vietnam Campaign Medal, Vietnam Cross of Gallantry, and the Nation Defense Service Medal. He was also qualified as an Instructor Pilot in the CH-47A-C and OH-6A. He holds a Commercial Helicopter Pilots License and has a type rating in the Boeing Vertol (BV) 234. Kounk graduated from Embry-Riddle Aeronautical University in 1976 with a BS in Aeronautics and an AS in Aviation Safety.

While assigned to the U.S. Army Computer Science School at Fort Benjamin Harrison in Indianapolis, IN he met and married the former Vicki L. Whitmyre. They have three Daughters (Lisa, Trisha, and Wendi) and between them six Grandchildren (Brayton, Brandon, Brenden, Cortney, Emma and Annabelle).

Kounk has continuously served the U.S. Government since retirement in 1986 as a contractor where he is employed today by the Northrop Grumman Corporation and works as a Microsoft Systems Engineer for the Missile Defense Agency (MDA) at Schriever Air Force Base in Colorado Springs. Kounk holds numerous Microsoft Certifications.

NEIL A. KROGER joined the Army in November 1963. After completing basic training at Fort Knox, Kentucky, he was transferred to C Co 5Bn 3d Bde, Fort Ord, CA for AIT. Upon completion of AIT, Neil was transferred to HQCO USAG & LSOE at Camp Roberts, CA. In September 1964, he was transferred to Hq & HqCo 4th Bn 3d Bde at Fort Ord. In November 1965, PFC Kroger was transferred to 55th Co (OC) 5th Stu Bn TSB, Fort Benning, GA for officer training. On May 13, 1965, Neil graduated from Officer Candidate School. Since childhood he had wanted to be a Soldier.

Second Lieutenant Kroger then entered Ranger Training, completing this training on July 15, 1965. Lieutenant Kroger was then transferred to C Company, 1st Battalion, 7th Cavalry Regiment, First Cavalry Division (Airmobile). On Aug. 16, 1965, the 1st Battalion, 7th Cavalry, First Air Cavalry Division boarded the *USNS Maurice Rose* for deployment to Vietnam.

The First Cavalry Division arrived at their An Khe base in mid September, 1965. On Nov. 14, 1965, Lieutenant Kroger, as part of 1st Battalion, 7th Cavalry, flew into landing zone X-Ray in the la Orang Valley.

After repelling the afternoon attack of the North Vietnamese 7th Battalion on Nov. 14, Lieutenant Kroger's 1st platoon and Lieutenant Jack Geoghegan's 2nd platoon were attacked at 7:15 AM on Nov. 15, 1965 by three companies of North Vietnamese regulars. They stood with their men and fought to the last man. Second Lieutenant Neil A. Kroger was killed in action while "holding the line" of C Company, 1st Battalion 7th Cavalry, First Air Cavalry Division, in the Battle of the la Orang Valley. (Read *We Were Soldiers Once ... And Young.*)

Neil was buried with military honors in our family grave site at Mount Carmel Cemetery in Hillside, IL. Neil was survived by his parents, Mr. and Mrs. Carl H. Kroger, his sisters, Nancy and Martha, and his little brother, Jeff. After my mother received the ceremonial flag, the sparkle went out of her eyes. She was never the same. I was left to wonder how, after all that training, Neil would be killed after two months in Vietnam.

Second Lieutenant Neil A. Kroger received the Bronze Star Medal with V device, for valor, the Purple Heart Medal, Ranger Tab, Combat Infantry Badge, Presidential Unit Citation, National Defense Service Medal, Good Conduct Medal, Vietnam Service Medal, Vietnam Campaign Medal, and the Vietnam Cross of Gallantry with palm.

Neil wanted to be a career Army officer, and friends of his who survived the war have said he would have made a good one. Many things could have been! He missed being my best man and I missed being his. My kids missed having his kids for cousins. It took meeting the men Neil died for, at 15 la Drang Dinners, for me to accept his death and the fact that he was meant to be a warrior and I was meant to be a teacher and Gold Star brother. My name is Jeff Kroger, and I will always be Second Lieutenant Neil Kroger's "little brother."

MIGUEL A. LABOY was drafted from Yabucoa, Puerto Rico and sworn in on Feb 1, 1973 at Fort Buchanan, P.R. He spoke no English and only had $17.00 in his pocket at that time. He completed BCT at Fort Jackson, SC and graduated as the Honor Graduate of the Radio Teletypewriter Operator Course Fort Gordon, Ga. He was promoted from PV2 to Specialist (held PFC for one day) for his accomplishments.

Upon graduation, Laboy was assigned to Fort Riley, KS (HHC, 1st BN, 28th Infantry) as a TTY operator. He participated in numerous exercises including two REFORGERS, and also graduated from the NCO academy during this tour. He was next assigned to the 167th Signal Company, Caserma Ederle, Vicenza, Italy (SETAF) and promoted to Sergeant. As a Team Chief, he completed real world classified missions and was appointed a Platoon Sergeant. Laboy's next assignment was to HHB, 3rd BN, and Fort Knox, KY, where he graduated from ANCOC, served as Training NCO, Supply Sergeant, Communications Chief and applied for and was selected to become a Drill Sergeant. He was subsequently assigned to A Co, 8th Bn, 2nd Infantry Training Brigade, Fort Benning, GA, and graduated from the Drill Sergeant Course. Upon graduation, he was assigned to train infantrymen (11B) in basic skills at Fort Benning.

Laboy's next assignment was as a Platoon and later First Sergeant of Delta Company, 57th Signal Battalion, 3rd Signal Brigade. He deployed his company in support of Desert Shield/Storm and upon his return attended and graduated for the First Sergeant's Course at Fort Bliss, TX. In 1993, he attended and graduated from the Sergeant's Major Academy and subsequently served as the Training NCOIC, HHC, 3rd Signal Brigade; Communications Chief 1st Brigade, 2nd Infantry Division, Camp Casey, South Korea, and was selected as Sergeant Major and Senior Advisor to the Army National Guard (SRAAG) New York with units in the Bronx, Harlem, Brooklyn and Queens. His last two positions were as Chief Signal NCO (G6), 122nd Signal Battalion, Camp Red Cloud, South Korea and as the S3 Operations, acting CSM (while the battalion was deployed to Bosnia) and G6, 1st Cavalry Division.

During his tenure, he supported and participated in numerous humanitarian missions (earthquake and floods), several deployments (NTC, REFORGER, CPXs, FTXs).

He is grateful for all of God's blessings, his family, the U.S. Army and the USA for giving him the opportunity to achieve the American dream. Also, he is grateful for the trust and support given to him by his leaders and the superb Soldiers that he had the honor to serve with. They say that "no Army marches forward without the cook", and he believes that no Soldier receives promotions, decorations, leadership positions without the support of his Soldiers, great leaders and loving family. He is honored, proud, and humbled to have served with so many outstanding Soldiers.

SIDNEY L. "SID" LADOW joined the US Army in 1957, two weeks after graduating from high school in LaMonte, MO. His basic training was with the 9th Infantry Division in Fort Carson, CO. From there he went to Fort Belvoir, VA for Engineer training then on to Germany for three years. He was reassigned to Fort Jackson, SC until 1963, then on to Korea. During the Fort Jackson tour, his MOS was changed to Infantryman after he graduated from the 3rd Army NCO Academy.

In Korea, he was assigned as a squad leader with Company "E," 20th Infantry. After a year, he was assigned to the 2nd Armored Division at Fort Hood, TX where he was promoted to Staff Sergeant in an Infantry Battalion. In 1966 Sid attended Officers Candidate School and was commissioned a 2nd Lt. in the Ordnance corps. He attended the Maintenance Officers course at Aberdeen Proving Grounds and upon completion was reassigned back to the 2nd Armored Division as the Maintenance Officer of a Tank Battalion. After six months, he was transferred to an Infantry Battalion in the 1st Armored Division as a Test Officer with the Division Logistics Systems Test.

He was promoted to 1st Lt. in October of 1967 and went to Vietnam where he assumed command of "A" Detachment, 27th Maintenance Battalion supporting the 1st Brigade at Quang Tri and later at Tay Ninh. He was promoted to Captain in October 1968 and returned to the US in July 1969 to attend the Ordnance Officer's Career Course. After graduation, he was transferred to Fort Bragg, NC and was the Executive Officer of the 3rd Army Command Maintenance Management Team until being assigned the following year to command the 563rd Heavy Equipment Maintenance Company supporting the 18th Airborne Corps and assigned units. Sid also served as the State Maintenance Advisor to the Kentucky National Guard for a year. He was promoted to Major in 1978.

His last assignment before retiring was with the 377th Theater Army Area Command, an Army Reserve Logistical Command unit in New Orleans, LA where he was the Maintenance Plans and Policies Officer. He participated in a Reforger Exercise in Germany and later in the United Arab Republic of Egypt as part of Exercise "BrightStar."

His decorations include the Bronze Star, Meritorious Service Medal, Air Medal, Army Commendation Medal and numerous other awards and decorations. Sid and his wife, Sue, enjoy cruises in the Caribbean, Bluegrass Festivals and antique tractor shows. Sid is a graduate of the University of Central Florida. They have three children, five grandchildren and two great grandchildren. Sid enjoys volunteering at the Palm Bay Florida Police Department as a Cold Case Investigator.

FRANCIS "FRANK" LAFFERTY enlisted in June 1963 as Providence, RI. Following Boot Camp at Fort Dix, he had training in Avionics/ Bell helicopter. Frank was stationed at Fort Gordon, Fort Benning and Vietnam. He was involved in LZ S-Ray, LZ Albany and Ia Drang Valley.

For his service, he was awarded the BSM W/V and AM / 11 cluster. Memorable experiences were the battles of LZ X-Ray and Albany.

Frank was discharged in August 1966 at Oakland, CA with the rank of E5.

He is affiliated with the VFW, American Legion and 1st CAV Association.

Since retiring in 2005 he plays golf, is a VA Volunteer and works with the VFW.

He and Carol have four children – Mike, Paul, Patricia and Kathlee. Grandchildren are Martin, Joey, Leam, Mason, Julia, Gina and Tony.

GENERAL LEON J. LAPORTE is a native of Providence, Rhode Island and a 1964 graduate of Mount Pleasant High School where he was a scholar and athlete. He entered the University of Rhode Island in the fall of 1964. During his senior year, he was a Cadet Battalion Commander and graduated as a Distinguished Military Graduate and he was commissioned as a Second Lieutenant of Armor. General LaPorte served in the US Army for 38 years, rising to the rank of 4-star General.

General LaPorte served in worldwide operational assignments where he commanded at every level from Lieutenant to General. In 1971, he served as a Gunship Pilot and Platoon Commander for the 238th Aerial Weapons Company in the Republic of Vietnam and received several awards for valor.

Colonel LaPorte served as the G3 Operations Officer, Chief of Staff and 3rd Brigade Commander in the First Cavalry Division. He deployed and fought with in Southwest Asia during Operations Desert Shield and Desert Storm. In 1995, Major General LaPorte returned to Fort Hood where he commanded the First Cavalry Division until July 1997. During this period, he deployed elements of the 1st Cav Division worldwide on operational missions in area such as Kuwait, Korea and Europe.

In August 1998, Lieutenant General LaPorte assumed command of the III Armored Corps and Fort Hood, Texas, where he served until August 2001. During this period, III Corps had the mission to train and deploy forces to Bosnia and Herzegovina for Peace Stability Operations. In May 2002, General LaPorte assumed command of United Nations Command, Combined Forces Command, and the United States Forces Korea, located in Seoul, South Korea. He held this command for four years until his retirement from active duty in April 2006. General LaPorte was a vital force in restoring the confidence of the ROK-US Alliance and revolutionizing its ability to deter or defeat an attack from North Korea. General Leon J. LaPorte was awarded the Korean Tong-Il Medal, the highest of the five medals under the Order of National Security, by South Korean President Roh, Moo-hyun for his four years of dedicated leadership and service to the Republic of Korea/United States Alliance.

Some of General LaPorte's awards include the Defense Distinguished Service Medal, Distinguished Service Medal with one OLC, Legion of Merit with three OLC, Distinguished Flying Cross, Bronze Star, Meritorious Service Medal with with two Oak Leaf Clusters, Air Medal with "V" device, Army Commendation with "V" device and Oak Leaf Cluster, Vietnamese Cross of Gallantry with Palm Parachute Badge, Aviator Badge and Ranger Tab. General LaPorte was awarded the Honorary Doctor of Laws degree from the University of Rhode Island in May 2004.

Since his retirement from active duty, General LaPorte continues to be a staunch supporter of the Army and the First Cavalry Division. The distinctive accomplishments of General Leon J. LaPorte culminate a distinguished career in the service of his country and reflect great credit upon himself, his family and the United States of America.

General LaPorte and his wife Judy reside in San Antonio, Texas.

NORMAN DEE LAUB was born Jan. 6, 1924 in Enterprise, UT and enlisted in November 1942 at Salt Lake City, UT. After Boot Camp at Fort Douglas, UT he had additional training at Fort Riley, KS.

Laub was stationed at Camp Strathpine, Australia. He was engaged in battles in New Guinea; Admiralty Islands; Leyte, Philippines and the liberation of Santa Tomas.

He was awarded a Bronze Star, Purple Heart and Manila, PI.

Norman was discharged at Salt Lake City, UT as a Corporal.

Laub spent his civilian life in farming. He was affiliated with the Utah Young Farmer of the Year.

Prior to his death in 2002, he had served two missions for the LDS Church in Oregon and Montana.

Norman and Barbara Ruth (Jensen) had eight children – Craig, Janet, Lynnette, Larry, Laurie, LaDel, Jody Lynn and Caylon. Grandchildren are: Jody Corbett; Merril, Jared, Justin and Mattew Campbell; Megan Everett; Robert, Nathan, Scott and Emily Judd; Michelle Peterson; Andrea, McCall, Jessie and Ben Ovard; Suzy Mortenson; Milton, Travis, Kevin, D.J., Mandy, Tanner, Parker, Maddison, Spencer, Allie Jo, Varon, Rylon and Sharah Lamb. They have 47 great-grandchildren.

CARL H. LAWRENCE enlisted at Wilmington, DE in September 1959 and took Basic Training at Fort Jackson, SC. Additional training was A.I.T., NCO Academy, Jungle School, Drill Sgt. School and NCO Adv. Course

He was stationed Fort Knox, KY; Korea, DMZ Police 1/9th Cav. 1st Cav. Div.; Munich, Germany; Fort Carson, CO; Panama; RVN 12th CAV/5th CAV, 1st CAV Div, Fort Polk, LA; RVN; Fort Benning, GA and Crailsheim, Germany.

He was awarded CIB, SS, two BS, MSM, two AM, ARCOM, Good Conduct, National Defense, RVN Service, Korean Service, RVN Crss of Gall, RVN Campaign, Drill Sgt. Badge and Jungle Expert Patch.

Lawrence was discharged on Oct. 31, 1979 at Fort Knox, KY as MSGE-8.

He was a JROTC teacher for 11 years and a tour bus driver for 17 years. In retirement he travels, attends church and a DAV van driver.

Carl and Catherin have two children, Jacqueline and Richard, and two grandchildren, Heather and Brittany.

CRAIG LAWSON was born in 1949 in Morrisville, VT. He graduated from Peoples Academy in 1967.

Lawson enlisted at Anchorage, AK and took basic training at Fort Lewis, WA. Additional training was MP at Fort Gordon, GA.

After being stationed at Fort Ord and Camp Gorvad, Vietnam, he was discharged in California with the rank of SP4.

COLONEL KIRBY LAWSON was commissioned a Second Lieutenant of Infantry upon graduation from Bucknell University as a distinguished military graduate in 1960.

Completing Ranger and Airborne schooling he served as an infantry platoon leader and company executive officer with the 1st Battle Group, A Co, 5th Cavalry, 1st Cavalry Division in Korea. He then volunteered for Army Flight Training earning his wings in 1963. He served in 1966 with the First Infantry Division in Vietnam in both infantry and aviation positions, logging over 800 combat hours.

He returned to Vietnam for a second year in 1969, commanding Charlie Company "Ghostriders" and as executive officer of the 227th Assault Helicopter Battalion of the First Air Cavalry Division. Colonel Lawson led the first air assault formation of helicopters into Cambodia at first light on May 1, 1970. During this tour of duty he logged his 1500th combat hour.

For his service in Vietnam, Colonel Lawson was decorated with the Silver Star, 3 awards of the Distinguished Flying Cross, 3 Bronze Stars and 54 Air Medals, two for Valor, Army Commendation Medal for Valor, to mention a few.

In the years following Vietnam, Colonel Lawson attended the Air Force Command and Staff College while earning an MPA from Auburn University. Later he served in numerous command and staff positions including Executive Officer 3rd Brigade 4th Inf. Div., Commander 7th Combat Aviation Bn and as G-3 Operations of the 7th Infantry Div.

Following graduation from the Army War College, he served on the Army staff in the Pentagon in the office of the Deputy Chief of Operations G-3, and later as Aviation Officer of US Army Europe and Commander 2nd Basic Training Brigade, Fort Jackson, S.C.

During his last tour Colonel Lawson was Deputy Assistant Commandant of the Army Aviation School and Garrison Commander, Fort Rucker, AL. He earned the coveted Air Assault Badge and was awarded the Legion of Merit (2nd award) upon his retirement as a Master Army Aviator with over 3300 flying hours in 1989.

Colonel Lawson currently lives in the space coast of Viera, FL with his wife of 53 years, Barbara. He has served as Chairman of the Board of Directors for the Indian River Colon Club, a retired military resort community of 773 homes and golfing country club.

PAUL A. LINK was born March 18, 1929 in Attica, OH. After graduating from St. Paul's Catholic High School in 1948, he enlisted in January 1949 and took basic training at Fort Knox, KY.

Link was in Germany twice, twice in Korea and in Vietnam from 1965-1966. While in Korea (1958), he had a cart "Links U Haul." He didn't talk too much about his service. He was a member of 11th Air Assault Division Association.

Link received the Good Conduct Medal (5th award). He was discharged on April 30, 1969 at Fort Benning, GA as E-6.

Link retired in 1990 after working 22 years for Bellevue Manufacturing Co. He was active in American Legion, as Sherman, Huron County, Ohio Township Trustee, and Knights of Columbus until his death.

Paul and Juanita M. had one daughter, Paula Jeane Link-Cockie and two grandchildren, Andrew G. and Sarah A. Cockie.

RONALD F. LIVINGSTON was born in Durango, Colorado. Livingston was raised on a dry land farm 22 miles north of Cortez, CO. Livingston graduated from Montezuma Cortez High School in May 1965 then went to Southern Colorado State College, studying machine shop and graduating with an Associate of Applied Science Degree in May 1967.

Livingston entered the U.S. Army on 4 March 1968 and attended basic training at Fort Polk, Louisiana completing the training on 10 May

1968. Livingston went to Warrant Officer Rotary Wing Aviator Course in Fort Wolters, TX for Primary Helicopter Training for 20 weeks. Advanced Helicopter Training was for an additional 16 weeks at Fort Rucker, Alabama. Upon completion of this training Livingston was appointed a WO1 and was awarded the Army Aviation Badge on 10 February 1969.

Livingston served in Vietnam with the 1st Cavalry Division; 1st Squadron 9th Cavalry Regiment; A Troop in Tay Ninh, Vietnam. Livingston was assigned to the Weapons Platoon to fly helicopter gunships. A Troop was receiving more Cobra Gunships to phase out the Huey Gunships so more Cobra qualified pilots were needed for the Cobra. Livingston was selected to attend the Cobra Transition course in Vung Tau, Vietnam. Livingston was made Aircraft Commander in the Cobra a few weeks after his return to the unit.

During Livingston's time in the Army he was awarded the Army Aviation Badge; National Defense Service Medal; Vietnam Service Medal; Vietnam Campaign Medal with 60 Device; Bronze Star; Distinguished Flying Cross; Air Medal with 39 OLC; Vietnamese Cross of Gallantry with Palm; and Army Commendation Medal for Heroism. Campaigns include Vietnam War/Tet 69 Counteroffensive Campaign 23 February to 8 June 1969; Vietnam War/Summer-Fall 1969 Campaign 9 June to 31 October 1969; Vietnam War/Winter-Spring 1970 Campaign 1 November 1969 to 30 April 1970.

Livingston returned to the U.S. and was stationed at Fort Carson, Colorado with the Fifth United States Army; Troop D; 4th Squadron; 12th Cavalry. Livingston went to a special project at Fort Hunter Liggett in California, testing Cobra gunships against F-4 Phantom Jets from the U.S. Navy. Livingston returned to Fort Carson, Colorado and was discharged from service on Dec. 15, 1970.

After being discharged from the Army Livingston worked for Rocky Mountain Helicopters, Inc. flying helicopters for approximately a year and a half. From 1975 to 1994 Livingston owned and operated helicopters, having eight helicopters at one point. Most of the flying was for oil exploration, wild land firefighting and power line construction. From 1994 to 2004 Livingston worked for the U.S. Department of Transportation (FAA); Department of Agriculture (Wildlife Services); and Department of the Interior (BLM). Livingston was an Aviation Safety Inspector for the FAA and Wildlife Services and a Program Manager for the Large Air tankers Structural Integrity program. Currently Livingston is a consultant for aviation businesses as well as a Designated Airworthiness Representative for the FAA.

Livingston is married to Bequi L. Livingston. Livingston has four children and one granddaughter. Livingston's children are Mendee Ray Livingston, Kyle Ray Livingston, Amity Francis Livingston, and Parker Dee Livingston. Granddaughter Penelope Janae Nicolace (Mendee's daughter) and a daughter in-law, Savannah Livingston, married to Kyle Livingston. Kyle Livingston and Savannah Livingston are both Blackhawk Helicopter Pilots in the U.S. Army. They have both completed tours in Afghanistan. Savannah was with the 1st Cavalry Division in Afghanistan and Kyle was with the 25th Infantry Division. Kyle is a CW3 and Savannah is a Captain and both are currently assigned to Fort Rucker, Alabama.

ALBERT M. "MIKE" LORBER enlisted in October 1966 and entered basic and advanced training at Fort Ord, CA. Upon graduation, he was sent to Vietnam in April 1967 and assigned as company clerk to HHC, 3rd Brigade (7th Cav.) of the 1st Air Cavalry Division. Lorber served on several landing zones (LZs) in 1 Corps and in the Hue area during the Tet Offensive. He was responsible for submission of operational readiness reports to division headquarters. Lorber completed his tour in Vietnam in April 1968 with the rank of SP5, E-5.

Stateside, Lorber served with the Judge Advocation General's office at the Oakland Army Base performing administrative legal duties, including criminal and conscientious objectors proceedings. Lorber was then transferred to Fort McArthur in San Pedro, CA where he completed his military service in September 1969.

In addition to the Army Commendation Medal for meritorious service in Vietnam, Lorber received Vietnam Service Medal, Vietnam Campaign Medal, National Defense Service Medal and Army Valorous Unit Award for operations against an armed enemy during the period Oct. 1, 1967 through Oct. 31, 1968.

After discharge, Lorber received his undergraduate degree from California State University at Los Angeles and graduate degrees from Michigan State University and Aurora University. After many years of service for the State of Illinois in the departments of Mental Health, Children and Family Services and Human Services, he retired with the Department of Corrections as Unit Superintendent in Joliet, IL in 2002.

Mike married Susan Lorber in 1987. The Lorbers have two wonderful children, Sarah and Stephen. Mike and Susan reside in Mt. Pleasant, WI.

BILL LORD enlisted in the Army in 1954 and served four years as a paratrooper in the 11th Airborne Division. Upon leaving active duty in 1958, he served six years in the Army Reserves. He was commissioned into the Chaplain Corps as a Reservist in 1962.

Called to active duty as a Chaplain in 1964, he participated in the Air Mobile Division Test at Fort Benning. He was assigned to the 1st Battalion, 12th Cavalry (Airborne) and shipped with the First Brigade airborne battalions to Vietnam in August 1965.

During Operation Shiny Bayonet in October, earned the first Silver Star given to an Army Chaplain during the Vietnam War for rescuing 17 wounded men under extreme enemy fire and at great risk to his life.

He also was invited to the White House to be part of the presentation of the Presidential Unit Citation awarded to the 1st Cavalry Division (Air Mobile).

In 1968 he returned to Vietnam to serve with infantry and air cavalry units of the 101st Airborne Division and again in 1970 to help establish the Drug Detoxification Centers while on TDY from the Office of the Chief of Army Chaplains.

His later assignments included establishing the first Clinical Pastoral Training program on an installation at Fort Leonard Wood. He also served as the 82nd Airborne Division Chaplain and the Deputy XVIII Airborne Corps Chaplain at Fort Bragg. He was then sent to Germany where he served as the Community Staff Chaplain in Munich and in Nuremberg, Germany where he retired as a Colonel in 1984.

Chaplain Lord's decorations and awards include: The Silver Star, two Bronze Stars, two Air Medals, The Legion of Merit, two Meritorious Service Medals, two Army Commendation Medals, the Presidential Unit Citation (for participating in the battles along the la Drang River in November 1965), The Master Parachutist Badge and the 11th Air Mobile Air Assault Badge.

Upon retiring from the Army, he became a Consultant in the Corporate Training industry. He led a training program for managers and supervisors, which focused on following the "golden rule" at work (where it is the most difficult). He later wrote a similar training program for Law Enforcement Supervisors, which took him to Police Academies and Sheriffs training from coast to coast.

He fully retired in 2006 because of health issues and volunteered his time and energy into founding and building The US Army Chaplain Corps Regimental Association. He also pursued his hobby of fly fishing and has almost completed his "bucket list" of fishing in the 100 best trout streams in America. He and his wife live in Springfield, MO.

Chaplain Lord married Bettye Ellis in 1957. They have three children - Patrick, Darlene and William and four grandchildren - Susie Gray, Michael Weiss, Evan Lord, Erica Ballard and four great-grandchildren.

GEORGE LUKETIC enlisted at Kittanning, PA. He took Boot Camp at Fort Bliss, TX with Cannon Troop, 7th Cav. Regt. 1 Cav. Div. He had additional training as a Heavy Machine Gunner 605.

Luketic was engaged in battles GO33 & WD 45 in New Guinea, Bismarck Archipelago, Southern Philippines and Luzon.

He was awarded the Purple Heart, Good Conduct Medal, Philippines Liberation Ribbon with two Bronze Stars, Asiatic Pacific Service Medal with four Bronze Stars and one Bronze Arrowhead and the Combat Infantry Badge.

George Luketic was discharged on Oct. 20, 1945 at Indiantown Gap, PA with the rank of corporal.

In civilian life he was a coal miner and affiliated with the United Mine Workers of America. After retirement in 1982 he enjoyed hunting and fishing.

George and Betty L. (Tarr) Luketic had four children – George Jr., Mary, John and Joseph.

Luketic passed away on Nov. 19, 2008.

TONY LUPO began his military career after graduating from Seattle University in 1971 as a Second Lieutenant in the Military Police Corps. After several military police assignments in Germany and stateside he served as the 1st Cavalry Division Provost Marshal from June 1990 to June 1992. He deployed to Saudi Arabia for Desert Shield/Desert Storm. After deploying to the Division Rear at

AA Horse, he established MP patrols along the major MSR providing MP support for transiting convoys. During Desert Storm he assisted with the division's Refuel on the Move (ROM) as the division moved into Iraq.

After returning to Ft Hood, he was selected for Battalion Command of a CID Bn at Ft Lewis, followed by selection to Colonel, attendance at the Army War College, and assignment as the Deputy Chief of Staff for Support, Criminal Investigation Command (CID) Headquarters.

After retirement from active duty, Lupo served nearly 16 years as the US Army Medical Command Provost Marshal at Ft Sam Houston, TX. In this capacity he was responsible for all physical security, law enforcement and antiterrorism programs/oversight for all Army hospitals worldwide.

In 1979 Lupo married Martha Coenen, an active duty Army nurse (also a retired Colonel) and they have four sons, John, Judd, Tony and Andrew, along with one granddaughter, Maggie.

RANDALL "RANDY" L. LUSK was born Oct. 2, 1960 in Tampa, FL and graduated from New Hanover High School in 1978. He enlisted at AFEES Station, Raleigh, NC. Basic training at Fort Benning, GA (1978), was followed by training in Infantry, Airborne, Ranger and Special Forces.

He was stationed at Fort Bragg, Fort Benning, Fort Hood, Camp McKall, Fort Campbell, Fort Stewart, HAAF and MacDill AFB. He was in battles in El Salvador, Grenada, Lebanon, Panama – Operation Just Cause, Desert Shield/Storm and Bosnia.

He was awarded the CIB, Master Parachutist Badge with Star, Pathfinder Badge, Scuba Badge, Ranger Tab, and SF Tab.

Lusk was discharged in 1996 at MacDill AFB, Florida as a Master Sergeant.

He is affiliated with VFEW, AL, DAV, TREA, 75th RRA, 1st Cavalry Association, 82nd Association, 101st Association, CIA and now volunteers with Veterans Associations.

Randy and Julie have three children: Jacob, Tonya and Jennifer. Their grandchildren are Alexius, Jewell, Jesse, Memphis and Emma.

ROGER L. "DOC" LUTZ was born July 14, 1947 in Watsonville, CA, and graduated from Armona Union Academy, and later, California Polytechnical (SLO) IT/IA. He received AIT at Fort Sam Houston (Combat Medic 91B), and was also stationed at An Khe, Phan Thiet, Bong Song, Hue, Camp Evans, Khe Sanh, A Shau Valley, Quon Loie, and the Iron Triangle.

Doc fought in numerous engagements throughout I Corps, II, Corps, and III Corps, including Operation Jeb Stuart ('68), Tet Offensive – Battle of Hue and Quan Tri – New Year's, Operation Pegasus, Battle of Khe Sanh, Operation Toan Thang, Operation Comanche Falls II, Operation Navajo Warhorse, Ashau Valley, Quon Loi, and others.

He received the Bronze Star with V, Air Medal, Air Force Commendation Medal, Army Commendation Medal, Air Force Outstanding Unit Award, Combat Readiness Medal, Good Conduct Medal, Air Reserve Forces Meritorious Service Medal, Defense Service Medal, Vietnam Service Medal, Southwest Asia Service Medal with 2 Bronze Service Stars, Air Forces Reserve Medal, Air Force Training Ribbon, Republic of Vietnam Gallantry Cross with Device, and Republic of Vietnam Campaign Medal.

He was discharged from the Army in 1969 at Fort Lewis, WA with the rank of E-5. He later joined the U.S Air Force, where served in Operation Desert Storm January 2 – June 24, 1991. He retired from the Air Force in 2000 at Travis AFB with the rank of CMS (E-9).

He is currently active in professional life as a Water Engineer, CEO of Oakville Pump Service, and a farmer. Lutz is married to Marlys with three children – Roger Lutz III, Wesley Lutz, and Nicholas Lutz, and seven grandchildren – Kaiza, Andrew, Asher, Ava, Machelle, Kayla, and Abby.

ROBERTO TUDELA MAAÑAO enlisted into the Army on Feb. 5, 1968 in Naval Station, Guam. Flying and leaving home for the first time, headed for Fort Ord, CA for basic training. After basic training in April 1968 he then headed east to Fort Rucker, AL for his Helicopter Mechanic and Door Gunner training. His first unit assignment in June 1968 was in Fort Knox, KY, by late November of 1968 he was further transferred to Budingen. Germany assigned to 3112th Cavalry Troop and was immediately assigned to crew an OH-13 helicopter. By July 1969 he received orders for Republic of Vietnam. He then was sent to Fort Lewis, WA for a week of Vietnam jungle training.

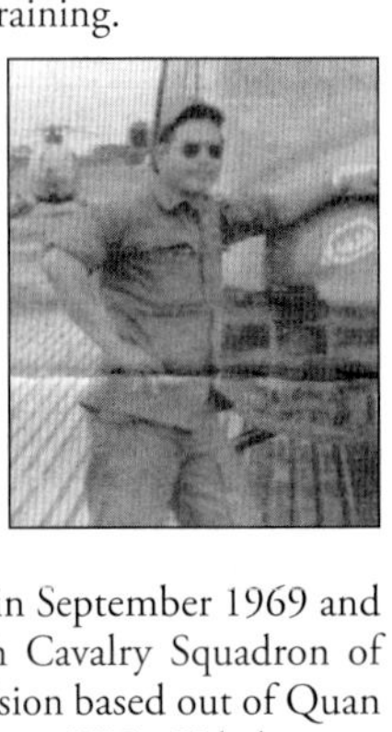

He arrived in Vietnam in September 1969 and assigned to B Troop 1/9th Cavalry Squadron of 1st Cavalry Airmobile Division based out of Quan Loi. He again was assigned as a UH-1H helicopter to crew chief within two days after arriving in the unit. Being a new guy, he got the worst condition helicopter. The helicopter had vibration issues that were never resolved and Roberto crashed for the first time on Oct. 10. The helicopter was destroyed in place where it crashed; fortunately the crew only obtained minor bruises and cuts. By the following day he started crewing another helicopter that just completed a major repair and maintenance schedule. He flew 24/7 until he and crew were shot down burning during an ammo resupply mission for a US Special Forces leading Laotian Army Infantry Company at night. They had picked up a Soldier that was hitching a ride for Ben Hoa processing center, because his time was up and was going home. Because they did not have a place to land, the ammo supply was kicked out by the crew chief, gunner and hitchhiker. This all happened on Nov. 10, 1969, which was noticed by all the helicopter crewmembers. It was decided that Roberto would no longer crew on combat missions on the 10th of the month. The Maintenance Officer made it a point to have Roberto crew the maintenance helicopter on the 10th of the month.

MICHAEL N. MANTEGNA was born into a family of Italian immigrants in Newark, NJ. Graduating at the top of his class from Newark's East Side Vocational and Technical High School, Mike attended Rutgers University's College of Arts and Sciences, where he majored in sociology with minors in psychology and economics. He also voluntarily participated in the Air Force ROTC program for two years. He graduated from Rutgers in 1964 with a Bachelor of Arts degree.

Mike enlisted in the US Army on July 1, 1964. After successfully completing Basic and Advanced Infantry Training at Fort Gordon, GA, he attended Infantry Officer Candidate School at Fort Benning. Commissioned a Second Lieutenant, he volunteered in the Second Infantry Division, which later was converted into the 1st Cavalry Division (Airmobile). In August 1965 President Lyndon Johnson ordered the "First Team," including its Light Brigade to Vietnam. Mike was the First Platoon Leader of Alpha Company, 2nd Battalion, 7th Cavalry.

Returning from Vietnam in August 1966, as a First Lieutenant, Mike was reassignment to Fort Benning, where he volunteered to return to Officer Candidate School as a Senior Tactical Officer.

After three and a half years on active duty, Mike went to Detroit, MI, to attend law school under the G.I. Bill. While a fulltime student at Detroit College of Law, Mike also volunteered to serve in the Michigan Army National Guard as Executive Officer of a mechanized infantry company.

For his almost six years of military service, Mike received numerous awards, decorations and commendations, including: the Bronze Star Medal, the Army Air Medal, the Combat Infantryman Badge, the National Defense Service Medal, the Vietnam Service Medal, the Presidential Unit Citation, the Republic of Vietnam Campaign Medal, the Distinguished Service Award, the Michigan State Service Medal, the Armed Forces Reserve Medal, Expert Qualification Badges for the M 14 and M16 Rifles, the M60 Machine Gun and the .45 Calibre Pistol, plus numerous letters and certificates of appreciation and commendation from his many unit commanders.

After graduation from law school with a Juris Doctor degree in 1970, Mike resigned his Army commission and returned to Georgia, where he started his own private law practice in Atlanta.

Mike currently resides with his wife, Sarah, in Alpharetta. He has a son, Michael Brian, and a daughter, Lara Kathleen Eddleman from a previous marriage, and a step-daughter Bonnie.

Now retired from the practice of law, Mike conducts a successful internet mail order business selling investment-quality postage stamps and coins and other collectibles.

OSCAR DANIEL MARSHALL was born Dec. 28, 1937 in Luverne, AL and graduated from Park College. He enlisted at Epselanta, MI and took Boot Camp at Fort Knox, KY. Additional training was Lacrosse Fire (1959), non-Commissioned Officer Academy (1960), Unit Cadre (1969), MAP-TOE (1973), Senior Non-Commissioned Officer Command & Staff (1973), Basic Airborne (1963) and Initial Enter Training-Cadre Training (1981).

Decorations for his service were National Defense Service Medal, Army Commendation Medal, Bronze Star Medal, Air Medal, Vietnam Service Medal with four Bronze Service Stars, Vietnam Campaign Medal with 60 Device, Vietnam Cross of Gallantry with Palm, Combat Infantryman Badge, Expert Infantryman Badge, Army of Occupation Medal (Berlin), Purple Heart with one OLC, Master Parachute Badge, Army Service Ribbon, Overseas Service Ribbon (second award), Non-Commissioned Professional Development Ribbon with 2nd Device, Good Conduct Medal (10th award) and Meritorious Service Medal. Marshall was honorably discharged at Fort Jackson, SC with the rank of 1SG E8.

Oscar and wife, Eartha, have four children – Alan, Oscar Jr., Lisa and Shannon. Sharon Wilson is their grandchild.

LARRY "STAN" MARTIN enlisted on March 21, 1968 at Harrisburg, PA. After basic training at Fort Gordon, he received additional training in Air Frame Repair and Air Frame Welding.

Martin was stationed at Fort Gordon, Fort Eustis, Phu Loi, Phouc Vinh, Quan Loi and Hunter Army/Airfield. He served in Vietnam 3 Corps.

Martin received the NDSM, VSM, VCM with 60 device, 1 O/S Bar, VN Cross of Gallantry with Palm and Sharpshooter (M16).

His memorable experience was being struck twice by lightning in Vietnam.

E-4 Martin was discharged on March 22, 1971 at Hunter Army Airfield.

He worked 35 years as Morgan Corp Buyer-Planner, retiring in 2016. His retirement activities are travel and Corvettes.

Larry and Josephine Martin have two children, Lawrence and Colleen.

MICHAEL C. MARTIN was born Sept. 17, 1947 in Albany, NY and graduated from Troy High School. He enlisted at Albany, NY in 1966 and took Boot Camp at Fort Carson, CO.

From January 1967 to January 1968, he served in Vietnam, C Company, 2nd of 5th Cavalry.

He was awarded the Bronze Star Medal, Meritorious Service Medal (2nd award), Air Medal, Army Commendation Medal (2nd award), Army Achievement Medal, Valorous Unit Award, Army Good Conduct Medal (6th award), Army Reserve Components Achievement Medal (5th award), National Defense Service Medal (2nd award), Vietnam Service Medal (2nd award), Armed Forces Reserve Medal, Noncommissioned Officer's Professional Develop; Ribbon with Numeral 4, Army Service Ribbon, Overseas Service Ribbon (2nd award), Republic of Vietnam Gallantry Cross Unit Citation with palm, Sharpshooter Marksmanship Qualification Badge with Rifle Bar, Combat Infantryman Badge and Army National Guard Recruiter Badge.

E8 Martin was discharged in May 1998 at Fort Drum, NY. He now spends time camping and traveling.

Michael and Kathryn have two children, Michelle and Melissa, and two grandchildren, Olivia and Nolan.

ELISEO "ED" V. MARTINEZ was born Nov. 24, 1932 in Roswell, NM and graduated from Roosevelt High School in East Los Angeles. He enlisted on August 8, 1950 in Los Angeles, CA, followed by Boot Camp at Camp Carson, CO.

Martinez says he was proud to have served under 1st Lt. Donald Moore, Arcadia, CA.

Martinez was awarded the Combat Infantry Badge, Korean War and UN.

Memorable experiences were five Martinez's in Co. "L", 8th Cavalry, 1st Cavalry Division in 1951 and an Honor Guard during the Korean Peace Talks at Punmunjom.

PFC Martinez was discharged on Oct. 10, 1953 at Fort Lewis, WA.

Ed retired in 1993 after being a driver, belonging to the Teamsters. Retirement activities are art and gardening.

Ed and Violet (Gotingco) have two children, Katherine and Hazel and three grandchildren – Julia, Victoria and Francisco.

ROBERTO "BOB" MATULAC was born Sept. 1, 1935 in San Francisco and graduated from George Washington High School in 1953. He enlisted Dec. 1, 1953 at San Francisco, CA. After Boot Camp at Fort Riley, KS he received additional training as COMMO SPECIALIST, Ansbach, Germany; Non Commissioned Officer School, Bad Tolz, Germany; Small Arms Firing School, and Intermediate Radio Operator Course, Fort Lewis, WA; and Pre commission Course, Fort Benning, GA.

He was stationed at Fort Riley, KS; Schweinfurt Germany; Fort Benning, GA; Kirchgoens, Germany; Fort Bliss, TX; Fort Lewis, WA; Wolmido Island, Korea; Yongsan, Korea; Fort Carson, CO; Camp Radcliff, Vietnam; Camp Holloway Pleiku, Vietnam; Aschaffenburg, Germany; Di An, Vietnam; Fort Hood, TX; Hanau, Germany and Fort Ord, CA.

Matulac was in Binh Dinh Province, Anh Lao Valley, LZ Byrd, LZ Hammond, Kontum. Vietnam Counter Offensive, Phase II, Vietnam Counter Offensive Phase III, Tet counter Offensive, Operation Irving, in the valley bordered by Phu Cat mountains and Nui Mieu mountains and Operation Thayer.

He received the Good Conduct Medal 7th award, National Defense Service Medal with Oak Leaf Cluster, Vietnam Service Medal, Vietnam Campaign Medal, Vietnam Cross of Gallantry with Palm, Air Medal, Purple Heart, Bronze Star Medal with 2 Oak Leaf Cluster, Combat Infantry Badge, Arm Commendation Medal with V Device, with 1 Oak Leaf cluster

Memorable experiences included Searching and engaging enemy forces throughout the Central Highlands with A Company, 5th Battalion, 7th Cavalry, 1st Cavalry Division and teaching MAT teams prior to their deployment in the field and designing and constructing Instructional aids, while serving with MACV team 15, USARV Adviser School, An Khe, Vietnam.

Matulac was discharged Jan. 31, 1978 at Fort Ord, CA.

He retired in 2010 after working as an electrician, maintenance supervisor at Monterey Peninsula College and track coach, Monterey, CA High School.

Retirement activities include distance running over 200 marathons, 100 miles in one day. He took up golf when he turned 70.

"Bob" and Loida Asis have three children: Desiree Pettas, Roberta and Sean, and two grandchildren, Nathaniel and Dylan.

DOUG MATZE, JR. entered the U.S. Army on May 6, 1969 in Roanoke, VA. He completed basic training at Fort Bragg, NC; advanced infantry training at Fort McClellan, AL; Non-Commissioned Officer Candidate School at Fort Benning, GA; & OJT at Fort Polk, LA. Shortly thereafter, he arrived in Vietnam at the time of the Cambodian Invasion and was assigned to the 1st Cavalry Division at Bien Hoa. While awaiting further assignment, he volunteered for Company H (Ranger) 75th Infantry (Airborne). The unit was located at Phuoc Vinh. He was one of four in a class of twenty-five to complete the rigorous training course. He was awarded the National Defense Service Medal; Vietnam Service Medal; Vietnam Campaign Medal; 1 O/S Bar; Expert Badge Machine Gun M 60; Sharpshooter Badge Rifle M 16. He completed his active duty at Fort George G. Meade, MD receiving an honorable discharge.

After discharge, he attended Danville Community College for two years and transferred to Elon College where he graduated in 1975. His career included employment with Rose's Stores, Inc., Universal Leaf Tobacco Co., McGuire V. A. FCU, Virginia Credit Union League, and Richmond Postal Credit Union where he retired as Vice President of Finance in 2010.

In 1990 he married Debbie Ratledge and began the most wonderful experience of his life. Their children are Melissa Ratledge, Ben Pellum (USMC), and Holly Pellum.

COLONEL JOHN W. MAYHEW was selected for Battalion command duty with the 1st Cavalry Division at Fort Hood, TX in 1972. His first assignment was as the Executive Officer of the Division Support Command. Here he met Command Sergeant Major (CSM) Barnes, one of the finest NCO's he had the pleasure of serving with.

His new unit, the 34th Support Battalion, was identical to that of the division support command with the exception that its units were companies as compared to battalions in the support command.

About six months into his assignment they were alerted to move with the 6th Brigade to the White Sands training, north of El Paso, TX for a lengthy training exercise in the desert. They prepared and moved, without incident. Once in place they set up mobile support systems using an abandoned airport as home base. Over the next several weeks they provided on site logistical and maintenance support to the units of the brigade. One of their most creative ventures was obtaining freezers mounted in 3/4 ton trucks, which they filled with ice cream bars which were distributed to the Troopers of the Brigade. That action got them a loud hand at the closing critique.

They returned to Fort Hood to win the division field day trophy and field a baseball team that was to be reckoned with. Their readiness ratings grew, they passed all their tests with ease and AWOL and disciplinary stats were among the best in the division. All in all, they turned over a top notch unit to a new commander and, now on the full Colonels promotion list, Mayhew headed to the Pentagon for duty with the JCS.

TERRY A. McCARL received a commission through Army ROTC at South Dakota State University in 1967 and entered the Army in January 1968 at Fort Sam Houston, TX where he attended Medical Service Corps Officer Training.

His next assignment was the 714th Preventive Medicine Unit at Ft. Bragg, NC from May-October 1968. He arrived in Vietnam in November 1968, and was assigned to HSC, 15th Medical BN, 1st Cavalry Division as the Sanitarian for the Division. He was stationed at Camp Gorvad (Phuoc Vinh Base Camp) for his entire one-year tour.

He assisted the Division Preventive Medicine Officer primarily in water supply, food service sanitation, waste disposal, insect and rodent control, and malaria control. His duties involved travel by helicopter to all 1st Cav base camps and landing zones.

He was awarded a number of medals including a Bronze Star and Air Medal.

Upon return from Vietnam in November 1969, he was discharged and returned to South Dakota State University to obtain an M.S. in Environmental Engineering in 1971. He lived in the Omaha, NE area from 1971-2011 working in the area of water supply and wastewater treatment. He retired in 2011.

WILLIAM "BILL" L. McCARRON was born March 21, 1940 in Kelty, Fife, Scotland, and graduated from Warwick High School in Newport News, VA, in 1959. He later earned a Bachelor of Arts degree from Frederick College, Portsmouth, VA.

McCarron enlisted on March 29, 1964 in Richmond, VA. After Boot Camp at Fort Jackson, SC additional training was: Officer Candidate School, Class 10-64; Airborne, 1965; Ranger, 1965; Drill SGT Familiarization, 1965; Instructor Training Course, 1967; Intelligence Research Officers Course, 1968; Military Intelligence Officers Advance Course, 1969; Vietnamese Language, 1969; Armed Forces Staff College, 1978 and Military Operations Familiarization Course 1983.

McCarron was stationed at Fort Jackson, SC; Fort Benning, GA (twice); Fort Ord, CA; 1st Cavalry Division, Republic of Vietnam; Fort Holabird, MD; IV Corps, Republic of Vietnam; Rock Island Arsenal, IL; UNC/USFK/EUSA Republic of Korea (twice); Norfolk Naval Base, VA; Intelligence Center Pacific, HI; Fort Meade, MD and Pentagon, Washington, DC.

Awards received were Silver Star, Legion of Merit, Bronze Star with OLC, Purple Heart, Defense Meritorious Service Medal with OLC, Army Meritorious Service Medal, Air Medal with OLC, Presidential Unit Citation with OLC, National Defense Service Medal, Joint Service Commendation Medal, Armed Forces Reserve Medal, Vietnam Service Medal, Korean Service Medal, Vietnamese Campaign Medal, Vietnam Cross of Gallantry with Palm, Army Service Ribbon, Overseas Service Ribbon with 3 OLC, Joint Meritorious Service Unit Award with OLC, Combat Infantry Badge, Parachute Badge, Ranger Tab and Defense Intelligence Meritorious Medal.

Bill and Constance "Connie" have three children – Lonnie, Randy and Russ. Their grandchildren are Loni, Scott, Bennett, Hunter, Hailey, Sophia, and their great-grandson is Liam.

N.L. "MAC" McCARTNEY was born Oct. 12, 1923 in Jameson, MO, and graduated from Jameson High School. He obtained an MBA from Syracuse University and an MBA from George Washington University. "Mac" enlisted in 1944 at Fort Leavenworth, KS. In addition to Boot Camp at Camp Callan, CA, he attended Industrial College of the Armed Forces.

McCartney served in Europe during World War II, in Korea and Vietnam.

He was awarded the LOM, BS, Purple Heart (three) and CIB with Star.

Mac was discharged at the Pentagon in 1972 as a Colonel.

In civilian life he served as the Mayor of Springfield, MO. Professional affiliations include District Governor for Rotary, Missouri.

Mac and Helen (deceased) have three children: Patricia, Deborah and Patrick, and two grandchildren, Hannah and Rebecca.

RICHARD H. McDANIEL entered the US Army at Ft Knox, KY in 1961. Following basic training, he was transferred to Ft Lee, VA for Quartermaster training. He was then transferred to Ft Campbell, KY to undergo Airborne Training with the 101st Airborne Division. He also attended the 101st Recondo School. He was transferred to the 82nd Airborne Division in 1963. He deployed to the Dominican Republic with the 82nd.

After returning to Ft Bragg, NC, he volunteered for the newly formed 11th Air Assault Division at Ft Benning, GA. 1st Cavalry colors were returned to Fort Benning to replace the 11th Air Assault Division and he deployed to Vietnam with the 1st Battalion (Airborne) 12th Cavalry of the 1st Cavalry Division in 1965. After returning from Vietnam he was assigned to the 101st Airborne again. He deployed to Vietnam again with the 3rd Battalion 506th (Airborne) Infantry. He was wounded at Phan Thiet Vietnam in 1968 and recovered from his wounds in the 12th EVAC hospital in Cam Rahn Bay. After departing Vietnam he was assigned to the US Army Infantry School in Ft. Benning as an Airborne Instructor. His next assignment was in Ft Wainwright, AK with the 4th Battalion 9th (Airborne) Infantry 172nd Arctic Light Infantry Brigade. After Alaska he returned to Ft. Benning as an Airborne Instructor once again. He remained as an instructor until he injured his back during a parachute jump and had to terminate his jump status. His next assignment was Operations NCO of the Infantry Officers Basic Course followed by a tour in Korea as the NCOIC of an Aviation Direct Support Supply unit. His last army assignment prior to retirement in 1981 was the NCOIC of 24th Infantry Division Supply Requisition Processing Unit at Ft Stewart, GA.

After retirement he became an instructor for Central Texas College teaching Army Logistics to Officers and Enlisted Soldiers. He joined the Department of Defense Civil Service Corps in 1985 as a Logistics Management Specialist and served in that position until his retirement in 2012.

McDaniel has been awarded the Combat Infantry Badge, Expert Infantry Badge, Master Parachutist Badge, Pathfinder Badge, Ranger Tab, Meritorious Service Ribbon, Purple Heart, Bronze Star with V device, Bronze Star with Oak Leaf, Army Commendation with Oak Leaf, Good Conduct (sixth award), Air Medal with numeral 21, Korea Defense Service Ribbon, Army Valorous Unit Award, Presidential Unit Citation with Oak Leaf, Army Expeditionary Medal, Vietnam Service Campaign ribbon with 60 device, Vietnam Service Medal, Vietnam Cross of Gallantry with Palm.

He is married to Sandra L. McDaniel and has one son, Christopher.

DONALD MATHIS "BUZZ" McKAY enlisted on March 31, 1957 at Americus, GA. From 1957 to 1960, he attended Georgia Army National Summer Guard camps. Buzz served as an enlisted man until commissioned as 2LT of Infantry on Sept. 8, 19862 upon graduation from Georgia Tech, Atlanta, GA. He entered active duty Sept. 11, 1962 at Fort Benning, GA, was ROTC Distinguished Military Student and Graduate. He took an RA commission.

In his 31 years and three months of service he received 32 separate medals/ribbons. Key ones are Silver Star, Bronze Stars (two for valor and one for meritorious service), two Army Commendation Medals (one for valor), two Legions of Merit, three Meritorious Service Medals, one Air Medal and one Joint Service Commendation Medal. He also received 36 separate qualification badges/patches. A number were for qualification with various weapons, both individual and crew served, both US and foreign. Key ones are Combat Infantryman's Badge, Expert Infantryman's Badge, Novice Parachute Badge, Senior Parachute Badge, Master Parachute Badge (147 static line jumps), Air Assault Badge, plus foreign awards of Parachute Badges from Thailand (twice), Vietnam, Canada (twice), Panama and Korea. Buzz is also dual classified as Infantry (13B) and Special Forces (18B).

Buzz and Nancy Patricia "Pat" (Maughon) McKay have three children – Donald M. III, Michael Britt and Nancy Christian. Grandchildren are Dylan and Emily McKay, Colton and Chason McKay and Morgan and Joseph Ewing.

JOHN J. "JACK" McNIFF served as a Captain with the 1st Air Cavalry Division in Vietnam. He was Assistant G-2 Air from July 1966 to April 1967 coordinating aerial intelligence activities during Operations Nathan Hale (Tuy Hoa area), Paul Revere II (Pleiku area), Thayer (Binh Dinh Province), Irving (Bong Son area) and Pershing (Binh Dinh Provence). The primary intelligence aircraft for the lst Cav Division was the Mohawk, with its forward looking cameras, belly cameras, Side Looking Airborne Radar (SLAR) and infrared cameras. The Div Hq was located in Tuy Hoa, An Khe, Pleiku and Bon Son.

From April to June 1967 he was the S-3 Air for the 2nd Bn (Abn), 8th Cavalry in the Bong Son Plain and An Lao Valley areas. He coordinated air assault aircraft requests, air requests and USAF Air Requests. He spent most of his time on LZ Santana and LZ Geronimo.

His second Vietnam tour was with the 4th Infantry Division in Pleiku. He is a graduate of the US Army Command and General Staff College and the US Air Force War College. He retired from the Army, retired again after another twenty years as a Department of the Army Civilian, and volunteered with the Maryland Defense Force of the Maryland National Guard.

His awards and decorations include the Legion of Merit, the Bronze Star with OLC, the Meritorious Service Medal, the Air Medal, the Army Commendation Medal with OLC, the Combat Infantryman's badge, the Parachute Badge and the Maryland National Guard Distinguished Service Medal, His DA Civilian Awards include the Superior Civilian Service Medal, the Commanders Award for Civilian Service Medal, and two Outstanding Supervisor Awards from the Baltimore Federal Executive Board. He received a BA degree from Providence College in 1961 and a MS degree in human resource management from the University of Utah.

Colonel McNiff has been on the 1st Cav Div Association Board of Governors since 2005. He has attended most Reunions since 1990, including the Covered Wagon Train Ride in Billings, MT in 1992 that ended on Last Stand Hill at the Custer Battlefield.

LOUIS S. MEHL was born October 25, 1915 in Massachusetts and attended college at The Ohio State University. He enlisted at Boston, MA (or nearby) and worked his way through the ranks to become a lieutenant colonel upon his retirement in Tampa, FL.

Mehl received the following awards during his distinguished career: Silver Star, Distinguished Flying Cross, Bronze Star, Purple Heart, Air Medal, Joint Service Commendation Medal, Army Commendation Medal, Asiatic-Pacific Campaign Medal, European-African-Middle Eastern Campaign Medal, World War II Victory Medal, Army of Occupation Medal with Japan Clasp, National Defense Service Medal, Korean Service Medal with Bronze Star attachment (single) and Silver Star attachment (single), Armed Forces Reserve Medal with Hourglass Device (bronze), Combat Infantryman Badge (1st award), United Nations Service Medal, Honorable Service Lapel Button (World War II), and Marksman Badge (carbine and machine gun bar).

He passed away in November 2008 and had two children.

JAMES "JIM" K. MELLOW enlisted in October 1946. After Boot Camp at Fort Dix, NJ he was sent to Fort Lewis, Seattle to ship to Japan.

Jim was stationed with 1st Cavalry at Camp Drake, Asaka and Tokyo, Japan. He was with the 1st Signal Troop during the Occupation of Japan and the editor of *The Signalman*, a company newspaper.

Mellow was the only American to witness Emperor Hirohito promulgate the new Japanese constitution at the Japanese National Diet in Tokyo, Japan in 1947.

Jim served 40 years as executive vice president of Liberty Foundry Company in St. Louis, MO, retiring in 1993.

Jim and Mary Virginia have four children – Jim Jr., Ann, Lucy and Tom. Their grandchildren are Stephen, David, Sarah, Emily and Madilyn.

ANDREW J. MICHEL enlisted in the Army on March 28, 1952 and was assigned to the Aberdeen Proving Grounds. After basic training he attended ordnance training for Light Artillery Repair. After training he joined the 747 Ordnance Maintenance Company in Camp Crawford. In June 1953 orders came for him to report for transfer to the "Far East."

After a short stay at home, he took a train to the West Coast to board the *General MM Patrick* to Japan. After arriving in Yokohama on July 7, 1953 he was assigned to Company B, 27 Ordnance Battalion of the First Cavalry Division in Camp Crawford on the island of Hokkaido. In February 1955, he departed Japan to Fort Knox, where Sgt. Michel received an honorable discharge on March 23, 1955.

Back in civilian life he used the GI Bill to go to college. The first two years were at the University of Akron and the remaining two at the University of Arkansas, graduating with a degree of Bachelor of Science in Electrical Engineering,

His first job after college was with the Federal Aviation Agency (FAA) in Fort Worth, TX. After five years he left the FAA for a job with Central Moloney Corporation in Pine Bluff, AR as an electrical design engineer. A downturn in the economy forced Central Moloney to downsize so he rejoined the FAA at FAA headquarters in Washington, DC until he retired on Jan. 3, 2003.

He married Shirley Michel in 1968 and they have three children, Katrina, Richard, John and three grandchildren, Katie, Mary, and Grayson.

DALLAS MILLS was born in 1943 in Laredo, WV. He graduated from Wayne High School in 1960. He attended Moody College, Vincennes College and Bethany College.

On Jan. 19, 1961 he enlisted. In addition to Boot Camp at Fort Knox, KY he also received training in ABN/S.F.

Mills was stationed at Fort Knox, Fort Bragg three times, Fort Benning twice, Fort Jackson and in Germany three times.

CSM Mills as discharged on Sept. 31, 2001. In retirement he is a minister.

Dallas and Carolyn have two children, Jennifer and Chris. Their grandchildren are Jacob, Mollie, Micah, Luke, Jenna, Malaki and Levi.

DAVID PHILMORE MINTER enlisted for Korea in December 1965 and entered service Jan. 17, 1966. He took Basic training and AIT at Fort Jackson, SC, and finished AIT in May 1966.

Minter arrived in Korea in May 1966 and was assigned to the 7th Cavalry B Troop 4/7. He was trained by the 7th Cavalry to drive the M114-A1, M106, M48-A medium tank (Patton) and M151 Jeep. He drove this equipment while in Korea. He drove the M114-A1 and M48-A tanks on missions on the Korea DMZ during the Korea DMZ conflict 1966 through 1967. He was awarded the Imjin Scout Insignia and Driver and Mechanic Badge for this service.

He returned to the United States in June 1967. He went to Fort Gordon, GA and was sent to Fort McClellan, AL to Drill Sergeant school, after the training returned to Fort Gordon, GA and trained troops until leaving service Jan. 16, 1969. He was awarded the good conduct medal for that service.

After returning to Martinsville, VA, he went to work as an electrician in 1969, and was named foreman in 1974. He was working on a Zero Motion Detection System and got a patent for the system in 1995.

He has just finished helping the Bassett Historical Center with a Korean War Memorial Bench for the 50th anniversary of the DMZ conflict. The bench will be at the Bassett Historical Center in Bassett, VA.

He has received a letter from the Government of South Korea thanking him for his service to their country.

He has been married to Julia Francis Minter since married July 18, 1987. They have one son, John David Minter.

JAMES L. MOBLEY, the son of a farmer, was drafted into the Army Jan. 9, 1951. He was assigned to Neckarsulm, Germany as a field artillery Soldier working with the 155 Howitzer. After 23 months he was honorably discharged and began farming. Now married with a son, in 1955 Hurricane Hazel wiped out his crops so he returned to the Army that November.

Initially Mobley was a cook but cross trained into helicopter maintenance, graduating with honors. He was part of the crew that brought the first UH1 "Huey" helicopters to Fort Bragg, NC. It was on one of his four tours in Vietnam that he first joined the 1st CAV DIV. While in Vietnam, Mobley participated in six campaigns, received the Air Medal with 18 OLC and was awarded the Bronze Star Medal for Heroism.

Mobley retired in 1974 with over 24 years of service. He built six houses on "Easy Lane." He is active in the Anderson Creek Ruritan Club and a member of Pleasant Hill Advent Christian Church. Mobley and his wife, Mable, will celebrate their 64th wedding anniversary this year. They have four children, three grandchildren and one great-grandchild with two more on the way.

JAMES H. MONTGOMERY was born Feb. 4, 1950 in Conway, AR, and graduated from Conway High School in 1968. He attended the United States Military Academy at West Point, NY, graduating in 1972. Other training included Airborne School, CG & SC, and he earned a Masters of Strategic Studies from Army War College in 2000.

Montgomery was stationed at Fort Hood, TX, Fort Benning, GA, Fort Clayton in the Panama Canal Zone. He participated in Operation Desert Storm/Desert Shield with the 25th RAOC assigned to the XVIII Airborne attached to the 3rd ACR. He earned the Parachutist Badge, Bronze Star, and MSM. Memorable experiences include moving with the 3rd ACR into Iraq during Desert Storm.

He retired from active duty in October 1979 and entered the Arkansas Army National Guard, from which he retired on June 7, 2002 with the rank of Colonel. He later worked as a staff training consultant, retiring in 2015.

He is married to Patty, and they have two children, Katy and Travis, and two grandchildren, Alex and Charlotte.

KENNETH "KEN" D. MOORE was commissioned a 2nd Lieutenant of Infantry through Army ROTC at the University of Iowa, June 6, 1969. He graduated with a BA in History from the University of Iowa in 1969.

He attended IOBC at Fort Benning, GA reporting on Nov. 9, 1969 followed by Organizational Maintenance Officer Course at Fort Knox, KY. He completed Infantry Advance Course, Logistics Executive Development Course and Command and General Staff College. He also received his MBA from Edgewood College, Madison, WI in 1992.

After an assignment to Grafenwoehr, Germany, he was sent to Vietnam and the 3rd Bde (Sep) 1st Cav. Division in Bien Hoa. He was Platoon Leader for 1st Platoon, C Co., 1st Bn 12th Cav. with action in War Zone D. When the 3rd Bde returned to the US he became 1st Platoon Leader, B Co., 1st Bn 7th Cav., Task Force Garry Owen. When the 7th Cav. stood down in August he was assigned as Deputy Regimental Advisor to the 10th Regiment 7th Infantry Division (ARVN) until returned to the United States in March 1973.

Other assignments were 101st Airborne Division, (C Company Commander 2/327th) Fort Campbell, KY; ROTC at Western Illinois University, Macomb, IL; 2nd Infantry Division in Korea; 4th Infantry Division, Fort Carson, CO and 5th Army as a National Guard Advisor.

He received the Bronze Star Medal (1 OLC), Air Medal (3) with V Device, Meritorious Service Medal (3 OLC), Army Commendation Medal (1 OLC), National Defense Service Medal, Vietnam Service Medal Vietnam Campaign Medal, Vietnamese Cross of Gallantry with Palm and Bronze Star, Vietnamese Air Service Medal, Armed Forces Reserve Medal Army Service Ribbon, Overseas Service Ribbon (2), Combat Infantry Badge, Expert Infantry Badge, German Marksmanship Badge - Bronze and Jungle Warfare Badge.

Moore was discharged in December 1989 at Madison, WI as a Major.

Memorable experiences for Moore were working directly for General Colin Powell at Fort Carson, CO as Division Training Management Officer; commissioning his son as a second lieutenant in the Army Armor Branch; and having his son follow him in the 1st Bn, 7th Cav. as his initial duty assignment at Fort Hood, TX.

Moore worked for the State of Wisconsin Bureau of Apprenticeship Standards for 21 years as the Chief of Field Operations. During that time he spent 17 years as the national chair/co-chair of the Apprenticeship and OJT Committee for the National Association of State Approving Agencies (NASA) for the GI Bill approving Apprenticeship and OJT programs for Veterans. He was recognized by his peers and elected to the Wisconsin Apprenticeship Hall of Fame shortly after his retirement from state service.

Retiring in June 2013, his activities now are traveling the world, reading and cooking.

Kenneth married Cynthia Blaesing on August 24, 1968 in Muscatine, IA. They have three children: Col. Matthew P., Louise and Stephen W. Moore. Their grandchildren are Mary Margaret "Maggie," Shelby, Payton, Ryan and Parker.

FRIEDRICH H. MORAWIETZ was born in 1939 in Germany. He immigrated to the United States in 1950 and grew up in Lackawanna, NY. He enlisted in the U.S. Army in October 1957 and completed basic training at Fort Knox, KY. Following basic training, he was transferred to Ft. Bragg, NC and completed advanced infantry and basic Airborne training with the 82nd Airborne Division.

In late 1958, the 1/504 Airborne Battle Group of the 82nd Airborne Division to which Morawietz was assigned, received orders to deploy to Germany. He served five years in Germany. During that timeframe, he was married and experienced the birth of his daughter, Patricia. At the end of 1963, he was transferred to the 101st Airborne Division at Ft. Campbell, KY and in 1965, was re-assigned to Ft. McClellan, AL. In August 1965, his son Frederick was born, and in October of that same year, he was promoted to Staff Sergeant (E6).

In February 1968, Morawietz received orders for an assignment in South Viet Nam. He was assigned to Bravo Company, 1st Battalion 7th Cavalry, 1st Cavalry Division. When he arrived at Bravo Company, he was assigned to the Mortar Platoon. Due to a shortage of Senior Non-Commissioned Officers and Junior Officers, he was given the responsibilities of both Platoon Sergeant and Platoon Leader, positions he occupied nearly throughout his entire tour.

Upon his return from Viet Nam, Morawietz volunteered to attend Drill Sergeant School, followed by assignments at several training centers. In 1970, he again received orders for an assignment in Vietnam. During this tour of duty, he would serve as an advisor to South Vietnamese Ranger Units.

For much of the final years of his 30-year military career, he served as 1st Sergeant and/or Command Sergeant Major at various units and locations. Morawietz received five Bronze Star Medals, Purple Heart, Combat infantry Badge, Air Medal, Meritorious Service Medal, Army Commendation Medal among other awards.

After retirement from the U.S. Army in 1986, he earned both bachelor and graduate degrees, and began teaching. Health issues forced his full retirement in 1998 and since then, he and his wife, Kristine, enjoy traveling.

JAMES MULLENS entered military service at Fort Knox, KY on May 31, 1961. Basic Training, Combat Inf. Training, Medical School, Co. B 2nd Bn. Med. 2nd Inf. Div., Fort Benning, GA, 45th Field Hospital, Italy Ambulance Driver, Med. Det.

Redstone Ambulance Al, HHC 2nd BDE 1st Cav. Div. Co. C 1st/5th Cav. Plt. Medic RVN, Det US-AHF Fort Campbell, KY Ward Spec, 606 Med Co. C 5th/12 Inf. 199 Light Inf. BDG Co., NCOIC Hospital Det. Fort Campbell, KY Plains and Training, NCO School Class 3, Fort Sam Houston, TX, NCOIC HHC Troop Clinic NCOIC Drug and Alcohol Germany, 2/8 Fort Ord, CA NCOIC health clinic, Acting 1st Sgt. NCOIC Clinic Disp. Spec. Food Insp., Fort Greeley, AK. He retired at Fort Leonard Wood, MO.

He was awarded RVN Cross of Gallantry (with Palm) Unit Citation Badge, Bronze Star Medical with V Device, Good Conduct Medal with clasp silver with one loop, Combat Medical Badge, Combat Infantry Badge, Army Commendation Medal with First Oak Leaf Cluster 3rd, Presidential Unit Emblem, Meritorious Unit Emblem, National Defense Service Medal, Vietnam Service Medal with three Bronze Stars and one Silver Service Star, Republic of Vietnam Campaign Ribbon with Citation Badge, Republic of Vietnam Civil Action Honor Medal, First Class Unit Citation Badge, Driver Badge with Bar, Sharpshooter M1, 2nd Class M60, PUC.

Mullens worked as a CNA – LPN, retiring on May 31, 1981.

Children of James and Mary C. (Harrell) Mullens are James III, Charles, Sherri, Stacy, John, Joshua, Patrick and Andrew. Their grandchildren are Matty, Colton and Jason.

DON B. MUNSON was born August 27, 1938 in Indianapolis, IN, and graduated from Biloxi High School in 1956. He received his Bachelor of Arts degree and Regular Army commission from Tulane University, New Orleans, LA. He is a graduate of the Infantry Officer Advance Course (Fort Benning, GA), Army Command and General Staff College (Fort Leavenworth, KS), Defense Language Institute (Monterey, CA), and the Russian Area Studies program at Georgetown University, Washington, DC.

Following graduation and commissioning from Tulane University, he served as Infantry Platoon Leader, 2nd Battalion, 504th Airborne Battle Group, 82nd Airborne Division, at Fort Bragg, North Carolina; and Infantry Company Commander, 2nd Battalion, 504th Airborne Battle Group, 82nd Airborne Division, at Fort Bragg, North Carolina. Later assignments included: Assistant G-3 Operations, 18th Airborne Corps, Fort Bragg; Aide-de-Camp to Commanding General, 7th Army Support Command, Germany; Commander, Detachment A-26, 10th Special Forces, Germany; Commander, Company B, 1st Battalion, 7th Cavalry Regiment, 1st Cavalry Division, Viet Nam; Operations Officer, 2nd Battalion, 7th Cavalry Regiment, 1st Cav Div, Viet Nam; Assistant Professor, Senior ROTC Detachment, University of Delaware; Commander, Company B, US Army Special Forces, Lop Buri, Thailand; Foreign Exchange Officer, University of Belgrade, Yugoslavia; Chief, Current Intell Division, Defense Intelligence Agency, the Pentagon; Commander, 1st Battalion, 507th Airborne Regiment, Fort Benning, Georgia; Deputy Commander, US Army Ranger Department, Fort Benning, Georgia; Analyst, Studies and Analysis Agency, Office of the Chairman, Joint Chiefs of Staff, the Pentagon.

LTC Munson has been awarded the Silver Star, Distinguished Flying Cross, Bronze Stars with V and Oak Leaf, 11 Air Medals, Purple Heart, 5 Meritorious Service Medals (DA, DOD, JCS), Master Parachutist Badge, and Parachutist Badges from Germany, Belgium, Viet Nam, and Thailand.

He retired as a Lieutenant Colonel after 22 years of active duty service, and currently lives in Coppell, TX, a suburb of Dallas.

GLEASON J. "JACK" MURRAY was born July 12, 1926 in Erie, PA and graduated from Oil City High School, and later Welches Business College. He enlisted in September 1944, followed by Boot Camp at Fort Riley, KS.

Murray at right, Philippines, 1944.

Jack served in Luzon, Philippines and also remembers going around the USS *Missouri* during the Japanese surrender.

Murray earned the ICB, Bronze Star and eight more medals for his service.

Memorable experience for Jack was doing jungle patrols in Luzon, Philippines as an 18 year old.

PFC Murray was discharged in 1946 at Fort George Mead.

He served as a driver and foreman for Keystone Lawrence, retiring in 1971. In retirement he owns five businesses.

Jack has eight children, 22 grandchildren and 27 great-grandchildren.

JAMES L. NEELEY left Rice University and was inducted into the U.S. Army in July 1967. He took basic and advanced infantry training at Fort Polk, LA and went to Vietnam in December 1967, where he was assigned to "D" Company, 1st Battalion, 12th Cavalry, 1st Cavalry Division.

He went to I Corps for the Tet Offensive, was involved in the relief of Khe Sanh and wounded by U.S. Air Force in the A Shau Valley. He attended 1st Cavalry Combat Leader's Course and promoted to Sergeant as top graduate in his class.

Neeley was wounded north of Quan Tri by a booby trap in August 1968, flown to Japan and then to Brook Army Hospital in San Antonio, TX for treatment. He finished his tour of duty at Fort Carson, CO, and was discharged in July 1969.

He received the Purple Heart with oak leaf cluster, Bronze Star, National Defense Service Medal, Combat Infantryman Badge, Air Medal, and Vietnam Service Medal with Bronze Service Star.

After discharge he returned to west Texas to raise cotton in Dawson and Gaines Counties, and became active in the Masonic Lodge. He retired in 2005 and married Sandra Harris Osborne in 2002.

RONALD Q. NICHOLS was born August 23, 1943 in Minot, ND, and graduated from Stanley High School, later earning a BA (1966) and MS (1971) from North Dakota State University.

Nichols enlisted from the 5/66 ROTC (NDSU), serving boot camp at Ft. Lewis, WA, with additional training at Artillery School at Ft. Sill, OK. He was a member of the 6/16 Arty, 1st Armored Division at Ft. Hood, TX, before assignment to Vietnam from May 1968-May 1969, where he was a Arty FO with the A 2/12 CAV, FDOC 1/77 Arty, and XOC Btry 1/77 Arty.

He received the Bronze Star, Bronze Star with V, Air Medal with oak leaf cluster, and others.

Memorable experiences are serving as XO C 1/77 Arty during ground attacks on LZ Grant, Spring 1969 near Nui Ba Den. He was discharged in May 1969 with the rank of 1st Lieutenant.

Nichols worked for the Transportation Institute – NDSU, the North Dakota Legislative Council, Loan Officer (1986-2008), farmer/rancher, and a member of the North Dakota Legislature from 1991-2005.

He married to Sue (Midgarden) in November 1966 and they have four children — Kimberly, Kelly, Desiree, and Heidi — and 13 grandchildren — Jacob, Jeseb, Grace, Gunnar, Joshua, Katarina, Lucas, Joel, Gabe, Adrianna, Jack, Caleb, and Ainsley.

ALLEN O. NORRIS graduated from college in December 1967 and joined the Army in 1968 to avoid being drafted. His active duty was from April 22, 1968 to Jan. 16, 1971.

After Basic Training at Fort Leonard Wood, MO he attended AIT and OCS at Fort Sill, OK, being commissioned March 11, 1969.

Duty assignments included Instructor for US Army Artillery and Missile School, Office Candidate Brigade, S-3 (March 1969 – January 1970) and Forward Observer (FO), Liaison Officer (LNO), Fire Direction Officer (FDO), First Cavalry Division: B Battery, 2nd Battalion, 19th Field Artillery, Jan. 12, 1970 – Jan. 11, 1971 USARVN

Norris received the Bronze Star Medal with three OLC, 1st and 2nd award with V), two Air Medals, Army Commendation Medal with V, National Defense Service Medal, Vietnam Service Medal with two campaign stars, Vietnam Campaign Medal, Valorous Unit Citation and Vietnam Gallantry Cross with Palm.

After the Army he continued as a textile chemist in the textile dyeing and finishing business. For over 30 years with two companies he was in technical service, market research, product management, supply chain management and sales. Norris changed professions in 2002 to the paper industry and retired in 2015.

Allen and the former Cathleen Judkins married in 1974. Cathy and Allen have three children (Jean, Jessica and Douglas) and six grandchildren (Amie, Devin, Libby, Joshua, Jack and Ryan).

RICHARD M. O'BRIEN was born June 4, 1947 in Chicago, IL, and graduated from Fenton High School in 1966, later attending St. Xavier University, Roosevelt, earning his MBA. He enlisted on Aug. 25, 1966 in Chicago, and went through basic training at Ft. Lewis, WA, and AIT at Ft. Polk before transitioning to An Khe, Vietnam with the 1st Cav.

O'Brien fought in Operation Pershing and received the CIB and Purple Heart with OLC. He was wounded twice, and lost his right leg below the knee. He was discharged in Feb. 1968 at Walter Reed Hospital, with the rank of E-3.

In civilian life, he was a Materials Manager for Pfizer, retiring in 2003. He likes to golf and is a member of the VVA and Society of the Purple Heart.

Rich and Kathy have two children, Michael and Jill, and two grandchildren, Ansley and Ellie.

JOSEPH P. O'CONNOR JR. graduated from the United States Military Academy at West Point in 1968 as an Infantry 2LT. After Ranger School, O'Connor was assigned to the 82nd Airborne Division for six months as a Weapons Platoon Leader and held many additional duties, e.g., 2nd Brigade Trial Counsel (special courts martial prosecutor).

He arrived in Vietnam in July 1969 and was assigned as a Rifle Platoon Leader with Bravo Company, 1/7 Cavalry. After two months, O'Connor was named Company XO. He then served as the Battalion Reconnaissance Platoon Leader from November 1969 to June 1970 in Binh Long and Phuoc Long Provinces of III Corps as well as in Cambodia. After a few weeks as Echo Company CO, O'Connor went on 30-day leave, as he had extended six months in Vietnam for the opportunity to be a 1/7 Cav Rifle Company CO. When he returned in July 1970, the whole Battalion had reorganized and there were no vacancies, so O'Connor become CO of Charlie Company, 1/12 Cavalry. He then served as CO, HHC, 11th Combat Aviation Group from November 1970 to February 1971.

After leaving Vietnam, O'Connor switched branches to Military Intelligence (MI), attended the last Counterintelligence Officers Course at Fort Holabird and was assigned to the 112th MI Group's Fort Bliss Field Office in June 1971. In October 1972, he was assigned to the Defense Investigative Service's El Paso Field Office, serving as Field Office Commander in 1974 prior to taking the MI Officers Advanced Course at Fort Huachuca. While in El Paso, O'Connor earned his Master of Arts in Economics from The University of Texas at El Paso (UTEP). He was then assigned in January 1975 as S2, 307th Army Security Agency Battalion in Germany, handling both security and some operational matters for this SIGINT/EW unit supporting VII Corps. While at Garmisch-Partenkirchen for an AFRC Learn-to-Ski Week, O'Connor met his future wife, Mary, who was a Department of Defense Education System teacher in Germany.

Looking for greater challenges, O'Connor left active duty in 1976, joined the Army Reserve and Pfizer Inc. in Human Resources (HR) in New York City, and married Mary. He spent 25 years in HR with such companies as Pfizer and Monsanto. O'Connor finished his career as Vice President & Global HR Leader for Actuant Corporation, a Fortune 500 corporation based in Milwaukee. In 2002, he started his third career as a doctoral student at the University of Wisconsin-Milwaukee and earned his Ph.D. in Management Science (Organizations and Strategy) in 2005. O'Connor then returned to UTEP as an Assistant Professor of Management as UTEP had started a new Ph.D. in International Business program. His first assignment was leading the Doctoral Seminar in Strategy for eleven doctoral students. O'Connor spent 11 years as a management professor, teaching strategic management and organization development courses at the undergraduate, MBA and doctoral levels. He retired from UTEP in 2016 at age 70.

O'Connor served in the Army Reserve in a variety of assignments: 24th MI Battalion (Aerial Reconnaissance Support) Battalion S2/3 and Detachment Commander; 10th PSYOPS Battalion Battalion XO; and various staff assignments with the 90th and 102nd Army Reserve Commands, and with the Deputy Chiefs of Staff, Intelligence for FORSCOM, INSCOM, and DA. He graduated with honors from the Command and General Staff College. O'Connor retired from the Army Reserve as a Lieutenant Colonel in 1991 to devote more time as an adult leader in his son Michael's Boy Scout Troop and in his daughter Kathleen's Girl Scout Troop. Mike later earned his Eagle Scout and Katie earned her Eagle-equivalent Gold Award.

Before Vietnam, O'Connor was awarded the Parachutist Badge and Ranger Tab. During Vietnam, he was awarded the Combat Infantry Badge, Air Medal, ARCOM with V device, and two Bronze Stars. After Vietnam, O'Connor earned two more ARCOMs, one Joint Service Commendation Medal and two Meritorious Service Medals.

FREDERICK N. OLSON was born on April 23, 1936 in Northfield, Jackson County, WI, to Fred. M. and Sylvia V. (Aske) Olson. He was commissioned a Second Lieutenant in the Army Infantry on Jan. 20, 1959 upon completion of the Reserve Officers Training Corps (ROTC) at the University of Wisconsin, Madison, WI. Fred retired from the Army on the 31 October, 1981, after almost 23 years of active duty.

After completing his Infantry Officer's Training Course in Fort Benning, GA, Fred was assigned to a Training Regiment in Fort Dix, NJ, to train Army recruits. In July 1959, he entered the Rotary Wing Army Aviator's Course, completing the course in Feb. 1960, thus commencing his career as an Infantry Officer and Aviator.

During his Army career, Fred served two long terms in German, one with the 3rd Armored Division, and one with the 1st Armored Division, two tours in Vietnam with the 1st Cavalry Division (Airmobile), a tour in the Pentagon with the Office of the Deputy Chief of Staff for Operations (ODCSOPS), a tour as Director of ROTC at Georgetown University, two tours at the Army Aviation School, and a tour with the Director of the Army Material Readiness Command (DARCOM). He commanded a Mechanized Infantry Company, two Air Cavalry Troops, and a Mechanized Infantry Battalion. He also served in staff assignments from battalion to Department of the Army level and in several instructional assignments.

Fred earned the Expert Infantrymen's Badge, the Combat Infantryman's Badge, the Master Army Aviator's Badge, and the General Staff Identification Badge. His awards for combat service and valor include the Silver Star, Distinguished Flying Cross with Oak Leaf Cluster, Bronze Star Medal with OLC, and Air Medal with 35 OLC. His awards for service include the Legion of Merit, Meritorious Service Medal, and Army Commendation Medal with OLC.

Fred married DeAnete Johnson from Humbird, WI, in August 1958, and they have three children: Lynne, Lori, and Lisa.

MICHAEL E. O'NEIL was enlisted from 1962 – 1967, graduated from Infantry OCS in 1968, was commissioned 2nd Lieutenant, earned his Army helicopter flight wings in 1969 and went on to transition and fly the AH-1 Cobra helicopter. In Feb. 1970 O'Neil was sent to Vietnam and upon checking in at the 97th Replacement he was asked to choose three units/divisions where he wanted to go, he chose 1st Cav, 1st Cav, 1st Cav. His request was granted and his 1st unit was D company 227 AHB in Lai Khe, 3 Corps Vietnam, where he flew gun cover for 6-8 combat assaults a day for 7 months.

One of the most memorable experiences occurred when the 1st Cav Division led the incursion into Cambodia on May 1, 1970, O'Neil was in the lead Cobra when 200 slick UH-1 helicopters and 22 Cobras invaded Cambodia. O'Neil received the Distinguished Flying Cross for his actions that day.

In September 1970 D/227 became E Troop 1/9 Cav (Provisional), O'Neil went to D/229th in Dau Tieng, as Aircraft Commander and in December 1970 D/229th became F Troop 1/9 Cav (Provisional) stationed in Bear Cat, Vietnam. While in the 1/9 Cav O'Neil flew Hunter/Killer Teams for 8-10 hrs. a day which was an exciting mission which resulted in many memorable experiences. By the time O'Neil left Vietnam he had accumulated

1,250 combat flying hours in the AH-1 Cobra. After Vietnam, Captain O'Neil was stationed in Italy as XO of the 6th Aviation Detachment in Vicenza, Italy. After 12 years of service Captain O'Neil resigned his commission to become test pilot for the Shah of Iran, working for Agusta Bell in Teheran, Iran, coming back to the U.S. in the late 1970s.

O'Neil received the Distinguished Flying Cross Medal, the Bronze Star with Oak Leaf Cluster, the Air Medal with 42 Device, Army Commendation Medal with Oak Leaf Cluster, Vietnam Service Medal, Vietnam Campaign Medal with 60 Device, Vietnam Cross of Gallantry with palm, and Army Aviation Badge.

Today as a retired real estate entrepreneur, O'Neil lives in Southern California with his wife of over 40 years, Beverley. They have a son Timothy, daughter Dawn-Marie, and two grandchildren, Kendyll and Alex.

BOB ORKAND, an Infantry officer commissioned from OCS in 1955, served with the 1st Battalion (Airmobile), 7th Cavalry from September 1967 to late January 1968. Because of casualties, he was the battalion's only major, serving simultaneously as XO and S-3 during fighting in the An Lao Valley, Que Son Valley and elsewhere in the northern provinces.

Bob was drafted into the Army in 1954 during his senior year at Columbia University. After graduating from Infantry OCS, he became a heavy mortar platoon leader with the 17th Infantry Regiment in Korea, serving 16 months north of the 38th Parallel.

After commanding a basic training company at Fort Ord, CA, Bob was selected as aide-de-camp to post commander Maj. Gen. William M. Breckinridge, who had been assigned as Eighth Army chief of staff in Seoul, Korea. Bob remained with Gen. Breckinridge during the general's subsequent assignment in Washington as chief of the Army Security Agency, the Army component of NSA.

After leading an ROTC detachment in Rockford, IL, Bob was assigned to West Berlin, where he became spokesman for the US Commander, Berlin during peak days of the Cold War. He volunteered for duty in Vietnam and became media spokesman for all terrorist actions in the Saigon metropolitan area on his initial RVN assignment.

As a lieutenant colonel, Bob was editor/publisher of *INFANTRY* magazine at Fort Benning, was deputy director of the Infantry School's Weapons Department, and served as executive officer of the 197th Infantry Brigade at Benning when it became the prototype unit for creation of the all-volunteer Army in the early 1970s. As CO of the brigade's 1,000-man 1st Battalion (Mechanized), 58th Infantry, he helped train the unit while also being responsible for recruiting volunteers from North and South Carolina.

In his final assignment, he was spokesman for the secretary of the Army on many personnel matters, including the volunteer Army, and was Pentagon spokesman on the illness and subsequent death in 1974 of Army chief of staff General Creighton W. Abrams.

After retirement, Bob joined the *Miami Herald* and worked for the next 12 years for Knight-Ridder Newspapers, becoming president and publisher of the company's newspaper in State College, PA. He later taught high school English and social studies in Houston and Huntsville, TX, where he and his wife Belinda reside.

Bob's awards and decorations include CIB, EIB, BSM (two awards), Air Medal, Meritorious Service Medal (three awards), Army Commendation Medal (two awards), Valorous Unit Commendation, etc.

JOSE R. ORTIZ was drafted into the US Army in April 1968. From San Juan, Puerto Rico, he traveled to Fort Benning, GA and then to Fort Sam Houston in Texas where he served as a subsistence supply specialist. In 1969 Spc Ortiz was deployed to Korea to the 348 S&S Company. He was then transferred to supply point #49 Daejeon, Korea. After his tour of service he returned home to San Juan. In 1976 he joined the Army ROTC program at the University of Puerto Rico, where he would go on to graduate with a degree in economics. After graduation in 1976, Lieutenant Ortiz went to officer basic course in Fort Lee, VA. Once passing this course he was assigned to the 3/10 Cav S&S Company 1st Cavalry Division in Fort Hood, TX. The 3/10 Cav was part of the division restructuration study and was dismantled in 1979. At the time 1Lt Ortiz was transferred to the 15th S&S Battalion where he served as an executive officer of A company.

Following his discharge from active duty he joined the US Army Reserve to continue his service. Maj. Ortiz served in numerous assignments in the reserves including Fort Ord, CA; Panama; Honduras; Fort Sam Houston and several tours at Fort Lee, VA where he served as Logistics Staff Officer and combat service support reactor during LOGEX. By then he had been promoted to Major. On his last assignment in the U.S. Army reserves in 1996/1997, he served as Senior Logistics Staff Officer at Fort Shafter, HI Logistic Division OCDSLOG US Army Pacific, where he helped to prepare, analyze and coordinate input to USAPA COM and USARPAC OPLANs, compiled MOBPLANs for logistical Concepts, combat Service structures, resupply sustainment and Time Phase Force deployment Data (TPFDD). He served also as a member of USARPAC Crisis Action Staff.

DONALD "DON" R. PAGE graduated from McGregger Military School and enlisted in 1964. He took Basic Training at Fort Ord, CA and many other courses. Page was stationed at Fort Bragg, NC; Fort Benning, GA; Fort Huachuca, AZ; Fort Hood, TX; Fort Meade, MD and Hunter AAF/GA. He was in Vietnam twice and in Germany (USAEUR) twice. Memorable experiences were in TET in 1968 and Cambodia in 1970.

Page was awarded CIB and EIB. In 1972 he was discharged in Germany as a First Lieutenant.

From Golden West College, Huntington Beach, CA he earned an Associate of Arts (1974) and a BS from California State University in Long Beach (1977).

Page is affiliated with VFW, American Legion, VVA, USPA and AOPA.

He retired in 2010 from FAA Inspection Authorization. In retirement he enjoys skydiving and renovating VW buses.

Don and Gloria have three children: Rebeca, Sharon and Rachel. Grandchildren are Emma, Graciela and Penelope.

WILLIAM P. "SGT SMOKE" PAGE was born Nov. 25, 1945 in Pulaski, TN. He graduated from Pensacola Adult in 1963 and attended PJC Criminal Justice for one year.

He enlisted in December 1964 at Pensacola, FL. After Boot Camp at Fort Gordon, GA he had Basic Airborne and Truck Vehicle training.

Page was stationed at Augsburg, Germany. After that he was assigned to An Khe, South Vietnam to the 1st Cavalry Air Mobile D Company 2nd Battalion 5th Cavalry. After extending his tour, SSG Page was reassigned to AES Company Airborne 15th S&S Battalion. After tour was over in October 1968 he was reassigned to the 82nd Airborne Division, Fort Bragg, NC. From there he was reassigned to the 118th MP Company, 18th Airborne Corps.

He was awarded a Bronze Star, Purple Heart and Air Medal Commendation.

In December 1968 after a stay in Womack Army Hospital, Fort Bragg, NC convalescent leave was given and he went home to Cantonment, FL and married his wife, Sue. SSG Page was honorably discharged in April 1969. Together they have two sons, four grandchildren and one great grandchild.

After working at Monsanto for 19 months he was laid off in 1971, then worked for L&N railroad (later named CSX) as a train engineer, retiring in 2005 after 33 years. SSG Page is active in the Masonic Lodge as a 32nd degree Mason. His hobbies include working on his Smoky Mountain cabin and traveling, especially on cruise ships.

JOHN S. PARKER was born Sept. 1, 1948 in Gastonia, NC, and graduated from Kings Mountain High School in 1967. He enlisted at Gastonia on April 1, 1968 and did Boot Camp at Ft. Bragg, NC. He was stationed with the 82nd Airborne Division at Fort Bragg, NC (1968-1969). He was then sent to Vietnam in March 1969. He thought he was going as a replacement for someone in the 82nd that was due to come back from Vietnam. John arrived in Bien Hoa then to Pleiku. He was initially was to go the 173rd Airborne Brigade, but the 1st Cavalry Division need replacements. Parker was assigned to C Btry, 2/19 FA as an assistant gunner on a 105mm howitzer. A few weeks later he was assigned to Co D 1/8 Cavalry as a Recon Sergeant. John was to be the assistant to the forward observer.

About midway through his tour, he was reassigned back at A artillery battery. John spent the last part of his tour with A Btry, 1/21 FA as a gunner on a 105mm howitzer. Parker ended his tour in April 1970. His next assignment was with C

Btry, 6/10 FA in Bamberg, Germany. John was a gunner on an 8in SP Howitzer. John says he was proud to have served in the 1st Cavalry Division. He says, "While I was in Germany I wore that big yellow 1st Cavalry Division on my right shoulder with pride."

John received the Bronze Star, Purple Heart, and Air Medal. In retirement he was a letter carrier for the US Postal Service, retiring on May 1, 2013. He is a member of the 82nd Airborne Division Association and 1st Cavalry Division Association.

John is married to Judy Wallace Parker and has two daughters: Natasha Parker Yarbro and Ginger Parker Spiller, with five grandchildren.

EDSEL "ED" C. PARNELL was born Sept. 22, 1945 in New Orleans, LA and graduated from Jefferson High School in 1963. He enlisted in 1963 in New Orleans, LA. In addition to Boot Camp at Fort Polk, he attended Aviation School and Communications.

Parnell was stationed at Fort Polk, Fort Rucker, Fort Benning, US Boxer Vietnam, Fort Eustis and with Michigan Army National Guard (1967 to 1969).

He served in Vietnam and was awarded the Air, Combat Infantry Badge, Good Conduct, Vietnam Medal, Rifle Expert, Marksman and Efficiency Honor and Fidelity.

Memorable experiences include continual memories of Vietnam.

In 1967 SP4 Parnell was discharged at Fort Eustis, VA.

He retired in 2008 from working in car sales and parts. He now enjoys restoring old cars and making birdhouses.

"Ed" and Janet (DeSloover) have two children, Tracy Parnell Kubricht and Edsel Jr. Grandchildren are Katherine, Lauren, Evan, Elliot, Olivia and Ethan. Step-grandchildren are Devin, Chase, Morgan, Nicholas and Corinne. Step-great-grandchildren are Olivia, Nicholas and Lily.

GLENWOOD N. "MICKEY" PARRISH was commissioned 2nd Lieutenant upon graduating as a distinguished military graduate from the University of Virginia in 1955 with a BS degree in education/history. He was awarded the Marshall Award for outstanding ROTC student.

In 1955 he completed the Artillery Basic Officer Course in El Paso, TX. In 1963-65 he completed the 11th Air Assault 1st Cavalry Division - 1st Team at Fort Benning, GA. In 1967 he was in the graduating class of the US Army Command and General Staff College at Fort Leavenworth, KS. In 1970-71 he served his second tour of duty in Viet Nam as a battalion leader and was the helicopter liaison officer during the battle of la Drang Valley near Cambodia. He was one Soldier who will forever be memorialized in the book written by Lt. Gen. Harold Moore and writer Joseph Galloway, *We were Soldiers Once...and Young*.

Mickey served 30 years in a variety of commands, staff and aviation positions throughout the US, Korea, Germany and two tours in Viet Nam. He was a Transportation Corps Senior Army aviator. Mickey retired as full Colonel in 1985. He has numerous awards, including the Legion of Merit, Bronze Star with one OLC, Air Medal with 13 OLC and V device, and the Army Commendation Medal with two OLCs.

Mickey and his high school sweetheart, Anna Snider, married 57 years, have four children, eight grandchildren and eight great-grandchildren. In December 1993 the 1st Cavalry Division Association sponsored an Ia Drang Scholarship Program in which so far seven of his grandchildren have benefited. Mickey retired to his hometown of Staunton, VA where he spent his retirement playing golf, travelling and was a dedicated member of his church volunteering where needed. He also gave blood monthly for over 40 years.

Mickey died on October 10, 2010 from ischemic heart disease. He was buried in Thornrose Cemetery in Staunton, VA.

ROBERT PATRIZIO was born Nov. 12, 1948 in Brooklyn, NY and graduated from Franklin K. Lane High School in 1966. He reported to Fort Hamilton in Brooklyn, NY on May 21, 1968, where he was drafted into the Army and assigned to Fort Gordon in Georgia for basic training and A.I.T. Infantry. After graduation he went to Fort Benning for Jump School.

He received his orders for Viet Nam after Jump School and arrived in Viet Nam Dec. 17, 1968, assigned to Co. A 1/12 Cav. as a rifleman. About four months in country, he became the company commander's radioman until September when he was transferred to Fire Base Grant where he finished out his time in Viet Nam as Company Rep.

Patrizio received the Combat Infantry Badge, Purple Heart, Air Medal, Army Comm. Medal with D Device, Army Comm. Medal, Parachute Badge, Viet Nam Service Medal, Viet Nam Campaign Medal with 60 Device, Viet Nam Cross of Gallantry with Palm Device, and Viet Nam Wound Award.

Returning to the world, he finished his hitch in the Army at Fort Rucker, AL.

Patrizio married Nuris "Cindy" Pinero in June 1972 and had three children: Anthony (deceased), Thomas and John. They have four grandchildren: Justin, Kimberly, Katelyn and Kelly and two great-grandchildren, Jordan and Isiah.

LAURA JEAN PARUNAK was born Feb. 1, 1981 in Boone, NC, and graduated from Beaver Creek High School in 1999. She earned a B.S. in Mathematics (minor in military science) from North Carolina State University in May 2003, and a masters in equine industry management from Texas A&M University in May 2017.

She was commissioned as a Second Lieutenant into the Aviation branch from North Carolina State University ROTC program in May 2003. After completing the Officer Leadership Course at Fort Lewis, WA, she went on to Fort Rucker, AL, for all Aviation and Officer training. Additional training included: Airborne School (Fort Benning); Initial Entry Rotary Wing Course, Aviation Basic Course (Honor Graduate), Flight School XXI AH-64-D Longbow Qualification Course, and SERE (B) Course (all at Fort Rucker).

Stations include Camp Page and Camp Eagle, South Korea (Platoon leader in 1-2 Attack Battalion); Fort Hood, TX (S-1 Officer for 1-227 ARB); Balad Air Base, Iraq (Airborne Communications Battle Staff, 77th Expeditionary Airlift Squadron, 332nd Expeditionary Operations Group, 332nd Air Expeditionary Wing); Camp Taji, Iraq (Asst. Operations Officer & Battle Captain for 1-227 ARB, and later Shops Platoon Leader for 615th Aviation Support Battalion, 1ACB); and Conroe, TX (Charlie Co. Commander for 1-558th Attack Reconnaissance Battalion).

She served during OIF 06-08 (15-month deployment during the "Surge" was a memorable experience), OIF 09-10, and multiple engagements as an Apache helicopter pilot. She received the Distinguished Flying Cross, Air Medal (with 2 device), Meritorious Service Medal, Army Commendation Medal with three OLC, Army Achievement Medal, Meritorious Unit Commendation, National Defense Service Medal, Iraqi Campaign Medal (with three campaign stars), Global War on Terrorism Service Medal, Korean Defense Service Medal, Army Service Ribbon, Overseas Service Ribbon, Combat Action Badge, Army Aviator Badge, and Parachutist Badge.

Paraunak received an honorable discharge from active duty in November 2010, and from Army Reserves in November 2013 (both in Texas), with the rank of Captain. She served as a high school math teacher from January 2012-July 2015, was a graduate student at Texas A&M University from August 2015-May 2017, and is now involved in equine related activities for Veterans.

JACK WALTER PELLINGTON received notice to report to his draft board in Morristown, NJ in 1965, which he did on 10 November along with other draftees. From Morristown, they were bussed to the induction center at Fort Dix, NJ. Once at Fort Dix, a dozen or so were pulled from his group. They were selected to stay and do basic training right there at Fort Dix, while the rest of them remained at the induction center until a location for basic training was determined. The buildup for Vietnam was taking place, which inevitably created mass confusion. The army did not know where to send them. While waiting, they had to fall into formation three times a day, which continued for a week or so before receiving their assignments. Half the group was sent to the state of Washington for training; the other half, including Jack, went to Fort Hood, TX.

While at Fort Hood, he was assigned to 1st Platoon, Company A, 2nd Battalion, 66th Armor, 2nd Armor Division "Hell on Wheels". Throughout basic training, he served as an acting Corporal and carried the company guidon. He finished basic and went home on leave 31 January 1966. At the end of his leave, he traveled to Fort Bragg, NC for Advanced Individual Training (AIT). His report date was 18 February 1966. Once at Fort Bragg, he was assigned to communications with the 503rd Military Police Battalion, Headquarters Company. He completed AIT on 16 June 1966 and then returned home for leave, once again.

His leave was up on 3 July 1966. He then flew from Newark Airport to California, where he boarded a military cargo plane heading to a tropical paradise known as Vietnam. On 8 July 1966, after a twenty-two or twenty-four hour flight, he landed at Pleiku, Vietnam. Once arrived, he and the other newly-arrived Soldiers reported to the 526th Replacement Company. The next day they were trucked to the 1st Cavalry Division base camp located at An Khe. From there, he was assigned to Charlie Battery, 1st Battalion, 77th Artillery, 1st Cavalry Division, Airmobile.

On 5 August 1966, he was assigned as an RTO (radio telegraph operator) with the forward observation (FO) section that was attached to A Company, 2nd Battalion, 12th Cavalry, 1st Cavalry Division, Airmobile. He initially started out carrying the radio for the recon sergeant, who was going home in several weeks and that he was his replacement; therefore, he had to start on the job training. In less than thirty days, he had to learn how to call in and adjust artillery and air support whenever Alpha Company 2nd of the 12th was in a firefight with the NVA or Viet Cong. Five days later, 10 August 1966, they were involved in a four-hour firefight in the Ia Drang Valley. He lived in and patrolled the jungles with Alpha Company from 5 August 1966 until 6 June 1967. Their area of operation was in the Central Highlands from the South China Sea to the Cambodia border. While in Vietnam, he was involved in ninety-four different engagements, encountering everything from sniper fire to a three-day firefight. He and his RTO were always on the first helicopters to land at a landing zone and we walked the sixth and seventh man in the column daily. Whenever there was even the remote possibility of being attacked during extraction, they would wait to leave on the last helicopter so that no one would ever chance being left on the ground without artillery support. Throughout his tour, his call signs were Concrete 3-6 Mike, Top Kick 3-6 Mike, and Lightning Bolt 6-2 Mike. Some of the operations in which he participated were Paul Revere II, Thayer, Irving, Thayer II, and Pershing. Ironically, both his first and last firefight were in Pleiku. On 6 July 1967, my tour in Vietnam was over; he departed the tropical paradise and headed home.

His next duty station was Fort Benning, Georgia, where he was assigned to B Battery, 2nd Battalion, 10th Artillery, 197th Infantry Brigade. While with the 19th, his job was to work on the ranges while Second Lieutenants were learning how to call in and adjust artillery rounds on targets. These Lieutenants would become the new forward observers heading to Vietnam. Fort Benning was his last duty station. He received my discharge from the Army on 9 November 1967. In the two years he was in the Army, he obtained the rank of Sergeant (E-5), and served as a section chief in both Vietnam and Fort Benning.

He received the National Defense Service Medal, Vietnam Service Medal with two Bronze Service Stars, Republic of Vietnam Campaign Medal with Device 1960, Army Commendation Medal, Air Medal, Good Conduct Medal, Expert Marksmanship Badge with Rifle Bar, Republic of Vietnam Gallantry Cross with Palm, Unit Citation Badge, and two Overseas Bars. While in Vietnam he was also recommended for the Silver Star Medal and three Bronze Star Medals; however, the recommendation paperwork was lost when the 1st Cavalry Division relocated north from An Khe in 1967. Therefore, he never received the medals.

After leaving the Army, he was a factory worker for one year, a rear axle line feeder at the Ford Assembly Plant in Mahwah, New Jersey for one year, and then a cable splicer, airman, and cable troubleshooter for New Jersey Bell Telephone and then Bell Atlantic. He retired from the telecommunications industry in June 2000 after 31 years of service.

On 21 June 1969, he married Charlene Travers. They have two children, John and Dawn; five grandchildren, Mackenzie, Jack, Johnathan, Reagan, and Walter; and one great granddaughter, Olivia.

MIKE PERRY was in the 1st Cavalry Division Vietnam Class of 1970-71, then on to Fort Hood from 1971-73.

While in Vietnam, his first five months was with the 3rd Bgd Recon Platoon at Fire Base Mace, then Scout Platoon B Troop 1/9, then to Fort Hood CSC 2/7, Scout Motorcyle Pit. Scouts Out.

JOHN ROBERT PETERSON, at six feet four inches, was known as "Big John" on the battlefield and on the job. John was in the Iowa National Guard before being called up. He was a .50 cal. machine gunner. On the march he had the "Ma Deuce" over his shoulder. As MacArthur was always giving accolades to "his" Marines, the Army's First Cav. was right in the thick of the fighting alongside them.

Prior to the "advance in a different direction" John's 1st Cav. was at the front when the first human was attempted to wash over them. As the first wave of driven civilians and some North Korean Soldiers advanced, most dressed inadequately and unarmed, the Ma Deuces and rifles began to chatter. Bodies piled up. The second wave was mostly armed consisting of some civilians and largely N. Korean Soldiers. Bodies continued to pile up. The third wave was all armed N. Koreans and some Chinese Regulars. The last wave added to the wall of dead that rose between 12 and 15 feet high. While barrels heated up needing replacement it was always known that new barrels were available to the rear. John survived the advance to the rear in the bitter cold. He participated in seven major battles in Korea.

John had an affinity for guns and target shooting. After the Army, John spent a few years in business in payroll departments. He had a calling and joined the California State Police and was assigned to the California Governor's Office where he provided security to many dignitaries. He served the California State Police from the late 1950s until 1972, when he retired. Retirement found him buying properties through tax liens. He never married, but was visited often by his friends and nieces and nephews. He died in February 2011 while recovering from a fall and a broken hip.

MERLE J. "PETE" PETERSON was born Jan. 20, 1931 in Blooming Prairie, MN and graduated from Blooming Prairie High School in 1948, later earning his BS (1955) and MS (1965) from Winona State University.

He enlisted on Dec. 7, 1948 at Mankato, MN. After basic training at Fort Riley, KS he took Advanced Infantry training at Fort Benning, GA. He was discharged Dec. 6, 1951 at Camp Edwards, MA, having served in the Korean War (August 1950 – July 1951) with 3rd Bn., 7th Cav. Regt., 1st Cav. Div. He was in Task Force Lynch – Breakout of Pusan Perimeter, Sept. 16, 1950.

Memorable experiences were Task Force Lynch – 123 miles in enemy territory in 23 hours and Breakout of Pusan Perimeter.

Peterson was awarded CIB, KSM – 5 campaign stars and ROK Pres. Unit Citation.

In 1956 he was commissioned in Reserve Duty and retired in 1991 as Colonel. From 1972-2012 he was West Point Liaison Officer.

Peterson retired in 1986 after being a Minnesota schoolteacher for 31 years.

Merle and Betty have four children, 10 grandchildren and one great-grandson.

GEORGE H. PHILLIPS, JR. was drafted into the Army at Camp Robinson, AR May 1, 1945 and then transferred to Camp Hood, TX, for Tank Destroyer Basic Training. After completing basic training, he was transferred overseas and assigned to the 1st Cavalry Division Band at Camp Drake, Japan.

During his military service, he served with Army Bands in Japan, Germany, France, Hawaii and the Continental United States.

After retirement, he was employed by the American National Red Cross and served in Vietnam. After returning to the States he was employed by the Federal Civil Service as a Program Analyst at Fort Leonard Wood and Zweibruecken. During that service, he obtained his bachelor's and master's degrees.

Phillips' awards include the Army Commendation Medal while serving with the 4th Armored Division Band at Goeppingen, the Medal for Humane Action while serving with the American National Red Cross at Vietnam and the Commanders' Award while serving with the 517th Maintenance Battalion (TMDE) at Zweibruecken.

He completed 21 years of military service and 21 years of civil service.

Phillips married Marianne Kollmuss in 1952 while serving at Munich, Germany. They have three children, three granddaughters and one great-granddaughter.

RONALD "RON" H. PIATEK was a member of the 115th MPC, RING. He did basic at Ft. Jackson and AIT at Dix.

In May 1968, the five officers and one hundred twenty-one enlisted men of the 115th Military Police Company, RING, were mobilized for active duty and stationed at the USMA, West Point, NY. The men were to act as a personnel pool, under the Levy System, to fill slots in major combat divisions in Vietnam. Special training included night infiltration and reconnaissance, with field maneuvers against the 82nd Airborne.

Ron was one of three (along with SSG Corsair (McGroarty) & Specialist Nicholson) who served with the 1st Cav. Airmobile, RVN.

In February 1969 he was assigned to the 2nd of the 12th, Headquarters Company, of the 1st Cav, in Tay Ninh, where he served as Motor Sergeant. He processed out of Country in Nov69 and rejoined the 115th MPC at USMA, ending his service in RI, Dec69 when the Company returned to State control.

Piatek's awards and decorations include the Bronze Star, Combat Air Medal, Vietnam Service and Vietnam Campaign Medal, along with the Vietnamese Cross of Gallantry with Palm, Army Valorous Unit Award and Presidential Unit Citation Division awards. Three Combat Stars for "Tet 69 Counteroffensive", "Vietnam Summer-Fall 1969" and "Vietnam Winter-Spring 1970."

Ron settled in Scituate, Rhode Island and summered in Barrington, RI. He passed away peacefully on Wednesday, February 29, 2012. He was the beloved husband of Gail A. (Cabral) Piatek for 33 years. Born in Providence, he was the proud 2nd generation proprietor of Piatek Machine Co., Inc. Ron was an avid boater and enjoyed fishing, traveling and gardening, but especially spending time with his two grandsons. Besides his loving wife, he leaves a daughter, Tracy Greenlaw and her husband, Brian along with his two grandsons, Chad and Chase.

STEPHEN P. POULOS graduated from the City College of New York with a B.A. in Russian and was commissioned as a Regular Army 2LT, Infantry, in June 1968. Following Infantry Officers Basic Course, Ranger and Airborne Schools at Fort Benning, GA, he was assigned to the Berlin Brigade for 14 months before being deployed to Vietnam in 1970.

Poulos served with the 1st Battalion, 5th Regiment, 1st Cavalry Division (Airmobile) in Vietnam and Cambodia as an Infantry Platoon Leader, Company Commander and as Acting Battalion Commander he brought his Battalion's colors back to Fort Hood, Texas in 1971. He was then assigned to Fort Benning to attend the Infantry Officer's Advanced Course and after graduation, was the Distinguished Honor Graduate of his class at both Jumpmaster and Pathfinder Schools. His next assignment in 1973 was with the ROTC Detachment at Loyola College, Baltimore, MD while pursuing his M.A. at Georgetown in Russian Area Studies, which he earned in 1976.

In 1976, Poulos then became an Individual Mobilization Augmentee (IMA), initially serving as a Reserve Training School Instructor. While an IMA, Poulos worked as a Budget Director and Corporate Planner for two corporations and during this time he earned an MBA in 1989 at the Loyola Graduate School of Business in Baltimore, MD. In 1990 he was invited into the Reserve Component (RC) Foreign Area Officer (FAO) Program and was assigned for 10 years at the Office of Deputy Chief of Staff, Intelligence, at the Pentagon. His final 5 years at the Pentagon was with the Office of Deputy Chief of Staff, Operations, as Chief of the RC FAO Accession Branch.

Poulos retired after 36 years of total service in 2004 as a Colonel (O-6), and over the course of his career received 3 Bronze Stars (1 for Valor), 2 Air Medals (Airmobile assignment), Meritorious Service Medal, 2 Army Commendation Medals, Vietnam Service Medal, Vietnam Campaign Medal w/60 Device, World War II Occupation Medal (Berlin assignment), National Defense Service Medal, Vietnam Cross of Gallantry w/Palm, Army Valorous Unit Award (1st Cav, Cambodia Incursion), Combat Infantryman's Badge, Airborne Badge and Pathfinder Badge. He has been working for IBM as a Project Executive since 1999 and is currently planning his second retirement.

Poulos, who was married to Carol, has one child (Candace), five grandchildren (Stephen, Jordan, Carissa, Victoria and Sophia) and one great-grandchild (Luke).

JOHN W. POWELL was born Sept. 1, 1946 in Macon, GA, and graduated from Sidney Lanier High School in 1964. He started his career in the U.S. Army in 1966. After being commissioned as a second lieutenant, he subsequently became a rotary winged aviator, and served for eight years on active duty, including a tour of duty in the Republic of South Vietnam as a helicopter pilot with the 1st Squadron, 9th Cavalry, First Cavalry Division.

In 1974, he left active duty and spent the next 10 years as a consumer-marketing manager with the Hershey Chocolate Co. He joined the Virginia National Guard in 1978, and in 1984 was recalled to active duty and retired in 1995 with the rank of Lieutenant Colonel. LTC (R) Powell has 71 military decorations, including two awards of the Distinguished Flying Cross, two awards of the Air Medal for Valor, the Vietnamese Cross of Gallantry, the Bronze Star, three awards of the Meritorious Service Medal, the Legion of Merit, and thirty-three (33) Air medals for combat air missions.

After retirement, he was the National Membership Director for AMVETS until 2002. He is now the Director of Operations for Military Historical Tours, and serves as the Secretary/Treasurer for the Vietnam Helicopter Pilots Association. He is married to Angie; they have one child and two grandchildren.

JAMES G. PRATT was born in 1946 in Whiteman, MA. He graduated from Whitman-Hanson Regional High School in 1964.

He enlisted in December 1965 and attended basic training at Fort Polk, LA. He completed flight training as a helicopter pilot at Fort Rucker, AL and was appointed a Warrant Officer on Jan. 10, 1967. He served his first tour in Vietnam with Bravo Troop, 1/9 Cav., a reconnaissance unit, flying in the lift section. In his words, "I took some very brave men into some very bad places and took them out again." Following his first tour he was an instructor pilot at Fort Wolters, TX, but he returned to Vietnam as a Chinook Pilot, serving with the 196 ASHC. During his military service he was awarded numerous medals, including two Distinguished Flying Crosses, two Bronze Stars, Army Commendation Medal, and the Air Medal with 27 OLC for the 750 hours of combat flying he accrued.

He left the Army in November 1969 and entered law enforcement. He retired from the City of Hialeah Police Department in 1994. He resides in Tallahassee, FL and spends his time fishing with his daughter, Amy, and traveling with his girlfriend, Lou.

PHILIP "PHIL" A. PRYOR was born 26 Aug. 1936 in Washington, D.C. and enlisted in June 1954. Additional training was ABN, Ranger, Pathfinder, Jungle, etc.

Pryor served three RVN tours, 1st ID, 1st Cavalry and VN Abn Adv. He was the Commander 2/12 Cavalry, July 1970 to March 1971.

He received the Def. Sup. Svc, LOM, DFC, BSV and AM (23) for his service.

Pryor was with the first permanent US unit to land in RVN, July 1965, B Company, 1/18th, 1st ID.

He received a B.S. degree from USMA in 1958, graduated from Naval War College in 1972, and earned his MBA from Tulane University in 1973. After 28 years, Colonel Pryor was discharged in 1986.

He was a business development executive, retiring in 2006. In retirement he enjoys golf, is a wine instructor/collector and has traveled to 60+ countries.

He and wife, Lynn, have two children, Janet and Penny and two grandchildren, Dana and Amanda.

HALIDAY M. PULLUM was born May 5, 1947 in Brooklyn, NY and graduated from Medford

High School in 1966. He enlisted in the US Army during April 1966 with the intent of going to Officer Candidate School (OCS). After successfully completing Basic Training (Fort Dix) and Advanced Infantry Training (Fort Gordon), he attended Artillery OCS at Fort Sill. He successfully graduated with Class 17-67 on May 9, 1967. After a short tour with the 82nd Airborne Division, he was sent to Viet Nam in February 1968. Arriving during TET Pullum was assigned to I Field Forces and then to the 1st Battalion, 30th Artillery. During June of 1968 the Battalion was assigned to the 1st Cavalry Division. While in the Viet Nam he served with both A and C Batteries of the 30th Artillery and with Division Artillery.

Pullum went on to serve in the US Army for over 20 years. Some of the organizations he served in were the 59th Ordnance Group, 820d Airborne Division, 2nd Infantry Division and XVIII Airborne Corps. He also attended Jumpmaster School at Fort Bragg and graduated on Dec. 19, 1978; earlier in his career he had attended basic airborne school. A few years later Pullum earned his Master Parachute wings. Also, during his time in the US Army he earned his under graduate degree and graduate degree and graduated Command & General Staff School.

RAYFIELD MARK PURNELL graduated from Mergenthaler Vocational Technical High School in 1985 and enlisted on Nov. 13, 1986, with basic training at Fort Knox, KY. He completed the Basic Recruiters Course, Primary Leadership Course, Basic NCO Course, and Sr. Leaders Course.

His assignments include: Fort Hood, TX (Black Jack); Fort Richardson, AK; Fort Jackson, SC; USAEUR HQ; HRC St. Louis; MEPCOM; USAREC; and Camp Casey, Korea. He has received the following awards: Joint Service Commendation Medal, MSM (2), Army Commendation (6), Army Achievement Medal (6), Meritorious Unit Commendation Medal, Valorous Unit Award, Army Unit Superior Award (2), Army Good Conduct Medal (8), National Defense Service Medal (2), South West Asia Service Medal (3 BS), Gloal War on Terrorism Service Medal, Korean Defense Service Medal, Noncommissioned Officer Professional Development Ribbon (3), Overseas Service Ribbon (5), Kuwait Liberation Medal (Saudi Arabia), Kuwait Liberation Medal (Kuwait), Gold Recruiter Badge (3 sapphires), Recruiting Ring of Excellence and the Glenn E. Morrell award.

He was discharged on March 31, 2012, with the rank of Sergeant First Class. He currently works as a Social Service Assistant and enjoys traveling.

He is married to Rosalie Purnell. Their children are Natasha, Marques, Whitley, Malaya, Mark, Erica, and Elayka. Grandchildren include: Ziyon, Eli, Olivia, Elijah, and Jillian.

MATTHEW "MATT" S. QUAY was born Dec. 28, 1929 in Altoona, PA. He enlisted in the US Army in April 1945 at the age of 15, later receiving his GED. He attended boot camp at Camp Wheeler, GA. Later stateside stations included Fort Dix, NJ; Camp Pickett, VA and Fort Sill, OK.

Matt served tours in World War II, the Korean War and the Vietnam War, during which he was awarded the Bronze Star and European Theater medal. Memorable experiences include serving as a special escort guard at the Nuremberg Trials in Germany. He went to Korea as a member of the 77th Field Artillery. He was discharged at Fort Sill, OK on Sept. 30, 1971 with the rank of CSM.

Following the service, Matt worked as a real estate broker, retiring in 1980. Following retirement he was on the Board of Directors for the Area Agency on Aging, also serving as its Director for two years.

He is married to Elizabeth and has five children from a previous marriage - Debra, Bret, Valerie, Pandora and Susan – and seven grandchildren – Matthew, Hannah, Emma, Halle, Megan, Christina and Rebecca. Matt and Elizabeth live in Ellsinore, MO.

JOHN "TINO" RANGEL JR. was born May 28, 1937 in Oakland, CA and graduated from Washington Union High School in 1956. He enlisted in June 1956 at Hayward, CA. After Boot Camp at Fort Ord, CA, he spent 10 weeks of Infantry training.

He was stationed at Fort Ord and served in Vietnam (1965) LZ-Ray and Ia Drang, Valley.

Rangel was awarded a Purple Heart, Bronze Star with Device and Presidential Citation.

Memorable experiences were being a guest of his Platoon Leader, receiving the Medal of Honor in Washington, DC.

SFC Rangel was discharged at Fort Gordon, GA.

He retired in 1980 after working in civil service.

"Tino" and Shirley B. Rangel have four children: Steve, David, Billy and Danny. Their grandchildren are Ashley, Jordon, Genel, Evan, Garrett and Gaven.

WILLIAM "HATCHET" REED was born in Buffalo, NY, on Oct. 11, 1942 and was raised on a diary farm in northern Pennsylvania. He was drafted into the Army in January 1968. His basic training was at Fort Benning, with advanced infantry at Fort Polk, back to Fort Benning for N.C.O. School, then to Fort Polk again as a training sergeant.

He arrived in Viet Nam in January 1969. In country at Long Bien, Assigned to 1st Cavalry Division, arrived at Cav. headquarters in An Kay — one week Cav. training and assignment. Assigned to 2nd of the 7th Company C. Out to company by chopper. Since he was the only E-5 left in company, he was given a squad to lead. With the help of the "Old Guys" and a great 1st. Lt. John Gillory and his growing up in the Pennsylvania forests, he was able to spend 10 months as a squad leader in the boonies and only losing one fellow grunt and a few wounded. He was on many LZ s and areas, ending up on LZ Jamie near Tai Ninh. After being a grunt for 10 months he was sent TDY to Mac V in Saigon. He was then part of a Special Services Band, the Nashville Cats. With four other service personnel and some Red Cross Donut Dollies, they performed shows on many fire bases and permanent installations. At the end of the TDY his year in Viet Nam was over.

Reed received the Bronze Star, Combat Infantry Badge, Air Medal, Viet Nam Service Medal, Pres. Unit Citation and other awards from Special Services Music Entertainment Division.

After returning home, he married Louise Schmidt on Sept. 4, 1971 and they had two sons, Earl William Reed and Mathew Arlington Reed.

Reed spent his working years as a welder, mechanic, and heavy equip operator. He says he values his time in the 1st Cav. greatly and will never forget the "GUYS" as long as he lives.

RICHARD H. "REGGIE" REGULA was born July 11, 1924 in Northville, MI, and graduated from Cooley High School in 1943. After high school, he began his military service at Fort Riley in the horse cavalry. Later he volunteered for a secret and dangerous mission behind Japanese lines.

Richard Regula in in the front row, leaning far right.

The varied 3,000 volunteers left on a troop ship for India, where they became "Merrill's Marauders" in the CBI Theater, led into the jungles of Burma by General Merrill to open the Burma Road so that the Chinese could get supplies through.

Dick was a mule skinner and his unit WALKED over the mountains and through the mud. If the mules had difficulty navigating the mountains, the men carried the mules' burdens (usually guns and ammo) on their own backs. Supplies were air dropped – food for the mules, ammo and G.I. rations.

The monsoon and Japs they encountered made the journey even more difficult. The wounded were airlifted out one at a time when the small planes could find a spot to land. Richard was very proud of his service. He finally received the Bronze Star 60 years later. His outfit was to receive the Presidential Citation but he never did.

They have two sons, four granddaughters and a great-grandson. Richard owned a printing and office supply business, a home in Beverly Hills, MI and a cottage on Lake Charlevoix, MI. His hobbies were fishing and pheasant hunting.

Dick passed away in 2009, a month before their 59th anniversary.

JAMES C. RICHARDS, CW03 RET. started his military career in the Navy on Oct. 21, 1965. He went to boot camp at Great Lakes and his first assignment was to Attack Squadron 72 (VA-72) flying A-4E Skyhawks as a Plane Captain. In February 1966 he was transferred to Patrol Squadron 18 (VP18), flying in the P2V-7 Neptune. While there he completed aircrew training as an Aviation Ordnanceman.

In March 1967 he volunteered for Vietnam service with Project TRIM (Naval Air Special Ops) flying in modified P2V-7 aircraft. All ASW gear was removed and the Aero 11A-2 twin M-3 20mm cannons with an Image Intensifier gun sight was installed in the tail where he flew. After much training they were sent to Cam Ranh Bay Naval Air Facility, South Vietnam. August of 1968 Project TRIM was decommissioned and they became Heavy Attack Squadron 21, VAH-21 that same day. He left the squadron in March of 1969 and went to the *USS F.D. Roosevelt CVA-42* at Mayport, FL. He was on this great ship until May 1969 and then was transferred to the *USS John F. Kennedy, CV67*. He took the "Big John" on its first Med Cruise and left the Navy in October 1969.

He joined the Navy Reserve program and was recalled to active duty as a TAR (Training/Administration of Reserves) in February 1975. He went to refresher training on the P2V7 and on the P-3A1B Orion patrol plane, then on to Patrol Squadron 94 (VP-94), in New Orleans, LA. He transferred to Patrol Squadron 69 (VP-69) at Whidbey Island, WA in January 1979. While there he completed certification as Aircrew Trainer on the P-3 Orion. He transferred to Helicopter Attack Light Squadron 4 (HAL-4) (Naval Air Special Ops) at Norfolk, VA in February 1981 and flew as Crew Chief and Door Gunner, on the HH-1K helicopter until September 1982 when he was accepted in the Army Warrant Officer Flight Program at Fort Rucker, AL. He left the Navy with over 3,000 aircrew flight hours. He graduated from the program in September 1983 as a WO-1. His first Army assignment was to "C" Troop, 4/6th Cav., 1st Cav Div, Fort Hood, piloting the UH-1H Huey. In February 1984 he was trained in the AH-1 Cobra back at Fort Rucker. He was then assigned to "C" Troop, 227th Avn Reg, 1st CAV Div, flying both the UH-1 and AH-1. During this time he was involved in many overseas assignments including Honduras, Nicaragua, El Salvador, Panama and Guatemala. In May of 1987 he was transferred to the Army Helicopter Maintenance Officer Training Course at Fort Eustis, VA and became a Maintenance Test Pilot on the UH-1H and AH-1. In September 1987, he was assigned to the 268th Avn Batt. at Fort Lewis, WA flying UH-1H, AH-1 helicopters. In January 1989 he was transferred to "C" Troop 1/9h Cav, Fort Lewis, WA flying the same type aircraft. During this timeframe he was an Aviation Liaison Officer during Operation Just Cause on Ancon Hill, Panama. His final assignment was with "C" Company 224th Avn Batt, who flew the CH-47D Chinook helicopters.

He retired on August 1, 1991 as a CW3 with over 1500 Army flight hours and 26 years of service. He currently resides in Olympia, WA with his wife, Kathi, son Adam and daughter Kyla.

WILLIAM A. (BILL) RICHARDSON joined the Army in July, 1940, as a mounted Soldier patrolling the Mexican border in the 7th US Cavalry in Ft. Bliss, TX. In 1943 the 1st Cav Division changed from a horse cavalry to dismounted infantry and deployed to Australia for further infantry training. In December they sailed for New Guinea and in March, 1944, made an assault landing on the Admiralty Islands before moving on to the Philippines, Leyte and then Luzon. On Luzon, they advanced directly to Manilla to liberate the Filipino civilians interned there. When the war ended, the 1st Cav served as the occupying division in Tokyo.

In 1945, Bill sailed for home in Texas. Briefly mustering out of the Army before reenlisting, he returned to Japan and the 7th Cav as a technical sergeant. Gen. MacArthur commissioned him a 2nd Lieutenant in December, 1946.

Next Bill was posted to Ft. Bliss, Germany, and Ft. Meade, MD. He transferred to Army Security Agency at Arlington Hall Station, VA in 1956. In 1958 he served a year's unaccompanied tour to Korea. Bill retired as a major at Vint Hill Farms Station, Warrenton, VA, in February, 1961, having earned the Bronze Star, Army Commendation Medal, Combat Infantry Badge, WWII Victory Medal and Medals for the Occupation of Japan and of Germany. Bill continued to work with the Army at Vint Hill in a civilian role with ASA and INSCOM, retiring in 1984, from the Civil Service.

Bill loved Warrenton, volunteering as a tutor with a literacy group and co-founding the local chapter of Habitat for Humanity where he served a term as president and for years helped build new houses.

Bill's greatest passion, next to his family and country, was the First Cavalry Division Association. Seventy-three years ago in the Admiralty Islands, Bill and some fellow Cav Soldiers decided that if they should survive the war, they would meet yearly to keep their friendship going. That agreement was the start of the First Cavalry Division Association with its numerous regional chapters. Bill served a term as Association President and was a member of its Board of Governors. He also served as President and President Emeritus of the 7th Cavalry Association. A yearly highlight was his and his wife Eva's attendance at the annual 1st Cavalry Reunions, over the decades, missing very few.

A plank member of the local Cav chapter, Bill treasured the chapter's activities on behalf of the Wounded Warriors of Walter Reed Hospital. For several years Bill was honored each November to lay the First Cav's memorial wreath at the WWII Memorial on Veterans Day. In 2014 the local metro chapter was renamed to honor Bill's participation and steadfast dedication; it is now the William A Richardson National Capital Region Chapter.

Besides his love of the Cav, Bill also loved playing the guitar. In retirement he decided to build his own guitars and studied with a luthier, returning home to build a guitar shop. Well into his eighties, he delighted in meticulously crafting and selling his beautiful guitars.

In 1942 Bill lovingly made Eva Ulias an Army wife and they celebrated their 73rd wedding anniversary in 2015. They had two daughters, Sheron (Hume) and Carol (Dandy) and four grandsons, Mark, Shannon, Kevin and Matthew. After bravely battling cancer, Bill died peacefully with his family by his side on November 29, 2015. He was 94 years old.

KENNETH C. RISLEY grew up in Kansas City, KS where in 1962, he joined the Kansas National Guard. In October 1963, Risley left the Guard and enlisted in the Army; was sent to Fort Leonard Wood then to Fort Benning in the 2nd Infantry, 2/38th. He trained in the 11th Air Assault (Test).

June 1965 found him in the 1st Cavalry Division, Company D 2/5th Cavalry and in September 1965 he landed with the Division in Vietnam. Risley was promoted to Sergeant in October 1965, just days after his 20th birthday.

November 1965, Risley saw action as a mortar gunner at LZ X-ray after air assaulting into the "hot" LZ with others of Company D 2/5th and Recon Units.

After LZ X-ray, Risley served as a forward observer until June 1966 when he contacted malaria and was sent to Camp Zama, Japan, then to the US for discharge in August 1966.

Risley was awarded the Air Medal, Presidential Unit Citation, National Defense Service Medal, Vietnam Service Medal with 3 stars, Combat Infantryman Badge, Republic of Vietnam Campaign Ribbon with Device, Expert Badge with Mortar and Rifle Bars, Sharpshooter Badge with Pistol Bar, and Republic of Vietnam Gallantry Cross with Palm.

A pitcher with the Brigade ball team at Fort Benning, Risley continued playing on local Kansas City teams. He worked as machinist for Santa Fe Railroad until a workplace accident forced early retirement. He built racing engines for stock cars and go-carts.

After his wife, Mary Elizabeth Teague, died in 1993, Risley married Martha "Lou" Ala in 1996 and they were together in Overland Park, KS until his sudden death in 2012. He also left two children and three grandchildren.

DOUG RITCHEY was drafted into the Army in April 1969, trained at Fort Polk graduating with the MOS of 11H, heavy weapons infantry (recoilless rifle). He joined A Co, 2/12 Cav, 1st Air Cav in September 1969. At that time A Co, known as Ace High, was trying to stop the infiltration of the NVA along the Ho Chi Minh Trail on the Cambodian border. Typical duty consisted of 15 or more days out on patrol, listening posts or ambushes followed by 3 to 5 days of duty on one of about 20 landing zones that popped up near the border.

The months of May and June of 1970 were very different as the company moved to Cambodia and began work at the largest ammo cache of the war, named Rock Island East. Through all of this he worked closely with Steve Conley and today they are strong friends still. Doug and Steve met with about 60 Ace High vets of the Cambodian Incursion last year and keep in touch often.

Doug is retired, living in West Virginia, and received the Bronze Star, Air Medal, Arcom with "V" and the Combat Infantry Badge.

GEORGE G. "SGT. BLUE" ROBERTSON was born June 13, 1943 in McAlester, OK and graduated from Hardin High School in 1963. He enlisted on Dec. 23, 1964 and took Boot Camp at Fort Leonard Wood, MO with additional training at Fort Sill, OK. He was stationed at 13E20 and 13E40. He served in Korea (moonsonie) and Alaska, Fort Wainwright.

He was awarded the National Defense, Army Forces Expedition, Sharpshooter Badge, Good Conduct – two orders) and Korea Defense Medal.

Memorable experience was the travel to see how other people lives.

Sgt. E5 Robertson was discharged in May 1969 at Fort Lewis, WA.

He worked as a cowboy ranch hand and spent 30 years as a propane truck driver, retiring in 2013.

Retirement activities include Custer Re-enactor, VFW Post 1849 and American Legion Post 39.

George and Diana Mae have two children, Daniel Lee and Marcus Wendell and three grand-children: Brittnay, Sean and Summer.

CAPTAIN WINSTON T. ROBINSON was born Nov. 15, 1942 in Rector, AR, graduated from Rector High School in 1960, and later graduated as a Distinguished Military Graduate and received a Regular Army Commission from Arkansas State University in May 1964.

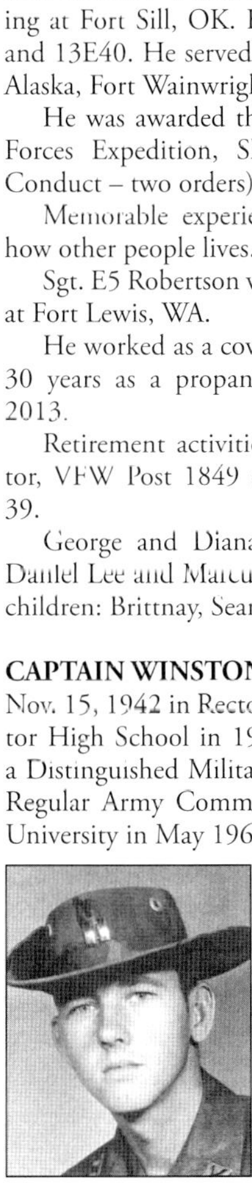

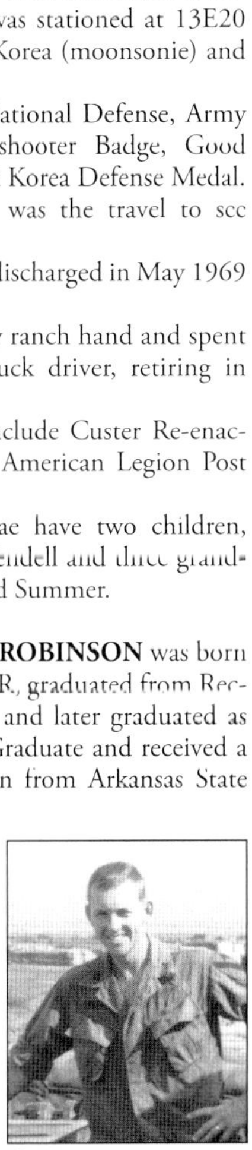

He attended Infantry Officer Basic Schooling and Airborne Training at Fort Benning, GA.

Robinson was assigned with Hq. and Hq. Company, 2nd Battalion, 46th Infantry, Fort Hood, TX from April 1965 until January 1966.

He completed nine months helicopter pilot training at Fort Wolters, TX and Fort Rucker, AL from January to September 1966.

In Viet Nam, October 1966 to September 1967, he was assigned to 2nd Battalion, 20th Aerial Rocket Artillery in the First Cavalry Division. He attended PACAF Jungle Survival School in February 1967.

Captain Robinson was killed in Viet Nam on Sept. 6, 1967.

He was awarded the Distinguished Flying Cross, the Bronze Star and the Air Medal (First through 24th OLC).

Winston and Renee have one son, Winston Scott Robinson and two grandchildren, Seth and Sophie Robinson.

JOHN ROGERS was a ROTC Distinguished Military Graduate (DMG) and was commissioned in the Field Artillery Corps in 1965 after graduating from the University of North Alabama, Florence, AL. His military education includes the Army Command and General Staff College (1974) and the US Army War College (1984).

In 1968 he served with the 1st Cavalry Division first as a Fire Direction Officer in Division Artillery (DIVARTY) and subsequently with the 2d BN, 19th Artillery as a Brigade LNO to the 1st BDE of the First Team. In 1969 he was branch transferred to Air Defense Artillery. As an "air defender" he had over five years of Army command experience culminating as Commander, 11th Air Defense Artillery Brigade.

Rogers received the Legion of Merit with two OLC, Bronze Star Medal, Meritorious Service Medal with four OLC, Air Medal with 9 Num, Army Commendation Medal and VN service awards. He was awarded the Parachutist Badge and Ranger Tab.

From 2003-2013, Rogers served as a Civilian Aide to the Secretary of the Army (CASA), Alabama-North having been appointed by the Hon orable Thomas White.

Rogers was extremely active with the Association of the United States Army (AUSA) and served as President of the Redstone Huntsville Chapter of AUSA and as AUSA 3rd Region President.

He is married to the former Cheri A. Duggar of Florence, AL.

JAMES R. ROLLINS was born in Longview, Texas, on 26 July 1954. After entering the United States Military Academy on 3 July 1972 and graduating on 25 June 1976 with a Bachelor of Science, he was commissioned as a Second Lieutenant of Armor.

After attending Ranger School, Armor Officer Basic Course, and the Motor Officer Course, LT Rollins received an assignment to the 11th Armored Cavalry Regiment at Bad Hersfeld, Germany. During his tour with the 3d Squadron, 11th Armored Cavalry Regiment, he served as a cavalry platoon leader, tank platoon leader, tank company executive officer, and assistant squadron operations officer.

Captain Rollins departed Germany in June 1980 to attend the Armor Officer Advanced Course. After graduating, he was assigned to Fort Bragg, North Carolina, as the assistant G3 Air, XVIII Airborne Corps. CPT Rollins was next assigned as the adjutant for 4th Battalion (Airborne), 68th Armor, 82d Airborne Division, in October 1982.

Captain Rollins received an assignment to 1st Armored Division in October 1983. During his tour with 3d Battalion, 34th Armor at Erlangen, Germany, he served as the battalion maintenance officer and then commanded Company A.

Captain Rollins was assigned in June 1986, as a Ground Liaison Officer with the United States Army Europe and 7th Army Liaison Group attached to United States Air Force Europe with duty at Royal Air Force Base Upper Heyford, United Kingdom, home of the 20th Tactical Fighter Wing. Not only was Captain Rollins, later Major Rollins, expected to perform the duties as the Army advisor to the Air Force, but also performed flying duties in the F-111E aircraft.

In December 1987, Major Rollins was assigned to the Defense Nuclear Agency, Alexandria, Virginia, as the Armor Staff Officer in the Electromagnetic Applications Division, working on electromagnetic weapons systems for offensive and defensive operations.

Major Rollins was next assigned, in June 1989, as an Action Officer and Executive Officer for the Resource Analysis and Integration Office for the Deputy Chief of Staff for Operations, Headquarters, Department of the Army, at the Pentagon, Washington, D.C. It was while assigned to this office he received orders for temporary duty with the 1st Cavalry Division in Southwest Asia as an operations officer in the G4 section from February through April 1991. He departed the Pentagon in June 1991.

LTC Rollins was assigned to Fort Hood, Texas, from June 1991 to June 1993 where he served as the Assistant Chief of Staff, G5 for Civil-Military Operations, 1st Cavalry Division, and Adjutant, 3d (Grey Wolf) Brigade, 1st Cavalry Division.

In June 1993, LTC Rollins became an exchange officer assigned to Australia where he graduated from the Australian Joint Services Staff College, at Canberra, Australia, and received a Graduate Degree in Strategic Studies in December 1993. He was then assigned to Victoria Barracks in Sydney, where he served as the Staff Officer One for the Training Plans Section, Training Branch, Land Headquarters, until December 1995.

LTC Rollins returned to Fort Hood, Texas, in January 1996, where he served as the Assistant Chief of Staff, G5 for Civil-Military Operations, 1st Cavalry Division, until his retirement from the United States Army on 30 November 1997, in the grade of Lieutenant Colonel. He now resides in Lufkin, Texas, with his wife, the former Donna Trimble, daughter Robin and son Jeffrey.

In October 1997, LTC (Ret) Rollins became an employee of Angelina College as a procurement counselor with the Angelina College Procurement Assistance Center. On 1 February 2000, he became the Senior Procurement Counselor of the Angelina College Procurement Assistance Center and in August 2004, he became the Director. Additionally, he earned his Masters of Business Administration from the University of Colorado at Colorado Springs in May 2001 and an Associate of Science Degree in Business from Angelina College in August 2002.

JAMES R. ROMINGER was born Dec. 18, 1932 in Milport, AL, enlisted at Columbus, MS and took Boot Camp at Camp Chaffee. Additional training was in Communication, Electronics and Intelligence. He was stationed at Fort Knox, Fort Sill and Camp San Luis Obispo, CA.

Rominger was engaged in seven battles in Korea and four in Vietnam.

He received the MSM and ACMW/2 oak leaf cluster medals.

CSM Rominger was discharged at Fort Hood, TX.

He was a comptroller with BDM. Professional affiliations are CSM, 9 ARTY, 41 ARTY GP, 13 SIG BN, 122 SIG, 1st Field Forces ARTY, 1st CAV DIV ARTY, BDM Master TCATA.

He and Cosia Burke have one child, James R. Rominger, Jr.

RICHARD "RICK" K. ROWE entered military service at Niagara Falls, NY as an enlisted Soldier in February 1966 attending basic training and parachute school with the 3/187th Inf., 101st Airborne Division. In April 1967, commissioned 2d Lt. Armor and attended flight school. He was assigned to A Troop 1/9th Air Cavalry Squadron, 1st Cavalry Division October 1968 through November 1969; as an AH1G pilot; serving six months as Weapons Platoon Leader. He was released from active duty in 1974.

In 1977 joined the 100th Division USAR as a rotary wing aviator with various command and staff assignments to include Division CofS retiring in 1998. In April 1989, Rowe was selected for Battalion Command to activate and train a USAR Cobra Aviation Attack Battalion, 8th Bn 229th Aviation Regiment.

Colonel Rowe's Decorations and Awards include LOM, DFC 2 OLC, Bronze Star, Air Medal with "V", Air Medal 33 OLC, Master Aviator Wings, and Order of Saint Michael. He holds a Bachelor of Science in Commerce from the University of Louisville. Beginning his civilian career in 1974, he served as an SVP in Wealth Management Group, PNC Bank, Louisville, Kentucky, retiring in 2012.

He and his wife, Kay, reside in Prospect, Kentucky.

HURLEY L. RULON was born August 6, 1928 in Mozier, IL and graduated from Hardin Community High Schol in 1946. He enlisted at Carrolton, IL on Sept. 9, 1948, was examined and sworn in on the same date at St. Louis, MO. That day, he traveled by train to Fort Knox, KY for basic training – Third Armed Division. After graduation and 10 days leave at home, he traveled to Camp Stoneman, Pittsburg, CA, Placement Depot in December 1948.

January 1949 he left for Yokohama, Japan and on to Tokyo, becoming a member of Heavy Motor Company of the 7th US Cavalry. He was in Japan 18 months. Maneuvers on Mt. Fuji were as Cadre of NCO Leadership School. Then he was moved to Camp Drake where the 8th Cavalry as. On June 25, North Korea attacked South Korea. On July 22, 1950, he made an amphibious landing. His most memorable experience was the breakout of the Pusan Parameter. He was in Korea 10 months, then in Truman's Extension, served in H Company as School Troops for eight months.

He has two Letters of Appreciation from Leadership School, one from South Korean Government plus Korean Service Medal, Combat Infantry Badge, United Nations Medal and Silver Star, National Defense, one Arrowhead and five Combat Stars.

He worked in fertilizers and seed corn, then finally realized his dream and got a 160-acre farm. At this time he has sold 120 acres and moved back to 40 acres.

Hurley and his wife have been married 63 years, they have two children and three grandchildren.

GEORGE H. "SANDY" SANDERSON JR. was commissioned in ROTC as an Army Chemical Corps Officer. After Chemical Officer's Basic at Fort McClellan, AL he volunteered for Korea where he served in the First Cavalry Division. Then he was put in command of the troops at the 5th Army Chemical Depot. The parents asked him to start a Boy Scout Troop, which he did. The Boy Scouts started a night school where they taught the farmers to read and write Korean. When they could read Farm Journals, they planted wheat and rye up high where they couldn't grow rice. That freed rice for export to Japan in return for industrial equipment so they could put their refugees to work.

At Fort Ord Chemical Office, he put together a two week AIT Program for a 91st Division Truck Company, which had been re-designated chemical and joined it. He taught a Company Officers' Course for the Army Reserve School while at Command and General Staff College, then taught C & GS.

He taught state radiological defense to volunteer firemen who could then apply for the paid fire department. Certificate caused the state to equip fire trucks with radiological equipment.

Now he is a docent at the Veterans Museum.

ROBERT M. SANTRY, M.D., PhD served 17 years in the US Navy (including seven years with the US Marine Corps as a naval officer)-1971 to 1989. He started his military career as a Navy doctor. He went to Vietnam in 1973 aboard the *USS Mt. Whitney* and worked with repatriated military personnel and prisoners of war. When he returned to California, he served as a medical missionary and served immigrant farm workers as a general practitioner without an internship (1973-1977).

Dr. Santry completed an internship at Letterman Army Medical Center, San Francisco (1977-1978). He completed a residency in psychiatry at Walson Community Hospital Fort Dix, NJ, 1985-1988.

Dr. Santry transferred to the US Army in January 1989 as a Chaplain Corps member. He was the first married man ordained deacon and priest for the Diocese of Honolulu under the pastoral provision program (former Anglican clergymen seeking admission into the Catholic Church and ordination to the priesthood). He made history as the first married man to serve as a Catholic Chaplain in the military.

Following the US Army Basic Officer course for chaplains, Dr. Santry was assigned to HHC, Aviation Brigade, First Cavalry Division (April 1989). He honorably served members of the First Team and also provided psychiatric consultations for the medical community.

Dr. Santry deployed with the First Team to Southwest Asia in 1990. The Brigade Commander asked him to assume the position as Civil-Military Affairs Officer (S5) as well as serve as the unit chaplain. Dr. Santry did the CMA training, studied Arabic and provided multiple combat multipliers as a physician and chaplain who engaged in contract negotiations, engagement with village chieftans and providing medical-dental-vision services to people in many villages. Dr. Santry entered into relationships with the Saudi Royal Family and negotiated services to US military personnel to support them during their tour in Southwest Asia. Dr. Santry was granted an honorary membership in the Royal Saudi Medical Society.

The division chaplain asked Dr. Santry to go to an ammunition depot and talk to three Iraqi Chaldean Catholics and ask them to surrender. During his intervention, an explosion occurred. Dr. Santry covered their bodies and saved them. The three Iraqi Soldiers surrendered to US authorities afterwards and credited Dr. Santry as the reason for their surrender.

Dr. Santry received the Bronze Star with Valor as well as other theater awards.

Upon re-deployment to home station, Dr. Santry attended the Army Officer Advanced Course (Chaplain Corps) and served in Europe for 10 years. He served as the international staff chaplain to the Supreme Allied Commander of NATO (1995-1997) as well as the senior mental health advisor to NATO for the Bosnia operation.

Dr. Santry completed his service at Fort Benning, Fort Rucker and US Army Garrison Darmstadt before retirement in 2005. Dr. Santry completed Command and Staff College and Air War College before retirement.

STEPHEN D. SAUNDERS was born June 8, 1947 in Monroe, WI, and graduated from Brodhead, WI High School in 1965, received a BA at the University of Wisconsin in 1972, and earned a Law Degree at Creighton University in 1975.

He enlisted in the US Army in June 1965, attending basic training at Ft. Knox, KY and then airborne infantry advanced training at Ft. Gordon, GA. He graduated from basic airborne school at Ft. Banning, GA in December 1965 and was stationed in Ft. Campbell, KY with the 101st Airborne Division and Ft. Bragg, NC in the 82nd Airborne Division in the States.

In June 1966, he began a tour in Vietnam with C/2/8 (Abn), 1st Cavalry Division as a machine gunner and squad leader until DEROS in

June 1967. He was discharged in June 1968 at Ft. Bragg, NC.

He received the Bronze Star, Air Medal, Good Conduct Medial, Vietnamese Cross of Gallantry with Palm, National Defense Medal, Vietnam Service Medal, Vietnam Campaign Medal, Parachute Badge and Combat Infantryman's Badge.

In 2005, he authored and published a memoir of my war experiences, *Breaking Squelch, A Vietnam Introspective.* In recent years he has been privileged with several formal speaking engagements, the subject of which are my Infantryman's perspective of the Vietnam War.

From 1975 until retirement in 2013, he was engaged in the private practice of law in Elkader, IA. He has been married to Denise Albert Saunders since 1967. They have three daughters and seven granddaughters.

EDISON E. "ED" SCHOLES, served 35 years in the US Army in key leadership positions from platoon leader to deputy commanding general of XVIII Airborne Corps, Third US Army and a major NATO command. He has served in Infantry, Airborne Infantry, Special Forces, and Ranger units, to include four combat tours in three conflicts. Primary theater of interest since 1980 has been Middle East. Retired from active military in 1996 as Major General to assume position as Program General Manager of Army supervised contract to provide training and support to Saudi Arabian National Guard. After six and a half years in Saudi Arabia, returned to US in 2002 as private consultant. Since June 2002, worked as private contractor for several US firms, which involved defense related work in Iraq, Afghanistan, Jordan, Algeria, Columbia, Peru, Bolivia and the United States.

He was awarded the following medals: Bronze Star Medal with Valor Device and one Oak Leaf Cluster, Bronze Star Medal for Combat Service and two OLC, Purple Heart with Oak Leaf Cluster, Meritorious Service Medal with Oak Leaf Cluster, 6 Air Medals, Army Commendation Medal with Valor Device and Oak Leaf Cluster, National Defense Service Medal with Bronze Star, Armed Forces Expeditionary Medal, Vietnam Campaign Medal with six Campaign Stars, Southwest Asia Service Medal with three Campaign Stars, Humanitarian Service Medal, Army Service Ribbon, three Overseas Service Ribbons, Vietnamese Gallantry Cross Medal with Silver Star and Bronze Star, Vietnam Service Medal, Kuwait Liberation Medal (Kingdom of Saudi Arabia and Kuwait), Joint Meritorious Award, Army Superior Unit Medal and Vietnamese Gallantry Cross Med al with Palm Unit Award.

Scholes was inducted into the University of North Georgia Hall of Fame in 2003, into the RANGER Hall of Fame in 2007 and into the GEORGIA MILITARY VETERANS Hall of Fame (for Valor) in 2015.

Ed and wife, Elva, have three children – Kim, Tracy and Mike.

RICHARD LEON SCHRODER was born in Topeka, Kansas, and attended Topeka High School. After completing college work at Washburn University, he enlisted in the U.S. Army as a medical corpsman, went on active duty on June 6, 1968, and attended Basic Training at Ft. Leonard Wood, MO. After basic, he was assigned to Ft. Sam Houston Medical Center for Medical Corpsman training. He applied for and was accepted into the Clinical Specialist Program (91C) at Ft. Lewis, Washington, graduating in 1969. After Ft. Lewis, he was assigned to the Republic of Viet Nam, arriving in country in November 1969.

In Viet Nam, he was assigned to B Co., 15th Med. Bn., 1st Cavalry Division, at FSB Buttons at Song Be, Phouc Binh Province. His duties included Civilian Med Cap operations in the Song Be area, pharmacist, sanitation inspections and medical operations. While at FSB Buttons, he worked with three fantastic physicians, Captains Jon Lundquist, John Henderson and Paul Parkey. He returned to the states in October, 1970, and was assigned to Darnell Army Medical Center at Ft. Hood, Texas. He was discharged from the U.S. Army in 1971.

After discharge, he returned home to work as an LPN and attended grad school at Ft. Hays State University, after which he moved to Kansas City. He had a brief tour of duty with the Kansas National Guard, and then upon moving to the Kansas City area, joined the 325th General Hospital, USAR, and was a member of that organization for 21 years. His final three years in the military was with the 5039th USAR School teaching 91Bs. He retired in 1995 with 26.5 years of service.

While in the military, he received the Bronze Star Medal, Combat Medical Badge, Army Commendation Medal, Vietnam Service Medal, Vietnam Campaign Medal, National Defense Service Medal and Expert (Rifle).

As a civilian, after active duty, he worked as an LPN, was involved in medical research and, in 1991, he graduated from Nursing School. He worked in a variety of nursing duties including teaching until he retired in 2009.

Schroder married Patricia Schroder in 1969 and have two sons, William and Steven along with six grandchildren.

JOHN T. SCHULTZ attended Boot Camp at Fort Bliss, TX. He took FA Basic Officer training and FA Career Course.

Schultz was stationed at Bien Hoa – FSB Melanie. He was engaged in battles in RVN.

For his service he was awarded the BSM, AM, ARCOM with V Device.

Major John Schultz was medically retired on Dec. 19, 1981 at Fort Polk, LA.

In retirement he enjoys hunting, fishing and following the South Dakota State University Jack Rabbits.

John has two children, J. Thomas Burton Schultz and James Michael Schultz. His grandchildren are Liam, Kailee, Luke, Chris and Larkin.

GEORGE M. SHANNON was a recent enlistee when the Korean War began on 26 June 1950, and he was assigned to A Company, 1st Battalion, 5th Cavalry Regiment, 1st Cavalry Division. On 31 October 1950, Shannon's unit was near P'yonyang, just north of the 38th Parallel when they were surrounded and came under intense fire by Chinese forces suffering heavy losses. Shannon eluded death or capture, making his way back to U.S. forces. For his service in Korea, Shannon earned a Purple Heart, Korean Campaign Ribbon, National Defense Ribbon, U.N. Ribbon, and the Combat Infantry Badge.

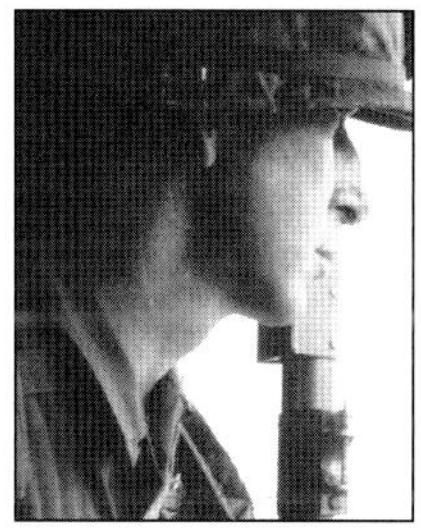

After a variety of other assignments domestically and abroad, Shannon again served with the 1st Cav when in October 1966; he was assigned as a Platoon Sergeant in A Company, 2nd Battalion, 5th Cavalry Regiment in the Republic of Viet Nam. During this first of two tours of duty in Viet Nam, Shannon distinguished himself by exceptionally valorous action when, near the Nui Mieu Mountain complex, his unit came under intense hostile fire and the commanding officer was killed. Though wounded, Shannon took command of the company. Shannon refused medical treatment until all of the wounded were evacuated and contact with the enemy was broken. For his actions on June 20, 1967, Shannon was awarded the Silver Star, his second Purple Heart, second award of the Combat Infantry Badge and was offered a battlefield commission.

Shannon's twenty-four year military career wound down with instructor assignments for Purdue University's Senior ROTC followed by the Junior ROTC program at A.D. Johnston High School in Bessemer, Michigan. He received the Bronze Star (his second) for Meritorious Service and the Army Commendation Medal while at Purdue and the respect and appreciation of Bessemer for transforming the high school's probationary ROTC program into an Honor Unit with Distinction.

Shannon married in 1958 and has four children, Roswitha, Michael, Eileen and Patricia and six grandchildren, Jessica, Jacob, Matthew, Aman da, Mark and Molly and three great grandchildren, Breanna, Sawyer and Derek. Shannon resides in his home town, Milwaukee Wisconsin.

JONATHAN D. "DOC SHOCK" SHOCKLEY was born Feb. 20, 1952 in Cleveland, OH, and graduated from John F. Kennedy High School, Class of 1972. He was drafted in October 1972 in Ohio and took Boot Camp at Fort Polk, Louisiana, Alpha 4/1. He was stationed at Fort Polk, LA; Bamburg, Germany-188th dispensary; Fort Sam Houston, Texas-BAMC Hospital; Kitzigen, Germany-HHC 1/15 Infantry and 3/63 Armor; Fort Carson, Colorado 4/61 ADA; Gelnhausen, Germany; Fort Hood,

Texas; and Gulf War, Iraq during Operation Iraqi Freedom.

His awards and medals include Army Commendation Medal, Army Achievement Medal, Good Conduct Medal, NCO Professional Development Ribbon, Army Service Ribbon, Overseas Service Ribbon, Combat Medical Badge, Expert Badge Rifle, Expert Badge Pistol, German Armed Forces Marksmanship Award in Bronze, National Defense Service Medal with 3 Bronze Service Stars, Kuwait Liberation Medal.

His most memorable experiences include: while working in the ER at Fort Sam, he was able to assist with all types of trauma, including burns, shooting and stabbing victims; he was able to deliver three babies while in Germany — two in the back of ambulances and one in the back of a Volkswagen. With the good memories I too carry the bad. I will never forget the loss of several Soldiers from my platoon, whom were involved in a motorcycle accident at Fort Carson.

He was discharged at Fort Hood, TX, November 1992, with the rank of E6 PLT SGT HHC 1/5 CAV. In civilian life, he worked with UPS parcel delivery, was a care provider to children with special needs, and US Post Office Assistant Maintenance Manager/retired. He is a member of VFW, Wounded Warrior, New Mexico YAFL Football Board Member, and 1st CAV Division 5th Regiment VP.

Shockley is married to Cherry L. Their children include Shavon Shockley, Micah Feser, Jonathan D. Shockley II, Tiffany Shockley, Tara Shockley, with grandchildren, Roquelle Butler, Addison Shockley, Jameson Feser, and Jonathan D. Shockley III.

HOOVER "HOOT" SHORT enlisted on June 14, 1949 at attended Boot Camp at Fort Jackson, SC following by AG School at Fort Benning.

He was stationed at Camp Leroy John, LA, Austin, TX and Fort Sill, OK.

Short was engaged in battles in Korea and Vietnam. He received a Bronze Star.

WO2 Hoover Short was discharged on July 31, 1969.

Short retired in 1989 from Bank of America as AVP.

In retirement he enjoys golf.

Hoover and Joan W. Short have two children – Roger and Brook. Grandchildren are Scott, Dianne, Rachel, Jessie and Joey.

CECIL LYNN SHRADER (COLONEL, US ARMY RETIRED) was born 16 Dec. 1935 in Ashley, WV, and graduated from Salem High School in Salem, WV, later graduating from the United States Military Academy at West Point, NY, Class of 1958. He is a distinguished graduate of The Naval War College, and earned a MS in aerospace engineering from the University of Arizona.

Following West Point, he was commissioned in the Armor Branch, then attended fixed wing school and received his wing in June 1959 and interment qualification in August 1959. He received rotary wing aircraft qualification in 1961.

He served as C Troop Weapons Commander in 1966-67; C Troop Commander, 1969; and thought the men he served with in the 1/9 were the very best. Shrader was a member of the Ft. Hood Chapter, 1st Cavalry Division Association.

He was awarded the Distinguished Service Medal, Silver Star with 1 OLC, Legion of Merit, Distinguished Flying Cross with 1 OLC, Bronze Star with 1 OLC, Air Medal (50), Army Commendation Medal with V device and 1 OLC, and Presidential Unit Citation with 1 OLC.

Shrader retired from active service at Fort Knox in January 1988 with the rank of Colonel. He worked for B.D.M. in Williamsburg, VA, and then Teledyne Brown Engineering in Huntsville, AL, before retiring to Georgetown, TX, in Dec. 1997. He was active in MOWW and First Presbyterian Church.

He married Joan Welch on 5 Sept. 1959. They had three children, Laura, Mark, and Scott, and six grandchildren: Allen (died May 2016), Brian, Courtney, Natalie, Zachary, and Kharon Marie. Col. Shrader passed away on 6 May 2016 in Georgetown, TX.

DANIEL "DANNY" H. SIEN enlisted on Oct. 20, 1966 and attended Boot Camp at Lackland Air Force Base, TX.

Sien was stationed at Travis, U-Tapal, Korat, Thailand; and Westover.

His memorable experience was a trip to Bangkok.

3rd Class Sien was discharged on Oct. 20, 1970.

He is a videographer in Video Productions.

Danny has two children, Michelle and Gregory and two grandchildren, Savannah and Gemma.

BENJAMIN "BEN" S. SILVER was born in Maryland Aug. 22, 1922; graduated from Havre de Grace High School in 1939 and University of Maryland, 1943 by working his way through.

Enlisted May 19, 1942 in the Army at Fort Meade; graduated from Officers Candidate School (OCS) a Second Lieutenant Infantry 1944; fought in Europe World War II, North and South Korea, Vietnam twice and fought against the Insurrection at Oxford, MS. He served at Forts Benning, Devens, Campbell, Sill and Hood; graduated from The Infantry Advance Course, Command General Staff College, Liaison Pilot School, Navy War College, served four years on the Army General Staff, Pentagon and Assistant Division Commander, First Cavalry.

Silver received Combat Infantry Badge, Master Aviation Badge, Silver Star, Legion of Merit and three OLC, Bronze Star with "V" and three (OLC), Bronze Star with "V" and three OLC, Air Medal with 16 OLC, Army Commendation Medal, Vietnam Campaign Medal, National Defense Medal and Vietnam Cross of Gallantry with Palm.

Colonel Silver retired at Fort Hood, TX April 1, 1974.

He published *Ride At a Gallop* (military history) and Silver Family History.

Silver married Frances Bowen in 1946. They had Sharon and Sandra along with grandchildren Dale, Brice, Jonathan, Casey and Sarah. Frances died in 1992. He remarried in 1994 to Kyoko Jones, who had a son, Wayne.

RICHARD SIMMONS entered the Army in August 1966. Basic training was at Fort Gordon, GA and AIT was in Tigerland at Fort Polk. He was assigned to the 54th Infantry Detachment, 1st Cavalry Division. Simmons arrived in Viet Nam one month before the Tet Offensive.

After discharge he worked at IBM for over 32 years as a systems engineer, retiring in 1995. Richard then became the information technology manager for the West Point Federal Credit Union at the USMA in West Point

The 54th Infantry Detachment received Presidential Unit Citation. Simmons also received the VCM, VSM, CIB, ARCOM, 1 O/S Bar.

Richard has two sons, Jeffrey and Scott and three grandchildren – Emma, Rome and Titan.

CHARLES L. SKIPPER was born July 14, 1946 in Lake Wales, FL, where he attended school. On May 26, 1967, he was drafted into the U.S. Army and sent to Fort Benning, GA. There on Sandhill, he took basic training and was immediately sent to Fort Polk, LA, going through AIT at Tiger Land (jungle training) — so from day one he knew where his destination was to be.

In mid-October 1967, after a three-week leave, he stepped off a plane at Cam Rhan Bay, Vietnam, into a well of intense heat with a bad smell. A week later he was flown to An Khe, assigned to D Co., 5th BN, 7th Cavalry, First Cavalry Division. He fought in Operation Pershing, Operation Jeb Stuart, the Battle of TT Woods, Operation Pegasus, and Operation Delaware.

On May 19, 1968, his squad walked into a minefield, killing two and sending him on a medevac plane to the States after an eight-month tour. He was later assigned to B Co., 5th BN, 31st Inf., 197th Inf Bde., and was discharged on May 25, 1969.

Charles received the following awards: Vietnam Service Commemorative, Combat Service, American Defense, Air Combat Action, Presidential Citation, United States Army Service, Cold War Victory, Overseas Service, and the Purple Heart. He is a lifetime member of the 1st Cavalry Division Association and the 5th Battalion, 7th Cavalry Association.

Following the service, he worked for Progress Energy in Florida and retired after 35 years. He is the father of two sons, one daughter, and one stepson, and makes his home in Lake Wales with his wife, Kathryn.

DENNIS LEE SMITH was born Nov. 12, 1942. He took Boot Camp at Fort Jackson, SC and was discharged with the rank of 1SG.

Smith was a lab technician with General Motors and later was the CFO/COO for 3c Home Care.

In retirement he enjoys hunting and fishing.

Dennis and Lorraine have two children, Lori and Jason. Grandchildren are D.J., Cade, Connor and Religh.

GREGG A. SMITH enlisted in the Navy in January 1969, completing boot camp in San Diego, CA, having grown up in the suburbs of Los Angeles. After serving as a Drum Major of the boot camp drum bugle corps, he was transferred to Great Lakes Naval Training Center and graduated as a Machinist Mate. He completed the Naval Nuclear Power School, serving aboard the USS *Sacramento* (AOE-1), USS *Midway* (CVA-41), and the USS *Kilauea* (KE-26)

After four combat tours in Vietnam, Gregg left the Navy to attend North Dakota State University, where in 1978 he graduated with degrees in zoology and mathematics, including serving with the U.S. Army ROTC. After graduation and training at Aberdeen Proving Ground, MD, he was transferred to the 1st Maintenance Battalion, with duty at the 78th Maintenance Company as a Platoon Leader, then as the Shop Officer with the 586th Maintenance Company, and then with battalion HQ as Battalion S-1 (Adjutant) and Company Commander.

Gregg returned to Aberdeen Proving Ground for further training, again serving as a company commander for HHC School Brigade at the Army Ordnance Center and School. While there, he completed the Infantry Officers' Advance Course and received a MBA, specializing in logistics and finance.

He was assigned as an assistant professor of military science at Seattle University, with duty at Pacific Lutheran University in Spanaway (Tacoma), Washington, and later as Executive Officer and Secretary of the General Staff (SGS) at the 4th ROTC Region, Fort Lewis, WA. After completing Command and General Staff School (CGSC), Greg services as Materiel Officer (MATO), and Executive Officer with units in the 2d Infantry Division at Camp Casey, Tongduchon, South Korea.

Following that, he was transferred to the 43d Corps Support Group at Fort Carson, CO. There Gregg was initially assigned as the Maintenance Analysis Officer, and later became the Group S-4 (Logistics Officer). Upon the outbreak of Operation Desert Shield, Gregg helped organize railroad and ship transportation as the Group moved to a cement plant outside of Dhahran, Saudi Arabia. Within days, the Group joined the 1st Cavalry Division in October 1989 at TAA (Tactical Assembly Area) Windy.

In January 1990, the Group moved to LB (Logistics Base) Provider outside King Khalid Military City (KKMC) for initial preparations for the coming 1st Cavalry's assault into Kuwait. Relocating again, the Group moved to a wadi near Hafr Al-Batin for final preparations for the assault. During the assault into Kuwait, Gregg served as the logistics officer for the task force supporting 1st Cavalry's attacks deep into Kuwait. At the conclusion of Operation Desert Storm, Gregg relocated to Khubar Towers in Dhahran to prepare for return to Fort Hood and ultimately Fort Carson.

Upon returning to Fort Carson, Gregg served as the Maintenance Officer, Directorate of Logistics (DOL). He retired in 1992, having earned many honors including a Bronze Star Medal, and completed five combat deployments during Vietnam and the Persian Gulf War, taking him to many countries in Asia and Europe.

Gregg worked as a business analyst, a technical writer, a software development project manager, and a Red Cross office director. Gregg's other interests include collecting wine, cooking, woodworking, and cars. He has worked in a vineyard, as a grape harvest chef, a Salmon Bake team member at the White House, and numerous International Pinot Noir Celebrations (IPNC) events in Oregon, and as a team member cooking at the James Beard House in New York City.

In 1970, he marred Kris Dana Jensen. The Smiths currently live in Rochester, WA. Gregg and Kris have two adult children, Jason and Kara living in Rhododendron, Oregon and Tumwater, Washington, respectively, and five grandchildren.

MITCHELL LEE SMITH was born in Dillon, SC on Sept. 24, 1950. He graduated from McColl Fletcher Memorial High School in 1970, where he earned a 4-year degree in small engine repair. He enlisted in the Army in Bennettsville, SC on May 12, 1971. He completed boot camp and Advanced Individual Training at Fort Jackson, SC.

He was deployed in December 1971 with the 7th Cavalry Division to Vietnam. In 1972, the 7th Cavalry Division was recalled back to the US, and he was reassigned to the 2/8 Cavalry Division as an Assistant Machine Gunner at Fire Base Melanie. His nickname was "Snuffy," but a lot of guys called him "Carolina." In May 1972, the Army trained them on the TOW missiles that were mounted on the back of Jeeps and they were deployed to the Battle of Kontum.

During deployment in Vietnam, he received several awards including Combat Infantryman's Badge, Bronze Star Medal, Gallantry Cross with Bronze Star, Vietnam Service Medal with one Bronze Star, Republic of Vietnam Campaign Metal, Overseas Service Medal, National Defense Service Medal, Presidential Citation Award and Marksman Badge.

Smith was reassigned to A Troop 1st Squadron 4th Cavalry Infantry Division at Fort Riley, KS. While there, he received the Croix De Guerre Unit Citation Award with the Big Red One. Their Division also participated in multiple war games in Germany.

In 1973 while in Kansas, he met and married Linda Case. They have two children, Brenda and Mitchell Smith Jr. along with six grandchildren: Kasey, Christopher, Brandon, Cayden, Nickolas, Riley and one great-grandchild, Trevor.

Smith was honorably discharged from Fort Riley in February 1974 with the rank of SP/4. After that he joined the Army National Guard in South Carolina until he was honorably discharged in September 1974. He then joined the National Guard in Michigan and also worked as a steel laborer. He was honorably discharged from the National Guard in September 1975.

Even though retired now, he stays very active with the V.F.W. and Rolling Thunder. He also loves spending time with family and going hunting and gold prospecting.

"Our brothers will never be forgotten."

ORA ARLAN "CHIEF" SMITH was born 9 January 1948 in Warren County, TN, and graduated from Centertown School in 1966; the same building was used for grades 1-12. He also attended the University of Maryland, Pepperdine University, Northern Virginia Community College, and earned an AA degree in Real Estate from Los Angeles Metropolitan College (1978).

He enlisted in Nashville, TN, and went through basic training at Fort Jackson, SC. Additional training included Morse Intercept, Traffic Analyst (PMOS), Photographic Laboratory Specialist (SMOS), and Army Finance Specialist. His bases/stations include: Ft Jackson, SC; Ft Devens, MA; USAFS Two Rock Ranch Station, Petaluma, CA; USAFS Kuma Station, Chitose (Hokaido), Japan; USAFS Vint Hill Farms Station, Warrenton, VA; 6993 AF Security Sqdrn San Antonio, TX; USAFS Torii Station, Okinawa, Japan; HQ USAINSCOM, Arlington Hall Station, Arlington, VA; US Army Finance Center, Ft Benjamin Harrison, IN; USAFS Diogenes Station, Sinop, Turkey; US Army Signals Warfare Laboratory, Vint Hill Farms Station, Warrenton, VA.

Republic of Vietnam Service: 330th RRC, Pleiku, Jul. 1967/Jan. 1968; 371 RRC, An Khe, Jan.1968/Feb.1968 Camp Evans Feb. 1968/May1968; Quangtri, Jul. 1968/Nov. 1968; Phouc Vinh, Nov. 1968/Feb. 1969; Sep. 1970/Mar. 1971; 175 RRFS Bien Hoa, Mar.1971/Sep.1971.

Awards/Medals Received: National Defense Service Medal, Meritorious Unit Citation (2), Vietnam Campaign Medal with 60s device, Vietnam Service Medal, Vietnam Cross of Gallantry with Palm, Presidential Unit Citation (2), Army Commendation Medal (5), Air Force Commendation Medal, Good Conduct Medal (6), Bronze Star Medal, Expert Badge (Grenade), Sharpshooter Badge (Rifle), and Marksman Badge (Pistol).

He was discharged from service on 1 October 1986 at VHFS, Warrenton, VA, with the rank of MSGT. In civilian life, he worked for the U.S. Immigration and Naturalization Service, Detroit Metro Airport, from June 1991-March 2003, and U.S. Customs and Border Protection from March 2003-Oct. 2011, when he retired as CBP Chief Officer.

In 2002, he had the honor of testifying in both houses of the U.S. Congress about border security on the Northern U.S. Border, and to the best of his knowledge, is the only Immigration Officer to testify in both the House of Representatives and the Senate.

He is married to Sally R. (Turberville) Wright-Smith (1991) and has one son, Paul S. Wright

(SS), and two grandchildren, Alex Michael White and Kelsey Grace Wright.

WALTER (WALT) CLIFTON SMITH was born Dec. 10, 1942 in Lakeland, FL, and graduated from Lakeland Senior High School in 1961, later receiving his BS in Accounting from Florida State University (1965) and an MBA from Jacksonville State University (1972). He was commissioned a 2LT (USAR) in Artillery through DMG Florida State University ROTC, 1965.

Smith entered active service on Jan. 1, 1966 at Ft. Sill, OK, and was assigned Tactical Officer Transportation OCS, Ft. Eustis, VA, through Dec. 1966. Assigned PCS 1967-68 First Cavalry (Airmobile) Div. RVN, then B/1/21st FA as FO, LNO, FDO, and XO. He applied and accepted 2LT (RA) in field artillery in 1967; PCS to 1/320th FA (Glider), 82d Abn. Division, Ft. Bragg, NC, 1968-69, FDO, BC; PCS Ft. Sill, OK Officer Advance Course, 1969; PCS MACV III Corps HQ, 74th Vietnam Ranger Bn, Loc Ninj Camp, 1970-71; PCS back to the world with tours in AL ROTC, language school DC, FRG, Ft. Leavenworth, Ft. Knox, Hawaii NG, Pentagon OJCS, and Hurlburt Fld FL Army.

He retired from service on July 31, 1989 as Lieutenant Colonel. His second career was as a bank officer, insurance agent METLIFE, and accountant with Polk Co. government, later retiring to rural Holt in Florida's northwest panhandle to farm small acreage north of Eglin AFB.

Smith is married to Glenda with three children – Jennifer, Susanna, and Clifton – and grandchildren Nickolas, Annalisa, Kimberly, and Westin.

LARRY DALE SNYDER volunteered for the draft at the age of 18 and entered military service at Fort Bliss, TX in February 1966. He received Advanced Infantry Training at Fort Polk, LA before serving in Vietnam. Snyder served with the 7th Air Cav., Co. B, 2nd Platoon as an ammo bearer, M60 carrier and a squad leader.

Snyder was wounded by mortar fire on LZ Orange and spent 20 days in the hospital in 1966. He was wounded a second time in 1967 at Phan Thiet, LZ Betty.

He received the following medals: CIB, Bronze Star, Purple Heart with Oak Leaf Cluster, Air Medal, President's Unit Citation, Vietnam Service Medal, Vietnam Company Medal and National Defense Service Medal.

After returning to the States, Snyder taught land navigation at Fort Polk, LA. He received his discharge February 1968 and returned to Westville where he and his wife purchased a ranch and raised cattle and chickens.

Snyder has two boys, Bart and Todd and seven grandchildren: Travis, Larod, Tyler, Taylor, Shayder, Sarah and Timberlyn and two wonderful daughters-in-law, Lori and Shawna.

An avid outdoorsman, Snyder was thrilled when he, Gary Power and Sergeant Morgan were able to harvest a deer in Vietnam where they provided fresh meat for the men.

JOHN F. STEBBINGS was born in 1940 in Kansas City, MO. He graduated from St. Louis University High School, and in 1970 earned his bachelor's degree in civil engineering from the University of Arizona.

He enlisted July 18, 1960 at Phoenix, AZ and received Atomic Demolitions Training at Fort Belvoir, VA.

Stebbings was stationed at Fort Lewis, WA; Germany, Korea and Vietnam, being in engagements in Vietnam Central Highlands.

He was awarded the Bronze Star, Vietnam Service Medal, Vietnam Campaign Medal, Soldiers Medal and Air Medal.

Memorable experience was the day in Vietnam when a sniper almost got him, but he tripped and fell just as she fired.

SSG. Stebbings was discharged at US Army Personnel Center at Oakland, CA.

He was a Civil Engineer, Davis-Monthan AFB; Branch Head NAVAIR System Command, DOD, Department of the Navy.

He is a Life Member of VFW, VVA and TAU-BETA PI.

His retirement interests include coaching youth soccer teams and performating volunteer trail maintenance work on the Colorado Trail.

John and Maurie have two children, Eric Stebbings and Carol Lawrence and three grandchildren: Preston, Piper and Parker Lawrence.

DANIEL E. "IRON DUKE" STEELE was born April 13, 1929 in Minatare, NE, graduating from Minatare High School in 1946. He joined the service at Grand Island Army Air Base, NE, on June 17, 1946, with boot camp at Ft. McClellan, AL. He also attended the NCO Academy, WO Introduction School, and passed Airborne Jump School at the age of 38.

He was stationed in Bad Kreuznach, Germany, Trieste, Italy, An Khe, Vietnam (1966-1967), and Bien Hoa (1969-1970), among other stations.

Awards include Expert Badge (Rifle & Carbine), Good Conduct Medal, Army of Occupation Medal (Germany), National Defense Service Medal with 1 OLC, Vietnam Service Medal, Vietnam Campaign Medal, World War II Victory Medal, Bronze Star Medal with 4 OLC, Parachute Badge, and 6 Overseas Service Bars.

Steele retired from service on July 31, 1976 at Ft. Hamilton, NY, with the ranks of CW3 (USAR) and CW2 (RA). Following the service, he worked at Kiri Kiri, Nigeria (Material Control & Maintenance) from 1978-83 and (Director, Aeromaritime) 1987-89.

He is married to Clara and they have five children: Charles, Robert, Daniel Jr., Margherita, and Isabella.

ROBERT "BOB" G. STEIN graduated from Cotter High School in 1960 and graduated after four years from University of Minnesota. He enlisted in 1965 at Minneapolis, MN. After Boot Camp at Fort Leonard Wood he trained at Airborne, Recondo School and Officer Candidate School.

In 1967, Lt. Bob Stein arrived at Pleiku Air Base in South Vietnam and was assigned to the First Cavalry Division as a platoon leader in the Fifth Cavalry Regiment (B-1-5). During the next twelve months, he was in frequent combat, and sometimes daily gunfights, surrounded by exceptional American warriors who were fighting veterans of the North Vietnamese army.

In the battle of Vien Thien (3) on June 21, 1967, his cavalry company clashed with the 7th Battalion, 18th NVA Regiment. Stein was the only lieutenant left in the field since the other three lieutenants and most senior non-commissioned officers were dead or seriously wounded. Two men of his company (Carmel Bernon Harvey, Jr. and Edger Lee McWethy, Jr.) were awarded the Medal of Honor for their actions on that day. Stein received the Silver Star.

In November, 1967, he was selected as the 4th Platoon's leader for a new Long Range Patrol Company being formed in-country principally with battle-hardened combatants volunteering from the 101st Airborne Division. He participated in a night combat jump, rowed a raft from a Navy Riverine patrol boat that inserted a Special Forces team, and was at Camp Enari in the Central Highlands on January 30, 1968 for the massive Tet Offensive.

His platoon's seven six-man teams usually patrolled along the Cambodian border and provided intelligence as they reported enemy movements on the Ho Chi Minh resupply route from North Vietnam. About half of those patrols ended in gunfights requiring extraction under fire. Normally Stein was found in the Command and Control helicopter inserting and recovering his brave men from deep inside the enemies' domain.

Army Ranger units had been disbanded in 1959, but his teams' successes as well as those of another Long Range Patrol Company and Long Range Reconnaissance Patrol units, prompted the Army to re-flag them on February 1, 1969 creating today's Army Rangers. Following his stint in the Army, Stein worked for the Marriott Corporation for thirty-three years and retired in 2007.

Stein is the author of the popular book, *Ghost Warriors*, which includes a detailed description of the battle of Vien Thien (3).

For his service he was award the Army Commendation Medal, Vietnam Service Medal, Vietnam Campaign Medal, Presidential Unit Citation, Silver Star, Bronze Star and Air Medal. First Lt. Stein was discharged at Minneapolis, MN.

For 33 years he was National Sales Vice President for Marriott Corporation, retiring in 2010.

Bob and Virginia Grace have three children – Meredith, Hillary and Michael. Grandchildren are Reaghan, Will, Timothy, Madeline and Henry.

GODFREY J. "STEW" STEWART was born Sept. 15, 1950 in South Milwaukee, WI, and graduated from South Milwaukee High School in 1968. He was drafted on April 9, 1970 and was shipped to Ft. Campbell, KY, for basic training, later receiving 67V20 Crew Chief training for the OH-6A helicopter. He spent time at Ft. Eustis, VA, and Ft. Hood, TX, and served with Troop A, 1/9, 1st Cavalry Division in Vietnam from Sept. 1970 – June 1971, at Song Bey and Tay Ninh.

While in Vietnam besides being an OH-6A Crew Chief and seven months later becoming a Line Chief, he flew as a Torque (Door Gunner) on a Scout Helicopter. Their mission was with the High Bird (Cobra-Snake) and us the Low Bird (LOH). The LOH Mission was to draw fire from the enemy and snake was to provide more support and fire power. Stew was shot down in Cambodia on March 7, 1971 and survived.

He was awarded the National Defense Service Medal, Vietnam Service Medal with 1 Bronze Service Star, Aircraft Crewman Badge, Republic of Vietnam Campaign Medal, Purple Heart, Army Commendation Medal, Air Medal, and Expert (Rifle M-16).

He was discharged at Ft. Hood, TX, with the rank of E-5.

In civilian life, he was a maintenance mechanic supervisor, retiring in 2013. He enjoys hunting, fishing, hobby gunsmithing, motorcycle repair, and touring. He is married to Nancy.

STEVEN D. STEWART enlisted for the Aviation branch as a 680 Powertrain Repairman, entering military service in Houston, TX on Oct. 24, 1974. Following basic and advanced individual training he was assigned to his first permanent party unit, O Troop, 1st Squadron, 9th Cavalry (Blue Max) at Fort Hood, TX. It was here, working with and trained by 1st Cavalry Division combat Veterans, he began to learn rotary wing aircraft maintenance.

Stewart attended Warrant Officer Entry Course 25 August 1988, UH-1 Maintenance Manager/Maintenance Test Pilot Course (Honor Graduate) Dec. 16, 1988, OH-58A/C Maintenance Manager/Maintenance Test Pilot Course Jan. 31, 1989, AH-l Aircraft Armament Maintenance Tech Course April 19, 1989, AH-64 Aircraft Armament Maintenance Tech Course 2 April 1993, Army Aviation Warrant Officer Advanced Course July 18, 1997, OH-58D Aircraft Armament Maintenance Tech Course (Distinguished Graduate) June 9, 1998, Radiological Safety Course Aug. 22, 2000 and Warrant Officer Staff Course Aug. 2, 2002.

He served as Armament Platoon Leader, A Company, 404th Aviation Support Battalion, 4th ID, deploying with and assigned to the 4th Aviation Brigade, 1st CD to Camp Comanche, Bosnia during SFOR 5 1999 and his final permanent party assignment, Armament Platoon Leader, A Company, 615th Aviation Support Battalion, DISCOM, deploying to Camp Cooke, Iraq, OIF II 2004, in support of the Aviation Brigade Combat Team, 1st CD, redeploying and retiring on Dec. 31, 2004 after 30 years active duty service.

Stewart received the Legion of Merit, Meritorious Service Medal (3rd Award), Army Commendation Medal (6th Award), Army Achievement Medal (3rd Award), Meritorious Unit Commendation, Army Superior Unit Award, Global War on Terrorism Expeditionary Medal, Global War on Terrorism Service Medal, Army Good Conduct Medal (4th Award), National Defense Service Medal (2nd Award), Armed Forces Expeditionary Medal, Southwest Asia Service Medal with two Bronze Service Stars, Korea Defense Service Medal, Noncommissioned Officer's Professional Development Ribbon with Numeral 3, Army Service Ribbon, Overseas Service Ribbon (6th Award), NATO Medal, Kuwait Liberation Medal, Kuwait Liberation Medal (SA), Master Aircraft Crewman Badge.

After retirement, he moved to Lake Tawakoni, TX in 2005 and in 2009 was selected by the Lake Tawakoni Sabine River Authority and granted the position, duties and responsibilities of Commercial Operator for the White Deer Landing Manufactured Home/Recreational Vehicle Community where he serves that community today.

Stewart married Edna Aleman in 1975 and is happily divorced. He has four children: Jericho, Aaron, Nathan and Candace and two grandchildren, Analysa and Jake.

WILLIAM E. STEWART was born June 24, 1930 in Dallas, TX, and graduated from Terre Haute Wiley High School in 1948. He received basic training and AIT at Fort Knox, and fought in five major battles in Korea from July 18, 1950 – Nov. 1, 1951, with additional stays at Camp Drew, Japan and Yuma Test Station, Yuma, AZ. He received the UN Ribbon w/5 Battle Stars, Korean President Citation, and US President Unit Citation.

He was discharged from active service at Fort Bliss, TX, on June 23, 1952 with the rank of SFC E-6, and from the Army Reserves in 1981 at Terre Haute, IN, with the rank of 1SG E-8. Stewar worked for Weston Box Factory in Terre Haute as a machine operator, from 1953-1992.

He is a lifetime member of the VFW, member of the American Legion and Loyal Order of the Moose, coordinator of the 61st FA annual reunions, and United States Bowling Congress.

He is married to Patricia. They have four children, Dale, Mike, Billy and Nancy, and 12 grandchildren.

CHARLES F. "STONEY" STONE was born June 21, 1947 in Lyons, NY and graduated from Lyons Central School in 1965. He went to the draft board to push his number up. They handed him an envelope with his notice that would have been mailed that day – largest draft of the Vietnam War. He was then inducted Sept. 19, 1966 at Syracuse, NY.

Boot Camp and Advanced Individual Training, 1/29th Field Artillery, 5th Division, Fort Carson, CO.

He received the Bronze Star Medal, National Defense Medal, Vietnam Service Medal with three Campaign Stars, Vietnam Campaign Medal, Good Conduct Medal, Army Presidential Unit Citation, Army Meritorious Unit Citation, Army Valorous Unit Citation, Republic of Vietnam Gallantry Cross Unit Citation, Sharpshooter Badge, two Overseas Bars and the New York Conspicuous Service Cross.

He joined the 42nd Infantry Division of the New York National Guard in 1976 and served until 1983. He graduated from the New York Military Academy as Staff Sergeantt. He was awarded the New York Military Commendation Medal, the New York National Guard Achievement Medal and three other ribbons for service during the New York State Prison Guard strike and time served.

He retired in 2010 after hauling petroleum products for 40 years.

Charles and Patricia were married in 1969. They have two children, Scott and Amy and two grandchildren, Cassandra and Zachary.

COLONEL JAMES L. STONE was born in Pine Bluff, AR, but moved frequently throughout his youth. Before his death on Nov. 9, 2012 he lived with his lovely wife, Mary Lou, in Arlington, TX. He was buried with Full Military Honors, at DFW National Cemetery in Dallas County, which was where he wanted to be laid to rest. His 29 years-plus involved a career which was most rewarding and demanding. His duty assignments included considerable command experiences, high-level staff planning, multi-million dollar programming, advisory functions to two foreign countries, administration and command in the Army ROTC Program and active participation in sport activities.

Colonel Stone was commissioned through Army ROTC, University of Arkansas, Fayetteville, AR. He entered military service on Oct. 14, 1948 at Fort Ord, CA and was assigned as Platoon Leader, Company I, 12th Infantry Regiment, 4th Division. Approximately nine months later, he was placed on detached duty at Fort Lewis, WA and Schoffield Barracks, HI, involving umpire duties with rifle companies of the 2d Infantry Division. He returned to Fort Ord and was assigned as Executive Officer and later as Company Commander of Company M, 12th Infantry. He was promoted to First Lieutenant in August 1950.

Colonel Stone was reassigned to Korea in March 1951 and joined Company G, 8th Cavalry Regiment, 1st Cavalry Division. After a few months as a rifle platoon leader, he was sent to Company F as Executive Officer. Colonel Stone was captured at a platoon outpost in November 1951 and remained in a Chinese POW camp until September 1953. He was repatriated through operation "BIG SWITCH" with other American military personnel.

Colonel Stone was assigned to Headquarters Company, Sixth Army, Presidio of San Francisco as

Executive Officer. He was promoted to Captain in June 1954 and later assumed duties of Company Commander. He received orders for the Advance Course, US Army Infantry School, Fort Benning, GA, during the summer of 1955 and graduated in June 1956.

Colonel Stone joined the 3d Division in late June 1956 as Company Commander, Company E, 15th Infantry, Fort Benning, GA. During the months that followed, he was assigned to umpire duties at Forts Hood, Polk and Stewart, but always returning to Fort Benning as Company Commander. During July 1957 the 3d Division was reorganized and Colonel Stone again performed the duties of Company Commander, Company D, 2d Battle Group, 4th Infantry.

During March 1958, he gyroscoped with the 3d Division to Bamberg, Germany. Colonel Stone was selected to serve as the Combat Support Company Commander and in October 1958 he was assigned to position of Battle Group S-2 and remained in that capacity until April 1960. During this time he participated extensively in the evaluation duties from squad level to the NATO maneuvers in the Grafenwohr - Hohenfels training complexes. He was reassigned to the 7th Army NCO Academy, Bad Toelz, Germany. After serving as Company Commander and assistant Student Director, he departed Europe in the summer of 1961.

Colonel Stone attended the Regular Course, Command and General Staff College, Fort Leavenworth, KS during 1961-62 and graduated in June. He was promoted to Major in October 1961. He was assigned as Professor of Military Science, ROTC Unit, Fort Worth High Schools, Fort Worth, TX for a period of three years.

During July 1965, Colonel Stone received orders to serve as Counterinsurgency Advisor, Armish MAAG, Tehran, Iran. In addition to his primary role, he served as an advisor to the 2d Division, Imperial Iranian Army. During November 1965, Colonel Stone was promoted to Lieutenant Colonel and assumed the duties of the Combat Arms Advisor. In February 1966, he was reassigned to the position of Military Assistance Programs Officer, J-5 section, Joint Staff, Armish MAAG. He departed Iran in December 1967.

Colonel Stone's next tour of duty occurred at Fort McPherson, GA. He served in the Office of the Deputy Chief of Staff, ROTC, Third US Army, as Operations Officer.

During August 1970, orders were received for the Republic of Vietnam and in September he was promoted to Colonel. His tour in Vietnam consisted of advisory duties or as Senior Advisor, RVNAF National NCO Academy. In addition, extensive trips were conducted to the field to determine the true combat effectiveness of the Vietnamese Army. He departed Vietnam in September 1971 and was assigned as Senior Unit Advisor, 72d Separate Infantry Brigade (Mechanized), Texas Army National Guard, Dallas, TX.

In August 1974 orders were received transferring Colonel Stone to the VIII US Army Readiness Command, Fitzsimmons Army Medical Center, Denver, CO. He served as Infantry Coordinator. His duties were to coordinate, evaluate, and supervise training activities of all Army National Guard and Army Reserve Infantry units within a total of 10 states.

On Dec. 1, 1977 Colonel Stone was retired from military service.

After being retired from military service, he moved to Arlington, TX where he became active in First United Methodist Church and enjoyed being retired. In June 1989 he met his wife, Mary Lou and they were married in December 1989. They continued to reside in their Arlington, TX home until his passing in November 2012.

JOSEPH STOTSKI was born May 26, 1945 and graduated from Bishop Canevin High School, 1963; Ohio State University with a BCS in education, 1967; Ohio State University, MA in adult education, 1970 and Indiana University, EdD in adult education, 1973.

Military service was ROTC, Ohio State University; active duty 1967-1969; November 1967 to May 1968 — Fort Lee, VA Quartermaster Officer and Quartermaster POL Courses; June to August 1968 — Fort Bragg, NC, 83rd Maintenance Bn.; Aug. 29, 1968 to Aug. 25, 1969 — 1st Air Cav. Div. – Division POL Officer – I Corps – Phu Bai; September to October 1968 — III corps – various base camps, November 1969 and Bien Hoa, December 1968; January to August 1969 — Platoon Leader, 3rd Forward Support Platoon, 3rd Bde base camp, Quan Lois (aka LZ Andy). From 1970 through 1995 (with short breaks), he served in the Ohio National Guard, Indiana National Guard and the 83rd Army Reserve Command.

Stotski retired in 1995 with 20 years of service with the rank of Major.

He was awarded: Bronze Star Medal, Meritorious Service Medal, Air Medal, Army Commendation Medal, National Defense Service Medal with one Oak Leaf Cluster, Army Reserve Components Achievement Medal, Vietnam Service Medal, Vietnam Campaign Medal, Armed Forces Reserve Medal, Army Service Ribbon, Army Overseas Ribbon, Meritorious Unit Commendation and Vietnamese Cross of Gallantry.

He retired in 2007 after working at Wittenburg University, Ohio Dominican College, Children's Hospital in Columbus Ohio and Jess Howard Electric Company.

His children are Eric, Marc and Lara. Grandchildren are Kristin and Angela, and great-grandchildren are Amelia and Jude.

JOHN C. SULLIVAN was born Feb. 27, 1945 in Louisville, KY, and graduated from St. Xavier High School in 1963. He later received a degree in business administration from Bellarmine University in 1968.

Sullivan entered the service on August 12, 1968 in Louisville, and was sent to Fort Knox, KY for basic training. His special training was as an OST Clerk Typist. He was stationed at Fort Gordon, GA, and Vietnam, and was discharged on June 2, 1970 in San Francisco, CA, with the rank of SP5.

He was a production supervisor and manager for KitPak, retiring in 2009. He is married to Donna, and they have two children, Sean and Tara, and five grandchildren, Patrick, Ryan, Nate, Evan, and Olivia.

JAMES W. "SURB" SURBER was born March 13, 1947 in Lebanon, IN and graduated from high school in 1965. He was drafted in October 1966; boot camp was at Fort Leonard Wood, followed by AIT at Fort Polk.

Surber was stationed at An Khe and Fort Campbell, KY; serving in TET – HUE.

He was awarded a Bronze Star and Soldiers Medal.

Memorable experience was flying over Nam.

Surber was discharged in October 1968 at Fort Campbell with the rank of E-5Sgt.

He retired in 2009 after working at Rock Island Refinery (24 years) and Eli Lilly (18 years). Retirement activities include boating and travel.

His children are Nikki, DeDe and Kari. Grandchildren are Quinn, Cole, Jack, AJ, Hudson, Brooklyn, Ben, Maddie, Aiden and Prim.

DONALD SWAN volunteered for the Army and Vietnam, serving with the 1st Cavalry Division (Airmobile) 1967-1968 in An Khe and Bong Son as a Combat Correspondent and a DJ with AFVN, witnessing part of the battle and its aftermath in Northern Binh Dinh Providence, 20 Mar '67, that culminated in the Medal of Honor for medic Charles Hagemeister 1/5 Cav; a highlight in his 12-month tour.

Swan was medically retired as a SSG (P)* and used the GI bill to earn a BA and MA in the Communication Arts from the University of Denver. He was a popular DJ in the Mile High City before pivoting to more secure employment in Civil Service, where he served as a senior Public Affairs Officer (GM-13) with the USAF.

He was a successful semi-pro racecar driver and received the "Hard Charger" award. Lately Swan's been writing about Veterans and his articles, including a feature on a 92-year-old former POW from World War II, have been widely published.

He lives in Northern California with his wife and three dogs in a cottage overlooking the Pacific. His most recent accomplishment was having his bio end at exactly 200 words.

**Note: This designation is not widely known, (P) stands for promotable; he would have attained the rank of SFC had he remained in the Army a few months longer.*

JOHN B. SWIFT received an ROTC commission in 1956 from Dickinson College and reported into the Infantry Officers Schoolhouse at Ft Benning where he also earned his jump wings.

Fixed Wing Army Aviation School followed later along with a 3-year tour in Germany. He returned to another Ft Benning Schoolhouse tour and later assigned to 1st Bn 7th Cavalry of the 1st Cavalry Division unit mobilizing for Vietnam in 1965.

Swift was BN Adjutant and later Bn Hq Co Cmdr with participation in the Ia Drang Valley campaign at LZ Falcon. Still in country he returned to Army Aviation and transitioned into the Division's 17th Aviation Co's CV-2 Caribou, finishing his Vietnam tour six months later.

At his return, Swift left active duty but remained in the USAR until retirement in 1976 as a Major. He was hired by American Airlines in

1966 for a 27-year career, where he flew BAC1-11, B-727, B-707 and DC-10 aircraft.

Swift received the Combat Infantry Badge, Sr. Army Aviator Badge, Parachute Badge, Bronze Star Medal, Air Medal with 5 OLC, Vietnam Service Medal with 3 campaign stars, Vietnam Campaign Medal, National Service Medal, Vietnam Cross of Gallantry with Palm, and Presidential Unit Citation.

In 2016 John and Nancy celebrated their 56th wedding anniversary and have five children and 11 grandchildren.

JOHN E. TAYLOR enlisted in the U.S. Army on December 3, 1986. His first duty assignment was at fort Ord, California in 1987. He was assigned to the 2/9 Cavalry recon squadron. This would be a recurring theme of being assigned to Cavalry units throughout his military career.

He was assigned to 4/2 ACR, 5/17th, 1/ 4, and 1/7 Cav at Ft. Hood, TX, where he served as 1SG in E Troop. Upon the 1st Cavalry Division call to arms in 2002, 1SG Taylor was assigned to C Company 1/227th ARB. 1SG Taylor served in C and D company 1/227th until his selection as the CSM for 1/227th ARB in 2009. He served with the Regiment until 2010 where upon his return from Iraq he was assigned to the 1/291st at Ft Hood as a Maintenance trainer and observer for National Guard Unit and reserve Apache battalions. SGM Taylor retired on 31 December 2011.

Upon retirement, he received his Airframe & Power plant license. Mr. Taylor currently resides on an island called Kwajalein Atoll. He continues to support the U.S. Army, NASA, and other government agencies in support of our nation's defense for the Space Missile Defense Command (SMDC) as a contractor.

PHILLIP DAVID TAYLOR enlisted at St. Joseph, MO on July 3, 1968. After Boot Camp at Fort Leonard Wood, additional training was Unit/Org. Supply and Small Arms Repair and Advanced NCOS at NCO Academy.

He was stationed at Fort Lee, VA, Vietnam-Thailand, Okinawa, Fort Knox, KY, Korea, Fort Hood, Hawaii and Fort Campbell, KY. He served in Vietnam, 1 & 12 Cav.-HHC from March 1969-Sept. 1970 and January-August 1972.

He received the Army Achievement, Korean Defense Medal, Good Conduct Medal, Bronze Star, Air Medal, Army Comm. Medal, National Defense SV, US Vietnam SV and Vietnam Campaign with 60 Device.

Memorable experiences were bonding with fellow Soldiers, being able to travel and meeting people and learning their customs.

SSG Taylor was discharged at Fort Campbell, KY on July 31, 1988.

For 10 years, he worked as a correctional officer for Missouri Department of Corrections, retiring in October 2009.

COLONEL ERNEST P. TERRELL JR. was born Oct. 18, 1929 in Stamps, AR. His parents were Mrs. Lucille H. Terrell, R.N. and Dr. (M.D.) Ernest P Terrell (both deceased). He graduated from high school in Chickasha, OK in 1947 and attended the University of Oklahoma in Norman in 1947 and 1948. He graduated with a BA in History from Saint Benedict's College, Atchison, KS in 1965.

Colonel Terrell enlisted in the Army in July, 1948 at the age of 18, and was commissioned a Second Lieutenant, Field Artillery, OCW, Fort Riley, Kansas, Aug. 12, 1949. After completing the Officer Basic Course at Fort Sill, OK, he was assigned to the 11th Field Artillery, 24th Infantry Division, first in Japan, then in Korea 1950-1951 as Battery Executive Officer, Air Observer and Battery Commander. From 1951 through 1955, he commanded several different battery-size units ranging in caliber from 105 mm to 8-inch towed and graduated from the Field Artillery Advanced Course at Fort Sill in 1956.

His next assignments were as a Battalion Advisor to the 49th Infantry Division, California National Guard and the Secretary, Cold Weather and Mountain School; Fort Greely, AK. Upon return to CONUS, Colonel Terrell served as Battalion Executive Officer and Battalion Commander, 1st Battalion, 14th Field Artillery, 2nd Armored Division, Fort Hood, TX from 1960 to 1963.

Upon graduation from the Command and General Staff College, Fort Leavenworth, KS in 1964, he was the G-3 Plans Officer, III Corps, Fort Hood and FFVI, RVN 1965. He was subsequently selected as Battalion Commander, 1st Battalion, 21st Field Artillery, 1st Cavalry Division, January to August 1966. He was the Chief Staff Officer for the US Army Recruiting Command and Armed Forces Examining and Entrance Stations, ODC-SPER, Pentagon 1966-1968.

General Harold K. Johnson, Chief of Staff, US Army, selected Colonel Terrell to join the Province Senior Advisor Program for RVN and he served as Province Senior Advisor of Kien Tuong Province, RVN 1969-1970. He graduated from Industrial College of the Armed Forces, Fort McNair, DC 1971. He served as Commander, 214th Field Artillery Group, Fort Sill, 1972-1973.

Colonel Terrell's last active duty assignment was Deputy Commander, V Corps Artillery, Darmstadt and Frankfurt, FRG, for a period of 39 months, and he retired from active service on Dec. 1, 1976.

His awards and decorations include the Distinguished Service Cross, the Second highest award for Valor, the Legion of Merit with oak leaf cluster, the Bronze Star, the Purple Heart, the Meritorious Service Medal, the Air Medal with 9 OLC, the Army Commendation Medal, the Occupation Medal, the National Defense Service Medal w/oak cluster, the Korean Service Medal with 5 battle stars, the Vietnam Service Medal with 7 battle stars, the Vietnam Cross of Gallantry with silver and gold stars, the United Nations Medal, the Vietnamese Service Medal (RVN), the Combat Infantryman's Badge, the Aircraft Crewman's Badge, General Staff Identification Badge, Distinguished Unit Citation, Korean Presidential Unit Citation, and Vietnamese Unit Citation with Palm.

Colonel Terrell was originally inducted as Honorary Colonel of the 21st Field Artillery Regiment at Fort Hood, TX on June 29, 1989 by Major General William F. Streeter, Commanding General 1st Cavalry Division. He was an active member of the 1st Cavalry Division Association and served on the Board of Trustees from 1990 till 2002. He served as President of the Association in 1995-1996. Colonel Terrell was also a member of the 24th Infantry Division Association and Legion of Valor. He accepted an appointment in November 1995 to the Executive Council of the US Field Artillery Association and served till 2002.

Colonel Terrell was President of Falconhead Men's Golf Association, Falconhead Christian Fellowship, Marietta, OK Lion's Club and Southern Oklahoma Retired Officers Association.

Colonel Terrell married the former Allene White in Chickasha, OK in 1956. They have one son, Ernest, two daughters, Teresa and Linda and five grandchildren.

Colonel Terrell passed away June 2009. He is buried at Fort Sill National Cemetery.

JAMES "LARRY" THOMAS was born January 17, 1947 in Lee County, NC, and graduated from Boone Trail High School in 1965, later receiving his BS from Campbell University in 1972. He was drafted on Feb. 14, 1968 at Lillington, NC. After Boot Camp at Fort Bragg, he also received 13 weeks of Air Traffic Control, USAKAFB in 1968. Larry was also stationed at Fort Leavenworth, KS.

He was engaged in battles with HHC 11th AVN GP, Phouc Vinh, various fire bases, LZs Luxan, Loc and Melai.

Thomas received the Air Medal, Bronze Star, VN Service and VN Campaign Medal.

Memorable experiences were the day he arrived in Vietnam the day he left Vietnam and Bob Hope USO Christmas Show in 1969.

SPC 5 Thomas was discharged on Feb. 6, 1970 at Oakland.

Professionally he was the Division I Project Manager for ACE Hardware Corp, Oakbrook, IL, retiring in 2011.

After retirement he became the Board Chairman of Welcome Home Veterans, Inc, Mooresville, NC; USO Volunteer – Charlotte – Douglas airport.

Larry and Nikki Thomas have two children, Brian and Jamie.

COMMAND SERGEANT MAJOR ROY THOMAS was born in Dallas, TX, on Aug. 28, 1948. He entered into the Army on Dec. 2, 1968 and was sent to Fort Bliss, TX for Basic Combat Training. He then attended Advanced Individual Training at Fort Eustis, VA and upon completion was assigned to the Republic of Vietnam.

His major assignments include: 540th Transportation Company, Republic of Vietnam; B Company, 1-66 Armor, 2AD, Fort Hood, TX, as a Tank Commander; 25th Transportation Company, Korea, as a Shop Foreman, while there promoted to SSG; C Company, 1-8 Cavalry, ICD, Fort Hood, TX as a Tank Platoon Sergeant; C Company, 1-33 Armor, 3AD, Gelhausen, Germany, as a Tank Platoon Sergeant and Operations Sergeant, while there promoted to SFC and inducted into the Sergeant Morales Club. He served as Senior Instructor for the Reserve Officer Training corps, University of Richmond, Richmond, VA; 2-1 Cavalry, 2AD, Fort Hood, TX as the Operation sergeant Major and First Sergeant of C Troop and HHT. He was then assigned to the Apache Training Brigade, Fort Hood, TX as the Operations Sergeant Major. He was promoted to Sergeant Major while attending the Sergeants Major Academy at Fort Bliss, TX and upon completion was assigned to the 2d Infantry Division in Korea. He served as the Operations Sergeant Major in the 2d Battalion, 72nd Armor. Upon his return from Korea, he was assigned as the operations Sergeant Major in the 4th squadron, 3d Armored Cavalry Regiment. He was appointed to Command Sergeant Major and assigned to the 1st Squadron, 3d ACR, his assignment as Command Sergeant Major of the 2d Brigade, ICD, Fort Hood, TX (June 1995-August 1997), he was last assigned as Command Sergeant Major, TEXCOM. His retirement was Dec. 31, 1999.

His awards and decorations include the Legion of Merit, Meritorious Service Medal with fourth oak leaf cluster, Army Commendation Medal with third oak leaf cluster, Army Achievement Medal with one oak leaf cluster and numerous other awards and certificates. He is a member of the prestigious Sergeant Morales Club and was inducted as a member of the Order of St. George for honorable service to Armor and Cavalry.

He earned a degree in business from Southern Nazarene University in Oklahoma. After retiring from the Army he has worked at Met Life as a Broker, AOL and AT&T as a manager and now is currently working as a Leadership Trainer at American Fidelity.

Command Sergeant Major Roy Thomas is married to the former Maria Elena Garcia of El Paso, TX. They have five children: Paul, Chris, George, Francisco and Mariana, 10 grandchildren and two great grandsons.

SGT. WILLIAM "BILL" A. THOMASON was born Nov. 15, 1927 in Maysville, AR, and graduated from Southwest City High School in Missouri in 1946. He was drafted into the military service on Sept. 26, 1950.

He served in Btry "C" 99 F.A. Bn. 1st Cavalry Division in the Korean War. He was honorably discharged on July 1, 1952.

After his military service, he attended LeTourneau Institute of Mechanical Technology (now LeTourneau University). He graduated with a B.S. in Machine Science. He was employed with Dresser Industries from 1958 until 1987 as a tool designer.

After retirement he and wife, Francis, traveled all over the US and foreign countries, among them Russia and China

He enjoyed fishing in Colorado, Wyoming and Montana. He was a great gardener. He could grow everything.

He fathered two children – William Alan and Larry K. He had five grandchildren. On Dec. 12, 2014 he passed away at the age of 87.

GEN. JOHN H. TILELLI JR. (USA, RET.) was commissioned a 2Lt. in 1963 through ROTC. He attended Armor Officer Basic and Advanced Courses, US Marine Corps Command and Staff College and US Army War College.

He advanced through the ranks and by July 1994 was promoted to General.

Memorable experience was as Commanding General, 1st Cavalry.

Tilelli was awarded the Defense Distinguished Service Medal with OLC, Distinguished Service Medal with three OLC, Navy Distinguished Service Medal, Legion of Merit, Bronze Star Medal with "V" Device, Bronze Star Medal with OLC, Meritorious Service Medal with three OLC, Air Medal, Army Commendation Medal with two OLC, Combat Infantryman Badge, Parachutist Badge, Office of the Secretary of Defense Identification Badge, Joint Chiefs of Staff Identification Badge, Army Staff Identification Badge.

General Tilelli retired in January 2000 after 30 years of service. He is married to Elise with three children: Christine, Margaret, and Jeanne.

JONATHAN P. TOMES was commissioned a 2nd Lieutenant in 1968 as a Distinguished Military Graduate of the University of Cincinnati's ROTC program. Following Infantry Officer Basic and Airborne Training at Fort Benning, GA, he was assigned as a mechanized infantry platoon leader and company executive officer. After that assignment and Jungle Warfare School in Panama, he joined the 1st Cavalry Division in Vietnam. While he was an Infantry platoon leader there, he was awarded a Silver Star and other medals in Alpha Company 1/8th Cavalry.

Upon returning to CONUS, he reverted to his basic branch, Military Intelligence, and attended the Area Intelligence Course at Fort Holabird, Dundalk, MD. After graduation, he commanded the 8th Military Intelligence Detachment in support of the 8th Infantry Division (Airborne) in Bad Kreuznach, West Germany, and then served as East German Branch Chief in the 430th Military Intelligence in Munich, where he supervised clandestine operations in East Germany during the Cold War.

The Army then selected him to go to law school. He graduated first in his class at Oklahoma City University School of law, and during the periods when school was not in session, he won all six of the courts-martial that he either prosecuted or defended.

After graduation, he served in the office of the Staff Judge Advocate at Fort Knox, KY. There, he served as the Chief Trial Counsel, Chief Defense Counsel, Chief of Administrative Law, Military Law Instructor at the Armor School, and Command Judge Advocate, 194th Armored Brigade, often performing in two or three of these positions simultaneously. He was the first captain to be awarded a Meritorious Service Medal upon completion of his tour.

His next assignment was as a military judge at Fort Campbell, KY, where he received an oak leaf on his Meritorious Service Medal.

Following that tour, he was selected to attend the U.S. Army Command and General Staff College, Fort Leavenworth, KS, where he was an honor graduate. The College then retained him as the Military Law Instructor. While on the CGSC faculty, he wrote a law review article that the U.S. Supreme Court cited in the most important case concerning military criminal jurisdiction in the last 50 years.

His final assignment was as the Chief of Special Claims, U.S. Army Claims Service, Fort Meade, MD. Upon his retirement, he was awarded the Legion of Merit.

Since retiring, he has continued to represent service members before courts-martial, administrative discharge boards, the Boards of Correction of Military Records, Discharge Review Boards, and physical evaluation boards.

Since his retirement, he has taught law at IIT Chicago-Kent College of Law, where he was awarded the Professor of the Year by the students. He has continued to represent service members before courts-martial, administrative discharge boards, the Boards of Correction of Military Records, Discharge Review Boards, and physical evaluation boards. He has written and has had published more than 60 books, including *The Servicemembers' Legal Guide* (now in its 5th edition) and as many articles. A recent article titled "Practical Problems with Reforming the Military Justice System," earned him a letter of appreciation from the General Counsel of the Department of Defense, who said that he was going to have his lawyers use the article to rebut clueless Congresspersons who have never served a day in the military from taking over the military justice system.

He has also published military fiction, *Lawful Orders* and *JAGC-Off: a Politically Incorrect Mem-*

oir of the Judge Advocate Generals Corps, both available through Amazon.

Jon has a son and grandson with his first wife, Marilyn, who was a Trooper when he served in 'Nam and with whom he has remained friends. Jon and his current wife, Kenda, have an adopted daughter from Thailand, Aree. They live in Kansas City, MO, where Jon has a HIPAA consulting business, emrlegal.com, and a small publishing company, www.veteranspress.com.

His awards include the Silver Star, Legion of Merit, Bronze Star, Air Medal, Meritorious Service Medal with Oak Leaf Cluster, Army Commendation Medal, Combat Infantry Badge, Airborne Wings, Jungle Expert Patch, and various service awards. He considers his greatest life achievement to have been that he led U.S. troops in combat as an Infantry platoon leader and didn't get any of them killed through any act of stupidity on his part. He greatest wish is to be 21 again and an Infantry platoon leader so that he could lead a platoon of American sky Troopers from the 1st Cav to go fight ISIS.

GREGORIO P. TORRES was born May 19, 1945 and graduated from Edgewood High School in 1964. He enlisted on May 3, 1966 and was sent to Fort Polk, LA for basic training, and Tiger Land for AIT before shipping to Viet Nam.

He proudly served with the 1st Air Cavalry (1966-67) assigned to Co. D, 2/7 Garry-Owen, Republic of Vietnam. He was always scared to death while in Viet Nam, serving as rifleman, radio operator, and machine gunner. He arrived in An Khe and spent most of his tour in the combat fields, plus a little time in Camp Drake, Japan, for a knee injury from jumping out of helicopters. Memorable experiences include finding out that most of his "squad and Delta Company made it back to the world!"

Torres was awarded the Combat Infantryman Badge, Vietnam Service Medal with 1 Bronze Star, Republic of Vietnam Gallantry Cross with Palm Unit Citation Badge, and Presidential Unit Citation Badge.

He was discharged from service on March 3, 1967 in Oakland, CA, with the rank of E-1. He then spent 31 years with the United States Postal Service and Kelly Field Air Base, retiring in May 5, 2001.

Torres is married to Alma S. Torres. They have two children, Omar and Griselda, and seven grandchildren, Matthew, Gina, Calvin, Bethanie, Joe, Emma, and Mille.

MICHAEL A. TORRES enlisted in the infantry on January 1977. He conducted and completed basic training at Fort Dix, NJ, and Advance Individual Training at Fort Benning GA in 1977. In 1978, Michael's first duty station was with A Company 1st Bn. 4th IN, 3rd Infantry Division, Aschaffenburg, West Germany and served as a gunner, M-60 machine gunner, and fire team leader. In early 1981, Michael now a sergeant, transferred to Fort Hood, TX, assigned to A Company 1st Bn. 5th Cav, First Cavalry Division as a TOW section sergeant. Michael's section won several TOW competitions and selected on numerous occasions as NCO of the month and NCO of the quarter awards.

In 1984, Michael attended Drill Sergeant School at Fort Sill, OK, and was assigned to B Company 7th Training Bn. Michael won numerous Drill Sergeant of the Cycle Awards and marching competitions while at Fort Sill. In 1987, Michael returned to Fort Hood, and assigned to E Company 1st Bn. 5th Cav, First Cavalry Division. Michael now a Sergeant First Class served as acting company first sergeant and platoon leader. Michael was also inducted into the Sergeant Audie Murphy Club in 1989. Michael served with the First Cavalry Division during Operation Desert Shield and Desert Storm as a platoon sergeant in an anti-tank company and participated in Operation Night Strike I into Iraq. In 1992, Michael was assigned to Prairie View A&M University, Prairie View, TX, as a military science instructor. In 1995, Michael returned to Fort Hood assigned to 1st Bn. 22nd IN. 4th Infantry Division, serving as an infantry company first sergeant for Task Force XXI, and in December 1997, Michael retired from active duty after 20 years of loyal service.

Michael has received numerous awards and decorations including the Meritorious Service Medal, Army Commendation Medal (5th award), Combat Infantrymen Award, Army Valorous Unit Award, Southwest Asia Service Medal, Saudi Arabia Liberation of Kuwait Medal, and Kuwait Liberation of Kuwait Medal, Drill Sergeant Identification Badge, and Basic Parachutist Badge.

After retiring Michael obtained his Graduate Degree from Tarleton State University, Stephenville, TX, and is currently a lieutenant with the Office of the Texas Attorney General's Office, Houston District Office.

Michael is married to Yolanda and has three sons, Michael Jr., Miguel and Marc.

COL. ROBERT B. TULLY was born in 1923, graduated in 1942, and graduated from USMA in 1946. He enlisted in June 1946 and after Boot Camp at Fort Benning, GA, he took Basic Infantry, Airborne and Pathfinder courses.

Tully served in Korea (1950-1951) and in Vietnam being discharged at Fort Benning, GA.

He was awarded the Bronze Star and Silver Star.

His memorable experiences were serving with 1st Cavalry Division, 2nd BN. 5th Cavalry.

After military service, he worked with Bell Helicopter Iran, retiring in 1976.

Robert and Patricia have four children: Robert, Charles, Michael and Elizabeth. Their grandchildren are Robert, Caroline, Emily, Isaac, Ian, Catherine, Marie, Hannah, Claire and Mark.

GARY LEE ULLOM enlisted for the Corps of Engineers in December 1958 and entered service at Fort Knox, KY on Dec. 31, 1958. Following basic training, March 1959 he was transferred to Fort Leonard Wood, MO for Combat Engineer training. On completion of training he was assigned to the Engineer Foreman's Course. August he was transferred to Fort Benning, GA assigned to the 2d Infantry Division, Company "C" 2d Engineer Battalion as a light truck driver. December 1959 he was transferred to Company "A" 317th Engineer Battalion as a Combat Demolition Specialist and truck driver in Hoechst, Germany.

In May 1962 Gary was assigned to Company "B" 27th Engineer Battalion, as a Combat Demolition Specialist. Transferred in August 1963 to 82d Engineer Battalion, Atomic Demolition Specialist, later as Squad Leader. July 1966 he was transferred to the 537th Atomic demolition at Fort Campbell, KY as Squad Leader. November 1966 the 537th was transferred to Fort Belvoir, VA, attached to the 91st Engineer Battalion. Transferred in October 1967 he was transferred to the Atomic Demolition Platoon, 317th Engineer Battalion, Eschborn, Germany, as Squad Leader and later as Platoon Sergeant. July 1970 was transferred to Fort Lewis, WA for Vietnam training. Upon completion was assigned to 1st Cavalry Division, Company "C" 8th Engineer Battalion as Platoon Sergeant, at Quan Loi. Company "C" was later transferred to Fire Support Base Mace. In August 1971 Company "C" was redesignated 501st Engineer Company (SEP), 3rd Brigade, 1st Cavalry Division.

Transferred in November 1971 to 10th Engineer Battalion, Atomic Demolition Platoon, 3rd Infantry Division as Platoon Sergeant. Transferred in June 1974 to 537th Atomic Demolition, 600th Engineer Company, Fort Belvoir, VA as Platoon Sergeant. Transferred November 1967 to 62d Engineer Company, Vicenza, Italy as Platoon Sergeant, later as Housing Manager, Vicenza Community. June 1980 transferred to III Corps Engineer, attached Facility Engineers, Fort, Hood, TX. January 1981 transferred to 62d Engineer Battalion, Company "B" as First Sergeant. He was discharged from service in August 1981.

Ullom received the Bronze Star Medal, Air Medal, three Army Commendation Medal's, Seven Good Conduct Medal's, National Defense Service Medal, Vietnam Service Medal with 60 device, Vietnam Cross of Gallantry with Palm.

After discharge, Ullom worked for the Arizona Department of Corrections as a correctional service sergeant.

Ullom married Dolores Jean Ullom in 1962. They have three children: Gary II, Joseph and Deborah, along with seven grandchildren: Krystal, Joseph II, Kendra, Kayla, Jay, Laura and Heather. Their great-grandchildren are Joshua, Matthew, Joseph III Riley, and in November 2016, Ariel.

ED VARNHAGEN enlisted in Combat Engineering on 21 January 1967 and entered military service at Fort Wayne, Detroit, MI. Following BCT training and Combat Engineering he was assigned to Post Engineers at Fort Leonard Wood, MO and then onto Fort Sheridan, IL. On 1 Nov. 1967 while at Fort Sheridan he was assigned to Co. A 8th Engr. Bn. 1st CAV DIV. On 22 Dec. 1967, he received orders to Vietnam and deployed to LZ English towards the end of Operation PERSHING.

In late January 1968, he began to move north and was relocated to Camp Evans in the Quang Tri Province. This was during the TET offensive, which proved to be a very dangerous time and was the beginning of Operation JEB STUART I. While there he went out on a multitude of missions that included demolitions, blowing LZ's for various CAV units, built the Division Tactical Operations Center, swept QL1 highway for mines daily as well as many other operations. At A Loui he blew up the airfield and then turned around and re-built it.

In April, he was involved in Operation PEGASUS. This was an operation that took him into Khe Sanh to relieve the Marines who had been surrounded and besieged by the enemy. In the summer of 1968 he took part in destroying caches of weapons and military equipment in the A Shau Valley. Also at the A Shau Valley while up in the mountains destroying com lines he saw a C-130 cargo plane piloted by Major L. R. Stow fly into the valley to drop off re-supplies. The plane was attacked by anti-aircraft and he saw the plane crash and burn. All on board were lost. This made a major impact on him and gave him an even more determined resolve in his mission. On 11 August 1968, his mission being completed was leaving the LZ Ann when hostile action caused him to be struck with shrapnel in his neck. A couple of weeks later he returned to Camp Evans and in October 1968 the whole division moved again to Tay Ninh where he continued his job. He returned to the states on 17 December 1968 where he was reassigned to Fort Leonard Wood, MO.

Varnhagen received the Purple Heart, Air Medals, Army Commendation Medal, Vietnam Service Medal with one Silver Service Star, Republic of Vietnam Gallantry Cross with Palm Unit Citation Badge, Vietnam Campaign with 60 Device, Meritorious Unit Commendation, Presidential Unit Citation, Certificate of Recognition, Vietnam Combat Certificate, Expert Qualifications Badge with Rifle & Grenade Bar.

After his discharge on 20 January 1970 he returned to Michigan, where he worked at Ford Motor Co., then joined the Peace Corps for two years. While in the Peace Corps he went to Swaziland in Africa and taught his counterpart surface blasting as well as various land development operations. He joined the Michigan National Guard and the California National Guard. In 1979 he moved to California. He began working at the Naval Weapons Center, China Lake as an engineering technician. He retired in 2001.

Varnhagen married Lucia Varnhagen in 1987, and they have two children, Aaron and Megan.

SAMUEL R. VEER entered the service in September 1969 from Freeport, IL, and took the oath in Chicago. Basic training was at Ft. Campbell, KY, with AIT at Ft. Polk, LA.

He was with A. Co 1/12 1st Cav. Div. In 70-71 as a M60 machine gunner. He was going to D Co 2/12 when they were then told that A Co 1/12 had taken casualties; they were there as replacements, first going to LZ Buttons, then to the field. When they arrived it was mostly over, just mopping up.

The worst firefight he was in was being pinned down all night in Cambodia, and having to have napalm dropped so we could walk through to escape. He didn't think it affected him that much at the time. After eight months in the bush, he was sent to a mortar platoon, and then home.

Even though he came from a family of 14 and had lots of friends, he was still alone, an alcoholic, going from job to job, divorced, and from one relationship after another. Then he was facing a 2-10 year sentence for hitting a cop in a bar fight. The man he worked for helped and changed his life. He only had to do 90 days work release, and he quit drinking. He didn't know it at the time, but he was the stereotypical Nam Vet.

Veer received the Air Medal, Good Conduct, VSM, VCM, Meritorious Unit, National Defense, RVN Gallantry Cross, and RVN Civil Action Ribbon. After the service he worked in construction, as a lineman for a cable company, and in factories, retiring in October 2014. He belongs to the VietNow Freeport Chapter, 1st Cavalry Division Association, Last Patrol POW/MIA activist group, and First Church of the Nazarene of Freeport, IL.

He is married to Sandy Veer. Their children are Sheri, Tammy, Dawn, and Corey, with 13 grandchildren and four great-grandchildren.

GLEN VELA was born in Dallas, Texas. He volunteered for service and took the oath of enlistment on 18 January 1985 and, subsequently completed Basic Training at Fort Jackson, South Carolina and Advanced Individual Training at Fort Eustis, Virginia.

His past assignments include Command Sergeant Major, US Army Aviation and Missile Command (AMCOM) Redstone Arsenal, Huntsville, Alabama; Command Sergeant Major, 166th Aviation Brigade, Fort Hood, Texas; Command Sergeant Major, 1st Air Cavalry Brigade, 1st Cavalry Division, Fort Hood, Texas; Command Sergeant Major, 615th Aviation Support Battalion, 1st Cavalry Division, Fort Hood, Texas; III Corps, CMMC Aviation Maintenance Sergeant Major, Fort Hood, Texas; First Sergeant, Headquarters and Headquarters Company, 4th Brigade, 4th Infantry Division, Fort Hood, Texas; First Sergeant, C Company 1-4 Aviation Regiment, 4th Infantry Division, Fort Hood Texas; Attack NCO Trainer, National Training Center, Operations Group, Fort Irwin, California; Aviation Maintenance Manager, 3rd Armored Cavalry Regiment, Fort Carson, Colorado; Platoon Sergeant, Q Troop 3rd Armored Cavalry Regiment, Fort Carson, Colorado; Platoon Sergeant, A Company, 1-1 Aviation Regiment, 1st Infantry Division, Katterbach, Germany; AH-64 Apache Aircraft Technical Inspector, 3rd Infantry Division, Katterbach, Germany and Crew Chief, A Company 1-4 Aviation Regiment, 4th Infantry Division, Fort Carson, Colorado. His deployments include Operations Iraqi Freedom 01, Operation Iraqi Freedom 06-08, Operation Iraqi Freedom 09-10 and Operation Enduring Freedom 11-12.

Command Sergeant Major Vela's military and civilian education includes Advanced Individual Training MOS 67Y1O and 67R1O, Primary Leadership Course, Basic Noncommissioned Officer Course, Advanced Noncommissioned Officer Course, First Sergeant Course, Aviation Accident Prevention Course, Equal Opportunity Representative Course, and the Army Retention Course. Additionally, he completed the Executive Leader Course, Sergeants Major Course Class 55 and holds an associate's degree in applied science in administration management from Excelsior College.

His awards and decorations include the Distinguished Service Medal, Legion of Merit with OLC, Bronze Star Medal with three OLC, Meritorious Service Medal with four OLC, NATO Medal, Air Medal (Numeral 3), Army Commendation Medal with one Oak Leaf Cluster, Army Achievement Medal with eight OLC, Good Conduct Medal Ninth award, National Defense Service Medal with Bronze Star, Afghanistan Campaign Medal with two Campaign Stars, Iraqi Campaign Medal with four Campaign Stars, Global War on Terrorism Expeditionary Medal, Global War on Terrorism Service Medal, NCO Professional Development Ribbon (Numeral 4), the Army Service Ribbon, the Overseas Service Ribbon (Numeral 6), the Combat Action Badge, and the Master Aviation Badge.

Command Sergeant Major Vela is married to the former Kathryn A. Brown from Oklahoma City, Oklahoma. They have two children: Melinda, 25 and Andrew, 21.

PABLO "PAUL" VELEZ-SANCHEZ was born July 24, 1947 and enlisted at Fort Hamilton, Brooklyn, NY.

He was stationed at USAREUR, Germany (Jan. 10, 1967 – Sept. 10, 1968) and USARPAC Vietnam (October 25, 1968 to July 15, 1969). He was with the B Btry. 1st Bn. 77th Artillery, 1st Cavalry Division.

Velez-Sanchez was awarded the Vietnam Campaign Medal, Air Medal, Army Commendation Medal, Vietnam Service Medal, Sharpshooters M-14, two Overseas Bars, National Defense Service Medal.

Memorable experiences were LZ Dolly, LZ Grant and losing a friend, Med. 1/5 Cav. at Tay Ninh.

SP4 Velez-Sanchez was discharged at Fort Dix, NJ on July 16, 1969.

He retired in 1996 after being a NYC corrections officer.

Paul and Isabel have four children: Paul, Maritza, Coretta and Samanthen and grandchild Paul.

ALBERT WALKER was born Oct. 20, 1947 in Cartersville, GA, and graduated from Dallas High School (GA) in 1966. He entered the service on Nov. 15, 1966 in Atlanta, with basic training at Fort Benning and AIT at Fort Pope. During his tour in Vietnam, he received the following awards: National Defense Service Medal, Sharpshooter (MG M-60), Sharpshooter (Rifle M-14), Marksman (Rifle M-16), Vietnam Campaign Medal with Device 1960, Vietnam Service Medal with two Bronze Stars, Army Commendation Medal, Air Medal, and Combat Infantryman Badge.

He was discharged on Nov. 15, 1968 at Fort Benning, with the rank of Sergeant E5. Al was the owner of Al Walker Interiors from 1992-2014, at which time he retired.

On June 27, 1969, Al married the love of his life, Diane Thomason Walker, who passed away on Feb. 5, 2015 after 45 years of marriage. They have two children, Kim Walker Moore and Kristie Walker Boatright, and seven grandchildren: Erin, Dillon, Courtney, Garrett, Amber Grace, Ashlynn, and Autumn.

NATHANIEL P. WARD IV took a RA commission from VMI in 1965. After Armor Basic, Airborne and Ranger School, he had to have a one-year troop duty and took a tank assignment in Korea south of the DMZ. Then January 1967 he was able to arrange for an Infantry assignment with the First Cavalry Division at An Khe, RSV. With the 1 Bde, 2/8 Cav., he reported to "D" Co. in command of the Reconnaissance Platoon. When not in the bush, he was air assaulted to wherever there was a downed US aircraft. His duty was to secure the craft and crewmen. If any were captured, he would track them to secure their release.

After five months, the BTN wanted him back as XO. After three days back, his request was granted and he was reassigned to "C" Co. with another Recon Platoon. When the call came in May that the 2/8 Cav was to deploy to Khe Sanh as a relief force re the Marines, he was air assaulted as a Jump Command Post. En route after landing, he encountered an explosion that tore off a leg, paralyzed the other and a hand that was scheduled to be amputated.

After two years at Walter Reed Army Hospital, he was returned to active as the FIRST AMPUTEE TO DO SO IN THE VIETNAM WAR. After three more assignments, he medically retired as a Captain in August 1973 after the war was over. He moved to San Diego, CA and practiced law for 30 years. Additionally he was the Executive Officer of the Mekong Education Foundation for 30 years, which worked in northern Laos on the recovery of US downed crafts.

He and his wife, Diane, have been married for 52 years with two sons and five grandkids.

DOUG WARDEN was born April 14, 1941 in Prague, OK, and graduated from Prague High School in 1964. He was drafted in June of 1966, with basic training at Fort Bragg, NC and Advanced Infantry Training at Fort Ord, CA. While serving in Germany, he volunteered for jump school at Mainz, Germany and shortly thereafter, he volunteered for Vietnam.

Warden arrived in Vietnam in May 1967 as a PFC and served with C Company, 1st BN (ABN), 12th Cavalry, as a rifleman. He also was an RTO, Squad leader, Platoon Sergeant and Platoon leader, attaining the rank of SSG as a draftee. He participated in the Battle of An Qui in the Bong Son Plain, operations in Kontum, Oak To, the Battle of Tam Quan and was at Quang Tri for Tet in 1968.

Warden received the Combat Infantry Badge, Parachutist Badge, Silver Star with 1st OLC, Soldiers Medal, Bronze Star with V, Purple Heart with 2nd OLC, Air Medal, Good Conduct Medal, Vietnam Service Medal, Vietnam Campaign Medal with four bronze stars, National Defense Medal, Valorous Unit Award and Vietnamese Cross of Gallantry.

He re-enlisted in October 1969 and served with the 1st Special Forces Group on Okinawa. He received the Special Forces Tab and Army Commendation Medal during this enlistment. He was medically retired in March 1973 after a parachute tower accident. After his medical discharge, he returned to college, graduating from Webster College in St. Louis, MO in 1980.

He worked for AT&T as an area manager and the Gartner Group before retirement in 2006.

He married Marty Warden in 1968 and they have two children, Rob and April, along with five grandchildren: Jordan, Cole, Sam, lily and Molly. Warden has been a member of the 1st Cavalry Division Association since 1967. He has served in the 12th Cavalry Regiment Association as President, Vice-President, Treasurer, Webmaster and Historian. In 2011, he was honored as a Distinguished Member of the 12th Cavalry Regiment.

DENNIS E. WEBSTER was born in Wisconsin and entered the Army from Arkansas in April 1972. He graduated from Mountain Home High School In 1969 and was a student at Arkansas State University for two years. He attended BCT at Fort Polk, Louisiana, followed by AIT as an Armor Crewman at Fort Knox, Kentucky.

CSM Webster's assignments include numerous positions in Armor and Cavalry units from tank loader to Tank Platoon Sergeant in the United States and Germany; Drill Sergeant at Fort Knox, Kentucky; Professional Development NCO at the Military Personnel Center in Alexandria, Virginia; CSM of Support Squadron, 3d Armored Cavalry Regiment at Fort Bliss and during Operation Desert Shield/Storm; CSM of 3d Squadron, 3d ACR; and Regimental CSM of the Brave Rifles. He served as Regimental CSM of the 11th ACR, Fort Irwin, California and as the Division CSM of the 1st Cavalry Division, Fort Hood, Texas from 1996 to 1998.

He retired after his final assignment as the CSM of III Corps and Fort Hood, Texas in 2002. He served as the Executive Director of the 1st Cavalry Division Association from 2002-2016. He and his wife, Sandra, live in Copperas Cove, Texas.

RONALD F. WELLER was born July 9, 1936 in Yakima, WA and graduated from West Seattle High School in 1955. He enlisted in the Army National Guard at the age of 17, in Seattle in 1954. He entered active duty in February 1956 and did his Basic Training at Fort Ord, CA. He was sent to the 530th AAA Battalion in Rapid City, SD. In December 1956 he was sent to Fort Lewis, WA for deployment overseas.

He left the Seattle Army Terminal on the *Frederick Funkson*, a troop ship, for a 16-day voyage to Yokohama, Japan. At the "Repo-depot" in Tokyo he was assigned to the 545th M.P. Company, 1st Cavalry Division as a security guard and courier. In August 1957 the 1st Cavalry Division was sent to the Bong Il Chong area of Korea. Ronald was sent home on the troop ship *General Mann* in February 1958 and discharged at Fort Lewis, WA.

Ronald settled in the Seattle area and worked for the Seattle Fire Department and later sold logging equipment and rock crushing machinery. He married Rachel Weatherstone on the Opening day of the 1962 Seattle World's Fair and has three children: Randal, Ryan and Robin, and 11 grandchildren.

STEVEN "KIRK" WERNER was born July 13, 1952 in Wilson, OK, and graduated from Duncan High School in 1970.

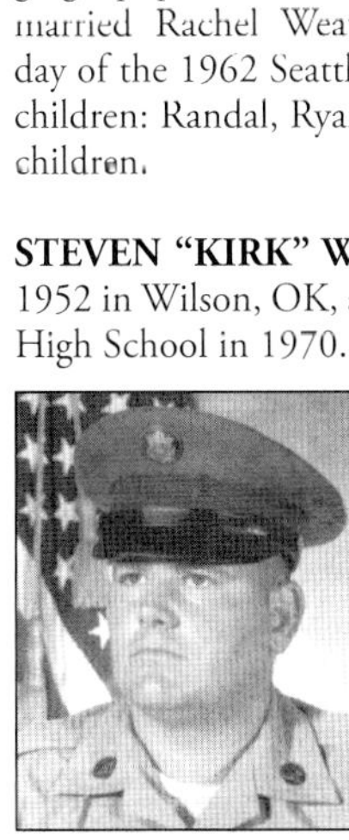
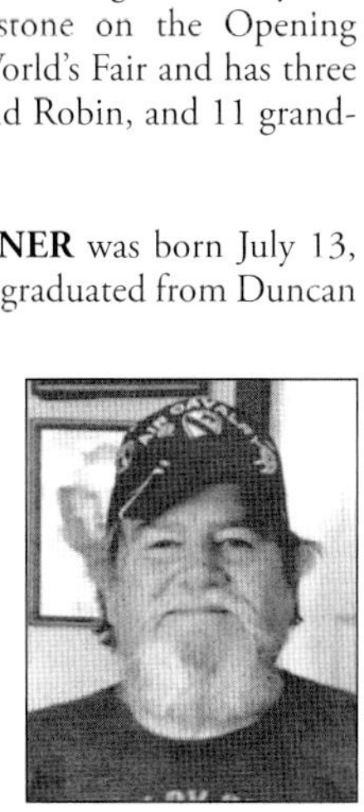

He entered service at Ft. Leonard Wood, MO in 1973, then to Ft. Polk, LA, for AIT Tigerland, the last class of 11. Nov. 1973 to Ft. Hood, TX CSC 2/7 assigned to GS and DS Mortar Plt, to Motorcycle Scoots Mtr, Sgt. Attended BLC, NCO Ach. Unit Armor, PLL. Transferred to ACO ½ for Bde 75 move to Wildflecken, Germany, got E1B. Transferred to Berlin Bde 1977, assigned B

3/6 Inf. Sq. Leader, promoted to SSG/E6, 1979. Berlin Boxing Coach when they were three time USAGR Boxing Champs.

In 1980 transferred to 101st Abn. A 1/501 as PSQ. Did training in Panama for Jungle School, Winter Training in Alaska, marched for President Reagan's inauguration, Air Assault School, conducted 1st Miles ARTEP at Ft. Gordon, GA, 1981. Transferred to Ft. Sill, OK 4/31st Inf. for support of Arty OCS, ETS on June 14, 1982 at Ft. Sill.

He was awarded the Good Conduct Medal three times, Occupation Medal, Expeditionary Medal, NCO Ribbon, Overseas Ribbon, National Defense Medal, Gold Schuchnur, Jungle Expert, and other awards.

In civilian life he worked in civil service and as a butcher, retiring in 2014. He is a Past Master Mason, 32 degree Scottish Rite Mason, and Shriner Clown. He married Debra Sue Werner on April 23, 1973 and they were together 42 years until her death on Oct. 7, 2013. Their children are Travis, Joe Bob, and Tiffany, with grandchildren Cheyenne, Michael, Dalton, and Gailey.

EDWARD C. WEST graduated from West Point on 6 June 1950 and married Marcy that same day. His first assignment was to Japan, and Marcy was to accompany him. Thirteen days later, the Korean War started. Ed was soon on his way to Korea, where he joined the 1st Cavalry Division as a platoon leader in the Cav's 8th Combat Engineer Battalion. After 15 adventurous months, Ed had climbed to battalion S-3 and was returning to Marcy and the US. To this day, those 15 months are right at the top of his fascinating Army career. Ed retired from the Army in 1972 to manage a new, challenging position in the budding field of environmental engineering.

During 22 years in the Army, Ed earned Masters degrees in Civil Engineering and Business Administration. He also commanded an active construction battalion; served on the personal staff of Gen. Westmoreland when "Westie" was U.S. Army Chief of Staff; commanded an organization responsible for all contract construction for U.S. services in France (by French contractors) for three years (during which time Ed, Marcy and their two little girls became fluently bilingual); taught engineer subjects at the Infantry School at Fort Benning, GA; commanded a teaching group at the Engineer School at Fort Belvoir, VA; and served as District Engineer of the Pittsburgh District of the Army Corps of Engineers. That much of his Army career should give you a feel for the rest.

The ensuing career in environmental engineering has been equally challenging and interesting in a much different way. Suffice it to say, he is still working full time at the tender age of 88. Concentration at present is on composting organic waste and creating electricity from waste instead of conventional fuels.

NORMAN "RALPH" WEST was born May 18, 1941 in Miami, FL and graduated from Miami Sr. High in 1960. He enlisted on Dec. 12, 1963 and took Boot Camp at Fort Jackson. He took AIT at Fort Benning, GA.

He was in battles the Central Highlands, Vietnam, LZ-XRAY, 1965.

For his service he was awarded the CIB, Vietnam Service, Expert Rifle, Sharpshooter and Pistol Air Assault Wings.

E-4 West was discharged on Dec. 11, 1965.

Ralph was a farrier (horse shoer) for Eastern Airlines until retiring in 2009. In retirement, he hunts, fishes, makes crafts and enjoys his grandchildren.

Ralph and Lois A. West have four children: Lisa Barrera, Ralph Eric West, Michelle Rush and Shelly A. Zambo. Grandchildren are Matt, Vinnie, John, Ron, Meagan, Brianna, Troy, Chase, Tony, Rihanna, Chloe, Brienna and Olivia.

DONALD A. WESTABY was born 16 June, 1947 in Stanley, WI and enlisted in the Army on 6 October 1966 at Minneapolis, MN. He attended basic training at Fort Bliss, Tx. Following boot camp, he attended training at Fort Sill, OK to be a Howitzer Gunner. Westaby was shipped to Vietnam where he was assigned to the 1st Cavalry Division as a Recon. Sgt.

Westaby received the National Defense Medal, Vietnam Campaign Medal, Vietnam Service Medal, Air Medal, Bronze Star, and Good Conduct Medal.

Westaby was honorably discharged on 2 February 1972 in Oakdale, PA. After discharge he returned to Minnesota where he attended vocational school to be a diesel mechanic. He worked as a mechanic at Crystal Farms until he accepted a position at Belgrade Steel Tank. He worked there from 1978 until his retirement in 2007. In retirement he enjoys fishing, camping, and hunting.

Westaby and his wife, Sandra, have four children. Michael, Lisa, Tracey and Tara along with six grandchildren Travis, Bailey, Quinn, Jesse, Bree, and Jackson.

WALTER GARY WESTERNOFF, at 17, graduated from Encinal High, Alameda, California and enlisted on July 16, 1959. Following basic training at Fort Ord, California he was transferred to Fort Bliss, Texas and deployed to Korea as a sentry dog handler and reassigned to the 21st field Artillery of the 1st Cavalry Division as a forward observer. He returned to the US and honorably discharged on July 13, 1962 receiving the good conduct medal, expert (pistol and carbine), and sharpshooter (rifle).

After discharge, using the GI bill, he earned associate and bachelor degrees in architecture and construction management from San Francisco State University in 1968. Following graduation he advanced from architectural draftsman to vice president of Planning and Construction for Fortune 500 companies until starting his own company planning and building projects throughout the United States.

After retiring in 1999 he taught college courses in construction management, wrote and published *Construction Management Made Easy* and launched Constructionplace.com. He was past president of his Rotary club and is an Aloha Shriner.

Westernoff married Peggy Westernoff in 1966, and have two sons, Tom and John, along with two grandsons Troy and Tristan. Following Peggy's death from cancer in 2004, Westernoff married Taemi Westernoff in 2005.

MARK T. WHEELER was born Jan. 19, 1974 in Columbus, OH, and graduated from Lawrence County High School in 1992. He joined the service on July 11, 1996 at Beckley, WV, and was sent to Fort Knox, KY for basic training. Other stations include Fort Eustis, VA; Fort Hood, TX; and Camp Commanche, Tuzla, Bosnia. He was part of Operation Joint Forge.

Wheeler received the Armed Forces Expeditionary Medal, Army Service Ribbon, NATO Medal, Expert Marksmanship Badge with Rifle Bar and Grenade Bar, Aircraft Crewman Badge and Army Commendation Medal. He was discharged on Oct. 18, 1999 at Fort Hood, with the rank of Specialist.

Since March 2004, he has worked for the Lawrence County (KY) Sheriff's Office, serving as a deputy sheriff and now chief deputy. He and his wife, Kerry, have two children, Allyson and Andrew.

NEAL C. WHETSEL JR. enlisted on June 24, 1966 for the Army College Option Program to attend Officer Candidate School. He entered active army service at Fort Knox, KY, following graduation from East Tennessee State University. He completed Basic Training at Fort Knox and Advance Individual Training as Infantry (11B MOS) at Fort Ord, CA, and then graduated from Officer Candidate School at Fort Lee, VA.

He was commissioned as a 2nd Lieutenant, U.S. Army, Quartermaster Corp. on May 4, 1967 with assignment to the Quartermaster Petroleum Supply Officer's Course at Fort Lee, VA. Upon graduation, he was assigned to the 540th Quartermaster Battalion at Fort Lee, with a future report date for duty in the Republic of Vietnam.

He reported for duty to the 15th Supply and Service Battalion, 1st Cavalry Division (Air mobile) at An Khe, RVN in March 1968 assigned as the Division Petroleum Supply Officer until March 15, 1969. He provided petroleum logistic support under the direction of the G4 for Division operations Jeb Stewart (68 Tet Offensive), Pegasus (68 Tet Counter Offensive), Delaware (A Shau Valley campaign), Liberty Cannon and Tay Ninh Province operations.

He was released from active duty on March 29, 1969 with transfer to the U. S. Army Reserves (RCPAC) assigned to the troop program, 3292 USAR School Knoxville, Tennessee. He served on the school staff as the S4 and MOS Assistant Director and completed both the Officer Advance Course and Command and General Staff College. He became an instructor assigned for the inactive duty course phase after completion of each course. He accepted assignment to the Forces Command Individual Mobilization position in the Supply and Service section for Garrison at Fort Campbell, KY. He transferred to the 3290th USAR School in Nashville, Tennessee from 1983 to 1985 as an instructor for Command and General Staff College. He was assigned to the 125th Army Reserve Command (Tennessee and Kentucky Reserve Units) in 1985 as Chief of the Supply and Service Division. He transferred to the U. S. Army Reserve Personnel Center as assigned until retirement on June 12, 2003.

Medals and Awards: Bronze Star, Meritorious Service, Air Medal, Army Commendation, Army Achievement, Army Reserve Component Achievement with Bronze Cluster, National Defense Service with Bronze Cluster, Vietnam Service/two campaigns, Armed Forces Reserve with hour glass, Army Service Ribbon, Vietnam (RVN) Gallantry Cross with palms, Army Meritorious Unit Citation.

Upon release from active duty in 1969, he was employed by the Right of Way Division, Tennessee Department of Transportation (TDOT). He worked for the Department Knoxville Region One as the Chief of Acquisition to acquire land for public road construction projects. He accepted the position of Civil Engineer Specialist in TDOT Right of Way Headquarter Office to manage the statewide right of way acquisitions, relocation assistance/property management functions and coordination of eminent domain for land acquisition as required with the State of Tennessee Deputy Attorney General.

Following retirement from TDOT/State he established Real Estate Acquisition Management Company. As owner/corporate president from 1994 to 2014, he expanded the company to include Maple Ridge Nursery and Lakeway Landscaping. He concurrently accepted employment with Vaughn and Melton Consulting Engineers in 1998 as Principal Right of Way Agent to establish the Corporate Right of Way Operation to acquire land in Kentucky, Tennessee, Virginia, North Carolina and South Carolina.

He retired from Vaughn and Melton Consulting Engineers in 2014. He has continued in right of way consulting work as a private contract consultant to state, city and public agencies.

JEFF WHITE enlisted in the Massachusetts Army National Guard in 1989 as a combat engineer. In 1992, he was commissioned a Second Lieutenant in the Regular Army as an Engineer Officer after graduating from the University of Massachusetts/Amherst and was assigned to the 17th Combat Engineer Battalion, 2nd Armored Division, Fort Hood, TX. As a combat engineer, he served as a line platoon leader, support platoon leader, and assistant S3 (Operations).

In May 1995, Colonel White transferred into Army Aviation, where he completed the Initial Entry Rotary Wing Course, the AH-64A Aircraft Qualification Course, and the Aviation Advanced Course (Captains Career Course) while at Fort Rucker, AL. His first assignment as an Army Aviator was in the Republic of Korea from 1997-1999 where he commanded Headquarters and Headquarters Company (HHC), 6th Cavalry Brigade, followed by an attack helicopter company command of Bravo Troop, 1st Squadron, 6th Cavalry Regiment.

Upon return from Korea, Colonel White served as an Aviation Observer/Controller (OC) on the Eagle Team at the National Training Center (NTC) from 1999-2001. Following NTC, he was selected as the Aide-de-Camp to the Commanding General, U.S. Army Aviation Center and Fort Rucker, where he served from 2001-2003. After graduating from the Air Command and Staff College at Maxwell Air Force Base, he was assigned to the 101st Airborne Division (Air Assault), Fort Campbell, KY and served as the S3 Operations Officer and Executive Officer (XO) in 1st Battalion, 101st Aviation Regiment, and then Brigade XO in the 101st Combat Aviation Brigade (CAB). While serving in the 101st CAB, COL White deployed to Iraq in support of Operation Iraqi Freedom (OIF) 05-06.

Following Fort Campbell, Colonel White transitioned to the Joint Unmanned Aircraft Systems Center of Excellence located at Creech Air Force Base, NV. He served there from 2007 to 2009 as a Joint Staff Project Officer and XO to the Commander. Colonel White was then assigned to the 1st Air Cavalry Brigade (ACB), 1st Cavalry Division in 2009 where he served as the Deputy Brigade Commander during the unit's OIF 09-10 deployment to Iraq. After being selected for tactical command, Colonel White assumed command of 4th Battalion, 227th Aviation Regiment, 1st ACB at Fort Hood. While in command, he trained and deployed a reconfigured multi-function Aviation Task Force (Task Force Guns) to Afghanistan and led the unit during OEF 11-12.

Upon redeployment in June 2012, Colonel White changed command and was re-assigned back to the NTC at Fort Irwin, CA serving as the Senior Aviation Trainer (Eagle 07) until July 2013. After NTC, he attended the U.S. Army War College as a resident student. Upon graduation in June 2014, he was assigned back to the U.S. Army Aviation Center of Excellence at Fort Rucker where he finished his career serving as the Director, U.S. Army Training and Doctrine Command (TRADOC) Capability Manger for Reconnaissance and Attack (TCM-RA). Colonel White retired on Sept. 30, 2017 after 28 years of service in the United States Army.

Colonel White is a graduate of the Engineer Officer Basic Course, Air Assault School, Airborne School, Ranger School, Sapper Leader's Course, Aviation Captain's Career Course, Combined Arms Services Staff School, Air Command and Staff College, the U.S. Army War College, the AH-64A and AH-64D Aircraft Qualification Courses. His awards include the Legion of Merit, Bronze Star Medal (3), Defense Meritorious Service Medal, Meritorious Service Medal (6), Air Medal (2), Army Commendation Medal (2), Joint Service Achievement Award, Army Achievement Award (4), and Combat Action Badge. He is a Senior Army Aviator qualified in the OH-58A/C and AH-64A/D helicopters.

Colonel White is married to the former Sara Miller, and they have two daughters, Caylee and Abigayle.

JAMES L. WIGGINS was born August 13, 1946 in Savannah, GA, and graduated from Albany High School in Albany, GA, in 1964. He attended Auburn University from 1964-66, graduated from Armstrong State College in Savannah, GA, in 1972, and graduated from the Walter F. George School of Law, Mercer University, Macon, GA, in 1975.

He enlisted at Atlanta, GA, in 1966, with Boot Camp at Fort Polk, LA; Helicopter Flight School, Ft. Wolters, TX and Ft. Rucker, AL, 1966; and Advanced Cobra Training at Hunter Army Air Field, Savannah, GA, 1967. In December 1967 he was assigned to Delta Co., 229th Assault Helicopter BN, 1st Cav. Division, Vietnam, and participated in the Battle of Khe Sanh (1968), Battle of Hue/Tet (1968), and the Battle of A Shaw Valley (1968)/Operation Delaware.

He was awarded the Silver Star for gallantry in action while engaged in military operations in Vietnam on Sept. 3, 1968; three Bronze Star medals for gallantry in action; and five Air Medals with "V" device. He was discharged at Savannah, GA, 1970, as a CWO, UH1 Instructor Pilot.

Jim served as District Attorney for the Oconee Judicial Circuit of GA from 1980-96; was a United States Attorney for the Middle District of Georgia in Macon, 1996; and a private practice attorney in Eastman, GA, until retiring in April 2014. He is a member of the Board of Governors State Bar of Georgia.

He married Kitty Tabb in October 1967. They have two children, Kitten Katrina and Meredith Auburn, three grandchildren, Coty, Stoney and Merebelle, and two great grandchildren, Payton and Walker.

JAMES L. WIGINTON was born Oct. 15, 1941 in Iuka, MS, and graduated from Belmont High School in 1961. He was drafted into the US Army Feb. 17, 1966 and sent to Fort Polk, LA for basic training.

After a short leave, he was sent to the Republic of Vietnam where he was assigned to D Company, 227th Assault Helicopter Battalion where he was assigned Crew Chief on Huey Gunship. He served with 1st Cav. Division, 227 Assault Helicopter Battalion, Vietnam, Sept. 1, 1966-August 31, 1967.

He was wounded in December 1966 during Operation Pershing. He saw action in Bong Son, An Loe Valley, VC Valley and Duc Pho. James also spent some time at LZ Dog, LZ Oasis, LZ Uplift, LZ English, LZ Bird and LZ Pony.

He was awarded the Purple Heart for injuries received at Operation Pershing and during time with Cavalry was awarded Air Medal with 18 Clusters.

He left Vietnam in September 1967 and returned home to his wife, Brenda, in Cicero, IL. Son Larry was born in 1968, son Benji was born in 1971. Both sons served in the US Army as Airborne Officers.

He has been self-employed for 48 years. Jim is a Life Member of Order of Purple Heart, VFW and Viet Now and served on the Boards of all of these organizations

Wiginton is the proud grandfather of eight.

DONALD E. "DON" WILLIAMS enlisted in the U.S. Army in August 1960 to be a small arms repairman. After basic at Fort Ord, CA, his first duty station was later at Fort Lewis, WA, where he attained the rank of SP4 and in 1962 Giessen and Hanau, Germany. While in Germany, duty was changed from small arms repairman to company clerk and he was promoted to E5. In 1965, he was transferred to Fort Benning, GA and continued working as a company clerk.

He applied for and was accepted into Warrant Officer Rotary Wing Aviator Class 67-11 at Fort Wolters, TX. Initial training was in the OH-23D. Upon graduation, he served in the 543rd Assault Helicopter Co. at Bearcat, Vietnam, flying to Fort Rucker, AL as an instructor pilot in the "Contact" phase of flight school in the A, B, B, with a 540 rotorhead (later became the C model), and H models of the UH-1 helicopter. In 1970, he accepted a commission as a 1LT in Field Artillery.

He attended the Field Artillery Officers Basic Course at Fort Sill, OK, en route to Vietnam for a second tour. A further en route school was at Fort Stewart, GA for AH-1G Cobra gunship transition. He again was at Bearcat in B Troop, 1/9 Cavalry, 1st Cavalry Division Flying Cobras in and later transferred to D Co., 229th Aviation Bn (a Cobra equipped gun company), which was later converted to F Troop 1/9 Cavalry – still at Bearcat.

After a second full tour in Vietnam, he was sent to 1st Battalion, 5th Field Artillery (Hamilton's Cannoneers) at Fort Riley, KS, where he served as Liaison Officer, S-2 Officer, and S-1 Officer. He was RIF'ed in late 1975.

He immediately reentered the U.S. Army as a SGT and was sent to White Sands Missile Range, NM as a Field Artillery Fire Direction NCO, then immediately promoted to SSG (while also serving as a reserve Captain). He participated in testing of the Field Artillery TACFIRE Computer System, the Battery Computer System, and FADAC Artillery Tape Revision testing.

After 21 years of service in the U.S. Army, he retired as the recipient of the Basic Aviator Badge, Distinguished Flying Cross with 2 OLC, Bronze Star, Distinguished Service Medal, Air Medal with "V" device and 77 OLC, Good Conduct Medal with 3 knots, National Defense Service Medal, Vietnam Campaign Medal with 6 campaign stars, Reserve Medal, Vietnam Cross of Gallantry with Palm, and the Vietnam Service Medal with "60" device. He retired as a Field Artillery Captain.

Upon retirement, he worked as a Department of the Army Civil Servant at White Sands Missile Range, NM, on the Mortar Ballistic Computer, the Lance Missile System, Copperhead Artillery projectile, the Pershing I and II missiles, the Multiple Launch Rocket System (MLRS) and Army Tactical Missile System (ATACMS) missiles, the Japanese CHU-SAM missile, and Line-of-sight Anti-Tank (LOSAT) missile system.

He retired in 2004 after 23 years with Civil Service, and now resides in Las Cruces, NM with interest in genealogy, photo restoration, travel, several fraternal organizations, as well as charitable, patriotic and Veteran organizations. He has developed an absolute love for mini-dachshunds.

He met and married Ursula in 1964 while in Germany and had four children: Steven E., Donald M., James R., and Elizabeth A. Ursula died in 1979 of cancer. He married Rebecca in September 2016 in Las Cruces, NM.

CLIFFORD "WILL" D. WILSON JR. enlisted at Morganton, NC. After basic training at Fort Bragg, he took AIT training at Fort Polk, LA.

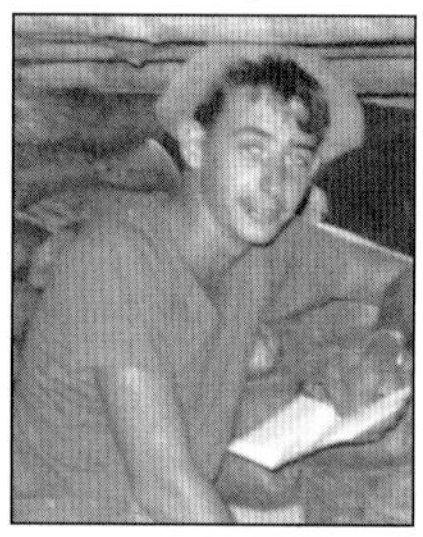

He served at A Shau Valley, Tay Ninh City, Black Virgin Mtn.

Wilson was awarded the Vietnam Campaign Medal M-60 Device, CIB, Badge, Bronze Star, Vietnam Service Medal with two Bronze Stars and Air Medal.

Memorable experiences were Freedom Bird home and his brothers.

Wilson was discharged as E-5 at Fort Benning, GA.

He retired in 2002 after working at Corning Cable for 31 years.

"Will" and Sharon (Zimmerman) Wilson have one child, Dana S. Wilson.

JACK H. WILSON was born April 10, 1945 in Maryville, Blount County, TN, and enlisted on June 3, 1969 with boot camp in Fort Ord, CA. In addition to Fort Ord, he served at Song Bay, Vietnam.

For his service, Wilson was awarded the Vietnam National Defense Service Medal, Vietnam Service Medal, Vietnam Campaign Medal, Army Commendation Medal and Bronze Star Medal.

Memorable experiences for Wilson were survival and meeting a lot of good people.

He was discharged on March 23, 1971 with the rank of SP4.

Wilson retired on April 1999 after 35 years as a truck driver for Arrowhead Water Co.

Jack and Anna R. Wilson have one child, Dusty D. Wilson Curry and one grandchild, Gunner Curry.

TERRY WILSON enlisted in the U.S. Army in April 1967. He attended basic Training at Sand Hill, Fort Benning, GA, and AIT at Southeastern Signal School Fort Gordon, GA.

Wilson received orders to Vietnam and arrived in-country in February 1969. He was assigned to 13th Signal Battalion, Camp Evans, located outside of Phon Dien Province about 30 miles north of the ancient city of Hue, along the Perfume River. Wilson was honorably discharged from the Army, Fort Huachuca, AZ in April 1970.

He had significant difficulty adjusting to civilian life, so, he enlisted in the U.S Navy in October 1973. He completed 12 years of service with the Navy and received an honorable discharge for a service-connected disability in June 1985. Wilson was employed for an additional 20 years as a Department of Defense civilian, first for the Department of the Army and later Department of the Navy. In total, he gave 34 years of service to the U.S. Department of Defense (DOD), which included 14 years of active duty.

He retired in 2005 at the Naval Submarine Base, Kings Bay, GA, pay grade GS-1152-11. He is a retired member of the Federal Managers Association, life member of the First Cavalry Division Association, and a life member of Disabled American Veterans (DAV).

He and his wife of 42 years, Mary, now live in Kingsland, GA. He is the founder and director of "First Strike Ministries," a Christ-centered nonprofit corporation that provides tools for military Christians, specifically to U.S. and British Armed forces. Their primary ministry tool is the "Combat Life Deployment Kit." They have provided thousands of kits to British and American troops at no cost to them over the last 10 years. Recently they expanded their ministry to include the law enforcement community.

PAUL PATTON "WINK" WINKEL JR. was born July 10, 1931 in Chicago, IL and graduated high school in Vienna, Austria. He graduated from the USMA in 1956 with a BA in Military Science & Engineering, then received an MA in Foreign Affairs from American University.

Winkel entered service with the 1802d Regt. at West Point, NY, and later went through Ranger, Airborne, Senior Army Aviation, OPNS Research/System Analysis, Command & Control Systems, and Research & Development training. During his career he spent time at Ft. Benning, GA, Ft. Bragg, NC, Europe, and Vietnam, including the Pleiku campaign (six battle stars), Ia Drang, LZ X-Ray, Albany, and others.

In addition to other medals, he was awarded Silver Star and Bronze Star.

Winkel was discharged on June 30, 1986 as Colonel (06) after 31-1/2 years of service. He is married to Rita with two children, Paul III and Heather, and four grandchildren.

JOHN M. "SOUP" WITTS was born Sept. 2, 1946 in Olewine, IA, and graduated from Peken Community High School in 1964. He enlisted on Feb. 13, 1966 at Pekin, IL. After basic training at Fort Polk, LA he trained as a Huey Engine Technician.

He was stationed at Fort Eustis, VA and Fort Benning, GA. From 1966 to 1967 he served at An Khe.

Photograph at left: John Witts (left) and Sgt. Kelley

Memories include Sept. 3, 1966, a day he will remember – two KIA, 15 TC Company, Camp Radclif, Vietnam.

On Feb. 14, 1969, Witts was discharged as E-5 at Fort Benning.

He served with the Peoria Air Guard for 26 years, retiring on Sept. 29, 2001. He is affiliated with Engine Tech. IO-360, PW 100 and 200 Eng., CJ-85, T-56-501 Allison.

In retirement he is teaching aviation at Lincoln Land Community College.

John and Carol L. were married in June 1974. They have one son, Ryan J. Witts

He says "Army 1st Cav. gave me my start in aviation. Thank you!"

GERALD "JERRY" C. WOOD was born January 12, 1931 in Stamford, CT, and graduated from Stamford High School. He enlisted at age 17 on July 29, 1948 in Connecticut. After Boot Camp at Fort Knox, KY he attended Tanker School. He was Tank Gunner and then promoted to Sergeant First Class Tank Commander. The tanks were Sherman M4A3E8.

Jerry was based at Pusan, Tague, Seoul, South Korea and Fort Knox, KY. All major battles he was involved in were fought in the Korean War.

For his service, he was award the Good Conduct Medal, Korean Service Medal with five Campaign Stars, Distinguished Unit Citation, Republic of Korea War Service Medal, National Defense Medal, State of Connecticut Foreign War Service Medal.

Memorable experiences were the lead tank platoon from Seoul to Pyongyang, crossing the 38th Parallel and fighting to Unsan by the Yellow River and meeting his older brother, Ken Wood, on the battlefield in Korea.

SFC (Tank Commander) Wood was discharged at HQ the Armored Center, Fort Knox, KY.

He worked as a book binder for Thrush Press and as a machinist for Conde Nast Publications.

He is affiliated with VFW 9617 and American Legion Post 3.

Retirement activities include gardening, trips to Vermont with his family and building things at home.

He and Barbara have one son, Jason.

ROY WOOD was born in Rocky Mount, NC, 1941, and graduated from Fayetteville High School in 1959, later receiving his BS from NC State University in 1964. He enlisted in April 1964 at Fayetteville, NC. Additional training was in Atomic Demolition Munitions. He was stationed at Fort Belvoir, VA and Fort Benning, GA.

He was engaged in battles in Vietnam, Ia Drang Valley and Masher/White Wing – Bong Son.

Roy received the Air Medal, Commendation Medal, Presidential Unit Citation, Meritorious Unit Citation, Army Good Conduct Medal, Armed Forces Expedition Medal, National Defense Medal, Vietnam Service Medal, Republic of Vietnam Campaign Medal, Vietnam Presidential Unit Citation and Vietnam Cross of Gallantry with palm.

1Lt. Wood was discharged in April 1966 at Oakland, CA.

Memorable experience was being responsible for three BN Equipment Platoons during Deployment and Operations in 1965.

He is presently President of the North Carolina Chapter, First Cavalry Division Association.

STEPHEN L. WORKMAN enlisted on April 3, 1961 in Beckley, WV. After Boot Camp at Fort Knox, KY, he had additional training at Fort Benning, GA.

In 1965 he was engaged in battles at LZ XRAY, Vietnam.

He was awarded the Bronze Star and Purple Heart.

Memorable experience was servicing with General Moore and CSM Plumbey in LZ XRAY in 1965.

After service, he was with Civil Service at Fort Campbell, KY.

Stephen married Cathy (Bolton) Workman, and his stepchildren are Kim Conrad and Travis Bolton. Grandchildren are Jack and Sam Conrad.

JAMES D. WRIGHT was born Nov. 9, 1947 in Minneapolis, MN, and graduated from Osseo Senior High School in 1965. He received basic training at Ft. Campbell, KY, with AIT in Military Intelligence and POW Interrogation. He was stationed at Ft. Campbell, KY; Ft. Bragg, NC; and Vietnam.

He was sent to Vietnam in late June 1968 and after processing out of Binh Hoa was sent to the 1st Cavalry at Camp Evans, where he was assigned to the 191st MI Detachment, 3rd Brigade team in support of the 7th Cav, responsible for interviewing POWs to get strategic information to help units in the field. He left Vietnam the first week of July 1969.

He was awarded the Bronze Star, Air Medal, Good Conduct Medal, Nation Defense, VN Service Medal with Bronze star attachment, Republic of Vietnam Campaign with device (60), Expert Badge with rifle bar, and Sharpshooters Badge with auto rifle bar.

Wright was discharged on Jan. 21, 1970 at Ft. Bragg, with the rank of E-5. He spent his entire professional career in banking (44 years), retiring at the age of 62 in 2009. He is also a show promoter for gun and knife shows in the Minneapolis-St. Paul, MN, area.

He and Patricia have been married for 50 years (March 2017) and has two children — Jason (27-year Army Veteran and pilot of the Blackhawk and Chinook) and Dana (pilot for Southwest Airlines) — and six grandchildren.

RAYMOND "RAY" J. WRIGHT was born August 23, 1936 in Frederick, MD and graduated from Frederick High School in 1954. He was commissioned ROTC in 1958 at Western Maryland College. He attended the Infantry Officer Basic Course at Fort Benning, GA in addition to Airborne, Pathfinder, Special Forces, Infantry Officer Career Course and Command and General Staff training.

Ray was stationed at Fort Leonard Wood, Fort Meade, Fort Bragg, University of Hawaii and Fort Benning. He serviced in Vietnam from July 1967 – July 1968.

He received the BSM, Purple Heart, Combat Infantry Badge and MSM medals.

Memorable experience was serving under LTC John Wickham 5/7 Cav, who later became Chief of Staff of US Army.

In 1988, Col. Wright was discharged at 97th ARCOM.

Professionally he was Director of Budget Analysis for the State of Maryland, retiring in 1998.

He is a life member of National Association of State Budget Officers.

In retirement he is volunteering and staying active.

Ray and Arlene have three children: William, Jennifer and Andrew. They have seven grandchildren: Joshua, Megan, Jonah, Maddy, Drew, Kelleigh and Ben.

DARRIEL R. YOUNG was drafted into the US Army on June 23, 1969 and entered the Army for basic training at Fort Polk, LA.

Upon completion of basic, he continued his AIT at Tigerland at North Fort Polk, LA. After graduating from AIT, he was sent to Fort Knox, KY for M113 APC driver's training.

Young was assigned to the First Cavalry Division in Vietnam in January 1970. He would serve in Company C, First Battalion, 12th Cavalry Regiment until leaving Vietnam in late December 1970. He would be assigned to 1st Platoon, 1st Squad, where he was first a Grenadier and later RTO. Young would be part of the Cambodian Campaign in May-June 1970.

Young received the Bronze Star Medal, Air Medal, Army Commendation Medal, Good Conduct Medal, as well as the Combat Infantry Badge, Presidential Unit Citation, Valorous Unit Citation and Meritorious Unit Citation.

After ETS, he completed his BSE degree at Henderson State University. He was an educator for 36 years, retiring in 2010.

Young joined the Army Reserve in 1971 and retired at the rank of CSM in June 2004. He married Brenda in 1968. They have two children, Christy and Clint, five grandchildren and one great-grandchild.

1SGT. HOWARD DAVID ZINGRAF was born August 21, 1942 and attended Downers Grove High School. He enlisted in the Field Artillery January 1964. After AIT, he went to 2/3 FA in Germany. He was trained as a Recon Sgt. OJT. In January 1966, he re-enlisted for Vietnam. He arrived in March 1966 and was assigned to 2/32nd FA II Field Forces. Zingraf volunteered for the 1st Cav. Division. He went to 1/77th FA and was attached to the 1/5th Cav. as a Recon Sergeant. His tour was extended for six months. He departed Vietnam in November 1967 to Fort Sill, OK.

In January 1972 Zingraf returned to Vietnam and requested assignment to the 3rd Bde. (Sep.) 1st Cav. He was assigned to 1/21st FA as Fire Direction Center Chief. They were very involved in the Easter Offensive. His unit performed the evacuation of ARVN Artillery guns, troops and civilians from An Loc as it was being overrun by the NVA. When the 3rd BDE left Vietnam many of them stayed and became Task Force Garry Owens. He was with F Btry. 26th FA. They stood down in late August 1972 and returned to the United States.

Zingraf continued his military career with assignments to Fort Knox, KY; Fort Sill, OK (Drill Sergeant duty); and Germany with the 8th Inf. Div. as a 1st Sergeant. He went to Fort Bliss, TX for the US Army Sergeant Major Academy. His last assignment was as a 1st HHB 2/34 FA at Fort Sill, OK. He retired in August 1984 at Fort Sill, OK.

After retirement he was a Realtor for five years, then became self-employed as a ceramic tile installer, which he is still doing.

Zingraf married Patricia in February 1968. They have three children: Denise, Diana and David, and 10 grandchildren: Gerald, Sean, Christopher, Rachel, Kyle, Mikaela, Samantha, Daniel, Venelin and Maisen.

COL (RET.) ERVAN E. ZOUZALIK was born on Sept. 24, 1936 in Flatonia, TX. He received the "Outstanding Athlete Award" in his 1955 graduation class at Flatonia High School.

Colonel Zouzalik was a "Distinguished Military Graduate" at Texas A&M University and received a Regular Commission in the US Army. He was the first student to graduate with a BA/BS in Journalism/Industrial Education from Texas A&M University. He attended the Artillery Basic Course at Fort Sill and his first assignment was in Schwabisch Hall, Germany in the 37th Field Artillery, a towed 8" Artillery unit with a nuclear capability. He then reverted to his basic logistical branch of Quartermaster Corps. The Army sent Colonel Zouzalik to the University of Texas at Austin, where he graduated with a MBA degree. He also was a graduate of the Army War College in 1981.

During his first tour in Vietnam in 1966-1967, he was Commanding Officer of the 74th Repair Parts Company, with over 100,000 line items in the Cam Rahn Bay Depot. The Commanding Officer of the Battalion was LTC Art Gregg, who had 18 companies in the battalion. Colonel Zouzalik would later worked for him when he was a LTG and was the HQDA, ODCSIOG of the Army. His first assignment with the 1st Cavalry Division was during his 2nd tour in Vietnam as the Operations Officer of the 15th S&S Battalion in 1969-1970.

Colonel Zouzalik would again be assigned to the 1st Cav. Division both as the G-4 and Battalion Commander of the 15th S&T Battalion at Fort Hood in a three-year tour beginning in 1975. Part of the time MG Julius Becton was the commander of the division when Colonel Zouzalik had both jobs. He would later make LTG and would command the 7th Corps in Germany.

The names of LTG Art Gregg and LTG Julius Becton are important because years later they would send letters of recommendation for Colonel Zouzalik to be inducted into the "Hall of Fame in the Quartermaster Corps" and this honor was achieved at Fort Lee, VA on June 5, 2015.

He commanded a Brigade (DISCOM) in the 2nd Infantry Division in Korea. The Division was under the command of MG Jim Johnson. He was then assigned to Fort Hood as the III Corps G-4. After six months, the 0-6 assignments officer stated that he was selected to command the Defense Property Disposal Service (DPDS) in Battle Creek, MI, which was a Major General position and included about 4,000 civilians and about 200 military. He left Fort Hood but the III Corps Commander was not happy. The command was spread over 227 military installations in 20 countries.

Colonel Zouzalik retired from the US Army in 1984 after 24 years of service in the Army and returned to his hometown to get involved in banking. His father and father-in-law worked for the Flatonia State Bank for many years and he would spend the next 28 years in the banking business. He got involved in the Independent Bankers Association of Texas (IBAT) and served on their Board of Directors for 14 years, including one year as chairman. He also served on the Texas Independent Bankers (TIB) board for six years.

Flatonia State Bank created a holding company and began to expand. When they had eight locations and Zouzalik was President/CEO, they merged with a bank that was also in Fayette County and created the name of State Bank. Zouzalik became Chairman of the Board due to his age and when they had 43 locations they sold to Prosperity Bancshares. Zouzalik became a Director of Prosperity Bancshares until his second retirement in 2013.

His awards include: Defense Superior Service Medal, Legion of Merit, Meritorious Service Medal, Bronze Star Medal with two OLC, Army Commendation Medal with two OLC, Air Medal, National Defense Service Medal, Vietnam Service Medal, Vietnam Campaign Medal with 60 Device, Vietnamese Cross of Gallantry with Palm, Army Service Ribbon, Overseas Service Ribbon and the Meritorious Unit Commendation.

He has been married to his wife, Jeanette, for 60 years on July 1, 2016. They have five children – Michael, John, Gregory, Brenda and Elizabeth – and 14 grandchildren.

Members of the 1st Cavalry Division Association

SP5 Raymond P. Aakjar
SSG Michael S. Aalsburg
SFC (Ret) Garroll L. Aamodt
SGT Frank L. Aamold
SPC John W. Aaron
SPC James M. Abada-O'Malley
SSG Jose Abarca
SGT Larry H. Abarr
PFC Michael Abascal
COL (Ret) Claude W. Abate
SPC Charles J. Abbey
2LT John P. Abbey
SGT Cecil M. Abbott
SGT Jesse H. Abbott
MSG (Ret) Robert E. Abbott
SPC Robert J. Abbott
CW4 (Ret) Terence S. Abbott
SGT William M. Abbott
SPC Nader Abdel Maseih
SGT Brian G. Abel
SGT Reiders Abel
CH (Ret) Steven Abel
SPC Lester W. Abele
SPC (Ret) Richard B. Abell
1SG (Ret) Allan F. Abels
SFC (Ret) Arthur Abendschein
SPC Gary R. Abernathy
SGT George D. Abernathy
SSG Donald T. Abernethy
PVT Jody C. Abner
COL (Ret) Joseph E. Abodeely
MRS. Alan J. Abraham
SFC Richard L. Abraham
SGT James E. Abram
SPC James P. Abram
SPC James W. Abram
CPL Robert Abram
CPT Timothy Abram
COL (Ret) Benjamin L. Abramowitz
SP5 Ronald Abramowitz
SFC (Ret) Herve A. Abrams
1SG (Ret) Robert W. Abrams
PV2 Miguel Abreu
CPL Francis J. Abril
SGT Charles J. Abt
CPL Ruben S. Abundis
PFC Bennar M. Acac
CPT Joseph Ace
SSG Armando L. Acevedo
1SG (Ret) Fernando Acevedo
SSG Ramiro Acevedo
SGT Ramon R. Acevedo
SGT Vincent Acevedo
MAJ Edgardo Acevedo Sanchez
SGT Shihiah R. Achmad
PFC Gerri Achtenberg
MSG Michael H. Achy
LTC (Ret) Raymond A. Acker
CPL Mark J. Ackerman
LTG (Ret) Michael W. Ackerman
SPC Richard R. Ackerman
SGT Aaron D. Acosta
MRS. Effen Acosta
MR. Luis Acosta
SFC (Ret) Osvaldo L. Acosta
SSG Priscilla M. Acosta-Barron
SSG Alfred Acovio
MSG Charlie C. Acuna
CPL Bradley D. Adair
SGT George W. Adair
SGT Anthony E. Adams
1SG Anthony W. Adams
SGT Beverly Adams
SFC Billie L. Adams
SPC Brandon W. Adams
MR. Bruce F. Adams
MSG (Ret) Charles Adams
PVT Charles L. Adams
CPL Clyde E. Adams
PFC Daniel A. Adams
PVT David Adams
SPC David C. Adams
SGT David S. Adams
MRS. Earl W. Adams
1LT Evan N. Adams
CPT Gail B. Adams
COL (Ret) Gary L. Adams
CPL (Ret) Gary L. Adams
PFC George F. Adams
1LT Guy W. Adams
LTC James R. Adams
MAJ John A. Adams
CSM John F. Adams
CPT John T. Adams
SPC John W. Adams
SPC Julian C. Adams
SGT Kevin M. Adams
1SG Larry L. Adams
SGT Leroy Adams
CPT Lonnie B. Adams
SP5 Lynn R. Adams
SPC Mathew Adams
SSG Michael W. Adams
SGT Nick R. Adams
MR. Ray H. Adams
SSG Raymond A. Adams
SGT Robert A. Adams
TSgt Robert J. Adams
SPC Robert R. Adams
SGT Robert W. Adams
SSG Rocky A. Adams
CPL Roger D. Adams
SPC Russell E. Adams
CSM (Ret) Samuel E. Adams
SGT Stephen C. Adams
SFC Stephen P. Adams
CPT Terry R. Adams
SGT Thomas E. Adams
SGT Thomas G. Adams
SPC Vester Adams
SP5 W. Howard Adams
SGT Walter Adams
CSM (Ret) Warren E. Adams
LTC William G. Adams
SGT David F. Adcock
CPT Paul Adcock
WO1 James K. Addington
SFC (Ret) Samuel J. Addison
SGT Peter Addorisio
SPC Omololu Adeyemi
SGT Scott Adie
1SG (Ret) Allen R. Adkins
SP5 David L. Adkins
CPT Eric W. Adkins
SGT James A. Adkins
SGT James H. Adkins
SGT Robert L. Adkins
SFC Scott Adkins
SSG Wilmer W. Adkins
MRS. Charles A. Adkinson
MSG Daniel Adle
SGT George A. Adler
SP5 Michael Adler
SPC Paul H. Adler
COL Ronald L. Adolphi
SGT Rodney L. Adolphson
SGT Seth Yaw Adomako-Adjei
PVT Ralph S. Adorno
SGT Neemia Afoa
SGT James D. Agan
LTC Jim Agar
SGT Robert T. Agee
SFC (Ret) Annette Agin
SSG Damon L. Agnew
LTC Jack S. Agnew
SPC Winfield S. Agonoy
SPC Brad N. Agorastos
SGT Larry M. Agosta
2LT Francis J. Agresta
1LT Hypolitus Agu
CSM Kenneth Agueda
SSG Frank H. Aguiar
SPC Aribey J. Aguilar
LT Juan C. Aguilar
SGT Kenneth M. Aguilar
SPC Reymundo Aguilar
SPC Steven A. Aguilar
SSG Matthew Aguilera
SSG Aldo S. Aguirre
1SG (Ret) Don V. Aguirre
2LT John Michael Aguirre
SPC Lorraine Aguirre
WO1 Ralph Aguirre
LTC Ralph G. Aguirre
SPC Santiago Aguirre
CPT Gerald G. Agustin
TSgt Arnold Ahders
SPC Daniel F. Ahearn
SGT James B. Ahearn
CPT John W. Ahearn
SPC Frank Ahern
SSG Fred G. Ahern
SPC Richard Ahern
SGT Robert M. Ahern
CPT Sandra Leilani Ahinga
LTC Neil W. Ahle
SFC Herman A. Aho
CPL Bill Ahrenberg
MR. William Ahrens
SGT Albert Aiello
2LT Thomas L. Aiello
SGT Lee E. Aikey
CW4 (Ret) Henry E. Ainsworth
PFC Joe R. Airsman
TSgt Aleck F. Aizint
COL (Ret) Robert B. Akam
SFC Karl Akama
SP5 Robert Akanewich
SGT Lisiate M. Akau
SPC Raymond A. Akerley
CPT Scott J. Akerley
SP5 Bud J. Akers
PVT Lance R. Akers
SSG Raymond Akers
PFC Roland T. Akers
CPT Robert C. Akervick
SGT John E. Akey
CPT Robert Akin
CPT Thomas S. Akin
SPC Thomas Akins
MAJ Amanda Akins-Vornholt
SPC Anyetei Nii Akofio-Sowah
SPC Ruben Alaniz
MR. Henry Alarid
SPC Juan L. Alba
PFC Salvatore Albanese
SGT Michael N. Albee
MAJ (Ret) Wayne C. Alberg
SPC Paul M. Albert
MR. Rallin R. Albert
SPC Richard A. Albertson
SGT (Ret) Roger D. Albertson
SPC Dennis Albrecht
SGT Travis Albrecht
SPC Otto L. Albright
LTC Robert H. Albright
SSG Ronald L. Albright
SPC John P. Albrycht
MR. John A. Alcantara
SGT Andrew Alcares
SGT Michael J. Alcorn
SSG Dana J. Alden
PFC Devin Alderman
CPL Virgil Alderman
SSG Bradley D. Alders
SSG Michael S. Aldi
LTC (Ret) Buck Aldrich
SGT Earl F. Aldrich
1SG Jonathan G. Aldrich
SGT Alex D. Aldridge
SGT Charles B. Aldridge
CPL Donald W. Aldridge
SSG Francis Aleck
1SG Alvin Alejandro
SSG Rene Alejandro
SPC David Aleman
SGT Francisco Aleman
LTC Christopher G. Aleshire
MSG (Ret) Carl T. Alessandra
SFC (Ret) Willie J. Alex
SFC Aaron Alexander
SFC Armond Alexander
SPC Brian P. Alexander
1LT David R. Alexander
SGT Delio Alexander
MAJ George Alexander
SGT Glen R. Alexander
SPC Herman K. Alexander
PFC Homer F. Alexander
SGT Hoppie Alexander
SPC James Scott Alexander
SFC Jimmy J. Alexander
SPC John T. Alexander
SSG La Tisha Alexander
SSG Leroy Alexander
SGT Lonnie D. Alexander
SFC (Ret) Michael J. Alexander
PFC Michael R. Alexander
SGT Pat P. Alexander
CPT R. B. Alexander
SSG Robert N. Alexander
COL S. Blake Alexander
SSG (Ret) Terry L. Alexander
SSG (Ret) William Alexander
CPL William Alexander
SPC Fabio Alexis
SPC Clifford R. Alexson
SSG Mario R. Alfaro
MR. Paul I. Alfaro
PVT Tony Alfaro
MRS. Richard C. Alfieri
1LT Thomas J. Alfonsi
SSG Brandon W. Alford
SFC Larry J. Alford
SPC Michael B. Alford
SGT Paul A. Alford
PFC James L. Alfred
MAJ Robert M. Algermissen
1LT Robert E. Ali
SPC John Alia
SP5 Ralph G. Aliberti
SPC Salvatore Alice
SGM (Ret) Felix C. Alicea
PFC Robert M. Alicea
MAJ (Ret) John A. Alicki
SPC Benny J. Aliroo
CW4 (Ret) John L. Allan
SFC Timothy L. Allbee
SPC Gerald L. Alldredge
2LT Jerry K. Alldredge
SSG Richard E. Allebach
SGT Robert J. Allegretti
SPC Alan J. Allen
CPL Alton M. Allen
MR. Andrew C. Allen
SP5 Ashby L. Allen
SPC Bradley C. Allen
1SG Brian K. Allen
LTC Bruce E. Allen
SPC Cecil J. Allen
SGT Charles Allen
BG (Ret) David J. Allen
CW2 David L. Allen
SSG David W. Allen
PFC Delmar L. Allen
SGT Dennis S. Allen
PFC Donald J. Allen
MR. Floyd D. Allen
SPC Frederick G. Allen
MSG Gilbert L. Allen
SPC Glen L. Allen
PFC Graham H. Allen
SGT Gregory L. Allen
CPT Harold L. Allen
SP5 James E. Allen
CPT Jerome M. Allen
SFC Justin Allen
SFC Keith Allen
SFC (Ret) Kenneth W. Allen
MAJ (Ret) Kenneth W. Allen
SGT Lance J. Allen
CW4 Leroy D. Allen
SSG Louis E. Allen
SPC Mel J. Allen
SFC Michael L. Allen
1SG (Ret) Michael R. Allen
PVT Neiman M. Allen
PFC Pamela R. Allen
SGT Robert O. Allen
CPT Samuel Allen
CPT Stanley Allen
SPC Stephen S. Allen
SGT Steve Allen
SGT Terry D. Allen
CW3 Terry M. Allen
PVT Timothy W. Allen
CW4 (Ret) Valton Allen
SFC Walter R. Allen
SPC Wendell Wayne Allen
SPC William A. Allen
CPT William C. Allen
MG (Ret) William F. Allen
SSG Zelpha A. Allen
SPC Kenneth Allenbrand
SSG Robert Allendorf
SPC Michael R. Allexenberg
1LT Jesse L. Alley
SGT Wayne R. Allgaier
PFC Danny S. Alligood
SGT Paris Alligood
SPC Stan L. Alligood
SP5 Larry K. Allin
SGT Wilmer B. Allinder
SFC Benjamin W. Allison
SGT Joseph Robert Allison
PFC Melvin R. Allmon
SP5 Myron J. Allquist
SSG Donald R. Allred
SPC William L. Allred
SPC Roy R. Allsopp
CPT Michael Allsup
CPT Michael A. Allums
SP5 Dennis D. Allward
SGT Gary B. Allwardt
GEN Daniel B. Allyn
1LT Hugh R. Allyn
PVT Richard P. Almaguer
SGT Edward A. Almanza
SFC (Ret) Arturo Almaraz
SSG Hugo Almaraz
SPC Roberto Almaraz
CW2 Edgar J. Almazol
SPC Mark B. Almendares
CW2 Michael L. Almgren
PVT Moises Almonte
SFC Frank H. Almy
MRS. Rita T. Alongi
SGT Lisa Alonso
PVT Frank A. Alonzo
SGT Kristina Alonzo
SFC (Ret) Steve Alpaugh
COL (Ret) Donald E. Alsbro
SGM Mathew D. Alsman
SPC William R. Alt
2LT David A. Altenburg
SGT Thomas Altersitz
SFC Rae M. Althiser
SPC Nicholas A. Altieri
SGT (Ret) Donald Altizer
SP5 Dennis Altman
LTC John M. Altman
PFC Warren Altman
MAJ Rob Altmann
CPL Salvatore Altomare
SFC Jose Alva
CW3 Antonio J. Alvarado
CPL Procopio Alvarado
SGT Rafael E. Alvarado
SSG Ricardo Alvarado
SFC Augusto Alvarez
SGT Enrique M. Alvarez
PFC Gilbert J. Alvarez
SSG Jose J. Alvarez
MR. Luis Alvarez
PVT Richard S. Alvarez
MR. Rolando Alvarez
LTC (Ret) Frank L. Alverson
SFC Ivan J. Alvira
PVT Marcos Alzati
CSM Chris Amagliani
CPL Giovanni Amar
SGT Dominic Amaral
SSG Richard J. Amason
PVT Louis J. Amati
SPC John R. Amato
SPC Rene Omar Amaya
SPC Sabas Amaya
SFC Elmer M. Ambat
2LT Amirah Ambekisye
CPT John W. Amberg
SP5 Frank H. Ambrose
LT G. Alex Ambrose
SPC George D. Ambrose
SSG John P. Ambrose
SPC Terry J. Ambrose
PVT Luther C. Amburgey
SGT Paul W. Amburgey
SGT Brandt Ameigh
SPC Landon Ames
PFC Larry B. Ames
1LT William M. Ames
PFC Farrell J. Ami
LTC (Ret) Richard C. Amme
SP5 Raymond W. Ammon
SPC Aubrey Ammons
SPC Christopher H. Ammons
SGT Paul F. Amnhein
SPC Michael A. Amodio
SGT Joseph E. Amos
PFC Louis Amos
PV2 Stephen R. Amos
SGT Steve L. Amos
SGT Tonna'sheka N. Amos
SPC Dale E. Amsbaugh
SPC Richard J. Amsden
1SG William L. Amundson
SPC Jichen An
PFC Daniel T. Anaye
MAJ (Ret) Leonard J. Anchor
CPT Gregg E. Anderle
SGT Sean Andermann
SGT Stephen Anders
TSgt Carl M. Andersen
SGT (Ret) Charles B. Andersen
MRS. Robert V. Andersen
SPC Andria Anderson
SPC Andy Anderson
SGT Arden E. Anderson
SFC Ashley C. Anderson
SPC Barry C. Anderson
PVT Bill E. Anderson
LTC (Ret) Bobby Tim Anderson
SFC C. B. Anderson
PFC Carl A. Anderson
COL (Ret) Cecil T. Anderson
SFC Charles Anderson
MG (Ret) Charles A. Anderson
SSG Christopher Anderson
BG (Ret) Clinton T. Anderson
SGT Craig A. Anderson
SGT Dale A. Anderson
MSG (Ret) Dan D. Anderson
SP5 David Anderson
SPC David L. Anderson
PFC Donald L. Anderson
SSG Douglas W. Anderson
MAJ Earideth E. Anderson
SGM Edward W. Anderson
CPT Eldon D. Anderson
SGT Elray F. Anderson
CPL Ennis A. Anderson
PVT Eugene D. Anderson
SGT Frank R. Anderson
MR. Gair M. Anderson
CPT Garrett V. Anderson
1SG Gary L. Anderson
PVT Gregory P. Anderson
CPT Harley B. Anderson
MRS. Hattie M. Anderson
PFC Herman Anderson
LTC Howard P. Anderson
SGT Howard P. Anderson
SSG James A. Anderson
MR. James A. Anderson
CW4 James D. Anderson
1SG James E. Anderson
SGT James Joseph Anderson
SPC James Preston Anderson
SPC Jeffrey W. Anderson
WO1 Jere D. Anderson
CPT Jesse Anderson
SPC Jim G. Anderson
SFC (Ret) Joe E. Anderson
1LT John D. Anderson
SPC John E. Anderson
SGT John F. Anderson
SFC John J. Anderson
COL (Ret) John K. Anderson
PFC John L. Anderson
SGT Keith W. Anderson
SPC Ken Anderson
PV2 Kenneth S. Anderson
SP5 Larry C. Anderson
MSG (Ret) Leroy Anderson
TSgt Les Anderson
MSG Lynn E. Anderson
SPC Marion R. Anderson
SSG Martin E. Anderson
MSG (Ret) Marvin L. Anderson
SGT Matthew A. Anderson
CPT Matthew W. Anderson
SGT Michael J. Anderson
2LT Michael J. Anderson
SP5 Myron L. Anderson
SP5 Nathaniel L. Anderson
PFC Orange L. Anderson
SGT Patrick Anderson
SFC Patrick A. Anderson
SGT Paul D. Anderson
CW4 (Ret) Peter C. Anderson
MAJ Ransome W. Anderson
SGT Richard B. Anderson
SGT Richard I. Anderson
SPC Richard L. Anderson
SPC Richard S. Anderson
PFC Robert E. Anderson
1LT Robert J. Anderson
1SG Robert P. Anderson
PFC Rodney L. Anderson
SGT Roger D. Anderson
PFC Roland Anderson

SFC Ronald T. Anderson
SPC Sydney R. Anderson
SGT Sylvester Anderson
SGT Timothy S. Anderson
MSG Walter E. Anderson
SGT (Ret) Wayne L. Anderson
SPC William H. Anderson
LTC William H. W. Anderson
SFC William R. Anderson
SGT Vanessa Andou
SGT Martin Andre
PV2 Scott W. Andre
LTC Robert G. Andree
LTC Mark C. Andres
SGT Alfred D. Andrew
CPT Robert B. Andrew
MR. David Andrews
CPL David R. Andrews
SGT Earl W. Andrews
SP5 Gary E. Andrews
SFC Henry B. Andrews
PFC Jerry D. Andrews
SPC Jimmy Andrews
SP5 John W. Andrews
SFC Robert J. Andrews
SGT Stephen P. Andrews
CPL Thomas R. Andrews
COL (Ret) William E. Andrews
SFC Arthur Andrike
LT David Andros
SPC Joseph M. Androshick
CSM Ivan L. Andrus
SGT Ronald M. Andrus
SGT Robert Joseph Anetz
SPC John P. Angaiak
CW3 Frank B. Angarola
SPC Gene E. Angell
SPC Maxwell P. Angell
SGT Joseph M. Angelo
SGT Richard F. Angelo
SPC Alexander Angeloff
SGT Igorco Angelov
CW2 Terry S. Anglesey
2LT Travis J. Anglin
SFC Ramon M. Angulo
CPT Joseph W. Angyal
WO1 Tommy Ankenbauer
SGT Robert D. Ankeney
SGT Larry R. Ankney
MRS. Robert C. Ankony
SGT Johnny Ankrom
SPC Donald E. Annala
LTC David M. Annen
CPL Anthony T. Annicelli
SPC Terry Annis
1SG Michael G. Anslinger
SGT Larry L. Anstett
1SG (Ret) Albert N. Antaki
SGT Terry G. Antee
SPC Daniel Antelo
PFC Danny R. Anthony
SPC Douglas W. Anthony
SP5 Herman Anthony
LTC James R. Anthony
SGT Lanice Anthony
MSG (Ret) Manuel Anthony
SGT Robert W. Anthony
SPC Vernon T. Anthony
CPL Eugene B. Antley
SPC Michael P. Antoncich
SPC Pasquale M. Antonellis
TSgt Daniel P. Antonietti
TSgt Frank E. Antonio
SGT Carmen Antonucci
1LT Joseph J. Antosh
SPC Wayne Antrican
LTC Richard C. Antross
SPC Richard Anuskiewicz
SP5 George V. Anzelmo
SGT Dennis Apana
MSG (Ret) Lionel W. Apana
SPC Joseph H. Aparo
SPC Ruby M. Apgwilym
1SG Ramon E. Aponte-Velez
SFC James D. Apple
PVT Larry F. Apple
LTC David N. Appleby
SFC David E. Applegate
MAJ Gregory S. Applegate
SGT John K. Applegate
LTC Larry W. Applewhite
SPC Christopher Apsey
SFC Jorge Aquino
COL Juan Q. Aquino
SGT Joseph Aragon
SSG Lucas M. Aragon
1SG (Ret) Luis M. Aragon
SSG (Ret) Richard M. Aragon
SGM Nicholas J. Araiz
SPC Jaime F. Arancibia
SGT Clovis Aranda
MR. Ignacio Aranda
SPC Roberto V. Aranda
MAJ Jose E. Aranes
MR. Edward J. Arayaes
SGT Anthony J. Arbanas
SPC Bob Arbasetti
SGM Thomas W. Arbaugh
SPC Rolando Arce
SPC Amanda Arceneaux
CSM (Ret) Leroy A. Arceneaux
SGT Roland H. Archambault
PFC Troy Archambeault
SGT Alfred Archer
CW3 Dale L. Archer
SP5 Marion E. Archer
SFC Robert A. Archer
SPC Hunter L. Archibald
SPC James A. Archibald
SPC Jay N. Archibald
SSG (Ret) Brian H. Archie
PFC Jose J. E. Archuleta
SSG Orlondo S. Archuleta
SSG Wayne Archuleta
SP5 Willard J. Archuleta
SPC Warren H. Ard
SPC Lawrence Ardoin
SPC Thomas Ardsey
PVT Eli Arebalo
MRS. Helen Aregood
MSG Fernando Arellano
SPC Maria V. Arellano
SPC Salvatore A. Arena
SFC Vincent M. Arena
PFC Aloysius P. Arend
PFC Alvin E. Arends
1LT Joel A. Arends
SFC Paul M. Arends
MRS. Harold J. Arendt
SGT Orville F. Arendt
SPC Stanley Arendts
PFC Michael H. Arett
SGT John Arevian
SFC Walter Argentieri
SGT Kenneth L. Argue
SGT Frank Arguello
PFC Marcos N. Arguello
MR. Bob Argumosa
SGT Spero G. Argyris
CW3 (Ret) Roy D. Arian
SPC Frank L. Arias
SGT Robert J. Armagno
SP5 Jesus F. Armenta
MAJ (Ret) Raymond B. Armer
SGT Samuel H. Armes
SPC Davonna E. M. Armijo
1SG James E. Armour
SSG Rickey C. Armstead
MAJ Charles S. Armstrong
SGT David C. Armstrong
LTC (Ret) Frank H. Armstrong
PFC Fred T. Armstrong
SGT Gerald Armstrong
SPC Harold S. Armstrong
SGT Jeremy D. Armstrong
2LT Joe E. Armstrong
CW2 Paul T. Armstrong
LTC Richard N. Armstrong
SGT Ronald Armstrong
SGT Roy L. Armstrong
SGT Thompson L. Armstrong
SPC Timothy M. Armstrong
MRS. Harold Arndt
SPC Ralph John Arneson
CPT William J. Arneson
PFC Chester E. Arnett
SPC Richard L. Arnett
LTC (Ret) Truman R. Arnett
LTC Rolfe G. Arnhym
SGT Barry J. Arnold
SPC Cassandra Arnold
CPT Cheryl L. Arnold
MSG Darrell T. Arnold
SGT F. Frank Arnold
SSG George H. Arnold
SGT James F. Arnold
SSG (Ret) Michael Arnold
SSG Ron Michael Arnold
SFC Scott Arnold
SGT W. Michael Arnold
SFC William M. Arnold
SP5 Robert P. Arnoldt
PFC Joseph J. Arnopel
PFC John P. Arnot
MR. Stephen A. Arntz
MRS. Curtis R. Aronson
SPC David E. Aronson
SGT Frank B. Arostegui
SSG (Ret) John W. Arp
SPC Ken Arpan
SPC James F. Arpey
PFC Vincent A. Arpino
PFC Juan A. Arredondo
SFC Domingo Arreguin
PVT Joseph F. Arrigo
CSM Rodney Arrowood
CPL Clynton M. Arrowwood
CSM (Ret) Clarence Arruda
1LT Nino Arsena
PFC John L. Arshen
SPC Tisha S. Arther
SGT Ed Arthur
SPC Hazel Arthur
SGT Richard L. Arthur
1SG Lekeith L. Artis
SSG Rose Artis
1SG Cornelius A. Arvin
CPL Miguel Arvizu
DR. Herbert A. Asch
SPC Jason Aschenbrenner
PFC Jonathan Asencio
SSG Alan J. Ash
SPC Chase N. Ash
1LT Emil J. Ash
PFC John J. Ash
SPC Michael T. Ash
MSG Larry F. Ashby
SPC Michael Ashby
SGT Rodney T. Ashby
MR. Steve W. Ashby
SPC William L. Ashby
CPT Al S. Ashcraft
SSG Chad Ashe
SGT Douglas E. Asher
PVT Harris W. Asher
CPL Norman Asher
SGT Ronald A. Ashford
SPC Nazar H. Ashjian
SSG Chandra K. Ashley
MR. Charles Ashley
MRS. Charles L. Ashley
SGT Richard L. Ashman
MAJ William C. Ashmore
1LT Donald B. Ashton
SPC Jonathan V.K. Ashton
SFC Archie Ashworth
SFC Jason Ashworth
COL (Ret) Kenton L. Ashworth
SSG Henry Askew
CPT John M. Askew
CPT Mark Askew
CW2 Byron W. Aslett
SGT Theodore C. Asp
PFC Ralph H. Aspell
MAJ (Ret) Gary W. Aspera
SPC Charles Assad
CPT Charles L. Assadourian
SGT Thomas K. Asselta
PFC Adrian Astorga
SPC Chadwick E. Aswell
CW3 Bolivar Atanasio
CSM (Ret) William E. Atchley
SPC Donald Ater
MAJ Kenneth S. Ates
SPC David J. Athas
SP5 John J. Atherton
SGT Shelby Atherton
MAJ David G. Athey
SPC Robert M. Atkeson
SSG B. F. Atkins
CPT Carl D. Atkins
SP5 Gary Randle Atkins
MSG (Ret) Horace C. Atkins
2LT Ian P. Atkins
PV2 John W. Atkins
LTC Mark Atkins
SGT Paul A. Atkins
MAJ Robert M. Atkins
TSgt William J. Atkins
PFC William P. Atkins
MSG Willie A. Atkins
SGT Edward C. Atkinson
MAJ Jason C. Atkinson
CPL Thomas D. Atkinson
LTC (Ret) Thomas J. Atkinson
CW4 (Ret) William Atkinson
1LT William F. Attardi
SGT Jack W. Attig
SPC Winifred Atwell
1LT Cheryl B. Aubas
CW2 Joseph L. Aubee
SPC Jason S. Aubin
MAJ Darrell Aubrey
1LT Nicholas Auck
SP5 Albert R. Audette
SSG Joseph M. Audia
SGT Franklin H. Aue
SPC Harry W. Auffinger
PFC Harold Augbon
1LT Harvey J. Auger
CPT John D. Auger
SPC Robert L. Auger
SPC Timothy R. Augustine
SPC Aaron Augustus
2LT Nicholas M. Auletta
LTC (Ret) Samuel W. Ault
SPC Bobby R. Aultman
SGT Paul W. Ausbun
SFC Ron Austiff
MRS. Billy G. Austin
SP5 Charles R. Austin
MSG Daniel J. Austin
SGT Gary A. Austin
CPT Gene Austin
CPL Henry A. Austin
PFC John F. Austin
LTC (Ret) Larry L. Austin
SSG Richard Austin
SGT Richard W. Austin
CSM Stephen L. Austin
WO1 Timothy R. Austin
SPC Walter B. Austin
SPC Howard Austraw
WO1 William H. Auten
LTC Edward E. Authier
PFC Nicholas D. Autin
SSG Jimmie E. Autmon
SFC Jeffrey M. Auton
SFC Charles L. Autry
SGT Carlos Avalos
SPC Mary T. Avalos
CSM (Ret) Enrique Avalo-Simo
SPC Jose Avelar
SSG Jose A. Avelar
PFC Anthony F. Avellino
LTC John B. Avera
SP5 J. C. Averett
CW2 Kindrick Averett
SSG Arthur D. Averitt
PV2 Charles E. Avery
SGT Don P. Avery
SGT Donovan Avery
SPC Jimmy D. Avery
SPC Richard Avery
SP5 Arthur M. Avila
SGT Donald M. Avila
SFC (Ret) Henry V. Avila
CPL Mark Jason R. Avila
MR. Brad A. Axell
LTC Harold Axelrod
SFC (Ret) Thomas R. Axley
PFC Abraham Ayala
PFC Elias Ayala
SGT Oscar Ayala
SPC Ricardo Ayala
SPC Victor M. Ayala-Alers
MAJ Charles L. Aycock
LTC Christopher Aycock
MAJ Michael Aycock
SGM Michael E. Aycock
SGT Fred D. Ayer
CPT Larry W. Ayers
SFC Thomas Ayers
1LT Dennis P. Aylward
1LT Julliet O. Ayodele
SP5 Paul J. Ayotte
CW2 William Ayotte
SPC Kenneth A. Ayres
SGT Delron Aytch
1SG Carlos Ayub
SGT Wayne M. Ayudan
TSgt Thomas Azar
SPC Stanley Azaravich
PFC Fred Azbill
MR. Reza Mohammad Aziz Bayat
SPC Pedro R. Azuero
CPL Francis X. Azzopardi
MAJ John Azzopardi
SGT Eric M. Baarck
SFC Billy J. Babb
SPC David H. Babcock
SPC Donald Babcock
CSM (Ret) Robert D. Babcock
CW2 Wayne R. Babcock
SPC John M. Babich
SP5 Wilhelm T. Babin
SPC Nolan J. Babineaux
MAJ Alexander Babington
SGT David A. Babinski
SGT Jerome Thomas Babor
SGT John P. Baca
SSG William S. Baca
SPC Matthew A. Bacak
CPT Clark Baccay
LT Michael P. Baccellieri
SGT Keith L. Bach
1SG Kenneth Bach
LTC Robert M. Bach
CPL Edward S. Bachar
SGT Casper D. Bachler
COL Clayton J. Bachman
CPT Chris H. Bachmann
MRS. Lyle J. Backen
PVT Ragan J. Backstrom
MR. Joe W. Backus
MSG James B. Bacon
SSG Michael R. Bacon
LTC Stanley Bacon
SSG Terry A. Bacon
CPT John P. Bacot
SPC Dan Bader
PV2 Wesley G. Bader
SGT Aileen K. Badgett
SSG Jeremy Badgett
SSG Miguel Badillo
1LT Clellon Baeder
SP3 Donald F. Baer
CPT Douglas C. Baer
SGT Bolivar Baez
PFC Frankie Baez
SFC Daniel Baeza
SGT Carl J. Bafs
1LT Durwood R. Bagby
SPC Kenneth W. Bagby
PV2 Robert Bagby
LTC (Ret) Douglas G. D. Bagdasarian
SSG Dominador A. Baggao
CPL John L. Bagge
SPC Charles Baggett
PFC Talmage S. Baggett
SGT Charles E. Baggott
LTC Chris L. Baggott
SGT Clark Bagley
SPC John M. Bagley
SPC Joseph P. Bagley
1LT Louis G. Baglietto
PFC Robert Baglin
SGT Fatoumata Bah
SPC Roger Bahls
MR. Carl B. Bahnlein
LTC (Ret) Margaret M. Bahnsen
CPL Fred D. Baier
PFC Alfred D. Bailey
CW3 Arnold R. Bailey
SPC Arthur C. Bailey
SGT Brian Bailey
SSG Charles W. Bailey
SGT Eddie D. Bailey
CPT Edward G. Bailey
SSG (Ret) James C. Bailey
CPT James E. Bailey
SFC Jeffrey P. Bailey
SPC John A. Bailey
MR. John A. Bailey
SP5 John E. Bailey
SrA John S. Bailey
MAJ (Ret) Junior C. Bailey
PFC Kenneth G. Bailey
SGT Kurt Bailey
SPC Larry G. Bailey
SPC Larry J. Bailey
1SG (Ret) Mack G. Bailey
LTC (Ret) Paul F. Bailey
SGT Phillip Bailey
SFC Raymond A. Bailey
SPC Richard C. Bailey
SGT Richard E. Bailey
SGT Richard J. Bailey
PV2 Ronald D. Bailey
SPC Thomas Bailey
LTC Thomas C. Bailey
SP5 Timothy G. Bailey
CW3 William E. Bailey
SP5 William L. Bailey
CSM (Ret) David Baillie
SSG Shane E. Bails
SPC James R. Bain
SSG Jon A. Bain
MRS. Shirley K. Bain
SGT William R. Bain
SGM Charles E. Baine
CPT Kevin Baird
CW4 Robert L. Baird
SSG Willis G. Baird
SGT Ken Baisden
SPC James Baisley
MSG Alberto Baiza
SPC Lionel Bajana
1SG Albert L. Baker
CW2 Bill Baker
PV2 Bryan Baker
TSgt Carl A. Baker
COL (Ret) Charles R. Baker
PVT Daniel C. Baker
SPC David R. Baker
WO1 Donald N. Baker
SrA Earle C. Baker
PFC Edward F. Baker
SP5 Eugene K. Baker
SGT Frank J. Baker
SGT Fredrick B. Baker
CW2 Grandyon W. Baker
SPC Gregory Baker
MR. Hugh C. Baker
SFC James C. Baker
SGT James R. Baker
SSG James R. Baker
CPL James R. Baker
1LT John M. Baker
MR. John R. Baker
1SG (Ret) Joseph C. Baker
SGT Larry Baker
MSG (Ret) Leon A. Baker
SGT Leslie L. Baker
LTC (Ret) Malcolm H. Baker
MR. Mark Baker
CPT Michael J. Baker
SGT Percy B. Baker
COL Phillip Baker
SSG Prince E. Baker
SPC Ralph W. Baker
SGT Richard Baker
SGM (Ret) Richard A. Baker
SPC Richard C. Baker
PFC Robert Baker
CSM (Ret) Robert A. Baker
CW2 Robert D. Baker
1SG (Ret) Robert W. Baker
CPT Roger C. Baker
SP5 Ronald M. Baker
SGM Rose M. Baker
COL (Ret) Rudolph Baker
CPT Scott R. Baker
SPC Steven L. Baker
MR. Terrald L. Baker
SSG Thomas V. Baker
SPC Timothy M. Baker
MSG (Ret) Tony Baker
SFC Tracey L. Baker
MR. Walter J. Baker
MSG Wayne E. Baker
SGT William Charles Baker
PFC William E. Baker
MSG William R. Baker
SGT Michael J. Bakkie
CPT Peter A. Baktis
SFC Ceny A. Balagat
SGT Jeffrey M. Balandra
CPL Apolonio R. P. Balboa
MAJ Mark Balboni
CSM (Ret) Michael M. Balch
SP5 Michael E. Balchin
SFC (Ret) H. Mike Balcombe
SGT Paul Baldassano
SSG Derrick Balderas
SPC James Balderas
SPC Armando Balderrama
MR. Leon T. Balderson
CPT Larry G. Baldridge
CPL Basil L. Baldwin
SPC David L. Baldwin
SGT Edward R. Baldwin
SGT Edward R. Baldwin
CPL Garland Lee Baldwin
SGT Larry R. Baldwin
SFC Leonard F. Baldwin
CSM Leroy Baldwin
PFC Lewis G. Baldwin
SGT Mark E. Baldwin
SPC Michael J. Baldwin
MAJ Page M. Baldwin
CW2 Reginald A. Baldwin
MRS. Robert F. Baldwin
SGT John J. Balek
SGT Robert R. Balicki
LTC (Ret) Joseph M. Balint
CPL A. C. Ball
2LT Charles E. Ball
SFC Clarence R. Ball
LTC Daniel L. Ball
SPC Delbert Ball
SGT Elgin W. Ball
SP5 Geoffrey G. Ball
SGT Harold Jess Ball
2LT James Ball
SPC James S. Ball
SGT Kenneth W. Ball
CPT Norman H. Ball
MR. William Ball
1SG (Ret) Jerry R. Ballantyne
CSM Ray E. Ballantyne
COL Christopher S. Ballard

SSG Mark L. Ballard
SGT Michael C. Ballard
CPL Walter G. Ballard
SSG Wilbur C. Ballard
LT David J. Ballenger
SGT Ronald E. Ballenger
SFC Cynthia Ballinger
PV2 Dawna D. Ballinger
1LT Peter Ballo
SGT Christopher A. Ballou
1LT Eric Balough
SFC (Ret) Walter Balsavage
MSG (Ret) Noel E. A. Baltier
MR. Niles C. Baltrusitis
PFC Jerry L. Bambauer
PV2 William Bamford
SGM (Ret) George F. Bammert
SFC (Ret) Franklin D. Bamsey
SGT Don Banaitis
SPC Douglas R. Banar
PFC Richard W. Banasiak
SSG Michael Banaszak
SP5 Emmanuel B. Banawa
SGT Tom Banda
SGT Gregory L. Baney
SPC Russell D. Bangerter
SPC John Banicki
PVT Tommie L. Bankhead
SGT Stephen T. Banko
PVT Charles J. Banks
SFC Kenneth L. Banks
SGT Larry P. Banks
SGT Jason J. Bankston
LTC Ray Banning
LTC (Ret) James D. Bannister
SGT George F. Bannon
SPC Dennis D. Banta
PFC Gildardo E. Barajas
1SG (Ret) Jesse B. Barajas
SPC Rafael Barajos
MAJ Albert J. Baraniak
SGT Michael Baranuk
SGT Frank L. Baranyai
SGT William Barba
SPC Gary L. Barbaro
SPC Alex J. Barber
SFC Cheyenne Barber
2LT Garrett Barber
SPC Jacob Barber
SSG James C. Barber
SPC James F. Barber
SGT Jeffery D. Barber
CPT Kenneth Barber
CPT Louie A. Barber
MRS. Melvin E. Barber
SP5 Michael W. Barber
PFC Paul E. Barber
SGT William J. Barber
SGT Dennis P. Barberie
WO1 Bernardo Barbero
SrA Celestino Barbero
MAJ Michael Barbero
COL Richard J. Barbero
SGT Charles Barbour
SGT Donald E. Barbour
SGT Elmon Alfred Barbour
CPT Jerome A. Barbour
CPL Joseph S. Barca
SSG Cesar C. Barcelon
MRS. Evalena Barcus
SGT Joseph C. Barcus
MR. Clair L. Bard
2LT Daniel T. Bard
TSgt William J. Bardalamas
SPC John E. Bardes
SGT Ron Bardnell
SPC Kenneth L. Bardo
PV2 Jeremiah Bardsley
CW3 David E. Bare
TSgt (Ret) Jerry Barela
SSG Michael W. Barfield
SPC Sonny D. Bargala
SGM (Ret) Gerald L. Barger
MRS. Martha Barger
SSG Bret L. Barham
CPL Richard E. Barham
SGT Frederick L. Barhorst
SGT Michael Barile
2LT Dan Baringer
SGT Dennis Barios
SFC (Ret) Delynn H. Barkdull
SFC Allen N. Barker
SFC Aussie Barker
CPL Carmont Barker
SGT Dave Barker
SPC Donald T. Barker
SFC Joe S. Barker
CPL John C. Barker
LTC (Ret) Robert L. Barker

SGT Terry L. Barker
SSG Timothy W. Barker
SGT Vernon R. Barker
SGT Cedrick Antonia Barkley
SPC Weaver J. Barkman
SPC Barry G. Barlow
MAJ Benjamin R. Barlow
SGT Bobby W. Barlow
SSG Edward C. Barlow
MSG (Ret) Ernest E. Barlow
2LT Joseph B. Barlow
PFC Jack G. Barmore
SGT Leonard W. Barnard
MSG Joseph J. Barnas
PFC Andrew J. Barnes
SGT Bruce D. Barnes
LTC Cyril A. Barnes
LTC Daniel Barnes
MAJ Daniel R. Barnes
MSG (Ret) Danny C. Barnes
SFC (Ret) David A. Barnes
SP5 David H. Barnes
SSG David L. Barnes
SGT David L. Barnes
SSG David P. Barnes
SPC Donald T. Barnes
CPL Edward K. Barnes
PFC George R. Barnes
MRS. Grady Barnes
SPC Jeremy D. Barnes
CPT Jerry R. Barnes
SGT John L. Barnes
SGM (Ret) John R. Barnes
SSG Keith L. Barnes
SPC Lloyd N. Barnes
SFC Ray A. Barnes
PVT Robert L. Barnes
CPT Terrance L. Barnes
CW2 Wesley D. Barnes
CPL William E. Barnes
PFC Carson Barnett
SGT Danny K. Barnett
CSM (Ret) Ernest Barnett
SGT Larry S. Barnett
SGT Lonnie M. Barnett
SGT Marion Barnett
1LT Michael Harrison Barnett
SGT Richard Barnett
SPC Roger A. Barnett
SP3 Sargent D. Barnett
CPT William A. Barnett
PFC Allen D. Barney
LTC Charles F. Barney
CPL Fred R. Barney
SP5 Ford H. Barnhardt
SPC Clovis E. Barnhart
SP5 Robert M. Barnhart
SPC Vernon M. Barnhouse
MSG (Ret) Franklin Barnum
PFC John A. Baron
CPT Allyn J. Barr
SP5 Gerald W. Barr
CPL Mark Richard Barr
SSG Martin A. Barr
SPC Phillip Barrancotta
1LT William S. Barratt
SGT Alejandro M. Barraza
CPT James E. Barren
MSG (Ret) Noe Barrera
SGT Raymond G. Barrera
PFC David R. Barret
PVT Bryan Barrett
SGT Carleton W. Barrett
SP3 David D. Barrett
SSG Earl W. Barrett
COL (Ret) Frederick T. Barrett
SGT James Barrett
SPC James H. Barrett
SGT James M. Barrett
1LT John L. Barrett
SPC John L. Barrett
CPL Paul C. Barrett
CPT Paul S. Barrett
SPC Ronald F. Barrett
PFC Vernon W. Barrett
SPC Wendell Barrett
SFC William Barrett
SPC Douglas W. Barrick
PVT Jeremy Barrientes
SSG Erik Barrientos
CPL Robert S. Barrientos
SP5 Roger D. Barrier
MRS. Francisco Barrios
SGT Ray Barrios
LTC Melvin J. Barrois
SGT Craig Barron
SGT David L. Barron
CSM Donald J. Barron
COL (Ret) Michael C. Barron

SFC Michael P. Barros
SGT Ronald W. Barrow
SSG Fred W. Barrowman
MRS. Arthur A. Barry
CPT Edward J. Barry
COL (Ret) John F. Barry
COL (Ret) Lawrence M. Barry
SP5 Patrick R. Barry
SPC Richard W. Barry
SSG Keith A. Bart
1LT Jeff Barta
CSM Andrew L. Barteky
SSG Tommy L. Barter
SGT Brian Bartes
MAJ Aaron T. Barth
SPC James Barth
MR. Robert J. Barth
MAJ Ken Bartholomew
SPC Bradley Bartlett
PFC Eugene O. Bartlett
SGT Marc Bartlett
SGT Robert D. Bartlett
CPT Robin B. Bartlett
SFC George M. Bartley
SSG (Ret) Arthur P. Bartol
SPC Patrick J. Bartolomeo
SFC Carl Barton
SSG Compton G. Barton
SGT Dennis P. Barton
CPT Donald Barton
SGT James Barton
TSgt James T. Barton
SGT Jeremy A. Barton
SPC Joseph Barton
SFC L. Don Barton
SP5 Manly G. Barton
SPC Randall B. Barton
SGT Robert H. Barton
CPT Ronald F. Barton
PSG Roy L. Barton
SGT Steven A. Barton
SSG Byron Bartosh
SP5 Bruce J. Bartram
SPC Vernon Wayne Barts
SFC (Ret) Wade R. Barttels
SP5 Robert T. Bartunek
LTC (Ret) Robert J. Bartusch
CSM (Ret) John W. Barvenik
SPC James R. Barzyk
SSG (Ret) Adam R. Basaldua
SGT Robert Basaldua
SGT Paul Basballe
PFC Eric Napoleon Basco
SGT Robert O. Basham
SGT Ray R. Bashaw
1LT Janny J. Basil
SGT Bobby L. Basinger
PVT Rick Baskett
SFC (Ret) Claud Baskin
SFC Archie Bass
MAJ (Ret) David Bass
SFC (Ret) David S. Bass
MRS. Evelyn H. Bass
SSG John L. Bass
MAJ (Ret) Silas W. Bass
MAJ Thomas L. Bass
SSG William W. Bass
SPC Carl S. Bassett
1LT Thomas J. Bassett
CPT Michael K. Bassi
SPC Gary Basso
SPC Gerald L. Bast
CW4 David C. Bastedo
CPL John Bastjancic
CW5 James Michael Baswell
SPC Paul D. Bataille
PFC David K. Batchelder
MSG (Ret) Clinton D. Batcheller
SPC Jay C. Batchelor
SPC Jim Batchelor
CW2 Bobby Bateman
SSG Carey N. Bateman
LTC Robert L. Bateman
MRS. Almon R. Bates
SSG Billy R. Bates
SGT Bobby G. Bates
MRS. Charles A. Bates
SGT (Ret) David L. Bates
SFC (Ret) Don M. Bates
SPC George W. Bates
SSG Jamel Bates
SSG James A. Bates
SPC Jessica Bates
PVT Jonathan Bates
SGT Michael E. Bates
COL (Ret) Phillip H. Bates
SGT Richard E. Bates
SGT Ron Bates
MAJ Ryan D. Bates

MSG (Ret) Steve Bates
1SG (Ret) Thomas Bates
SGT Thomas E. Bates
PFC James G. Batey
MSG (Ret) Noel C. Bath
SGT Darrel H. Bathurst
SGT Kenneth V. Batie
MG (Ret) John R. Batiste
PFC Bruce S. Batistig
LTC (Ret) Botond G. Batizy
SGT James F. Batman
SSG John D. Batt
COL Philip F. Battaglia
MAJ (Ret) James W. Battcher
CPT David P. Batten
SSG Michael S. Batterman
SPC Joseph M. Battiste
CSM Donald Battle
1LT Ernie F. Battle
SGT John T. Battle
SFC Kendrick M. Battle
SGT Matthew B. Battle
CSM (Ret) Morris E. Battle
CW3 Alan K. Battles
MR. Fred C. Battles
PFC David W. Batts
MAJ Randall G. Baucom
SP5 Archie A. Bauer
SGT Harold G. Bauer
WO1 Keith N. Bauer
SGT Kenneth W. Bauer
SPC Leonard E. Bauer
SGT Michael J. Bauer
SGT Michael K. Bauer
PFC Peter M. Bauer
CPT Richard L. Bauer
SrA Robert A. Bauer
SGT Timothy Bauer
PFC William Bauer
MR. Daniel Baughman
SGT Floyd F. Baughman
SGT John G. Baughman
MR. Ray L. Baughman
SSG Alan C. Baum
SFC Daniel Baum
SFC Donald C. Baum
PSG Jack Bauman
SGT Paul Bauman
LTC (Ret) Mike Baumann
COL Richard E. Baumer
SPC Mark E. Baumgardner
SPC Barry C. Baumgartner
SPC Gerardo R. Bautista
CPL Joel C. Bautista
SPC Ryan A. Bautista
CW2 Robert Bavier
SSG James D. Baxendale
SP5 Gary L. Baxman
SPC Joe E. Baxter
MR. John P. Baxter
SPC Justin Baxter
SPC Willie B. Baxter
SSG Edison R. Bayas
CPL David Bayer
SGT Franklin L. Bayer
SFC George H. Bayer
LTC (Ret) James W. Bayer
SGT Dell D. Bayles
PFC Cloman J. Bayless
CPL Francis Baylock
SGT Russell S. Bayly
SSG Michael E. Bayne
SGT William F. Bazemore
PFC Christopher Bazhaw
MR. Roger Beabout
CPL Charles F. Beach
SP5 James Edward Beach
SFC (Ret) Javone J. Beach
MRS. Howard W. Beacom
LTC Richard S. Beahm
SGT Robert E. Beal
SGT Robert M. Beal
MRS. Thomas L. Beale
COL (Ret) Bruce Beals
MR. Horace E. Beaman
CPL Richard Beamesderfer
SPC Thomas J. Beamon
PFC Charles I. Bean
SGT Dale R. Bean
MR. John L. Bean
CPT Robert E. Bean
TSgt Raul F. Beanes
SP5 Robert O. Bear
PFC Christopher C. Beard
SFC Fletcher H. Beard
SSG John R. Beard
SGT Larry J. Beard
SFC Mevil M. Beard
SGT Robert L. Beard

SGT Robert N. Beard
PFC Ronald Beard
2LT Steven Beard
SPC Nathan H. Bearden
MAJ Steven R. Bearden
LTC (Ret) Stephen G. Beardsley
SSG Howard A. Bearse
SFC Arnold R. Beasely
SGT Brandon Beasley
PFC Carlton F. Beasley
SGT Charlie R. Beasley
SSG Danny W. Beasley
SSG Jesse R. Beasley
LTC (Ret) Michael D. Beasley
CPT Thomas W. Beasley
PFC Ronald P. Beatty
MR. Jerry M. Beaty
SGM Charles H. Beauchamp
1SG James T. Beauchamp
MAJ Stephen E. Beauchamp
SGT Jason M. Beaudre
1SG Keith W. Beaulieu
SGT Thomas C. Beaulieu
CW2 Harvey M. Beaupied
SGT J. Robert Beaver
SSG William J. Beaver
SFC Buddy R. Beavers
SPC Raymond L. Beavers
CPL Timothy D. Bebee
1SG (Ret) Marco Becerra
PVT Rudy G. Becerra
SFC Paul W. Bechberger
COL Charles M. Bechtel
PVT Darlene M. Beck
SPC Frederick L. Beck
SGT James C. Beck
CPL James D. Beck
SP5 James P. Beck
LTC (Ret) John R. Beck
PVT Louis C. Beck
MR. Monroe L. Beck
1LT Robert B. Beck
SGT Stuart D. Beck
SPC William A. Beck
LTC (Ret) Charles E. Beckel
SGT Harley E. Beckelhymer
SGT Carl E. Becker
PV2 Cody Becker
SGT Dale G. Becker
SGT Daniel Becker
1LT Edward P. Becker
1LT James A. Becker
MR. Lawrence J. Becker
LTG (Ret) Quinn H. Becker
COL (Ret) Ronald C. Becker
SP5 Tyssen W. Becker
CPL Virgil H. Becker
SPC Kord M. Beckerdite
SGT Donald R. Beckermann
CPT Christopher H. Beckert
SGT Oris Glenn Beckett
CPL David L. Beckey
SPC Andrew A. Beckham
COL (Ret) Earnest A. Becking
SGT George W. Beckley
SGT Glendal M. Beckley
CW4 (Ret) Martin P. Beckman
CSM Walter Beckman
CPL Frank J. Beckmann
SPC Robert Beckom
PVT Errol B. Beckum
LTG (Ret) Julius W. Becton
SP5 George E. Bedard
MAJ Jonathan P. Beddall
SFC William Beddard
SGT Aaron T. Beddingfield
SGT Daniel C. Bedford
SPC Ryan Bedford
SGT Keith A. Bedillion
SPC Ray Bedingfield
SGT Edward A. Bednar
LTC (Ret) Gregory Pul Bedrosian
COL (Ret) William K. Bedsole
SSG Dwight J. Bedwell
LTC Ben Bedzis
SFC Robert L. Bee
MR. Howard Beebe
SP5 Paul A. Beebe
SGT Timothy L. Beebe
SGT Joseph L. Beegle
SPC Thomas Joseph Beeh
SPC Lawrence Beek
CPT James R. Beeler
PVT Charles E. Beeman
MRS. Harold R. Beeman
MAJ (Ret) Joseph R. Beeman
SGT Leonard F. Beenick
SGT Roy C. Beer
CPL Edward J. Beers

SPC Harold E. Beers
SFC (Ret) Lemoine D. Beers
CSM William B. Beever
SGT Charlysa R. Begay
LTC R. C. Begay
CPL Dennis D. Beggren
CPL Wilbur C. Beghtol
SP5 Kevin F. Begley
SGT Richard Begrin
SGT Alfred Pat Beharelle
CW4 Philip R. Behler
SGM Henry N. Behnfeldt
SPC Eric Behnke
SPC Gary L. Behrnes
SGT Dennis P. Behselich
MSG Robin A. Behymer
1LT John N. Beidler
SGT Dale F. Beierman
SSG Mark A. Beirich
SPC John F. Beirne
CPL William M. Beisel
SP5 Frank E. Beishline
PVT Gregory C. Beitenman
LTC Richard T. Beitz
SGT Manny Bejar
SPC Margarito R. Bejarano
SP5 James V. Belair
SPC Paul H. Beland
SPC Joseph A. Belanger
MR. Robert M. Belch
SGT Alan Belcher
PFC Bruce H. Belcher
SGT Chris O. Belcher
CPT Chuck Belding
SFC (Ret) Robert D. Belew
LTC Sunset Belinsky
1SG Danny G. Belk
SGT Andrew T. Bell
SGT Bruce E. Bell
CPL Calvin S. Bell
CPT Charles E. Bell
SGT Don Juan O. Bell
CPL Eddie C. Bell
SGT Gary W. Bell
CPT Gerald L. Bell
SGT Harold K. Bell
SFC Harrison C. V. Bell
PFC James F. Bell
SSG Joseph C. Bell
SPC Joshua Scott Bell
SGT Kenneth Bell
BG (Ret) Leroy C. Bell
CW3 (Ret) Leslie D. Bell
1LT Lyle Bell
MRS. Malra C. Bell
SSG Merl J. Bell
LTC Michael S. Bell
MSG Paul R. Bell
SSG Ralph F. Bell
SPC Raymond E. Bell
SGT Rosalynn N. Bell
SPC Stanley E. Bell
MSG Stephen Bell
SP5 Thomas H. Bell
SSG Thomas J. Bell
SPC Troy E. Bell
SSG Warren "Ollie" W. Bell
CPT William Bell
SGT William Bell
PFC (Ret) Jonathan D. Bella
1LT Earle D. Bellamy
SGT Richard V. Bellamy
SFC August J. Bellardine
SGT Charles E. Bellemare
PFC Jerry Bellerose
SFC Roland J. Belletete
SFC (Ret) Robert W. Bellin
BG (Ret) Mark A. Bellini
SPC Christopher S. Bellmore
SFC Tracey Bellotte
CW2 Gary A. Belmore
SGT Carl E. Below
CW2 Joseph H. Belsha
SPC Harry N. Belt
1LT Daumants Belte
SPC William C. Beltram
SGT Raul Beltran
PV2 Ruben S. Beltran
SSG Victor P. Beltran
MG (Ret) Richard D. Beltson
SSG Donald J. Belz
SGT David C. Benaides
SPC Eric Benavides
SFC Julian Benavides
SPC Keren-Happuch Benavides
1SG Juan Benavidez
LTC Darrell E. Bench
SPC Fred W. Benchwit
SGT Darrell F. Bencken

CPL Robert J. Benda
CPL Marvin Bendel
SGT Marvin E. Bendele
SP5 Frank C. Bender
1LT Richard P. Bender
COL (Ret) John C. Bendyk
SGT Gerald Benedick
SGT Bobby L. Benedict
CPT Leith A. Benedict
MRS. Richard J. Benedict
PFC Ward N. Benedict
COL (Ret) William G. Benedict
PVT Zachery Benefield
1LT Marcus Benford
SPC Michael Benham
SPC Gary P. Benjamin
SPC Matthew Benjamin
SGT Stephen L. Benjamin
MR. Matt Benn
1LT Steve M. Benner
MSG (Ret) Benford A. Bennett
SPC Chad Bennett
SFC Charles Bennett
SPC David L. Bennett
1SG David W. Bennett
CSM (Ret) Douglas W. Bennett
SSG Glenn W. Bennett
SPC J. C. Bennett
SFC Jack L. Bennett
CPT James B. Bennett
SPC Keith A. Bennett
SGT Kenneth E. Bennett
LTC Mark J. Bennett
SGT Max L. Bennett
SGM Michael L. Bennett
SFC Paul D. Bennett
1LT Robert F. Bennett
1SG Robert M. Bennett
SPC Robert O. Bennett
SFC Stevie Bennett
MRS. Will Bennett
CPL William A. Bennett
SP5 William G. Bennett
SSG William P. Bennett
SGT Craig Bennington
SGT Armond J. Benoit
MAJ Christopher P. Benoit
1LT (Ret) Clifford E. Benoit
SPC Clyde D. Bensenhaver
SSG Bill Benson
SFC Billy J. Benson
CPT Brad Benson
COL (Ret) Kevin C. M. Benson
SPC Patrick H. Benson
2LT Richard H. Benson
SPC Richard J. Benson
PVT Thomas R. Benson
COL William E. Benson
MR. Patrick H. Bentley
SSG Paul E. Bentley
SFC (Ret) Steven R. Bentley
SGT William H. Bentley
MSG (Ret) William J. Bentley
CPL (Ret) Francis Bento
SPC David L. Benton
SFC (Ret) Edward C. Benton
SGT Kyl Benton
1SG Randall B. Benton
SFC Ronald H. Benton
SGT Danny L. Bentz
SGT Glen A. Bentz
PFC Russell L. Benus
SFC Gerna G. Benz
SGT Dominic S. Beran
PFC Domenick Berardi
SGT NicoLino Berardi
MSG (Ret) Bill Bercaw
MAJ Linden J. Bercegeay
SP3 Leonard Berdal
SGT Charles B. Berg
CPT Lukas B. Berg
SPC Marshall F. Berg
MAJ Paul Berg
SGT Raymond G. Berg
SPC Stephen E. Berg
CPT Robert P. Bergeman
2LT Justin Bergen
SPC Steven C. Bergenty
PFC Andrew Berger
SPC Durien Berger
SGT Eugene P. Berger
MSG (Ret) John H. Berger
SPC Richard Bergeron
LTC Robert Bergeron
CPT Frederic A. Bergerson
CPL Lloyd L. Bergfeld
PFC Jerry Berggren
SSG Timothy M. Bergholtz
SP5 Jan L. Berghult

SGT (Ret) Wayne C. Berglund
MR. John P. Bergman
SGT Matthew P. Bergmann
SGT Gordy Bergquist
CPL Clarence R. Bergsing
CPT Brian M. Bergson
COL (Ret) Albion A. Bergstrom
SFC (Ret) Bruce A. Bergstrom
SPC Jeff Bergstrom
SGT Jerry L. Berkstresser
SGT William H. Berls
CW2 Ronald J. Bermel
SPC J. Douglas Bermingham
SPC Alberto L. Bermudez
PV2 Pasaqual Bermudez
COL Sean C. Bernabe
SPC Daniel Bernal
SPC George Bernal
MR. Edmund A. Bernard
SPC James P. Bernard
PFC Mark Travis Bernard
SGT Michael F. Bernard
PFC Rocco Bernard
SGT Thomas Bernard
1SG (Ret) William H. Bernard
SGT William J. Bernardini
SSG George A. Bernardo
SFC Roque B. Bernardo
SPC Bruce P. Bernath
SPC Raymond C. Berndt
SGT Edwin M. Berner
MRS. Betty J. Bernett
CPT Donn H. Berney
SGT Eugene C. Berney
SPC Gene Bernhardt
1SG (Ret) Luther K. Bernhart
CPT Robert L. Bernhart
CPT Steven A. Bernier
SFC Ralph G. Bernotas
SGT William J. Berns
COL (Ret) Charles P. Bernstein
SGT Thomas F. Bernstein
PFC Daniel Berreth
PVT Tobbie Berrian
PFC John R. Berrie
SSG Kenneth P. Berrios
PFC Joseph R. Berru
SGT Alan Berry
CPT Alan R. Berry
CPL Bill S. Berry
SPC Charles R. Berry
MAJ Dale W. Berry
SPC David W. Berry
SPC Gregory L. Berry
LTC (Ret) Joe D. Berry
SGT Joseph A. Berry
SPC Kenneth R. Berry
SGT Lashaun T. Berry
CW2 Richard F. Berry
1LT Robert K. Berry
SPC Ronnie H. Berry
1LT Russell T. Berry
SGT Tanya Berry
MSG (Ret) Gordon C. Berryessa
COL (Ret) Frank Q. Bertagnolli
PV2 Jonathan A. Berthiaume
MR. Gene G. Berthod
SGT Richard C. Bertola
PVT Peter F. Bertollini
SGT Charles Berton
SPC Gerald Bertone
SGT Urban G. Bertrand
SGT Leonard M. Bertuli
SPC George W. Bertz
SPC Donald J. Berube
SSG Ruben B. Berumen
SFC (Ret) James T. Bescheinen
LTC (Ret) Kenneth H. Besecker
LTC Steven A. Beseda
SGT Michael J. Beshore
SPC John E. Besk
SPC Adrian G. Bess
CSM Gary Bess
PFC Guy F. Bess
CPL James A. Bess
SFC Lyman J. Bessellieu
CPT Christopher S. Besser
CPT Nick Bessette
COL (Ret) David M. Best
SP3 John R. Best
MAJ (Ret) Joseph A. Best
PFC Joseph Edward Best
CPT Malcolm T. Best
SGT William Best
SGT Fernando Betancourt
CSM Willie J. Bethay
LTC Robert L. Bethea
MRS. Parnell W. Bethune
MR. Art Betker

SPC Anthony N. Betrus
SPC Chris Bettelyoun
SGT Anthony Bettencourt
CPL John S. Bettencourt
MRS. Fred Betteridge
SPC Aaron Betts
MSG Emerson H. Betts
SPC Paul R. Betts
MAJ Russel Betts
SPC Tom E. Betts
MR. Fred A. Beutel
SPC Sean Bevan
SPC Ronald G. Bevans
SGT Franklin N. Bevel
CPL Leo Bevelaqua
CPL Joseph J. Bever
SGT Ronald Beverly
CPL Ralph Bevins
1SG Michael P. Bey
COL (Ret) Eugene A. Beyer
SFC Michael R. Beyer
SFC (Ret) Glenn Beyerling
PFC Rebekah Beyers
COL (Ret) Terry W. Beynon
SGT Michael D. Bezdziecki
SGT Richard Francis Bezinski
MAJ (Ret) George M. Bezou
SGT Alfred M. Biagi
SPC Thomas Biagioni
PFC Michael L. Bialik
SPC James E. Bialy
1LT Matthew I. Bialy
CPT Bernardo F. Bianco
SGT Joseph R. Bianculli
MRS. Ralph Bianculli
LTC Maria A. Biank
SP5 Jerry E. Bias
SPC Rick A. Bias
SSG Philip R. Bibb
SSG Reynard Bibbins
SSG Robert J. Biberston
SGT Kenneth H. Bice
SGT Merle P. Bice
SFC Richard L. Bice
SGT Mindy Bickal
MSG (Ret) Gerald J. Bickford
SSG Vernon Bickford
SPC David S. Bickler
CPL James J. Bickley
LTC Dwyke A. Bidjou
PFC William Bidner
SPC Edward L. Bidwell
2LT John M. Bidwell
SP5 Peter Bie
SPC Carl Gustave Biebrich
SPC Arthur E. Bieker
SGT Donald M. Biel
CPT Charles R. Bielinski
SFC (Ret) Patrick M. Bieneman
CPL Albert J. Bierly
SGT Kurt Biermann
SPC Stephen J. Biernacki
SPC James O. Bierwirth
SPC Frank R. Biesel
CPT Robert D. Biestek
SGM (Ret) James W. Bieze
SGT James K. Bigbie
SGT Lisle E. Bigelow
SSG Robert C. Biggar
CPT Clinton R. Bigger
PVT Darryl W. Biggs
PFC Roy H. Biggs
SGT William S. Biggs
SPC Joseph M. Biglin
SPC Bob Bigos
LTC George M. Bilafer
LTC Gary R. Bill
SPC Ramon O. Billalobos
MR. Allen C. Biller
LTC Gary E. Billick
SPC Isaac Billie
MAJ Mathew J. Billings
PFC Gale E. Billington
SGT Keith E. Billington
CPT Bryant R. Billiot
SPC Eric W. Billman
SPC Harold J. Billow
SSG J. C. Bills
SGT Thomas N. Bills
SSG Bruce J. Billstrand
SSG (Ret) Timothy Billue
BG (Ret) William C. Bilo
SGT Francis E. Bingham
SGT Larry J. Bingham
COL (Ret) Raymond L. Bingham
SFC Chasity C. Bingley
SFC Herman Bingley
PVT Louis John Bini

CPL Billy T. Binion
PVT Harry O. Binion
PFC Mark R. Binkley
PFC Merle W. Birch
SPC Richard L. Birch
SSG Samuel A. Birchfield
SSG Adren J. K. Bird
COL Carl D. Bird
SSG (Ret) Kevin A. Bird
SFC (Ret) Lawrence Bird
SPC Martin W. Bird
SP5 Stephen W. Bird
LTC William W. Bird
SSG Tyron J. Birdsong
SGT Larry Birkett
PVT Gregory P. Birkmeyer
SGT Alan R. Bisaillon
MR. Patrick Bish
CH (COL) Brenson P. Bishop
PFC David G. Bishop
SGM Harold E. Bishop
SGT Isabel Bishop
SGT Larry J. Bishop
SSG Mark K. Bishop
SGT Peter L. Bishop
SPC Terrence L. Bishop
SSG William Bishop
SGT Gilbert Biskupski
SSG Richard Bissett
SPC Jonathan M. Bisson
SPC Robert E. Bisterfeldt
SP5 Rod Bitz
COL (Ret) Courtland C. Bivens
PFC Angelo J. Biviano
PFC Timothy L. Bixler
MR. Chester C. Black
SGT Dave Black
SPC Dennis F. Black
CW1 Donnie Black
SSG G. T. Black
SPC Henry W. Black
CPT Hugh M. Black
MRS. James M. Black
SGT James W. Black
CPT Kevin T. Black
SPC Lewis H. Black
SGT Rick Black
CW2 Ronald M. Black
SPC Shannon Black
SP5 Travis M. Black
SP5 Wayne R. Black
SPC Wilfred E. Black
COL (Ret) William M. Black
PVT William W. Black
SGT T. Jay Blackbird
SGT Gather Wayne Blackburn
MRS. Glenn G. Blackburn
SPC Joel Blackburn
SPC Raymond E. Blackburn
SGT Melvin L. Blackford
PV2 Loy E. Blackketter
SPC David E. Blackman
PVT Harvey E. Blackman
SP5 Jeffrey Blackman
SSG Keith Blackman
PVT Melvin Blackmon
SFC Willie Blackmon
SGT Robert S. Blackston-Lyons
SPC Duane Blackwelder
SPC Tony H. Blackwelder
PVT Jan D. Blackwell
SPC Marcus L. Blackwell
PFC Voren R. Blackwell
SGT Richard D. Blackwood
SGT Michael D. Bladen
SPC Larry L. Blades
CW2 Ronnie Blagg
COL Thomas E. Blagg
LTC John M. Blaine
SGT Donald D. Blair
SrA Jerry W. Blair
SPC Keith Blair
SGT Lewis P. Blair
SGT Maurice G. Blair
SGT Merl E. Blair
CW2 Scott Blair
CW4 Timothy B. Blair
CPL Winfred Blair
CPT Banaise P. Blake
CPL Clifford E. Blake
PVT Frank L. Blake
SSG Marrell L. Blake
SSG Michael Blake
SSG Paul F. Blake
COL (Ret) Phillip L. Blake
LTC (Ret) Stephen Blake
SP5 Bruce Blakeslee
SFC Robert Blakey
SPC Linwood T. Blalock

CPL Thomas D. Blalock
SGT Harold Blanc
SGT Anthony R. Blancett
MAJ Charles E. Blanchard
SP5 John W. Blanchard
CPL Larry N. Blanchard
SSG Mark S. Blanchard
2LT Matthew Blanchard
LTC (Ret) Robert C. Blanchard
SFC Israel L. Blanco
PFC Roger L. Blanco
SFC Sergio Blancomartinez
SPC David A. Bland
SSG Delbert E. Bland
SSG (Ret) Glen W. Bland
SPC John M. Bland
1SG (Ret) Ronald K. Bland
MR. Steve Bland
SPC Thomas R. Bland
SPC Chavawya Z. Blanding
PFC Charles M. Blanken
LTC (Ret) Paul N. Blankenbeckler
SGT Wayne L. Blankenbiller
MRS. Mitch F. Blankenburg
1LT Bobby J. Blankenship
SPC Clyde D. Blankenship
SPC Donnie Ray Blankenship
SPC Glenn R. Blankenship
SFC Jackie Lee Blankenship
COL Robert Leroy Blankenship
SPC Thomas E. Blankenship
CPL John M. Blanti
SSG Lawrence Blanton
SFC Tommy Blanton
MAJ Larry Blasingame
SPC Rodney H. Blaylock
PFC Robert Blechman
SPC James L. Bledsoe
CPT Jason A. Bledsoe
SFC Winfield S. Bledsoe
SFC John Blehm
COL Scott Bleichwehl
SGT Dennis D. Blessing
CPT Steven L. Blessing
CPL Michael Paul Blette
SFC Arthur L. Blevins
LTC (Ret) Dean Blevins
CPL Drexel Blevins
SGT Jerry W. Blevins
SGT Phillip M. Blevins
SPC Patrick A. Blewett
SGT John E. Bliefernich
SGT Robert W. Bline
SSG Eugene F. Blink
CPL Doug K. Bliss
CW4 Herman C. Bliss
PFC Robert A. Blixt
SGT Alan P. Block
SP5 Bob Block
SGT Cecil Edward Block
PVT Clayton R. Blocker
SSG George R. Blocker
CPT Christopher L. Blockhus
SSG Norman Blodgett
CPL Edmund S. Blome
SGT Richard Blonde
1LT Edward Bloom
CW4 (Ret) George F. Bloom
SGT Jeffrey M. Bloom
SSG Vernal R. Bloom
SGM (Ret) Malcolm Bloomer
LTC (Ret) Kenneth M. Blose
SSG Robert W. Bloss
SSG John Curtis Blosser
SFC George S. Blossingham
LTC John M. Blough
1SG (Ret) David A. Blouin
1SG George B. Blount
LTG (Ret) John B. Blount
CPL (Ret) Richard A. Blowers
LTC John R. Bloyd
SPC Lance E. Bloyd
SSG Clay P. Bloyer
CPL Daniel C. Blubaugh
SGT Arbe D. Blue
1LT Billy Blue
SPC Gilbert E. Blue
SGT Joseph C. Blue
2LT Krista M. Blue
SFC Stevie Blue
CPT (Ret) William Deer Hawks Bluestone
COL (Ret) Raymond K. Bluhm
SGT Howard W. Blum
SGT Terry R. Blumberg
MR. Joseph O. Blume
PVT Tyler Blumenstock
SPC Jim F. Blunt

SGT Michael J. Blymyer
1LT Nathan W. Blythe
SGT Coran R. Boardingham
SGT Coran R. Boardingham
PFC Charles T. Boardman
CPT (Ret) Phillip C. Boatner
SSG Marwin Bob
PFC George K. Bobbitt
2LT Joe Bobbitt
SPC Duane P. Bobby
SPC Anthony S. Bobo
SGT Timothy J. Bobula
WO1 Esteban I. Bocanegra
SPC Xavier H. Bocanegra
CPT W. Maria Bochat
SPC David L. Bock
SSG (Ret) Gilbert E. Bocock
CPL William H. Bocock
SGT Gregory R. Boddy
SGM (Ret) George C. Bode
SGT Carlton J. Boden
2LT Matthew J. Bodie
SPC Keith M. Bodine
SGT Michael Bodnar
SGT Stephen D. Bodwell
SPC Ralph M. Boeckers
MSG Robert Boeckman
CPL Richard Boedecker
MR. Richard C. Boeger
LTC Wilbur J. Boegli
CW4 (Ret) Geoffrey M. Boehm
2LT David Boehmker
CPL Paul W. Boen
SPC Johnny Boeneman
SMSgt (Ret) Hans F. Boensel
SPC John Boesch
MAJ Diane R. Boese
SPC George A. Bogan
PFC Rick Bogar
SP5 David L. Bogart
2LT Pete Bogart
SGT Rodney L. Bogart
2LT Alexander B. Bogaski
1LT Ronald C. Bogay
SPC Roger L. Bogdan
SGT Walter Bogdanovich
MAJ Michael Bogdue
SFC Junior F. Bogenschutz
SGT John W. Bogg
PFC James A. Boggan
SPC Heinrich J. Boggess
SPC Michael J. Boggess
MSG (Ret) Lawrence G. Boggio
SPC Gary W. Boggs
2LT Jay W. Boggs
SGT Leighton J. Boggs
SPC Randall L. Boggs
MAJ Everett Bogle
WO1 Jeff D. Bogue
MAJ George W. Boguslawski
PFC Thomas A. Bohall
CSM (Ret) Alfred Z. Bohannon
CPL Otto R. Bohlender
SP5 John F. Bohn
CPT (Ret) Peter N. Bohn
LTC Edward T. Bohnemann
SP6 Richard Bohnemann
MRS. Francis Bohnert
CPL Ervin L. Bohnstengel
SSG Horace Boies
SPC Gerard J. Bois
MAJ James C. Boisselle
SGT Roland Boisvert
PFC Mome Bojkovski
2LT Mainor Bojorquez
SPC Richard Bojorquez
1LT Seth P. Bokmeyer
1LT Wayne Bokorney
SPC David Bolanos
SFC Milo G. Bold
SGT Gerald E. Boldenow
SFC Lee A. Bolding
SPC Michael Bolen
CPL James E. Boles
SPC Robert E. Boles
LTG (Ret) Daniel P. Bolger
MAJ (Ret) Daniel C. Bolhouse
SGT James Bolibrzuch
SFC William M. Bolicki
SP5 Roger S. Bolin
SGT James R. Boling
SGT Skipper D. Bollar
CPT Steve C. Bolling
MR. Brian G. Bollinger
SPC Stephen Bollinger
SGT John Bolsteins
SFC James W. Bolt
COL (Ret) David E. Bolte
SGT John B. Bolton

CPL Joseph M. Bolton
SSG Kent H. Bolyard
WO1 Ryan A. Bomar
SGT Theodore P. Bombardier
1LT Vincent P. Bommarito
SFC (Ret) Fred A. Bomysoad
SGT Christopher Bonaparte
CPL Paul Bonaquest
PFC Edward Bonczyk
2LT Christopher M. Bond
SSG Curtis L. Bond
SPC Frank Bond
MAJ George E. Bond
CPT James J. Bond
LTC (Ret) John S. Bond
SPC Kenneth B. Bond
CPT Michael W. Bond
SPC Rachel Bond
SSG Randy C. Bond
COL Richard E. Bond
SPC Robert R. Bond
LTC Madeline T. Bondy
SGT Duke Bone
MRS. Joseph F. Bonetti
SFC Mathew Bonham
CPT Christopher J. Bonheim
SrA Lawrence Bonifanti
CW4 Luis Bonilla
SGT Gregory Bonine
SGT David A. Bonkoski
SP5 Henry L. Bonn
MSG Clyde Bonnelycke
PVT Randy D. Bonner
1LT Tyler Bonner
CPT Mary Eva Bonnetty
SGM Shane G. Bonney
SGT G. Raymond Bono
CW2 (Ret) William J. Bono
SPC John C. Bonse
SP5 Arnie Bontrager
SPC Frank J. Bonura
1LT Michael Bonville
SFC (Ret) Brent Boodoo
SFC Jerry L. Booker
PFC John E. Booker
CSM Robert Booker
1SG (Ret) Robert G. Bookheimer
SPC James E. Bookless
LTC Todd M. Bookless
LTC Douglas A. Boom
COL (Ret) Douglas A. Boone
CW2 Steven L. Boone
2LT Richard M. Boonisar
PVT Michael Boose
SPC Christopher Booth
MSG (Ret) Daniel T. Booth
CPL David J. Booth
WO1 Edwin D. Booth
SPC James Booth
SFC James E. Booth
CW4 James R. Booth
COL (Ret) James W. Booth
SFC John C. Booth
SPC Jonah B. Booth
COL Lance E. Booth
SPC Lawrence D. Booth
SPC Roger D. Booth
CSM (Ret) Willard E. Booth
SGT Quentin Boothe
SPC Philip L. Boots
SSG Brian S. Boozel
PFC Louis E. Boozer
SSG Kenny M. Boquin
CPT Adam Borah
SPC Mark A. Borchardt
SGT David F. Borchers
SFC Kenneth E. Borchers
SSG Douglas Bordelon
SGT Harry E. Borden
CPT Joseph L. Borders
CW2 Ronald M. Borders
SFC Peter C. Borella
SGT Jeffery D. Boren
CPT David C. Borgeson
SPC James Borgmann
SPC Thomas Borjas
SPC Gary L. Borkowski
CW4 David F. Borland
SPC Wayne T. Bormann
SGT Douglas M. Bornemeier
MR. Henry R. Boros
LTC (Ret) Marvin R. Boroski
PFC Ziggy Borowik
SPC Ronald J. Borr
SGT David L. Borrego
SGM (Ret) Weber J. Borrell
SGT Edwin L. Borsari
PFC Francis M. Borso
SPC James A. Borsos

CPT Barry C. Bort
1LT Daryl L. Bortel
MR. Larry G. Borth
MSG James W. Borum
SGT Dennis L. Bos
LTC Joseph W. Boscia
SPC Kimberly R. Bosco
SSG Larry Boshens
SFC Robert P. Bosher
SPC Craig T. Bosley
SSG Bob Bosma
LTC (Ret) Stephen F. Bosma
CPL Eugene J. Boso
SFC Reinaldo Bosques
SGT Wayne W. Boss
SPC Al B. Bosse
SGT Donald J. Bosse
MAJ Byron C. Bosshardt
MR. David L. Bost
CSM (Ret) Michael S. Bost
SPC Larry Bostick
LTG (Ret) Thomas P. Bostick
SGT (Ret) Alfred Boston
CPT Brett Boston
LTC Gerald A. Boston
SGT Jerice M. Boston
SFC Larry Boston
PVT Michael A. Boston
SGT Noah Boston
SSG Bill J. Bostrom
CPT Robert B. Bostwick
CPL Robert Berry Bostwick
PVT Kevin S. Boswell
SGT Christie Botello
SSG (Ret) Rocky Botsford
1LT William L. Bott
PFC Butch X. Bottimore
MR. John O. Botts
LTC (Ret) Stanley E. Botts
SSG Kathleen S. Botwinick
SSG Markus B. Botwinick
SGT Wickens J. Bouch
CPL George W. Bouchard
SSG Kenneth L. Bouche
1LT Dodd W. Bouchillon
SGT Patrick L. Boudreau
1LT John J. Boudreaux
MAJ (Ret) Roy J. Boudreaux
SPC Timothy Boudreaux
SPC Nathaniel Boulanger
SGT Jim Boulden
SGT Ronald Bouley
SPC David R. Bourbeau
SPC Don E. Bourcier
MRS. Elvis Bourdon
WO1 Jason Bourdon
SFC Dan Bouren
SPC Eugene F. Bourgeois
MR. J. E. Bourgeois
SSG John H. Bourgeois
CPT Mark Bourgery
SPC George Bourliea
LTC (Ret) Harold O. Bourne
SPC Lynn L. Bourne
SGT Frank E. Bovee
CW2 James Bowden
SFC Aaron S. Bowen
PV2 Barrett H. Bowen
CPT Gregory W. Bowen
SGT James F. Bowen
SGT James R. Bowen
COL (Ret) Joseph S. Bowen
SFC Paul M. Bowen
SPC Richard W. Bowen
SGT Stefen Bowen
SGT Thomas O. Bowen
PFC Tony W. Bowen
CPT William S. Bowen
SGT Alan Bower
1LT David L. Bower
SGT Ivan Bower
SPC Larry Bower
SPC William J. Bower
PV2 Charles L. Bowers
SSG Jack E. Bowers
MAJ (Ret) James J. Bowers
SFC John M. Bowers
CPL John N. Bowers
SGT Kurtis Dane Bowers
CPL Michael Bowers
SPC Owen Richard Bowers
SSG Richard C. Bowers
1LT Victor J. Bowers
PFC (Ret) Wallace C. Bowers
PFC Michael Bowersox
MAJ Catherine Mary Ann Bowery
SSG (Ret) Donald B. Bowes
1LT Charles Bowie

MSG Fred R. Bowie
SGT Michael W. Bowie
SGT Garry Bowles
1LT John Bowles
CPL John F. Bowles
MR. Robert J. Bowles
SSG Wayne A. Bowles
CSM (Ret) Clifford R. Bowlin
CPT Andrew Bowling
PFC Charles E. Bowling
MR. Dennis “Rob” Robert Bowling
CPL A. Jimmy Bowman
CW1 Bernard J. Bowman
SSG Carter R. Bowman
2LT David J. Bowman
LTC Donald C. Bowman
SSG Gary D. Bowman
SGT Gordon E. Bowman
SFC Jim Bowman
SGT John W. Bowman
SGT Mary M. Bowman
PFC Michael L. Bowman
SMSgt (Ret) Steven J. Bowman
MRS. Vera Bowman
SFC William B. Bowman
SGT Benjamin A. Bowser
PVT Lawrence A. Bowser
SGT Philip A. Bowsher
2LT Joseph H. Box
SPC Barbara Boxley
SSG Clifford R. Boxley
SGT (Ret) Gene E. Boxx
1LT William J. Boyan
CPL Edward F. Boyce
SFC Mark Wiley Boyce
PVT Mary Elaine C. Boyce
SFC Ben Boyd
SPC Dwight D. Boyd
SFC Gean G. Boyd
CPT George F. Boyd
SPC Jackie L. Boyd
PV2 James P. Boyd
CSM (Ret) Jess W. Boyd
CPT John F. Boyd
SPC Jonathan Boyd
2LT Samuel J. Boyd
SPC Thomas E. Boyd
PFC William Boyd
CPT Kunio F. Boydston
SGT Ken Boyer
SPC Richard W. Boyer
SGT Wendell C. Boyer
SGT George M. Boyette
SGT John M. Boyette
CSM (Ret) Kim D. Boyink
SSG James W. Boykin
SFC William P. Boykin
SFC John Boyle
COL Patrick J. Boyle
SPC Ray N. Boyle
SGT William R. Boyles
1LT John T. Boyt
SP5 Gerald D. Bozarth
SGT Andrew G. Bozeman
PFC Robert D. Bracci
CW3 (Ret) James P. Bracewell
CPL Robert E. L. Bracewell
CPL Charles A. Bracey
CSM (Ret) Donald Bracht
SFC Jacob Brack
SSG Harry Bracken
SPC James M. Brackett
SSG Nicholas B. Brackett
SGM Chuckie Brackins
MSG Billy W. Bradberry
SGT Charles Bradberry
SSG Michael Scott Bradberry
SGT Heiner G. Bradburn
SGT Marshall E. Bradburn
SGT Richard E. Bradbury
PFC Dwight Braden
SSG Paul R. Braden
MR. Thomas H. Braden
CW2 James Braderman
SGT George E. Bradfield
SSG Antonio Bradford
SPC Clarence K. Bradford
SFC Raven Bradford
SPC Darcus Bradley
LTC Darryl M. Bradley
SSG Desiree D. Bradley
SFC Dominic P. Bradley
MAJ John B. Bradley
LTC Kevin D. Bradley
MAJ Kevin N. Bradley
MAJ Larry R. Bradley
SPC Michael Bradley
SGT Michael J. Bradley

SGT (Ret) Mitchell L. Bradley
MSG (Ret) Nedom E. Bradley
SPC Richard R. Bradley
2LT Tiffany Bradley
MSG (Ret) William Dave Bradley
CW4 (Ret) Peter Bradsell
SPC Danny Bradshaw
PVT Jason Bradshaw
SGT Levi Bradstream
PVT Albert W. Brady
CPL Archie M. Brady
SGT Barry Brady
MR. James R. Brady
MG (Ret) Morris J. Brady
SGT Randy Brady
SGT Sye Brady
SSG Terence Patrick Brady
SPC James L. Braga
LTC (Ret) Rexford T. Bragaw
MR. Danny E. Bragg
CPT Earl G. Bragg
MAJ Keith W. Bragg
1LT Stephen J. Bragg
SGT James A. Bragger
PV2 Jeffrey R. Braggs
SPC Terence M. Brain
SGT Michael D. Brainard
1LT Michael C. Braine
SSG (Ret) Tracy Braley
SP5 Richard W. Braly
COL (Ret) Eric W. Braman
CW3 Patrick D. Braman
CPT Thomas J. Bramanti
SGT James L. Bramble
SGT (Ret) Edward A. Brambrick
BG (Ret) James T. Bramlett
SGT Nicholas E. Brammeier
SP5 Jack G. Branam
SPC Jim Branan
CSM (Ret) Terry A. Branan
SGM (Ret) Thomas A. Branard
2LT Anthony Brancato
SGM (Ret) Bernard C. Branch
SFC Caleb Branch
TSgt Clinton L. Branch
SPC Destry Branch
MAJ Jackson A. Branch
SSG Michael E. Branch
1SG Robert L. Branch
SFC Anthony M. Brand
SPC George R. Brand
1SG (Ret) Ira Brand
CPL Joel Brand
MR. John H. Brand
SPC Billie L. Brandenburg
SSG James K. Brandenburg
SGT Robert F. Brandenburg
COL (Ret) Bruce D. Brandes
SGT Robert N. Brandin
SPC Ronald Y. Brandl
SSG George L. Brandon
1SG Daniel C. Brandt
WO1 David H. Brandt
SFC (Ret) Don C. Branford
MAJ Marvin E. Branham
SFC Omer T. Branham
SGT Michael S. Brannan
MSG Dennis J. Brannon
SPC Devon Brannon
SGT Homer Brannon
MAJ (Ret) Joe Brannon
SSG Tom Brannon
SPC Elbert G. J. Branscum
SPC Joe Don Branson
SPC Carl R. Branthoover
MR. Bobby T. Brantley
MRS. Heidi K. Brantley
SSG Randall E. Brantley
SSG Max H. Branyon
SPC Ronald Brasfield
SGT Stephen A. Brasher
SP5 Claude M. Brashier
SPC Anthony Brasile
SFC (Ret) Hubert L. Brast
SPC Oscar L. Braswell
MAJ (Ret) Vernon S. Braswell
SFC Kenneth F. Bratcher
CMSgt (Ret) George A. Bratina
PFC John C. Bratland
CPL De Loris E. Braton
MAJ Magnus Bratt
CW2 Bruce D. Brattain
SGT Steve Brattis
SPC Hilmar R. Braun
SGT James E. Braun
SP5 James M. Braun
SGT Paul Braun
SPC Dirk R. Braune

1LT Paul F. Brauneis
SFC Edward P. Bravchok
SSG Angel A. Bravoserrato
SGT Bob Brawdy
SP5 Charles W. Brawn
PFC Perry Braxton
SGT Vernon T. Bray
SP5 Lanny M. Braybrook
PFC Trevor Braye
SFC Brian S. Brazee
SGT Edward E. Brazelton
CPT Daniel S. Brazil
SFC Roboam Brea
SFC Pearlise J. Breaux
SSG Pierre P. Breaux
SGT Thomas L. Breaux
SFC Inger Breaux-Sherman
CPT (Ret) Truitt D. Breazeale
CPT T. Ulrich Brechbohl
SPC Jeremy J. Brecken
SPC John R. Bredahl
1LT Fred L. Bredhoeft
CPT Harry M. Breeden
SGT Sherman Breeden
SFC (Ret) Howard C. Breedlove
SPC Darren K. Breen
SGT James F. Breen
1SG (Ret) Joseph B. Breen
SFC Richard L. Breiding
MAJ Benny Breimar
SSG Chad Breit
SGT Paul G. Breitfeld
SSG Jamal Breland
SGT Charles L. Bremer
1LT James Breneman
CW4 (Ret) Joseph P. Breneman
SFC Edward Brennan
PFC Erica Brennan
MSG (Ret) James J. Brennan
CW4 (Ret) James P. Brennan
COL (Ret) Michael J. Brennan
1LT Patrick J. Brennan
1LT Thomas J. Brennan
SFC (Ret) Marcel F. Brenneis
CPT Franz Brenner
SPC (Ret) John A. Brenner
SGT John W. Brenner
SGT Robert W. Brenner
MR. Geoffrey W. Brereton
1LT (Ret) Arthur W. Bresciani
SP5 James W. Breslain
SGT David A. Bresnahan
2LT Albert R. Bresnik
PFC Otto Bresocnik
MAJ (Ret) Edward F. Bressinck
1LT Edward J. Bresson
SPC Calvin Brett
CSM George M. Brett
COL (Ret) Thomas H. Brett
SPC George W. Bretz
SGT Norman Bretz
1SG (Ret) Larry J. Breukelman
PVT Sherrick Brevard
MAJ (Ret) Alvie L. Brewer
CW4 (Ret) Casto Leland Brewer
CH (COL) Dewayne L. Brewer
LT Donald U. Brewer
SGT Forrest W. Brewer
SP5 Jerry Jason Brewer
SGT John W. Brewer
SGT Joseph Brewer
SP5 Randell J. Brewer
SGT Richard H. Brewer
TSgt Theressa K. Brewer
SFC Thomas E. Brewer
MAJ Howard K. Brewington
MSG Christopher Brewton
PV2 Richard R. Breyman
CPT (Ret) Adrian B. Brian
PFC Bernard C. Brice
PFC Brian D. Brice
SSG (Ret) Alejandro L. Briceno
SPC Brian Brickey
PFC Kenneth D. Bridge
SSG James Bridgers
SPC Larry V. Bridges
BG Mike Bridges
SSG (Ret) Ronald C. Bridges
PFC Stacey M. Bridges
PFC Edward Bridgett
CPT Lyndell Bridgewater
SGT Frank T. Brigantino
SFC Christopher Brigdon
CPL Arnold Briggs
LTC (Ret) James B. Briggs
SGT Kenneth M. Bright
SPC Shural J. Bright
SGT Ray Brightman
MR. Alessandro Brignole

CPL Joseph M. Brignolo
SGT Chester D. Brilowski
LTC (Ret) Douglas L. Brimmer
MR. Michael E. Brinchek
SGT Jordan Brindley
SFC James Brinegar
SGT Kent D. Bringhurst
SGT Gerrit J. Brink
1SG Mickey J. Brinker
PFC Glenn Brinkley
SFC Henry D. Brinkley
MAJ (Ret) Steven E. Brinkman
SPC James J. Brinkworth
PV2 Burnie G. Brinn
CPL David O. Brinson
SFC Eldred D. Brinson
SPC Joe Nathan Brinson
SPC Loren Brinson
SGT George F. Brinton
CPT Juan Briones
SPC Linwood J. Brisbane
CSM (Ret) Byron Briscoe
SPC Robert T. Briscoe
SGM Javier Briseno
SGT Robert E. Brison
COL (Ret) Alan A. Brister
1SG Donald D. Brister
SPC Micah Jon Bristol
SGT Travis Bristol
CPT David Briten
SGT James E. Britt
SPC John Wesley Britt
LTC (Ret) Ronald E. Britt
SPC Kenneth P. Brittain
SPC Timmie O. Brittan
SP5 Richard T. Brittsan
SSG Eric A. Brixius
CPT (Ret) Robert Broadnax
LTG (Ret) Colby M. Broadwater
PV2 Darnell Broadwater
SSG Donald R. Broadwater
SFC William H. Broadway
MRS. Beverly L. Brock
CSM (Ret) Freddie L. T. Brock
SPC Kenneth W. Brock
SGT Mark L. Brock
SFC Vincent E. Brock
CPT Walter R. Brock
LTC Doug Brockhard
CW3 Robert F. Brockington
CPL Bernard A. Brockling
SGT Lloyd J. Brockney
MRS. Glenda Broderick
1LT Jared A. Broderick
CPT Matthew A. Broderick
CPL Thomas A. Broderick
PFC Gregory A. Brodeuer
CSM (Ret) Albert J. Brodeur
SFC (Ret) James F. Brodie
SSG Dan Brodt
SPC Mark L. Broeffle
SPC Robert L. Broeker
COL (Ret) Duane R. Brofer
SGT John G. Brogan
SFC Scott T. Brogan
SPC Shawn M. Brogan
CW2 Paul B. Bromley
SGT David Bromm
SSG Frederick L. Bromwell
CSM (Ret) Gilbert Broner
PFC (Ret) Edwin R. Broneske
SPC Stephen Bronke
SSG Leon B. Bronson
SGT Philip M. Brooker
SSG Bernie Brooks
COL (Ret) Billy T. Brooks
SP5 Bobby W. Brooks
1LT Brian S. Brooks
SFC Danny R. Brooks
SPC David A. Brooks
SPC Dennis Brooks
SPC Douglas A. Brooks
MR. Gary Brooks
MSG Gene D. Brooks
CPT (Ret) Jerry R. Brooks
SGT Kenneth A. Brooks
2LT Lamont Brooks
LTC Paul T. Brooks
SFC Philip E. Brooks
SPC Robert V. Brooks
CW2 Robert W. Brooks
SGT Stephen F. Brooks
SP5 Steve Larry Brooks
MR. Thomas M. Brooks
MR. Thurman S. Brooks
SPC Tom R. Brooks
SPC William Brooks
PFC Willie K. Brooks
COL Winston P. Brooks

SSG Horace F. Broom
SGT Johnny S. Broomas
1SG (Ret) Lee E. Broome
SPC Gerald Broomfield
LTC (Ret) Stephen B. Broomfield
SGT Edward Brosky
PVT Robert E. Brosnahan
CPT (Ret) Patrick J. Brosnan
LTC (Ret) Stephen W. Bross
SPC Andrew Brosseit
CPL Gerhard C. Brostrom
PFC Andrew B. Brothers
SGT Robert Brothers
SGT Robert H. Brothers
SPC Ralph E. Brotherton
LTC Mervin G. Brott
SSG Harvey A. Brough
SPC John Brougham
1LT Robert L. Broughton
SFC William Henry Broughton
COL (Ret) Douglas S. Brouillette
SSG (Ret) Paul E. Brouillette
SFC (Ret) Thomas F. Brouse
SPC Cecil W. Broussard
MAJ David Broussard
PFC Raymond M. Broussard
CPL Ray J. Broussard
SPC Bruce F. Browder
SGT Richard J. Brower
SGT William M. Brower
1LT Aaron Brown
MR. Abraham Brown
PFC Alexander Brown
SPC Allen Brown
SPC Allen J. Brown
MAJ (Ret) Allen S. Brown
CPL Amos J. Brown
SSG Arthur M. Brown
MSG Bernard B. Brown
LTC Billy C. Brown
SFC Bobby Brown
SGT Cal W. Brown
SGT Carl A. Brown
CPT Charles Brown
SPC Charles A. Brown
PFC Charles E. Brown
SPC Charles L. Brown
MG (Ret) Charles P. Brown
SSG Charlie Brown
SFC Christopher Brown
CPL Cletus V. Brown
CPL Clyde D. Brown
SGT Courtney D. Brown
SGT Daniel A. Brown
PFC Daniel P. Brown
CPT David A. Brown
MAJ David M. Brown
MSG (Ret) David P. Brown
SP5 David P. Brown
SFC Deborah Brown
MR. Delmar C. Brown
SGT Dennis A. Brown
SGT Dennis H. Brown
SPC Diana M. Brown
SPC Dock H. Brown
SPC Douglas E. Brown
LTC Edmond M. Brown
MR. Edward Brown
SGT Edwin L. Brown
SPC Eric Edward Brown
CPT Eric J. Brown
SP5 Forrest E. Brown
CPL Frank Brown
CPT G. Alan Brown
SSG Gale Brown
CPL Garold L. Brown
SP5 Gary L. Brown
LTC (Ret) Gene E. Brown
SP5 George R. Brown
SGT Gerald Brown
SPC Gerald E. Brown
SPC Hardy D. Brown
TSgt Harold Wilson Brown
SPC Harry G. Brown
PFC Harry W. Brown
CSM Headirick Brown
SSG Henry A. Brown
SFC Hero M. Brown
COL (Ret) Howard F. Brown
SP5 Jack M. Brown
SPC James Brown
SGT James A. Brown
SGT James E. Brown
SSG (Ret) James H. Brown
MAJ (Ret) James L. Brown
LTC (Ret) James L. Brown
LTC James M. Brown
CPT James R. Brown
SSG James T. Brown

SPC Jared M. Brown
1LT Jeffrey W. Brown
CPT Jeffrey W. Brown
SPC Jeremy W. Brown
PFC Jessie F. Brown
SGT Jimmie L. Brown
SFC (Ret) Joan Brown
1LT Joel R. A. Brown
PFC John Brown
MSG John A. Brown
SGT John H. Brown
SGT Jonathan Brown
PFC Kenneth T. Brown
PFC L. David Brown
CW3 Lach I. Brown
COL (Ret) Larry G. Brown
SGT Larry R. Brown
CPL Lawrence E. Brown
MSG (Ret) Leonard J. Brown
PFC Leslie R. Brown
SPC Lloyd E. Brown
MAJ Melvin Brown
CPT (Ret) Michael A. Brown
1SG Michael D. Brown
PFC Michael D. Brown
SFC Michael L. Brown
SP5 Michael L. Brown
PFC Michael L. Brown
PFC Michael R. Brown
LTC (Ret) Milt Brown
LTC (Ret) N. G. Brown
SFC Nancy Brown
PVT Noel Simeon Brown
SSG Oscar L. Brown
PVT Oscar Wayne Brown
LTC Otis L. Brown
SGT Paul F. Brown
SGT Paul J. Brown
PFC Phillip A. Brown
CPT Randal Edward Brown
SPC Raymond Brown
SGT Raymond H. Brown
CPL Richard R. Brown
SPC Robert L. Brown
TSgt Robert L. Brown
SGT Robert L. Brown
SGT Robert Michael Brown
PVT Robert S. Brown
SGT Robert S. Brown
PFC Rodney G. Brown
SGT Rogelio F. Brown
SPC Roger L. Brown
SPC Roger L. Brown
SGT Ronald B. Brown
SSG Ronald Dean Brown
SP5 Roy A. Brown
SGT Roy C. Brown
SFC (Ret) Samuel B. Brown
CPL Samuel E. Brown
CSM (Ret) Stanley A. Brown
SGT Stanley H. Brown
SSG Stephan Brown
SGT Stephanie Brown
CPT Stephen M. Brown
CW2 Stephen P. Brown
SGT Terry E. Brown
1LT Timothy B. Brown
SP5 Timothy J. Brown
SPC Tobias Brown
SGT Tom R. Brown
MSG Torrence T. Brown
SGT Walter Brown
SPC William Brown
LTC William A. Brown
SFC William D. Brown
SFC (Ret) William Edward Brown
CPT William R. Brown
SFC Willie A. Brown
SFC Zamain D. Brown
SGT Donald A. Brown-Denning
MSG Ann S. Browne
SFC Linda D. Browne
CPT William Brownell
MR. Clearn Browning
SSG Lynn J. Browning
SFC (Ret) Randall J. Browning
LTC (Ret) Richard R. Browning
PFC Michael Brownlee
PFC Milton Brownlow
MSG (Ret) Sylvia R. Brownlow
SSG Jimmy L. Broyles
SPC Daniel E. Brubaker
1SG Brian W. Bruce
SPC Clarence L. Bruce
SGT Mario A. Bruce
SFC Shaun T. Bruce
SPC Zane Bruce
SGM Lewis W. Bruchey

CPL Garry Bruckner
SGT Eugene H. Brueckner
PFC Ronald C. Bruellisauer
SGT Milton E. Bruemmer
CPT Gerald P. Bruening
CPT Carl E. Bruer
CPL Joseph A. Bruesch
PV2 John S. Bruggeman
MRS. Carl F. Brugmann
SSG Christopher E. Brumback
LTC Timothy A. Brumfiel
SSG Randall D. Brumfield
CPT Tyrone T. Brumfield
CW4 (Ret) Garl Brumit
SFC Newman W. Brumlow
SP5 William P. Brumme
SPC Bewel J. Brummett
SPC Coy P. Brummett
SFC (Ret) John S. Brunato
MS. Erma Brunckhorst
SFC Jeffrey S. Brundage
COL (Ret) Warren H. Brune
CPT Thomas Bruneau
SGT Bruce N. Bruner
SSG Don W. Bruner
SGT Kieth Bruner
SGT Danyel Brunger
SSG Edward W. Bruning
SPC Joseph D. Bruning
SGT Thomas C. Brunkow
SGT Harry J. Brunn
CPL Charles Bruno
SP5 Gary M. Bruno
SP5 Tom Bruno
SFC Jack O. Bruns
SSG Arthur L. Brunson
SFC Timothy A. Brust
PFC Richard R. Brustowicz
SPC Adam Bruton
SSG (Ret) Arthur L. Bryan
PFC Billy Bryan
SGT Claiborne Bryan
CW4 Daniel Bryan
MRS. Don C. Bryan
SPC Edward M. Bryan
SPC Jerry R. Bryan
SGT Jouanna S. Bryan
SP5 Ronald F. Bryan
MAJ (Ret) Charles E. Bryant
SSG Cynthia Bryant
SGT David Bryant
CPL Edward L. Bryant
SSG Gregory W. Bryant
CPL Harold J. Bryant
MR. James A. Bryant
SGT James E. Bryant
MAJ James W. Bryant
SGT Joe M. Bryant
SGT John Bryant
SPC Joseph A. Bryant
SPC Larry G. Bryant
SPC Louis Bryant
SSG Martin L. Bryant
SGT Michael P. Bryant
1LT Roberts S. Bryant
CW2 Roland Bryant
SGT Stephen Bryant
MAJ William O. Bryant
SGT Willie Bryant
SP5 Addie M. Bryant-Pinckney
SPC Joshua Bryars
MSG Joe H. Bryce
SGT Marc T. Brydges
DR. Harold S. R. Brydy
SP3 H. Bob Bryman
SFC Ryan L. Bryner
CH (LTC) (Ret) George T. Bryon
SSG David A. Bryson
SPC John S. Brzozinski
SPC David Brzozowski
SGM Francis J. Brzyski
SFC Thomas F. Bubanich
1LT Frank J. Bubb
SFC (Ret) John L. Bubela
PVT Mark A. Bubendorf
SGT Barry N. Bucchioni
1LT Anthony C. Buchanan
SGT Bobby W. Buchanan
CPL Bruce G. Buchanan
PFC Clarence Buchanan
COL (Ret) Crawford Buchanan
SFC Howard A. Buchanan
SGT Percy F. Buchanan
SPC Samuel R. Buchanan
SSG Brandon Bucher
SGT John Bucherich
SPC Michael Buchinski
SPC Robert Bucholtz
COL Todd A. Buchs

SP5 Frank S. Buchvalt
PFC Carlos Bucio
SFC Anthony Ray Buck
MAJ Chris Buck
PFC Greydon L. Buck
MSG (Ret) Howard J. Buck
SFC Paul R. Buck
SFC Wesley H. Buckalew
SPC Preston Buckallen
CW4 (Ret) Steven A. Buckey
SP5 Paul Buckholdt
MR. Kenneth M. Buckler
CW4 Gary Buckles
SFC Arthur W. Buckley
COL (Ret) Benjamin C. Buckley
SPC David Buckley
SPC Gary J. Buckley
SSG James J. Buckley
SFC Joseph C. Buckley
MRS. Silas T. Buckley
LTC (Ret) James L. Buckner
SSG (Ret) Larry J. Buczinski
SP5 Arthur J. Budek
SPC Brandon D. Budfuloski
MG (Ret) Larry D. Budge
SGT John Budlong
SGT Steven D. Budnick
SPC Terry L. Budreau
SSG Andrew John Budzina
MR. Dennis Budzinski
SPC Lawrence E. Buehner
MR. Donald Buehrly
PV2 Javier Buendia
1SG Jose C. Bueno
SPC Robert C. Buenzly
SSG Steve Buero
SSG Rodney Buffaloe
SPC John D. Buffer
MSG Paul O. Buffington
SFC William J. Buffton
SPC Ralph Bugamelli
SGT Jerry J. Bugenski
SrA James D. Bugher
CPT Carl M. Buick
SP5 Edmund Buis
SFC Rickey E. Buis
SFC Ruben Buitron
SPC Michael J. Bukovcik
LTC (Ret) Robert J. Bukowczyk
SP5 Lawrence J. Bukowski
1LT Edward Bulewich
CPL Gerald Bullard
CSM (Ret) Howard Bullard
SFC (Ret) Robert L. Bullard
SPC Wayne B. Bullard
SGT Lee R. Bulleigh
SSG Diane Bullington
SPC Emmanuel S. Bullo
1SG Jennifer Diana Bullock
LTC (Ret) John H. Bullock
SPC Louis Bullock
SGT Michael Bullock
SSG Robin Bullock
PFC Sammie L. Bullock
BG (Ret) Roger C. Bultman
SGT Richard Bulvid
SSG Ronald Bumann
1SG (Ret) Wallace R. Bumbalough-Polk
SGT Arthur C. Bumgardner
SSG (Ret) Crystal E. Bumgardner
SPC Stephen G. Bumgarner
1LT Gary R. Bunch
LT Shaunta Bunch
PV2 Kenneth W. Bundrum
CSM George E. Bundy
SGT Harvey Bundy
PFC William B. Bunes
SGT John H. Buneta
SPC Galen Bungum
MR. Dean L. Bunnell
SGT Ronald Bunston
CPT Jay Bunte
CPT Charles Buntin
SGT Ronald K. Buntin
SPC Charles Bunton
SSG Charles F. Bunyard
LTG (Ret) Jerry Max Bunyard
CPT Paul P. Buonaccorsi
SGT Johnson A. Buquet
GEN (Ret) Edwin H. Burba
CPT Howard N. Burbank
SGT Samuel Burbank
SPC David Burch
MRS. Elfriede R. Burch
BG (Ret) Harold E. Burch
COL (Ret) John C. Burch
SFC Ronald M. Burch
COL (Ret) Jerry J. Burcham

PSG (Ret) Francis J. Burchick
LTC Marland J. Burckhardt
SSG Charles E. Burden
SPC Ennis Burden
MAJ (Ret) Wyndell E. Burden
BG (Ret) William B. Burdeshaw
SGT C. Ray Burdette
SFC Marion O. Burdette
SFC Gene A. Burdick
MR. Richard O. Burdick
SPC Robert Burdiss
CPL David D. Burds
PFC Jack C. Burdsall
SGT Kenneth W. Burdwood
SPC David Burdyck
CPT Matthew M. Buretz
SGT John M. Burford
CSM (Ret) William Burford
LT William B. Burford
SPC Clarence L. Burgan
SPC Bruce B. Burgar
SPC John Charles Burge
SGT Leanne M. Burge
SSG Paul Burge
CPT Robert P. Burge
LTC Eric Burger
LTC Addison Burgess
SPC Clyde E. Burgess
SPC John W. Burgess
1SG Kerry A. Burgess
SGT Lee Burgess
SFC (Ret) Leroy Burgess
SPC Paul C. Burgess
SPC Steven N. Burgess
1SG (Ret) James A. Burgin
SPC John H. Burgner
CPT Matthew W.P. Burgoon
SGT Kenneth D. Burington
CPL Arnold R. Burk
LTC Stephen A. Burk
SSG (Ret) Andrew H. Burke
LTC (Ret) Christopher J. Burke
SGT Gaumal O. Burke
SPC (Ret) Henry J. Burke
SGT Johnny J. Burke
SPC Kevin J. Burke
SP5 Kirby Burke
SPC Michael Burke
MSG Patrick M. Burke
COL (Ret) Paul F. Burke
MRS. Pierce J. Burke
SPC Raymond D. Burke
CPT Richard K. Burke
SFC Robert E. Burke
SGT Ronald Burke
SPC Steve Burke
SGM (Ret) Steven T. Burke
MAJ (Ret) David H. Burkes
SPC Allen W. Burkett
SGT James F. Burkett
MAJ Ray W. Burkett
LTC Robert P. Burkey
SFC Charles W. Burkham
SGT Bill Burkhard
SPC John B. Burkhardt
SGT Robert James Burkhardt
LTC William A. Burkhardt
TSgt Joseph R. Burkhart
SP5 Raymond H. Burkhart
SGT Larry G. Burks
SGT Jonathan J. Burleigh
SPC H. Taylor Burleson
SGT Roy J. Burlew
SPC Randall E. Burley
MAJ Terry D. Burlingame
SP5 James T. Burn
SP3 Robert Burnam
SSG Brenda L. Burnett
SGT Bruce G. B. Burnett
COL (Ret) Clark A. Burnett
SGT Dan Burnett
SPC Danny J. Burnett
SGT Ed Burnett
SGT Harvetta Burnett
PVT Robert Kevin Burnett
MR. Robert N. Burnett
SGT U. Jean Burnett
SPC Edwin L. Burnette
SGT Ray C. Burnette
MAJ Ron Burnette
BG (Ret) John C. Burney
SSG Nicholas D. Burney
SSG Wesley Bruce Burnham
CW2 Alan I. Burnor
SPC Carrie Burns
1LT Charles K. Burns
SPC Charles R. Burns
PFC Curtis E. Burns
CPT Devin D. Burns

LTC Francis B. Burns
CPT Furlton M. Burns
COL (Ret) George T. Burns
SPC Gregory Walter Burns
LTC Hugh R. Burns
SPC James E. Burns
SFC James E. Burns
SPC James L. Burns
PVT James T. Burns
SGT John F. Burns
SGT Kevin A. Burns
CPT Mark A. Burns
SGT Michael Burns
SPC Michael W. Burns
SGT Patrick J. Burns
LTC Phil Burns
SFC Phillip A. Burns
SGM Richard E. Burns
1SG (Ret) Richard R. Burns
LTC Robert A. Burns
1LT Robert L. Burns
SGT Thomas E. Burns
SGT William D. Burns
SPC William D. Burns
PSG (Ret) Richard C. Burnside
PVT Curtis L. Burr
SGT Frank Burr
PV2 Michael Burr
CPL Carroll R. Burras
CPT Cathleen Burrell
SPC John A. Burrell
SGT Tommy L. Burrell
SGT Donald F. Burris
SGT Joe W. Burris
SSG Latoyia Burris
SGT Samuel S. Burriss
SFC (Ret) Elmer R. Burroughs
MSG Lloyd A. Burroughs
SSG Michael R. Burroughs
MAJ Stephen Burroughs
COL (Ret) George D. Burrow
LTC William O. Burrow
1LT Amy L. Burrows
PFC Jerry W. Burrows
SP5 Robert E. Burrows
SSG Marion Tom Burrus
SSG Calvin Burt
CPT Robert B. Burtch
SGT Robert S. Burtch
1LT Bruce D. Burton
1LT Edward E. Burton
LTC Emory A. Burton
PFC George W. Burton
BG (Ret) James B. Burton
PFC James E. Burton
SGT James P. Burton
MRS. Jimmie R. Burton
SSG John A. Burton
MG (Ret) Jonathan R. Burton
PFC Lamonte Burton
1LT William L. Burton
SSG William R. Burton
SGT Mark J. Burwell
SFC Chester J. Burzenski
PFC Chris Busboom
SFC Frank Busch
SFC George B. Busch
SPC Lloyd W. Busch
SPC Russ T. Busch
SGT Edward F. Buscher
PVT Brandon Buscio
SFC Dennis W. Buse
SGT Brad Busekrus
2LT Chris R. Busenkell
PFC Billie G. Bush
MRS. Charles H. Bush
SP5 Douglas W. Bush
1SG Elton Bush
PVT Fred S. Bush
PFC Gary Lee Bush
SGT Gordon S. Bush
PFC Johnny J. Bush
MSG (Ret) Keith W. Bush
SGT Martin H. Bush
SGT Patrick J. Bush
PVT Timothy D. Bush
CW2 William D. Bush
CPL Edward D. Bushey
CW4 Clair L. Bushnell
1LT Christopher E. Busic
1SG (Ret) Harry C. Busick
CPL Lawrence J. Busini
SGT Gary B. Bussart
CPL Francis O. Busse
SSG Patrick Bussell
1SG (Ret) Robert Bussell
SPC James E. Bussey
1SG Anthony Wayne Bussler
SPC Timothy C. Bussone

SGT Carl W. Bussow
SFC Joseph R. Bustamante
2LT Elias Busuego
CPT Dorothy E. Butala
COL (Ret) Brian J. Butcher
SPC Gary B. Butcher
LTC (Ret) Steve W. Butcher
CPT John J. Butkovich
SFC Arnetta Butler
PFC Benjamin Butler
2LT Brian A. Butler
MAJ Brian D. Butler
SFC (Ret) Charles L. Butler
SGT Dennis L. Butler
CSM (Ret) John C. Butler
MRS. Kenneth A. Butler
SGT Kevin Butler
SGT Lloyd Butler
CW4 Michael D. Butler
SGT Neil H. Butler
SGT Paul J. Butler
COL (Ret) Philip R. Butler
BG (Ret) Remo Butler
MR. Robert H. Butler
CPT Ryan K. Butler
SPC Tony M. Butler
SFC Warren J. Butler
CPL William L. Butler
CW3 Darrell L. Butlett
A1C Frank Butoryak
SSG David C. Butow
SGT Michael Butry
SGM John T. Butt
CPT Matthew D. Butt
SFC Hector Butter
BG Richard L. Butterfield
SPC Luis E. Butter-Pagan
SPC Brian D. Butti
SPC Richard J. Buttone
SGT Carlis G. Buttram
CPT Beau Butts
SPC James L. Butts
1SG Sedrick Buxton
SFC Stephanie Buxton
1LT Angela Buysman
SPC Ken Buysse
CPL Ralph J. Buzbee
CW3 (Ret) Ted L. Buzbee
CPT (Ret) Richard L. Buzen
SFC (Ret) Hugh L. Buzzell
PFC Clifford R. Byars
COL Jack L. Byas
SGT John A. Byerly
SPC Charles Byers
SFC Mark A. Byers
CPL Rickie R. Byers
SGT Rocky D. Byers
SSG James Byington
2LT Lakito T. Bynom
SFC John D. Bynum
LTC (Ret) William R. Bynum
SP5 Leonard Byram
SPC Adam L. Byrd
PVT Alvin Lee Byrd
PFC Corey J. Byrd
SFC Gilbert O. Byrd
SFC Homer E. Byrd
SFC J. H. Byrd
CPL Richard E. Byrd
1SG Tony L. Byrd
SFC Victor Lee Byrd
SPC William A. Byrd
SSG William A. Byrd
SPC John A. Byrley
MAJ John E. Byrn
TSgt (Ret) Clair C. Byrne
MAJ Marcus Byrne
SPC Matthew J. Byrne
SGT Patrick M. Byrne
LTG (Ret) Kevin P. Byrnes
PFC William J. Byron
MAJ Vaughan Byrum
SGT Michael Bys
SSG Nicholas R. Byse
SPC German D. Caballero
SGT Billy Cabaniss
MAJ Lewis R. Cabe
SGT Richard S. Cable
MRS. Robert C. Cable
SGT Freddy Cabral
SFC Daniel L. Cabrera
CSM Jim Cabrera
MSG (Ret) Elilu C. Cabreros
SPC Jim Caccavo
SSG Rubiel M. Cadavid
SP5 Richard K. Cade
SSG Stephen R. Cade
SP5 James Cadieux
SSG Edwin C. Cadle
COL Richard E. Cadorette
MSG (Ret) Edward F. Cadwallader
SPC Michael O. Cady
SGT Roger G. Cady
MSG Patrick James Caesar
MRS. Rodney B. Caesar
SGT Michael B. Cagle
MAJ Norman A. Cagle
SPC Michael J. Cahalan
PFC Patrick Cahalan
CPL Roy E. Cahall
SGT John A. Cahill
SFC Robert K. Cahill
SGT Gary L. Cahoon
SGT Bruce Cain
SSG (Ret) Jason P. Cain
CW4 Vaughn H. Caine
SGT Ernest L. Cairns
PFC Jesse R. Cajas
SPC Francis T. Calabrese
SPC Gerard A. Calabrese
SGT Peter S. Calabrese
CPT Brian Caladra
SGT Richard N. Calarie
2LT Gabrielle Caldara
SP5 Hector Caldera
SPC Julian Calderon
CPL Dominick F. Calderone
SPC E. Bruce Caldie
SP5 Curtis E. Caldwell
SFC (Ret) David A. Caldwell
SPC James E. Caldwell
SFC Joe L. Caldwell
CPL Kenneth M. Caldwell
SFC Michael N. Caldwell
CPT Michael R. Caldwell
SP5 Michael W. Caldwell
SPC Lloyd L. Calease
MSG Dwight M. Caler
SGT Gary P. Calhoun
SPC Leamon W. Calhoun
SGT Lynn P. Calhoun
SSG Victor W. Calhoun
SFC (Ret) James C. Calibro
CPT Jaime Calica
SFC George M. Calicchia
PFC Christopher A. Califano
SGT Alix A. Calixte
SPC Victor M. Calixto
PFC Donald W. Calkins
CSM (Ret) Thomas Calkins
SPC George H. Call
MRS. Glenn P. Call
SPC Robert L. Call
MR. Hank Callaghan
SFC Charles A. Callahan
SSG Donald O. Callahan
LTC Edwin J. Callahan
SFC Herman M. Callahan
CPT Jody Kyle Callahan
SP5 Micheal F. Callahan
SPC Richard M. Callahan
SrA Charles L. Callaway
MRS. Jack G. Callaway
SFC Stanley T. Callaway
MR. Michael Calleia
SGT Gerald G. Callen
COL (Ret) Jan E. Callen
COL Jeffrey M. Callin
CPL Glenn W. Callow
SFC (Ret) James E. Callow
SFC (Ret) John J. Calo
SGT Henry W. Calonhey
SGT Gary G. Calpito
SGT Warren R. Caltabiano
SPC Don L. Calvano
PFC Jason Calvelage
SGT Chester H. Calvert
LTC Kreg C. Calvert
BG Paul T. Calvert
SPC Aaron B. Calvin
PFC Joseph Calvitti
1LT Charles C. Calvo
SPC Anthony Camacho
SGT Castulo Camarillo
MR. Steven Cambio
SGT Douglas R. Camden
SGT Carmen J. Camerato
SPC George R. Cameron
SGT Jason K. Cameron
SPC Ossie B. Cameron
MG (Ret) Richard D. Cameron
SFC Robert F. Cameron
SGT Robert J. Cameron
CW4 (Ret) Maurice E. Cammack
SSG Anthony D. Camp
SPC David H. Camp
SPC James E. Camp
MR. Lawrence B. Camp
SP5 Ronlad Wayne Camp
MSG (Ret) A. M. Campa
SGT Brett A. Campa
SFC (Ret) Frank M. Campa
PFC Jovanny Campa
SFC Aaron Campanella
SGM Albert L. Campbell
SPC Allen L. Campbell
SGT Andrew Campbell
MR. Anthony D. Campbell
MAJ Anthony D. Campbell
SPC Arthur Campbell
PVT Brian D. Campbell
SFC Charles E. Campbell
SFC Christopher N. Campbell
SP5 Clarence K. Campbell
2LT Daniel Campbell
SGT Develand C. Campbell
CSM (Ret) Donald A. Campbell
SGT Donald D. Campbell
SGT Donald D. Campbell
PFC Donald J. Campbell
SGT Donnell Campbell
SPC Douglas E. Campbell
SGT Earnest Campbell
SPC Francis S. Campbell
SFC Howard Campbell
1LT James H. Campbell
SSG Jaree L. Campbell
SSG Jeffrey W. Campbell
MAJ Jim Campbell
SGT John H. Campbell
SGT John W. Campbell
PFC Joseph P. Campbell
MR. Michael A. Campbell
PFC Patrick G. Campbell
SPC Randy Campbell
DR. (1LT) Richard W. Campbell
SSG Robert Campbell
PFC Robert S. Campbell
LTC (Ret) Robert W. Campbell
PFC Robert W. Campbell
TSgt Ronald G. Campbell
1LT Ronald L. Campbell
SGT Ronald L. Campbell
SFC Shawn Campbell
PV2 Stephen A. Campbell
CPL Terrence W. Campbell
SSG Thomas A. Campbell
MRS. Thomas J. Campbell
SFC William L. Campbell
CPL William L. Campbell
SP5 William M. Campbell
PV2 William S. Campbell
PFC Zachary R. Campbell
SGT Donald J. "Frenchy" Campeau
CPL Russell A. Campeau
SFC Clifford D. Camphor
1LT Jasper A. Campise
1SG Carlos Campos
SP5 John Campos
PFC John P. Campos
MSG Jose Campos
SGT Ysidro U. Campos
CPT David C. Camps
MR. Adidas Campus
SSG Darin S. Canaday
MSG (Ret) Daniel L. Canady
SGT Lawrence Duane Canales
SPC Louis P. Canarelli
1LT Adrian R. Cancel
PVT Richard C. Candiff
SGT Gary Candy
COL (Ret) James D. Canfield
MSG Alfred D. Canipe
SPC Dennis L. Canipe
1SG (Ret) Ralph H. Canitz
SPC Dennis Cannarella
SGT C. R. Cannella
SPC Tracy H. Canniff
SGT Bradley A. Cannon
1SG (Ret) Carl R. Cannon
MG (Ret) Charles C. Cannon
CPL Coy R. Cannon
SGT Henry L. Cannon
SGT James E. Cannon
LTC (Ret) M. Clinton Cannon
CPL Ocie L. Cannon
MR. Robert A. Cannon
SPC Robert H. Cannon
SFC Noe Cano
CW3 Mel L. Canon
SPC Marcus Canseco
PFC Richard L. Cantal
PFC Todd Canter
CPT Hector Cantillo
SPC Jim Cantillo
COL Cameron Cantlon
SGT Charles Cantrell
SFC Charles R. Cantrell
SPC Clifford Cantrell
MAJ (CH) Howard F. Rick Cantrell
LTC Frank Cantu
SP5 Juan Eric Cantu
SSG Rene Cantu
SPC Vincent F. Cantu
SGT Gary L. Cantwell
CPT Michael Canty
1LT Michael E. Canty
CSM Gilbert Canuela
SPC Jeffrey A. Capalar
SPC Francesco L. Capaldi
SPC Michael R. Capehart
SSG Francis S. Capella
CW3 (Ret) Gene H. Capen
2LT Angela M. Capetillo
1LT Charles R. Caplinger
SGT Anthony T. Caponigro
COL (Ret) Frank J. Caponio
SGT Anthony J. Capparelle
SPC William T. Capps
MAJ Kevin Capra
TSgt Joseph D. Caprara
SSG Dennis E. Capron
SGM (Ret) Jimmy F. Capshaw
SGT Jimer Carambas
SSG Harold M. Caraway
SGT Michael J. Caraway
SPC Charles B. Carbaugh
MRS. Thomas M. Carberry
1LT Christopher Carbone
1SG (Ret) Winston A. Carbonneau
SFC Eddie Carcamo
SFC Charles B. Card
SGT Jerry L. Carda
PFC Walter A. Cardell
SPC James M. Cardenas
PFC Jessica Cardenas
SP5 John Carder
SFC Daniel Cardiel
SSG Richard J. Cardillo
MAJ Richard M. Cardillo
SSG Leo Cardinale
CPT Gil Cardona
MSG (Ret) Nelson Cardona
PVT Rick Cardona
SGT Luis E. Cardozo
SPC Anthony Carella
SGT Peter E. Carello
SPC James T. Carew
SGT Edward J. Carey
SPC James R. Carey
PFC Lowell E. Carey
SPC Nathanael R. Carey
CPT Stephen D. Carey
SPC Timothy Carey
SGT William T. Carey
MR. Stephen J. Carfora
1LT Rudolpho Cariaga
SPC Joey L. Carico
SPC Frank Carilli
SGT Jackloid M. Carino
1SG Terence W. Carl
SFC Don Carley
SPC Gary A. Carlile
LTC (Ret) James A. Carlile
SFC Monica L. Carlile
SPC Howard S. Carlin
SGT Thomas O. Carlin
SP5 Alfred W. Carlisle
SPC Jeff Carlisle
SGT Anthony M. Carlock
CPL Christian M. Carlson
SPC D. Murray Carlson
SPC Lance E. Carlson
MRS. Margery P. Carlson
PV2 Mark A. Carlson
1LT Raymond Carlson
PFC Shannon Carlson
PFC Shannon Kelly Carlson
SGT Warren W. Carlstedt
1LT Randy Carlton
1SG Russell C. Carmack
SSG Herman Carman
CPL Doyle V. Carmody
LTC (Ret) Frank T. Carmody
SPC Joseph A. Carmona
MRS. Douglas E. Carnahan
1LT Patrick L. Carnahan
SGT John R. Carnako
CPT Patrick B. Carneal
SP5 James Alfred Carnes
SPC Wesley L. Carnes
SPC Vittorio Carnevale
SGT Dennis B. Carney
SPC Joseph M. Carney
PVT Matt Carnley
SPC David Carnline
SFC Arthur Caro
SP5 Joseph F. Carolin
MSG (Ret) Paul L. Caron
SPC Thomas M. Caron
MAJ John J. Caronna
COL Steven Carozza
1LT Albert H. Carpenter
SPC Bobby Ray Carpenter
SGT Dale A. Carpenter
2LT David L. Carpenter
SGT David Lee Carpenter
SGT Dennis F. Carpenter
CPL Donald G. Carpenter
CPT Edwin S. Carpenter
CPT Forrest L. Carpenter
CPT Joe M. Carpenter
PFC Joseph J. Carpenter
MR. Larry Carpenter
1SG (Ret) Luther A. Carpenter
SGT Mathew Carpenter
CSM (Ret) Quintin L. Carpenter
CW4 Ralph A. Carpenter
SGT Richard E. Carpenter
MAJ Scott W. Carpenter
MAJ Steve Carpenter
SFC Terry R. Carpenter
SSG Thomas S. Carpenter
SPC William D. Carpenter
SGT L. Steven Carper
SGT Anthony R. Carpita
COL (Ret) Eldon D. Carr
SPC Fred H. Carr
LTC (Ret) Glenn P. Carr
SFC (Ret) John D. Carr
1LT John D. Carr
PFC John P. Carr
SFC Lowry T. Carr
SSG Mark Carr
CSM Melvin Carr
SGT Melvin L. Carr
SGT Richard F. Carr
1SG (Ret) Robert L. Carr
CSM Rocky Carr
CPL Roger E. Carr
MSG (Ret) Ronald L. Carr
SFC Roxana I. Carr
SPC Thomas E. Carr
SPC William Carr
MR. Joel Carranza
MSG (Ret) Lee Roy Carranza
CPT Robert Allan Carrara
SP5 Robert D. Carrel
SFC David W. Carrell
SGT Fred W. Carrell
SSG Lawrence Carreon
MAJ (Ret) Luis Carreras
CPT Victor J. Carreras
SSG Rodrigo Carreras Adorno
SGT Miguel Carretero
SGT George L. Carretto
MR. Thomas A. Carrick
LTC Jason A. Carrico
SPC Ted J. Carrico
SFC Danny R. Carrier
PFC Jon P. Carrier
SGT Raymond N. Carrier
MSG (Ret) James Allen Carrigan
SGT Robert N. Carriger
SFC (Ret) Jesus E. Carrillo
SSG Jesus E. Carrillo
SSG Jesus M. Carrillo
SPC John A. Carrillo
SPC Miguel Carrillo
PVT Anthony L. Carrington
SGT Jose C. Carrion
1SG (Ret) Luis T. Carrion
1SG (Ret) Pete Carrion
SFC Jorge Carrisalez
SPC Angel S. Carrisoza
SPC Fredrick L. Carrizales
PV2 Sam Carrizales
PFC Andrew Carroll
PFC Anthony K. Carroll
COL Chad G. Carroll
LT D. Frederic Carroll
MAJ Donald E. Carroll
SPC Gary D. Carroll
PV2 Jason A. Carroll
PFC John F. Carroll
PFC John J. Carroll
SFC (Ret) Lavoid Carroll
1LT Max Carroll
CPT Paul L. Carroll
PFC Rayford J. Carroll
SSG (Ret) Robert E. Carroll
1LT Robert W. Carroll
SP6 (Ret) Roger H. Carroll
SGT Russell L. Carroll
PV2 Sean Patrick Carroll
SGT Truman D. Carroll
1LT Tyrie Carroll
MR. William S. Carroll
CSM Douglas R. Carron
SSG Don W. Carroway
SPC Robert D. Carroway
MSG Scott M. Carry
SFC Casey A. Carson
SPC Earl N. Carson
SGT Michael J. Carson
SP5 Randolph B. Carson
1LT Richard J. Carson
SGT Robert L. Carson
TSgt Russell J. Carson
CPL Tremayne R. Carson
1LT William D. Carson
COL Joseph E. Carstens
SFC Richard L. Cart
COL John B. Cartafalsa
CPT Samuel Cartee
SPC Bill Carter
MAJ Brian S. Carter
SPC Charles A. Carter
SFC (Ret) Charles H. Carter
SPC Charles H. Carter
MRS. Cleo Carter
1LT David B. Carter
SSG Elijah J. Carter
MR. Eugene Carter
LTC Florentino L. Carter
SSG Freddie C. Carter
1SG Gerald Carter
SGT Henry J. Carter
CPT Herbert R. Carter
CSM Howard L. Carter
PFC James A. Carter
SFC James C. Carter
PFC James E. Carter
SGT John G. Carter
MRS. King W. Carter
SFC Langston Carter
SGT Larry W. Carter
SPC Leonard Carter
SP5 Michael D. Carter
CSM (Ret) Moses Carter
PFC Orville W. Carter
SPC Robert L. Carter
MSG Robert W. Carter
SPC Robert Weston Carter
PFC Ronald Carter
SPC Ronald Carter
COL (Ret) Rosemary M. Carter
SGT Stanley Carter
SGT Stephen A. Carter
SPC Tedford H. Carter
CW2 Warren G. Carter
SSG Wayne T. Carter
WO1 William F. Carter
SSG Devester L. Carthan
SGT Dennis Carthew
SSG Gregory Cartledge
CPT Ernest Cartmill
SGT Albert H. Carton
SPC Joseph A. Cartonia
1LT John H. Cartwright
SSG Norman L. Cartwright
MR. Richard R. Cartwright
CW3 Robert L. Cartwright
SPC Rollon Cartwright
SGT Edward R. Carty
SFC Lauren Carty
SGT Philip Caruana
SGT Thomas Carvalho
COL (Ret) Richard K. Carver
PFC Taylor M. Carver
SPC Donald C. Carverick
LTC (Ret) Kenneth C. Cary
SPC William T. Cary
SPC Louis J. Casa
CPL Tony S. Casaccio
MRS. Thomas Stephen Casagrande
SPC Arthur Casale
SGT Julio Casarez
SFC Miguel L. Casarez
SPC Aaron F. Casas
SPC Fabian M. Casas
PFC Louis R. Casazza
SPC Jerry T. Casbon
CPT Thomas J. Cascio
PVT Bruce A. Case
SGT Dawson R. Case
SSG Eric Brent Case
COL (Ret) H. Michael Case

SGT Edumnd Casebeer
CW3 (Ret) Dennis James Casey
SGM (Ret) Dennis R. Casey
PFC Derrick Casey
GEN George W. Casey
SSG George W. Casey
CPL James Casey
SPC Jason Casey
CSM John J. Casey
SPC Kevin Casey
LTC (Ret) Leonard R. Casey
1LT Thomas J. Casey
CPT William L. Casey
SPC Dennis E. Cash
SGT Melton D. Cash
PVT Ronald D. Cash
SSG Terry W. Cashatt
SPC Curtis Cashio
MR. Charles H. Cashman
SPC James A. Casler
SSG Christopher Casper
SGT Robert C. Casper
SGT Bill Cassel
SSG Augustus V. Cassell
CPT Charles M. Cassidy
PFC John F. Cassidy
SPC Vincent W. Cassidy
SPC John W. Cassie
CSM (Ret) Ben Castaneda
SGT Gino M. Castaneda
PFC Louis Castellanos
SGT Robert J. Castelli
PVT Richard R. Castellon
SGT Marimer Castelow
SGT Celerino Castillo
PVT Domingo A. Castillo
MR. Guadalupe Castillo
SPC Jose Castillo
SSG Kervin A. Castillo
SSG Michael Castillo
SGT Ralph E. Castillo
1SG (Ret) James M. Castle
CPL Victor P. Castle
SPC Fred Castner
SPC Eugene C. Caston
SPC Rodney D. Caston
MR. Vincent J. Castor
SPC Luis M. Castorena
SSG Ray Castorena
SGT Armando Castro
SGT Carlos Castro
SPC Christopher Castro
SGT Gordon J. Castro
SGT Juan Castro
SPC Juan E. Castro
PVT Juvenal Castro
CPT Kyle M. Castro
SSG Louis Castro
SFC Luis Castro
1LT Ruben R. Castro
PFC Augustus M. Casucci
WO1 Duane A. Caswell
PFC Randolph S. Caswell
CPL William R. Catanese
MR. Jim Catania
1LT Arthur F. Cataw
SPC James A. Cate
SPC George T. Catencamp
LT Aaron Cater
PFC Dennis Cater
1LT John E. Cater
CSM (Ret) David L. Cates
SPC John E. Cathcart
MR. Robert L. Catherman
SGT Greg L. Catherwood
MSG Robert A. Cathey
LTC Robert H. Cathey
SFC Jimmy Catiro
SPC George Catloth
PVT Jesse Catrett
SGT Oliver J. Catterson
SPC John Lee Cauble
CPT David A. Caudill
PV2 David Steven Caudill
PFC Timothy Caudle
SSG Grant F. Cauffman
CW2 James L. Caufman
SGT (Ret) William J. Caulder
SGT Floyd A. Cauley
MSG John E. Cauley
1LT William R. Caulk
PVT Raqeeb Causey
MR. Ken Cauthern
SSG Stephen D. Cava
SSG Gerald Cavagnaro
SPC Dominic Cavalieri
SPC Danny Cavanaugh
SFC Dennis Cavanaugh
SGT Patrick Cavanaugh
SPC Randy L. Cavanaugh
SPC Sidney A. Cavanaugh
1LT Thomas A. Cavanaugh
SGT (Ret) Tom Cavanaugh
SPC Robert T. Cavaness
SGT Carmon W. Cave
PFC Oliver D. Cavendish
SSG Robert Lance Caver
LTG (Ret) Dennis D. Cavin
LTC (Ret) Russell D. Cavin
LTC Lloyd Paul Caviness
SSG Joshua P. Cavins
SGT Ralph Cavito
SGT Michael C. Cavitt
CPL Guy R. Cawley
MRS. James P. Caylor
CSM (Ret) Richard B. Cayton
SGT Stanley W. Cazier
CPL Daniel Ceballos
PFC Pedro Ceballos
SMSgt (Ret) Ronald Cebulski
SPC John Cecere
SPC Rex L. Cecil
SGT Harry E. Cedar
SSG Chester K. Cejnowski
SGT Kenneth F. Cellilo
SGT Dominick J. Cello
MR. Joseph Cellucci
SPC Chi Wen Cen
SPC Scott Centrell
SGT Juan Cerda
SSG (Ret) Kenneth A. Cerka
MR. Francis R. Cerrone
1LT Michael J. Cervera
MAJ John M. Cervetti
PFC Ricardo H. Cesar
TSgt William A. Cesario
SGT George L. Cesena
SSG Joseph R. Cevallos
SFC Tou S. Cha
SPC Oscar Chabrier
CPT Jonathan L. Chace
SPC Douglas A. Chacho
PFC Steven T. Chaco
SGT Ray D. Chacon
LTC (Ret) Harold M. Chadick
SPC Holly E. Chadwick
1SG Joe C. Chadwick
SGT Phil Chaffey
SPC David W. Chaffin
COL (Ret) Jimmie M. Chaffin
SSG Bobby D. Chafin
BG Bela J. Chain
SGT Ronald P. Chaisson
MAJ Charles Chalfort
CPL Maynard Challinor
CPL Don J. Challman
CPL Bryce C. Chalquist
CPT Patrick Scott Chamberlain
CPT Tammy L. Chamberlain
CPT Ty Chamberlain
SSG Raymond Chamberland
SPC Calvin D. Chambers
MAJ Christopher W. Chambers
SSG Cinnamon T. Chambers
SPC Clarence J. Chambers
SP5 Enos E. Chambers
SGT Jerry L. Chambers
SFC Paul Chambers
SGT Richard A. Chambers
SGT Robert Chambers
SPC Robert D. Chambers
SPC Sterling J. Chambers
CW2 William R. Chambers
SSG (Ret) Max R. Chamblee
1LT Michael D. Chambless
SPC Charles Chambliss
CPT Christopher B. Chambliss
MRS. Delmar Champ
COL Brian P. Champagne
PFC Joseph J. Champagne
SPC Jack A. Champion
SPC Leo K. M. Chan
SPC Ying Chan
SFC David W. Chance
SSG Don E. Chancy
SGT Charles V. Chandler
SGT David L. Chandler
CW2 Don R. Chandler
PFC Donald J. Chandler
SPC Fred L. Chandler
PFC Howard C. Chandler
PV2 James S. Chandler
SP5 Joe A. Chandler
SPC John E. Chandler
1LT Mark T. Chandler
COL Norman P. Chandler
SMA Raymond F. Chandler
SGT Stanley M. Chandler
SPC Bill Chaney
SGT Harold D. Chaney
SSG James E. Chaney
1SG James L. Chaney
SPC James S. Chaney
LTC (Ret) Mark R. Chaney
SP5 Victor E. Chaney
1LT Bertram J. Channick
PFC Christopher Chaparro
MAJ Thomas Chapeau
SFC (Ret) Ronald B. Chapell
1LT William R. Chapin
CPL Kenneth Chaplin
SPC David A. Chapman
SGT Dennis Chapman
SrA Dennis L. Chapman
LTC (Ret) George G. Chapman
PVT Guy M. Chapman
SGT James J. Chapman
1SG Landon L. Chapman
SPC Michael C. Chapman
CPT Pete Chapman
SFC (Ret) Sam Chapman
2LT Timothy D. Chapman
SP5 Louis J. Chapoton
SGT David M. Chappel
SPC Charles G. Chappelear
SGT Donald Chappell
SP6 Elton B. Chappell
SGT Steve W. Chappell
MSG Lucian L. Chappelle
PFC (Ret) Federico S. Chappins
SPC Michael E. Characky
MAJ Peter Charbonneau
PV2 Christopher Charles
CPL John Charles
SFC Jose G. Charles
SSG Terry L. Charlett
COL (Ret) Darrel T. Charlton
1LT Nicholas Charlton
SPC Armand H. Charpentier
SGT Dennis Charron
1SG (Ret) Kenneth L. Charters
SGT Aaron Chase
SPC Allen D. Chase
WO1 (Ret) Aretis Chase
SGT Bruce A. Chase
LTC David W. Chase
CPT Joel K. Chase
SPC Ken Chase
COL (Ret) Michael T. Chase
CPT Richard D. Chase
SP5 Robert J. Chase
COL (Ret) Santo A. Chase
SPC Aaron S. Chassells
SPC James P. Chassie
CPT Jerry S. Chastain
CW2 Michael Chastain
MG (Ret) Ronald S. Chastain
MAJ Carl A. Chasteen
CPL James A. Chasteen
SPC Jerry D. Chastine
SGT Keith Chatelain
SSG (Ret) James D. Chatham
CPL Allen T. Chatman
SGT Willie J. Chatman
MSG Charles W. Chatterton
SGT Dennis R. Chattin
1SG Eloy G. Chavarria
PVT Albert Chavez
CPL Alex Chavez
SGT Carlos B. Chavez
SSG Daniel J. Chavez
CSM (Ret) Daniel M. Chavez
SGT David R. Chavez
SFC (Ret) Eladio C. Chavez
SSG Francisco Chavez
SPC Gene Michael Chavez
SGT Gregory T. Chavez
SGT Lorenzo Chavez
SP5 Roy J. Chavez
CPL Steven A. Chavez
SPC Clifford Chavis
CW3 (Ret) Lyle E. Cheadle
COL (Ret) Jesse R. Cheatham
SFC Bobby G. Cheatom
SGT Joshua A. Chebret
SGT Bill Cheek
MSG James D. Cheek
SPC Loyd R. Cheek
SGT Peter P. Cheek
2LT T. Kent Cheeseman
SGT Oscar J. Chelf
SSG Eric E. Cheney
SPC Gilbert Cheney
SGT Michael Cheney
SPC Nelson W. Cheney
SGT Thomas M. Chenvert
CSM Philip A. Chepenik
PV2 Dwayne Chermaine
SPC James K. Cherry
SGT Paul Cherry
CW4 Jerry Cheselka
CPL Theodore J. Cheski
PVT Scott D. Chesler
CW4 (Ret) John W. Chesnut
LTC (Ret) Conrad F. Chesser
CPT Richard K. Chesson
LTC James D. Chestnut
1LT Siu Cheung
SFC David A. Chevalier
SGT Leroy C. Chevis
CPT Eric Chewning
SGT Chanthorl Jem Chhem
SGT Thomas Chiappone
SGT George A. Chiaramello
GEN (Ret) Peter W. Chiarelli
SGT Frank J. Chiarello
SSG Nigil G. Chichester
SSG (Ret) John Chick
SSG Daniel J. Chiego
SP5 Bruno J. Chiesa
PVT Michael M. Chikar
MRS. Ted C. Chilcote
1LT Robert J. Child
CPT Aaron W. Childers
SGM James R. Childers
SGT Joseph E. Childers
SGT W. S. (Bill) Childers
COL William W. Childers
MR. Allen L. Childress
SSG Joel Childress
SSG Michael A. Childress
MAJ (Ret) Ralph S. Childress
SGT William G. Childress
SFC Carl N. Childs
CPT Norman R. Childs
PFC James D. Chile
MR. James D. Chiles
SPC Wesley Chim
SGT Al Chimoski
LTC Chongkin Chin
CW4 James Chin
LTC Darryl K. H. Ching
CPL Frank C. Chiodo
SGT Lavonne M. Chipman
MSG (Ret) James F. Chisholm
CW2 Harold L. Chism
SGT Stephen Jim Chism
PFC Melvin Chisolm
COL (Ret) Warde P. Chittenden
SPC Dave Chivers
MR. Michael A. Chlarson
MSG Andrew Chmiel
CPT Andrew J. Chmiel
SSG Edward J. Chmura
SFC Marty R. Choate
SPC Michael G. Choate
MRS. Ralph S. Choffo
CPL Peter T. Chokola
LTC (Ret) Hilbert H. Chole
PVT George Choma
CPT Michael Chon
MR. Edward L. Chong
PVT Raymond Chong
1LT Ali M. Chouhdry
MAJ Louis W. Chow
MS. Susan G. Rose Chriscoe
SGT Douglas F. Christ
COL (Ret) Linda D. Christ
PV2 Nick Christ
PFC Robert P. Christansen
SP5 David E. Christen
2LT Derek P. Christensen
MRS. John S. Christensen
SGT Mel H. Christensen
1LT Pearl H. Christensen
PVT Bernard A. Christian
MAJ (Ret) John K. Christian
SPC Kenneth A. Christian
CPT Patrick M. Christian
SPC Richard M. Christian
SGT Ronald Christian
CPL Ronald E. Christian
SSG Andreas H. Christiansen
SGT (Ret) Charles T. Christianson
SGT David L. Christianson
PFC Raymond Christianson
LTC (Ret) Donald H. Christie
MAJ Norman Christie
CPT Stuart Christie
SGM Thomas S. Christie
LTC Eric P. Christinsen
SGT David L. Christman
SPC H. Ray Christman
SGT Jason E. Christman
CPL Jerry A. Christman
MRS. Allen Scott Christmas
CPL John F. Christoff
SGT Timothy A. Christoff
SPC Albert C. Christopher
MRS. Joe M. Christopher
SGT Mark G. Christopher
SFC (Ret) Ronald L. Christopher
SGT Alan T. Christy
SSG (Ret) Lyle M. Christy
LTC (Ret) Michael B. Christy
SFC (Ret) Douglas A. Chubb
SP5 Paul L. Chumbley
SPC William G. Chumbley
SSG Bobby G. Chumley
1SG Donald L. Chumley
MR. Charles C. Chun
SGT Hwasup Chung
MRS. Andrew P. Chura
SGT Charles D. Church
SGT Harry A. Church
LT Jerome E. Church
SGM Randy T. Church
SPC Thomas Church
PV2 Zachary W. Church
TSgt Carter Churchill
SPC Richard S. Churchill
SP5 Sydney S. Churchill
MSG Winston Churchill
PFC Michael W. Chytracek
PFC James S. Ciara
1LT Peter Cibula
LTC Carmine Cicalese
SGT Harold Ciccotti
PFC Leonard J. Cich
PFC George A. Cicharz
SGT Christopher M. Cichocki
SSG Kurt J. Cicinelli
PVT Anthony R. Cicolini
SGT Richard J. Cifelli
SFC Patrick J. Ciferri
SGT Loren Cigar
SP5 Michael E. Cimoli
SSG Albert F. Cinqmars
SGT (Ret) Angelo J. Cinquegrana
SPC Juan R. Cintron
CPT Lucas J. Cioffi
PFC David A. Ciosek
CSM (Ret) Neil L. Ciotola
SPC Anthony G. Cirabisi
SPC John Ciraolo
SPC Joseph Cirigliano
SFC Bryan Cisco
SGT Mark S. Cisek
SP5 William Cisko
LTC Guillermo Cisneros
MS. Jenny L. Cisneros
SPC Jose B. Cisneros
MAJ John H. Cisney
CPL R. Ken Cisson
SPC Joseph Cistone
SGT Kenneth J. Citelli
CW3 Joseph N. Civitarese
CPL Michael E. Civitello
SP5 Jerry Claassen
SFC John M. Clabaugh
SPC Michael A. Claiborn
1LT Kevin Claiborne
1LT Ronald G. Claiborne
TSgt Alfred B. Clair
1LT James F. Clancy
CPT James T. Clancy
SFC John W. Clancy
SSG Anthony Clapp
1SG Robert A. Clapp
CPT George K. Clardy
CPT Allen B. Clark
PFC Barbara A. Clark
PVT Bryan V. Clark
SGT C. W. Clark
PVT Calvin Clark
TSgt Carl C. Clark
SFC Charles W. Clark
CPT Clarence E. Clark
SGT Cleve Clark
PFC Dajuan Clark
LTC (Ret) Danny D. Clark
SPC David A. Clark
LTC (Ret) Denzel L. Clark
CH (COL) (Ret) Donald D. Clark
SP5 Donald E. Clark
SGT (Ret) Donald Richard Clark
SGT Douglas H. Clark
SGT Douglas M. Clark
1SG (Ret) Earl Clark
SGT Elliott K. Clark
SSG Emmitt L. Clark
MRS. Frank D. Clark
1LT Gary M. Clark
SP5 George A. Clark
SGM (Ret) Gordon G. Clark
CW4 Harold Clark
SSG Howard E. Clark
SGT James K. Clark
SPC James M. Clark
SGT James R. Clark
SGT Jeffery C. Clark
SGT Jerry L. Clark
SP5 Jimmy Y. Clark
SGM Joe Clark
SGT John B. Clark
SPC John M. Clark
SPC John P. Clark
MSG Kevin M. Clark
SFC Leighton E. Clark
SGT Michael Clark
CPL Michael A. Clark
LTC (Ret) Michael B. Clark
2LT Michael E. Clark
CW3 (Ret) Milton S. Clark
LT Nathaniel Clark
SPC Noel Tom Clark
SGT Philip R. Clark
CPT Ray K. Clark
1SG Richard D. Clark
SGT Richard E. Clark
MR. Richard E. Clark
CPL Richard J. Clark
SGT Roger D. Clark
MSG (Ret) Ron Clark
SFC Stacie Clark
SFC Stanley T. Clark
SPC Stephen V. Clark
PFC Thomas E. Clark
1SG Toby L. Clark
SPC Travis Clark
MSG (Ret) Val D. Clark
SPC Victor D. Clark
SGT Wallace J. Clark
SPC Wesley Clark
GEN (Ret) Wesley K. Clark
SPC Albert E. Clarke
PFC Carlo J. Clarke
1LT David Clarke
CPL Douglas J. Clarke
SFC (Ret) James L. Clarke
WO1 John W. Clarke
MG (Ret) Mary E. Clarke
MAJ Natasha S. Clarke
MR. Robert W. Clarke
PFC Stephen Clarke
CPL Michael L. Clary
SGT Patrick M. Clary
MAJ Timothy Clauss
SGT Jack Clavey
CPT (Ret) Donald E. Clawson
MRS. Thomas F. Clawson
SGT Benjamin C. Claxton
SPC Lee W. Claxton
SSG Albert H. Clay
SGT Billy Kirk Clay
1LT David A. Clay
SPC David L. Clay
MRS. Richard A. Clay
SGT Ronald Clay
SPC Russell D. Clay
SPC William S. Clay
SSG Harvey G. Claypool
SGT Harvey J. Claypoole
MRS. Bobbie Clayton
SGT Charles S. Clayton
SSG (Ret) Daniel R. Clayton
SGT Donald A. Clayton
SGT Harry G. Clayton
SPC James D. Clayton
SPC Larry D. Clayton
SPC Phillip D. Clayton
2LT Brendan O. Cleary
SSG Diane E. Cleary-Vernon
SPC Edward E. C. Clebsch
PFC James Ken Clegg
COL (Ret) Thomas E. Cleland
SGT John T. Clellan
MAJ (Ret) Judd L. Clemens
1LT Gerald A. Clement
SGT James A. Clement
PVT Leroy J. Clement
SGT Blake Clements
SPC Keith A. Clements
COL (Ret) Michael R. Clements
PFC Richard L. Clements
SP5 Robert M. Clements
SFC (Ret) Ralph O. Clemings
SGT George N. Clemmens
SPC Charles R. Clemmer
SGT George W. Clemmer
CPL Arron J. Clemons

CSM (Ret) David W. Clemons
MAJ Tim Cleveland
CPT Torrance G. Cleveland
SGM (Ret) Joseph F. Clever
SP5 Ronald L. Clever
SFC Daniel Cliatt
SGT Ronald W. Cliffin
SPC James H. Clifford
CW2 James R. Clifford
SFC (Ret) Patrick L. Clifford
CPT Sean L. Clifford
COL Claude E. Clifton
PFC Lawrence M. Clifton
MR. Ron W. Clifton
PFC William Wesley Clifton
CW4 (Ret) David A. Clinansmith
MAJ Sharman Clincy
PVT Cecil L. Cline
CSM (Ret) Danny C. Cline
SGT Glenn W. Cline
SGT John A. Cline
PFC John F. Cline
SSG Mitchell A. Cline
LTC (Ret) R. T. Cline
CW2 Stuart L. Cline
1SG Brett Clingan
PFC John Franklin Clingan
CPL Wayne D. Clingman
PFC Donald V. Clites
SSG (Ret) Michael Clifford
SPC Larry B. Clopton
CPT Robert J. Close
MSG (Ret) Roger W. Closinski
PV2 John B. Closson
SPC Donald J. Clostio
SP5 Billy N. Clothier
MRS. Samuel E. Cloud
SP5 Alan S. Clough
SP3 Paul Joseph Cloutier
SGT Raymond W. Cloutier
SGT Glen L. Clover
SPC Daniel E. Clow
PFC Arthur L. Clowney
CPT William W. Cloyd
SGT Richard Clubine
SGT Jim L. Cluckey
LTC (Ret) James M. Clune
SFC Robert E. Clutts
SPC Gail Coakley
SSG Jacob W. Coan
PFC Rex A. Coando
CPT David L. Coate
SGT Bill Coates
SGT Charley B. Coats
CPL Howard N. Coats
PFC John A. Coats
CPT Adam M. Cobb
SPC Clayton E. Cobb
SGT James D. Cobb
COL Jerald M. Cobb
SPC Jonathan Cobb
SPC Mark A. Cobb
MRS. Maylon M. Cobb
CPT Robert G. Cobb
SGT Tony R. Cobb
SGT Edward L. Cobbler
SGT Howard L. Coble
SSG James D. Coble
SSG (Ret) James F. Coble
PFC Donald R. Coblentz
SPC Jeffrey A. Coburn
PVT Larry R. Coburn
2LT Thomas M. Coburn
A1C Thomas E. Cocain
SSG Clifford D. Cochran
1LT D. Woodrow Cochran
1SG David Cochran
SGT Donald D. Cochran
1LT Gill Cochran
MSG Marshall C. Cochran
CW4 (Ret) Thomas C. Cochran
SGM (Ret) Thomas M. Cochran
MAJ Richard B. Cochrane
CPL Rowland E. Cochren
MAJ Kenneth G. Cockerham
SPC Thomas Emanuel Cockrell
PFC Rhett J. Cockrill
SGT Larry L. Cockrum
PFC Leon L.C. Cockrum
SSG W. Dean Cockrum
MSG John T. Codd
CPL Eugene T. Cody
SGT Jerry Cody
SGT John Michael Cody
PFC Michael J. Cody
PV2 Patrick Cody
GEN Richard A. Cody
SPC Kevin M. Coe

CPL Leo Coe
SFC Phillip S. Coe
SPC Sidney Coe
SPC Timothy R. Coenen
SSG Shannon W. Coey
PVT Michael T. Cofell
2LT George Coffee
SPC David Coffelt
SGT Robert E. Coffey
SSG Andrew J. Coffin
LTC (Ret) Raymond D. Coffin
SSG Terry L. Coffindaffer
SPC (Ret) Earnie W. Coffman
2LT Edward M. Coffman
MSG Richard A. Coffman
PFC Edward Cofrancesco
SPC Leslie Cogdell
SGT Tracy S. Cogdill
SGT Charles F. Coghill
COL (Ret) James J. Coghlan
COL Christopher M. Coglianese
SGT Joseph A. Cognitore
CW2 (Ret) Theodore L. Cogut
2LT Cary Cohan
SFC (Ret) William R. Cohea
SFC Anthony L. Cohen
1SG (Ret) Conrad H. Cohen
SPC (Ret) I. Michael Cohen
SGT Jerome H. Cohen
CPL Jerome L. Cohen
MR. Merlin L. Cohen
COL Richard Cohen
SSG (Ret) Robert S. Cohen
2LT Angel M. Coic
SPC Patrick M. Coignard
MRS. Clytus E. Coil
MR. Gale C. Coil
SFC Chester Coker
SSG W. L. Coker
COL Jimmie P. Cokinos
SFC Lawrence Colabucci
SPC Harold C. Colander
SGM Louis P. Colantoni
SPC Michael J. Colarusso
COL Christopher Colavita
LTC (Ret) Henry Colavita
SPC Arthur Colbert
LTC (Ret) Harold M. Colbert
SGT Anna M. Colburn
SFC John M. Colburn
CW3 Mary L. Colburn
SPC Michael A. Colby
SPC Larry W. Colclasure
PVT James D. Coldiron
SGT Corey Cole
MR. David Cole
MRS. David L. Cole
SGT Dennis M. Cole
SGT Donald Cole
1SG (Ret) Duffie E. Cole
SPC Edward M. Cole
PFC Hershel F. Cole
SGT James F. Cole
SGM (Ret) John E. Cole
SGT John S. Cole
1SG (Ret) Millard B. Cole
SSG Peter C. Cole
SGT Richard D. Cole
SPC Richard E. Cole
LTC (Ret) Robert L. Cole
SPC Robert W. Cole
SPC Robert W. Cole
PFC Ronald W. Cole
MRS. Stephen M. Cole
SFC (Ret) William H. Cole
PFC Peter L. Colegrove
SPC Aaron R. Coleman
PFC Arthur P. Coleman
CPL Bobby W. Coleman
1SG Charles C. Coleman
SGM (Ret) Charles L. Coleman
CPT Derrick G. Coleman
SPC Donald O. Coleman
SPC Frank K. Coleman
CPL Garry N. Coleman
SP5 Gerald Coleman
SP5 Herbert L. Coleman
PFC Herbert R. Coleman
MRS. J. D. Coleman
SFC James Coleman
PFC James Earl Coleman
SGT (Ret) James M. Coleman
MR. James M. Coleman
CW2 Jim Coleman
MR. Jimmy D. Coleman
SGT John A. Coleman
PFC Joseph F. Coleman
PV2 Kevin R. Coleman
SGM Lester W. Coleman

SPC Lionel A. Coleman
SFC Mark A. Coleman
SPC Mark D. Coleman
SGT Mattie Coleman
SPC Michael A. Coleman
MRS. Ray R. Coleman
COL (Ret) Rex L. Coleman
MAJ Rickey L. Coleman
SGT Ronald A. Coleman
MSG Stacey C. Coleman
1LT Tommie Coleman
SGT Tron Coleman
SGT Vicki L. Coleman
SPC Ernest J. Colern
SPC Douglas D. Coles
SPC Philip N. Coles
SPC Andrew Coley
PV2 David K. Coley
COL (Ret) Eugene D. Colgan
MSG (Ret) Robert M. Colgrove
PFC James R. Colignon
SFC Luis F. Colindres
MR. David C. Coll
CPL Walter H. Coll
CPL Gilbert W. Collamore
MR. Timothy E. Collar
MAJ Nelson B. Collard
COL (Ret) Carlos M. Collat
MAJ (Ret) Juan R. Collazo
SGM Myles Colleran
MRS. Walter L. Collett
SPC Aaron J. Collette
SFC Robert J. Collette
SPC Donald R. Colley
SGT Viola K. Colley
1LT Ann Collier
SPC Edward L. Collier
SSG Glenn R. Collier
MR. John C. Collier
SSG John E. Collier
MRS. Leon L. Collier
SPC William H. Collier
COL (Ret) William P. Collier
SPC Harry A. Collin
SFC Steven L. Collinge
MAJ (Ret) Mark A. Collinger
MR. Allen M. Collins
SSG Arthur J. Collins
SGT Brandon Justyce Collins
MSG (Ret) Charles R. Collins
SSG David A. Collins
MAJ David R. Collins
SPC Elliott James Collins
MR. Floyd Collins
SGT G. Martin Collins
PFC George W. Collins
1SG Homer T. Collins
SPC Howard J. Collins
SPC James Bradley Collins
SGT Jerry L. Collins
SPC Jerry P. Collins
CPT Jesse Collins
MRS. John J. Collins
SFC Keith B. Collins
SPC Kevin B. Collins
SP5 Larry R. Collins
SPC Laurence Collins
SPC Mathew S. Collins
SGT Michael A. Collins
CPL Milton E. Collins
PFC Paul A. Collins
MRS. Paul K. Collins
SSG Raymond James Collins
MR. Sammie Collins
SGT Scotty T. Collins
LTC (Ret) Warren J. Collins
SGT Wesley L. Collins
SPC William C. Collins
SGT William R. Collins
MR. William R. Collins
SFC William T. Collins
MR. Ron W. Collis
CPT Clayton T. Colliton
SPC Charley A. Collum
MSG (Ret) Henry J. Colman
SGT Andre Coln
MAJ Anibal Colon
SGT Ismael Colon
SGT Mauricio Colon
1SG Nestor E. Colon
SGT Rosa M. Colon
SGT Steven Colon
MR. Victor W. Colon
SPC Julio C. Colon-Bermudez
PFC Joseph Colonna
SPC Miguel A. Colorado
MR. Renoldo Colorosa
SSG Anthony Colozzi
CPL Arnold R. Colpitts

SGT Jerrell Colquette
SSG John S. Colquhoun
CPL Clifford V. Colson
LTC Carl W. Coltrane
1LT Christopher Columbres
SGM Charles R. Colvin
CPL Frank R. Colvin
LTC David Colwell
PV2 Edwin D. Colwell
PFC James M. Colwell
SPC Lute Colwell
MRS. Ozon A. Colwell
MS. SPC Terry L. Colwell
MS. Christina Combs
SPC Clyde Combs
CW4 (Ret) George J. Combs
SGT James Combs
PV2 Jerry B. Combs
1LT Jim Combs
MR. Lawrence Combs
SGT Michael W. Combs
SGT Phillip V. Combs
CW4 Thomas Combs
SGT Thomas W. Combs
SPC Al Comeau
SFC Gerard E. Comeau
COL (Ret) William C. Comee
SGT Randolph John Comegys
CPT Darrell L. Comer
SGT James C. Comer
SGT Randy Comer
SPC Robert E. Comer
LTC (Ret) Troy Comer
SSG Joseph T. Comerford
SPC James M. Commander
SFC (Ret) Martin A. Commander
SPC Justin Comne
CPT Darrell S. Compas
MAJ Joel D. Compeggie
MR. David H. Compo
SPC Scott A. Compo
PFC Gerald B. Compton
SP5 Jack Compton
SPC Ryan P. Compton
MG (Ret) James Comstock
CPT James M. Comstock
SFC Roger K. Comstock
SPC Brian Conant
MRS. Donald L. Conant
SSG Heath Conaway
PFC Carl N. Concha
SGT Robert M. Condela
MR. Raymond R. Condell
SSG William R. Conder
SP5 James E. Condon
SPC Jerome P. Condon
PFC William J. Condrick
SPC Joseph R. Condroski
SPC Stanley Cone
SPC Robert A. Conetta
CPT Al J. Conetto
SPC Joe H. Conic
SPC Michael A. Coniglio
PVT Timothy M. Conkle
PV2 Richard Conklin
1LT Booker Conley
CSM Brunk W. Conley
SSG Roger A. Conley
SPC Michael Conn
SPC James Connally
SGT Donald T. Connell
SGT Robert Connell
CPT Brent Connelly
SGT Kevin C. Connelly
SFC Matthew Connelly
SMA (Ret) William A. Connelly
SPC Demetrion J. Conner
MRS. James H. Conner
SPC Jeffery R. Conner
CPT Michael H. Conner
CPT Roger N. Conner
SGT Roy Conner
PFC Timothy A. Conner
CPT William D. Conner
SPC William R. Conner
LTC Thomas J. Conneran
PVT Bryan K. Connerly
SPC Marc D. Conners
SPC Chad S. Connolly
SPC George M. Connolly
SGT Joseph M. Connolly
CSM Paul T. Connolly
SGT Robert J. Connolly
SPC Timothy D. Connolly
COL (Ret) Arthur W. Connor
SPC Gilbert Connor
SPC Glenn M. Connor
SSG (Ret) John R. Connor

PFC Robert A. Connor
SPC Russell Connor
LTC Timothy M. Connor
CW5 Timothy M. Connor
1LT William M. Connor
LTC (Ret) Francis X. K. Connors
SSG Joseph M. Connors
LT Lawrence E. Connors
LTC Gregory B. Conover
CSM (Ret) George D. Conrad
CPL George H. Conrad
SPC Malcolm N. Conrad
MG (Ret) Michael J. Conrad
SP5 Richard K. Conrad
CSM (Ret) Jackie E. Conroe
MR. Frank E. Conroy
1LT Matthew R. Considine
1SG Calvin C. Constable
SPC John G. Constant
SPC William K. Conter
SPC James T. Conti
CPT Christopher L. Contino
SPC Dean L. Contover
SSG Adam Contreras
PVT Andrew Contreras
SGT Fabian Mariscal Contreras
SFC (Ret) Juan P. Contreras
SSG Rodrigo Contreras
PFC Stephen W. Contreras
CPL Frank K. Conway
SGT John B. Conway
CPT Michael J. Conway
CW4 William H. Conway
SGT Patrick E. Conwell
CPL Phillip A. Conybear
SGT Ronnie M. Conyer
SGT David L. Coody
PFC Alonzo Cook
SSG Bryan J. Cook
MAJ Carl K. Cook
SPC Charles R. Cook
SGT Clifford C. Cook
MR. Daniel V. Cook
1SG (Ret) Don Cook
CPL Donald J. Cook
SFC Glenn Cook
COL (Ret) Holly Cook
SPC Howard J. Cook
SGT Ira George Cook
SPC James L. Cook
MR. James M. Cook
SGT Jimmy M. Cook
1LT Joe D. Cook
SFC John A. Cook
SPC John R. Cook
1LT (Ret) Jonathan L. Cook
PVT Kenneth D. Cook
CPT Leonard Cook
MAJ Michael Cook
SGT Michael G. Cook
SGT Nicholas E. Cook
MR. Ramon H. Cook
SFC Robert L. Cook
PFC Robert R. Cook
1LT Robert W. Cook
1SG (Ret) Sam R. Cook
SSG Steven E. Cook
SPC Terry Cook
MAJ Thomas J. Cook
SGT Thomas J. Cook
SPC Tommy A. Cook
SFC (Ret) Vincent Raymond Cook
SFC W. D. Cook
SGT William F. Cook
1LT (Ret) William O. Cook
CPT James Cooke
SPC Jay P. Cooke
SGT Michael A. Cooke
CSM (Ret) Michael K. Cooke
LTC Thomas M. Cooke
SGT Virgil B. Cooksey
CW3 Maurice A. Cookson
SGT Charles L. Coole
SSG Earl W. Cooley
1SG (Ret) Robert H. Cooley
CPT Robert A. Coombs
SSG Robert V. Coombs
SGT Edwin K. Coon
MR. Robert B. Coon
SPC Douglas E. Coonce
CW2 Richard L. Coonce
1SG James T. Cooney
MSG Lawrence W. Coonrod
SGT Larry Coonts
SPC Benton R. Cooper
PFC Brian Cooper
SPC Christopher W. Cooper
SPC Daniel L. Cooper

MSG David A. Cooper
SGT David M. Cooper
SGM (Ret) Edward L. Cooper
CPT Emerson A. Cooper
SFC Eric V. Cooper
TSgt George A. Cooper
SGT Giles S. Cooper
CPT H. Ed Cooper
SPC Harvey Cooper
SPC James Cooper
CPT John M. Cooper
SGM (Ret) Kendall O. Cooper
PFC Kennedy A. Cooper
SFC Marion Cooper
LTC (Ret) Mark A. Cooper
PFC Marshall T. Cooper
MRS. Robert P. Cooper
SGT Sherman O. Cooper
1LT Stephen B. Cooper
PVT Joseph Cooperwood
CPT Douglas W. Copeland
CSM (Ret) George W. Copeland
SFC James T. Copeland
SSG James W. Copeland
MR. Jimmy W. Copeland
MRS. John F. Copeland
SSG Lloyd E. Copeland
CW3 Loren V. Copeland
CSM (Ret) Otto M. Copeland
CSM Charles L. Copello
SSG William Bart Copes
SFC Randall L. Copiskey
SGT Donald D. Copley
CPT (Ret) Jay C. Copley
SFC Larry C. Coppala
SSG William A. Coppedge
MSG (Ret) James R. Coppeler
PFC M. B. Coppock
1LT Paul J. Coppola
SGT Jeff Copsetta
SPC Charles E. Copson
SFC (Ret) Dale A. Corbett
LTC (Ret) Richard L. Corbett
SGT Timothy D. Corbett
SFC (Ret) Don R. Corbin
SFC Donald R. Corbin
SGT James P. Corbin
SSG Michael Lewis Corbin
CPT Starr Corbin
PFC James E. Corbitt
SSG Tom Corbutt
SGT Eugene Corcino
COL (Ret) Edward F. Corcoran
SGT John E. Corcoran
PFC John E. Corcoran
SFC (Ret) Mervin L. Corder
SP5 Robert B. Corder
MSG Enrique Cordero
SPC Gonsalo Cordero
1SG Jose R. Cordero
SFC Manuel Cordero
SFC Renee Cordero
CPT Cary B. Cordes
SPC Christopher G. Cordi
SPC Larry L. Cordle
SGT Augustine Santiago Cordova
PSG Bevallin F. Cordova
SFC (Ret) Dagoberto Cordova
MSG (Ret) Jose B. Cordova
TSgt Vincent G. Cordova
SPC Bernard L. Corella
MAJ (Ret) Richard H. Coreno
2LT Daniel R. Corey
SGT Leo B. Corey
SPC Thomas H. Corey
SFC James E. Corke
SGT August B. Corley
MR. Johnnie W. Corley
CPL Gregory E. Cormany
SPC Larry Cormier
SPC Robert J. Cormier
SP5 Larry Corn
SFC Richard L. Cornachia
LTC (Ret) Terry C. Corneil
SP5 Fabian B. Cornejo
SGT Ronald D. Cornell
SPC Cindy L. Cornell-Pettey
1SG (Ret) Charles M. Cornett
MR. Dana Roy Corney
1SG Michael J. Corning
SGT Barry K. Corno
SGM Derek J. Cornwall
1LT James A. Cornwell
SGT Robert J. Cornwell
SSG Edward J. Corona
SPC Ramon C. Corona
SPC Diego Coronado
SSG George Coronado

SGT Clinton E. Corpe
SrA George E. Corpuz
MAJ Nicholas Corrao
PVT Abiel A. Correa
SSG Anibal C. Correa
COL (Ret) Arnaldo L. Correa
SPC Robert A. Correa
TSgt Jack Correll
SPC Leslie D. Corrie
LTC (Ret) James T. Corrigan
SPC David A. Corriveau
LTC (Ret) Lawrence E. Corser
SPC John J. Corso
SPC Richard A. Cortell
SGT Angel M. Cortez
SSG Dennis Cortez
LTC Elward P. Cortez
CPT George Cortez
SFC Henry B. Cortez
SSG Ricky J. Cortez
SGT Miguel A. Cortina
CPT Tyler W. Cortner
SSG Vincent R. Corzo
SPC Kavin D. Cosay
MSG Glen J. Cosby
SSG Jason Cosby
SGT Ralph M. Cosby
SPC Thomas Cosby
SFC (Ret) Anthony F. Coscione
2LT Daniel Cosentino
PVT Ben Cosgrove
LTC (Ret) Charles A. Cosgrove
LT William R. Cosh
SFC (Ret) Donald J. Coshey
SFC Julius R. Cosma
SGT Alejandro Cosme
SGT Rafael Cosme-Ortiz
CPL Gilbert R. Cosner
CSM David Costa
SGT Gerald Costa
SPC Lenny Costa
COL Charles Costanza
SGT Jay M. Costanzo
1LT Charles H. Costello
SGT Harold L. Costello
SPC Michael D. Costello
SGT Steven M. Costello
SSG Richard E. Costo
CPL Raul M. Cota
COL (Ret) Albert H. Cote
SPC Frederick R. Cote
SGT Stan Cotner
MSG Joseph A. Cotropia
SPC James R. Cottam
SGT H. Tucker Cotten
SGT Craig J. Cotter
SPC Jason Cotter
MR. John Cotterell
SFC Gregory A. Cottle
1SG Robert M. Cottle
CSM (Ret) A. C. Cotton
SGT Charles R. Cotton
CSM (Ret) Niles E. Cotton
SSG (Ret) Patrick L. Cotton
CPT Reginald Cotton
SSG Arthur A. Couch
2LT Christopher Monroe Couch
PFC Freddie L. Couch
SPC Matthew D. Couch
SFC (Ret) Ralph E. Couch
SGT John Couffer
SPC Christopher Coughlin
SGT Christopher F. Coughlin
SPC James V. Coughlin
SPC Richard B. Couitt
SGT William Coulson
SPC Neil C. Coulston
1LT Charles J. Coulter
SGT Daniel F. Coulter
COL (Ret) Joseph S. Coulter
PFC Derrick L. Countryman
SGT Randolph Counts
SGT John M. Couper
SGT David C. Courchane
SP5 Jerry D. Courington
SGT Christopher J. Coursey
SGT Daniel Courtney
SGT Daniel M. Courtney
SSG James D. Courtney
MSG (Ret) John Courtney
CSM (Ret) Larry T. Courtney
SGT Andrew Courtright
LTC Michael P. Courts
SGT Jonathan Courville
SGM (Ret) Alexander E. Cousart
CPT William Griffith Couser
SGT Joseph R. Cousineau
PFC Rafael E. Cousins
SGM (Ret) Thurman C. Cousins
SPC Merritte M. Coussons
SPC Gustavo Coutin
MR. Richard P. Couture
SGT Erasmo Covarrubias
PVT Robert E. Covault
MR. Robert Covert
WO1 Michael T. Covey
COL (Ret) E. D. Covington
CPT James L. Covington
SPC Sidney A. Covington
PVT Alfredo M. Covos
SPC Richard L. Cowan
SSG Robert Cowan
SGT Ronnie E. Cowan
SGT Richard Cowand
LTC Jack E. Coward
SPC Jason Coward
CPT Robert K. Cowart
MR. Eldon R. Cowden
COL (Ret) Claiborne W. Cowgill
PFC Leonard M. Cowherd
MRS. Betty Cox
MSG Bryan Cox
SPC Calvin B. Cox
CPT Charles W. Cox
MAJ Chris Cox
SSG Damon Cox
SPC Dennis J. Cox
MSG Emmett F. Cox
SSG Erick M. Cox
SP5 Frank L. Cox
SPC James Andrew Cox
SPC James Mykel Cox
SGT Jerry Joe Cox
CPT John L. Cox
PVT Justin Cox
MG Kendall P. Cox
1LT Norman J. Cox
SFC Pearl W. Cox
MR. Robert L. Cox
SGT Steven K. Cox
MSG (Ret) Troy A. Cox
SFC (Ret) Walter D. Cox
PVT William C. Cox
SPC Henry J. Coyle
PVT Joseph M. Coyne
MAJ (Ret) Richard J. Coyne
LTC (Ret) John W. Cozart
SPC Earl J. Crabtree
MSG (Ret) Earl W. Crabtree
SGT James D. Crabtree
MSG Keith E. Crabtree
CPT Philip E. Crabtree
SGT Thomas L. Crabtree
CW4 (Ret) Alfred B. Craft
SFC (Ret) Charlie N. Craft
SGT Edwin T. Craft
MRS. Renate Craft
SSG (Ret) William E. Craft
SFC (Ret) Charles H. Cragg
SSG Arthur J. Craig
PVT Darryl M. Craig
SPC Edward Omar Craig
SFC Franklin A. Craig
SSG Henry E. Craig
SSG Jesse A. Craig
CPT John D. Craig
PFC Joseph R. Craig
SPC Kelly Craig
CPT Mark B. Craig
SGT Mark E. Craig
MR. Raymond L. Craig
CMSgt (Ret) Robert C. Craig
PVT Robert K. Craig
SGT William H. Craig
SPC John Craigen
SGT Richard E. Crain
MAJ William F. Crain
PFC Lynn G. Craine
LTC Maury S. Cralle
MAJ Paul D. Cramer
SPC Barry C. Crandall
COL (Ret) Bruce P. Crandall
SPC Floyd E. Crane
MRS. Frederick A. Crane
SPC James Crane
LTC Kit C. Dean Crane
CW2 Richard A. Crane
CPT Ronald T. Crane
SPC Jerry L. Cranford
SSG Jamie Crankfield
MR. Joe Crankshaw
PFC George H. Cranswick
SP5 Gary Crapser
MAJ (Ret) Clinton W. Crass
SGT Robert D. Cravello
SGT Ray E. Cravens
MR. Theodore R. Cravens
SGT Joseph D. Cravey
LTC C. M. Crawford
SGT Craig Crawford
CW2 David A. Crawford
SGT David M. Crawford
PFC Dennis R. Crawford
SPC Douglas J. Crawford
SSG Eric Crawford
LTC (Ret) Francis M. Crawford
CPT George Crawford
LTC (Ret) George S. Crawford
CW4 Harold W. Crawford
CPL Hugh Crawford
LTC James C. Crawford
SGT John David Crawford
SGT John S. Crawford
LTC Kenneth J. Crawford
MAJ Kenneth T. Crawford
SGT Nick Crawford
SFC Randy M. Crawford
SGT William S. Crawford
CPT Jesse Crawford-Mancini
SGT Walter G. Crawley
SPC Jason L. Cray
SPC Gene A. Crayne
SPC Paul J. Crayton
SFC James M. Creager
LTC Paul E. Creal
MAJ Shawn Creamer
SPC David Crecelius
MRS. Bernard J. Creed
SPC Bonny Creed
SGT Gary W. Creed
SPC Ollie L. Creed
SGM Charles E. Creek
PFC Brendan Creighton
CPT George E. Creighton
1LT James M. Creim
SPC Philip R. Cremins
MSG (Ret) Herbert L. Crenshaw
MR. James L. Crenshaw
SFC John J. Crespi
SSG Alberto Crespo
SSG Aaron L. Cress
1LT Gordon P. Cress
SGT Rodney G. Cress
PFC Lane Cressonie
SPC Edward B. Creutzberger
SGT Darrell E. Crews
CPL Robert R. Crews
CPT Thomas L. Crews
MRS. Joseph P. Cribbins
SPC Michael W. Cricco
SGT Glenn F. Crider
PFC Rayburn L. Crider
CW3 Jesse C. Crimm
SSG Joseph E. Crimmins
1LT Christopher J. Crisafi
SP5 Patrick S. Crisafulli
SGT Thomas J. Criser
MSG George T. Crisp
SFC Jeremy Crisp
SPC John O. Crisp
SGT Joseph J. Crispino
SPC Edward E. Criss
SPC Kevin Michael Criss
COL Douglas C. Crissman
CPL Edward Crist
MR. John C. Crist
SFC Greg Crochran
SP5 Donald E. Crocker
SPC H. Joseph Crocker
CPT John A. Crocker
PFC Robert Earl Crocker
SGT Lawrence R. Crockett
SFC Thomas Crockett
SGT Bruce Croel
SPC Vernon Croffoot
MAJ Ira L. Crofford
SGT Wayne M. Crofford
SGT Richard T. Crogan
SSG Anthony B. Crognale
LTC (Ret) Gordon W. Crom
SGT Raymond W. Crombe
CPT Raymond E. Cromer
2LT Amy Cronin
CW4 (Ret) Eugene C. Cronin
SGT Philip Cronin
SGT Robert D. Cronin
COL Robert M. Cronin
CW2 Gregory Cronos
SFC Edward P. Crook
SGT Arthur Crooker
CPL Leo Crosariol
LTG (Ret) John S. Crosby
MR. John W. Crosby
SGT Marcus Crosby
SSG Thomas E. Crosby
MR. Layfayette Crosier
CW5 (Ret) Richard E. Crosley
SFC Booker T. Cross
SPC Dennis Cross
COL Dennis D. Cross
TSgt Gerald D. Cross
MAJ Joel R. Cross
CPL Michael L. Cross
SPC Tommy L. Cross
SPC Vanessa R. Cross
PFC Vernon E. Cross
SGT Vernon L. Cross
2LT Jim Crossley
PFC Ernest C. Crosson
MAJ Peter Crosthwaite
SPC Charles C. Crotts
SSG Brad S. Crouch
SFC Myron L. Crouch
SSG Paul Stewart Crouch
SSG Troy E. Crouch
SPC Raymond L. Croucher
SGT M. Lamar Crouse
SSG Arthur E. Crouse
SPC Eldon D. Crouse
SSG William Crouthamel
SPC Brian L. Crow
CW2 Carl V. Crow
MAJ Mason W. Crow
1LT (Ret) Michael P. Crow
SFC Robert D. Crow
1SG (Ret) Samuel A. Crow
MAJ William A. Crow
SGT Charles Crow Flies High
PSG John D. Crowden
SPC Don D. Crowder
PFC Ernest L. Crowder
SSG Gerald L. Crowder
MR. William C. Crowder
SFC D. L. Crowell
SFC Joshua Crowell
PFC Arthur V. Crowley
SGT Ronald D. Crowley
SPC Thomas J. Crowley
SGT Josh Crownover
PV2 James Cruey
SGT Kenny V. Cruise
SPC Gary M. Crull
CPT Anthony B. Crumbey
SPC John A. Crumbley
SFC (Ret) James D. Crumpton
LTC Joseph A. Cruse
SPC Kevin M. Crusilla
SGT John F. Crussard
COL (Ret) Michael H. Crutcher
SPC Patrick Crutchfield
SGT William Earl Crutchfield
PV2 Allen M. Cruz
SPC Arthur P. Cruz
SSG Duane C. Cruz
SFC Edward T. Cruz
1SG Jaime Cruz
CPL Larry Cruz
SSG Luis Cruz
SGT Manuel Cruz
SGT Pedro Cruz
SGT Ricardo Cruz
SGT Ricardo A. Cruz
SP5 Robert A. Cruz
1SG (Ret) Ruperto Cruz
SPC Toby F. Cruz
SGT Angel E. Cruz Cova
SSG Jose A. Cruz-Ortiz
SFC Kerry C. Cryer
PFC Andrew Csaszar
CPT C. E. Gene Cubbage
COL (Ret) Joseph T. Cuccaro
MG Anthony A. Cucolo
SSG Larry L. Cuddy
MRS. Dywane D. Cude
PFC Trevor E. Cudjoe
CPL Cruz G. Cuellar
SGM (Ret) Lawrence F. Cuellar
SPC Filbert H. Cuesta
SGT Jose Cuestas
SPC David Cuevas
SPC Elias S. Cuevas
SGT Marjan Cukarski
SGT Charles M. Culbertson
SPC John H. Culbertson
CPT Jamie L. Culbreath
SP5 Gerald E. Culler
SPC Franklin Culp
CPT Trygve H. Culp
SFC (Ret) Fred E. Culpepper
COL (Ret) John W. Culton
SGM (Ret) Armando Cumba
1SG Donald P. Cumm
SFC (Ret) Dannie L. Cummings
SP5 David G. Cummings
COL (Ret) Frank Cummings
SGT Frank J. Cummings
SGM Harry J. Cummings
MAJ J. Bruce Cummings
LTC Maryann B. Cummings
PFC Michael L. Cummings
CPL Roger L. Cummings
LTC Steve Cummings
SGT Eugene H. Cummins
MSG Frank W. Cummins
SGT John P. Cummins
WO1 Joe L. Cundiff
SP5 Alfred Cuneo
SrA Vernon F. Cunha
CPT George T. Cunkelman
SGT Adam C. Cunningham
MRS. Alfred J. Cunningham
1SG (Ret) Benjamin B. Cunningham
SSG Damion Earl Cunningham
MR. Harold A. Cunningham
SSG Jerry J. Cunningham
SSG (Ret) Jerry M. Cunningham
SGT John Cunningham
PFC Paul Cunningham
COL Robert A. Cunningham
LTC (Ret) Roger D. Cunningham
MAJ Thomas J. Cunningham
SPC Thomas J. Cunningham
PFC Charles G. Cunningham
1SG Jerry Cupp
MSG Robert L. Cupp
SFC Dwight Curb
SPC Lance Curci
SGM James Cureton
SPC Jerome Curiale
1LT David R. Curiel
SSG Diane Curley
MR. Earl P. Curling
1SG Daniel Curnan
CPT Donald P. Curnutte
PVT James W. Curram
LTC Gerard P. Curran
SGT Ray Curran
SPC Frederick Currie
SGT Ted B. Currier
PVT Anthony P. Curry
CPT Donald E. Curry
SFC (Ret) James D. Curry
1SG Phelan A. Curry
PFC Ronald Curry
SGT Steve Curry
SPC Timothy L. Curry
MAJ (Ret) Aaron E. Curtis
PFC Charles A. Curtis
SGT Christopher A. Curtis
SGT Daniel L. Curtis
SGT David L. Curtis
PFC Edward F. Curtis
PFC Eugene R. Curtis
CMSgt Gilbert Curtis
PFC Harold E. Curtis
CSM (Ret) James E. Curtis
CSM Kevin T. Curtis
SGT (Ret) Lawrence M. Curtis
SGT Patch Curtis
SSG Paul D. Curtis
1SG Paul S. Curtis
1SG (Ret) Richard Curtis
SGT Russell Curtis
LTC Samuel W. Curtis
1LT Alfred P. Curty
PFC George R. Cusher
LTC John Cushing
BG (Ret) Thomas S. Cushing
CPL Jack Lewis Custer
SGT Marc J. Custer
SSG Edward D. Cutlip
SGT Markus Cuttino
PFC Chris M. Cuttlers
CSM Derek Cuvellier
MAJ Matthew P. Cuviello
SPC Patrick J. Cybert
CPL William P. Cybula
SPC Joseph M. Cybulski
MAJ (Ret) Charles M. Cychosz
CPT Cornell J. Cypress
CPT Brian Cyr
SGT Lionel J. Cyr
CPL Maurice E. Cyr
SPC Michael John Cyran
SPC Kert C. Cyrille
SGT David W. Cyrulik
WO1 James T. Cyrus
COL (Ret) Walter R. Cyrus
CPT John R. Czapko
SPC Mike Czaplewski
SPC Eugene R. Czaplicki
SGT Matthew W. Czaplicki
SPC Edward J. Czarnecki
SSG Frank J. Czech
SGT Dave Czerniakowski
SPC Philip E. Czuper
PFC Larry S. Czyscon
SPC Kenneth B. Czyz
MRS. James H. Da Foe
SSGT John Da Ponte
PV2 Bryan M. Dabbs
PFC Christopher Dabney
MSG (Ret) Stanley A. Dabrowski
SGT Ralph Dagenhart
SP5 Bruce V. Dagilis
SPC Jon Dagostino
BG (Ret) James J. D'Agostino
CPT Anthony D'Aguillo
LTC Anthony A. D'Aguillo
SPC Darry L. Dahl
SGT Ralph R. Dahl
1SG (Ret) Roy C. Dahl
SGT Duane J. Dahlstrom
SPC Edward W. Dahse
SPC Tony Dai
SPC Ronald J. Daigle
MSG Joseph A. Dailey
SPC Milton R. Dailey
SP5 Rick Dailey
SGT Wendell L. Dailey
PFC William J. Dailing
SP5 Bruce E. Daily
COL (Ret) James I. Daily
SPC Anthony Daisy
SGT Gary W. Dake
SGT Don W. Dalby
COL (Ret) Ronald P. Dale
MRS. Francis B. D'Aleo
SGT Bridgette M. Daley
SPC Don Daley
SPC Eileen M. Daley
SFC (Ret) John I. Daley
SPC Marcus E. Daley
DR. Robert Daliessio
SPC Stephen F. Dalrymple
SSG (Ret) Gerald E. Dalton
MR. Herbert L. Dalton
SGT Kenneth J. Dalton
SPC Larry G. Dalton
SSG Michael C. Dalton
CPT Stewart G. Dalton
SGT Anthony E. Daly
SPC Franklin E. Daly
SrA John J. Daly
SPC Joseph J. Daly
LTC (Ret) Michael P. Daly
PFC Raymond D. Daly
PFC Robert F. Daly
SFC Robert G. Daly
SPC William E. Daly
MR. Patrick H. D'Amico
SPC (Ret) Thomas J. Damore
SPC Richard H. Dampman
SGT Edward T. Damron
SGT Russell Irving Damskov
MS. Amy Damveld
SPC Merlin K. Dana
SSG Marion R. Danak
MR. John P. Danckaert
CW3 Peter R. Dancy
PSG Claude D. Danders
SP5 Ron E. D'Andre
MR. Andrew Arthur Dane
SPC Gary Danford
SGT Daniel G. Danforth
SGT Dan A. D'Angelo
SFC (Ret) Leon J. D'Angelo
SPC Paul A. D'Angelo
MR. John C. D'Angelone
SSG Bailey Daniel
PFC Branson Daniel
1SG Dale D. Daniel
SFC Harold K. Daniel
MSG Jack L. Daniel
SPC James Daniel
MAJ James Steve Daniel
SPC Jerry L. Daniel
SPC Jerry W. Daniel
SGT Joshua L. Daniel
PFC Marvin C. Daniel
SSG Jason J. Danielecki
LTC Barry E. Daniels
SPC Bruce E. Daniels
PVT Grante C. Daniels
CSM James P. Daniels
SSG Kendrick J. Daniels
SFC Larry Daniels
SGT Mark E. Daniels
CPL Robert L. Daniels
MR. Thomas Edward Daniels
PFC Thomas S. Daniels
SP5 William Daniels

MRS. Theodore S. Danielsen
MRS. Dennis A. Danielson
MAJ James D. Danielson
SPC Gary C. Danjou
CPL Thomas F. Dankert
SPC Steven G. Danks
SFC Rocky A. Danners
MR. Billy R. Dansby
PFC Danny Dansby
SGT Daniel D. Danton
LTC (Ret) William Dan Dantzler
SGT Frank Danulevith
MAJ David A. Danzeiser
1SG Juan Darby
SSG Jackie Darden
SPC Ronnie Lee Darden
SPC Steven D. Darden
SPC Jessica L. Dareing
SPC Phillip W. Darity
SSG Peter A. Darling
SGT Richard R. Darling
SFC Robert J. Darling
SPC Michael Darmstedter
REV. Thomas W. Darnall
SGT Gary R. Darnell
SSG James A. Darnell
SSG John E. Darnell
CW4 Robert L. Darnell
SFC Ross Darnell
CPL William S. Darnell
SPC Seward J. Darr
TSgt Donald G. Darrah
SPC John Michael Darrah
SPC Frederick E. Darris
SGT (Ret) Hubert Darrisaw
CPT Joel L. Darrow
SGT Kim D. Dary
1LT Thomas E. Dasenbrock
COL (Ret) Michael E. Dash
PVT Sean E. Dasho
SGT Robert J. Datish
PV2 David Datra
SGT Vincent F. Dattoli
MR. David Daugette
SGT George M. Daugherty
MR. Gerald L. Daugherty
1SG Hubert W. Daugherty
LTC Timothy J. Daugherty
SPC Johnny L. Daughtry
CW4 (Ret) Roy E. Daughtry
SGT Donald J. Daujatas
SSG Gerald Daulton
SPC Michael G. Daum
SGT Robert L. Daumiller
SGT Albert Vincent D'Autorio
SGT Luc R. Dauvin
PFC William Davenhall
SPC Douglas C. Davenport
SSG Jimmy R. Davenport
MAJ (Ret) Leon Davenport
SPC Michael D. Davenport
2LT Robert F. Davenport
SGT Terry Davenport
SPC Travis Davenport
PFC Walter Davenport
CPL Joseph T. Daversa
SSG Charles J. Davey
2LT George W. Davey
SGT George M. David
COL (Ret) Ronald C. David
1LT Warren O. David
SSG Ric Davidge
SGT A. Dave Davidson
SGT Gerald Davidson
SFC James C. Davidson
CPT James P. Davidson
SFC James P. Davidson
LTC (Ret) Jay P. Davidson
LTC John C. Davidson
SSG John H. Davidson
MR. John R. Davidson
COL (Ret) Lonnie M. Davidson
SPC Robert C. Davidson
MAJ Robert E. Davidson
SPC Robert Davie
1SG (Ret) Robert M. Davie
SSG Daniel C. Davies
SPC Duane L. Davies
CPL Jason P. Davies
PFC Russel J. Davies
PV2 Sackie S. Davies
WO1 David J. Davighi
SGT Joseph R. Davila
SPC Richard A. Davila
SGT Ruben Davila
SPC Alexander Davis
CPT Allen F. Davis
SFC Anthony Davis
LTC Archie P. Davis
PFC Arthur R. Davis
SGT Bennie E. Davis
MRS. Bennie F. Davis
SGT Bob G. Davis
SGT Bobby Davis
MAJ (Ret) Bruce A. Davis
SSG Bruce D. Davis
SP5 C. Raymond Davis
2LT Calvin Davis
SGT Carl G. Davis
SSG Carthais D. Davis
CPL Cecil M. Davis
SSG (Ret) Charles F. Davis
SPC Charles L. Davis
2LT Charles M. Davis
SPC Clarence R. Davis
SGT Claude L. Davis
CPL Clifford A. Davis
MRS. Clifford R. Davis
SPC Clifton Davis
SSG Clyde W. Davis
CPL Curtis E. Davis
SGT Darrell Davis
PVT David Earl Davis
1LT David P. Davis
SGT David W. Davis
SGT Dennis W. Davis
SSG Domonic V. Davis
PFC Donald L. Davis
SSG Donald L. Davis
MRS. Donald R. Davis
SGT Doyle Davis
MAJ (Ret) Duane J. Davis
SSG Edward R. Davis
SGT Elmer A. Davis
SFC (Ret) Eugene R. Davis
MR. Evan W. Davis
PV2 Francis E. Davis
SFC Freddie J. Davis
SGT Gary D. Davis
SSG George M. Davis
PFC Gerald D. Davis
SSG Gerald E. Davis
MSG Gordon L. Davis
MAJ Hal M. Davis
1SG (Ret) Harold D. Davis
SSG Harold K. Davis
MR. Harry E. Davis
SFC Huey L. Davis
PFC Jalexus Davis
SPC James Davis
SPC James Davis
SGT James C. Davis
PFC James E. Davis
CPT James G. Davis
SSG James M. Davis
SPC James R. Davis
2LT James R. Davis
SSG (Ret) James R. Davis
SFC Jennings B. Davis
SGT Jerry C. Davis
SGT Jesse Davis
LTC Jim Davis
1SG Jim Davis
SFC Joe Davis
SPC John D. Davis
SSG Johnie R. Davis
SFC Johnny F. Davis
SGM (Ret) Johnny K. Davis
SGT Jonathan Davis
1LT Jonathan Davis
CSM Joseph Davis
SFC Joseph E. Davis
SFC Joseph L. Davis
LTC (Ret) Joseph P. Davis
SGT Juan B. Davis
SSG Justin S. Davis
SPC Kermit A. Davis
SFC Laddie F. Davis
SGT Lawrence Davis
MRS. Lola Davis
SPC Louis C. Davis
SPC Louis W. Davis
SPC Luke M. Davis
PVT Michael A. Davis
SSG Michael D. Davis
SGT Michael L. Davis
2LT Nadine B. Davis
1LT Nathaniel M. Davis
SSG Orgene Franklin Davis
SFC Palmer D. Davis
SPC Patrick R. Davis
CW2 Paul S. Davis
MRS. Preston M. Davis
CPL Ray Davis
SFC Reginald L. Davis
MS. Reginald N. Davis
LTC Reginald R. Davis
SPC Rex Davis
MAJ Richard A. Davis
SSG (Ret) Robert E. Davis
COL (Ret) Robert E. Davis
SGM (Ret) Robert K. Davis
2LT Robert W. Davis
CW4 Roger W. Davis
SPC Ronald A. Davis
SFC Ronald W. Davis
SSG Ronald W. Davis
PFC Roy T. Davis
SGT Russell I. Davis
MAJ Sean P. Davis
SFC Sheila R. Davis
MAJ (Ret) Standley H. Davis
SPC Steven Davis
1SG Steven A. Davis
SPC Steven L. Davis
SGT Terrence L. Davis
SGT Terry L. Davis
SSG Thomas A. Davis
SSG Timothy A. Davis
SPC Timothy A. Davis
SPC Timothy W. Davis
SSG Tracy H. Davis
SGT Van F. Davis
CPT (Ret) Vann B. Davis
SPC Vernon E. Davis
1SG Walter B. Davis
SGT William E. Davis
SGT William S. Davis
SPC Willie Davis
SGT Willie A. Davis
TSgt Curtis P. Davison
MR. John Davison
SPC Lowell D. Davison
SFC (Ret) Charles W. Davitz
CPT Brandon B. Dawalt
PFC William C. Dawdy
PFC Jeffrey Dawe
SPC Emery W. Dawes
SSG James E. Dawkins
SPC Ronald R. Dawkins
2LT Brian J. Dawson
SGT Bruce W. Dawson
SGT Charles W. Dawson
MSG Dean Dawson
MR. John E. Dawson
SFC Joseph L. Dawson
SPC Michael A. Dawson
SFC (Ret) Michael C. Dawson
COL Michael T. Dawson
SFC Robert Dusty Dawson
SPC Robert E. Dawson
SGT Ronald W. Dawson
1SG Scott Dawson
COL Stephen Dawson
SFC (Ret) Tae Dawson
SPC Thomas J. Dawson
SGT Johnny Dawyd
COL (Ret) Arnold Daxe
SP5 Al Day
SGT Barbara J. Day
SPC Danny Day
SGT Dennis R. Day
PFC Elmer G. Day
MAJ Eugene R. Day
SP5 Francis E. Day
SP5 James C. Day
SSG Joe H. Day
SGT Randy C. Day
PFC Raymond E. Day
SPC Ronald D. Day
SPC Howard Daymude
SFC (Ret) David B. Dayton
SGT Robert Dayton
PFC Thomas T. Daywalt
MAJ Philip De Aguilera
SGT (Ret) Joe De Alejandro
LTC Zane E. De Amaral
SPC Ernie De Anda
COL (Ret) A. J. De Angelis
SGT Vincent F. De Berardinis
SGM Robert R. De Blois
MSG John De Borde
CPL Doc Courtney J. De Bruin
MSG Hansel De Busk
SPC James M. De Carlo
SGT Leonard De Clue
SPC Merlyn Lewayne De Coster
SFC Daniel R. De Criscio
CPT Joseph A. De Croce
LTC Brian L. J. De Davenport-Stuart
SGT John F. De Fazio
CPL Richard A. De Fazio
2LT Robert J. De Fea
SGT Frank A. De Fino
CPL Francesco De Fronzo
1SG (Ret) Peter J. De Gaetano
PFC Philip P. De Garis
SFC Jay R. De Garmo
CPT (Ret) Anthony A. De Gennaro
SFC Patrick J. De George
SGT Salvatore De George
PFC Roger W. De Graff
CPT Robert F. De Groff
SPC Andres De Haro
MR. John De Hart
SSG Michael L. De Hart
SP5 Emmett A. De Harty
SPC Charles De Herrera
PFC Leon A. De Herrera
CPT Clarissa De Jesus
SSG Pablo De Jesus
SFC Jose A. De Jesus Benn
SSG Archie De John
SPC Shawn A. De Journett
SGT Tiberio P. De Julio
SSG Carlos De La Llata
SPC Anthony De La Pena
SGT Frank De La Puente
SFC Robert De La Rosa
SPC Dennis B. De Laire
LTC (Ret) Charles J. De Lancey
PFC Gerard F. De Lang
SGT James De Lauder
SGT Arturo De Le Garza
SSG Esteban S. De Leon
PV2 Frank J. Diaz De Leon
SPC Richard R. De Leon
CW4 Roland De Leon
SGT Pearlstine De Loach
MR. Pearlstine De Loache
SFC Ralph A. De Lome
SP5 Daniel R. De Long
SPC Walter De Long
SPC Peter De Lorenzo
SSG Augustin S. De Luna
SSG Carlos De Luna
COL Vincent J. De Maggio
MAJ (Ret) Alfred S. De Mailo
SPC Samuel Paul De Mars
CPT John De Martini
SPC Marcus J. De Matos
SPC Anthony De Mayo
1LT Nelson R. De Mille
SPC Michael De Moss
SGT Domenick De Nuzzio
COL William A. De Palo
SPC Anthony P. De Pasquale
SPC Frank T. De Passio
LTC (Ret) John F. De Perro
SPC James P. De Persia
SGT Salvatore De Petro
SSG Lane W. De Priest
SPC Daniel De Prima
PVT William D. De Primeo
BG (Ret) John F. De Pue
1SG Francisco De Ramirez
SSG Gary De Rigne
SPC Stephen J. De Rouco
MR. James P. De Salvo
MR. Michael B. De Sanctis
SGT Edward F. De Santis
SGT Frank Patrick De Santo
WO1 Benjamin De Shields
COL (Ret) Charles E. De Shields
PFC Alfred J. De Siano
1LT Jeffrey A. De Stefano
SGT Joseph S. De Vargas
PV2 Jacob De Vault
PFC Phillip H. De Villers
SPC Louis A. De Vito
LTC Tim De Vito
COL (Ret) Paul T. De Vries
SPC Walter F. De Vries
SFC Michael S. De Wilde
MSG Austin De Witt
LTC (Ret) Clyde H. De Witt
SGT Robert B. De Wolf
PFC John P. De Young
MR. Thomas J. De Young
MR. James J. Deah
MR. Timothy A. Deah
SP5 William F. Deakins
2LT Dennis J. Deal
MRS. Kenneth W. Deal
PFC Michael E. Deal
SGT Bernard J. Deamicis
SPC Arthur Ray Dean
LTC Benjamin P. Dean
SP5 David Dean
SGT George F. Dean
PFC Howard O. Dean
SGT James M. Dean
MR. John T. Dean
SPC Lawrence Grant Dean
WO1 Paul M. Dean
MAJ Robert C. Dean
CW2 Timothy W. Dean
SGT Walter T. Dean
SP5 Wendel C. Dean
SGM (Ret) William E. Dean
SGM Timothy W. Deane
SFC Lawrence A. Dearborn
PVT Branden D. Deardorff
MR. Carl E. Dearth
CPL James A. Deaton
SGT Robert T. Deaux
SFC E. G. Deaven
SGT Winston Deblanc
SGT David P. Debyl
SFC (Ret) Terry A. K. Decamp
CPT Peter J. Decareau
PFC Gary A. Decesaro
PFC Gary R. Dechaine
SP3 Richard L. Deck
MR. Marvin Deckard
CW1 Clayton G. Decker
SGT Forrest E. Decker
SFC Gerald E. Decker
SFC Homer A. Decker
SPC James R. Decker
SPC Jan A. Decker
PFC Jay Decker
SSG Matt Decker
SGT Paul J. Decker
MR. Richard Decker
SGT Terry A. Decker
SGT Leonard R. Deckert
SGT William Deckert
SGT Ron J. Decktor
SPC Edward L. Decoito
SGT Gary D. Decoteau
SPC Carl L. Dednam
SFC Charles J. Dedrick
MR. Everard E. Dedrick
SP5 John L. Dees
PFC Taylor C. Dees
SFC (Ret) Gerald H. Deffenbaugh
SFC Michael A. Deforest
SGT Frank J. Defusco
SSG Hector Degado Vega
PFC Christopher Degaetano
COL (Ret) Delano E. Degeneffe
SFC David E. Degenhardt
SFC James R. Degenkolb
SPC Roger R. Deglow
SGT James W. Degner
CW5 Troy A. Degolyer
CPL Donald W. Degood
SSG Dominic Degrado
SGT Kenneth J. Degruy
PFC Garry D. Dehart
SGT Raymond C. Dehart
SP5 William J. Dehart
SPC Alvino Y. Deimes
SSG Victor S. Deines
SGT Robert Deisbeck
SPC Edward A. Deissroth
SPC Jimmie E. Deiter
PFC William F. Deitler
SPC Jeremy Deitz
SFC Cesar Dejesus
COL (Ret) Gary F. Dekay
PFC John D. Dekoskie
LTC (Ret) George Del Carlo
MAJ (Ret) Frank R. Del Gregg
SPC D. J. Del Signore
SPC Anthony J. Del Sordo
MSG Richard Dela Cruz Bernardo
SFC Aida S. Delacruz
MAJ (Ret) Bernard J. Delahunty
SSG (Ret) David J. Delancey
CPL Dale E. Delaney
SFC David Delaney
SGT Duane Delaney
1LT John W. Delaney
1SG (Ret) Joseph Delaney
SPC Robert J. Delaney
SGT Philip W. Delano
PFC Robert R. Delao
SSG Frederick Delap
SGT Christopher Delara
SGT Larry Delashmit
COL (Ret) Patrick N. Delavan
PV2 Joseph Delbiacovo
SPC Robert O. Deleon
SGT Kole Delev
MR. Antonio M. Delgado
PVT Jon Delgado
SFC Jose I. Delgado
SPC Joseph Delgado
SPC Julio R. Delgado
CPL Tomas M. Delgado
SGT William K. Delgado
CSM (Ret) Robert M. Delia
SFC Luis Delima
SGT Richard Delisio
SPC James V. Della Silva
PFC David Dellatto
SFC (Ret) Joseph Delle
SP5 Norman A. Delligatti
CPT Aaron P. Dellinger
MR. Donald Rex Delong
SPC Lewis L. Delong
SPC Cyprian J. Delorme
SSG Aaron Delossantos
SPC George W. Delph
SGT Donald A. Delsing
PFC Brian K. Delzeit
MR. John A. Demairo
SGT George A. Demarco
SSG Armando Demartino
PFC Daniel L. Demaskie
TSgt Edward Dembeck
SP5 Donald J. Demchak
PFC Michael Demchuk
MRS. Paul J. Demcoe
SGT Bobbie J. Dement
SGT David L. Dement
1LT Jennifer L. Dement
SPC Everett W. Demeritt
SPC Robert C. Demerson
CPL Dan G. Demetry
MSG Norman R. Demeule
SP5 Peter J. Demianych
SGT Michael Deming
PFC Johnathan Demmons
SFC (Ret) Charles J. Demons
SP5 Richard M. Demoro
CPT Lekisa Dempsey
SGT Philip D. Dempsey
PFC Robert P. Dempsey
PFC Richard A. Demski
MAJ (Ret) Peter A. Dencker
CPL Brett A. Dendler
SFC Mark E. Deneault
PFC Danny L. Deneteclaw
SGT James M. Denholm
SGT Keith H. Denison
SGT Jerry P. Denissen
SPC Rodney C. Denius
MS. Joyce Denke
SPC Frank Denman
1LT James W. Denman
PFC John D. Denman
MAJ Shevin Denmark
PFC Brian F. Dennehey
SP5 William Harold Denner
SGT Jonathan Denney
MAJ Phillip R. Denney
PFC James J. Dennigan
SPC Jeffery A. Denning
SGT Johnny K. Denning
SPC Richard V. Denning
CPL Todd A. Denning
SGT David L. Dennis
CW5 (Ret) Donald W. Dennis
PVT Harold G. Dennis
PFC Jonathan M. Dennis
SSG (Ret) Mark E. Dennis
1LT Michael L. Dennis
SFC Robert A. Dennis
SPC Theodore B. Dennis
SFC Thomas E. Dennis
SGT Joseph M. Dennison
SSG Charles Dennisten
SP5 Billy D. Denny
1LT Stephen E. Denny
BG (Ret) Kerry G. Denson
SGT Malcolm Garnelle Dent
PFC Glenn D. Dentan
SGT (Ret) David D. Dentinger
SPC Merle Dentino
SPC Clarence F. Denton
SPC Doreen S. Denton
SGT Jack M. Denton
CPL Jimmie C. Denton
SPC John C. Denton
SPC Mark K. Denton
1LT Ronnie Denton
MSG Tamatha L. Denton
SP5 Anthony J. Depassio
MR. Jack B. Depew
SSG John H. Depew
MR. John H. Deppe
SPC Dale Deprez
CSM (Ret) James L. Depriest
CPT Stephen J. Derbes
SPC Jeremiah P. Derek
MAJ Thomas H. Deren
SPC Ron Derouen

MR. Stephen J. Derousse
SPC Garrett L. Derr
LTC (Ret) Stanley Derr
SSG Robert A. Derrick
SPC Chris Dertz
1LT Karl Derums
MR. Ed. J. Des Jardin
2LT Matthew J. Desarno
CPL Eugene J. Desaunoy
SGT Paul Deschamp
SGT Brian D. Deschenes
SGT Jerry Desert
PFC Tyrone Deshields
SPC Wilbur L. Deshields
SGT David J. Desloover
PFC Patrick Desmarais
PFC James M. Desmone
SP5 Arthur T. Desouza
SFC (Ret) Leon T. Desper
SSG Larry Dessner
PFC Robert C. Detert
SPC Curtis Dethample
SPC Michael Detrick
SPC Thomas G. Dettman
SP5 Marion E. Dettmer
SGT Colin E. Detty
PFC Raymond M. Detty
CSM Duane A. Detweiler
CPL Ronald L. Detweiler
PFC Frank Deutsch
COL (Ret) Thomas M. Devanney
SGT Joseph Devenero
PFC Frederick Devens
LTC (Ret) Ben Dever
SGT Charles R. Dever
SGT Billy R. Devereaux
SFC Bart Devine
SP5 Donald W. Devine
2LT Thomas A. Devine
SP5 John Devitt
SPC Joe Devlaeminck
LTC (Ret) Alan E. Devney
SPC David Devon
PFC Dwight H. Devore
PFC Tyler Devore
CW1 Jim T. Dew
MR. Robert M. Deweese
PFC James R. Dewell
PFC Mitchell D. Dewey
MAJ George G. Dewitt
1SG (Ret) Johnnie L. Dewitt
PFC Matthew Dewitt
SPC Ralph E. Dewitt
PFC Allen Deyo
MSG George D. Dhane
SPC Rod J. Dhone
SP5 Michael Dhunjishah
SGT Frank Di Battista
SGT Joseph Di Bella
MR. Dana W. Di Biase
SSG Raymond J. Di Caprio
PVT Jimmy T. Di Carlo
SPC Joseph P. Di Clementi
LTC (Ret) Louis M. Di Donato
PFC Jeffrey T. Di Giorgio
SPC Mario S. Di Giovanni
PFC Joseph D. Di Lossi
MR. V. J. Di Maiolo
MAJ Louis A. Di Marco
SP5 Barry Di Maria
1SG (Ret) John P. Di Maria
SGT Joseph Di Martino
CPL Pasquale R. Di Mattio
MAJ (Ret) Frank A. Di Muccio
SPC Richard Di Natale
SGT Arthur Di Spirito
SGT Michael F. Diaferio
SP5 Edward T. Dial
MSG (Ret) Roy B. Dial
SPC Sherwin A. Dial
SPC Wilkie Dial
COL (Ret) Thomas A. Dials
LTC Eugene M. Diamond
SPC Richard D. Diamond
SP5 Alberto Diaz
SGT Cesar Diaz
PFC David R. Diaz
PVT Deo D. Diaz
SGT Faustino Diaz
SGT Henry J. Diaz
SGT John R. Diaz
SGT Jose M. Diaz
PFC Juan J. Diaz
SGT Miguel A. Diaz
SPC Ramon L. Diaz
SGT Raul N. Diaz
SPC Victor Diaz
SPC Ricardo Diaz Amezcua
SGT Raquel Diaz-Suarez
CW3 Stephen Dibenedetto
SSG Jackie Dick
SPC Jerry L. Dick
CPL Alfred B. Dickens
1LT Brad C. Dickens
MAJ W. J. Dickens
MR. Bernard W. Dickerson
1SG Bobby R. Dickerson
CSM Ira L. Dickerson
SGT James L. Dickerson
CPL John R. Dickerson
SPC Leon R. Dickerson
CPL Peter L. Dickerson
SSG Richard R. Dickerson
SGT Sherwood Dickie
SPC Devin Dickinson
PFC Earl W. Dickinson
SFC Charles Dickison
MRS. Terrance L. Dickison
SGT Arthur W. Dickman
SPC George H. Dickman
COL Carroll Dickson
CPT Daniel Dickson
SPC Harold R. Dickson
LTC James M. Dickson
CPL James J. Dicus
SGT Harry J. Diebner
MR. Jeffrey S. Diehl
SP5 Robert E. Diehl
MR. Steve Diehl
CPL (Ret) Richard W. Dielen
SPC David Diemer
SPC Waymon Diemer
MAJ Khanh Diep
CPT Gary V. Diers
PFC Max J. Diers
SSG Jerry G. Diersing
CPT Kenneth P. Dies
SPC Michael Diesso
SGT Richard L. Dieterle
CPT Neil D. Dietrich
CPT Gary M. Dietz
CW3 Kevin L. Dietze
1SG Connie C. Diggs
CPT Curtis A. Diggs
COL John P. Digiambattista
SFC Robert E. Dike
1SG Jerald H. Dilge
CPT Peter T. Dilillo
MRS. George D. Dill
SP5 Jimmy G. Dillard
PFC Neheniah Dillard
PVT Rudolph Dillard
CPT George E. Dille
CPT Jeffrey Dillemuth
CW2 Ronald E. Diller
SGT Garry B. Dilley
1SG Marion E. Dilley
SPC Dwight F. Dillivan
SP5 Calvin Lee Dillon
COL (Ret) Gregory P. Matt Dillon
SGT Joseph D. Dillon
SFC Robert C. Dillon
SSG Stanley A. Dillon
SPC Travis Dillon
SPC John E. Dills
SPC Robert J. Dimatteo
SGT Gregory T. Dineas
COL (Ret) James W. Dingeman
SSG Dean L. Dinger
CPT Frank S. Dinger
PFC Ronald L. Dinger
SSG Curtiss M. Dingess
SGT Darrin Dingey
SPC John Dingman
SFC Timothy J. Dingman
LTC Hung Q. Dinh
CPT David Dinkelman
MR. John Dinkelmeyer
SGT Kenneth D. Dinkins
SGT Robert W. Dinsmore
SSG Anthony D. Dinwiddie
LTC (Ret) Richard W. Dinwiddie
PFC Ralph Dioguardi
SGT Jeremy Dionida
MAJ Dom Dionne
SGT Louis P. Dionne
LTC (Ret) Frank H. Dippo
CPT Desiree Dirige
MAJ Desiree Dirige
SP5 Thomas R. Dirmyer
2LT Zach Disbrow
SGT Dennis F. Disch
SPC Michael M. Dishaw
SGT Michael D. Dishon
SPC Yvanronex E. Disla
MAJ William T. Dismuke
SPC Harold J. Disney
SP5 Richard Disney
CW2 Ronald W. Disney
MR. Edward M. Dison
SP5 Eric A. Distad
PFC Andre J. Ditimus
SFC Brian D. Ditzler
MR. Vern C. Divine
SGT George V. Dix
SGT Adrian E. Dixon
SGT Anthony P. Dixon
CPL Clark N. Dixon
CPT Dan Dixon
SPC David Miller Dixon
MSG Elwood L. Dixon
SFC (Ret) Federico M. Dixon
SPC Hobert G. Dixon
MR. James L. Dixon
SGT Jerry W. Dixon
MSG John N. Dixon
CW2 Justin W. Dixon
SSG Levie C. Dixon
SGT Oscar Dixon
SSG Ralph Dixon
SFC Robert E. Dixon
SSG Robert J. Dixon
SPC Roland H. Dixon
SPC Samuel C. Dixon
PFC Terry V. Dixon
PV2 Timothy Dixon
1SG (Ret) Van Dixon
PFC Willie J. Dixon
SFC Gilbert S. Dobak
PFC Jerry R. Dobbe
MRS. Gilbert F. Dobbins
1SG (Ret) Bobby W. Dobbs
SGT Gary Ray Dobbs
SGT Jackson J. Dobbs
SGT John M. Dobbs
SSG William R. Dobbs
CW2 Dale Dobesh
SP5 John M. Dobrenick
CPL Oscar Dobrow
PFC Donald W. Dobson
SSG E. Marie Dockery
SPC Rodney D. Dockstader
SFC (Ret) Mark A. Dockter
PV2 Vernon R. Docter
1SG (Ret) Alan S. Doctor
MR. Bobby Dodd
CW3 Charles E. Dodd
SGT John K. Dodd
SPC John M. Dodd
SGM (Ret) John F. Dodds
COL (Ret) Griffin N. Dodge
SGT John E. Dodge
SFC James W. Dodgen
SPC James Henry Dodson
COL (Ret) Jonathan B. Dodson
SPC Melissa D. Dodson
SFC (Ret) Robert W. Dodson
SP5 Edward J. Doerr
SP5 Samuel P. Doerr
LTC (Ret) Charles E. Doesburg
SGT Robert P. Doescher
PV2 Allen Doggett
MR. Bill Doherty
SPC Dennis Doherty
SPC Jim Doherty
CPT John C. Doherty
SGT Richard Dohle
MAJ (Ret) Glenn F. Dohrmann
SGT Donald A. Dohse
2LT Edwin J. Dojka
SPC Donald W. Doke
PFC Jerry Dokken
SGT James Dolan
CPT Jerome A. Dolan
SPC Michael J. Dolan
LTC Michael J. Dolan
LTC William T. Dolan
SFC (Ret) Arthur W. Dolaway
SSG (Ret) Donald O. Doles
COL Eugene Dolfi
MAJ Michael D. Dolge
SSG Clifford L. Dolick
MAJ Garry F. Dolin
MSG (Ret) William A. Dolinger
CPL Mark E. Dollar
SPC April E. Dollison
SGT Chad M. Dollison
MSG (Ret) Gerald W. Dolloff
CPL James C. Dolly
SGT Henry J. Dolny
SGT Richard F. Dolock
SPC Daniel Dominguez
SGT Jesus V. Dominguez
SGT Lupe Dominguez
SGT Manuel Dominguez
SSG Robert F. X. Dominicus
SFC Christopher H. Domont
1LT Harvie A. Domsalla
SFC Steven Domser
CPL John A. Donaghue
LTC Glynn R. Donaho
SGT Charles E. Donahoo
SGT James W. Donahue
SSG Jeremy D. Donahue
PV2 Randolph J. Donahue
SGT Thomas M. Donahue
SSG James P. Donald
SGT John D. Donaldson
PFC Steven R. Donalson
MRS. Thomas Donatelli
CPT Timothy Donelson
SFC (Ret) George R. Donlow
SSG Christopher A. Donmoyer
CSM (Ret) Wayne H. Donn
SPC George Donnad.io
SPC James A. Donnay
CPT Tyler R. Donnell
MRS. Donald R. Donnelly
SGT Horace L. Donnelly
SFC Bernard F. Donnerstag
CPT Neal D. Donohue
CW4 (Ret) Robert P. Donohue
SGT Dick Donovan
SGT Kevin P. Donovan
MRS. Louis W. Donovan
SGT Patrick S. Donovan
SGT Mike Donschietz
SGT Nicholas W. Donvito
CPT James K. Dooghan
MR. Jack R. Dooley
SPC James D. Dooley
SGT Patrick Dooley
SGT William D. Dooley
SP5 Edward E. Doolittle
SPC (Ret) John E. Doolittle
SFC Steven Doolittle
MR. William G. Dooly
MR. Frank Doran
1LT Leo M. Doran
CW2 Michael G. Doran
SGT Paul Doran
MAJ Robert L. Doran
SPC Brian J. Dorben
SPC Michael J. Dorchack
SGT Oliver Dordievski
SFC (Ret) Troy Doremus
SPC Judy B. Dorgler
MR. Joseph M. Dorio
SGT Fred R. Doriot
MG Jeffrey J. Dorko
1SG (Ret) Arthur J. Dorn
CPT (Ret) Richard M. Dorn
1LT Richard W. Dornan
SP5 Frank E. Dorner
SFC Douglas J. Dorney
SGT Brian Dorr
SFC Wayne E. Dorr
LTC (Ret) Gerald O'Neal Dorroh
1LT V. Peter Dorsett
COL John C. Dorsey
SGT Richard Dorsey
SP5 (Ret) Tommy L. Dorsey
COL (Ret) Brian L. Dosa
SSG Billy D. Doss
SPC Christopher R. Doss
SFC Clifford D. Doss
CPL Dewey A. Doss
SSG Franklyn L. Doss
MSG Edward A. Dossett
SPC Rickey Heath Doster
LTC Jerry L. Dotey
SPC Benjamin E. Dotson
SGT James G. Dotson
CPL George W. Dotterer
PFC Nicholas A. Dottore
PFC Darwin D. Doty
1LT Jack B. Doty
CSM (Ret) Leon B. Doubek
2LT John E. Doubet
CSM (Ret) Harold L. Doucet
SPC Charles W. Dougherty
1SG Robert J. Dougherty
SPC Steven W. Doughty
PFC Barry E. Douglas
SGM Clevester Douglas
PV2 Elvis L. Douglas
SGT John Henry Douglas
SFC (Ret) Kay Douglas
MSG Marcus L. Douglas
LTC Robert N. Douglas
MAJ William K. Douglass
SSG William L. Doutaz
CPL Lavoy A. Douvikas
MAJ Jeffrey M. Douville
MSG Mario A. Dovalina
SGT Dwayne Dove
SGT Dwayne R. F. Dove
1LT George F. Dove
1SG Gerald T. Dove
MAJ Alan J. Dover
MSG (Ret) Michael P. Dover
SSG William E. Dover
CPL David C. Dow
LTC Richard J. M. Dow
SGT John J. Dowd
SSG William M. Dowdy
MRS. Richard K. Dowell
MSG (Ret) Billy F. Dowers
SP5 Ronnie Dowlin
SSG David W. Dowling
WO1 Donald L. Dowling
CW5 John Mike Dowling
SSG Robert C. Dowling
1SG (Ret) Charles O. Downard
SPC Freddy C. Downard
1SG Carl G. Downey
LTC (Ret) Scott A. Downey
SFC Arthur Downie
CPT Lynn E. Downie
SP5 Cecil E. Downing
SGT Dennis Downing
SGT Edward C. Downing
1LT Jack D. Downing
SFC Jason E. Downing
SGT Ricky Downing
SPC Thomas C. J. Downing
SGT Daniel C. Downs
PFC David W. Downs
1LT Douglas Downs
SPC Gary D. Downs
SGT Robert A. Downs
MR. Ronald N. Downs
PFC Anthony F. Doyle
PFC Billy G. Doyle
1LT Christopher J. Doyle
1LT Daniel G. Doyle
SSG Dennis A. Doyle
MR. Donald T. Doyle
MSG Herbert S. Doyle
MSG James A. Doyle
CSM Larry R. Doyle
SFC (Ret) Maurice Doyle
2LT Michael J. Doyle
SPC Michael L. Doyle
SGT Michael Theodore Doyle
CSM (Ret) Ralph E. Doyle
SP5 Scott Drabant
SGT Diedrich L. Drafz
CPL Matthew A. Dragicevic
SSG Arthur S. Drago
MAJ Randal A. Dragon
SSG David B. Drake
SGT Mark A. Drake
CPT Melvin William Drake
1LT Paul Drake
PFC Wayne B. Drake
2LT Winona Drakeford
SPC Rhett Henry Draluck
SGT Steven P. Drapala
SPC David A. Draper
PV2 Lacie Draper
COL Leo Draper
SFC Milton E. Draper
SGT Oscar C. Draper
SGT Steve Draper
GS-11 Steven C. Draper
1SG Michael R. Draughn
MAJ Timothy H. Draves
1SG (Ret) Earl W. Dreher
SPC George T. Drenski
SPC Robert L. Drenth
CPT James R. Dresbach
CPT Brian D. Drescher
SPC Erica Drew
CPT John T. Drew
CPT Michael Drew
PVT Seth Drew
SP5 Carl F. Dreyer
SGT William M. Dreyer
SPC James H. Driggers
MSG Stanley Driggers
CW3 Tim Driggers
PV2 Walter T. Dright
TSgt James S. Dripps
MAJ John J. Driscoll
PFC John J. Driscoll
1LT Kevin P. Driscoll
SSG Herman Drobish
SGT Marvin R. Droege
SPC Robert L. Droesch
SPC Anthony Drogos
CPT Kenneth W. Drombosky
SPC Cecil Phillip Drone
PFC Jack W. Droneburg
CSM Henry Dronet
SGT Martin A. Drop
COL Allen E. Dross
SGT Keith O. Druckrey
SP5 Donald R. Drumheller
CPL Jack Drummey
PFC James C. Drury
MSG (Ret) Leonard L. Drury
1LT Donald J. Dryer
LTC (Ret) Ronald E. Du Bay
SPC James E. Du Bois
SGT Peter J. Du Bois
SPC Seth Gabriel Du Bois
CW4 James C. Du Bose
SFC (Ret) Larry J. Du Bose
MAJ James S. Du Pre
SSG C. J. Duke Du Shane
SSG Hector Duante
SGT Armando Duarte
SPC Carlos N. Duarte
SP5 Dennis J. Duarte
SPC Enrique Noriega Duarte
1SG (Ret) Robert M. Duarte
SPC Larry M. Duba
CPT John A. Duban
SGT Thomas J. Dubasik
PFC Patrick Dubbs
SP5 Jack S. Dube
SPC Timothy N. Dube
SSG Bryce Dubee
LTC Donald H. Dubia
LTG (Ret) James M. Dubik
SSG Simon S. Dubik
DR. John T. Dubinski
CSM (Ret) Adam Dubois
SSG Antwone Dubose
SGT Ben W. Dubose
SSG Johnny Dubose
SGT Dennis J. Dubrowa
TSgt William J. Duby
SGT Leonard H. Duchene
CPL Anthony J. Duchinsky
SSG Robert W. Ducker
PFC Dustin Duckett
CPL Kenneth M. Duckman
MR. David C. Duckworth
SGT Jerry Duckworth
SSG Michael J. Ducommun
SPC Alphonse Ducre
MSG Ted E. Dudek
PFC James R. Dudley
SPC Roger G. Dudley
WO1 (Ret) William R. Dudley
SSG Daniel F. Duenas
CPL Hugo Duenez
SGT Martin C. Duesel
SP5 Joseph L. Duey
PV2 Curtis E. Duffield
SSG Stephan M. Duffing
SGT James Duffy
CPL Robert L. Duffy
PFC Thomas J. Duffy
SSG Keith Allen Dufort
SPC Dennis R. Dugan
SPC Larry V. Dugan
SP5 Paul E. Dugan
CPT Timothy J. Dugan
1LT Timothy P. Dugan
SSG Wayne D. Dugan
1LT William L. Dugan
SPC Chester C. Dugas
SGT Leo Dugdale
SGT Francis J. Duggan
CPT Gerald F. Duggan
CPL James Duggan
CSM (Ret) Kalub D. Duggins
TSgt Donald R. Duggleby
CPL Michael A. Duka
SSG (Ret) Dwight Duke
SPC James L. Duke
COL (Ret) Steven Duke
2LT Charles E. Dukes
SGM James Dukes
MSG James Dukes
PV2 James Albert Dukes
SGT Joseph T. Dukes
SPC Stephen D. Dukes
CW4 (Ret) Jones R. Dula
SPC Ronald A. Dula
CW2 Andrew W. Dulay
PFC Cleod L. Dulin
Rev. Frank R. Dulzer
SGT Richard R. Dumais
SPC Stephen Duman
SPC Philip A. Dumas
SSG James E. Dumdie
SSG John C. Dumdie
SPC Barbara S. Dumke

SGT Kenneth L. Dunahee
1LT Alan Dunaway
SGT Jeanette Dunaway
PVT David L. Dunbar
PFC David L. Duncan
SSG (Ret) Eddie J. Duncan
SFC Edmond R. Duncan
SGT Fred R. Duncan
SSG James B. Duncan
CSM (Ret) Johnny D. Duncan
MRS. Kenneth E. Duncan
SPC Kenneth G. Duncan
SSG Kurtis Duncan
SPC Lee T. Duncan
SPC Mark Lemuel Duncan
CPL Michael W. Duncan
CPT Peter E. Duncan
CW2 Randall L. Duncan
MAJ Richard L. Duncan
SGT Robert Duncan
SPC Scott Duncan
SGT Terry L. Duncan
1SG Todd Duncan
WO1 Robert Dundas
SP5 James A. Dundon
SPC Mike Dunfold
SPC Michael J. Dunford
SP5 Steven D. Dungan
CW2 Susan E. Dungan
SGM Dewey L. Dunham
SGT John H. Dunham
MSG Lloyd A. Dunham
SGT Gary M. Dunigan
SGT Jerry D. Dunivan
PFC John F. Dunkerly
1LT Edgar B. Dunkle
LT Jonathan K. Dunkleberger
MAJ Nigel C.W. Dunkley
MAJ (Ret) Gerald W. Dunklin
SSG Isaiah Dunklin
LTC Kevin R. Dunlap
SFC Leland E. Dunlap
SFC (Ret) William L. Dunlap
1SG Richard A. Dunlop
SPC Garry N. Dunlow
SP5 Arthur E. Dunn
SPC Bryant E. Dunn
SFC Calvin G. Dunn
CPL Dale L. Dunn
SGT Douglas M. Dunn
1LT Henry L. Dunn
SFC (Ret) Lester T. Dunn
SGT Max L. Dunn
CSM (Ret) Michael A. Dunn
CPT Patrick Dunn
SGT Robert J. Dunn
SPC Robert J. Dunn
SPC Robert L. Dunn
CSM Sean M. Dunn
SSG Steven Dunn
SGM Thomas E. Dunn
SPC Thomas R. Dunn
SGT William F. Dunn
SPC Craig R. Dunna
MR. Gary D. Dunnagan
CPT Gary L. Dunnam
CPT Bob Dunne
MR. Dennis A. Dunne
SPC John B. Dunne
SPC Lindsay J. Dunne
SGT Morgan R. Dunne
SGT James B. Dunnigan
MR. Craig Lee Dunning
SSG Gary M. Dunning
2LT Herbert Dunnington
SGT Ralph L. Dunshee
CSM Antonio Dunston
SPC David A. Dunzik
SSG John O. Dupla
SFC (Ret) Howard D. Dupont
SPC Warren C. Dupre
MSG (Ret) Samuel M. Dupreast
2LT Annie P. Dupree
CW2 Devin C. Dupree
MRS. Mavis Dupree
SGT William S. Dupree
2LT Darren G. Dupuis
SPC Michael C. Dupuy
PFC Glenn N. Duque
SP5 Thomas L. Duquette
SSG Antonio E. Duran
SSG Edward Andrew Duran
SGT Frank H. Duran
MR. Jose A. Duran
CPL Omar Duran
PFC Andres R. Durand
CSM Theodore Durand
CSM (Ret) Gary Durant
PFC George W. Durant
SGT Francis J. Durante
SSG Raymond H. Durate
PFC Donald D. Duray
SGT Daryl I. Durbin
LTG (Ret) Robert E. Durbin
SGT James R. Durborow
SGT Joseph J. Durco
SP5 John H. Durda
SFC (Ret) Charles J. Duren
SFC Anthony T. Durham
SSG Julius C. Durham
SFC Kevin M. Durham
SSG Robert Durham
SGT Craig S. Duritza
PFC Joseph P. Durkin
SPC Ryan Durmisevich
SP5 Peter J. Durno
PVT Raymond S. Duron
SSG Rolander Durr
SPC David C. Durrance
SGT David Durrant
SPC Miles P. Durrant
COL (Ret) Lyman C. Duryea
SGT John F. Duscher
SGT Steve Duske
SGT Frederick R. Dusseault
SPC Mark R. Dusso
SPC James Duszynski
SGT Nathan Dutch
1LT Michael M. Dutcher
PFC Dennis W. Dutney
SPC John H. Dutram
PFC Donald C. Dutton
SGT Brandon Duvall
PVT Malcolm F. Duvall
MRS. Fred A. Duve
MR. Don Duvjatas
CPT Beth Duynslager
PFC Lee C. Dworshak
LTC James C. Dwyer
SPC Jeffrey H. Dwyer
SFC Kenneth G. Dwyer
SPC William F. Dwyer
SPC James Dyckman
PFC Devin Dyer
1SG (Ret) James B. Dyer
SGT Joseph Dyer
CSM Kristopher Dyer
SSG Lawrence D. Dyer
SPC Richard A. Dyer
SGT Richard Tim Dyer
SGT Thomas M. Dyer
SPC Charles W. Dykes
SGT Hayward Dykes
SFC (Ret) James A. Dykes
SSG Clifford E. Dykstra
SPC Robert Dykstra
SGT Robert W. Dykstra
MAJ Harold B. Dyson
SGT Jeffrey A. Dyson
SGT Thomas A. Dyson
SSG Alex J. Dziekonski
CW3 Ronald M. Dzierzawic
SGT Stanley Dziewa
PFC Jimmy L. Eades
MR. James M. Eads
SPC Richard E. Eads
SGT Alton Eady
SGT Cliff Eagerton
SPC Bradley N. Eagle
PFC Claude E. Eakins
PFC Anthony C. Ealey
SPC John Ealons
SSG John E. Eargle
SPC Arnold B. Earl
MAJ (Ret) Robert J. Earl
SPC George J. Earle
COL (Ret) Jeffrey R. Earley
SFC Richard L. Earls
SPC Charles Early
SGT Merlin E. Earlywine
SPC Coty L. Earnest
PFC Ivan L. Earnest
MR. Max M. Earnheart
MRS. John Sidney Earp
CW5 Charles M. Earwood
1SG Franklin D. Easley
CW2 (Ret) Emory Allen Eason
TSgt Robert E. Eason
SFC Herman D. East
SGM (Ret) William C. Easten
CPT Kevin L. Eastep
PFC Dalton Easter
PFC James Easter
1SG Bobby J. Easterling
SGT Charles Easterling
CPT Dale A. Easterling
SGT James L. Easterling
CPL Wesley L. Easterly
SPC Leonard J. Easterwood
PFC Kenneth G. Eastham
SGT R. Bearwallow Eastman
PFC Marvin T. Easton
SPC Robert Easton
MRS. Robert L. Easton
SGT William Jay Eastridge
SP5 John E. Eastwood
SSG Mathew B. Eastwood
CW4 Gordon F. Eatley
CW2 Charles A. Eaton
CPL Douglas J. Eaton
SGT Henry J. Eaton
SGT Jerel F. Eaton
SGT Johnathon Eaton
SGT Larry Eaton
SGT Leroy W. Eaton
SPC Lynn A. Eaton
SPC Michael A. Eaton
SPC Joel T. Eaves
PV2 Susan C. Eaves
SPC Steve E. Ebaugh
CPT Anthony Ebbing
CPT Jeremy Ebdrup
PV2 Keith J. Ebel
MR. Terry M. Ebeltoft
CPT Jeff Eberhart
PVT Jason Eberline
SSG Randall Eberling
MRS. Harry S. Eberly
CPL Roy L. Eblen
SPC Robert L. Echola
MR. C. C. Echols
SSG Michael J. Echterling
SPC Bradley M. Eckard
SPC William A. Eckart
1SG (Ret) David D. Eckel
SGT James C. Eckel
SSG Mark Eckenrode
PFC Edwin B. Ecker
SGM Gerald C. Ecker
PFC R. Scott Ecker
SGT Randy A. Ecker
SPC Jerome R. Eckerle
SPC Alton Eckert
SGT Earl T. Eckert
COL (Ret) Kenneth R. Eckert
SGT Michael G. Eckert
MRS. Billy Eckhardt
CPT John L. Eckhardt
SFC (Ret) Richard J. Eckhardt
SGT Alfred L. Eckhart
2LT David C. Eckley
SGT Floyd E. Ecklor
WO1 John C. Eckroat
BG (Ret) Joseph L. Ecoppi
MR. Bradford J. Edblom
SGT Broadus R. Eddings
SGT Charles David Eddins
SGM Clarence Eddy
PFC Jackie R. Eddy
MSG Leon Eddy
CPL Nelson R. Eddy
CPT Lawrence A. Edell
SGT Raymond A. Eden
PFC Anthony Edenburn
SPC G. R. Edenburn
CPT Frankie Edens
LTC (Ret) Michael W. Edgar
1LT Liston L. Edge
CPT Raymond A. Edge
SSG Byron L. Edgecomb
1SG (Ret) Frank J. Edger
SGT Erik L. Ediger
SSG Jacques Edmond
PFC Robert Edmond
CPT James T. Edmonds
SFC Marvin E. Edmonds
MG (Ret) Maurice O. Edmonds
CPL Tracie E. Edmonds
MAJ William H. Edmonds
SPC Patricia L. Edmonson
SGT Ian R. Edmonston
SGT Guy M. Edmunds
CW4 (Ret) John D. Edmunds
SPC John G. Edmunds
PFC Stephen D. Edquist
CSM (Ret) Annie G. Edwards
CSM Ashmore O. Edwards
SGT Bernard O. Edwards
MAJ Boyce L. Edwards
MRS. Carolyn Edwards
SGT Charles A. Edwards
CPT Daniel J. Edwards
SGT David R. Edwards
CPT Dwayne A. Edwards
SPC Dwight D. Edwards
SP5 Eric L. Edwards
CW2 Gary H. Edwards
PFC George J. Edwards
SGT Gerald L. Edwards
SFC Harry J. Edwards
SPC Harry L. Edwards
SGT Heather Edwards
SGT Herbert L. Edwards
MSG (Ret) James L. Edwards
SSG James P. Edwards
CPT Jason Edwards
SFC John T. Edwards
SGT Johnnie L. Edwards
MSG Kenneth R. Edwards
SPC Larry Edwards
1LT Leonard E. Edwards
SSG Lyle P. Edwards
SGT Melvin R. Edwards
LTC Michael C. Edwards
PVT Nehemiah M. Edwards
MSG Orval M. Edwards
PFC Phil C. Edwards
PVT Raford B. Edwards
COL (Ret) Robert H. Edwards
SGT Roger L. Edwards
SSG Ronny D. Edwards
PVT Skyler C. Edwards
MR. Stanley D. Edwards
PVT Treveen Edwards
LTC William J. Edwards
SGT George Michael Egan
SFC Kyle P. Egan
LTC Margaret Egan
MAJ Dag Egede-Nissen
SPC Katrina Yvonne Eggen
MR. Elmer Egger
LT Richard F. Eggers
SGT Joseph D. Eggert
SPC Wayne D. Eggert
MSG Lawrence V. Eggie
SPC Chase T. Eggleston
MR. Michael A. Eggleston
SPC Jeff S. Ehl
SGT Charles Ehlers
SFC Roy Joseph Ehlers
CW2 Ronald Ehmann
1SG Charles E. Ehredt
SPC Carl W. Ehresman
SPC Malcolm P. Ehrhardt
CPT Theodore C. Ehrlich
SGT Albert H. Ehrman
TSgt Arnold W. Ehrsam
PFC Paul C. Eibeck
SGT Randolph W. Eichelberg
MR. Bill Eichelberger
MSG (Ret) Daniel R. Eichelberger
SPC Robert Eichelberger
SPC Dean Allen Eichenberger
SGT Robert E. Eichler
SPC Larry R. Eicholtz
PFC James Eiden
CPT Lawrence S. Eiden
MRS. David W. Einsel
CPL Thomas B. Einwechter
SSG Gregory F. Eisenhauer
SPC Peter Eisentrager
PFC James M. Eisner
SSG Eka A. Eka
SGT Francis Ekudi
MR. Albert El
SGT James M. Elam
CPL John D. Elden
SPC Kevin J. Elder
CPT Lindsey Elder
PFC Robert C. Elder
SGT Thomas P. Eldredge
SGT Johnny W. Eldreth
SPC David W. Eldridge
SGT Eric Paul Eldridge
CPT Kyle T. Eldridge
SSG Murray E. Eldridge
MAJ (Ret) Peter B. Eldridge
SPC Rick Elftmann
1LT Mark Elfving
SPC Ronald E. Elge
SGT Harold G. Elgin
TSgt Alexander Elia
SP5 Richard T. Elias
2LT Cory Elich
MAJ Russell J. Elizondo
1LT E. D. Elkenberry
SGT Richard H. Elkins
SSG Roger M. Elkins
SFC Thomas D. Elkins
CPT Walter H. Elkins
SFC Harry S. Ellenberger
MSG Hugh L. Eller
SGT Jack M. Eller
CSM (Ret) Jerry F. Eller
SGT Justin P. Eller
DR. Thomas J. Eller
CW2 Sammy J. Ellerbee
SSG Arthur E. Ellerson
MSG (Ret) Archie E. Ellinger
SGT Bill F. Elliott
SSG Bobby R. Elliott
CPL Carroll L. Elliott
SGT Charles Lee Elliott
SGT Ed Elliott
LTC (Ret) Edwin Elliott
SGT Frank W. Elliott
SPC George Elliott
SGT James Elliott
PVT Jeffery D. Elliott
SPC John Elliott
1LT John R. Elliott
CPT Jon L. Elliott
SFC Michael C. Elliott
SSG (Ret) Michael L. Elliott
SPC Mike P. Elliott
SPC Robert C. Elliott
1SG (Ret) Ronald Elliott
SPC Ronald W. Elliott
1LT (Ret) Ward Elliott
PVT Allon Ellis
SGT Bill Ellis
SGT Billy R. Ellis
SGT Charles E. Ellis
SPC Charles J. Ellis
CW3 Charles L. Ellis
TSgt Charles L. Ellis
SGT Dale L. Ellis
SFC Earl D. Ellis
MSG (Ret) Ernest E. Ellis
MR. Ester H. Ellis
SGT Gregory S. Ellis
SGT Harry J. Ellis
MAJ (Ret) Jack R. Ellis
MAJ James Ellis
CPT Jeff Ellis
SSG Jeremy Ellis
SSG Joe T. Ellis
SPC Leon Ellis
CSM Lincoln H. Ellis
SP5 Mark S. Ellis
SPC Michael D. Ellis
SPC Michael M. Ellis
PVT Robert L. Ellis
CPT Sanquanetta Ellis
WO1 Steven C. Ellis
CW2 Thomas C. Ellis
SPC William L. Ellis
SGT Gary W. Ellison
CDR Greg Ellison
MAJ Gregory W. Ellison
MSG Harry L. Ellison
SSG Tommy E. Elmore
SFC Valesita Elmore
CPT James W. Elrod
SPC Tammy K. Elrod
SPC Robert E. Elsasser
SGT Glenn Elsing
CPL Harold F. Elsner
SPC Dan D. Elston
SSG Harry E. Elston
PFC Mike Elston
LTC (Ret) Robert G. Elton
SGT Jerry A. Elwell
CPL Daniel A. Emanuel
SPC Daniel R. Emblen
SGT Reed B. Embley
SP5 William M. Embree
CPT (Ret) James L. Embrey
SSG (Ret) Edward C. Emenhiser
CSM (Ret) Kenneth R. Emerson
SGT Orville Emerson
PFC Harold S. Emery
SPC Robert L. Emery
SGT Scott A. Emery
SGT Darrell W. Emily
SSG George W. Emmens
PFC Edward W. Emond
SGT Harold L. Empett
SSG Espy L. Encalade
SFC Tawana V. Encalade
SGM (Ret) Manuel J. Encarnacao
1LT Conrad J. Encarnacion
SSG Jesus A. Encinas
SSG Steven Encinias
MSG Marco A. Endara
PFC James M. Enderli
SPC Hubbard Malcolm Endicott
MR. James A. Endicott
SSG Anthony G. Endl
SPC David J. Endler
SPC Greg Endres
MAJ (Ret) Michael A. Endres
MRS. Raymond E. Engbring
SPC George R. Engebretson
PFC Peter J. Engel
SPC Alan G. England
SSG Gregory P. England
SP5 James A. Engle
MR. Larry A. Engle
CPL Robert W. Engle
MAJ Walter D. Engle
SFC William J. Engle
MS. Adele B. Englebert
SFC (Ret) Ellis Englebert
SFC (Ret) Ronald J. Englehart
SPC John J. Englert
SGT Robert P. Englert
SSG George V. Englis
CSM (Ret) Arnold R. English
SFC (Ret) Edward E. English
SFC (Ret) Gregory Scott English
MSG (Ret) Joseph L. English
1SG Michael A. English
CPL Robert E. English
SSG Talmadge G. English
SGT Thomas English
MSG Thomas J. English
SPC Kimberly D. English-Brown
CPT Eric Martin Engquist
SGT Andrew Ennes
CPT Brian P. Ennesser
CPT Paul Eno
SP5 Warren Enoch
SGM Norbert K. Enos
SPC Richard G. Enright
SP5 James Entwisle
MAJ Andrew Entwistle
SGT David M. Enyart
MAJ Erik Enyart
LTC John D. Enyart
CSM Ernest A. Epley
SPC James O. Epperson
CW4 (Ret) Richard E. Eppler
SGT Robert R. Eppler
SGT Ronald K. Epps
1LT Allan J. Epstein
MRS. Marvin A. Epstein
PVT Herbert M. Erb
SGT Emil A. Ercolano
SPC Jason B. Erekson
SGT Alton E. Ergle
SPC Andrew Erich
SSG Brant L. Erickson
SP5 Dale R. Erickson
SSG Dean A. Erickson
CPL Francis G. Erickson
LTC James M. Erickson
SFC (Ret) Kenneth W. Erickson
PFC Larry E. Erickson
PFC Laurel D. Erickson
SGT Mark L. Erickson
MAJ Robert Alan Erickson
LTC Steven A. Erickson
PFC Willard W. Erickson
SGT Eldon Erlenbach
2LT Christopher Erler
SP5 Douglas R. Erne
MR. Joseph F. Ernest
SPC Malcolm B. Ernisse
PVT Kerry W. Ernsberger
LTC Joey Errington
SPC Anthony Erskin
SSG James E. Ertle
SGT Arlan Ervasti
LTC (Ret) Charles P. Ervin
SFC (Ret) David L. Ervin
SFC Kevin D. Ervine
LTC (Ret) Douglas K. Erway
SPC Antonio Erwin
SFC Robert E. Erwin
LTC Paul E. Eschina
SGT William Esack
PFC Jesus J. Escabedo
SPC Alex Escalante
SGT Fred Escalante
SFC (Ret) Kyler S. Escalera
MR. Paul Escamilla
MR. Vincent J. Escandon
CPL Alexander Escarsega
SPC Paul A. Eschbacher
PVT Joshua Escobedo
1SG Manuel Escobedo
CSM (Ret) Natividad Escobedo
SSG William W. Eskew
CSM Paul N. Eskridge
CPT Delino M. Eslinger
SGT Reinaldo Espada
SFC Juan M. Espaillat
MR. Alberto Esparza
1SG Francisco Esparza
SPC Joseph M. Esparza
SGT Raymond Esparza

PV2 Ricky Esparza
SPC William R. Espe
PVT Isael P. Espinosa
SPC Jereme S. Espinosa
SSG Robert Espinosa
SPC Dionisio Espinoza
SGT Eduardo Espinoza
CSM Norberto F. Espitia
CW3 (Ret) Vincent Esponilla
SGT John B. Esposito
SGT Edward A. Esposti
SSG Dionicio Esquivel
PVT Eric Esquivel
CPL Gilbert Esquivel
SP5 Richard L. Esquivel
SPC Randall D. Esry
SGT Edward C. Essary
SFC (Ret) Raymond J. Essenmacher
CPL William J. Esser
PFC William A. Essex
CPL Harold W. Essig
SP5 Thomas W. Essig
CPL Gordon L. Essington
SSG Robert P. Estabrook
SPC Ronald J. Estabrook
SFC Charles W. Estell
SFC Kelvin Estell
SFC Lawrence L. Estell
CW2 Lydia E. Estell
1LT Alben B. Estep
CPT Corey D. Estep
COL (Ret) James Estep
SP5 Lester E. Estep
SGT Robert A. Estep
PFC William H. Estepp
SGT Bill E. Estes
SGT David A. Estes
LTC Gregory L. Estes
SPC Joseph F. Estes
SGT Lindel Estes
SGT Michael G. Estes
SGT Paul L. Estes
LTC (Ret) Richard D. Estes
SP5 Sam L. Estes
PFC Tracy W. Estes
CW4 Vernon L. Estes
LTC (Ret) William H. Estey
SGT Mark J. Estopare
SGT Art Estrada
SPC Christopher Estrada
SGT David Estrada
CPT David E. Estrada
1LT Frank W. Estrada
1LT Jesus M. Estrada
SGT Jorge Estrada
SGT Omar Estrada
SP5 Rudolf C. Estrada
SGT Craig Etchison
PVT Gary Ethan
SSG Christopher Michael Etheridge
MR. Don Etheridge
CW3 Parry Willis Etheridge
PVT Walter E. Ethier
SGT Harle B. Ethridge
SSG Jackie Etienne
SFC Albert L. Etris
PFC David L. Ettelman
SPC Larry E. Etts
SGT Robert L. Etzwiler
SSG Charles F. Eubanks
MRS. Hal D. Eubanks
MAJ Kevin Eubanks
SFC (Ret) Ronnie Eubanks
CPL Darwin C. Eucker
CSM (Ret) James M. Euell
CSM (Ret) Michael G. Eugster
SPC Michael T. B. Eull
MSG George S. Evanko
SP6 Belmont S. Evans
SGT Benjamin H. Evans
SGT Billy W. Evans
LTC Boyce H. Evans
SPC Callie Evans
SGM (Ret) Charles H. Evans
SPC Clifford L. Evans
1SG (Ret) Dan J. Evans
SGT Darryl R. Evans
CPL David E. Evans
SFC (Ret) Detroit L. Evans
SGT Donald E. Evans
SGT Donald L. Evans
CW4 Douglas Evans
MSG Douglas W. Evans
SGT Eddie Evans
SFC George P. Evans
SFC Guy C. Evans
SGT Harmon L. Evans
PFC Harry E. Evans
SFC Jack S. Evans
CPL James E. Evans
SPC James Glenn Evans
SFC (Ret) James J. Evans
SSG James L. Evans
CW2 (Ret) James R. Evans
PFC James R. Evans
PFC Jerry A. Evans
SGT (Ret) John B. Evans
CPT John M. Evans
SSG Jonathan Evans
MSG (Ret) Joni L. Evans
LTC (Ret) Larry D. Evans
SSG Larry D. Evans
SPC Maraya Evans
SPC Mark A. Evans
MAJ (Ret) Michael E. Evans
SPC Norman W. Evans
SGT Otney M. Evans
SGT (Ret) Paul L. Evans
SGT Quanita Evans
SPC Robert Evans
MAJ Robert D. Evans
MR. Robert J. Evans
1SG Robert R. Evans
SPC Ronald L. Evans
SPC Stephanie L. Evans
SSG Steven P. Evans
CPL Thomas J. Evans
PFC Wilbert C. Evans
SSG Wilburn M. Evans
PFC Willi T. Evans
SFC (Ret) William C. Evans
SFC (Ret) John H. Evarts
CPT Daniel J. Everett
SGT David E. Everett
COL (Ret) Michael W. Everett
LTC Patrovick G. Everett
TSgt Richard J. Everett
1SG Wayne L. Everett
SSG (Ret) Carroll G. Everist
SPC Joe L. Everitt
MSG Joel H. Everitt
SFC (Ret) Edward S. Evers
CPL Marlin B. Evers
SFC Lawrence A. Eversole
SGT Kevin W. Everson
SFC (Ret) Harry M. Everth
SPC John J. Evorik
COL (Ret) Michael A. Ewens
SPC Austin Z. Ewing
PV2 Brian J. Ewing
1LT John A. Ewing
SGT Willie Edward Ewings
SPC Thomas G. Exterkamp
PFC Robert J. Eyer
MR. William Eymann
SPC Jackie L. Ezell
CPT James J. Ezell
CPT Keith R. Ezell
LT Michael Ezell
PFC Ollie Ezell
SPC Prentiss R. Ezelle
SGT Robert J. Faasse
SPC John E. Faber
SGT Peter J. Faber
SPC Donald J. Fabre
CPT Jauita Facion
MSG Perfecto Facundo
CPT Raymond D. Faczan
SSG Julia K. Fadell
PFC Ernest B. Fadness
MR. John Fadorsen
LTC (Ret) Henry F. Faery
2LT Clifford R. Fagan
SPC Kelly Fagan
MSG Arthur Fagen
SGT George Fagerstrom
SP5 Donald W. Fagundes
SSG Fred Fah
SGT Dale A. Fahrnow
2LT Mary Ann Faias
SPC Lonnie W. Faile
SSG Johnnie J. Fair
SFC (Ret) Ken J. Fair
SSG Robert L. Fair
LTC (Ret) Richard L. Fairall
SGT David L. Fairbairn
1SG (Ret) Douglas A. Fairbanks
SP5 James E. Fairchild
CPT Lorna L. Fairchild
SGT Clayton S. Faircloth
1LT David A. Faircloth
LTC (Ret) Michael P. Fairhead
LTC (Ret) Richard C. Fairlamb
SSG Richard Fairley
SGT Kenneth W. Fairly
PVT Lancer D. Fairman
PV2 Wilbert A. Faison
SPC William Faison
1LT Richard L. Fajen
SPC Tajudeen Fakoya
SGT Howard G. Falardeau
SP5 Harry T. Falck
SPC Robert N. Falco
SFC Eduardo Falcon
SPC Christopher Falcone
SGT Larry Falconer
CPT Michael P. Falkowski
SPC Leonard W. Fallscheer
MG (Ret) Vincent E. Falter
1LT W. Patrick Falvey
CPL Frank S. Famiglietti
SrA William A. Fancher
SPC Kathleen M. Fanella
SPC David G. Fangman
SGT Russell J. Fankell
SPC Michael P. Fanning
MR. Arlington P. Fant
MR. Vincent J. Fantasia
SPC Sam P. Fantino
MAJ David C. Faragher
SSG Steven E. Farber
CSM (Ret) Jesus G. Farias
SPC Jose Farias
SGT Gerald J. Farkasofsky
SP5 John V. Farless
PVT Ronald D. Farley
SFC Charles K. Farlow
LTC (Ret) David Farlow
SP3 Dennis L. Farmer
SSG Francis Edwin Farmer
SPC Gary A. Farmer
SFC Jamie L. Farmer
CSM Jerry W. Farmer
SPC Levi Farmer
MSG Wilson L. Farmer
PV2 Timothy B. Farnell
SGT George T. Farnum
SPC John W. Farnum
SPC Anthony B. Farr
1LT Quenton L. Farr
SFC (Ret) James Farran
MAJ Dale Farrand
1SG Lawrence R. Farrar
PFC James E. Farrell
MR. Kevin M. Farrell
PVT Roy H. Farrell
MR. Walter A. Farrell
MRS. James L. Farrer
SSG John W. Farrier
SPC Johnny M. Farrior
LTC (Ret) Billy D. Farris
SPC James O. Farris
SPC James R. Farris
SPC Jason Farris
SPC Rickey J. Farris
SGT Robert Lee Farris
MAJ Roger E. Farris
SSG Gerald R. Farrow
SPC Ronald R. Farthing
SPC Robert J. Fashbaugh
PFC Jacob M. Fassold
MR. Earl T. Fatlan
SSG Glen J. Faughnan
SPC Gary L. Faulk
SPC Jimmy Wade Faulkenberry
MRS. John C. Faulkenberry
PFC Rodney Faulkenbery
MR. Bill Faulkner
SPC James E. Faulkner
SSG James S. Faulkner
SPC Robert Fauls
SPC Terry M. Fauquher
SP5 Pete Fauske
SSG Clarence E. Faust
CPL Rickey F. Faust
LT Heather Fauvell
SSG Thomas Glen Faux
1SG Ronald Favela
SPC Daniel M. Favreau
SGT Bruce H. Fawcett
SGT David R. Fawcett
SPC Michael T. Fayard
SSG Jose Angel Faz
SSG (Ret) Gary D. Fazenbaker
MAJ Michael J. Fazio
MSG Darrald G. Feaker
SP5 Joseph A. Feasel
SPC Jonathan Thomas Feaster
SSG Melvin L. Feather
SPC Aaron Featherston
MAJ (Ret) Jimmy J. Featherston
CPT Steven F. Featherston
CPT Kirk M. Fechter
MSG Jon G. Fecteau
SSG George P. Feehan
MR. Francis M. Feeley
SPC James R. Fehrenbacher
LTC Edward P. Feigenbaum
COL (Ret) Terry T. Feild
1SG Ramiro P. Fejeran
CSM (Ret) Tomas P. Fejeran
SGT Brian K. Fejfar
SPC Michael L. Felder
CPL Donald Feldman
SPC Eugene Feldman
MAJ Albert R. Feliciano
SFC Eric E. Feliciano
2LT Juan P. Feliciano
CPT Luis A. Feliciano
SFC Miguel A. Feliciano
PVT Adrian Feliz
SGT Rene Felizardo
SPC Daniel L. Felker
SPC John D. Fella
CPL David Feller
SPC John L. Feller
CPL Marion G. Fellers
PFC Terry Felowtiz
CPT Edwin H. Felsher
CSM (Ret) Donald Felt
PFC William E. Felter
SPC Bobby N. Felts
MSG (Ret) John L. Fencl
PFC Stacy M. Fender
SFC Cally J. Fenner
MSG James I. Fenton
SGT Robert K. Fenton
SP5 Robert R. Fenton
CPL Charles H. Fergason
SPC William Fergeson
SPC John C. Fergurson
CPL Richard K. Fergus
CPT Andrew T. Ferguson
SFC Bernard H. Ferguson
PSG Billie Jay Ferguson
MR. Edward C. Ferguson
PV2 Frank S. Ferguson
MAJ (Ret) Frederick E. Ferguson
COL (Ret) Gerald E. Ferguson
CPL Henry M. Ferguson
SGM (Ret) John H. Ferguson
PFC Kristopher G. Ferguson
MAJ Marion M. Ferguson
SGT Marvin Ferguson
CPT Tim Ferguson
1SG (Ret) William A. Ferguson
MSG Gloria A. Ferguson Krauklis
SGT Carlos M. Fernandes
SSG Duarte Fernandes
CPL Alex D. Fernandez
SPC Alfred J. Fernandez
1SG Eduardo Fernandez
1SG Ferdinand Fernandez
SFC Filiberto Fernandez
SPC Juan Fernandez
LT Larry Fernandez
SPC Michael R. Fernandez
CPL Thomas J. Fernandez
MAJ John M. Fernas
SPC David Ferrance
SSG Carmine A. Ferrandi
SGT Michael F. Ferrara
COL (Ret) Albert J. Ferrea
SGT (Ret) Stephen A. Ferreira
SGT Walter Ferreira
CPL John Ferrell
CPT Keith Ferrell
SSG Norbert Ferrell
CPL William Ferrell
SPC Jack L. Ferrenburgh
SPC Jeremy Ferriell
LTC Donald V. Ferrier
SP5 Robert T. Ferrier
SPC William W. Ferrill
PFC Leslie D. Ferris
SPC Ralph H. Ferris
PFC Richard W. Ferris
2LT Evan Fertel
SGT Nicholas A. Ferzacca
PFC Walter. Feszchak
PFC Kevin D. Fettel
2LT Benjamin Fetter
MRS. George A. Fetter
LTC (Ret) Mark Fetter
SPC Richard A. Fetterman
SPC Terrance Fetterman
SPC Aaron Fetters
PFC Arthur J. Fettig
CPT Ryan M. Feuge
SSG Richard D. Feuling
PFC Richard Fey
BG (Ret) William C. Feyk
SPC George E. Fichter
SSG (Ret) Thomas E. Fichter
CPL Miller L. Fickett
SSG Garvin M. Ficklin
SGT James G. Fickling
PFC Thomas P. Fickus
SPC Libris Rk Fidelis
CPL John M. Fidler
MRS. Corrine Fiefer
SPC James Fiefer
1LT John R. Fiegel
PFC Albert A. Field
MRS. Patricia F. Field
LTC (Ret) Terry S. Fielden
SGT Eric Donnie Fielder
SFC Jack E. Fielding
MAJ Robert J. Fielding
SPC Bruce F. Fields
CPT Cody Fields
SGT Douglas A. Fields
CPL Gary E. Fields
SGT Glenn R. Fields
LTG (Ret) Harold T. Fields
LTC (Ret) James L. Fields
MAJ (Ret) Joe E. Fields
CPT Marcus B. Fields
SGT Raphael Fields
SGT Lionel A. Fierro
SFC Michael A. Fierro
PFC Rafael L. Fierro
SGT Robert Fierro
SFC Robert J. Fifield
PVT Regan B. Fighter
PFC Abilio Caldas Figueiredo
SFC (Ret) Arlinda D. Figueredo
SFC Alexander R. Figueroa
1LT Arturo J. Figueroa
1SG Carlos E. Figueroa
SGT George Figueroa
CW2 Luis A. Figueroa
CPT T. Chris Figueroa
CW4 (Ret) Jerry A. Figures
SPC Kenneth Fikes
MG (Ret) Joseph F. Fil
1LT Theodore E. Filandrianos
SPC James F. Filip
SGT Thomas A. Filipiak
PFC Robert J. Filkosky
SPC Richard L. Fillmer
SPC Charles M. Fillmore
MR. Walter T. Fillyaw
PFC Franklin Filmon
MS. Ellen R. Finch
CW3 Robert A. Finch
CW3 Robert J. Finch
SPC Samuel D. Finch
CPT Donald E. Fincher
SPC Gary Fincher
COL (Ret) H. Thomas Fincher
PFC Lewis R. Fincher
CW5 Jess L. Findley
PFC John J. E. Finel
SGT George M. Finger
SGT Earl B. Fink
MAJ JK Fink
SPC John R. Fink
WO1 John S. Fink
SGM Ronald M. Fink
COL Jon E. Finke
SSG Jerome W. Finkelstein
SSG Allison R. Finley
SSG J. C. Finley
MAJ Michael Finn
SGT Ryan Finn
CW2 Thomas C. Finnegan
CW4 (Ret) Francis H. Finnerty
MRS. John J. Finnessy
SPC William E. Finney
PFC William E. Finnimore
SGT Thomas A. Fino
SGT Anthony J. Finocchio
SGM (Ret) Stephen S. Fintak
1LT Ronald Fiocca
SPC John B. Fiore
SPC Vincent A. Fiore
SP5 Calsidonia Fiorella
SFC Thomas A. Fiorillo
COL (Ret) John E. Firth
PFC Ira Fisch
SFC Clifford O. Fischer
SPC Gregory Fischer
LTC (Ret) James C. Fischer
CPT Michael C. Fischer
SSG Michael E. Fischer
COL (Ret) Richard L. Fischer
SSG Robert F. Fischer
CPL Wallace R. Fischer
PFC William F. Fischer
CW2 Aaron K. Fish
SP5 John E. Fish
SGT Richard F. Fish
SP5 Dennis L. Fishar
SSG Thomas L. Fishbaugher
MSG John R. Fishburn
PVT Arthur J. Fisher
SPC Charles A. Fisher
LTC (Ret) Charles M. Fisher
SFC (Ret) David A. Fisher
SGM (Ret) Earl H. Fisher
MR. Gilbert D. Fisher
SGT Gordon M. Fisher
SPC Howard Fisher
LTC Kenneth F. Fisher
MAJ Mark Fisher
LTC (Ret) Paul Fisher
SFC (Ret) Thomas L. Fisher
SPC Tyler R. Fisher
CPT James M. Fisk
LTC Kelly F. Fisk
SGT Phillip Fisk
CSM Richard Fisk
SGT Richard P. Fisk
CPT Roger A. Fiske
SGT L. John Fisken
PFC Ronald K. Fiskum
SGT David Fitch
CPT Gerald Fitch
SGT John G. Fitch
CPL Robert K. Fitch
SSG Coy D. Fitts
MG (Ret) William H. Fitts
PV2 Todd H. Fitz
SGT Arthur M. Fitzgerald
SSG Carlton W. Fitzgerald
CPT Chad Fitzgerald
SGM (Ret) Charles E. Fitzgerald
PFC Gerald Fitzgerald
SSG Gerald J. Fitzgerald
SGT James Fitzgerald
LTC James G. R. Fitzgerald
LTC (Ret) Jerry E. Fitzgerald
SGT John A. Fitzgerald
SGT Joseph M. Fitzgerald
1LT Lemuel W. Fitzgerald
CPL Robert M. Fitzgerald
1LT Thomas J. Fitzgerald
MR. William H. Fitzgerald
PFC William T. Fitzgerald
SGT Jerome J. Fitzmaurice
CPT Thomas I. Fitzpatrick
CPT Ronald R. Fitz-Randolph
PFC James F. Fitzroy
SGT Darwood Lee Fix
SFC Fellotain S. Fizer
MSG (Ret) Peter M. Fizer
SGM Carl J. Fjelstad
CPT James R. Flack
SGT Delmer V. Fladwood
SP5 Robert L. Flaherty
SPC Thomas Flaherty
SFC Daniel P. Flake
PFC Junior Flamar
SPC James W. Flamm
PFC Robert C. Flamm
SPC (Ret) Jim Flanagan
MAJ (Ret) John E. Flanagan
CW2 Phillip R. Flanagan
LTC (Ret) Joseph Norris Flanders
SGT Richard E. Flanders
1SG (Ret) Sherman C. Flanders
MRS. Lewis D. Flanigan
2LT Michael D. Flanigan
SP5 Thomas A. Flanigan
PFC Patrick E. Flannery
1SG John P. Flannigan
MR. Larre R. Flannigan
PVT Patrick G. Flannigan
SGT Barry H. Flashner
TSgt Morton Flashner
SGT Paul Norman Flaten
SSG David L. Flatt
SPC George Flavin
MRS. Frances D. Fleeman
SPC Gary E. Fleeson
CPT Richard Fleischauer
1SG Thomas L. Fleischhauer
MRS. William J. Fleischman
SPC Nelson Fleishman
COL (Ret) Blaine T. Fleming
SSG (Ret) Don R. Fleming
SPC James Fleming
SFC (Ret) James R. Fleming
SGT John Fleming
SGT John E. Fleming
1LT Joseph A. Fleming
SPC Mark Fleming
SGT Mary J. Fleming
LTC Matthew W. Fleming
SP5 (Ret) Miles D. Fleming

2LT Stephen P. Fleming
CW4 (Ret) William T. Fleming
SSG Steven P. Flemister
LTC Michael Ac Flemming
1LT Warren Flenniken
LTC (Ret) Franklin A. Flesher
PVT Andrew Fletcher
PVT Archie Fletcher
SFC Arvis H. Fletcher
SGT Carroll L. Fletcher
MAJ Douglas M. Fletcher
PFC Erwin Fletcher
1SG (Ret) Gene C. Fletcher
SGT Jason D. Fletcher
SFC Jim Fletcher
MRS. John T. Fletcher
SPC Micah Fletcher
SGT Michael E. Fletcher
SPC Ronald A. Fletcher
SGT Troy Lee Fletcher
MAJ (Ret) Edward W. Fleuren
LT George L. Flick
SSG Jack R. Flick
SGT James L. Flinchum
COL Edward L. Flinn
LTC (Ret) Edward A. Flippen
SPC Otis C. Flippin
SPC Willard A. Flippin
SFC William H. Flohr
MSG Marshall J. Flood
SGT Scott Flood
PFC Lawrence Flora
SGT William C. Flora
SPC Alfonso Flores
SPC Armando R. Flores
SFC (Ret) Carl H. Flores
TSgt Claudio Flores
SSG Elisandro Flores
SGT Felipe Flores
CSM Fernando Q. Flores
SPC Francisco A. Flores
SPC Francisco J. Flores
CW2 Frank A. Flores
MR. Frank V. Flores
MSG Humberto Flores
SPC Israel A. Flores
CPL Jesse C. Flores
SGT Joe Flores
MAJ Jon A. Flores
CPL Jose L. Flores
CPL Louis C. Flores
PV2 Oscar G. Flores
SGT Ricardo F. Flores
SGT Richard A. Flores
PFC Robert V. Flores
SFC (Ret) William J. Flores
SPC Edwin Flores-Oritiz
SPC Michael I. Floress
PFC Alonzo R. Florez
SGT Gregorio R. Florez
1LT Leo E. Flower
SSG Derrick Flowers
MAJ Frankie L. Flowers
CW2 Grover A. Flowers
CW2 J. W. Flowers
PFC James W. Flowers
SPC Jimmy C. Flowers
SPC Bobby L. Floyd
SPC David B. Floyd
SGT James K. Floyd
SGT John David Floyd
MSG (Ret) Robert H. Floyd
SSG Mitchell A. Flud
COL (Ret) Eugene C. Fluke
SGT John Flukes
SP5 Edward Flynn
SGT Edward F. Flynn
MR. James J. Flynn
CPT John S. Flynn
PFC Kenneth J. Flynn
SGT Patrick W. Flynn
BG (Ret) Ronald B. Flynn
COL Vernon M. Flynn
MSG Joe E. Flynt
CPT Rocco Foderaro
SP5 Robert E. Foerster
SPC Kyle W. Fogarty
CPL Lawrence H. Fogerty
SGT Charles P. Fogg
PFC Robert Foggiato
SPC Tony R. Fogle
PFC Francis M. Fogner
SFC Donald R. Foisie
SP5 Marc Folden
SP5 Larry M. Folds
SGT Alfred C. Foley
LTC (Ret) Ed Foley
LT Joseph Foley
SGT Joseph W. Foley
MRS. Michael J. Foley
SPC Robert E. Foley
COL (Ret) William A. Foley
SPC Joseph Folk
SGT Keever Folk
SPC James R. Folker
SGT Eldon J. Folkerts
SGT Melvin J. Folkertsma
SGM (Ret) Eugene Folks
MSG (Ret) Michael W. Follis
SFC Emmit W. Folsom
LTC Philip G. Fonde
SSG Antonio J. Fonseca
1SG Bruce A. Fontaine
1SG James M. Fontaine
CPT Matthew E. Fontaine
SGT John Fontana
MAJ Joseph F. Fontanella
MAJ Sharon K. Fontanella
SSG (Ret) Clarence J. Fontenot
SP5 David B. Fontenot
CPT Doyle A. Fontenot
SGT Michael P. Fontenot
1LT Rusty Fontenot
SGT Wade P. Fontenot
SPC Steven M. Fontes
CPL Victor Fontes
SGT Thomas L. Foor
SSG (Ret) Edward Foos
CW4 Louis Foote
SFC Michael B. Foote
PFC Ramon G. Foote
SGT Terry L. Foote
SSG John D. Footman
PFC Ernest J. Foppes
SSG Booker J. Forbes
SGT James G. Forbes
PFC Michael J. Forbes
MRS. Ralph L. Forbes
CPL Robert Forbes
SGT Thomas J. Forbes
SP5 Tony D. Forbes
CPT Chris D. Ford
SPC Curtis Ford
SPC (Ret) Daniel Ford
SGM Eddie Ford
CPL Floyd E. Ford
SSG George Ford
MR. Henry H. Ford
PFC James A. Ford
PFC James A. Ford
SPC James L. Ford
PFC John J. Ford
MRS. Lee Ford
CPT Marion L. Ford
SSG Shannon P. Ford
1LT Stephen E. Ford
MR. Tom Ford
SSG William R. Ford
LTC (Ret) James R. Foreman
SP5 Leeland E. Foreman
CPL Roy J. Foreman
2LT Lewis Forero
MR. Darrell P. Forest
SSG Frank P. Forest
COL (Ret) Ronald P. Forest
LTC (Ret) Frank D. Forestiere
SPC Timothy P. Forget
SGT Joseph D. Forgione
COL (Ret) Michael D. Formica
SPC Vincent V. Formisano
CW3 (Ret) Thomas L. Formy-Duval
SSG (Ret) William W. Fornaro
SPC James Joseph Fornes
SGT Charles H. Forney
SPC Richard T. Forney
1SG (Ret) Delwin I. Forrest
LTC (Ret) George G. Forrest
SGT Robert A. Forrest
MR. Robert O. Forrest
COL Robert W. Forrester
SP5 Ron Forrester
PFC Ronnie L. Forrester
SP5 Steven R. Forrester
PFC Lloyd N. Forry
CPL Walter E. Forsha
LTC Charles E. Forshee
MAJ Karl M. Forster
2LT Anthony Forstner
CPT David J. Forsyth
SFC Harry R. Forsythe
SPC John W. Fort
CSM (Ret) Monte R. Forte
SSG Paul G. Fortenberry
PV2 Marc D. Fortier
SPC David L. Fortin
CPL Placido S. Fortino
MSG Rex Fortner
SPC Timothy B. Fortner
SFC Jesse F. Fortson
PFC Richard G. Fortson
CSM (Ret) John W. Fortune
SFC Bradley K. Fosdick
CPT Shane D. Foshee
SSG (Ret) Art Foss
GEN (Ret) John W. Foss
SGT Allan F. Foster
MAJ Chad R. Foster
SGT Charles L. Foster
1SG (Ret) Claude D. Foster
SSG Coley Foster
SGT Daryle E. Foster
SPC David L. Foster
CW2 Edmond K. Foster
CPT Edward N. Foster
LTC (Ret) Hugh F. Foster
SGT Jack B. Foster
SPC James D. Foster
SSG James Edward Foster
CPT Jeffrey Lee Foster
SFC (Ret) Jerald B. Foster
SFC Jesse Foster
SGT Joe Ray Foster
SGT Kevin Foster
SSG Kevin R. Foster
LTC (Ret) Leland C. Foster
CPT Raymond T. Foster
PFC Robert M. Foster
SPC Ron R. Foster
2LT Ronnie D. Foster
SGT Thomas A. Foster
CPT Joe Fosterik
2LT Matthew C. Fouch
TSgt Leonard L. Fougere
SP6 James E. Fought
SGT Paul Foulkes
SFC Donald R. Fountain
SPC Edward H. Fountain
SGT James G. Fountain
SGT Terry L. Fountain
CSM Dennis L. Fountaine
MAJ Paul H. Fournia
SGT Claude H. Fourroux
SFC Enrique Fourzan
LTC (Ret) Scott D. Fouse
COL (Ret) Richard J. Fousek
SSG Aaron Fowler
SPC (Ret) David W. Fowler
1SG Eric J. Fowler
LTC (Ret) Gary Sterling Fowler
MR. James F. Fowler
CPT James H. Fowler
CPT Jeffrey Fowler
SP5 Marc J. Fowler
SPC Robert A. Fowler
SPC Thomas C. Fowler
SP5 Valton Dwayne Fowler
SP5 Alan G. Fox
CW4 Carl U. Fox
SSG Christopher E. Fox
2LT Darryl T. Fox
SGT David H. Fox
SGT (Ret) Edward B. Fox
PFC Emery K. Fox
COL (Ret) Eugene A. Fox
CPL Garry J. Fox
CW3 (Ret) George S. Fox
SGT Harold L. Fox
SPC James M. Fox
CPT Jeffrey Fox
SGT Jerry L. Fox
SGT Justin G. Fox
SSG Larry V. Fox
CW3 Marianne Fox
CPT Matthew M. Fox
1LT Michael W. Fox
CPL Ronald V. Fox
CSM (Ret) Stanley Lee Fox
SPC Stephen L. Fox
SPC Steven A. Fox
SPC Timothy Fox
CPT Todd M. Fox
SGT William R. Fox
SGT Louis A. Foy
MSG (Ret) William J. Foy
SPC Manuel Fraga
SPC Eric L. Fragoso
CSM (Ret) Jose Fragoso
PVT Jerry F. Fragoza
PFC Craig U. Fraley
SPC Herbert A. Fralix
CPT Charles L. Frame
SP5 Larry D. France
SPC Robert P. Franch
MRS. George F. Francioni
SPC Jeffrey R. Francis
SFC Larry E. Francis
SFC Mark Francis
SGT Michael Francis
SGT Phillip N. Francis
1LT Sam W. Francis
CPT William H. Francisco
SGT Dean T. Franciskovich
SPC Larry Franco
SGT Roneldo Franco
SGT Warren D. Franco
COL David Francvilla
MRS. Benny Frank
SPC Charles L. Frank
SSG Dwight Frank
MR. James Frank
SPC (Ret) James R. Frank
CPT Michael J. Frank
PFC Thomas Frank
COL (Ret) A. Wayne Franke
CW4 (Ret) Carl G. Franke
1SG Henry G. Franke
SGT Kenneth A. Frankenberry
SP5 Benjamin F. Franklin
SSG Bobby G. Franklin
2LT Charles J. Franklin
CSM (Ret) Joseph H. Franklin
SPC Leonard C. Franklin
SFC Lewis Franklin
1SG Lewis A. Franklin
CSM Richard E. Franklin
LTC (Ret) William W. Franklin
SPC Willie C. Franklin
SGT Floyd E. Franks
SGT Jimmy D. Franks
COL (Ret) Robert F. Franks
1LT Robert S. Franks
1SG Scotty R. Franks
GEN (Ret) Tommy R. Franks
PFC Martin L. Fransen
SP5 David L. Frantz
SGT George Frantz
MSG (Ret) Robert L. Frantz
MRS. Thomas W. Franz
CPT Jonathan Christoffer Fraser
1LT Bruce L. Frasier
SSG Cedric S. Frasier
LTC Ralph C. Frates
SGT (Ret) Earl T. Frawley
SPC James S. Frazer
SFC Stanley P. Frazer
CW3 William C. Frazer
MR. Charles Frazier
MSG Eugene B. Frazier
SPC James D. Frazier
SPC James P. Frazier
SGT John Frazier
MSG Robert A. Frazier
SPC Rudolph Frazier
MSG (Ret) Wesley E. Frazier
A1C Wilson L. Frazier
SGT Thomas N. Fread
LTG (Ret) Benjamin C. Freakley
SSG Michael S. Freas
SGT Jerry E. Frease
CDR J. Fredas
CPL Robert F. Frede
MR. Dale G. Fredenburg
SGT Donald L. Fredenburg
SSG Clifton Frederick
SGT Donald W. Frederick
SSG John P. Frederick
COL (Ret) Jonathan E. Frederick
SFC Yves Frederique
SGM Christopher Frediani
MSG Mark D. Fredrickson
SP5 Delbert A. Free
SPC Stanley D. Freeborn
SSG David Freece
SPC Timothy R. Freed
MAJ David A. Freel
COL (Ret) Albert W. Freeland
SFC Alphine H. Freeman
SGT (Ret) Charles E. Freeman
MSG Donald J. Freeman
CPT James M. Freeman
SSG Jason Freeman
PFC Jess Freeman
MRS. John K. Freeman
SP5 John M. Freeman
SGT Kenneth Freeman
CPT Robert V. Freeman
1LT Ronald V. Freeman
SSG Scot A. Freeman
SSG Thomas Freeman
1LT Tommie L. Freeman
MRS. Diane L. Freeman-Holloway
SrA Charles Freer
SPC Ralph J. Freese
CSM Paul V. Freiday
MRS. Henry M. Freidinger
SGT Victor M. Freilich
PFC Robert G. Freker
1SG James Freman
CW2 Clyde B. French
CPT Jeffrey W. French
1SG John C. French
SPC Kenneth J. French
COL (Ret) Mark R. French
PVT Melvin B. French
CPT Richard L. French
CSM (Ret) Stephan Frennier
SPC Michael A. Fressola
SPC Larry L. Fretwell
SSG Arthur Fretz
PFC Glen Freudenburg
1LT Donald J. Frey
1SG Luis Freyre
CPT Gerald Freytag
1LT Frank A. Friar
CW3 Manuel S. Frias
COL (Ret) John Fricas
CPT Robert S. Frick
SGT Dennis J. Friday
SPC Edgar F. Friday
SGT Richard Friday
MAJ Mitchell H. Fridley
SP5 Robert A. Fridrych
LTC Kent Friederich
PFC Daniel G. Friedline
SGT Mike W. Friedrichs
PFC Theodore R. Frields
1LT Daniel Friend
1LT Kathleen K. Friend
SPC Paul J. Friese
MAJ Michael C. Friess
PV2 Richard C. Friess
CPT Jonathan C. Fristoe
1LT Joseph F. Frisz
1LT Basil W. Frith
1SG Daniel A. Fritz
SGT Frank J. Fritz
SP5 William C. Fritz
COL William H. Fritz
SFC Jack Frizzell
PFC Gary A. Frizzi
SGT Kevin Froehler
PFC Christopher P. Froelich
CPT (Ret) George H. Froemke
SGM Gregory A. Froggatt
PVT Dennis J. Froh
SPC Fred F. Fronczek
SPC John J. Frongillo
SSG Michael Frongillo
SSG David G. Fronius
SP6 Joseph B. Frosch
SGT Cullen D. Frost
SGT Jack E. Frost
MR. Leonidas Frost
SPC Matthew C. Frost
MSG Joseph A. Fruzzetti
COL (Ret) Ernest M. Fry
MR. James Fry
SSG Michael Fry
SFC William D. Fry
SSG Gary L. Frye
SGT Joseph C. Frye
PFC Joseph E. Frye
LTC (Ret) Thomas F. Frye
PFC Briggs L. Fryer
MRS. Lowell H. Fryer
LTC (Ret) Michael J. Fucci
SGT David Fuentes
SFC Efrain Fuentes
SPC Jimmy Fuentes
SGT R. Alan Fuentes
SFC Ruben R. Fuentes
SPC Jose E. Fuentes-Roche
PVT Joseph Fuentez
SSG Timmie T. Fuewell
MR. William Fugelsang
CPT Patrick G. Fugere
MR. Robert J. Fuggiti
1SG Robert H. Fugitt
PFC Keith T. Fujimoto
MAJ George J. Fukumoto
MAJ David E. Fulbright
CPL Robert D. Fulbright
SPC Johnnie M. Fulcher
CPL Jack G. Fulfer
PFC (Ret) Edward R. Fullam
MR. Lester M. Fullen
SPC Archie D. Fuller
SrA Charles A. Fuller
SFC Doralo Fuller
1SG Douglas R. Fuller
CPL Gerald R. Fuller
SGT James W. Fuller
MSG Jerry Fuller
SP5 John H. Fuller
MSG John R. Fuller
SFC (Ret) Michael B. Fuller
1SG Michael E. Fuller
SSG Michael R. Fuller
SSG Randall L. Fuller
MSG (Ret) Thomas W. Fuller
SGT (Ret) William B. Fuller
COL (Ret) Robert J. Fullerton
SPC Dennis A. Fullshire
2LT Scott C. Fulmer
SPC Ricky L. Fulps
1SG Robert C. Fulps
LTC (Ret) Charles F. Fulton
SP5 Dennis A. Fultz
SP5 Alvin M. Funge
MAJ (Ret) Jack Funk
MR. Mark Funk
LTG (Ret) Paul E. Funk
BG Anthony C. Funkhouser
SPC Robert Fuquay
COL (Ret) Bartley W. Furey
MR. Steve P. Furlan
SGT James D. Furlong
MR. Robert A. Furmanek
SPC John C. Furnas
SFC (Ret) Jimmie L. Furr
SGT John P. Furst
SPC David L. Futch
PFC Ebenezer Fynn
WO1 Samuel A. Gabara
PVT Michael R. Gabaree
MR. James Gabbamonte
1SG Robert E. Gabe
CPT Wilfried E. Gabel
LTC W. F. Gabella
SPC Jeffrey C. Gable
SPC John A. Gable
SGT Louis M. Gabor
BG Douglas M. Gabram
MAJ Robert D. Gabriel
SPC Roland P. Gacayan
SGT Stojan Gacov
PFC Wade L. Gadberry
SP5 Jeffrey H. Gadbois
PV2 Clyde R. Gadd
MR. Albert Gaddis
SSG Calvin J. Gaddis
PFC Jerome A. Gaddis
SGT John Gaddis
SGM Melvin L. Gaddis
SGT Rick P. Gaddis
PVT Terri A. Gaddy
SFC Henry S. Gadsden
1SG Michael D. Gadzinski
SGT Harold J. Gaertner
1LT Steve Gaertner
CW2 (Ret) John F. Gafeller
SPC Don Gaffney
CPT James A. Gaffney
SPC Patrick A. Gaffney
SP5 Michael L. Gafford
SSG Bradley Gage
MAJ Phillip K. Gage
PFC Joseph Gaglio
PFC David L. Gagne
SFC Glen C. Gagnier
SPC Douglas C. Gagnon
SGT Jessica Gagnon
CPL Stephen A. Gagnon
CPT Dennis L. Gahagen
PVT Kevin M. Gahring
COL (Ret) Gerry Gaida
SFC Robert C. Gailey
SGT John R. Gailfoil
CW4 William L. Gaillard
SSG Steven D. Gain
SGT Ronnie A. Gainer
CPL Walter J. Gainer
SPC Columbus Gaines
SGT Edward I. Gaines
SFC Timothy Gaines
SGT William Gaines
SP5 Cecil L. Gainey
CSM (Ret) Juan E. Gaitan
SP5 Merse Gaitan
SFC (Ret) James E. Gaither
PVT John H. Gaither
PFC Robert C. Galante
SPC Reginald Galanto
SPC Arnold H. Galaviz
PVT Alexander J. Galban
WO1 Gary C. Galbraith
SPC Glenn W. Galbraith
LTC William S. Galbraith
SPC Ernest E. Galbreath
SSG Albert L. Galbreth
SPC Anthony Charles Gale
PFC Anthony Galella

SPC Fred J. Galemore
PFC Gordon T. Galfo
SFC Rafael Galiano
SSG Gabriel Galindo
PFC Gabriel I. Galindo
SGT Michael Galindo
SSG Omar Galindo
SGT Ralph G. Galindo
SSG Roberto L. Galindo
CPL Gene O. Gall
SPC Donald F. Gallagher
SGT Francis David Gallagher
SP5 Gene F. Gallagher
SP5 Joseph C. Gallagher
SP5 Kenneth Gallagher
SPC Michael Gallagher
MSG William J. Gallagher
SSG Phillip C. Gallardo
SFC (Ret) Victor A. Gallardo
SGT Manuel Gallareta
PFC (Ret) James Gallas
LTC John W. Gallaspy
PFC Gerald L. Galleano
SP5 Benirito Gallegos
SGT Felipe R. Gallegos
PVT Jose S. Gallegos
SGT Leonardo Gallegos
CPT David A. Galles
MRS. Anne Galligan
COL John P. Galligan
SGT Henry Gallimore
CPL Richard Gallina
1LT Charles P. Gallion
SGT Stephen D. Gallion
COL James Gallivan
COL James J. Gallivan
CPT (Ret) John K. Gallman
CPT (Ret) David T. Gallo
SPC Jeremy A. Gallo
MR. Juan Gallo
SPC Kale W. Gallo
SPC Nicholas G. Gallo
PFC Vito John Gallo
SSG Michael J. Gallob
PVT Joseph A. Gallos
COL Michael S. Galloucis
MAJ Byron A. Galloway
SPC Dennis Galloway
SGT Dennis M. Galloway
SPC Earl Galloway
MR. Joseph L. Galloway
MR. Kenneth Galloway
SPC Matthew A. Galloway
SGT Roger A. Galloway
PFC Michael J. Gallucci
MSG Joseph Galluzzo
SSG Fabio A. Galo
CW3 (Ret) Gayle Galvan
SGT Richard Galvan
SPC Peter M. Galvin
MAJ Richard J. Galvin
MAJ (Ret) Thomas P. Galvin
SPC Walter F. Gamache
PFC Matthew Gambardella
SGT James J. Gambatese
SPC Harold D. Gambill
1SG Joe Gambino
LTC Alphonso L. Gamble
SGT Carol D. Gamble
MR. Hal B. Gamble
SPC John H. Gamble
MS. Marietta Gamble
CPL Philip E. Gamblin
PFC Lloyd Gambling
SGT Robert M. Gambrell
1LT Henry E. Game
MAJ Ben R. Games
SPC Arthur R. Gamez
SGT Rafael S. Gamez
CPT Jonathan B. Gamm
SGT Jeffrey N. Gammel
CSM Roy C. Gammell
SSG Dewayne L. Gammill
MRS. Kathy Gammill
PFC Anthony Gandara
MRS. Hazel Gander
CSM James I. Gandy
SSG James W. Gandy
CSM (Ret) L. A. Gandy
BG (Ret) Raymond E. Gandy
CPT Loyd R. Ganey
PVT Joseph G. Gange
SP5 Donald T. Gangell
PFC Dennis M. Ganley
SGT Billy R. Gann
SGM Jerry Gann
SGM (Ret) Jerry W. Gann
MR. Terry L. Gann
PFC Raven Gannaway
SFC James F. Gano
MR. Benny Gant
SGT Larry W. Gant
SGT Robert L. Gant
SPC Alonzo Ganther
MAJ Kenneth D. Gantt
SGT Ernest Ganz
SPC Julian C. Gaona
SFC Geraldo Gapol
MR. George Garbacz
SGT Robert W. Garbacz
SGT Paul C. Garber
MR. Dennis J. Garboski
SFC (Ret) David F. Garceau
SFC Refugio Garces
SPC Adalberto M. Garcia
PFC Alberto Garcia
SFC Alex S. Garcia
SPC Anivar J. Garcia
SGT Anthony Garcia
SGT Antonio C. Garcia
SFC Arthur Garcia
SGT Daniel P. Garcia
SGT David Garcia
SFC David J. Garcia
PVT Eduardo Garcia
SPC Eduardo Garcia
SPC Edward E. Garcia
SSG Ernesto Garcia
CPT Esteban Antonio Garcia
SP3 Eugene Delano Garcia
SGM (Ret) Frank S. Garcia
SSG Gabriel Garcia
SPC Gabriel G. Garcia
SSG George M. Garcia
SGT George S. Garcia
PV2 Gilbert Garcia
SGT Gilberto A. Garcia
SSG Isidoro Garcia
2LT James Garcia
CW4 Javier Garcia
SGT (Ret) Jesse Romero Garcia
SSG Jesus E. Garcia
SSG Joe Garcia
SFC John Garcia
LTC John J. Garcia
PV2 Juan Garcia
SGT Juan B. Garcia
WO1 Juan J. Garcia
MSG Juan J. Garcia
SPC Juan M. Garcia
SSG Julio C. Garcia
SGT Lino L. Garcia
PVT Luis E. Garcia
SFC Luis R. Garcia
CPL Manuel B. Garcia
SP5 Margarito Garcia
SPC Michael B. Garcia
SSG Miguel Thomas Garcia
SFC Mike Garcia
SGT Nathan G. Garcia
SGT Nicolas Garcia
SGT Norma L. Garcia
SGT Olga M. Garcia
SFC Orlando Garcia
PVT Orlando A. Garcia
LTC Paul Garcia
CSM (Ret) Raul G. Garcia
SPC Robert Garcia
SPC Robert M. Garcia
SGT Roberto A. Garcia
PVT Rodolfo Garcia
SFC Saul G. Garcia
MSG (Ret) Simon G. Garcia
MR. Tedosio A. Garcia
1SG Victor M. Garcia
MSG Rafael Garcia-Rivera
SGT David D. Gardiner
MR. Ferd Gardiner
SPC Kenneth W. Cisco Gardiner
PFC Anthony Gardner
PFC Brenden R. Gardner
SGT Calvin Gardner
SGT David L. Gardner
1LT Eric J. Gardner
CW3 Eugene Gardner
CPT Gavin J. Gardner
MSG (Ret) George M. Gardner
MSG (Ret) Gordon M. Gardner
SGT John Timothy Gardner
PFC Ora O. Gardner
SSG Paul L. Gardner
SGM Richard H. Gardner
SPC Rob Gardner
1SG Robert M. Gardner
LTC (Ret) Roland L. Gardner
MAJ James J. Gardon
SGT David S. Gardonio
LTC Craig R. Gardunia
SGT Luis A. Garera
SFC (Ret) Willie R. Garfield
CSM (Ret) Paul Gargis
SPC Steve Garlan
MAJ Jeri C. Garland
SGT Ronald A. Garland
CSM (Ret) Michael G. Garlanger
2LT Christian S. Garlitz
1LT John W. Garmong
SGT Douglas Garn
SPC Jeffrey K. Garnand
SPC Michael B. Garneau
1LT Thomas W. Garnella
SFC Billy J. Garner
1LT Christian Garner
PVT David L. Garner
SGM (Ret) Donald E. Garner
MAJ George Garner
SPC Jack E. Garner
SrA Walter Garner
SPC Stanley E. Garnhart
SPC Steven D. Garnhart
SPC Frank R. Garofalo
SPC Brian K. Garon
SGT Allen Garr
SPC Brian Garraty
SFC Joslin C. Garraway
SSG Aldrick S. Garrett
SPC Anthony M. Garrett
CPT Benjamin L. Garrett
CSM (Ret) Dale W. Garrett
SPC Eugene T. Garrett
SGM (Ret) James G. Garrett
SGT Jerry Garrett
MRS. Jim Garrett
SSG John W. Garrett
SGT Johnny L. Garrett
SSG Kareem Garrett
SGM Karl K. Garrett
MAJ Kenneth C. Garrett
MSG Louis A. Garrett
SSG Mark A. Garrett
CW4 Robert H. Garrett
MR. Robert L. Garrett
SSG Scott Garrett
SGT George L. Garretto
CPL John E. Garrido
SPC James G. Garrigan
SGT Glen Garris
SFC Randy Garris
PFC Charlie W. Garrison
SFC Donald T. Garrison
PVT Dwayne T. Garrison
SP5 Harry J. Garrison
SGT John L. Garrison
MS. Margaret A. Garrison
SP5 Millard Garrison
SSG Tony Garrison
MAJ William G. Garrison
PFC Daniel J. Garrity
SPC Richard J. Garrity
MRS. Gladys Gartrell
LTC (Ret) Jack T. Garven
CPT Brian Garvey
SPC John A. Garvey
REV. Enos V. Garvin
SGT James E. Garvin
SFC Anselmo Garza
SPC Carlos Antonio Garza
SPC Demetrio Garza
SGM Guadalupe Garza
CSM (Ret) Homer M. Garza
SSG Jesus Garza
MR. Joe L. Garza
1SG Matias Garza
SPC Max Garza
CW3 (Ret) Pedro C. Garza
SPC Rolando Garza
SGT Simon V. Garza
SFC Earl A. Gascho
SPC Bruce E. Gasdaska
PFC Thomas D. Gaskins
BG George W. Gaspard
SGT Tylor J. Gaspard
SP5 Nicholas J. Gasparre
SPC Russell Gasser
MR. David B. Gassman
MRS. Walter R. Gassman
SGT K. Paul Gassner
SGT Henry Gast
CPT O. Raymond Gaster
TSgt Arnold E. Gaston
CSM James W. Gaston
SSG Lawrence M. Gaston
SFC Timothy A. Gaston
COL (Ret) Mark D. Gatanas
PFC Dale J. Gatehouse
SPC Robert W. Gatenby
SFC (Ret) Otis Gates
SP5 Vaughn A. Gates
CPT Kim A. Gatewood
SP5 Richard L. Gatewood
TSgt Robert B. Gatewood
MRS. Thomas B. Gatewood
CPT Gregory Steven Gatrell
LTC Jacob W. Gatrell
CPL Roy L. Gatson
MSG Al Gatto
MR. George D. Gaucker
SGT Jules Gaudet
SGT Jose Felipe Flores Gaudin
LTC Derek Gaudlitz
COL (Ret) Ralph C. Gauer
CPL Henry W. Gauger
SGT Francis Gaule
LTC Edward H. Gaulin
SP5 Richard E. Gauthier
MAJ Robert W. Gautier
SPC Kenneth M. Gauvreau
CPT Sean E. Gavan
SGT Francis P. Gavin
SGT Kirkland J. Gavin
MSG (Ret) Michael J. Gavin
MAJ William A. Gawthrop
SPC Chuck Gay
SPC John M. Gay
CPL Kenneth F. Gay
SFC (Ret) Kenneth R. Gay
SPC Robert C. Gay
CW2 Rocky Gay
CW2 Sherri Gayden
COL Patrick L. Gaydon
1LT Glen M. Gayheart
CPT Ronald D. Gayler
SGT John S. Gayman
SGT Martin Gaymon
CPT Luis N. Gaytan
PFC Freddie J. Gazaway
SGT Thomas S. Gdovin
PV2 Gerald A. Gdula
MR. Benjamin F. Gearhart
SPC Michael S. Geary
PV2 Vanessa Gebhart
SSG John A. Gedick
CSM (Ret) Charles M. Gee
MRS. Wanda Gee
PVT Howard D. Geer
SFC (Ret) James W. Geer
SFC Kenneth C. Geers
PVT Otto L. Gehant
PVT Tyler Gehlhausen
SSG Duane W. Gehling
COL Emroy M. Gehlsen
PFC Ryne Gehring
1LT Fritz Geibel
SGT Roy Geigen
SGT Alan L. Geiger
SGT Bryan Geiger
CPT Grace M. Geiger
SGT Joseph C. Geiger
SGT Joseph J. Geiger
SPC Nathaniel Wayne Geiger
SGT William F. Geiger
SFC (Ret) Douglas P. Geis
MR. John L. Geis
BG (Ret) John P. Geis
SGM Charles R. Geisewite
MRS. Paula A. Geisler
SGT Rodney Geisler
SrA Carroll Geist
CPT Joseph L. Gelinas
CPT Louis Gelling
SSG Anthony J. Gelose
SGT Bernard N. Gemelli
SFC (Ret) Michael A. Gemignani
SGT Richard J. Gendek
SGT Peter E. Genecki
PFC Luther A. Genes
CPL Harry C. Gennaro
SFC (Ret) Albert A. Gensiejewski
SPC Ronald L. Gent
SPC Vincent Gentile
1LT Sylvio M. Gentili
SPC Bennie O. Gentry
MSG Howard D. Gentry
SPC James B. Gentry
LTC (Ret) Joseph W. Gentry
COL Paul Gentry
PVT Paul A. Gentry
PFC Rick Gentry
LTC (Ret) Robert K. Gentry
MAJ (Ret) Roy C. Gentry
SGT Travis Gentzler
SSG Robert W. Geoffrion
MR. Mick Geoghegan
MSG Charles W. George
1SG (Ret) Curt H. George
SSG Delbert L. George
MSG (Ret) Denroy C. George
SFC Edward J. George
1SG James S. George
SPC Michael George
SGT Michael W. George
MAJ Milan George
PFC Miquel L. George
PFC Paul M. George
MSG Percy L. George
SGT Stormy George
MAJ Thomas W. George
SGT Walt George
SGT William R. George
PFC Joseph Gephart
CPT (Ret) John J. Geraghty
SSG (Ret) Anselmo Jerry Gerard
SSG Paul Wayne Gerard
CW3 Charles M. Gerber
LTC Christopher P. Gerdes
SGT James C. Geren
COL (Ret) John G. Gergulis
LTC Robert Gerhardt
MR. Carl H. Gerke
SPC Steven E. Gerke
SFC Kevin G. Gerken
SPC Leonard L. Gerlach
LT Jack R. Germain
SGT Barton T. Germaine
MRS. Michael J. Germano
SFC Dale Germany
SGT Michael Germany
MR. Charles R. Germeck
COL (Ret) George F. Germond
SSG Thomas Germuga
PFC Randall S. Germundson
SPC James R. Gerner
MR. R. E. Gerow
SGT Andrew Gerrier
SGT John F. Gerrish
PFC Michael Gershon
MAJ (Ret) Roy Gersten
CPT David L. Gerstenlauer
SGT Fred L. Gerstner
WO1 Brian Geschke
COL (Ret) Joseph M. Gesker
LTC (Ret) Robert Gesner
SGT John W. Gestes
PFC Brian J. Gettle
SGT Kurt R. Getz
SSG Larry D. Getz
SFC (Ret) Leroy C. Getz
SGT William C. Getz
2LT Daniel L. Geu
SPC Timothy A. Geyer
SPC Asghar Ghafoor
CPT John R. Ghere
MAJ Edward M. Ghiz
SFC Frank Giaimo
SGT Nick Giamarino
PFC Panfilo Edward Giammarco
SPC John P. Giampia
SP5 Frank J. Giancola
SGM Alfred M. Giann
CPT Eric M. Giannaris
CPL Joseph N. Giannoccora
SPC Frank A. Giaquinto
MSG (Ret) Roy Gibbens
SGT Cartan L. Gibbons
SPC John M. Gibbons
SFC (Ret) Kenneth C. Gibbons
MR. Kevin S. Gibbons
SFC Lawrence M. Gibbons
SGT Michael W. Gibbons
SPC Robert D. Gibbons
MR. Edward Y. Gibbs
SGT Joe R. Gibbs
SPC Larry A. Gibbs
CPT Lexie R. Gibbs
SFC Lyle R. Gibbs
SGT Murray Gibbs
SSG Willard W. Gibbs
MR. Dennis Gibby
SGT Lee Gibelyou
CPL Angelo Gibilterra
SGT James David Giblin
LTC Cristine Gibney
SPC Larry G. Gibreal
SPC Bart Gibson
SGT Brian L. Gibson
SPC Carl W. Gibson
SGT Charles J. Gibson
SGT David Wayne Gibson
MR. Donald M. Gibson
SGT Donald T. Gibson
CPL Edwin L. Gibson
CPL Eugene Gibson
SGT Floyd A. Gibson
SSG Harold L. Gibson
PFC Herman A. Gibson
SFC James A. Gibson
SGT James P. Gibson
SPC Lewis Gibson
SFC Ralph H. Gibson
SSG Robert E. Gibson
SGT Ronald E. Gibson
SGT Scott A. Gibson
PFC Shannon J. Gibson
SGT Terry A. Gibson
SGT Walter A. Gibson
SPC Bobby L. Giddens
CPT Paul J. Giddens
SP3 Richard O. Gideon
SGT Ivan P. Gierich
SGT Richard W. Giertz
DR. T.H. Giese
CPL Floyd E. Gieseke
SPC Randolph M. Giesen
LTC Charles Gietz
SGT Roy Giffin
SGT Arthur D. Gifford
PVT Craig N. Gifford
SFC Danny Gifford
PFC Douglas M. Gifford
MAJ (Ret) Michael W. Gifford
MR. Myron L. Gifford
CPT Thomas C. Tim Gifford
SP5 Joseph N. Gigandet
SPC John A. Gigante
CPL Donald R. Gilardi
SPC John M. Gilardi
SPC Daniel L. Gilbert
PFC Eldred G. Gilbert
SGT Emanuel Gilbert
CSM (Ret) Horace Eddie Gilbert
SGT James H. Gilbert
PV2 Jimmy L. Gilbert
SPC John Lee Gilbert
1SG (Ret) Lawrence R. Gilbert
SPC Michael A. Gilbert
CPL Thomas J. Gilbert
SGT Wendell L. Gilbert
SFC Jeff Gilbertson
TSgt John T. Gilboy
SGT Dana G. Gilbreath
SGT Joseph L. Gilchrest
MR. Elton C. Gilchrist
LTC Malcolm S. Gilchrist
PFC Richard M. Gile
SPC Bobbie J. Giles
MAJ Carl L. Giles
SSG Morris L. Giles
SPC William Jacob Giles
CSM (Ret) William H. Gilkey
CSM (Ret) Darryl Gill
2LT David R. Gill
LTC Michael M. Gill
MR. Rexford E. Gill
PFC Richard H. Gill
SGT Robert C. Gill
CPT Sherman A. Gill
CW4 (Ret) Thomas Gill
SSG Travis Gill
MR. William F. Gill
SSG William J. Gill
SGT William J. Gill
SSG Don L. Gillam
SGT Paul E. Gilland
COL Steve Gilland
COL (Ret) Richard D. Gillem
TSgt August Gilleskie
SGT Brian F. Gillespie
1SG Charles D. Gillespie
SPC Jimmy Gillespie
LTC (Ret) Vernon W. Gillespie
SPC Albert A. Gillette
LTC (Ret) William P. Gillette
CPL Robert C. Gilley
SGT Michael P. Gillhoolley
CPL Peter J. Gilli
SSG Harold L. Gilliam
MAJ John Gilliam
SGT Linville D. Gilliam
LTC (Ret) Richard D. Gilliam
SPC Richard L. Gilliam
MR. Robert A. Gillie
SFC Ronald Dale Gilliland
CPL Casandra Gillinger
SGT Carey L. Gillis
COL (Ret) Aaron P. Gillison
MSG (Ret) Daniel P. Gillotti
SPC Donald Gillotti
MAJ Scott D. Gilman
2LT Robert F. Gilmartin
SGM Franklin Gilmore
MAJ (Ret) George H. Gilmore
SrA Jack V. Gilmore
1LT Lloyd W. Gilmore
TSgt Robert T. Gilmore

SPC Larry L. Gilpin
SGT Gregory Gilreath
MRS. Larry M. Gilreath
SP5 Rickey E. Gilson
1SG Roger Gilson
SPC Ryan Gilson
SPC Aaron T. Gilstrap
PFC James W. Gilstrap
SSG Larry L. Gilstrap
SGT Jerry H. Ginder
SFC Leland W. Ginger
CPL Gerald D. Gingery
CPT William T. Ginn
SGT Thomas Ginop
CW2 Geoffrey Ginos
CPL (Ret) Arthur S. Ginsberg
SPC Ted Ginsburg
CPT Philip J. Gioia
SGT Anthony Giordano
MRS. Augustine Giordano
SGT Frank U. Giordano
SGT Gregory E. Giordano
SGT Phillip Gipson
PVT Joseph A. Girard
1SG (Ret) Paul A. Girard
CPL (Ret) Terrance P. Girard
MRS. Gerald J. Girens
CW3 (Ret) Gaetano A. Girone
SSG Glenn A. Girton
PVT James Tich Girvan
SSG Joe Gist
1LT (Ret) Cass I. Gittins
SGT John A. Giunco
SFC (Ret) H. Wayne Givens
SPC James T. Givens
PFC Robert D. Givens
PFC Robert S. Givens
SSG James F. Gladden
PVT Michael J. Gladis
MR. Joseph Gladue
CPT Jerome S. Gladysz
MAJ Jesse W. Glance
SP5 Roy M. Glancy
SGT Clark O. Glaser
MR. David C. Glasgow
PFC Larry Glasgow
CW2 (Ret) Edward J. Glasheen
MSG Jeffery E. Glasper
CW2 Charles R. Glass
CPT Gary B. Glass
LTC (Ret) Patrick R. Glass
PFC Rexford L. Glass
MSG Jeffrey L. Glassco
SPC Albert Brad Glasscock
MR. Larry E. Glaze
SFC Victor J. Glaze
CPT David Glazebrook
CPT Jeffrey D. Gleasman
DR. Bruce Gleason
SGT Paul Daniel Gleason
SFC (Ret) George J. Gleissner
CSM Roland Glenister
TSgt Albert Glenn
CW2 James C. Glenn
1LT Lawson W. Glenn
SSG Maxell Glenn
MAJ Michael B. Glenn
CPT (Ret) Ora L. Glenn
MSG Randell Glenn
CPL Erica Glidewell
SGT Samuel Lee Glidewell
1LT Arthur D. Glikin
SGT Richard P. Glisinski
SP5 F. G. Glisson
SGT Milton E. Glisson
1SG (Ret) Dick Gloar
MR. Peter F. Globuschutz
MR. Michael Gloden
SGT Raynaldo D. Gloria
SGT Don Glover
MR. Howard L. Glover
SGT Jason M. Glover
SGT John Alfred Glover
SSG John W. Glover
PFC Joseph W. Glover
SGT Kenneth T. Glover
SGT Reece M. Glover
SGT Thurman Lee Glover
SGT Charles R. Glowzenski
LT Larry J. Glozier
CPT (Ret) Brion P. Gluck
SP5 Dennis D. Glumack
MSG George F. Glycenfer
MR. Richard M. Gnagy
CPT Jeffrey Gniffke
CPT Michael Andrew Salvatore Goba
CPL Robert B. Goben
MRS. Roy Dee Gober
SFC Marcel N. Gobeth
MSG Robert D. Goble
1SG (Ret) Jerry Godbee
SGT Zachary B. Godbee
SGT Thomas D. Godbold
CPT Willie J. Godchaux
SGT Alfred W. Goddard
SGT Jack L. Goddard
PFC Butch Godfrey
SSG Dewan D. Godfrey
CPT J. Frank Godfrey
SSG James G. Godfrey
SFC (Ret) James T. Godfrey
SGT (Ret) Norman J. Godfrey
COL (Ret) Thomas G. Godfrey
MR. Tim Godfrey
SPC David Godkin
PFC Richard P. Godley
SPC Anrae Godley-Cooper
CPL James C. Godwin
CPT William Godwin-Stremler
SPC Jonathan C. Goecke
PVT Gerard P. Goeden
CPL Francis Goedken
1SG Leslie J. Goehner
SPC Larry W. Goehring
CPT James S. Goemmer
SPC Delbert Goerlitz
SSG Jared Goertzen
SPC Jason L. Goerz
SGT David L. Goetchius
SGT Kenneth R. Goethe
SGT Jessica Ann Goettl
SPC Jamie R. Goettle
SPC Kenneth F. Goetz
COL Barron L. Goff
CPT Christopher Goff
SSG Donald R. Goff
SGT James E. Goff
MR. Ken Goff
SGT Kevin Goff
SSG David K. Goffinet
LTC Keith M. Gogas
SPC Charles E. Goggin
CW2 (Ret) Warren Charles Gohl
SGT Kenneth Gohr
SP5 (Ret) Steven Goin
SPC T. Clayton Goings
MRS. Carl B. Goins
SGT Clarence R. Goins
COL Morris T. Goins
SGM Michael J. Golabek
CPL Cody Kevin Golant
SGT Alan S. Gold
PFC James T. Gold
SPC Paul J. Gold
SPC Mark B. Golde
LTC (Ret) Alonzo J. Golden
PV2 Casey Golden
SFC Dearl Golden
SGT Lanny R. Golden
CW4 (Ret) Robert T. Golden
PFC William M. Golden
SPC John G. Goldin
LTC (Ret) Eugene C. Goldner
SGT David M. Goldrick
CW4 James O. Goldsberry
PFC Kenneth F. Goldsmith
CPL Erwin Goldstein
MSG (Ret) Leonard M. Goldstein
CW4 (Ret) Lloyd I. Goldston
SFC (Ret) Thomas H. Goldsworthy
1LT Robert A. Goldwin
SP5 Dominick J. Golio
CW4 David W. Gollem
SSG John Y. Gollero
SPC Wilmer H. Gollman
LTC Orval J. Golphenee
SGT Dorothy J. Golphinsyas
COL Ellis W. Golson
SGT Manuel Gomes
PFC Tony Gomes
SPC Alexander Gomez
TSgt Alfred L. Gomez
MR. Angel H. Gomez
SFC Carlos Gomez
1SG (Ret) Claude O. Gomez
CSM Fidel Gomez
MRS. Flora Gomez
SSG Jacinto V. Gomez
PFC Joe Gomez
MSG Joseph Lupe Gomez
2LT Justin B. Gomez
SP5 Manuel F. Gomez
SPC Marco A. Gomez
PFC Max A. Gomez
PFC Ming Y. Gomez
SGT Patrick H. Gomez
PFC Reynaldo Gomez
SSG Robert A. Gomez
LT Roy Gomez
SGT Steven Gomez
1SG Tracy A. Gomez
PFC George E. Gonder
SGT Mark Gondola
SFC Peter K. Gong
BG Ryan Gonsalves
SGT Abel A. Gonzales
SFC Anthony J. Gonzales
SGT Antonio O. Gonzales
SSG Armando O. Gonzales
MAJ Arthur J. Gonzales
PFC Augustine M. Gonzales
SGT Benny J. Gonzales
SSG Gilbert Gonzales
SGT Ian M. Gonzales
SP5 Ismael M. Gonzales
SPC John Gonzales
SGT Juan Carlos Gonzales
MR. Luis Gonzales
PFC Miguel Gonzales
MR. Patrick J. Gonzales
SSG Phillip Gonzales
SPC Raul R. Gonzales
SSG Richard G. Gonzales
SPC Richard T. Gonzales
1SG Robert Gonzales
SFC (Ret) Roy Gonzales
SGT Sammy Gonzales
SSG Victor B. Gonzales
SSG Willie G. Gonzales
1SG Angel F. Gonzalez
CPT Anthony E. Gonzalez
SSG Conrado Gonzalez
2LT Daniel Gonzalez
SFC Donald R. Gonzalez
MRS. Emilio S. Gonzalez
SGT Enrique G. Gonzalez
PV2 Eric A. Gonzalez
SSG Fernando Luis Gonzalez
SPC George Gonzalez
SPC Gilberto S. Gonzalez
SPC Gustavo Gonzalez
PV2 Jesus F. Gonzalez
SFC Jesus M. Gonzalez
SPC Jose Carlos Gonzalez
CPL Jose V. Gonzalez
1LT Leticia Gonzalez
SPC Louis A. Gonzalez
PVT Luis A. Gonzalez
SFC Luis E. Gonzalez
1SG Manuel Gonzalez
CPT Manuel Gonzalez
SPC Matthew Gonzalez
PFC Melton Gonzalez
SPC Michael Gonzalez
SGT Noe Gonzalez
SPC Ollicia Gonzalez
SSG Patrick A. Gonzalez
PFC Ramiro V. Gonzalez
SGT Roberto Gonzalez
SPC Ruben M. Gonzalez
SPC Alberto Gonzalez Alers
SSG Edgardo A. Gonzalez-Arauz
SSG Marilyn Gonzalez-Velez
SPC Joseph C. Gooch
SGT Mike R. Gooch
SPC Ralph W. Gooch
SGT Barry Good
MRS. Benjamin F. Good
MAJ (Ret) Bob Good
PFC James R. Good
MS. Jane Good
SPC Jerry W. Good
SPC Stanley R. Good
MR. George E. Goodall
SPC James E. Goodbred
SGT Brenda Goode
MSG Clyne A. Goode
SGT David W. Goode
PFC Deniz Goode
SFC Elliott L. Goode
COL Franklin C. Goode
SGT James J. Goode
MAJ Keith Goode
SSG Maria L. Goode
SPC Wayne A. Goode
LTC (Ret) Ronald R. Goodell
CSM (Ret) James H. Gooden
SP5 Arthur T. Goodhall
SPC Paul F. Goodhue
MAJ (Ret) Donald K. Goodin
SP5 Edwin E. Gooding
COL (Ret) Mike Gooding
CW2 Richard Gooding
SPC Katharine Goodland
MSG Michael Goodley
SPC Charles Goodloe
SSG Tracy Goodloe
CPL David Goodman
CPT Frank Goodman
CPL Frank J. Goodman
SSG John D. Goodman
PFC Neal M. Goodman
SGT Stephen J. Goodman
SSG William Goodman
SGT John L. Goodpaster
SPC William J. Goodreau
MRS. Wilma P. Goodrich
1LT James P. Goodridge
SGT Richard G. Goodson
SGT Mitchell Goodspeed
CPT Gregory G. Goodwiler
MRS. Barbara Goodwin
CPT Brandon Goodwin
MRS. Harold L. Goodwin
SP5 Jeff L. Goodwin
SGT John A. Goodwin
CPT (Ret) John W. Goodwin
CPL Lynn R. H. Goodwin
CPL M. J. Goodwin
CW4 Parker R. Goodwin
COL (Ret) Richard C. Goodwin
LT Travis Wayne Goodwin
CPT Eric Gooley
SP5 Charles W. Goolsby
SFC L. Weldon Goolsby
PFC Willie H. Goolsby
SSG Brian J. Goosby
SGT John R. Goosman
SPC Marshall I. Gorden
SSG Alberto Gordillo
SPC John Gordish
LTC Bob F. Gordon
LTC Brett Gordon
1SG (Ret) Carl R. Gordon
SGT Daniel C. Gordon
PV2 Darryl L. Gordon
LTC David W. Gordon
SPC Edward Gordon
CW2 Glenn A. Gordon
PFC Harry W. Gordon
CPL Jack E. Gordon
SSG John Gordon
SPC John H. Gordon
SGT Johnny G. Gordon
SPC Joseph Gordon
MR. Joseph Gordon
MR. Joseph T. Gordon
MRS. Kenneth V. Gordon
SPC Larry W. Gordon
SFC Marlon D. Gordon
SGT Steven R. Gordon
SFC Troy E. Gordon
MAJ (Ret) William B. Gordon
CPT William H. Gordon
MAJ Daryl Gore
CPT G. Matthew Gore
SPC Jerry T. Gore
SP5 Kent W. Gore
MRS. Larry G. Gore
SGT Ronald D. Gore
SSG Wallace B. Gore
COL (Ret) William W. Gore
MR. Stan M. Gorecki
SGT Daniel R. Gorman
PFC Michael J. Gorman
SPC Robert K. Gorman
SSG (Ret) Thomas N. Gorman
SGT Troy E. Gorman
PFC William S. Gorman
SPC Gerald F. Gormas
SGT Ronald F. Gornick
MAJ Charles S. Gorton
MR. Fredrick Gose
PFC David L. Goshay
PFC Jimmie L. Gosnell
SPC Edward A. Goss
SPC John M. Goss
CW3 Robert C. Gosselin
SPC Stanley E. Gossett
SPC George M. Goswick
SSG (Ret) Ken A. Gotshalk
SPC Harold Gottesman
LTC Michael T. Goudeau
SPC Carl L. Goudy
SSG (Ret) Harlan Gough
MR. Harvey Gough
PVT Ian E. Goulbourne
SGT Charles O. Gould
SPC Don M. Gould
CSM Raymond S. Gould
CW4 Roger K. Gould
SP5 Thornton J. Gould
SGT William T. Gourley
1LT Bruce J. Gourlie
SPC George M. Govitz
CPT Katherine Gowel
MR. Orville E. Gower
1SG Warren Gower
MAJ Melvin L. Gowing
SGT Roger L. Goze
SPC John M. Gozelski
MR. Kenneth E. Graber
SSG Thomas M. Graber
CPT Timothy Graber
SFC (Ret) Eugene G. Grabill
CPT Lloyd Grable
SGT Edgar G. Grace
SGT Hugh James Grace
CPL James A. Grace
SGT Sean Grace
SFC Waymond J. Grace
SGT Michael Gracey
PFC Louis W. Grade
CPT (Ret) Bernard E. Grady
CPT Charles M. Grady
MSG (Ret) John C. Grady
SSG Kenneth E. Grady
SFC (Ret) Kenneth G. Grady
SPC Patrick J. Grady
PFC Joseph Graffagnino
SGT Michael P. Graffis
1LT Andrew F. Graham
CSM (Ret) Charles S. Graham
SPC David C. Graham
MR. David G. Graham
SGT Dennis Graham
SP5 Donald E. Graham
SPC Donald Hugh Graham
PVT Donnie Graham
SPC Edward K. Graham
CSM (Ret) Ernest G. Graham
MSGT (Ret) Frank A. Graham
SPC John W. Graham
CPT Lacy T. Graham
SPC Larry W. Graham
CW3 Lawrence C. Graham
SSG Lee O. Graham
LTC (Ret) Leonard T. Graham
SGT Leslie Graham
MSG (Ret) Michael A. Graham
CW2 Nelson M. Graham
SGT Parker L. Graham
MRS. Raymond E. Graham
MAJ Richard D. Graham
SGT Robert E. Graham
MSG (Ret) Vernon W. Graham
SFC Willie Earl Graham
SSG Jack M. Graichen
LT Charles S. Grainger
SSG James Richard Grainger
SGT Christopher Gral
PV2 Lawrence G. Gralewski
SFC Robert T. Gram
PFC Arturo T. Granado
MSG Daniel K. Granado
SFC Eduardo Granado
SPC Thomas Granai
COL (Ret) Carl W. Granberry
SGT Jeffrey S. Granberry
1SG Michael C. Grand
SSG Sharon Ann Grand
SSG (Ret) Randolph Grandberry
SGT Frank Grandinetti
1LT James A. Grandowicz
PFC Edwin A. Grandy
SGT Paul H. Grandy
SFC (Ret) Bruce P. Graner
CPT Scott E. Granger
LT Casey Granillo
LTC (Ret) Douglas D. Gransberg
SFC Bobby R. Grant
SGT Cleveland A. Grant
SGT Dennis C. Grant
LT Elliot Grant
SSG Ernest M. Grant
SSG Fzelle Grant
LTC (Ret) Gordon E. Grant
PVT Jason L. Grant
SGT Leonard Grant
1LT Wiley Grant
SGT William H. Grant
SGT Anthony L. Grantham
MAJ Edwin A. Grantham
SFC (Ret) Ivey W. Grantham
SGT Joseph Grantham
SPC Jordan L. Granum
SP5 Bruce I. Granzow
SGT Anthony T. Grasso
COL Len Grasso
CW4 Robert H. Gratkowski
SGT Lloyd W. Gratz
SPC Daniel S. Graves
SSG (Ret) Jerry W. Graves
MSG Johnny Robert Graves
LTG (Ret) Richard G. Graves
CPT Richard P. Graves
CPT Seth Graves
MSG Thomas Graves
SPC Allen R. Gray
PVT Basil E. Gray
SSG Billy E. Gray
CW4 (Ret) David J. Gray
SPC Derrick M. Gray
1SG (Ret) Douglas Gray
MSG (Ret) Franklin B. Gray
SGT Gary R. Gray
SGT Jerry C. Gray
SGT Jerry M. Gray
CPL John L. Gray
SFC Kevin D. Gray
SGT Lawrence W. Gray
SGT Loren Gray
SFC Michelle Gray
MAJ Nelson Gray
CW3 Otis B. Gray
PFC Randall Gray
SPC Randy D. Gray
LTC (Ret) Richard W. Gray
SP5 Robert A. Gray
PFC Robert A. Gray
SFC Robert W. Gray
SSG Teresa M. Gray
MSG (Ret) Virgil L. Gray
MR. Warren Sandy Gray
SP5 Wayne A. Gray
MRS. Willard L. Gray
PFC William A. Gray
MAJ William C. Gray
SSG Willie Marion Gray
SSG Carl D. Grayson
1SG Elbert L. Grayson
COL (Ret) Eugene H. Grayson
SPC Joseph E. Grayson
CPT Alexander C. Graziano
SFC (Ret) Frank F. Graziano
PFC Thomas Graziosetta
SGT (Ret) Edwin V. Grecious
SP3 Richard Greco
PVT Raymond D. Greedy
1LT Michael S. Greek
SPC Dominique Greeley
SSG Aaron M. Green
SPC Albert B. Green
SSG Alvin Green
SPC Anthony C. Green
SFC Celester Green
MRS. Charles Green
WO1 Christopher S. Green
SGT Dan Green
SGT Daniel J. Green
2LT Darrell R. Green
SPC David G. Green
CPL Edward A. Green
MR. Edward E. Green
CW3 F. Jack Green
MR. Gary L. Green
PVT (Ret) Gerald L. Green
PVT Herman L. Green
SPC James E. Green
SSG James O. Green
SSG John E. Green
TSgt John F. Green
MSG (Ret) John G. Green
MSG (Ret) Johnnie D. Green
CW3 Joseph Green
1LT Joseph E. Green
PV2 Joshua R. Green
1LT Leslie K. Green
SFC Levi L. Green
SFC Melvin Green
SFC Michael Green
LTC Morris M. Green
SP5 Paul W. Green
1SG Phyllis Y. Green
PFC Randolph Green
SPC Richard C. Green
1SG Ritchey V. Green
SGT Robert A. Green
CPL Robert L. Green
SGT Timothy W. Green
COL Tobin L. Green
1LT Walton T. Green
CPL Wheeler Green
SGT William Green
SPC William C. Green
SP5 William E. Green
SPC William R. Green
PFC John J. Greenan
SPC Martin B. Greenbaum
SPC Robert Greenblatt
MAJ Channing M. Greene

SGT Charles D. Greene
SGT Clinton Edward Greene
CSM Douglas K. Greene
MR. Edward Greene
SPC Gary D. Greene
SSG John L. Greene
SGT Ken Greene
SPC Lawrence Greene
SPC Leonard J. J. Greene
CW2 (Ret) Robert L. Greene
SGT Ronald J. Greene
CPL Seymour Greene
PFC Stephen F. Greene
SGT William K. Greene
MAJ William N. Greene
CW3 (Ret) William S. Greene
PFC Douglas E. Greenfield
CW2 Christopher Greenhill
SGT William D. Greenhood
CSM Maurice S. Greening
COL (Ret) Patrick J. Greenlaw
SPC Frank T. Greenleaf
SGT Michael A. Greenlee
MR. Darwin K. Greenley
TSgt (Ret) L. Jack Greenley
1SG Timothy A. Greenly
SPC Ronald L. Greenslade
SPC Charles D. Greenville
SPC Jeremy Greenwald
SGT Thomas J. Greenway
PVT Bruce Greenwood
COL (Ret) Everett O. Greenwood
SGT Wesley G. Greenwood
CH Blake J. Greer
MSG Curtis A. Greer
MAJ James K. Greer
SP5 Larry W. Greer
SPC Ronald C. Greer
SSG Stephen R. Greer
PFC William W. Greer
1SG (Ret) David J. Greger
SPC Galen E. Gregerson
SFC Dennis J. Gregg
PVT John Gregg
SP5 Walter Gregg
SFC Donald R. Gregor
CPT John P. Gregor
SP5 Ralph Gregor
SGT Russell H. Gregor
SGT Albert W. Gregori
SGT Doug Gregory
MR. Finley T. Gregory
SPC Garry L. Gregory
SFC John E. Gregory
SPC (Ret) Melvin L. Gregory
SFC Michael O. Gregory
MSG (Ret) Milton F. Gregory
MRS. Norman D. Gregory
COL (Ret) Robert J. Gregory
CPL Robin Gregory
PFC Roger D. Gregory
CPL Wayne May Gregory
CPT (Ret) William B. Gregory
MAJ Jessica L. Gregris
1LT Gorden M. Gregson
SPC Larry Greidanus
SPC Richard Greimann
MRS. John W. Greiner
CW2 Neal Q. Greiner
PFC David W. Greissinger
CPL Brett E. Grenvall
COL (Ret) Stanley E. Grett
PV2 Raymond Grewe
SGT John L. Grewell
SFC David K. Grey
SPC Gordon M. Grey
COL (Ret) Thomas E. Greyard
LTC Jeffrey S. Gribschaw
MAJ (Ret) Johnny Grice
CPL Edgar L. Grider
MAJ (Ret) Dave L. Grieger
MRS. William M. Grier
COL (Ret) David S. Grieshop
SP5 J. B. Griffeth
GEN (Ret) Benjamin S. Griffin
SSG Cecil R. Griffin
SGT Daniel Griffin
CPT Danielle Griffin
SP5 Delbert D. Griffin
SFC Gary W. Griffin
CPT George L. Griffin
SSG Horace E. Griffin
SSG James Griffin
CPT James A. Griffin
SPC James E. Griffin
SGT Jesse L. Griffin
MR. Joseph H. Griffin
SFC Lartim Griffin

PFC Michael J. Griffin
SGT Paul E. Griffin
SFC Robert Griffin
SFC (Ret) Robert W. Griffin
TSgt Thomas J. Griffin
SGT Adam K. Griffith
SPC David L. Griffith
CPL F. Don Griffith
SGT Francis G. Griffith
CSM Henry Griffith
COL (Ret) J. Samuel Griffith
MR. James Griffith
SGT John W. Griffith
SSG Mikel H. Griffith
GEN (Ret) Ronald H. Griffith
SSG Tony Griffith
1LT William E. Griffith
SP5 D. Edward Griffiths
SGT Eugene R. Griffiths
MRS. Donald E. Grigg
SSG (Ret) Douglas F. Grigg
SGM Barbara Griggs
SGT Melvin Dale Griggs
PFC David Grigsby
CPT Joseph B. Grigsby
PFC Melvin S. Grigsby
SFC Paul E. Grigsby
SGT William M. Grigsby
SPC Timothy F. Grillo
SPC Philip A. Grim
PFC Scott Grim
SGT David A. Grimaldi
LTC (Ret) Dan S. Grimes
SPC George Grimes
SSG Leonard Grimes
SP5 Roger L. Grimes
CPL Raymond W. Grimm
SP5 William W. Grimm
PV2 Joseph W. Grimmer
PFC Roger Grimsby
SP5 Don F. Grimsley
SGT Ronnie V. Grin
LTC Jay W. Grinnell
SPC Thomas H. Grinnell
SP5 John M. Grinton
SGT Douglas W. Gripp
MR. Mario D. Grisanti
SSG James C. Grisham
SP5 Graylin Grissett
SGT Richard L. Grissom
1LT Charles M. Grist
MAJ Charles G. Griswold
SGT Brian A. Grob
SGT Stanley J. Grochowina
CPT Heather J. Grodin-Putman
CPT Philip W. Groenweghe
PVT Joshua D. Groetsch
SSG Kelsey J. Groff
CPL Edward S. Groft
MSG (Ret) Arthur M. Grogan
MR. James Grogan
SFC (Ret) William J. Grogan
SPC Herman B. Groman
CW4 (Ret) Lance S. Gromme
SSG Lawayne D. Gronau
SGT George Grondin
CW2 (Ret) Charles E. Groner
MAJ Robin W. E. Gronovius
MSG Alfred J. Gronroos
SGT Michael E. Gronseth
PFC Ralph G. Groom
SSG James S. Gropper
PV2 Brandon S. Gross
LTC (Ret) Donald W. Gross
COL Gregg E. Gross
SFC John E. Gross
1LT Joseph Grossman
1LT Peter C. Grossnickle
1LT Stanley H. Grote
1SG (Ret) Ted M. Groupe
SSG (Ret) Gary M. Grove
SGT Gary Groves
SGT Jess G. Groves
SSG James D. Grubb
SPC Ralph J. Grubb
CPT Stephen B. Grubb
SFC (Ret) Dennis L. Grubbs
SSG Vance E. Grubbs
MRS. Dick D. Grube
WO1 Brent Gruber
SGT John J. Grudzien
PFC Robert M. Gruen
CSM Peter Gruener
SGT William Grueschow
COL Edward C. Gruetzemacher
COL Friedrich L. Gruetzmacher
SGT Michael R. Grunblatt
SGT Joseph Gruttolori
PFC Anthony M. Grybowski

SGT John L. Grznar
SPC Stephen D. Grzych
SPC Raymond Grzywaczewski
PFC Robert H. Gsell
SPC Jorge L. Guadalupe
SPC Vincent D. Guarino
LTC Albert Guarnieri
MR. Alfred B. Guaydacan
1SG Lance L. Guderian
MR. Hiram G. Gudgeon
SPC Gerry Gudinas
CPL David Guebara
SSG Michael R. Guedea
MAJ Brian Guenthenspberger
SGT Lonnie Guenther
PFC Savino Guercio
SPC Kevan A. Guerin
SGM (Ret) Ronald J. Guerin
SGT David Guerra
SFC Rene Guerra
SPC Arthur Guerrero
MAJ Eddie Guerrero
SPC Freddy S. Guerrero
1LT Jaciel J. Guerrero
TSgt Tito Guerrero
SGT Antonio Guerriero
SGT Armand E. Guertin
SGM (Ret) Isaac Guest
SPC Jose Guevara
SPC Ricaldo Guevara
SGT Paul D. Guffey
LT James Guggenheim
SSG Paul S. Guglietta
CPL Daniel J. Guider
SSG Joseph Guidice
SGT Henry L. Guidotti
LT Byron J. Guidroz
SP6 Dwayne J. Guidry
MAJ Peter V. Guidry
SGT Christopher J. Guilbault
PFC Earl T. Guilbault
LT Dennis J. Guill
CPL Jose E. Guillen
CPT Rivera Guillermo
SGT David G. Guillory
1LT John Guillory
PFC Mick Guinan
SGT Gregory Guinea
SSG George C. Guinn
SGT James Pat Guinn
1SG James R. Guinn
SFC Larry Guinn
SGT Tommy D. Guinn
SSG Jesus E. Guinto
SGT David J. Guitron
SFC Henry W. Guitznow
SFC Larry S. Guizar
MR. Allon Guldman
SPC Hans C. Gulden
MR. Alberto Gulisao
SGT David O. Gullette
CW4 Dan S. Gulley
1LT James M. Gulley
SPC William A. Gulley
PFC Howard D. Gumaer
CPL Raymond G. Gunderman
CPL Glenn L. Gunderson
CPT John A. Gunderson
SPC Mel W. Gunderson
COL (Ret) James B. Gunlicks
PVT David Gunn
SPC Richard Gunn
MR. Carl Gunter
1LT Dixon M. Gunther
MAJ Heather Gunther
SGT Walter Gurbisz
SP5 Thomas Gurchinoff
SGT Lee S. Gurley
WO1 William R. Gurley
CPT Dennis E. Gurnea
PVT Singh Gurvir
SPC Edward J. Gusbar
CPT Eric Gust
MR. Dan M. Gustafson
SGT Dan M. Gustafson
CPL G. L. Gustafson
SGT Glenn A. Gustafson
SP5 Jay H. Gustafson
CPL (Ret) John O. Gustafson
LTC (Ret) Kurt A. Gustafson
SPC Eric Gustafsson
MAJ Carl W. Gustke
SGT Mark B. Guth
LTC (Ret) Bennett M. Guthrie
SP5 Dennis G. Guthrie
SSG Christian O. Gutierrez
MSG (Ret) Duane Gutierrez
PFC Efrain Gutierrez
PVT Giovannie Gutierrez

PFC John R. Gutierrez
MAJ Jonathan K. Gutierrez
CW4 Joseph F. Gutierrez
SGT Jovie S. Gutierrez
SGT Luis E. Gutierrez
CPT Patrica A. Gutierrez
SFC (Ret) Victor Gutierrez
SPC William F. Gutierrez
PFC Ebenezer Guttenball
TSgt David Gutterman
SP5 Joe Gutzmann
SSG Chris A. Guy
SFC Daniel E. Guy
SP5 Kenneth C. Guy
CW4 Richard Guy
CPL Terry W. Guy
SPC Wesley J. Guy
SPC Gregory Guyer
SPC Ronald W. Guyer
SFC Michael D. Guynn
SPC Richard Guzek
SFC (Ret) Andy Guzman
SSG Daniel Guzman
SPC Edwin Guzman
SPC Herman Guzman
SSG Jaime Arthur Guzman
SSG Lorenzo Guzman
SSG Wilfredo Guzman
PVT Luis A. Guzman Liquet
SGT Gerardo Guzman-Rentas
MAJ Steven Gventer
SFC Theodore N. Gwillim
CPT (Ret) S. Lawrence Gwin
SSG Larry L. Gwinn
SSG Richard Earl Gwinn
MAJ Yi Se Gwon
SFC (Ret) Harold J. Haack
SSG Christopher R. Haag
SFC Lee E. Haag
LTC Anthony E. Haager
CW3 Michael A. Haar
SPC Karl F. Haartz
SP5 Albert H. Haas
SSG Brendan L. Haas
SSG Harold L. Haas
SPC Albert E. Gene Haase
SGT John H. Haase
MS. Shirley Haase
SGT Terry L. Haase
COL Fredrick Haberman
SPC Robert L. Haberman
PFC Mena G. Habib
PFC Bob Habisch
PFC Thomas H. Hacha
SPC Kamal A. Hack
PFC James E. Hackbarth
SGT James M. Hackbarth
SGT Charles Hackenmiller
SGT Forrest Hacker
SSG (Ret) Gerald L. Hacker
1LT Mathew F. Hacker
SPC Steven C. Hacker
PFC Thomas E. Hacker
COL Michael W. Hackerson
MG (Ret) Craig D. Hackett
SPC James F. Hackett
SSG Kevin A. Hackett
MRS. Lawrence J. Hackett
COL (Ret) Edward C. Hackney
SPC Frederick C. Hackney
SSG Robert A. Hackney
SPC Les Hackworth
SGT Donald L. Hadala
SSG Almer L. Hadaway
SSG Steven A. Hadder
PVT Roy S. Haddix
SGT Charles H. Haddock
SFC James M. Haddox
SSG William A. Hadfield
MR. Bobby G. Hadley
SGT Steven Hadt
SGT Matt Haeffner
SGT Robert J. Haegele
SFC (Ret) Alfred A. Haener
LTC (Ret) George H. Haertel
SGT Kawika M. Hafoka
SFC Edward H. Hagadorn
SPC James D. Hagan
CPT James L. Hagan
CPT Michael Hagan
SPC Richard L. Hagan
SGT Ronald Hageft
MSG Donel R. Hagelin
LTC (Ret) Charles C. Hagemeister
SSG John A. Hagen
MRS. Marjorie Hagen
SGT Raymond A. Hagen
SSG Fred Hager

SGT John H. Hager
SGT Richard F. Hager
LTC Stephen J. Hager
SGT Thomas B. Hager
SGT Thomas M. Hager
MRS. Wiley S. Hagerman
MRS. Joe H. Hagerty
SP5 Hanson Doug Haggard
SPC Henry Nathan Haggard
SP5 John J. Haggerty
MR. Lee W. Haggerty
2LT Richard T. Haggerty
MAJ Warren L. Haggray
SGT Carl R. Hagins
SFC Gregory L. Haglerjones
SFC Ricky Hagood
MAJ (Ret) Samuel Hagood
COL William B. Hagood
MAJ Allen Hahn
SPC Sean F. Hahn
2LT William Haig
SPC Russell E. Haigh
SGT Ernest L. Haight
CW4 (Ret) Warren J. Haight
SGT Dorsey R. Hailey
PFC Dennis L. Hainline
SSG Billie J. Hair
SGT Johnnie D. Hairel
PFC Dennis Hairston
1SG (Ret) Robert T. Hairston
SFC (Ret) Eugene S. Haislip
SGT Benjamin Hajovsky
SFC James V. Hakes
CW4 (Ret) Michael Hakola
SPC Rachelle Halaska
SPC Rodney Halbach
CPL Alvin H. Halcomb
MR. Monty Halcomb
1LT Ray L. Haldeman
CSM Brouston Hale
SGM (Ret) David O. Hale
SFC (Ret) Henry Lee Hale
LTC Henry S. Hale
SGT Hoyt H. Hale
SGT Joel Alan Hale
CPT Patrick D. Hale
SFC Robert S. Hale
SSG Jervon Hale-Bates
SPC Bernard Haley
PFC Cody Haley
CPT Jay W. Haley
MAJ John C. Haley
SSG Raymond P. Haley
1SG (Ret) Rodney L. Halford
PFC Anthony L. Hall
SPC Anthony L. Hall
CPT Aubrey C. Hall
MR. Aubury L. Hall
SFC Avery W. Hall
CPT Brian T. Hall
SPC Calvin L. Hall
SPC Cecil M. Hall
SGT Charles Hall
CPL Charles A. Hall
SPC Cory Hall
SPC Daniel J. Hall
CPL Darrell J. Hall
CW4 David Hall
SSG David L. Hall
SGT David N. Hall
SFC (Ret) David W. Hall
CPL Dillard R. Hall
2LT Dion Hall
SPC Don W. Hall
MSG Donald C. Hall
SPC Donald F. Hall
SPC Floyd A. Hall
CSM (Ret) Frank H. Hall
CPL Gary L. Hall
SGT Gary L. Hall
SGT (Ret) George W. Hall
CPT Henry L. Hall
CW4 James D. Hall
SP3 James D. Hall
1SG (Ret) James W. Hall
SGT James Wilfied Hall
2LT Jonathan A. Hall
PFC Joseph Michael Hall
MAJ Justin R. Hall
SFC Kenneth Hall
CW2 Kenneth R. Hall
SFC Lewis Hall
SGT Linwood A. Hall
SGT Maurice C. Hall
SFC (Ret) Mcarthur Hall
SSG Milborn E. Hall
PV2 Peter J. Hall
SSG Quion T. Hall
SSG Ralph Hall

SPC Rhett E. Hall
SGT Rhoderick D. Hall
SFC (Ret) Richard M. Hall
MAJ (Ret) Robert Hall
MR. Robert H. Hall
SPC Robert R. Hall
SGT Ronald C. Hall
PFC Ronald D. Hall
SP5 Ronald F. Hall
SGT Ronald L. Hall
CPT Sanci M. Hall
LT Scott Hall
SGT Sequoyah Hall
SPC Terry E. Hall
SGT Theodorer Hall
SGT Tim W. Hall
SGT Timothy J. Hall
SGT Tom Edward Hall
2LT Whitney Hall
SGT William L. Hall
1SG (Ret) William R. Hall
SGT John M. Hallam
LTC (Ret) Charles H. Hallden
MS. Joyce A. Hallenbeck
PFC Fred C. Haller
SGT Thomas C. Haller
SPC John J. Halley
SGT Thomas J. Hallinan
SGT Harry Halliwell
CSM Robert L. Hallman
SGT Steven M. Hallman
CPL Scott T. Hallock
SGT Douglas D. Halls
MAJ Charles E. Hallyburton
LTC Wayne J. Halpern
MR. Kenneth M. Halstead
CPL Marvin L. Halstead
PFC Harold S. Haltiwanger
SP5 John K. Halvorson
SPC Werner R. Halvorson
SGT David D. Ham
1SG Charles D. Hamberger
SGT Robert D. Hamblen
CPT Harold Hamblet
PFC Dale L. Hamblin
COL Ken Hamburger
SGT Dennis Hamby
CPT James R. Hamby
MAJ Tyrone A. Hamby
SPC Ronald J. Hamel
SSG Alegray Hamer
SPC Darrel L. Hamer
CSM (Ret) George H. Hamill
PFC Alfred Hamilton
PFC Andrew R. Hamilton
SFC (Ret) Billy R. Hamilton
CPL Bobby Hamilton
CPL Clifford E. Hamilton
SFC (Ret) Daniel R. Hamilton
SP5 Donald J. Hamilton
SPC Douglas V. Hamilton
SGT Eric Hamilton
MRS. Helen Hamilton
CPL James F. Hamilton
CW3 James R. Hamilton
SGT Joe R. Hamilton
PFC Johnnie G. Hamilton
SPC Jordan Hamilton
SPC Larry L. Hamilton
MR. Richard J. Hamilton
CW4 (Ret) Robert L. Hamilton
MAJ Sharon R. Hamilton
SPC James R. Hamler
PFC Weldon R. Hamlett
PFC Bryan Hamlin
SP5 Richard J. Hamlin
SSG Tyrone D. Hamlin
SSG Fred L. Hamm
SGT John Hamm
1LT Larry W. Hamm
MR. Orval A. Hamm
SSG Bernard O. Mike Hammer
SPC Richard V. Hammer
SFC Ronald C. Hammerly
MR. Tom Hammersley
MAJ Tony J. Hammes
CPL Daniel F. Hammett
CPL Carl J. Hammill
SGT Ronald E. Hammon
MSG Geroge Hammond
MG (Ret) Jeffery W. Hammond
CPT Joseph R. Hammond
PVT Kevin L. Hammond
SPC Steve Hammond
SPC Tyler Hammond
CPT David M. Hammons
SSG Mark Hammons
SPC Patrick Joseph Hammons
SSG Michael Elliott Hamovitz

LTC Joseph J. Hampl
SGT Richard C. Hampsher
SPC Charles R. Hampton
PSG (Ret) Cortez J. Hampton
SGT Danny R. Hampton
SFC George Hampton
1LT Gregory G. Hampton
MRS. Jack N. Hampton
SSG Jayson Hampton
CW2 John R. Hampton
PFC Joshua Hampton
SSG Leandrew Hampton
SPC Michael Hampton
SSG William K. Hampton
MR. Allen Hamrick
PFC James D. Hamrick
MAJ Matt Hamrick
SSG (Ret) William Hamrock
SGT Michael M. Hamus
CPL James W. Hanawalt
1SG (Ret) Franklin E. Hance
PSG (Ret) Owen E. Hanchey
MR. Charles Hancock
1SG David L. Hancock
SP5 James W. Hancock
COL (Ret) Jay R. Hancock
CPT P. Lain Hancock
SPC Scott E. Hancock
SGT Thomas Eddie Hancock
PFC Peter J. Hand
SGT William T. Hand
SP5 Mike J. Handley
SPC Mark R. Handrahan
SPC Robert Martin Hands
PFC John A. Handy
COL (Ret) Malvin L. Handy
SPC Rick Haneline
SFC (Ret) Bernie Hanenberger
SPC Donald S. Hanes
LTC Richard F. Hanesworth
CPL Aubrey J. Haney
CSM (Ret) Elton W. Haney
SGT Lowell Haney
SPC Russell H. Haney
SSG (Ret) Paul E. Hanisch
SFC Pierce A. Hankal
SPC Larry J. Hankerson
SFC Curtis O. Hankins
SSG Eldon A. Hankins
CPT Guy L. Hankins
SSG Jerry I. Hankins
SFC Jimmy J. Hankins
MR. Leslie R. Hankins
SSG Michael W. Hankins
MR. Randy H. Hankins
CPT Robert S. Hankins
PVT William M. Hankins
SGT Daniel David Hanley
SPC Richard M. Hanley
SPC W. Earl Hanley
SGT James E. Hanlon
1LT John B. Hanlon
SGT Michael A. Hanlon
CW3 (Ret) Thomas J. Hanlon
LTC (Ret) Patrick D. Hanly
PFC Barkley S. Hanna
SSG (Ret) Billie D. Hanna
TSgt Daniel D. Hanna
SGT Thomas Hannafin
SPC George W. Hannaford
SPC Billy L. Hannah
SPC James Vernon Hannah
CPL Richard E. Hannah
SGT Samuel R. Hannah
SFC Timothy M. Hannah
MSG (Ret) Calvin L. Hannan
2LT Schuyler M. Hannan
COL Robert Hannas
SPC James A. Hannatt
SPC Jason Hanneken
MSG Charles L. Hanneman
SP5 Donald D. Hanneman
SGT Michael S. Hannigan
SSG Max T. Hanning
PFC John Hannula
SGT Kenneth D. Hanrahan
SPC Thomas M. Hanrahan
SSG Richard J. Hans
SGT William D. Hansel
PFC Bob Hansen
MAJ Brian M. Hansen
CPL Charles W. Hansen
LTC David L. Hansen
1SG Dieter F. Hansen
SPC Donald R. Hansen
MR. Harold Hansen
PV2 Harold H. Hansen
SP5 Hillery M. Hansen
SPC Howard Hansen
SPC Jarrett Hansen
MR. Jeffrey L. Hansen
SPC John C. Hansen
SPC John C. Hansen
SPC John T. Hansen
2LT Jonathan R. Hansen
MAJ Richard L. Hansen
SGT Robert A. Hansen
MSG Scott A. Hansen
LTC Steven R. Hansen
MR. Bob E. Hanson
SPC David E. Hanson
SGM (Ret) Don Hanson
SPC Dustin Hanson
CPL Eugene S. Hanson
CPT James R. Hanson
PVT Joseph Hanson
SSG Mervin R. Hanson
SGM (Ret) Paul D. Hanson
CPT Paul T. Hanson
SFC Robert A. Hanson
SPC Robert I. Hanson
LTC Stephen A. Hanson
PFC Steven G. Hanson
SGT Todd M. Hanson
SSG William A. Hanson
1LT David Alan Hansz
LTC (Ret) Russell C. Hantke
MRS. Lawrence H. Hanus
MS. Leona Hanus
SFC (Ret) Hans L. Hanwalter
PVT James J. Hanzel
1SG Glen D. Hapney
PFC Bernard C. Happel
SGT Gary C. Happel
1SG (Ret) Jimmie Happney
MRS. Debora M. Hara-Eull
SSG Charles E. Haralson
SP5 Kenneth E. Harbaugh
SGT Richard F. Harbaugh
SFC William A. Harbert
SPC Dale Harbitz
CW2 Jerral D. Harchenko
1LT Christopher Hardee
CW4 Harvey J. Hardeman
CPT Jesse Harden
SSG Edward J. Harder
SP5 Larry K. Harders
SFC Duane E. Hardesty
COL Duane E. Hardesty
1SG (Ret) Edward Hardesty
SFC John W. D. Hardesty
PFC Merlyn Hardesty
1SG George T. Hardge
MR. Bill Hardin
SFC Bobby Hardin
SSG James F. Hardin
PFC James L. Hardin
PV2 John W. Hardin
SGT Lynn E. Hardin
MAJ (Ret) Robert E. Hardin
SSG Robert J. Hardin
PFC Theodore R. Hardin
SFC Charles Bruce Harding
SGT Daniel A. Harding
SSG Edwin A. Hardwick
MAJ Bradley J. Hardy
SPC David J. Hardy
SPC Etienne J. Hardy
SSG George M. Hardy
CSM (Ret) Harold L. Hardy
SGT Jimmie L. Hardy
SGT Michael G. Hardy
MRS. Owen Hardy
SPC Robert W. Hardy
SPC William R. Hargesheimer
SPC Joe Hargett
LTC Allen P. Hargis
1SG (Ret) Jay Hargis
SSG Randy H. Hargis
CPT Kellie Hargreaves
CPL Andrew Hargrett
SGT Bobby R. Hargrove
SGT Samuel F. Hargrove
SSG Thomas M. Hargrove
PFC Monroe J. Harjo
SPC Philip G. Harker
LTC (Ret) Wilburn C. Harkey
PFC William T. Harkins
SFC (Ret) Greg K. Harkness
MAJ (Ret) Jimmy W. Harkness
SPC Thomas W. Harkness
MSG (Ret) Val E. Harkness
PSG (Ret) Richard W. Harkrider
MR. Dennis Harley
SPC George Harley
LT Adam J. Harm
MG (Ret) George H. Harmeyer
SFC Brian C. Harmon
CPT Bryan A. Harmon
TSgt Charles L. Harmon
SPC Christopher W. Harmon
CPL Corey S. Harmon
CPT Fred R. Harmon
1LT Lawrence H. Harmon
MR. Nathaniel Harmon
SSG (Ret) Ralph F. Harmon
SFC (Ret) Richard V. Harmon
LTC Robert T. Harmon
LTC (Ret) Thomas D. Harmon
COL Victor M. Harmon
2LT William T. Harmon
1SG Zachary Harmon
SPC Gerald H. Harms
SGT Albert Paul Harne
MAJ Karl Harness
CPT Matthew T. Harney
PFC Thomas D. Harney
CW3 Thomas J. Harnisher
CPT Jose A. Haro
SPC Gary C. Harold
SGM (Ret) Robert L. Harold
WO1 George E. Harp
SGT Gregory B. Harp
MSG Jerry L. Harp
SFC John R. Harp
SPC Kenneth Mark Harp
SPC Albert Harper
MR. Charles B. Harper
SFC Chuck Harper
MAJ (Ret) Dallas H. Harper
PFC Daniel T. Harper
1SG (Ret) Jeffrey C. Harper
SGT Joseph L. Harper
PV2 Kevin M. Harper
MR. Lee Harper
SGT Mack L. Harper
SGT Patrick D. Harper
1LT (Ret) Philip V. Harper
SSG Randolph Harper
CSM Raymond Harper
SFC (Ret) Rickey L. Harper
SPC Rodney R. Harper
MAJ (Ret) Stephen D. Harper
CPT Thomas W. Harper
PFC William F. S. Harper
2LT Willie Harper
PFC Norman Harpole
SFC Rusty K. Harr
CPT Floyd B. Harrell
MR. Lenzie L. Harrell
PV2 Mikale L. Harrell
SGT Phillip A. Harrell
SPC Robert G. Harrell
SFC Stanley E. Harrell
SPC (Ret) William D. Harrell
2LT Eric W. Harrelson
SFC Patrick Harrelson
MRS. Wallace L. Harrier
SSG David E. Harrill
SPC George Harriman
BG (Ret) Edward M. Harrington
SFC Kelly Harrington
SPC Lynn Harrington
SSG Reginald L. Harrington
SPC William J. Harrington
MSG Alvin D. Harris
COL Brian C. Harris
SGT Carlos E. Harris
SPC Charles N. Harris
1SG Dale E. Harris
1LT Dennis L. Harris
SPC Dennis W. Harris
SFC Donald E. Harris
CPT Douglas J. Harris
COL (Ret) Earl D. Harris
PVT Earl William Harris
SFC Eddie L. Harris
SP5 Emil V. Harris
CSM Geoffrey Harris
SSG Gilbert W. Harris
SGT Herman J. Harris
SFC James B. Harris
1LT James G. Harris
PVT James M. Harris
SPC James N. Harris
SGT James Randy Harris
SPC Jason Harris
MAJ Jeffrey T. Harris
SFC John L. Harris
SSG Kevin L. Harris
1LT Leroy Harris
SPC Lucious M. Harris
SGT Madison Harris
SPC Marcellous Harris
CPT Michael K. Harris
SGT Michael Scott Harris
CPL Milton Harris
SGT Orrealus Harris
CSM (Ret) Oscar Harris
LTC (Ret) Randall D. Harris
MS. Rebecca Harris
PV2 Richard M. Harris
CW4 Robert A. Harris
SGT Robert A. Harris
SFC Robert C. Harris
CW2 Roy Harris
SPC Rulon R. Harris
COL (Ret) Sam E. Harris
SSG Shelby W. Harris
SGT Thomas H. Harris
MRS. Thomas Pressley Harris
SPC Thomas S. Harris
PFC Thomas V. Harris
MSG Tommy H. Harris
PVT Tyree Harris
SGT Wade J. Harris
MSG Walter Harris
SPC William C. Harris
MG (Ret) Ben L. Harrison
SFC Celester Harrison
1LT Charles A. Harrison
CPT Donald T. Harrison
CPT Frank L. Harrison
SPC Gregory Harrison
SSG Homer Harrison
SPC Jimmy Dwight Harrison
CPL John T. Harrison
SPC Jonathan F. Harrison
PFC Joseph Harrison
SGT Joseph J. Harrison
COL Kent E. Harrison
SFC Kevin K. Harrison
SGT Larry D. Harrison
SGT Larry D. Harrison
SGT Michael Harrison
PFC Richard E. Harrison
SPC Ronald Harrison
MAJ Brian P. Harrity
SSG (Ret) Herbert A. Harrod
MR. Lyle Harrold
CPL Curtis E. Harry
SGT Leroy E. Harshberger
SGT Danny A. Hart
SGT David A. Hart
MRS. Donald L. Hart
SP5 George J. Hart
CSM Humberto Hart
SGT James G. Hart
SSG James W. Hart
LTC Joe P. Hart
SPC John W. Hart
CW4 (Ret) John W. Hart
SPC Leslie J. Hart
PFC Raymond M. Hart
SPC Richard Hart
LTC Steven D. Hart
SFC Richard N. Hartel
CPT Michael L. Harter
SP5 Clarence Hartfield
SSG Weldon Hartgrove
1LT Thomas E. Hartin
MRS. Eugene A. Hartle
MR. Woodrow W. Hartle
SP5 Anthony J. Hartley
PVT Christy Hartley
SFC Donald T. Hartley
SFC Henry A. Hartley
SGT Joe L. Hartley
SGT John Hartley
1LT Thomas M. Hartley
MR. David L. Hartline
CPT Andrew J. Hartman
CPL Arthur E. Hartman
PFC Dale T. Hartman
SSG Daniel R. Hartman
SGT George L. Hartman
SFC Jay Hartman
SGT Josh Hartman
LTC Richard C. Hartman
PV2 Russell E. Hartman
SGT Samuel E. Hartman
SPC William A. Hartmann
SPC Cory Harton
SGT Daniel G. Hartsfield
CPL Jerry W. Hartsock
CW4 (Ret) Donald O. Hartson
SPC Roger W. Hartter
SFC Donald J. Harty
2LT Matthew D. Hartzell
SGT William R. K. Harvest
MSG Darrell A. Harvey
SGT David Wilson Harvey
CPL Don Harvey
SFC Homer L. Harvey
SGT Jacob B. Harvey
SGT Joel E. Harvey
SPC Lakristie Shohtae Harvey
LTC Michael Harvey
PFC Michael Harvey
SPC Nathan Harvey
CW5 Ralph C. Harvey
SGT Richard B. Harvey
SSG (Ret) Robert C. Harvey
SSG Rodney A. Harvey
SPC Samuel M. Harvey
SGT Travis J. Harvey
CPT Warren A. Harvey
PFC William D. Harvey
SFC Leonard W. Harviel
CPT (Ret) Bruce K. Harwood
CPL Richard T. Harwood
SPC Russell D. Harwood
PV2 James Richard Hasbrouck
SPC Jerry E. Haselden
SSG Marvin Hasenak
PFC Kenneth C. Hasenaner
SPC James M. Hash
MAJ (Ret) John W. Haskell
SFC Clifton G. Haskins
LTC Heinz Haskins
SPC Samuel R. Haskins
SFC David Haslach
1LT James E. Haslitt
MSG Samuel I. Haspel
SP5 Cornell Eugene Hassan
SFC Michael Hassenfelt
SPC Alain V. M. Hasson
SSG Joseph Hasson
SPC Larry D. Haste
SGT Dan R. Hastings
CPT David Hastings
SSG Erik Hastings
2LT Patrick J. Hastings
CPT Scott Hastings
2LT Derek T. Hasty
SSG James D. Hasty
LTC (Ret) Alden E. Hatch
SFC Lawrence J. Hatch
SSG Neil Hatch
SGT Ralph W. Hatchell
MAJ John M. Hatcher
CPT John W. Hatcher
CPT Towyanger Hatcher
SPC Arlen R. Hatfield
SGT Emsley E. Hatfield
SPC Michael L. Hatfield
SGT Michael L. Hatfield
SPC Scott R. Hatfield
PFC Stanely H. Hatfield
SGT Willis F. Hatfield
2LT Eric V. Hathaway
CPT Peter N. Hathaway
SP5 Robert R. Hathaway
SGT Ralph C. Hathcock
SFC (Ret) Guy W. Hathorn
SFC Robert Hatke
SPC Gary R. Hatley
SGM Charles J. Hatten
CPL Eaften A. Hatten
SPC Jessie J. Hatton
SFC Rhonda Hatton
SGT Leo L. Haubenschild
SGT William J. Haubert
PFC David A. Hauck
PFC Mark K. Hauck
COL (Ret) Ralph A. Hauenbeck
SPC Henry D. Hauge
SGT Leland Mark Haugen
MRS. Hubert H. Haugh
SGT (Ret) Charles Haughey
PFC Henry Robert Haught
PFC Willliam D. Haught
SPC Doug Haughton
MR. Larry Haun
SPC Greg Haupt
SFC Steve Hauschildt
LTC David W. Hause
SPC David L. Hausechild
LTC Clifford E. Hauser
SFC (Ret) Gary P. Hauser
CPT Jack W. Hauser
LTC Robert J. Hauser
SP5 Harold Hauver
SSG Leslie Neal Havard
SSG Andrew Havay
SGT George W. Havelock
LTC Charles J. Haven
SGT Harry Haverkamp
SPC Raymond E. Havey
SGT Martin J. Havran
SGT Terrance M. Havrilla
SPC Donna M. Hawe
SPC John F. Hawes
1LT Donald W. Hawk
SGT Howard L. Hawk
CPT Michael Hawkes
MAJ (Ret) William F. Hawkinberry
PV2 Alvin T. Hawkins
SGT Charles A. Hawkins
2LT Chris Hawkins
SPC Clyde L. Hawkins
SFC Ellis R. Hawkins
SGT Ernest M. Hawkins
SSG George W. Hawkins
SGT Gordon W. Hawkins
MR. Harley M. Hawkins
SSG Lynn R. Hawkins
MR. R. M. Hawkins
SPC Rayvon T. Hawkins
SGT Richard Hawkins
1SG Richard L. Hawkins
CW2 Robert J. Hawkins
SSG Ronald D. Hawkins
SGT Robert L. Hawkinson
1LT James Hawks
1SG (Ret) Bruce C. Hawley
SGT Jonathan Hawley
LTC Leonard R. Hawley
PFC Paul V. Hawley
BG (Ret) Robert C. Hawlk
MRS. Lewis W. Hawn
SSG Isaac Hawthorne
SGT Louise B. Hawthorne
SGM (Ret) Robert Hawthorne
SGT James P. Hay
MR. W. Morgan Hay
SSG Aaron Haycox
SPC Arthur Hayday
SGT Patrick A. Hayday
SFC (Ret) Arnold J. Hayden
SFC Bennie R. Hayden
PFC Billy F. Hayden
SPC Gary A. Hayden
CPT George F. Hayden
SSG Monte L. Hayden
SGT Robert L. Hayden
MRS. Thomas D. Hayden
SFC Russell S. Haye
CPT Joseph Hayek
LTC (Ret) Arthur J. Hayes
MAJ Chris Hayes
TSgt Donald E. Hayes
CSM (Ret) Douglas B. Hayes
LTC Douglas J. Hayes
PFC Eugene B. Hayes
SFC Floyd Hayes
SP5 George Ralph Hayes
SGT James Allen Hayes
LTC Jason Michael Hayes
MSG John Hayes
MR. John A. Hayes
SPC John E. Hayes
SPC Kevin F. Hayes
SP5 Michael David Hayes
SGT Michael J. Hayes
PFC Paul H. Hayes
SSG (Ret) Robert I. Hayes
SGT Ronald C. Hayes
SFC Shawn K. Hayes
SGT Walter F. Hayes
SGT Walter M. Hayes
CPT Shawn Y. Hayes-Davis
CPT Donald K. Hayfron
MR. Michael B. Haygood
SGM Charles C. Hayhurst
SSG Michael K. Hayman
SPC John Haymond
SSG Charles Haynes
2LT Dillon B. Haynes
SGT Gary B. Haynes
SSG James Michael Haynes
MSG John A. Haynes
SPC Matthew Haynes
SFC Matthew Haynes
PFC Robert E. Haynes
CPL T. J. Haynes
SPC William M. Haynes
CPT John M. Haynicz
SGT Carl F. Hays
SPC Donald E. Hays
SGT Harvey E. Hays
SP5 James R. Hays
SGT Michael L. Hays
CPT Ronald J. Hays
SFC (Ret) Wilbur P. Hays
SPC Loran L. Hayslip
SGT Jacky L. Haywood
MRS. Ronnie D. Hayworth
SP5 Calvin W. Hazlett
MR. Walter C. Hazzlerig
SPC Darrell G. Heaberlin
SGT Donald Head
SGT Jack Headrick

PFC Burton R. Heagy
MR. G.E. Heal
MR. Jerry Heal
SPC Daniel J. Heald
SPC Thomas E. Heald
SPC Joseph W. Healy
1LT Richard P. Healy
PFC Bernard A. Heaney
1LT Michael K. Heany
CW4 (Ret) Artie A. Heape
MRS. Charles Neal Heape
MAJ Glen Heape
LTC (Ret) George L. Heard
SGT Donald Bruce Hearn
LTC Forrest Hearn
CPT Stephen E. Hearn
SGT Larry J. Hearnen
LTC Robert W. Hearon
SPC Edward C. Heary
MAJ Andrea J. Heater
CPL Charles P. Heater
SFC (Ret) Harry J. Heater
SPC Bobbie Heath
SGT Brian T. Heath
1LT Chris Heath
CPL Harold L. Heath
2LT John W. Heath
SPC Kenneth Heath
MR. Preston Heath
MR. Ralph L. Heath
SFC John R. Heathcoat
MAJ Chris Heatherly
SPC Ronald R. Heavner
SPC Thomas C. Heavrin
MRS. Clayton Hebert
SGT Melvin J. Hebert
CPL Rodney P. Hebert
SPC Stephen J. Hebert
MRS. Charles C. Heck
SPC Larry A. Heck
PV2 Levi H. Heck
1LT Albert C. Hecker
SGT Joachim W. Heckert
SSG Rich P. Heckler
CPL Robert Heckler
SGT Lee A. Heckman
SFC Robert J. Heckman
SPC Steven T. Heckman
SGT Willie A. Heckstall
SGT Gene L. Hedberg
SGT Carl L. Hedden
SPC Ryan J. Hedgcoth
LT Richard Hedgecock
SSG James E. Hedgepeth
SGT Bob D. Hedges
SPC Michael W. Hedges
1LT Kenneth R. Heebner
CPL Mark W. Heenan
TSgt Paul D. Heeren
SGT Francis D. Heesakker
LTC William R. Heflin
SGT Raymond A. Hegarty
SFC Jim E. Hegelman
SPC Brian D. Heglund
MR. Marvin A. Heibult
SGT Alan L. Heidbreder
MRS. Gerald W. Heide
MSG (Ret) Frank T. Heidel
1LT Clark H. Heidelbaugh
SFC Jerome R. Heideman
SGT Mazin A. Heiderson
LTC Richard E. Heidt
MSG Joseph J. Heil
SFC Randy A. Heil
SGT Roger P. Heilig
COL (Ret) John P. Heilman
SFC (Ret) Dennis A. Heim
PFC Harry V. Heim
SFC (Ret) Wendell D. Heim
SP5 Daniel A. Heiman
PFC Gerald D. Heiman
SPC Wallace H. Heimbach
SGT John F. Heimerman
PFC Richard Heimes
SGT Donald Hein
SGT Kenneth C. Hein
SP5 Michael K. Hein
SPC Simon Heine
SPC Kenneth J. Heinen
SPC Matthew G. Heinen
1SG Rhody S. Heinen
SPC David L. Heiner
MS. Mary Heinle
SGT Gregory C. Heinlein
SFC Lloyd Heinrichs
MAJ (Ret) Milton H. Heins
SGT Robert S. Heintz
SGT James M. Heintzel
1LT Terry M. Heintzman
SFC Jerry R. Heinz
SGT Thomas J. Heinz
SGT Kody Heinze
SPC Michael S. Heinze
CSM Roger L. Heinze
SPC Dean W. Heise
SPC William R. Heiser
SGT Peter M. Heisey
SSG Jared D. Heisler
SGT Steven Heismann
MAJ Eric T. Heist
COL (Ret) James A. Heiter
SPC David K. Heitman
CW3 (Ret) Robert F. Heitmann
1LT Terrance Edward Heitter
SPC James E. Heitz
SSG (Ret) Louis J. Heitz
SPC Michael L. Heitz
MRS. Allan L. Hejcl
LTC (Ret) Donald J. Hejna
SFC Daniel K. Helber
SGT Todd D. Held
SPC Daniel J. Helfrich
SFC Brian E. Helgren
SSG Melvin E. Heller
SFC Roger Lee Heller
PFC Jay B. Hellwege
CPL Harold Helm
SPC Don Helmick
COL (Ret) Michael R. Helmick
SGT Tom Helminger
CW4 (Ret) Norman L. Helmke
CSM (Ret) Felix L. Helms
SP5 James E. Helms
SPC Leonard W. Helms
SGT Robert J. Helmsing
SPC James Helton
SGT John D. Helton
SGT Keith E. Helton
MRS. Edward Helwig
SSG John C. Hemauer
SGT Alfred Hembd
SPC Carl Hemenway
MSG Keith David Hemenway
SPC Tom Hemmelgarn
SPC Chuck Hemmer
1SG Norman L. Hemminger
SP5 Lawrence F. Hempfling
CSM Donald F. Hemphill
MG (Ret) John A. Hemphill
SGT Thomas N. Hemphill
MR. Joseph R. Hems
MRS. John Hencke
SFC Jesse G. Hendershot
SGT Alfred W. Henderson
LTC (Ret) Berry H. Henderson
1LT Billy J. Henderson
PFC Clarence J. Henderson
1SG (Ret) Clifford D. Henderson
SSG Clyde M. Henderson
SSG Craig Henderson
SP5 Ernest L. Henderson
SP5 Gene Henderson
SFC (Ret) Howard S. Henderson
MSG Howard W. Henderson
PFC James A. Henderson
SPC James G. Henderson
MAJ John H. Henderson
SPC John S. Henderson
SPC Jyrel W. Henderson
SSG Kacy Henderson
COL Kevin T. Henderson
SGT Lee O. Henderson
MSG Norvell Henderson
SPC Rickey L. Henderson
1LT Ryan Henderson
COL Wm Darryl Henderson
SFC (Ret) Charles A. Hendricks
SGT Todd J. Hendricks
LTC (Ret) Alan C. Hendrickson
SP5 Chester M. Hendrickson
LTC Daniel E. Hendrickson
SGT David L. Hendrickson
CSM Robert J. Hendrickson
MRS. Sandra J. Hendrickson
SPC Norman R. Hendrie
MRS. James C. Hendrix
SPC James C. Hendrix
CPT Jeffrey A. Hendrix
MAJ (Ret) Phillip L. Hendrix
MSG (Ret) Steven L. Hendrix
COL (Ret) Cecil B. Hengeveld
SPC James L. Henicke
CPT Michael B. Heninger
SPC Richard Cole Henington
SP5 Edward D. Henk
SFC Ken Henkemeyer
CPT Darryl E. Henley
MRS. Wilburn E. Henley
PVT Bruce Henn
MR. Michael Hennegan
SGT Peter Hennen
SGT Robert J. Hennessy
CPT (Ret) James E. Hennig
MAJ (Ret) Mac K. Hennigan
1LT Theresa Hennigan
SPC Christopher F. Henning
SGT Rodney W. Henning
SGT Jeffrey Henningsen
SSG (Ret) Richard A. Henningsen
SPC Michael Henrie
SFC Tracy Henrikson
LTC Richmond B. Henriques
SSG Joaquin Henriquez
SFC Ulises Henriquez
SGT Alfred Charles Henry
SPC Cecil Henry
SFC Christopher C. Henry
COL (Ret) Edwin H. Henry
MRS. Emma Lee Henry
SPC Fred A. Henry
LTC (Ret) James Pat Henry
CPT James R. Henry
SFC Jason M. Henry
SGT Jeremy Henry
MSG Kenneth R. Henry
SGT Larry L. Henry
SGT Larry P. Henry
SGM Merle C. Henry
CPT Myles D. Henry
CPT Peter B. Henry
1SG (Ret) Richard J. Henry
MAJ Robert J. Henry
CPL Ronnie R. Henry
SPC Sammie L. Henry
MR. William R. Henry
SPC Emily S. Henshaw
SGT Steve Henshaw
SFC William E. Henshaw
SSG Harold A. Henslee
CPT Chuck Hensley
SPC David B. Hensley
CPT Edward L. Hensley
SPC John H. Hensley
SPC Michael H. Hensley
LTC Robert B. Hensley
SFC Ronald L. Hensley
2LT William R. Hensley
SGT Erick P. Henson
MR. Harold D. Henson
PFC James H. Henson
TSGT Richard E. Henson
PFC Stephen E. Henson
CSM Ted L. Henson
1SG William L. Henson
PFC Paul A. Henthorn
SP5 Robert Hentschel
SSG Robert S. Henzerling
SGT WaLT W. Henzi
CPL Aquirrie P. Hepler
MAJ (Ret) Ferdinand Heppf
SPC Neal R. Heppler
MAJ Michael S. Hequembourg
PFC Zachary A. Herb
SFC John R. Herbert
SSG (Ret) Joseph E. Herbert
SSG Maurita R. Herbert-Phelps
SGM (Ret) Eugene A. Herbest
SSG David L. Herbst
SGT Luke Herbst
MR. Marc Herdegen
CPL Troy E. Herdman
SPC Albert Heredia
SPC Jose M. Heredia
CPT Matthew S. Hergenroeder
LTC (Ret) Craig N. Herget
CW2 Robert W. Herington
CPL Melvin Herink
SSG Gracia Herisse
LTC Arthur L. Herman
PV2 Duane A. Herman
CPT John A. Herman
SGT Jack A. Hermann
MR. John R. Hermann
MSG Dwayne R. Hermans
1LT Tom Hermansen
PFC Robin M. Hermes
SPC John D. Hermesmann
SPC Adam Hernandez
SGT Andrew M. Hernandez
SPC Antonio C. Hernandez
SSG Carlos Hernandez
SPC Celestino Hernandez
SPC Daniel A. Hernandez
SPC Emil G. Hernandez
SGT Esequiel Hernandez
SGT Ezequiel Hernandez
SGT Faustino Hernandez
SPC Fernando Hernandez
SPC Francisco Hernandez
MR. Frank Hernandez
SP3 Genaro Hernandez
WO1 Gerardo Hernandez
MAJ Jeffrey R. Hernandez
MSG (Ret) Jesus Hernandez
SSG Joe A. Hernandez
SGT John M. Hernandez
SSG Jose Hernandez
CSM (Ret) Jose A. Hernandez
PFC Jose A. (Joseph) Hernandez
SSG Jose L. Hernandez
SPC Jose L. Hernandez
SGT Juan Hernandez
SGT Juan C. Hernandez
LTC (Ret) Juan J. Hernandez
CSM (Ret) Juan J. Hernandez
SGT Juan M. Hernandez
1SG Julio M. Hernandez
SPC Lawrence N. Hernandez
SFC Manuel P. Hernandez
1SG Mario M. Hernandez
PVT Martin Hernandez
SGT Nicolas Hernandez
SFC Oscar S. Hernandez
2LT Paul A. Hernandez
SPC Pedro H. Hernandez
CSM (Ret) Richard Hernandez
CW3 (Ret) Robert Hernandez
SGT Robert B. Hernandez
PVT Rodrigo G. Hernandez
CPL Santiago C. Hernandez
SSG Victor M. Hernandez
PFC Jose H. Hernandez Ramirez
CPL Robert G. Herr
SPC Marlin C. Herrboldt
MSG (Ret) Leslie E. Herrell
SSG Deryl V. Herren
COL (Ret) John D. Herren
SSG Prentice A. Herren
SGT Albert Joseph Herrera
SPC Carlos Herrera
SSG Gilberto A. Herrera
MSG Gregory Herrera
PVT Gustavo M. Herrera
SGM (Ret) Herman J. Herrera
SSG Jesse Herrera
SGT John Herrera
CPT John David Herrera
SSG Michael Herrera
SSG Paul I. Herrera
SGT Roger E. Herrera
SP5 David L. Herrick
SGT John Herrick
SPC Louis C. Herrick
SFC Clifford B. Herrin
SFC (Ret) Bobby J. Herring
SFC Daniel W. Herring
CPT John Herring
SSG Linwood Herring
SPC Timothy T. Herrington
SGT Bob Herrmann
SGT Charles Herrmann
SGT Gerald E. Herron
MSG Harry L. Herron
SFC Isiah Herron
LTC John T. Herron
SPC John David Hershberger
SP5 John E. Hershberger
SFC (Ret) Paul J. Hershberger
MAJ (Ret) Roger L. Hershberger
2LT Howard Hershey
SPC Kenneth L. Hershman
1LT Ray B. Hersman
1LT Richard A. Herster
MAJ William Hertel
CPL Larry J. Hervey
SFC Katrina M. Herzfeld
PVT Philip H. Herzig
SPC Charles A. Hesleitner
SSG John M. Hesley
SGT (Ret) Charles R. Hess
CW5 (Ret) Gerald L. Hess
CW3 Herman L.W. Hess
SGT Larry L. Hess
SPC Peter L. Hess
CPT Robert G. Hess
SPC Robert M. Hester
CPT Ryan G. Hester
SGT Walter A. Hester
CPT Terry M. Hestilow
CPT Donald G. Heth
CPT Douglas B. Hetrick
SGT Kenneth Heute
SGT Jim Hevelone
SSG (Ret) William C. Heverling
SFC (Ret) Thomas W. Hewell
PFC Billie D. Hewitt
1SG Nelden D. Hewitt
SGT Robert S. Hewitt
CSM (Ret) Southern Hewitt
SGT Tom Hewitt
MAJ William D. Hewitt
SPC Thomas P. Hewson
MAJ George D. Hey
SSG Ryan W. Hey
CPT Thomas E. Heydinger
MSG Dwayne A. Heyward
MAJ (Ret) James E. Hibbitts
SPC Virgie Hibbler
PFC William G. Hibbs
COL (Ret) Arville L. Hickerson
SPC John A. Hickey
SFC Robert C. Hickey
SPC Arthur L. Hickman
SFC Gregory K. Hickman
SP6 Howard C. Hickman
SGT James E. Hickman
1LT Jerry Hickman
SSG Patrick M. Hickman
MSG Patrick Hickok
SSG Ben C. Hicks
SGT Dennis W. Hicks
SrA Elmer L. Hicks
SGT Gerald A. Hicks
SPC James L. Hicks
2LT Jonathan Hicks
SPC Joshua M. Hicks
CPT Kevin A. Hicks
MAJ (Ret) Mark S. Hicks
SFC Michael A. Hicks
SGT Paul S. Hicks
SPC Rickey Hicks
CPL Stuart C. Hicks
SSG Tamma T. Hicks
CW3 (Ret) Thomas J. Hicks
SGT Timothy Hicks
SPC Tom Hicks
SGT Lloyd H. Hickscolon
PVT Eduardo Hidalgo
LTC (Ret) Jose A. Hidalgo
CPT Michael J. Hidalgo
SFC Jay F. Hidano
SPC Thomas F. Hiett
1SG Luther Higdon
CPT Chad A. Higginbotham
SPC Eston Higginbotham
SFC Hobert D. Higginbotham
CPL Richard Higginbotham
SGT Sherman L. Higginbottom
MR. Bill Higgins
CPT Daniel L. Higgins
SGT Frank S. Higgins
1SG James R. Higgins
SSG John P. Higgins
SP5 Kenneth Higgins
1SG Lee Higgins
PFC Preston S. Higgins
SPC Sean M. Higgins
SPC Alberto T. Higgs
SPC (Ret) Ellis H. Higgs
1LT William G. Higgs
SP5 (Ret) Raymond V. High
MSG James M. Highberg
SGT Christopher J. Highe
PVT Robie L. Highfield
SPC Gary D. Hight
CSM (Ret) Steven D. Hight
SPC Gary Hightower
SSG Samuel B. Hightower
LTC (Ret) Thomas K. Hightower
SFC Bruce R. Higley
SPC George W. Hikade
2LT Kirk E. Hilbrecht
SP5 Dwight W. Hilburn
PFC Gary P. Hildebran
SPC Steve Hildebran
SGM Donald L. Hildebrand
SPC Paul C. Hildebrand
SGT James A. Hildebrandt
CPT Scott B. Hildebrandt
PFC Richard R. Hildenbrand
MR. William Walter Hilgris
SPC Allen D. Hill
SPC Andrew Hill
SGT Andrew A. Hill
1SG Anthony Hill
SSG Arron M. Hill
SFC (Ret) Bobby Hill
CPL Carl M. Hill
PFC Charles T. Hill
MAJ Chetwood R. Hill
MAJ Chris Hill
SPC Clarence E. Hill
CPT Donald E. Hill
SGT Donny J. Hill
SGT Edward J. Hill
1LT Edwin E. Hill
MRS. Emil D. Hill
SGT Ernest A. Hill
SFC Everett L. Hill
SGT Harry L. Hill
COL (Ret) Howard D. Hill
COL (Ret) Howard D. Hill
SGT Ian Hill
SPC James A. Hill
1LT James M. Hill
MSG James Richards Hill
GEN (Ret) James T. Hill
PV2 Jason Hill
SPC John P. Hill
PFC Kaple L. Hill
SGT Kermetris Hill
PFC Kevin H. Hill
SSG Larry Hill
PFC Leroy E. Hill
SPC Michael Hill
SSG Michael R. Hill
SGT Phillip O. Hill
MRS. R. G. Hill
SGT Ray Lynn Hill
SPC Robert E. Hill
SGT Robert E. Hill
1SG Robert L. Hill
CPT Robert M. Hill
1SG Teddy A. Hill
1SG (Ret) Tonja A. Hill
SSG Walter C. Hill
SPC Wesley Hill
PFC William B. Hill
SGT William F. Hill
LTC (Ret) William H. Hill
SGT William H. Hill
SPC Ronald Hilla
PFC Kenneth Hillas
SP5 W. V. Hille
PFC Kurt A. Hillebrand
SGT Samuel R. Hillegas
PVT Barry L. Hillen
SPC Paul A. Hillenbrand
SGT Robert A. Hillerby
MAJ E. Wayne Hilliard
SGT Fred D. Hilliard
COL (Ret) Henry C. Hilliard
SFC Raymond L. Hilliard
PFC Terry Lee Hilliard
SGT Mark S. Hilliker
MAJ David B. Hilling
SP5 John H. Hillis
MAJ Idamaria Hillkjonaas
MR. Campbell W. Hillman
SPC Wayne C. Hillman
SFC William A. Hillman
CPT Heather Hills
PFC John K. Hillyer
PFC Raymond C. Hillyer
CPT Andrew C. Hilmes
LTC Lance K. Hiltbrand
LTC Bradley C. Hilton
PFC John C. Hilton
MSG (Ret) Larry G. Hilton
CW2 (Ret) Mark H. Hilton
MAJ Myrna L. Hilton
MAJ James M. Hilts
2LT Gerald E. Himes
CW3 (Ret) John M. Himes
SGT Terry W. Himes
SPC Daniel J. Himmelman
MR. Joseph Himmelstein
CPT Joseph Himpelmann
CW4 George W. Hinchliffe
CPT Douglas R. Hinckley
SPC Richard Hinds
CW3 Francis M. Hines
SPC George B. Hines
CW2 Joseph A. Hines
SGT Todd Hines
SFC Woodrow N. Hines
1SG Conrad C. Hinkel
PFC Edward Brad Hinker
SPC Barry P. Hinkle
2LT Jack K. Hinman
SFC Gilbert Hinnant
SP3 Robert J. Hino
SGT Jorge V. Hinojosa
SPC Charles Hinote
LTC (Ret) Ralph W. Hinrichs
SPC Gregg P. Hinrichsen
LTC James S. Hinrichsen
MR. Arthur J. Hinsch
MRS. Jesse Hinson
PFC Stephen C. Hinson
MAJ William C. Hinson
MRS. William L. Hinson
SGT Bill M. Hinton

SGT Joseph C. Hinton
CPT Leon J. Hinton
SSG Richard W. Hinton
MS. Sandra Hinton
SPC Stephen J. Hinton
SGT Theodore G. Hinton
SPC Barry J. Hinytz
CPT James W. Hinz
SGT Mark E. Hipp
SP5 Percy Delmar Hipple
SGT James W. Hippmann
SP5 Glenn Hipps
SP5 Larry Hipshire
SPC Mervyn Hiramoto
SSG Brian Hirayama
CPT Freddie Hires
SFC (Ret) Carl Franklin Hirlston
SSG Paul Hirsch
SSG Sandy Hirsch
LTC Mark R. Hirschinger
SSG Timothy C. Hirshberg-Schuman
COL (Ret) Herbert L. Hirst
SPC Thomas Hirst
SGT Jeanne M. Hisek
CW2 Francis A. Hiser
SGT John R. Hiser
CPT Charles Matthew Hitchcock
SGT Joe B. Hitchcock
MRS. Karol Lynn L. Hitchens
MR. Lloyd Hitchens
SGT John R. Hite
MR. Leonard K. Hiteshew
MR. Leonard K. Hitshey
SSG (Ret) La Marse E. Hitson
PSG (Ret) George A. Hitzman
CPL Mark R. Hitzner
PFC Zachary Hixon
SFC Elmer J. Hixson
MSG (Ret) Odean E. Hjelter
SGT Dave Hjerpe
CPT Paul M. Hlas
SSG Conrad L. Hlavacek
LTC Nicholas G. Hlywa
SPC (Ret) Donald P. Hoag
MAJ Insoon G. Hoagland
PVT Randal R. Hoagland
COL Samuel L. Hoard
SGT Paul E. Hoban
PVT Kyle Aaron Hobart
MSG James L. Hobaugh
CPT Arthur M. Hobbs
SP5 Earl B. Hobbs
SPC James Hobbs
1SG James Y. Hobbs
1LT Michael D. Hobbs
SGT Robert W. Hobbs
PFC Thomas Hobbs
SSG Wallace N. Hobbs
MAJ (Ret) Jesse L. Hobby
1LT Michael B. Hobgood
MAJ (Ret) Gary R. Hobin
LTC (Ret) George Hobson
SGT James E. Hobson
SGT Leonard T. Hobson
MAJ Richard Hobson
SGT Arnold G. Hoch
PVT Justin Hoch
CPL Ernst N. Hochberger
SPC Glenn A. Hocher
CPT Gerald J. Hock
SSG Conrad M. Hockaby
SSG Richard A. Hockenberry
SGT Jay W. Hockenbury
CPT Mitchell C. Hockenbury
SPC Joe D. Hockersmith
MR. Carl Hockett
SGT David S. Hockett
MAJ Keith Hockman
SGT Ottie E. Hockman
MRS. John T. Hodes
MR. Brian Hodge
PFC David Hodge
SGT Duane Hodge
CPT (Ret) John D. Hodge
SPC Ryan Hodge
PFC Thomas E. Hodge
SGT Timothy A. Hodge
CSM (Ret) Brent L. Hodges
MR. Charles M. Hodges
SGT Clyde H. Hodges
SSG Gerald M. Hodges
CPL James E. Hodges
SSG Joseph S. Hodges
SGT Lee W. Hodges
SPC Marc Hodges
SSG Ralph K. Hodges
2LT Sheldon Hodges
SPC Thomas J. Hodges
MSG Willie E. Hodges
PFC Jerry J. Hodgin
MAJ Dave Hodne
SSG Leaton Wayne Hodnett
1SG Joseph Hodonsky
SGT Terry A. Hodous
SGT John M. Hodson
COL (Ret) Gary L. Hoebeke
CPL Gary E. Hoefler
SSG Robert G. Hoeft
CPT Howard H. Hoege
CPL Ronald F. Hoehn
MSG Philip R. Hoelscher
MR. Raymond J. Hoelzl
CW2 David W. Hoepf
SPC Gail M. Hoerner
SGT Louis J. Hoerner
PFC Charles B. Hoessel
CSM (Ret) John A. Hoetker
CSM (Ret) Jeffery A. Hof
SPC Paul B. Hofer
CPL Clinton L. Hoferman
SSG Glen Hoffa
SGT Charles L. Hoffman
SGT Christopher S. Hoffman
LT Daniel Hoffman
1LT David Hoffman
PFC Eugene C. Hoffman
SPC James Hoffman
PFC Jeffery D. Hoffman
CPL Joseph Hoffman
LTC (Ret) Louis E. Hoffman
SPC Michael W. Hoffman
MR. Paul Hoffman
MR. Paul E. Hoffman
COL Peter D. Hoffman
SPC Richard D. Hoffman
MR. Robert L. Hoffman
SFC Robert L. Hoffman
SP5 Roy A. Hoffman
SSG Rudolph H. Hoffman
SPC Seth Hoffman
SPC Virgil A. Hoffman
MSG (Ret) Walter G. Hoffman
SP6 William J. Hoffman
SSG Conrad A. Hoffmann
PVT David A. Hoffmann
SGT John K. Hoffmann
CPT Kenneth R. Hoffmann
SP5 Leland C. Hoffmann
PFC Joseph W. Hoffner
SGT Ernie A. Hoffstetter
SFC James M. Hofling
SGT Theodore C. Hofsiss
LT Gary F. Hogan
2LT Jason P. Hogan
SGT Jerry Hogan
MSG Nathaniel I. Hogan
LTC Roderick L. Hogan
SPC Sean L. Hogan
CPL Elmer Hogarth
SPC John F. Hogate
CPT James F. Hoge
SP5 Thomas A. Hoge
SGT Rod Hogevoll
SGT Jack Hogge
SSG Robert T. Hogston
SGT Richard L. Hogue
SP5 James A. Hohman
SGT Duane D. Hohvart
SPC Joseph Hoinski
SSG Eric D. Hoke
SPC Santonio A. Hoke
SGT Ted Hoke
SPC Larry J. Hoksch
LTC Angelia K. Holbrook
LTC Gary G. Holbrook
SPC Stewart B. Holbrooke
SGT Larry D. Holbrooks
CW4 Brian S. Holcomb
PVT Edwin T. Holcomb
SPC Frank E. Holcomb
SPC Thomas Teddy Holcomb
CPL Arnold Holcombe
PVT Gregory H. Holcombe
1LT James H. Holcombe
SGT John W. Holcombe
SGT Thomas S. Holcombe
BG (Ret) Ronald M. Holdaway
SPC Gordon Holdburg
SPC Mark H. Holden
LTC (Ret) Parker Holden
LTC (Ret) Rich L. Holden
CPT Scott E. Holden
CPT Timothy H. Holden
CPL Jeremiah Holder
PFC Lawrence S. Holder
CPL Marvin S. Holder
SGT William H. Holder
SGT Donavon N. Holderread
SPC Christoper Allen Holdren
COL David R. Holdsworth
PFC Michael D. Hole
SFC (Ret) Stanley D. Holewa
SGT Gregg Holgate
CPT David R. Holguin
CPL Kristopher R. Holien
SFC Robert Holifield
PFC John J. Holihan
PVT Colson W. Hollan
SGT Minor L. Hollan
MAJ Christopher A. Holland
SFC David J. Holland
PFC Donald J. Holland
COL (Ret) F. Barry Holland
1SG Harold Holland
SGT Howard S. Holland
SSG (Ret) James E. Holland
SGT Jerry O. Holland
CW2 John K. Holland
LTC Joseph C. Holland
MR. Mark Holland
MAJ Robert G. Holland
CSM (Ret) Roland Holland
CSM Jimmie R. Hollander
SGT Chester Holleman
LTC John H. Holler
SSG Joseph V. Holler
2LT James P. Holley
SGT William E. Holliday
SFC Deljuan Hollingshead
SGT Eddie Hollingshead
CPT James J. Hollingsworth
2LT Joshua P. Hollingsworth
MAJ (Ret) John F. Hollins
TSgt Virland D. Hollins
PFC Norman R. Hollister
SPC Tom Hollobaugh
CPT Alfred M. Holloway
CPT Charles H. Holloway
PVT Curtis J. Holloway
MR. David H. Holloway
SGT Gregory R. Holloway
SSG James S. Holloway
SPC Joseph C. Holloway
SGT Kenneth Ray Holloway
MAJ Ralph L. Holloway
SGT (Ret) Robert K. Holloway
SPC W. Earl Holloway
COL George C. Hollwedel
1LT Benjamin H. Holly
CSM (Ret) Lawrence G. Holly
CPT Brent W. Holman
MR. Curtis Holman
SPC Miranda Holman
SSG Richard P. Holman
LTC (Ret) Robert E. Holman
SGT Nicholas L. Holmberg
COL James L. Holmer
PFC Abraham Holmes
SSG Connie M. Holmes
CPT Donald J. Holmes
SPC Edward S. Holmes
SGT George Holmes
MAJ Gregory R. Holmes
SP5 Jason E. Holmes
PV2 Latimore Holmes
LTC Lawrence B. Holmes
SGT Lyman F. Holmes
SFC (Ret) Marvin A. Holmes
SPC Mason Holmes
CPT David B. Holobaugh
SSG Leonard W. Holsman
CPT James J. Holstein
PFC Anthony Holt
MR. David W. Holt
SPC Donald A. Holt
MRS. Erma Holt
MR. Jeffrey K. Holt
SPC Robert L. Holt
SGT Steven Holt
SFC (Ret) Thomas W. Holt
MR. Ron Holte
PFC Donald W. Holthauser
CPL Robert C. Holtkamp
SPC Walter W. Holtmeyer
MR. F. Michael Holton
SPC Kerry D. Holton
1LT Joseph F. Holtslag
SGT Charles L. Holtz
SSG Dave E. Holtzendorff
LTC John A. Holtzman
CPT Ralph D. Holweck
SPC Gary A. Holyoke
MAJ John C. Holz
PFC Ron Holz
SPC David F. Homan
LTC Dwight F. Homann
PVT Adam D. Homerston
PFC Jonathan D. Homeyer
MAJ Michael D. Homiller
SSG Mike Honea
PVT Stephen T. Honeycutt
MAJ Eric Hong
CPL Paul Honor
LTG (Ret) Russel L. Honore
SGT Joseph E. Honzo
SPC Bruce A. Hood
MR. Charles Hood
LTC (Ret) Colin L. Hood
SGT David W. Hood
SPC Gordon H. Hood
SP5 Gregory A. Hood
SSG Leon T. Hood
SPC Robert E. Hood
MRS. Wallace W. Hood
SPC Kristopher A. Hoogerworf
SSG Bryan L. Hook
SP5 Harlan F. Hooker
SPC Wayne B. Hooker
SP5 Daniel J. Hooks
SGT Erik L. Hooks
PV2 Kevin B. Hooks
SFC Robert Hooks
SPC Michael D. Hoopaugh
SSG Bernie N. Hooper
SGT Charles Hooper
MR. Robert L. Hooper
SGT James P. Hooser
SP5 Chuck Hoover
SGT David A. Hoover
MR. Harold H. Hoover
SSG Mary C. Hoover
SGT Matthew R. Hoover
SGT Richard J. Hoover
SGT Thomas J. Hoover
CW2 Ronald E. Hope
MSG Donald D. Hopke
SFC Daryl K. Hopkins
PV2 Douglas R. Hopkins
SP5 Howard E. Hopkins
MR. Paul Hopkins
SPC Terry Hopkins
PFC Theodore W. Hoppenrath
1SG Earnest O. Hopper
MSG Jerry R. Hopper
CPT Matthew D. Hopper
SSG Justin A. Hopple
SPC Richard E. Hopson
SGM James A. Horace
SPC Rudy J. Horak
CW4 (Ret) George B. Horan
MS. Morriah Holly Horani
SGT Thomas Horas
LTC (Ret) Richard Hore
SPC Dennis R. Horin
SSG Martin E. Horinek
SGT Charles R. Horn
COL Douglas L. Horn
1SG Roland E. Horn
CPT Shelby Paul Horn
SGT Tyson R. Horn
1LT Dave Hornbarger
SPC William F. Hornbuckle
1LT Court R. Horncastle
SGT Eugene B. Horne
CPT Garth M. Horne
SGT James R. Horne
SP5 Jim R. Horne
1SG William Horne
LTC Robert C. Horneck
SFC Cornelius J. Horner
SGT George E. Horner
SGT Howard R. Horner
SPC Raymond E. Horner
COL Thomas A. Horner
SGT Frank P. Hornik
SPC Laymon C. Hornsby
PFC Michael J. Horon
MAJ Naomi J. Horowitz
SGT Ralph Horowitz
SPC Michael A. Horrall
CPT Paul M. Horrigan
CPT Thomas H. Horrigan
MR. Bennie R. Horton
COL (Ret) George C. Horton
SPC Gerald Horton
SPC Irvin A. Horton
1SG James M. Horton
SPC Obbie J. Horton
CW2 (Ret) Max W. Hosafros
PFC Frank Hose
SP5 Gary L. Hosfelt
SFC (Ret) Richard L. Hosking
SSG Bernie Hoskins
SPC Ralph L. Hoskins
1LT David Hosna
SFC (Ret) Larry W. Hostetler
SP5 Mark A. Hostetler
2LT Andrew T. Hotaling
CW2 Mark Hotchkiss
SGT Ross Hottman
MRS. Roma L. Houchin
SPC Samantha Houck
1SG (Ret) Darrell D. Hough
SGT Daniel W. Houmes
SFC (Ret) Carl S. House
CPT Charles S. House
SGT Jeremy D. House
CPT John C. House
LTG (Ret) Randolph W. House
SGT Walter L. House
SGT Lorrin H. C. Housh
SPC Richard P. Housh
SSG Robert J. Housholder
SPC Gary A. Houska
SP5 Dean P. Houstman
SSG Edward Houston
SPC Fred Michael Houston
MR. James E. Houston
COL Jerry B. Houston
SGT Lemuel Nelson Houston
PVT Leroy R. Houston
SGT Ocie L. Houston
SGT R. Clinton Houston
SFC Wayne J. Houston
SPC John B. Hovde
MSG (Ret) John O. Hovdenes
PVT Andrew J. Howard
SPC Bruce B. Howard
MAJ (Ret) David D. Howard
SGT Eric Howard
MSG (Ret) Fred Howard
SP3 (Ret) Hugh C. Howard
MRS. John R. Howard
PV2 Keith E. Howard
PSG (Ret) Lee E. Howard
MAJ Lowell E. Howard
SSG (Ret) Marcus V. Howard
SFC Michael Howard
SGT Randolph M. Howard
SSG Reginald Howard
SPC Richard Astorga Howard
SFC Robert C. Howard
SSG Robert L. Howard
MAJ Sidney D. Howard
SFC Sixto T. Howard
MAJ Steven R. Howard
1LT Steven Ty Howard
SSG Thomas Scott Howard
SGT Dean M. Howarth
SGT Edward Howe
1LT John R. Howe
SPC Darin Howell
SGT David C. Howell
PVT Donald L. Howell
SGT Donald S. Howell
CW3 Dwayne Howell
SSG Glenn K. Howell
SGT Jerry L. Howell
MRS. Jessie M. Howell
CPL John E. Howell
PVT Kevin Howell
2LT Richard A. Howell
SGT Robert G. Howell
SSG Robert M. Howell
MSG (Ret) Samuel Howell
MAJ Scott L. Howell
SSG (Ret) Harold L. Howerter
LTC (Ret) Robert A. Howes
PFC James A. Howison
SSG Chris Howlett
SPC Carlos W. Howley
MAJ Shawn Howley
PFC William F. Howorth
SGT Kenneth G. Howser
SGT Clinton T. Hoy
SP5 George L. Hoy
MAJ James R. Hoy
PFC John Hoy
SSG John R. Hoy
CPT Timothy J. Hoy
CPT Jonathan Mark Hoyle
SSG Weldon S. Hoyle
SGT George T. Hoyt
MR. Robert L. Hoyt
SGT James Curtis Hozey
SPC Zbigniew F. Hrabik
PFC Raymond E. Hrach
SFC Daniel G. Hreha
CPT Christopher A. Hric
SSG Ron Hrydziuszko
SGT David S. Hrynda
SGT (Ret) Daniel Hubbard
SPC Danny Hubbard
SGT Dennis O. Hubbard
CPL Gary W. Hubbard
PFC Jim Hubbard
SFC Joe W. Hubbard
1SG Kim A. Hubbard
SGT Larry Hubbard
CPT Michael Shane Hubbard
SGT O. H. Hubbard
SFC William H. Hubbard
SGT Wilson G. Hubbell
1SG (Ret) David N. Hubbert
SPC John Hubbs
SPC Jerry Huber
COL (Ret) Joseph E. Huber
PVT Thomas Hubert
SGT Gary L. Hubler
SGT Edward L. Huckabee
MSG James Huckabee
SFC (Ret) Robert L. Huckaby
SPC Edward L. Huckman
SPC Michael Huculak
SP5 William J. Hudachek
SGT Allen W. Huddleston
PVT Kendal W. Huddleston
PV2 Mark R. Hudgens
CPL James M. Hudik
SGT Mike A. Hudnall
LTC (Ret) Andrew J. Hudson
SGT Caven Hudson
PFC David M. Hudson
SGT George M. Hudson
CPL James Edward Hudson
SGT James W. Hudson
CPT Jay Hudson
MSG John L. Hudson
MAJ (Ret) Larry G. Hudson
SPC Steven B. Hudson
PFC Swanson N. Hudson
MSG Willie M. Hudson
SSG Willis E. Hudson
CPL Willis N. Hudson
SGT Michael E. Hudzinski
PVT Michael A. Huebenthal
CPT Robert E. Huebner
SGT Thomas J. Huelsmann
CPL Sal V. Huerta
SGT Hector L. Huertas
MAJ (Ret) Gary C. Huested
PVT Christopher J. Huettl
PVT Douglas L. Huey
SPC Herbert N. Huey
PFC Richard C. Huey
SFC (Ret) Bill J. Huff
MR. Fred Huff
MSG (Ret) John A. Huff
SFC John E. Huff
CPL John W. Huff
SGT T. J. Huff
MAJ Timothy C. Huff
LTC William H. Huff
SGT Gerald W. Huffman
MR. James D. Huffman
SPC Jerry Huffman
COL John Bruce Huffman
SFC (Ret) Matthew L. Huffman
CPL Richard Huffman
SGT David E. Huffmaster
PFC James S. Hufnall
1LT Jack Hugele
SSG David L. Hughart
MAJ (Ret) John H. Hughen
COL (Ret) Algin J. Hughes
SPC Billy H. Hughes
SGT Christian J. Hughes
SGT Clifford Hughes
SGT Danny R. Hughes
COL (Ret) David R. Hughes
CPL Eugene Hughes
SP3 George L. Hughes
MAJ (Ret) George W. Hughes
PFC Gerard J. Hughes
SPC Greg J. Hughes
SP5 Howard E. Hughes
CPT Huber C. Hughes
CW2 Jack E. Hughes
CW3 (Ret) Jack E. Hughes
SGT Jim Hughes
SGT John M. Hughes
CSM Kelvin A. Hughes
MR. Kevin C. Hughes
SPC Michael W. Hughes
MAJ (Ret) Norman F. S. Hughes
SGT Richard G. Hughes
SP5 Richard L. Hughes
SPC Riley L. Hughes
SSG Robbin Hughes
MSG Roy M. Hughes
SPC William M. Hughes
SGT Willie Hughes
SGT Richard A. Hughey

SGT Ed Hugley
PVT Scott R. Huguenin
SP5 Jack William Huguley
PVT Cody Huiet
SP5 Laddie E. Hula
SPC Robert R. Hulbert
SGT Gary G. Hulett
CPL Charles L. Hull
SGT Cory Hull
SFC (Ret) David C. Hull
SFC (Ret) Douglas B. Hull
SPC Gregory J. Hull
SGT James J. Hull
CW4 (Ret) James O. Hull
SGT Michael A. Hull
SPC (Ret) Richard L. Hull
SFC (Ret) Robert C. Hullihen
SGT Larry A. Huls
LTC (Ret) Andrew Hulse
SGT Billy R. Hulse
PFC James C. Hulsey
MRS. Venus (Woody) Hulsey
COL (Ret) William R. Humbaugh
CW5 Marvin P. Humble
MSG Michael E. Hume
MAJ Shannon S. Hume
CPL Harold M. Humes
SGT Melvin Humes
SP5 William R. Humes
1LT Peter F. Humm
SPC David Hummel
SGT Dennis Hummel
SGT Theresa M. Hummel
SSG Charles A. Hummer
SGT Glenn Hummer
SPC Lawrence H. Hummer
SGT Steven C. Hummer
CW2 Bill Humphrey
SPC Clare Humphrey
MRS. Floyd V. Humphrey
MSG Richard G. Humphrey
SGT William Humphrey
MAJ (Ret) Michael A. Humphreys
2LT Frederick W. Humphries
PFC Joshua E. Humphries
SSG Newell Humphries
PV2 Charles R. Hunchman
SP5 Charles D. Hund
SPC Glen Hundley
MSG Stephen W. Hundley
MRS. Hans Hundsberger
1SG David S. Hungerford
MRS. William D. Hungerford
PFC Robert S. Hungerpeler
CPT Bryan Joshua Hunsaker
SGT James L. Hunsberger
CPL Lonnie J. Hunsucker
CPT Bill Hunt
SPC Buddy Hunt
MR. Daryl L. Hunt
MRS. David E. W. Hunt
MAJ D'hania Hunt
SGT Douglas L. Hunt
MRS. George L. Hunt
COL Henry L. Hunt
SGT John W. Hunt
SGT Laddie Hunt
SSG Lee Hunt
SPC Marvin H. Hunt
PFC Phillip G. Hunt
SGT Richard A. Hunt
SFC (Ret) Ronald L. Hunt
1LT Russell L. Hunt
SFC Ryan Hunt
COL (Ret) Wallace G. Hunt
SPC Abraham Hunter
SPC Arthur Hunter
MSG Arvil D. Hunter
PFC Carolyn L. Hunter
SGT Cornelius B. Hunter
SSG David W. Hunter
MSG Douglas A. S. Hunter
LTC (Ret) Jack M. Hunter
SGT James J. Hunter
SPC Leslie E. Hunter
MSG (Ret) Otis H. Hunter
PFC Pamela Hunter
SGT Ralph L. Hunter
SMSgt (Ret) Richard D. Hunter
SGT Shaun M. Hunter
2LT Shawn M. Hunter
CW3 (Ret) Walter E. Hunter
SPC Randall Huntes
SPC Christopher Hunthrop
TSgt Robert L. Huntley
LTG David H. Huntoon
LTG (Ret) Kenneth Hunzeker
CPL Kenny Hupy
PFC Michael K. Hurder
SGT Jeffery Hurell
COL Daniel Hurlbut
TSgt Frederick Hurlbutt
CSM (Ret) Henry Fulton Hurley
CW3 (Ret) Jack E. Hurley
SGT James H. Hurley
SPC James L. Hurley
1SG (Ret) John A. Hurley
CPT John K. Hurley
SGT John P. Hurley
SFC Scott Hurley
SPC Max Hurrelbrink
SGT John G. Hursh
SSG Charles M. Hurst
MR. Daniel V. Hurst
SGT Fred C. Hurst
SPC James R. Hurst
SPC Jessie Hurst
PFC Joseph M. Hurst
SP5 William A. Hurst
SGT William R. Hurst
SFC Chad Hurt
PFC Danny E. Hurt
SGT James C. Hurtado
SGM Gilbert D. Hurte
CPL Edward J. Hurysz
SSG Joe F. Husband
PFC Aloyouis A. Huschka
CPT Thomas D. Huse
SPC David Huser
MSG Jody K. Huskey
COL (Ret) Stephen E. Huskey
DR. (MAJ) Arnold M. Huskins
PFC Benjiman R. Husman
PSG Archie P. Huss
PFC Edwin L. Huss
SPC Martin Huss
SPC Rodney D. Huss
PFC Gurney L. Husser
SPC Leon T. Hussey
PFC Rodney P. Hussey
CPT Matthew D. Hustead
MAJ Robin-Desty Husted
SGT Travis Husted
SGT Chuck Hustedt
SPC Leslie C. Huster
CPL James F. Hutchcraft
1LT Jerry Hutchens
SPC Dudley Hutcheson
MR. Loyal D. Hutchetson
PFC Billy G. Hutchings
SPC Robert C. Hutchings
PFC Francis M. Hutchins
SGT Larry J. Hutchins
PFC Jack Hutchinson
SGT James S. Hutchinson
SPC Ronald L. Hutchinson
CPT Walter W. Hutchison
SGT Thomas M. Hutka
SPC Richard B. Hutson
SSG John E. Hutter
SPC Richard G. Hutting
SPC Cecil Ray Hutto
COL (Ret) James E. Hutton
SGT Kenneth D. Hutton
WO1 Jason L. Huvar
SP5 Calvin W. Hyatt
SGT Claude Hyatt
SPC David M. Hyatt
SPC Robert J. Hyche
SPC Larry T. Hyde
CSM (Ret) Mark A. Hyde
LTC (Ret) Orion J. Hyde
MSG (Ret) Franklin Hyke
SPC Amanda Hyler
CPL Alpha V. Hylton
SPC Alton L. Hyman
SPC David Hyman
SPC Kiana Hymer
PFC Emil Hynek
SPC Edward F. Hynes
LTC (Ret) Robert F. Hynes
SPC Pasquale R. Iagana
SGT Kim Iampietro
MG (Ret) Francis A. Ianni
SPC Scott Ianno
SPC Joseph S. Iannuzzi
SSG Hector J. Ibarra
SGT Richard R. Ibarra
CSM Walter J. Ibbotson
LTC Donald A. Ice
SSG Olen B. Ice
SPC Kenneth E. Ickes
PFC Donald J. Iddings
SGT Thomas R. Idema
LTG Anthony Ierardi
SPC Ezra A. O. Ifie
SSG Jack P. Iglesias
MRS. Abraham K. Ignacio
SGT William H. Ihnat
CPT Kevin Ike
SGT Gary C. Iker
MSG (Ret) William R. Ikner
LTC (Ret) George A. Iler
CPT Goran Ilioski
MR. Dennis W. Imka
SSG Elvis R. Imus
SGT Jhampier Inchaustegui
MSG Howard K. Inderdahl
MR. Robert Indermuehle
LTG (Ret) Joseph R. Inge
CPT Christopher Ingels
SP5 (Ret) Jimmy E. Ingersoll
SP5 Paul M. Ingevaldson
PFC James W. Ingham
SSG Gary S. Ingle
PFC James E. Ingle
MAJ George Ingleright
SPC Kenneth Inglis
MAJ Charles L. Ingraham
SSG Al Ingram
MAJ Bernd L. Ingram
SGT Daniel J. Ingram
SSG Daniel M. Ingram
CPT Darren E. Ingram
SGT Donald R. Ingram
SSG Earnest John Ingram
PFC Ellis Ingram
SPC (Ret) Glenn L. Ingram
SPC Keatron N. Ingram
SPC Michael K. Ingram
1SG Michael P. Ingram
SGT Robert E. Ingram
SGT Ronald D. Ingram
1SG William F. Ingram
SGT D. C. Inman
SSG Michael Inman
CSM (Ret) Paul M. Inman
MSG Phillip W. Inman
SPC Robert A. Inman
SGT William L. Inman
SPC George C. Innis
SPC Samuel B. Interrante
SSG Archangelo Iovanne
CPT (Ret) Ray D. Irby
SGT Thomas L. Irby
CPL Joe Ireland
MRS. Orville F. Ireland
SGT Blaine S. Irish
1SG Richard Irizarry
PVT Shane C. Irons
SSG Jerry A. Irvin
LT John Irvin
SFC Tasheema A. Irvin
MS. Liz Irvine
MAJ Michael M. Irvine
SSG Ted G. Irvine
SGT John D. Irving
CW3 Ronald P. Irving
COL (Ret) Wilburt J. Irwin
CSM Aaron B. Isaac
SGT Fred H. Isaack
SGT Clinton Dale Isbell
SPC George A. Isenbart
CPT James P. Isenhower
CPT Karl H. Isern
CPT Joshua Ishibashi
SFC Howard T. Ishikawa
SPC Ronald L. Ishmael
SP5 Stephen Iskowitz
COL (Ret) John A. Islin
PFC Timothy J. Isom
MR. Lewis M. Ison
SGT Larry D. Israel
SFC (Ret) Michael S. Israel
SGT John E. Issitt
SGT Jeffery Istre
SPC (Ret) Wayne Istre
SPC Donald A. Ivanoski
MAJ Harry A. Ivarie
SGT Raymond W. Iversen
SGT Gordon D. Iverson
MR. Ralph W. Iverson
MR. Jesse J. Ivery
SPC Geoffrey P. Ives
SSG Joshua Wayne Ives
SGT Richard David Ivester
SFC Anthony P. Ivey
SSG Charlie R. Ivey
SSG Tom J. Ivey
CPL James A. Ivison
CPL Clarence W. Ivy
SPC Earl I. Iwamoto
SSG Guadalupe Izaguirre
PFC John P. Izett
CSM (Ret) Herbert H. Izumi
SGT Anthony Izzo
1SG (Ret) John L. Izzo
MR. Robert M. Izzo
PFC Dennis W. Jack
CPT Jason Jack
CPT Benjamin Jackman
SFC Frederick Jackman
SPC Robert E. Jackman
COL Timothy Jackman
PVT Andre Jackson
MSG Andrew Jackson
CSM (Ret) Andrew L. Jackson
SFC Andy Jackson
SSG (Ret) Benjamin Jackson
1SG (Ret) Bobby Jackson
CPT (Ret) Bobby J. Jackson
1LT Bruce D. Jackson
SGT Byron Jackson
SPC Charles E. Jackson
SFC Dale K. Jackson
SPC Daniel K. Jackson
SGT Danny F. Jackson
SGT David Jackson
2LT David A. Jackson
SFC Deann Jackson
CPT Dewey M. Jackson
CPL Donald L. Jackson
SPC Elliott C. Jackson
PFC Eric L. Jackson
PVT Ernest J. Jackson
SPC Felton Jackson
SP5 Floyd F. Jackson
SPC Frankie L. Jackson
SPC George R. Jackson
SSG George W. Jackson
PFC Herbert Jackson
SPC Ivory Jackson
SFC James D. Jackson
PVT James R. Jackson
SSG Jeffery M. Jackson
PVT Jeffrey O. Jackson
2LT Jeramie G. Jackson
MAJ Jerry D. Jackson
SGT Jon S. Jackson
PFC Joseph Jackson
SGT Keith J. Jackson
SGT Lavern Jackson
SGT Lavern R. Jackson
SPC Lennie P. Jackson
SGM Leonard Jackson
SFC Les Jackson
SP5 Lloyd N. Jackson
PVT Malcolm M. Jackson
PV2 Mark Jackson
CSM Maurice Jackson
SSG Michael Jackson
CPT Oliver S. Jackson
CPT Patricia A. Jackson
SP3 Richard B. Jackson
SPC Robert G. Jackson
SGT Robert G. Jackson
PFC Robert Lee Jackson
SPC Ronald R. Jackson
LTC Scott A. Jackson
SSG Shilreds Jackson
SFC Terrance Jackson
SGM (Ret) Terry E. Jackson
COL (Ret) Thomas M. Jackson
CPT Wade M. Jackson
SSG Walter L. Jackson
SP5 Whitney T. Jackson
COL (Ret) Wilfred A. Jackson
1SG William Jackson
SGM (Ret) William A. Jackson
SPC William Larry Jackson
CPT William P. Jackson
SGT William R. Jackson
SPC David J. Jacob
CPT James C. Jacob
CPT Jack L. Jacober
SGT Albert W. Jacobs
CPT Arthur R. Jacobs
SGT Brad R. Jacobs
SGT Douglas M. Jacobs
SSG (Ret) Robert E. Jacobs
SGT Robert L. Jacobs
CW2 Robert T. Jacobs
SGT Ronald Jacobs
SPC Tom A. Jacobs
MSG Willie N. Jacobs
SGT Alan T. Jacobsen
SSG William T. Jacobsen
SGT David J. Jacobson
MAJ Douglas Jacobson
SPC Frederick Gary Jacobson
CPL Melvin R. Jacobson
CPL Ronald Jacobson
CPT Vincent G. Jacot
CPT John F. Jacques
SPC Ricardo A. Jacques
SFC William E. Jacques
SFC Daiwin F. Jadan
SFC (Ret) Gerald P. Jaeger
CPL Jeffrey L. Jaeger
SGT Kenneth H. Jaeger
SPC Jason A. Jaffe
2LT Jerry Jaime
PFC Kenneth J. Jaker
MSG Jimmie Jakes
SPC James J. Jaklin
SSG Edwin Jakubowski
PFC Edwin J. Jakubowski
SSG Thomas W. Jakubowski
SSG Tim Jalbert
SFC Reynaldo Jallorina
MAJ (Ret) Bennie B. Jamerson
SPC (Ret) Anthony R. James
SPC Bradley James
CPT Brian J. James
PV2 David M. James
SPC Donald W. James
1LT Frank M. James
SSG Frederick A. James
MSG Gerry L. James
SPC Grover Q. James
COL (Ret) James D. James
SSG Jeffrey James
PVT Jesse James
SPC Larry B. James
PVT Lorenza A. James
SPC Lori K. James
LTC (Ret) Lynn M. James
CPT Norma Ann James
MSG Olanda James
SFC Paleamon L. James
SP5 Richard James
PFC Richard E. James
SFC Robert A. James
2LT Robert G. James
SGT Robert R. James
SGT Timothy James
MSG William T. James
SGT Willie James
SGT Zachary James
SGT Charles C. Jamieson
SGT Gerald D. Jamieson
SSG Jason Jamieson
SP5 Lawrence W. Jamison
PVT Robert E. Jamison
SSG Frank C. Jancosek
PV2 Chase R. Janecku
SPC Stanley H. Janeczko
SSG Ralph A. Janek
SPC Robert W. Janelle
MAJ (Ret) Kenneth A. Janes
LTC (Ret) Ray H. Janes
SGT Robert Janes
SPC Wendell Janke
SSG (Ret) Edward J. Jankowiak
2LT Raymond A. Jankowski
SPC Thomas S. Janowski
SPC Steven R. Jansen
PFC Donald E. Janssen
SGT Jason Janssen
LTC Linda Jantzen
WO1 Lyman Jantzen
CPL Walter Janus
SPC Frank S. Janusczak
CW2 (Ret) Kenneth E. Jaques
SPC Stephen V. Jarahian
PSG Raul A. Jaramillo
SSGT (Ret) Santiago R. Jaramillo
MR. John L. Jarboe
SP5 Joseph Craig Jarboe
SPC Grady Jared
SPC Arthur D. Jarman
1LT Harry H. Jarnagan
SP5 William J. Jarousky
SGT Michael T. Jarrard
MAJ David L. Jarratt
COL Richard S. Jarrett
SFC Scottie L. Jarrett
SFC (Ret) Jeffrey M. Jarriel
PFC Darin Jarvis
SSG John R. Jarvis
PVT Joseph W. Jarvis
SPC Stephen W. Jarvis
1SG (Ret) Robert Jarzynkowski
PFC Joshua Jasie
SPC Tom Jaskiewicz
MAJ Michael D. Jason
PFC Charisse Jasper
SSG Richard L. Jasper
1SG Scott Jasper
CPT Chris Jauch
LTC Thomas G. Jauquet
SPC Joe J. Jauregui
CPT Igor Javonov
COL (Ret) Joseph J. Jaworowski
SGT Larry E. Jay
SGT Robert L. Jay
SPC Gregory G. Jayne
COL (Ret) Robert K. Jayne
SP5 Thomas Jaynes
SGT Andrew Jeamise
1LT (Ret) Robert J. Jeanette
SGT Dan Jeannerat
SGT Darrell F. Jeanotte
MAJ Nick Jeffers
SFC Robert A. Jeffers
CPT Charles W. Jefferson
SSG Debre R. Jefferson
SFC Jimmie L. Jefferson
SPC Nicholas D. Jefferson
SGT Richard Thom Jefferson
SFC Rodney Jefferson
SPC RooseveLT Jefferson
CPT David L. Jeffery
CPL Charles W. Jeffrey
MSG Michael A. Jeffrey
CW2 Tillman L. Jeffrey
MRS. Alex S. Jekel
SGT James G. Jeleski
SPC Curley Jeli
SGT Al Jelten
SFC Howard L. Jemison
MRS. Robert Jemison
SGT Alan W. Jenest
PV2 Charles Jenkins
PV2 Clayton Jenkins
CW4 Clifton E. Jenkins
SSG Eddie J. Jenkins
COL Gregory R. Jenkins
1SG (Ret) Jerry L. Jenkins
LTC (Ret) John D. Jenkins
SPC John Q. Jenkins
PFC Joshua R. Jenkins
LTC Leon C. Jenkins
SPC Matthew Lee Jenkins
SGT Matthew P. Jenkins
SPC Merrill W. Jenkins
1SG Michael S. Jenkins
LTC Plez A. Jenkins
SGT Preston A. Jenkins
SGT Richard P. Jenkins
SPC Thomas W. Jenkins
SPC Troy C. Jenkins
CPT William R. Jenkins
CW2 (Ret) Scott C. Jenkinson
SGT James A. Jenne
SGT James M. Jenner
SGT David A. Jennette
SPC Arthur Thurman Jennings
SFC Darren Jennings
MRS. Delbert O. Jennings
LTC Dwight C. Jennings
MAJ (Ret) George W. Jennings
CPT Harley Jennings
CPL James P. Jennings
CPT Kevin N. Jennings
COL Richard M. Jennings
LTC (Ret) Robert H. Jennings
LTC Thomas J. Jennings
PFC Alan P. Jensen
SGT Arne Kenny Jensen
SGT Chad R. Jensen
SPC David F. Jensen
SGT David H. Jensen
SFC (Ret) David S. Jensen
SGT Donald G. Jensen
PVT James C. Jensen
SPC Jeffery R. Jensen
2LT Mark W. Jensen
SGT Marvin D. Jensen
SSG Mathew T. Jensen
SPC Michael V. Jensen
PFC Raymond E. Jentz
SGT Norman G. Jepson
SSG (Ret) Gary Oliver Jerald
MAJ Loren B. Jerlow
COL (Ret) Cecil L. Jernigan
LTC David S. Jernigan
SPC Jeffrey N. Jernigan
CW2 Jonathon G. Jervis
CPL Frank S. Jerz
SPC Thmothy D. Jesky
1LT Charles F. Jesse
LTC James L. Jester
LTC (Ret) James R. Jester
MRS. Cora Jeter
SPC Scott W. Jeter
CPT Arthur C. Jetter
SSG Don A. Jewell
CPT Gregory R. Jicha
1SG Alex R. Jimenez
SP5 Alfredo A. Jimenez
SGT Anthony Jimenez

SGT Joe Jimenez
SGT Juan C. Jimenez
PFC Peter Jimenez
1LT Ramon Jimenez
SGT Richard R. Jimenez
SPC Robert Jimenez
SFC Steven P. Jimenez
SSG Jack L. Jines
CPL Ronald L. Jingles
SFC James Raymond Jinks
PFC George T. Job
MR. Dennis L. Jobe
CW2 Robert W. Jobe
MR. Robert J. Jock
MAJ Norbert B. Jocz
LTC (Ret) Richard A. Jodoin
SSG Faron V. Joe
SPC Timothy H. Joeckel
1LT Ivan Joens
2LT Andrew Johanson
SSG Bryan John
MSG Lee Edward John
LTC Eric Johnagin
CSM (Ret) Philip F. Johndrow
SSG Allen M. Johns
CPT Bradley N. Johns
CSM (Ret) William H. Johns
CPT Frederick J. Johnsen
SGT Jeff Johnsen
COL Nicholas R. Johnsen
SSG Aaron Johnson
SGT Aaron Johnson
SFC Aaron E. Johnson
SGT Albert A. Johnson
MR. Albin J. Johnson
SGT Aldrick Johnson
PFC Alexander E. Johnson
CPT Alicia J. Johnson
COL (Ret) Alvin B. Johnson
SSG Amos Johnson
SSG Anthony Johnson
SPC Benjamin Johnson
SSG Bertyl V. Johnson
SFC Billy R. Johnson
SGT Bobby Lane Johnson
SSG Bonnie M. Johnson
SGT Brandon Johnson
SPC Brian E. Johnson
SGT Bruce F. Johnson
MR. Byron E. Johnson
MR. Carl H. Johnson
LTC Carl H. Johnson
SGT Carl T. Johnson
SPC Charles Johnson
SPC Charles A. Johnson
1SG (Ret) Charles E. Johnson
MAJ (Ret) Charles F. Johnson
SSG Charles S. Johnson
CSM Charles V. Johnson
SFC (Ret) Charles W. Johnson
PFC Chester E. Johnson
MAJ Christian Johnson
CPT Christopher B. Johnson
SPC Clifford Johnson
SP3 Clyde Johnson
SGT Colon Johnson
CPT Cornelius Johnson
SFC Craig T. Johnson
SPC Dale Alan Johnson
SFC Danielche Johnson
LTC Darfus L. Johnson
SPC Darin P. Johnson
SPC Darrel G. Johnson
1LT David E. Johnson
MAJ David G. Johnson
PFC David L. Johnson
MSG David L. Johnson
SP5 Deane L. Johnson
SSG Dennis D. Johnson
SPC Dennis K. Johnson
SGT Derek R. Johnson
SPC Donald A. Johnson
PSG Donald D. Johnson
1LT Donald M. Johnson
SGT Donald R. Johnson
SSG Donielle Johnson
SFC (Ret) Doran A. Johnson
MR. Douglas L. Johnson
SGT Douglas L. Johnson
SP5 Douglas R. Johnson
SPC Douglas R. Johnson
LTC (Ret) Douglas V. Johnson
SGT Edward A. Johnson
SGM Edward G. Johnson
CSM (Ret) Edward L. Johnson
1LT Edward V. Johnson
CSM Edward W. Johnson
SPC Elias Johnson
SSG Elmer Johnson

SGT Elmer R. Johnson
CPT Eric B. Johnson
SSG Eric F. Johnson
MSG Eugene Johnson
MRS. Faye Johnson
SGT Forrest Johnson
SPC Fred W. Johnson
MAJ Fredrick E. Johnson
1LT Gary Glenn Johnson
SGT Gary L. Johnson
SPC Gary L. Johnson
SPC Geoffrey M. Johnson
SPC George Johnson
SPC (Ret) George Johnson
MAJ George C. Johnson
SSG George H. Johnson
SFC Gerry P. Johnson
MAJ Gregory L. Johnson
SPC Gregory W. Johnson
PFC Harry L. Johnson
SSG Harvey Johnson
SGT Henry A. Johnson
SGM Jack T. Johnson
SSG James Johnson
SP5 James A. Johnson
1LT James C. Johnson
SGT James H. Johnson
LTC (Ret) James K. Johnson
SPC James L. Johnson
SPC James L. Johnson
SPC James P. Johnson
SPC Jeremy Johnson
SGT Jerry L. Johnson
SGT Jill E. Johnson
SGT Jimmy D. Johnson
CPT John E. Johnson
SSG John H. Johnson
REV. John T. Johnson
CW3 Johnny W. Johnson
SGT Jon M. Johnson
PVT Jon P. Johnson
SPC Joseph R. Johnson
CPT Julius M. Johnson
SPC Kenneth D. Johnson
SFC (Ret) Kenneth D. Johnson
PFC Kenneth R. Johnson
PFC Kimberly Johnson
MSG Kimberlyn Johnson
SPC Kyle W. Johnson
SPC Larry E. Johnson
SPC Larry K. Johnson
SGT Larry P. Johnson
MSG Le Vetrice Johnson
SFC (Ret) Lloyd A. Johnson
PVT Lloyd C. Johnson
CW2 Martin Johnson
CPT Matthew Johnson
PFC Matthew C. Johnson
GS-13 Michael R. Johnson
SSG Mildred Johnson
SGT Milton Johnson
MRS. Minnie Johnson
MRS. Monte D. Johnson
SPC Otto Johnson
PV2 Patrick Johnson
2LT Peter E. Johnson
SGM Philip J. Johnson
SPC Phillip E. Johnson
PVT Ralph C. Johnson
SPC Ralph W. Johnson
SFC Randall L. Johnson
PFC Randy V. Johnson
PFC Raymond H. Johnson
1LT Richard E. Johnson
SGT Richard E. Johnson
SGT Richard Earl Johnson
SPC Richard L. Johnson
SGT Richard M. Johnson
SPC Robert A. Johnson
CW4 Robert B. Johnson
MR. Robert E. Johnson
PVT Robert L. Johnson
SPC Robert L. B. Johnson
SP5 Rodney W. Johnson
SPC Roger D. Johnson
SPC Roger L. Johnson
SFC Russell E. Johnson
SPC Ryan A. Johnson
SPC Salvador Johnson
CPL Samuel G. Johnson
SGT Shannon L. Johnson
CPL Steven D. Johnson
SGT Steven M. Johnson
CPT Sylvester C. Johnson
MR. Taylor D. Johnson
PFC Theodore Johnson
CW2 Thomas E. Johnson
SGT Thomas E. Johnson
SGT Thomas J. Johnson

SGT Thomas L. Johnson
SGT Thomas L. Johnson
CW4 Thomas M. Johnson
SPC Thomas M. Johnson
1SG Timothy S. Johnson
CW2 Tom A. Johnson
COL Tone Johnson
SSG Urcel L. Johnson
MR. Vernon E. Johnson
COL (Ret) Walter A. Johnson
SPC Walter L. Johnson
SSG Walter W. Johnson
LTC Wayman J. Johnson
SPC Wayne A. Johnson
SGT Wilbur H. Johnson
CPL William B. Johnson
SGT (Ret) William F. Johnson
SSG William J. Johnson
COL (Ret) William M. Johnson
SGT William N. Johnson
CW3 William R. Johnson
SSG Willie Lee Johnson
SFC (Ret) Woodrow Johnson
1LT Charles C. Johnston
CW4 David Johnston
SSG David M. Johnston
SPC Diane M. Johnston
SPC Douglas L. Johnston
CPL Edward B. Johnston
SGT Floyd D. Johnston
CPT Gerald S. Johnston
1SG Herbert Johnston
MAJ James H. Johnston
SPC James J. Johnston
CW4 (Ret) Jimmy B. Johnston
SPC Jody D. Johnston
MAJ Joel Johnston
SPC John Johnston
CPT Michael D. Johnston
CPL Micheal I. Johnston
MR. Myron T. Johnston
SPC Rex Johnston
MAJ Richard A. Johnston
1LT Robert J. Johnston
SPC Ronald D. Johnston
SPC Stephen Kent Johnston
CPL Thomas Johnston
BG (Ret) Homer Johnstone
SGT S. Wayne Joiner
SGT Larry D. Jokl
SPC William P. Jolin
1LT Bob L. Jolley
COL Alan F. Jones
SPC Alex Jones
1SG (Ret) Alonzo Jones
SGT Angelica Jones
SGT Archie B. Jones
MR. Arle Jones
SGT Arlena M. Jones
SGT Barney B. Jones
CSM Benjamin Jones
SPC Billy E. Jones
SSG Billy J. Jones
SPC Billy L. Jones
MSG Billy W. Jones
PFC Brian H. Jones
SPC Bruce M. Jones
SFC Burton E. Jones
PVT Carl L. Jones
SGT Charles E. Jones
SPC Charles Ernest Jones
SP5 Charles G. Jones
CPT Charles L. Jones
SFC (Ret) Clarence T. Jones
SP5 Claude L. Jones
SSG Clayton D. Jones
SGT Clinton F. Jones
SPC Clovis Jones
1SG (Ret) Clyde W. Jones
1SG Curtis Jones
SSG Danny Ray Jones
PFC David A. Jones
MR. David E. Jones
SFC (Ret) David E. Jones
CPT David P. Jones
SGT David W. Jones
SPC Dennis Jones
SGT Dennis H. Jones
PVT Donald L. Jones
SGT Donald R. Jones
LTG (Ret) Donald W. Jones
SPC Dorothy K. Jones
CPT Doug Jones
LTC (Ret) Douglas E. Jones
SGT Edward C. Jones
SGT Edward D. Jones
PV2 Elijah U. Jones
SPC Emmett D. Jones
SFC Eric C. Jones

MR. Ernest K. Jones
1LT Fred M. Jones
SGT Freddie Jones
CPT Freddie L. Jones
SFC Frederick A. Jones
MAJ Gerard H. Jones
SGT Gordon E. Jones
SFC Gregory C. Jones
SGT Gregory T. Jones
MSG (Ret) Harold D. Jones
SPC Harold G. Jones
MAJ Harry Jones
SP5 Henry C. Jones
SPC Herbert H. Jones
MRS. Hillery D. Jones
SPC Hosea James Jones
SP5 Howard D. Jones
COL Isaac R. Jones
CPL Jack R. Jones
SFC Jacqueline D. Jones
SFC James Jones
SPC James Jones
SFC James A. Jones
SGM James E. Jones
SPC Jamie B. Jones
[illegible]
PFC Jayden Jones
SSG Jereld C. Jones
PV2 Jerry E. Jones
MSG Jimmy D. Jones
COL (Ret) Joel D. Jones
1SG John A. Jones
SFC John P. Jones
1LT Jon M. Jones
PV2 Jonas Jones
CPT Jonathan Jones
SPC Jonathan P. Jones
COL Jordan T. Jones
SFC Joseph Jones
SSG Joseph D. Jones
SPC Justin T. Jones
SFC (Ret) Kenneth P. Jones
SFC Kennis Jones
SPC Larry J. Jones
SGT Larry L. Jones
CPT Latonya Jones
SGT Lindsay E. Jones
SGT MAJor Jones
SGT Mark Jones
SSG Marlin D. Jones
SPC Matthew L. Jones
MG (Ret) Michael D. Jones
PFC Michael H. Jones
MR. Mickey Jones
SFC Mike Jones
PVT Myria Jones
TSgt Olon O. Jones
CPT Omar J. Jones
LTC (Ret) Paul L. Jones
SGT (Ret) Paul R. Jones
MAJ Peter M. Jones
CPT R. T. Jones
MR. Ralph H. Jones
SFC (Ret) Ralph T. Jones
SGM Ray Jones
MAJ Raymond L. Jones
MAJ Richard Jones
SGM Richard Jones
CPT Richard F. Jones
SGT Richard H. Jones
SPC Richard Q. Jones
SGT Riley C. Jones
SGT Robert B. Jones
MRS. Robert E. Jones
CPL Robert M. Jones
CW2 (Ret) Robert M. Jones
SPC Robert R. Jones
SFC Ronald C. Jones
SGT Ronald L. Jones
CPT (Ret) Ronnie K. Jones
SGT Ronnie L. Jones
SGT Roy R. Jones
PFC Rudolph Jones
SGT Rudy Jones
SGT Sammy R. Jones
1LT Samuel P. Jones
SPC Scott F. Jones
LTC (Ret) Steve L. Jones
SFC Ted F. Jones
SSG Terence Jones
SGT Theodore Jones
SGT Thomas L. Jones
SSG (Ret) Tommie E. Jones
SGT Tommy W. Jones
CW2 Walker A. Jones
SGT Walter Jones
SGT Wayne L. Jones
SP5 Will M. Jones
LT William L. Jones

PFC William S. Jones
SGT Willie Jones
SPC Willie J. Jones
SPC Robert L. Jones Spencer
SSG Andre Jordan
SSG Charles Jordan
LTC (Ret) Charles Jordan
SGT Clayton D. Jordan
SSG Cullie Jordan
PV2 Curtis E. Jordan
SGT Danny G. Jordan
SPC Ebony Jordan
SGT Frank Jordan
PFC James N. Jordan
SFC James Wolf Jordan
SFC (Ret) Kenneth V. Jordan
PFC Leroy Jordan
SSG Leslie Jordan
SFC (Ret) Louis E. Jordan
WO1 Ramsey T. Jordan
CPL Randy W. Jordan
SGT Richard W. Jordan
MSG Richard W. Jordan
1LT Robert J. Jordan
CPL Royce L. Jordan
[illegible]
SFC (Ret) Ervin W. Jorgensen
SPC Gary L. Jorgensen
SSG Kregg P. J. Jorgenson
SPC Robert F. Jory
SFC (Ret) Juan Jose
SPC Alex Joseph
CSM (Ret) Annette Joseph
CSM Clinton L. Joseph
SFC Frank A. Joseph
CSM (Ret) Mark D. Joseph
SGM Rowan N. Joseph
CPT Tiara Joseph
CPT Donald E. Josephs
MRS. Annie V. Josey
LTC (Ret) Christopher A. Joslin
SPC (Ret) Charles C. Josselyn
SGT David Josselyn
SPC Gary M. Jostes
SSG James H. Journey
TSgt Eli Jovich
1LT Jason Jowers
SPC Robert K. Joy
TSgt Charles R. Joyce
SSG Corey Allen Joyce
SGT Festus Joyce
PV2 Michael J. Joyce
SGT Thomas R. Joyce
CPL Timothy J. Joyce
COL James N. Joyner
PVT Jeffrey S. Joyner
CPT Lambert S. Joyner
SPC Robert Joyner
COL (Ret) James T. Darrah Jr.
PFC Donnie W. Juan
PVT Guadalupe Juarez
SPC Jeremy Juarez
SSG Miguel Juarez
MAJ Miguel A. Juarez
SFC Rudy F. Juarez
SFC Norman F. Jubilee
MAJ Dexter K. Judd
MSG James H. Judd
CW3 Johnny W. Judd
COL David J. Judge
SFC Yamileth D. Judge
SSG Bruce W. Judkins
PFC Richard S. Judkins
SFC William K. Judy
SPC Lyle E. Juffs
SPC Albert L. Julian
SSG (Ret) Casey H. Julian
CPT Lanny Julian
COL (Ret) Robert A. Julian
PFC James A. Julien
CPL Christian M. Julius
SPC Codye A. Jumping Wolf
CW3 Keith Junas
SGT Roger F. Jundt
1LT Alexis Jung
CPT (Ret) Erwin O. Jung
2LT Matthew Jung
MAJ Richard G. Jung
1LT Teoyoung Jung
PFC Herbert L. Jungwirth
COL (Ret) Susan L. Junker
SP5 John D. Junkersfeld
BG (Ret) Arthur J. Junot
MAJ Michael A. Junot
MR. James L. Jupina
SPC Carl B. Juran
MAJ (Ret) Dale Jurgensen
SGT Joel Jusino
PV2 Darron D. Justice

CPL Edward E. Justice
SP5 Rich Justice
MRS. Robert E. Justice
SGT Ronald D. Justice
CW2 Ronald E. Justice
CPL James C. Justus
CW2 Peter Francis Jutras
MSG John F. Kaasch
PFC Steven R. Kaatz
PFC Michael Kachnoskie
SGT Stephen Kaczmarski
SGT David L. Kadell
SSG (Ret) Norman W. Kadunc
SPC William R. Kaempf
1LT Wayne L. Kaff
SSG Charles G. Kaffenberger
LTC (Ret) Herman G. Kafura
PFC Dennis C. Kahl
CW5 (Ret) Fritz E. Kahley
MSG (Ret) Charles C. Kaiser
SSG Darell W. Kaiser
SP5 Edward A. Kaiser
MAJ John J. Kaiser
SPC Matthew Kaiser
SPC Tim Kaiser
[illegible]
1LT Herbert H. Kajihara
SGT Howard Kalachman
SGT Harry J. Kalamon
SGT Edmund A. Kalaola
SSG Michael H. Kalata
CPT Tony Kalbli
SP3 Raymond G. Kalef
MAJ Alexander J. Kaleta
MR. Sam Kalfas
PFC Robert A. Kalich
1LT Michael J. Kalik
SPC Anthony D. Kalinowski
COL (Ret) William J. Kalinowski
COL (Ret) George Kalinski
2LT Donald W. Kalkman
SPC Robert W. Kallio
LTC (Ret) Aaron E. Kalloch
PFC Scott W. Kalman
SPC Myron Kalwinski
SP5 Joe Kamalick
SFC Charles Kaminski
PFC Francis H. Kaminski
SPC Wesley J. Kaminsky
SFC Rasool Kamma
SPC Scott P. Kammer
CPT Derek V. Kammerzell
CPL James S. Kamoto
SPC Douglas Kamphuis
CPL Anthony Kamps
SGT Steve Kanaly
CSM Robert M. Kanardy
SSG Gary L. Kanarr
SPC Thomas B. Kanawyer
PFC Charles H. Kane
2LT Christopher J. Kane
SSG Daniel R. Kane
SGM (Ret) Francis A. Kane
SPC Patrick M. Kane
PFC Ryan J. Kane
PVT Gilbert L. Kanesta
PFC Seung M. Kang
MR. Carl E. Kanipe
DR. Ferdinand Kann
SFC Brian Kanoa
CPT Edwin D. Kansler
SPC Dennis R. Kantner
SPC Robert F. Kapalo
SGT Ronald Kapaun
SPC Mark S. Kapinos
SP5 Edward D. Kaplan
TSgt Norman J. Kaplan
1LT Warren G. Kappenberg
CPL James J. Kapucinski
CW3 Thomas L. Kapugia
PV2 Mitchell F. Kaquatosh
SPC Andrew S. Karabinos
PFC Michael R. Karas
SGT Paul P. Karavas
SPC Wesley E. Karber
MR. Lawrence A. Karcher
COL (Ret) Timothy M. Karcher
CPL Eugene A. Karcz
SGT Gene M. Karenbauer
MRS. Edward V. Karl
SGT Michael Karlin
SPC Wayne G. Karlstad
2LT Andrew J. Karnes
CPL Tommie F. Karns
SGT (Ret) Charles Karotseris
SGT David R. Karp
CPT Jerry L. Karr
SGT Kermit D. Karr
LTC (Ret) Mike Karr

2LT Stephen Karr
CPL Egbert Kars
MRS. Arthur C. Karstens
SFC (Ret) Norbert J. Kartak
CPT John Kasel
SFC Howard Kaser
SPC Robert J. Kash
PFC Samuel Kash
SGT James Kasmer
SPC James T. Kasper
PFC Richard J. Kasprovic
SSG John Kasprzak
SGT Phillip D. Kastner
SP5 Robert A. Kastner
PV2 John R. Katchko
SGT John E. Katherman
PVT Steve Katkics
SGT Robert L. Kator
SPC Howard M. Katz
SGM Sidney M. Katz
PFC Irwin S. Katzman
SPC John Kaufenberg
CPL Jerry Kauffman
SSG Lisle J. Kauffman
SPC Alan J. Kaufman
SPC Daniel I. Kaufman
SFC David Kaufman
MRS. Evelyn Kaufman
CPT Gerald Kaufman
LTC Matt Kaufman
SSG Vance S. Kaup
PVT Cory Kaus
CW4 (Ret) Dan H. Kauth
MSG Kim G. Kavanaugh
CPL Roger L. Kavanaugh
SGT Robert G. Kaverman
SGT Adam Kawaguchi
SPC Mitchell Kawalec
SGT Jesse A. Kay
LTC (Ret) Richard A. Kaye
CW2 O. J.R. Kays
SGT (Ret) Robert C. Kazmierczak
SGT Larry Keaffaber
SGT Danny R. Kean
SPC Joshua M. Keane
COL (Ret) Patrick J. Keane
MS. Lucille L. Keanini
SGT Larry L. Kearney
SSG Philip J. Kearney
CPT Bill Kearns
LTC (Ret) John A. Kearns
SPC Marc S. Kearns
1LT Thomas J. Kearns
MAJ (Ret) Charles F. Keating
CPL Martin K. Keating
SGT Patrick J. Keating
PFC Theodore F. Keating
CSM (Ret) Garland E. Keaton
SGT Rowland E. Keaveney
SFC (Ret) James A. Keay
MR. C. Allan Keck
SFC Dennis Keck
MAJ Harold D. Keck
MR. James Keck
SP5 Richard Keck
PFC David M. Kedroske
CPT (Ret) James W. Keefe
SP5 John Keefe
LTC (Ret) John L. Keefe
MAJ Sandy Keefer
MR. Francis Keegan
SGT Tracie L. Keegan
CPT David L. Keel
PFC Zachary D. Keel
SPC Michael F. Keele
SGT Michael Keeler
SGT Thomas B. Keeley
SGT Charles J. Keeling
SPC Billy C. Keen
SGT Michael R. Keen
CPL Michael C. Keena
SSG Dennis E. Keene
MSG Jeremy T. Keene
SGT Lloyd D. Keene
SSG Michael S. Keene
CPL Robert J. Keene
SGT Robert A. Keener
SSG Don A. Keeney
SGT Harold Fred Keepes
SPC Mark A. Kees
MAJ Christopher Keeshan
1SG (Ret) Donald R. Keesler
1SG Timothy D. Keesling
CPL Howell Keeter
PFC Charlie Thaxton Keeton
CPT Douglas W. Keeton
SPC Joe W. Keeton
SSG Richard W. Keeton
1SG (Ret) Thomas H. Keeton
SGT Joseph R. Keezer
CPT Clarence W. Kehoe
SPC Edward A. Kehoe
SPC Thomas F. Kehres
MAJ (Ret) Roger L. Kehrier
SPC August M. Keifer
MRS. Bill Keijzer
LTC (Ret) Paul T. Keil
SFC George F. Keillor
SPC (Ret) Manfred Keim
LTC (Ret) Herbert L. Keister
MS. Bobbie Keith
SGM (Ret) James David Keith
SGT John P. Keith
SGM (Ret) Peter L. Keith
SPC Robert E. Keith
CW5 Dennis H. K. Kekona
MRS. Dorothy S. Kelbus
CSM Daniel D. Kelch
SSG Jerome Keliihoomalu
SPC Christopher Kell
SFC Marvin L. Kellam
2LT Robert L. Kellam
SPC Robert R. Kellams
COL Robert S. Kellar
CW4 (Ret) William C. Kellaway
SSG Patrick H. Kelleher
SFC Charles C. Keller
CSM Donald G. Keller
CW3 (Ret) John L. Keller
MAJ Joseph E. Keller
SGT Mark E. Keller
SPC Paul Edward Keller
PVT Roy W. Keller
SGT Stephen E. Keller
PFC Stephen H. Keller
SP5 William N. Keller
PFC William T. Keller
SGT Steven E. Kellerhals
PFC Ronald W. Kellerman
PFC Charles W. Kelley
SSG David Kelley
LTC David J. Kelley
SPC David K. Kelley
SSG Elmer F. Kelley
SSG Eugene F. Kelley
1SG Fillmore Kelley
SPC James Kelley
PFC James Kelley
SSG James W. Kelley
MAJ John W. Kelley
1SG (Ret) Loyd W. Kelley
SPC Marion Kelley
SP5 Michael A. Kelley
SP5 Michael L. Kelley
SFC Nathan R. Kelley
SGT Peter G. Kelley
SSG Ronald D. Kelley
CSM (Ret) Ronnie R. Kelley
SPC Scott Kelley
SGT Shane Kelley
SGT Thomas J. Kelley
PVT Timothy J. Kelley
MR. Lester R. Kelliher
LTC (Ret) George H. Kelling
SFC James E. Kelling
MAJ David M. Kelln
SPC Juan P. Kellogg
SPC Andrew Kelly
MAJ Andrew J. Kelly
MAJ Clarence S. Kelly
SFC (Ret) Daniel J. Kelly
SGM David E. Kelly
PFC Dennis F. Kelly
SGT Dennis W. Kelly
COL (Ret) Edward J. Kelly
1SG (Ret) Edward M. Kelly
SGM Euguene Kelly
SPC George N. Kelly
SFC Gwin Kelly
SGT John E. Kelly
SPC Joseph F. Kelly
CW4 (Ret) Lawrence D. Kelly
SFC (Ret) Malcolm W. Kelly
SPC Nathalie Kelly
MAJ Patrick Kelly
SGT Paul N. Kelly
CW2 Robert W. Kelly
SPC Stephen Kelly
SPC Thomas P. Kelly
1LT Timothy D. Kelly
1SG (Ret) William W. Kelly
SFC Willie B. Kelly
SPC Robert B. Kelman
SGT Gregory M. Kelsch
PFC John F. Kelsch
MAJ (Ret) Thomas C. Kelso
SPC Vernon Kelson
PFC Harry W. Kemble
SPC Keith H. Kemmer
SPC Marion Lloyd Kemmerlin
PFC Gus Kemmerling
1LT Eric Michael Kemner
LTC Albert L. Kemp
SFC James C. Kemp
SPC James R. Kemp
PVT Lloyd C. Kemp
SP5 William B. Kemp
1SG (Ret) Paul R. Kemper
SGT Gordon B. Kempkers
PFC Austin M. Kemple
SGT Bill O. Kemppainen
PVT Curtis D. Kempton
SSG Latesha M. Kenan
MR. Daniel W. Kendal
SPC Bernard C. Kendall
SP5 William D. Kendall
CPT U. R. "Al" Kendree
SGT Elvin Kendrick
CSM (Ret) Garry O. Kendrick
MAJ Scott T. Kendrick
SGT Ron L. Kenerson
SPC Thomas R. Kenna
TSgt Arthur R. Kennedy
SPC Bayard F. Kennedy
PFC Bob Kennedy
MR. Charles W. Kennedy
SFC Clinton Kennedy
LTC (Ret) David R. Kennedy
1SG (Ret) Dennis E. Kennedy
SPC Dwayne T. Kennedy
LTC Ed Kennedy
LTC (Ret) Edmund J. Kennedy
SP5 George M. Kennedy
MR. Glenn A. Kennedy
SGT Janet E. G. Kennedy
PFC Jerry A. Kennedy
CPL Jesse C. Kennedy
2LT Joshua Kennedy
MAJ Kerry M. Kennedy
MAJ Kevin E. Kennedy
SGT Michael Douglas Kennedy
SPC Richard D. Kennedy
MRS. Robert F. Kennedy
SPC Samantha Kennedy
SSG Steven D. Kennedy
SPC Tommie L. Kennedy
SSG William J. Kennedy
CPT Harry C. Kennemer
MSG Charles M. Kennemore
SGT Lawrence L. Kenney
LTC (Ret) Edward R. Kennington
LTC (Ret) Robert L. Kennison
MAJ Raymond C. Kenny
SGT Billy W. Kent
SGT Edward C. Kent
SSG (Ret) Henry L. Kent
LTC (Ret) James E. Kent
MAJ John C. Kent
DR. Lawrence Kent
PFC Permelia Kent
SPC Richard E. Kent
COL (Ret) Richard S. Kent
SSG Robert W. Kent
1LT Stanley C. Kent
PVT Robert H. Kenworthy
SSG James R. Keown
SSG James M. Kephart
SGT Samuel Reid Kepler
SGT Gregory Kepner
SGT James E. Keppel
PVT Kenneth J. Keppel
1LT John K. Keppler
LTC Alberto Kercado
LTC (Ret) Lester R. Kerfoot
SGT Charles H. Kerkhove
PFC Anthony M. Kern
1SG (Ret) Larry D. Kern
CPT Patrick M. Kern
PVT Charles E. Kernan
SFC (Ret) Thomas A. Kernan
SGT Steven P. Kernek
2LT Elijah Kern-Ruesink
SPC Dale B. Kerns
MR. Paul B. Kerns
TSgt James A. Kerr
SPC John W. Kerr
PFC Richard B. Kerr
2LT Spencer Kerr
PFC John M. Kerrick
1LT James F. Kerschner
SP5 David Kersey
SFC Mark W. Kersh
SSG Bryan Kershaw
PFC Oland J. Kershaw
1LT Kenneth Eugene Kershner
SGT David A. Kesler
SGT Richard L. Kesler
SPC Barry Kessler
SPC Tom Kessler
2LT Justin Todd Kesterson
SGT Ernie Ketchum
SGT Jerry R. Ketchum
SGT James L. Ketrow
1LT Tommy Ketterer
SPC Lloyd M. Kettle
SGT Thomas E. Kettles
CW3 Fredrick W. Ketz
SP5 Howard J. Ketzner
1LT Robert L. Kevan
SGT Charles Kevern
SP5 Edward E. Kexel
SGT Howard A. Key
SPC Michael A. Key
PFC Robert L. Key
SPC Toby Shane Key
MRS. Elizabeth D. Keyes
PFC John Keymel
SSG Daniel Keys
SSG James E. Keys
SSG John R. Keys
CSM David R. Keyser
SPC Kartar Khalsa
SGM (Ret) Henry A. Khan
SPC Brian James Kibbe
SGT David D. Kibbe
SGT George E. Kibler
SFC Donald C. Kichline
PFC Joshua F. Kichta
SPC Joseph S. Kicklighter
SPC Gary R. Kidd
SSG Robert J. Kidd
CW4 (Ret) Benjamin R. Kidder
MR. Wilbur L. Kidder
SPC Michael Kidwiler
SPC Michael G. Kiefer
MSG (Ret) Ralph G. Kiefer
PVT Irving L. Kiehn
MAJ Michael W. Kielpinski
MR. David W. Kierstead
SFC (Ret) Alford G. Kies
COL (Ret) Robert H. Kies
SPC John D. Kieslar
SGT Gerald R. Kietzman
SPC William E. Kiger
2LT Chad Kijewski
CPT Richard Kijowski
PFC Jon Kilburn
SFC Dallas Kilby
SSG Raymond J. Kildisas
LTC (Ret) Rodney E. Kilduff
PVT John A. Kiley
SPC Richard L. Kiley
1LT Brian Keith Kilgore
2LT Daniel K. Kilgore
SGT Edward S. Kilgore
SSG Michael D. Kilgore
SGM William B. Kilgore
SSG Christian R. Killam
SSG Donald F. Killam
LTC Sidney E. Killebrew
MAJ Haston T. Killgore
CW2 Fred Killian
CW3 (Ret) Ronnie L. Killingsworth
SGT Thomas Killingsworth
SSG James Killough
SFC Gary Kilmer
DR. (SPC) Alan T. Kilpatrick
SPC George Michael Kilpatrick
LT Chong H. Kim
SFC Douglas K. Kim
CPT Hyeon-Joong Kim
SFC Kap Kim
LT Steve Y. Kim
SFC Yong K. Kim
LTC (Ret) Alan M. Kimball
CPT Alvion R. Kimball
CPT John W. Kimball
CPT Mark D. Kimball
SGT Ronald L. Kimball
SGM (Ret) Troy F. Kimbell
CPL James E. Kimberlin
PFC Mark E. Kimberlin
CMSgt (Ret) Warren C. Kimberlin
CPL Delmar D. Kimbro
PFC Donald R. Kimbrough
SPC Karl S. Kimbrough
CW4 (Ret) Gerald D. Kimel
MAJ Robert Kimmel
SGT Nelson W. Kimmey
1LT Eunyi Kim-Murphy
SPC William P. Kimrey
MSG Jay Kimsey
CPT Kevin A. Kimzey
CPT Curtiss L. Kinard
SP5 Earl D. Kinard
SPC Jared M. Kinard
SGT Charles E. Kincaid
CPL Fred M. Kincaid
CPT (Ret) Phillip A. Kincy
LTC Scott Kindberg
MAJ (Ret) James E. Kindel
CW3 (Ret) Brady L. Kinder
PSG (Ret) Robert E. Kinder
SP3 Robert T. Kinder
SSG Jackie P. Kindle
SGT Lester Kines
SGT Wade K. Kines
SP5 Charles F. King
LTC Charles H. King
PVT Christopher A. King
CPL Daniel J. King
CSM Dennis James King
SPC Don King
SSG Donnie King
CPL Earl D. King
SSG Eugene King
CPL Fletcher G. King
SGM Gene A. King
CPL George King
SGT Herbert D. King
SSG Ivet R. King
MAJ James King
SPC (Ret) James B. King
1LT James C. King
SFC (Ret) John G. King
SSG John M. King
MG (Ret) John Q. T. King
2LT Jordan King
SPC Kenneth C. King
1SG Les D. King
SGT Mark P. King
SSG Michael King
SGT Michael R. King
SFC Morris E. King
SGT Nicolas King
MSG (Ret) Patrick J. King
CPL Pete H. King
SFC Reginald E. King
SFC (Ret) Richard Franklin King
PFC Robert E. King
MSG (Ret) Robert P. King
SGT Roger C. King
SPC Roy W. King
PV2 Roy W. King
1LT Stetson King
SSG (Ret) Vance D. King
CPT Will King
CPT William King
CPL William E. King
1SG (Ret) William H. King
CPL William J. King
CW2 William K. Kingdollar
COL (Ret) Arthur J. Kingdom
2LT Anna King-Mc Crillis
SGT Philip R. Kingsbury
SFC George W. Kingston
MS. Julie Kink
SGT Gary R. Kinkade
LTC Matthew Kinkead
SSG Kyle Kinkel
MR. Robert L. Kinkoff
MAJ Eddie Kinley
SGT William C. Kinnaman
SGT Allan N. Kinney
1LT Gregory D. Kinney
CPL Michael L. Kinney
SP5 Robert L. Kinney
MR. Rodney K. Kinney
CPT Charles R. Kinnie
SPC James R. Kinsey
SGT Walter Kinsey
SGT Arthur F. Kinsley
CPT Milton Kinslow
SGT Larry J. Kintz
SPC Michael M. Kinyanjui
SGT Steve D. Kinzer
MAJ Russell Kinzie
SPC John F. Kinzinger
SPC Richard E. Kipker
SFC (Ret) John A. Kipp
SFC Kenneth R. Kipple
SSG Bill Kirby
COL Charles G. Kirby
SGT Jaudon Kirby
COL John D. Kirby
SPC Kenneth E. Kirby
CPL Kevin L. Kirby
PFC Michael Kirby
SSG Randy Kirby
SGT Richard B. Kirby
MSG Robert M. Kirby
SFC Russell W. Kirby
SPC Michael Kirchgessner
CPL Richard Kirchoff
SGT David M. Kirk
SP5 Jerry Kirk
PV2 Kelsey Kirk
SFC Jeremiah Kirkland
SP5 Charlie W. Kirkley
SSG Edward V. Kirkley
BG Ronald Kirklin
CPT Charles D. Kirkpatrick
MAJ Michael R. Kirkpatrick
CDR Gregory S. Kirkwood
CSM (Ret) Joe J. Kirven
SGT Timothy J. Kirwan
CW3 Joseph A. Kisa
SGT Gerald L. Kisabeth
CW4 Andrew J. Kisela
CPL Dwayne F. Kiser
CPT Mike Kiser
PFC Reuben E. Kiser
SPC Robert S. Kish
CPT Richard Kishur
SGT Andrew F. Kisik
SGT Joseph J. Kisko
MSG Richard G. Kisling
COL John S. Kistler
1SG William D. Kitchens
PVT Lyle H. Kittleson
CW4 Hadley F. Kittredge
CPT David M. Kitzman
SGT Norman F. Kivette
COL (Ret) John Kizirian
CPT Thomas W. Kjos
1SG Mark Klaas
SGT William K. Klaiber
CPL Larry F. Klang
SGT Jerry D. Klatt
1LT James R. Klaus
PFC Roger R. Klaus
PFC Frank M. Klauser
SGM (Ret) S. J. Klava
MR. Ralph A. Kleekamp
CPL Alfred A. Klein
LTC (Ret) Dale E. Klein
2LT Gary J. Klein
LT Gary M. Klein
SPC James T. Klein
SSG James W. Klein
SGT Jerold A. Klein
SPC Kenneth J. Klein
SSG Kimberly J. Klein
SPC Mark A. Klein
MRS. Ruth H. Klein
CW2 Samuel R. Klein
SGT William S. Klein
SPC David A. Kleindorfer
SGT Richard Kleinheksel
SGT James D. Kleinhenz
CPL Dennis G. Kleitz
CPL Henry Klemm
SPC Lorin G. Klemm
LTC Keith A. Klemmer
SPC Jon C. Kleppe
SFC Carl G. Klepper
PFC Orville R. Klepper
COL Duane A. Kleven
LTC Thomas W. Klewin
SGT David J. Klimek
MR. Emil C. Klimek
SGT Richard H. Klimkiewicz
1SG (Ret) Charles H. Kline
SPC David A. Kline
SSG Donald H. Kline
SPC Larrie C. Kline
SGT Thomas R. Kline
1SG (Ret) Timothy F. Kline
SPC Jerald D. Klinetobe
MSG Cynthia Kling
SPC Garry E. Kling
SPC Terry L. Kling
CPL (Ret) William J. Klingenberg
CPL Kent A. Klinger
SFC Robert D. Klinger
CPT Michael E. Klingler
PFC Kenneth F. Klinkert
SPC Terrence J. Klise
SPC Vernon H. Klock
CPT Stephen J. Klocko
COL (Ret) Ronald G. Kloet
COL (Ret) John C. Kloke
SPC Richard Klopp
SGT John L. Klotz
SPC Robert C. Klug
CPL Theodore G. Klug
PVT Joseph Klukaczynski
CPL Arthur Klunk
SPC David J. Klym

SSG Chuck Knabusch
SPC James C. Knafel
1LT Terrence D. Knafl
SGT Dennis Knapp
MAJ Gerold Ed Knapp
CPT Kevin E. Knapp
SFC Stanley L. Knapp
SPC Tom Knapp
SFC (Ret) William K. Knarr
SGT Ken Knecht
SSG Charles Kneeland
SFC Eric A. Kneffler
2LT Jason Kneib
SGT Joseph Knell
SPC Stacey L. Kness
SPC Steven Kniffin
CPT Arthur Knight
PFC Bryan Knight
CW3 Buford W. Knight
SFC Charles R. Knight
SPC David Knight
PV2 Emerson T. Knight
SGT Erv Knight
MSG Eugene J. Knight
SSG Evan Knight
COL (Ret) Kenneth R. Knight
COL (Ret) Lee F. Knight
WO1 Leonard G. Knight
SPC Randell W. Knight
SGT Rickey J. Knight
1SG Robert D. Knight
SSG Robert K. Knight
SPC Roger A. Knight
SGT Thomas D. Knight
CPL Wylie Knight
1SG (Ret) William F. Knipe
SrA Robert R. Knipp
CH (CPT) Gregory Knippa
SPC David P. Knippel
MR. Robert B. Knisely
CSM James L. Knobel
MAJ Tommy L. Knobel
PFC John W. Knoblock
PFC Richard E. Knodel
CPT Kurt S. Knoedler
CPL Robert E. Knoerzer
LTC (Ret) Roger A. Knopf
TSgt Cornelius C. Knorr
SGT Robert C. Knott
MSG (Ret) Alan W. Knotts
SPC David D. Knouse
PFC Robert J. Knouse
LTC (Ret) Charles B. Knowlen
MAJ Foster E. Knowles
TSgt Melbourne E. Knowles
SP5 Patrick Sam Knowles
SPC Paul Knowles
LTC Robert G. Knowles
SPC Dallas Knowlton
CW5 Richard W. Knowlton
SGT Frank J. Knowski
SP5 Benny J. Knox
SPC Charlie A. Knox
LTC Dean W. Knox
SPC Dennis Knox
SGT Kenny D. Knox
SPC Ray C. Knox
SPC Taylor O. Knox
SFC Terry Knox
SPC David P. Knudsen
SPC Howard J. Knudson
MSG Karl Knudson
SPC Howard D. Knudtson
DR. Duane C. Knutson
SPC Greg Knutson
SP5 Kenneth A. Knutson
SP5 Richard A. Knutson
CPL William D. Koapke
CPL Paul Koban
SPC Jerry R. Kobbeman
PV2 Daniel J. Kobis
LTC David M. Kobs
SGT Clifford E. Koch
SSG (Ret) Jacob J. Koch
SP5 James C. Koch
SPC Jeffrey Koch
SP5 Joe Koch
1SG John A. Koch
MSG John S. Koch
SFC Kevin J. Koch
SFC Ralph A. Koch
MR. Roy Koch
PFC Sanford J. Koch
SPC Joseph Kochanski
LTC Robert W. Kocher
SGT Timothy Kochert
SP5 John L. Koedel
SP5 Keno W. Koehl
SGT Arthur J. Koehler
SPC Christopher Koehler
SP5 Glenn Koehler
SGT John A. Koehler
MAJ Kevin R. Koehler
SGT Marvin Koehler
MR. Thomas G. Koehly
SPC Benjamin R. Koehn
CW2 Richard C. Koehnen
CPT Bernard F. Koelsch
MSG Peter H. Koenen
SGT Daniel J. Koenig
SGT Henry J. Koenig
SSG Michael F. Koenig
SGM (Ret) William F. Koepp
PFC Frank R. Koerbacher
SGT Christopher S. Koerner
MSG Verdell C. Koerwiz
SGT Charles A. Koester
CPL Daniel J. Koffler
SFC John H. Koffski
PFC Edmunde Kofman
SGT Joseph Kogut
MR. Arnold G. Kohl
SPC Robert Gary Kohl
SFC Robert Kohlberg
CPL Raymond A. Kohler
CPT Walter J. Kohls
CPL Robert F. Kohn
1LT Sean M. Kohnke
CSM Roger W. Kohout
PSG Charles T. Koker
SGT David E. Kolb
SGM Donald L. Kolb
1SG Leland E. Bud Kolberg
SGT Joseph P. Kolceski
MSG (Ret) Orval W. Kolden
MAJ John Kolessar
PV2 Richard P. Kolinsky
PFC Harman F. Kolk
SGT Harold R. Kollars
MAJ James L. Kollenberg
SPC Robert R. Kolling
SPC Richard P. Kolodi
2LT Jerome F. Koltz
CW4 (Ret) Lee C. Komich
CPT Chris Komisarjevsky
SPC Alan Komperda
SGT Robert T. Kon
SSG Craig R. Koncal
SGT Andrew Kondracki
PFC Conrad A. Kondratowico
SPC Samuel Jason Konecny
SPC Robert C. Koneful
1LT Brian W. Kong
MRS. Charles A. Kongro
SPC Thomas L. Koniarz
MAJ Elias Koniditsiotis
SGT Mark A. Konietzko
BG (Ret) Thomas J. Konitzer
1LT Robert J. Konrardy
SPC Joseph W. Kontos
MAJ Joseph M. J. Kools
SGT Bennie F. Koon
SGT Glenn L. Koonce
MR. Gerald P. Koondel
CSM (Ret) Daniel L. Koonter
MRS. Donald L. Koontz
MR. Edwin Steve Koops
SPC Joseph J. Kopac
CPT Michael J. Kopacko
1LT Michael M. Kopaczewski
SPC Dennis M. Kopchinski
SP5 Gregory Kopec
LTC (Ret) Julius L. Kopec
CPT R. Joseph Kopec
1LT Richard J. Kopec
MS. Mary Lou Kopecky
MRS. Geoffrey Koper
SGT Anthony L. Kopf
SSG Donald M. Kopis
CW3 Richard J. Kopitskie
SGT James D. Kopkie
MR. Richard Kopytko
PFC Julius Korczynski
1LT Henry Tony Koren
COL (Ret) Rolland A. Koreski
1LT Jeffrey Kornbluth
CPT William C. Korner
PFC Julius Korry
SGT John P. Korsan
SP5 Reginald R. Kosarek
SFC Edward Kosbab
SPC William R. Koscher
SSG Joseph Koschman
SPC Gary Kosiba
SPC Timothy F. Kosinski
CPT Dustin Blu Kostelich
SFC John Kostoulas
SPC Joseph J. Kosyla
SPC Edward C. Kotch
1LT Robert Kotecki
PFC Vlade Koteff
SFC Robert C. Koths
SPC Stanley Kotkiewicz
SPC James C. Kotsonis
SPC Christopher A. Kotz
SPC John Kotzian
MAJ (Ret) Clinton M. Kounk
SGT Dean Kouvavas
SGT James C. Kovach
SPC (Ret) John C. Kovach
SFC Andrew Kovacsy
1SG (Ret) Joseph F. Kovalcik
CW3 Jason M. Kovatchitch
SPC Alois M. Kowalczyk
SSG Christopher Kowalczyk
SFC Christopher Kowalewski
SPC (Ret) Frank J. Kowalewski
CPL Fred J. Kowalka
PFC Edward J. Kowalski
SPC Henry Kowalski
PVT Dennis A. Kowalzek
SGT Nelson Koyl
SP5 Chester P. Kozdra
SGT Michael A. Kozemczak
SSG Jason Kozeniesky
SPC Ron Kozima
CW2 Joseph Kozlowski
1LT Liam Kozma
SP5 John L. Kozyra
SFC Keith Kraatz
SPC Thomas E. Kraemer
MR. Brian J. Kraft
SPC Charles F. Kraft
SGM (Ret) J. Walter Kraft
SFC Reginald J. Kraft
SGT Stanley E. Kraft
SSG William D. Krahl
1SG Freddy W. Krail
SGT Alex J. Krajewski
SFC (Ret) Michael Krakowiak
CSM (Ret) Robert A. Kral
SP5 Clifford Kramer
SGT Earl D. Kramer
CPL Edward F. Kramer
SFC Gilbert L. Kramer
MR. John C. Kramer
CPL Leroy Kramer
SGT M. James Kramer
CW2 Michael J. Kramer
SP5 Philip H. Kramer
SSG (Ret) Robert E. Kramer
PFC Ronald F. Kramerich
SPC Paul W. Kramlich
CPT Donald K. Kramlinger
SGT John F. Kranyak
SPC Larry Kranz
SPC Robert L. Krasean
SPC William F. Krasovec
SFC (Ret) Eugene L. Krattli
MR. Jerald W. Kratz
SFC Sean M. Kratz
LTC (Ret) Guy N. Kratzer
SGT Crystal A. Kraus
SP5 Daniel E. Kraus
SP5 Larry D. Kraus
SGT Paul J. Kraus
SPC Rich Kraus
TSgt Frank M. Krause
SPC Richard Krause
SPC Robert J. Krause
SPC Sean Krause
PFC John W. Krawczyk
LT Michael Alexander Krayer
SGT William J. Krean
SP5 Robert M. Krebs
MS. Mary Krebs Devine
CPT John W. Kredo
SPC Simon P. Kregar
SPC Ramon Kreher
PFC Carl D. Kreider
COL (Ret) Raymond F. Kreiner
SPC Thomas J. Kremer
SGT Richard Krenzer
1LT Larry R. Kreps
COL (Ret) Milton Kresse
SGM (Ret) Samuel H. Kretzer
CPT Timothy R. Kreuttner
SPC Warren Kreutziger
PFC George F. Krieger
PFC Joseph O. Kriemelmeyer
SFC (Ret) John N. Krier
SFC Robert Krikava
SSG John E. Krise
SGT James E. Kristof
PFC Richard W. Kritlow
CPL John P. Kritzer
SGT (Ret) George Kritzman
CPL William F. Krobath
SPC (Ret) Henry A. Kroeger
SPC William H. Kroeplin
1LT John L. Kroesser
MR. Ted A. Krogen
MR. Jeffrey Kroger
SPC Louis Kroh
SGT Kenton M. Krohlow
LTC (Ret) Charles A. Krohn
MR. David Krohn
1LT Chester A. Krokoski
SPC Philip Krolczyk
2LT Timothy J. Kroll
SPC John R. Kromer
PVT Jason A. Kroncke
SPC Jon C. Kronenberg
SPC Robert Kronenberg
MRS. John F. Kronenberger
SGT Donald J. Kroohs
CSM Bryan D. Kroontje
SGT Robert Krowech
SPC Samantha L. Kruczynski
SSG David Richard Krueger
SGT Dennis S. Krueger
SP5 Gary A. Krueger
SPC John A. Kruetzkamp
SGT Thomas W. Kruger
SSG Arthur Kruithof
CW2 James A. Krull
PFC John R. Krull
PFC Peter D. Krumbhaar
SPC Daniel J. Krupa
SPC Gerald J. Krupa
SPC Alvin L. Krus
SGT Michael P. Kruse
CPT Robert L. Kruse
SPC Ralph F. Krusey
CPL Richard T. Kruske
LTC Mark A. Krzeczowski
SFC Ervin W. Krzewinski
SSG Edmund C. Krzywicki
SSG Alfred R. Krzywosinski
SGT Dennis Kubicki
SPC Gerald H. Kubik
CPT Louis J. Kubus
MRS. Eugene A. Kuca
CPT John M. Kucharo
SPC Robert E. Kuchenbaker
SPC Dennis L. Kuchenmeister
SGT Joseph B. Kucza
SGT Kent Kuddes
CPL Francis L. Kudla
1SG Terrence T. Kudravy
SP5 John Kudyk
MR. Darryl Kuecker
SGT Dennis C. Kuecker
MR. Forrest Kuecker
1LT John C. Kuehl
SPC Samuel A. Kuehn
SFC (Ret) George A. Kuehne
PFC Timothy Kuensting
MAJ Kevin Kugel
SP5 Stanley Z. Kugler
SPC Urban V. Kuhl
SPC Robert P. Kuhlberg
SGT William A. Kuhlin
PFC Douglas Kuhlman
SGT Richard Kuhlmen
SPC Danny L. Kuhn
SPC Donald J. Kuhn
1LT James J. Kuhn
1LT Jim Kuhn
SGM Joseph F. Kuhn
SGT Lester J. Kuhn
SGT Ronald R. Kuhn
1LT Scott M. Kuhn
SFC (Ret) Steve E. Kuhn
1LT William Robert Kuhn
SSG William H. Kuhnke
SGM (Ret) David W. Kuhns
CPT Ronald D. Kuhns
1SG (Ret) William W. Kuhns
LTC Gregory S. Kuhr
SPC Richard Kuhr
SGT George G. Kuiper
CPT Richard L. Kuiper
1SG (Ret) Stan (Ike) Kujawski
SGT Scott Allen Kukas
SP5 Barnett V. Kukta
SGT Paul Kukuk
SFC Joseph Kulig
SGT Mark A. Kulikowski
SGT Robert A. Kulin
SFC (Ret) August G. Kulms
SFC (Ret) Francisco M. Kumangai
PFC Jack Kume
SPC Joseph S. Kumpel
CPL Joseph M. Kunder
CPL Jerome A. Kunicki
CW2 Robert Kunicki
SFC Wade M. Kuniyoshi
2LT Kaname Kuniyuki
PFC Barney R. Kunkel
SPC Robert E. Kunkel
SSG Jerry R. Kunkle
CPT Yukio A. Kunmuki
PFC Daniel R. Kuntz
PFC John M. Kuntzman
SP5 Michael W. Kuopus
SGT Kyle J. Kurk
1LT Amberle Kurkowski
SGT Norbert Kurle
SGT Nick J. Kurns
CPL John Kurtenbach
SGT Hazen R. Kurth
SGT Bernard Rusty Kurtz
COL (Ret) James H. Kurtz
COL (Ret) Richard G. Kurtz
SGT Pawel Kuryj
SPC James A. Kuschel
MRS. Susan L. Kuschmirz
1SG (Ret) Zan A. Kushmaul
COL Floyd Hal Kushner
SGT Stanley L. Kusmierczyk
SGT Donald T. Kusz
SSG Robert J. Kuta
LTC Robert B. Kuth
SSG (Ret) Lloyd P. Kuykendall
SGT Richard D. Kuykendall
SGT William G. Kuykendall
LTC (Ret) Thomas O. Kuypers
CPL David H. Kvarnes
MAJ Allen R. Kyle
SPC Richard Keith Kyle
PFC William H. Kyle
MR. Hung La
SGT Bruce A. La Barr
MR. Francis La Belle
SP5 Lloyd K. La Bombard
CPT Angelica La Boone
1SG (Ret) Harold J. La Borde
MAJ Matt La Chance
SSG Sheridan G. La Chapelle
SSG John W. La Chase
MR. Pete L. La Combe
SGM Terry A. La Croix
CW2 John J. La Due
SGT James B. La Farlette
PV2 Keith M. La Fauci
SFC Richard W. La Flamme
PFC Charles D. La Fleur
SrA Richard La Fleur
SPC Earl M. La Follette
MRS. Jerry A. La Follette
SPC Herman A. La Force
SGT Dennis L. La Forest
SPC Gerald P. La Fountain
1SG Les La Fountain
CW2 Richard H. La Freniere
SPC Guy La Gioia
MRS. Rosa La Grand
SPC Aaron L. La Grange
SFC (Ret) William J. La Guardia
MAJ William G. La Mai
SPC Justin Matthew La Marine
1SG Chris La Noue
PFC Milton F. La Pine
SPC David L. La Plante
SPC Joseph La Point
SGT Robert C. La Porta
SPC Daniel P. La Porte
SGT James Russell La Porte
SP5 (Ret) Joseph J. La Porte
GEN (Ret) Leon J. La Porte
COL Ryan J. La Porte
CPL John D. La Prairie
SGT Donald E. La Reau
1SG Bernard J. La Roche
SGT Stephen E. La Roche
CPL Kenneth J. La Rue
SPC Walter H. La Rue
MR. Arthur J. La Selle
LTC William G. La Sorsa
SSG Barry A. La Vigne
PVT Robert L. La Vine
SGT Joseph K. Laa
MSG Henry Laarman
PFC Robert L. Labak
LTC Pierre D. Labat
SGT Thomas W. Laberge
MRS. John J. Labin
SGM Miguel A. Laboy
SGT Leon W. Labrador
PFC David C. Labrelque
MRS. Richard S. Lacey
MAJ Robert J. Lacey
COL William J. Lacey
SSG Joseph E. Lacheney
MR. Mario Lachica
SGT Klaus W. Lachmann
CW2 Gary Lackey
COL Jimmie R. Lackey
SGT Michael J. Lacombe
SFC John E. Laconico
MR. Jean Lacoste
SGT Gerald Lacrosse
CPL Patrick S. Lacy
SFC Stephony C. Lacy
CW2 Willie Lacy
COL (Ret) Eddie B. Ladd
SGT Jessie B. Ladd
SGM Peter J. Ladd
PVT William J. Ladd
SPC Theron P. Ladner
SFC (Ret) Wilfred J. Ladoux
MAJ (Ret) Sidney L. Ladow
2LT Austin Laetsch
SFC Pierre Lafaille
SGT William J. Laferriere
1SG (Ret) Francis T. Lafferty
SGT Michael J. Lafferty
SGM (Ret) William P. Lafferty
SP5 Thomas N. Laffey
SSG Kenneth A. Lafnear
SFC Carolynette Lagana
2LT Brian J. Lagarde
SFC Eddie Thomas Lagarez
LTC Jason J. Lageman
SPC Richard F. Lagoe
CPL Anthony Lagotta
SFC Rafael Laguerre-Rosa
MAJ Jose R. Laguna
CPT John W. Lahey
CPT Dennis W. Lahmann
1LT Walter E. Laich
MSG Joe D. Lail
SSG Ricky J. Lail
SPC Russell B. Laine
PFC Don C. Laing
MAJ James D. Laird
CW4 Kevin R. Laird
SGT Larry Gene Laird
SGT Thomas C. Laird
MRS. Maxine M. Lajko
MR. William J. Lakatos
SGT Brian C. Lake
SP5 James F. Lake
SGT Joseph F. Lake
SGT John S. Lakes
SGT Melvin E. Lakin
SGM (Ret) Roland D. Laliberte
PFC Ray A. Lally
SGT Anthony F. Lama
SPC Roger D. Lama
SSG Earnest Lamay
SP5 Don M. Lamb
PFC John Lamb
PV2 Myron B. Lamb
1LT Richard Lamb
CPT Richard A. Lamb
SGT Robert S. Lamb
SPC Shane D. Lamb
MAJ Steven F. Lamb
SGT Ted A. Lamb
MRS. Billie G. Lambden
SGT Robert E. Lamberson
SPC Albert T. Lambert
WO1 Allen D. Lambert
SSG Chaitanya M. Lambert
SSG Charles E. Lambert
2LT De Veilla Lambert
CPT Garrett R. Lambert
SSG Gary Lambert
SFC Harold A. Lambert
SSG Jeffrey T. Lambert
PFC Justin Lambert
SP5 Larry D. Lambert
SPC Larry E. Lambert
SPC Nicholas Lambert
CSM (Ret) Robert B. Lambert
MSG (Ret) Robert W. Lambert
SPC Tommy E. Lambert
1SG William Lambert
PSG William E. Lambert
SPC David J. Lamberti
SSG Harold F. Lambright
SPC Frank B. Lambson
2LT Owen P. Lamerson
SSG David P. Lamica
SPC David A. Lammert
PFC Joshua Lammert
PFC Norman J. Lamontagne
SPC Leon C. Lamp
SPC Thomas J. Lampa
SGT Donald R. Lampe
SP5 Robert Lampert

CPT Chad Lamphere
MSG Michael W. Lampkin
MR. Lawrence H. Lampley
PVT Shawn A. Lampman
SGT Gerard Lampo
CPL Bill Lampson
SPC David Lamson
SPC Michael A. Lana
1SG (Ret) John R. Lancaster
SGT Shad D. Lancaster
SGT Cody G. Lance
SGT Michael J. Lanctot
SFC Barrie Land
1LT Beverly C. Land
LTC Eric A. Land
CPT (Ret) Henry W. Land
SGT Howard L. Land
SFC Roland R. Land
COL (Ret) Vincent J. Land
SGT Kenneth Ed Landers
PVT James R. Landis
SSG Jeffrey Landolfi
CPL Anthony J. Landoll
SFC Steven Landon
SFC Aljay Landrum
SGT Jim Landrum
SPC Brian N. Landry
MAJ Harry J. Landry
CPT Scott Landry
SPC John T. Landstad
CPL Robert W. Landucci
SPC Michael R. Landy
PVT Andre D. Lane
SGT Bruce Lane
LTC (Ret) C. Dennis Lane
SPC Charles F. Lane
SPC David Lane
SGT Gary L. Lane
MAJ James F. Lane
1SG James R. Lane
SSG Jerry P. Lane
SFC Joe Lane
CPT Kent Lane
LTC Pearce Rocky Lane
SGT Robert Lane
SFC (Ret) Robert E. Lane
SGT Thomas K. Lane
SGT Eugene Lang
CPT Jared A. Lang
MSG Laurence Lang
SPC Michael Lang
SGT Norbert D. Lang
SGT Thomas A. Lang
SPC William R. Lang
SPC Bruce W. Langbein
SGT Richard D. Langdon
CPT Christopher Lange
SGT Frederick H. Lange
SPC Wesley E. Lange
SFC Stephen Langelier
PFC Michael G. Langer
CPL Joseph T. Langevin
COL David Langfellow
COL (Ret) Ollie L. Langford
PFC James L. Langley
SGT Lester E. Langley
SGT Lucas Langley
SSG Sheila Renee Langsam
SPC Roger L. Langsdorf
SFC Warren G. Langston
SPC Robert J. Langton
SPC Charles W. Lanham
CSM (Ret) Joel E. Lanier
PV2 Daniel B. Lanigan
SGT Joseph C. Lankelis
SFC Martin D. Lankford
SPC Joseph F. Lanman
SGT James Lee Lann
CPT Wayne Lannin
MAJ Donald A. Lannom
PFC John M. Lanoha
SSG Adrian Lanspeary
SP5 J. D. Lantz
1LT Thomas R. Lantzy
LTC (Ret) Robert E. Lanzotti
LT Michael W. Lapaglia
SGT Joseph M. Lapatka
LTC (Ret) George S. Lapinskes
SFC Rhonddo J. Lapointe
SGT Rubin Laposky
CPL James J. Laprise
MR. Bernardo A. Lara
MAJ Felipe Lara
SGT Hector G. Lara
SFC (Ret) Marcus M. Lara
PFC Richard Lara
MR. Salvador Lara
SSG R. F. Laramee
SGT Joseph D. Laratta
MR. Wayne Laraway
MR. Benjamin Larca
SGT John E. Larensen
SPC George W. Large
CW2 Seth Large
SPC Timothy R. Large
1LT Roderick Larios
CPL Martin Larioz
PV2 Anthony Larkin
SGM Joe W. Larkin
LTC (Ret) Thomas B. Larkin
CPT Rose Larkins
CPT James H. Larose
SPC Bernard G. Larrauri
PFC Lawrence E. Larry
SPC Chuck Larsen
MSG (Ret) David J. Larsen
MR. Harry Larsen
SP5 Kim R. Larsen
SPC Michael Larsen
SPC William S. Larsen
SPC Brian C. Larson
SPC Charles A. Larson
SPC Darryl M. Larson
WO1 David J. Larson
MR. David R. Larson
SFC (Ret) Edward M. Larson
SPC Elgin W. Larson
SSG Gerald A. Larson
SGT Gerald C. Larson
CPL John E. Larson
CPT Keith A. Larson
SGT Larry M. Larson
SGT Marvin E. Larson
PSG (Ret) Richard A. Larson
CPL Richard D. Larson
SSG Robert A. Larson
SPC Robert J. Larson
SSG Robert J. Larson
CPL Theodore S. Larson
SPC Adam J. Lasater
CPL Roy C. Lasater
CPL Charles F. Laseman
PVT Richard J. Lash
PFC Robert J. Lash
CW4 (Ret) James T. Lashley
SP6 Warren Lashley
MRS. Harold Wesley Lasiter
SSG Richard D. Lask
SGT Tom J. Laska
CW3 Christopher J. Laskey
MRS. Ernest N. Lasley
PFC James J. Lasley
SPC Jose D. Lasmarias
SP5 James K. Lassell
COL Earle F. Lasseter
SSG Kenneth C. Lasseter
CPT Norman E. Lassiter
CSM Luther L. Laster
SP5 Michael J. Lastoria
CPT Wayne A. Lasuzzo
SGT Fred L. Latham
MG (Ret) Willard Latham
MAJ Harold D. Lathrem
1LT Donald L. Lathrop
SPC Martin Latigue
1SG (Ret) Jack R. Latimer
SGT Lancelot S. Latouche
MAJ Kenneth C. Latta
SGT Rees W. Lattimer
SGT Jack A. Lattrel
MR. Arne J. Latvala
CPL George Latza
PVT Clayton C. Lau
PFC Joshua L. Laub
MRS. Normand D. Laub
PFC Robert E. Laubscher
SP5 David P. Lauck
SFC John E. Lauck
2LT Ethan S. Lauer
SGT Ronald W. Lauer
MSG (Ret) Jerry Laughland
MAJ Kevin Laughlin
MAJ Richard Laughlin
MR. Dennis Laumb
LTC (Ret) Norman G. Laumeyer
SP5 Dennis Launderville
SGT Charles S. Lauraine
1LT Jose D. Laureano
CPT (Ret) Vincent M. Laurich
SGT James T. Laurie
SSG Michael R. Lauster
SGT David J. Laux
SPC Robert B. Lauzon
SGT Gary Lavake
CW4 (Ret) Wayne Lavender
MAJ William H. Lavender
LT Albert J. Lavezzi
SPC Adam C. Laviolette
SGT Sam Lavoie
2LT Charles G. Law
LT David J. Law
PFC Dustin Law
MR. James Law
SSG Roy Law
SPC Thomas P. Law
SPC Charles W. Lawhead
SGT Cleo Lawhorn
SSG Fred J. Lawhorn
MR. Dennis F. Lawler
CPT B. A. Lawless
LT Chris Lawless
CPT E. J. Lawless
SFC (Ret) Timothy P. Lawless
SFC William A. Lawless
CPL John D. Lawlor
MSG (Ret) Carl H. Lawrence
CPL Chuck H. Lawrence
MAJ Cortez Lawrence
1LT James T. Lawrence
SPC Jeff Lawrence
SP5 Mark Lawrence
CPL Ralph E. Lawrence
1LT Stephen E. Lawrence
SFC (Ret) Bill R. Laws
SGT Charles Michael Laws
PFC Alexandra Lawson
SSG Bennett W. Lawson
SP5 Christopher M. Lawson
MR. Craig R. Lawson
SFC (Ret) Donald C. Lawson
COL E. Kirby Lawson
COL (Ret) Herbert L. Lawson
SPC Lan V. Lawson
SPC Larry K. Lawson
SFC William C. Lawson
SGT William J. Lawson
CPT Herbert L. Jim Lawton
PFC James T. Lawton
1SG James D. Layden
MG (Ret) Stephen R. Layfield
SPC Russell Laymance
SPC John D. Layne
SFC Fred P. Layoau
CPT Brian Layton
LTC Christopher E. Layton
LTC Joseph K. Layton
1LT Robert Colby Layton
CPT Darlene A. Lazard
PFC Larry R. Lazaro
SP5 Ronald R. Lazenby
SSG Robert C. Lazevnick
CPL William H. Le Barron
1SG (Ret) George F. Le Blanc
PFC Henry E. Le Blanc
SFC (Ret) Herman R. Le Blanc
PFC Jeffery A. Le Blanc
SPC Justin Jude Le Blanc
PFC Lee M. Le Blanc
SPC Robert J. Le Blanc
MAJ John Le Brun
SSG Roy A. Le Clair
MAJ Thomas J. Le Cleir
SGT Randall P. Le Fevre
CPT David J. Le Master
MSG (Ret) R. J. Le Master
LTC Robert W. Le May
SSG Dan H. Le Van
SPC Donald R. Leach
SPC Harold J. Leach
SGT Harry L. R. Leach
SSG James E. Leach
SGT Merriel J. Leach
LTC (Ret) P. Judson Leach
1LT Paula F. Leach
SGT Mark M. Leachman
LTC Jerry A. Leadabrand
SFC Michael J. Leahy
SSG Carlos M. Leal
SFC Leoncio F. Leal
SGT Manuel Leal
PFC Rafael C. Leal
SPC Robert Y. Leal
MR. Sherman M. Leamon
PFC (Ret) Anton J.C. Lear
SFC Gerald W. Lear
CPL Clinton B. Leary
SGT James C. Leary
SFC Lonnie L. Leary
CPL Michael C. Leary
LTC Sharon L. Leary
LTC William J. Leary
PVT Ronald H. Lease
SPC David I. Leathers
SFC (Ret) Jack Leathers
CPT Vaughn L. Leatherwood
PVT Maurice L. Leavell
SGT Charles B. Leavitt
SPC Gregory S. Leavitt
SGM Melvin A. Leavitt
1LT Roger E. Lebeau
SGM Ronald Leblanc
SGT Earl Lebold
SPC Arthur O. Leboo
SPC Gilberto Lebron
SGT Derek Lecheminant
PFC Joseph J. Lechman
SGT George J. Lechner
SGT Wayne D. Lechner
SSG (Ret) Thomas J. Lechowicz
SSG Till Lecian
SFC Joseph Lecklikner
SGT Robert L'ecuyer
1SG (Ret) Alfred B. Ledbetter
SSG Reynold L. Ledbetter
SPC William Lederman
1LT David M. Ledesma
SPC Juan M. Ledesma
MR. Leslie Ledger
SPC Raymond R. Ledoux
CPT Marc Leduc
SP5 Edward A. Ledwig
SGT Arthur R. Lee
SSG Bobby R. Lee
SGT Carl R. Lee
COL (Ret) Charles B. Lee
SGT Charles E. Lee
MR. Charles R. Lee
CW2 Christopher A. Lee
SGM Courtney C. Lee
COL (Ret) Curtis D. Lee
SGT Dawes D. Lee
SPC Don Boyd Lee
SGT (Ret) Douglas N. Lee
PFC Douglas S. Lee
MSG (Ret) Edward Lee
SGT Edwin W. Lee
SPC Gary M. Lee
PVT Gary T. Lee
SGT George E. Lee
SSG George T. Lee
SGT Homer V. Lee
SPC James Lee
CSM James F. Lee
SFC James H. Lee
LTG (Ret) James M. Lee
PFC James R. Lee
SGM (Ret) James R. Lee
SP5 James Y. Lee
PFC Jeff Lee
SGT Jesse F. Lee
SGT Jimmie O. Lee
SGT Joe D. Lee
1LT John P. Lee
SGT John W. Lee
COL (Ret) Jong-Hwan Lee
SGT Julian F. Lee
SSG Justin E. Lee
CPL Louis A. Lee
SFC Mark J. Lee
MRS. Marvin Lee
SGT Marvin C. Lee
SPC Michael E. Lee
CPT Peter Lee
SPC Randy D. Lee
SGT Richard C. Lee
SPC Robert E. Lee
SPC Robert E. Lee
PFC Robert E. Lee
1LT Robert M. Lee
CPT Royce N. Lee
SP5 Stanley E. Lee
SPC Thomas F. Lee
PVT Titus O. Lee
1SG William R. Lee
SGT William S. Lee
SGT Lonnie Leech
SPC Philip A. Leekley
SSG Scott A. Leenerts
SGT Craig Leerberg
SP5 Frederick Leerhsen
PFC John W. Lees
CSM (Ret) John M. Leese
PFC Christopher J. Lefebvre
SGT Michele Lefever
SGT Charles T. Lefevre
SSG Joseph L. Lefferts
MSG Roger L. Leftwich
MR. Bill Legan
SPC Joseph Legato
SGT James Lege
SPC Joseph W. Leger
SSG Bryan Legere
MAJ Daniel Legereit
SGT Billy J. Legg
SGT Phillip L. Legg
SPC Amanda Leggett
CH (MAJ) Charles A. Leggett
SGT David A. Legier
SPC C. R. Bob Lego
SGT Richard W. Legocki
SPC Amos G. Legrand
SPC Gregory P. Lehan
SPC Daniel P. Lehman
CSM Grover F. Lehman
1LT Richard A. Lehman
SGT Suzette Lehman
SSG William B. Lehman
LTC (Ret) Douglas K. Lehmann
1SG John P. Lehmann
PFC Kyle Lehmann
1SG Thomas D. Lehmann
PFC Ryan Lehmkuhle
SPC John W. Lehner
SGT Henry W. Lehnerer
CPL Carl Amos Lehr
CSM Lance P. Lehr
SPC George F. Leiby
PFC Joshua Leichty
SPC Thomas G. Leidemann
MR. Conrad Leighton
SPC Joseph R. Leighton
SPC David S. Leikam
LTC Cameron A. Leiker
MAJ (Ret) Robert C. Leinberger
SFC Peter R. Leinenweber
SrA Carl R. Leininger
1LT Donald C. Leins
1LT David L. Leinum
MR. Edward K. Leisengang
SPC Jerry L. Leisure
SPC Richard C. Leitgeb
MAJ Todd M. Leitschuh
CPL Charles A. Leitt
MSG Vernon J. Lejeune
SPC Greg James Lejune
SPC Doyle E. Lemaire
MR. Robert J. Lemanski
CPT James C. Lemaster
LTC (Ret) Robert E. Lemaster
SFC Tommy William Lemaster
SPC Raymond S. Lemasters
CPT Jessica Lemieux
CW4 Paul E. Lemieux
SGT Ronald Lemieux
MSG David J. Lemire
LTC Judith K. Lemire
SPC Gary G. Lemirur
SSG Morton J. Lemkau
PFC Levere Lemkelde
1LT Joseph M. Lemley
SPC Ernest L. Lemmerman
SSG (Ret) Albert L. Lemon
SGT Peter C. Lemon
CPL Michael G. Lemons
SPC James F. Lemos
SGT Luis S. Lemos
MRS. Edward R. Lemp
PV2 Astrid E. Lemus
SSG Timothy P. Lenahan
1SG David Shannon Lenard
SFC Jimmie D. Lendennie
CPT Joseph E. Lendo
MR. Carl C. Leneaugh
LTC Charles C. Leneten
CDR Derek J. Leney
SGT Jacob Matthew Lenhart
SP3 John F. Lenker
SGT Catherine A. Lennox
2LT Michael Lennox
SSG Ronald L. Lennox
LTC (Ret) Jim Lenon
SGT George T. Lenotte
SGT (Ret) Thomas D. Lent
MR. Bradley A. Lenth
MSG (Ret) Darryl G. Lentini
SGT Michael T. Lentino
CPT Robert C. Lentz
MRS. William D. Lentz
SPC Joseph Lenz
MR. William Leo
SGT Thomas Richard Leoffels
SFC Norberto A. Leon
SFC John M. Leon Guerrero
SGT Bruce T. Leonard
SGT James A. Leonard
CPT (Ret) Max S. Leonard
2LT Paul Leonard
SSG (Ret) Thomas H. Leonard
MR. Thomas J. Leonard
1LT Tiane R. Leonard
SPC Richard J. Leonberger
SPC James A. Leone
SGT Donald W. Leonhardt
SGT Dwight E. Leonhardt
SGT Larry W. Leonhardt
SSG Duncan N. Leonhardy
SSG Nelson E. Leopold
SGT Pedro F. Leos
MR. Raymond Leos
SPC Gary A. Lepley
SP5 John C. Leps
PFC Andrew Lequerique
SPC Richard L. Lercari
MR. Rey Lerma
CPL Bernard J. Lerner
SGT Marshall L. Lerner
SSG Stanley Lerner
SGT Richard C. Leroue
LTC (Ret) Burton A. Lesh
SGT Robert Leshan
SPC Carl W. Leslie
MSG (Ret) Edward L. Leslie
CPT Mark Leslie
SGT Don Lesser
PFC Fred A. Lester
1LT Hazen R. Lester
PFC John Lester
PVT Lewis W. Lester
SGT Joseph F. Letarte
LTC Ken Letcher
LTC (Ret) Robert Letchworth
COL (Ret) Gerald E. Lethcoe
2LT Scott T. Lethiot
SPC (Ret) Paul Letkiewicz
SGM Ronald J. Letrent
PFC Craig D. Lettington
SSG Junior L. Letts
LTC Frank N. Letzkus
SGT Joseph S. Leuch
SSG Thomas D. Leue
SP5 Ronald Leuenberger
MRS. James T. Leva
SSG Jason S. Levalley
LTC (Ret) Richard Levandovsky
SSG Joseph G. Levengood
LTC (Ret) Elliott I. Levenson
SGT Emanuel Leventelis
LTC Jerry Leverett
2LT Kelly C. Leverett
SGT Adam Levesque
SP5 Richard J. Levesque
1LT Frederick I. Levine
1SG (Ret) Owen J. Levine
1SG (Ret) Teig Levingston
MSG (Ret) James R. Levinson
1SG Kim S. Levitre
SGT Bob Levy
PVT Marc Levy
SPC Steven Levy
SPC Robert Lew
SPC Daniel Lewallen
MR. Lawrence E. Lewallen
COL (Ret) William H. Lewandowski
SGT Dan Lewanski
PFC Michael R. Lewellen
SPC Daniel Lewerenz
LTG (Ret) Bennett L. Lewis
SGT Bernadette L. Lewis
SPC Bradford Alexander Lewis
PFC Carlton R. Lewis
SFC (Ret) Charles E. Lewis
SPC Christopher Aron Lewis
PFC Curtis H. Lewis
PVT Dana Lewis
SPC Daniel L. Lewis
SPC David G. Lewis
MRS. Debbie Lewis
PVT Don M. Lewis
SGT Donald S. Lewis
PFC Douglas J. Lewis
PFC Dwayne Lewis
PFC Edward G. Lewis
MAJ Frank B. Lewis
SSG Freddie Lewis
SPC Frederick C. Lewis
PFC Garnet E. Lewis
SGT George Lewis
CPL George T. Lewis
MSG Gerald W. Lewis
CW2 Gregory A. Lewis
SPC Gregory D. Lewis
PFC Jacob B. Lewis
SPC James R. Lewis
SPC Jason Lewis
SGT Jerry E. Lewis
PFC John A. Lewis
CW2 Judd C. Lewis
SPC Kenneth D. Lewis
SGT Kenneth E. Lewis
SGT Kenneth H. Lewis
SGT Larry T. Lewis
CSM Lawrence E. Lewis
MSG Leonard W. Lewis

SPC Michael W. Lewis
CPL Mike Lewis
CW3 (Ret) Norman Kenneth Lewis
SGT Owen L. Lewis
SPC Raymond H. Lewis
1SG Richard W. Lewis
SFC Rick Lewis
SFC Robert W. Lewis
SPC Robert W. Lewis
SSG Sterling G. Lewis
SPC Steven E. Lewis
SGT Ted W. Lewis
TSgt Thomas J. Lewis
SSG Tom B. Lewis
MR. William C. Lewis
SSG William A. Lewright
SPC Moses Leyba
COL Craig H. Leyda
SPC Vern L'huillier
CSM Hans E. Li
SFC (Ret) Charles H. Libbey
SP5 George H. Libbey
SSG Leeirby Ray Libby
CPT John E. Liberg
SGT John D. Licavoli
MAJ Mark A. Lichak
CPT (Ret) John M. Lichtenfels
CW4 (Ret) Joseph R. Licina
SGT Eugene S. Licker
SFC (Ret) Michael Lidbetter
1LT James H. Liddell
SPC Gregory J. Liddle
SPC Justin Lidgett
PVT Kiara N. Lie
MAJ Leland A. Liebe
CPT Richard D. Liebert
SSG Robert M. Liebsch
CPT Todd R. Lietha
CPT Anthony S. Lieto
SGT Bob Lietz
CPT Hung N. Lieu
SPC Tung S. Lieu
COL (CH) Bernard H. Lieving
CPT Gregory H. Light
PVT Lisa A. Light
MAJ Eric B. Lightfoot
CPT Robin C. Lightfoot
CSM (Ret) Johnnie Lightsey
SGM (Ret) Freddie A. Lighty
SSG Dean H. Ligon
1LT Douglas C. Ligor
LTC Joseph W. Likar
SSG Siopesili P. Likio
SGT Richard W. Lillenthal
SPC Toby Lillard
COL Richard J. Lilley
PVT Jack L. Lillie
PVT Charles F. Lilly
SGT Donnie R. Lilly
SGT Michael W. Lilly
MSG Robert R. Lilly
MR. John E. Limburg
CPT Steve Lin
LTC William Lin
MSG (Ret) Juan R. Linan
SFC Gary S. Linard
SSG Abraham Lincoln
PVT Andrew Lincoln
2LT Christopher G. Lind
SPC John D. Lind
SPC Robert E. Lind
SPC Mindy K. Lindahl
SPC John Lindale
COL Brian S. Lindamood
SSG (Ret) Michael C. Lindberg
SPC John Lindemann
SGT Gerhard Lindenmayer
SP5 Rex Linder
TSgt Robert W. Linderman
SP5 John R. Lindermuth
SFC Dale R. Lindholm
SGT Lawrence A. Lindloff
MAJ William C. Lindner
SPC Dennis H. Lindquist
COL (Ret) Robert E. Lindquist
SGT Edward R. Lindsay
SGT Marvin L. Lindsay
SFC (Ret) Melvin F. Lindsay
SSG Henry Lindsey
SFC (Ret) James R. Lindsey
SPC Lewis A. Lindsey
SGT Ronald C. Lindsey
SGT Sam Lindsey
TSgt Walter F. Lindsey
PVT David S. Lindsley
MAJ Jack Lindstrom
CW2 Gary E. Lineberry
CPT Jerome F. Linenkugel
CW4 Jerry Liner
SSG Jesse L. Ling
1LT Scott D. Lingle
CW2 Stephen W. Linholm
SP5 Craig A. Link
MRS. Juanita M. Link
SGT James Linker
SGT Brandon M. Linn
SP5 Raymond Edwin Linn
SGT Rodney J. Linn
SGT Thomas G. Linn
1LT Bryon Laszlo Linnehan
CPT Edward Linneweber
SSG George P. Lino
SGT Lee A. Linscott
PV2 Loy M. Linscott
LTC (Ret) Bruce A. Linsley
MSG (Ret) Dennis F. Linster
CPL Troy Linthicum
SSG Jack Linton
CSM Ricky L. Linton
SSG Edgar D. Linville
PFC Bruce R. Linzy
MRS. Thomas Lioces
SPC John P. Liparula
SFC Ben R. Lipford
SFC Anthony J. Lipitt
PFC David S. Lipman
SGT Terance J. Lipnick
SGT Jim Lipp
SSG Joseph Lipp
PFC George R. Lipps
SPC Robert Lipps
CPT Jonathan D. Lipscomb
CPL Roy Lipscomb
SFC Leo J. Lipsie
TSgt Joseph J. Lipski
SSG Daniel T. Lis
PFC Robert Lisenby
SSG Melvin C. Lisher
MRS. Nicholas A. Lisi
LT Joseph P. Lisiecki
SGT Francis W. Lisieski
MSG (Ret) Glenn T. Liska
MSG Leslie E. Lisson
CSM (Ret) Jack H. List
MAJ (Ret) John J. Lister
SFC Paul J. Liszka
SPC Dale Litchford
SGT Viktor Litkewycz
MRS. Robert F. Litle
SGT Allan S. Litman
COL (Ret) Mark T. Littel
SPC Stephen A. Littel
SGT Michael D. Liltig
SFC (Ret) Carl C. Little
LTC (Ret) Charlie Little
PFC Erika Little
SPC John P. Little
SP5 Rolland R. Little
SGM Rommie L. Little
CPL Tim Little
SGT Wayne E. Little
SPC Robert E. Littlefield
SFC Oliver Littles
LTC (Ret) James L. Litton
1LT William Kent Litton
SFC David E. Littrell
SPC William M. Litvjak
SGT Anthony C. Litwin
SPC Donald Litz
SP5 Faustino Livas
SSG Thomas B. Lively
MSG Premas D. Liverpool
PVT Charles F. Livingston
SSG J. Ray Livingston
MRS. James E. Livingston
SSG (Ret) Jeremy Livingston
SGT Jerord Livingston
CPL Marvin Livingston
CW2 Ronald F. Livingston
SPC Alex Liwienski
SSG Ernest Lizakowski
SGT Cesario Lizarrago
SSG (Ret) Arthur A. Llacuna
SGT Wilfredo Llenza
SPC Henry S. Llewellyn
PVT Mitchell N. Llewellyn
CPL Arthur J. Lloyd
1LT J. Pat Lloyd
SFC Jerry M. Lloyd
PVT Michael M. Lloyd
SPC Richard K. Lloyd
CPL Robert A. Lloyd
SFC Robert E. Lloyd
CW4 (Ret) Robert W. Lloyd
SPC William T. Lloyd
CW2 Harold E. Llywelyn
SGM (Ret) Kin Lo
PFC Pasquale S. Lo Vullo
SGT Carl B. Lobaugh
COL (Ret) William E. Lobit
PFC Leo F. Lobsinger
MR. George B. Locatelli
1LT (Ret) Robert E. Locey
PFC Samuel R. Lochabay
SGT Anthony W. Lochard
PFC Jerry F. Locher
SGT Gary E. Lock
SGT Durwood Gene Lockamy
CSM Harry Lockamy
SP5 Robert Dwight Lockamy
SGT Victor T. Lockamy
SPC Doug Lockary
1SG Donald E. Locke
SGT Kenneth Lockhart
SSG Patrick Lockhart
CPT Paul G. Lockhart
SPC Don Locking
SPC Don H. Locking
MSG Baxton Locklear
PFC Osman Locklear
PFC Waymon L. Locklear
SGT Robert J. Locklin
CPL Millard E. Lockwood
SPC William K. Lockwood
SP5 Kenneth N. Lodding
SGT Rickey Lodico
SGT Garry P. Lodoen
SSG Thomas A. Loehr
SP5 Charles E. Loendorf
SP5 William Harry Loescher
LTC (Ret) George U. Loffert
SGT William Lofquest
1LT Christopher Loftin
SGT Mark Loftis
SPC Troy Lofton
PFC Clair W. Logan
SFC Jess Yvonne Logan
SPC John Logan
CPL John T. Logan
MSG Steven R. Logan
SGM Terry L. Logan
MS. Vicki Logan
PFC Derek Loggains
MRS. Gloria Logsdon
SGT John M. Logsdon
SGT Robert L. Logue
SSG (Ret) Wayne R. Lohaus
SSG (Ret) John R. Lohne
SPC George S. Lokey
SGT Stephen D. Lokken
SPC James R. Lollar
SPC Albert R. Loma
SGT James E. Loman
SPC Louis Fernandez Lomas
SPC Michael J. Lomax
BG (Ret) Rhoss C. Lomax
COL Reginald T. Lombard
MAJ Charles Lombardo
SGT Edward C. Lombardo
SSG Gerald A. Lombardo
SSG Samuel A. Lombardo
MAJ Harold E. Lomenick
1LT Carl W. Lomison
PFC Michael H. Lomker
MR. Cleo London
SSG Dennis C. London
MSG (Ret) Murphy L. London
PFC Carl K. Lones
SFC Amos A. Long
CPT Benjamin Long
SPC Claude F. Long
1LT Clint Long
SPC Daniel O. Long
PFC Felton Lyon Long
MAJ Gail M. Long
SGT Glennon M. Long
1SG James E. Long
SGT James R. Long
CPT Joel D. Long
COL (Ret) John M. Long
2LT Joseph E. Long
CPL Melvin E. Long
CSM Richard Long
SGT Thomas H. Long
CPL Tyrone R. Long
SGT Wendell Ray Long
SGT William Long
SGT Greg Longenbaugh
SGT Anatol Andy Longinow
SGT Alex Longoria
SSG Lawrence A. Longoria
PFC John T. Longshore
SGT Earl A. Longstreth
SPC George Longway
PFC Joe P. Lonigro
SPC John C. Looker
SPC James R. Lookingbill
SFC (Ret) Leon M. Loomis
CPT Thomas C. Loomis
SSG James P. Looney
SPC James Robert Looney
SPC Daniel A. Loop
1LT Don A. Loorz
SFC Jeffery B. Lopau
CPL Allen H. Lopenski
SSG Jerry Edward Loper
LTC Thomas Loper
SGT Alan Lopez
MRS. Antonio Lopez
SGT Baltazar Lopez
SSG Eddie Lopez
SGT Eliott J. Lopez
CPT Ernesto Lopez
SPC Frank A. Lopez
PFC Frank F. Lopez
SGM (Ret) Guadalupe Lopez
1LT Jacob J. Lopez
SGT Jesse C. Lopez
SPC Jesus Lopez
SSG John A. Lopez
CPT Jose Abraham Lopez
PVT Joshua Lopez
SPC Julio A. Lopez
2LT Justin J. Lopez
SGT Luis Lopez
CSM Natividad Lopez
SPC Ricardo E. Lopez
SGT Ruben C. Lopez
SGT Santiago Lopez
SFC Sergio Lopez
SSG Tomas C. Lopez
SPC Triny Lopez
SGT Jose Roberto Lopez Hernandez
SGT Jean P. Lopez Olavarria
2LT Mary Lopez-Dale
SP5 A. Michael Lorber
CH (COL) (Ret) Bill Lord
SGT Hodges Lord
1SG Matthew T. Lord
COL (Ret) Edward J. Lorentzen
LTC (Ret) Dwight L. Lorenz
CPL Eric Lorenz
SPC Eric E. Lorenz
SGT Gary T. Lorenz
SGT Robert E. Lorenz
SPC Anthony H. Lorenzi
SFC Longoria Lorenzo
CSM Marvin W. Loris
LTC (Ret) Norman E. Lorsung
PVT Angela T. Losardo
SFC Clyde V. Losasso
SPC Joseph Losievski
LTC (Ret) Raymond A. Lossing
MAJ Alfred D. Lott
LTC Claude W. Lott
CW3 (Ret) Dwaine S. Lott
SGT Preston Lott
CPT William Benton Lott
SPC Willie G. Loucas
MSG (Ret) Louis K. Louck
PFC Richard W. Louck
SGT Mike Louden
SPC Robert E. Lougee
LTC Thomas A. Loughlin
MRS. John A. Loughran
SPC Leo Loughran
SPC James R. Loughrey
PFC Alfred Louie
SFC (Ret) Bert Floyd Lovato
SPC Dennis R. Lovato
SP5 Lawrence F. Lovato
CPL Charles J. Love
PFC Charles L. Love
SFC Fredrick E. Love
1LT John D. Love
SGM (Ret) John H. Love
SGT Rodney A. Love
SPC Rober R. Lovejoy
PFC Stanley E. Lovekamp
CPL Robert N. Lovelace
SPC Norman E. Lovelady
COL (Ret) Kenneth Loveless
SPC Garner L. Lovell
PFC Kathleen G. Lovell
SPC Richard E. Lovell
LTC Troy L. Lovett
SPC Carl E. B. Lovgren
SSG Thomas Loving
LTC Bruce Lovins
SP5 Terrance E. Low
SPC Richard L. Lowder
MSG Herman E. Lowe
SSG Janea Lowe
SGT Jeffrey R. Lowe
COL (Ret) John W. Lowe
SGT Robert P. Lowe
MSG Jerry L. Lowenstein
CPL Albert J. Lowery
CW3 Chad Lowery
SGT Floyd Lowery
MR. Henery M. Lowery
CSM Patrick Lowery
SP5 Robert G. Lowery
CPL Steven J. Lowery
SSG Clarence Lowman
PVT William R. Lowman
SGT Lynne M. Lowney
PFC Larry W. Lowrey
MRS. James M. Lowry
MRS. Robert C. Lowry
SPC Ronald E. Lowry
MRS. Bruce S. Lowther
1SG (Ret) John P. Lowthorpe
LTC Eric M. Lowy
SFC (Ret) Duane L. Loy
1LT James R. Loy
SPC Leland J. Loy
SPC Emelia Loya
SSG Gene C. Loya
SFC Guadalupe Loya
SFC Efrain Lozano
SFC Manuel F. Lozano
CPT (Ret) Gary O. Lozier
PFC Edward J. Lozinski
1LT Ash Lubecke
SGT Richard H. Luby
SPC Matthew L. Luc
MAJ Thomas W. Lucario
SPC Chester R. Lucas
SPC David Lucas
SSG James C. Lucas
CPL Jerry Lucas
CPT Nick Lucas
SSG (Ret) Robert G. Lucas
SGT Robert J. Lucas
PFC Thurman E. Lucas
TSgt Harland C. Luce
LTC Christopher H. Lucier
SPC Christopher P. Lucine
SPC Ana L. Lucio
1LT Jason O. Luckey
SFC Michael Lucki
PFC David Lucus
SPC Donald Ludden
SSG Thomas A. Ludden
SGT Mike Ludwig
CPT Stephen L. Luebke
LTC Kirk Luedeke
SGT Barry L. Luedke
SGT Darrell E. Luedtke
CPT Joseph F. Luedtke
SP5 Richard A. Luemen
1SG Ricardo Lucra
MR. Bernard H. Luers
SGT Larry K. Lufcy
SP5 Abraham Lugo
SGT James Luhrs
CPT Norbert E. Luick
LT John J. Luik
SGT Brad Luis
SSG Francisco L. Lujan
SGT William Luka
PVT Louis A. Lukasiuk
SPC Charles L. Lukat
CPL Larry A. Luke
SSG Michael F. Lukeman
MR. George Luketic
SGT Milan L. Lukich
1LT William J. Lulves
SGT Gary C. Lumbard
PFC Ralph W. Lumbatis
MR. Ed Lumbert
SGT Lloyd E. Lumpkins
SGT Eduardo Luna
SPC Herberto Luna
CPT Frank P. Lunati
SGT Alvin C. Lund
PVT John C. Lund
SP5 Robert M. Lund
1LT Gregory T. Lundahl
1LT Tommy A. Lundberg
CPL Walter C. Lundberg
CPT Robert A. Lunde
MSG Paul A. Lundholm
SPC Gary Lundin
SSG Daniel E. Lundy
SPC Daniel E. Lundy
CSM (Ret) James D. Lundy
LTC Michael D. Lundy
SFC William L. Lundy
MR. George F. Lunn
CW3 Jack E. Lunn
SGT (Ret) Loney R. Lunsford
SPC William Lunsford
SFC Tai Luong
BG Viet Luong
SSG Allen Lup Place
SPC Ralph A. Lupkes
COL (Ret) Anthony T. Lupo
CPL Kenneth M. Lupp
SPC James M. Lupton
SSG Stephen Lusardi
COL (Ret) Perry M. Lusby
MR. Conrad Lushbaugh
MSG (Ret) Randall L. Lusk
MR. Andrew Lutgen
1LT David A. Lutgen
MS. Ellen M. Lutgen
MS. Emily R. Lutgen
SFC Stephen W. Luther
MAJ (Ret) William H. Luther
COL (Ret) Steven K. Lutter
MSG Benjamin A. Luttrell
CPL David W. Luttrell
SPC Douglas A. Lutz
LTC (Ret) Edwin C. Lutz
SFC James E. Lutz
SGM Roger Lutz
CPT William Lutz
SFC Billy Lycans
MRS. Paul T. Lyczak
CPT Travis Q. Lyday
MR. Woxie C. Lyday
MR. Jess B. Lydick
CPL James L. Lyle
CW4 (Ret) Joseph A. Lyle
CW2 Curtis O. Lyles
SGT John G. Lyles
MR. Laurence L. Lyles
PVT Shaquita M. Lyles
1SG (Ret) Allen J. Lynch
SPC B. Quinton Lynch
SGT Bob Lynch
CPT David M. Lynch
SFC Eugene R. Lynch
SGT Harold A. Lynch
SSG Harold O. Lynch
MAJ Ingrid W. Lynch
SPC James Lynch
SGT James Dupree Lynch
MAJ Joel F. Lynch
CPT John A. Lynch
1LT John E. Lynch
SP5 Kermit R. Lynch
SGT Larry E. Lynch
SGT Michael P. Lynch
SSG (Ret) Olden E. Lynch
LTC (Ret) Patrick E. Lynch
LTG (Ret) Rick Lynch
MR. Robert G. Lynch
SP5 Stephen Lynch
COL Thomas F. Lynch
MR. Wayne E. Lynch
MRS. William R. Lynch
SGT Paul Anthony Lynd
CPL Carl E. Lynn
SSG Louis A. Lynn
SFC Mark H. Lynn
PVT Richard S. Lynn
MG (Ret) Robert G. Lynn
PFC Craine Lynn G.
SPC Curtis H. Lyon
1SG (Ret) Charles Lyons
SFC Edward R. Lyons
SPC Frank W. Lyons
SGT Gerald L. Lyons
1LT Harold D. Lyons
SFC J. N. Lyons
PFC Joshua Lyons
CPT Matthew Lyons
SGT Michael R. Lyons
SGT Patrick J. Lyons
CPT Thomas A. Lyons
PFC Matthew Lyster
MR. J. L. Lytle
MRS. Joseph F. Lyttle
PVT Mohammad Z. Maali
SPC Edward A. Mabe
SPC Dennis L. Mabee
SFC Robert S. Mable
MAJ (Ret) Jon W. Mabrey
CPT (Ret) David L. Mabry
SGT Edward H. Mac Cabe
PFC Robert W. Mac Callum
MR. Edward W. Mac Dade
SGT Allan L. Mac Donald
SGT Donald W. Mac Donald
SGT Jack Mac Donald
SGT Jeffrey W. Mac Donald
PVT John Mac Donald
SPC Kevin Mac Donald
CW4 Michael F. Mac Donald

SP6 Steven G. Mac Donald
SGT Richard H. Mac Dougall
LTC Gerald D. Mac Dowell
SFC Donald J. Mac Farland
SGT Charles R. Mac Kay
SGT Wayne Mac Kay
PVT Michale T. Mac Kenzie
SGT Fred Mac Lennan
SGT Richard A. Mac Leod
LTC (Ret) Barbara J. Mac Millan
LTC (Ret) Dougald Mac Millan
2LT Thomas N. Mac Millin
SSG Thomas M. Mac Neil
BG (Ret) Don M. Mac Willie
COL Stephen S. Mac Willie
CPT Bronislaw Maca
LTC (Ret) Arturo P. Macaltao
PV2 Jose M. Macay
MAJ James Macdonald
COL Thomas D. Macdonald
SFC Kim A. Mace
SGT Sean Mace
SFC John E. Maceda
MRS. Cathleen M. Macfarlane
SSG Peter Macfarlane
CSM Bruce Machado
SGM Rafael Machado
1LT Norman R. Machelor
PFC William H. Machen
SSG Bruce C. Machia
SSG (Ret) Richard W. Machia
SGT James Machin
MSG Ruth Machine
MSG Jerry L. Machnic
SPC Steven R. Machuca
SP5 Joseph F. Machuga
SPC George M. Macias
PFC Richard M. Maciaszek
SGT Bob Mack
SGT Darrel E. Mack
2LT Devon M. Mack
MSG Harold D. Mack
CPT Jimmie L. Mack
SSG Joseph M. Mack
1SG Michael J. Mack
SGT Pete Mack
COL (Ret) Richard E. Mack
PFC Robert L. Mack
CPL William J. Mack
CPT Ronald A. Mackay
CPT John J. Mackel
1SG (Ret) Charlie Mackey
SGT Donald E. Mackey
PFC Erik L. Mackey
SPC Ross Lee Mackey
CPL John M. Mackie
SFC Edwin L. Mackinnon
SGT Michael J. Mackus
2LT Joshua T. Maclean
SGT Tyson James Maclean
SPC David Macrae
SGT Duncan Macrae
MSG Charles F. Macrelli
1SG Joseph Macri
1LT Terrell W. Macy
MSG (Ret) Billy R. Madden
SGT Clifford J. Madden
SPC Eric Madden
SPC James Ray Madden
SPC Mike Madden
SP5 Gary L. Maddox
PFC Philip M. Maddox
COL (Ret) William T. Maddox
CPT Drew Scott A. Maddry
MAJ Steven C. Maddry
SGT John M. Maddux
SGT Johnny M. Mader
SGT Thomas S. Mader
SPC Bruce D. Madison
1SG Darrick Madison
SSG (Ret) Joseph Madison
SSG Kenneth W. Madison
CPT Joshua David Madlinger
CPT Michael P. Madon
SFC Gordon E. Madore
MR. Richard Madore
CPL Alberto Madrid
SPC Elias Madrid
MAJ Orlando Madrid
SPC Jose R. Madrueno
SPC Dane R. Madsen
MS. Shirley Chris Madsen
SGT C.J. Maes
CPL Julio Maes
SP3 Eloy Maestas
PVT Joshua Mafnas
SFC Manuel Magana
SSG (Ret) Robert J. Magarrell
SSG Luis C. Magdaleno
SP5 Clayton F. Magee
LTC Kenneth J. Magee
SPC Lanell Magee
SGT Robert B. Magee
LTC Robert K. Magee
SSG Phyllis Magee-Lindsey
SGT Peter J. Magers
PFC Eddie R. Maggard
MSG Robert M. Maggard
SPC August Rhu Maggio
MAJ Christopher S. Maggio
SGT Greg Maggs
SPC William W. Magie
PFC Claude R. Magill
SGM Francis L. Magill
PFC Vincent A. Maglia
CW2 Richard W. Magner
SGT Myron C. Magnon
1LT Eric Magnuson
SGT Richard Wayne Magnuson
MR. Douglas E. Magruder
MRS. Robert L. Magruder
SSG Charles J. Maguire
SGT Frank E. Maguire
SFC Quincy Magwood
SGT James Mah
LTG (Ret) Charles S. Mahan
1LT Billy W. Mahaney
SPC Edward H. Mahar
CSM Cyril G. Maher
SSG Frank J. Maher
MRS. James C. Maher
SFC James N. Mahery
SGT Steve E. Mahn
SGT Cummins K. Mahoe
LTC (Ret) Daniel T. Mahoney
SGT Frank Mahoney
SGT Frederick L. Mahoney
SP5 Marvin L. Mahoney
SP5 Michael J. Mahoney
SPC Neil E. Mahoney
SP5 Maurice William Mahony
MAJ Michael F. Mahony
SPC Paul B. Mahony
SGT Donald H. Mahr
SP5 Edward R. Mahr
SPC Michael G. Mahr
CPT Chris Mahre
SFC Carlisle T. Mahto
SGT James R. Mahurin
SSG Kevin O. Mai
SPC Chris W. Maier
SPC Timmy C. Maier
CSM (Ret) Paul Mailou
SGT James W. Main
COL (Ret) Stephen C. Main
SSG Earl L. Maines
SSG Eloy A. Mainez
SGT Jerry F. Mainus
PFC Jake E. Maire
SGT (Ret) Charles Mais
PFC Ronald J. Maisano
SGT Kirk Maisenbacher
SGT Kevin Maitland
2LT Scott A. Maitland
LTC (Ret) Zbigniew M. Majchrzak
SPC Michael F. MAJors
SGM James E. Makamson
SPC Daniel M. Makarewich
SP5 Jerry W. Makin
SGT Emil Makish
MSG Scott Malan
SSG Elena Malautea
SPC Robert Malavet
MSG Veryl Malberg
SFC (Ret) Eddie P. Malbroue
SPC Elbert T. Malbrough
SGT Steven Bruce Malden
SPC Manuel Maldonaddo
SGT Angel R. Maldonado
SGT Charles L. Maldonado
SSG Hector L. Maldonado
PFC Higinio Maldonado
SSG Jesus S. Maldonado
CW2 Luis D. Maldonado
SGT Oswaldo Maldonado
SPC Randolph F. Maldonado
SGT Ricardo Maldonado
SSG Rogelio Maldonado
SSG Tony Maldonado
SPC Ron Maleti
SGT Robert E. Malick
SGT Patrick J. Malinka
SPC Robert F. Malinoski
CW4 (Ret) Shawn M. Malinowski
2LT Nathaniel Malise
CPT Frank Malkin
LTC (Ret) Virgil L. Mallard
CW4 (Ret) Garry B. Mallernee
CPL John Robert Mallernee
1SG (Ret) Lawrence Mallery
CSM (Ret) Albert Mallet
SFC (Ret) Stephanie Malley
SSG Charles F. Mallon
PFC Thomas C. Mallon
1LT Harold Mallory
CPT Nick Mallos
MR. Edward Malloy
1LT Michael J. Malloy
CSM Rory L. Malloy
1LT Chris V. Malmquist
SPC Donald Maloff
SFC (Ret) Howard A. Malone
MRS. Jimy M. Malone
SPC John Terrill Malone
LTC Marvin Shawn Malone
SP5 Paddy C. Malone
CPT Thomas D. Malone
PV2 William P. Malone
COL (Ret) Winfred F. Malone
SFC (Ret) Iman Malone-Dirige
SGT George Maloney
SGT James P. Maloney
SGT James T. Maloney
MS. Karleen Maloney
SPC Richard F. Maloney
CW2 Donald P. Maloof
CPT Mario J. Malpica
CSM (Ret) Raymond J. Malpica
TSgt Joe R. Malpiede
SP5 Terry L. Maltarich
PVT Freddie J. Malveaux
SSG Sam Mamolen
SGT Susan M. Mamp
CPT Rinaldo B. Manago
MSG (Ret) James D. Manahan
SFC Gerry M. Manalang
SPC Richard Mance
MR. Jose D. Mancha
SPC Christopher J. Mancilla
SGT Jesse B. Mancillas
SSG Daniel P. Mancini
SGT Guy Guido Mancini
SGT James A. Mancini
CPT (Ret) Thomas M. Mancini
2LT Michael G. Manculich
1SG Michael Mancuso
SGT Charles G. Manes
PFC Archie L. Maness
CPT Edward A. Maney
1SG Stephen R. Maney
PFC John Manfre
SGT Arthur C. Manfredo
1SG Frank A. Mangalavite
CPL Louis G. Mangieri
1LT Chris B. Manglicmot
MAJ Robert G. Mangrum
SPC Gary W. Mangum
SPC William L. Manion
SGT Ron K. Manjarrez
SGT Thomas W. Manley
SP6 (Ret) William E. Manley
LTC Hal G. Mann
2LT Joseph T. Mann
SPC Landon W. Mann
SPC Patrick Mann
SPC Stephen M. Mann
MR. Steven J. Mann
MAJ Travis D. Mann
SGT William H. Mann
SSG Robert A. Mannheimer
SGT Damon Manning
2LT Joseph Manning
MSG Leo A. Manning
CPT Ted Manning
SGT Thomas J. Manning
MRS. Roy P. Manring
SGT Justin Mansfield
SGT Rodney T. Manson
SGT Andrew Manss
SGT Ashlye Manss
1LT Michael N. Mantegna
SP5 Clinton H. Mantz
PFC Larry D. Manuel
SFC Marcus Manuel
LTC James C. Manuele
SSG James Manuelson
1SG Francis J. Manyen
SGT John E. Maphis
MSG William C. Mapp
SFC Butch Mara
CPL Kenneth Ted Marak
PFC Joseph A. Marakovits
CPT Stephen J. Maranian
MAJ Ashley Maranich
PVT Reubin M. Marble
CPL Curtis N. Marcano
SGT Stephen Marceau
SSG Robert March
PFC John A. Marchand
SPC Leo Marchand
SGT Frank T. Marchello
PFC Anthony Marciano
SPC Joseph Marciniak
SFC Bruce Marciszewski
SPC Louis J. Marcos
SGT (Ret) Phillip M. Marcucci
SSG Eugene Marcum
SGT Thomas Marcum
SGT Vernice Marcum
SGT Alan I. Marcus
SGT Jonathan D. Marcus
SPC Sidney O. Marcus
SGT Michael W. Marden
LTC James A. Marek
SSG (Ret) Larry Mares
SGT Rafael R. Marfil
COL (Ret) Rene S. Marfull
PFC Virgil Benjamin Margelofsky
SPC John Margenau
SPC Carmine Margiotta
PV2 Andrew Margolis
SPC David J. Maricle
MSG Paul Marietta
MR. Faustino M. Marin
SPC Jorge L. Marin
CPL Julio Marin
LTC Roberto E. Marin
SGT Marshall H. Maring
SGT Vince Marinkovich
CPL Peter J. Mariotti
PFC Jonathon J. Mariscal
LTC (Ret) Art Mark
CPT Robert D. Mark
PVT Robert M. Mark
MR. Roy Mark
SPC Alan G. Markell
SGM Chris A. Marker
SPC John Marker
BG (Ret) Edward M. Markham
SGT Johnny R. Markham
SGT Gary W. Markle
SGT Trajce Markov
SGT Dale M. Markovich
MR. Steven E. Markowski
SGT Andrew J. Marks
PFC Frank I. Marks
PFC Franklin C. Marks
COL (Ret) Jimmy C. Marks
SGT Michael J. Marks
PFC William S. Marks
1LT Bruce R. Markusen
SGM Robert C. Marler
SGT James E. Marley
COL John T. Marley
SPC Paul L. Marling
SGT James T. Marlow
CSM John B. Marlow
1LT E. Virgil Marlowe
COL (Ret) Walter J. Marm
SPC Juan E. Marmolejo
1SG Brian Marone
SSG John Maroney
MR. John J. Marovich
SGT Keith Marquardt
1SG (Ret) Edward Marquez
SSG Israel G. Marquez
SSG Jason L. Marquez
SGM (Ret) Joe G. Marquez
SGT Jose H. Marquez
PFC Jose S. Marquez
SFC Reyes Marquez
PFC Vince Bryan Marquez
MR. Bill Marquis
CPL (Ret) Leo H. Marquis
SGT David C. Marr
1SG Greg J. Marr
1LT Larry G. Marr
MR. James M. Marrinan
SSG Jack P. Marrone
CPT Francisco Z. Marroquin
SPC Jaime Marroquin
CSM (Ret) Douglas R. Marrs
SGT John R. Marschall
SGT Douglas L. Marsh
SPC Larry G. Marsh
SGT Loren D. Marsh
1LT Stephen E. Marsh
MAJ Vance Marsh
1SG William E. Marsh
1LT Ann T. Marshall
1SG Cambrel B. Marshall
1SG Charles Marshall
SPC Daniel C. Marshall
CW2 De Angelo C. Marshall
CPL Donald E. Marshall
SGT Herbert W. Marshall
SGT Howard Marshall
TSgt Irving S. Marshall
CSM (Ret) Jack H. Marshall
SPC John W. Marshall
MAJ (Ret) Klaus E. Marshall
SSG Lanny R. Marshall
SSG Larry R. Marshall
SSG Loyd W. Marshall
MSG (Ret) Oscar D. Marshall
CPT Patrick Marshall
CPT Rick Marshall
CPT Robert A. Marshall
SGT Robert J. Marshall
LTC (Ret) Robert W. Marshall
SGT Ronald J. Marshall
SPC Thomas R. Marshall
SPC Ugene Scott Marshall
CH (MAJ) Walter Marshall
SPC Walter M. Marshall
CPL Joseph P. Marshello
MR. William T. Marshman
SFC (Ret) Daniel Marsicek
MRS. William H. Marslender
CPT Gary F. Marstall
SGM (Ret) Floyd J. Marsteller
PV2 Ezequiel Marte
SPC Thomas W. Martel
SPC Kenny W. Marten
MRS. Margaret Marten
SGT Berl D. Martin
COL (Ret) Bobby J. Martin
SPC Charles E. Martin
CSM Clarence J. Martin
SPC Clifford B. Martin
SGT Clinton G. Martin
SPC Daryl E. Martin
SSG (Ret) David A. Martin
MR. David B. Martin
SGT David J. Martin
SPC Douglas S. Martin
CPL Edward S. Martin
SSG Gerald Martin
SPC James C. Martin
SP5 James H. Martin
SPC James M. Martin
CPT James M. Martin
COL (Ret) James R. Martin
SP5 John B. Martin
SSG John C. Martin
1LT John D. Martin
SGT John D. Martin
CPL John F. Martin
SGT John P. Martin
SGT John P. Martin
SSG John T. Martin
1SG Johnny L. Martin
SGT Joseph A. Martin
BG Joseph M. Martin
SPC Justin L. Martin
LTC Kenneth D. Martin
SPC Larry G. Martin
SP5 Lee R. Martin
SGT Luther A. Martin
CPT Lynn D. Martin
SFC Marcus L. Martin
SGT Mark A. Martin
SP5 Marshall W. Martin
SPC Michael Martin
SGT Michael Martin
SGT Michael A. Martin
MSG (Ret) Michael C. Martin
PV2 Nathan A. Martin
SFC (Ret) Norman W. Martin
SGT Patrick L. Martin
TSgt Randall D. Martin
SGT Raymond J. Martin
1LT Robert J. Martin
MAJ Robert N. Martin
1SG (Ret) Robert O. Martin
SGT Roger L. Martin
PFC Roger M. Martin
SPC Ron Martin
SGT Ronald H. Martin
SGT Ronald J. Martin
SGT Ronnie Martin
SSG Scammel Martin
SPC Sean C. Martin
SSG (Ret) Sharon F. Martin
SGT Stephen L. Martin
MR. Stephen T. Martin
SSG Steven L. Martin
SGT Terry A. Martin
CPT (Ret) Thomas E. Martin
SPC Thomas J. Martin
SFC Timothy L. Martin
SGT Tom Martin
CW3 Wayne A. Martin
SGT Wilfred C. Martin
SMSgt William C. Martin
SGT William F. (Doc) Martin
MSG (Ret) William H. Martin
MR. William L. Martin
MSG (Ret) William L. Martin
SGT William R. Martin
SGT Willie R. Martin
LTC (Ret) Michael Martindale
COL George J. Martindell
SSG Francis Martineau
SSG Abe Martinez
SGT Adam A. Martinez
MSG (Ret) Albert O. Martinez
SPC Alfred Martinez
SPC Alfredo Martinez
MAJ Alina C. Martinez
MR. Bernard Martinez
SPC Carlos Josue Martinez
SGT Cruz B. Martinez
SGT Daniel Martinez
SSG David O. Martinez
SSG Domingo Martinez
SFC Edgar Martinez
SGT Edwin N. Martinez
MR. Eliseo V. Martinez
PFC Eric S. Martinez
MR. Felipe Martinez
SPC George Martinez
PFC Ignacio E. Martinez
PFC Ivan Martinez
SSG Jaime C. Martinez
CPT Javier Martinez
PFC Joe A. Martinez
SFC Joe C. Martinez
1LT Joel Martinez
SPC John A. Martinez
1LT John J. Martinez
SPC Jose Martinez
SFC Jose D. Martinez
SPC Joseph Martinez
CPT Joseph H. Martinez
SP5 Juan Martinez
MR. Juan P. Martinez
SPC Julian Henry Martinez
SPC Julio A. Martinez
MSG Julio R. Martinez
SGT Leonel R. Martinez
MR. Manuel L. Martinez
SSG Marcos Martinez
SSG Matt Martinez
SSG Michael Martinez
SPC Michael E. Martinez
2LT Miguel A. Martinez
PVT Mike R. Martinez
PFC Nancy Martinez
SPC Oscar Martinez
1LT Paul Martinez
SPC Pedro R. Martinez
PFC Pete Martinez
SGT Rahmindah Pehnii Martinez
SPC Raul A. Martinez
SSG (Ret) Raymond D. Martinez
MAJ Remso Martinez
SGT Richard Martinez
SPC Robert A. Martinez
SGT Robert R. Martinez
SGT Robert V. Martinez
SSG Ruben R. Martinez
SGT Ruben R. E. Martinez
SFC Seferino Martinez
LTC Sonja R. Martinez
PVT Vincent Martinez
PVT William Martinez
PVT Xavier C. Martinez
SPC Tomas Martinez Quinones
SSG Gilberto A. Martinez-Diaz
SGT John Michael Martini
SGT Dominick A. Martino
MSG Frank Martino
SPC Michael Martino
CPL Eugene Martinson
1LT Anthony Martucci
SFC (Ret) Stephen G. Martucio
MAJ Edward J. Marty
SGT Ronald K. Martyn
SPC James E. Martz
SPC Lewis A. Marucci
PFC Frederick Marx
SPC Jeffrey Marzan
SPC Jason S. Marzette
SSG Vincent L. Marzo
SGT Dan Mascheck
1SG Scott Maschek
SGT Daniel J. Mascher
SSG William J. Masci
PFC Richard D. Masciocchi

SGT Nick Mascolo
SSG James V. Masi
SP5 William A. Masik
1LT Alvin Maslov
WO1 Daniel F. Maslowski
TSgt Alfred P. Mason
SSG Charles D. Mason
CPT Charles E. Mason
SSG (Ret) Corey V. Mason
MR. David Mason
CW3 David G. Mason
SPC David R. Mason
MSG Donald Mason
SPC Donald R. Mason
PFC Jimmie C. Mason
SGT John A. Mason
CPT Joseph B. Mason
SPC Joseph M. Mason
SGT Matthew Mason
PFC Patrick Mason
MS. Robert E. Mason
SSG Vernon E. Mason
SFC W. Lowell Mason
SGM Kenneth M. Masoner
SFC Michael Massarelli
SPC James E. Massengill
MR. Jimmy Massengill
MR. Billy Massey
SP5 Charles R. Massey
SGT Leroy Massey
MSG Robert H. Massey
PVT Timothy D. Massey
SGT Lewis B. Rusty Massie
CSM Charles K. Masters
MAJ (Ret) Michael J. Masterson
1SG (Ret) Richard M. Masterson
CPL Robert T. Masterson
SSG Wardner Mastin
SGT Lawrence Mastrella
SGT Michael F. Mastromatteo
SSG Joseph P. Mastrorilli
PFC Frank Sosa Masuda
SGT Johnny T. Masuda
SGT Mario G. Mata
MAJ Thomas J. Matason
MAJ Tom Matason
1SG Richard Matcher
SSG Edward L. Matchette
PV2 William Mateas
SFC Martin Edward Matelan
SGT David A. Mates
PFC Mark T. Matesich
SSG Robert A. Matheny
CPL Robert E. Matheny
PFC Charles H. Mathers
CPL Bennie F. Mathews
SSG Charles J. Mathews
SSG Claude C. Mathews
SGT David M. Mathews
1LT Kenneth J. Mathews
SPC Wilford F. Mathews
SFC William Z. Mathews
SGT Marvin P. Mathiak
CPL Alfred D. Mathias
CPT Anthony E. Mathias
MAJ David L. Mathias
SGT Judge Mathis
MSG Samuel Matias
SGT Ulises Matias
PFC George Matlock
1LT John C. Matousek
SP5 Alan T. Matsuda
SGT Estel Charles Matt
SGT David L. Matter
SSG (Ret) Charles W. Mattes
SSG John K. Matteson
SGT Paul Matteucci
CPT Peter Matthew
MAJ Allan L. Matthews
SGT David B. Matthews
SPC Edward Matthews
PFC Jason M. Matthews
2LT John C. Matthews
SGT Nathaniel Matthews
TSgt Robert J. Matthews
SPC Steve Allen Matthey
SPC David J. Matthias
SSG Henry N. Matthias
CPT Ray Mattia
SPC Terrence C. Mattia
SP5 Daniel L. Mattice
SGT Erich J. Mattice
SGT Raymond A. Mattícks
SFC Peter J. Mattie
MAJ Walter C. Mattil
PV2 Stephen J. Mattion
PSG George C. Mattison
SGT William B. Mattlin
PVT Jeff A. Mattsen
SGT David C. Mattson
SPC Paul A. Mattuccilli
PFC Adam Matuka
MAJ Joseph A. Matukonis
SFC (Ret) Roberto Matulac
1LT Frank Matulich
SSG Shay N. Matyja
MR. Darrell N. Matz
SGT Douglas B. Matze
CPT Norman K. Matzke
SGT Laverne Mauck
SPC David B. Maue
CPL Robert N. Mauger
CPT Bruce P. Mauldin
MR. Howard P. Mauldin
SSG Robert V. Maull
CSM Edwin K. Maunakea
CSM Emmett M. Maunakea
SFC Robert L. Maupin
CW4 (Ret) Alton F. Maurais
CPT Michel Paul Maurais
SGT Dana D. Maurer
SFC David A. Maurer
SGT Gregory J. Maurice
SPC Dominick Louis Mauro
SGT William J. Maus
MS. Betty Mause
SSG David W. Mauser
SP5 James M. Mauzey
SPC Don A. Mauzy
CW3 (Ret) Paul A. Maw
SFC Robert J. Maxie
SPC Darren Coy Maxwell
SSG Frederick E. Maxwell
1LT Gordon K. Maxwell
WO1 Judson L. Maxwell
SFC (Ret) Marvin D. Maxwell
PVT David M. May
COL (Ret) Elmer C. May
SPC Gary P. May
SFC (Ret) Gary R. May
CPL Gregory W. May
MR. Herbert P. May
1SG John R. May
SPC John Steven May
PFC Johnny May
SGT Nevin H. May
PVT Nicholas May
SPC Roger May
CW2 (Ret) Wayne D. May
CSM (Ret) William E. May
SGT David T. Mayberry
CPL Thaddeus Mayberry
SPC Richard E. Maybury
1SG Eddie R. Maycen
SGT Merrill A. Maye
CPT Carrie Mayer
CPL David A. Mayer
SPC David W. Mayer
PFC Ted H. Mayer
SGT Lawrence J. Mayers
SPC Andrew P. Mayes
MAJ Kelly L. Mayes
SPC Dennis V. Mayfield
MSG (Ret) Edward L. Mayfield
CPL Harold J. Mayfield
SSG Jason Mayfield
SFC Joseph A. Mayfield
1SG Paul C. Mayfield
PFC Brandon Mayhall
COL (Ret) John W. Mayhew
SGT Kevin Mayhew
SGT Howard L. Mayle
PFC A. Arnold Maynard
SPC James E. Maynard
MAJ Joseph D. Maynard
SSG (Ret) Keith O. Maynard
CSM Lawrence Maynard
SGT Michael Maynard
1LT Michael N. Maynard
SPC Alberto Maynez
SPC Clarence D. Maynor
SGT David Gerald Mayo
MAJ David Neal Mayo
SGT Dennis R. Mayo
1LT Mark Mayor
MSG Bernard Mays
SP5 Bobby K. Mays
MSG (Ret) Ed Mike Mays
CSM James H. Mays
SGT Johnnie Mays
SGT Ronald E. Mays
CPL Wilbur G. Mays
SGT Jack H. Mayse
SGT William A. Mazejko
CPL Frank B. Mazur
SPC Andrew Mazza
SPC Anthony Mazzamuto
SPC Cadmus Mazzarella
SPC Charles A. Mazzarella
SFC (Ret) Michael T. Mazzaro
SPC John A. Mazzeo
PFC Richard Mazzocca
1SG (Ret) Joseph J. Mazzola
1SG (Ret) John B. McAbee
CW2 Robert N. McAdams
CPT David R. McAdoo
SFC Dennis L. McAfee
COL (Ret) Lawrence S. McAfee
SSG Louis J. McAfee
SGT Russell McAfoose
PFC Barry McAlee
SGT John W. McAlhany
COL (Ret) Rodger L. McAlister
SP5 James A. McAllister
LTC (Ret) John M. McAllister
LTC Max F. McAllister
MAJ (Ret) Max W. McAllister
SGT Richard E. McAllister
SGT Terrence Marlon McAllister
DR. Barry L. McAlpine
CPT Robert W. McAlpine
MSG Monroe A. McAnally
SSG Joseph A. McAnany
PFC Matthew McAndrew
LTC (Ret) Tom McAndrews
SGT Michael P. McAnelly
CPL Langdon McAninch
SGT John G. McArdell
SPC Kevin B. McAree
SSG Antwan J. McArthur
PFC Robert C. McArtor
SPC Kenneth McAteer
2LT Brenton McAuley
SPC Robert W. McAuley
SSG Thomas S. McBriarty
CW2 Deon C. McBride
SFC (Ret) Jack E. McBride
SP5 Jim R. McBride
SFC John McBride
COL (Ret) Michael T. McBride
SGT Norman L. McBride
SGT Ralph C. McBride
SGT Raymond Dean McBride
LTC (Ret) Roger P. McBride
SGT William G. McBride
CPL E. V. McBroom
SSG (Ret) Timothy A. McBroom
SPC Michael E. McCabe
1SG Joseph A. McCadden
SGT Bryan C. McCaffery
SPC George McCaffery
GEN (Ret) Barry R. McCaffrey
MAJ Albert M. McCaig
SGT Jason D. McCaig
SGT Kenny McCain
PVT Mark M. McCain
SSG Ian R. McCalister
SGT Donald R. McCall
SPC Dustin Allen McCall
SPC Larry McCall
SP5 Malcom E. McCall
CPL Terrance E. McCall
PFC Clyde H. McCalley
SGT Gerald McCallister
SGT Gerald Wrenn McCallister
SSG James W. McCallister
MSG (Ret) Lawrence R. McCallister
MR. David J. McCallum
SP5 Wesley E. McCament
SPC James R. McCamey
MRS. Charles Mick McCann
2LT Jacob McCann
COL (Ret) John R. McCann
1LT Mitchell A. McCann
SGT Roy McCann
PFC Steven C. McCann
1LT Terry A. McCarl
LTC (Ret) Thomas J. McCarran
LTC (Ret) William L. McCarron
MR. John F. McCarson
SGT Kelly M. McCarthck
MSG (Ret) Asa L. McCarthy
CPT David J. McCarthy
PFC Donald McCarthy
SPC Gary L. McCarthy
SGT John J. McCarthy
PFC Laurence G. McCarthy
SPC Michael J. McCarthy
CPT Paul I. McCarthy
PFC Sydney L. McCarthy
MAJ Thomas D. McCarthy
SPC Timothy R. McCarthy
COL N. L. McCartney
SGT James McCartthy
SP5 Charles A. McCarty
SGT John M. McCarty
SPC Louis J. McCarty
COL Ray W. McCarver
SGT Sam H. McCaston
SSG Jay H. McCauley
SPC Radford C. McCauley
CPT Randall McCauley
CW2 Stanley C. McCaw
SPC Wendell E. McCellon
SGT Michael J. McClafferty
SGT Gregg A. McClain
SGT James E. McClain
SSG Jason M. McClain
SFC Robert E. McClain
CPL Willie C. McClain
SPC Anothony McClary
CPL Robert McClellan
COL (Ret) Kyle M. McClelland
SGM Thomas A. McClelland
CPT Dennis D. McClelland-Sherman
SGT Michael McClendon
SFC (Ret) Donald F. McClernon
CPT Donald E. McClintock
CW4 (Ret) Daniel M. McClinton
SSG Everett L. McClinton
CW2 Jared T. McClinton
SSG Corey McCloud
SGT Glenn McCloy
CPL Carl W. McClung
SPC Donald W. McClung
SGT Ronald G. McClung
SP5 William McClung
2LT Bryan S. McClure
WO1 Hugh M. McClure
MR. Jerry Wayne McClure
PVT Joe H. McClure
SSG Ronnie E. McClure
1LT William M. McClure
SGT Brian D. McCluskey
SPC James H. McCluskey
SPC Clint A. McCollough
SGT Robert McCollums
MAJ Clyde W. McComas
CPL Jerold W. McComas
PVT William Charles McComas
SSG William J. McComas
SSG Alex T. McComber
1LT Edward L. McCombs
SFC (Ret) Jason McCombs
SPC Fermin R. McConkey
SP5 James McConnaughey
LTC (Ret) Donald G. McConnaughhay
SSG Guy R. McConnell
SFC (Ret) James F. McConnell
MRS. Richard W. McConnell
COL (Ret) Robert M. McConnell
SPC Joshua McCool
CPL Paul D. McCord
1LT John L. McCorkle
WO1 Phillip E. McCorkle
1LT Andrew McCormick
SGT Andrew T. McCormick
SGT Don McCormick
MRS. Edna McCormick
SFC Homer C. McCormick
CW2 Jack P. McCormick
1LT James A. McCormick
CPT John E. McCormick
CPT (Ret) Olin F. McCormick
SPC Patrick L. McCormick
SP5 Philip J. McCormick
SGT Robert E. McCormick
MAJ Thomas J. McCormick
SGT Timothy J. McCormick
SSG Ulysses McCormick
MSG Vincent E. McCormick
SP3 Gary Michael McCourt
SSG Dana J. McCown
SSG Anthony McCoy
MSG Burl G. McCoy
SPC Dwight D. McCoy
SPC Harvey L. McCoy
SFC Johnny R. McCoy
WO1 Linc McCoy
CPT Mark W. McCoy
SSG Michael McCoy
PFC Robert G. McCoy
2LT Rosalyn R. McCoy
SGT Dan McCracken
SP5 Jeffery H. McCracken
CPL Merle A. McCracken
SSG Sean M. McCracken
MSG Jean F. McCrady
MAJ Scott E. McCraney
LTC (Ret) Joe R. McCray
MAJ Wiley W. McCray
CW3 (Ret) John C. McCrea
SPC Ryan McCready
SSG Amy C. McCreary
MAJ Christopher McCreery
SFC Jesse D. McCrocklin
SP5 Robert W. McCrory
SFC John McCroy
SGT Dennis W. McCulley
CPT Matthew Y. McCulley
MAJ Claire McCulliss
MRS. John H. McCulloch
SSG Bernard J. McCullough
SP5 Doug McCullough
SP5 Kirk W. McCullough
SGT Ulyless McCullough
MSG Jeffery McCummings
CW2 Richard J. McCune
CSM (Ret) William E. McCune
SGT Allie B. McCurdy
SPC Daniel L. McCurdy
PFC James L. McCurdy
SP5 Jonathan D. McCurdy
SPC Christopher P. McCurry
SPC James J. McCusker
SP5 Kent A. McCutchen
CPL (Ret) Alvin C. McDaniel
SPC (Ret) Billy D. McDaniel
COL Cecil D. McDaniel
1LT Danny Lee McDaniel
LTC Frederick McDaniel
SGT Gerald D. McDaniel
SFC Hydress Curtis McDaniel
CW2 John P. McDaniel
SPC Justin A. McDaniel
MR. Kenneth McDaniel
LTC Patricia J. McDaniel
MSG (Ret) Richard H. McDaniel
CPL Robert D. McDaniel
PVT Roy M. McDaniel
SPC Thomas A. McDaniel
SGT Timothy McDaniel
CPT William S. McDaniel
PV2 Jonathan M. McDermott
SFC (Ret) Paul C. McDermott
SGT Robert T. McDermott
MAJ Vincent A. McDermott
SGT Michael J. McDevitt
SGT Ron T. McDevitt
SFC (Ret) Arthur J. McDonald
SGT Booker T. McDonald
SFC (Ret) Elzye McDonald
CW2 (Ret) Garry N. McDonald
SGT Henry C. McDonald
PFC James Daren McDonald
SGT Jonathan McDonald
PVT Kreutanare McDonald
CPT McFerrin McDonald
SP5 Raymond P. McDonald
WO1 Robert T. McDonald
LTC Roger L. McDonald
SGT Roland W. McDonald
SP5 Roy J. McDonald
SPC Steve McDonald
MSG (Ret) Thomas P. McDonald
1LT Joseph McDonaugh
SGT Bryan McDonel
SFC Michael McDonel
MAJ (Ret) James J. McDonnell
SPC Kevin McDonnell
SGT Martin McDonnell
SGT George D. McDonough
SGT Michael D. McDougall
MRS. Michael E. McDougle
SP5 David L. McDowell
SGT Robbie McDowell
PFC Mark K. McElfresh
SPC Paul D. McElhannon
SP5 Don McElhattan
SSG (Ret) Robert M. McElhone
SPC Henry G. McElmurray
SGT William T. McElrath
SGT Larry B. McElreavy
SSG Rex M. McElroy
SSG William McElroy
LTG (Ret) John W. McEnery
MAJ Douglas W. McEniry
SPC Edward O. McEntee
SSG Edward P. McEvoy
SFC Ira L. McFadden
SPC Michael McFadden
SGT William F. McFadden
LTC (Ret) Ben P. McFall
CPT Ben P. McFall
PVT Alan McFarland
SGT Donna D. McFarland
MR. Douglas D. McFarland
SPC Dwayne A. McFarland
SSG Kenneth B. McFarland
SGT Kent A. McFarland
PFC Richard McFarland
SSG (Ret) William R. McFarland
1LT Anthony C. McFarlane Gonzalez
PFC John E. McFee
SGT William R. McFeeters
1LT Altee Craig McFellin
CPT Edward F. McGaffick
SGT Jimmy C. McGaha
SPC Thomas M. McGarey
1SG (Ret) Edward J. McGarvey
SGT James R. McGath
SGT Dean McGeath
COL J.P. McGee
MSG James H. McGee
MR. Johnny A. McGee
SPC Kerry McGee
SFC Matthew J. McGee
1LT Michael J. McGee
SSG Michael S. McGee
CPL Raymond J. McGee
SP5 Russell Lee McGee
SPC Terry L. McGee
SPC James M. McGettigan
SGT Albert W. McGhee
SGT David A. McGhee
SGT Harry G. McGhee
SSG Richard McGibeny
SP5 Gerald B. McGiffin
PFC Gary N. McGill
MAJ Robert E. McGill
SFC Robert L. McGill
SSG Rufus L. McGill
COL (Ret) William Dan McGill
CPT Luther McGinley
SFC Patrick T. McGinley
SGT John J. McGinn
SGT Joel R. McGinnis
PFC Mickey R. McGinnis
PFC John T. McGinty
SPC Thomas M. McGivern
LTC Hugh M. McGloin
PSG James McGlone
MSG (Ret) Paul V. McGonigle
SPC (Ret) Christopher J. McGorman
PFC James McGougain
SGT Charles M. McGovern
SPC Gerard McGovern
SSG James O. McGovern
SPC Joseph A .H. McGovern
MAJ Elizabeth McGovney
PFC Armand McGowan
SGT James F. McGowan
SGT James P. McGowan
CPT Robert S. McGowan
SPC Michael E. McGrail
SGT Bern J. McGrane
SP5 William J. McGrane
SPC April McGrath
CPT Daniel F. McGrath
SPC Gerald P. McGrath
1LT Michael J. McGrath
2LT Thomas M. McGrath
CPL William F. McGrath
CPL John M. McGraw
SGT Matthew D. McGraw
SGT William F. McGraw
CPT Robert L. McGreevy
SSG Charles R. McGregor
SGT Michael McGregor
PFC Randall McGregor
SPC Billy J. McGrew
SGT James E. McGriff
CSM (Ret) Willis M. McGriff
SSG William "Bill" Corsair McGroarty
CPL Charles F. McGuire
CPT David A. McGuire
SPC Dennis F. McGuire
SGT Mike J. McGuire
SSG Paul H. McGuire
SPC William M. McGuire
SPC Matthew McHaffey
SGT Charles L. McHenry
SFC (Ret) John L. McHoul
MR. Allen H. McIlravy
SPC Alan McIlvain
MR. Harry S. McIlvaine
SPC John E. McIlvoy
COL (Ret) Blake M. McIlwain
SGT Paul D. McInerny
SPC Noble M. McInnis
CPT William R. McInnis
SPC Lawrence J. McIntire
CPT James H. McIntosh
SPC Keith McIntosh
CW2 Larry McIntosh

CW4 Norman W. McIntosh
PFC Russell F. McIntosh
CPL Walter L. McIntosh
CPL Wilbert L. McIntosh
SPC Carrie J. McIntyre
SFC Floyd P. McIntyre
SGT James S. McIntyre
SGT (Ret) Philip D. McIntyre
MAJ Tyler J. McIntyre
LTC Timothy M. McKane
COL (Ret) Donald M. McKay
SPC Erin McKay
SGT George L. McKay
LTC (Ret) Ivor W. McKay
COL James C. McKay
LTC (Ret) Dewey E. McKee
CPT George W. McKee
SPC Henry McKee
SFC Isaac McKee
SPC James L. McKee
SPC (Ret) Orvel L. McKee
COL (Ret) Richard W. McKee
MAJ Stephen F. McKee
SPC Adam McKeever
1LT Chris J. McKeever
SGT Frank A. McKeever
LTC (Ret) Henry H. McKeithan
SSG Maurice McKellar
PVT Steven F. McKellips
SSG Theodore D. McKelvey
COL (Ret) Gerard M. McKenna
1LT Michael J. McKenna
SPC Murray P. McKenna
SGT (Ret) Donald C. McKenney
SPC Arthur N. McKenzie
SPC Gary W. McKenzie
MAJ Geoffrey McKenzie
SGT Joseph D. McKenzie
PFC Leon McKenzie
SPC Lyle L. McKenzie
LTC (Ret) Roger L. McKenzie
CW3 William E. McKenzie
SGT Ronald H. McKeown
SPC William G. McKeown
MSG (Ret) Robert W. McKey
MRS. A. J. McKibbens
MR. Edgar A. McKiddy
MR. Ronnie J. McKiddy
SGT William C. McKie
GEN (Ret) David D. McKiernan
SPC Francis P. McKiernan
PFC Daniel C. McKinley
CPT Francis R. Skip McKinley
SFC (Ret) Robert B. McKinley
SGT Russell McKinley
SSG Ben McKinney
SFC James W. McKinney
MRS. June David McKinney
SGT Michael McKinney
SGT Roman McKinney
SPC Roy C. McKinney
PFC Steven E. McKinney
SGT (Ret) Wallace L. McKinney
SP5 William Lynn McKinnie
SFC Bradford A. McKinnis
CPL Emmearl G. McKinnon
MSG Angela McKinzie
LTC (Ret) James D. McKissick
PVT Albert McKnight
CPL Harry C. McKnight
MAJ (Ret) James D. McKnight
SPC Jimmy L. McKnight
SPC Phillip W. McKnight
LTC Shawana J. McKnight-Brazzle
MR. Gary R. McKowen
CW4 (Ret) William N. McKown
CPT Cory T. McKoy
CW2 George McLachlan
SGT Gerald McLain
SFC Lester James McLain
CPT William H. McLain
SGT Ian R. McLauchlan
SGT Bob McLaughlin
CW3 Davin G. McLaughlin
LTC (Ret) Gary F. McLaughlin
SP5 Gordon E. McLaughlin
PVT James E. McLaughlin
SSG Joseph E. McLaughlin
SPC Preston E. McLaughlin
PFC Richard K. McLaughlin
CW4 (Ret) Richard L. McLaughlin
SP5 Richard W. McLaughlin
LTC Robert F. McLaughlin
SGT Bill McLean
CPT Daniel S. McLean
MSG Ernest E. McLean
MAJ Gregory W. McLean
2LT Jason McLean
1LT John L. McLean
SP5 John S. McLean
SSG John W. McLean
CW4 Neil N. McLean
CPL Rob Roy A. McLean
COL Scott D. McLean
SP5 Stephen H. McLean
SSG William McLean
CPL James S. McLeland
CPL John D. McLellan
CPT William W. McLemore
SGT Bruce J. McLeod
SPC Charles C. McLeod
LTC (Ret) Norman F. McLeod
1SG William K. McLeod
CW2 Dennis W. McLeroy
CPT (Ret) Douglas S. McLeroy
CPL Warren R. McLeroy
CPT George D. McLouth
SGT Guy A. McMahan
MAJ Kevin D. McMahan
1LT Michael K. McMahan
SSG (Ret) Ray J. McMahan
SSG Christopher McMahon
SGT Gerald M. McMahon
SSG James McMahon
SSG (Ret) James J. McMahon
CPT Robert W. McMahon
SFC (Ret) Robert E. McManamy
CPL William D. McMann
PFC Daniel P. McManus
MR. Edward D. McManus
CPL Edward J. McManus
MRS. Gerard J. McManus
SGT James J. McManus
SFC John B. McManus
2LT Kelly McManus
1LT Michael J. McManus
MAJ (Ret) William W. McManus
SPC Daniel McMaster
PFC Paul C. McMasters
SPC Willie J. McMeans
MRS. Elmer L. McMichael
SGT Howard W. McMichael
SGT Marvin D. McMichael
PFC Taijonna McMickens
SSG John H. McMilian
MAJ Elridge W. McMillan
SGT La'mark V. McMillan
SSG Ronald A. McMillan
2LT Tiffany McMillan
CPL William I. McMillan
MR. C.R. McMillen
SGT Patrick D. McMillen
LTC (Ret) Stanley D. McMillian
SGT Larry B. McMillin
MR. Mark McMonigle
SP5 Richard McMullen
1SG William J. McMullen
CSM (Ret) Donlie S. McMullin
PFC John H. McMullin
MSG (Ret) Matthew W. McMullin
MR. Levaniel McMurray
CSM (Ret) Thomas O. McMurtrie
SGT Bruce McNabb
PVT Jeffery D. McNabb
SSG Grant McNair
SPC Dan McNamara
CPT Homer C. McNamara
SPC John P. McNamara
SGT Danni McNaughton
1LT Thomas D. McNaughton
2LT Alonzo McNeal
SPC Dennis L. McNeal
SFC Glen E. McNeal
SPC Joe L. McNeal
CPT John T. McNeal
PVT Roosevett McNeal
MSG Sheldrick McNeal
MAJ (Ret) William D. McNeal
SGT Charles E. McNeave
SGT Charles J. McNeely
LTC Hugh R. McNeely
SGT Leo S. McNeely
SFC (Ret) Michael S. McNeely
CPT Walter J. McNees
SPC Charles R. McNeil
SSG Christopher S. McNeil
SFC Dale R. McNeil
SFC Durnell McNeil
PFC Kenneth W. McNeil
PFC Meredith W. McNeil
SPC Patrick James McNeil
SGT Brian E. McNeill
MAJ Daniel McNeill
SGT James L. McNeill
COL (Ret) Joseph M. McNeill
SGM (Ret) Norman G. McNeill
SPC Jerry McNelly
SGT Joshua McNett
SPC Robert McNichols
LTC Arick R. McNiel-Cho
COL (Ret) John J. McNiff
SPC Jerome E. McNinch
CPL Joseph J. McNulty
SFC Mark McNulty
CPT Meighan K. McNulty
1LT William E. McOwen
SGT Joseph H. McPeek
MSG Ralph B. McPhail
CPT (Ret) Robby McPhail
SSG Ballard D. McPherson
SSG George R. McPherson
CPT James K. McPherson
SP5 Ronald C. McPherson
SSG Seth McPherson
MAJ Slade A. McPherson
SSG Vernon McPherson
COL (Ret) William H. McPherson
SPC Carroll A. McQuaig
SGT William T. McQuaig
PFC Winston A. McQuaig
MAJ Anthony L. McQueen
SGT Clifton McQueen
MR. Jerome McQueen
CSM (Ret) Charles L. McQuerry
SPC Allan McQuilkon
SFC (Ret) Lewis McRae
COL (Ret) John B. McRaney
CPT June C. McRaney
1LT James A. McRell
SSG Eric P. McRoberts
MR. Michael H. McRoy
SGT (Ret) Thomas J. McShane
SGT Kenneth McSheehy
MR. Robert McSherry
SFC Ivan McStoy
SGT Dennis H. McSwain
1SG John H. McSwain
SFC Dock H. McSwane
SPC Richard McSweeney
1LT Erit B. McTernan
SP5 Tom McTigue
SPC Simon McTizic
SPC Phil McVay
COL (Ret) Andrew J. McVeigh
PFC Ronald S. McVey
SPC Vincent McVicker
1LT Thomas D. McWhinnie
LTC (Ret) Clint S. McWhorter
1SG (Ret) Danny R. McWilliams
SGT Heath David McWilliams
SGT John B. McWilliams
SFC Franklin G. Mead
SGT Richard T. Mead
SSG Timothy Mead
SGT Henry T. Meade
SGT Richard E. Meade
SPC Thomas W. Meade
SGT Grover C. Meador
SPC Robert J. Meadowcroft
SGM (Ret) Bobby E. Meadows
SGT Brian Meadows
SGT Charles J. Meadows
SPC Jesse W. Meadows
1SG Maynard Meadows
LTC (Ret) Robert C. Meager
MSG Peter E. Meagher
2LT Kandace D. Means
1LT Jonathan Mears
SSG Leland R. Mears
SSG Scott Mears
SPC Carl Mecca
PFC Vito Mecca
PFC Jeremy L. Meche
SPC Kyle Medeck
CW4 (Ret) Albert R. Medeiros
SP5 Manuel Medellin
SGT Victor Mederos
SGT Roland R. Medford
1LT Fernando A. Medina
CSM (Ret) Ismael Medina
SSG Jose R. Medina
2LT Ronnie Medina
SSG William Medina
SPC Michael W. Medlin
SPC Richard L. Medlock
SGT Adrian A. Medrano
SGT Carlos F. Medrano
MR. Daniel Medrano
CW4 Bill Medsker
SPC James F. Meechan
SSG Randol P. Meeds
SGT James L. Meegan
LTC (Ret) John J. Meehan
CPT (Ret) Shannon P. Meehan
MAJ Steven R. Meek
MAJ Jeffrey L. Meeker
SPC Samuel L. Meekins
TSgt Charles B. Meeks
SGT Henry Joe Meeks
MAJ Mark A. Meeks
SGT Roger D. Meeks
SPC Steven T. Meenaghan
LTC Daniel B. Megehee
SFC Eric J. Mehall
CPT Jason Meharg
MRS. Louis S. Mehl
SPC Luke D. Mehling
SPC Brian A. Mehrhof
PFC Bin Bin Mei
SGT Derek Bing Mei
CPL James F. Meicho
SPC John H. Meicht
PVT Alisa Meikle
SPC Patrick M. Meiluta
SGT Richard A. Meiners
SPC Lester E. Meinert
SPC John Meinhardt
SGT Thomas C. Meinhardt
SPC Robert L. Meinzer
PVT Steven L. Meisenhelder
SP5 Kenneth A. Meismer
SPC Ronald Meiss
LT Carl William Meister
SPC Harold G. Meister
SGT Rich Meister
CPT Tim Meitin
SSG Macario J. Mejia
SFC David A. Melancon
SSG Robert J. Melander
SGT Edward R. Melanson
SPC John C. Melasecca
CPT Alex Melbardis
LTG (Ret) David F. Melcher
SGT Douglas L. Melcher
SSG (Ret) Kristy Meldrum
COL Paul Mele
SGT Manuel Melendez
MR. Joe A. Melendrez
MR. Lawrence Meligro
SPC John A. Mellen
CSM James J. Mello
MAJ Eric Melloh
SGT Paul V. Mellone
SrA James K. Mellow
PFC William B. Melody
MRS. Guy S. Meloy
CPT James C. Melton
CSM Larry L. Melton
SGT Randy P. Melton
MAJ Robert L. Melton
SFC (Ret) Walter R. Meltz
SPC Barry L. Melvin
SSG (Ret) James F. Melzard
SSG Robert C. Memmer
SGT Cornell T. Menard
SGM Keith C. Menchey
MRS. Clarence A. Menchhofer
COL Cory Mendenhall
SPC Gilbert Mendez
CPL Henry Mendez
SGT Myles Mendez
SGT Thomas J. Mendez
SPC (Ret) Candido Mendez-Nevarez
COL (Ret) Billy J. Mendheim
MR. Umberto Mendia
SGT Jose E. Mendieta
SSG Anthony F. Mendiola
1SG (Ret) Isreal S. Mendiola
MSG Albert Mendoza
TSgt Angel L. Mendoza
MRS. Chelly P. Mendoza
SSG Edward Mendoza
SFC Harry H. Mendoza
SPC Hector R. Mendoza
MR. Joe K. Mendoza
CPT Joshua A. Mendoza
SGT Kissthopher Mendoza
PVT Martinez Mendoza
SPC Pedro Mendoza
SPC Priscilla Mendoza
PFC Samuel Mendoza
SPC Willard B. Menefee
SPC Howard Mensch
SSG Fred E. Mensing
MAJ Robert L. Menti
CSM Christopher Menton
SPC William R. Menzel
MAJ (Ret) Julius A. Menzoff
MAJ Matthew Mercadante
SPC Gerado Mercado
SGT Ralph Mercado
SPC Reinaldo J. Mercado
SPC William C. Merce
SFC (Ret) George W. Mercer
SPC Paul F. Mercer
SGT Willoughby Mercer
SGT John R. Merchant
LTC (Ret) Richard I. Merchant
CW2 Paul C. Mercready
SGT Eli A. Mercy
SGT Slave Merdzanovski
CPT Billy Meredith
CPT Casey L. Meredith
CPT Jon W. Meredith
SGT William B. Meredith
SGT William S. Mergenthal
CPT G. Jerry Merges
SPC Curtis J. Merkel
SFC (Ret) Dean R. Merkins
MAJ Jennifer Merkle
MAJ Scot Merkle
LTC James Merlo
PFC Richard E. Mero
PFC David Merrell
CPL Garrett L. Merrell
SGT Jeffrey Merrick
CSM Gerry N. Merrihew
SGT Gary Lee Merrill
SGT Paul D. Merrill
SGT Robert L. Merrill
PV2 Roy S. Merriman
CPL Jackie Eugene Merriott
CPL Donald S. Merritt
SPC Gerald R. Merritt
MR. Glenn R. Merritt
GEN (Ret) Jack N. Merritt
SGT Lu Merritt
MR. Nathaniel Merritt
SFC Roy M. Merritt
SSG Thomas E. Merritt
SGT Richard A. Merry
CPT Jeff Mersiowsky
1SG (Ret) Mick Merthen
SGT Edgar T. Mertz
SPC John I. Mertz
SPC Raymond L. Merz
SPC John Mesich
SSG Linda S. Messer
SPC Vinson F. Messer
CPT Virgil Marvin Messer
PFC Larry L. Messerschmidt
MR. Richard O. Messier
MAJ Betty J. Messmore
SFC Gracie Mestre
TSgt John R. Metcalf
SPC Kirk Metcalf
1SG Timothy M. Metcalf
MSG (Ret) William A. Metcalf
COL (Ret) Richard T. Metheny
CSM Tim Metheny
COL (Ret) James R. Methered
MRS. Robert D. Methven
SGT Andrew J. Metrando
SPC Alan Metz
PVT Meleeta Metzler
SPC Francis R. Meunier
SP5 Paul F. Meuse
MSG (Ret) Mathew G. Meverden
SPC Alexus Monique C. Mey
SGT Robert J. Meyd
SGT Carl H. Meyer
PFC Charles J. Meyer
MSG (Ret) David F. Meyer
SPC David P. Meyer
SPC Donald E. Meyer
GEN (Ret) Edward C. Meyer
LTC (Ret) James F. Meyer
MR. John Meyer
SPC John J. Meyer
SGT Neil T. Meyer
SGT Paul B. Meyer
SPC Stephen W. Meyer
MR. Ronald Mike Meyerhoff
MR. Dale Meyers
SGT (Ret) Edwin R. Meyers
SFC (Ret) John E. Meyers
SSG Raymond F. Meyers
SGT Richard E. Meyers
SGT Russell W. Meyers
CPT Scott L. Meyers
MSG Richard C. Meza
SGT E. Dwight Mhire
CPL Julius J. Mianecki
PV2 Robert Michael
SGT David M. Michalak
SFC (Ret) Iris B. Michaux
SGT Andrew J. Michel
TSgt Douglas M. Michel
SGM (Ret) Benjamin J. Michels
LTC Robert F. Michener
SGT Clare M. Michlin
SPC Joseph Michnowski
LTC (Ret) John B. Mickam
SPC Todd Mickelson
PV2 Robert L. Mickey
SFC (Ret) James V. Mickiewicz
CPT Ronald E. Micuch
PVT Alan D. Middaugh
SPC Howard P. Middaugh
MSG (Ret) Birdeye L. Middleton
CPT (Ret) Bryant E. Middleton
1LT Charles C. Middleton
SFC (Ret) Dudley A. Middleton
SPC Kevin B. Middleton
COL (Ret) Robert D. Middleton
COL Ted Middleton
MSG (Ret) William E. Middleton
SFC Ernie Midkiff
SFC (Ret) Norbert F. Miedowicz
MR. Craig E. Mielke
MRS. Myron W. Miels
SPC Matthew J. Mierzejewski
2LT Kurt A. Miesner
SGT Ronald J. Migut
SP5 John P. Mihal
CPT James R. Mijares
SSG Travis Mikel
SFC Bob D. Mikell
BG (Ret) Bruce T. Miketinac
MAJ Michael T. Miklos
SPC Richard J. Mikolajczyk
LTG (Ret) Paul T. Mikolashek
PFC Joseph Mikula
CPL J. T. Milam
SFC (Ret) Robert C. Milam
SP5 John M. Milano
CPL Joseph S. Milazzo
1SG (Ret) Vinton K. Milbank
SSG Paul Laurence Milburn
SP5 David J. Miles
SP5 Fred C. Miles
LTC (Ret) Joel Miles
SFC Keith R. Miles
SP5 Lawrence P. Miles
1LT Marshall C. Miles
SPC Richard K. Miles
PFC Matthew W. Milewski
SFC Glenn A. Miley
COL Jeffrey L. Milhorn
SFC (Ret) Andre Milhouse
MAJ Noel Milian
CPT Rebecca A. Milkowski
CPT Hugh C. Millar
SP5 William J. Millard
SFC John D. Millender
SGT Adam C. Miller
SGT Albert R. Miller
MR. Albin J. Miller
CW4 (Ret) Andrew W. Miller
SGT Arthur Miller
COL (Ret) Boulton B. Miller
SPC Bruce A. Miller
SPC Bruce T. Miller
1SG Bryan Miller
PVT Caleb D. Miller
MR. Carl Miller
SSG Charles H. Miller
PFC Charlie Miller
SGT Christopher O. Miller
MR. Clarence L. Miller
SSG Clayton Miller
SGT Cory D. Miller
SFC Dall H. Miller
SSG Daniel Miller
PFC Daniel E. Miller
SFC Daniel J. Miller
CPT Daniel W. Miller
SGT Daniel W. Miller
MRS. Danny J. Miller
PFC David A. Miller
PFC Don J. Miller
SGT Douglas L. Miller
SPC Doyle A. Miller
CPT Dwight W. Miller
LTC (Ret) Dyson Miller
PFC Earle G. Miller
LTC (Ret) Edward J. Miller
SFC Edwin P. Miller
1SG Floyd C. Miller
CSM (Ret) Frank L. Miller
MSG (Ret) Frederick E. Miller
MSG (Ret) Frederick W. Miller
MAJ (Ret) George C. Miller
SPC Glenn Miller
LTC (Ret) Guy E. Miller
MRS. Harvey R. Miller

BG Henry S. Miller
SFC Herbert A. Miller
SFC Howard Miller
SGT Jackie P. Miller
SGT James Miller
MSG James D. Miller
LTC James D. Miller
SPC James E. Miller
LTC (Ret) James F. Miller
SSG James Mike Miller
SSG James R. Miller
LTC (Ret) James S. Miller
1LT Jeffrey A. Miller
SGT Jerrod Miller
LTC Joe R. Miller
TSgt John E. Miller
SGT John W. Miller
1LT Joseph R. Miller
PVT Joshua Miller
SGT Justin Miller
1LT Justin L. Miller
MR. Kenneth C. Miller
2LT Kenneth W. Miller
MR. Kevyn Miller
CPT Kimberly K. Miller
COL (Ret) Kipp O. Miller
SP5 Larry E. Miller
CPT Larry G. Miller
SGT Lee Miller
1SG (Ret) Leo Miller
CW4 Lyle I. Miller
PFC M. Ross Miller
SGT Mark S. Miller
SGT Marvin Miller
CPT Michael Miller
SPC Michael C. Miller
SGT Michael L. Miller
MRS. Oscar A. Miller
MAJ Patrick W. Miller
MSG (Ret) Paul V. Miller
SFC Perry M. Miller
CW2 Peter A. Miller
CPL Ralph T. Miller
SSG Richard A. Miller
SPC Richard A. Miller
SSG Richard C. Miller
SPC Richard E. Miller
SGT Richard Gene Miller
PFC Robert C. Miller
CSM Robert G. Miller
CW2 Robert J. Miller
SGT (Ret) Robert W. Miller
SGT Rodney D. Miller
SPC Ronald Miller
SGT Ronald R. Miller
PVT Ronny C. Miller
CPT Ryan Miller
SSG Ryan Dean Miller
CPT Ryder Scott Miller
SSG Scott A. Miller
SP5 Stephen D. Miller
SGT Stephen D. Miller
PFC Steven E. Miller
SGT Swindle D. Miller
SGT Thad Miller
SPC Theodore R. Miller
SGT Thomas J. Miller
PFC Thomas L. Miller
SGT Thomas M. Miller
SPC Thomas M. Miller
SGT Thomas N. Miller
CW2 Todd A. Miller
SPC Triston W. Miller
SP5 Vernon L. Miller
SGT William A. Miller
MAJ William C. Miller
SPC William D. Miller
MR. William F. Miller
CW2 William H. Miller
CPT William J. Miller
SSG William J. Miller
SGT (Ret) Willie G. Miller
SSG (Ret) Willis S. Miller
SFC Zachary E. Miller
SFC Lee G. Millett
CPL Edward G. Milligan
SFC John W. Milligan
MSG Kevin D. Milligan
SSG William Robert Milligan
PFC Billy Devo Millikan
LTC (Ret) Rick Millikan
PFC William J. Milliken
PFC Cecil Milliner
SPC William K. Milliner
MR. Ken Millington
LTC Ronald T. Millis
CH (LTC) Charlie S. Mills
PV2 Dale G. Mills
CSM (Ret) Dallas O. Mills
CPT Darin W. Mills
CSM (Ret) David D. Mills
SSG (Ret) David H. Mills
PVT George Mills
SPC James B. Mills
SFC Jonathan A. Mills
SGT Kenneth M. Mills
SPC Mark S. Mills
SPC Peter E. Mills
LTC Richard L. Mills
MSG Robert Mills
MRS. Ronald L. Mills
PFC Ronnie Taylor Mills
MSG Stanley W. Mills
SPC Stephen D. Mills
SPC Todd Mills
SPC William C. Mills
CPL William C. Mills
1SG William E. Mills
SGT Willis E. Mills
SPC Arthur F. Milner
SSG David Milner
SP5 Toby V. Milroy
SPC Andreas Milsap
SFC (Ret) Andre V. Milteer
SGT Thomas L. Mims
CPL William M. Mincer
SSG J. Marshall Minchew
CPL George E. Minda
SPC Garvin T. Mindt
SPC Glenn Miner
SGT Jonathan A. Miner
SGT Norvall M. Miner
SSG Ralph G. Miner
SGT Tony A. Miner
1SG Gary W. Minerue
SPC Tyler Mines
CPT Edwin L. Minges
SPC James L. Minish
MR. John Minneci
PFC Dominic Minneti
LTC (Ret) Robert W. Minney
SGT James A. Minnichsoffer
SGT Allan R. Minns
1SG Gregory S. Minonno
SPC Carl R. Minor
SPC Earl Minor
MAJ Eric Minor
SGM (Ret) James D. Minor
SP5 James H. Minor
SPC John Minor
CSM (Ret) G. Frank Minosky
SPC Josh Minshew
SGT Richard J. Minski
SGT David P. Minter
1SG Dennis R. Minter
SGT Frank Minter
SGT Roy L. Minter
SFC William A. Mintmier
CSM (Ret) Billy F. Minton
1SG Jeffrey Minton
SGT Joseph A. Minton
1SG John V. Mintz
DR. Milton Mintz
2LT Oliver F. Mintz
PFC David Stephen Mirabella
SGT John J. Mirabella
CPT Joseph R. Mirabella
SP5 Paul L. Mirage
SPC Bruce D. Miranda
MRS. Carlos D. Miranda
SPC Edward Miranda
SGT Efrain Miranda
PVT Jaime Miranda
LTC (Ret) Jose M. Miranda
SSG Brian K. Miree
1SG (Ret) Andrew Mireles
SGT Eric W. Mirshak
SGT Bryan M. Mischler
SGT Guy W. Miser
SPC James H. Misfeldt
PFC Edmund Misiaszek
SFC John V. Misner
SP6 Bruce D. Mistelske
SPC Roland Mistral
SPC William G. Mitch
SGT John Mitchelides
SGT Arthur O. Mitchell
SPC Ben E. Mitchell
MSG Benjamin N. Mitchell
SGT Bradley S. Mitchell
PFC Charles Mitchell
SFC (Ret) Dan A. Mitchell
SP5 David C. Mitchell
MAJ David H. Mitchell
MSG (Ret) David S. Mitchell
1LT Frank B. Mitchell
PSG (Ret) George Mitchell
1SG Hector G. Mitchell
1SG (Ret) Herbert Mitchell
SPC Horace Lee Mitchell
SPC James E. Mitchell
MRS. James F. Mitchell
1LT Jeffrey C. Mitchell
SSG (Ret) Jimmy C. Mitchell
REV. (SGT) John M. Mitchell
LTC Korey O. Mitchell
SPC Lawrence C. Mitchell
MSG Leo T. Mitchell
SFC Marvin E. Mitchell
PFC Matthew G. Mitchell
SPC Michael J. Mitchell
SSG (Ret) Michael W. Mitchell
SGT Nora Mitchell
SFC Oscar Mitchell
SFC (Ret) Phillip J. Mitchell
SPC Ralph C. Mitchell
1SG (Ret) Rebecca L. Mitchell
CPL Richard J. Mitchell
SPC Robert T. Mitchell
SFC Robert T. Mitchell
SPC Robert T. Mitchell
LTC Stephen D. Mitchell
SP5 Teddy L. Mitchell
1LT Thomas H. Mitchell
SGT Victor R. Mitchell
PFC William A. Mitchell
TSgt Donald E. Mitcheltree
2LT Matthew Mitchiner
SGT Kenneth Mitchko
MAJ George A. Mitroka
MR. Raymond N. Mitulinski
PFC Harvey W. Mix
CW5 (Ret) Robert E. Mix
SGT Reuben Moses Mixsooke
COL (Ret) Myles M. Miyamasu
SGT Momi Mladenovski
PFC Clifford Mlincek
SPC Daniel M. Moats
SGT Mark H. Moberg
SPC Jessie S. Mobley
MRS. Joyce P. Mobley
SFC War E. Mobley
PVT Calvin W. Mock
2LT Seth Model
2LT Philip M. Modica
SGT Anthony H. Modock
SSG Richard J. Modolo
SGT (Ret) Warren H. Moe
SP5 Bill Moeller
SSG (Ret) Dwaine A. Moeller
MRS. Gene L. Moeller
SPC John Mangam Moeller
CPT Travis Moen
SFC (Ret) Cleveland A. Moffett
1SG Herbert R. Moffett
MRS. Hoy K. Moffett
COL Ralph V. Moffett
PVT Larry B. Moffitt
MAJ Gregory R. Mogavero
SSG Shoan I. Mohammed
PFC James M. Moher
CPT Larry D. Mohler
SSG Harold L. Mohn
MRS. Elsie C. Mohr
SSG Jerry A. Mohr
CPL Percy Mohr
SGT Thomas J. Mohr
SPC Vernon Mohr
SPC Willis Francis Mohr
1SG (Ret) Richard E. Mohs
SGT Pedro Hector Mojica
SGM Jesus M. Mojila
SPC Steve Mojonier
CPT Samuel E. Mokhiber
CPT Michael T. Mokrycki
WO1 Andrew S. Molchan
SPC John Moldthan
SSG Holland K. Moler
SGT Carlos H. Molina
SPC Daniel A. Molina
SFC Frank C. Molina
SPC Jose J. Molina
SPC Rafael M. Molina
SSG Ramiro Molina
SGT Ricardo L. Molina
SGT Jason L. Molinar
CPT Pete Molinari
CPT David W. Moline
MAJ Daniel Moll
1LT Richard A. Mollandor
MR. Norman R. Molloy
CPL Bill S. Molnar
SPC George A. Molnar
SP5 Charles E. Molner
SPC Joey I. Mols
PVT Juan D. Molyneaux
COL (Ret) John L. Momeier
SGT F. Donald Monaco
SP5 Gary L. Monaco
SGT Chantele A. Monares
SFC Romain E. Monarski
SGT Joe Monastro
SPC Ricky D. Monce
SP5 Gail M. Moncivais
SSG Forrest Moncrief
SSG Willie R. Moncrief
SPC Robert L. Monday
1SG (Ret) Marvin Mondy
1LT Mitchell D. Monette
CW4 (Ret) Robert J. Monette
CSM (Ret) Ernest R. Moneymaker
SFC Alfred Mongar
SFC Junior W. Mongold
SFC (Ret) James M. Monk
SGT Sam B. Monk
SGT Elzner C. Monks
SGT Tom Monnier
PFC Dan Monroe
CPL Gene S. Monroe
SPC James L. Monroe
2LT Rodney M. Monsees
LTC George N. Monsson
SFC Eugene M. Mont
SPC Frank J. Montagna
SGT Randolph V. Montagno
SGT Frank Montalbano
CSM Francisco Montalvo Ortiz
SSG Phillip P. Montanaro
SPC Jose L. Montanez
SGM (Ret) Victor Montanez
CW3 Charles A. Montano
SGT Leonard A. Montante
SPC Mario Z. Montecino
SGT Christopher Monteith
SGT David M. Montella
SPC Veronica Montenegro
SFC Liduvino Montero
SPC Elisa A. Montes
SGM Ricky J. Montet
SGT Ramon A. Montez
SSG Alfred B. Montgomery
CPT Charles L. Montgomery
CPT David L. Montgomery
COL (Ret) James H. Montgomery
SPC John T. Montgomery
SSG Larry E. Montgomery
MS. Rita Montgomery
CPT Robin Montgomery
SGT Ronald A. Montgomery
SGT Wes Montgomery
1LT William E. Montgomery
2LT William G. Montgomery
SFC Ramon E. Montijo-Carran
SGT Brett Montiville
SP5 John Montoveno
SPC Allan Montoya
SGT Carlos H. Montoya
SPC Christopher R. Montoya
MSG Harvey H. Montoya
SFC Louis Montoya
SFC Matthew Montoya
SGT Robert Montoya
SSG Ruben Montoya
MAJ (Ret) J. Eugene Montozzi
PFC Richard W. Montrose
SGT Bobby D. Moody
1SG Craig L. Moody
LTC Herbert E. Moody
SSG Jonathan K. Moody
CPL Michael W. Moody
CPL Montclair Moody
MAJ Paul M. Moody
PVT Sean Moogan
SP5 Donald Moon
SSG James Moon
SGT Melville Moon
1LT R. Michael Moon
SP5 Terry A. Moon
SGT Mark A. Mooney
LTC (Ret) Philip A. Mooney
SPC Shawn Mooney
LTC William K. Mooney
1SG (Ret) William T. Mooney
PVT Jason W. Mooneyham
COL (Ret) John D. Mooneyham
MAJ Alan Moore
SPC Alfred F. Moore
PV2 Algernon J. Moore
SSG Alvin E. Moore
SGM Anthony J. Moore
SPC Arthur L. Moore
CPT Arthur S. Moore
SGT Bill Moore
SGT Billy V. Moore
SGT Bruce G. Moore
SFC Cedric B. Moore
CPT Cesar A. Moore
SSG Chad W. Moore
SSG Charles W. Moore
SGM Cheryl A. Moore
SSG Craig Moore
PVT Curnie D. Moore
SGT Curtis C. Moore
PVT Cyrus D. Moore
PFC Dan Moore
SFC (Ret) Danny M. Moore
SPC David K. Moore
SGT David W. Moore
SGT Demico Moore
SGT Dennis L. Moore
SGT Dennis M. Moore
MSG Dwaine R. Moore
SP5 Edward A. Moore
SFC Gary L. Moore
MAJ Gary L. Moore
LTC Gerald P. Moore
SSG Gerald T. Moore
LTG (Ret) Harold G. Moore
CPL Harold R. Moore
SFC Herman Moore
SFC Howard W. Moore
CPT Jack Moore
SGT Jack L. Moore
SFC (Ret) Jack N. Moore
SSG James E. Moore
TSgt James E. Moore
SPC James J. Moore
PFC James L. Moore
SPC James R. Moore
SP5 James R. Moore
SSG Jason G. Moore
SPC Jerry Dean Moore
SGT Jimmy R. Moore
MAJ (Ret) Kenneth D. Moore
SSG Kenneth R. Moore
LTC Lance D. Moore
SGM Linsley R. Moore
SGM Nathaniel Moore
SSG Patrick A. Moore
SSG Paul Moore
CPT Ramey Moore
SGT Ray M. Moore
SPC Raymond K. Moore
CPT Rhonda P. Moore
MSG Richard Moore
SGT Richard C. Moore
SPC Robert C. Moore
SGT Robert D. Moore
PFC Robert J. Moore
LTC Robert J. Moore
CPT Robert W. Moore
SSG Ronald D. Moore
SP5 Ronald E. Moore
MR. Roy P. Moore
LTC Sidney R. Moore
PVT Stuart D. Moore
MAJ Thomas E. Moore
SSG Thomas G. Moore
LTC Timmy D. Moore
MRS. Vernon M. Moore
MSG Vincent A. Moore
CW4 Wayne F. Moore
SFC William E. Moore
CPL William F. Moore
SGT William I. Moore
PFC William J. Moore
SGT William J. Moore
PVT William L. Moore
SSG Wilson E. Moore
PVT Zackery Moore
1SG (Ret) Joseph Moores
SP5 (Ret) David Moorhead
SPC Christopher M. Moorman
SP5 Dale L. Moorman
MAJ John R. Moos
SPC Richard Moose
1SG Steven Moose
SGT Harvey G. Moquist
SSG Adolfo Mora
SGT Daniel Mora
SFC (Ret) Gonzalo Mora
SP5 David R. Morack
PFC Carlos Q. Morada
CPL Raymond S. Moraga
MR. Herbert Moragne
SSG Benjamin Morales
MSG (Ret) Carlos Morales
PFC Cesar V. Morales
SGT Francisco Morales
SSG Gabriela Morales
SPC George Morales
SGT James M. Morales
MAJ Louis W. Morales
1SG (Ret) R. Andres Morales
SFC (Ret) Refugio Morales
SSG Sammy Morales
MRS. Sandra Morales
COL (CH) David C. Moran
SGT Donald J. Moran
CPT James R. Moran
CPT John F. Moran
SPC Jorge D. Moran
PVT Joseph D. Moran
SGT Michael J. Moran
CPT Miguel Moran
SGT Patrick J. Moran
SSG Ralph Moran
SGM (Ret) Raymond J. Moran
PVT Robert L. Moran
SGT Thomas J. Moran
CSM (Ret) Friedrich H. Morawietz
CPT Norman A. Mordue
MSG Lee R. More
CPL David B. Morehead
LTC (Ret) Benjamin Moreira
WO1 Abigail Moreland
LTC R. L. Moreland
SGT Kim Morelock
SGT Joe Morelos
SPC Jack A. Moreman
PFC Michael A. Morena
MRS. Anastacio P. Moreno
SPC Angello A. Moreno
CPT Daniel Moreno
CPT Daron Moreno
MAJ (Ret) Francisco Moreno
SFC Marcos Moreno
SFC (Ret) Richard K. Moreno
SPC Rodolfo Moreno
PFC Donald C. Moretina
SGT Dennis Moreton
SGT Jim Morey
SFC Alfred C. Morgan
SPC Andrew Morgan
CPT Carl R. Morgan
SPC Charlie Morgan
SP5 David A. Morgan
MAJ (Ret) David R. Morgan
CPL Douglas H. Morgan
PV2 Gordon B. Morgan
LTC Greg Morgan
SGT Harold Morgan
SSG Herbert Morgan
SPC Herbert C. Morgan
SGM (Ret) James N. Morgan
LTC (Ret) Jerry T. Morgan
CPT John J. Morgan
CSM (Ret) Karl K. Morgan
SGT Kenneth R. Morgan
SGT Mathew M. Morgan
SFC Michael Morgan
SGT Michael A. Morgan
SPC Robert D. Morgan
SPC Robert J. Morgan
SGT Robert Jacob Morgan
CPT Rod Morgan
SPC Sidney D. Morgan
SPC Terrence Morgan
SPC William T. Morgan
SGT (Ret) David L. Morgen
SSG Donald P. Moriarty
COL (Ret) Donald P. Moriarty
SPC Daniel Morin
PVT Ernest Morin
SGT Keith Morin
PVT Paul A. Morin
PFC John T. Morio
PFC Clifford S. Moriyama
MAJ Troy Morken
SGT Freddy M. Morlan
CPL Greg Morlen
SP5 Clifford John Morley
PFC James L. Morley
MAJ (Ret) John C. Morning
SFC (Ret) Dale E. Morningstar
CPT Brian S. Moroney
1LT Carl V. Moroney
MSG (Ret) Heginio Morquecho
CPT Benjamin B. Morrill
PFC Brandon J. Morris
MSG (Ret) Bruce T. Morris
PVT Bruce W. Morris
SPC Casandra L. Morris
SPC Charles Morris
SGT Deandre L. Morris
MSG Donnell D. Morris
MSG Ernest B. Morris
PSG Garret A. Morris
SPC Gregory Morris
SP5 Harmon C. Morris
LTC (Ret) Hubert (Hugh) Morris

SFC (Ret) Jack H. Morris
SFC James Morris
MRS. James C. Morris
SGT James T. Morris
CPT Jeff Morris
BG (Ret) John K. Morris
CSM (Ret) Joseph A. Morris
SFC (Ret) Joseph H. Morris
SSG Joseph W. Morris
SSG (Ret) Kraig Michael Morris
SP5 Lauryn Morris
SP5 Leslie D. Morris
SGT Louis C. Morris
SGT Matthew J. Morris
SPC Paul C. Morris
SPC Richard Morris
1LT Richard A. Morris
SFC S. J. Morris
SPC Terry Morris
SPC Thomas L. Morris
SGT Timothy J. Morris
MR. Todd E. Morris
MSG (Ret) William A. Morris
MAJ William D. Morris
SP5 William T. Morris
CPL Roy C. Morrisette
MSG Austin D. Morrison
CPT Bradley Morrison
SGT Bryan Morrison
SP5 Charles N. Morrison
MRS. Claude B. Morrison
SSG David L. Morrison
SGT Dennis Morrison
SSG (Ret) Howard Lew Morrison
LTC (Ret) Jack L. Morrison
CPL Jack W. Morrison
CPL James O. Morrison
SP5 Jerry L. Morrison
PFC Jerry T. Morrison
SGT Jimmy A. J. Morrison
MG John B. Morrison
SPC Les Morrison
MSG (Ret) Louis Mark Morrison
SSG Matthew Morrison
CPL Paul G. Morrison
1LT (Ret) Richard A. Morrison
PFC Ruhnner Morrison
SPC Shane Morrison
1SG Wesley R. Morrison
MR. Jack Morrissey
SGT John P. Morrissey
LTC Kevin M. Morrissey
SGT Billy Ray Morrow
CPT David P. Morrow
SGT Deane Alan Morrow
LTC Mitchell Todd Morrow
CW2 Robert G. Morrow
SGT Carl F. Morse
SPC Timothy Dale Morsett
PFC Gary R. Mortensen
1LT Richard C. Mortensen
SPC Steven Mortenson
SGT Burnis E. Morton
SSG James Morton
LTC (Ret) John Riley Morton
SPC Johnny L. Morton
MRS. Julie Morton
SPC Kenneth M. Morton
CPT Robert Alan Morton
SPC Robert L. Morton
SGT Stephanie Morton
SGT William J. Moruzzi
SGT Tommy J. Morvant
MSG William Mosby
SGT Richard A. Moscatel
COL (Ret) Robert G. Moscatelli
SGT Robert W. Moscati
SGT Bradford A. Moseley
SGT Joe T. Moseley
SGT Larry Moseley
SPC Eddie Q. Mosely
LT Martin J. Mosen
SPC Jonathan Moser
CPT Steve Moser
CPL Tommy R. Moser
PV2 Wayne M. Moses
SP5 David C. Mosher
SPC Gerald Mosher
SGT Russell L. Mosier
SP5 William G. Moskal
SPC Earle W. Mosley
SFC Nora Mosley
SSG John T. Mosqueda
SGT Bob L. Moss
SGT Bradley E. Moss
SFC (Ret) David A. Moss
SPC Dennis W. Moss
MRS. Denverd H. Moss
SFC (Ret) Harry G. Moss
CSM (Ret) Homer R. Moss
CSM John C. Moss
WO1 John F. Moss
SGT Lawrence M. Moss
SFC (Ret) Raymond C. Moss
SGT Willie James Moss
SPC James A. Mosteller
SPC Leonard Motisi
SFC Tyrone L. Moton
SPC Harry J. Motschenbacher
SP5 James L. Mott
CSM Thomas A. Mott
CPT (Ret) Joseph E. Mottola
SPC Henry B. Motty
2LT Marc Motyleski
CPT Katie R. Moughon
PFC William F. Moul
PFC Brian M. Mount
MSG William L. Mount
1SG Michael Mouton
SGT George N. Mouzakiotis
SSG Frank L. Mowery
SFC Herbert L. Mowery
SFC (Ret) Robert S. Mowl
SGT Walter E. Moxham
MAJ Bernard L. Moxley
SGT Robert M. Moya
SPC Frank P. Moyer
SrA Harry C. Moyer
SPC John K. Moyer
SGT Keith P. Moyer
SGT Ronald L. Moyer
CPL Walter M. Moyer
SFC William C. Moyer
SPC Michael P. Moynihan
LTC William B. Mozey
SGT Terrance A. Mozingo
1LT David L. Mozley
SGT Terrance A. Mrachina
CPL Joseph J. Mroczka
SPC Stephen R. Mros
SPC John A. Mroz
PFC Patrick M. Mruczek
SFC Bruce W. Muckerson
SGT Lawrence A. Mudgett
SGT Bill Mueller
SGT John E. Mueller
MR. Leslie H. Mueller
SP5 Marty C. Mueller
PVT Michael Mueller
PFC Philip F. Mueller
SPC Virgil Mueller
SSG Pierre J. Muentnich
MAJ Christopher Mugavero
PFC Mueen Muhammad
SPC Gary L. Muhs
CPT Matt Mularoni
SP5 Leslie E. Mulcahy
SFC Jose A. Mulero
CPT (Ret) Peter L. Mulford
WO1 Timothy P. Mulhall
SGT David Mulhern
SFC (Ret) James A. Mulheron
SP5 Harry A. Mulhollan
SGT Thomas P. Mulkern
SP5 David B. Mullahy
SSG Dennis L. Mullaly
MS. Carol K. Mullane
SGT Gerard T. Mullaney
SGT Thomas J. Mullaney
LTC (Ret) Cassius J. Mullen
2LT Daniel J. Mullen
MAJ Edward J. Mullen
SGT Patrick Mullen
MR. James F. Mullens
CPL John V. Mullens
SGT Kenneth Muller
SGT Richard A. Muller-Thym
PV2 Nicholas Mulligan
SFC Robert E. Mullin
CPT Timothy D. Mullin
MR. Jon Mullinax
1LT Michael L. Mullinax
SGT (Ret) J. Mike Mullings
SPC Arnold Mullins
MRS. Bill L. Mullins
SGT Gilmer Mullins
SP5 J. Michael Mullins
CPL Jeffery Mullins
SPC Robbie G. Mullins
SPC Robert G. Mullins
SPC Boyd W. Mullis
CW4 Larry L. Mullis
PFC Zachary E. Muma
MRS. Ivan W. Mumaugh
SSG Earl Mummert
CPL John E. Mumper
SSG James V. Munday
SGT Galen G. Butch Mundy
SSG Fernando Munguia
SPC Joseph Muni
1LT Philip B. Munisteri
LTC David A. Muniz
SSG Edwin Muniz
SFC Jose R. Muniz
SP5 Miguel E. Muniz
PV2 Joseph Munizich
SP5 John M. Munn
CPT Pamela C. Munn
SPC David N. Munoz
PFC John Munoz
PFC Jose L. Munoz
SP3 Peter M. Munoz
1LT Rafael Angel Munoz
SPC Ricardo Munoz
CPL Arthur L. Munsell
SPC Derek C. Munson
LTC (Ret) Don B. Munson
SPC James A. Murdock
SGM Lonnie T. Murdock
SPC Robert Murdock
SPC Thomas J. Murdock
SPC Melanie A. Murguia
SGT Fred Murillo
SGT George Murillo
SSG Ruben Murillo
MR. Charles F. Murley
SGT John P. Murnane
CPL Adrian F. Murphy
SFC Anthony J. Murphy
SGT Bill Murphy
SSG Burke Murphy
CPT Christopher M. Murphy
SGT Clifford J. Murphy
SGT Frank Murphy
SSG George N. Murphy
CPL Isaac F. Murphy
CPT Jackie D. Murphy
LTC James Murphy
MR. James Murphy
PV2 James E. Murphy
SGT Jarco Murphy
SFC (Ret) John W. Murphy
SFC Lorenzo D. (Pat) Murphy
SPC Martin J. Murphy
1LT Maurice E. Murphy
MR. Melvin Murphy
SPC Michael D. Murphy
SGT Michael E. Murphy
SPC Michael K. Murphy
SFC Patrick Murphy
SGT Patrick A. Murphy
MSG Phillip C. Murphy
LTC Powell D. Murphy
PFC Richard Murphy
LTC (Ret) Richard L. Murphy
MR. Robert Murphy
SSG Robert J. Murphy
PFC Robert T. Murphy
SSG Rodney L. Murphy
SPC Ronald E. Murphy
SSG Ronald E. Murphy
LTC (Ret) Thomas G. Murphy
SGT Thomas L. Murphy
CPL Thomas W. Murphy
CPT Timothy Murphy
SGT Tyler Murphy
PFC Walter K. Murphy
SGT Wendell Lee Murphy
SGT William J. Murphy
SSG William J. Murphy
SGT William R. Murphy
PVT Adam Murray
SPC Chesley G. Murray
PFC Gleason J. Murray
SPC James C. Murray
CPT James E. Murray
CW4 John J. Murray
SSG Patrick T. Murray
PFC Paul Murray
MR. Sam G. Murray
SPC Sam J. Murray
1SG (Ret) Thomas B. Murray
MR. William E. Murray
SFC Dion R. Murrell
CW2 Lee A. Murrell
SSG Leonard Murrell
SPC James D. Murrie
SGT James H. Murry
SPC Robert C. Murry
CPL Donald G. Murtha
LTC (Ret) Paul E. Murtha
MSG (Ret) Walter J. Murzyn
SSG Larry Muse
1LT Eric Musgrave
SFC Albert O. Musgrove
SPC Donald B. Musgrove
SPC Lyn Musgrove
SFC (Ret) Joseph W. Musial
CPL Lynton D. Musick
SSG Louis Musilli
SSG (Ret) George E. Musselman
SGT Kenneth L. Musser
SPC Terry M. Musser
SGT Frank R. Musso
SGT Christopher L. Musson
SSG Thomas J. Rick Musticchi
CPT Gregory L. Muth
LTC Marcus W. Muth
CPL Fred C. Mutter
SFC Felipe C. Muzguiz
SSG Raymond Muzquiz
SPC Omari B. Mwayungu
CW3 Walter J. Myal
SPC Nicholas Mychajluk
LTC Anthony E. Myers
SGT Clinton E. Myers
CPT David P. Myers
MAJ Duane A. Myers
SP5 Edward Myers
LTC (Ret) James A. Myers
SFC James L. Myers
SGT Jeffery D. Myers
SGT Jeffrey D. Myers
MSG Jimmie C. Myers
SPC John Edwin Myers
CPL Kevin J. Myers
SSG Leon Myers
SPC (Ret) Merl R. Myers
CPT Michael D. Myers
SGT Michael E. Myers
SP5 Michael L. Myers
SPC Michael O. Myers
CPL (Ret) Millard E. Myers
CW4 (Ret) Richard E. Myers
SGT Robert R. Myers
MSG Ronald M. Myers
SGT Stephen A. Myers
SPC Warden B. Myers
SPC Wayne D. Myers
SFC Wesley G. Myers
SSG Mark A. Myler
MG (Ret) James R. Myles
SPC Kevan E. Mynderup
SFC Jacob C. Myres
PFC Eugene K. Naatz
LTC Kent S. Nabarrete
MR. Joe L. Nabor
COL (Ret) Ramon A. Nadal
SGT Wendell I. Nadal
CSM Christopher L. Nadeau
SGT DJ Nader
CW2 John Naegele
SPC Ronald J. Nagaj
SGT Henry H. Nagami
SPC David K. Nagatani
SP5 John R. Nagel
CPL Benjamin F. Nagle
PFC Kenneth E. Naglewski
SGT John Nagorka
PFC Alan Nagy
MR. Clayton H. Nagy
SP5 Frank J. Nagy
SGT Stephen T. Nagy
SGT Shawn M. Naiduk
SGT Lori Naifeh
CPL Harroll Nakagawa
SP5 Toshio Nakano
SPC Bruce K. Nakashima
CSM (Ret) Karl H. Nakaten
CW3 Steven D. Naley
SGT Dane Q. Nalley
PVT Kenneth R. Nalls
PFC Hubert Nally
SGT Rossie M. Nance
COL Roberto N. Nang
PFC Fred E. Napier
SGT Henry Napier
SGT Walter Napier
MRS. Michelle Napolitano
SPC Timothy Napolitano
SGT Neil J. Nappi
SSG Terrell A. Narcisse
LTC Carl J. Nardei
MR. Michael A. Nardella
SGT Patrick Nardi
CW4 Glen W. Nardin
SGT Paul V. Nardomarino
MG (Ret) Michael J. Nardotti
MAJ (Ret) Frank P. Nascimbeni
MRS. Florine Nash
SPC John Nash
SGT Keith R. Nash
SPC Lawrence D. Nash
SSG Max E. Nash
MAJ (Ret) Phillip A. Nash
SPC Todd H. Nash
LT Trevor Nash
SPC Tyde R. Nash
SPC Wayne E. Nash
SSG Joe Nasypany
SGT Nelson Nathaniel
PFC Frank A. Nati
PV2 Jeremy Nations
SFC Eric Nattrass
SP5 Karl E. Naugle
SFC Willis M. Naugle
SGM (Ret) Ronald J. Naujelis
SFC Robert E. Naukkari
TSgt Alfonso R. Nava
SFC Jose Navarrete
CPT Jaime Navarro
SPC Raymond L. Navarro
LT Silvie L. Nave
CPT Bridgette Navejar
CPL Claude Nay
SPC Dennis M. Nazarok
CPT Ralph Nazzaro
PVT Dennis D. Neal
1SG (Ret) Elias F. Neal
SFC (Ret) James H. Neale
MSG Ennis C. T. Nealy
MAJ Christian M. Neary
PFC Gerald E. Neatherlin
SFC Raymond S. Nebe
SPC Quinton Nedd
2LT Marcus P. Needham
SFC (Ret) Raymond C. Needham
SSG Terry M. Needham
1LT Michael Neel
SGT William Neel
PFC William M. Neelands
SGT James Neeley
PFC Eugene D. Neelsen
SGT Dan Neely
SP5 Jack Neely
SFC (Ret) Sidney L. Neely
1LT John B. Neese
SGT Randy A. Neff
CPT Teresa D. Nefflen
PFC Robert M. Negrete
PFC Steven B. Neice
CPL Robert Neighmond
SPC Aaron Lee Neilson
PFC Robert V. Neilson
SGT William Neilson
MAJ Patrick L. Neky
SFC (Ret) Albert K. Nelms
SGT Gerald F. Nelms
SSG James R. Nelms
SGT Joe Nelms
CPL William E. Nelms
SFC Andrew L. Neloms
CPT Stacy Nelsen
1LT Allen G. Nelson
SP5 Allen L. Nelson
CPT Andrew R. Nelson
CPT Blake W. Nelson
LTC Brent V. Nelson
SPC Brian H. Nelson
SGT Bruce M. Nelson
SSG Bruce W. Nelson
CPT (Ret) Carl J. Nelson
SGT Clifford A. Nelson
PFC Delmer D. Nelson
1LT Edward L. Nelson
CPT Ellis H. Nelson
SGT Frederick D. Nelson
SGT Gary L. Nelson
LTC (Ret) George J. Nelson
LTC (Ret) George R. Nelson
LTC George W. Nelson
SP5 Gerald J. Nelson
SGT James E. Nelson
MSG James F. Nelson
CPT James P. Nelson
SPC Jeff Nelson
SPC Jerome G. Nelson
SSG Jessie D. Nelson
MAJ Joe Nelson
SGT John Don Nelson
PV2 Joseph A. Nelson
SGT Kingston Nelson
SFC (Ret) Manuel E. Nelson
LTC (Ret) Martin E. Nelson
SGT Maxwell Nelson
CW2 Michael D. Nelson
SGT Michael D. Nelson
SGT Nils F. Nelson
SPC Oscar L. Nelson
SPC Perry A. Nelson
SGT Phillip Nelson
SGT Richard Nelson
CPT Richard A. Nelson
PFC Robert Nelson
MRS. Robert A. Nelson
MAJ Robert A. Nelson
MSG (Ret) Robert A. Nelson
PFC Robert D. Nelson
SFC Robert L. Nelson
SPC Steven Nelson
MAJ Steven Nelson
SPC Timon A. Nelson
SGT Tommy A. Nelson
COL (Ret) W. Tom Nelson
SGT Warren L. Nelson
SPC Nicholas A. Nelums
CPT Wales P. Nematollahi
SPC Donald Nemeth
PFC Edward A. Nemeth
SGT Gary A. Nemeth
LTC (Ret) Howard A. Nemetsky
SGT Alex Nergelovic
SGT Marc Ian E. Nero
SGM (Ret) David L. Nesbitt
CPL John W. Nesbitt
SPC David E. Nesky
LTC (Ret) Lonnie E. Nesrsta
MAJ Terry Ness
CPL Leon Netardus
PVT Kevin R. Netcott
MR. Matthew Nethercutt
SGT Wayne L. Nethers
SSG Billy J. Netherton
SPC David Netherwood
TSgt Hal D. Neugebauer
MAJ Michael A. Neulander
CW3 (Ret) William R. Neuman
SGT Raymond M. Neuse
WO1 Bill Neuss
SPC Michael Neuzil
SGT Merle J. Nevenhoven
SPC Michael E. Neveu
SFC Richard J. Neville
MR. William E. Nevitt
SSG William H. Nevius
SPC Carl Elsworth New
CPT David R. New
PVT Terry D. New
SPC Ronald R. Newberg
SGT James M. Newberry
MRS. Johnny V. Newberry
SPC Orbit G. Newberry
CPT Berton R. Newbill
SPC Charles Ryan Newbill
SPC Stanley L. Newbury
CPT Carl G. Newby
LTC (Ret) Claude D. Newby
SPC Jay P. Newcomb
MAJ (Ret) Nelson O. Newcombe
SGT Gary L. Newcomer
CPT Jeff Newell
CPT John L. Newell
SGT Larry L. Newell
CPL Walter R. Newell
SPC Aaron S. Newhart
SGT Richard M. Newhart
COL Eric J. Newland
SSG George A. Newland
SFC (Ret) Albert W. Newman
SFC David Newman
LTC (Ret) David A. Newman
WO1 Davis O. Newman
SGT Douglas R. Newman
SGT Ernest D. Newman
SPC Gary T. Newman
PVT Ken M. Newman
SFC (Ret) Kenneth R. Newman
CPT Raymond E. Newman
SPC Thomas R. Newman
CPL Wallace R. Newman
SGT Robert Gary Newsham
1LT Joel D. Newsom
CPL Ballard Newsome
CPT Robert R. Newstead
SPC Clement Newton
PFC John H. Newton
SGT Odell Newton
MR. Robert D. Newton
SGT Thomas W. Newton
MRS. W. Creighton Newton
SP5 Walter A. Ney
SPC Frank Ng
SPC Bryson E. Ngiratumerang
SFC Marcel N. Ngobeh
PV2 Makai Ngov
CPL Dai T. Nguyen
MSG (Ret) Hoanh Nguyen
SSG Lawrence H. Nguyen
MAJ (Ret) John Niamtu
CPL Lendol J. Nibbe
CPL Charles F. Niceley
SGT Dale E. Nicholas
SSG Earnestine Nicholas

SGT Milton D. Nicholas
MAJ Ronald F. Nicholl
1LT Alexander Nichols
CPT Alfred E. Nichols
PFC Bobby G. Nichols
SSG Claude V. Nichols
SGT Curtis E. Nichols
LTC Daniel R. Nichols
MSG George E. Nichols
SSG Howard R. Nichols
SFC (Ret) James Nichols
MRS. James H. Nichols
2LT Jared W. Nichols
1SG Jerome Nichols
SPC John Nichols
SP5 John O. Nichols
CPT Josh Nichols
SFC Larry W. Nichols
MSG Leon W. Nichols
SSG Orville Daniel Nichols
SSG Percy Nichols
MR. Richard Nichols
1LT Ronald Q. Nichols
SGT Sherod J. Nichols
PVT Sonya D. Nichols
MSG (Ret) Tex A. Nichols
CPL Thomas C. Nichols
SGT William J. Nichols
SPC Brandon Nicholson
SP5 Charles B. Nicholson
SPC David A. Nicholson
CPL Donald E. Nicholson
LTC R. W. Nicholson
SSG Ralph D. Nicholson
SSG Robert C. Nickel
SGT Robert A. Nickell
MAJ Jimmie H. Nickels
SPC Frederick L. Nickens
SP5 Alan J. Nickerson
SFC (Ret) August L. Nickerson
PFC Earl Nickerson
CSM Edward C. Nickerson
CW2 Robert Nickison
SPC John Nickl
CW3 (Ret) Lance R. Nickles
SPC Joseph W. Nickleson
TSgt Edward L. Nickless
LTC James D. Nickolas
2LT Ross A. Nickoley
SFC Thomas G. Nickson
SGT Gregory Nicol
SSG Theodore Nicolas
SPC William Nicolaus
SP5 Steve Nicolich
MRS. Angelo A. Nicolosi
1LT Thomas M. Niebling
SPC Thomas Niece
CPT David B. Niederauer
SFC (Ret) Frank Niederriter
SFC Douglas Nielsen
SPC John C. Nielsen
WO1 John R. Nielsen
MR. Kenneth Dale Nielsen
2LT Patrick Nielsen
SPC Richard F. Nielsen
MAJ Shannon Nielsen
SPC Ronald L. Nielson
MRS. Ulric C. Nielson
SPC Lloyd C. Nieman
SSG Donald J. Niemann
MRS. Walter A. Niemeyer
SPC Thomas Nienalt
SP5 Nicholas Niernberger
SP5 Richard U. Niesen
SSG Jose Nieto
SGT Miguel A. Nieves
SGT Keith R. Nightingale
SPC Peter J. Nigido
CSM (Ret) Guy R. Niles
SPC Richard H. Niles
MR. Michael A. Nimec
MR. Thomas M. Nimmich
SPC William Nink
SrA Sunny Nishimoto
MSG (Ret) John R. Nistler
SPC Ron Nistler
1LT Zane A. Nitzel
PVT Cameron K. Nix
SFC (Ret) Francisco J. Nix
SGT George Nix
SGT James R. Nix
SPC Nathan M. Nix
PFC Robert A. Nix
SP3 Ronald L. Nix
SPC Robert H. Nixon
SPC Robert M. Nixon
SSG Luther J. Nixson
SGT Andrew N. Njenga
PFC Johnson R. Noah

SGT Samuel C. Noah
1SG Tony L. Noakes
MAJ (Ret) William L. Noard
SGT Donald M. Noble
2LT Douglas A. Noble
SGT Floyd A. Noble
PFC Gary R. Noble
LTC Larry H. Noble
SSG David Nobles
SFC (Ret) Jerry C. Nobles
CW4 (Ret) Jesse M. Nobles
SPC Russell S. Noblet
PFC Thomas E. Noch
MR. Steven A. Noehren
CPL Donald E. Noel
COL (Ret) James M. Noel
SGT Corey P. Noeldner
MRS. Richard B. Nogle
LTC Gerald Nolan
SPC Andrew Noland
SGT Gary L. Noland
SGT Carlos S. Nolasco
SPC Chris W. Nolen
SPC Glen E. Nolen
MR. Glenn F. Nolen
MAJ (Ret) Joe Noles
SPC Wayne M. Noller
MR. Earl L. Nolte
SPC Glen C. Noma
SGT Ronald S. Nomura
PFC George E. Nonnemacher
SPC Chris Noonan
SGT Dan A. Noonan
CPT Gerard J. Noone
SGT Charles E. Nordan
CPT Christopher James Nordin
SFC (Ret) William Nordness
SGT Gary L. Nordstrom
SPC Leroy David Nordstrom
SP5 Robert Nordstrom
LTC (Ret) Luther N. Norene
CPT Michael J. Noriega
SGT Kyle R. Norlin
SPC Bobby C. Norman
LTC Geoffrey A. Norman
1LT Jack Norman
CSM (Ret) James P. Norman
SGT Keith Norman
CW2 Tonya Norman
MAJ Craig T. Normand
SGT Charles L. Norrell
SPC Thomas Norrie
1LT Allen O. Norris
CPT Benjamin Norris
SGT Bill R. Norris
SFC (Ret) Billie P. Norris
SPC Christopher A. Norris
SPC Dennis A. Norris
MAJ Glenwood Norris
SPC Jim O. Norris
LTC (Ret) Jimmy A. Norris
SP5 Kenneth A. Norris
PVT Phillip R. Norris
MSG Richard Norris
SPC Robert A. Norris
PFC Robert R. Norris
SFC Tom E. Norris
SGT Van Sherwood Norris
PFC Butch E. North
SGM Larry E. North
SPC Randall E. North
MR. Robert North
MAJ Steven North
SGT William F. North
SSG Troy Northcutt
SGT Richard H. Northorn
PVT Edward E. Northrop
SPC Colby Norton
LTC (Ret) Dunbar S. Norton
LTC (Ret) James A. Norton
SP5 Jerry Norton
SGT Phillip R. Norton
MR. Jeffrey Norwitz
PFC Ben Norwood
SGT Micah Norwood
1SG (Ret) William F. Nosen
SGT Giles C. Nossett
COL (Ret) Robert D. Nossov
SSG Ralph Nota
LTC (Ret) Michael B. Nott
SSG Paul L. Nouhan
SFC Anthony Nourse
TSgt Alan L. Novak
1LT Daniel T. Novak
CW2 (Ret) Frank J. Novak
SGT Paul J. Novak
1LT Philip A. Novak
SPC Walter M. Novak
1LT Edward J. Novakoski

CPL Johnny J. Novela
SPC Joe Novosielski
MRS. Albert H. Novotny
1SG (Ret) Allen D. Novreske
LTC James F. Novy
SPC John Nowa
1SG (Ret) Joseph M. Nowacki
SP5 Daniel A. Nowak
SGT Gregory F. Nowak
CW4 (Ret) Walter J. Nowakowski
SP5 Douglas S. Nowell
SPC Gerald Nowicki
SPC Leonard W. Nowicki
SPC Philip A. Nowlan
SGT John W. Nowling
COL (Ret) Dean A. Nowowiejski
SPC Charles E. Noyes
CPT Eric R. Noyes
PFC Francis M. Nucci
PVT Daniel Nuessle
PFC Joseph A. Nunes
MSG Richard R. Nunes
SSG Frank Nunez
MR. Peter Nunez
SGT Raul Nunez
PFC Bradley Nungester
SGT Carl W. Nunley
SFC (Ret) Friedrich Nunley
CSM David W. Nunn
SGT Thomas J. Nunn
SGT Dennis L. Nunnally
SFC Richard F. Nunnally
LTC (Ret) Stephens W. Nunnally
SGM (Ret) Paul Nussbaumer
SGT Maxine A. Nussman
CW4 Wayne C. Nutsch
MR. Veldon J. Nuttall
SPC Randall C. Nyberg
SGT Daniel T. Nye
SGT Lester D. Nyenhuis
SP5 Gerald L. Nygren
SFC Michael A. Nygren
CPL Henry R. Nylan
SPC Kenneth L. Nyswaner
SGT Thomas Oakden
SPC Gary A. Oakes
CPL Jonathan M. Oakes
SPC Robert T. Oakes
MR. Thomas J. Oakes
CW2 Donald H. Oakley
CPT Glenda Oakley
COL (Ret) Howard H. Oakley
MAJ (Ret) Lon D. Oakley
SFC Robert Oaks
PFC Harold J. Oas
SP5 Ayden J. Oates
LTG Michael L. Oates
SSG William R. Oaxaca
SP5 Thomas K. O'Barr
CW2 Ralph W. Obenauf
BG (Ret) Harry B. Oberg
SFC Paul W. Oberlies
SSG Richard J. Obershaw
TSgt Edwin A. Oberste
SPC Phil Obetts
LTC Kurt Obispo
SGT Ernest Obman
SPC Patrick H. Obrecht
SPC Arthur Obregon
PFC Joseph T. O'Brian
SFC William O'Briant
SGT Eugene P. OBrien
SP5 John T. O'Brien
SGT Michael Vincent O'Brien
SGT Patrick C. O'Brien
SSG Paul J. O'Brien
SPC Peter P. O'Brien
PFC Richard M. O'Brien
SGT Roger R. O'Brien
PFC Ronald E. O'Brien
SGT Wilbur D. O'Brien
SPC William O'Brien
SPC William M. O'Brien
1SG (Ret) Michael E. O'Bryen
SPC Jeremiah P. O'Carroll
SFC Cesar O. Ocasio
SGT Blas Ochoa
SGT Carlos Ochoa
SGT Gustavo R. Ochoa
SGT Richard D. Ochoa
1LT Edward J. O'Connell
SGT Larry G. O'Connell
BG (Ret) Michael G. O'Connell
SGT Richard O'Connell
SGT Wilbert J. O'Connell
SGT Denis R. O'Connor
SSG Frank X. O'Connor
SGT Iyanda S. O'Connor

PVT James E. O'Connor
MR. John F. O'Connor
1LT John P. O'Connor
LTC (Ret) Joseph P. O'Connor
1LT Joseph P. O'Connor
COL Jospeh W. O'Connor
SGT Neil J. O'Connor
LTC Ryan P. O'Connor
CPT Theodore R. O'Connor
2LT Thomas O'Connor
SGT Thomas V. O'Connor
SGT Todd K. O'Connor
SPC Fernando J. Ocontrillo
1SG (Ret) Robert M. O'Daniel
SSG Gerald Odefey
SPC Christopher O'Dell
SFC (Ret) Frank L. O'Dell
SPC George W. O'Dell
PFC Liana O'Dell
PV2 Roger D. Oden
CPL Ben E. O'Diam
PFC Jordan Odle
SFC Emmit C. Odom
SGT Kenneth W. Odom
SPC Neil H. Odom
CPL Hugh C. O'Donnell
CW3 (Ret) M. J. O'Donnell
CPT Magnus P. O'Donnell
SP5 Michael K. O'Donnell
SSG Patrick T. O'Donnell
MR. Ralph E. O'Donnell
WO1 Terrence J. O'Donnell
SPC Jeremiah O'Donovan
SGT (Ret) Ken W. O'Donovan
SPC Howard Odum
SPC Jimmy Odum
SPC Larry D. Odum
MRS. Carole O'Dwyer
COL (Ret) Dennis R. Oechsner
SPC Mark H. Oehler
CPT Carl S. Oelschig
MR. William Oelslager
SPC Haakan F. Oestlin
SGT Karl D. Oestreich
PFC Shawn D. O'Farrell
SSG Emmanuel Ogbolu
MR. Harold K. Ogden
PVT Patsy M. Ogden
SGT Elvin Ogg
CPT Olufunso S. Ogidan
MRS. Betty Ogle
SGT Chester H. Ogle
SPC David L. Ogle
CPL David P. Ogle
LTC (Ret) Glenn A. Ogle
SGT Roger Ogle
SGT Verlis Ogle
SPC James W. Oglesbee
LTC (Ret) George O'Grady
SGT Stephen R. O'Grady
SGT Stephen R. O'Grady
SPC Daniel F. O'Hagan
SGT Eugene F. O'Hara
SP5 George M. O'Hara
SGT Howard J. O'Hara
SSG Paul E. O'Hara
SPC Henry R. Ohlsen
TSgt Michas M. Ohnstad
SSG (Ret) Skip Ohrt
SGT Daniel W. Okada
SGT Joseph W. O'Keefe
CPT Kevin P. O'Keefe
CW2 Michael A. O'Keefe
CPT Michael F. O'Keefe
SGT Paul B. O'Kelley
CPT Shane M. O'Kelly
SGT A. Wayne Okken
SPC Richard Okner
SGT Anthony Okonji
MRS. John M. O'Kucian
1LT John J. O'Laughlin
SGT Robert Olcott
SGT Thomas L. Old
PFC Douglas V. W. Oldenburg
MAJ (Ret) Peter Oldfield
CPL John Oldham
CW3 Lance Oldham
SPC Leonard F. Oldland
LTC (Ret) Pat O'Lear
SSG Brian J. O'Leary
TSgt John M. O'Leary
PFC John W. O'Leary
1LT Joseph V. O'Leary
SSG Matthew O'Leary
CPT Michael S. O'Leary
SPC Michael Oleksiak
SGT Joseph J. Oleszkiewicz
SGT James Michael Olheiser
SFC Robert R. Olin

SFC John R. Olinger
SFC Eric J. Oliphant
CPT Jose Oliva
LTC John B. Olivar
SFC Jesse James Olivares
MR. Peter A. Olivas
SPC Thomas Oliveira
MAJ Antoime D. Oliver
LTC (Ret) Charles A. Oliver
LTC Daniel Oliver
SPC Gary A. Oliver
SSG Hugh M. Oliver
2LT Jeffrey E. Oliver
SGT Julia Oliver
SPC Kenneth Oliver
PV2 Mark D. Oliver
SPC Ronald C. Oliver
PV2 Xiomara Oliveras
LT Robert Olivi
SSG Roger D. Olivier
CPL Frank J. Olivio
2LT John R. Olivo
SGT Lawrence E. Olle
SPC Sean M. Ollek
SSG Charles M. Ollervidez
SPC Paul B. Ollila
SPC Robert E. Ollis
SGT Kenneth R. Ollison
LTC Douglas Ollivant
PV2 Matthew R. Olps
SPC Shaun S. Olsberg
CW2 Alan Olsen
SP5 Chris A. Olsen
LTC (Ret) Donald R. Olsen
SGT John R. Olsen
PFC Noel Olsen
LTC (Ret) Wesley R. Olsen
TSgt Myron G. Olsgaard
CPT John A. Olshefski
SPC David A. Olshove
SPC Arthur J. Olson
SGM Dallas D. Olson
SPC Donald D. Olson
PFC Donald G. Olson
CPL Floyd W. Olson
SPC Glen A. Olson
1LT Gregory A. Olson
CPL Harry Olson
PFC Henry Olson
SPC Kenneth G. Olson
SFC Matthew A. Olson
MR. Maynard L. Olson
SGT Roger G. Olson
SPC William P. Olson
PFC Dennis D. Olsonawski
SPC Edward Olvera
SFC William Olynyk
SPC Andrew E. O'Malley
SSG Eugene P. O'Malley
CPT F. Ward O'Malley
SPC Vance Edward Onderek
PVT Robert L. O'Neal
DR. Ruben M. O'Neal
1SG Terrance W. O'Neal
LT Mitchell L. O'Neel
SPC James M. O'Neil
SPC Joseph F. O'Neil
CPT Michael E. O'Neil
SGT Brian J. O'Neill
SGT Joseph P. O'Neill
1LT Steven J. O'Neill
SPC Charles T. Onellion
SPC Jeffrey K. Onest
PFC Theodore R. Onest
SP5 James J. Ong
SP5 Reon Onstine
CPT Bill M. Onstott
CPL James Ontano
CPT John L. Ontko
SFC David P. Opalewski
SGT Jose L. Opio
SGT Peter J. Opitz
CW2 James S. Opp
SP5 Ernest E. Oppenheim
SPC Karl Robert Oppermann
LTC Erhard P. Opsahl
2LT Luis R. Oquendo
SGT Arthur R. Orato
SPC Ronald E. Orazine
CSM John A. Orbe
PFC Ronald Ordonez
SPC Louis A. Oreamuno
1LT Altangerel Orgil
SPC Joseph T. Orient
SGT Anthony P. Orifici
LTC (Ret) Robert E. Orkand
SSG Pete Orlando
SFC Thomas J. Orlando
LTC (Ret) Frank T. Orlevitch

PFC Robert F. Orndorff
PFC Daryl L. Orns
SPC Charles O'Rourke
SGM Mike O'Rourke
LTC Morgan Dan O'Rourke
SPC Juan Orozco
MR. Jerry Orpen
TSgt Alton F. Orr
MAJ Ethan Orr
CPT Gary M. Orr
MSG John A. Orr
SGT Romer R. Orr
SGT William A. Orr
1SG Otto Orraca
CW4 Harry W. Orser
COL Jim A. Orsini
MSG George Ortega
PFC Javier A. Ortega
MR. L. J. Ortega
CPL Oscar G. Ortega
PFC Ruben S. Ortega
SSG Corey P. Ortego
SGT Vernon R. Ortenzi
SGT Paul Ortenzio
SGT Jesse J. Ortez
SPC William Orth
SSG Mario A. Ortigara
SSG Alberto Ortiz
SPC Antonio Ortiz
SSG Carlos Ortiz
CPL Donald C. Ortiz
MR. Ernesto Ortiz
CSM (Ret) Guillermo C. Ortiz
SSG Jose A. Ortiz
MAJ Jose R. Ortiz
SGT Luis A. Ortiz
SPC Nelson Ortiz
SGT Noe Ortiz
SGT Raymond Ortiz
SSG Reinaldo Ortiz
TSgt Robert M. Ortiz
CPT Ruben I. Ortiz
MSG (Ret) Ruben L. Ortiz
1LT Juan Ortiz-Rivera
SPC Brian S. Orto
SP5 Ronald Orton
SFC Stephen L. Ortwein
MRS. Mary Orvis
CPL Michael James Orwig
SPC Justin Orzechowski
SGT Charles S. Osborn
SGT Edward M. Osborn
SPC Ronald G. Osborn
CSM David A. Osborne
1SG David A. Osborne
SPC Dennis M. Osborne
SGT Earl H. Osborne
MR. George M. Osborne
SPC Major M. Osborne
CW2 Paul G. Osborne
SGT Raymond B. Osborne
MR. Robert Osborne
SGT Thomas A. Osborne
LTC (Ret) W. Herbert Osborne
CPT John C. Osbourn
LTC Tyler Osenbaugh
CPL Gene L. O'Shea
SGT Valor J. O'Shea
SGT Noble J. O'Shell
SP5 Clyde S. Oshiro
CPL Frederick F. Osmun
PVT David Osorio
SFC Wilfredo Osorio
SFC David Osornio
1SG (Ret) Daniel W. Ossa
SGT Henry J. Oster
SGT Howard A. Osterberg
SSG Robert Osterland
LTC Gary R. Ostrander
SGT Michael J. Ostroski
SPC Joseph B. Ostrowski
LTC (Ret) Peter O'Sullivan
SGT Victor Phillip Osweiler
MAJ George Oteiza
SSG Angel M. Otero
PFC Angel M. Otero
SSG Plinio G. Otero
SPC Roy P. Otero
SGT Steven R. Otey
SP5 Keith Otis
SFC Thomas E. Otis
SGT Walt Otolinsky
MAJ Elias D. Otoshi
SGT Shawn J. Ott
CPT David F. Ottavianelli
SGT Gary S. Otte
CPT Kenneth L. Otte
PFC John W. Otten
PFC Kenneth S. Otterstrom

SSG Jay Ottinger
SPC Wayne Ottinger
SPC William E. Ottis
CW2 James M. Ottman
SSG Jason E. Otto
PFC Matthew J. Otto
SPC Richard J. Otto
SP5 Jimmy C. Ottwell
SPC Colin M. Ouderkirk
SP5 Gilbert L. Ouellette
PFC Lee M. Ouellette
SGT Robert Ouellette
SPC Robert P. Ouellette
SGT Elmer G. Ours
SGT Dwight Ousley
PFC John A. H. Outhuijse
SSG Dan R. Outlaw
MAJ Darrell R. Over
MSG Steve Overby
SPC Frederick Overing
CPT William P. Overmohle
SP6 Maxey R. Overmyer
MAJ Richard E. Overmyer
PV2 Johnnie R. Overs
CSM Antoine B. Overstreet
SPC Joseph R. Overstreet
COL Charles D. Overton
MAJ James Doug Overton
CPT Robert O. Overton
SGT William B. Overton
LTC (Ret) Kenneth L. Overturf
PFC John M. Owada
MRS. Betty D. Owen
MSG (Ret) Calvin J. Owen
SSG (Ret) Dewey G. Owen
SSG Jeffrey S. Owen
SPC Joab Owen
LTC (Ret) Joseph K. Owen
MAJ (Ret) Larry L. Owen
SPC Philip A. Owen
SPC Thomas H. Owen
CPT A. A. Owens
SSG Alvin L. Owens
1SG Andre L. Owens
SGT Bart E. Owens
SGM Brad T. Owens
1SG Clifford L. Owens
MR. Dallas D. Owens
1SG (Ret) David T. Owens
SGT David W. Owens
SGT Desmond Owens
SSG Freddie J. Owens
SGT (Ret) Howard M. Owens
SGT James H. Owens
SGT James N. Owens
SSG James R. Owens
MAJ James R. Owens
SGT James W. Owens
CPT John J. Owens
CW4 (Ret) Marion F. Owens
MAJ Marland L. Owens
SSG Michael Owens
SGM (Ret) Paul J. Owens
SFC (Ret) Ray D. Owens
CSM (Ret) Ronald D. Owens
SSG Royce X. Owens
SGT William H. Owens
SFC Willis G. Owens
SGT Michelle V. Owens Martin
SGT Wayne K. Owings
CPL William J. Oxenford
MR. Larry E. Oxley
SSG Lawrence E. Oxman
CPL Tom S. Oyama
SPC Martin C. Oyer
PSG Alfred S. Oyler
MSG (Ret) Francis G. Oyler
CW4 Robert R. Ozier
SGT James M. Paar
CW5 Jeanne Y. Pace
SP5 John C. Pace
MAJ Vincent A. Pacelli
SFC Brig Pacheco
SPC Frank Pacheco
PFC Mathew Pacheco
MR. Tomas Pacheco
MAJ Jackie C. Packer
SP5 Robert D. Packham
CPT Michael Padar
SFC (Ret) Ronald Padavan
SPC Cannon Paddie
SPC David R. Paddock
SGT Dale L. Padgett
MR. Jeff M. Padgett
SGT Willis Padgett
SGT Felix R. Padilla
PFC Franklin Padilla
SPC Jody B. Padilla
SPC Terry Padovan
SPC Liliana B. Padromercade
SGT Michael M. Paestella
CSM (Ret) Gilbert Paez
SFC Sidney L. Pafford
1LT John Pagano
LTC Bertrand A. Page
SSG Donald R. Page
2LT Dwayne K. Page
SPC Harold Page
SSG Henry F. Page
CPT Jonathan Page
SPC Jonathan R. Page
SP5 Ronald F. Page
SGT Stephen M. Page
SSG Terry G. Page
SPC William B. Page
MG (Ret) William C. Page
SSG William P. Page
1SG (Ret) Willis Page
CPL Robert A. Pagillo
MR. John B. Paglia
PFC Deno A. Pagliai
PFC David L. Paige
SPC Kelley Paige
LT Jeffrey O. Paine
SSG Thomas S. Paine
SPC Sean M. Painter
SSG (Ret) Luis F. Paiz
SPC Jerry Pala
PV2 Julian H. Palacio
SPC Herbert B. Palacios
1SG (Ret) Gene Paladin
SPC John M. Palermo
2LT Joseph P. Palermo
PVT Alvin Paliani
PFC Kenneth L. Palicki
SP5 Armando A. Paliotta
CW2 Daniel G. Palivoda
CPT Eric T. Paliwoda
CPL Luke Palladino
MSG Elwood C. Palm
MR. Gennane Palma
SPC Nicholas Palma
SSG Raymond Palma
SFC Jocelyn E. Palmares
SGT Brian Palmer
LTC (Ret) Charles R. Palmer
SPC Daniel Palmer
MR. David William Palmer
SFC Donald Bruce Palmer
MAJ Frederick Palmer
SSG Gerald M. Palmer
MAJ Ian C. Palmer
SGT Jack W. Palmer
SPC John J. Palmer
PSG Leslie L. Palmer
SSG Lloyd Brent Palmer
MAJ Matthew Palmer
CPL Nicola J. Palmer
PFC Robert Palmer
SPC Robert L. Palmer
MRS. Tomoko Palmer
1LT Maxwell Palumbo
SSG Robert J. Palumbo
CPL Elea Pambuku
SGT Curtis Pandorf
SGT Ronald S. Pandos
1SG (Ret) Willie L. Pandy
SPC Carl W. Panetta
SPC Joel C. Panetta
1LT Frank Pangborn
PFC Ray A. Pangle
PVT Robert G. Paniagua
2LT David M. Panian
SPC Gregory A. Panik
SPC Randall J. Panke
LTC Mark L. Pankow
TSgt George Pannacciulli
SFC Norman Panther
SPC Joseph A. Panzardi
SGT Thomas G. Paoli
PFC Raymond J. Papp
CPL Gary Neal Paquette
SPC Robert G. Paquin
SGT Jose M. Paranal
PFC Michael J. Parchom
SGT John Pardee
CW2 Brian D. Pardo
SGT Isidros Pardo
CW4 Charles H. Pardue
SGT James B. Pardue
SPC Anthony Paren
SPC John J. Parente
CPL Byron L. Parfrey
PVT Gary V. Parham
SGT Gerald H. Parham
SFC Reginald Parham
SSG William Michael Parham
LTC (Ret) Edward J. Paris
COL (Ret) Howard S. Paris
MAJ William A. Paris
1SG Charles L. Parish
CPL Claude T. Parish
SSG Elden M. Parish
PFC Jason B. Parish
SPC Willard F. Parish
CPL Amedeo A. Parisi
MR. James R. Parisot
SSG Curtis L. Park
LTC Francis J. H. Park
SPC Oliver Park
SSG Thomas D. Park
PFC Alexander Parker
SPC Bobby D. Parker
SFC Brant Parker
SFC Brent Parker
MRS. C. W. Parker
1SG Charles R. Parker
PFC Chris D. Parker
SPC Claude Parker
SP5 Claude O. Parker
MAJ (Ret) David L. Parker
SPC Dean E. Parker
SFC (Ret) Earl L. Parker
SGT Gary A. Parker
MAJ James C. Parker
1LT Jason Parker
MAJ John R. Parker
SGT John S. Parker
SGT Joseph E. Parker
SPC Joseph L. Parker
CSM (Ret) Keyron J. Parker
SGT Larry B. Parker
SGT Larry D. Parker
CSM Larry D. M. Parker
SGM (Ret) Louis D. Parker
SrA Marvin C. Parker
CPL Michael Q. Parker
COL (Ret) Michael W. Parker
LTC (Ret) Neal G. Parker
SP5 Raynauld J. Parker
SGT Richard R. Parker
CPT Robert A. Parker
PFC Robert H. Parker
CPT Robert S. Parker
SPC Roger S. Parker
SFC Roman E. Parker
SSG (Ret) Russell Eugene Parker
PFC Stanley R. Parker
CW3 Stevan D. Parker
SGT Troy H. Parker
LTC (Ret) Wendell G. Parker
CPT (Ret) William Parker
2LT William J. Parker
SGT Michael G. Parkhill
CPL David L. Parkhurst
CPL Bernard W. Parkinson
SGT Douglas B. Parkinson
SPC George T. Parkinson
SPC John P. Parkinson
PFC Charles Parks
SP6 David E. Parks
SPC Edward D. Parks
SPC Larry Owen Parks
SFC Marlow Parks
LTC Robert R. Parks
SP5 Gerald W. Parnall
SPC Edsel C. Parnell
CW3 (Ret) Leslie D. Parnell
SSG Louis Parnell
CSM (Ret) Robert W. Parnell
MAJ (Ret) Gary K. Parr
CW4 Harry P. Parr
MAJ (Ret) Roland R. Parr
SGT Steven H. Parr
PFC William G. Parr
SFC Andrew A. Parra
SGT Wayne Parra
CPL Thomas C. Parramore
MSG Evaristo Parras
CSM (Ret) Ronald A. Parrett
CPL Roger A. Parrie
SGT Bobby A. Parris
MSG Eric E. Parris
PFC Matthew Parris
CSM Michael A. Parris
MRS. Glenwood N. Parrish
1LT Jeffrey J. Parrish
SFC Joseph H. Parrish
SPC Larry W. Parrish
LTC Robert D. Parrish
SGT Robert L. Parrish
SGT Robert Leon Parrish
SGM Ronald B. Parrish
SSG Ronald P. Parrish
SPC James M. Parrot
1LT Demetrius D. Parrott
SP5 Max F. Parrott
CPT Bruce E. Parry
SPC Matthew J. Parry
COL (Ret) William H. Parry
SGT Chandresh Parsaud
SSG William H. Parsonage
CSM Berk Parsons
CW4 (Ret) Gary F. Parsons
SGM James H. Parsons
SGT Jonathan C. Parsons
SSG Kenneth T. Parsons
SPC Mahlon Parsons
LTC Michael Parsons
SPC Michael L. Partee
SPC Thomas Partee
SPC Cory J. Parten
LT J. David Particelli
SSG Ed Partin
SPC Richard M. Partington
PFC Joseph David Partney
SGT Stanley Parvanoff
PVT Ronald Parzero
SSG Gregory Pascal
PFC Earnest C. Paschal
SFC (Ret) Karl E. Pasco
CSM (Ret) Henry Pascua
PV2 Chase Pasek
SGT Karl Pasero
LTC (Ret) Timothy L. Pasquarelli
CPT Matthew J. Passarell
SP5 Ralph D. Passero
SSG Frank T. Passini
CPT Mitchell G. Passini
SFC Alan A. Passmore
PFC Michael S. Passmore
SGT (Ret) George J. Passwater
MAJ John Pastella
SGT Paul J. Pasternak
SPC Armando Pastran
SGT Steven R. Patchen
SPC Kenneth L. Pate
MAJ Ralph Pate
SSG (Ret) Robert L. Pate
SPC Kenneth W. Patek
CPL Raymond M. Patella
PVT Eugene C. Pateman
SGT Joseph D. Paterwade
CPL Kenneth R. Patete
SSG Robert A. Patitucci
MSG (Ret) Donald H. Patrick
TSgt Homer Patrick
SGT Howard B. Patrick
SSG James R. Patrick
SGT James W. Patrick
SGT Walter Patrick
SGT Robert Patrizio
SPC George R. Patten
PV2 Bobby Patterson
SGT Charles Ray Patterson
PVT Charles W. Patterson
SPC Conrad L. Patterson
CPT Daniel K. Patterson
SSG David L. Patterson
CPL Donn D. Patterson
LTC Flint M. Patterson
SGT George J. Patterson
SGT Godwin E. Patterson
SGT Howard Patterson
SSG J. Robert Patterson
SPC James M. Patterson
MR. James R. Patterson
MRS. Kenneth M. Patterson
SSG Lawrence Patterson
SP5 Michael A. Patterson
MAJ Michael W. Patterson
CH (CPT) Robert Patterson
SFC Robert F. Patterson
SGT Robert J. Patterson
SPC Roger D. Patterson
SGT Ruben G. Patterson
SPC Thomas Patterson
1LT Thomas H. Patterson
PVT Willie G. Patterson
CPL J. E. Patteson
SGT Clifford Patton
2LT James P. Patton
SPC Jesse D. Patton
SPC Neil G. Patton
MR. Robert Patton
MAJ Robert S. Patton
CPT Scott Patton
SGT Vincent Patton
SPC W. Robert Patton
SrA Kenneth E. Pattrell
SPC Emery L. Paugh
SGT Allen E. Paul
CPL Brian Paul
SP5 Chuck Paul
CW3 (Ret) Delbert A. Paul
SP5 Gary M. Paul
SPC James A. Paul
SGT Kelly R. Paul
MSG Rex L. Paul
PFC William H. Paul
SPC Joao P. Paula
SPC Jack C. Paule
PVT Robin A. Paulette
PVT Henry John Pauley
PVT Curtis L. Paulhamus
SPC Joseph M. Paulik
SSG Clarence Paulk
MR. Roger G. Paulmeno
SGT Thomas M. Paulovitz
SSG Billy D. Paulsen
TSgt Clifford J. Paulsen
LTC (Ret) David D. Paulsen
1SG (Ret) James G. Paulsen
SSG (Ret) Duane R. Paulson
CPL Harry M. Paulson
MAJ John C. Paulson
SPC David J. Paulus
SGT Frankie Paulus
SPC Nicholas A. Paulus
SPC John Pavlik
CPL Paul J. Pavlik
MRS. Ivan R. Pavlovich
SPC Dennis A. Pavluk
SGT Robert H. Pavone
SFC (Ret) Martin D. Pawlak
TSgt Wadsworth H. Pawlik
SGT Larry P. Pawloski
CPT Aleksandr Pawluk
SPC Edwin P. Paxton
2LT Adrienne Payne
SGT Bennie F. Payne
PFC Coy C. Payne
SGT Forrest J. Payne
SP5 Gary F. Payne
SPC John C. Payne
PVT John C. Payne
SGT John L. Payne
PFC Larry D. Payne
MAJ Mack W. Payne
MAJ Robert Payne
CSM Samuel J. Payne
SFC Fred L. Payton
SGT Russell E. Payton
SSG Clement D. Peace
PFC Donald Peach
1LT William C. Peachey
1LT Patrick L. Peacock
SSG Robert Peacock
PFC William T. Peacock
CW4 Wyndell D. Peacock
MR. Darrel A. Peakes
SSG Jerry C. Peal
CPL Kenneth Peal
SSG James E. Peale
SPC James Pearce
LTC Jeffrey W. Pearce
SGT Richard Pearce
MR. William V. Pearce
MRS. Gerald Pearsall
WO1 Arnold C. Pearson
1LT Frank L. Pearson
MR. Ira F. Pearson
SPC James M. Pearson
SGM (Ret) James W. Pearson
PVT Joy L. Pearson
CW4 (Ret) Keith R. Pearson
MRS. Kenneth E. Pearson
SPC Zachariah J. Pearson
SGT Thomas R. Pease
CPL Michel J. Peat
GEN (Ret) J. H. Binford Peay
MAJ William J. Peberdy
SFC Jason E. Peck
SGT Roy Peck
MSG Wendell R. (Ray) Peck
1SG Michael Peckinpaugh
MSG Edgardo S. Pecson
SPC Billy R. Peden
1LT Marvin M. Peden
1SG (Ret) Orla T. Pedersen
1LT Randen Pederson
CSM (Ret) Walter H. Pederson
MR. Edward Pedraza
SPC Josean D. Pedraza Melendez
CPT Viterbo D. Pedregon
SPC Jimmie Peebles
CW2 John N. Peele
COL John A. Peeler
MAJ Patricia A. Peeler
SGT William C. Peevy
SPC Leroy E. Peffley
SFC (Ret) Richard K. Pegg
SSG Karla K. Pegues
SPC Reginald J. Peguese
CPL Thomas R. Peichert
MR. Bobby R. Peikert
MRS. Rodman H. Peil
SPC Manford C. Peins
SFC Vanessa M. Pelesasa
PFC Richard A. Pelfrey
CPL Frank J. Peljae
SGT David J. Pelkey
MRS. Frank Pellegrino
SP5 Samuel J. Pellegrino
SGT Samuel T. Pellegrino
MRS. Andy Pellerito
SPC Louis I. Pelletier
SPC Raymond N. Pelletier
SGT Jack W. Pellington
MRS. Mell S. Pelot
1SG (Ret) John J. Pelow
SPC Robert Peltak
SPC William R. Pelton
MAJ Greg Pelts
MSG David Peluso
SGT Travis K. Pelz
SGT James T. Pemberton
SPC Steve Pemberton
PFC William C. Pemberton
SPC David C. Pembroke
SGT Abelardo Pena
MRS. Delphino Pena
SGT Eloy C. Pena
SGT Elvis H. Pena
PFC James A. Pena
PFC Joe R. Pena
SGT Mario Anthony Pena
SSG Oracio Pena
SGT Oscar N. Pena
SSG Pablo Pena
SSG Ricardo P. Pena
PFC Richard R. Pena
SGT Roel Pena
MSG Kristian F. Penafiel
1LT (Ret) Albert L. Pence
CSM (Ret) Larry D. Pence
SPC Curtis A. Pendergraft
SPC Stephen M. Pendergrass
CPL Charles R. Pendleton
PFC David A. Pendleton
CPL Robert F. Pendleton
SP5 Verne H. Pendleton
1SG (Ret) Glenn M. Pendley
SPC Bernard B. Penfield
PFC Milton Penfield
SSG Paulo Penitani
CW2 Frank J. Penk
SGT Charles B. Penkunis
PFC (Ret) Burton M. Penn
PVT Eric D. Penn
LTC Kendall W. Penn
CPL Lester R. Penn
SFC Leon S. Pennepacker
SGT Charles E. Pennewell
SPC David E. Penney
SP5 Julius Penney
1SG Timothy Penning
MR. Anthony J. Pennington
SPC Douglas W. Pennington
MRS. John L. Pennington
MR. Jon Pennington
SGT Ronald D. Pennington
SPC Raymond Penninpede
SGT Forrest J. Pennison
SGT Keshnel S. Penny
MSG Richard L. Penny
SPC Thomas Penny
MAJ Clarence E. Penree
SGT Mike W. Penrod
SGT Christopher S. Pentilla
DR. (CPT) Elizabeth M. Pepe
MRS. Helen E. Pepe
SSG Matthew A. Pepe
SPC Robert Pepin
SPC Steve Pepin
CW4 (Ret) William L. Pepin
SFC (Ret) A. J. Pepper
SPC Adam W. Pepper
SSG (Ret) Charles W. Pepple
MR. James R. Pera
1SG (Ret) Frank J. Perales
SSG David Percivill
1SG Grady Perdue
MR. Francisco Pereda
SGT Roy Michael Pereira
CPL Richard G. Peres
SGT Romano M. Peretti
PFC Alfred G. Perez
SSG Antonio Perez
SGT Calistro Perez
SPC Danny Perez
SPC Eduardo A. Perez
CSM Eliodoro Perez
SGT Emilio J. Perez

SGT Ernest R. Perez
SSG Faith Perez
1SG (Ret) Felix M. Perez
PFC Francisco Perez
SPC Gabriel R. Perez
PFC Gerald J. Perez
SSG Henry Perez
SGT Javier A. Perez
SPC Jesus D. Perez
PFC Jose G. Perez
SSG Joseph M. Perez
SPC Juan D. Perez
1SG Juan L. Perez
1SG Kalep Perez
SPC Louie Perez
SFC Luis A. Perez
PVT Marcos Antonio Perez
LTC Mario Perez
SGT Michael Perez
SFC Norberto Perez
LTC Octavio Perez
1SG Paul E. Perez
1SG Raul Perez
SPC Rey Perez
SSG Richard Perez
SGT Robert R. Perez
SFC Sam Perez
SPC Santiago Perez
SGT Steven S. Perez
SSG Rosalba Perez Chavez
MR. Paul Perfelz
SPC Ernest L. Perham
SPC Adam L. Perkins
SGT Adolphos J. Perkins
CW3 Arland V. Perkins
MR. Carey L. Perkins
PFC Darrell W. Perkins
SFC Edgar R. Perkins
PVT Evan Perkins
SPC Gregory A. Perkins
SGT J. David Perkins
PFC James R. Perkins
SPC Jeffery A. Perkins
CW2 John P. Perkins
SPC Kenneth F. Perkins
CPT Kris N. Perkins
MR. Lamar S. Perkins
SSG (Ret) Marion W. Perkins
SGM Robert S. Perkins
SPC Ronald Perkins
PVT Thomas P. Perkins
SPC Christopher W. Perkowski
MS. Debra Pernice
SSG Kenneth L. Perrault
TSgt Adelard J. Perreault
PFC Frank P. Perreira
1SG Donald Perrier
MAJ (Ret) Peter H. Perrino
MSG Alvin B. Perry
SFC Anthony L. Perry
SGT Arthur W. Perry
1LT Bill J. Perry
SPC Charles E. Perry
1LT Charles R. Perry
SGT David R. Perry
SGT Edward G. Perry
PFC Eugene Perry
PFC Frederick J. Perry
SPC Gerald Perry
SSG Glen J. Perry
SSG Harry L. Perry
SFC (Ret) Henry M. Perry
LTC J. Shawn Perry
SGT James E. Perry
PFC James Lewis Perry
LTC Jeffrey C. Perry
MR. John Perry
SGT John A. Perry
1SG Lewis E. Perry
SSG Michael G. Perry
SGT Nicholas T. Perry
SPC Phil F. Perry
SGT Richard Perry
LTC (Ret) Richard Perry
SP5 Robert P. Perry
LTC Thomas A. Perry
SGT Thomas O. Perry
CPT Troy D. Perry
SSG William H. Perry
SGT Joseph Persaud
PFC Edward P. Pershing
SP5 Roland H. Perske
MSG Audie Person
CPL Lance Persson
SP5 Robert L. Peskey
SPC Tom Pessagno
SPC William M. Pestana
CW4 Terrence Pestel
SGT James Pestle
MAJ Jeffrey Pete
SFC David M. Peter
COL (Ret) Daniel Peterjohn
SPC Bryan Peterman
1LT Charles David Peterman
SSG Dennis Peters
SGT Devan Peters
SPC Dillon Peters
PVT Eva K. Peters
COL (Ret) Harry E. Peters
CPL John M. Peters
SGT John P. Peters
PVT Joshua Peters
1SG (Ret) Leon Peters
SSG Oliver H. Peters
PVT Paul T. Peters
SSG Randall V. Peters
CPL Roshelle S. Peters
MRS. Vern O. Peters
MR. Wallace Peters
SSG Edward E. Petersen
SGT Gary R. Petersen
CPL Harold J. Petersen
SP5 Paul A. Petersen
SPC Thomas Petersen
LTC (Ret) Bruce A. Peterson
SPC Charles Peterson
SGT David A. Peterson
SrA Dawn A. Peterson
SP5 Donald F. Peterson
MAJ Erik S. Peterson
SGT Gregory C. Peterson
SSG James A. Peterson
SGT James C. Peterson
MR. James W. Peterson
CPT Jay T. Peterson
SFC John E. Peterson
PFC John R. Peterson
LTG (Ret) Joseph F. H. Peterson
COL (Ret) Merle J. Peterson
MR. Nick Peterson
MAJ (Ret) Philip H. Peterson
SPC Robert A. Peterson
MAJ Robert A. Peterson
SPC Ronald J. Peterson
CPL Roy E. Peterson
SGT Samuel J. Peterson
MSG Stephen C. Peterson
SP5 Terry W. Peterson
SGT William E. Peterson
SSG William J. Peterson
CPT Zachary Peterson
SGT Charles G. Pethel
MSG Joseph J. Petka
SP5 Peter Z. Petr
SGT Nicholas A. Petracca
CW4 Jim Petraitis
SP5 Gary A. Petras
SPC Luigi Gino Petrella
SPC Bennie W. Petrey
MRS. Clifford L. Petrey
SPC Dennis L. Petrick
LTC (Ret) Richard J. Petronis
SGT James R. Petrosky
SGT Goce Petrov
PFC Ronald J. Petrovich
CW2 Michael G. Petrovick
MR. David C. Petruska
PFC William J. Petrula
SFC Eric Joseph Pettell
CPT Kristian Pettengill
SPC Donald B. Pettibone
SPC Charles L. Pettljohn
SGT Gregory G. Pettis
SP5 Russell Pettis
MR. Loney O. Pettit
SFC Richard A. Pettit
CPL Martin A. Pettrone
PVT Victor A. Pettus
MR. Franklin M. Petty
PVT Robert Petty
CSM (Ret) Sam J. Petty
CPT Paul A. Petzrick
SGT Benny Peveler
COL (Ret) Daniel B. Peyser
MR. Paul Peyser
MR. Gary W. Pezzuti
SFC Edgar P. Pfaff
PFC (Ret) George J. Pfaff
SPC Kenneth L. Pfau
SSG John W. Pfeiffer
1SG Hans J. Pfeil
SP5 Thomas L. Pfenningwerth
SGT Jeremy S. Pflaume
SGT Jason J. Pflugh
SPC Joseph D. Phalen
SGT Albert Pham
WO1 Hien Nhu Pham
SPC Khanhhung Pham
SGT Long Pham
SPC Patrick A. Pham
LTC Dam Van Phan
1LT Donald H. Phares
SGT Richard A. Pharney
SFC Christopher Phelps
COL (Ret) Lawrence P. Phelps
SFC (Ret) Michael A. Phelps
PV2 Richard P. Phelps
SGT William Philblad
SP3 Jack F. Philbrick
PFC Thomas Philip
PFC Gerard Philipp
COL (Ret) Ronald E. Philipp
PFC Mark L. Philips
SSG Antonio Phillips
SPC Arthur H. Phillips
SSG Charles A. Phillips
MR. Clyde W. Phillips
SPC David M. Phillips
LTC (Ret) Dean A. Phillips
PFC Frank G. Phillips
MSG (Ret) George H. Phillips
PFC Gordon B. Phillips
SFC Grant B. Phillips
PFC Howard R. Phillips
SGT James A. Phillips
SFC James F. Phillips
LTC (Ret) James H. Phillips
SGT James W. Phillips
SSG Jason J. Phillips
SP5 Jay H. Phillips
MG Jeffrey E. Phillips
SGT Jeremiah M. Phillips
MR. Jerry W. Phillips
LTC Jesse Phillips
CPT Jocolby Phillips
CPT Joe E. Phillips
SPC John T. Phillips
PVT John W. Phillips
SPC Johnnie L. Phillips
SGT Joseph Phillips
SGT Keith N. Phillips
SSG Michael C. Phillips
PFC Paul N. Phillips
SSG Richard Phillips
MSG (Ret) Richard P. Phillips
PVT Robert R. Phillips
SGT Ronald W. Phillips
SSG Steve H. Phillips
SGT William B. Phillips
SFC William F. Phillips
SGT Gerald D. Phillipy
SGT Roger L. Philo
SGT Gary Philpot
PFC Loren D. Phippen
2LT Brian F. Phipps
SGT Gerald D. Phipps
CSM Marlon B. Phipps
SSG (Ret) Michael A. Phipps
SFC Okey W. Phipps
PFC Stephen F. Phipps
SPC Dat K. Phun
SSG Daniel R. Piantaggini
SPC Mark A. Piasecki
SPC Victor A. Piaszik
SGT Ronald H. Piatek
PFC Robert H. Picano
SSG Thomas E. Picarella
SPC Louis J. Picariello
SPC Jack Picciolo
SPC Gerald W. Picha
MSG (Ret) William O. Pick
PFC Vincent G. Pickard
SGT James E. Pickell
SGT Ariana Pickens
SGT David M. Pickens
CPT Patton K. Pickens
PVT Troy S. Pickens
SGT Harry I. Pickering
SPC Randall A. Pickering
SP5 Craig Pickett
SPC George E. Pickett
SGT William H. Pickle
SSG Gerald L. Piehl
SPC Donald Pienkowski
CPT Greg Pieper
PFC Hamilton C. Pieper
1LT Kenneth L. Pieper
SGT John R. Piepowski
PFC George W. Pierce
SPC Harold Pierce
SGT Harold D. Pierce
2LT John M. Pierce
SFC Joseph L. Pierce
SP5 Kenneth M. Pierce
SPC Kenneth W. Pierce
SSG (Ret) Larry M. Pierce
PFC Leo Pierce
SSG Raymond L. Pierce
MSG Raymond R. Pierce
SGT Richard A. Pierce
SGT Ronald L. Pierce
SPC Thomas G. Pierce
CPT Wendy Pierce
LTC Wilbur R. Pierce
COL Fremont Piercefield
SPC David A. Pierman
SP5 Howard A. Pierson
CPT Matthew Pierson
SFC Roger D. Pierson
BG Aundre F. Piggee
SSG Victor Pignanelli
SPC Frank A. Pignataro
CW2 Michael G. Pignataro
PVT David L. Pike
SGT John E. Pike
SGT John R. Pike
MR. Reed Pike
SSG Walter John Pike
SP5 Wilber G. Pilgreen
CPT Chad M. Pilker
MR. Paul W. Pilkerton
MAJ Bryan K. Pillai
SFC Charles Pillers
MSG (Ret) Ronald A. Pilling
SPC Vernon C. Pilling
MAJ Harry Pillot
PVT James G. Pillsbury
SPC Kenneth Piltz
SSG James Pimental
CPL Larry V. Pimental
SGT Vannak Pin
SGM (Ret) Edmond A. Pinault
MAJ Kenneth D. Pindell
SGT Daniel Lee Pine
MRS. Edward H. Pine
CW4 (Ret) Carlos M. Pineda
CPT James A. Piner
1LT Derek K. Ping
SSG (Ret) James J. Pinget
SFC William Pingrey
CPT George E. Pinkerton
COL Kurt Pinkerton
SSG Albert Pinkham
SPC Franklin A. Pinkham
MR. Andrew P. Pinkos
SGT Donald Pinkston
PFC Alex A. Pino
SGT Manuel Pino
SGT Adrian Pinon
LTC (Ret) James W. Pinson
SGT Timmy Pinter
SPC Anthony J. Pinto
SFC Richaro Pinto
MAJ Cristian A. Pinzon
MR. Julius Piorkowski
MSG Arthur H. Piper
MSG (Ret) Robert F. Pipes
SPC Frank Pipitone
CPL Harry V. Pipkin
SSG James W. Pipkin
SPC Paul Pipo
SGT Herb Lee Pippin
CSM James D. Pippin
SFC Anthony J. Piraino
SSG Charles J. Piro
LTC Richard G. Piscal
SPC Joseph Pisciotta
1LT Roy R. Pistone
SP5 Fred Pisturino
SFC Bernie D. Pitcher
SSG Harvey A. Pitcher
CPL Gary J. Pitchford
CSM Eric Pitkus
CPL Lloyd Pitman
SGT Mark J. Pitman
SGT Cruz Pitre
SGT Tom Pitstick
COL (Ret) Ernest M. Pitt
PVT Popito Pitters
PFC Bennie M. Pittman
SGT Donald R. Pittman
MSG James L. Pittman
SSG Michael Pittman
PVT Richard L. Pittman
PV2 Timmy R. Pittman
SSG Wilfredo L. Pittman
PFC Daniel J. Pitts
PFC Dorman D. Pitts
MSG John B. Pitts
SPC Mark Pitts
MSG Ralph Pitts
COL (Ret) Russell N. Pitts
SPC Jeffrey Pitzen
SGT Charles A. Piwonski
BG (Ret) Allan G. Pixton
LTC (Ret) Christopher C. Pixton
CPT Dennise M. Pizarro
SPC Robert W. Pizzi
SPC Stephen J. Place
1LT David Plain
MR. James Plair
CPL Ecton J. Plaisance
MR. Ray Plaisted
PFC Alford B. Plamondon
PFC Val Ray V. Planer
PV2 John T. Planinshek
SPC Daniel H. Plant
SFC Steven M. Plante
MR. Eduardo G. Plascencia
SGT Alvin R. Plasek
CSM (Ret) Frank C. Plass
SSG Joseph E. Plasters
MR. Richard Plastine
SP5 Joseph R. Plata
MR. Peter W. Platt
SP5 Don C. Plattsmier
SGT Lyle D. Platz
PV2 Jimmie Pleasant
SSG (Ret) William Pleat
SSG (Ret) William T. Pleat
SGT Vanessa J. Pleban
CW4 Jerry Lewis Pledger
SGT Barry Plesser
LTC George D. Pletcher
SGT Tom Pleuss
SPC Jacob L. Plisek
SFC William Plotner
SPC Harry P. Plotycia
SPC James Plovanic
CPT Robert E. Plowey
1LT Michael T. Plowman
SFC Anthony J. Pluhar
SSG Bruce D. Plumb
SPC Harold E. Plumlee
CPT Comer Plummer
LTC (Ret) Gerrell V. Plummer
PVT Shane E. Plummer
LTC Thomas B. Plunkett
COL (Ret) Daniel B. Plyler
SFC Dewey C. Plyler
SP5 Steven R. Plyman
1LT Richard C. Pobgee
SFC (Ret) John P.S. Podgornik
CPL Thomas R. Podobnik
SGT Donald M. Podolak
SGT W. C. Podraza
SGT Elvis L. Poe
CW5 (Ret) Robert A. Poe
PV2 James R. Poellinger
SPC James E. Poelstra
SGT Charles R. Poff
CPT (Ret) Dennis S. Pogany
SGT Terry Pohl
SPC Bryan K. Pohlen
SPC Brandon Pohler
SPC Boddy A. Poirier
MRS. Lucien Poirier
SSG Analdo Polanco
SGT James A. Polanco
SGT Brian E. Poland
SPC Michael C. Poland
SPC Herbert Polchow
SGT Douglas J. Poldoski
SPC Clinton D. Poley
PFC Simon I. Polisky
CPL William F. Polites
SP5 Frank J. Polivka
PVT Anthony R. Polk
COL John F. Polk
CPT Kendal V. Polk
SGT Lacey L. Polk
LTC Patrick B. Polk
2LT Nicholas Pollacia
PFC Robert W. Pollack
SGT Stanley I. Pollack
MR. Vincent J. Pollak
SPC Barry N. Pollard
SPC Charles R. Pollard
SPC Darrell W. Pollard
LT David E. Pollard
SSG Lance Pollard
SGT Shed Pollard
SGT Gerald Pollay
SGT David L. Polley
CPL Roger W. Pollitt
1SG Earl A. Pollock
MSG Ronald D. Pollock
MRS. Monica Polnik
PVT Ray A. Polock
COL (Ret) Edmund H. Polonitza
MR. Frank J. Polsak
2LT Robert B. Polston
2LT Thomas D. Pomenti
1SG Tony Pomerlee
SGT James A. Pomeroy
PVT Steven G. Pomeroy
SSG (Ret) William A. Pomeroy
LTC (Ret) Stephen D. Pomper
SPC Christopher Ponce De Leon
SPC Donald A. Pond
MAJ Jeffrey R. Ponder
PFC Marcus N. Poneroy
PVT David L. Ponton
SPC James Pontz
SGT John L. Pool
MR. Robert B. Pool
SPC Pascal C. Poolan
LTC Richard W. Poole
SPC Ross G. Poole
SP5 Victor Poole
SFC Warren D. Poole
SGM (Ret) Willard G. Poole
MR. William F. Poole
SGT John E. Poor
SPC Holly N. Poore
MR. Cornel J. Popa
LTC (Ret) Arthur L. Pope
SSG Billie G. Pope
SPC Dakota Pope
SGT Evan Pope
SSG Gary L. Pope
SPC Jerry L. Pope
SGT Kenneth L. Pope
COL Thomas G. Pope
LTC (Ret) William A. Pope
COL (Ret) Roger E. Popham
MR. Joe Popielowski
SGT James L. Popik
SGT Donald W. Popp
CW4 (Ret) Kenneth Popp
SPC Victor Porchiazzo
MAJ David P. Porreca
PFC Harold N. Porstner
SSG Anthony J. Portelli
COL (Ret) Bruce Porter
MAJ (Ret) Gail F. Porter
SFC (Ret) James E. Porter
PV2 (Ret) Jeff A. Porter
1LT John M. Porter
SGT Mike Porter
SPC Ronn D. Porter
SGT Terry A. Porter
CSM (Ret) Terry J. Porter
LTC William D. Porter
SGT Gordon B. Porterfield
CPT Harry W. Porthouse
SPC Joseph S. Portugal
SPC James Posey
SGT Robert A. Poskocil
SPC David J. Posner
CSM Shane Pospisil
SPC Jerry D. Poss
CPT Mark T. Post
MSG Patrick Post
CPT Thomas D. Postema
SSG Timothy M. Postema
SP5 Albert M. Postma
2LT Jennifer A. Poston
MR. Michael Potpinka
1LT David W. Potter
MSG (Ret) Enoch I. Potter
SGT Gary P. Potter
SPC Jack Potter
SGT James A. Potter
MSG James G. Potter
SFC James H. Potter
SSG Orie R. Potter
SPC Terry L. Potter
SFC (Ret) James W. Potts
MRS. Jerry L. Potts
CPT John O. Potts
LTC (Ret) William L. Potts
WO1 Joseph M. Potvin
SPC Patrick J. Potvin
CW4 Robert F. Potvin
CPT Thomas K. Poulakidas
SPC Theodore P. Poull
COL (Ret) Stephen P. Poulos
LTC Michael L. Poumade
SSG Edwin A. Pounal
SGT Robert Poundstone
PFC Thomas Powalie
SPC Brian Powell
SGT Charles Powell
SPC Charles E. Powell
PFC (Ret) Charles E. Powell
SFC Douglas Powell
CPT Duncan D. Powell
WO1 (Ret) Edward Powell
SPC Floyd Powell
SFC Glennie M. Powell
SSG Jason Powell
SPC Jeffrey J. Powell
SPC Jerome Powell

SSG Joe Ell Powell
LTC (Ret) John W. Powell
MSG Lemuel N. Powell
MRS. Leo D. Powell
LTC Mark F. Powell
SPC Mike Powell
CW3 Neal W. Powell
CPL Oliver H. Powell
LTC (Ret) Raymond F. Powell
COL Richard L. Powell
SGT Richard S. Powell
COL (Ret) Robert Powell
SGT Thomas I. Powell
SSG Travis Powell
MSG William T. Powell
SGT Gary Power
CPL James V. Power
SGT Roger Power
1SG Kenny Powerlopez
1SG (Ret) Archie B. Powers
SPC Charles F. Powers
SP6 Hugh C. Powers
SPC James T. Powers
SPC Jimmy C. Powers
SGT Lloyd C. Powers
SGT Michael S. Powers
CPT Patrick H. Powers
1LT Richard A. Powers
SGT Robert Powers
SPC Robert K. Powers
SP5 (Ret) William J. Powers
CPT Russell Powledge
SPC Jack Poyner
1SG (Ret) Ray E. Poynter
SSG Robert A. Pozek
SGT Jack Poznansky
SPC Sim Pradhan
SGT Porfirio Prado
Sp Justin E. Pragel
PFC Fredrick L. Prahl
SPC Louis Praino
PFC James Prappas
PFC Norm Prasatik
SPC Jerry T. Prater
MRS. Morgan L. Prater
SPC Nyan B. Prater
CPT Stephen Prater
LTC (Ret) Tim Prater
1SG Ray D. Prather
CW2 James G. Pratt
SGM Jesse R. Pratt
SGM John N. Pratt
SGM Larry Pratt
COL (Ret) Michael W. Pratt
CPL Paul K. Pratt
CW4 Robert N. Pratt
SGT Walden J. Pratt
PVT Aaron C. Pratte
MAJ Brian W. Pray
SPC Myron A. Prchal
CPL Thomas Prchal
SSG Gregory Lyle Preast
PFC David E. Preble
SSG Thomas A. Preece
SP5 Ivan G. Preheim
PVT John G. Prendergast
SGT Christopher R. Prentice
SPC Lisa A. Prentice
MSG Monica Prescher
MSG (Ret) David E. Prescott
CPT Scott A. Prescott
SPC Charles W. Presley
MR. Walter Presley
SPC David W. Presnell
CPT Richard L. Pressley
CPT James L. Pressman
SPC George Presson
SFC George Presswood
SSG David D. Preston
MRS. James E. Preston
CPT Jeff Preston
MSG (Ret) John B. Preston
SPC Joseph Preston
SMA (Ret) Kenneth O. Preston
SPC Thomas D. Preston
CPL Walter F. Preston
CPL Wesley Preston
PFC Len Pretty
CPT Ronald G. Pretty
SPC William F. Prettyman
SP5 Jerry D. Prevatt
SGT Paul L. Prevatte
PFC Lawrence E. Prevette
2LT Andrew Prevost
SPC Jason L. Pribble
MRS. Ben S. Price
LTC Curtis Price
SPC Curtis W. Price
CPT David R. Price
SGT Eddie Price
SGT Edward Price
LTC (Ret) Eric R. Price
SSG Gerald Price
SPC Ivan Price
CPT J. Dave Price
CPT James A. Price
1SG James H. Price
LTC Joe Price
SGT John D. Price
SP5 John S. Price
MSG (Ret) Johnnie S. Price
SGT Kenneth R. Price
PFC Louis K. Price
LTC Martin L. Price
MAJ Michael H. Price
SGT Michael R. Price
SSG (Ret) Ollie B. Price
SFC Paul E. Price
SGT R. J. Price
CPT Richard A. Price
LTC (Ret) Robert D. Price
SPC Robert M. Price
CPL Ronald Price
SGT Ronald J. Price
SGT Ronald K. Price
SPC Walter L. Roy Price
SPC William G. Price
SGT Angela Price-Aman
CW3 Thomas H. Pride
SGM Van J. Prier
CPT Hardy W. Priest
MRS. John R. Priestner
SGT Alfred J. Prihoda
CPT Donald Prill
SFC Ramiro Primero
SP5 William D. Primrose
SGT Antonio B. Prince
MRS. Beatrice Prince
SPC Charmion M. Prince
MSG William B. Prince
SPC Mike Prindiville
1LT Paul R. Prindle
2LT Jefferson P. Pringle
CPL Donald C. Pringnitz
MR. Claus Prins
LTC Danny L. Prins
MRS. Sharon J. Priskorn
SPC Brent Pritchard
SGT Dennis G. Pritchard
SGT Gary L. Pritchard
SSG (Ret) Lewis Pritchard
PVT Michael Pritchard
SSG Graden Pritt
LTC William H. Privette
SPC Gene E. Proctor
PV2 Theron L. Proctor
SPC Fred J. Prokop
COL (Ret) John H. Prokopowicz
SGT Tom Propes
CPT Travis A. Propes
SGT Donald J. Protas
SSG James E. Proteau
SFC Gregory J. Protsko
SGT Dennis P. Proulx
SGT Sean Provart
CPL Anthony F. Provenzano
LTC Kerry Prowell
SSG (Ret) James Prpich
1LT Andrew S. Pruett
SGT (Ret) James Henry Pruett
PFC Dale R. Pruitt
COL (Ret) Earl E. Pruitt
SPC Garland W. Pruitt
MR. James D. Pruitt
SSG Rayburn A. Pruitt
MSG Roy R. Pruitt
SSG (Ret) Russell W. Pruitt
SSG Cynthia Pruitte
SGT Ronald F. Prushko
SGT Joseph K. Pruszinski
MRS. David H. Pryce
SPC Albert R. Pryor
SGT Charles E. Pryor
2LT Gabriel W. Pryor
TSgt Joseph W. Pryor
COL (Ret) Philip A. Pryor
SGT Paul Pryslopski
LTC (Ret) Edward C. Prytko
1SG David Przepiora
SrA Eugene J. Przybyl
SFC Felix J. Przybylowicz
SPC Walter J. Przybysz
SGT Bruce C. Publicover
SGT Daniel Puccetti
SPC Alexander A. Pucilowski
CSM Drury M. Puckett
SPC Joseph A. Puckett
SGT Ray A. Puckett
SGT Michael M. Puente
MAJ Carlos A. Puentes
GS-10 Joan L. Puffer Kotcher
CPL Donald Pugh
PFC Douglas N. Pugh
MR. Johnny D. Pugh
SGT Kary Lee Pugh
1SG (Ret) Thomas D. Pugh
1LT Walter Jim Pugh
PFC Tom Pugliese
SP5 Richard M. Puhan
CPT Enrique V. Pujals
SPC Emily Pules
CPL Jesus B. Pulido
CSM John P. Pulido
CPT Manuel F. Pulido
SPC Roger L. Pullan
MAJ (Ret) Joseph F. Pullano
SP5 Donald J. Pullen
SGT Robert T. Pullen
SGT Charles N. Pulley
1LT Doug A. Pulliam
COL Nathan M. Pulliam
SPC Ralph Pullin
MAJ (Ret) Haliday M. Pullum
SSG Maria Fedelez D. Puls
PV2 Tyrone Pulse
MRS. Bernard P. Pulvermacher
MRS. A. T. Pumphrey
MR. Armando Punceles
SSG Michael Puppolo
SGT Michael Puraty
PFC Darryle Purcell
SGT John M. Purcell
SGM Rick Purdin
PFC Melvin Purdy
SPC William L. Purdy
SPC Leonard Wayne Purinton
SSG Marc Purinton
SFC (Ret) Rayfield M. Purnell
1LT Michael S. Purtill
LTC J. Keith Purvis
SGT James N. Purvis
SPC Bobby W. Puryear
MRS. George W. Putnam
CW4 Ira W. Putnam
COL (Ret) Lawrence H. Putnam
CPT Thomas T. Putnam
CPL William R. Putnam
SSG (Ret) William R. Putnam
SPC Stanley J. Putra
SFC Eric Putt
SFC Robert M. Putzer
CPL Tony A. Pyara
SSG Rusty Pyatt
MR. R. Douglas Pye
LTC Dale M. Pyeatt
SPC Michael J. Pyfferoen
SSG Billy R. Pyle
SPC James M. Pyles
SPC Jonathan Pyles
SPC William P. Pylilo
SP5 Gregory James Pylman
MSG (Ret) Richard W. Pylypuw
SGT Kenneth P. Pymm
CPT Michael D. Pyott
SGT Daud K. Qawiyy
SSG Jason A. Quade
MG (Ret) Marilyn A. Quagliotti
PFC Edward H. Quail
CPT Gary F. Qualley
SGT Julian N. Qualley
SP5 Noris L. Qualls
SGT Roger M. Qualls
MRS. Allen J. Quam
CPT Rolland J. Quam
SSG Ronald A. Quam
MRS. James D. L. Quan
2LT Vincent V. Quarles
SSG Donald A. Quash
SSG Nicholas Quattrone
CSM (Ret) Matthew S. Quay
SSG Douglas J. Queen
CPL Kenneth Queener
SPC John Quello
SPC James E. Quesenberry
PFC Lee E. Quesenberry
SSG Joshua Quick
SPC Lisa A. Quick
SPC Daniel F. Quigley
SFC (Ret) Donald J.G. Quigley
SPC James E. Quigley
SPC Thomas Quigley
SPC Alec J. Quijano
SGT Donnie W. Quillen
SGT Vitus D. Quillet
SPC Ernest E. Quinn
SGT Gary Norford Quinn
PFC James S. Quinn
SSG John P. Quinn
CPT Patrick D. Quinn
SGT Stephen Quinn
LTC L. P. Pete Quinnell
SPC James R. Quinnett
SSG Jesse Quinones
SSG John Quinones
SSG Mariano Quinones
SGM Juan L. Quinones-Pagan
CPL Simon Quinonez
SP5 Robert L. Quintana
SPC Juan A. Quintanar
PFC Eric Quintanilla
SGT Jario A. Quintero
SPC Clifford Kalup Quinton
SGT Damon S. Quinton
SGT Lyle N. Quist
CPT Mark Quivers
MRS. Anne Parker Qureshi
MR. Robert J. Raab
SGT Gary A. Raabe
CSM (Ret) Leonardo B. Rabago
SFC Joseph Michael Rabas
MRS. Donald F. Rabb
SGT Michael D. Rabb
PFC Lyle M. Rabbitts
MR. Jimmie H. Raben
COL William S. Rabena
SPC Stanley Rabesa
1SG Marc Rabins
SGT Ted Rabkin
SGT David R. Rabon
LTC William T. Rachal
SGT (Ret) James E. Rachau
CPL Clifford R. Rachford
SPC Kevin C. Rachford
SPC Stanley J. Rachuba
LTC Armand E. Racine
SSG Al Rackley
COL (Ret) Duane Rackley
COL (Ret) James Thomas Rackstraw
CPT John J. Rada
MR. Michael J. Radcliff
SGT Marvin W. Radcliffe
SPC H. Philip Radecker
CPT Colin R. Rader
CPT Justin P. Rader
SGT Melvin Rader
CW4 (Ret) Samuel P. Rader
SGT Scott William Rader
CPT Stacy Rader
CSM (Ret) Tony Radetic
SPC Bruce T. Radford
SFC Roy Radke
SP5 Steven W. Radke
SP5 Wilhelm F. Radl
LTC Eden L. Rado
SPC Andrew T. Radtke
1LT Thomas J. Radwell
1SG John R. Rael
SSG Jerome J. Rafalski
SPC Frank P. Raffa
CPL Raymond L. Raffaelli
SSG Michelle Rafferty
MG (Ret) Frank P. Ragano
SP5 David L. Ragsdale
SPC Donald Ragsdale
SGT Gerald W. Ragsdale
TSgt Thomas E. Rahe
SPC Glenn A. Rahorst
CPL William F. Rahorst
SSG Brian C. Raine
SSG Dennis G. Raine
PFC Carl R. Raines
MR. James F. Raines
SPC William F. Raines
SFC Edward Rainey
PVT Marvin L. Rainey
CPT Michael B. Rainey
SP5 William H. Rainey
CPT (Ret) Jackie R. Rains
MRS. Joanne Rains
LTC (Ret) Ronald D. Rainville
SGT David Wayne Rainwater
LTC Ross A. Rainwater
SGT Roman V. Rajm
CPL Wilbur A. Rakow
1SG Jesse D. Raley
1LT (Ret) William P. Raley
TSgt Daniel Ralich
SPC Dan Rall
PFC Harold Ralph
PFC Bob N. Ralston
SFC Charles S. Ralston
SGT Creighton L. Ralston
MG (Ret) David C. Ralston
SGT Kevin Lee Ralston
SGM (Ret) Lyndon P. Ramage
CPT William Rambo
SGT William D. Rambo
SP5 Fred S. Rambur
SGT Agapito A. Ramirez
SGT Alfredo Ramirez
2LT Carlos A. Ramirez
CPT Carol Andrea Ramirez
1SG (Ret) Eduardo Ramirez
SGT Eugene A. Ramirez
MSG Frank H. Ramirez
SSG Gil Ramirez
SPC Gilbert T. Ramirez
SGT Harley Ramirez
1SG (Ret) Hector G. Ramirez
SPC Isack Ramirez
CPT Jason Ramirez
SGT John M. Ramirez
SSG Johnny Ramirez
CW3 Jose A. Ramirez
MSG (Ret) Joseph E. Ramirez
SSG Juan A. Ramirez
CPT Michael R. Ramirez
SSG Ramiro A. Ramirez
SFC (Ret) Raul Ramirez
SFC Rick Ramirez
SSG Santiago Ramirez
PFC Steve Ramirez
SPC Sylvia Ramirez
PFC Daniel W. Ramlow
1LT Rakesh Ramnarine
SGT Jesus Ramon
SFC Joseph D. Ramon
PFC Roberto P. Ramon
SPC Adrain Ramos
2LT Bruce Ramos
TSgt Carl S. Ramos
SGT Carlos G. Ramos
SGT Edison Ramos
SFC Erick Ramos
SGT Guadalupe Ramos
SFC John Ramos
SP5 (Ret) Leonardo Ramos
SFC Luis Ramos
2LT Meghan Ramos
CPL Reinaldo Ramos
CPT Richard Ramos
SSG Salvador D. Ramos
SPC Tracy A. Ramos
SFC Pedro J. Ramos Ramos
CPT William A. Rampmeier
SPC David M. Ramsay
DR. Stephen R. Ramsburgh
COL (Ret) John J. Ramsden
MR. Phillip Ramsell
PVT Clyde A. Ramseur
SPC Billy W. Ramsey
MAJ (Ret) James L. Ramsey
MSG James R. Ramsey
MR. Lenox Ramsey
SGT Lowell M. Ramsey
SPC Robert F. Ramsey
LTC Russell W. Ramsey
SGT Ryan Ramsey
SPC Steve Ramsey
SrA Stewart W. Ramsey
1LT Christian J. Ramthun
MSG (Ret) Lloyd P. Ranalli
SGT Cory Rand
SGT Gary M. Rand
SSG Walter Rand
CW4 Craig V. Randall
CPL Hilton K. Randall
SGT Nicholas K. Randall
MR. Tom Randall
SSG Frank E. Randant
SGT Tad Randell
SGT Thomas E. Randell
MAJ (Ret) Claiborne Randle
SGT Robert K. Randleman
SGT Richard L. Randol
SSG Jonathan Randolph
SGT Nancy R. Randolph
SGT William F. Randolph
SFC (Ret) John Rangel
1SG Nicolas Rangel
MAJ (Ret) Daetha J. Rankin
MAJ H. Michael Rankin
SGT Thomas W. Rankin
SPC Frank B. Rannie
SGT Steven E. Ransbottom
SGT John G. Ransome
PV2 Randell D. Ranson
CPT Kevin J. Rants
SPC Harish B. Rao
SPC John Anthony Raper
SPC Scott M. Raper
SGT Charles M. Raphael
MR. Henry F. Raposo
SPC Richard Rapp
SPC Alan Rappaport
SGT Joshua M. Rarick
1LT Eric K. Rasanen
DR. James J. Rascher
SGT Alvin James Raschke
SFC Richard R. Raschle
SPC Andre Rascoe
SGT William R. Rasely
SGT Ronnie Rash
CW2 Gordon Rask
SGT Michael R. Rasmussen
SFC James S. Rasnake
CPT James R. Rasnick
PFC Glenn O. Ratcliff
SSG Steven W. Ratcliff
SGT Hugh E. Ratcliffe
SSG William J. Rath
MR. Robert Rathburn
SPC Craig S. Rathjen
CPT John F. Rathman
SSG Earl R. Ratledge
2LT Abe R. Ratliff
SPC Dennis M. Ratliff
SGT Donald F. Ratliff
MR. L.W. Ratliff
SFC Larry Ratliff
SPC Neal F. Ratliff
SGT Randall B. Ratliff
SGT Vern Roger Ratliff
MG (Ret) Donald V. Rattan
SPC James M. Ratti
SGT Joseph Paul Ratti
SGT Norman J. Ratzlow
CPT (Ret) Merlin W. Rau
SP6 Harold D. Raub
PFC Blair D. Rauch
PFC Junior A. Rauch
CPL Oliver E. Rauch
SGT John M. Rauh
SPC Larry I. Rauh
CPT Contanya Ravin
PVT Thomas Ravinsky
1LT Richard Ravnsborg
MAJ (Ret) Joe H. Rawl
COL James S. Rawlings
SPC Shawndall R. Rawls
MR. Allen D. Ray
SGT Charles H. Ray
SGT Daniey Ray
SPC James E. Ray
PVT Jerome H. Ray
LTC John L. Ray
MSG Kenneth E. Ray
SGT Michael G. Ray
MR. Michael T. Ray
SGT Norman D. Ray
SPC Philip W. Ray
PFC (Ret) Richard A. Ray
MR. Robert D. Ray
COL (Ret) Robert L. Ray
1LT Waymond L. Ray
SPC William A. Ray
SGT Alvin K. Raycraft
CPL John C. Rayder
SFC Scott H. Rayman
COL James Herbert Raymer
SFC Alfred H. Raymond
SGT Daniel G. Raymond
SPC Kenneth C. Raymond
MAJ Robert K. Raynard
CPT Ashton J. Read
CPT B. John Read
CPT John P. Read
CPT Jack L. Reade
PFC Michael W. Readnour
CPL Adam Readout
MRS. Dorthy Reagan
SSG Michael Reagan
SSG Kenneth A. Real
SGT Joseph Reale
SGT Larry W. Ream
MR. Philip E. Reams
PFC John E. Reap
PVT Gordon A. Rearden
SGT James L. Reardon
SGT James W. Reardon
MR. Leo Reardon
LTC Myles Reardon
CPT Thomas L. Reardon
WO1 Andrew C. Rearick
1LT Scott Reasland
SFC (Ret) Hollis T. Reasons
SGT Bradley Reaves
SGT Timothy O. Reaves
CPT Darren M. Rebelez
SPC Rich Rebholz
1LT Ralph E. Rech
1LT Dwight L. Recht
CPL Delbert A. Reckart

CPT John J. Recke
CW4 (Ret) Gerald M. Reckman
MR. David L. Recob
SGT Glenn Record
SGT Ronald Ray Redalen
SGT Shemekia Redar
SPC Samuel W. Redburn
CSM Cassandra Redd
MR. Roger Redd
CW2 Dennis D. Reddix
SGT Craig G. Redman
MRS. William W. Redman
1SG (Ret) William Paul Redmon
SGT Gary E. Redmond
MSG James F. Redmond
SGT Mark S. Redmond
SGT Ryan D. Redner
1SG (Ret) James E. Reecamper
SGT Donald L. Reece
SFC (Ret) Earl Reece
CPL Frederick J. Reece
CPT Robert Reece
SGM Thomas E. Reece
PFC Tyler A. Reece
CPL Barry D. Reed
SPC Brian Reed
SGT Brian Reed
SFC Charles C. Reed
SSG Charles K. Reed
SPC Dana Reed
SGT Dave A. Reed
MAJ David M. Reed
SPC Del W. Reed
PFC Derek Reed
PFC Duane E. Reed
TSgt Ed Reed
1SG Frank V. Reed
LT Gregory Reed
SPC Gregory A. Reed
PVT Jack F. Reed
SSG Jack H. Reed
PFC Jacquain Reed
SPC Joe E. Reed
PFC John C. Reed
CW1 John H. Reed
SGT Joshua A. Reed
SGT (Ret) Marvin Reed
SGM Michael Reed
CPT Nathan T. Reed
SPC Richard C. Reed
MSG Robert Reed
PFC Robert H. Reed
PFC Robert M. J. Reed
SP5 Roger A. Reed
MR. Ronnie Lee Reed
MAJ (Ret) Stanley L. Reed
2LT Timothy L. Reed
SPC Wilbert D. Reed
CPL William C. Reed
SGT William Wayne Reed
SGT Brian Reeder
SGT Aubrey D. Reefer
SP5 Harold E. Reeg
CSM (Ret) Edmund L. Reel
SPC Larry Reel
MSG William L. Rees
SGT William W. Rees
MAJ David D. Reese
SP5 Donald E. Reese
MSG Elmer C. Reese
MSG James E. Reese
SSG Jerry Dayle Reese
PVT Kenneth L. Reese
MAJ Morgan Reese
SSG Robert H. Reese
SFC Roslyn E. Reesemoran
SSG Brian Ogden Reeve
LTC Daniel E. Reeves
SPC Isaac L. Reeves
SFC (Ret) Joseph R. Reeves
MAJ Mark Allen Reeves
SFC Morris Reeves
1LT Robert N. Reeves
SGT Wesley Reeves
CPL Richard Regalado
MSG (Ret) Richard T. Regalado
1SG Veronica B. Regalbuti
SGT Edward P. Regan
CSM (Ret) James P. Regan
SFC Jerry J. Regan
SPC Robert M. Regan
MR. Thomas Patrick Regan
SGT Donald W. Regenhardt
SGT James Reghi
SFC (Ret) Willie L. Regian
MRS. Richard Regimbald
CPT Christopher D. Rego
MRS. Richard H. Regula
SGT Richard B. Rehagen
SPC Robert Michael Rehard
SGT Timothy A. Rehg
SPC Harold A. Rehm
SP5 Bruce W. Rehmer
CPT Patrick G. Rehmet
MR. Willard E. Rehpohl
CPT Robert M. Reich
SP5 John J. Reichenberg
CPT Carl T. Reichert
CPT Dave Reichert
SP5 William Reichert
SPC Brian D. Reichner
1SG Archie Reid
COL (Ret) Carlton B. Reid
SPC (Ret) Clifford Reid
SFC David R. Reid
SGT Donald K. Reid
PFC Earl S. Reid
CW4 James S. Reid
SFC Michael Reid
MAJ Michele Reid
SP5 Miles T. Reid
MAJ (Ret) Ralph C. Reid
1LT Robert L. Reid
SP5 Robert W. Bill Reid
LTC (Ret) Ronald T. Reid
SGT Ben A. Reida
SPC Bruce Reidenbach
SSG Kenneth Reidy
SFC (Ret) Edward E. Reier
SPC John E. Reif
MRS. Richard D. Reiger
CPT Lindsay Reigrut
1LT George Reihner
SSG Robert F. Reiland
SPC Michael R. Reilly
PFC Patrick M. Reilly
MAJ Robert J. Reilly
LTC Stephen T. Reilly
SGT Thomas M. Reilly
SGT William Reiman
SGT Michael D. Reimers
SPC David J. Reimler
MR. Charles Reinecke
PFC Russell H. Reinecke
CPT Sam Reinert
CW2 Howard B. Reiney
SSG Robert W. Reinhardt
PFC Gerard W. Reinhart
LTC William H. Reinhart
SPC David J. Reinsch
2LT William Jay Reinstatler
MSG (Ret) Robbie Reinstein
TSgt Dan E. Reiss
PFC Ron Reiss
MAJ Paul Reist
LTC (Ret) Robert C. Reister
PVT Dennis H. Reiter
MR. George E. Reith
1SG Julius E. Reithoffer
SPC Louis Rekash
MAJ H. Jerome Rektorik
MR. John L. Rekward
MR. Archie N. Rembert
CPT Randy Remiker
SPC Brian Remillard
2LT Sean I. Remley
CPT Eric M. Remoy
MRS. James V. Remple
MRS. Glen W. Remsburg
SFC John F. Renaud
SPC Robert Francis Rendelman
SGM Mario E. Rendon
SFC Harold L. Reney
SSG Brandon Renfro
SGT Cal Renfro
SGT William A. Renfroe
SFC Dennis E. Renken
SGT Bruce D. Renner
CPL Vincent F. Rennich
SSG Ellis E. Reno
SPC William B. Reno
SPC Greg Renteria
CPT Mark A. Renteria
SPC Steven J. Renteria
SGT Robert E. Rentfro
CPT Rodger A. Renzulli
MAJ Michael J. Repasky
LTC (Ret) Edward J. Repetski
PFC Thomas Repta
SGT John Resio
SPC James T. Reskovac
SSG Alfred E. Ressico
CPL Larry N. Ressin
LTC (Ret) Karl D. Restall
PFC Joseph E. Restiano
PFC Peter Restivo
MR. Richard R. Restivo
SPC Daniel Resto
SSG Carl T. Restoff
MAJ (Ret) John M. Retterer
SFC Jon E. Rettmann
PFC Carmen Rettzo
MR. Henry F. Reusing
SGT Bill J. Reuter
SPC Brannon Revel
MAJ David L. Revell
SGT Joe L. Revels
SP5 William J. Revels
SGT Jeffery F. Revisky
MAJ Charles F. Rey
SPC Armando R. Reyes
SPC Charlotte Reyes
MR. Emmanuelle Reyes
1SG Hector N. Reyes
SSG Jeffrey B. Reyes
SSG Jesus C. Reyes
SGT Josue Reyes
SGT Mark Reyes
SGT Mauricio Reyes
SPC Paulo Reyes
CPT Rosalinda Reyes
SGM (Ret) Roy C. Reyes
SPC Saul A. Reyes
MSG Jose A. Reyes-Gonzalez
1LT Giovan A. Reyes-Mercado
PFC Faustino Reyna
SPC Juan R. Reyna
SPC Martin Reyna
SGT Oscar J. Reyna
SPC Severo Reyna
MAJ Steven Reynnells
PVT Billy R. Reynolds
SPC C. H. Reynolds
MR. Dean F. Reynolds
SSG Don A. Reynolds
SGT (Ret) Gale L. Reynolds
MSG Glenn V. Reynolds
MAJ James Reynolds
SFC (Ret) James H. Reynolds
CW2 James H. Reynolds
1LT John P. Reynolds
SSG (Ret) Johnny E. Reynolds
SGT Jonathan E. Reynolds
SPC Lanny R. Reynolds
SGT Louis W. Reynolds
SGT Mannie Reynolds
SFC (Ret) Paul G. Reynolds
PFC Ranse W. Reynolds
SSG Raymond T. Reynolds
LT Regan Reynolds
SFC Robert J. Reynolds
SGT Robert L. Reynolds
LT Robert W. Reynolds
SGT Steven L. Reynolds
SPC Thomas R. Reynolds
1SG (Ret) Wesley A. Reynolds
SSG (Ret) William Reynolds
PFC David Rezuke
LTG (Ret) Thomas G. Rhame
CPT James I. Rhiel
SFC David L. Rhine
SSG Harry Rhine
SFC (Ret) Jacob B. Rhines
SP5 Alan E. Rhoades
SFC Jeffrey A. Rhodan
PVT Jimmie L. Rhodd
SFC Lewis Rhoden
SPC Christopher B. Rhodes
1SG Daryl W. Rhodes
MSG Ernest F. Rhodes
SPC Gary L. Rhodes
SGT Harry W. Rhodes
SPC Jason P. Rhodes
MAJ (Ret) Jerry L. Rhodes
SSG R. J. Rhodes
SGT Stephen B. Rhodes
SFC Dennis A. Rhoney
MAJ (Ret) Peter J. Rhymer
COL (Ret) Robert B. Rhynsburger
CPT Rudolph R. Ribbeck
CPL Keith Ricciardi
SGT Michael A. Riccio
LTC (Ret) Arthur A. Rice
CPL Berkley M. Rice
2LT Curtis W. Rice
CPT David Rice
SP5 David R. Rice
SPC Edmund V. Rice
CSM Edward K. Rice
SPC Gary L. Rice
SP5 Gregory L. Rice
MR. Harry W. Rice
1LT Jesse A. Rice
SPC Joseph P. Rice
SPC Matthew Rice
SFC (Ret) Norman I. Rice
SPC Orrin L. Rice
CPT Robert R. Rice
SP5 Seth Michael Rice
1SG Torry Rice
SFC Veronica F. Rice
PVT Wendell D. Rice
SGT Ralph S. Ricedorf
SFC (Ret) Cecil W. Rich
SGT Craig C. Rich
1SG James A. Rich
SGT James A. Rich
CPL Jason E. Rich
TSgt Joseph T. Rich
MAJ Kenneth Rich
MRS. Nicholas J. Rich
SPC Ron Rich
CPL Charles Richard
SGT Damien Richard
CPL Emile D. Richard
WO1 Michael R. Richard
SGT Dick C. Richards
SFC Donald E. Richards
CW3 (Ret) James C. Richards
CPT James R. Richards
SGT Jerry R. Richards
SGT Richard C. Richards
SPC Rick R. Richards
SGT Terry Richards
SGT Thomas L. Richards
MAJ William I. Richards
SFC William J. Richards
SSG Arlie T. Richardson
MAJ Charles E. Richardson
SGT Christian J. Richardson
SSG Danny D. Richardson
MRS. Edward B. Richardson
MR. Elijah Richardson
SGT Etharl Richardson
SSG Floyd T. Richardson
DR. Francis H. Richardson
PSG Fred D. Richardson
SGT George L. Richardson
SGT Harvill P. Richardson
SGT Jamal Richardson
CPT John C. Richardson
CPL Keith M. Richardson
SFC Kiryenski Richardson
SGT Leo M. Richardson
SFC Matthew Richardson
SGT Merle E. Richardson
SGT Michael Richardson
CW2 Milton O. Richardson
CPT Nathan Richardson
SFC Oscar L. Richardson
SPC Phillip R. Richardson
SPC Raymond E. Richardson
SPC Raymond L. Richardson
SGT Robert J. Richardson
MAJ (Ret) Robert M. Richardson
CPT Robert W. Richardson
TSgt Theron D. Richardson
COL (Ret) Thomas C. Richardson
MRS. William A. Richardson
1LT William E. Richardson
COL (Ret) William J. Richardson
SPC Nathan Richer
SPC Frank Richey
SPC Harold Paul Richey
SP5 Stephen L. Richey
1SG Thomas Richey
2LT Chad Richman
1LT Brandon L. Richmond
CPL Charles E. Richmond
PFC Edward W. Richmond
MRS. Robert L. Richmond
PV2 Victor F. Richmond
PFC Charles A. Richter
SGT Don W. Richter
SP5 Robert A. Richter
CW2 Dennis L. Rick
COL (Ret) Daniel S. Rickard
CPT James H. Rickard
SPC David S. Rickett
SPC Clifton Ricketts
SFC George H. Ricketts
SSG Jeremy Ricketts
SGT William Ricketts
PFC James E. Ricks
MAJ (Ret) Ned B. Ricks
MAJ Ranson J. Ricks
MR. Steve E. Ricks
SPC Domingo Rico
SGT Matthew L. Rico
SFC Rodolfo Rico
MSG John F. Riddick
PVT Elmer A. Riddle
SFC (Ret) Jennifer L. Riddle
MSG Ronald G. Riddle
MR. William G. Riddle
1SG Antoinette Riddlespriger
CPT Alphonse T. Rideau
SSG (Ret) Charles H. Rider
MSG Paul W. Rider
SGT (Ret) Francis X. Ridge
SGT Albert J. Ridout
SFC Francis H. Rieckman
SGT Richard J. Riedman
CW4 (Ret) Arlie J. Riefer
SPC Michael J. Rieffer
PFC Henry Rieger
PFC John G. Rieger
1LT Timothy J. Riehl
SFC Priscilla Jean Riendeau
CPL Joseph Riepen
MAJ Miguel Riera
SGT H. Sam Rierson
SPC Gerald R. Rietfort
SFC (Ret) Barry C. Rietman
MR. Harold L. Rife
SPC Rex A. Rife
SPC Robert C. Rife
CPT Leland R. Riffel
1LT John R. Riffle
CPT James J. Rigelsky
SGM Annie R. Riggins
PFC Cameron P. Riggins
CPT Allan D. Riggs
LTC (Ret) Karen L. Riggs
SGT Robert Rightenour
SGT Ronald H. Righton
COL (Ret) Cecil H. Rigsby
SPC Robert Rigsby
1LT John S. Rike
SGT J. Craig Riker
SPC Clifford Riley
SPC Darlene M. Riley
CPT Darren Riley
SPC David Andrew Riley
CPT (Ret) David F. Riley
PFC Dennis G. Riley
SGT Franklin D. Riley
CW2 (Ret) Herbert D. Riley
SSG Herbert D. Riley
SFC John J. Riley
PFC John J. (Jack) Riley
SPC Kenneth G. Riley
CPT Kevin Riley
SSG Michael E. Riley
COL (Ret) Michael N. Riley
SFC Monroe Riley
LTC (Ret) Paul R. Riley
CPT Philip A. Riley
MR. Rufus F. Riley
SSG Kenneth D. Rimmer
PFC Mario Rincent
MS. Rhonda Rincon
SGT Paul C. Rineer
SGT Douglas J. Riney
SPC Billy N. Ring
SPC Terry A. Ring
SGT Michael L. Ringer
SGT Roger R. Ringgold
CPT Leonard E. Ringler
MR. Thomas J. Ringwald
CPL Thomas L. Rinn
PVT Roy S. Rio
SGT Joseph P. Riolo
SP5 Brian L. Riordan
1SG (Ret) Andres A. Rios
SP6 Gonzalo Rios
SPC Hector A. Rios
CPL Juvencio Rios
MR. O. L. Rios
MSG (Ret) Reyes Rios
SPC Ricardo Rios
SPC Roger M. Rios
SPC Brian D. Ripley
SSG David Ripp
LTC (Ret) Joe F. Rippetoe
CPT Allen R. Rippey
SGT Gerald J. Risch
PFC Latasha Risher
CPL Edward W. Rising
SSG Robert W. Risinger
MRS. Kenneth C. Risley
MR. Lawrence P. Rist
PFC Elmer F. Rister
MR. Doug Ritchey
SSG Johnnie H. Rittenberry
SP5 Jerry W. Rittenhouse
COL (Ret) William R. Rittenhouse
MRS. Ernest J. Ritter
CPL John R. Ritter
SPC Paul H. Ritter
SFC Robert L. Ritter
PFC Stuart Ritter
SGT Gene Rittman
SGT Otis E. Rittman
PSG Charles E. Ritz
MR. Morris A. Ritzel
SPC Karalyn Rivard
SGT David Rivas
SPC Christine Rivera
MAJ Cruz Rivera
SGT David Rivera
SPC David Rivera
CPT Gerardo Rivera
SPC Henry Bejarano Rivera
SGT Israel Rivera
SFC Joe M. Rivera
SGT John Rivera
SPC Johnnie Rivera
SGT Jorge Rivera
PFC Jose Rivera
PFC Julio E. Rivera
SSG Luis Rivera
SSG Luis D. Rivera
SGT Mark S. Rivera
SSG (Ret) Marta Luz Rivera
PFC Michael R. Rivera
SPC Nestor L. Rivera
SGM (Ret) Peter Rivera
SFC Peter Rivera
SGM Phillip W. Rivera
SGT Ramon Rivera
SSG Robert Ralph Rivera
SFC Rodney Rivera
MR. Stephen S. Rivera
SGT Thomas J. Rivera
SPC Victor M. Rivera
SGT Yany E. Rivera
PSG (Ret) Jose Rivera-Cosme
SSG Eddie Rivera-Jimenez
1SG (Ret) Luis Rivera-Lugo
CPT Leonardo Rivera-Rivera
SPC Herbert Rivero
SPC Bernard Rivers
MSG Dan W. Rivers
SGT Johnny Two Feather Rivns
SGT William C. Rizi
CPT Michael J. Rizzo
SPC James J. Roach
MAJ Joe D. Roach
CPT John H. Roach
MSG Thomas J. Roach
CSM (Ret) Willie J. Roach
LTC John C. Roadcap
SPC Timothy J. Roat
CPT John V. Rob
SP5 John (Jack) A. Robak
MR. Richard Robart
SGT James C. Robarts
SPC Albert J. Robb
SGT Alex Robbins
SPC Donald L. Robbins
PFC Frank Robbins
1SG (Ret) James M. Robbins
SPC Jerry D. Robbins
SGM Joe L. Robbins
CPT Michael A. Robbins
SSG Robert C. Robbins
MAJ Victor Wayne Robbins
SPC C. Randall Rober
PFC George Robere
CPL Harvey G. Roberge
1SG Normand Roberge
SP5 Clifford Roberson
SFC Curtis F. Roberson
MS. Dee Alberts Roberson
MR. Doug Roberson
1SG (Ret) Gary T. Roberson
MAJ James Roberson
SGT James O. Roberson
CPT John C. Roberson
PFC Juan D. Roberson
SGT Bruce L. Robert
SPC Jason Robertazzi
SFC (Ret) Alfred J. Roberts
SPC Anthony Lorren Roberts
SPC Barry Roberts
LTC Cassandra V. Roberts
SFC Christopher A. Roberts
PFC Christopher M. Roberts
SSG Daniel J. Roberts
SGT David H. Roberts
SSG Douglas E. Roberts
1LT Eddie B. Roberts
SFC Edrena Roberts
MRS. Elvy B. Roberts
SGT Harold Wayne Roberts
SPC James D. Roberts
SGT James E. Roberts
SPC James E. Roberts
SPC James R. Roberts
MRS. Joseph L. Roberts

MAJ Kenneth N. Roberts
MAJ Kurt Roberts
SGT Max Roberts
SFC (Ret) Olen F. Roberts
CPT Patricia J. Roberts
SGT Ralph Roberts
SGT Raymond E. Roberts
SPC Richard R. Roberts
SFC Robert D. Roberts
SGT Ronald W. Roberts
MSG Sammy Roberts
SPC Shaquoia Roberts
SSG Steve F. Roberts
CW2 Terrance J. Roberts
CSM Tommy R. Roberts
1LT Walker E. Roberts
SPC Walter B. Roberts
PFC Wayne Ten Roberts
PFC Willard T. Roberts
SGT William H. Roberts
CPT (Ret) William J. Roberts
SGT Charles E. Robertson
CPL Clinton L. Robertson
SPC David Robertson
SGT Donald L. Robertson
SPC Douglas Robertson
SGT Gary D. Robertson
SGT George G. Robertson
MR. Harold G. Robertson
SPC James G. Robertson
SPC Jesse H. Robertson
MAJ John W. Robertson
CPL Paul L. Robertson
CPL Robert J. Robertson
SPC Sadie A. Robertson
CW3 John Robeski
MRS. James E. Robey
SGT Harvey L. Robideaux
MRS. Andrew J. Robidoux
MAJ Edward J. Robillard
SGT Paul E. Robin
PVT Steven M. Robinette
SGT Fred J. Robins
SPC Ronald S. Robins
LTC Alan L. Robinson
SGT Alan R. Robinson
PFC Andre Robinson
2LT Anthony T. Robinson
CPT Brian L. Robinson
SGT Bruce L. Robinson
CSM Charles A. Robinson
LT Christopher H. Robinson
1SG Cliff M. Robinson
SGT Council Robinson
2LT David D. Robinson
SGT Dennis G. Robinson
SPC Dianne Robinson
SSG Dominic E. Robinson
CPT Dwayne H. Robinson
SSG Earl Keith Robinson
COL (Ret) Edward C. Robinson
SPC Edwin H. Robinson
LTC Edwin K. Robinson
2LT Elissa R. Robinson
MR. Frederick E. Robinson
SGT George Robinson
1SG George S. Robinson
SGT Gerald K. Robinson
CSM Glenn D. Robinson
MSG Harold Gilbert Robinson
PVT Herman Robinson
CPT J. Paul Robinson
CPT J. Wesley Robinson
SPC Jacob T. Robinson
MRS. James Robinson
SPC James A. Robinson
PVT James A. Robinson
PV2 Jeffery K. Robinson
SGT Jeffrey Robinson
SPC Jerry Ivan Robinson
MR. John Robinson
SGT John D. Robinson
SFC Johnny A. Robinson
COL Joseph P. Robinson
SGT Kurt A. Robinson
SPC Larry D. Robinson
CPL Larry G. Robinson
MSG Larry R. Robinson
SPC Leland Robinson
CSM (Ret) Leland L. Robinson
MRS. Maurice L. Robinson
2LT Michael A. Robinson
SPC Michael E. Robinson
SGT Mike Robinson
CPT Naryo Robinson
SGT Nicholas Robinson
SGT Paul A. Robinson
SSG Raymond E. Robinson
CSM Richard E. Robinson
PVT Robbie R. Robinson
SP5 Robert D. Robinson
1LT Robert E. Robinson
SP5 Robert E. Robinson
SPC Robert L. Robinson
CPT Roger H. Robinson
SSG (Ret) Ronald Robinson
SGT Sammy Lewis Robinson
SGT Scherwood Robinson
SSG Theodore E. Robinson
SSG Timothy M. Robinson
SPC Tyree B. Robinson
PVT Walter F. Robinson
CPT William T. Robinson
LTC Cecil M. Robison
CSM (Ret) Robert D. Robison
SGT Russell D. Skip Robison
SPC Timothy R. Robison
SSG Eric J. Robledo
SSG Marlon R. Roblero
PFC Angel E. Robles
MG (Ret) Josue Robles
SPC Katherine Robles
CPT Orlando Lxex Robles
MRS. Fred J. Robling
SGT Gene Robortson
PVT Jon M. Robson
SPC George D. Roby
SPC Samuel R. Rocci
SGT Joseph A. Rocco
TSgt James M. Rocha
SFC Larrie A. Rocha
SGT Paul A. Rocha
CSM (Ret) Richard Rocha
SFC Roberto R. Rocha
CPL Rodolfo R. Rocha
MRS. Louis J. Rochat
1LT Danny Roche
CPT Robert F. Roche
CPT Robert N. Rochell
SGT Richard S. Rock
SGT Gregory Rocker
CW2 C. Steven Rockett
SGT Chester Rockhill
SGT Donald D. Rockhold
SGT Rick Rockholt
MRS. Randolph A. Rockne
1LT Brenda F. Rockwell
SSG Dennis C. Rockwell
SGT James R. Rockwell
SGT Robert A. Rockwell
PFC Robert Rodarte
SPC Billy T. Rodden
1LT Kirk F. Roddie
COL Frederick L. Roddy
1LT Leslie M. Roddy
SPC Paul R. Roddy
PFC Robert H. Rode
SPC Edward T. Rodela
SPC David J. Roden
SGT Gary L. Roden
CPL A. L. Rodenhizer
SFC (Ret) Allen Rodesky
SPC Bruce A. Rodgers
PVT Earl Rodgers
CW3 (Ret) James T. Rodgers
SPC Martin A. Rodgers
MSG (Ret) Patrick Rodgers
SFC (Ret) Samuel A. Rodgers
WO1 Shawn Rodgers
1SG Terence L. Rodgers
SP5 John A. Rodland
PFC John O. Rodney
CPL Frank N. Rodono
SFC (Ret) Archie Rodrigue
SGT Ronnie J. Rodrigue
SSG Abel H. Rodriguez
1SG Agustin Rodriguez
SPC Alejandro Rodriguez
1SG (Ret) Alfredo Rodriguez
SSG Allain Rodriguez
PVT Andres Rodriguez
SPC Anthony Rodriguez
PVT Anthony Rodriguez
SSG Antonio Rodriguez
PV2 Armando Rodriguez
SGT Baldomero Rodriguez
1LT Bryan A. Rodriguez
SGT Chuck Rodriguez
SSG Daniel Rodriguez
SPC Daniel Cruz W. Rodriguez
SSG Danny Rodriguez
SPC Eddie M. Rodriguez
CSM Edwin Rodriguez
SP5 Ernie A. Rodriguez
CSM (Ret) Fernando Rodriguez
SGT Frank G. Rodriguez
SPC Fred Rodriguez
SGT Gil Rodriguez
PV2 Gregory Rodriguez
SGT Henry A. Rodriguez
CPL Heriberto Rodriguez
PSG Ismael Rodriguez
PVT Israel O. Rodriguez
SPC Jesus M. Rodriguez
PVT Jose L. Rodriguez
SFC Jose L. R. Rodriguez
SGT Jose N. Rodriguez
PFC Joseph Rodriguez
SSG Joshua Rodriguez
SSG Juan H. Rodriguez
PFC Juan M. Rodriguez
SPC Louis Rodriguez
SGT Manuel Rodriguez
LTC (Ret) Manuel A. Rodriguez
SPC Michael Rodriguez
MAJ Mike Rodriguez
SPC Monico Rodriguez
SFC Paul A. Rodriguez
SP6 Pedro P. Rodriguez
SP5 Peter O. Rodriguez
SGT Robert Rodriguez
SSG Ronald Rodriguez
SGT Rudy B. Rodriguez
SSG Sebastian Rodriguez
PVT Timmy L. Rodriguez
SPC Pedro A. Rodriguez Martinez
SGT Sergio Rodriguez Perez
SPC Miguel Rodriguez-Collazo
SSG Claudia A. Rodriquez
SGT Tiffany Rodriquez-Rexroad
SGT George Roeber
SGT Allen G. Roeder
1SG David E. Roeder
SPC Harlan L. Roeder
SGT Robert R. Roeder
2LT Theresa Roeder
SPC Anthony B. Roegiers
1LT James T. Roehm
LTC Fredric E. Roeming
PFC Randall E. Roen
SPC Douglas Roeschlein
MRS. Laura D. Roettger
SSG Arnold J. Roff
SPC David P. Roffers
SPC Adam P. Rogers
1LT Alfred W. Rogers
SGT Bobby J. Rogers
SPC Burton C. Rogers
SGT Dennis D. Rogers
SSG Dennis S. Rogers
SSG Dieter J. Rogers
SP5 Gary D. Rogers
SPC Gary L. Rogers
MSG (Ret) George H. Rogers
MR. H. A. Rogers
SFC James K. Rogers
COL (Ret) John B. Rogers
SGT John C. Rogers
SGT John J. Rogers
SGT John L. Rogers
MAJ John M. Rogers
SPC John T. Rogers
SGT Joshua Rogers
SP5 Leslie E. Rogers
PFC Mark W. Rogers
PFC Melbourne Leroy Rogers
SGT Michael K. Rogers
CPL Raymond P. Rogers
LTC (Ret) Richard W. Rogers
SFC (Ret) Thomas A. Rogers
SSG Tommie L. Rogers
LTC Travis L. Rogers
SGT Verlin N. Rogers
SGT Walter Rogers
1SG Walter P. Rogers
SGT Christian Rohde
CPL Cyril L. Rohde
SP5 Robert E. Rohde
PVT Walter D. Rohde
SGT Mark A. Rohlffs
CW2 Ed Rohner
PVT Dustin B. Rohr
PVT Danielle Rohrer
SSG Daniel C. Rojas
SGM Israel Rojas
SPC Reinaldo Rojas
SGT Rodolfo Rojas
SPC Gerald P. Rojek
SGT Max Rokita
SGT Keith Roland
SGT Johnny A. Roldan
SSG Ronald W. Rolen
CPL John M. Roles
SPC Benjamin D. Rolfe
CPL Clifford H. Roling
SPC Warren L. Roll
CPL Nathanial J. Rollin
SSG Barbara P. Rollings
CPL Angelo S. Rollins
CSM (Ret) Danny E. Rollins
LTC (Ret) James R. Rollins
SPC John P. Rollins
SPC Samuel T. Rollins
SPC Harry L. Rom
MAJ (Ret) Susan Roma
CPT Brian J. Roman
PV2 Jeffrey D. Roman
SGT Luis R. Roman
SGT Charles V. Romanenko
SSG Raul E. Roman-Mercado
COL Anthony P. Romano
PFC Phillip T. Romano
CW4 (Ret) Alfred J. Romaszewski
SPC Jason C. Rombold
SSG (Ret) Frank S. Romeo
CSM Clifford P. Romer
SGT Carlos E. Romero
SSG Carlos E. Romero
SGT Christopher Romero
SGT Ernest Romero
SGT Florindo Romero
SPC Ivan Romero
MR. Juan G. Romero
MSG Julian Romero
CPT Pia G. Romero
SPC Ricardo Romero
SFC Samuel D. Romero
2LT Christopher T. Romig
PFC Kevin Romine
SGT Robert Clark Romine
CSM (Ret) James R. Rominger
PFC Mark A. Rominger
CPT Robin L. Rominger
CPL George E. Romiti
SFC (Ret) Robert J. Romstadt
CPL Maurice J. Ronayne
LTC Monte L. Rone
2LT Ray C. Ronk
SGT Ole Ronning
MAJ Jae C. Rood
SPC Norman W. Rood
SGT (Ret) Robert A. Roof
SGT Timothy M. Roof
SGT James J. Rook
PVT Walter Junior Rook
SPC Richard Rooker
SGM (Ret) Lawrence F. Rooney
CPT Thomas J. Rooney
PFC Michael L. Root
CPT Peter G. Root
SPC Stephen S. Root
MAJ Adam T. Ropelewski
SSG Andrew T. Roper
LTC Butch Roper
LTC Glenn Roper
SSG Danny V. Rosa
SSG Jose I. Rosa
SPC Joseph Rosa
1LT Nicholas F. Rosa
SPC Edwin G. Rosado
SSG Michael J. Rosado
SPC Gilberto Rosalerjaime
SSG Gilbert L. Rosales
SFC Gwendolyn G. Rosales
SSG Jason G. Rosales
SPC Dolores Rosalez
CW2 Carl J. Rosapepe
SFC Edwin Rosario
CPT (Ret) Joseph J. Rosario
SGT Kenneth F. Rosario
SFC William Rosario
MSG (Ret) John Rosas
MRS. Raymundo Rosas
PFC Harlow Rosborough
SGT Frederick G. Roscoe
SPC Allen Roscovius
LTC (Ret) Alfred F. Rose
LTC Alvin Rose
PFC Benjamin Rose
SPC Billy Joe Rose
SSG (Ret) Bobby D. Rose
LTC (Ret) Charles H. Rose
PFC Charles J. Rose
SSG David W. Rose
LTC Harold L. Rose
PFC Jacob G. Rose
SPC Jason R. Rose
MR. John G. Rose
SGT Larry L. Rose
SGT Michael Leo Dale Rose
LTC (Ret) Michael W. Rose
SFC Milton W. Rose
SFC Newton A. Rose
1SG Ronald L. Rose
SFC Tonga Rose
SGT Tracy E. Rose
1LT James W. Rosebrough
PFC James Rosedahl
MSG Antonio G. Rosela
SPC Craig Rosen
CW4 (Ret) Jack S. Rosen
SGT Philip J. Rosen
SFC David K. Rosenbaum
MAJ Terry L. Rosenberg
COL (Ret) John D. Rosenberger
SPC Larry Rosencrans
SPC Joseph W. Rosenfield
SPC Steven Rosenow
CPT Elijah Rosenthal
SGT Cosmas J. D. Roserie
COL (Ret) Galen Rosher
SSG Melvin W. Rosiak
SPC Francis Keith Rosier
CW3 (Ret) Alexander Rosin
SFC Adam John Rosinski
MR. Kevin J. Rosinski
SFC George J. Rosko
SGT Albert H. Ross
SFC (Ret) Billy R. Ross
SFC Brian A. Ross
CPL Christopher E. Ross
SP5 Daniel D. Ross
CSM (Ret) Donald S. Ross
COL George M. Ross
CPL Gregory A. Ross
SSG Harold G. Ross
SGT James A. Ross
SGM James E. Ross
SGM (Ret) Jeffrey P. Ross
SFC John R. Ross
MR. John W. Ross
2LT Joseph R. Ross
MRS. Margaret F. Ross
SPC Marvin B. Ross
CPT Marvin L. Ross
SPC Michael E. Ross
CPL Philip G. Ross
SGT Robert E. Ross
SP5 Robert W. Ross
SPC Sidney Eugene Ross
MAJ Thomas H. Ross
SPC William G. Ross
SFC William L. Ross
PFC Francis J. Rossano
SGT Laurence L. Rossi
MR. Ronald Rossi
WO1 Steven J. Rossiter
MR. Peter F. Rossman
CW4 Gary Rossomme
CPT Sidney W. Rossuck
SPC Dave Roster
SPC Ditmar Rostig
SGT Derek Rotavera
SGT Derek Rotavera
SGT Kenneth A. Rotgers
CW3 George J. Roth
SGT Kara Roth
MR. Leo F. Roth
SGT Robert W. Roth
SPC Chad Rother
PV2 L. Kehl Rothermel
CPL Harvey Rothman
MG Roger L. Rothrock
PFC Craig H. Rotureau
SFC Jerome L. Roulhac
SP5 Frederick A. Rounds
SGT Michael D. Rounds
SP5 Buford Ray Roundtree
CW3 Robert Roundtree
CPT Jordan Roundy
CPT (Ret) John C. Rourke
SGT Harold C. Rouse
SGT Joe J. Rouse
CW2 (Ret) Kiplin A. Rouse
SGT Terry R. Rouse
SGT Lawrence W. Roush
CPL Roy J. Roush
SGT Richard J. Rousseau
SPC Eric Joseph Roux
SGM James J. Rovano
LT Philip S. Rovner
SPC Kenneth J. Rowan
SGT Jerry D. Rowe
SPC John Rowe
SPC Richard Rowe
CPL Richard J. Rowe
SPC Roscoe C. Rowe
SPC Delano B. R. Rowe Duke
SGT James M. Rowell
CPL Richard M. Rowinski
SPC Jeffrey Rowland
MSG (Ret) Jerry A. Rowland
CSM (Ret) Norman W. Rowland
SPC Roger E. Rowland
1SG (Ret) Ted Rowland
MRS. Glenn Rowley
SGT (Ret) Claude D. Roy
CPT Jeremy Roy
MAJ John Roy
MRS. John M. Roy
CPT Kenneth C. Roy
MSG Richard F. Roy
SPC Robert Roy
CPL Robert W. Roy
SSG Steven D. Roy
SPC Eddye J. Royal
MSG (Ret) Alejandro Roybal
MSG Fred L. Roybal
MR. Henry Roybal
PFC Sam Royer
PFC Samuel P. Royer
1SG Francisco Royos
SSG Jerry Y. Royston
SFC James Rozanski
SGT Richard L. Rozbicki
CPT Robert (Skip) L. Rozelle
MAJ (Ret) Thomas P. Rozga
SGT David Thomas Rozzell
1LT James M. Ruane
SGT Richard Carl Rubalcava
PFC Roger L. Rubear
SSG Alan M. Rubel
SP5 William Rubenstein
SFC Carl V. Rubin
MR. Ronald J. Rubin
A1C Edward A. Ruble
SSG Robert T. Rubley
SFC John R. Ruby
SP5 Gerald L. Rucker
SGT Robert D. Rucker
SPC Robert G. Rucker
CSM Theodore B. Rucker
SPC James M. Rucki
1LT Bradley S. Rudder
MSG Robbie S. Rudder
SFC Richard H. Rude
SFC (Ret) William R. Rudey
SGT Bruce J. Rudigier
SP5 Roy P. Rudl
PFC Donald E. Rudolph
PFC James W. Rudolph
PFC Howard W. Rudy
CW3 Mark Rudy
MRS. William J. Rudy
SGT Martin J. Rue
MAJ Daniel W. Ruecking
MAJ William P. Ruedel
LTC Matthew H. Ruedi
SGT James M. Ruegg
SSG Luis R. Ruelasvillanueva
SGT Henry Ruesing
SSG Stephen Rueter
PFC Dennis L. Ruff
SGT Edwarner Ruffin
PFC Jimmy Ruffin
SGT Patrick J. Ruffner
MRS. Daniel A. Rufo
MR. Edward Rufolo
SSG William W. Ruge
CPL Thomas M. Ruggeri
SGT Joseph J. Ruggiano
MR. RooseveLT Ruggs
MAJ John B. Ruhl
MSG Andres Ruiz
PFC Carlos C. Ruiz
SGT Domingo Ruiz
SFC Jose Carlos Ruiz
MR. Manuel Ruiz
SGT Robert Ruiz
SPC Robert F. Ruiz
SSG Simon R. Ruiz
SGT Fred D. Ruland
MR. Hurley Rulon
CPL Blair C. Rumble
SGT Bob F. Rumsey
MAJ Tyler Rund
SPC Marshall W. Rundell
PVT John B. Runk
SP6 John P. Runkel
SFC Steven J. Runnels
CPL Myron D. Runyon
SFC Steven C. Runyon
SSG James W. Rupert
MR. Robert B. Rupert
SGT Terry W. Rupholdt
PFC Gary R. Rupp
CH (LTC) Kenneth M. Ruppar
SPC Chris T. Ruppel
SFC Christopher Rush
SPC Christopher Rush
SGT Rodney A. Rush
SSG Thomas J. Rush

SPC Grover H. Rushing
CSM (Ret) Jack P. Rushing
MSG Michael J. Ruskovitz
CW2 Brian J. Russ
PVT Roger W. Russ
CW2 Allen F. Russell
SGT Ambrose Russell
SPC Craig A. Russell
SPC Daniel L. Russell
SPC David G. Russell
SFC (Ret) Douglas F. Russell
CW2 (Ret) Douglas G. Russell
COL (Ret) Eugene N. Russell
SP5 Frank Russell
1LT Guy P. Russell
MR. Henry E. Russell
SSG Henry M. Russell
PFC Howard V. Russell
SGT J. David Russell
SFC (Ret) James K. Russell
SGT Jeffrey T. Russell
SGT John Russell
SGT John D. Russell
SP5 John L. Russell
SSG (Ret) John L. Russell
CPT (Ret) Larry R. Russell
SGT Malcolm G. Russell
MRS. Marian G. Russell
MAJ Marvin N. Russell
LTC (Ret) Michael H. Russell
PFC Michael T. Russell
2LT Montrell Russell
SSG (Ret) Paul E. Russell
1LT Phillip C. Russell
1SG Robert Russell
SSG Robert G. Russell
SPC Ronnie Russell
MAJ Steven E. Russell
SGT William A. Russell
PFC John L. Russo
SPC Joseph F. Russo
SFC Hugh A. (Bert) Ruth
SPC Ken Ruth
CSM Jimmy Rutherford
PV2 Walter L. Rutherford
COL Wilson R. Rutherford
SSG Kevin M. Rutland
SPC Charles W. Rutledge
PVT Garry E. Rutledge
SPC William J. Rutolo
MAJ Paul H. Rutt
SFC (Ret) Gerald L. Ruud
2LT Aaron J. Ryan
SGT Albert M. Ryan
CPL Allan R. Ryan
SP5 Dennis P. Ryan
COL Diane M. Ryan
SSG (Ret) Earnest T. Ryan
PFC Francis Ryan
1LT Frank L. Ryan
PVT Frederick M. Ryan
MS. J. Stephania Ryan
LTC (Ret) James H. Ryan
SGM Jasper Ryan
SSG John L. Ryan
SGT John L. Ryan
LTC John T. Ryan
SPC Joseph D. Ryan
COL Karen L. Ryan
SGT Kevin P. Ryan
CPT Lawrence M. Ryan
SGT Michael Ryan
BG (Ret) Michael A. Ryan
SPC Michael D. Ryan
1LT Michael D. Ryan
CPT Terrence Ryan
SPC Tom Ryan
SFC (Ret) Willie Ryan
SPC Kurt A. Rychener
SFC Albert R. Rychlinski
SGT Kenneth J. Ryder
SPC Robert G. Rydzewski
MAJ James D. Rye
CPT Alex Rygas
SPC Ralph E. Ryker
SGT Lonnie J. Ryland
SGT John Rymas
PFC Polly A. Rymers
SFC Fred Rynkowski
CSM (Ret) Joseph M. Rynne
SPC David C. Ryon
SGT Raymond J. Rys
1LT Seung H. Ryu
SPC Newton Saarinen
CPL Lloyd T. Saathoff
CPT John W. Sabala
2LT John Sabat
MR. Leonard Sabia
SGT Jonathan Sablan
MRS. Harriet D. Sabo
SGT David L. Sabourin
SFC (Ret) Jameel H. Sabree
LTC John W. Sacca
SSG Dennis A. Sacco
PFC Greg Sacenti
MAJ Alphie Sachnik
2LT Philip Sacks
SP5 Anthony J. Sacowitz
SSG Gary A. Sader
PVT Christopher D. Sadler
SSG James R. Sadler
PFC Shawn R. Sadler
MG Thomas M. Sadler
SGT Daniel J. Sadley
SPC James E. Sadowski
SPC Richard J. Sadowski
SSG Kaofong Saelee
SPC Abel Martinez Saenz
CPL Alejandro Saenz
CPL Esequiel Saenz
1SG Jose G. Saenz
SGT Mike G. Saenz
PFC Raymond Saenz
SSG Douglas James Saffell
SGT Terry T. Saffron
SGT Harvey L. Saganov
CPL Allen H. Sager
SFC Anthony W. Sager
SGT James R. Sagerhorn
PFC Aldo E. Saggese
MSG Everett G. Sagraves
MSG (Ret) Joseph J. Sagucio
SFC (Ret) Gordon L. Saint
PFC Francisco L. Saiz
SP5 Ronald A. Saizon
CPT Gillian Sakai
COL (Ret) Robert E. Saksa
SGT Augustine G. Salacup
SGT Blaine Saladin
MR. Avelino R. Salamanca
SPC Jesus Jesse Salame
SPC Maria Salas
SGT Peter L. Salas
SGT Antonio Salazar
1SG Daniel Salazar
SGT Jose A. Salazar
PFC Juan G. Salazar
SGT Luis A. Salazar
PFC Manuel T. Salazar
CPT Michael B. Salazar
SPC Ramiro R. Salazar
PFC Robert Salazar
1SG Rodolfo R. Salazar
SPC Rolando A. Salazar
SGT Yadira V. Salazar
SPC Yrineo Salazar
SGT Jesse D. Salcedo
CPT Arturo S. Saldana
SGT Mario Victor Saldana
SGT Fred Salem
SSG Matthew O. Salerno
SP5 Michael J. Salerno
SPC Demetrius Sales
CPL Donald R. Sales
PFC James M. Sales
LTC Kevin Salge
SGT Fernando A. Salinas
PFC Fidel Salinas
PFC Fred Salinas
SPC Ruben Salinas
SFC Willie B. Salinas
SGT Laird W. Salisbury
CPT Robert L. Salling
SGT Darrell Salmon
MR. Gary D. Salmon
1SG Teresa Salmon
SFC Uhuru C. Salmon
SGT Daniel A. Salome
GEN (Ret) Leon E. Salomon
WO1 Joseph F. Salomone
2LT Stephen Salomone
SP5 Maurice Salomonsky
1LT Albert T. Saloom
CPL Samuel M. Saloom
SGT Dale E. Salsberry
SGT Leroy A. Salsbury
COL (Ret) William R. Salter
PFC Peter J. Salusha
SP5 Rodney E. Salvi
1LT Joseph L. Salvucci
SPC Luster Salyer
MAJ Edward A. Salzer
SPC Juan C. Samaniego
SFC Pedro Samaniego
CSM (Ret) Salvador Samano
1SG Ruben Samarripa
PVT Jacob H. Samborski
SGT Timoteo P. Sambrano
CSM Kenneth R. Sammons
COL Danny W. Sample
COL (Ret) Danny W. Sample
SPC Emily J. Samples
SP5 Clifford Sampson
MSG Clyde Sampson
CPT (Ret) Donald M. Sampson
MAJ John Sampson
1LT Tyrone L. Sampson
SSG Donald D. Sams
PV2 Erica L. Samson
SGT George D. Samson
SP5 James E. Samuels
2LT Joshua D. Samuels
1LT Julie-Ann Samuelson
CPT Demian William San Miguel
CPT Nyra Liz Sanabria Rivera
MR. Bruce Sanborn
1LT Carl H. Sanborn
1SG Alvaro Sanchez
SPC Andres Sanchez
WO1 Antonio Sanchez
CPT David R. Sanchez
SGT Edwardo Sanchez
SGT Eriberto Sanchez
SFC (Ret) Faustino C. Sanchez
SPC Fidel Sanchez
SGT Flavio Sanchez
MAJ Francisco Sanchez
SPC Gilbert S. Sanchez
SPC Hector Sanchez
SPC Javier M. Sanchez
SGT Jose A. Sanchez
PVT Jose M. Sanchez
SFC (Ret) Julio Sanchez
PV2 Kurt S. Sanchez
SPC Luis Sanchez
SFC Luis O. Sanchez
MR. Manuel R. Sanchez
SGT Michael D. Sanchez
SFC Pablo Sanchez
SPC Robert Sanchez
SGT Robert B. Sanchez
1SG (Ret) Salvador S. Sanchez
SPC Samuel C. Sanchez
SPC Sergio I. Sanchez
PVT Stefan A. Sanchez
2LT Steven Sanchez
CPT Luis A. Sanchez Raffucci
SPC Donald R. Sandberg
SSG Rufus A. Sanderlin
SSG Charles M. Sanders
PFC Charles N. Sanders
WO1 Christopher Sanders
COL (Ret) Donald A. Sanders
CSM (Ret) Donald R. Sanders
PV2 Ernest L. Sanders
SSG Fredrick Sanders
MR. Glen H. Sanders
SPC James H. Sanders
CPL Jerry D. Sanders
SFC (Ret) Perry Sanders
SFC (Ret) Ralph S. Sanders
SFC Robert M. Sanders
CPL Sylvanus Sanders
SPC Tommy D. Sanders
PFC Willie Odell Sanders
CPL Allan W. Sanderson
LTC (Ret) George H. Sanderson
CPT Scott R. Sandhoff
PFC Donovan B. Sandidge
SPC Sonja P. Sandidge
SPC Martin Sandiego
2LT James K. Sandifer
MSG Jimmie L. Sandifer
SFC Kirk D. Sandles
SP5 John Sandmore
CPL Benny Sandoval
MR. David Sandoval
CSM (Ret) David O. Sandoval
SPC Edward Sandoval
2LT Enrique E. Sandoval
SPC German Sandoval
SSG Jose E. Sandoval
CPL Joseph Sandoval
MSG Paul F. Sandoval
SPC Michael Sandretto
SSG Richard Sands
MAJ Thomas L. Sands
TSgt William A. Sands
1LT Verne C. Sandwall
CPT Stephen L. Sanetti
COL (Ret) Gary T. Sanford
SSG Norman L. Sanford
SFC Robert C. Sanford
1SG William Harold Sanford
SPC Robert Sangster
1LT Alan Sanner
MAJ Debra A. Sannwaldt
SGT Frank R. Sano
SFC Pedro L. Sanoja
SGT Robert M. Sans
CPT Steven Sans
SSG George Sansoucie
SGT Lawrence S. Sant
SGT Elliot A. Santaella
MAJ Julio C. Santa-Lopez
SGT Jose A. Santana
SFC (Ret) Manuel I. Santana
MR. Tim Z. Santana
SPC Dominic A. Santangelo
SGT Nicholas J. Santangelo
SPC Peter A. Santangelo
MRS. Robert J. Santelli
SGT John A. Santer
SPC Carla H. Santiago
1LT Cristobal Santiago
SFC Dianna Santiago
MSG Felix J. Estrada Santiago
1LT Fredrick Santiago
CPT Jose R. Santiago
MSG (Ret) Pedro C. Santiago
SPC Wilfredo Santiago
SPC Wilfredo Santiago
SSG William D. Santiago
SPC Jorge R. Santillan
SSG Deron G. Santiny
SPC James Santo
SGT Anthony Santos
CPT April Santos
PFC Bernardino Santos
CSM Jesse D. Santos
SPC Raul A. Santos
SGT Robert Santos
CW2 Siegfried Santos
SPC Yerimaller Santos
DR. Robert M. Santry
SSG Alphonse Santucci
SPC Jerome C. Santy
SSG John E. Santy
SGT Domingo E. Sapien
SPC Richard F. Saragoza
MR. Nicholas Evan Sarantakes
PFC Gene Sarcinello
SGM Alvin J. Sargent
SFC George C. Sargent
SPC James A. Sargent
CW4 Wellington H. Sargent
MR. William G. Sargent
SSG Ralph R. Sarmiento
COL Joseph D. Sarnicki
SFC (Ret) Francis A. Sarnowski
SPC William L. Sarro
LTC (Ret) Francis L. Sarsfield
SSG Barry M. Sartori
SP5 John R. Sarvella
SSG John R. Sarver
SFC (Ret) Norman E. Sarver
SP5 Robert Lee Sarver
PFC Charles E. Sasser
SSG John A. Satorius
SGT Vernon E. Satrom
SGT Dan Satterfield
SGT Ray Satterfield
SGM Jessie Saucedo
MAJ (Ret) Jose F. Saucedo
SGT Ray Saucedo
PFC Roberto S. Saucedo
SPC Rossi O'Neal Saucedo
MAJ Wayne A. Sauer
SPC John Sauerbier
SGT Ronald E. Sauers
SP5 Tom Saulino
SGT Charles G. Sauls
PVT Derek Saulsberry
PVT Milton E. Saulsberry
SGT Hank Saulters
CSM Franklin A. Saunders
MAJ James D. Saunders
SGT James M. Saunders
SGT James Russell Saunders
PFC Jason Saunders
SSG Lawrence E. Saunders
SP5 Richard Saunders
SPC Roger F. Saunders
SGT Stephen D. Saunders
PFC Joseph F. Sausville
SSG Andrew Sautkulis
SFC (Ret) Clyde Ernie Savage
MR. James W. Savage
SPC Joe Savage
SGT Nikitta Savage
SP5 Walter Jack Savage
SPC Gerald P. Savarese
CPT Bogdan Saveski
PFC Ilario N. Saviano
SSG Tim H. Savilisky
SFC (Ret) Douglas D. Saville
CPT Matthew Savoie
MAJ Philip A. Savoie
SPC Jonathon Savoy
SGT (Ret) Zara A. Sawi
LTC (Ret) Paul E. Sawyer
1LT Richard H. Sawyer
SPC Robert L. Sawyer
SGT Ronald Sawyer
CPT Sterling A. Sawyer
PFC Thomas C. Sawyer
SP3 James L. Sawyers
PFC Ransom F. Saxer
1LT Fred L. Saxton
SFC Robert D. Saxton
SFC (Ret) David L. Sayer
CPT Gerald B. Saylor
SPC Christopher G. Sayre
SSG Joseph E. Sayre
CPT Brian P. Sbertoli
SGT Elmer Scaggs
SPC Salvatore M. Scalato
2LT Maria L. Scales
SGT Napoleon N. Scales
SGT (Ret) Christopher J. Scalf
LTC (Ret) James J. Scalise
SPC Patrick V. Scallon
PFC Peter G. Scanlon
2LT Jennifer Scarboro
SGT Joe H. Scarborough
SPC Anthony Scarlata
SGT Robert G. Scarlavai
SP5 Joseph V. Scatena
SPC Lee A. Scerba
SGT Terry L. Schaack
SPC Ronald E. Schaadt
SGT Fred Schaaff
MAJ Eric O. Schacht
CPT (Ret) John H. Jack Schachte
PFC Edward J. Schad
SPC Charles T. Schadt
LTC Chester C. Schaefer
MAJ Chris Schaefer
MR. Don Jay Schaefer
SPC Gregory Layne Schaefer
SGT James A. Schaefer
SSG Jeffrey A. Schaefer
SP5 Kurt G. Schaefer
SPC Louie F. Schaefer
PFC Patrick G. Schaefer
SPC Walter L. Schaefer
SPC Will F. Schaefer
SPC Arthur Schaeffer
SPC Douglas D. Schaeffer
SGT I. S. Schaeffer
SSG Spencer D. Schaepman
SSG Frank P. Schaeppi
SFC Russel J. Schaeppi
SPC Rick R. Schaetzl
PFC John Schafer
MRS. Russell L. Schafer
CPT James B. Schaffer
1LT Fred B. Schaffert
SSG Ryan Schaffner
SGT James R. Schaller
SP5 John N. Schank
MR. Reece J. Schank
COL (Ret) Gregory J. Schannep
SFC (Ret) Joseph G. Schapatone
CSM (Ret) Fred L. Scharper
CPT Victor H. Scharstein
MR. Robert H. Schaubert
MR. Gary W. Schauer
PFC Adam P. Schebler
SPC Robert C. Scheel
SGT Allan C. Schefer
TSgt John E. Scheff
MRS. Pamela P. Scheffer
SGT Erik C. Scheffler
SPC Raymond W. Scheffler
LTC (Ret) Carlton L. Schelhorn
CPT Harold A. Schelin
MAJ (Ret) Charles P. Schell
CPT Joseph A. Schellings
SPC Henry F. Schemitz
TSgt Frederick Schemmer
PV2 Joshua Schenck
CPL Wilbur H. Schenerlein
SSG Edward W. Schenk
MSG Mark L. Schenk
SSG Dustin Schenstrom
SGT Theodore R. Scherck
2LT Aaron Scherffius
SPC Dale D. Schermerhorn
SPC George P. Schester
SPC Vincent A. Schettino
1LT Barry J. Schieb
1LT William J. Schiebler
SP5 Cleon H. Schiefer
SSG Melvin R. Schield
CPL Anthony C. Schienschang
LTC (Ret) Ronald A. Schier
LTC (Ret) James J. Schild
SGT John R. Schilling
SGT Kirk Schilling
SPC Len Schilling
SGT Matthew Schilling
SGT Thomas J. Schilling
CPL Wendell H. Schillinger
SGT Richard A. Schiltz
SPC Charles A. Schimmel
2LT Adam P. Schinder
CSM (Ret) Gerald R. Schindler
CPL James J. Schinker
SFC Thomas L. Schinskey
SGT Daniel L. Schipper
SGT Steven Schirmer
CPT James Schlaak
1LT Mark D. Schlageter
SSG Milo E. Schlaudraff
CPL George E. Schlegel
SGT Mike J. Schlemer
LTC (Ret) Austin Schlenker
CPL Cecil G. Schlesselmann
2LT Andrew G. Schlessinger
CPT David R. Schlichter
SGT Gregory A. Schlieve
SGT Richard H. Schlipp
SPC Erik D. Schlobohm
LTC (Ret) Jim Schlottman
CW3 (Ret) Frank W. Schlueter
CPL John C. Schlund
SGT Bill C. Schlutt
SGT Carl Schmeckpeper
SGT Edward R. Schmerder
LTC (Ret) Lloyd A. Schmid
SFC Otto Schmid
SGT Stuart R. Schmidgall
SPC Albert Schmidt
SPC Charles A. Schmidt
SGT David R. Schmidt
1LT Gary Schmidt
MR. Harold E. Schmidt
1LT Jeffrey S. Schmidt
SGT John Schmidt
SPC John F. Schmidt
MS. Katherine L. Schmidt
LTC (Ret) Kendall A. Schmidt
SGT Kenneth J. Schmidt
SFC (Ret) Kevin E. Schmidt
CPL (Ret) Leroy A. Schmidt
PV2 Matthew R. Schmidt
SPC Robert A. Schmidt
SGT Robert R. Schmidt
CSM Warren A. Schmidt
SSG Dennis P. Schmieder
SP5 Dalton T. Schmill
SGT Michael Schmit
SGT Pete Schmitt
SPC William T. Schmitt
SPC Christopher Schmittou
SGT Bruce J. Schmitz
CPL Charles R. Schmitz
LTC (Ret) Jim W. Schmitz
SPC Joseph A. Schmitz
SPC Jerry A. Schmotolocha
MAJ Nathan L. Schmutz
SPC Eric Schnabel
SGT Garland D. Schnack
SGT Thomas J. Schnackenberg
CW4 (Ret) Charles W. Schneck
SGT Fred Schneck
COL Gene A. Schneebeck
SGT Jon P. Schneewind
COL Edward T. Schneickert
SGT Carl P. Schneider
SPC Dale Schneider
COL (Ret) Lawrence Schneider
CPL Ray F. Schneider
1SG Robert R. Schneider
LTC Thomas F. Schneider
CPT Warren A. Schneider
CPL Sterling A. Schnell
SGT Ronald D. Schnelle
SGT Mike Schnetzer
LTC John H. Schnibben
PFC Logan G. Schnider
MR. Joseph M. Schoblocher
MSG Emil D. Schocknmyer
SPC William Schoebel
1LT Frank F. Schoelch
SGT Geoff Schoeman
1SG (Ret) Gary F. Schoen
MR. David H. Schoenbeck
PV2 Chad Schoenfelder
MSG Joseph E. Schoenholtz
SPC David G. Schoenrock
MAJ Garlan L. Schoenrock

SFC (Ret) Richard A. Schoenrock
SGT William T. Schoepf
MRS. Amelia Schoettle
PFC William Schoffstall
MG (Ret) Edison E. Scholes
SPC James E. Scholl
PFC Bradley E. Scholtens
SPC Raymond Schone
CSM (Ret) James J. Schonefeld
MR. Rodney Schonland
BG (Ret) Steven P. Schook
SPC David Schoolcraft
LTC David E. Schoolcraft
MR. Robert E. Schoon
PFC Raymond J. Schooner
CPT Steven M. Schopp
PFC William B. Schorn
SSG Matthew P. Schorr
PVT Raymond C. Schotanus
COL (Ret) Carl A. Schott
SPC David Schott
LTC Paul J. Schottenhamel
LTC Robert T. Schoville
SGT Lonny P. Schrade
CW4 (Ret) Walter J. Schramm
SGT Walter C. Schrank
LTC Charles R. Schrankel
LTC (Ret) Bertrand J. Schreibstein
SGT Dennis R. Schreiner
LTC George W. Schreiner
SPC Joseph K. Schriefer
SGT Robert L. Schrimper
LTC (Ret) John D. Schrimpf
MSG (Ret) Richard L. Schroder
SPC W. Frank Schroeck
SP5 Al Schroeder
2LT Carl Schroeder
SGT David L. Schroeder
MR. Fred W. Schroeder
SSG (Ret) Frederick Schroeder
SPC Jarod L. Schroeder
SPC Jerrold E. Schroeder
SGT Stephen P. Schroeder
MAJ Timothy M. Schroeder
MRS. Betty Schroedl
PFC Thomas Schroedl
1LT Edward J. Schroedter
LT Garrett Schubert
LTC Philip W. Schuck
CPL Edward W. Schuessler
PV2 Chad Schuette
SP5 Harold R. Schuette
MAJ James C. Schug
SGT Michael D. Schulberg
SSG Thomas L. Schulein
1LT Edward J. Schultz
SSG Eric W. Schultz
MR. Gary J. Schultz
LTC Gregory B. Schultz
SP5 John D. Schultz
MSG (Ret) John F. Schultz
MAJ (Ret) John T. Schultz
SPC Joseph S. Schultz
SSG Nicholas J. Schultz
SGT Richard O. Schultz
CW4 Robert L. Schultz
SGT Thomas J. Schultz
CPT Walter J. Schultz
SSG (Ret) Will J. Schultz
SPC Gary W. Schulwitz
SFC Eugene F. Schulz
SGT Gary J. Schulz
CPT Jerome Schulz
SFC John Schulz
SGT Richard D. Schulz
PFC John C. Schumacher
SPC Rollie E. Schumacher
CPT Scott Schumacher
SSG Steven Schumacher
SPC Victor Schumacher
PFC Ronald L. Schumacker
SP5 James R. Schumann
SPC John P. Schumski
SGT William J. Schuster
PFC Gerald G. Schute
SPC James R. Schutt
SSG Alfred J. Schutte
MR. Leland J. Schutte
LT Stephen Schwab
SPC Raymond Schwach
SGT Damen S. Schwalle
LT John H. Schwan
MR. Joseph P. Schwan
SGT Joseph R. Schwaninger
PFC Richard L. Schwarten
SP5 Dale L. Schwartz
SPC Fred A. Schwartz
PFC Harold Schwartz
MAJ James C. Schwartz
PFC James G. Schwartz
BG Mark C. Schwartz
TSgt Stanley A. Schwartz
MR. Wayne L. Schwartz
LTC (Ret) William L. Schwartz
SGT Fred H. Schwarz
CW2 John R. Schwarz
CPL Ryan M. Schwarz
SSG (Ret) Jamie D. Schweigert
PVT Thomad E. Schweigl
SPC Chris Schweitzer
SP5 Robert M. Schweitzer
PV2 Brian Schwettman
SPC Wally K. Schweitz
SGT Todd A. Schwickerath
SPC Paul Schwiegeraht
SGT George Schwimmer
CPT Carl J. Schwind
LTC (Ret) Michael W. Schwind
SSG Jeremy L. Schwindt
SSG Charles T. Schwinn
SFC (Ret) Joseph A. Sciuto
LT Anthony Sciuva
COL (Ret) Thomas C. Scofield
MR. Byron Scoggins
1SG (Ret) Gary L. Scoggins
PFC Tyrone Scoggins
SPC William Bert Scoggins
CPT Byron A. Scogins
SGT David E. Scoon
SGT Eric A. Scotson
SPC Albert A. Scott
LT Andrew J. Scott
CPT Artice Scott
SP5 Barron F. Scott
SGT Benjamin F. Scott
SPC Byron Thomas Scott
SFC Calvin E. Scott
SPC David B. Scott
SPC David D. Scott
CPT Dennis P. Scott
SSG Douglas James Scott
PFC Eddie Scott
1LT Gabriel Scott
SFC (Ret) George H. Scott
SGT Gordon C. Scott
CPT Jacob A. Scott
SPC John R. Scott
SGT Johnnie B. Scott
CPT Kelley O. Scott
PVT Kenneth C. Scott
SP5 Kenneth N. Scott
CPT Lawrence A. Scott
MAJ Lloyd M. Scott
SGT Loren L. Scott
SSG Marion R. Scott
SGT Mary A. Scott
SPC Michael L. Scott
SPC Patrick W. Scott
PFC Paul J. Scott
MR. Richard Scott
CW4 (Ret) Robert A. Scott
SSG Robert D. Scott
SPC Roland G. Scott
SPC Stephen W. Scott
MSG (Ret) Thomas J. Scott
CPT Timothy P. Scott
CPL Walter G. Scott
PSG (Ret) Wilburt B. Scott
COL (Ret) William A. Scott
SGT William V. Scott
MSG (Ret) Eldon D. Screws
1SG Albert Scrimsher
CPT William H. Scroggins
PFC John M. Scruby
SPC James Scudder
MRS. Michael J. Scullin
SGT Mark C. Scullion
2LT Daniel C. Scully
PFC Richard E. Scully
SPC Stephen H. Sea
SPC William Seabreeze
SPC Joseph A. Seager
SGT William Lee Seagraves
CPT Robert C. Seal
CPL Paul E. Sealand
SPC Robert Seale
SGT Loven V. Joe Seaman
SPC Ronald L. Seaman
1SG David Eugene Seamands
SPC Elmer L. Seamster
SSG Arturo G. Seanez
PFC Joe Searcy
SFC James A. Seargeant
COL (Ret) Thomas D. Seargeant
SPC Arthur H. Searle
SGT Michael B. Searles
SFC (Ret) Ralph W. Sebastian
1SG Daniel Sebeck
SPC F.R. Seccareccia
SPC Dale Sechler
CPT Kerrie Second
SPC Lynn Secules
CPT (Ret) Emanuel Sedacca
SPC Duane R. Sedler
SGT Edward P. Sedler
1LT Walter J. Seeba
LT Garry L. Seeburger
SP6 Douglas L. Seeds
SGT Glenn E. Seefeld
1SG (Ret) Daniel L. Seefeldt
MAJ Larry D. Seefeldt
PVT Keenan R. Seegobin
SFC John A. Seek
SGT Dennis M. Seel
MRS. Ann Glynis Seeley
SPC Laverne E. Seeley
CPL William H. Seeley
SSG Daniel W. Seemann
PFC Todd Seemann
SGT Brian C. Seery
SPC Agustin P. Segarra
SGT Eufemio Segarra
MAJ Kenneth A. Segelhorst
SPC Art Segers
SFC (Ret) George C. Segerstrom
1SG Mike S. Segovia
CPT David A. Segulin
PFC Ernest J. Segura
SSG Richard Lee Seher
SSG Thomas C. Seher
PFC Toby J. Seider
CW2 (Ret) Ronald W. Seifert
SPC Marvin Seigal
MAJ David T. Seigel
SPC Johnathen W. Seils
1LT Daniel Seiter
CPL Edwin W. Seith
MAJ (Ret) Ernest R. Seitz
SPC Leland Sekayumptewa
SGT Justin A. Selak
SGT Orbie J. N. Selby
SGT Randy R. Selby
SSG Clarence Michael Self
LTC (Ret) Dennis E. Self
PFC Jimmy R. Self
PFC Harvey W. Sell
SGT John L. Sell
SPC Russell C. Sell
CSM (Ret) Chris A. Sellards
SFC Jerry Sellari
1SG Elaine Sellars
SGT Rodney E. Sellars
SPC Patrick J. Selleck
2LT David M. Sellen
LTC Art Sellers
MRS. Billy R. Sellers
SGT Erika Sellers
MSG Fredrick H. Sellers
PFC Marty L. Sellers
CPT Olen Z. Sellers
SPC Richard D. Sellers
MR. Robert P. Sellers
SPC Stetson C. Sellers
SGT Harold V. Selley
SPC Donald G. Sellmann
SSG Barry V. Sells
MAJ Eugene W. Sells
SGT David D. Selmon
SP5 Charles F. Selph
CPT Guy Selsor
SGT Roger Semallie
SGT Frank J. Seman
TSgt Joseph J. Semancsin
SSG Toilolo Semel
PVT Daniel Semidey
SPC Robert C. Semrow
MR. Myron D. Semunchick
MAJ David C. Senay
SSG Susavan Sengvirat
1LT John G. Senor
SGT Robert W. Senske
CW2 Joseph M. Sepesy
SFC Martin Sepkowski
1LT Richard M. Sepulvado
CPT Carlos R. Sepulveda
SGT Romer S. Sepulveda
MAJ Oliver Sequeira
SPC Gregory P. Seraphine
SPC Arthur M. Serena
CW5 Terry P. Serface
SPC John P. Serini
1SG Sam Serna
2LT Dominick A. Serra
SSG Damaso Serrano
SPC Ignacio Serrano
SSG Camilo Serrano-Ramos
SGT (Ret) James Serras
SSG Lowell D. Serum
SGT James H. Server
SGT Warren E. Sessler
2LT Eric M. Setala
MRS. John I. Setelin
CPL Alan C. Setherley
1SG Ed Setliff
SPC Frederick Setterberg
SPC Larry W. Settles
SFC William W. Seuffer
LTC (Ret) Arthur E. Sevelius
SSG (Ret) Gary D. Severian
CPT (Ret) Gordon J. Severson
CPL Michael R. Severson
SSG Jerry R. Seward
SP3 Clifford C. Sewell
LT James Erik Sewell
SFC (Ret) Foster Sexton
SGT Keith P. Sexton
SFC Robert Seybold
1LT Thomas N. Seyfried
1LT Eric L. Seymore
CPT James D. Seymour
SGT James R. Seymour
SGT Robert J. Seymour
SSG Walter J. Seymour
MSG (Ret) William A. Seymour
CPT Raymond L. Shackelford
SFC Frank R. Shackleford
CPT Don Shacklette
PFC Brandon Shadden
SGT Donald W. Shadden
SFC Joe Shadrick
PFC Brian J. Shaefer
SPC Bobby J. Shafer
CPT Christopher J. Shafer
CPL Donald N. Shafer
CPT Paul E. Shafer
SPC Paul L. Shafer
LT Scott Shafer
PFC Tom Shaff
SSG James L. Shaffer
SGT Kevin W. Shaffer
SP5 Michael L. Shaffer
SSG Nathan D. Shaffer
PV2 John L. Shahbazian
SGM (Ret) Harry S. Shakes
SPC Sherif Z. Shalaby
SFC William R. Shales
SSG Steve A. Shamblin
COL William Shambora
2LT David A. Shamsi
COL (Ret) Daniel J. Shanahan
LTC Michael K. Shanahan
MR. Jerry Shane
SPC John W. Shane
SPC Mark Shane
SSG Sandra C. Shane Trovato
SFC (Ret) Eldo R. Shank
CPT Joel F. Shank
2LT Theodore G. Shank
MAJ Mark E. Shankle
CW4 (Ret) David M. Shanklin
1LT Bernard Shankman
MAJ Anne P. Shanks
LTC Wayne M. Shanks
SPC Phillip Ned Shanley
CPL Charles H. Shannon
LT Deborah D. Shannon
1SG (Ret) George M. Shannon
SPC Richard J. Shannon
SGT Kirby Shapiro
PFC Roger A. Shaputis
SGT William C. Sharbrough
SGT Scott P. Sharbutt
LTC Michael P. Sharer
SSG (Ret) Thomas G. Sharkey
SGT Don J. Sharon
SGT Abraham M. Sharp
TSgt Charles M. Sharp
PV2 Daryl A. Sharp
SGT David L. Sharp
SPC Derrick Sharp
SFC Douglas D. Sharp
SSG James P. Sharp
SP5 John Sharp
CPT Stephen E. Sharp
SGT Timothy D. Sharp
GEN (Ret) Walter L. Sharp
SGM (Ret) Wayne Sharp
CPT Christopher A. Sharpe
MAJ Gerald W. Sharpe
SSG John R. Sharpe
SFC Joseph T. Sharpe
SGT Neal Sharpe
SSG Ralph H. Sharpe
SGT Robert Sharpe
SSG Aric L. Sharper
SFC (Ret) Karl W. Sharples
SSG Stanley D. Sharrah
PFC Robert C. Sharrard
SGT John R. Sharrow
SGT Michael L. Shatley
SFC John R. Shatto
SSG George Shaughnessy
CW3 Ernest T. Shaut
CPT Charles Shaver
CPT Karen E. Shaver
1SG (Ret) Robert D. Shaver
SPC Russell Shaver
COL (Ret) A. Park Shaw
CPT Aaron T. Shaw
PV2 Ashley R. Shaw
SPC Catrina Shaw
SSG Charles Shaw
LTC (Ret) David R. Shaw
CPT Eric B. Shaw
PVT Floyd A. Shaw
SGT Harold E. Shaw
SPC Jeff H. Shaw
CW2 Jim Shaw
SPC John Floyd Shaw
SSG Jonathan C. Shaw
SPC Larry L. Shaw
SGT Marshall Shaw
SGT Michael A. Shaw
MAJ Peter J. Shaw
LTC (Ret) Ralph W. Shaw
CPT Robert C. Shaw
SPC Robert J. Shaw
SFC RooseveLT Shaw
SSG William E. Shaw
MR. Dennis Shea
CPT Matthew T. Shea
1LT Michael C. Shea
CW2 (Ret) Mitch Sheairs
SPC Steve Shear
PV2 William Shear
PFC Clyde L. Shearer
MAJ (Ret) Leonard B. Shearer
SFC (Ret) Sidney R. Shearing
SGT Glenn H. Sheathelm
SPC Charles H. Sheckells
SP5 Lynn Shedden
1SG (Ret) Bryan G. Sheehan
CPT Christopher Jon Sheehan
SPC Douglas T. Sheehan
PVT Lester Sheehan
SGT Timothy J. Sheehe
PFC Daniel J. Sheets
LTC Fredrick S. Sheets
SGT Michael C. Sheets
SSG Walter L. Sheffield
LT William F. Sheffield
CPL Patrick J. Sheffler
SP3 Harold Sheil
SGT Richard F. Shekey
LTC David H. Shelby
MRS. Selwyn Shelby
PFC Fred D. Shelden
CPL Carroll Sheldon
MSG Crispin M. Sheldon
SGT Donald R. Sheldon
MR. Dean L. Shell
SSG Sam O. Shell
SGT Anthony Shellenberg
PFC Daniel J. Shelley
MR. W. B. Shelley
SPC Don J. Shelton
SSG Francis J. Shelton
SGT Gary R. Shelton
PVT Kevin A. Shelton
PVT Robert D. Shelton
SGT Stephen Shelton
LTC Michael L. Shenk
SSG Robert D. Shepard
SSG Charles R. Shephard
1LT Brian Shepherd
SSG Dustin Shepherd
PFC John C. Shepherd
SFC (Ret) John M. Shepherd
SFC (Ret) Keith W. Shepherd
PFC Ron Shepherd
MAJ Samuel Shepherd
SPC William C. Shepherd
SSG William D. Shepherd
SGT David Sheppard
SGM Edgar A. Sheppard
SSG James E. Sheppard
SPC Jason Sheppard
CPL Robert F. Sheppard
SPC Wayne E. Sheppard
PFC William A. Sheppard
LTC (Ret) Robert O. Sherard
COL (Ret) John H. Sherburn
CH (COL) Barbara K. Sherer
MSGT (Ret) John N. Sherian
CW2 Ezekiel Sheridan
SGT George R. Sheridan
SP5 James M. Sheridan
1LT Philip H. Sheridan
SFC Robert J. Sheridan
SPC Christian B. Sherk
SPC Donald R. Sherman
SGT Gene Sherman
SGT Jack E. Sherman
MR. John P. Sherman
PVT Mark R. Sherman
SSG Michael Sherman
SSG Myer Sherman
PFC Ronald E. Sherman
MSG (Ret) Jerry L. Sherrill
SGT Ronald A. Sherrod
SGT David P. Sherwood
SGT Patrick J. Sherwood
MR. Peter Sherwood
SSG Richard R. Sherwood
SGT Ron Sherwood
SGT William G. Sherwood
CPT Raymond Y. Shetzline
SPC Conroy A. Shields
1LT Isaac S. B. Shields
SGT Richard J. Shields
PFC Thomas Shields
SSG Tony Shields
SPC John C. Shifflett
SGT James W. Shiflet
CPT Ernest W. Shillak
LTC Cary A. Shillcutt
PVT Larry D. Shilling
SGT Ronald J. Shilling
SFC (Ret) Ronal Shinault
MRS. Joyce Shindoll
1LT Bill L. Shine
SPC Kelly D. W. Shine
PFC Donald Shingleton
SP5 William J. Shink
GEN (Ret) Eric K. Shinseki
SP5 Donald C. Shipley
SSG Nicholas Shipley
1LT Stan J. Shipley
CPL Charles C. Shipman
SGT Don L. Shipman
SGM Donald R. Shipman
SFC (Ret) Kenneth M. Shipman
PV2 Spencer R. Shipman
CPL William M. Shipman
SPC Carl H. Shipp
CPT Elbert D. Shipp
CW2 Thomas P. Shipp
TSgt John H. Shippee
SGT Martin L. Shirk
MSG Aubrey B. Shirley
COL Eric P. Shirley
LTC (Ret) Roy T. Shishido
PFC Dylan Shively
CPT (Ret) Thurman W. Shivers
PFC Andrew Shoaf
1LT Eric P. Shockley
SSG (Ret) Jonathan D. Shockley
SPC Roger W. Shockley
SP5 William L. Shockley
PFC James D. Shockome
SGM (Ret) William G. Shoe
SPC Russell A. Shoebotham
PFC John M. Shoemaker
PFC Robert F. Shoemaker
GEN (Ret) Robert M. Shoemaker
LTC Thomas A. Shoffner
SPC Kenneth A. Shogren
SGT Melvin Shollenberger
SGT Michael N. Sholtz
SPC Micheal Shook
SPC Steven J. Shook
CPT Tommy Shook
SPC William W. Shook
SPC Carroll S. Shoopman
SSG Terry E. Shoopman
SSG Randy Shores
WO1 Hoover Short
SPC Leroy Short
SGT Marvin Short
CPL Ted W. Short
PVT Timothy J. Short
SGT Edward J. Shortall
MSG W. H. Shorter
LTC (Ret) Harold L. Shortnacy
SGT Richard H. Shortt
SGT James C. Shotwell
SGT William Clyde Shotwell
MSG Melvin L. Shoulders
SFC Samuel J. F. Shoults
MAJ (Ret) Tom Shoupe
CPT James G. Shover
SGT Richard Trent Showalter

LTC (Ret) Stephen A. Showalter
SGT William F. Showalter
MR. Robert Showers
SFC Barney N. Shows
SPC Dale Shows
SGT David G. Shows
MRS. Cecil L. Shrader
PFC Roger D. Shrader
SGT Garland P. Shreck
SGT William B. Shreckengost
SGT Joseph G. Shredl
CW3 Preston R. Shreve
SP6 Richard L. Shriver
LTC Terry W. Shroyer
MAJ Richard P. Shuey
PV2 Arnold A. Shufelt
SPC Samuel D. Shuff
1LT Edward L. Shufflebarger
SSG Cynthia Shula-Davis
SPC Harold R. Shuler
SPC Thomas O. Shuler
SSG Robert M. Shultz
MAJ Richard C. Shumard
1SG Jimmy T. Shumate
SFC (Ret) Vincent E. Shumate
PFC Bryant C. Shurley
SFC Harry K. A. Shuron
SGT Howard S. Shute
PFC Russell L. Shuts
SP5 Donald W. Shutt
SSG Arthur P. Shy
SGT Marion J. Siara
SPC Ted D. Sibley
CPL Lloyd E. Sichting
CPT David F. Siciliano
LTC Peter Sicoli
PFC Richard A. Sicotte
SGT David M. Siders
LTC Don Sides
CPL Cay Sidwell
SPC Shawn Siebold
MR. Randy Siebring
SPC Jason C. Sieg
SFC Anthony J. Siegel
SPC Paul H. Siegel
PFC Robert J. Siegel
PV2 Steven L. Siegel
SGT Gerald T. Siegert
SPC John T. Siegfred
CW4 (Ret) Donald W. Siegfried
PFC James J. Siegfried
LTC (Ret) William A. Siegling
1LT Robert W. Siemer
MR. Danny Sien
SGT Philip B. Sierer
SSG Richard Sierra
A1C Theodore T. Sierra
1SG Steven Sierras
SGT Kenneth W. Siers
CW2 Craig T. Sieting
SGT Asael M. Sievers
MAJ William H. Sievers
1LT John R. Sievert
SSG Donald Sifford
SGT Javier Sifuentes
MSG (Ret) Mario P. Sifuentes
SSG Timothy Sifuentes
SPC Reginald W. Sigers
1LT James M. Sigler
SSG Arthur C. Sigmon
SGT Drew J. Sigmund
LTC (Ret) David A. Sikes
SPC Paul Siko
PV2 Eric Silas
MR. Robert F. Silcock
SFC Richard M. Silcox
LT Frank E. Siler
MAJ (Ret) Michael J. Silipini
SFC Michael A. Siller
SGT William S. Sillery
CPL Gary L. Silliman
1SG John Silva
SPC Joseph M. Silva
SSG Josue Silva
SPC Kevin P. Silva
SGT Manuel Silva
CW2 Robert R. Silva
SPC Michael Lee Silvanic
1SG (Ret) Joe Silvas
SFC Benjamin Silver
CPT Marshall P. Silver
SGT Stanley S. Silverberg
COL (Ret) Gene S. Silverblatt
SPC Michael J. Silvernagel
CPL Myron D. Silvernagel
SFC Carl E. Silvers
1LT Andre K. Silvola
1LT Michael Sim
SPC Walter J. Simkus
CPL Harold Simlak
SFC Anthony D. Simmons
MSG Dana L. Simmons
MAJ Donald R. Simmons
CPL Franklin H. Simmons
SGT Gary L. Simmons
SFC George C. Simmons
LTC (Ret) Gerald R. Simmons
SGT Glenn F. Simmons
SFC J. W. Simmons
MG (Ret) James E. Simmons
COL Milton E. Simmons
SFC Paul T. Simmons
SPC Phillip Simmons
MR. Randy N. Simmons
SP5 Richard W. Simmons
CPT Robert Simmons
SGT Roger Dale Simmons
SPC Ross Simmons
SSG Stephen K. Simmons
PFC Terrell Simmons
SPC Thomas R. Simmons
SFC (Ret) Travis Simmons
SPC Walter L. Simmons
PVT Robert L. Simms
SGT Steven C. Simms
SGT Adam J. Simon
PFC Bernard Simon
SPC Bruce Simon
SGT Fred L. Simon
SPC Larry A. Simon
1SG (Ret) Mark A. Simon
CPT Matthew L. Simon
COL (Ret) Paul N. Simon
CW5 Tyrone Simon
SGT Roland Simoneaux
SFC (Ret) John C. Simones
SGT Stevce Simonov
SGT Eric V. Simons
SGT Frank D. Simons
PFC Gary E. Simons
CPL Merrill C. Simons
MAJ Jerry A. Simonsen
SGT Bruce G. Simonson
CPT Erik Simonson
SFC Lawrence B. Simonson
SPC Martin Simonson
MS. Virainia Simonson
LTC Dale L. Simpkins
SPC Alvin Guy Simpson
SPC Curtis L. Simpson
SGT Darrell D. Simpson
SGT Delton Simpson
SGT Don Simpson
SGT Eugene J. Simpson
1LT G. A. Simpson
PVT George F. Simpson
MR. Harry Simpson
LTC (Ret) Patrick J. Simpson
SGT Paul R. Simpson
SGM Ralph Simpson
SGT Robert F. Simpson
PFC Shawn M. Simpson
SGT Steve Simpson
PFC Thomas W. Simpson
SFC (Ret) Billy F. Sims
SPC Cory J. Sims
SPC David L. Sims
MAJ Eric Shelton Sims
SGT Gabriel U. Sims
PFC Jacob C. Sims
SSG Jerry D. Sims
CPT Mark C. Sims
SGT Marvin E. Sims
SFC Oscar L. Sims
CPT Paul E. Sims
PVT Vincent E. Sims
SGM Walter Sims
CPT Anthony C. Sims-Hall
PFC Hyunho Sin
SGT Navanny Sin
SGT Mile Sinadinoski
SFC Milo Sinapati
1LT Seth R. Sindel
SGT S. S. Sindelar
SPC William H. Sindelar
MR. Martin Sinderbrand
SGT Mark S. Siner
SGT Dennis M. Sines
LTC (Ret) Kenneth A. Sines
PFC Bikramjit Singh
PFC Gene Singh
PFC Jack W. Singleton
SGT Jacqueline Singleton
SPC James E. Singleton
MAJ (Ret) John R. Singleton
CW2 Kalonji Singleton
CPT Schnicka L. Singleton
SGT Bharat Sinha
SGT Joseph J. Sinisi
MRS. Martha Sink
1SG (Ret) Richard C. Sink
2LT Timothy Adam Sinks
SPC Charles Sinquefield
SFC Daniel T. Sipes
MSG Brian Sipp
CW2 John B. Sipple
SGT Russell Sirmans
CPT Thomas E. Sirois
SGT Farrell L. Sirovy
SPC (Ret) Daniel T. Sirr
SSG Jeremey S. Sisak
SPC Ross Sisinni
CW2 Robert W. Sisk
SFC (Ret) Manuel D. Sisneros
SFC Lanny J. Sisson
SGT Robert D. Sisson
SSG Travis Sisson
SGT John B. Sistek
PFC Jason N. Sites
SPC Ronald Sites
MR. Melvin E. Sitze
CPL Walter T. Siuley
SSG Damien O. Siwik
SPC Alvah Sizemore
SPC James J. Sizemore
CSM S. D. Sizemore
1SG (Ret) Scott L. Sjule
PVT Gregory D. Skaggs
CPL Hubert A. Skaggs
SGT James D. Skaggs
CPT Jerry R. Skaggs
SSG Terry Skaggs
PFC Marion R. Skains
SGT Thomas Skalecki
SPC Harry Skalla
PV2 Lyle V. Skalla
CPL James G. Skaltsakos
MR. William M. Skane
SGT Gary L. Skarphol
MR. Charles Skaulam
SPC Gerry Skelly
CPL Howard P. Skelly
PFC Patrick F. Skelly
SGT Thomas D. Skelly
MR. Clifford L. Skelton
PVT Merle Skelton
SPC James A. Skiba
MSG Bobby L. Skidmore
SGT James D. Skidmore
SPC Le Roy Skief
MR. John L. Skiff
PFC Charles D. Skiles
CPT (Ret) John C. Skillicorn
SSG Frank W. Skinner
MR. H. A. Skinner
PFC James E. Skinner
SGT John M. Skinner
LT Patrick L. Skinner
SFC Patrick N. Skinner
SPC Perry D. Skinner
SSG Ronald L. Skinner
SPC William Skinner
SGT Charles Skipper
1SG (Ret) Terrance A. Skipper
CPL John D. Skirvin
SPC Ronald L. Skirvin
SGT Leonard Skodje
1LT Joe Skoglund
1Sgt Robert Skole
SGT Wayne P. Skopek
1SG Ernest J. Skoropowski
SSG Sherby J. Skrantz
2LT Stephen J. Skriba
CPL John W. Skurka
PFC Paul H. Skwiera
SGT Charles W. Skyles
MR. Herbert J. Slack
SGT John R. Slack
1LT Richard C. Slack
PFC Andrae Slade
SGT James D. Slade
SSG Lisa C. Slade
MSG (Ret) John L. Slagel
SPC James A. Slager
MR. James E. Slaggy
SPC Robert S. Slagle
SPC Robert C. Slanicky
SSG Ken Slaten
SSG James Slaton
SGT Donald D. Slatter
SGT Joe Slaughter
PFC Daniel E. Slayden
SPC Norman E. Slead
SFC (Ret) Kirk V. Sledge
MR. John Slee
SGT Ronald G. Sleeis
SGT Eric C. Sleeper
SGT James Slevin
SGT John F. Sliger
SSG Daniel Slimp
SPC Michael J. Sliozis
SGT Alpheus Sloan
SPC Austin J. Sloan
CPT Bernard H. Sloan
SPC Calvin E. Sloan
SPC Rick A. Sloan
SPC Jeffrey Slocum
MR. Walter M. Slomienski
SPC Robert E. Slonaker
MSG Charles W. Slone
LTC (Ret) Michael E. Sloniker
PFC William E. Sloop
CPL Jack Slootweg
PFC Charles V. Sloper
1LT Brian Slotnick
MSG (Ret) Charles E. Sluder
SPC Dale A. Sluder
SPC Paul Slusarczyk
SGT Tony D. Slusarski
MAJ (Ret) Kenneth M. Slye
SSG Charles Small
SGT David Anthony Small
CSM (Ret) Stanley D. Small
MR. Leonard W. Smalley
SFC Lori Ann Smalley
SGT Roger W. Smalley
SSG Louis V. Smalls
CW2 Thomas H. Smallwood
LTC Cheryl L. Smart
1SG Daniel E. Smart
SP5 Frank M. Smart
MSG James H. Smart
1LT John D. Smart
SP5 Joseph Smart
PFC (Ret) Allen R. Smartt
SPC Nicky L. Smartt
MR. Michael J. Smaydy
SSG Joseph S. Smeck
MAJ (Ret) Daniel R. Smestad
SGT John R. Smiley
1SG Ronald Smiley
1LT Mike Smilnak
SSG Aaron T. Smith
CW2 Alfred C. Smith
SSG Algie Smith
CPT Anthony Smith
SPC Antony Smith
1LT Arthur W. Smith
MRS. Barton M. Smith
SGT Ben L. Smith
PFC Bennie R. Smith
SSG Betty J. Smith
SPC Billy E. Smith
MSG (Ret) Billy G. Smith
SPC Billy H. Smith
CPT Bob Smith
SFC Bobby E. Smith
SPC Bobby J. Smith
SPC Brandon Smith
2LT Brian J. Smith
SGT Brian K. Smith
SSG Brian T. Smith
SGT Brian W. Smith
CW3 (Ret) Bruce James Smith
CSM Bruce O. Smith
SPC Bryan Smith
SFC Bryan L. Smith
MSG Calhoun C. Smith
CW3 (Ret) Carl L. Smith
SGT Carl V. Smith
MAJ Cecil Smith
SP5 Charles C. Smith
SGT Charles G. Smith
MR. Charles J. Smith
MSG Charles K. Smith
MSG Charles R. Smith
MR. Charles S. Smith
MR. Charles U. Smith
MSG (Ret) Charles W. Smith
SSG Christopher F. Smith
SSG Christopher L. Smith
LTC (Ret) Clarence Alvin Smith
MR. Clarion L. Smith
PVT Cletis H. Smith
CSM Cornelius Smith
LTC Cory R. Smith
SFC Dale W. Smith
1LT Daniel Smith
1SG (Ret) Daniel J. Smith
SPC Danny L. Smith
SGT Darryl Smith
SGM (Ret) David Smith
SSG David A. Smith
1LT David A. Smith
SSG David A. Smith
LTC (Ret) David B. Smith
SSG (Ret) David C. Smith
LT David C. Smith
MR. David D. Smith
LT David L. Smith
LTC (Ret) David R. Smith
PFC Dayton Ralph Smith
SPC Delmor W. Smith
SFC Demetrius L. Smith
1SG Dennis L. Smith
SPC Dennis Lamarr Smith
SGT Dennis R. Smith
1SG (Ret) Deriek Smith
PFC Derrick Smith
SGT (Ret) Derrick H. Smith
SGT Dewey R. Smith
SSG Don W. Smith
SGT Donald Smith
BG (Ret) Donald B. Smith
SSG Donald E. Smith
SGT Donald J. Smith
TSgt Donald M. Smith
SSG Donald O. Smith
CPT Douglas J. Smith
SFC Doyle W. Smith
SFC Earlean Smith
SSG (Ret) Edgar J. Smith
COL Edgar L. Smith
SGT Edwin D. Smith
SPC Edwin E. Smith
CPT (Ret) Elmer Smith
CPL Emerson L. Smith
CSM (Ret) Emory L. Smith
SFC Erik W. Smith
SFC Ernest Smith
LTC Eugene C. Smith
SSG Eugene G. Smith
LTC (Ret) Everett A. Smith
SGT Frank M. Smith
1LT Frank T. Smith
SFC Franklin D. Smith
MSG Franklin R. Smith
SPC Fred Smith
SPC Fred D. Smith
1SG Freddie M. Smith
CPT Frederick Smith
SGT Frederick A. Smith
MR. Frederick P. Smith
SPC Gabriel Smith
SSG Gail W. Smith
SGT Garry David Smith
SPC George A. Smith
CW2 George A. Smith
COL George F. Smith
SPC George P. Smith
SFC Gerald D. Smith
CPL Gerald L. Smith
MAJ Gerald W. Smith
MR. Glenn C. Smith
CSM Glenn R. Smith
PFC Gordon Smith
MAJ Gregg A. Smith
COL (Ret) Harold Smith
CPL Harold E. Smith
SGT Harold Jesse Smith
SFC Harry L. Smith
LTC Horrell H. Smith
PFC Howard Dennis Smith
MAJ Howard T. Smith
SPC Ike Smith
SGT Iris F. Smith
SP5 Irvin W. Smith
SGT Jack C. L. Smith
PVT Jacob W. Smith
PVT Jadzia A. Smith
COL (Ret) James A. Smith
MR. James E. Smith
LTC James M. Smith
SFC James O. Smith
SSG James P. Smith
LTC James R. Smith
SSG (Ret) James R. Smith
PFC James V. Smith
PFC James W. Smith
SPC Jamie L. Smith
SPC Jason A. Smith
MAJ Jeffrey A. Smith
SSG Jeffry Smith
MSG (Ret) Jerry D. Smith
PFC Jerry L. Smith
PVT Jerry M. Smith
MR. Jerry R. Smith
SP5 Jerry W. Smith
SP5 Jessie L. Smith
SPC Jim Smith
1LT Jim C. Smith
CPL (Ret) Jim D. Smith
SSG John Smith
SGT John C. Smith
SGT John E. Smith
MAJ John T. Smith
SSG John T. Smith
SFC Joseph K. Smith
PFC Joseph R. Smith
PV2 Josh Smith
SGM Jurdy L. Smith
SGT Justin D. Smith
MR. Kenneth C. Smith
LTC Kenneth L. Smith
CPT Kenneth M. Smith
1SG Kevin Smith
MAJ Kevin G. Smith
SPC Kevin L. Smith
MAJ Kevin P. Smith
CSM Kevin R. Smith
CPL Kim E. Smith
1LT Lafe Z. Smith
SFC Larry G. Smith
SGT Larry J. Smith
SGT (Ret) Larry J. Smith
SPC Leo J. Smith
SGT Leroy Smith
SGT Lissette Smith
SGT Lonnie L. Smith
SGT Marcia Smith
CPT Marion K. Smith
SGT Mark A. B. Smith
MAJ Mark D. Smith
1LT Martin Smith
1SG (Ret) Martin J. Smith
SPC Marzellus W. Smith
MAJ Matthew L. Smith
SGM (Ret) Mc Kinley Smith
SP5 Michael A. Smith
CPL Michael A. Smith
CW2 Michael C. Smith
SPC Michael D. Smith
SGT Michael D. Smith
SPC Michael E. Smith
SSG Michael F. Smith
1SG Michael H. Smith
2LT Michael J. Smith
SSG Michael L. Smith
SGT Michael L. Smith
CPT Michael L. Smith
SPC Michael R. Smith
CW4 (Ret) Michael S. Smith
SGT Michael T. Smith
MR. Mitchell L. Smith
CPT Mushawn D. Smith
SSG Noel Smith
SSG (Ret) Olen M. Smith
SSG Oliver W. Smith
MSG (Ret) Ora A. Smith
SGT Owen F. Smith
1LT Patrick A. Smith
SGT Paul K. Smith
SPC Paul R. Smith
MG (Ret) Paul T. Smith
SP5 Paul V. Smith
LTC Philip J. Smith
COL Rayburn G. Smith
SP5 Raymond J. Smith
SGT Rexford L. Smith
PFC Richard H. Smith
SP5 Richard L. Smith
MRS. Richard L. Smith
SPC Richard N. Smith
SPC Robert Smith
SGT Robert Smith
SGT Robert A. Smith
PFC Robert D. Smith
1LT Robert H. Smith
SFC Robert J. Smith
SGT Robert L. Smith
SFC Robert L. Smith
SSG Robert L. Smith
PFC Robert S. Smith
SGT Robert W. Smith
LTC (Ret) Roddy L. Smith
SSG Roderick Smith
1LT Rodney E. Smith
SP5 Rodney L. Smith
SGT Romaine Kirton Smith
1SG Ronald W. Smith
MR. Roy J. Smith
SrA Roy L. Smith
MR. Rubin M. Smith
MAJ (Ret) Sam G. Smith
SGT Sammy E. Smith
SPC Samuel Alexander Smith
MG (Ret) Scott B. Smith
PFC Seneca S. Smith
SPC Shane Smith
SPC Shawn Smith
SPC Simon P. Smith
SGM Simon T. Smith
SPC Stephen Smith
SGT Steven A. Smith

SPC Steven P. Smith
PFC Ted Smith
SGT Terence J. Smith
SSG Terry Lee Smith
SSG (Ret) Thomas Smith
MRS. Thomas F. Smith
LTC (Ret) Thomas G. Smith
BG (Ret) Thomas G. Smith
SGT Thomas J. Smith
MRS. Thomas J. Smith
CW2 (Ret) Thomas L. Smith
SGT Thomas Lee Smith
SGT Thomas W. Smith
SPC Timothy J. Smith
PFC Tommy E. Smith
MSG Travion U. Smith
CPT Travis A. Smith
SGT Trey Smith
CPT Troy A. Smith
PV2 Vincent W. Smith
CPT Virgel L. Smith
MAJ Wade L. Smith
LTC (Ret) Walter C. Smith
DR. Warren L. Smith
PFC Wayne E. Smith
CPL Wayne L. Smith
LTC Wilbur P. Smith
SPC William Smith
SPC William A. Smith
SPC William A. Smith
CPL William D. Smith
SGT William D. Smith
SSG William F. Smith
LTC (Ret) William H. Smith
SFC (Ret) William Howard Smith
SP5 William J. Smith
1LT William P. Smith
SFC Willie T. Smith
SFC Zachary Smith
PFC Claude A. Smithey
CSM (Ret) Ocie L. Smithhart
SGT Heather L. Smith-Langs
SPC Robert V. Smitley
SSG (Ret) Robert M. Smocer
SFC David R. Smoker
SGT W. George Smokorowski
COL (Ret) Donald R. Smolinski
SPC Curtis K. Smoot
MR. Jack Smoot
SGT Alva Lloyd Smothers
SGT Earl R. Smothers
SGT Jimmie R. Smothers
PFC Jon M. Smothers
SPC Michael L. Smothers
MS. Nancy Smoyer
PFC Paul R. Smulian
CPL David K. Smyth
WO1 Fred C. Smyth
MR. Guy E. Smyth
MAJ (Ret) Hamilton C. Smyth
MR. Alvin Smythe
SPC Duane W. Smythe
1SG Mark Snair
SGT William L. Snead
SGT Donald W. Snedeker
SGT Richard W. Sneden
SGT Barber J. Sneed
MRS. David E. Sneed
SGT Paul H. Sneed
SGT Cassidy R. Snell
SPC Larry K. Snell
1SG Perry B. Snell
SPC Raymond J. Snell
PFC George Z. Snellings
CPL Alva H. Snider
SPC Byron C. Snider
MRS. Lucille A. Snider
SSG Melvin E. Snider
SGT Gerald S. Sniezyk
SFC (Ret) Fred G. Snipes
2LT Joe Ben Snipes
PFC Arlon K. Snoddy
SGT Harold M. Snoddy
CPT Raymond F. Snoddy
MSG (Ret) Gerald D. Snodgrass
SFC Henry C. Snodgrass
SSG Joseph L. Snook
LTC Marc R. Snook
MR. Charles R. Snow
SGT Dwayne Snow
LTC Joseph C. Snow
2LT Robert Snow
SPC Roger D. Snow
LTC Stephen J. Snow
MAJ Daniel Snowdall
SGT Dustin Snowdy
CW3 Bill O. Snyder
CPT David M. Snyder
LT Gary W. Snyder
SGM (Ret) George J. Snyder
LTC James W. Snyder
SGT John H. Snyder
CPL John W. Snyder
1LT (Ret) Joseph A. Snyder
MSG Kenneth L. Snyder
MR. Larry Dale Snyder
MAJ Michael L. Snyder
SPC Peter S. Snyder
SGT Richard W. Snyder
SPC Robert E. Snyder
1SG (Ret) Robert R. Snyder
SPC Ryan C. Snyder
MAJ Stephen D. Snyder
2LT Philip J. Sobiesk
SGT John T. Sobol
SPC Joseph T. Sobolak
COL (Ret) John E. (Jack) Sobraske
SGT Wilferd A. Sochor
MSG William M. Soda
MRS. Gudrun R. Soderstrom
SPC Joshua Soileau
SGT Don P. Sokolowski
SPC Cynthia Solano
SPC Jonathan Solas
SGT Donald J. Sole
SGM Gilberto G. Solis
MSG Jesus C. Solis
CSM Jose L. Soliz
MSG Roberto E. Soliz
SSG (Ret) Steve Soliz
CPL Earl W. Sollenberger
MSG (Ret) Robert D. Soller
SGT Kenneth W. Solley
1LT Patrick Sollo
SGT George Soloman
SPC Benji J. Solomon
MRS. Chet H. Solomon
SPC Michael Solomon
PFC Morgan P. Solomon
SGT Nathan Solomon
SFC Nathaniel Solomon
LTC Mark E. Solomons
SPC Ashleigh Solorzano
SPC Ronald J. Solorzano
CSM (Ret) Richard G. Soloway
SPC Jeffrey P. Solt
PFC Edward F. Soltis
SP5 Raymond Somers
MSG Spurgeon R. Somers
SP5 Darrel R. Somerville
SPC Edward L. Sommer
SSG Henry G. Sommers
CW4 Jerry C. Sommers
SGT Frederick F. Sona
SPC Monty W. Sondrol
SGT Alan Keith Sones
SFC Jim C. Song
SGT Phillip M. Sonn
LTC Scott Sonsalla
SGM Brian G. Soper
SGT Edward L. Sorace
CPL James J. Sorce
COL Kenneth R. Sorenson
MR. Mark A. Sorg
SGT Thomas J. Sorge
SGT Raymond Soria
SGT Mike Soroski
1SG Charles Sorrell
CPT Steven G. Sorrell
MR. David C. Sorrells
SSG Earl L. Sorrells
SSG Ronald B. Sorrells
CW2 William D. Sorrenson
SPC Larry R. Sosa
MRS. Betty Sosbe
MAJ Javier E. Sostre
CPL Jose Sotelo
SPC Raul N. Sotelo
SPC Angel L. Soto
PFC Dustin J. Soto
SPC Frank A. Soto
SPC Jose J. Soto
1SG Jose J. Soto
SSG Jose L. Soto
SSG Julian Soto
SGT Keith Soto
SGM Manuel C. Soto
SFC Robert Soto
SSG Robert Soto
SPC Tomas Soto
CSM Carlos R. Soto-Bonilla
1SG (Ret) Julio Soto-Perez
MSG Frederic B. Soules
CW2 Joseph D. Sours
1LT Brian N. Souter
MR. J. M. Souter
SGT Donald South
CPT James Roland Southall
MAJ Jarrell D. Southall
MAJ Joseph A. Southcotti
PVT (Ret) Dale L. Southerland
CPL Gary Southerland
SGT James W. Southerland
PVT Jim L. Southwell
SPC William Southwood
1LT Jason R. Souza
SFC John P. Souza
SPC Ronald D. Sovell
CPT Jerome M. Sovich
SGT Louis H. Sowders
SPC Chad Sowers
CPT Tim R. Soyars
SP5 Henry Soza
SPC John J. Spada
PFC Ron Spada
PFC Ralph Spadafora
SSG Lucy A. Spade
SGT Fred W. Spading
SPC John A. Spagnotti
SP5 Donald E. Spahr
SPC Todd R. Spain
1LT Fredd S. Spainhouer
SGT Michael R. Spainhour
SSG Thomas W. Spalding
PFC Nicholas Spalinger
SGT Thomas J. Spampinato
SPC Matthew Karl Spangenberg
SGT Orville L. Spangler
PFC Robert W. Spangler
SPC Timothy W. Spangler
SGT John C. Spaniol
LTC (Ret) Patrick J. Spann
SSG Claude E. Spargur
2LT Michael Brent Sparkes
SPC Allen Ryan Sparks
PVT Andrew Sparks
CPT Bishop Sparks
LTC Dick Sparks
CPT Earl C. Sparks
1SG (Ret) General S. Sparks
CSM (Ret) John D. Sparks
SGT John W. Sparks
1SG (Ret) Philip T. Sparks
CPT Thomas W. Sparks
SSG William A. Sparks
SGT William D. Sparks
SSG Richard G. Sparta
SGT Stephon Michael Spates
SP5 John C. Spatig
MR. James Spatny
SGT Dannie K. Spaulding
LTC (Ret) Fredrick L. Spaulding
SGT John P. Spaulding
CW4 (Ret) Kyle J. Spaulding
SSG Vencie E. Spaw
LTG (Ret) Stephen M. Speakes
CPL (Ret) Harold J. Speakman
SGT Irvin L. Speakman
CSM (Ret) Robert E. Speakman
SFC Johnny L. Speaks
2LT Mark A. Spear
PFC Paul W. Spear
COL (Ret) Ralph S. Spear
SP5 Randall S. Speare
SPC Stacey Spearmon
SSG Christopher Michael Spears
1LT Daaron Spears
SGT David A. Spears
SFC Ernest R. Spears
SGT Gary W. Spears
SPC Gilbert Wayne Spears
MAJ Jeff Spears
LTC Joseph M. Spears
LTC Michael R. Spears
SPC Reginald M. Spears
SPC Shane Allan Spears
CPL Richard L. Speas
SGT Ascenzio J. Speca
SPC Matthew D. Speciale
LTC Daniel J. Speck
SSG David M. Specking
SGM Jason E. Speede
LTC (Ret) Richard L. Speedman
LT Brian L. Speer
SPC Frank D. Speer
SP5 Gary Speer
COL (Ret) William L. Speer
LT Francis X. Speh
SGT Michael A. Spehar
SPC Gordon Speidel
SFC Jonathan M. Speidel
TSgt Leonard M. Speier
1LT Lynna M. Speier
LTC William Speier
SGT Michael W. Speights
SGT John H. Speigner
LTC (Ret) Robin G. Speiser
SGT Tyke Spells
1LT C. J. Spence
MG (Ret) Clyde W. Spence
2LT Dale A. Spence
1LT Kenneth A. Spence
MAJ Sean Spence
COL (Ret) Thomas H. Spence
MAJ (Ret) William R. Spence
CPL Francis R. Spencer
SPC Jack L. Spencer
CPT Jason G. Spencer
SPC Jim Spencer
CSM (Ret) Jimmie W. Spencer
SSG John Spencer
CW2 John I. Spencer
MR. Jon F. Spencer
MAJ Kenneth H. Spencer
CPT Patricia Spencer
SGT Quentine C. Spencer
SGT Randall Spencer
SPC Richard F. Spencer
PFC Stephen P. Spencer
SFC William W. Spencer
SGT Jeffrey E. Spenzer
SPC Christopher A. Sperry
PFC Floyd G. Spice
CPT Marland R. Spicher
SSG John F. Spickler
SGT James P. Spies
SGT Anthony L. Spiewak
LTG (Ret) Michael F. Spigelmire
SGT Gerald Spigelmyer
SSG Hal D. Spiller
1LT Lewis W. Spiller
COL (Ret) Robert E. Spiller
CPT Gordon Spillinger
SFC John W. Spilman
SGT Joseph C. Spinner
SGT Jimmie Spino
WO1 James Spiri
1SG (Ret) Boris R. Spiroff
SPC Thomas A. Spittal
PFC Dick Spittler
SP5 Charles W. Spitz
CSM Scott A. Spiva
SPC William T. Spivey
LTC Christopher J. Spohn
SP5 Clyde E. Spohn
MAJ Warren E. Sponsler
PFC Staci Lee M. Spooner
PFC Arnold D. Spoonmore
SPC Fred L. Sporar
MAJ Nick Sporinsky
SPC Michael J. Sporlein
SPC Chucksey Spotts
COL (Ret) Rodney W. Spotts
CPL Ernest Spradley
PVT Robert C. Spradley
CSM Grover E. Sprague
SSG James R. Sprague
SGT John S. Spranza
1LT Ronald C. Spranzani
SPC Jeffery A. Spratt
SFC Billy J. Spray
LTC (Ret) James M. Sprayberry
SGT Brian D. Sprehn
SGT Montie F. Spriggs
SPC Robert Spring
CPT Carl D. Springer
SGT Patrick K. Springer
SPC Robert E. Springer
COL (Ret) Robert M. Springer
SPC Thomas Springer
SPC Willard J. W. Springer
1LT William P. Sprinkel
SGT Basil L. Sprinkle
SSG Rodney E. Sprinkle
1SG Glenn P. Sproles
PVT Michael A. Sprong
SPC Richard Sprowl
MRS. Alfred E. Spry
SSG Lorraine Spry
SGT Michael S. Spry
SGT Ronald Spurgeon
CPL Jerry W. Spurlock
CPL William J. Spych
PFC Luby Squier
SGT Ernest R. Squire
CW4 William R. Squire
SSG (Ret) Charles St Andrews
SSG Carl R. St Clair
SGM (Ret) Gary L. St Clair
SSG Michael A. St Clair
SPC Norman L. St Clair
SFC (Ret) Leo G. St Cyr
SPC John T. St George
SGT Thomas P. St Germain
SGT Ronald J. St Jean
CPT Don H. St John
MS. Ida M. St John
MSG Jennifer St John
SGT Joseph H. St John
SGT Raymond St John
PVT Mitchell St Julien
SFC E. Larry St Laurent
SGT Richard St Leger
SGM (Ret) Della St Louis
MG (Ret) Robert J. St Onge
SPC Virgil C. Staab
SGT Dillon W. Staas
CW3 (Ret) Jerry D. Staatz
SPC Dewey J. Stabler
SSG Frederick W. Stacey
MAJ Stephen C. Stacey
PVT Brent Stackhouse
SPC Thomas F. Stacy
PVT Patrick L. Stadelbacher
MG (Ret) Gerald P. Stadler
MSG Warner J. Stadler
SPC Donald J. Staffeld
MAJ (Ret) Donald W. Staffon
SSG David B. Stafford
1LT Ernest M. Stafford
SGT Harold H. Stafford
MAJ (Ret) John E. Stafford
SPC Thomas Stagg
LTC B. G. Staggs
SP5 John M. Stagi
SSG Earnest Stahl
CPT Frank B. Stahl
SGT George A. Stahl
MR. Hunter Stahl
PFC Lloyd E. Stahl
SPC Ronald L. Stahl
SGT David V. Stahley
SFC John M. Stahlschmidt
CPL Leland R. Staker
SPC Matthew Stalans
CPT Gerald J. Stalder
SGT Chad J. Stallings
SGT Coy L. Stallings
CPT J. D. Stallings
PFC John W. Stallings
CW3 (Ret) Steven Stallings
SGT Tony Stallings
PFC Donald L. Stallman
LTC (Ret) Charles W. Stam
MAJ Paul Stambaugh
MR. Leon Stamp
MR. Donald E. Stamper
SPC Donald E. Stamper
SSG Raleigh W. Stamps
CPT William H. Stancer
CW4 (Ret) Zug G. Standing Bear
MAJ John M. Standley
SFC William C. Stanfel
SPC Eddie Stanfield
SGT Thomas Raymond Stanfield
SGT John R. Stanfill
CPL Christopher B. Stanford
PVT Clyde Stanford
MAJ Harold D. Stanford
MRS. James W. Stanford
SPC Kevin A. Stanford
MAJ Scott Stanger
LTC (Ret) Anthony M. Stanich
LT Jovan Stanikevski
1SG (Ret) Donald Stanley
CPT Gary P. Stanley
CPT James David Stanley
CSM (Ret) Joseph W. Stanley
MAJ Matthew Stanley
SGT Robert W. Stanley
CW4 William P. Stanley
MR. William S. Stanley
CW2 Wm. Robert Stanley
PFC Zachary Stanley
CW3 (Ret) Harry J. Stansbury
SSG (Ret) Jack R. Stansfield
CPT John Stanton
SGT Roy L. Stapleford
SSG Hubert D. Stapler
MAJ Clinert R. Staples
SP5 James A. Stapleton
SPC Robert Stapleton
CPT David R. Stapp
SGT Terry Starai
CW4 (Ret) Lawrence E. Starbuck
SPC (Ret) James E. Starcher
SGT Billy Stark
PVT Cecilia Stark
CPL Duane V. Stark
PVT Joseph W. Stark
PV2 Nathan A. Stark
SGT Ralph E. Stark
SP5 Richard W. Stark
SGT Robert H. Stark
CPL William D. Starkey
1LT Alvin D. Starks
SGT Corey Starks
SSG Walter A. Starling
SFC (Ret) William M. Starnes
MR. Joe Starns
SGT Earl J. Starr
CSM (Ret) Sam W. Starr
CPL Arthur J. Starrick
COL (Ret) Michael D. Starry
CW2 Kestutis A. Stasaitis
CW3 Sean C. Staton
SSG Sydney D. Staton
PFC Brian Joseph Staub
1LT Steven D. Stauch
PFC James E. Staude
SFC (Ret) Robert Stauffacher
SFC Rick L. Stauffer
LTC (Ret) Wallace J. Stauffer
CPL John W. Stausmire
1LT Edward J. Stawowczyk
SGT Terrence A. Steadman
SPC Spencer S. Stearns
SSG John F. Stebbings
MSG (Ret) Charles E. Stebbins
SPC Joseph V. Stec
LTC (Ret) Chester J. Steckel
SGT Patrick M. Stedl
MAJ (Ret) Charles D. Stedman
MR. Michael C. Stedman
MRS. Carlee Steed
MR. James J. Steed
MS. Rebecca D. Steed
SPC Troy D. Steed
CPL Denver W. Steel
PFC James A. Steel
WO1 Bob D. Steele
CW3 (Ret) Daniel E. Steele
COL (Ret) Edgar W. Steele
SSG Harold G. Steele
SPC J. Mike Steele
SSG Kenneth S. Steele
SPC Max B. Steele
1SG Ray T. Steele
SSG Robert D. Steele
SFC Robert Lee Steele
SPC John Steelman
SPC Thomas G. Steen
SGM William M. Steen
SPC Terence C. Steer
SGT William C. Steever
SP5 (Ret) Gary J. Stefanini
SGT Jan P. Steffen
SPC James S. Steffenhagen
SP5 Henry Steffes
CPL Wayne E. Steffey
SGT Raymond Steich
SGT Elvin Steierwald
PFC Alfred E. Steiger
COL William A. Steiger
CPL Adam E. Stein
SP5 Donald M. Stein
SP5 Ed Stein
COL (Ret) Henry J. Stein
1LT Meghan S. Stein
SGT Paul E. Stein
1LT Robert Gerald Stein
CPT Stephen H. Stein
PFC Matthew M. Steinbach
SFC W. Jeff Steinbach
MR. Harry Steinberg
SP5 Philip M. Steinbrick
LTC (Ret) Joel R. Steine
MAJ (Ret) Carl F. Steiner
2LT John M. Steiner
SP3 Roland Steingraber
SPC James D. Steinhauer
SP5 Michael E. Steinhilper
SSG (Ret) Richard A. Steinhoff
MSG Virgil Steinhorst
1LT John E. Steinkrauss
SPC Gregory P. Steinman
SPC Robert William Steinmetz
MR. William E. Steir
PFC Thomas J. Stelma
SGT Bradley Lane Stemple
CPL William T. Stenberg
CW3 Thomas F. Stenehjem
SGT John R. Stenger
SPC David W. Stenman
SPC Lance J. Stepek
SP5 Lee C. Stephans
SPC Bobbie E. Stephens
PVT Clarence B. Stephens
SP5 Donald J. Stephens
SFC Douglas C. Stephens
SPC Ira T. Stephens

SSG Jack W. Stephens
SP5 James H. Stephens
SGT James L. Stephens
SPC John L. Stephens
WO1 Lee J. Stephens
SGM (Ret) Raymond E. Stephens
SPC Sam Stephens
2LT Scott Lee Stephens
2LT Tod Stephens
PFC William M. Stephens
SSG Willond L. D. Stephens
SPC Daniel Stephenson
PVT Jesse Stephenson
CPT Wayne W. Stepniewski
SPC Hubert A. Stepp
MAJ John M. Stepp
MR. Robert Stepp
SSG Theresa Stepp
SGT Paul D. Sterbenz
SGT William P. Sterbenz
MAJ Sorin A. Sterea
CPT Greg Sterley
CPT Anthony K. Sterling
SGT Douglas Sterling
CPL Guy Sterling
SGT Richard F. Sterling
MAJ Jeremy Stermer
SGT Clifford G. Stern
SSG Elroy R. Stern
LTC (Ret) Jack K. Sterne
SGT Claude Douglas Sterner
SPC Karl A. Stetler
MRS. Karl A. Stettmeier
SGT Edward J. Steurer
SGT Barry L. Stevens
LTC Charles H. Stevens
SSG (Ret) Charles T. Stevens
SGT Cody Stevens
TSgt Dale J. Stevens
PFC Dana D. Stevens
SSG Jerry Lee Stevens
MRS. Jessie L. Stevens
SFC John T. Stevens
SSG Joseph A. Stevens
SPC Marcel T. Stevens
MSG Matthew Stevens
MAJ Michael J. Stevens
SP5 Peter R. Stevens
PV2 Randy G. Stevens
PFC Robert J. Stevens
MG (Ret) Story C. Stevens
SPC Arthur Stevenson
SSG Jack T. Stevenson
PFC Larry D. Stevenson
SGT Ricardo P. Stevenson
CPT Robert Stevenson
SPC Michael J. Stever
SGT Borce Stevkovski
LTC (Ret) Hal D. Steward
PFC Rayfort J. Steward
SFC Antione Stewart
SGT Brian K. Stewart
SPC Bruce Allen Stewart
PFC Calvin Stewart
SPC Carl A. Stewart
COL (Ret) Carolyn A. Stewart
COL (Ret) Claude C. Stewart
SFC Curtis Stewart
MS. Deonna S. Stewart
SPC Donald R. Stewart
SGT Douglas Stewart
SSG Eugene Stewart
1LT Frank G. Stewart
LTC (Ret) George A. Stewart
SP5 Gilbert O. Stewart
SGT Henry L. Stewart
SGT Jack C. Stewart
SPC James C. Stewart
PFC James E. Stewart
SGT James R. Stewart
MSG (Ret) James S. Stewart
SPC Jeffrey W. Stewart
SP5 Jerry L. Stewart
SP5 John A. Stewart
CPT Kelly Jay Stewart
SSG Kevin W. Stewart
SPC Kim A. Stewart
SPC Kyle R. Stewart
CW2 Lance E. Stewart
SGT Mark A. Stewart
CPT Martha M. Stewart
MSG Meredith B. Stewart
LTC Michael J. Stewart
CPT Montieth A. Stewart
SP5 Paul L. Stewart
SGT Raymond L. Stewart
SPC Robert E. Lee Stewart
CW4 (Ret) Steven D. Stewart
SPC Steven M. Stewart
CW2 Wayne M. Stewart
1SG (Ret) William C. Stewart
SP5 William E. Stewart
1SG (Ret) William E. Stewart
CDR (Ret) William J. Stewart
MAJ Abe G. Stice
PFC Robert J. Sticken
MR. Harry L. Stickle
PFC Craig A. Stickley
CPT Douglas P. Stickley
SGT Terry J. Stickradt
SPC (Ret) Warren D. Stidham
SSG Karl Ellington Stiefel
MRS. Sidney Stiefler
CSM Robert J. Stiefvater
SGT Mark F. Stieren
SSG Donald N. Stiffler
MSG Joseph N. Stilchen
PVT Walter Stiles
SFC Grady W. Stilley
COL (Ret) Frank E. Stillman
PVT Howard M. Stillwagon
SFC Edward E. Stilwell
SGT Gary P. Stine
PFC Luther H. Stines
SFC (Ret) Bobby R. Stinson
CSM Robert L. Stinson
PFC William R. Stinson
SGT Danny R. Stire
SPC Robert M. Stirling
MSG Edward L. Stites
SGT Gary L. Stites
1LT Timothy L. Stith
MAJ (Ret) Robert C. Stitt
SGT Don R. Stivers
SSG Wesley Stobaugh
SFC Robert K. Stober
CW3 (Ret) Norbert W. Stocker
CPT John A. Stockhaus
SGT Ronnie Stocks
SGT Leon A. Stockton
PFC Robert R. Stockton
MAJ Erik F. Stoeckle
SGT D. Glenn Stoecklin
SPC Lawrence G. Stoffel
SGT Gerald Stofko
SGT Horace N. Stogner
MSG Boban Stojadinovski
SGT Goran Stojanovski
SGT James R. Stokely
CPT Albert W. Stokes
SGT Gregory Stokes
SPC O. King Stokes
LTC (Ret) Ronald J. Stokes
1SG (Ret) Vernell A. Stokes
MAJ Willie J. Stokes
1SG (Ret) Tom Stokesberry
CPT Eric Stolle
SSG Christopher J. Stoltie
SGT E. Greg Stoltz
MRS. Elizabeth Sue Stoltz Rathbun
SGT John Calvin Stoltzfus
MR. Charles F. Stone
CW2 Damian Stone
SGT Daniel T. Stone
1LT David K. Stone
CPL Floyd L. Stone
PVT Gerald E. Stone
COL Gregory A. Stone
MRS. James L. Stone
PVT James W. Stone
SP5 Jeffrey A. Stone
SPC Jimmy Stone
SPC Kenneth Elmer Stone
SGT Larry I. Stone
SSG Leo Samal Stone
SGT Roy E. Stone
SP3 Russell C. Stone
SPC James D. Stoneburner
SGT Don Stonemetz
CPT David Stoner
SGT Donald W. Stoner
SGT James L. Stoner
PV2 Eric Stoodley
CW3 (Ret) Walter P. Stook
SP5 Thomas E. Stookey
SP5 Harry L. Stoops
SPC Jared Stoops
SPC Michael Stoops
PFC Larry E. Stopper
SPC Ronald W. Storad
SGT Ed Storer
SGT James R. Storey
CPT (Ret) R. A. Storey
2LT William D. Storey
1LT Alvin A. Storm
SGT Thomas Ken Storm
SGT Dennis A. Stormer
PFC Charles Storms
CPL Frank Storno
SPC Louis A. Stortenbecker
CW2 Dennis Story
MR. Michael W. Story
SPC Stephen F. Stotler
MAJ (Ret) Joseph Stotski
CPT (Ret) James D. Stotts
SSG Johnny Stough
SGT Bobby Lane Stout
PFC Cecil C. Stout
PFC Fred T. Stout
SSG John L. Stout
SGT Keith Stout
SFC Patrick Stout
SFC John B. Stoute
SSG Eric D. Stoutenburg
SPC Ronald E. Stoutzenberger
CPL Berman Stovall
SSG Gilbert B. Stovall
SGT Jeffery Stovall
SPC Jerry L. Stovall
SSG Nikiki L. Stovall
1SG Andrei Stover
SPC Clifford G. Stover
SFC (Ret) John L. B. Stover
LTC (Ret) Lynn G. Stover
CW3 (Ret) Walter H. Stover
SSG (Ret) Calvin C. Stoves
2LT Jeffrey N. Stowe
SSG Chad C. Stowers
PV2 Dennis G. Strabel
MSG Elian C. Strachan
SPC Steve A. Strahotsky
MR. Dallas Strait
SPC Robert S. Strand
SPC James L. Strande
CPT David A. Strange
LTC John J. Strange
1LT Joseph L. Strange
SPC Michelle Strange
SPC Charles G. Stranger
SP5 Steven L. Strasburg
SGT Harold Strassberg
CPL David L. Straten
MSG Eugene R. Stratmoen
CPL John L. Stratton
MR. Richard E. Stratton
LTC David A. Strauss
SSG Vicki L. Straw
CPL Fred Strawson
1LT Edward L. Strawther
SGT Charles A. Strayer
SFC Justin W. Strayer
SFC Emmett W. Street
PFC Caydon W. Street
LTC (Ret) Robert W. Street
SGT Donald J. Streeter
SGT Eddie J. Streeter
MG (Ret) William F. Streeter
1SG John H. Streetman
SPC Gerald Streett
SPC David Streible
SFC Brian Streigle
SGT Thomas R. Strempka
SPC Jason W. Strength
PFC William Streppone
PFC James E. Stricker
SGT James W. Strickland
SGT Jesse M. Strickland
SSG John W. Strickland
CPT Nathan L. Strickland
SFC Ross R. Strickland
LTC (Ret) Sidney L. Strickland
SPC Jeffrey D. Stricklin
PFC Pete M. Stride
SPC H. Carl Strieker
SSG Lawrence E. Stringberg
SPC James Stringer
CSM (Ret) Lilburn O. Stringfield
SPC Matthew C. Stritch
TSgt Michael F. Strivelli
PFC Raymond C. Strobel
SPC Paul E. Stroessner
CPL George J. Strohm
SSG Jason Strom
MRS. Robert F. Strom
SPC Elroy R. Stromeyer
SSG Albert Strong
SPC Lawrence Strong
1SG Patrick D. Strong
CPT Richard M. Strong
MR. Elmer C. Stroschein
SGT Robert J. Strosser
SSG Douglas R. Strother
PVT Timothy B. Strother
SGT John Stroube
SGT Dennis M. Stroud
SSG Paul E. Stroud
LTC William L. Stroud
SPC James W. Strouse
SPC Kameren P. Strouse
PFC Adrian L. Strowder
PVT Edward H. Strowder
MR. Joseph G. Strub
SPC Ron D. Strub
PVT Jeffrey R. Struble
SGT Jerome L. Struemke
SSG (Ret) John A. Strugala
SPC James H. Strunk
PFC Robert W. Strunk
PFC Bernard W. Struntz
SGT Clarence W. Struska
SGT Douglas P. Struthers
CPL Carl R. Stryker
CW2 Thomas A. Stryker
PFC John Jay Stuart
LTC Ted R. Stuart
SPC William J. Stuart
MR. Charles A. Stubblefield
PFC Tommy Stubblefield
MR. Clair E. Stubbs
SGT Jon A. Stubbs
MAJ Jonathan Stubbs
SPC Kenneth R. Stuber
PFC Frederick Stuckey
CPT Matthew S. Stuckey
SGM Rick M. Stuckey
SGT John P. Studebaker
PFC William F. Studley
SGT David J. Studstill
SPC William T. Studstill
CPL George P. Studt
SPC Richard W. Stueber
SPC Fred Stuessi
PV2 Christopher Stull
SSG Marlin K. Stumbo
CPT Gary D. Stump
MR. John M. Stumpf
SGT Theodore J. Stupariu
PVT Jimmie A. Sturdivant
MAJ Mervin Sturdivant
CPT Vontrese Sturdivant
SSG Daniel T. Sturgell
LTC (Ret) Charles E. Sturgeon
PFC James J. Sturgeon
SFC Joseph L. Sturgeon
SSG Gary L. Sturgill
SGT Ronald J. Stuttler
SSG Jerry S. Stutz
SPC Tim Stutzman
MAJ Howard T. Styron
MR. Glen G. Suaren
SPC Edwin P. Suarez
2LT Ignacio A. Suarez
1SG (Ret) Steve Suavia
1LT Frank T. Suber
SGT John A. Succo
SGT Anthony T. Succese
SGT Walter J. Suchowiecki
SP5 Robert E. Suchy
SGT Mark Suckfiel
MSG (Ret) Stephen A. Suddith
MAJ Greg Sudman
COL Ramon Q. Sudo
PFC Sidney T. Sue
1SG Lawrence J. Sueppel
1LT Ryan M. Suerth
CPT Michael B. Suessmann
PFC Steve Sufilka
MR. Steven Sufilka
SSG (Ret) Nicholas P. Sugar
CPT Joel E. Sugdinis
CPL Jess Sugg
SSG (Ret) Claude C. Suggs
SSG Larry D. Suggs
MAJ (Ret) Eugene W. Suhr
COL (Ret) Thomas W. Suitt
PFC Andrew L. Sulak
PFC James R. Sulcer
SSG Yusef Sulieman
2LT Joey J. Sullinger
COL Palmer Sullins
SPC Brian Sullivan
PFC Charles T. Sullivan
CW4 (Ret) Daniel M. Sullivan
SSG Derrick Sullivan
CPT Emmet R. Sullivan
SSG Emmett W. Sullivan
PFC Harold P. Sullivan
MR. Howard C. Sullivan
SPC James D. Sullivan
SGT John C. Sullivan
SGT John F. Sullivan
COL John L. Sullivan
1LT John L. Sullivan
2LT Joseph Sullivan
SGT Kelvin Sullivan
MSG (Ret) Kenneth M. Sullivan
SGT Kevin D. Sullivan
SGT (Ret) Michael P. Sullivan
SPC Mike Sullivan
SGT Patrick F. Sullivan
SPC Patrick G. Sullivan
CPT Paul J. Sullivan
SFC Raymond Eugene Sullivan
SP5 Raymond R. Sullivan
LTC Robert D. Sullivan
COL (Ret) Roy F. Sullivan
SPC Steve Sullivan
SGT Thomas J. Sullivan
MR. Thomas M. Sullivan
PFC Timothy P. Sullivan
SFC Veral Sullivan
SGT Willis B. Sullivan
CPL Daniel M. Sulsberger
SPC Kenneth Sulser
SSG Verlin E. Sulser
SSG Arthur Sumler
PFC Randall D. Summerford
2LT Lee I. Summerlin
BG (Ret) Russell E. Summerlin
PVT Barry R. Summers
SSG Charles D. Summers
PVT Corry Summers
CPL Donald H. Summers
SPC Harry Lee Summers
2LT Kevin R. Summers
TSgt Paul L. Summers
SGT Raymond D. Summers
MS. Yolanda M. Summers
SPC William L. Summerville
SGM (Ret) Floyd D. Sumner
SFC (Ret) Lawrence R. Sumrall
SGT Micheal Sumrall
SPC Walter W. Sumrall
SSG George Sumrow
SPC Duane A. Sundberg
CPL James N. Sundblom
MAJ Eiven Sunde
CPT Kelly K. Sunderland
SPC Scott Sunford
SGM Edward L. Surbaugh
SP5 James W. Surber
SPC Samuel Surgeon
SGT Farah Surin
LTC Nathan S. Surrey
SGT Edward B. Surritt
PVT Mark S. Susoeff
SPC Frank Suszka
PFC Terry Suter
MR. Thomas Sutera
COL Russell J. Suther
COL (Ret) David W. Sutherland
MRS. Dennis R. Sutherland
SPC Michael G. Sutherland
SGT Robert W. Sutherlin
MRS. William L. Sutphin
SPC Leland Sutter
MSG (Ret) Jack A. Suttmiller
LTC C. Kenneth Sutton
MSG Cash E. Sutton
SPC Charles Sutton
LT Clayton P. Sutton
CPL Ernest L. Sutton
SGT Eugene H. Sutton
SPC Frank A. Sutton
PFC John E. Sutton
MR. John H. Sutton
MAJ Johnny R. Sutton
SFC (Ret) Randy X. Sutton
MSG (Ret) Robert L. Sutton
SGT Ronald G. Sutton
SPC William W. Sutton
SGT T. J. Svaren
SPC Zac L. Svedberg
SFC Scott D. Sveter
SPC Danny R. Svoboda
CPL Patrick S. Swafford
CPT John F. Swahn
LTC Kenneth R. Swaim
SFC Jason D. Swain
MSG (Ret) Martell Swain
MRS. Richard A. Swain
CPT Robert J. Swain
SSG Garry L. Swales
SGT Tracy L. Swales
SSG David A. Swallow
SSG (Ret) Donald Swan
SPC Duane A. Swan
SGT James A. Swan
1SG Lloyd V. Swan
SP5 Tommy J. Swaney
CW4 (Ret) Brian M. Swann
SFC Shelly Swann
CW3 Clarence Swanson
PFC Gerald E. Swanson
LTC Harold M. Swanson
SGT Joe Swanson
SPC Kenneth S. Swanson
MSG (Ret) Lannie D. Swanson
COL Paul A. Swanson
SGT Phillip C. Swanson
SGT Rod Swanson
MRS. Sandee Swanson
1LT Scott A. Swanson
TSgt Hubert L. Swantek
SFC (Ret) Robert C. Swantek
CPT John J. Swart
PFC Timothy S. Swartz
CPT Virgil L. Swartz
SGT Neal T. Swayne
SSG John T. Sweat
1SG (Ret) Richard L. Sweat
SPC Norman Benny Swecker
SPC Douglas G. Swede
SGT Walter S. Sweder
SrA Thomas J. Sween
MR. Anthony T. Sweeney
MAJ (Ret) Charles P. Sweeney
SPC Hugh Sweeney
SSG John J. Sweeney
MR. Richard Sweeney
LTC (Ret) Richard L. Sweeney
COL (Ret) Robert N. Sweeney
SGT Ronald C. Sweeney
SPC Timothy M. Sweeney
SGT Ryan C. Sweesy
CPL Clarence A. Sweet
SGT William R. Sweet
1LT Robert L. Sweetland
SGT Buford Y. Sweeton
SGT William C. Sweitzer
CW2 Richard Swendig
SGT Gary P. Swenson
SGT Gordon Swenson
MAJ Karl Swenson
1LT Terrance P. Swenson
SPC Todd A. Swenson
SPC John W. Swett
CPL La Roi B. Swick
SPC Jamie Swidecki
SPC Garry A. Swierenga
SSG Arnold B. Swift
PFC David M. Swift
CH (MAJ) Douglas C. Swift
SP5 Gerald Swift
MAJ (Ret) John B. Swift
MRS. Elza Swindell
SGT Michael L. Swink
LTC Kelvin Swint
TSgt (Ret) Reuben V. Swisher
SP5 Richard A. Switzer
CPT (Ret) William A. Switzer
COL (Ret) Robin N. Swope
CPL David L. Swoyer
PFC David O. Swoyer
SGT Harrison Sydnor
CSM (Ret) Michael C. Syfert
SFC (Ret) Alexander T. Sykes
PFC John E. Sykes
SGM George J. Sykora
SGT Ashner Sylvain
SPC Ronald A. Sylvain
LTC (Ret) John B. Sylvester
PV2 Joshua A. Sylvester
CPT Richmond Sylvester
1LT Robert M. Symes
MR. Alister A. Symon
SFC Raymond F. Symonds
MAJ Rodney W. Symons
MSG Alan N. Syndergaard
PFC Harvey J. Sytsma
MR. Jule Szabo
MAJ Michael Szalma
SSG Walter F. Szarek
SPC Joseph J. Szatkowski
SSG Reginald T. Szatny
1SG Daniel E. Szczepankiewicz
SPC Dennis Szczygielski
SGT Leslie J. Szell
SPC Stephen Szever
SGT Marvin H. Szidon
CPL Andrew Szilay
SFC Michael M. Szot
PFC George Szpunar
MR. Damian Szumski
SPC Richard Szutenbach
SGT Michael A. Szwaczkowski
SGT Peter N. Szymczyk
CW4 (Ret) Donald S. Taber
1SG Rene Taber
SFC Robert W. Taber
SGT Robert B. Tabers
SPC Elbert A. Taboada

CPT Raul E. Taboada
SPC Richard L. Tabor
PFC Robert Tabor
MR. Vernon M. Tabor
SGT Benjamin H. Tackett
SGT William C. Tackett
SPC Dominic P. Tacla
SSG David L. Taddy
CW3 (Ret) Robert G. Tadlock
SPC Danny Taff
SPC Robert W. Taft
SGT Phillip B. Taggart
PFC (Ret) William H. Taggart
SPC Randy Tagupa
CW3 Roman P. Taijeron
SGM (Ret) Vicente B. Tainatongo
SSG Travis Tait
SSG Franklin J. Taitano
SPC Richard L. Taival
SPC Frank G. Takacs
SGT Jack L. Taksa
SSG Victorio H. Talaoc
CPT Jose M. Talavera-Toso
SSG Chester L. Talbert
MR. Larry E. Talbert
COL Asa R. Talbot
SGT David G. Talbot
SGT Jeffery M. Talbot
1LT John D. Talbott
PFC Michael J. Tallarito
MRS. Howard G. Tallau
MAJ Hugh B. Talley
MRS. Jack H. Talley
SPC Jeremy K. Talley
SGT Walter L. Talley
CPL Merle J. Tallman
SP5 Edward Vance Tallon
LTC (Ret) George M. Talmadge
COL (Ret) Roger S. Talmadge
SPC Thomas E. Talton
1LT Ken Tamberg
SGT Thomas N. Tamburro
CPT Carlos Tamez
SGT Emilio R. Tamez
SGT Thomas Tamsett
PV2 Tei Tus A. Tanihu
MAJ Walter T. Tanimoto
SGT Randolph D. Tankerley
SPC James E. Tann
SGT Craig W. Tanner
SPC Larry E. Tanner
SSG Mark A. Tanner
SPC Ray E. Tanner
COL (Ret) John A. Tanzi
MAJ John R. Tapia
SPC Jonah J. Tapia
SGT Peter G. Tapia
SGT James Tapin
SPC Matthew Tapin
MRS. George M. Tapley
SGT Mack A. Taplin
SSG Otto C. Tapp
CW3 (Ret) Manfred Tappe
PVT David D. Tapper
COL (Ret) Charles P. Tappero
1LT Karl E. Tappert
SGT Alexander Tarazona
SGT Bruce A. Tardif
SGT Robert A. Tardif
SGT Chris A. Tardiff
SGT Larry Targosh
MR. Larry G. Targosh
SFC Wm. E. Tarkington
SPC Michael D. Tarpey
SPC William R. Tarpey
SGT Eric Christopher Tarr
SGT Jay P. Tarr
SGT Daniel J. Tarver
SFC Dezia Tarver
SPC Nace Cohen Tasby
CW4 Larry L. Tasker
PFC Aaron R. Tassler
SPC Nicholas L. Tassone
CPL Vincent A. Tassone
SGM Bobby Tate
CSM (Ret) Carl N. Tate
PFC Charles O. Tate
MRS. Dottie Tate
SFC Jackson L. Tate
1SG James A. Tate
CPL Johnathan Tate
SPC Larry W. Tate
PV2 Paul F. Tate
SGT Robin Wartell Tate
CPT Terry Tate
SGT William E. Tate
MR. Kenneth Tatham
SFC (Ret) Alva Tatom
SGT Peter Tattersall
SFC (Ret) Bobby J. Tatum
SFC Clinton L. Tatum
SPC Franklin B. Tatum
SPC James Taube
CPT James H. Taumoepeau
SFC (Ret) Tommy J. Tauro
COL Richard M. Taus
CPT Todd N. Tauscheck
SGT Jerry M. Tausz
SSG Ronald E. Tavalero
COL (Ret) H. Sprague Taveau
MAJ Horatio S. Taveau
SPC Frank N. Tavern
MSG Kevin P. Tayes
SSG Edmar R. Taylan
SSG Adarius Taylor
CSM Allen Taylor
LTC Allen E. Taylor
SSG Allen Junior Taylor
1SG Alonso Taylor
1SG (Ret) Alton D. Taylor
SSG Antonio D. Taylor
PVT Bert A. Taylor
SGT Bob J. Taylor
SFC Charles D. Taylor
SPC Christopher Taylor
PFC Craig C. Taylor
2LT Curtis D. Taylor
SSG Daniel L. Taylor
SGT David Taylor
SPC David A. Taylor
SPC David B. Taylor
MAJ David J. Taylor
SGT Dean Taylor
SP5 Donald J. Taylor
SGT Donald W. Taylor
SGT Dowell W. Taylor
1LT Dwight D. Taylor
SGT Fred Taylor
1LT Fred E. Taylor
SPC Frederick A. Taylor
SPC Glenn Taylor
PFC Harold L. Taylor
MAJ Harold W. Taylor
LTC Harry O. "Skip" Taylor
SPC Henry W. Taylor
CW2 (Ret) Hollis W. Taylor
LTG (Ret) Horace G. Taylor
MR. James E. Taylor
SPC James E. Taylor
MSG James E. Taylor
CPT James M. Taylor
MG (Ret) James R. Taylor
SPC Jason E. Taylor
1LT Joe Taylor
MAJ (Ret) Joe C. Taylor
PFC John H. Taylor
PFC John M. Taylor
SPC John R. Taylor
MAJ John W. Taylor
MAJ Johnathan H. Taylor
CPL Joseph Taylor
SGT Joshua Taylor
SPC Kenneth R. Taylor
SPC Kent Taylor
SFC Lorenzo Taylor
1LT Lyssa Taylor
SGM Mark A. Taylor
PVT Mark A. Taylor
1LT Mark C. Taylor
SSG Mark W. Taylor
SSG Marlin C. Taylor
CPL Marlyn D. Taylor
SPC Marvin E. Taylor
SPC Marvin L. Taylor
SPC Marvin W. Taylor
SGT Michael J. Taylor
SGT Michael J. Taylor
MRS. Myron D. Taylor
SGT Peter A. Taylor
1SG Phillip D. Taylor
MR. Randy W. Taylor
COL (Ret) Richard H. Taylor
CPT Richard I. Taylor
1SG Robert Taylor
SGT Robert M. Taylor
1SG Robin B. Taylor
CPL Roy Taylor
SSG Sabrina Taylor
1LT Scott Taylor
SSG Shane Taylor
MAJ Stacy Taylor
SPC Stuart Taylor
PFC Thomas E. Taylor
CPT Thomas J. Taylor
SGT Trevor Taylor
SSG Victor S. Taylor
CPT Wendell B. Taylor
SFC William E. Taylor
SPC William F. Taylor
COL William W. Taylor
SP5 Cecil J. Tayse
SGT Leonard F. Te Poel
SFC Robert H. Teachout
COL (Ret) Glenn E. Teague
SPC Hobert F. Teague
MR. Jay W. Teague
SPC Roger Neale Teague
LTC Tim Teague
SGT Jackie D. Teakell
SSG Bryan Teal
SPC Graymon R. Teal
SFC Mark E. Teal
SGT David A. Tederick
SPC David H. Tedford
SP5 Gary Teed
SSG Wayne Teegardin
SP5 John J. Teel
WO1 William John Teeple
SGT Jerry Teeson
PFC Jennifer L. Teeter
PFC Jimmie E. Teeter
SSG Shane R. Teeter
CW3 John B. Teetsel
PV2 Shawn B. Tegenkamp
SSG Kevin A. Teinert
SGT Victor M. Tejera
SP5 Edward V. Tellado
SPC Thomas R. Telles
CSM (Ret) Stephen E. Telless
SGT Arthur Tellez
SP5 George A. Temme
SPC Larry C. Temperato
COL Nicholas R. Temperley
SSG Herschel G. Temple
CSM (Ret) Raymond P. Temple
CPT Roger A. Temple
MR. Lyle Templeton
MSG (Ret) Cleo F. Templin
SGT Lowell L. Templin
LTC Max M. Tenberg
SGT Daliborco Tenev
MR. Guillerma Teniente
SGT David E. Tenley
SPC Larrie A. Tennant
2LT Matthew Tennant
1LT Robert J. Tennant
SPC Eric Tennison
SGT William R. Tennyson
MSG Steve H. Teresko
CPT Richard O. Ternosky
CPL Eldon R. Terrell
MRS. Ernest P. Terrell
MAJ Patrick R. Terrell
SPC Paul Terrell
LTC (Ret) Richard D. Terrell
SPC Robert L. Terrell
CW4 Shane Terrell
PV2 Willard L. Terrell
PFC Donald P. Terrien
SGT Danny T. Terrio
SGT Charles G. Terry
PVT Grady L. Terry
MRS. Hortense M. Terry
CPL John T. Terry
SGT Joseph L. Terry
SFC Randy Terry
SSG Robert L. Terry
MSG Timothy Jay Terry
SFC (Ret) Tommy L. Terry
COL (Ret) William F. Terry
CW4 (Ret) William L. Terry
SGT Joseph A. Teruel
SPC Kenneth C. Teske
SPC William H. Tesmer
SSG (Ret) Pablo M. Teso
CW3 (Ret) Larry D. Tessmer
SGT Charles R. Teter
MSG David Tetrault
SPC Arthur L. Tetreault
SSG Robert L. Tetreault
LTC Donald C. Tettelbach
SSG Richard Teunis
PFC Billy J. Thach
SGT Gary J. Thaler
SP5 Kenneth L. Thames
1LT Bruce K. Thatcher
CPL Robert Thaut
SPC Joie Thaxton
CW3 Robert L. Thaxton
SPC Gary Lee Thayer
SGT Hugh C. Thayer
1LT James E. Thayer
SGT Martin E. Thayer
LTC Ronald L. Thayer
SGT Tom Theakston
PFC Frank A. Theall
SFC Lloyd J. Theard
CPT Hugh A. Theiler
2LT Sean H. Theiss
SPC Filipczuk Theodre
SGT Dennis Theuret
SGT George V. Thibault
PFC Joseph C. Thibault
PFC Raymond A. Thibodaux
SFC John Thibodeau
SPC Sylvio M. Thibodeau
SSG (Ret) John E. Thiel
1LT Todd V. Thiel
PFC Jacob Thielbar
SGT John L. Thielemann
SPC Thomas John Thielen
PFC Joseph A. Thienel
PFC Lee E. Thies
SSG William D. Thigpen
LTC Michael D. Thimblin
CPL Wesley Thoma
SSG Aaron W. Thomas
PVT Alan C. Thomas
SFC Anthony L. Thomas
SPC Brian Taylor Thomas
SSG Carroll R. Thomas
2LT Casey Z. Thomas
1LT Charles R. Thomas
SPC Chester Thomas
SSG Dana R. Thomas
SGT Daniel Thomas
PFC David G. Thomas
CW2 David M. Thomas
SGT Donald E. Thomas
SP5 Dorsey O. Thomas
SGT Earl L. Thomas
MR. Eddie L. Thomas
SPC Edgar R. Thomas
SSG Eric Thomas
PVT Ferle B. Thomas
SFC (Ret) Frederick L. Thomas
SGT (Ret) Gary M. Thomas
MR. Gary M. Thomas
SPC George Thomas
SGT George H. Thomas
LTC (Ret) Grant Thomas
SFC Gregory A. Thomas
CPT Herman L. Thomas
SGT J. Gerard Thomas
MSG James L. Thomas
SP5 James L. Thomas
MSG (Ret) James L. Thomas
SGT James Russell Thomas
CSM Janet F. Thomas
CPT Jason M. Thomas
MRS. Jesse L. Thomas
SSG Jimmie O. Thomas
SSG John A. Thomas
2LT John C. Thomas
SFC (Ret) John W. Thomas
SGT John W. Thomas
SFC Joseph D. Thomas
CW3 Kenneth Thomas
SSG Kenneth E. Thomas
SFC Kevin A. Thomas
CPT Kralyn R. Thomas
PVT Laden L. Thomas
SFC (Ret) Larry Thomas
PFC Larry D. Thomas
SGT Lloyd E. Thomas
SSG (Ret) Marlon L. Thomas
CSM Matthew A. Thomas
SGT Michael M. Thomas
SPC Michael P. Thomas
SPC Michael S. Thomas
SSG Michell Thomas
MS. Nancy Thomas
PFC Norman A. Thomas
SPC O. T. Thomas
SP5 Paul L. Thomas
SPC Rick L. Thomas
SGT Robert Thomas
SFC Robert L. Thomas
MRS. Robert T. Thomas
COL (Ret) Robert W. Thomas
SFC Ronald J. Thomas
CSM (Ret) Roy Thomas
SGT Stephen J. Thomas
1SG Stephen T. Thomas
CPT Steven K. Thomas
PFC Theodore R. Thomas
SGT Tolbert J. Thomas
COL (Ret) Tom W. Thomas
SPC Tony M. Thomas
CPT Vincent A. Thomas
SPC Willie Thomas
1SG Willie B. Thomas
1SG Willie L. Thomas
SFC (Ret) Wren A. Thomas
SGT H. Clinton Thomason
SPC James Allen Thomason
CPT Jerald O. Thomason
PFC John S. Thomason
MRS. William A. Thomason
SPC Gerald F. Thomes
2LT Lamar Thompkins
SGT Alan L. Thompson
SGT Angelo L. Thompson
SPC Aves D. Thompson
MAJ Carl V. Thompson
SSG Charles E. Thompson
SPC Dana E. Thompson
SSG Daryl R. Thompson
SGT David J. Thompson
SGT Demarco L. Thompson
SP5 Don G. Thompson
SGT Donald F. Thompson
MR. Duane S. Thompson
SGT Dwight Thompson
SFC Emmett S. Thompson
SGT Fred Thompson
SGT Frederick Scott Thompson
SPC Gary M. Thompson
SPC Gary R. Thompson
SGT Gary W. Thompson
SGT George C. Thompson
PSG George W. Thompson
CPL Gregory R. Thompson
CPT Hollie J. Thompson
SPC Horace Thompson
LTC (Ret) Jack H. Thompson
SPC James A. Thompson
SSG James M. Thompson
SFC James O. Thompson
WO1 (Ret) James R. Thompson
SFC (Ret) James W. Thompson
SGT Jamie C. Thompson
PVT Jeffrey L. Thompson
SGT John E. Thompson
SSG John H. Thompson
SFC John P. Thompson
MR. John W. Thompson
SGT Joseph Thompson
SPC Kyle Thompson
SPC Larry Thompson
PVT Lawrence P. Thompson
PFC Mark Anthony Thompson
SGT Martin Thompson
SGT Michael A. Thompson
PFC Mitchell Thompson
LTG (Ret) Nathaniel R. Thompson
SPC Patrick L. Thompson
CSM Paul E. Thompson
PFC Phillip A. Thompson
SFC (Ret) Raymond G. Thompson
MAJ Richard B. Thompson
CPL Robert Thompson
CW4 Robert D. Thompson
CPT Robert J. Thompson
SGT Robert L. Thompson
SGT Rodger E. Pete Thompson
CPT (Ret) Roger L. Thompson
MSG (Ret) Roland L. Thompson
SPC Ronald G. Thompson
CPT Ronald J. Thompson
SGT Stephen L. Thompson
WO1 Stuart D. Thompson
WO1 Thomas W. Thompson
SGT Timothy Thompson
2LT Todd E. Thompson
PFC Tony R. Thompson
SFC Willie Thompson
PFC Walter L. Thoms
SGT Joshua S. Thomsen
CPL Tom Thomsen
MG John C. Thomson
SGT Travis Thomson
PV2 Michael Thonen
MRS. Eugene W. Thorn
MR. Thomas H. Thorn
WO1 James Thornberry
SP5 Paul B. Thornblad
SFC Aaron E. Thorne
CPL George R. Thorne
MR. James R. Thorne
SGT Ernest D. Thornhill
MAJ (Ret) Franklin T. Thornhill
PFC Buddy Thornton
CPL Carl D. Thornton
SGT Jackie R. Thornton
MRS. Jerry A. Thornton
SGT Koblar D. Thornton
CPT Michael Thornton
SGT Richard L. Thornton
MAJ Victor A. Thornton
SSG Laverne P. Thorp
SFC (Ret) Melvin M. Thorpe
SP5 William A. Thorpe
PVT Jeremy Thorsted
CPT Mervin Thorwald
SPC James R. Thrane
SGT Larry L. Thrash
SGT Christopher M. Thrasher
SSG James M. Threatt
SGT James L. Threehouse
SPC James A. Threlkeld
SPC Robert E. Throckmorton
MSG (Ret) Marion F. Throne
1LT Lee A. Thurbee
PV2 Richard A. Thurber
PFC James L. Thurgood
SPC Roger B. Thurman
MAJ James F. Thurmond
MR. Walter A. Thurston
SGT Gerald W. Tibbetts
SSG Robert John Tibbetts
PVT J. Edward Tichenor
1LT Myron H. Tichenor
MR. William C. Tickle
CPL Edward N. Tidmore
MAJ (Ret) Ronald V. Tieken
MR. Vernon G. Tielemann
MAJ Timothy Tielking
CPL George P. Tielsch
SGT Nathan Tiemeier
SPC David J. Tierney
CPT Ingrid Tighe
MR. Rafaael Tijerina
PVT Reynaldo Tijeriwa
SSG (Ret) Eugene B. Tijing
SGT Russell E. Tikey
LT Mark D. Tilch
GEN (Ret) John H. Tilelli
PVT Robert M. Tilghman
LTC (Ret) G. Gordon Tillery
SGT Jim Tillery
SPC Don Tilley
SPC Michael B. Tilley
SFC Richard D. Tilley
SGT Thomas N. Tilley
SGT C. L. Tillison
SGT Bobby W. Tillman
SGM Jennifer M. Tillman
PFC John W. Tillman
SGT Lance M. Tillman
SPC Perry Tillman
SGT Robert Allen Tillman
MRS. Ronald C. Tillman
LTC (Ret) Philip R. Tilly
MAJ Dennis A. Tilson
SGT Michael Tilson
1LT George N. Tilton
SPC Robert Tilton
SFC Miguel R. Timarky
CPL James D. Timberlake
SPC Edward L. Times
SPC Clifford Timke
SPC Jacob D. Timm
SPC Greg Timmons
MAJ Tommy G. Timmons
SGT William R. Timmons
SPC Reginald Timms
SSG David W. Tincher
MR. Michael R. Tincher
SPC Ernie Tindell
SSG Carl Tindle
SSG Gregory W. Tindoll
MR. Martin Tingey
COL (Ret) Earl L. Tingle
COL (Ret) William A. Tingler
CPT Jack Tingley
MR. Paul Tinsley
SGT Phillip G. Tinsley
SPC John J. Tinti
SPC Dale Tippin
CSM (Ret) Billy J. Tippins
PFC Chuck Tippit
SGT Christopher Tipton
MSG Gary Tipton
PFC James T. Tipton
SSG Kenneth A. Tipton
PVT Curtis L. Tisby
MR. Augustine Tiscareno
SPC James G. Tischler
CPT Basil D. Tisdale
MR. Clarence A. Tish
SGT Allen C. Tiska
LTC John M. Tisson
SFC Wallace D. Titchenell
SGT James O. Titus
MR. John R. Titus
SP5 Ollie Lynn Titus
SGT (Ret) Thomas W. Titus
SGT Ronald C. Tjaden
SPC Michael M. Tkach
SGT Frederick C. Tobeler

SFC Mark D. Tobey
SSG Marion L. Tobin
CPL Robert E. Tobin
SPC Walter J. Tobin
SP5 George Tobuck
CPT C. Dean Todd
SFC Charles Todd
SGT Christopher Todd
SGT James L. Todd
SSG Jeffrey B. Todd
SP5 Kenneth L. Todd
CSM Robert G. Todd
SFC Tyrone Todd
MG (Ret) W. Russell Todd
SGT William R. Todd
SGT Goran Todoroski
SPC Matthew J. Todt
COL (Ret) A. E. Toepel
SPC Lee Toftner
SPC Kalauta Toilolo
SSG Richard Tokar
SGT John C. Tokarcik
1SG Terry B. Tolar
SPC Arnold Gray Tolbert
CSM Donald L. Tolbert
MR. Everett Tolbert
MRS. Maynard A. Tolbert
SFC Robert A. Tolbert
SFC (Ret) Thomas A. Tolbert
PVT Wallace N. Tolbert
SSG Francisco Toledo
1SG Alfred Tolentino
1LT John L. Toler
CSM (Ret) Frank E. Toles
SPC Michael J. Toles
SFC Charles D. Toliver
SGT John D. Tolle
MRS. Doris Tollefsrud
CSM (Ret) Gordon C. Tolleson
SPC Daniel G. Tollis
1SG Frederick D. Tolliver
SGT Joe R. Tolosa
CPT Clarke S. Tolton
1SG David C. Tolver
SGT Gary V. Tom
1LT Jeremy S. Tomaino
SGT Cosmo R. Tomanelli
SPC John R. Tomaro
CPL John W. Tomascheski
SSG Jesse Tomasek
1LT Charles Tombras
MR. Joseph J. Tomcavage
SFC Stephen R. Tomczek
LTC (Ret) Jonathan P. Tomes
SGT Roger D. Tominski
PFC Terry L. Tomlin
CSM Thomas R. Tomlin
SGT Wilbern E. Tomlin
SGT James O. Tomlinson
CPT Robert H. Tomlinson
SFC Gust G. Tompary
MSG Alan H. Toms
MR. Paul Tondini
SGT Daniel L. Toney
SSG Jack Toney
CSM (Ret) James W. Toney
SFC Leroy Toney
PVT William T. Toney
MAJ Andrew J. Tong
SGT John J. Tong
CSM (Ret) Leon R. Tonini
SP5 Craig Tonjes
SPC Ronald Tooker
SGT Patrick Tooman
PFC Dean Norval Toombs
COL (Ret) Sacksiam Toommanon
MR. Daniel L. Toothman
SSG Deborah E. Tootle
COL John A. Topper
PFC Ricardo E. Toppin
PFC Harold J. Topping
SPC Randy Lee Toppins
SGT Edmund A. Torbeck
SGT Richard R. Torbert
LTC Al Torgerson
SGT Derrick R. Torgerson
LTC (Ret) Scott R. Torgerson
CPL Jim Torinese
SGT John Torkelson
SSG Nathan D. Tormala
COL (Ret) Ernest A. Torok
MR. Richard R. Torrens
SGT Alexander M. Torres
1SG Anthony S. Torres
SGT Arthur S. Torres
1SG Benito Torres
SPC Carlos Torres
SFC Carlos R. Torres
SPC Carlos V. Torres
PFC (Ret) Cecilio Torres
CPT Christian E. Torres
SPC Daniel Torres
SGT Edward G. Torres
SFC Edwin Torres
MSG (Ret) Eusebio Torres
1SG (Ret) Gilberto Torres
PVT Gregorio P. Torres
PFC Hector Torres
CPL Jake Torres
SGT Jim Torres
SGT Jose M. Torres
SPC Luis Torres
CSM Marco Torres
SFC (Ret) Margarito S. Torres
1SG (Ret) Michael A. Torres
PVT Omar Torres
SPC Orlando Torres
PFC Salvador G. Torres
MSG (Ret) Teodoro Torres
SGT Veronica Nicole Torres
SFC Rene Torres-Diaz
SSG Geraldo A. Torres-Luna
SGT Jose A. Torres-Luna
CPL David S. Torrez
CPT Robert Tortolani
MR. Anthony L. Toskas
SGT Michael E. Tostenson
SGT John D. Totemeier
MR. Joseph E. Toth
SFC (Ret) Steven P. Toth
COL (Ret) James P. Totten
PVT Douglas A. Totton
SGT Larry Touchstone
CPT John E. Touchton
SGM James C. Tourgee
SFC (Ret) James Tousley
SFC Veronica Tovar
SP5 John A. Towarnicki
SGT Cliff L. Towe
PFC Nulion Towe
SSG Raymond W. Towe
1SG William R. Tower
SFC Logan R. Towery
CW3 Gerald A. Towler
SPC Nicholas Towler
SPC Robert L. Towles
CPL Howard M. Town
SGT Kenneth D. Towne
SGT Eddie W. Townley
SPC Jacob Townley
SPC Darrell L. Townsen
PVT Elzo Townsend
SGT Holmes L. Townsend
LTC (Ret) Marshall O. Townsend
SGT Paul E. Townsend
1LT H. William Townsley
SPC Dick Tracy
CPL Joseph Tracy
CW3 Kermit Frank Tracy
SPC Robert L. Tracy
SGT Walter B. Tracy
LTC (Ret) Anthony J. Traficante
SPC Joseph S. Tragna
MRS. Don Trahan
PFC Howard J. Trahan
MSG John M. Trahan
CPL Kimberly S. Trahan
SGT James E. Trainer
SGT James E. Trainham
MSG Esperanza M. Traino
CSM (Ret) Grady Trainor
1SG William Tramel
MSG Jermal Trammel
SSG Katara L. Trammel
1LT Erica Tramontano
PFC Joseph D. Tramontano
CH (MAJ) Xuan N. Tran
CPT Johns S. Transve
MRS. Franklin W. Trapnell
CPL Louis F. Trapolino
SPC Anthony P. Trapp
SPC Gary W. Trapp
SPC Russell H. Trapp
SGT Brian E. Trask
SGT Wayne H. Trask
CSM (Ret) Samuel G. Tratt
MR. Charles R. Travers
SFC James Travers
MAJ Brian M. Travis
SSG (Ret) Charles V. Travis
SGT James B. Travis
SSG (Ret) Levi F. Travis
SGT Charles B. Traxler
CPT Gene C. Trayer
MAJ (Ret) Mark A. Traylor
CSM (Ret) Martin Traylor
COL Richard K. Treacy
SGT Denny Treadway
SPC Paul E. Treadway
LTC (Ret) David O. Treadwell
LTC (Ret) Ralph A. Treat
MRS. Robert N. Tredway
LTG (Ret) Richard G. Trefry
SPC Peter A. Treglia
CPT Jacqueline R. Tregre
MR. Ulysse Trehan
SFC Harold D. Trent
CW4 Mark Trepanier
SGT Michael R. Trepkowski
PFC Arnulfo R. Trevino
CW3 Carlos Trevino
SFC Daniel Trevino
SSG Jesse Trevino
SP5 Taurino J. Trevino
SFC Alfonso Triana
SPC James R. Tribble
SGT Andrew J. Tridento
SGT Robert D. Trigg
2LT Joshua P. Trigo
1LT Bob Trimble
SPC Gary N. Trimble
SPC Robert Trimble
1SG (Ret) Robert J. Trimble
SFC Saverio Trinca
SGT Simon Trinh
MR. Claude E. Triplett
SGT Gary W. Triplett
SGT David S. Tripp
COL (Ret) Edwin A. Tripp
MAJ Vencent W. Tripp
CW4 William J. Tritt
SGT Jerry Trivisonno
MG (Ret) Edward L. Trobaugh
CPL Alfonso G. Troisi
CW3 (Ret) John S. Trolinger
SGT Jerry S. Trombley
COL Thomas H. Trombley
SSG Robert J. Troncone
SGT Paul Troop
SP5 Cosimo H. Tropeano
PVT Anthony Trosper
SGT Charles F. Trott
1SG (Ret) James G. Trott
SPC Morris M. Trott
1LT John J. Trotta
SGT Gary R. Trotter
2LT Jerry L. Trotter
MS. Nelda J. Trotter
SGT Billy W. Trout
SGT Thomas A. Trout
SPC Darrell G. Troutt
COL (Ret) Clarence A. Trowbridge
PFC Thomas Jeffrey Trowbridge
PFC Shane Troxell
SGT Leslie K. Troyan
SP5 William J. Truax
CW3 (Ret) Michael Truchon
SGT Louis J. Trudeau
SPC Greg Trudell
LTC Martha J. Trudo
SGT David E. True
SPC David N. True
SSG Ronald K. Trueblood
SGT Michael D. Truesdell
SGT William B. Truesdell
CW2 Lewis R. Truhan
SSG Roy J. Truick
SP5 Harold P. Truitt
SFC Joyce D. Truitt
MR. Larry W. Truitt
SGT Sybil Truitt
1SG Gregorio T. Trujillo
SFC Henry M. Trujillo
SSG Toby Antonio Trujillo
SrA Victoriano Trujillo
SGT John A. Trumbull
SGT Ronnie Trumps
SGT Kevin S. Trundy
SPC Bruce Trunnell
CPL Frank Truskowski
PV2 Kevin D. Truttling
CPL Robert R. Tryon
PFC Thomas C. Tsareff
SSG Daniel J. Tsatsanis
PVT Matthew T. Tsue
1LT Alvis W. Tubaugh
SrA Jerry Tucci
CSM (Ret) Michael A. Tucci
CPT Ralph E. Tucci
MR. Raymond J. Tuchner
2LT Albert H. Tucker
SGT Carl O. Tucker
SGT Frank Tucker
COL (Ret) George G. Tucker
MR. Hoyle S. Tucker
SGT James L. Tucker
SPC John P. Tucker
SSG Kurt L. Tucker
SPC Larry E. Tucker
SFC Larry Gene Tucker
SGT Lawrence Dean Tucker
SPC Leonard G. Tucker
SFC Michael Tucker
CW3 Ronald L. Tucker
MSG Rowan Tucker
MSG (Ret) Stanley G. Tucker
SFC Thomas H. Tucker
MSG (Ret) William H. Tucker
MSG David B. Tucy
SSG Clarence H. Tuenge
SPC Theodore R. Tuerke
SP5 John A. Tufano
LT Danielle M. Tufts
CPT Bennie E. Tuggle
SFC (Ret) Troy L. Tuggle
PVT Laupisi D. Tuitama
PFC Larry Tuley
SFC Magno B. Tulfo
SPC William Howard Tulloh
PFC Oscar Tullos
SP5 Larry Dean Tully
SGT Heyward E. Tumbleston
SGT Mark Tummett
SSG Daniel J. Tunison
SGT Eugene P. Tunney
SFC James D. Tunstall
PFC (Ret) Gabriel E. Tuono
SGT Gerald Turczyn
SGT Charles Turdo
COL Jack L. Turecek
SPC Edward O. Turek
SFC Joseph A. Turella
SGT Dixon Turk
SGT Fred D. Turk
PFC Jack R. Turk
MR. B. Turkla
CW4 William Turkoski
PFC Dennis R. Turland
SGT Ashlin Turley
SPC Johnney E. Turley
CSM Archie Turner
CW2 Barrie H. Turner
PFC Bradford F. Turner
SPC Branden Turner
SPC Brian A. Turner
MR. Charles Turner
1LT Charles C. Turner
SPC Curtis A. Turner
SP5 Danny R. Turner
SPC Dennis Turner
SPC Franklin K. Turner
SPC Gary L. Turner
SPC George M. Turner
SP5 James D. Turner
SGT John Turner
SFC (Ret) John A. Turner
SGT John E. Turner
SFC John P. Turner
PFC Joshua Turner
SPC Karachi P. Turner
SGT Lafayette Devere Turner
SGT Mark Stephen Turner
SFC Patrick L. Turner
SFC (Ret) Ray L. Turner
SGT Ray P. Turner
SGM Reginald Turner
SPC Richard J. Turner
SSG Rodney Turner
SFC Silas Turner
CPT Thomas M. Turner
SPC Walter R. Turner
MAJ William Turner
MR. William B. Turner
SP5 William S. Turner
MR. Willis D. Turner
SGT James L. Turney
SGT Robert G. Turney
SGT Dean W. Turpin
SPC Marion W. Turpin
SGT Mario J. Tursini
CPT Douglas F. Turtzo
2LT Jeffrey L. Tussey
SPC Barry Tutin
SGT Ralph Tutrani
MR. Paul Tutterow
PFC John L. Tuttle
MAJ Michael R. Tuttle
SGT Nelson J. Tuttle
PFC Timothy J. Tuttle
SPC Paul L. Tuzzolino
CPT Edward S. Twaddell
LTC (Ret) Francis J. Twarog
TSgt Morris T. Tweeten
CW4 J. D. Twenter
SGT John Two Stars
SSG Kevin W. Twyeffort
MSG (Ret) Marie C. Tyalor
MAJ Coley D. Tyler
2LT Daniel E. Tyler
SGT Dorsey A. Tyler
PFC John C. Tyler
LTC Matthew Tyler
SGT Robert E. Tyler
WO1 Michael L. Tymensky
SFC (Ret) Carl V. Tyozandlak
SPC Anthony H. Tyree
MSG (Ret) Elzie Tyree
1LT Richard L. Tyree
SP5 Thomas D. Tyree
CSM (Ret) Paul R. Tyrrell
SSG (Ret) James H. Tyson
SSG (Ret) Vernon A. Tyson
COL (Ret) Wallace S. Tyson
COL (Ret) Douglas L. Tystad
SPC John Tyz
SPC Robert Uccello
SGT Richard Udden
SSG Alden W. Udell
SPC Michael S. Udell
SGT Jesse Ugalde
PFC Clarence E. Uhlman
CPT John R. Ulbinsky
SPC Culum R. Ulechong
PVT Rodman L. Ullery
SGM (Ret) John C. Ulloa
MSG Walter G. Ulloa
MSG Gary L. Ullom
CPL Raymond E. Ulmer
MAJ Stiles C. Ulmer
SPC Gerald E. Ulrich
PFC Mark A. Ulrick
SPC Safauc Ulufaleilupe
SP5 William B. Ulwelling
SPC James Underhill
PFC Matthew Underhill
LTC (Ret) Cone S. Underwood
SSG Dewey L. Underwood
SP5 Glen E. Underwood
SP5 Julian Russ Underwood
SrA Robert D. Underwood
SGT William Underwood
CW4 William J. Underwood
MAJ Timothy P. Ungaro
COL (Ret) Guinn E. Unger
MR. Alvin D. Ungerleider
SGT William P. Unkalhaeuser
CW3 Donald L. Unmussig
MAJ Craig S. Unrath
PFC Albert R. Unsworth
1LT Chris Upchurch
SPC Arnold M. Upshaw
SGT Bradley B. Upson
SGT Billy Matthew Upton
SFC Jeffrey Upton
SGT Michael Upton
SPC Theresa R. Upton
MR. William J. Upton
SGT John J. Urban
SPC Ronald A. Urban
MRS. Donald Urbank
SSG Gregory Urbano
MSG Douglas Urbanski
PFC Marshill W. Urdiutez
MSG Carlos Uresti
PVT Alberto Uribe
SSG Benito Uribe
SSG Jason A. Urie
CPL Alan K. Urschel
SGT Louis C. Urso
SSG Gary M. Urton
LTC Joe A. Usrey
SFC Keith T. Ussery
MRS. Rosalie Ussery
CPT Chet Uszynski
SSG Tom Uthe
SPC Kurtis Utt
COL George B. Utter
PFC Tovia Utu
SPC Arnold Utz
CPT Todd Utz
MR. Kenneth T. Uyeda
SPC William J. Vadalabene
CPL Richard Vagts
SGT Gary Vail
SSG Andrew Valadez
SGT Robert R. Valadez
MAJ Timothy Valadez
1LT Peter M. Valane
MR. Robert Valdemar
SGT Alberto Valdez
SPC Alfonso Valdez
PVT Arcenio G. Valdez
SSG Carlos M. Valdez
SGT Eric A. Valdez
SGT Freddy Valdez
SPC Jorge A. Valdez
SPC Victor S. Valdez
MAJ Robert Valdivia
SFC Edgardo Valdiviavizcara
SSG Daniel Valdivieso
PFC Pedro J. Valencia
SGT George Valente
1SG Matthew V. Valente
SPC Vittorio V. Valente
COL (Ret) Fred Valenti
1LT Michael A. Valenti
1SG Allen L. Valentine
1SG Terry L. Valentine
SGT Terry M. Valentine
CPL Leonardo Valentino
SSG Bryan J. Valenzuela
PVT Allan D. Valeri
SP5 James W. Valinoti
CPL Andrew Valladares
CPL Frank C. Valle
LTC Gonzalo A. Vallecillo
SPC Caleb Vallembois
SGT Dave Vallen
SPC Christopher A. Vallerga
MR. Rich G. Valles
PV2 Rudolph Valles
MR. Sebastian Rodolfo Valles
SPC William M. Valley
SFC Emery A. Vallier
SPC Ronald B. Valliere
CPT Gregory S. Valloch
SPC William Valls
SSG Emilio P. Valverde
SPC Dino C. Valvero
SGM Robert D. Van Aken
SGT Leo A. P. Van Allen
SGT Larry D. Van Beest
PV2 John T. Van Belleghem
MS. Christine Van Bemmel
1LT Jeremy Van Boening
SPC Alan L. Van Dan
SSG Roy W. Van De Velde
SPC Richard J. Van Deurzen
SPC Michael M. Van Dreumel
SGT Norman Van Duinen
PFC Lowell K. Van Duzee
SGT Jack D. Van Dyke
SPC John S. Van Dyke
SP5 Ralph Joseph Van Dyke
PFC Sherman Van Dyke
SGT Robert Van Effen
1LT Joshua Van Epps
SGT Gerald L. Van Fossan
MR. Martin Van Gelder
PFC Harry R. Van Giesen
SPC John J. Van Horn
SGT Robert Van Hytte
CPT Dirk Van Ingen
CPL Jacob Van Kekrix
SGT Albert C. Van Kirk
SSG Michael L. Van Kirk
LTC (Ret) George R. Van Laethem
1LT Christina Van Langenberg
PFC Dudley P. Van Meter
LTC (Ret) William L. Van Nuys
COL Kirk Van Pelt
SPC Arlen Van Ravenswaay
SGT Ron Van Rossam
SP5 Peter L. Van Til
MR. John W. Van Vlack
PFC Dean Van Vorst
MR. Steven R. Van Vranken
SSG Jefferson Van Wey
MG (Ret) Hans A. Van Winkle
CPT James C. Van Winkle
SGT William A. Van Winkle
SFC Charles Ray Van Zandt
SGT David H. Van Zandt
SGT Bryan C. Van Zile
SGT Eugene T. Vanasse
SGT Michael L. Vanatta
1LT James H. Vanbuskirk
SGT Bobby Vance
SFC (Ret) Charles Vance
SGT Clarence E. Vance
SFC Donald R. Vance
SP5 James Vance
1LT Johnny M. Vance
MAJ Pamela A. Vance
SGT Alan Vandekieft
CPT Jeff Vanden Brock
SSG Charles H. Vandenplas
SGT Richard Vander Clute
CW4 (Ret) Richard W. Vander Henst
SGT Michael D. Vander Putten

CPL Al Vander Woude
SGT Gene Vander Zwaag
SGT Hubert M. Vanderbilt
SPC Robert J. Vanderhoff
CH (LTC) Elwin C. Vanderland
CSM (Ret) Joe C. Vanderlip
CPL Fred Vandermeer
SGT Eddie D. Vanderpool
SGT James Vanderpool
SPC Richard J. Vandersande
SPC Gary M. Vanderslice
MAJ Alexander Vandevelde
PFC John A. Vandeven
MAJ Gilmer L. Vandiver
SPC Billy W. Vandre
CSM Bernard W. Vandry
PVT Kayliegh Vandygriff
SPC James Vanecek
SGT James R. Vaness
LTC (Ret) Philip E. Vangorp
SSG Paul Vanlandingham
CPL Berle D. Vanley
SP5 Bobby J. Vanmeter
LTC Jonathan J. Vannatta
MSG (Ret) Roy A. Vannatter
MSG Hale Vannoy
SGM (Ret) James G. Vannoy
LTC Jack E. Vantress
CPL Norbert J. Vanyo
SGT R. Gil Vanza
MAJ Robert Varela
SGT Rosendo Varela
SP5 Wayne E. Varga
SSG William E. Varga
SGT Carlos Vargas
LTC Carlos A. Vargas
SSG Juan P. Vargas
SGT William Vargas
SP5 Arthur J. Varian
SGT Tawana Varice
CPT Mark L. Varljen
SFC Tharo Varnado
1LT Donnie R. Varnell
SSG John E. Varner
PFC Craig W. Varney
SP5 Edward G. Varnhagen
SPC Richard J. Varriale
SPC Gregory V. Vartanian
SPC Joseph P. Vasil
SGT William L. Vasil
SPC (Ret) Daniel A. Vasquez
SPC David G. Vasquez
SGT Eduardo Vasquez
PV2 Eric Vasquez
1SG Fernando Vasquez
1LT Jaime Vasquez
SGT John Vasquez
CSM Jorge L. Vasquez
1SG Jose G. Vasquez
SPC Juan Carlos Vasquez
SGT Michael Vasquez
SPC Richard Vasquez
MSG Santiago Vasquez
SGT James T. Vastano
CPT Frederick J. Vath
SGT Albert Edward Vaughan
SSG Brian G. Vaughan
SPC John P. Vaughan
2LT Kevin Vaughan
CW3 Lad Vaughan
PFC Richard L. Vaughan
SSG Robert Vaughan
SGT Anthony P. Vaughn
CPL Floyd Carlton Vaughn
SPC G. H. Vaughn
CPT Jack M. Vaughn
2LT Jason Anthony Vaughn
COL Jeffry D. Vaughn
SGT Randolph R. Vaughn
SSG Ronald C. Vaughn
SPC Ronnie L. Vaughn
SPC Steven M. Vaughn
PFC Vinson V. Vaughn
SSG Stevens D. Vaughns
SFC (Ret) Terry Vaught
SGT Angel Joel Vazquez
SPC Christina Vazquez
PVT Christopher Vazquez
SPC Dulce A. Vazquez
SFC Jose Vazquez
MSG Jose M. Vazquez
SPC Julio Vazquez
SGT Julio C. Vazquez
MSG Raul Vazquez
SPC Luis Vazquez-Contes
SGT Albert H. Veal
CSM Steven Veazey
MR. Wesley Veazey
SPC Cliff Veazie
SGT Jack G. Veazy
PFC Ted W. Vecchione
PFC Edwin P. Vecera
SPC Samuel R. Veer
SFC Elvin A. Vega
CPT Rex Vehrs
A1C I. B. Veillon
SGT Atilano Vela
1SG (Ret) Diego Vela
SPC Eugene O. Vela
CSM (Ret) Glen Vela
SPC Jose L. R. Vela
SGT Pedro R. Vela
SFC Ruben H. Vela
SSG Mike A. Velarde
SSG Peter J. Velardo
SGT Michael J. Velasco
MSG (Ret) Ismael Velasquez
CPL Tony Velasquez
1LT Javier R. Velazquez
1SG Nelson Velazquez
SGT James J. Velesky
SSG Cirilo Velez
CPL Israel Velez
CPT Richard Velez
SPC Pablo Velez Sanchez
MSG Miroslav Veljanovski
SGT Igor Velkovski
COL Frank P. Vellela
SSG John Veltri
SGT Richard A. Vena
SGT Michael L. Venable
CPT John Vencius
SGT Richard Venditti
SGT Douglas F. Vendola
CW4 Gerry F. Ventrella
SGT Anthony L. Ventura
PVT Joseph Venutto
SFC Eloy Vera
CW2 Aurelio Veralopez
SFC Ian M. Verasammy
CW4 Gerald D. Verbeek
PFC Robert A. Verbonitz
SP5 Charles L. Verby
PFC Alejandro Verdal
SFC Angel Verdejo
SGT Lawrence L. Verdekal
SGT Thomas Verderber
SPC Sam Verdini
SPC Mark A. Verdoni
SSG Joe F. Verdugo
CPT Miguel Vergara
PVT Michael H. Verissimo
SFC Sharon E. Vermillion
SPC Vincent L. Vermillion
CPL Alfred Verner
MAJ (Ret) Frederick G. Vernon
SGT J. Fred Vernon
CPL John M. Vernon
SPC Richard G. Vernor
CPL Ralph P. Verran
MR. Roger Verschueren
SGT Thomas J. Verstraete
SPC Donald Verucchi
CPT Frank Veselicky
SPC Donald A. Vess
CPT Patrick A. Vess
LTG (Ret) Dale A. Vesser
1LT Bruce Veteto
PFC Holley E. Vetterkind
MR. Arthur Veysey
SSG Norman Vialle
CPT Mark M. Viani
PFC J.G. Viau
1LT Michael L. Vice
SFC Royce A. Vick
SSG Gary A. Vickers
LTC (Ret) George F. Vickers
SSG James A. Vickers
SFC (Ret) Jimmy R. Vickers
CPT Eric L. Vickery
SGT G. Keith Victor
MRS. Silvan Videtic
SGT Jean Noel Vieira
MAJ Joseph F. Vieira
SGT Arthur J. Viera
MAJ Craig W. Vieth
MAJ Andre Vige
SP5 Joe Viggiano
SGT Edward Vigil
MSG (Ret) Eloy E. Vigil
TSgt Gilbert A. Vigil
SGT Joseph J. Vigil
SPC Rogerio Vigil
LT Ronald A. Vigil
SGT Stephen Vigil
CPT Ronald L. Vigue
SGT Carlos Manuel Vila
PFC Kenneth L. Viles
PFC Frank K. Villa
PVT George G. Villacis
SFC (Ret) Carlos F. Villafane
CPT Omar Villafane
MR. Joseph P. Villagomez
SPC Nathan Villagomez
SPC Elley Villalobos
SGT Jose Villalobos
PVT Joseph Villalobos
PVT Steven Villalobos
SGT Ader E. Villalta
CPT Peter Villaluz
SPC James E. Villanti
SPC Anthony M. Villanueva
SFC Matt Villanueva
MAJ Tito M. Villanueva
COL (Ret) Raul G. Villaronga
SPC Arturo Villarreal
SPC Juan Villarreal
MR. Leonel Villarreal
SFC Miguel Villarreal
1LT Ovid Villarreal
LTC Victor M. Villarreal
MR. Andres Villegas
SPC Hiram Villegas
CW4 Atelano Villon
SGT Murray E. Vilven
CSM (Ret) Isaia T. Vimoto
SSG Bruce A. Vinacco
SGT Dale Vincent
SGT Donald K. Vincent
CPT Douglas G. Vincent
CSM Gerald G. Vincent
SGT Michael S. Vincent
PFC Robert C. Vinci
COL Christopher Vine
MSG (Ret) Harry E. Vines
MAJ Natalie C. Vines
1SG Willie A. Vines
SP5 Donald L. Viningre
SPC Stewart E. Vint
SSG Dustin Vinyard
SGT John W. Viol
MSG Arthur Viola
MSG (Ret) Anthony D. Violino
SP5 Charles W. Virgin
SPC David Viscarra
2LT Thomas Visel
SGT Stephen Vitale
SGT John P. Vitchoff
SPC William P. Vitiello
SGT Mario Vittiglio
SSG Scott M. Vittorio
MAJ (Ret) S. Stephen Vitucci
SGT Loren O. Vixic
LTC (Ret) Seymour Vladimer
SGT Richard J. Vnuk
SPC Joelle Vo
SFC (Ret) Glen E. Vobeda
SFC Salvatore A. Voccia
PFC Richard A. Vocke
MAJ David Vodarick
SGT Shawn Vodenik
SGT Albert P. Voelkel
SP5 Charles Voeltz
SGT Carl V. Vogel
SGT Weldon A. Vogel
SP5 Gary K. Vogt
2LT Richard Vogt
SP5 Stephen Vogt
SPC Colin Voigt
MR. Robert A. Vokes
MG Gary J. Volesky
MAJ James Volheim
PFC Edward A. Volk
1LT Wayne S. Volk
1LT Thomas C. Volkenner
PFC Anthony J. Volkl
MSG (Ret) Edward J. Volkmann
SPC Gary Vollenweider
PFC Chris P. Vollmer
SSG Theodore L. Volovick
MAJ Michael F. Volpe
SGT David P. Volz
CPL Jan C. Volz
1SG (Ret) Frederick C. Von Gortler
MAJ Gail W. Vonderheid
SPC Thomas L. Vonderhey
SPC Larry J. Vondra
SSG Clinton G. Voorhees
PFC Thomas J. Vorgias
CPL William F. Vornkahl
SP5 Martin Voskamp
BG (Ret) Leonard F. Vosmeier
CPT Bob Voss
SSG Jason Voss
COL (Ret) Francis C. Vossen
SrA Emil J. Votava
MR. Ray Votzmeyer
SPC Robert S. Vought
COL (Ret) William O. Vowell
CPT Brian Vowinkel
SPC Jim R. Voytilla
SGT (Ret) Ronald V. Vrabel
1LT Michael F. Vrahnos
1LT William E. Vredenburgh
SGT Russell C. Vroman
SPC John J. Vuillemot
SFC Michael A. Vuolo
GEN (Ret) Carl E. Vuono
LTC Timothy A. Vuono
PVT William A. Vuto
PVT Roderick E. Vyse
CPL Sverre Waagen
CPL Fred T. Wackerman
DR. David M. Waddell
1SG (Ret) Jennings L. Waddell
SPC Michael J. Waddell
CPT Sharon Towle Waddell
SGT Travis L. Waddell
SFC (Ret) William W. Waddell
SPC Christopher B. Wade
CPT Jacob H. Wade
SGT James E. Wade
SGT Jerrell L. Wade
PSG John P. Wade
SSG Kenneth D. Wade
SSG Nicholas J. Wade
CW2 Richard S. Wadleigh
PFC Arthur Wadstrom
SSG Brian L. Wadsworth
SPC Joseph E. Wagel
CPT Tyler J. Wagenmaker
SPC Darrell G. Wagenman
SSG Cliff Wages
SGT Louis A. Wages
SPC Rodger D. Wages
SGT Terry J. Wages
SGT Carson N. Waggoner
SGM Timothy R. Wagley
SSG Alan Wagner
MR. Alfred C. Wagner
1SG Anthony M. Wagner
SPC Bruce K. Wagner
PVT Charles L. Wagner
SPC Charles R. Wagner
1LT Dan Wagner
SGT Danny Wagner
PFC Dennis Wagner
SFC (Ret) Donald E. Wagner
SFC Elisha Wagner
LTC Frank H. Wagner
SGT James Edward Wagner
SPC John A. Wagner
CPL John R. Jack Wagner
SFC Michael J. Wagner
SPC Richard E. Wagner
SrA Richard J. Wagner
SGT Richard W. Wagner
SSG (Ret) Robert J. Wagner
SFC Robert L. Wagner
MSG Stefan Wagner
1LT Thomas G. Wagner
1SG (Ret) Travis A. Wagner
SPC Gerald P. Wagoner
SPC Roy D. Wagstaff
CPT Darick Waguespack
SPC Kaare L. Wahl
SFC Michael Wail
1SG (Ret) Ralph P. Wainright
SPC Allen W. Wainwright
SGT Casey D. Wainwright
PVT Donavan Wainwright
SPC Jeffrey L. Waitt
SPC Michael Wajda
CPL B. J. Wakefield
PFC Bryce M. Wakefield
SPC Kenneth Wakefield
LTC (Ret) Christopher Walach
SSG Robert G. Walburg
SGT Gary W. Walden
SPC Keith T. Walden
SPC Melanie R. Waldman
MAJ Olen E. Waldrip
SGT Terry L. Waldrip
SPC Bob Waldron
CPT Joseph A. Waldron
SSG Augustus T. Waldsachs
SGT Ken Wales
CPL Slaney W. Walford
SGT Gerald Walk
SGM Willie Walk
SGT Albert L. Walker
SGT Claude W. Walker
SPC Clay Walker
MRS. Conrad N. Walker
MAJ Dennis W. Walker
MR. George M. Walker
SSG Glenn Walker
SGT Harold D. Walker
SGT J. Lowell Walker
MAJ Jacques D. Walker
SGT James A. Walker
CSM (Ret) James A. Walker
CPL James F. Walker
SPC Jason E. Walker
CPT Jeffrey M. Walker
SGT Jimmy Walker
MRS. Jo Ann Walker
SSG Jonathan C. Walker
SFC Joseph T. Walker
1SG Karen J. Walker
LTG Keith C. Walker
PFC Kourtnie A. Walker
SPC Melvin Dimitri Walker
1SG Michael L. Walker
SSG Paul Walker
SP5 Paul W. Walker
SSG Quintin A. Walker
MSG Raymond E. Walker
PV2 Revel Walker
MR. Richard W. Walker
SFC Ricky J. Walker
COL (Ret) Robert E. Walker
PFC Robert W. Walker
SFC (Ret) Stan Walker
SSG Stanton Walker
SPC Steven T. Walker
1LT Thomas F. Walker
SPC Thomas M. Walker
CSM Trevor C. Walker
SSG Troy Walker
SFC (Ret) Vance Walker
SFC Walter L. Walker
LTC (Ret) Walter M. Walker
MAJ William T. Walker
SFC (Ret) William T. Walker
SPC William T. Walker
SGT Willie J. Walker
SFC Willie J. Walker
SGT Joseph A. Walkup
SPC Stanley B. Walkup
SPC Delbert L. Wall
LTC James P. Wall
SSG Jeffery L. Wall
SGT Rand A. Wall
MRS. Richard J. Wall
CW2 Terry L. Wall
SGT Anthony James Wallace
CPL Bobby J. Wallace
SP5 David Wallace
LTC David R. Wallace
TSgt Dillon D. Wallace
SPC Edward T. Wallace
2LT Ellery R. Wallace
SSG (Ret) Harry C. Wallace
CPT (Ret) Jacob Wallace
2LT John C. Wallace
CW5 (Ret) John D. Wallace
LTC John K. Wallace
COL John W. Wallace
SGT John W. Wallace
SSG Jose A. Wallace
PFC Joseph S. Wallace
SPC Josh Wallace
SPC Kenneth Francis Wallace
1SG (Ret) Lavelle W. Wallace
SGT Michael A. Wallace
1LT Michael J. Wallace
SGT Milburn E. Wallace
MR. Randall B. Wallace
CSM Ricky Wallace
1SG Ricky B. Wallace
SPC Terry Wallace
SPC Terry Wallace
COL (Ret) Thomas R. Wallace
WO1 Tracey E. Wallace
SGM (Ret) William B. Wallace
SPC Brian F. Walleman
SP5 Jon W. Wallenius
MSG Ellis Guy Waller
COL Robert E. Waller
SPC William F. Waller
MRS. Tom Walley
CPT Ernest W. Wallhausen
CW2 Glenn A. Wallick
SGT Donald A. Wallin
SGT Micheal R. Wallin
SP5 Baily W. Walling
SSG Steven H. Walling
SSG George Wallinger
CPL Donnie E. Wallis
SGT Stanton L. Wallis
SGT Dennis Wallot
SGT Richard Walls
CPT Gregory A. Wallsten
CPT James M. Wallsten
PFC Dustin K. Walmer
MR. Phillip Waln
CPL Marion C. Walrath
SGT Jack N. Walraven
LTC (Ret) Bob Walsh
SPC Bob Walsh
PV2 David A. Walsh
SFC Edward Walsh
SGT Gerard P. Walsh
CPT Guy J. Walsh
PFC James S. Walsh
1LT John T. Walsh
PVT Joseph W. Walsh
SSG Ludmila Walsh
CPT Luke Walsh
COL (Ret) Martin W. Walsh
SP5 Maurice H. Walsh
SGT Michael F. Walsh
SPC Patrick M. Walsh
CPL Robert E. Walsh
LTC (Ret) Stephen M. Walsh
SFC Thomas Walsh
SPC Thomas J. Walsh
MRS. William J. Walsh
SPC William J. Walsh
MR. William K. Walsh
SPC Eric Walston
SFC Gisela K. Walston
SPC Casey Walter
SSG Charles Walter
MR. Dennis J. Walter
COL (Ret) Frank J. Walter
SGT George M. Walter
SPC Jerrod W. Walter
SGT Peter Walter
SGT Peter L. Walter
MRS. Richard D. Walter
SSG (Ret) William J. Walter
SGT Charles E. Walters
1LT Edward W. Walters
CPL Gerald R. Walters
1SG (Ret) Larry D. Walters
MR. Loy A. Walters
MRS. Marleen D. Walters
SFC Phillip S. Walters
MAJ (Ret) Russell T. Walters
PFC William F. Walters
COL William P. Walters
MAJ Eric M. Walthall
SGT Charles Walther
1SG Clyde J. Waltman
SPC Russ Waltman
SPC Andrew Walton
SPC Anthony Walton
SPC Anthony Walton
SGT Bill Walton
SSG Donald Walton
MAJ (Ret) Douglas E. Walton
CPT James V. Walton
SFC John W. Walton
SP5 Merlin B. Walton
SGT Ralph E. Walton
LTC (Ret) Richard C. Walton
SSG William A. Walton
SPC William R. Walton
PFC Edwin M. Waltz
SFC Glenn T. Waltz
SSG Michael E. Walulik
SP5 Michael C. Walvatne
MR. Jess Walz
SPC Richard L. Wamboldt
SGT Terry A. Wanish
CPL Robert L. Wanke
SSG Stephen Wanstall
SFC Bryan J. Ward
SGT Chris D. Ward
CW4 Clark H. Ward
SP5 David Ward
SGT Dennis M. Ward
SGT Donald J. Ward
SGT Donald Lynn Ward
SFC Edward Ward
SGT Edward N. Ward
SSG Edward R. Ward
CPL Franklin D. R. Ward
CW4 (Ret) Gerald B. Ward
SGT Gerald J. Ward
SGT Glen Ward
PFC Hosie L. Ward
SFC Jeffrey W. Ward
TSgt Jerry Ward
MAJ John E. Ward
SPC Joseph R. Ward
SSG (Ret) Les Ward
SGT Lisa Ward
SPC Mykel D. Ward
CPT (Ret) Nathaniel P. Ward
SFC Navan Ward

SFC Neil J. Ward
SGT Ralph J. Ward
TSgt Richard J. Ward
SFC Rickey Ward
SGT Robert L. Ward
SPC Russell D. Ward
SGT Ted Ward
1LT Ted Ward
MR. Theodore G. Ward
SPC Thomas W. Ward
SFC Wayne C. Ward
1LT William A. Ward
MG (Ret) William F. Ward
SSG (Ret) Douglas J. Warden
TSgt Russel L. Warden
SP5 Thomas F. Warden
SPC William Charles Warden
1LT Larry K. Wardle
SPC Daniel E. Wardzala
SGT Jerry L. Ware
SGT John S. Ware
SP5 Leigh E. Ware
PFC Robert Ware
SFC (Ret) Otto M. Warenskjold
SGT Bruce E. Warf
SGT William L. Warfield
SP5 Paul Warhanik
SGT Lisa D. Waring
CPL Chester E. Warix
SGT Daniel W. Warmbier
SPC Jason H. Warne
MR. Alexander H. Warner
LTC Donald W. Warner
SSG (Ret) Frank G. Warner
SPC George S. Warner
1LT Joseph Warner
SSG Paula A. Warner
SPC Richard R. Warner
LTC (Ret) Samuel H. Warner
CPL Walter W. Warner
SPC Whesley Warner
SPC Carl E. Warnick
PFC James W. Warrell
MS. Betty J. Warren
SPC Bradford M. Warren
SFC (Ret) Clinton Warren
2LT Colin Warren
PFC Donald J. Warren
PV2 Donald R. Warren
LTC (Ret) Harold M. Warren
SSG James G. Warren
SGT James L. Warren
SSG John J. Warren
SPC John L. Warren
WO1 Kenneth C. Warren
SP5 Louie Warren
CPT Rashaun Warren
COL Robert J. Warren
SP5 Robert V. Warren
SSG Shaun Warren
CW4 Stephen E. Warren
SPC Steve Warren
SGT Wayne L. Warren
MRS. Jerome K. Warren-Harders
SP5 Russell L. Warriner
MSG Richard S. Warring
SPC George Wasenko
PFC Thomas D. Wash
LTC (Ret) Ronald G. Washburn
COL (Ret) Jack N. Washburne
SGT Demetrius D. Washington
SSG Donald C. Washington
SPC Herbert L. Washington
MR. James W. Washington
SP5 John A. Washington
SPC Jonathan Washington
PFC Mona Y. Washington
SPC Paul M. Washington
MRS. Richard J. Washington
PVT Steven D. Washington
COL (Ret) Joseph E. Wasiak
LTC James B. Waskom
SFC (Ret) James T. Wasney
PFC Stephen Wassie
SFC Christian C. Wasson
PFC George A. J. Watanabe
CPT James Watanabe
CPT Gary E. Waterhouse
SPC Edward Q. Waterman
1LT Brent A. Waters
SFC (Ret) Dennis E. Waters
CW4 (Ret) Jack D. Waters
SP5 Jerry Waters
SSG Johnnie L. Waters
SGT Joseph C. Waters
SGT Louis E. Waters
LTC Mark Waters
SP5 Maurice E. Waters
2LT Roslyn A. Watford

SGT Butch Watkins
CSM (Ret) Earnest Watkins
SGT Gary N. Watkins
SPC John J. Watkins
CSM (Ret) John W. Watkins
SPC Keith A. Watkins
SGT Pierre A. Watkins
1SG (Ret) Stephen H. Watkins
SFC Wayne Watkins
SSG William D. Watkins
CSM Ronnie L. Watlington
SSG Clifford D. Watson
SPC Daniel G. Watson
SPC David A. Watson
CW2 David R. Watson
CPL Duane P. Watson
SPC Frank D. Watson
SPC Howard F. Watson
SP5 Jack Watson
SGT James A. Watson
SPC James E. Watson
SP5 James E. Watson
PFC James Ken Watson
LTC (Ret) James L. Watson
SGT Janet M. Watson
1SG Jerry S. Watson
1SG John T. Watson
MSG Kenneth Watson
2LT Mark C. Watson
1LT Michael Watson
SGT Michael Watson
SFC Michael J. Watson
SPC Patrick W. Watson
MRS. Robert W. Watson
CPT Sherman Watson
SSG Teddy E. Watson
CPT Thomas E. Watson
CPL Tommy Watson
PFC Warren W. Watson
SPC William G. Watson
SPC William R. Watson
LTC Gregory A. Watt
CPT James D. Watt
SGT Earl Watters
CW2 (Ret) Harold L. Watters
SPC Charles T. Watts
SPC Donald J. Watts
SGT Ernest S. Watts
SGT Jason Dontae Watts
SGT Raymond Watts
CPL Roland A. Watts
SGT Stephen L. Watts
CPT Velerick Watts
SPC William A. Watts
PFC John N. Waugh
SPC Stephen A. Waugh
SPC Freddie E. Wauneka
SFC Billy A. Way
SPC Fred Way
SPC James H. Way
COL (Ret) David H. Wayne
SGT Robert S. Waz
1SG (Ret) Charles S. Weable
SP5 Michael Weadon
SP5 Larry D. Weakland
SP5 Ronald J. Weakland
CPL Richard A. Weakley
SGT Ayleet J. Wease
SFC Benjamin Weatherall
MR. Mitch Weatherly
SPC Daniel A. Weathers
PFC Kevin G. Weathers
CSM (Ret) Freddie L. Weatherspoon
PVT Martin Weatherspoon
SFC Timothy Weatherspoon
SP5 Bernard D. Weaver
1LT David W. Weaver
SFC Jackie F. Weaver
SGT Kenneth A. Weaver
COL (Ret) Kurt A. Weaver
MAJ Kyle B. Weaver
CPL Mahlon C. Weaver
LTC Mark C. Weaver
SFC Mark D. Weaver
SGT Randy A. Weaver
SGT Richard E. Weaver
SFC (Ret) Robert A. Weaver
MRS. Robert L. Weaver
SSG Seaborn L. Weaver
MR. Ted R. Weaver
PFC Travis Anthony Weaver
SGT William L. Weaver
SP5 Billy D. Webb
CW2 Gary S. Webb
CPT Guy Webb
LTC Mark P. Webb
SGT Robert M. Webb
CPT Stephen A. Webb

MSG Thomas Webb
MG (Ret) William L. Webb
SP5 William Z. Webb
PFC Eugene R. Webber
SGT Gordon Webber
SSG (Ret) Henry R. Webber
CPT Tim Webber
PFC Chalmers R. Weber
MAJ Ethan T. Weber
MR. Gregor A. Weber
SGT James J. Weber
MSG John D. Weber
MRS. John H. Weber
SPC Joseph D. Weber
SPC Philip A. Weber
MRS. Rosemarie Hoyt Weber
SPC William R. Weber
MR. Albert Webster
CW5 Bruce Webster
LTC (Ret) Charles P. Webster
MR. Dale A. Webster
PFC David M. Webster
CSM (Ret) Dennis E. Webster
MR. Douglas W. Webster
LTC George K. Webster
SGT Glen R. Webster
COL Kelly Webster
SPC Kenneth W. Webster
SPC Larry G. Webster
MSG (Ret) Larry L. Webster
COL (Ret) Noel Webster
SGT Richard Wayne Webster
LTG (Ret) William G. Webster
SGT William M. Webster
SSG (Ret) Christian O. Weding
MR. Kenneth S. Wedmore
SGT Terry L. Wedmore
1SG Aaron E. Weed
SFC (Ret) Franklin J. Weed
SGT Jerry W. Weed
PFC Robert B. Weed
SPC Larry Darnell Weeden
SPC Elmer L. Weeks
1LT Robert A. Weeks
PSG (Ret) Clarence W. Weems
SFC Lionel Weems
SGT Earl Weertz
SGT D. C. Weese
SGT William F. Wegner
SPC Phillip W. Wehlitz
SGM (Ret) Wayne F. Wehrheim
CW5 Dan P. Weiberg
SPC Jack L. Weichal
CPL Jack Weichmann
PVT Gary Weickert
SPC James P. Weidener
SGT James F. Weidlich
PFC George Weidner
SPC Gordon J. Weidner
PFC Donald H. Weigand
SSG Earl H. Weigel
SPC James H. Weigelt
SSG Dennis J. Weigl
SFC Julien Weil
SGT Robert A. Weiler
SGT Brian A. Weimer
COL (Ret) Michael B. Weimer
LTC (Ret) Edward L. Weinberg
LTC (Ret) Richard A. Weinberg
SSG Richard J. Weindel
SGT Kenneth Weindl
PFC Kenneth J. Weinert
SP5 Charles T. Weinrich
SPC Stanley A. Weinstein
MRS. Donna Weintraub
CW2 Chuck Weinum
CW2 Dale L. Weir
CPT Garry K. Weir
SSG Steven Weiser
SPC Alfred G. Weiss
SPC Glen Weiss
SPC (Ret) Jerry L. Weiss
SPC Larry Weiss
MR. Larry L. Weiss
CPT Ronald J. Weiss
SGT Stephen Wayne Weiss
LTC Thomas J. Weiss
SPC Charles R. Weitlauf
PVT David W. Weitnauer
SGT James D. Welborn
CPT Aaron S. Welch
COL (Ret) Arthur J. Welch
PFC (Ret) Charles A. Welch
PFC David E. Welch
MSG Dean A. Welch
SSG Franklin D. Welch
SPC Fred R. Welch
SGT George B. Welch
SGT James F. Welch

SGT Jason B. Welch
SP5 John Welch
SPC Michael C. Welch
SSG Paul Welch
1LT Raymond C. Welch
LTC Richard D. Welch
SGT Timothy D. Welch
PFC William F. Welch
SSG Zachary W. Welch
SPC Greg Welcome
SGT James L. Weldon
SPC Richard J. Weldon
MRS. Virgil E. Weldon
CSM James B. Weldy
1SG (Ret) Earle A. Welker
CPT (Ret) Mark A. Welker
SGT John M. Wellenreuther
SGT Foster M. Weller
PFC Ronald F. Weller
CPT Shane Weller
MS. Kay H. Wellinger
SSG David Wellington
SGT Robert E. Wellmaker
SGT Lynn M. Wellman
SGT Rickie A. Wellman
SGT David A. Wellner
MSG Bernard J. Wells
MAJ (Ret) Charles Wells
SGT Charles R. Wells
CPT Craig A. Wells
SGT Eric W. Wells
LTC Gabriel D. Wells
SFC Glenn A. Wells
CPL Harold L. Wells
SP5 Jonathan F. Wells
LTC K. Brock Wells
1SG (Ret) Larry G. Wells
SGT Lennette A. Wells
PFC Leslie D. Wells
1SG Leslie H. Wells
SSG Marshall H. Wells
SPC Mike Wells
SFC Ricky A. Wells
SGT Robert Wells
SGT Steven Wells
SFC (Ret) Thomas L. Wells
SPC Walter E. Wells
MRS. Willis C. Wells
MSG (Ret) Donald R. Welsh
CPL James V. Welsh
PFC Stewart Welter
SGT Theodore G. Wempe
WO1 Michael T. Wendel
MSG Danny Wendell
PFC Steven D. Wendell
PFC Thomas P. Wendell
SSG Benjamin R. Wendland
CPL Manfred H. Wendland
SPC Thomas C. Wendland
SGT Paul L. Wendt
LTC (Ret) Robert L. Wendt
CSM (Ret) Donald A. Weng
SGT Harold L. Weninger
MAJ Chris Wenner
SGT Robert F. Wenner
SPC Joshua E. Wensel
SGM (Ret) Dennis J. Wenthe
COL (Ret) Eugene G. Wentworth
SGT John Wentworth
SFC William Donald Wentworth
SP5 David F. Wenzel
SPC Gerald Wenzel
SPC Mike Wenzel
CPL Robert M. Wenzel
2LT Alexander Werner
SGT Bruce A. Werner
CW3 Floyd S. Werner
PFC James A. Werner
SPC Michael L. Werner
SSG Steven Kirk Werner
SGT William T. Werner
MR. Edward Werwinski
SGT Bruce T. Wesley
SGT Patric Wesley
SPC Shane R. Wesley
SPC Walter J. Wesley
SPC Rudolph J. Wesselhoft
SGT Wilbur Wesselius
CPL Herman J. Wessels
SGT Robert T. Wessels
MAJ (Ret) Paul H. Wessman
SSG Lyle F. Wesson
COL Billy J. West
COL (Ret) Edward C. West
SGT Floyd E. West
SSG Francis W. West
CPT Fred D. West
SPC Gary W. West

LTC (Ret) Grover C. West
MRS. Jackie Lee West
SSG James L. West
PFC Jerry M. West
SGT John H. West
SPC (Ret) John J. West
SGT John K. West
SGT John L. West
SSG Joseph D. Jim West
SGT Kenny E. West
SGT Larry E. West
CPL Lester G. West
1SG Max E. West
SPC Michael R. West
SPC Norman Ralph West
SPC Robert D. West
MR. Ronald L. West
SGT Shannon West
LTC Stephen K. West
SGT Donald Allen Westaby
SGT Bruce R. Westall
MRS. Michael Westberg
SFC John Westcott
SP5 Richard D. Westenbarger
SGT Wayne Robert Westenberger
SFC Robert O. Wester
SGT Joseph W. Westerfer
PFC David A. Westerfield
MR. Walter Gary Westernoff
MRS. Chester R. Westervelt
SGT Arnold G. Westfall
MAJ David L. Westfall
SSG Harry E. Westfall
SGT Lewis C. Westfall
SGT Robert Westfall
1LT Andrew C. Westin
SFC Nathaniel Westly
DR. Charlie Westman
SGT Robert O. Westman
CSM (Ret) Haskel B. Westmoreland
MAJ (Ret) James A. Westmoreland
SFC Brent D. Weston
CW3 Grant M. Weston
MAJ Ian M. Weston
SGT Robert C. Weston
LTC Roderick Wetherill
SP5 Paul H. Wetherington
2LT John T. Wettack
1LT Jim Wettengel
SPC Clyde Weycker
SGT David Weygant
BG (Ret) Paul T. Weyrauch
PFC Alphonsa Whalen
SPC Matt Whalen
SGT Richard A. Whalen
SPC Yvonne Whalen
SPC Candace Whaley
SSG Nathan D. Whaley
SGT Patrick L. Whaley
PVT Steven E. Whaley
PFC Walter C. Whaley
LTC (Ret) Zachary H. Whaley
2LT Terron Wharton
PFC (Ret) Joseph H. Whatley
1LT Richard E. Whatley
SGT Erik Wheat
CSM (Ret) Walter E. Wheat
CPT Walter L. Wheatfall
SSG Alex F. Wheatley
SGT Clyde S. Wheaton
SGM Billy W. Wheeler
SGT Brandon Wheeler
SSG Cecil D. Wheeler
LTC Chrisopther S. Wheeler
SGT Daniel K. Wheeler
MAJ Douglas E. Wheeler
SGT Gene Wheeler
MR. George M. Wheeler
CPT Gordon L. Wheeler
SFC (Ret) H. William Wheeler
PFC James W. Wheeler
SGT Lavell D. Wheeler
PVT Leon A. Wheeler
SPC Mark T. Wheeler
CW4 (Ret) Michael J. Wheeler
SFC Riley G. Wheeler
SGM (Ret) William D. Wheeler
TSgt Thomas O. Wheeless
SP5 Larry A. Whelan
PFC Jerry A. Whelchel
LTC Neal C. Whetsel
SGT Jack D. Whidden
SPC Tyrone Whieler
CW3 Charles E. Whigham
PFC Ross Whigham
SFC (Ret) Zebedee Whindleton

CPT Thomas T. Whipple
SPC Richard A. Whiskin
PFC Caroline A. Whisman
SSG Eugene H. Whitacre
COL David O. Whitaker
CSM (Ret) Ivory Whitaker
SGT Jim T. Whitaker
SFC Mario D. Whitaker
SP5 Wayne Whitaker
SPC William M. Whitaker
SFC John E. Whitcher
LTG (Ret) R. Steven Whitcomb
SGT Roger W. Whitcomb
MR. Abel White
2LT Alex White
SPC Allan J. White
SGT Arnold Gene White
SGT Barry White
CW4 Baxter I. White
SGT Carl D. White
SSG Carl E. White
SrA Carl L. White
CPT Charles E. White
2LT Christian White
SPC Christopher L. White
PFC (Ret) Curtis R. White
SPC Dale E. White
LT Daniel Nelson White
CW3 (Ret) Danny O. White
SPC David White
SSG David C. White
SFC Dennis White
LTC (Ret) Dennis M. White
MR. Donald F. White
SFC Donald J. White
PFC (Ret) Donald L. White
SFC Elester White
CPT Eric L. White
1SG (Ret) George A. White
PFC George F. White
SPC Grant White
MSG Greg White
SGT Jack A. White
PVT Jacob White
CPT James A. White
SPC James C. White
CW2 James G. White
SPC Jerome White
SFC Jerry D. White
CPT Jerry D. White
PFC Jimmy R. White
SPC Joe White
CW2 John A. White
SGT John C. White
DR. John N. White
CW3 (Ret) John T. White
MR. Johnny White
CW2 Katrina White
SSG Keith F. White
SP5 Kenneth P. White
CSM (Ret) L. B. White
SSG (Ret) Larry White
SP5 Lester White
MSG Lucian C. White
SSG Matthew M. White
SFC Michael N. White
SFC Neil J. White
CPT Nicholas D. White
SSG Nikki L. White
SPC Paul L. White
SGT Quincy White
SGM Ralph M. White
LTC (Ret) Richard R. White
SPC Robert E. White
TSgt Robert L. White
MR. Robert L. White
SPC Robert L. White
SGT Rodger L. White
SPC Samuel E. White
1LT Stephen H. White
SGT Stephen L. White
SGT Steven White
SFC Steven L. White
MR. Thomas H. White
SSG William W. White
SGT John S. Whited
CPT Larry K. Whitefield
COL (Ret) Curtis G. Whiteford
SGT Robert M. Whiteford
SGT Eric Whitehead
SSG Gerald W. Whitehead
SPC Joseph A. Whitehead
SPC Keith J. Whitehead
SPC Paul Whitehead
SSG Daniel Whitehill
SFC Raymond L. Whiteley
CPL John Whitescarver
SGM Nathan Whitesell
SGT (Ret) Fred H. Whiteside

COL (Ret) Jerry E. Whiteside
SFC (Ret) Jay D. Whitfield
COL Dean L. Whitford
SSG Harvy L. Whitford
SGT Bruce Whitish
SGT Charles R. Whitley
MSG Joe L. Whitley
CW2 Kenneth Whitley
SGT (Ret) Ray E. Whitley
SSG Willie Mark Whitlock
SFC (Ret) Ray W. Whitlow
SGT Terry L. Whitlow
SPC Larry D. Whitman
1LT Scott D. Whitman
PFC Jerry Whitmore
SFC Paul M. Whitmore
SFC Walter B. Whitmore
SSG Edwin R. Whitney
SGT Dan L. Whitson
SP5 Dennis W. Whitson
SPC John Whitson
SPC Louis E. Whitson
LTC (Ret) Christopher J. Whittaker
1LT Jim Whittaker
SPC Lucas M. Whittaker
LTC Marvin E. Whittaker
SP5 Michael D. Whittaker
SPC Michael L. Whittaker
SGT Ulysses A. Whittaker
SGM William T. Whittaker
MSG (Ret) Dale E. Whittam
CPL Kenneth D. Whitteaker
1SG Nathaniel Whitted
DR. Robert G. Whittemore
SGT David Whitten
MAJ Stan Whitten
LTC (Ret) Allan R. Whittingham
SPC Charles W. Whittington
SSG Jonathan Whittington
CW2 Edd Whittle
BG Robert Whittle
COL (Ret) William A. Whittle
PVT Matthew Whorton
SSG Jamie Whyte
SP5 Thomas P. Wianecki
SGT Larry K. Wibbeler
GEN (Ret) John A. Wickham
SGT Spencer H. Wickham
PFC Virgil E. Wicklund
WO1 (Ret) Leo G. Wickman
SGT Lee Nelson Wicks
MAJ James G. Wideman
COL (Ret) Larry E. Widener
PFC Charles Widmann
MR. Gary N. Wiechart
PFC Gary B. Wiedeburch
CPL Richard L. Wiegerink
MSG Brenda Wiegert
SPC Keith K. Wiegman
SGT Richard B. Wiens
SPC Nicholas Wieringa
SPC David Wierwenga
SGT A. F. Wiese
SPC Carl R. Wiesjahn
CW3 Kenneth F. Wiggers
PFC Charlie L. Wiggins
SFC Daniel K. Wiggins
SFC (Ret) James Wiggins
SPC Jerry Wiggins
SFC (Ret) Jerry Mack Wiggins
SSG Victor V. Wiggins
SP5 William B. Wiggins
SSG Yolanda Wiggins
SPC Marcus D. Wiggs
SFC (Ret) Fred R. Wight
CW2 Leland S. Wight
CSM (Ret) Edward J. Wightman
2LT John Dave Wightman
SGT James L. Wiginton
SGT James L. Wiginton
CPT David C. Wigle
2LT Michael Wigley
2LT Samuel L. Wigley
SGT Roy Wiik
SPC Thomas J. Wiita
SSG Harvey A. Wike
SPC Neil L. Wiktor
MAJ Christopher Wilbeck
MR. Edwin J. Wilber
SPC Scott Wilbern
MR. Victor C. Wilbourne
SGT Edward H. Wilbur
PVT Keith E. Wilbur
SPC Dekete Wilburn
SSG (Ret) John Peter Wilch
SGT Clarence Dennis Wilcox
CPT Robert W. Wilcox
CPL Roger W. Wilcox
COL (Ret) Timothy J. Wilcox
SPC Wendell N. Wilcox
SSG Virgil O. Wilcutt
SPC Walter Wilczak
LTC (Ret) Brent A. Wildasin
1LT Kyle Wilde
CPL Leonard L. Wilde
SGT Stephen B. Wilde
PVT Dennis A. Wilder
2LT Jonathan Seth Wilder
SFC Lorenza S. Wilder
COL (Ret) W. Bruce Wilder
COL (Ret) W. Bruce Wilder
COL (Ret) W. Bruce Wilder
COL (Ret) William B. Wilder
SGT James O. Wildonger
SPC Jerry D. Wilemon
SGT Alan Wilenken
SFC Donald R. Wiles
LTC (Ret) David D. Wiley
CPL Dennis C. Wiley
SPC Gus O. Wiley
CPL James H. Wiley
CSM (Ret) Norman A. Wilfong
SGT A. P. Wilganoski
1SG (Ret) Joe Wilgeroth
SFC (Ret) Robert H. Wilgus
SPC Christopher Wilhelm
PV2 Christopher Wilhelm
CW2 Jay S. Wilhelm
CW2 James M. Wilhite
SPC Edward G. Wilhusen
SGT Michael J. Wilk
SGT Charles D. Wilke
SPC Richard A. Wilke
PFC Robert Wilkerson
SPC Ronnie E. Wilkerson
SPC Russell D. Wilkerson
2LT Thomas D. Wilkerson
CPT William T. Wilkerson
SPC Richard E. Wilkie
PFC Benjamin T. Wilkins
MRS. Henry J. Wilkins
CSM Roderick B. Wilkins
SSG Dee L. Wilkinson
SGT Gary D. Wilkinson
1SG (Ret) George Ben Wilkinson
SPC Jadon J. Wilkinson
MR. James E. Wilkinson
2LT Kevin R. Wilkinson
1LT Robert L. Wilkinson
SSG Shaun M. Wilkinson
SGT Richard J. Wilkos
SGT David C. Wilkowski
SSG Scott L. Wilks
PVT Skyler Will
SPC Billy H. Willard
SPC Bryan Lee Willard
SPC Gaylan P. Willard
SP5 Glenn D. Willard
SPC Timothy S. Willard
SP5 William T. Willard
LTC (Ret) James H. Willbanks
CPT Adam Willcoxon
CW2 Trason Willemin
PFC Charles J. Willen
MRS. James Willenburg
SGT George E. Willet
COL William D. Willett
SPC William P. Willett
SP5 K. Steven Willey
SGT Donald William
SPC Robert H. William
SGT Adam C. Williams
SGT Alan H. Williams
PFC Alfred H. Williams
1LT Alfred L. Williams
CPL Angela Williams
SGT Annie A. Williams
SGT Anthony Williams
SGT Anthony Williams
MRS. Arian B. Williams
1SG (Ret) Arlen J. Williams
MR. Arlon T. Williams
LTC (Ret) Billie G. Williams
SPC Brent E. Williams
SGT Brian Williams
MR. Carl D. Williams
SFC Caroline Williams
2LT Charles Williams
CSM Charles E. Williams
CPL Charles N. Williams
SSG Claude Peursell Williams
PFC Cody K. Williams
CPT Curtis Williams
SSG Curtis L. Williams
SSG (Ret) Dale D. Williams
SPC Daniel J. Williams
SPC Daniel J. Williams
SSG Daniel L. Williams
CW2 David Williams
SPC David Williams
SPC David A. Williams
MRS. David C. Williams
MAJ (Ret) David E. Williams
MR. David L. Williams
CPT David M. Williams
CW2 David S. Williams
SPC Denny Williams
SPC Donald B. Williams
SGM Donald W. Williams
SGM (Ret) Douglas R. Williams
1LT E. F. Williams
PFC Earl Williams
CSM (Ret) Earl J. Williams
SGT Edward C. Williams
COL (Ret) Edward H. Williams
PFC Emmett R. Williams
SFC Erwin L. Williams
SFC Fiedrick D. Williams
SGT Franklin Williams
SPC Gary D. Williams
SGT Gary D. Williams
SGT Gary L. Williams
CPT (Ret) Gene A. Williams
SGT Gene L. Williams
SPC George E. Williams
MS. Georgia P. Williams
SGT Gerald F. Williams
SGT Gerald L. Williams
SPC Gregory P. Williams
CPL H. Lyle Williams
MSG Hallie Williams
CPT Harold D. Williams
MSG Howard Williams
SFC Isaac Williams
PFC Jack C. Williams
SGT James B. Williams
SGT James C. Williams
SGT James D. Williams
MSG (Ret) James D. Williams
SGT James E. Williams
CPT James J. Williams
SPC James L. Williams
SPC James L. Williams
1LT Jason C. Williams
CPL Jasper E. Williams
CW2 Jennee Williams
SPC Jerrod B. Williams
SSG Joe C. Williams
SSG John A. Williams
CW4 John A. Williams
SGT John A. Williams
MAJ John D. Williams
SGT John D. Williams
SGT John E. Williams
SPC John M. Williams
SSG John P. Williams
SGT John P. Williams
MR. Jon H. Williams
LTC Jonathan M. Williams
SFC Jonathen Williams
SPC Joseph Williams
1LT Joseph J. Williams
CPT Joseph L. Williams
SP5 Joseph M. Williams
SGT Kathryn E. Williams
CPT Keith Williams
CW2 L. Michelle Williams
SGT Larry D. Williams
CPL Larry D. Williams
1SG Lee Williams
MR. Leighton D. Williams
SGT Leo E. Williams
CPL Leroy T. Williams
SPC Louis J. Williams
PFC Lucian B. Williams
SFC Mark A. Williams
COL Mark A. Williams
MAJ Matthew N. Williams
SGT Michael Williams
1SG Michael C. Williams
1LT Michael S. Williams
SPC Michael T. Williams
SFC Michele Williams
LTC Murray W. Williams
SGT Nathaniel Williams
COL (Ret) Nevin R. Williams
SSG Nichols E. Williams
CPL Norman D. Williams
SGT Paul E. Williams
SSG Percy L. Williams
SPC Randel Williams
MR. Rex Williams
SFC Rex E. Williams
SPC Robbie Williams
PFC Robert Williams
1LT Robert Williams
CPL Robert A. Williams
SFC Robert B. Williams
SSG Robert E. Williams
MRS. Robert L. Williams
PFC Robert W. Williams
CW3 Robin Pr Williams
PV2 Rona L. Williams
SPC Ronald R. Williams
TSgt Roy L. Williams
MSG Sam F. Williams
SPC Stephen B. Williams
SGT Stephen T. Williams
SP5 Steve A. Williams
SFC Steven L. Williams
SFC (Ret) Terry L. Williams
2LT Thomas B. Williams
DR. Thomas J. Williams
CSM Thomas M. Williams
SGT Thomas O. Williams
PFC Thomas S. Williams
SGT Tiffany Williams
SPC Tony Williams
SGM Travis L. Williams
MS. Trinece A. Williams
2LT Tyler D. Williams
PVT Tyrone Williams
SPC Walter D. Williams
CPT Wayne G. Williams
CPL Wendell Williams
SFC Wendell T. Williams
SGT Wesley Williams
CW2 William G. Williams
CW5 (Ret) William W. Williams
MSG Willie E. Williams
MSG Laura Williams Coleman
MR. Dallas Williams-Cox
MRS. Bobby W. Williamson
SGT C. Boyd Williamson
SGT Chris Williamson
PFC David B. Williamson
MR. Doug Williamson
SPC Gregory Alonzo Williamson
1SG (Ret) James A. Williamson
1SG (Ret) Jerry L. Williamson
CPL Kenneth E. Williamson
SPC Martin L. Williamson
SPC Michael Williamson
MSG (Ret) Raymond J. Williamson
MRS. Richard Williamson
MAJ (Ret) Robert J. Williamson
MR. Samuel Williamson
SGT Terry L. Williamson
SGT Anthony Willinghan
SFC (Ret) Carlie O. Willis
SGT Charles L. Willis
SGT David R. Willis
MRS. James E. Willis
SGT Jeremy D. Willis
SGT Jimmy Willis
SGT Kenneth W. Willis
SFC Lloyd Willis
SGT Shaun A. Willis
PFC Stephen L. Willis
SPC William Willis
SP5 William E. Willis
SPC William R. Willmann
SGT Gary M. Willmon
SSG Arthur Willoughby
SSG Brent Willoughby
SFC Earl L. Willoughby
SGT Walter H. Willoughby
LTC Christopher W. Wills
SGT Donald E. Wills
SSG Joseph B. Willson
MR. Arthur C. Wilming
SSG Dusty Wilmore
CW3 (Ret) Kirk W. Wilmore
MR. Al Wilson
CPT Albert E. Wilson
PV2 Anthony Wilson
1SG (Ret) Anthony Wilson
CW5 (Ret) B. Scott Wilson
SPC Calvin L. Wilson
MAJ (Ret) Charles L. Wilson
1SG (Ret) Charles R. Wilson
MSG Chester R. Wilson
MAJ Christopher A. Wilson
MR. Clifford Danny Wilson
SPC Clifford E. Wilson
SSG Clint Wilson
PVT Colt Wilson
SPC David W. Wilson
SPC Delbert W. Wilson
SPC Dennis Lane Wilson
MSG Edward P. Wilson
SGT Eldrod Wilson
1LT Emmett A. Wilson
MAJ Gordon L. Wilson
SGT Harry M. Wilson
SFC (Ret) Harry S. Wilson
SPC Harvey L. Wilson
CW2 Henry A. Wilson
MR. Howard Wilson
SPC Jack D. Wilson
SPC Jack H. Wilson
CPT James A. Wilson
SSG James A. Wilson
MSG James E. Wilson
CPT James R. Wilson
CPL James S. Wilson
CPL Jesse R. Wilson
CPL John Wilson
CW3 (Ret) John C. Wilson
SPC John M. Wilson
CPT John M. Wilson
SPC John Philip Wilson
SPC John R. Wilson
SFC Johnie R. Wilson
SFC Johnny L. Wilson
1SG Jonathan Wilson
MSG (Ret) Keith G. Wilson
CPL Larry S. Wilson
CPT Laurance A. Wilson
CSM (Ret) Lawrence K. Wilson
MR. Leland E. Wilson
SPC Leonard C. Wilson
LTC Martin J. Wilson
SGT Myrtis L. Wilson
SGM Nathan Wilson
PFC Norman E. Wilson
CPT Peter F. Wilson
PFC Philip H. Wilson
SPC Randall W. Wilson
SFC Raymond D. Wilson
SFC (Ret) Richard C. Wilson
SGT Ricky A. Wilson
CPT Robert B. Wilson
CSM (Ret) Robert E. Wilson
CPL Robert J. Wilson
CPL Robert W. Wilson
SPC Ronald Wilson
SPC Ronnie D. Wilson
SPC Russell L. Wilson
SGM Sammy L. Wilson
SPC Stanley P. Wilson
MR. Stephen R. Wilson
SPC Steven E. Wilson
MR. Terry N. Wilson
MAJ Thomas G. Wilson
SPC Thomas P. Wilson
SPC Thomas R. Wilson
MR. Thomas W. Wilson
1SG Todd A. Wilson
1SG (Ret) Van R. Wilson
SPC Wayne Wilson
SGT William Wilson
CPT William W. Wilson
SPC Willie Charles Wilson
SFC Willie E. Wilson
SSG Woodrow D. Wilson
SSG John Wilt
SSG Howard Wimbrough
SPC Jesse W. Winans
SGT John P. Winans
SFC Mark Winans
SGT Edward G. Winbourne
SGT John D. Wincz
1LT Robert J. Windell
SSG Charles D. Windham
SFC Douglas Windham
SGT Eddie L. Windham
SP5 James C. Windham
COL Robert E. Windham
SPC Tamara M. Windham
CSM David Windom
PFC Walter W. Windorff
1SG Aaron E. Windsor
SPC Richard E. Windsor
SP5 Patrick J. Winegar
CPT Patrick J. Winegerter
SP5 James W. Wines
PFC Walter C. Winfield
SGT Orville C. Winfrey
SGT Thomas Winfrey
SGT Karl A. Wing
TSgt Melvyn D. Wingard
SGT Robert Wingate
SPC Larry M. Winge
CPT James M. Winger
SGT James Wingerson
SP5 John W. Wingo
COL (Ret) Paul P. Winkel
COL W. Todd Winklbauer
SGT Robert L. Winkle
CW3 David A. Winkler
SPC Larry Winkler
SP5 Thomas F. Winkler
PFC W. S. Winkler
SPC James R. M. Winkles
SGT William J. Winn
SPC Virgil Winner
CW3 Patrick M. Winnert
SPC Michael J. Winney
CPL Kenneth L. Winship
COL Brian E. Winski
SFC Gale N. Winslow
SGT Dennis Winstead
SSG Reginald Winston
SP5 Wesley B. Winston
TSgt Eugene W. Winter
SGT Thomas D. Winter
SGT John J. Winterman
CPL Stan Winterroth
CPT Tracy J. Winton
SGT Andrew G. Wintz
LTC (Ret) Barry L. Winzeler
SPC Ray Wiora
PFC Dan P. Wire
SGT Carl Wireman
MR. Wayne L. Wirkus
SGT Daniel A. Wirt
MR. C. S. Wirth
MRS. Herman L. Wirth
SPC Thomas Wirth
LTC (Ret) Floyd R. Wirthlin
SSG Michael Wirtz
SGT Walter Wisby
SSG (Ret) Gary M. Wise
SFC James W. Wise
CPT Matthew B. Wise
CSM Randall Wise
MAJ Robert J. Wise
CPT Robert J. Wisham
SPC David R. Wishart
LTG (Ret) Leonard P. Wishart
CPL Jerry R. Wiskotzil
SPC Travis Wisley
CPL Robin S. Wisner
CPL Chester T. Wisniewski
MR. Paul Edward Wisniewski
SGT Richard J. Wisnlewski
SGT Robert C. Wissman
1LT William O. Wissman
SSG David E. Wister
SP3 Richard O. Wisti
SPC Robert A. Wistrom
CPL Thomas P. Witherow
SPC John N. Withers
2LT Shadrike Witherspoon
LTC Edward L. Witsell
SGT Dennis M. Witt
CW2 Robert D. Witt
MSG Hoss K. R. Witte
SFC James Witte
SFC (Ret) Jerry L. Wittkop
SMSgt (Ret) John M. Witts
SPC Gregory L. Witzler
SP5 Michael Wlodarczak
CPT (Ret) Robert L. Wlodarski
CPL Bartosz Wloka
SGT John Wnek
CPT John K. Wohlever
SPC Lowell A. Wohlk
SP5 William R. Wohlwend
PVT Edward J. Wojcik
MG (Ret) Walter Wojdkakowski
CPT Matthew M. Wojick
SGT Robert G. Wolaver
2LT Courtlandt D. Wolbe
CPT Kevin A. Wolf
CPT Marvin J. Wolf
SGT Neal F. Wolf
MAJ Ralph R. Wolf
SPC Richard N. Wolf
SGT Thomas Jared Wolf
CPL William A. Wolf
CPL Alden B. Wolfe
SPC Barry L. Wolfe
SPC Clifford F. Wolfe
SP5 Dennis L. Wolfe
MRS. Irene H. Wolfe
COL (Ret) James B. Wolfe
SGT Marcus C. Wolfe
SPC Robert D. Wolfe
1SG (Ret) Robert H. Wolfe
BG (Ret) Rodney D. Wolfe
PV2 Sarah Wolfe
SGT William C. Wolfe
SFC Earl Wolfenberger
PFC Greg A. Wolff
SGM Michael Wolff
SGT Nicholas Ryan Wolff
SGT Larry L. Wolfgram
PVT Timothy Wolfgram
SFC (Ret) Bob Wolford
CPT Gerald Alex Wolford

SP5 Kenneth R. Wollard
MAJ T. J. Wolner
SPC William Woloshyn
MAJ (Ret) Harry W. Wolstenholme
CPT Thomas C. Wolters
SGT T. Eugene Womach
CPT Alton W. Womack
MAJ Carl E. Womack
SFC Fletcher R. Womack
1LT Kenneth Roland Womack
SGT Larry D. Womack
PFC Robert E. Womack
COL (Ret) Donald R. Wong
1LT Jeffrey S. Wong
SFC Myron F. Wong
SFC Randall Wong
MAJ Robert Y. Wong
CPT John K. Woo
SPC Robin D. Woo
TSgt Arlie D. Wood
MR. Artie L. Wood
COL (Ret) Billy R. Wood
SSG Daniel D. Wood
PFC Daniel G. Wood
SGT Dennis L. Wood
SFC Derek A. Wood
CPT Donald N. Wood
MSG Edwin J. Wood
CSM (Ret) Frank C. Wood
MRS. Gerald C. Wood
CPT Jack E. Wood
SSG James D. Wood
SPC Jerry D. Wood
SGT Jerry E. Wood
SPC Joe Wood
1LT John A. Wood
CPT Jonathan Wood
SPC Joshua L. Wood
SSG (Ret) Kenneth W. Wood
MSG (Ret) Lawrence A. Wood
MAJ Luther L. Wood
MAJ (Ret) M. Douglas Wood
1LT Parker F. Wood
SSG Paul C. Wood
SGT Richard J. Wood
LTC (Ret) Richard W. Wood
SPC Robert Wood
LTC Roger M. Wood
SSG Ronald J. Wood
MR. Ronald R. Wood
MSG Roy A. Wood
1LT Roy L. Wood
SPC Ryan Wood
SGT William A. Wood
SSG Harold L. Woodall
SGT Danny R. Woodard
SPC S. P. Woodard
SSG Terrence Woodard
SFC Willie C. Woodard
SPC William S. Woodbury
SGT Johnny Wooden
SSG Michael C. Wooden
SGT Chester N. Woodford
SPC Michael J. Woodford
MR. Richard W. Woodke
SPC Douglas M. Woodland
SGT (Ret) Clinton A. Woodley
CPT Shane R. Woodley
MS. Shari Ann Woodley-Bankston
LTG (Ret) John W. Woodmansee
COL Robert A. Woodmansee
SPC Byron S. Woodruff
1LT David B. Woodruff
MAJ David C. Woodruff
PFC John H. Woodruff
SGT John J. Woodruff
CPT Mike Woodruff
SGT Thomas R. Woodruff
SSG (Ret) Alvin L. Woods
SSG Arthur L. Woods
SPC Dale R. Woods
SGT Dennis E. Woods
PFC Edward R. Woods
SGT Felix Woods
SPC Jim D. Woods
2LT Kevin M. Woods
SGT Lakecia Woods
SGT Laurence W. Woods
SFC Lisa Woods
SFC Michael G. Woods
SPC Michael J. Woods
SPC Raymond L. Woods
SPC Richard G. Woods
CPL Robert Woods
SPC Sam L. Woods
SGT Stephen R. Woods
PV2 Terryl L. Woods
CPT Timothy C. Woods
CPL William J. Woods
SGT William R. Woods
PVT Dewaine Woodson
SPC Lawrence R. Woodson
1LT Robert M. Woodson
SFC Scott H. Woodsz
SFC Carvel Woodward
SSG F. Woodward
SSG Forrest Woodward
CPL John E. Woodward
SPC Kenneth R. Woodward
SGT Michael Woodward
CPT Richard H. Woodward
SPC Wallace M. Woodward
SGT Jay Woodworth
SGT Matthew Woodworth
SPC Robert L. Woodworth
SGT (Ret) Carl E. Woody
SPC Charles H. Woody
SPC Donald H. Woody
SSG James A. Woody
1SG Marcus Q. Woody
PVT John J. Wool
SGT Kenneth Woolcock
SGT Burl D. Wooldridge
SGT Edward S. Woollen
CPT James P. Woolnough
1SG Curtis Woolsey
SSG William R. Woolsey
1LT David B. Woolverton
MAJ Colin Wooten
SGT Edward I. Wooten
SPC La-Dell V. Wooten
SSG Sherrie Wooten
SPC Joseph E. Wooton
SPC Timothy P. Wopinek
SGT Lee Worcester
MR. Felix Worchesik
CPT Gregory J. Worden
SGT James K. Workman
PVT Joseph D. Workman
PVT Orald F. Workman
MSG (Ret) Stephen L. Workman
SGT Timothy L. Workman
LTC (Ret) Joe R. Worley
CPT Seward C. Worley
SGT William R. Worley
SGT Terry L. Worrell
SGT Jason E. Worsdale
1LT Christopher Worshek
CPT Phil Worsley
CW3 Dennis L. Worthington
MRS. Gerald R. Worthington
SGT Ivan R. Worthington
CPL Marvin L. Worthington
SPC Bill Worthman
MRS. Ronald A. Wotring
SP5 Steven A. Wowk
SPC Lyday Woxie
SPC Glenn G. Wozniak
1SG (Ret) Leon S. Wozniak
MSG Donald D. Wratton
2LT Robert M. Wray
SGT Walter E. Wray
WO1 Danny Wreay
SGT Terry L. Wrench
SFC Bruce K. Wrenn
SPC Richard A. Wressell
1LT Kristopher Wrieden
PV2 Andrea Wright
SP5 Carle Vaughn Wright
CW3 (Ret) Danny Wright
SP5 Danny R. Wright
MAJ David E. Wright
PFC Dennis L. Wright
SGT Donald R. Wright
1LT Erik R. Wright
SPC Eugene Wright
SFC (Ret) Francis A. Wright
CPT Geoffrey R. Wright
COL Harold Russell Wright
SPC James Wright
SP5 James D. Wright
LTC (Ret) James E. Wright
SSG James M. Wright
CW2 James R. Wright
PFC Jeffrey Wright
2LT Jeffrey S. Wright
PFC John R. Wright
SPC Kimberly R. Wright
SSG Larry Wright
PFC Louis Wright
SPC Marshall E. Wright
2LT Mathis F. Wright
SSG Michael Wright
CPT Michael A. Wright
SPC Michael H. Wright
SGT Michael J. Wright
PFC Norman E. Wright
SFC Philip J. Wright
PFC Philip S. Wright
SSG Quenton S. Wright
COL (Ret) Raymond J. Wright
SGT Raymond L. Wright
COL (Ret) Richard K. Wright
LTC Robert Wright
COL (Ret) Robert A. Wright
SGT Rodney J. Wright
PVT Ronald E. Wright
SPC Timothy J. Wright
SPC Tom M. Wright
CPT Torre D. Wright
LTC (Ret) Walter G. B. Wright
CPT Will A. Wright
CW3 (Ret) William M. Wright
MS. Nance Wright-Beasley
SPC Walter B. Wrightstone
SGT Waverly Wrim
PVT David L. Wrisley
1LT Edward F. Wrubluski
LTC Joseph A. Wucik
MAJ (Ret) Marc J. Wuensch
CW4 (Ret) Kenneth W. Wuest
PV2 Robert R. Wuestenberg
SPC Erwin J. Wuestenhager
SGT Fred M. Wukich
SGT Richard Wulff
SPC Benjamin Wurtz
PFC Jeffrey L. Wyant
MSG Anita Lee Wyatt
SSG Carl E. Wyatt
SGT David O. Wyatt
SGT (Ret) Erick Wyatt
WO1 John M. Wyatt
CW3 (Ret) Melvin E. Wyatt
CPT Paul K. Wyatt
SPC Robert Wyatt
SPC Ronald V. Wyatt
SPC Steven M. Wyatt
CW2 Tolbert E. Wyatt
SFC John L. Wyche
1SG (Ret) Dara Wydler
1LT Patrick W. Wyffels
LT Thomas O. Wylie
SPC James M. Wyman
CPT Scott L. Wyman
SGT Joseph C. Wynder
SGT Donald Wyne
MSG (Ret) Anthony J. Wynn
SGM David L. Wynn
MAJ (Ret) Dennis M. Wynn
SPC Karon J. Wynne
MSG Edward L. Wynns
CW2 Bruce V. Wyrwitzke
SSG Christopher Wyss
1LT Yan Xiong
PV2 Anthony Yaba
CPT Stuart H. Yablon
SGT Adxable T. Yabut
WO1 Paul Yacobucci
MR. Arnold W. Yaden
SPC Thomas R. Yakowicz
SGT Dean C. Yamane
MSG (Ret) Yoshiharu Yamase
SFC Bob Yanacsek
CPT Leon H. Yancey
MR. S. Foster Yancey
LTC (Ret) Joseph Yanchar
SPC Peter F. Yancick
SPC Regal Craig Yaney
SPC Javier Yanez
SPC Chianeng Yang
SSG William C. Yankausky
PVT Sammy L. Yankaway
SGT Joseph S. Yannetta
SPC John M. Yannie
MSG (Ret) Amos L. Yarborough
LTC (Ret) Neill A. Yarborough
1SG Christopher Yarbrough
MR. Lonnie B. Yarbrough
MAJ Robert L. Yarbrough
MRS. Samuel K. Yarbrough
PVT Stephen Yarbrough
PV2 Everett E. Yarger
SFC Selcuk Yargici
SPC David L. Yarnall
SPC Stephen Loren Yarnell
SSG Matt Yarom
SPC T. J. Yarsh
SGM (Ret) Harry Yasson
PFC Ben Yasukochi
PFC John J. Yasurek
SGT Glenn M. Yata
SGT Bruce R. Yates
SSG Eddie D. Yates
SGT Gene Nolan Yates
MSG (Ret) Maxie E. Yates
SFC (Ret) Melvin C. Yates
MSG Olen R. Yates
SFC (Ret) Robert E. Yates
SFC Robert M. Yates
LTC (Ret) David A. Yatto
COL (Ret) Joseph S. Yavorsky
MAJ Richard N. Yaw
SFC Beneto Ybarra
SPC Mark A. Ybarra
2LT Rene Ybarra
1SG (Ret) Ricardo Ybarra
MR. Robert S. Ybarra
SGT Ricardo F. Ybarra-Weckmann
SPC Charles C. Yeager
SGT Gregg D. Yeager
SFC William R. Yeaman
SGT Gregory Lee Yeary
SPC Joseph C. Yeater
PFC Eric M. Yeats
SSG Robert J. Yelinek
2LT Guy Yelverton
1LT Robert J. Yencha
MAJ Jason B. Yenrick
SGT Herman W. Yentz
MRS. John J. Yeosock
SPC Johnny R. Yepes
SPC Johnny R. Yepes
SPC Cory A. Yerdon
SGT Robert B. Yesia
CPT Joseph A. Yessen
CPT Nicholas R. Yetman
SFC Stuart B. Yetman
SGT John S. Yevonishon
LT George C. Yezak
PFC Yong P. Yi
CPL Donald S. Yingling
SSG Ervin E. Ylitalo
SP5 Raymond M. Ynostroza
MR. Clyde Yoakum
SGT George A. Yocum
CW2 Jackie B. Yoder
SPC Dennis M. Yodsnukis
LTC Mark Q. Yoling
SGT Martin A. Yommer
SPC Patrick Yonak
1LT Robert Yonts
PFC Billy York
COL (Ret) Dennis J. York
CPT George M. York
SGT John York
SP5 John W. York
SGT Joshua M. York
SGT Vance A. York
CPL William D. York
SGT Ted M. Yoshimura
CPL G. Jack Yost
SPC Matthew Youmans
SSG Alan Young
SP5 Alan D. Young
SPC Carl G. Young
LTC (Ret) Charles D. Young
MAJ (Ret) Chester D. Young
SGT Daniel L. Young
CSM (Ret) Darriel R. Young
SPC David A. Young
SSG David E. Young
SGT David R. Young
SSG Dennis L. Young
SGT Dennis S. Young
SFC Donald D. Young
CPT Douglas A. Young
LTC (Ret) Earl W. Young
SPC Edward C. Young
SGT Frank S. Young
SFC Franklin Young
SGT George Young
SPC Gregory Young
CSM Herbert W. Young
SPC James C. Young
SGM Jerry W. Young
SP5 Jimmy Ray Young
1LT John L. Young
SPC Joseph D. Young
SGT Justin Young
LTC K. Malia Young
PFC Larry D. Young
SP5 Larry E. Young
CPL Larry P. Young
SFC Maurice P. Young
LT Michael S. Young
MR. Michael W. Young
SGT (Ret) Nichelle Renee Young
SSG Nicholas A. Young
PFC Ray A. Young
CPT Raymond A. Young
1SG (Ret) Richard Young
SSG Robert Young
SSG Robert A. Young
PFC Robert A. Young
SFC Robert Charles Young
SPC Scott A. Young
SGT Shannon R. Young
1LT Stephen Young
SGT Steven P. Young
SGT Terry Young
PV2 William Young
SGT Earl D. Youngblood
1LT Nicholas Youngerman
SPC James L. Youngman
MR. Richard Youngman
PFC David Youngs
SGT Bob E. Younis
SPC Donald H. Yowell
SGT Felix E. Ysais
CPL Gary R. Ysker
SPC Byung Yu
PFC Dennis R. Yuergens
WO1 James K. Yuille
MSG John M. Yunckes
SPC Brandon Yund
SPC Nicholas Yund
PFC John G. Yunker
MRS. Joseph P. Yurkovich
LTC (Ret) William B. Zabicki
SGT Nevin R. Zacharias
SSG Brian M. Zacher
SPC Frank A. Zacherson
PFC James F. Zack
SFC Wayne C. Zack
1LT Christopher Zaczyk
PFC Joe Zadell
PFC John J. Zagata
LTC Karen Zahm
CW2 Randy R. Zahn
SPC Jason Zahnley
CPL Fritz L. Zainer
SGT Andrew Zak
PV2 James J. Zak
SGT Louis P. Zalusky
SPC George Tom Zamaria
SPC Joe A. Zamarripa
SPC Josue M. Zamarron
SPC Anthony J. Zambito
CW2 (Ret) Anthony N. Zammarrelli
SGT (Ret) Donald L. Zammit
SPC Frank X. Zamora
CSM George Zamudio
SGT Joseph B. Zanco
SGT (Ret) L. Richard Zander
SrA Carl J. Zanella
SFC Eugene L. Zanon
CPL Louis T. Zanoni
SSG (Ret) James E. Zanotelli
CSM (Ret) Hector C. Zapata
SSG Salvador Zapata
SGT Ronald H. Zapka
CW3 Raul Zarco
SGT Gary A. Zarilla
SSG (Ret) Robert Zarowitz
CPL Christopher D. Zarth
SGT Gary Zarubick
SPC Glen R. Zastrow
PFC Herman W. Zastrow
SPC Troy A. Zastrow
PFC Daniel S. Zatsick
SGT Robert Zawacki
PFC Timothy E. Zazula
SPC Brian Zbiegien
SGT Jerome Michael Zdancewicz
SPC Daniel C. Zdroik
SSG Keith E. Zech
SGT Ray Zedlar
SGT Frank C. Zehner
PFC Allan Zeigler
SGT Natorial Zeigler
SGT Owen Zeigler
SPC Ray Zeigler
SSG Al Zeller
SGT Ron Zeller
LTC Walter G. Zeller
MRS. Phillip C. Zemke
SPC Walter Zemrock
SP5 Jessie Zendejas
MR. Edward L. Zenk
SGT Kenneth M. Zenk
SGM (Ret) Ernest O. Zenker
SP5 Donald J. Zennie
MRS. Lillian C. Zent
SGM (Ret) Franklin A. Zepp
SGT Milton Zernich
SGT Timothy A. Zerr
PFC Zhiqiang Zhang
PFC Hongning Zhong
1LT Jay M. Ziegler
MAJ Richard J. Ziegler
SSG James D. Zieglmeier
SGT John W. Zielny
SGT Monte R. Zierke
MR. George Zietz
SSG David Zilka
SPC Greg Zilka
CPT (Ret) Richard K. Zilka
SP5 Joseph J. Zima
TSgt (Ret) Joseph W. Zimmerman
SGT Michael Zimmerman
SPC Tim Zimmerman
SGT William A. Zimmerman
SGT Dan Zimmerschied
1SG (Ret) Howard D. Zingraf
1SG (Ret) Lawrence A. Zink
CPT Rebecca Zinnante
1LT Chad M. Zinnecker
SSG Hanz Zinsman
SGT Paul Zinzella
PFC Richard A. Zipperer
TSgt Louis R. Zlokovich
SPC Damian Zoida
SGT Benedict L. Zollo
PFC Kayla Zook
CPT Phillip M. Zook
SP5 Richard C. Zook
COL (Ret) William E. Zook
SPC Russell M. Zornes
COL (Ret) Ervan E. Zouzalik
CPT John R. Zsido
SPC Joseph G. Zub
CPL Henry P. Zubrowski
SPC Dennis R. Zuege
CPL Keith R. Zuhlke
SPC Joseph N. Zuk
PFC Jennifer Zukas
SGT Jose Zulaica
SGT Leonardo Zumaran
SPC David James Zumbrunnen
COL Maria Zumwalt
SFC Jesus G. Zuniga
CPT (Ret) Alexander M. Zupsich
SGT Joseph S. Zurawski
SPC Christopher A. Zwayer
MR. John B. Zweigart
MR. Mark Zwerling
CPL Daniel A. Zwiefka
PFC Theodore Zwies
LTC Richard M. Zygadlo

INDEX

The Roster is not included in the index since it is in alphabetical order in its respective section.

Taji R&S, May 30, 2
Courtesy of Carl

B Co., 2-8 CAV, 1st Brigade, 1st Cavalry Division, Camp Buehr
Kuwait, Christmas 2011. Courtesy of Tom Ketterer.